PENGUIN  CLASSICS

PENGUIN ENGLISH POETS
GENERAL EDITOR: CHRISTOPHER RICKS

JOHN MILTON: THE COMPLETE POEMS

JOHN MILTON was born in 1608. The son of a scrivener (a notary and money-lender), he was educated by private tutors and attended St Paul's School and Christ's College, Cambridge. He left Cambridge in 1632 and spent the next six years in scholarly retirement. *A Masque* and *Lycidas* belong to this period. Following his Italian journey (1638–9), he took up the cause of Presbyterianism in a series of hard-hitting anti-prelatical pamphlets (1641–2). His divorce pamphlets (1643–5), written after his first wife had temporarily deserted him, earned him much notoriety and contributed to his breach with the Presbyterians. In 1649 he took up the cause of the new Commonwealth. As Secretary for Foreign Tongues to the Council of State, he defended the English revolution both in English and Latin – and sacrificed his eyesight in the process. He risked his life by publishing *The Ready and Easy Way to Establish a Free Commonwealth* on the eve of the Restoration (1660). His great poems were published after this political defeat. A ten-book version of *Paradise Lost* appeared in 1667, and *Paradise Regained* and *Samson Agonistes* were published together in 1671. An expanded version of his shorter poems (first published in 1646) was brought out in 1673, and the twelve-book *Paradise Lost* appeared in 1674, the year of his death.

JOHN LEONARD has taught at the universities of Cambridge, Ottawa and Western Ontario. He has published widely on Milton, and his book *Naming in Paradise* (Clarendon Press, 1990) was a co-winner of the Milton Society's James Holly Hanford Award. He is a Professor of English at the University of Western Ontario, where he has taught since 1987.

JOHN MILTON

THE COMPLETE POEMS

edited with a preface and notes by
JOHN LEONARD

PENGUIN BOOKS

PENGUIN BOOKS

Published by the Penguin Group
Penguin Books Ltd, 27 Wrights Lane, London w8 5TZ, England
Penguin Putnam Inc., 375 Hudson Street, New York, New York 10014, USA
Penguin Books Australia Ltd, Ringwood, Victoria, Australia
Penguin Books Canada Ltd, 10 Alcorn Avenue, Toronto, Ontario, Canada M4V 3B2
Penguin Books (NZ) Ltd, 182–190 Wairau Road, Auckland 10, New Zealand

Penguin Books Ltd, Registered Offices: Harmondsworth, Middlesex, England

First published 1998
10 9 8 7 6 5 4 3 2

Set in 10/11.5 pt Monotype Ehrhardt
Typeset by Rowland Phototypesetting Ltd, Bury St Edmunds, Suffolk
Printed in England by Clays Ltd, St Ives plc

CONTENTS

TRANSLATIONS FROM THE PROSE WORKS

PARADISE LOST

PARADISE REGAINED

SAMSON AGONISTES 463

THE LATIN AND GREEK POEMS

PREFACE

The present text represents a partial modernization. Spelling has been modernized, italics removed, and most capitals reduced. Contractions have for the most part been preserved, for they provide a guide to Milton's prosody. I have modernized punctuation only when the original pointing might impede a modern reader. Most of my changes are from a comma to a semi-colon or full-stop. An example is *Lycidas* 128–32, which the editions of 1645 and 1673 point as follows:

> Besides what the grim Wolf with privy paw
> Daily devours apace, and nothing said,
> But that two-handed engine at the door,
> Stands ready to smite once, and smite no more.

The comma after 'said' is potentially confusing, for it gives the momentary signal that the 'two-handed engine' is something that the bad shepherds said. I have printed a full-stop. In this instance I have the support of the 1638 edition, which also has a full-stop. John Creaser has argued for the virtues of eclecticism in choosing between variants such as these.[1] Convinced by his arguments, I have drawn on the punctuation of all the texts produced in Milton's lifetime. Occasionally I have modernized against all early texts.

I have not modernized any punctuation that in my judgement conveys a deliberate ambiguity. An example is *Paradise Lost* v 77–81:

> Taste this, and be henceforth among the gods
> Thyself a goddess, not to earth confined,
> But sometimes in the air, as we, sometimes
> Ascend to Heav'n, by merit thine, and see
> What life the gods live there, and such live thou.

Many editors change the comma after 'we' to a semi-colon and so remove a suggestive ambiguity. As Zachary Pearce noted in 1733, Satan's 'as we' is placed so as to refer either to 'Ascend to Heav'n' or 'in the air'. William Empson discerns 'a natural embarrassment' in the fallen Satan's implied doubt as to whether 'he could go to Heaven himself'.[2] It is not always easy – and is sometimes impossible – to decide when a poet is being deliberately ambiguous, but it is an editor's responsibility to make difficult decisions.

Variations of punctuation are too numerous to be recorded in the notes (though I have drawn attention to a few cases). I have recorded more verbal variations between the early texts, though constraint of space has forced me to be selective – especially with the early poems, which are extensively reworked in the Trinity manuscript.

Attention should be drawn to a liberty I have taken in my use of capitals. The early editions usually capitalize 'Heaven', and they make no typographical distinction between God's empyreal Heaven and the stellar heavens of the created universe. I have used the upper case for God's Heaven and the lower case for the heavens below the *primum mobile*. The justification for this typographical distinction is that it can serve the modern reader as a helpful guide (see e.g. *Paradise Lost* ii 1004–6 and vii 162–7). Modern-spelling editions invariably make such a distinction between 'God' and 'god', even though the early texts use the upper case for pagan gods as well as God.

My prime purpose in the notes has been to elucidate Milton's biblical, classical, historical and other allusions. I have also attempted to illustrate Milton's verbal inventiveness by frequent recourse to the *Oxford English Dictionary*. Like Shakespeare, Milton added many words and phrases to the language. Many of these have become so integrated into standard English that the modern reader is not surprised by them; yet Milton may have meant them to surprise. Some of Milton's coinages have become clichés, and we must make an imaginative effort to hear them afresh. 'Pandaemonium' is the most famous example. Others are less well known, but no less significant. Lost in the woods at night, the Lady in *A Masque* catches a glimpse of the moon behind a cloud and asks:

> Was I deceived, or did a sable cloud
> Turn forth her silver lining on the night? (221–2)

This is the *OED*'s earliest instance of what has since become a hackneyed metaphor.

In my notes I have marked Milton's neologisms with an asterisk. When the *OED* credits Milton with the first use of a word, I place the asterisk immediately before the word, as in my note to *Paradise Lost* i 548:

> *serried pressed close together, shoulder to shoulder.

When the *OED* credits Milton with using an existing word in a new sense, I place the asterisk before the sense, as in my note to *Paradise Lost* ii 439:

> *unessential *possessing no essence (*OED* 1).

I have checked every word in Milton's English poems against the *OED*, but my asterisks should still be used with caution. Although the editors of the *OED* attempted to record the first use of every word, they inevitably made some errors. William B. Hunter has identified some of these in his seminal essay 'New Words in Milton's English Poems'.[3] Hunter nevertheless found the *OED* to be reliable in the vast majority of cases. Out of more than one thousand words and senses 'apparently original in some sense with Milton', Hunter found only twenty-eight cases where the *OED* was in error. Hunter was writing in 1954. Preparing my edition in the 1990s, I have been able to use the enormous searching-power of the *OED* on CD ROM. With just a few keystrokes it has been possible to check Milton's putative neologisms against all quotations in the *OED*. Sometimes the *OED* credits Milton with a new word, not knowing that it is quoted in an earlier text elsewhere in the dictionary. The *OED* credits Milton with coining 'loquacious' in *Paradise Lost* x 161, but a global search of all *OED* quotations finds an earlier instance from 1656. Sometimes Milton antedates the *OED*'s first instance. The *OED*'s earliest instance of 'self-esteem' is from 1657, but Milton had used the term in *An Apology for Smectymnuus* (1642). In my note to *Paradise Lost* viii 572 I accordingly mark 'self-esteem' with an asterisk and note that Milton may have coined the term in his prose. I have silently omitted any neologism that the *OED* falsely accredits to Milton.

The *OED* can also alert the modern reader to words that have changed or narrowed their meaning since Milton's time. English is rich in words that mean the opposite of themselves, and Milton loves to pun on words of this kind. In one case an entire poem hinges on such a word. The poem is Sonnet XII ('I did but prompt the age to quit their clogs'). Milton wrote it in 1646, after his divorce pamphlets had caused a scandal. The Presbyterians – Milton's erstwhile allies against the Bishops – called on Parliament to suppress his tracts. Sonnet XII has traditionally been read as Milton's embittered response to this rejection, but some critics have argued that the poem is really aimed at the radical sects who embraced Milton's views too enthusiastically. The disputed lines are these:

> But this is got by casting pearl to hogs;
> That bawl for freedom in their senseless mood,
> And still revolt when truth would set them free. (8–10)

Critics often ask how the Presbyterians can be said to 'revolt' when they wanted to reaffirm the conservative divorce laws. Such critics assume that 'revolt' has its modern meaning, and so must refer to the radical sects. The modern sense of 'revolt' did exist, but so did the opposite sense: 'draw back from a course of action, return to one's allegiance' (*OED* 2b). 'Still revolt' might therefore mean 'continually backslide'. This sense suits the Presbyterians, who had bawled for freedom from episcopacy, but shrank from reforming the divorce laws when God offered them the freedom they had asked for. This is not to deny that the modern sense of 'revolt' also asserts itself. Milton plays the two meanings against each other to imply that his conservative foes are the real rebels – against truth. Such a pun on 'revolt' is characteristic of Milton. He often uses it in his prose, and the Presbyterians are always his target.

The scholarly tradition of noting biblical and classical allusions in Milton's poetry began in 1695 with Patrick Hume's *Annotations on Milton's 'Paradise Lost'*. Hume's notes have a special claim to our attention, for they provide an insight into how an educated seventeenth-century reader responded to Milton's epic. Other valuable early editions include those of Zachary Pearce, the Jonathan Richardsons, and Thomas Newton. The greatest edition of recent decades is that of Alastair Fowler and John Carey. Every new edition is indebted to its predecessors, and the present text is no exception. It would be a mistake, however, to suppose that all of the analogues and allusions in the editorial tradition are the straightforward accumulation of centuries of disinterested inquiry. Recognizing an allusion is inescapably an interpretative act. Milton's editors, consciously or unconsciously, have privileged those analogues that most evidently support the poems' orthodox morality. The result is that Milton's allusive art has been made to seem more univocal than it really is. Editors and critics alike have tended to place too exclusive an emphasis on analogues that are safe. This is a pity because Milton's poetry draws much of its power from analogues that are unsafe. Sometimes an analogue will seem troublingly out of place. At other times, two or more analogues will compete for the same space. Obviously there is a danger of subjectivity here. Not everyone will agree about the pertinence of every supposed allusion. But it is not the case that safe allusions are always more obvious and accessible. Often it is the unsafe or problematic analogue that lies more readily to hand. In the notes to this edition I have tried to be open to problematic analogues in the belief that they invite interesting and liberating questions.

An example of a problematic analogue may be found in *A Masque* when the Second Brother expresses the fear that his sister might fall victim to sexual assault. The Elder Brother (who believes that virgins enjoy supernatural protection against assault) tries to assure his brother that there is nothing to worry about. At the climax of his speech he asks a rhetorical question:

> What was that snaky-headed Gorgon shield
> That wise Minerva wore, unconquered virgin,
> Wherewith she freezed her foes to cóngealed stone?
> But rigid looks of chaste austerity,
> And noble grace that dashed brute violence
> With sudden adoration, and blank awe. (447–52)

Merritt Hughes and John Carey both cite Natali Conti's *Mythologiae* IV v as the source for this allegorical interpretation of Minerva's shield. According to Conti, Minerva 'wore the Gorgon's head on her breast, because no one can turn his eyes against the light of the sun or against wisdom and remain unharmed'. One can see why editors would cite this reassuring analogue – even though 'wisdom' is something different from 'chaste austerity'. But the Elder Brother's rhetorical question invites more than one answer. The Elder Brother never names Medusa, but her story is immediately relevant both to Minerva's shield and to the debate between the two brothers. In *Metamorphoses* iv 790–803 Ovid relates that Medusa was a lovely maiden with beautiful hair until Neptune raped her in Minerva's temple. Outraged at the sacrilege, Minerva transformed Medusa into a Gorgon. The Elder Brother could hardly have chosen a less propitious mythical analogue. In the same breath that he mentions Medusa's shield, the Elder Brother mentions Diana's bow. He assumes that both weapons guarantee the inviolability of chaste persons, but a seventeenth-century reader might recall that in Claudian's *De Raptu Proserpinae* ii 204–8 the combined forces of Minerva's shield and Diana's bow failed to deter Pluto from ravishing Proserpine.

These analogues are of interest because they open the possibility that Milton might not have shared the Elder Brother's idealistic but naive views (views that are forgivable, even likeable, in an eleven-year-old boy, but alarming in a twenty-five-year-old man). Even if we prefer to see them as a subtext that infiltrates *A Masque* in Milton's despite, the analogues from Ovid and Claudian are still worth an editor's attention. They open possibilities, and invite critical questions, that are pre-empted if an editor hedges Milton's text with safe analogues drawn from such pedestrian sources as Conti.

Even when the traditional analogues are far from dull, they can present a one-sided perspective. Satan utters the following lines in a soliloquy when he first sees Adam and Eve:

> Hell shall unfold,
> To entertain you two, her widest gates,
> And send forth all her kings; there will be room,
> Not like these narrow limits, to receive
> Your numerous offspring.   (iv 381–5)

Most critics assume that Satan in these lines is being cruelly ironic. Editors usually (and quite rightly) note the suggestive echo of Isaiah's prophecy of the fall of Babylon:

> Hell from beneath is moved for thee to meet thee at thy coming: it stirreth up the dead for thee, even all the chief ones of the earth; it hath raised up from their thrones all the kings of the nations. (Isa. 14. 9)

This analogue does make Satan sound malevolent, but ironic statements (as William Empson always maintained) have no point unless they are true, to some degree, in both senses. Empson notoriously believed that Satan was sincere in offering Adam and Eve high honour in Hell.[4] Empson points out that the devils are able to live 'comfortably' in Hell, so Satan might not know that Hell will be a place of excruciating torture for human beings. Empson concludes that the irony in Satan's lines 'belongs only to the God who made Hell' (68).

Miltonists usually dismiss Empson's reading, but his intuition draws some support from a second possible allusion – one that editors have not noted. Satan echoes Isaiah, but he also echoes Pluto in Claudian's *De Raptu Proserpinae*. As Pluto carries Proserpine off in his chariot, he tries to console her by describing the honours that await her in Hades. He tells her not to miss the earth, for Hades is roomy (*immensum*), and even has its own sun and stars. This is close to Satan's contrast between earth's 'narrow limits' and Hell's 'room'. Pluto concludes: '*sub tua purpurei venient vestigia reges*', 'To thy feet shall come purple-robed kings' (ii 300). The resemblance between this line and 'send forth all her kings' is just about as close as that between Milton and Isaiah. Both analogues are appropriate to the moment, but they call forth different responses. The biblical echo makes Satan seem cruel; the classical one complicates the feeling because it suggests that Satan is capable of finer feelings even when he knowingly commits a wrong.

The Claudian analogue is not far-fetched. Only one hundred lines earlier Milton had likened Paradise to

> that fair field
> Of Enna, where Prosérpine gath'ring flow'rs
> Herself a fairer flow'r by gloomy Dis
> Was gathered.   (iv 268–71)

After this beautiful and memorable simile, it takes only a nudge to make us see Satan as Pluto (Dis), and Eve as Proserpine. Empson pushes Satan's soliloquy too far in the direction of generosity, but there is real insight in his intuition. Certainly, we cheapen the poem if we write Satan's speech off as mere 'sarcasm'.

From the foregoing examples it should be clear that the noting of analogues is a difficult and delicate task. This is especially true of the similes, many of which are borrowed from earlier epics, and so enter Milton's poem with a cluster of associations – some

excitingly troublesome. At the end of book iv of *Paradise Lost*
Milton likens the good angels (who are preparing to fight Satan) to
wind-tossed corn:

> th' angelic squadron bright
> Turned fiery red, sharp'ning in moonèd horns
> Their phalanx, and began to hem him round
> With ported spears, as thick as when a field
> Of Ceres ripe for harvest waving bends
> Her bearded grove of ears, which way the wind
> Sways them; the careful ploughman doubting stands
> Lest on the threshing floor his hopeful sheaves
> Prove chaff. (iv 977–85)

'It certainly makes the good angels look weak,' Empson remarks of
this simile[5] – and epic precedent supports his view. Homer, Apol-
lonius Rhodius, Ariosto and Tasso all compare armed warriors to
wind-tossed grain, and in every case the army so described is
demoralized, routed, or about to be cut down. Homer uses the
simile of the Greeks when they rush to their ships in despair of
conquering Troy:

> As when the west wind moves across the grain deep standing,
> boisterously, and shakes and sweeps it till the tassels lean, so all of
> that assembly was shaken, and the men in tumult swept to the ships.
> (*Iliad* ii 147–50)[6]

Milton's angels intend to stand and fight, but the words 'which way
the wind / Sways them' do not inspire much confidence in their
prowess. A seventeenth-century reader might recall that Tasso had
used the simile of wind and cornfield to describe Rinaldo cutting
down his enemies. Milton's wording directly recalls Edward Fair-
fax's translation of 1600:

> He brake their pikes, and brake their close array,
>   Entred their battaile, feld them downe around,
> So winde or tempest with impetious sway
>   The eares of ripened corn strikes flat to ground.
> (xx 60)

Editors have been reluctant to acknowledge these analogues. Fowler
briefly notes that 'the comparison of an excited army to wind-stirred

corn is Homeric', but he omits the detail that Homer's Greeks are deserting, and he makes no mention of Tasso. For Fowler, the real heart of Milton's simile is not the cornfield but the threshing-floor. Noting that this was a biblical metaphor for divine judgement, Fowler pertinently cites Jeremiah 51. 33: 'Babylon is like a threshing-floor, it is time to thresh her: yet a little while, and the time of her harvest shall come'. From this analogue, Fowler concludes that God as ploughman 'is *careful* that the final judgement, and the final reckoning with Satan, should not be premature'. Attractive as this reading is, it encounters an obstacle in Milton's words 'ripe for harvest' which suggest that the time of reckoning is now, not later. Pursuing the notion of judgement, Roy Flannagan sees an allusion to Matthew 3. 12 where John the Baptist prophesies Christ's final separation of the wheat from the chaff. To this we might add Psalm 1. 4 where 'the wicked' are 'as chaff which fanned / The wind drives' (Milton's translation). Yet even these analogues run into the difficulty that Milton has likened the *good* angels to 'a field / Of Ceres', so it is they, not Satan, who are in danger of becoming chaff.

Milton's analogues often work like this. Much as we editors would like to police them, they escape our control. My own candidate for a safe analogue (were I forced to choose one), would be Phineas Fletcher's *The Apollyonists* ii 40. Fletcher, like Milton, is describing Satan, who has just broken out of Hell, accompanied by a host of devils. These descend on our world as when the South wind

> sweeps with his dropping beard
> The ayer, earth, and Ocean; downe he flings
> The laden trees, the Plowmans hopes new-eard
> Swimme on the playne.

The connection with Milton is fortified by the ploughman, who here represents the peaceful world threatened by Satan's invasion. Critics have often tried to identify Milton's ploughman with God or Satan, but I suspect that Milton intended him to have much the same significance as Fletcher's. This does not mean that Fletcher's simile can drive all subversive possibilities from Milton's. Whatever Milton's conscious intentions, the classical and biblical analogues complicate his simile in ways that both trouble and enrich it. Throughout this edition I have endeavoured to annotate Milton's analogues in such a way as to permit rather than prohibit difficult questions. I do this not because I am determined on indeterminacy, but because I want to provide readers with the materials that will enable them to determine interpretative matters for themselves.

Throughout my notes I have assumed that Milton wrote the *De Doctrina Christiana*, even though William B. Hunter has argued that the traditional ascription of that work to Milton is unsafe.[7] Although I am unpersuaded by Hunter's arguments, I think they are valuable both for their own sake and for the excellent replies they have elicited from (among others) Christopher Hill, Maurice Kelley, Barbara Lewalski and John Shawcross.[8]

In preparing this edition I have received valuable help and guidance from many learned colleagues, as well as from graduate and undergraduate students at the University of Western Ontario. I owe a special debt to Gordon Campbell, John Creaser, Roy Flannagan, and Christopher Ricks, both for their own work as editors and for their advice on numerous points of detail. I have also received generous assistance from Christopher Brown, Gardner Campbell, Dennis Danielson, Richard Green, John Hale, Jeremy Maule, Diane McColley, Earl Miner and Alan Rudrum. My work has been greatly assisted by a grant from the Social Science and Humanities Research Council of Canada. To the Council I extend my sincerest thanks.

Notes

1. John Creaser, 'Editorial Problems in Milton', *RES* 34 (1983) 279–303 and *RES* 35 (1984) 45–60.
2. William Empson, *Some Versions of Pastoral* (1935) 163.
3. Hunter's essay was first published in *Essays in Honor of Walter Clyde Curry* (1954). It is reprinted in *The Descent of Urania: Studies in Milton, 1946–1988* (1989), 224–42.
4. Empson makes the point in all three of his major works on Milton. See *Milton's God* (1961) 68, *Some Versions of Pastoral* (1935) 168, and *The Structure of Complex Words* (1951) 103,
5. *Some Versions of Pastoral* (1935) 172.
6. *The Iliad of Homer*, trans. Richmond Lattimore (1951).
7. Hunter makes his case against Milton's authorship of the *De Doctrina*

Christiana in *SEL* 32 (1992), 129–42, *SEL* 33 (1993), 191–207, and *SEL* 34 (1994), 195–203.

8. For the replies by Lewalski and Shawcross, see *SEL* 32 (1992), 143–54 and 155–62. For the replies by Hill and Kelley, see *SEL* 34 (1994), 165–93 and 195–203.

TABLE OF DATES

Unless otherwise stated, Milton's works are listed by date of publication.

1608 (9 December) M. born in his father's house, Bread Street, Cheapside, London.

1615 (24 November) Brother Christopher born.

1620 (?) Enters St Paul's School. Friendship with Charles Diodati begins. Thomas Young begins to tutor M. at home at about this time.

1625 (12 February) Matriculates at Christ's College, Cambridge. March: Charles I becomes King.

1626 Probably rusticated (suspended) from Cambridge for part of the Lent term.

1629 (March) BA degree. December: writes *On the Morning of Christ's Nativity*.

1632 *On Shakespeare* published in second Shakespeare folio. July: MA degree.

1632–8 Life of scholarly retirement at family homes in Hammersmith and Horton.

1633 William Laud becomes Archbishop of Canterbury.

1634 (29 September) *A Masque* performed at Ludlow Castle.

1637 *A Masque* published. 3 April: mother dies. 30 June: Bastwick, Burton and Prynne lose their ears for writing anti-prelatical pamphlets. They are confined in prison ships on the Irish Sea throughout the autumn. 10 August: M.'s classmate Edward King drowns on the Irish Sea. November: writes *Lycidas*.

1638 (April)–1639 (August) Continental tour.

1638 *Lycidas* published in a volume of elegies for Edward King. August: Charles Diodati dies.

1639 (March) War with Scotland (First Bishops' War).

1639–40 Settles in London where he takes pupils, including his nephews Edward and John Phillips.

1640 (August) Second Bishops' War. 3 November: Long Parliament convened. Laud and Strafford impeached.

1641 Publication of first anti-prelatical pamphlets: *Of Reformation, Of Prelatical Episcopacy, Animadversions upon the Remonstrant's Defence*. Rebellion in Ireland.

1642 More anti-prelatical pamphlets: *The Reason of Church Government, An Apology for Smectymnuus*. May–June: marries Mary Powell, who left him a month or two later. 22 August: Civil War begins.

1643 *The Doctrine and Discipline of Divorce* (first edition).

1644 (February) *The Doctrine and Discipline of Divorce* (second edition). Thomas Young, M.'s old tutor, warns Parliament against advocates of 'digamy'. June: *Of Education*. August: *Judgement of Martin Bucer Concerning Divorce*. Herbert Palmer denounces M. in sermon before Parliament. Further attacks from the Stationers' Company, from Prynne and other Presbyterians. November: *Areopagitica*. December: M. summoned before the House of Lords, but soon dismissed.

1645 *Tetrachordon* and *Colasterion* published. June: Cromwell's New Model Army victorious at Naseby. July or August: M.'s wife returns. September(?): moves to a larger house in the Barbican.

1646 (January) *Poems of Mr. John Milton* published (dated 1645). 29 July: daughter Anne born.

1647 (13 March) Father dies.

1648 (25 October) Daughter Mary born. 6 December: Colonel Pride's Purge of Long Parliament.

1649 (30 January) Charles I executed. *Eikon Basilike* (then given out as by the King) published one week later. 13 February: *The Tenure of Kings and Magistrates*. March: M. appointed Secretary for Foreign Tongues by the Council of State. 11 May: Salmasius's *Defensio Regia* appears in England. 16 May: *Observations on the Articles of Peace*. 6 October: *Eikonoklastes* (M.'s answer to *Eikon Basilike*).

1651 (24 February) *Pro Populo Anglicano Defensio* (M.'s answer to Salmasius). 16 March: son John born.

1652 Becomes totally blind. 2 May: daughter Deborah born. Wife dies three days later. June: son John dies.

1653 (20 April) Cromwell forcibly dissolves Rump Parliament.

FURTHER READING

Editions

Richard Bentley, *Milton's 'Paradise Lost'*, 1732.

Cleanth Brooks and J. E. Hardy, *Poems of Mr. John Milton: the 1645 Edition with Essays in Analysis*, Harcourt, Brace, 1951.

Douglas Bush, *Milton: Poetical Works*, Oxford University Press, 1966.

Gordon Campbell, *John Milton: Complete English Poems, Of Education, Areopagitica*, Dent, 1990.

John Carey and Alastair Fowler, *Poems of John Milton*, Longman, 1968; revised 1980.

Scott Elledge, *John Milton: 'Paradise Lost'*, Norton, 1975; 2nd edn, 1993.

Roy Flannagan, *John Milton: 'Paradise Lost'*, Macmillan, 1993.

Harris F. Fletcher, *Milton's Complete Poetical Works in Photographic Facsimile*, 4 vols., University of Illinois Press, 1943–8.

Fowler. See above, under 'Carey'.

E. A. J. Honigmann, *Milton's Sonnets*, Macmillan, 1966.

Merritt Y. Hughes, *John Milton: Complete Poems and Major Prose*, Odyssey, 1957.

P[atrick] H[ume], *Annotations on Milton's 'Paradise Lost'*, 1695.

David Masson, *The Poetical Works of John Milton*, 3 vols., 1893.

Thomas Newton, *'Paradise Lost': a Poem in Twelve Books*, 1749.

Stephen Orgel and Jonathan Goldberg, *The Oxford Authors: John Milton*, Oxford University Press, 1990.

Zachary Pearce, *A Review of the Text of 'Paradise Lost'*, 1733.

F. T. Prince, *Milton: 'Samson Agonistes'*, Oxford University Press, 1957.

Jonathan Richardson, sen. and jun., *Explanatory Notes on 'Paradise Lost'*, 1734.

Christopher Ricks, *John Milton: 'Paradise Lost' and 'Paradise Regained'*, Signet Classics, 1968.

John T. Shawcross, *The Complete Poetry of John Milton*, Anchor-Doubleday, 1971.

John Smart, *The Sonnets of Milton*, Maclehose, Jackson, 1921.

S. E. Sprott, *John Milton, 'A Maske': the Earlier Versions*, University of Toronto Press, 1973.

Thomas Warton, *Poems upon Several Occasions . . . by John Milton*, 1791.

Don M. Wolfe (general ed.), *The Complete Prose Works of John Milton*, Yale University Press, 1953–82.

Biographies

Cedric Brown, *John Milton: a Literary Life*, St Martin's Press, 1995.

Helen Darbishire (ed.), *The Early Lives of Milton*, Constable, 1932; repr. Scholarly Press, 1972.

David Masson, *The Life of John Milton: Narrated in Connexion with the Political, Ecclesiastical, and Literary History of His Time*, 7 vols., Macmillan, 1859–94.

William Riley Parker, *Milton: a Biography*, 2 vols., Oxford University Press, 1968.

Critical Studies

Sharon Achinstein, *Milton and the Revolutionary Reader*, Princeton University Press, 1994.

Robert M. Adams, *Ikon: John Milton and the Modern Critics*, Cornell University Press, 1955.

Don Cameron Allen, *The Harmonious Vision: Studies in Milton's Poetry*, Johns Hopkins Press, 1954.

Michael Bauman, *Milton's Arianism*, Lang, 1987.

Joan Bennett, *Reviving Liberty: Radical Christian Humanism in Milton's Great Poems*, Harvard University Press, 1989.

Cedric Brown, *John Milton's Aristocratic Entertainments*, Cambridge University Press, 1985.

Dennis Burden, *The Logical Epic: a Study of the Argument of 'Paradise Lost'*, Harvard University Press, 1967.

Thomas N. Corns, *Milton's Language*, Basil Blackwell, 1990.

John Creaser, 'Editorial Problems in Milton', *Review of English Studies* n.s. 34 (1983), 279–303 and 35 (1984), 45–60.

Dennis Danielson, *Milton's Good God*, Cambridge University Press, 1982.

——, 'Through the Telescope of Typology: What Adam Should Have Done', *Milton Quarterly* 23 (1989), 121–7.

William Empson, *Milton's God*, Chatto & Windus, 1961, rev. edn 1965.

——, *Some Versions of Pastoral*, Chatto & Windus, 1935.

J. Martin Evans, *'Paradise Lost' and the Genesis Tradition*, Clarendon Press, 1968.

——, *The Road from Horton: Looking Backwards in 'Lycidas'*, University of Victoria Press, 1983.

——, *Milton's Imperial Epic: 'Paradise Lost' and the Discourse of Colonialism*, Cornell University Press, 1996.

Stephen M. Fallon, *Milton among the Philosophers*, Cornell University Press, 1991.

Stanley Eugene Fish, *Surprised by Sin: the Reader in 'Paradise Lost'*, St Martin's Press, 1967; University of California Press, 1971.

Christopher Hill, *Milton and the English Revolution*, Faber and Faber, 1977.

William B. Hunter, *The Descent of Urania: Studies in Milton, 1946–1988*, Bucknell University Press, 1989.

—— 'Milton's Arianism Reconsidered', in *Bright Essence: Studies in Milton's Theology*, ed. William B. Hunter, C. A. Patrides and J. H. Adamson, University of Utah Press, 1971.

Maurice Kelley, *This Great Argument: a Study of Milton's 'De Doctrina Christiana' as a Gloss upon 'Paradise Lost'*, Princeton University Press, 1941.

William Kerrigan, *The Sacred Complex: on the Psychogenesis of 'Paradise Lost'*, Harvard University Press, 1983.

Watson Kirkconnell, *The Celestial Cycle: the Theme of 'Paradise Lost' in World Literature with Translations of the Major Analogues*, University of Toronto Press, 1952.

F. M. Krouse, *Milton's Samson and the Christian Tradition*, Princeton University Press, 1949.

Edward Le Comte, *Milton and Sex*, Columbia University Press, 1978.

John Leonard, *Naming in Paradise: Milton and the Language of Adam and Eve*, Clarendon Press, 1990.

——, 'Saying "No" to Freud: Milton's *A Mask* and Sexual Assault', *Milton Quarterly* 25 (1991), 129–39.

Barbara K. Lewalski, *Milton's Brief Epic*, Brown University Press, 1966.

——, *'Paradise Lost' and the Rhetoric of Literary Forms*, Princeton University Press, 1985.

C. S. Lewis, *A Preface to 'Paradise Lost'*, Oxford University Press, 1942.

Michael Lieb, *Poetics of the Holy: a Reading of 'Paradise Lost'*, University of North Carolina Press, 1981.

——, *Milton and the Culture of Violence*, Cornell University Press, 1994.

David Loewenstein, *Milton and the Drama of History*, Cambridge University Press, 1990.

Isabel MacCaffrey, *'Paradise Lost' as Myth*, Harvard University Press, 1959.

Hugh MacCallum, *Milton and the Sons of God*, University of Toronto Press, 1986.

Leah Sinanoglou Marcus, 'The Milieu of Milton's *Comus*: Judicial Reform at Ludlow and the Problem of Sexual Assault', *Criticism* 25 (1983), 293–327.

Harinder S. Marjara, *Contemplation of Created Things: Science in 'Paradise Lost'*, University of Toronto Press, 1992.

Charles Martindale, *John Milton and the Transformation of Ancient Epic*, Barnes & Noble, 1986.

Louis Martz, *Milton: Poet of Exile*, Yale University Press, 1980; second edn, 1986.

Diane K. McColley, *Milton's Eve*, University of Illinois Press, 1983.

R. G. Moyles, *The Text of 'Paradise Lost': a Study in Editorial Procedure*, University of Toronto Press, 1985.

Annabel Patterson, 'That Old Man Eloquent', in *Literary Milton: Text, Pretext, Context*, ed. Diane Trevino Benet and Michael Lieb, Duquesne University Press, 1994.

John Peter, *A Critique of 'Paradise Lost'*, Columbia University Press, 1960.

Elizabeth Pope, *'Paradise Regained': the Tradition and the Poem*, Johns Hopkins Press, 1947.

William Porter, *Reading the Classics and 'Paradise Lost'*, Nebraska University Press, 1993.

F. T. Prince, *The Italian Element in Milton's Verse*, Oxford University Press, 1954.

David Quint, *Epic and Empire: Politics and Generic Form from Virgil to Milton*, Princeton University Press, 1993.

Mary Ann Radzinowicz, *Toward 'Samson Agonistes': the Growth of Milton's Mind*, Princeton University Press, 1978.

Balachandra Rajan, *'Paradise Lost' and the Seventeenth-Century Reader*, Chatto & Windus, 1947.

Stella Purce Revard, *The War in Heaven: 'Paradise Lost' and the Tradition of Satan's Rebellion*, Cornell University Press, 1980.

Christopher Ricks, *Milton's Grand Style*, Clarendon Press, 1963.

John P. Rumrich, *Matter of Glory: a New Preface to 'Paradise Lost'*, University of Pittsburgh Press, 1987.

——, *Milton Unbound: Controversy and Reinterpretation*, Cambridge University Press, 1996.

Ashraf A. Rushdy, *The Empty Garden*, University of Pittsburgh Press, 1992.

Regina Schwartz, *Remembering and Repeating: Biblical Creation in 'Paradise Lost'*, Cambridge University Press, 1988.

John M. Steadman, *Epic and Tragic Structure in 'Paradise Lost'*, University of Chicago Press, 1976.

Arnold Stein, *Answerable Style: Essays on 'Paradise Lost'*, University of Minnesota Press, 1953.

Kester Svendsen, *Milton and Science*, Harvard University Press, 1956.

John S. Tanner, *Anxiety in Eden: a Kierkegaardian Reading of 'Paradise Lost'*, Clarendon Press, 1993.

Rosemond Tuve, *Images and Themes in Five Poems by Milton*, Harvard University Press, 1957.

A. J. A. Waldock, *'Paradise Lost' and its Critics*, Cambridge University Press, 1947.

R. H. West, *Milton and the Angels*, University of Georgia Press, 1955.

Arnold Williams, *The Common Expositor: an Account of the Commentaries on Genesis 1527–1633*, University of North Carolina Press, 1948.

Joseph Wittreich, *Interpreting 'Samson Agonistes'*, Princeton University Press, 1986.

A. S. P. Woodhouse, 'Theme and Pattern in *Paradise Regained*', *UTQ* 25 (1956), 167–82.

On the Morning of Christ's Nativity. Composed 1629.

I
This is the month, and this the happy morn
Wherein the Son of Heav'n's eternal King,
Of wedded maid, and virgin mother born,
Our great redemption from above did bring;
5   For so the holy sages once did sing,
        That he our deadly forfeit should release,
And with his Father work us a perpetual peace.

II
That glorious form, that light unsufferable,
And that far-beaming blaze of majesty,
10   Wherewith he wont at Heav'n's high council table,
To sit the midst of trinal unity,
He laid aside; and here with us to be,
        Forsook the courts of everlasting day,
And chose with us a darksome house of mortal clay.

III
15   Say Heav'nly Muse, shall not thy sacred vein
Afford a present to the infant God?
Hast thou no verse, no hymn, or solemn strain,
To welcome him to this his new abode,
Now while the heav'n by the sun's team untrod,
20   Hath took no print of the approaching light,
And all the spangled host keep watch in squadrons bright?

IV
See how from far upon the eastern road
The star-led wizards haste with odours sweet:
O run, prevent them with thy humble ode,
25   And lay it lowly at his blessèd feet;

Have thou the honour first, thy Lord to greet,
  And join thy voice unto the angel choir,
From out his secret altar touched with hallowed fire.

The Hymn

I

It was the winter wild,
30 While the Heav'n-born-child,
    All meanly wrapped in the rude manger lies;
Nature in awe to him
Had doffed her gaudy trim,
    With her great Master so to sympathize:
35 It was no season then for her
To wanton with the sun her lusty paramour.

II

Only with speeches fair
She woos the gentle air
    To hide her guilty front with innocent snow,
40 And on her naked shame,
Pollute with sinful blame,
    The saintly veil of maiden white to throw,
Confounded, that her Maker's eyes
Should look so near upon her foul deformities.

III

45 But he her fears to cease,
Sent down the meek-eyed Peace;
    She crowned with olive green, came softly sliding
Down through the turning sphere
His ready harbinger,
50   With turtle wing the amorous clouds dividing.
And waving wide her myrtle wand,
She strikes a universal peace through sea and land.

IV

No war, or battle's sound
Was heard the world around:
    The idle spear and shield were high up hung;
The hookèd chariot stood
Unstained with hostile blood,
    The trumpet spake not to the armèd throng,
And kings sat still with awful eye,
As if they surely knew their sov'reign Lord was by.

V

But peaceful was the night
Wherein the Prince of Light
    His reign of peace upon the earth began:
The winds with wonder whist,
Smoothly the waters kissed,
    Whispering new joys to the mild Oceán,
Who now hath quite forgot to rave,
While birds of calm sit brooding on the charmèd wave.

VI

The stars with deep amaze
Stand fixed in steadfast gaze,
    Bending one way their precious influence,
And will not take their flight,
For all the morning light,
    Or Lucifer that often warned them thence;
But in their glimmering orbs did glow,
Until their Lord himself bespake, and bid them go.

VII

And though the shady gloom
Had given day her room,
    The sun himself withheld his wonted speed,
And hid his head for shame,
As his inferior flame,
    The new-enlightened world no more should need;
He saw a greater Sun appear
Than his bright throne, or burning axle-tree could bear.

VIII

85 The shepherds on the lawn,
Or ere the point of dawn,
   Sat simply chatting in a rustic row;
Full little thought they then,
That the mighty Pan
90   Was kindly come to live with them below;
Perhaps their loves, or else their sheep,
Was all that did their silly thoughts so busy keep.

IX

When such music sweet
Their hearts and ears did greet,
95   As never was by mortal finger strook,
Divinely-warbled voice
Answering the stringèd noise,
   As all their souls in blissful rapture took:
The air such pleasure loath to lose,
100 With thousand echoes still prolongs each Heav'nly close.

X

Nature that heard such sound
Beneath the hollow round
   Of Cynthia's seat, the airy region thrilling,
Now was almost won
105 To think her part was done,
   And that her reign had here its last fulfilling;
She knew such harmony alone
Could hold all Heav'n and earth in happier union.

XI

At last surrounds their sight
110 A globe of circular light,
   That with long beams the shame-faced night arrayed;
The helmèd Cherubim
And sworded Seraphim,
   Are seen in glittering ranks with wings displayed,
115 Harping in loud and solemn choir,
With unexpressive notes to Heav'n's new-born heir.

XII

Such music (as 'tis said)
Before was never made,
   But when of old the sons of morning sung,
120 While the Creator great
His constellations set,
   And the well-balanced world on hinges hung,
And cast the dark foundations deep,
And bid the welt'ring waves their oozy channel keep.

XIII

125 Ring out ye crystal spheres,
Once bless our human ears,
   (If ye have power to touch our senses so)
And let your silver chime
Move in melodious time;
130   And let the base of heav'n's deep organ blow,
And with your ninefold harmony
Make up full consort to th' angelic symphony.

XIV

For if such holy song
Enwrap our fancy long,
135   Time will run back, and fetch the age of gold,
And speckled Vanity
Will sicken soon and die,
   And lep'rous Sin will melt from earthly mould,
And Hell itself will pass away,
140 And leave her dolorous mansions to the peering day.

XV

Yea Truth, and Justice then
Will down return to men,
   Orbed in a rainbow; and, like glories wearing,
Mercy will sit between,
145 Throned in celestial sheen,
   With radiant feet the tissued clouds down steering,
And Heav'n as at some festival,
Will open wide the gates of her high palace hall.

XVI

But wisest Fate says no,
150 This must not yet be so,
    The babe yet lies in smiling infancy,
That on the bitter cross
Must redeem our loss;
    So both himself and us to glorify:
155 Yet first to those ychained in sleep,
The wakeful trump of doom must thunder through the
    deep.

XVII

With such a horrid clang
As on Mount Sinai rang
    While the red fire, and smould'ring clouds out brake:
160 The agèd earth aghast
With terror of the blast,
    Shall from the surface to the centre shake;
When at the world's last sessïon,
The dreadful Judge in middle air shall spread his throne.

XVIII

165 And then at last our bliss
Full and perfect is,
    But now begins; for from this happy day
Th' old Dragon under ground
In straiter limits bound,
170   Not half so far casts his usurpèd sway,
And wrath to see his kingdom fail,
Swinges the scaly horror of his folded tail.

XIX

The oracles are dumb,
No voice or hideous hum
175   Runs through the archèd roof in words deceiving.
Apollo from his shrine
Can no more divine,
    With hollow shriek the steep of Delphos leaving.

No nightly trance, or breathèd spell,
180 Inspires the pale-eyed priest from the prophetic cell.

XX
The lonely mountains o'er,
And the resounding shore,
    A voice of weeping heard, and loud lament;
From haunted spring, and dale
185 Edged with poplar pale.
    The parting Genius is with sighing sent,
With flow'r-inwoven tresses torn
The nymphs in twilight shade of tangled thickets mourn.

XXI
In consecrated earth,
190 And on the holy hearth,
    The lars and lemures moan with midnight plaint;
In urns, and altars round,
A drear, and dying sound
    Affrights the flamens at their service quaint;
195 And the chill marble seems to sweat,
While each peculiar power forgoes his wonted seat.

XXII
Peor, and Baälim,
Forsake their temples dim,
    With that twice-battered god of Palestine,
200 And moonèd Ashtaroth,
Heav'n's queen and mother both,
    Now sits not girt with tapers' holy shine;
The Libyc Hammon shrinks his horn,
In vain the Tyrian maids their wounded Thammuz
        mourn.

XXIII
205 And sullen Moloch fled,
Hath left in shadows dread,
    His burning idol all of blackest hue;

In vain with cymbals' ring,
They call the grisly king,
210   In dismal dance about the furnace blue;
The brutish gods of Nile as fast,
Isis and Orus, and the dog Anubis haste.

XXIV
Nor is Osiris seen
In Memphian grove, or green,
215   Trampling the unshow'red grass with lowings loud:
Nor can he be at rest
Within his sacred chest,
    Naught but profoundest Hell can be his shroud,
In vain with timbrelled anthems dark
220   The sable-stolèd sorcerers bear his worshipped ark.

XXV
He feels from Judah's land
The dreaded infant's hand,
    The rays of Bethlehem blind his dusky eyn;
Nor all the gods beside,
225   Longer dare abide,
    Not Typhon huge ending in snaky twine:
Our babe to show his Godhead true,
Can in his swaddling bands control the damnèd crew.

XXVI
So when the sun in bed,
230   Curtained with cloudy red,
    Pillows his chin upon an orient wave,
The flocking shadows pale,
Troop to th' infernal jail,
    Each fettered ghost slips to his several grave,
235   And the yellow-skirted fays,
Fly after the Night-steeds, leaving their moon-loved
        maze.

XXVII
But see the virgin blest,
Hath laid her babe to rest.
      Time is our tedious song should here have ending;
240   Heav'n's youngest teemèd star,
Hath fixed her polished car.
      Her sleeping Lord with handmaid lamp attending.
And all about the courtly stable,
Bright-harnessed angels sit in order serviceable.

A Paraphrase on Psalm 114

*This and the following Psalm were done by the author at
fifteen years old.*

When the blest seed of Terah's faithful son,
After long toil their liberty had won,
And passed from Pharian fields to Canaan land,
Led by the strength of the Almighty's hand,
5   Jehovah's wonders were in Israel shown,
His praise and glory was in Israel known.
That saw the troubled sea, and shivering fled,
And sought to hide his froth-becurlèd head
Low in the earth; Jordan's clear streams recoil,
10   As a faint host that hath received the foil.
The high, huge-bellied mountains skip like rams
Among their ewes, the little hills like lambs.
Why fled the ocean? And why skipped the mountains?
Why turnèd Jordan toward his crystal fountains?
15   Shake earth, and at the presence be aghast
Of him that ever was, and ay shall last,
That glassy floods from rugged rocks can crush,
And make soft rills from fiery flint-stones gush.

Psalm 136

Let us with a gladsome mind
Praise the Lord, for he is kind,
   For his mercies ay endure,
   Ever faithful, ever sure.

5   Let us blaze his name abroad,
For of gods he is the God;
   For, &c.

O let us his praises tell,
10 That doth the wrathful tyrants quell.
   For, &c.

That with his miracles doth make
Amazèd heav'n and earth to shake.
15   For, &c.

That by his wisdom did create
The painted heav'ns so full of state.
19   For, &c.

That did the solid earth ordain
To rise above the wat'ry plain.
   For, &c.

25 That by his all-commanding might,
Did fill the new-made world with light.
   For, &c.

And caused the golden-tressèd sun,
30 All the day long his course to run.
   For, &c.

The hornèd moon to shine by night,
Amongst her spangled sisters bright.
35   For, &c.

He with his thunder-clasping hand,
Smote the first-born of Egypt land.
39   For, &c.

And in despite of Pharaoh fell,
He brought from thence his Israël.
        For, &c.

45   The ruddy waves he cleft in twain,
Of the Erythraean main.
        For, &c.

The floods stood still like walls of glass,
50   While the Hebrew bands did pass.
        For, &c.

But full soon they did devour
The tawny king with all his power.
55   For, &c.

His chosen people he did bless
In the wasteful wilderness.
59   For, &c.

In bloody battle he brought down
Kings of prowess and renown.
        For, &c.

65   He foiled bold Seon and his host,
That ruled the Amorean coast.
        For, &c.

And large-limbed Og he did subdue,
70   With all his over-hardy crew.
        For, &c.

And to his servant Israël
He gave their land therein to dwell.
75   For, &c.

He hath with a piteous eye
Beheld us in our misery.
79   For, &c.

And freed us from the slavery
Of the invading enemy.
       For, &c.

85   All living creatures he doth feed,
And with full hand supplies their need.
       For, &c.

Let us therefore warble forth
90   His mighty majesty and worth.
       For, &c.

That his mansion hath on high
Above the reach of mortal eye.
95   For his mercies ay endure,
         Ever faithful, ever sure.

The Passion

I
Erewhile of music, and ethereal mirth,
Wherewith the stage of air and earth did ring,
And joyous news of Heav'nly infant's birth,
My Muse with angels did divide to sing;
5   But headlong joy is ever on the wing,
         In wintry solstice like the shortened light
Soon swallowed up in dark and long out-living night.

II
For now to sorrow must I tune my song,
And set my harp to notes of saddest woe,
10   Which on our dearest Lord did seize ere long,
Dangers, and snares, and wrongs, and worse than so,

Which he for us did freely undergo.
    Most perfect hero, tried in heaviest plight
Of labours huge and hard, too hard for human wight.

III

15 He sov'reign priest stooping his regal head
That dropped with odorous oil down his fair eyes,
Poor fleshly tabernacle enterèd,
His starry front low-roofed beneath the skies;
O what a mask was there, what a disguise!
20   Yet more; the stroke of death he must abide,
Then lies him meekly down fast by his brethren's side.

IV

These latter scenes confine my roving verse,
To this horizon is my Phoebus bound.
His Godlike acts, and his temptations fierce,
25 And former sufferings otherwhere are found;
Loud o'er the rest Cremona's trump doth sound;
    Me softer airs befit, and softer strings
Of lute, or viol still, more apt for mournful things.

V

Befriend me Night best patroness of grief,
30 Over the pole thy thickest mantle throw,
And work my flattered fancy to belief,
That heav'n and earth are coloured with my woe;
My sorrows are too dark for day to know:
    The leaves should all be black whereon I write,
35 And letters where my tears have washed a wannish white.

VI

See see the chariot, and those rushing wheels,
That whirled the prophet up at Chebar flood;
My spirit some transporting Cherub feels,
To bear me where the towers of Salem stood,
40 Once glorious towers, now sunk in guiltless blood;
    There doth my soul in holy vision sit
In pensive trance, and anguish, and ecstatic fit.

VII

Mine eye hath found that sad sepulchral rock
That was the casket of Heav'n's richest store,
45 And here though grief my feeble hands uplock,
Yet on the softened quarry would I score
My plaining verse as lively as before;
    For sure so well instructed are my tears,
That they would fitly fall in ordered characters.

VIII

50 Or should I thence hurried on viewless wing,
Take up a weeping on the mountains wild,
The gentle neighbourhood of grove and spring
Would soon unbosom all their echoes mild,
And I (for grief is easily beguiled)
55   Might think th' infection of my sorrows loud,
Had got a race of mourners on some pregnant cloud.

*This subject the author finding to be above the years he had, when
he wrote it, and nothing satisfied with what was begun, left it
unfinished.*

On Time

Fly envious Time, till thou run out thy race,
Call on the lazy leaden-stepping hours,
Whose speed is but the heavy plummet's pace;
And glut thyself with what thy womb devours,
5 Which is no more than what is false and vain,
And merely mortal dross;
So little is our loss,
So little is thy gain.
For when as each thing bad thou hast entombed,
10 And last of all, thy greedy self consumed,
Then long eternity shall greet our bliss
With an individual kiss;

And joy shall overtake us as a flood,
When everything that is sincerely good
15   And perfectly divine,
With Truth, and Peace, and Love shall ever shine
About the súpreme throne
Of him, t' whose happy-making sight alone,
When once our Heav'nly-guided soul shall climb,
20   Then all this earthy grossness quit,
Attired with stars, we shall for ever sit,
     Triumphing over Death, and Chance, and thee O Time.

Upon the Circumcision

Ye flaming Powers, and wingèd warriors bright,
That erst with music, and triumphant song
First heard by happy watchful shepherds' ear,
So sweetly sung your joy the clouds along
5   Through the soft silence of the list'ning night;
Now mourn, and if sad share with us to bear
Your fiery essence can distil no tear,
Burn in your sighs, and borrow
Seas wept from our deep sorrow;
10   He who with all Heav'n's heraldry whilere
Entered the world, now bleeds to give us ease;
Alas, how soon our sin
     Sore doth begin
          His infancy to seize!
15   O more exceeding love or law more just?
Just law indeed, but more exceeding love!
For we by rightful doom remédiless
Were lost in death, till he that dwelt above
High throned in secret bliss, for us frail dust
20   Emptied his glory, ev'n to nakedness;
And that great cov'nant which we still transgress
Entirely satisfied,
And the full wrath beside
Of vengeful justice bore for our excess,

25   And seals obedience first with wounding smart
        This day, but O ere long,
            Huge pangs and strong
                Will pierce more near his heart.

At a Solemn Music

        Blest pair of Sirens, pledges of Heav'n's joy,
        Sphere-borne harmonious sisters, Voice, and Verse,
        Wed your divine sounds, and mixed power employ
        Dead things with inbreathed sense able to pierce,
5   And to our high-raised fantasy present,
        That undisturbèd song of pure concent,
        Ay sung before the sapphire-coloured throne
        To him that sits thereon
        With saintly shout, and solemn jubilee,
10   Where the bright Seraphim in burning row
        Their loud uplifted angel trumpets blow,
        And the Cherubic host in thousand choirs
        Touch their immortal harps of golden wires,
        With those just spirits that wear victorious palms,
15   Hymns devout and holy psalms
        Singing everlastingly;
        That we on earth with undiscording voice
        May rightly answer that melodious noise;
        As once we did, till disproportioned sin
20   Jarred against Nature's chime, and with harsh din
        Broke the fair music that all creatures made
        To their great Lord, whose love their motion swayed
        In perfect diapason, whilst they stood
        In first obedience, and their state of good.
25   O may we soon again renew that song,
        And keep in tune with Heav'n, till God ere long
        To his celestial consort us unite,
        To live with him, and sing in endless morn of light.

An Epitaph on the Marchioness of Winchester

This rich marble doth inter
The honoured wife of Winchester,
A viscount's daughter, an earl's heir,
Besides what her virtues fair
5   Added to her noble birth,
More than she could own from earth.
Summers three times eight save one
She had told; alas too soon,
After so short time of breath,
10   To house with darkness, and with death.
Yet had the number of her days
Been as complete as was her praise,
Nature and fate had had no strife
In giving limit to her life.
15   Her high birth, and her graces sweet,
Quickly found a lover meet;
The virgin choir for her request
The god that sits at marriage feast;
He at their invoking came
20   But with a scarce-well-lighted flame;
And in his garland as he stood,
Ye might discern a cypress bud.
Once had the early matrons run
To greet her of a lovely son,
25   And now with second hope she goes,
And calls Lucina to her throes;
But whether by mischance or blame
Atropos for Lucina came;
And with remorseless cruelty,
30   Spoiled at once both fruit and tree:
The hapless babe before his birth
Had burial, yet not laid in earth,
And the languished mother's womb
Was not long a living tomb.
35   So have I seen some tender slip
Saved with care from winter's nip,

The pride of her carnation train,
Plucked up by some unheedy swain,
Who only thought to crop the flow'r
40   New shot up from vernal show'r;
But the fair blossom hangs the head
Sideways as on a dying bed,
And those pearls of dew she wears,
Prove to be presaging tears
45   Which the sad morn had let fall
On her hast'ning funeral.
Gentle lady may thy grave
Peace and quiet ever have;
After this thy travail sore
50   Sweet rest seize thee evermore,
That to give the world increase,
Shortened hast thy own life's lease;
Here, besides the sorrowing
That thy noble house doth bring,
55   Here be tears of perfect moan
Wept for thee in Helicon,
And some flowers, and some bays,
For thy hairs to strew the ways,
Sent thee from the banks of Came,
60   Devoted to thy virtuous name;
Whilst thou bright saint high sitt'st in glory,
Next her much like to thee in story,
That fair Syrian shepherdess,
Who after years of barrenness,
65   The highly favoured Joseph bore
To him that served for her before,
And at her next birth much like thee,
Through pangs fled to felicity,
Far within the bosom bright
70   Of blazing majesty and light;
There with thee, new-welcome saint,
Like fortune may her soul acquaint,
With thee there clad in radiant sheen,
No marchioness, but now a queen.

Song. On May Morning

Now the bright morning star, day's harbinger,
Comes dancing from the east, and leads with her
The flowery May, who from her green lap throws
The yellow cowslip, and the pale primrose.
5   Hail bounteous May that dost inspire
     Mirth and youth, and warm desire;
     Woods and groves are of thy dressing,
     Hill and dale doth boast thy blessing.
Thus we salute thee with our early song,
10 And welcome thee, and wish thee long.

On Shakespeare. 1630

What needs my Shakespeare for his honoured bones,
The labour of an age in pilèd stones,
Or that his hallowed relics should be hid
Under a star-ypointing pyramid?
5 Dear son of Memory, great heir of fame,
What need'st thou such weak witness of thy name?
Thou in our wonder and astonishment
Hast built thyself a live-long monument.
For whilst to th' shame of slow-endeavouring art,
10 Thy easy numbers flow, and that each heart
Hath from the leaves of thy unvalued book,
Those Delphic lines with deep impression took,
Then thou, our fancy of itself bereaving,
Dost make us marble with too much conceiving;
15 And so sepúlchred in such pomp dost lie,
That kings for such a tomb would wish to die.

On the University Carrier

Who sickened in the time of his vacancy, being forbid to go to London, by reason of the plague.

Here lies old Hobson, Death hath broke his girt,
And here alas, hath laid him in the dirt;
Or else the ways being foul, twenty to one,
He's here stuck in a slough, and overthrown.
5   'Twas such a shifter, that if the truth were known,
Death was half glad when he had got him down;
For he had any time this ten years full,
Dodged with him, betwixt Cambridge and the Bull.
And surely, Death could never have prevailed,
10   Had not his weekly course of carriage failed;
But lately finding him so long at home,
And thinking now his journey's end was come,
And that he had ta'en up his latest inn,
In the kind office of a chamberlain
15   Showed him his room where he must lodge that night,
Pulled off his boots, and took away the light:
If any ask for him, it shall be said,
Hobson has supped, and 's newly gone to bed.

Another on the Same

Here lieth one who did most truly prove,
That he could never die while he could move;
So hung his destiny never to rot
While he might still jog on and keep his trot;
5   Made of sphere-metal, never to decay
Until his revolution was at stay.
Time numbers motion, yet (without a crime
'Gainst old truth) motion numbered out his time;
And like an engine moved with wheel and weight,
10   His principles being ceased, he ended straight;

Rest that gives all men life, gave him his death,
And too much breathing put him out of breath;
Nor were it contradiction to affirm
Too long vacation hastened on his term.
15 Merely to drive away the time he sickened,
Fainted, and died, nor would with ale be quickened;
Nay, quoth he, on his swooning bed outstretched,
If I may not carry, sure I'll ne'er be fetched,
But vow though the cross doctors all stood hearers,
20 For one carrier put down to make six bearers.
Ease was his chief disease, and to judge right,
He died for heaviness that his cart went light,
His leisure told him that his time was come,
And lack of load, made his life burdensome,
25 That even to his last breath (there be that say't)
As he were pressed to death, he cried more weight;
But had his doings lasted as they were,
He had been an immortal carrier.
Obedient to the moon he spent his date
30 In course reciprocal, and had his fate
Linked to the mutual flowing of the seas,
Yet (strange to think) his wain was his increase:
His letters are delivered all and gone,
Only remains this superscription.

L'Allegro

Hence loathèd Melancholy,
    Of Cerberus, and blackest Midnight born,
In Stygian cave forlorn
    'Mongst horrid shapes, and shrieks, and sights unholy,
5   Find out some uncouth cell,
    Where brooding Darkness spreads his jealous wings,
And the night-raven sings;
    There under ebon shades, and low-browed rocks,
As ragged as thy locks,
10   In dark Cimmerian desert ever dwell.

But come thou goddess fair and free,
In Heav'n yclept Euphrosyne,
And by men, heart-easing Mirth,
Whom lovely Venus at a birth
15 With two sister Graces more
To ivy-crownèd Bacchus bore;
Or whether (as some sager sing)
The frolic wind that breathes the spring,
Zephyr with Aurora playing,
20 As he met her once a-Maying,
There on beds of violets blue,
And fresh-blown roses washed in dew,
Filled her with thee a daughter fair,
So buxom, blithe, and debonair.
25 Haste thee nymph, and bring with thee
Jest and youthful Jollity,
Quips and Cranks, and wanton Wiles,
Nods, and Becks, and wreathèd Smiles,
Such as hang on Hebe's cheek,
30 And love to live in dimple sleek;
Sport that wrinkled Care derides,
And Laughter holding both his sides.
Come, and trip it as ye go
On the light fantastic toe,
35 And in thy right hand lead with thee,
The mountain nymph, sweet Liberty;
And if I give thee honour due,
Mirth, admit me of thy crew
To live with her, and live with thee,
40 In unreprovèd pleasures free;
To hear the lark begin his flight,
And singing startle the dull night,
From his watch-tower in the skies,
Till the dappled dawn doth rise;
45 Then to come in spite of sorrow,
And at my window bid good morrow,
Through the sweet-briar, or the vine,
Or the twisted eglantine.

While the cock with lively din,
50 Scatters the rear of darkness thin,
And to the stack, or the barn door,
Stoutly struts his dames before,
Oft list'ning how the hounds and horn,
Cheerly rouse the slumb'ring morn,
55 From the side of some hoar hill,
Through the high woods echoing shrill.
Some time walking not unseen
By hedge-row elms, on hillocks green,
Right against the eastern gate,
60 Where the great sun begins his state,
Robed in flames, and amber light,
The clouds in thousand liveries dight.
While the ploughman near at hand,
Whistles o'er the furrowed land,
65 And the milkmaid singeth blithe,
And the mower whets his scythe,
And every shepherd tells his tale
Under the hawthorn in the dale.
Straight mine eye hath caught new pleasures
70 Whilst the landscape round it measures,
Russet lawns, and fallows grey,
Where the nibbling flocks do stray,
Mountains on whose barren breast
The labouring clouds do often rest:
75 Meadows trim with daisies pied,
Shallow brooks, and rivers wide.
Towers, and battlements it sees
Bosomed high in tufted trees,
Where perhaps some beauty lies,
80 The Cynosure of neighbouring eyes.
Hard by, a cottage chimney smokes,
From betwixt two agèd oaks,
Where Corydon and Thyrsis met,
Are at their savoury dinner set
85 Of herbs, and other country messes,
Which the neat-handed Phyllis dresses;

And then in haste her bower she leaves,
With Thestylis to bind the sheaves;
Or if the earlier season lead
90   To the tanned haycock in the mead,
Sometimes with secure delight
The upland hamlets will invite,
When the merry bells ring round,
And the jocund rebecks sound
95   To many a youth, and many a maid,
Dancing in the chequered shade;
And young and old come forth to play
On a sunshine holiday,
Till the livelong daylight fail,
100   Then to the spicy nut-brown ale,
With stories told of many a feat,
How faery Mab the junkets ate;
She was pinched, and pulled she said,
And he by friar's lantern led,
105   Tells how the drudging goblin sweat,
To earn his cream-bowl duly set,
When in one night, ere glimpse of morn,
His shadowy flail hath threshed the corn
That ten day-labourers could not end,
110   Then lies him down the lubber fiend,
And stretched out all the chimney's length,
Basks at the fire his hairy strength;
And crop-full out of doors he flings,
Ere the first cock his matin rings.
115   Thus done the tales, to bed they creep,
By whispering winds soon lulled asleep.
Towered cities please us then,
And the busy hum of men,
Where throngs of knights and barons bold,
120   In weeds of peace high triumphs hold,
With store of ladies, whose bright eyes
Rain influence, and judge the prize
Of wit, or arms, while both contend
To win her grace, whom all commend.

125 There let Hymen oft appear
In saffron robe, with taper clear,
And pomp, and feast, and revelry,
With masque and antique pageantry;
Such sights as youthful poets dream
130 On summer eves by haunted stream.
Then to the well-trod stage anon,
If Jonson's learned sock be on,
Or sweetest Shakespeare, Fancy's child,
Warble his native wood-notes wild.
135 And ever against eating cares,
Lap me in soft Lydian airs,
Married to immortal verse
Such as the meeting soul may pierce
In notes, with many a winding bout
140 Of linkèd sweetness long drawn out,
With wanton heed, and giddy cunning,
The melting voice through mazes running;
Untwisting all the chains that tie
The hidden soul of harmony.
145 That Orpheus' self may heave his head
From golden slumber on a bed
Of heaped Elysian flow'rs, and hear
Such strains as would have quite set free
His half-regainèd Eurydice.
150 These delights, if thou canst give,
Mirth with thee, I mean to live.

Il Penseroso

Hence vain deluding joys,
    The brood of Folly without father bred,
How little you bestead,
    Or fill the fixèd mind with all your toys;
5   Dwell in some idle brain,
    And fancies fond with gaudy shapes possess,
As thick and numberless

As the gay motes that people the sunbeams,
Or likest hovering dreams,
10   The fickle pensioners of Morpheus' train.
But hail thou goddess, sage and holy,
Hail divinest Melancholy,
Whose saintly visage is too bright
To hit the sense of human sight;
15   And therefore to our weaker view,
O'erlaid with black staid Wisdom's hue.
Black, but such as in esteem,
Prince Memnon's sister might beseem,
Or that starred Ethiop queen that strove
20   To set her beauty's praise above
The sea-nymphs, and their powers offended;
Yet thou art higher far descended,
Thee bright-haired Vesta long of yore,
To solitary Saturn bore;
25   His daughter she (in Saturn's reign,
Such mixture was not held a stain).
Oft in glimmering bow'rs and glades
He met her, and in secret shades
Of woody Ida's inmost grove,
30   While yet there was no fear of Jove.
Come pensive nun, devout and pure,
Sober, steadfast, and demure,
All in a robe of darkest grain,
Flowing with majestic train,
35   And sable stole of cypress lawn,
Over thy decent shoulders drawn.
Come, but keep thy wonted state,
With even step, and musing gait,
And looks commercing with the skies,
40   Thy rapt soul sitting in thine eyes:
There held in holy passion still,
Forget thyself to marble, till
With a sad leaden downward cast,
Thou fix them on the earth as fast.
45   And join with thee calm Peace, and Quiet,
Spare Fast, that oft with gods doth diet,

And hears the Muses in a ring,
Ay round about Jove's altar sing.
And add to these retired Leisure,
50   That in trim gardens takes his pleasure;
But first, and chiefest, with thee bring,
Him that yon soars with golden wing,
Guiding the fiery-wheelèd throne,
The Cherub Contemplatïon,
55   And the mute Silence hist along,
'Less Philomel will deign a song,
In her sweetest, saddest plight,
Smoothing the rugged brow of Night,
While Cynthia checks her dragon yoke,
60   Gently o'er th' accustomed oak;
Sweet bird that shunn'st the noise of folly,
Most musical, most melancholy!
Thee chantress oft the woods among,
I woo to hear thy even-song;
65   And missing thee, I walk unseen
On the dry smooth-shaven green,
To behold the wand'ring moon,
Riding near her highest noon,
Like one that had been led astray
70   Through the heav'n's wide pathless way;
And oft, as if her head she bowed,
Stooping through a fleecy cloud.
Oft on a plat of rising ground,
I hear the far-off curfew sound,
75   Over some wide-watered shore,
Swinging low with sullen roar;
Or if the air will not permit,
Some still removèd place will fit,
Where glowing embers through the room
80   Teach light to counterfeit a gloom,
Far from all resort of mirth,
Save the cricket on the hearth,
Or the bellman's drowsy charm,
To bless the doors from nightly harm:

85 Or let my lamp at midnight hour,
    Be seen in some high lonely tow'r,
    Where I may oft outwatch the Bear,
    With thrice-great Hermes, or unsphere
    The spirit of Plato to unfold
90 What worlds, or what vast regions hold
    The immortal mind that hath forsook
    Her mansion in this fleshly nook:
    And of those daemons that are found
    In fire, air, flood, or under ground,
95 Whose power hath a true consent
    With planet, or with element.
    Sometime let gorgeous Tragedy
    In sceptred pall come sweeping by,
    Presenting Thebes, or Pelops' line,
100 Or the tale of Troy divine.
    Or what (though rare) of later age,
    Ennobled hath the buskined stage.
    But, O sad virgin, that thy power
    Might raise Musaeus from his bower,
105 Or bid the soul of Orpheus sing
    Such notes as warbled to the string,
    Drew iron tears down Pluto's cheek,
    And made Hell grant what love did seek.
    Or call up him that left half-told
110 The story of Cambuscan bold,
    Of Camball, and of Algarsife,
    And who had Canace to wife,
    That owned the virtuous ring and glass,
    And of the wondrous horse of brass,
115 On which the Tartar king did ride;
    And if aught else, great bards beside,
    In sage and solemn tunes have sung,
    Of tourneys and of trophies hung;
    Of forests, and enchantments drear,
120 Where more is meant than meets the ear.
    Thus Night oft see me in thy pale career,
    Till civil-suited Morn appear,

Not tricked and frounced as she was wont,
With the Attic boy to hunt,
125 But kerchiefed in a comely cloud,
While rocking winds are piping loud,
Or ushered with a shower still,
When the gust hath blown his fill,
Ending on the rustling leaves,
130 With minute drops from off the eaves.
And when the sun begins to fling
His flaring beams, me goddess bring
To archèd walks of twilight groves,
And shadows brown that Sylvan loves
135 Of pine, and monumental oak,
Where the rude axe with heavèd stroke,
Was never heard the nymphs to daunt,
Or fright them from their hallowed haunt.
There in close covert by some brook,
140 Where no profaner eye may look,
Hide me from Day's garish eye,
While the bee with honeyed thigh,
That at her flow'ry work doth sing,
And the waters murmuring
145 With such consort as they keep,
Entice the dewy-feathered Sleep;
And let some strange mysterious dream,
Wave at his wings in airy stream,
Of lively portraiture displayed,
150 Softly on my eyelids laid.
And as I wake, sweet music breathe
Above, about, or underneath,
Sent by some spirit to mortals good,
Or th' unseen Genius of the wood.
155 But let my due feet never fail,
To walk the studious cloister's pale,
And love the high embowèd roof,
With antique pillars' massy proof,
And storied windows richly dight,
160 Casting a dim religious light.

There let the pealing organ blow,
To the full-voiced choir below,
In service high, and anthems clear,
As may with sweetness, through mine ear,
165   Dissolve me into ecstasies,
And bring all Heav'n before mine eyes.
And may at last my weary age
Find out some peaceful hermitage,
The hairy gown and mossy cell,
170   Where I may sit and rightly spell,
Of every star that heav'n doth show,
And every herb that sips the dew;
Till old experience do attain
To something like prophetic strain.
175   These pleasures Melancholy give,
And I with thee will choose to live.

Sonnet I

O nightingale, that on yon bloomy spray
   Warblest at eve, when all the woods are still,
   Thou with fresh hope the lover's heart dost fill,
   While the jolly Hours lead on propitious May;
5 Thy liquid notes that close the eye of day,
   First heard before the shallow cuckoo's bill
   Portend success in love; O if Jove's will
   Have linked that amorous power to thy soft lay,
Now timely sing, ere the rude bird of hate
10   Foretell my hopeless doom in some grove nigh:
   As thou from year to year hast sung too late
For my relief, yet hadst no reason why:
   Whether the Muse, or Love call thee his mate,
   Both them I serve, and of their train am I.

Sonnet II

Donna leggiadra il cui bel nome onora
   L'erbosa val di Reno, e il nobil varco,
   Ben è colui d'ogni valore scarco
   Qual tuo spirto gentil non innamora,
5 Che dolcemente mostrasi di fuora
   De' suoi atti soavi giammai parco,
   E i don', che son d'amor saette ed arco,
   Là onde l'alta tua virtù s'infiora.
Quando tu vaga parli, o lieta canti
10 Che mover possa duro alpestre legno,
   Guardi ciascun agli occhi, ed agli orecchi
L'entrata, chi di te si trova indegno,
   Grazia sola di sù gli vaglia, innanti
   Che'l disio amoroso al cuor s'invecchi.

Lovely lady, whose fair name[1] honours the grassy Reno valley and the famous ford,[2] that man must be wholly worthless who is not moved to love your gentle spirit, which sweetly reveals itself (bounteous in gracious looks and favours that are the arrows and bow of Love) there[8] where your high virtue blooms. When, in your beauty, you speak, or joyously sing (which might move tough mountain trees),[10] let every man who is unworthy of you guard the portals of his eyes and ears.[11] Only grace from above can prevent amorous desire from becoming inveterate in his heart.

Sonnet III

Qual in colle aspro, a l'imbrunir di sera,
   L'avvezza giovinetta pastorella
   Va bagnando l'erbetta strana e bella
   Che mal si spande a disusata spera
5 Fuor di sua natia alma primavera,

Così Amor meco insù la lingua snella
Desta il fior novo di strania favella,
Mentre io di te, vezzosamente altera,
Canto, dal mio buon popol non inteso,
10   E'l bel Tamigi cangio col bel Arno.
Amor lo volse, ed io a l'altrui peso
Seppi ch'Amor cosa mai volse indarno.
Deh! foss'il mio cuor lento e'l duro seno
A chi pianta dal ciel sì buon terreno.

As on a rugged hill at dusk, a youthful shepherdess, brought up there, waters a strange and beautiful plant which can scarcely spread its leaves in the alien clime, far from its bounteous native springtime; so Love awakens on my ready tongue the new flower of a foreign speech as I sing of you, graciously proud Lady, not understood by my own good countrymen, and exchange the fair Thames for the fair Arno.[10] Love willed it, and I knew from the distress of others that Love never willed anything in vain. Ah, that my sluggish heart and hard breast were as good a soil to Him who plants from heaven!

Canzone

Ridonsi donne e giovani amorosi
M'accostandosi attorno, e perchè scrivi,
Perchè tu scrivi in lingua ignota e strana
Verseggiando d'amor, e come t'osi?
5   Dinne, se la tua speme sia mai vana,
E de' pensieri lo miglior t'arrivi;
Così mi van burlando, altri rivi,
Altri lidi t'aspettan, ed altre onde
Nelle cui verdi sponde
10   Spuntati ad or, ad or a la tua chioma
L'immortal guiderdon d'eterne frondi:

Perchè alle spalle tue soverchia soma?
    Canzon dirotti, e tu per me rispondi:
Dice mia donna, e'l suo dir è il mio cuore,
15   Questa è lingua di cui si vanta Amore.

Young men and women[1] in love gather round me, laughing:
'Why, why do you write love poems in a strange and unknown
language? How dare you? Tell us, so that your hope may
never be in vain, and the best of your wishes may come true.'
Thus they tease me: 'Other streams[7] and other shores await
you, and other waves, on whose green banks the immortal
guerdon of unfading leaves is already growing for your hair.
Why add an excessive burden to your shoulders?'
    Canzone, I will tell you,[13] and you answer for me: my lady
says, and her words are my heart, 'This is the language of
which Love is proud.'

Sonnet IV

Diodati, e te'l dirò con maraviglia,
    Quel ritroso io ch'amor spreggia soléa
    E de' suoi lacci spesso mi ridéa,
    Già caddi, ov uom dabben talor s'impiglia.
5   Nè treccie d'oro, nè guancia vermiglia
    M'abbaglian sì, ma sotto nova idea
    Pellegrina bellezza che'l cuor bea,
    Portamenti alti onesti, e nelle ciglia
Quel sereno fulgor d'amabil nero,
10   Parole adorne di lingua più d'una,
    E'l cantar che di mezzo l'emisfero
Traviar ben può la faticosa luna;
    E degli occhi suoi avventa sì gran fuoco
    Che l'incerar gli orecchi mi fia poco.

Diodati[1] – and I tell you with amazement – I, the reluctant
one, who used to scorn Love, and often laughed at his snares,
have now fallen where a good man sometimes gets entangled.

It is not golden tresses or a rosy cheek that thus dazzles me, but strange beauty, modelled on a new form,[6] which delights my heart: modest pride in her bearing, a serene radiance of lovely black in her eyes, speech that is graced by more than one language, and singing that might well lure the labouring[12] moon from the midst of the sky; and such bright fire flashes from her eyes that sealing my ears with wax would be of little use.[14]

Sonnet V

Per certo i bei vostr' occhi, donna mia,
    Esser non può che non sian lo mio sole;
    Sì mi percuoton forte, come ei suole
    Per l'arene di Libia chi s'invia,
5 Mentre un caldo vapor (nè sentì pria)
    Da quel lato si spinge ove mi duole,
    Che forse amanti nelle lor parole
    Chiaman sospir; io non so che si sia:
  Parte rinchiusa e turbida si cela
10 Scossomi il petto, e poi n'uscendo poco
    Quivi d'attorno o s'agghiaccia, o s'ingiela;
  Ma quanto agli occhi giunge a trovar loco
    Tutte le notti a me suol far piovose
    Finchè mia Alba rivien colma di rose.

In truth, my lady, your beautiful eyes can only be my sun; they smite me as powerfully as the sun beating down on a traveller in the Libyan sands; meanwhile a warm vapour (such as I never felt before) bursts from that side[6] where my pain is. Perhaps lovers in their language call it a 'sigh'; I do not know what it might be. Part of it, confined and troubled, hides itself away in my shaking breast; then a little escapes into the surrounding air where it is either frozen or congealed. But that part that finds a place in my eyes makes every night rainy for me, until my Dawn returns brimming with roses.

Sonnet VI

Giovane piano, e semplicetto amante
    Poichè fuggir me stesso in dubbio sono,
    Madonna a voi del mio cuor l'umil dono
    Farò divoto; io certo a prove tante
5 L'ebbi fedele, intrepido, costante,
    Di pensieri leggiadro, accorto, e buono;
    Quando rugge il gran mondo, e scocca il tuono,
    S'arma di se, e d'intero diamante,
Tanto del forse, e d'invidia sicuro,
10 Di timori, e speranze al popol use
    Quanto d'ingegno e d'alto valor vago,
E di cetra sonora, e delle Muse:
    Sol troverete in tal parte men duro
    Ove amor mise l'insanabil ago.

Young, simple and artless lover that I am, since I am in doubt about how to fly from myself, I will devoutly offer the humble gift of my heart to you, my lady. In many trials I have proved it faithful, brave, and constant; fair, wise and good in its thoughts. When the whole world roars and the thunder crashes, it arms itself with itself, in complete adamant, as safe from chance and envy, and common hopes and fears, as it is eager for genius and lofty worth, the sounding lyre and the Muses. You will find it less hard only in that place where Love has fixed his incurable dart.

Sonnet VII

How soon hath Time the subtle thief of youth,
    Stol'n on his wing my three and twentieth year!
    My hasting days fly on with full career,
    But my late spring no bud or blossom shew'th.

5   Perhaps my semblance might deceive the truth,
      That I to manhood am arrived so near,
      And inward ripeness doth much less appear,
      That some more timely-happy spirits endu'th.
   Yet be it less or more, or soon or slow,
10   It shall be still in strictest measure even
      To that same lot, however mean, or high,
   Toward which Time leads me, and the will of Heaven;
      All is, if I have grace to use it so,
      As ever in my great task-master's eye.

Sonnet VIII

Captain or colonel, or knight in arms,
   Whose chance on these defenceless doors may seize,
   If deed of honour did thee ever please,
   Guard them, and him within protect from harms;
5   He can requite thee, for he knows the charms
      That call fame on such gentle acts as these,
      And he can spread thy name o'er lands and seas,
      Whatever clime the sun's bright circle warms.
   Lift not thy spear against the Muses' bower:
10   The great Emathian conqueror bid spare
      The house of Pindarus, when temple and tower
   Went to the ground; and the repeated air
      Of sad Electra's poet had the power
      To save th' Athenian walls from ruin bare.

Sonnet IX

Lady that in the prime of earliest youth,
   Wisely hast shunned the broad way and the green,
   And with those few art eminently seen,
   That labour up the hill of Heav'nly Truth,
5   The better part with Mary, and with Ruth,

Chosen thou hast; and they that overween,
   And at thy growing virtues fret their spleen,
   No anger find in thee, but pity and ruth.
Thy care is fixed, and zealously attends
10   To fill thy odorous lamp with deeds of light,
   And hope that reaps not shame. Therefore be sure
Thou, when the bridegroom with his feastful friends
   Passes to bliss at the mid hour of night,
   Hast gained thy entrance, virgin wise and pure.

Sonnet X

Daughter to that good Earl, once President
   Of England's Council, and her Treasury,
   Who lived in both, unstained with gold or fee,
   And left them both, more in himself content,
5 Till the sad breaking of that Parliament
   Broke him, as that dishonest victory
   At Chaeronea, fatal to liberty
   Killed with report that old man eloquent,
Though later born, than to have known the days
10   Wherein your father flourished, yet by you
   Madam, methinks I see him living yet;
So well your words his noble virtues praise,
   That all both judge you to relate them true,
   And to possess them, honoured Margaret.

Arcades

Part of an entertainment presented to the Countess Dowager of Derby at Harefield by some noble persons of her family, who appear on the scene in pastoral habit, moving toward the seat of state, with this song.

I. Song

Look nymphs, and shepherds look,
What sudden blaze of majesty
Is that which we from hence descry
Too divine to be mistook:
5   This this is she
To whom our vows and wishes bend,
Here our solemn search hath end.

Fame that her high worth to raise,
Seemed erst so lavish and profuse,
10   We may justly now accuse
Of detraction from her praise;
     Less than half we find expressed,
     Envy bid conceal the rest.

Mark what radiant state she spreads,
15   In circle round her shining throne,
Shooting her beams like silver threads:
This this is she alone,
     Sitting like a goddess bright,
     In the centre of her light.

20   Might she the wise Latona be,
Or the towered Cybele,
Mother of a hundred gods?
Juno dares not give her odds;
     Who had thought this clime had held
25   A deity so unparalleled?

*As they come forward, the Genius of the Wood appears, and
turning toward them, speaks.*

Genius. Stay gentle swains, for though in this disguise,
I see bright honour sparkle through your eyes;
Of famous Arcady ye are, and sprung
Of that renownèd flood, so often sung,
30   Divine Alpheus, who by secret sluice,
Stole under seas to meet his Arethuse;
And ye the breathing roses of the wood,
Fair silver-buskined nymphs as great and good,
I know this quest of yours, and free intent
35   Was all in honour and devotion meant
To the great mistress of yon princely shrine,
Whom with low reverence I adore as mine,
And with all helpful service will comply
To further this night's glad solemnity;
40   And lead ye where ye may more near behold
What shallow-searching Fame hath left untold;
Which I full oft amidst these shades alone
Have sat to wonder at, and gaze upon:
For know by lot from Jove I am the pow'r
45   Of this fair wood, and live in oaken bow'r,
To nurse the saplings tall, and curl the grove
With ringlets quaint, and wanton windings wove.
And all my plants I save from nightly ill,
Of noisome winds, and blasting vapours chill.
50   And from the boughs brush off the evil dew,
And heal the harms of thwarting thunder blue,
Or what the cross dire-looking planet smites,
Or hurtful worm with cankered venom bites.
When evening grey doth rise, I fetch my round
55   Over the mount, and all this hallowed ground
And early ere the odorous breath of morn
Awakes the slumb'ring leaves, or tasselled horn
Shakes the high thicket, haste I all about,
Number my ranks, and visit every sprout
60   With puissant words, and murmurs made to bless;
But else in deep of night when drowsiness

Hath locked up mortal sense, then listen I
To the celestial Sirens' harmony,
That sit upon the nine enfolded spheres,
65 And sing to those who hold the vital shears,
And turn the adamantine spindle round,
On which the fate of gods and men is wound.
Such sweet compulsion doth in music lie,
To lull the daughters of Necessity,
70 And keep unsteady Nature to her law,
And the low world in measured motion draw
After the heavenly tune, which none can hear
Of human mould with gross unpurgèd ear;
And yet such music worthiest were to blaze
75 The peerless height of her immortal praise,
Whose lustre leads us, and for her most fit,
If my inferior hand or voice could hit
Inimitable sounds; yet as we go,
Whate'er the skill of lesser gods can show,
80 I will assay, her worth to celebrate,
And so attend ye toward her glittering state;
Where ye may all that are of noble stem
Approach, and kiss her sacred vesture's hem.

II. Song

O'er the smooth enamelled green
85 Where no print of step hath been,
Follow me as I sing,
And touch the warbled string.
Under the shady roof
Of branching elm star-proof,
90 Follow me,
I will bring you where she sits,
Clad in splendour as befits
Her deity.
Such a rural Queen
95 All Arcadia hath not seen.

III. Song

Nymphs and shepherds dance no more
   By sandy Ladon's lilied banks.
On old Lycaeus or Cyllene hoar,
   Trip no more in twilight ranks;
100 Though Erymanth your loss deplore,
   A better soil shall give ye thanks.
From the stony Maenalus,
Bring your flocks, and live with us;
Here ye shall have greater grace,
105 To serve the Lady of this place.
   Though Syrinx your Pan's mistress were,
   Yet Syrinx well might wait on her.
     Such a rural Queen
   All Arcadia hath not seen.

Lycidas

In this monody the author bewails a learned friend, unfortunately drowned in his passage from Chester on the Irish Seas, 1637. And by occasion foretells the ruin of our corrupted clergy then in their height.

Yet once more, O ye laurels, and once more
Ye myrtles brown, with ivy never sere,
I come to pluck your berries harsh and crude,
And with forced fingers rude,
5 Shatter your leaves before the mellowing year.
Bitter constraint, and sad occasion dear,
Compels me to disturb your season due:
For Lycidas is dead, dead ere his prime,
Young Lycidas, and hath not left his peer.
10 Who would not sing for Lycidas? he knew
Himself to sing, and build the lofty rhyme.
He must not float upon his wat'ry bier
Unwept, and welter to the parching wind,

Without the meed of some melodious tear.
15   Begin then, Sisters of the sacred well,
That from beneath the seat of Jove doth spring;
Begin, and somewhat loudly sweep the string.
Hence with denial vain, and coy excuse;
So may some gentle Muse
20   With lucky words favour my destined urn,
And as he passes, turn
And bid fair peace be to my sable shroud.
For we were nursed upon the self-same hill,
Fed the same flock, by fountain, shade, and rill.
25   Together both, ere the high lawns appeared
Under the opening eye-lids of the morn,
We drove afield, and both together heard
What time the grey-fly winds her sultry horn,
Batt'ning our flocks with the fresh dews of night,
30   Oft till the star that rose, at evening, bright
Toward heav'n's descent had sloped his westering wheel.
Meanwhile the rural ditties were not mute,
Tempered to th' oaten flute,
Rough satyrs danced, and fauns with cloven heel
35   From the glad sound would not be absent long,
And old Damoetas loved to hear our song.
    But O the heavy change, now thou art gone,
Now thou art gone, and never must return!
Thee shepherd, thee the woods, and desert caves,
40   With wild thyme and the gadding vine o'ergrown,
And all their echoes mourn.
The willows, and the hazel copses green,
Shall now no more be seen,
Fanning their joyous leaves to thy soft lays.
45   As killing as the canker to the rose,
Or taint-worm to the weanling herds that graze,
Or frost to flowers, that their gay wardrobe wear,
When first the whitethorn blows;
Such, Lycidas, thy loss to shepherd's ear.
50   Where were ye nymphs when the remorseless deep
Closed o'er the head of your loved Lycidas?
For neither were ye playing on the steep,

Where your old Bards, the famous Druids lie,
Nor on the shaggy top of Mona high,
55   Nor yet where Deva spreads her wizard stream:
Ay me, I fondly dream!
Had ye been there – for what could that have done?
What could the Muse herself that Orpheus bore,
The Muse herself, for her enchanting son
60   Whom universal nature did lament,
When by the rout that made the hideous roar,
His gory visage down the stream was sent,
Down the swift Hebrus to the Lesbian shore.
     Alas! What boots it with uncessant care
65   To tend the homely slighted shepherd's trade,
And strictly meditate the thankless Muse?
Were it not better done as others use,
To sport with Amaryllis in the shade,
Or with the tangles of Neaera's hair?
70   Fame is the spur that the clear spirit doth raise
(That last infirmity of noble mind)
To scorn delights, and live laborious days;
But the fair guerdon when we hope to find,
And think to burst out into sudden blaze,
75   Comes the blind Fury with th' abhorrèd shears,
And slits the thin-spun life. But not the praise,
Phoebus replied, and touched my trembling ears;
Fame is no plant that grows on mortal soil,
Nor in the glistering foil
80   Set off to th' world, nor in broad rumour lies,
But lives and spreads aloft by those pure eyes
And perfect witness of all-judging Jove;
As he pronounces lastly on each deed,
Of so much fame in Heav'n expect thy meed.
85   O fountain Arethuse, and thou honoured flood,
Smooth-sliding Mincius, crowned with vocal reeds,
That strain I heard was of a higher mood:
But now my oat proceeds,
And listens to the herald of the sea
90   That came in Neptune's plea.
He asked the waves, and asked the felon winds,

What hard mishap hath doomed this gentle swain?
And questioned every gust of rugged wings
That blows from off each beakèd promontory:
95   They knew not of his story,
And sage Hippotades their answer brings,
That not a blast was from his dungeon strayed;
The air was calm, and on the level brine
Sleek Panope with all her sisters played.
100   It was that fatal and perfidious bark,
Built in th' eclipse, and rigged with curses dark,
That sunk so low that sacred head of thine.
      Next Camus, reverend sire, went footing slow,
His mantle hairy, and his bonnet sedge,
105   Inwrought with figures dim, and on the edge
Like to that sanguine flower inscribed with woe.
Ah! who hath reft (quoth he) my dearest pledge?
Last came, and last did go,
The pilot of the Galilean lake;
110   Two massy keys he bore of metals twain,
(The golden opes, the iron shuts amain).
He shook his mitred locks, and stern bespake,
How well could I have spared for thee, young swain,
Enow of such as for their bellies' sake
115   Creep, and intrude, and climb into the fold!
Of other care they little reck'ning make,
Than how to scramble at the shearers' feast,
And shove away the worthy bidden guest.
Blind mouths! that scarce themselves know how to hold
120   A sheep-hook, or have learnt aught else the least
That to the faithful herdsman's art belongs!
What recks it them? What need they? They are sped;
And when they list, their lean and flashy songs
Grate on their scrannel pipes of wretched straw;
125   The hungry sheep look up, and are not fed,
But swoll'n with wind, and the rank mist they draw,
Rot inwardly, and foul contagion spread:
Besides what the grim Wolf with privy paw
Daily devours apace, and nothing said.
130   But that two-handed engine at the door,

Stands ready to smite once, and smite no more.
   Return, Alpheus, the dread voice is past,
That shrunk thy streams; return, Sicilian Muse,
And call the vales, and bid them hither cast
135 Their bells, and flow'rets of a thousand hues.
Ye valleys low, where the mild whispers use
Of shades, and wanton winds, and gushing brooks,
On whose fresh lap the swart star sparely looks,
Throw hither all your quaint enamelled eyes,
140 That on the green turf suck the honied showers,
And purple all the ground with vernal flowers.
Bring the rathe primrose that forsaken dies,
The tufted crow-toe, and pale jessamine,
The white pink, and the pansy freaked with jet,
145 The growing violet,
The musk-rose, and the well-attired woodbine,
With cowslips wan that hang the pensive head,
And every flower that sad embroidery wears:
Bid amaranthus all his beauty shed,
150 And daffadillies fill their cups with tears,
To strew the laureate hearse where Lycid lies.
For so to interpose a little ease,
Let our frail thoughts dally with false surmise;
Ay me! whilst thee the shores, and sounding seas
155 Wash far away, where'er thy bones are hurled,
Whether beyond the stormy Hebrides,
Where thou perhaps under the whelming tide
Visit'st the bottom of the monstrous world;
Or whether thou to our moist vows denied,
160 Sleep'st by the fable of Bellerus old,
Where the great vision of the guarded mount
Looks toward Namancos and Bayona's hold;
Look homeward angel now, and melt with ruth.
And, O ye dolphins, waft the hapless youth.
165   Weep no more, woeful shepherds, weep no more,
For Lycidas your sorrow is not dead,
Sunk though he be beneath the wat'ry floor,
So sinks the day-star in the ocean bed,
And yet anon repairs his drooping head,

170   And tricks his beams, and with new-spangled ore,
      Flames in the forehead of the morning sky:
      So Lycidas sunk low, but mounted high,
      Through the dear might of him that walked the waves,
      Where other groves, and other streams along,
175   With nectar pure his oozy locks he laves,
      And hears the unexpressive nuptial song,
      In the blest kingdoms meek of joy and love.
      There entertain him all the saints above,
      In solemn troops, and sweet societies
180   That sing, and singing in their glory move,
      And wipe the tears for ever from his eyes.
      Now, Lycidas, the shepherds weep no more;
      Henceforth thou art the Genius of the shore
      In thy large recompense, and shalt be good
185   To all that wander in that perilous flood.
            Thus sang the uncouth swain to th' oaks and rills,
      While the still Morn went out with sandals grey;
      He touched the tender stops of various quills,
      With eager thought warbling his Doric lay:
190   And now the sun had stretched out all the hills,
      And now was dropped into the western bay;
      At last he rose, and twitched his mantle blue:
      Tomorrow to fresh woods and pastures new.

A Masque of the Same Author
Presented at Ludlow Castle, 1634
before the Earl of Bridgewater
then President of Wales

The Persons

The Attendant Spirit, afterwards in the habit of Thyrsis.
Comus, with his crew.
The Lady.
1. Brother.
2. Brother.
Sabrina the Nymph.

The chief persons which presented, were
The Lord Brackley,
Mr. Thomas Egerton his brother,
The Lady Alice Egerton.

The first scene discovers a wild wood.
The Attendant Spirit descends or enters.

Before the starry threshold of Jove's court
My mansion is, where those immortal shapes
Of bright aërial Spirits live insphered
In regions mild of calm and sérene air,
5   Above the smoke and stir of this dim spot
Which men call earth, and with low-thoughted care
Confined, and pestered in this pinfold here,
Strive to keep up a frail and feverish being
Unmindful of the crown that Virtue gives
10   After this mortal change, to her true servants
Amongst the énthroned gods on sainted seats.
Yet some there be that by due steps aspire
To lay their just hands on that golden key
That opes the palace of eternity:
15   To such my errand is, and but for such
I would not soil these pure ambrosial weeds
With the rank vapours of this sin-worn mould.
      But to my task. Neptune besides the sway
Of every salt flood, and each ebbing stream,
20   Took in by lot 'twixt high, and nether Jove,
Imperial rule of all the sea-girt isles
That like to rich and various gems inlay
The unadornèd bosom of the deep,
Which he to grace his tributary gods
25   By course commits to several government,
And gives them leave to wear their sapphire crowns
And wield their little tridents; but this isle
The greatest and the best of all the main
He quarters to his blue-haired deities;
30   And all this tract that fronts the falling sun
A noble peer of mickle trust and power

Has in his charge, with tempered awe to guide
An old and haughty nation proud in arms:
Where his fair offspring nursed in princely lore
35   Are coming to attend their father's state,
And new-entrusted sceptre. But their way
Lies through the pérplexed paths of this drear wood,
The nodding horror of whose shady brows
Threats the forlorn and wand'ring passenger.
40   And here their tender age might suffer peril
But that by quick command from sov'reign Jove
I was despatched for their defence, and guard;
And listen why, for I will tell ye now
What never yet was heard in tale or song
45   From old, or modern bard in hall, or bow'r.
     Bacchus, that first from out the purple grape
Crushed the sweet poison of misusèd wine,
After the Tuscan mariners transformed,
Coasting the Tyrrhene shore, as the winds listed,
50   On Circe's island fell (who knows not Circe
The daughter of the Sun? Whose charmèd cup
Whoever tasted, lost his upright shape,
And downward fell into a grovelling swine).
This nymph that gazed upon his clust'ring locks
55   With ivy berries wreathed, and his blithe youth,
Had by him, ere he parted thence, a son
Much like his father, but his mother more,
Whom therefore she brought up and Comus named,
Who ripe, and frolic of his full-grown age,
60   Roving the Celtic, and Iberian fields,
At last betakes him to this ominous wood,
And in thick shelter of black shades embowered,
Excels his mother at her mighty art,
Off'ring to every weary traveller,
65   His orient liquor in a crystal glass,
To quench the drouth of Phoebus, which as they taste
(For most do taste through fond intemperate thirst)
Soon as the potion works, their human count'nance,
Th' express resemblance of the gods, is changed
70   Into some brutish form of wolf, or bear,

Or ounce, or tiger, hog, or bearded goat,
All other parts remaining as they were;
And they, so perfect is their misery,
Not once perceive their foul disfigurement,
75 But boast themselves more comely than before,
And all their friends, and native home forget
To roll with pleasure in a sensual sty.
Therefore when any favoured of high Jove
Chances to pass through this advent'rous glade,
80 Swift as the sparkle of a glancing star
I shoot from Heav'n to give him safe convóy,
As now I do: but first I must put off
These my sky robes spun out of Iris' woof,
And take the weeds and likeness of a swain,
85 That to the service of this house belongs,
Who with his soft pipe, and smooth-dittied song,
Well knows to still the wild winds when they roar,
And hush the waving woods; nor of less faith,
And in this office of his mountain watch,
90 Likeliest, and nearest to the present aid
Of this occasion. But I hear the tread
Of hateful steps, I must be viewless now.

*Comus enters with a charming-rod in one hand, his glass in the
other, with him a rout of monsters headed like sundry sorts of wild
beasts, but otherwise like men and women, their apparel glistering;
they come in making a riotous and unruly noise, with torches in
their hands.*

Comus. The star that bids the shepherd fold,
Now the top of heav'n doth hold,
95 And the gilded car of day,
His glowing axle doth allay
In the steep Atlantic stream,
And the slope sun his upward beam
Shoots against the dusky pole,
100 Pacing toward the other goal
Of his chamber in the east.
Meanwhile welcome joy, and feast,

Midnight shout, and revelry,
Tipsy dance, and jollity.
105   Braid your locks with rosy twine,
Dropping odours, dropping wine.
Rigour now is gone to bed,
And Advice with scrupulous head,
Strict Age, and sour Severity
110   With their grave saws in slumber lie.
We that are of purer fire,
Imitate the starry choir,
Who in their nightly watchful spheres,
Lead in swift round the months and years.
115   The sounds, and seas with all their finny drove,
Now to the moon in wavering morris move,
And on the tawny sands and shelves,
Trip the pert fairies and the dapper elves;
By dimpled brook, and fountain brim,
120   The wood-nymphs decked with daisies trim,
Their merry wakes, and pastimes keep:
What hath night to do with sleep?
Night hath better sweets to prove,
Venus now wakes, and wakens Love.
125   Come let us our rites begin
'Tis only daylight that makes sin,
Which these dun shades will ne'er report.
Hail goddess of nocturnal sport
Dark-veiled Cotytto, t' whom the secret flame
130   Of midnight torches burns; mysterious dame
That ne'er art called, but when the dragon womb
Of Stygian darkness spits her thickest gloom,
And makes one blot of all the air,
Stay thy cloudy ebon chair,
135   Wherein thou rid'st with Hecat', and befriend
Us thy vowed priests, till utmost end
Of all thy dues be done, and none left out,
Ere the blabbing eastern scout,
The nice Morn on the Indian steep
140   From her cabined loophole peep,
And to the tell-tale sun descry

Our concealed solemnity.
Come, knit hands, and beat the ground,
In a light fantastic round.

The Measure in a wild, rude and wanton antic

145   Break off, break off, I feel the different pace
Of some chaste footing near about this ground.
Run to your shrouds, within these brakes, and trees;
Our number may affright: some virgin sure
(For so I can distinguish by mine art)
150   Benighted in these woods. Now to my charms
And to my wily trains; I shall ere long
Be well stocked with as fair a herd as grazed
About my mother Circe. Thus I hurl
My dazzling spells into the spongy air,
155   Of power to cheat the eye with blear illusion,
And give it false presentments, lest the place
And my quaint habits breed astonishment,
And put the damsel to suspicious flight,
Which must not be, for that's against my course;
160   I under fair pretence of friendly ends,
And well-placed words of glozing courtesy
Baited with reasons not unplausible
Wind me into the easy-hearted man,
And hug him into snares. When once her eye
165   Hath met the virtue of this magic dust,
I shall appear some harmless villager
Whom thrift keeps up about his country gear;
But here she comes, I fairly step aside
And hearken, if I may, her business here.

The Lady enters.

170   *Lady.* This way the noise was, if mine ear be true,
My best guide now; methought it was the sound
Of riot, and ill-managed merriment,
Such as the jocund flute, or gamesome pipe
Stirs up among the loose unlettered hinds,

175   When for their teeming flocks, and granges full
      In wanton dance they praise the bounteous Pan,
      And thank the gods amiss. I should be loath
      To meet the rudeness, and swilled insolence
      Of such late wassailers; yet O where else
180   Shall I inform my unacquainted feet
      In the blind mazes of this tangled wood?
      My brothers when they saw me wearied out
      With this long way, resolving here to lodge
      Under the spreading favour of these pines,
185   Stepped as they said to the next thicket side
      To bring me berries, or such cooling fruit
      As the kind hospitable woods provide.
      They left me then, when the grey-hooded Ev'n
      Like a sad votarist in palmer's weed
190   Rose from the hindmost wheels of Phoebus' wain.
      But where they are, and why they came not back,
      Is now the labour of my thoughts; 'tis likeliest
      They had engaged their wand'ring steps too far,
      And envious darkness, ere they could return,
195   Had stole them from me, else O thievish Night
      Why shouldst thou, but for some felonious end,
      In thy dark lantern thus close up the stars,
      That Nature hung in heav'n, and filled their lamps
      With everlasting oil, to give due light
200   To the misled, and lonely traveller?
      This is the place, as well as I may guess,
      Whence even now the tumult of loud mirth
      Was rife, and perfect in my listening ear,
      Yet nought but single darkness do I find.
205   What might this be? A thousand fantasies
      Begin to throng into my memory
      Of calling shapes, and beck'ning shadows dire,
      And airy tongues, that syllable men's names
      On sands, and shores, and desert wildernesses.
210   These thoughts may startle well, but not astound
      The virtuous mind, that ever walks attended
      By a strong siding champion Conscïence.—
      O welcome pure-eyed Faith, white-handed Hope,

Thou hovering angel girt with golden wings,
215 And thou unblemished form of Chastity,
I see ye visibly, and now believe
That he, the Súpreme Good, t' whom all things ill
Are but as slavish officers of vengeance,
Would send a glist'ring guardian if need were
220 To keep my life and honour unassailed.
Was I deceived, or did a sable cloud
Turn forth her silver lining on the night?
I did not err, there does a sable cloud
Turn forth her silver lining on the night,
225 And casts a gleam over this tufted grove.
I cannot hallo to my brothers, but
Such noise as I can make to be heard farthest
I'll venture, for my new enlivened spirits
Prompt me; and they perhaps are not far off.

Song

230 Sweet Echo, sweetest nymph that liv'st unseen
        Within thy airy shell
    By slow Meander's margent green,
And in the violet-embroidered vale
    Where the love-lorn nightingale
235 Nightly to thee her sad song mourneth well.
Canst thou not tell me of a gentle pair
    That likest thy Narcissus are?
        O if thou have
Hid them in some flow'ry cave,
240   Tell me but where,
    Sweet queen of parley, daughter of the sphere.
So may'st thou be translated to the skies,
And give resounding grace to all heav'n's harmonies.

Comus. Can any mortal mixture of earth's mould
245 Breathe such divine enchanting ravishment?
Sure something holy lodges in that breast,
And with these raptures moves the vocal air
To testify his hidden residence;

How sweetly did they float upon the wings
250   Of silence, through the empty-vaulted night,
At every fall smoothing the raven down
Of darkness till it smiled: I have oft heard
My mother Circe with the Sirens three,
Amidst the flow'ry-kirtled Naiades
255   Culling their potent herbs, and baleful drugs,
Who as they sung, would take the prisoned soul,
And lap it in Elysium; Scylla wept,
And chid her barking waves into attention,
And fell Charybdis murmured soft applause:
260   Yet they in pleasing slumber lulled the sense,
And in sweet madness robbed it of itself,
But such a sacred, and home-felt delight,
Such sober certainty of waking bliss
I never heard till now. I'll speak to her
265   And she shall be my queen. Hail foreign wonder
Whom certain these rough shades did never breed –
Unless the goddess that in rural shrine
Dwell'st here with Pan, or Sylvan, by blest song
Forbidding every bleak unkindly fog
270   To touch the prosperous growth of this tall wood.
Lady. Nay gentle shepherd, ill is lost that praise
That is addressed to unattending ears;
Not any boast of skill, but éxtreme shift
How to regain my severed company
275   Compelled me to awake the courteous Echo
To give me answer from her mossy couch.
Comus. What chance good Lady hath bereft you thus?
Lady. Dim darkness, and this leavy labyrinth.
Comus. Could that divide you from near-ushering guides?
280   *Lady.* They left me weary on a grassy turf.
Comus. By falsehood, or discourtesy, or why?
Lady. To seek i' the valley some cool friendly spring.
Comus. And left your fair side all unguarded Lady?
Lady. They were but twain, and purposed quick return.
285   *Comus.* Perhaps forestalling night prevented them.
Lady. How easy my misfortune is to hit!
Comus. Imports their loss, beside the present need?

Lady. No less than if I should my brothers lose.
Comus. Were they of manly prime, or youthful bloom?
290   *Lady.* As smooth as Hebe's their unrazored lips.
Comus. Two such I saw, what time the laboured ox
In his loose traces from the furrow came,
And the swinked hedger at his supper sat;
I saw them under a green mantling vine
295   That crawls along the side of yon small hill,
Plucking ripe clusters from the tender shoots;
Their port was more than human, as they stood;
I took it for a faery vision
Of some gay creatures of the element
300   That in the colours of the rainbow live
And play i' th' plighted clouds. I was awe-strook,
And as I passed, I worshipped; if those you seek,
It were a journey like the path to heav'n
To help you find them.
Lady.   Gentle villager
305   What readiest way would bring me to that place?
Comus. Due west it rises from this shrubby point.
Lady. To find out that, good shepherd, I suppose,
In such a scant allowance of star-light,
Would overtake the best land-pilot's art,
310   Without the sure guess of well-practised feet.
Comus. I know each lane, and every alley green,
Dingle, or bushy dell of this wild wood,
And every bosky bourn from side to side
My daily walks and ancient neighbourhood,
315   And if your stray attendance be yet lodged,
Or shroud within these limits, I shall know
Ere morrow wake, or the low-roosted lark
From her thatched pallet rouse; if otherwise
I can conduct you Lady to a low
320   But loyal cottage, where you may be safe
Till further quest.
Lady.   Shepherd I take thy word,
And trust thy honest offered courtesy,
Which oft is sooner found in lowly sheds
With smoky rafters, than in tap'stry halls

325 And courts of princes, where it first was named,
    And yet is most pretended: in a place
    Less warranted than this, or less secure
    I cannot be, that I should fear to change it.
    Eye me blest Providence, and square my trial
330 To my proportioned strength. Shepherd lead on. –

The Two Brothers

Elder Brother. Unmuffle ye faint stars, and thou fair moon
    That wont'st to love the traveller's benison,
    Stoop thy pale visage through an amber cloud,
    And disinherit Chaos, that reigns here
335 In double night of darkness, and of shades;
    Or if your influence be quite dammed up
    With black usurping mists, some gentle taper
    Though a rush candle from the wicker hole
    Of some clay habitation visit us
340 With thy long levelled rule of streaming light,
    And thou shalt be our star of Arcady,
    Or Tyrian Cynosure.
    Second Brother.   Or if our eyes
    Be barred that happiness, might we but hear
    The folded flocks penned in their wattled cotes,
345 Or sound of pastoral reed with oaten stops,
    Or whistle from the lodge, or village cock
    Count the night watches to his feathery dames,
    'Twould be some solace yet, some little cheering
    In this close dungeon of innumerous boughs.
350 But O that hapless virgin our lost sister,
    Where may she wander now, whither betake her
    From the chill dew, amongst rude burs and thistles?
    Perhaps some cold bank is her bolster now
    Or 'gainst the rugged bark of some broad elm
355 Leans her unpillowed head fraught with sad fears.
    What if in wild amazement, and affright,
    Or while we speak within the direful grasp
    Of savage hunger, or of savage heat?
    Elder Brother. Peace brother, be not over-exquisite

360 To cast the fashion of uncertain evils;
    For grant they be so, while they rest unknown,
    What need a man forestall his date of grief,
    And run to meet what he would most avoid?
    Or if they be but false alarms of fear,
365 How bitter is such self-delusïon!
    I do not think my sister so to seek,
    Or so unprincipled in virtue's book,
    And the sweet peace that goodness bosoms ever,
    As that the single want of light and noise
370 (Not being in danger, as I trust she is not)
    Could stir the constant mood of her calm thoughts,
    And put them into misbecoming plight.
    Virtue could see to do what virtue would
    By her own radiant light, though sun and moon
375 Were in the flat sea sunk. And Wisdom's self
    Oft seeks to sweet retired solitude,
    Where with her best nurse Contemplatïon
    She plumes her feathers, and lets grow her wings
    That in the various bustle of resort
380 Were all to-ruffled, and sometimes impaired.
    He that has light within his own clear breast
    May sit i' th' centre, and enjoy bright day,
    But he that hides a dark soul, and foul thoughts
    Benighted walks under the midday sun;
    Himself is his own dungeon.
385 *Second Brother.*   'Tis most true
    That musing meditation most affects
    The pensive secrecy of desert cell,
    Far from the cheerful haunt of men, and herds,
    And sits as safe as in a senate-house;
390 For who would rob a hermit of his weeds,
    His few books, or his beads, or maple dish,
    Or do his grey hairs any violence?
    But beauty like the fair Hesperian tree
    Laden with blooming gold, had need the guard
395 Of dragon watch with unenchanted eye,
    To save her blossoms, and defend her fruit
    From the rash hand of bold incontinence.

You may as well spread out the unsunned heaps
Of miser's treasure by an outlaw's den,
400   And tell me it is safe, as bid me hope
Danger will wink on opportunity,
And let a single helpless maiden pass
Uninjured in this wild surrounding waste.
Of night, or loneliness it recks me not,
405   I fear the dread events that dog them both,
Lest some ill-greeting touch attempt the person
Of our unownèd sister.
Elder Brother.   I do not, brother,
Infer, as if I thought my sister's state
Secure without all doubt, or controversy:
410   Yet where an equal poise of hope and fear
Does arbitrate th' event, my nature is
That I incline to hope, rather than fear,
And gladly banish squint suspicïon.
My sister is not so defenceless left
415   As you imagine; she has a hidden strength
Which you remember not.
Second Brother.   What hidden strength,
Unless the strength of Heav'n, if you mean that?
Elder Brother. I mean that too, but yet a hidden strength
Which if Heav'n gave it, may be termed her own:
420   'Tis chastity, my brother, chastity:
She that has that, is clad in cómplete steel,
And like a quivered nymph with arrows keen
May trace huge forests, and unharboured heaths,
Infamous hills, and sandy perilous wilds,
425   Where through the sacred rays of chastity,
No savage fierce, bandit, or mountaineer
Will dare to soil her virgin purity:
Yea there, where very desolation dwells,
By grots, and caverns shagged with horrid shades,
430   She may pass on with unblenched majesty,
Be it not done in pride, or in presumption.
Some say no evil thing that walks by night
In fog, or fire, by lake, or moorish fen,
Blue meagre hag, or stubborn unlaid ghost,

435 That breaks his magic chains at curfew time,
No goblin, or swart faery of the mine,
Hath hurtful power o'er true virginity.
Do ye believe me yet, or shall I call
Antiquity from the old schools of Greece
440 To testify the arms of chastity?
Hence had the huntress Dian her dread bow,
Fair silver-shafted queen for ever chaste,
Wherewith she tamed the brinded lioness
And spotted mountain pard, but set at nought
445 The frivolous bolt of Cupid; gods and men
Feared her stern frown, and she was queen o' th' woods.
What was that snaky-headed Gorgon shield
That wise Minerva wore, unconquered virgin,
Wherewith she freezed her foes to cóngealed stone?
450 But rigid looks of chaste austerity,
And noble grace that dashed brute violence
With sudden adoration, and blank awe.
So dear to Heav'n is saintly chastity,
That when a soul is found sincerely so,
455 A thousand liveried angels lackey her,
Driving far off each thing of sin and guilt,
And in clear dream, and solemn visïon
Tell her of things that no gross ear can hear,
Till oft converse with Heav'nly habitants
460 Begin to cast a beam on th' outward shape,
The unpolluted temple of the mind,
And turns it by degrees to the soul's essence,
Till all be made immortal: but when lust
By unchaste looks, loose gestures, and foul talk,
465 But most by lewd and lavish act of sin,
Lets in defilement to the inward parts,
The soul grows clotted by contagïon,
Embodies, and imbrutes, till she quite lose
The divine property of her first being.
470 Such are those thick and gloomy shadows damp
Oft seen in charnel vaults, and sepulchres
Lingering, and sitting by a new-made grave,
As loath to leave the body that it loved,

And linked itself by carnal sensualty
475 To a degenerate and degraded state.
Second Brother. How charming is divine philosophy!
Not harsh, and crabbed as dull fools suppose,
But musical as is Apollo's lute,
And a perpetual feast of nectared sweets,
Where no crude surfeit reigns.
480 *Elder Brother.*   List, list, I hear
Some far-off hallo break the silent air.
Second Brother. Methought so too; what should it be?
Elder Brother.   For certain
Either some one like us night-foundered here,
Or else some neighbour woodman, or at worst,
485 Some roving robber calling to his fellows.
Second Brother. Heav'n keep my sister. Again, again, and
            near.
Best draw, and stand upon our guard.
Elder Brother.   I'll hallo;
If he be friendly he comes well, if not,
Defence is a good cause, and Heav'n be for us.

The Attendant Spirit habited like a shepherd

490 That hallo I should know, what are you? Speak;
Come not too near, you fall on iron stakes else.
Spirit. What voice is that, my young lord? Speak again.
Second Brother. O brother, 'tis my father's shepherd sure.
Elder Brother. Thyrsis? Whose artful strains have oft
            delayed
495 The huddling brook to hear his madrigal,
And sweetened every muskrose of the dale,
How cam'st thou here good swain? Hath any ram
Slipped from the fold, or young kid lost his dam,
Or straggling wether the penned flock forsook?
500 How couldst thou find this dark sequestered nook?
Spirit. O my loved master's heir, and his next joy,
I came not here on such a trivial toy
As a strayed ewe, or to pursue the stealth
Of pilfering wolf; not all the fleecy wealth

505 That doth enrich these downs, is worth a thought
To this my errand, and the care it brought.
But O my virgin Lady, where is she?
How chance she is not in your company?
Elder Brother. To tell thee sadly shepherd, without blame,
510 Or our neglect, we lost her as we came.
Spirit. Ay me unhappy then my fears are true.
Elder Brother. What fears good Thyrsis? Prithee briefly
show.
Spirit. I'll tell ye. 'Tis not vain or fabulous
(Though so esteemed by shallow ignorance)
515 What the sage poets, taught by th' Heavenly Muse,
Storied of old in high immortal verse
Of dire Chimeras and enchanted isles,
And rifted rocks whose entrance leads to Hell,
For such there be, but unbelief is blind.
520   Within the navel of this hideous wood,
Immured in cypress shades a sorcerer dwells
Of Bacchus and of Circe born, great Comus,
Deep skilled in all his mother's witcheries,
And here to every thirsty wanderer,
525 By sly enticement gives his baneful cup,
With many murmurs mixed, whose pleasing poison
The visage quite transforms of him that drinks,
And the inglorious likeness of a beast
Fixes instead, unmoulding reason's mintage
530 Charáctered in the face; this have I learnt
Tending my flocks hard by i' th' hilly crofts
That brow this bottom glade, whence night by night
He and his monstrous rout are heard to howl
Like stabled wolves, or tigers at their prey,
535 Doing abhorrèd rites to Hecate
In their obscurèd haunts of inmost bow'rs.
Yet have they many baits, and guileful spells
T' inveigle and invite th' unwary sense
Of them that pass unweeting by the way.
540 This evening late, by then the chewing flocks
Had ta'en their supper on the savoury herb
Of knot-grass dew-besprent, and were in fold,

I sat me down to watch upon a bank
With ivy canopied, and interwove
545   With flaunting honeysuckle, and began
Wrapped in a pleasing fit of melancholy
To meditate my rural minstrelsy
Till fancy had her fill; but ere a close
The wonted roar was up amidst the woods,
550   And filled the air with barbarous dissonance,
At which I ceased, and listened them a while,
Till an unusual stop of sudden silence
Gave respite to the drowsy-frighted steeds
That draw the litter of close-curtained Sleep.
555   At last a soft and solemn breathing sound
Rose like a steam of rich distilled perfumes,
And stole upon the air, that even Silence
Was took ere she was ware, and wished she might
Deny her nature, and be never more
560   Still to be so displaced. I was all ear,
And took in strains that might create a soul
Under the ribs of Death. But O ere long
Too well I did perceive it was the voice
Of my most honoured Lady, your dear sister.
565   Amazed I stood, harrowed with grief and fear,
And O poor hapless nightingale thought I,
How sweet thou sing'st, how near the deadly snare!
Then down the lawns I ran with headlong haste
Through paths, and turnings often trod by day,
570   Till guided by mine ear I found the place
Where that damned wizard hid in sly disguise
(For so by certain signs I knew) had met
Already, ere my best speed could prevent,
The aidless innocent Lady his wished prey,
575   Who gently asked if he had seen such two,
Supposing him some neighbour villager;
Longer I durst not stay, but soon I guessed
Ye were the two she meant; with that I sprung
Into swift flight, till I had found you here,
But further know I not.
580   *Second Brother.*   O night and shades,

How are ye joined with Hell in triple knot
Against th' unarmèd weakness of one virgin
Alone, and helpless! Is this the confidence
You gave me brother?
Elder Brother.   Yes, and keep it still,
585   Lean on it safely; not a period
Shall be unsaid for me: against the threats
Of malice or of sorcery, or that power
Which erring men call Chance, this I hold firm,
Virtue may be assailed, but never hurt,
590   Surprised by unjust force, but not enthralled,
Yea even that which mischief meant most harm,
Shall in the happy trial prove most glory.
But evil on itself shall back recoil,
And mix no more with goodness, when at last
595   Gathered like scum, and settled to itself
It shall be in eternal restless change
Self-fed, and self-consumed. If this fail,
The pillared firmament is rottenness,
And earth's base built on stubble. But come let's on.
600   Against th' opposing will and arm of Heav'n
May never this just sword be lifted up.
But for that damned magician, let him be girt
With all the grisly legïons that troop
Under the sooty flag of Acheron,
605   Harpies and Hydras, or all the monstrous forms
'Twixt Africa and Ind, I'll find him out,
And force him to restore his purchase back,
Or drag him by the curls to a foul death,
Cursed as his life.
Spirit.   Alas good vent'rous youth,
610   I love thy courage yet, and bold emprise,
But here thy sword can do thee little stead;
Far other arms, and other weapons must
Be those that quell the might of Hellish charms;
He with his bare wand can unthread thy joints,
And crumble all thy sinews.
615   *Elder Brother.*   Why prithee shepherd
How durst thou then thyself approach so near

As to make this relation?
Spirit.   Care and utmost shifts
How to secure the Lady from surprisal
Brought to my mind a certain shepherd lad
620 Of small regard to see to, yet well skilled
In every virtuous plant and healing herb
That spreads her verdant leaf to the morning ray;
He loved me well, and oft would bid me sing,
Which when I did, he on the tender grass
625 Would sit, and hearken even to ecstasy,
And in requital ope his leathern scrip,
And show me simples of a thousand names
Telling their strange and vigorous faculties;
Amongst the rest a small unsightly root,
630 But of divine effect, he culled me out;
The leaf was darkish, and had prickles on it,
But in another country, as he said,
Bore a bright golden flower, but not in this soil:
Unknown, and like esteemed, and the dull swain
635 Treads on it daily with his clouted shoon,
And yet more med'cinal is it than that Moly
That Hermes once to wise Ulysses gave;
He called it haemony, and gave it me,
And bade me keep it as of sov'reign use
640 'Gainst all enchantments, mildew blast, or damp
Or ghastly Furies' apparition;
I pursed it up, but little reck'ning made
Till now that this extremity compelled,
But now I find it true; for by this means
645 I knew the foul enchanter though disguised,
Entered the very lime-twigs of his spells,
And yet came off: if you have this about you
(As I will give you when we go) you may
Boldly assault the necromancer's hall;
650 Where if he be, with dauntless hardihood,
And brandished blade rush on him, break his glass,
And shed the luscious liquor on the ground,
But seize his wand. Though he and his cursed crew
Fierce sign of battle make, and menace high,

655 Or like the sons of Vulcan vomit smoke,
   Yet will they soon retire, if he but shrink.
   Elder Brother. Thyrsis lead on apace, I'll follow thee,
   And some good angel bear a shield before us.

*The scene changes to a stately palace, set out with all manner of
deliciousness: soft music, tables spread with all dainties. Comus
appears with his rabble, and the Lady set in an enchanted chair,
to whom he offers his glass, which she puts by, and goes about to
rise.*

   Comus. Nay Lady sit; if I but wave this wand,
660 Your nerves are all chained up in alabaster,
   And you a statue; or as Daphne was
   Root-bound, that fled Apollo.
   Lady.   Fool do not boast,
   Thou canst not touch the freedom of my mind
   With all thy charms, although this corporal rind
665 Thou hast immanacled, while Heav'n sees good.
   Comus. Why are you vexed Lady? why do you frown?
   Here dwell no frowns, nor anger, from these gates
   Sorrow flies far: see here be all the pleasures
   That fancy can beget on youthful thoughts
670 When the fresh blood grows lively, and returns
   Brisk as the April buds in primrose season.
   And first behold this cordial julep here
   That flames, and dances in his crystal bounds
   With spirits of balm, and fragrant syrups mixed.
675 Not that Nepenthes which the wife of Thone
   In Egypt gave to Jove-born Helena
   Is of such power to stir up joy as this,
   To life so friendly, or so cool to thirst.
   Why should you be so cruel to yourself,
680 And to those dainty limbs which Nature lent
   For gentle usage, and soft delicacy?
   But you invert the cov'nants of her trust,
   And harshly deal like an ill borrower
   With that which you received on other terms,
685 Scorning the unexempt condition

By which all mortal frailty must subsist,
Refreshment after toil, ease after pain,
That have been tired all day without repast,
And timely rest have wanted; but fair virgin
This will restore all soon.
690   *Lady.*   'Twill not false traitor,
'Twill not restore the truth and honesty
That thou hast banished from thy tongue with lies;
Was this the cottage, and the safe abode
Thou told'st me of? What grim aspécts are these,
695   These ugly-headed monsters? Mercy guard me!
Hence with thy brewed enchantments, foul deceiver;
Hast thou betrayed my credulous innocence
With vizored falsehood, and base forgery,
And wouldst thou seek again to trap me here
700   With lickerish baits fit to ensnare a brute?
Were it a draught for Juno when she banquets,
I would not taste thy treasonous offer; none
But such as are good men may give good things,
And that which is not good, is not delicious
705   To a well-governed and wise appetite.
Comus. O foolishness of men! that lend their ears
To those budge doctors of the Stoic fur,
And fetch their precepts from the Cynic tub,
Praising the lean and sallow Abstinence.
710   Wherefore did Nature pour her bounties forth
With such a full and unwithdrawing hand,
Covering the earth with odours, fruits, and flocks,
Thronging the seas with spawn innumerable,
But all to please, and sate the curious taste?
715   And set to work millions of spinning worms,
That in their green shops weave the smooth-haired silk
To deck her sons, and that no corner might
Be vacant of her plenty, in her own loins
She hutched th' all-worshipped ore, and precious gems
720   To store her children with; if all the world
Should in a pet of temperance feed on pulse,
Drink the clear stream, and nothing wear but frieze,
Th' All-giver would be unthanked, would be unpraised,

Not half his riches known, and yet despised,
725 And we should serve him as a grudging master,
As a penurious niggard of his wealth,
And live like Nature's bastards, not her sons,
Who would be quite surcharged with her own weight,
And strangled with her waste fertility;
730 Th' earth cumbered, and the winged air dark with plumes,
The herds would over-multitude their lords,
The sea o'erfraught would swell, and th' unsought
        diamonds
Would so emblaze the forehead of the deep,
And so bestud with stars, that they below
735 Would grow inured to light, and come at last
To gaze upon the sun with shameless brows.
List Lady be not coy, and be not cozened
With that same vaunted name Virginity;
Beauty is Nature's coin, must not be hoarded,
740 But must be current, and the good thereof
Consists in mutual and partaken bliss,
Unsavoury in th' enjoyment of itself.
If you let slip time, like a neglected rose
It withers on the stalk with languished head.
745 Beauty is Nature's brag, and must be shown
In courts, at feasts, and high solemnities
Where most may wonder at the workmanship;
It is for homely features to keep home,
They had their name thence; coarse complexïons
750 And cheeks of sorry grain will serve to ply
The sampler, and to tease the huswife's wool.
What need a vermeil-tinctured lip for that,
Love-darting eyes, or tresses like the morn?
There was another meaning in these gifts,
755 Think what, and be advised, you are but young yet.
Lady. I had not thought to have unlocked my lips
In this unhallowed air, but that this juggler
Would think to charm my judgement, as mine eyes,
Obtruding false rules pranked in reason's garb.
760 I hate when vice can bolt her arguments,
And virtue has no tongue to check her pride:

Impostor do not charge most innocent Nature,
As if she would her children should be riotous
With her abundance; she good cateress
765 Means her provision only to the good
That live according to her sober laws,
And holy dictate of spare Temperance:
If every just man that now pines with want
Had but a moderate and beseeming share
770 Of that which lewdly-pampered Luxury
Now heaps upon some few with vast excess,
Nature's full blessings would be well-dispensed
In unsuperfluous even proportion,
And she no whit encumbered with her store;
775 And then the Giver would be better thanked,
His praise due paid, for swinish gluttony
Ne'er looks to Heav'n amidst his gorgeous feast,
But with besotted base ingratitude
Crams, and blasphemes his feeder. Shall I go on?
780 Or have I said enough? To him that dares
Arm his profane tongue with contemptuous words
Against the sun-clad power of Chastity,
Fain would I something say, yet to what end?
Thou hast nor ear, nor soul to apprehend
785 The súblime notion, and high mystery
That must be uttered to unfold the sage
And serious doctrine of Virginity,
And thou art worthy that thou shouldst not know
More happiness than this thy present lot.
790 Enjoy your dear wit, and gay rhetoric
That hath so well been taught her dazzling fence,
Thou art not fit to hear thyself convinced;
Yet should I try, the uncontrollèd worth
Of this pure cause would kindle my rapt spirits
795 To such a flame of sacred vehemence,
That dumb things would be moved to sympathize,
And the brute earth would lend her nerves, and shake,
Till all thy magic structures reared so high,
Were shattered into heaps o'er thy false head.

800 *Comus.* She fables not, I feel that I do fear
　　　Her words set off by some superior power;
　　　And though not mortal, yet a cold shuddering dew
　　　Dips me all o'er, as when the wrath of Jove
　　　Speaks thunder, and the chains of Erebus
805 To some of Saturn's crew. I must dissemble,
　　　And try her yet more strongly. Come, no more,
　　　This is mere moral babble, and direct
　　　Against the canon laws of our foundation;
　　　I must not suffer this; yet 'tis but the lees
810 And settlings of a melancholy blood;
　　　But this will cure all straight, one sip of this
　　　Will bathe the drooping spirits in delight
　　　Beyond the bliss of dreams. Be wise, and taste.—

*The Brothers rush in with swords drawn, wrest his glass out of
his hand, and break it against the ground; his rout make sign of
resistance, but are all driven in; the Attendant Spirit comes in.*

　　　Spirit. What, have you let the false enchanter 'scape?
815 O ye mistook, ye should have snatched his wand
　　　And bound him fast; without his rod reversed,
　　　And backward mutters of dissevering power,
　　　We cannot free the Lady that sits here
　　　In stony fetters fixed, and motionless;
820 Yet stay, be not disturbed, now I bethink me,
　　　Some other means I have which may be used,
　　　Which once of Meliboeus old I learnt,
　　　The soothest shepherd that e'er piped on plains.
　　　　There is a gentle nymph not far from hence,
825 That with moist curb sways the smooth Severn stream,
　　　Sabrina is her name, a virgin pure;
　　　Whilom she was the daughter of Locrine,
　　　That had the sceptre from his father Brute.
　　　She guiltless damsel flying the mad pursuit
830 Of her enragèd stepdame Guendolen,
　　　Commended her fair innocence to the flood
　　　That stayed her flight with his cross-flowing course;

The water nymphs that in the bottom played,
Held up their pearlèd wrists and took her in,
835 Bearing her straight to agèd Nereus' hall,
Who piteous of her woes, reared her lank head,
And gave her to his daughters to imbathe
In nectared lavers strewed with asphodel,
And through the porch and inlet of each sense
840 Dropped in ambrosial oils till she revived,
And underwent a quick immortal change
Made goddess of the river; still she retains
Her maiden gentleness, and oft at eve
Visits the herds along the twilight meadows,
845 Helping all urchin blasts, and ill-luck signs
That the shrewd meddling elf delights to make,
Which she with precious vialed liquors heals.
For which the shepherds at their festivals
Carol her goodness loud in rustic lays,
850 And throw sweet garland wreaths into her stream
Of pansies, pinks, and gaudy daffodils.
And, as the old swain said, she can unlock
The clasping charm, and thaw the numbing spell,
If she be right invoked in warbled song,
855 For maidenhood she loves, and will be swift
To aid a virgin, such as was herself
In hard-besetting need; this will I try
And add the power of some adjuring verse.

Song

Sabrina fair,
860   Listen where thou art sitting
Under the glassy, cool, translucent wave,
      In twisted braids of lilies knitting
The loose train of thy amber-dropping hair;
      Listen for dear honour's sake,
865   Goddess of the silver lake,
          Listen and save.

Listen and appear to us
In name of great Oceanus,
By th' earth-shaking Neptune's mace,
870 And Tethys' grave majestic pace,
By hoary Nereus' wrinkled look,
And the Carpathian wizard's hook,
By scaly Triton's winding shell,
And old sooth-saying Glaucus' spell,
875 By Leucothea's lovely hands,
And her son that rules the strands,
By Thetis' tinsel-slippered feet,
And the songs of Sirens sweet,
By dead Parthenope's dear tomb,
880 And fair Ligea's golden comb,
Wherewith she sits on diamond rocks
Sleeking her soft alluring locks,
By all the nymphs that nightly dance
Upon thy streams with wily glance,
885 Rise, rise, and heave thy rosy head
From thy coral-paven bed,
And bridle in thy headlong wave,
Till thou our summons answered have.

Listen and save.

Sabrina rises, attended by water-nymphs, and sings,

890 By the rushy-fringèd bank,
Where grows the willow and the osier dank,
    My sliding chariot stays,
Thick set with agate, and the azurn sheen
Of turkis blue, and emerald green
895   That in the channel strays,
Whilst from off the waters fleet
Thus I set my printless feet
O'er the cowslip's velvet head,
    That bends not as I tread;
900 Gentle swain at thy request
    I am here.
Spirit. Goddess dear

We implore thy powerful hand
To undo the charmèd band
905 Of true virgin here distressed,
Through the force, and through the wile
Of unblest enchanter vile.
Sabrina. Shepherd 'tis my office best
To help ensnarèd chastity;
910 Brightest Lady look on me,
Thus I sprinkle on thy breast
Drops that from my fountain pure,
I have kept of precious cure;
Thrice upon thy finger's tip,
915 Thrice upon thy rubied lip,
Next this marble venomed seat
Smeared with gums of glutinous heat
I touch with chaste palms moist and cold,
Now the spell hath lost his hold;
920 And I must haste ere morning hour
To wait in Amphitrite's bower.

Sabrina descends, and the Lady rises out of her seat.

Spirit. Virgin, daughter of Locrine
Sprung of old Anchises' line,
May thy brimmèd waves for this
925 Their full tribute never miss
From a thousand petty rills,
That tumble down the snowy hills:
Summer drought, or singèd air
Never scorch thy tresses fair,
930 Nor wet October's torrent flood
Thy molten crystal fill with mud,
May thy billows roll ashore
The beryl, and the golden ore;
May thy lofty head be crowned
935 With many a tower and terrace round,
And here and there thy banks upon
With groves of myrrh, and cinnamon.
Come Lady while Heaven lends us grace,

Let us fly this cursèd place,
940   Lest the sorcerer us entice
With some other new device.
Not a waste, or needless sound
Till we come to holier ground;
I shall be your faithful guide
945   Through this gloomy covert wide,
And not many furlongs thence
Is your father's residence,
Where this night are met in state
Many a friend to gratulate
950   His wished presence, and beside
All the swains that there abide,
With jigs, and rural dance resort,
We shall catch them at their sport,
And our sudden coming there
955   Will double all their mirth and cheer;
Come let us haste, the stars grow high,
But Night sits monarch yet in the mid sky.

The scene changes presenting Ludlow Town and the President's Castle, then come in country dancers, after them the Attendant Spirit, with the two Brothers and the Lady.

Song

Spirit. Back shepherds, back, enough your play,
Till next sunshine holiday,
960   Here be without duck or nod
Other trippings to be trod
Of lighter toes, and such court guise
As Mercury did first devise
With the mincing Dryades
965   On the lawns, and on the leas.

This second song presents them to their father and mother.

Noble Lord, and Lady bright,
I have brought ye new delight,

Here behold so goodly grown
Three fair branches of your own;
970 Heav'n hath timely tried their youth,
Their faith, their patience, and their truth.
And sent them here through hard assays
With a crown of deathless praise,
To triumph in victorious dance
975 O'er sensual folly, and intemperance.

The dances ended, the Spirit epiloguizes.

Spirit. To the Ocean now I fly,
And those happy climes that lie
Where day never shuts his eye,
Up in the broad fields of the sky:
980 There I suck the liquid air
All amidst the gardens fair
Of Hesperus, and his daughters three
That sing about the golden tree:
Along the crispèd shades and bow'rs
985 Revels the spruce and jocund Spring;
The Graces, and the rosy-bosomed Hours,
Thither all their bounties bring,
That there eternal Summer dwells,
And west winds, with musky wing
990 About the cedarn alleys fling
Nard, and cassia's balmy smells.
Iris there with humid bow,
Waters the odorous banks that blow
Flowers of more mingled hue
995 Than her purfled scarf can show,
And drenches with Elysian dew
(List mortals, if your ears be true)
Beds of hyacinth, and roses
Where young Adonis oft reposes,
1000 Waxing well of his deep wound
In slumber soft, and on the ground
Sadly sits th' Assyrian queen;
But far above in spangled sheen

Celestial Cupid her famed son advanced,
1005 Holds his dear Psyche sweet entranced
After her wand'ring labours long,
Till free consent the gods among
Make her his eternal bride,
And from her fair unspotted side
1010 Two blissful twins are to be born,
Youth and joy; so Jove hath sworn.
    But now my task is smoothly done,
I can fly, or I can run
Quickly to the green earth's end,
1015 Where the bowed welkin slow doth bend,
And from thence can soar as soon
To the corners of the moon.
    Mortals that would follow me,
Love Virtue, she alone is free,
1020 She can teach ye how to climb
Higher than the sphery chime;
Or if Virtue feeble were,
Heav'n itself would stoop to her.

ENGLISH POEMS ADDED IN 1673

On the Death of a Fair Infant Dying of a Cough
Anno aetatis 17

I

O fairest flower no sooner blown but blasted,
Soft silken primrose fading timelessly,
Summer's chief honour if thou hadst outlasted
Bleak Winter's force that made thy blossom dry;
5   For he being amorous on that lovely dye
      That did thy cheek envermeil, thought to kiss
But killed alas, and then bewailed his fatal bliss.

II

For since grim Aquilo his charioteer
By boist'rous rape th' Athenian damsel got,
10   He thought it touched his deity full near,
If likewise he some fair one wedded not,
Thereby to wipe away th' infámous blot
      Of long-uncoupled bed, and childless eld,
Which 'mongst the wanton gods a foul reproach was held.

III

15   So mounting up in icy-pearlèd car,
Through middle empire of the freezing air
He wandered long, till thee he spied from far;
There ended was his quest, there ceased his care.
Down he descended from his snow-soft chair,
20   But all unwares with his cold-kind embrace
Unhoused thy virgin soul from her fair biding-place.

IV

Yet art thou not inglorious in thy fate;
For so Apollo, with unweeting hand
Whilom did slay his dearly-lovèd mate

25   Young Hyacinth born on Eurotas' strand,
Young Hyacinth the pride of Spartan land;
    But then transformed him to a purple flower;
Alack that so to change thee Winter had no power.

V

Yet can I not persuade me thou art dead

30   Or that thy corse corrupts in earth's dark womb,
Or that thy beauties lie in wormy bed,
Hid from the world in a low-delvèd tomb;
Could Heav'n for pity thee so strictly doom?
    O no! for something in thy face did shine

35   Above mortality that showed thou wast divine.

VI

Resolve me then O soul most surely blest
(If so it be that thou these plaints dost hear),
Tell me bright spirit where'er thou hoverest,
Whether above that high first-moving sphere

40   Or in the Elysian fields (if such there were),
    O say me true if thou wert mortal wight,
And why from us so quickly thou didst take thy flight.

VII

Wert thou some star which from the ruined roof
Of shaked Olympus by mischance did fall;

45   Which careful Jove in Nature's true behoof
Took up, and in fit place did reinstall?
Or did of late Earth's sons besiege the wall
    Of sheeny heav'n, and thou some goddess fled
Amongst us here below to hide thy nectared head?

VIII

50 Or wert thou that just maid who once before
Forsook the hated earth, O tell me sooth,
And cam'st again to visit us once more?
Or wert thou [Mercy] that sweet smiling youth?
Or that crowned matron, sage white-robèd Truth?
55   Or any other of that Heav'nly brood
Let down in cloudy throne to do the world some good?

IX

Or wert thou of the golden-wingèd host,
Who having clad thyself in human weed,
To earth from thy prefixèd seat didst post,
60 And after short abode fly back with speed,
As if to show what creatures Heav'n doth breed,
      Thereby to set the hearts of men on fire
To scorn the sordid world, and unto Heav'n aspire?

X

But O why didst thou not stay here below
65 To bless us with thy Heav'n-loved innocence,
To slake his wrath whom sin hath made our foe,
To turn swift-rushing black perdition hence,
Or drive away the slaughtering pestilence,
      To stand 'twixt us and our deservèd smart?
70 But thou canst best perform that office where thou art.

XI

Then thou the mother of so sweet a child
Her false imagined loss cease to lament,
And wisely learn to curb thy sorrows wild;
Think what a present thou to God hast sent,
75 And render him with patience what he lent;
      This if thou do he will an offspring give,
That till the world's last end shall make thy name to live.

At a Vacation Exercise in the College, part Latin, part English
Anno aetatis 19

The Latin Speeches ended, the English thus began

Hail native language, that by sinews weak
Didst move my first endeavouring tongue to speak,
And mad'st imperfect words with childish trips,
Half unpronounced, slide through my infant lips,
5   Driving dumb silence from the portal door,
Where he had mutely sat two years before:
Here I salute thee and thy pardon ask,
That now I use thee in my latter task:
Small loss it is that hence can come unto thee,
10 I know my tongue but little grace can do thee.
Thou need'st not be ambitious to be first,
Believe me I have thither packed the worst:
And, if it happen as I did forecast,
The daintiest dishes shall be served up last.
15 I pray thee then deny me not thy aid
For this same small neglect that I have made:
But haste thee straight to do me once a pleasure,
And from thy wardrobe bring thy chiefest treasure;
Not those new-fangled toys, and trimming slight
20 Which takes our late fantastics with delight,
But cull those richest robes, and gay'st attire
Which deepest spirits, and choicest wits desire:
I have some naked thoughts that rove about
And loudly knock to have their passage out;
25 And weary of their place do only stay
Till thou hast decked them in thy best array;
That so they may without suspect or fears
Fly swiftly to this fair assembly's ears;
Yet I had rather, if I were to choose,
30 Thy service in some graver subject use,
Such as may make thee search thy coffers round,
Before thou clothe my fancy in fit sound:

Such where the deep transported mind may soar
Above the wheeling poles, and at Heav'n's door
35   Look in, and see each blissful deity
How he before the thunderous throne doth lie,
Listening to what unshorn Apollo sings
To th' touch of golden wires, while Hebe brings
Immortal nectar to her kingly sire:
40   Then passing through the spheres of watchful fire,
And misty regions of wide air next under,
And hills of snow and lofts of pilèd thunder,
May tell at length how green-eyed Neptune raves,
In Heav'n's defiance mustering all his waves;
45   Then sing of secret things that came to pass
When beldam Nature in her cradle was;
And last of kings and queens and heroes old,
Such as the wise Demodocus once told
In solemn feasts at King Alcinous' feast,
50   While sad Ulysses' soul and all the rest
Are held with his melodious harmony
In willing chains and sweet captivity.
But fie my wand'ring Muse how dost thou stray!
Expectance calls thee now another way;
55   Thou know'st it must be now thy only bent
To keep in compass of thy Predicament:
Then quick about thy purposed business come,
That to the next I may resign my room.

Then ENS *is represented as father of the Predicaments his ten*
sons, whereof the eldest stood for SUBSTANCE *with his Canons,*
which ENS *thus speaking, explains.*

Good luck befriend thee son; for at thy birth
60   The fairy ladies danced upon the hearth;
Thy drowsy nurse hath sworn she did them spy
Come tripping to the room where thou didst lie;
And sweetly singing round about thy bed
Strew all their blessings on thy sleeping head.
65   She heard them give thee this, that thou shouldst still
From eyes of mortals walk invisible,

Yet there is something that doth force my fear,
For once it was my dismal hap to hear
A Sibyl old, bow-bent with crookèd age,
70 That far events full wisely could presage,
And in time's long and dark prospective glass,
Foresaw what future days should bring to pass;
Your son, said she, (nor can you it prevent)
Shall subject be to many an Accident.
75 O'er all his brethren he shall reign as king,
Yet every one shall make him underling,
And those that cannot live from him asunder
Ungratefully shall strive to keep him under;
In worth and excellence he shall outgo them,
80 Yet being above them, he shall be below them;
From others he shall stand in need of nothing,
Yet on his brothers shall depend for clothing.
To find a foe it shall not be his hap,
And peace shall lull him in her flow'ry lap;
85 Yet shall he live in strife, and at his door
Devouring war shall never cease to roar:
Yea it shall be his natural property
To harbour those that are at enmity.
What power, what force, what mighty spell, if not
90 Your learned hands, can loose this Gordian knot?

The next, QUANTITY *and* QUALITY, *spake in prose, then*
RELATION *was called by his name*

Rivers arise; whether thou be the son,
Of utmost Tweed, or Ouse, or gulfy Dun,
Or Trent, who like some Earth-born Giant spreads
His thirty arms along th' indented meads,
95 Or sullen Mole that runneth underneath,
Or Severn swift, guilty of maiden's death,
Or rocky Avon, or of sedgy Lea,
Or coaly Tyne, or ancient hallowed Dee,
Or Humber loud that keeps the Scythian's name,
100 Or Medway smooth, or royal-towered Thame.
The rest was prose

Sonnet XI

A book was writ of late called *Tetrachordon*;
    And woven close, both matter, form and style;
    The subject new: it walked the town a while,
    Numb'ring good intellects; now seldom pored on.
5 Cries the stall-reader, Bless us! what a word on
    A title page is this! and some in file
    Stand spelling false, while one might walk to Mile-
    End Green. Why is it harder sirs than Gordon,
Colkitto, or Macdonnel, or Galasp?
10   Those rugged names to our like mouths grow sleek
    That would have made Quintilian stare and gasp.
Thy age, like ours, O soul of Sir John Cheke,
    Hated not learning worse than toad or asp,
    When thou taught'st Cambridge and King Edward
        Greek.

Sonnet XII

On the same

I did but prompt the age to quit their clogs
    By the known rules of ancient liberty,
    When straight a barbarous noise environs me
    Of owls and cuckoos, asses, apes and dogs.
5 As when those hinds that were transformed to frogs
    Railed at Latona's twin-born progeny
    Which after held the sun and moon in fee.
    But this is got by casting pearl to hogs;
That bawl for freedom in their senseless mood,
10   And still revolt when truth would set them free.
    Licence they mean when they cry Liberty;
For who loves that, must first be wise and good;
    But from that mark how far they rove we see
    For all this waste of wealth, and loss of blood.

Sonnet XIII

To Mr H. Lawes, on his Airs

Harry, whose tuneful and well-measured song
    First taught our English music how to span
    Words with just note and accent, not to scan
    With Midas' ears, committing short and long,
5   Thy worth and skill exempts thee from the throng,
    With praise enough for envy to look wan;
    To after age thou shalt be writ the man
    That with smooth air couldst humour best our tongue.
Thou honour'st verse, and verse must lend her wing
10   To honour thee, the priest of Phoebus' choir
    That tun'st their happiest lines in hymn, or story.
Dante shall give Fame leave to set thee higher
    Than his Casella, whom he wooed to sing
    Met in the milder shades of Purgatory.

Sonnet XIV

When Faith and Love which parted from thee never,
    Had ripened thy just soul to dwell with God,
    Meekly thou didst resign this earthy load
    Of death, called life; which us from life doth sever.
5   Thy works and alms and all thy good endeavour
    Stayed not behind, nor in the grave were trod;
    But as Faith pointed with her golden rod,
    Followed thee up to joy and bliss for ever.
Love led them on, and Faith who knew them best
10   Thy handmaids, clad them o'er with purple beams
    And azure wings, that up they flew so dressed,
And spake the truth of thee on glorious themes
    Before the Judge, who thenceforth bid thee rest
    And drink thy fill of pure immortal streams.

Sonnet XV

On the Late Massacre in Piedmont

Avenge O Lord thy slaughtered saints, whose bones
   Lie scattered on the Alpine mountains cold;
   Ev'n them who kept thy truth so pure of old
   When all our fathers worshipped stocks and stones,
5 Forget not: in thy book record their groans
   Who were thy sheep and in their ancient fold
   Slain by the bloody Piedmontese that rolled
   Mother with infant down the rocks. Their moans
The vales redoubled to the hills, and they
10 To Heav'n. Their martyred blood and ashes sow
   O'er all th' Italian fields where still doth sway
The triple Tyrant: that from these may grow
   A hundredfold, who having learnt thy way
   Early may fly the Babylonian woe.

Sonnet XVI

When I consider how my light is spent,
   Ere half my days, in this dark world and wide,
   And that one talent which is death to hide,
   Lodged with me useless, though my soul more bent
5 To serve therewith my Maker, and present
   My true account, lest he returning chide,
   Doth God exact day labour, light denied,
   I fondly ask; but patience to prevent
That murmur, soon replies, God doth not need
10 Either man's work or his own gifts; who best
   Bear his mild yoke, they serve him best; his state
Is kingly. Thousands at his bidding speed
   And post o'er land and ocean without rest:
   They also serve who only stand and wait.

Sonnet XVII

Lawrence of virtuous father virtuous son,
    Now that the fields are dank, and ways are mire,
    Where shall we sometimes meet, and by the fire
    Help waste a sullen day, what may be won
5 From the hard season gaining? Time will run
    On smoother, till Favonius re-inspire
    The frozen earth; and clothe in fresh attire
    The lily and rose, that neither sowed nor spun.
What neat repast shall feast us, light and choice,
10 Of Attic taste, with wine, whence we may rise
    To hear the lute well touched, or artful voice
Warble immortal notes and Tuscan air?
    He who of those delights can judge, and spare
    To interpose them oft, is not unwise.

Sonnet XVIII

Cyriack, whose grandsire on the Royal Bench
    Of British Themis, with no mean applause
    Pronounced and in his volumes taught our laws,
    Which others at their bar so often wrench;
5 Today deep thoughts resolve with me to drench
    In mirth, that after no repenting draws;
    Let Euclid rest and Archimedes pause,
    And what the Swede intend, and what the French.
To measure life learn thou betimes, and know
10 Toward solid good what leads the nearest way;
    For other things mild Heav'n a time ordains,
And disapproves that care, though wise in show,
    That with superfluous burden loads the day,
    And when God sends a cheerful hour, refrains.

Sonnet XIX

Methought I saw my late espousèd saint
   Brought to me like Alcestis from the grave,
   Whom Jove's great son to her glad husband gave,
   Rescued from death by force though pale and faint.
5 Mine as whom washed from spot of child-bed taint
   Purification in the old Law did save,
   And such, as yet once more I trust to have
   Full sight of her in Heaven without restraint,
Came vested all in white, pure as her mind:
10 Her face was veiled, yet to my fancied sight,
   Love, sweetness, goodness, in her person shined
So clear, as in no face with more delight.
   But O as to embrace me she inclined,
   I waked, she fled, and day brought back my night.

The Fifth Ode of Horace, Lib. I

Quis multa gracilis te puer in rosa

*Rendered almost word for word without rhyme according to the
Latin measure, as near as the language will permit.*

What slender youth bedewed with liquid odours
Courts thee on roses in some pleasant cave,
   Pyrrha? For whom bind'st thou
   In wreaths thy golden hair,
5 Plain in thy neatness? O how oft shall he
On faith and changèd gods complain: and seas
   Rough with black winds and storms
   Unwonted shall admire:
Who now enjoys thee credulous, all gold,
10 Who always vacant always amiable
   Hopes thee; of flattering gales
   Unmindful? Hapless they

To whom thou untried seem'st fair. Me in my vowed
Picture the sacred wall declares t' have hung
15   My dank and dropping weeds
       To the stern god of sea.

On the New Forcers of Conscience under the Long Parliament

Because you have thrown off your prelate lord,
    And with stiff vows renounced his liturgy
    To seize the widowed whore plurality
    From them whose sin ye envied, not abhorred,
5 Dare ye for this adjure the civil sword
    To force our consciences that Christ set free,
    And ride us with a classic hierarchy
    Taught ye by mere A.S. and Rutherford?
Men whose life, learning, faith and pure intent
10   Would have been held in high esteem with Paul
    Must now be named and printed heretics
By shallow Edwards and Scotch What-d'ye-call:
    But we do hope to find out all your tricks,
    Your plots and packings worse than those of Trent,
15   That so the Parliament
May with their wholesome and preventive shears
Clip your phylacteries, though balk your cars,
                        And succour our just fears
When they shall read this clearly in your charge:
20 New *Presbyter* is but old *Priest* writ large.

PSALM PARAPHRASES ADDED IN 1673

Psalm I

Done into Verse, *1653*

Blest is the man who hath not walked astray
In counsel of the wicked, and i' th' way
Of sinners hath not stood, and in the seat
Of scorners hath not sat. But in the great
5   Jehovah's Law is ever his delight,
And in his Law he studies day and night.
He shall be as a tree which planted grows
By wat'ry streams, and in his season knows
To yield his fruit, and his leaf shall not fall,
10   And what he takes in hand shall prosper all.
Not so the wicked, but as chaff which fanned
The wind drives, so the wicked shall not stand
In judgement, or abide their trial then,
Nor sinners in th' assembly of just men.
15   For the Lord knows th' upright way of the just,
And the way of bad men to ruin must.

Psalm II

Done *August 8, 1653*. Terzetti

Why do the Gentiles tumult, and the nations
   Muse a vain thing, the kings of th' earth upstand
   With power, and princes in their congregations
Lay deep their plots together through each land,
5   Against the Lord and his Messiah dear?
   Let us break off, say they, by strength of hand
Their bonds, and cast from us, no more to wear,

Their twisted cords: he who in Heaven doth dwell
Shall laugh, the Lord shall scoff them, then severe
10 Speak to them in his wrath, and in his fell
And fierce ire trouble them; but I, saith he
Anointed have my king (though ye rebel)
On Sion my holy hill. A firm decree
I will declare; the Lord to me hath said
15 Thou art my Son, I have begotten thee
This day; ask of me, and the grant is made;
As thy possession I on thee bestow
The heathen, and as thy conquest to be swayed
Earth's utmost bounds: them shalt thou bring full low
20 With iron sceptre bruised, and them disperse
Like to a potter's vessel shivered so.
And now be wise at length ye kings averse,
Be taught ye judges of the earth; with fear
Jehovah serve, and let your joy converse
25 With trembling; kiss the Son lest he appear
In anger and ye perish in the way,
If once his wrath take fire like fuel sere.
Happy all those who have in him their stay.

Psalm III

August 9, 1653

When he fled from Absalom

Lord how many are my foes,
    How many those
That in arms against me rise.
    Many are they
5   That of my life distrustfully thus say,
No help for him in God there lies.
But thou Lord art my shield, my glory;
    Thee through my story
Th' exalter of my head I count;

10   Aloud I cried
      Unto Jehovah; he full soon replied
And heard me from his holy mount.
I lay and slept, I walked again,
      For my sustain
15   Was the Lord. Of many millions
      The populous rout
      I fear not though encamping round about
They pitch against me their pavilions.
Rise Lord, save me my God for thou
20   Hast smote ere now
      On the cheek-bone all my foes,
      Of men abhorred
      Hast broke the teeth. This help was from the Lord;
Thy blessing on thy people flows.

Psalm IV

August 10, 1653

Answer me when I call,
God of my righteousness;
In straits and in distress
Thou didst me disenthrall
5   And set at large; now spare,
      Now pity me, and hear my earnest prayer.
Great ones how long will ye
My glory have in scorn,
How long be thus forborne
10   Still to love vanity,
To love, to seek, to prize
      Things false and vain and nothing else but lies?
Yet know the Lord hath chose,
Chose to himself apart
15   The good and meek of heart
(For whom he chose he knows);
Jehovah from on high

Will hear my voice what time to him I cry.
Be awed, and do not sin,
20   Speak to your hearts alone,
    Upon your beds, each one,
And be at peace within.
Offer the offerings just
    Of righteousness and in Jehovah trust.
25 Many there be that say
Who yet will show us good?
Talking like this world's brood;
But Lord, thus let me pray,
On us lift up the light,
30   Lift up the favour of thy count'nance bright.
Into my heart more joy
    And gladness thou hast put
    Than when a year of glut
Their stores doth over-cloy
35 And from their plenteous grounds
    With vast increase their corn and wine abounds.
In peace at once will I
    Both lay me down and sleep,
    For thou alone dost keep
40 Me safe where'er I lie;
As in a rocky cell
    Thou Lord alone in safety mak'st me dwell.

Psalm V

August 12, 1653

Jehovah to my words give ear,
    My meditation weigh;
The voice of my complaining hear,
My King and God, for unto thee I pray.
5   Jehovah thou my early voice
        Shalt in the morning hear;
    I' th' morning I to thee with choice

Will rank my prayers, and watch till thou appear.
    For thou art not a God that takes
10   In wickedness delight;
    Evil with thee no biding makes;
Fools or mad men stand not within thy sight.
    All workers of iniquity
        Thou hat'st; and them unblest
15   Thou wilt destroy that speak a lie;
The bloody and guileful man God doth detest.
    But I will in thy mercies dear,
        Thy numerous mercies, go
    Into thy house; I in thy fear
20 Will towards thy holy temple worship low.
    Lord lead me in thy righteousness,
        Lead me because of those
    That do observe if I transgress;
Set thy ways right before, where my step goes.
25   For in his falt'ring mouth unstable
        No word is firm or sooth;
    Their inside, troubles miseráble;
An open grave their throat, their tongue they smooth.
    God, find them guilty, let them fall
30   By their own counsels quelled;
    Push them in their rebellions all
Still on; for against thee they have rebelled;
    Then all who trust in thee shall bring
        Their joy, while thou from blame
35 Defend'st them; they shall ever sing
And shall triúmph in thee, who love thy name.
    For thou Jehovah wilt be found
        To bless the just man still,
    As with a shield thou wilt surround
40 Him with thy lasting favour and good will.

Psalm VI

August 13, 1653

Lord in thine anger do not reprehend me,
   Nor in thy hot displeasure me correct;
Pity me Lord for I am much deject,
   Am very weak and faint; heal and amend me,
5 For all my bones, that even with anguish ache,
   Are troubled, yea my soul is troubled sore
And thou O Lord how long? turn Lord, restore
   My soul, O save me for thy goodness' sake,
For in death no remembrance is of thee;
10   Who in the grave can celebrate thy praise?
Wearied I am with sighing out my days,
   Nightly my couch I make a kind of sea;
My bed I water with my tears; mine eye
   Through grief consumes, is waxen old and dark
15 I' th' midst of all mine enemies that mark.
   Depart all ye that work iniquity.
Depart from me, for the voice of my weeping
   The Lord hath heard, the Lord hath heard my prayer;
My supplication with acceptance fair
20 The Lord will own, and have me in his keeping.
Mine enemies shall all be blank and dashed
   With much confusion; then grow red with shame;
They shall return in haste the way they came
   And in a moment shall be quite abashed.

Psalm VII

August 14, 1653

Upon the words of Chush the Benjamite against him

Lord my God to thee I fly;
Save me and secure me under
Thy protection while I cry,
Lest as a lion (and no wonder)
5   He haste to tear my soul asunder,
Tearing and no rescue nigh.

Lord my God if I have thought
Or done this, if wickedness
Be in my hands, if I have wrought
10   Ill to him that meant me peace,
Or to him have rendered less,
And not freed my foe for naught;

Let th' enemy pursue my soul
And overtake it, let him tread
15   My life down to the earth and roll
In the dust my glory dead,
In the dust and there outspread
Lodge it with dishonour foul.

Rise Jehovah in thine ire,
20   Rouse thyself amidst the rage
Of my foes that urge like fire;
And wake for me, their fury assuage;
Judgement here thou didst engage
And command which I desire.

25   So th' assemblies of each nation
Will surround thee, seeking right;
Thence to thy glorious habitation

Return on high and in their sight.
Jehovah judgeth most upright
30   All people from the world's foundation.

Judge me Lord, be judge in this
According to my righteousness
And the innocence which is
Upon me: cause at length to cease
35   Of evil men the wickedness
And their power that do amiss.

But the just establish fast,
Since thou art the just God that tries
Hearts and reins. On God is cast
40   My defence, and in him lies,
In him who both just and wise
Saves th' upright of heart at last.

God is a just Judge and severe,
And God is every day offended;
45   If th' unjust will not forbear,
His sword he whets, his bow hath bended
Already, and for him intended
The tools of death, that waits him near.

(His arrows purposely made he
50   For them that persecute.) Behold
He travels big with vanity,
Trouble he hath conceived of old
As in a womb, and from that mould
Hath at length brought forth a lie.

55   He digged a pit, and delved it deep,
And fell into the pit he made;
His mischief that due course doth keep,
Turns on his head, and his ill trade
Of violence will undelayed
60   Fall on his crown with ruin steep.

Then will I Jehovah's praise
According to his justice raise,
And sing the name and deity
Of Jehovah the most high.

Psalm VIII

August 14, 1653

O Jehovah our Lord how wondrous great
   And glorious is thy name through all the earth!
So as above the heavens thy praise to set
   Out of the tender mouths of latest birth,

5   Out of the mouths of babes and sucklings thou
   Hast founded strength because of all thy foes
To stint th' enemy, and stack th' avenger's brow
   That bends his rage thy providence to oppose.

When I behold thy heavens, thy fingers' art,
10   The moon and stars which thou so bright hast set
In the pure firmament, then saith my heart,
   O what is man that thou rememb'rest yet,

And think'st upon him; or of man begot
   That him thou visit'st and of him art found?
15   Scarce to be less than gods, thou mad'st his lot,
   With honour and with state thou hast him crowned.

O'er the works of thy hand thou mad'st him Lord,
   Thou hast put all under his lordly feet,
All flocks, and herds, by thy commanding word,
20   All beasts that in the field or forest meet,

Fowl of the heavens, and fish that through the wet
  Sea-paths in shoals do slide, and know no dearth.
O Jehovah our Lord how wondrous great
  And glorious is thy name through all the earth.

April, 1648, J.M.

Nine of the Psalms done into metre, wherein all but what is in a different character are the very words of the text, translated from the original.

Psalm LXXX

1 Thou Shepherd that dost Israel *keep*,
    Give ear *in time of need*,
  Who leadest like a flock of sheep
    Thy lovèd Joseph's seed,
5   That sitt'st between the Cherubs *bright*
    Between their wings outspread,
  Shine forth, *and from thy cloud give light,*
    And on our foes thy dread.

2 In Ephraim's view and Benjamin's,
10   And in Manasseh's sight,
  Awake* thy strength, come, and *be seen*   *Gnorera
    To save us *by thy might.*

3 Turn us again, *thy grace divine*
    To us O God *vouchsafe*;
15 Cause thou thy face on us to shine
    And then we shall be safe.

4 Lord God of Hosts, how long wilt thou,
    How long wilt thou declare
  Thy *smoking wrath *and angry brow*   *Gnashanta
20   Against thy people's prayer?

5   Thou feed'st them with the bread of tears,
      Their bread with tears they eat,
      And mak'st them *largely drink the tears   *Shalish
      Wherewith their tears are wet.

25   6   A strife thou mak'st us *and a prey*
      To every neighbour foe;
      Among themselves they *laugh, they *play,   *Jilgnagu
      And *flouts at us they throw.

      7   Return us, *and thy grace divine,*
30   O God of Hosts *vouchsafe*;
      Cause thou thy face on us to shine,
      And then we shall be safe.

      8   A vine from Egypt thou hast brought,
            Thy free love made it shine,
35   And drov'st out nations *proud and haught*
      To plant this *lovely* vine.

      9   Thou didst prepare for it a place
      And root it deep and fast
      That it *began to grow apace,*
40   *And* filled the land *at last.*

      10   With her *green* shade *that* covered *all,*
      The hills were *overspread*;
      Her boughs *as high as* cedars tall
            Advanced their lofty head.

45   11   Her branches *on the western side*
      Down to the sea she sent,
      And *upward* to that river *wide*
      Her other branches *went.*

      12   Why hast thou laid her hedges low
50   And broken down her fence,
      That all may pluck her, as they go,
            With rudest violence?

      13   The *tuskèd* boar out of the wood
      Upturns it by the roots,
55   Wild beasts there browse, and make their food
            Her grapes and tender shoots.

14 Return now, God of Hosts, look down
    From Heav'n, thy seat divine,
Behold *us, but without a frown*,
60   And visit this *thy* vine.

15 Visit this vine, which thy right hand
    Hath set, and planted *long*,
And the young branch, that for thyself
    Thou hast made firm and strong.

65 16 But now it is consumed with fire,
    And cut *with axes* down;
They perish at thy dreadful ire,
    At thy rebuke and frown.

17 Upon the man of thy right hand
70   Let thy *good* hand be *laid*,
Upon the Son of Man, whom thou
    Strong for thyself hast made.

18 So shall we not go back from thee
    To ways of sin and shame,
75 Quicken us thou, then *gladly* we
    Shall call upon thy name.
Return us, *and thy grace divine*
    Lord God of Hosts *vouchsafe*,
Cause thou thy face on us to shine,
80   And then we shall be safe.

Psalm LXXXI

1 To God our strength sing loud, *and clear*,
    Sing loud to God *our King*,
To Jacob's God, *that all may hear*
    Loud acclamations ring.

5 2 Prepare a hymn, prepare a song,
    The timbrel hither bring;
The *cheerful* psaltery bring along
    And harp *with* pleasant *string*;

  3 Blow, *as is wont*, in the new moon
10   With trumpets' *lofty sound*,
        Th' appointed time, the day whereon
          Our solemn feast *comes round*.

  4 This was a statute *giv'n of old*
        For Israel *to observe*,
15   A law of Jacob's God, *to hold*
         From whence they might not swerve.

  5 This he a testimony ordained
        In Joseph, *not to change*,
        When as he passed through Egypt land;
20   The tongue I heard, was strange.

  6 From burden, *and from slavish toil*
        I set his shoulder free;
        His hands from pots, *and miry soil*
         Delivered were *by me.*

25 7 When trouble did thee sore assail,
        On me then didst thou call,
        And I to free thee *did not fail*,
         And led thee out of thrall.
        I answered thee in *thunder deep   **Besether ragnam*
30   With clouds encompassed round;
        I tried thee at the water *steep*
         Of Meriba *renowned.*

  8 Hear O my people, *hearken well*,
        I testify to thee
35   *Thou ancient stock of* Israel,
        If thou wilt list to me,

  9 Throughout the land of thy abode
        No alien god shall be,
        Nor shalt thou to a foreign god
40   In honour bend thy knee.

10 I am the Lord thy God which brought
        Thee out of Egypt land;
        Ask large enough, and I, *besought*,
        Will grant thy full demand.

45 11 And yet my people would not *hear*,
            Nor hearken to my voice;
        And Israel *whom I loved so dear*
            Misliked me for his choice.

    12 Then did I leave them to their will
50   And to their wand'ring mind;
        Their own conceits they followed still,
            Their own devices blind.

    13 O that my people would *be wise*
            To serve me *all their days*,
55   And O that Israel would *advise*
            To walk my *righteous* ways.

    14 Then would I soon bring down their foes
            That now so proudly rise,
        And turn my hand against *all those*
60   *That are* their enemies.

    15 Who hate the Lord should *then be fain*
            To bow to him and bend,
        But *they, his people, should remain*,
            Their time should have no end.

65 16 And we would feed them *from the shock*
            With flour of finest wheat,
        And satisfy them from the rock
            With honey *for their meat*.

Psalm LXXXII

     1 God in the *great *assembly stands   *Bagnadath-el*
            Of kings and lordly states;
        †Among the gods on both his hands   †*Bekerev*
            He judges and debates.

5   2 How long will ye *pervert the right   *Tishphetu gnavel*
            With *judgement false and wrong,
        Favouring the wicked *by your might*,
            Who thence grow bold and strong?

3   *Regard the *weak and fatherless,   *Shiphtu-dal
10   *Despatch the *poor man's cause,
        And †raise the man in deep distress
        By †just and equal laws   †Hatzdiku

4   Defend the poor and desolate,
        And rescue from the hands
15   Of wicked men the low estate
        Of him *that help demands.*

5   They know not nor will understand,
        In darkness they walk on;
        The earth's foundations all are *moved   *Jimmotu
20   And *out of order gone.

6   I said that ye were gods, yea all
        The sons of God most high;

7   But ye shall die like men, and fall
        As other princes *die.*

25 8   Rise God, *judge thou the earth *in might,*
        This *wicked* earth *redress,   *Shophta
        For thou art he who shalt by right
        The nations all possess.

Psalm LXXXIII

1   Be not thou silent *now at length,*
        O God hold not thy peace,
        Sit not thou still O God of *strength,*
        We cry and do not cease.

5   2   For lo thy *furious* foes *now* *swell
        And *storm outrageously,   *Jehemajun
        And they that hate thee *proud and fell*
        Exalt their heads full high.

3   Against thy people they †contrive   †Jagnarimu
10   Their †plots and counsels deep;   †Sod
        *Them to ensnare they chiefly strive   *Jithjagnatsu gnal
        *Whom thou dost hide and keep.   *Tsephuneca

4   Come let us cut them off say they,
     Till they no nation be,

15   That Israel's name for ever may
     Be lost in memory.

5   For they consult †with all their might,   †*Lev jachdau*
     And all as one in mind
     Themselves against thee they unite

20   And in firm union bind.

6   The tents of Edom, and the brood
     Of *scornful* Ishmael,
     Moab, with them of Hagar's blood
     That in the desert dwell,

25 7   Gebal and Ammon *there conspire*,
     And *hateful* Amalek,
     The Philistines, and they of Tyre
     Whose bounds the sea doth check.

8   With them *great* Ashur also bands
     And doth confirm the knot;

30   *All these have lent their armèd hands*
     To aid the sons of Lot.

9   Do to them as to Midian *bold*
     That wasted all the coast,

35   To Sisera, and as *is told*
     Thou didst to Jabin's *host,*
     When at the brook of Kishon *old*
     They were repulsed and slain,

10   At Endor quite cut off, and rolled

40   As dung upon the plain.

11   As Zeb and Oreb evil sped
     So let their princes speed;
     As Zeba, and Zalmunna *bled*
     So let their princes *bleed.*

45 12 *For they amidst their pride* have said
     By right now shall we seize
     †God's houses, and *will now invade*
     †Their stately palaces   †*Neoth Elohim bears both*

13   My God, O make them as a wheel,
50   *No quiet let them find*,
     Giddy and *restless* let *them reel*
     Like stubble from the wind.

14   As *when* an *aged* wood takes fire
          Which on a sudden strays,
55   The *greedy* flame runs higher and higher
          Till all the mountains blaze;

15   So with thy whirlwind them pursue,
          And with thy tempest chase;

16   And till they *yield thee honour due,   *They seek thy*
60   Lord fill with shame their face.   *Name.* Heb.

17   Ashamed and troubled let them be,
          Troubled and shamed for ever,
     Ever confounded, and so die
          With shame, *and 'scape it never*.

65   18   Then shall they know that thou whose name
          Jehovah is alone,
     Art the most high, *and thou the same*
          O'er all the earth *art one*.

Psalm LXXXIV

1   How lovely are thy dwellings fair!
         O Lord of Hosts, how dear
    The *pleasant* tabernacles are!
         Where thou dost dwell so near.

5   2   My soul doth long and almost die
         Thy courts O Lord to see;
    My heart and flesh aloud do cry,
         O living God, for thee.

3   There ev'n the sparrow *freed from wrong*
10   Hath found a house of *rest*;
    The swallow there, to lay her young
         Hath built her *brooding* nest;

Ev'n *by* thy altars Lord of Hosts
They find their safe abode,
15 *And home they fly from round the coasts*
Toward thee, my King, my God.

4 Happy, who in thy house reside
Where thee they ever praise;
5 Happy, whose strength in thee doth bide,
20 And in their hearts thy ways.

6 They pass through Baca's *thirsty* vale,
That dry and barren ground,
As through a fruitful wat'ry dale
Where springs and show'rs abound.

25 7 They journey on from strength to strength
With joy and gladsome cheer
Till all before *our* God *at length*
In Sion do appear.

8 Lord God of Hosts hear *now* my prayer,
30 O Jacob's God give ear;
9 Thou God our shield look on the face
Of thy anointed *dear.*

10 For one day in thy courts *to be*
Is better, *and more blest*
35 Than *in the joys of vanity,*
A thousand days *at best.*

I in the temple of my God
Had rather keep a door,
Than dwell in tents, *and rich abode*
40 With sin *for evermore.*

11 For God the Lord both sun and shield
Gives grace and glory *bright*;
No good from them shall be withheld
Whose ways are just and right.

45 12 Lord *God* of Hosts *that reign'st on high*,
That man is *truly* blest,
Who *only* on thee doth rely,
And in thee only rest.

Psalm LXXXV

1   Thy land to favour graciously
      Thou hast not Lord been slack;
      Thou hast from *hard* captivity
        Returnèd Jacob back.

5   2   Th' iniquity thou didst forgive
        That wrought thy people woe,
      And all their sin, *that did thee grieve*
      Hast hid *where none shall know.*

   3   Thine anger all thou hadst removed,
10   And *calmly* didst return
      From thy †fierce wrath which we had   †Heb. *The burning*
        proved   *heat of thy wrath*
      Far worse than fire to burn.

   4   God of our saving health and peace,
      Turn us, and us restore;
15   Thine indignation cause to cease
      Toward us, *and chide no more.*

   5   Wilt thou be angry without end,
      For ever angry thus?
      Wilt thy frowning ire extend
20   From age to age on us?

   6 Wilt thou not *turn, and *hear our voice*,   *Heb. *Turn to*
      And us again *revive,   *quicken us*
      That so thy people may rejoice
      By thee preserved alive.

25   7   Cause us to see thy goodness Lord,
      To us thy mercy show;
      Thy saving health to us afford
      And life in us renew.

   8   *And now* what God the Lord will speak
30   I will *go straight and* hear,
      For to his people he speaks peace
      And to his saints *full dear;*

To his dear saints he will speak peace,
  But let them never more
35 Return to folly, *but surcease*
  To trespass as before.

9 Surely to such as do him fear
  Salvation is at hand,
And glory shall *ere long appear*
40 *To* dwell within our land.

10 Mercy and Truth *that long were missed*
  Now *joyfully* are met;
Sweet Peace and Righteousness have kissed
  And hand in hand are set.

45 11 Truth from the earth *like to a flow'r*
  Shall bud and blossom *then*,
And Justice from her Heavenly bow'r
  Look down *on mortal men.*

12 The Lord will also then bestow
50   Whatever thing is good;
Our land shall forth in plenty throw
  Her fruits *to be our food.*

13 Before him Righteousness shall go
  His royal harbinger,
55 Then *will he come, and not be slow;   *Heb. *He will set his*
  His footsteps cannot err.   *steps to the way*

Psalm LXXXVI

1 Thy *gracious* ear, O Lord, incline,
  O hear me *I thee pray*,
For I am poor, and almost pine
  With need, *and sad decay.*

5 2 Preserve my soul, †for I have trod   †Heb. *I am good,*
  Thy ways, and love the just;   *loving, a doer of good*
Save thou thy servant O my God   *and holy things*
  Who *still* in thee doth trust.

3 Pity me Lord for daily thee
10   I call; 4 O make rejoice
Thy servant's soul; for Lord to thee
        I lift my soul *and voice*;

5 For thou art good, thou Lord art prone
        To pardon, thou to all
15 Art full of mercy, thou *alone*
        To them that on thee call.

6 Unto my supplication Lord
        Give ear, and to the cry
Of my *incessant* prayers afford
20   Thy hearing graciously.

7 I in the day of my distress
        Will call on thee *for aid*;
For thou wilt *grant* me *free accéss*
        And answer, *what I prayed.*

25 8 Like thee among the gods is none
        O Lord, nor any works
Of all that other gods have done
        Like to thy *glorious* works.

9 The nations all whom thou hast made
30   Shall come, *and all shall frame*
To bow them low before the Lord,
        And glorify thy name.

10 For great thou art, and wonders great
        By thy strong hand are done;
35 Thou *in thy everlasting seat*
        Remainest God alone.

11 Teach me O Lord thy way *most right*;
        I in thy truth will bide;
To fear thy name my heart unite,
40   *So shall it never slide.*

12 Thee will I praise O Lord my God
        Thee honour, and adore
With my whole heart, and blaze abroad
        Thy name for evermore.

45 13 For great thy mercy is toward me,
        And thou hast freed my soul,
        Ev'n from the lowest Hell set free,
        From deepest darkness foul.

   14 O God the proud against me rise
50   And violent men are met
        To seek my life, and in their eyes
        No fear of thee have set.

   15 But thou Lord art the God most mild,
        Readiest thy grace to show,
55   Slow to be angry, and *art styled*
        Most merciful, most true.

   16 O turn to me *thy face at length*,
        And me have mercy on;
        Unto thy servant give thy strength,
60   And save thy handmaid's son.

   17 Some sign of good to me afford,
        And let my foes *then* see
        And be ashamed, because thou Lord
        Dost help and comfort me.

Psalm LXXXVII

   1 Among the holy mountains *high*
        Is his foundation fast;
        There seated in his sanctuary,
        His temple there is placed.

5 2 Sion's *fair* gates the Lord loves more
        Than all the dwellings *fair*
        Of Jacob's *land, though there be store,*
        And all within his care.

   3 City of God, most glorious things
10   Of thee *abroad* are spoke;
   4 I mention Egypt, *where proud kings*
        Did our forefathers yoke;

I mention Babel to my friends,
    Philistia *full of scorn*,
15 And Tyre with Ethiop's *utmost ends*:
    Lo this man there was born.

5   But *twice that praise shall in our ear*
    Be said of Sion *last*:
    This and this man was born in her,
20   High God shall fix her fast.

6   The Lord shall write it in a scroll
    That ne'er shall be outworn,
    When he the nations doth enroll,
    That this man there was born.

25 7   Both they who sing, and they who dance
        With sacred songs are there;
    In thee *fresh brooks and soft streams glance
    And* all my fountains *clear*.

Psalm LXXXVIII

1   Lord God that dost me save and keep,
        All day to thee I cry;
    And all night long, before thee *weep*
        Before thee *prostrate lie*.

5   2   Into thy presence let my prayer
        With sighs devout ascend;
    And to my cries, that *ceaseless are*,
        Thine ear with favour bend.

3   For cloyed with woes and trouble store
10   Surcharged my soul doth lie;
    My life *at death's uncheerful door*
        Unto the grave draws nigh.

4   Reckoned I am with them that pass
        Down to the *dismal* pit;
15 I am a *man, but weak alas   *Heb. *A man without
        And for that name unfit.   manly srength*

5 From life discharged and parted quite
    Among the dead *to sleep*,
  And like the slain *in bloody fight*
20   That in the grave lie *deep*,
  Whom thou rememberest no more,
    Dost never more regard:
  Them from thy hand delivered o'er
    Death's hideous house hath barred.

25 6 Thou in the lowest pit *profound*
    Hast set me *all forlorn*,
  Where thickest darkness *hovers round*,
    In horrid deeps *to mourn*.

  7 Thy wrath *from which no shelter saves*
30   Full sore doth press on me;
  *Thou break'st upon me all thy waves,
  *And all thy waves break me.

                                  *The Heb.
                                   bears both*

  8 Thou dost my friends from me estrange,
    And mak'st me odious,
35 Me to them odious, *for they change*,
    And I here pent up thus.

  9 Through sorrow, and affliction great
    Mine eye grows dim and dead;
  Lord all the day I thee entreat,
40   My hands to thee I spread.

  10 Wilt thou do wonders on the dead?
    Shall the deceased arise
  And praise thee *from their loathsome bed
    With pale and hollow eyes*?

45 11 Shall they thy loving kindness tell
    On whom the grave *hath hold*,
  Or they *who* in perdition *dwell*
    Thy faithfulness *unfold*?

  12 In darkness can thy mighty *hand*
50   *Or* wondrous acts be known?
  Thy justice in the *gloomy* land
    Of *dark* oblivion?

13   But I to thee O Lord do cry
           Ere yet my life be spent,
55   And *up to thee* my prayer *doth hie*
           Each morn, and thee prevent.

14   Why wilt thou Lord my soul forsake,
           And hide thy face from me,

15   That am already bruised, and †shake   †Heb. *Prae*
60   With terror sent from thee;   *Concussione*
       Bruised, and afflicted and *so low*
           As ready to expire,
       While I thy terrors undergo
           Astonished with thine ire.

65 16   Thy fierce wrath over me doth flow,
           Thy threat'nings cut me through.

17   All day they round about me go,
           Like waves they me pursue.

18   Lover and friend thou hast removed
70   And severed from me far.
       They *fly me now* whom I have loved,
           And as in darkness are.

UNCOLLECTED ENGLISH POEMS

On the Lord General Fairfax at the Siege of Colchester

Fairfax, whose name in arms through Europe rings
    Filling each mouth with envy, or with praise,
    And all her jealous monarchs with amaze,
    And rumours loud, that daunt remotest kings,
5 Thy firm unshaken virtue ever brings
    Victory home, though new rebellions raise
    Their Hydra heads, and the false North displays
    Her broken league, to imp their serpent wings,
O yet a nobler task awaits thy hand;
10 For what can war, but endless war still breed,
    Till truth, and right from violence be freed,
And public faith cleared from the shameful brand
    Of public fraud. In vain doth valour bleed
    While avarice, and rapine share the land.

To the Lord General Cromwell, May 1652,

On the Proposals of Certain Ministers of the Committee for Propagation of the Gospel

Cromwell, our chief of men, who through a cloud
    Not of war only, but detractions rude,
    Guided by faith and matchless fortitude
    To peace and truth thy glorious way hast ploughed,
5 And on the neck of crownèd Fortune proud
    Hast reared God's trophies and his work pursued,
    While Darwen stream with blood of Scots imbrued,
    And Dunbar field resounds thy praises loud,

And Worcester's laureate wreath; yet more remains
10   To conquer still; peace hath her victories
      No less renowned than war, new foes arise
Threat'ning to bind our souls with secular chains:
      Help us to save free conscience from the paw
      Of hireling wolves whose Gospel is their maw.

To Sir Henry Vane the Younger

Vane, young in years, but in sage counsel old,
      Than whom a better senator ne'er held
      The helm of Rome, when gowns not arms repelled
      The fierce Epirot and the African bold:
5   Whether to settle peace or to unfold
      The drift of hollow states, hard to be spelled,
      Then to advise how war may best, upheld,
      Move by her two main nerves, iron and gold,
In all her equipage; besides to know
10   Both spiritual power and civil, what each means,
      What severs each, thou hast learnt, which few have done.
The bounds of either sword to thee we owe;
      Therefore on thy firm hand religion leans
      In peace, and reckons thee her eldest son.

To Mr Cyriack Skinner upon his Blindness

Cyriack, this three years' day these eyes, though clear
      To outward view, of blemish or of spot;
      Bereft of light their seeing have forgot,
      Nor to their idle orbs doth sight appear
5   Of sun or moon or star throughout the year,
      Or man or woman. Yet I argue not
      Against Heaven's hand or will, nor bate a jot
      Of heart or hope; but still bear up and steer

Right onward. What supports me dost thou ask?
10   The conscience, friend, to have lost them overplied
In liberty's defence, my noble task,
Of which all Europe talks from side to side.
This thought might lead me through the world's vain
            masque
Content though blind, had I no better guide.

'Fix Here'

Fix here ye overdated spheres
That wing the restless foot of time.

TRANSLATIONS FROM THE PROSE WORKS

From Of Reformation Touching Church Discipline in England *(1641)*

(i)   Ah Constantine, of how much ill was cause
Not thy conversion, but those rich domains
That the first wealthy Pope received of thee.

Dante, Inferno xix 115–17

(ii)   Founded in chaste and humble poverty,
'Gainst them that raised thee dost thou lift thy horn?
Impudent whore, where hast thou placed thy hope?
In thy adulterers, or thy ill-got wealth?
Another Constantine comes not in haste.

Petrarch, Rime cxxxviii 9–13

(iii)   Then passed he to a flow'ry mountain green,
Which once smelt sweet, now stinks as odiously;
This was that gift (if you the truth will have)
That Constantine to good Sylvestro gave.

Ariosto, Orlando Furioso xxxiv 80

From The Reason of Church Government *(1641)*

(iv)   When I die, let the earth be rolled in flames.

From An Apology for Smectymnuus *(1642)*

(v)   Laughing to teach the truth
         What hinders? As some teachers give to boys
         Junkets and knacks, that they may learn apace.
                              Horace, *Satires* I i 24–6.

(vi)   Jesting decides great things
         Stronglier, and better oft than earnest can.
                              Horace, *Satires* I x 14–15.

(vii) 'Tis you that say it, not I; you do the deeds,
         And your ungodly deeds find me the words.
                              Sophocles, *Electra* 624–5.

From the title-page of Areopagitica *(1644)*

(viii) This is true liberty, when freeborn men
         Having to advise the public may speak free,
         Which he who can, and will, deserves high praise;
         Who neither can nor will, may hold his peace;
5   What can be juster in a state than this?
                              Euripides, *Supplices* 438–41

From Tetrachordon *(1645)*

(ix) Whom do we count a good man, whom but he
         Who keeps the laws and statutes of the Senate,
         Who judges in great suits and controversies,
         Whose witness and opinion wins the cause;
5   But his own house, and the whole neighbourhood
         Sees his foul inside through his whited skin.
                              Horace, *Epistles* I xvi 40–45.

From The Tenure of Kings and Magistrates *(1649)*

(x)   There can be slain
        No sacrifice to God more ácceptáble
        Than an unjust and wicked king.

                            Seneca, *Hercules Furens* 922–4

From The History of Britain *(1670)*

(xi)   Goddess of shades, and huntress, who at will
        Walk'st on the rolling sphere, and through the deep,
        On thy third reign the earth look now, and tell
        What land, what seat of rest thou bidd'st me seek,
5   What certain seat, where I may worship thee
        For ay, with temples vowed, and virgin choirs.

(xii)   Brutus far to the west, in th' ocean wide
        Beyond the realm of Gaul, a land there lies,
        Sea-girt it lies, where giants dwelt of old;
        Now void, it fits thy people; thither bend
5   Thy course, there shalt thou find a lasting seat,
        There to thy sons another Troy shall rise,
        And kings be born of thee, whose dreaded might
        Shall awe the world, and conquer nations bold.

(xiii) Low in a mead of kine under a thorn,
        Of head bereft li'th poor Kenelm king-born.

PARADISE LOST

The Verse

The measure is English heroic verse without rhyme, as that of Homer in Greek, and of Virgil in Latin; rhyme being no necessary adjunct or true ornament of poem or good verse, in longer works especially, but the invention of a barbarous
5   age, to set off wretched matter and lame metre; graced indeed since by the use of some famous modern poets, carried away by custom, but much to their own vexation, hindrance, and constraint to express many things otherwise, and for the most part worse than else they would have expressed them. Not
10 without cause therefore some both Italian and Spanish poets of prime note have rejected rhyme both in longer and shorter works, as have also long since our best English tragedies, as a thing of itself, to all judicious ears, trivial and of no true musical delight; which consists only in apt numbers, fit quan-
15 tity of syllables, and the sense variously drawn out from one verse into another, not in the jingling sound of like endings, a fault avoided by the learned ancients both in poetry and all good oratory. This neglect then of rhyme so little is to be taken for a defect, though it may seem so perhaps to vulgar
20 readers, that it rather is to be esteemed an example set, the first in English, of ancient liberty recovered to heroic poem from the troublesome and modern bondage of rhyming.

BOOK I

The Argument

This first book proposes, first in brief, the whole subject, man's disobedience, and the loss thereupon of Paradise wherein he was placed: then touches the prime cause of his fall, the serpent, or rather Satan in the serpent; who revolting from God, and drawing to his side many legions of angels, was by the command of God driven out of Heaven with all his crew into the great deep. Which action passed over, the poem hastes into the midst of things, presenting Satan with his angels now fallen into Hell, described here, not in the centre (for heaven and earth may be supposed as yet not made, certainly not yet accursed) but in a place of utter darkness, fitliest called Chaos: here Satan with his angels lying on the burning lake, thunder-struck and astonished, after a certain space recovers, as from confusion, calls up him who next in order and dignity lay by him; they confer of their miserable fall, Satan awakens all his legions, who lay till then in the same manner confounded; they rise, their numbers, array of battle, their chief leaders named, according to the idols named afterwards in Canaan and the countries adjoining. To these Satan directs his speech, comforts them with hope yet of regaining Heaven, but tells them lastly of a new world and new kind of creature to be created, according to an ancient prophecy or report in Heaven; for that angels were long before this visible Creation, was the opinion of many ancient Fathers. To find out the truth of this prophecy, and what to determine thereon he refers to a full council. What his associates thence attempt. Pandaemonium the palace of Satan rises, suddenly built out of the deep: the infernal Peers there sit in council.

Of man's first disobedience, and the fruit
Of that forbidden tree, whose mortal taste
Brought death into the world, and all our woe,
With loss of Eden, till one greater man
5   Restore us, and regain the blissful seat,
Sing Heav'nly Muse, that on the secret top
Of Oreb, or of Sinai, didst inspire
That shepherd, who first taught the chosen seed,
In the beginning how the heav'ns and earth
10 Rose out of Chaos: or if Sion hill
Delight thee more, and Siloa's brook that flowed
Fast by the oracle of God; I thence
Invoke thy aid to my advent'rous song,
That with no middle flight intends to soar
15 Above th' Aonian mount, while it pursues
Things unattempted yet in prose or rhyme.
And chiefly thou O Spirit, that dost prefer
Before all temples th' upright heart and pure,
Instruct me, for thou know'st; thou from the first
20 Wast present, and with mighty wings outspread
Dove-like sat'st brooding on the vast abyss
And mad'st it pregnant: what in me is dark
Illumine, what is low raise and support;
That to the heighth of this great argument
25 I may assert Eternal Providence,
And justify the ways of God to men.
    Say first, for Heav'n hides nothing from thy view
Nor the deep tract of Hell, say first what cause
Moved our grand parents in that happy state,
30 Favoured of Heav'n so highly, to fall off
From their Creator and transgress his will
For one restraint, lords of the world besides?
Who first seduced them to that foul revolt?
Th' infernal Serpent; he it was, whose guile
35 Stirred up with envy and revenge, deceived
The mother of mankind, what time his pride
Had cast him out from Heav'n, with all his host
Of rebel angels, by whose aid aspiring
To set himself in glory above his peers,

40   He trusted to have equalled the Most High,
      If he opposed; and with ambitious aim
      Against the throne and monarchy of God
      Raised impious war in Heav'n and battle proud
      With vain attempt. Him the Almighty Power
45   Hurled headlong flaming from th' ethereal sky
      With hideous ruin and combustion down
      To bottomless perdition, there to dwell
      In adamantine chains and penal fire,
      Who durst defy th' Omnipotent to arms.
50   Nine times the space that measures day and night
      To mortal men, he with his horrid crew
      Lay vanquished, rolling in the fiery gulf
      Confounded though immortal: but his doom
      Reserved him to more wrath; for now the thought
55   Both of lost happiness and lasting pain
      Torments him; round he throws his baleful eyes
      That witnessed huge affliction and dismay
      Mixed with obdúrate pride and steadfast hate:
      At once as far as angels' ken he views
60   The dismal situation waste and wild,
      A dungeon horrible, on all sides round
      As one great furnace flamed, yet from those flames
      No light, but rather darkness visible
      Served only to discover sights of woe,
65   Regions of sorrow, doleful shades, where peace
      And rest can never dwell, hope never comes
      That comes to all; but torture without end
      Still urges, and a fiery deluge, fed
      With ever-burning sulphur unconsumed:
70   Such place Eternal Justice had prepared
      For those rebellious, here their prison ordained
      In utter darkness, and their portion set
      As far removed from God and light of Heav'n
      As from the centre thrice to th' utmost pole.
75   O how unlike the place from whence they fell!
      There the companions of his fall, o'erwhelmed
      With floods and whirlwinds of tempestuous fire,
      He soon discerns, and welt'ring by his side

One next himself in power, and next in crime,
80 Long after known in Palestine, and named
    Beëlzebub. To whom th' Arch-Enemy,
    And thence in Heav'n called Satan, with bold words
    Breaking the horrid silence thus began.
        If thou beest he; but O how fall'n! how changed
85 From him, who in the happy realms of light
    Clothed with transcendent brightness didst outshine
    Myriads though bright: if he whom mutual league,
    United thoughts and counsels, equal hope
    And hazard in the glorious enterprise,
90 Joined with me once, now misery hath joined
    In equal ruin: into what pit thou seest
    From what heighth fall'n, so much the stronger proved
    He with his thunder: and till then who knew
    The force of those dire arms? yet not for those,
95 Nor what the potent Victor in his rage
    Can else inflict, do I repent or change,
    Though changed in outward lustre, that fixed mind
    And high disdain, from sense of injured merit,
    That with the mightiest raised me to contend,
100 And to the fierce contention brought along
    Innumerable force of Spirits armed
    That durst dislike his reign, and me preferring,
    His utmost power with adverse power opposed
    In dubious battle on the plains of Heav'n,
105 And shook his throne. What though the field be lost?
    All is not lost; the unconquerable will,
    And study of revenge, immortal hate,
    And courage never to submit or yield:
    And what is else not to be overcome?
110 That glory never shall his wrath or might
    Extort from me. To bow and sue for grace
    With suppliant knee, and deify his power
    Who from the terror of this arm so late
    Doubted his empire, that were low indeed,
115 That were an ignominy and shame beneath
    This downfall; since by Fate the strength of gods
    And this empyreal substance cannot fail,

Since through experience of this great event
In arms not worse, in foresight much advanced,
120 We may with more successful hope resolve
To wage by force or guile eternal war
Irreconcilable, to our grand Foe,
Who now triúmphs, and in th' excess of joy
Sole reigning holds the tyranny of Heav'n.
125 So spake th' apostate angel, though in pain,
Vaunting aloud, but racked with deep despair:
And him thus answered soon his bold compeer.
O Prince, O chief of many thronèd Powers
That led th' embattled Seraphim to war
130 Under thy conduct, and in dreadful deeds
Fearless, endangered Heav'n's perpetual King;
And put to proof his high supremacy,
Whether upheld by strength, or Chance, or Fate;
Too well I see and rue the dire event,
135 That with sad overthrow and foul defeat
Hath lost us Heav'n, and all this mighty host
In horrible destruction laid thus low,
As far as gods and Heav'nly essences
Can perish: for the mind and spirit remains
140 Invincible, and vigour soon returns,
Though all our glory extinct, and happy state
Here swallowed up in endless misery.
But what if he our Conqueror, (whom I now
Of force believe Almighty, since no less
145 Than such could have o'erpow'red such force as ours)
Have left us this our spirit and strength entire
Strongly to suffer and support our pains,
That we may so suffice his vengeful ire,
Or do him mightier service as his thralls
150 By right of war, whate'er his business be,
Here in the heart of Hell to work in fire,
Or do his errands in the gloomy deep;
What can it then avail though yet we feel
Strength undiminished, or eternal being
155 To undergo eternal punishment?
Whereto with speedy words th' Arch-Fiend replied.

Fall'n Cherub, to be weak is miserable
Doing or suffering: but of this be sure,
To do aught good never will be our task,
160   But ever to do ill our sole delight,
As being the contrary to his high will
Whom we resist. If then his Providence
Out of our evil seek to bring forth good,
Our labour must be to pervert that end,
165   And out of good still to find means of evil,
Which oft-times may succeed, so as perhaps
Shall grieve him, if I fail not, and disturb
His inmost counsels from their destined aim.
But see the angry Victor hath recalled
170   His ministers of vengeance and pursuit
Back to the gates of Heav'n: the sulphurous hail
Shot after us in storm, o'erblown hath laid
The fiery surge, that from the precipice
Of Heav'n received us falling, and the thunder
175   Winged with red lightning and impetuous rage,
Perhaps hath spent his shafts, and ceases now
To bellow through the vast and boundless deep.
Let us not slip th' occasion, whether scorn,
Or satiate fury yield it from our Foe.
180   Seest thou yon dreary plain, forlorn and wild,
The seat of desolation, void of light,
Save what the glimmering of these livid flames
Casts pale and dreadful? Thither let us tend
From off the tossing of these fiery waves,
185   There rest, if any rest can harbour there,
And reassembling our afflicted powers,
Consult how we may henceforth most offend
Our Enemy, our own loss how repair,
How overcome this dire calamity,
190   What reinforcement we may gain from hope,
If not what resolution from despair.
        Thus Satan talking to his nearest mate
With head uplift above the wave, and eyes
That sparkling blazed; his other parts besides
195   Prone on the flood, extended long and large

Lay floating many a rood, in bulk as huge
As whom the fables name of monstrous size,
Titanian, or Earth-born, that warred on Jove,
Briareos or Typhon, whom the den
200   By ancient Tarsus held, or that sea-beast
Leviathan, which God of all his works
Created hugest that swim th' Océan stream:
Him haply slumb'ring on the Norway foam
The pilot of some small night-foundered skiff,
205   Deeming some island, oft, as seamen tell,
With fixèd anchor in his scaly rind
Moors by his side under the lee, while night
Invests the sea, and wishèd morn delays:
So stretched out huge in length the Arch-Fiend lay
210   Chained on the burning lake, nor ever thence
Had ris'n or heaved his head, but that the will
And high permission of all-ruling Heaven
Left him at large to his own dark designs,
That with reiterated crimes he might
215   Heap on himself damnation, while he sought
Evil to others, and enraged might see
How all his malice served but to bring forth
Infinite goodness, grace and mercy shown
On man by him seduced, but on himself
220   Treble confusion, wrath and vengeance poured.
Forthwith upright he rears from off the pool
His mighty stature; on each hand the flames
Driv'n backward slope their pointing spires, and rolled
In billows, leave i' th' midst a horrid vale.
225   Then with expanded wings he steers his flight
Aloft, incumbent on the dusky air
That felt unusual weight, till on dry land
He lights, if it were land that ever burned
With solid, as the lake with liquid fire,
230   And such appeared in hue; as when the force
Of subterranean wind transports a hill
Torn from Pelorus, or the shattered side
Of thund'ring Etna, whose combustible
And fuelled entrails thence conceiving fire,

235   Sublimed with mineral fury, aid the winds,
And leave a singèd bottom all involved
With stench and smoke: such resting found the sole
Of unblest feet. Him followed his next mate,
Both glorying to have 'scaped the Stygian flood
240   As gods, and by their own recovered strength,
Not by the sufferance of supernal power.
    Is this the region, this the soil, the clime,
Said then the lost Archangel, this the seat
That we must change for Heav'n, this mournful gloom
245   For that celestial light? Be it so, since he
Who now is sov'reign can dispose and bid
What shall be right: farthest from him is best
Whom reason hath equalled, force hath made supreme
Above his equals. Farewell happy fields
250   Where joy for ever dwells: hail horrors, hail
Infernal world, and thou profoundest Hell
Receive thy new possessor: one who brings
A mind not to be changed by place or time.
The mind is its own place, and in itself
255   Can make a Heav'n of Hell, a Hell of Heav'n.
What matter where, if I be still the same,
And what I should be, all but less than he
Whom thunder hath made greater? Here at least
We shall be free; th' Almighty hath not built
260   Here for his envy, will not drive us hence:
Here we may reign secure, and in my choice
To reign is worth ambition though in Hell:
Better to reign in Hell, than serve in Heav'n.
But wherefore let we then our faithful friends,
265   Th' associates and copartners of our loss
Lie thus astonished on th' oblivious pool,
And call them not to share with us their part
In this unhappy mansion; or once more
With rallied arms to try what may be yet
270   Regained in Heav'n, or what more lost in Hell?
    So Satan spake, and him Beëlzebub
Thus answered. Leader of those armies bright,
Which but th' Omnipotent none could have foiled,

If once they hear that voice, their liveliest pledge
275   Of hope in fears and dangers, heard so oft
In worst extremes, and on the perilous edge
Of battle when it raged, in all assaults
Their surest signal, they will soon resume
New courage and revive, though now they lie
280   Grovelling and prostrate on yon lake of fire,
As we erewhile, astounded and amazed,
No wonder, fall'n such a pernicious heighth.
    He scarce had ceased when the superior fiend
Was moving toward the shore; his ponderous shield
285   Ethereal temper, massy, large and round,
Behind him cast; the broad circumference
Hung on his shoulders like the moon, whose orb
Through optic glass the Tuscan artist views
At evening from the top of Fesole,
290   Or in Valdarno, to descry new lands,
Rivers or mountains in her spotty globe.
His spear, to equal which the tallest pine
Hewn on Norwegian hills, to be the mast
Of some great ammiral, were but a wand,
295   He walked with to support uneasy steps
Over the burning marl, not like those steps
On Heaven's azure; and the torrid clime
Smote on him sore besides, vaulted with fire;
Nathless he so endured, till on the beach
300   Of that inflamèd sea, he stood and called
His legions, angel forms, who lay entranced
Thick as autumnal leaves that strow the brooks
In Vallombrosa, where th' Etrurian shades
High overarched embow'r; or scattered sedge
305   Afloat, when with fierce winds Orion armed
Hath vexed the Red Sea coast, whose waves o'erthrew
Busiris and his Memphian chivalry,
While with perfidious hatred they pursued
The sojourners of Goshen, who beheld
310   From the safe shore their floating carcasses
And broken chariot wheels. So thick bestrown
Abject and lost lay these, covering the flood,

Under amazement of their hideous change.
He called so loud, that all the hollow deep
315 Of Hell resounded. Princes, Potentates,
Warriors, the flow'r of Heav'n, once yours, now lost,
If such astonishment as this can seize
Eternal Spirits: or have ye chos'n this place
After the toil of battle to repose
320 Your wearied virtue, for the ease you find
To slumber here, as in the vales of Heav'n?
Or in this abject posture have ye sworn
To adore the Conqueror? who now beholds
Cherub and Seraph rolling in the flood
325 With scattered arms and ensigns, till anon
His swift pursuers from Heav'n gates discern
Th' advantage, and descending tread us down
Thus drooping, or with linkèd thunderbolts
Transfix us to the bottom of this gulf.
330 Awake, arise, or be for ever fall'n.
        They heard, and were abashed, and up they sprung
Upon the wing, as when men wont to watch
On duty, sleeping found by whom they dread,
Rouse and bestir themselves ere well awake.
335 Nor did they not perceive the evil plight
In which they were, or the fierce pains not feel;
Yet to their General's voice they soon obeyed
Innumerable. As when the potent rod
Of Amram's son in Egypt's evil day
340 Waved round the coast, up called a pitchy cloud
Of locusts, warping on the eastern wind,
That o'er the realm of impious Pharaoh hung
Like night, and darkened all the land of Nile:
So numberless were those bad angels seen
345 Hovering on wing under the cope of Hell
'Twixt upper, nether, and surrounding fires;
Till, as a signal giv'n, th' uplifted spear
Of their great Sultan waving to direct
Their course, in even balance down they light
350 On the firm brimstone, and fill all the plain;
A multitude, like which the populous North

Poured never from her frozen loins, to pass
Rhene or the Danaw, when her barbarous sons
Came like a deluge on the South, and spread
355   Beneath Gibraltar to the Libyan sands.
Forthwith from every squadron and each band
The heads and leaders thither haste where stood
Their great Commander; godlike shapes and forms
Excelling human, Princely dignities,
360   And Powers that erst in Heaven sat on thrones;
Though of their names in Heav'nly records now
Be no memorial, blotted out and razed
By their rebellion, from the Books of Life.
Nor had they yet among the sons of Eve
365   Got them new names, till wand'ring o'er the earth,
Through God's high sufferance for the trial of man,
By falsities and lies the greatest part
Of mankind they corrupted to forsake
God their Creator, and th' invisible
370   Glory of him that made them to transform
Oft to the image of a brute, adorned
With gay religions full of pomp and gold,
And devils to adore for deities:
Then were they known to men by various names,
375   And various idols through the heathen world.
Say, Muse, their names then known, who first, who last,
Roused from the slumber on that fiery couch,
At their great Emperor's call, as next in worth
Came singly where he stood on the bare strand,
380   While the promiscuous crowd stood yet aloof?
The chief were those who from the pit of Hell
Roaming to seek their prey on earth, durst fix
Their seats, long after, next the seat of God,
Their altars by his altar, gods adored
385   Among the nations round, and durst abide
Jehovah thund'ring out of Sion, throned
Between the Cherubim; yea, often placed
Within his sanctuary itself their shrines,
Abominations; and with cursèd things
390   His holy rites, and solemn feasts profaned,

And with their darkness durst affront his light.
First Moloch, horrid king besmeared with blood
Of human sacrifice, and parents' tears,
Though for the noise of drums and timbrels loud
395 Their children's cries unheard, that passed through fire
To his grim idol. Him the Ammonite
Worshipped in Rabba and her wat'ry plain,
In Argob and in Basan, to the stream
Of utmost Arnon. Nor content with such
400 Audacious neighbourhood, the wisest heart
Of Solomon he led by fraud to build
His temple right against the temple of God
On that opprobrious hill, and made his grove
The pleasant valley of Hinnom, Tophet thence,
405 And black Gehenna called, the type of Hell.
Next Chemos, th' óbscene dread of Moab's sons,
From Aroer to Nebo, and the wild
Of southmost Abarim; in Hesebon
And Horonaim, Seon's realm, beyond
410 The flow'ry dale of Sibma clad with vines,
And Elealè to th' Asphaltic pool.
Peor his other name, when he enticed
Israel in Sittim on their march from Nile
To do him wanton rites, which cost them woe.
415 Yet thence his lustful orgies he enlarged
Even to that hill of scandal, by the grove
Of Moloch homicide, lust hard by hate;
Till good Josiah drove them thence to Hell.
With these came they, who from the bord'ring flood
420 Of old Euphrates to the brook that parts
Egypt from Syrian ground, had general names
Of Baälim and Ashtaroth, those male,
These feminine. For Spirits when they please
Can either sex assume, or both; so soft
425 And uncompounded is their essence pure;
Not tied or manacled with joint or limb,
Nor founded on the brittle strength of bones,
Like cumbrous flesh; but in what shape they choose
Dilated or condensed, bright or obscure,

430   Can execute their airy purposes,
       And works of love or enmity fulfil.
       For these the race of Israel oft forsook
       Their Living Strength, and unfrequented left
       His righteous altar, bowing lowly down
435   To bestial gods; for which their heads as low
       Bowed down in battle, sunk before the spear
       Of déspicable foes. With these in troop
       Came Astoreth, whom the Phoenicians called
       Astarte, queen of Heav'n, with crescent horns;
440   To whose bright image nightly by the moon
       Sidonian virgins paid their vows and songs,
       In Sion also not unsung, where stood
       Her temple on th' offensive mountain, built
       By that uxorious king whose heart though large,
445   Beguiled by fair idolatresses, fell
       To idols foul. Thammuz came next behind,
       Whose annual wound in Lebanon allured
       The Syrian damsels to lament his fate
       In amorous ditties all a summer's day,
450   While smooth Adonis from his native rock
       Ran purple to the sea, supposed with blood
       Of Thammuz yearly wounded: the love-tale
       Infected Sion's daughters with like heat,
       Whose wanton passions in the sacred porch
455   Ezekiel saw, when by the vision led
       His eye surveyed the dark idolatries
       Of alienated Judah. Next came one
       Who mourned in earnest, when the captive ark
       Maimed his brute image, head and hands lopped off
460   In his own temple, on the grunsel edge,
       Where he fell flat, and shamed his worshippers:
       Dagon his name, sea-monster, upward man
       And downward fish: yet had his temple high
       Reared in Azotus, dreaded through the coast
465   Of Palestine, in Gath and Ascalon
       And Accaron and Gaza's frontier bounds.
       Him followed Rimmon, whose delightful seat
       Was fair Damascus, on the fertile banks

Of Abbana and Pharphar, lucid streams.
470 He also against the house of God was bold:
A leper once he lost and gained a king,
Ahaz his sottish conqueror, whom he drew
God's altar to disparage and displace
For one of Syrian mode, whereon to burn
475 His odious off'rings, and adore the gods
Whom he had vanquished. After these appeared
A crew who under names of old renown,
Osiris, Isis, Orus and their train
With monstrous shapes and sorceries abused
480 Fanatic Egypt and her priests, to seek
Their wand'ring gods disguised in brutish forms
Rather than human. Nor did Israel 'scape
Th' infection when their borrowed gold composed
The calf in Oreb: and the rebel king
485 Doubled that sin in Bethel and in Dan,
Lik'ning his Maker to the grazèd ox,
Jehovah, who in one night when he passed
From Egypt marching, equalled with one stroke
Both her first-born and all her bleating gods.
490 Belial came last, than whom a Spirit more lewd
Fell not from Heaven, or more gross to love
Vice for itself: to him no temple stood
Or altar smoked; yet who more oft than he
In temples and at altars, when the priest
495 Turns atheist, as did Eli's sons, who filled
With lust and violence the house of God.
In courts and palaces he also reigns
And in luxurious cities, where the noise
Of riot ascends above their loftiest tow'rs,
500 And injury and outrage: and when night
Darkens the streets, then wander forth the sons
Of Belial, flown with insolence and wine.
Witness the streets of Sodom, and that night
In Gibeah, when the hospitable door
505 Exposed a matron to avoid worse rape.
These were the prime in order and in might;
The rest were long to tell, though far renowned,

Th' Ionian gods, of Javan's issue held
Gods, yet confessed later than Heav'n and Earth
510   Their boasted parents; Titan Heav'n's first-born
With his enormous brood, and birthright seized
By younger Saturn, he from mightier Jove
His own and Rhea's son like measure found;
So Jove usurping reigned: these first in Crete
515   And Ida known, thence on the snowy top
Of cold Olympus ruled the middle air
Their highest heav'n; or on the Delphian cliff,
Or in Dodona, and through all the bounds
Of Doric land; or who with Saturn old
520   Fled over Adria to th' Hesperian fields,
And o'er the Celtic roamed the utmost isles.
All these and more came flocking; but with looks
Downcast and damp, yet such wherein appeared
Obscure some glimpse of joy, to have found their chief
525   Not in despair, to have found themselves not lost
In loss itself; which on his count'nance cast
Like doubtful hue: but he his wonted pride
Soon recollecting, with high words, that bore
Semblance of worth, not substance, gently raised
530   Their fainting courage and dispelled their fears.
Then straight commands that at the warlike sound
Of trumpets loud and clarions be upreared
His mighty standard; that proud honour claimed
Azazel as his right, a Cherub tall:
535   Who forthwith from the glittering staff unfurled
Th' imperial ensign, which full high advanced
Shone like a meteor streaming to the wind
With gems and golden lustre rich emblazed,
Seraphic arms and trophies: all the while
540   Sonórous metal blowing martial sounds:
At which the universal host upsent
A shout that tore Hell's concave, and beyond
Frighted the reign of Chaos and old Night.
All in a moment through the gloom were seen
545   Ten thousand banners rise into the air
With orient colours waving: with them rose

A forest huge of spears: and thronging helms
Appeared, and serried shields in thick array
Of depth immeasurable: anon they move
550   In perfect phalanx to the Dorian mood
Of flutes and soft recorders; such as raised
To heighth of noblest temper heroes old
Arming to battle, and instead of rage
Deliberate valour breathed, firm and unmoved
555   With dread of death to flight or foul retreat,
Nor wanting power to mitigate and swage
With solemn touches, troubled thoughts, and chase
Anguish and doubt and fear and sorrow and pain
From mortal or immortal minds. Thus they
560   Breathing united force with fixèd thought
Moved on in silence to soft pipes that charmed
Their painful steps o'er the burnt soil; and now
Advanced in view they stand, a horrid front
Of dreadful length and dazzling arms, in guise
565   Of warriors old with ordered spear and shield,
Awaiting what command their mighty chief
Had to impose: he through the armèd files
Darts his experienced eye, and soon traverse
The whole battalion views; their order due,
570   Their visages and stature as of gods,
Their number last he sums. And now his heart
Distends with pride, and hard'ning in his strength
Glories: for never since created man,
Met such embodied force, as named with these
575   Could merit more than that small infantry
Warred on by cranes: though all the Giant brood
Of Phlegra with th' heroic race were joined
That fought at Thebes and Ilium, on each side
Mixed with auxiliar gods; and what resounds
580   In fable or romance of Uther's son
Begirt with British and Armoric knights;
And all who since, baptized or infidel
Jousted in Aspramont or Montalban,
Damasco, or Morocco, or Trebizond,
585   Or whom Biserta sent from Afric shore

When Charlemagne with all his peerage fell
By Fontarabbia. Thus far these beyond
Compare of mortal prowess, yet observed
Their dread commander: he above the rest
590 In shape and gesture proudly eminent
Stood like a tow'r; his form had yet not lost
All her original brightness, nor appeared
Less than Archangel ruined, and th' excess
Of glory obscured: as when the sun new ris'n
595 Looks through the horizontal misty air
Shorn of his beams, or from behind the moon
In dim eclipse disastrous twilight sheds
On half the nations, and with fear of change
Perplexes monarchs. Darkened so, yet shone
600 Above them all th' Archangel: but his face
Deep scars of thunder had intrenched, and care
Sat on his faded cheek, but under brows
Of dauntless courage, and considerate pride
Waiting revenge: cruel his eye, but cast
605 Signs of remorse and passion to behold
The fellows of his crime, the followers rather
(Far other once beheld in bliss) condemned
For ever now to have their lot in pain,
Millions of Spirits for his fault amerced
610 Of Heav'n, and from eternal splendours flung
For his revolt, yet faithful how they stood,
Their glory withered. As when Heaven's fire
Hath scathed the forest oaks or mountain pines,
With singèd top their stately growth though bare
615 Stands on the blasted heath. He now prepared
To speak; whereat their doubled ranks they bend
From wing to wing, and half enclose him round
With all his peers: attention held them mute.
Thrice he assayed, and thrice in spite of scorn,
620 Tears such as angels weep, burst forth: at last
Words interwove with sighs found out their way.
    O myriads of immortal Spirits, O Powers
Matchless, but with th' Almighty, and that strife
Was not inglorious, though th' event was dire,

625   As this place testifies, and this dire change
      Hateful to utter: but what power of mind
      Foreseeing or presaging, from the depth
      Of knowledge past or present, could have feared,
      How such united force of gods, how such
630   As stood like these, could ever know repulse?
      For who can yet believe, though after loss,
      That all these puissant legions, whose exile
      Hath emptied Heav'n, shall fail to reascend
      Self-raised, and repossess their native seat?
635   For me be witness all the host of Heav'n,
      If counsels different, or danger shunned
      By me, have lost our hopes. But he who reigns
      Monarch in Heav'n, till then as one secure
      Sat on his throne, upheld by old repute,
640   Consent or custom, and his regal state
      Put forth at full, but still his strength concealed,
      Which tempted our attempt, and wrought our fall.
      Henceforth his might we know, and know our own
      So as not either to provoke, or dread
645   New war, provoked; our better part remains
      To work in close design, by fraud or guile
      What force effected not: that he no less
      At length from us may find, who overcomes
      By force, hath overcome but half his foe.
650   Space may produce new worlds; whereof so rife
      There went a fame in Heav'n that he ere long
      Intended to create, and therein plant
      A generation, whom his choice regard
      Should favour equal to the sons of Heav'n:
655   Thither, if but to pry, shall be perhaps
      Our first eruption; thither or elsewhere:
      For this infernal pit shall never hold
      Celestial Spirits in bondage, nor th' abyss
      Long under darkness cover. But these thoughts
660   Full counsel must mature: peace is despaired,
      For who can think submission? War then, war
      Open or understood must be resolved.
        He spake: and to confirm his words, out flew

Millions of flaming swords, drawn from the thighs
665 Of mighty Cherubim; the sudden blaze
Far round illumined Hell: highly they raged
Against the Highest, and fierce with graspèd arms
Clashed on their sounding shields the din of war,
Hurling defiance against the vault of Heav'n.
670   There stood a hill not far whose grisly top
Belched fire and rolling smoke; the rest entire
Shone with a glossy scurf, undoubted sign
That in his womb was hid metallic ore,
The work of sulphur. Thither winged with speed
675 A numerous brígade hastened. As when bands
Of pioneers with spade and pickaxe armed
Forerun the royal camp, to trench a field
Or cast a rampart. Mammon led them on,
Mammon, the least erected Spirit that fell
680 From Heav'n, for ev'n in Heav'n his looks and thoughts
Were always downward bent, admiring more
The riches of Heav'n's pavement, trodden gold,
Than aught divine or holy else enjoyed
In vision beatific: by him first
685 Men also, and by his suggestion taught,
Ransacked the centre, and with impious hands
Rifled the bowels of their mother Earth
For treasures better hid. Soon had his crew
Opened into the hill a spacious wound
690 And digged out ribs of gold. Let none admire
That riches grow in Hell; that soil may best
Deserve the precious bane. And here let those
Who boast in mortal things, and wond'ring tell
Of Babel, and the works of Memphian kings,
695 Learn how their greatest monuments of fame,
And strength and art are easily outdone
By Spirits reprobate, and in an hour
What in an age they with incessant toil
And hands innumerable scarce perform.
700 Nigh on the plain in many cells prepared,
That underneath had veins of liquid fire
Sluiced from the lake, a second multitude

With wondrous art founded the massy ore,
Severing each kind, and scummed the bullion dross:
705   A third as soon had formed within the ground
A various mould, and from the boiling cells
By strange conveyance filled each hollow nook,
As in an organ from one blast of wind
To many a row of pipes the sound-board breathes.
710   Anon out of the earth a fabric huge
Rose like an exhalation, with the sound
Of dulcet symphonies and voices sweet,
Built like a temple, where pilasters round
Were set, and Doric pillars overlaid
715   With golden architrave; nor did there want
Cornice or frieze with bossy sculptures grav'n;
The roof was fretted gold. Not Babylon,
Nor great Alcairo such magnificence
Equalled in all their glories, to enshrine
720   Belus or Serapis their gods, or seat
Their kings, when Egypt with Assyria strove
In wealth and luxury. Th' ascending pile
Stood fixed her stately heighth, and straight the doors
Op'ning their brazen folds discover wide
725   Within, her ample spaces, o'er the smooth
And level pavement: from the archèd roof
Pendent by subtle magic many a row
Of starry lamps and blazing cressets fed
With naphtha and asphaltus yielded light
730   As from a sky. The hasty multitude
Admiring entered, and the work some praise
And some the architect: his hand was known
In Heav'n by many a towered structure high,
Where sceptred angels held their residence,
735   And sat as princes, whom the súpreme King
Exalted to such power, and gave to rule,
Each in his hierarchy, the orders bright.
Nor was his name unheard or unadored
In ancient Greece; and in Ausonian land
740   Men called him Mulciber; and how he fell
From Heav'n, they fabled, thrown by angry Jove

Sheer o'er the crystal battlements: from morn
To noon he fell, from noon to dewy eve,
A summer's day: and with the setting sun
745   Dropped from the zenith like a falling star,
On Lemnos th' Aégean isle: thus they relate,
Erring; for he with this rebellious rout
Fell long before; nor aught availed him now
To have built in Heav'n high tow'rs; nor did he 'scape
750   By all his engines, but was headlong sent
With his industrious crew to build in Hell.
Meanwhile the wingèd heralds by command
Of sov'reign power, with awful ceremony
And trumpets' sound throughout the host proclaim
755   A solemn council forthwith to be held
At Pandaemonium, the high capital
Of Satan and his peers: their summons called
From every band and squarèd regiment
By place or choice the worthiest; they anon
760   With hundreds and with thousands trooping came
Attended: all accéss was thronged, the gates
And porches wide, but chief the spacious hall
(Though like a covered field, where champions bold
Wont ride in armed, and at the Soldan's chair
765   Defied the best of paynim chivalry
To mortal combat or career with lance)
Thick swarmed, both on the ground and in the air,
Brushed with the hiss of rustling wings. As bees
In springtime, when the sun with Taurus rides,
770   Pour forth their populous youth about the hive
In clusters; they among fresh dews and flowers
Fly to and fro, or on the smoothèd plank,
The suburb of their straw-built citadel,
New rubbed with balm, expatiate and confer
775   Their state affairs. So thick the airy crowd
Swarmed and were straitened; till the signal giv'n,
Behold a wonder! They but now who seemed
In bigness to surpass Earth's Giant sons
Now less than smallest dwarfs, in narrow room
780   Throng numberless, like that Pygméan race

Beyond the Indian mount, or faery elves,
Whose midnight revels, by a forest side
Or fountain some belated peasant sees,
Or dreams he sees, while overhead the moon
785 Sits arbitress, and nearer to the earth
Wheels her pale course: they on their mirth and dance
Intent, with jocund music charm his ear;
At once with joy and fear his heart rebounds.
Thus incorporeal Spirits to smallest forms
790 Reduced their shapes immense, and were at large,
Though without number still amidst the hall
Of that infernal Court. But far within
And in their own dimensions like themselves
The great Seraphic Lords and Cherubim
795 In close recess and secret conclave sat
A thousand demi-gods on golden seats,
Frequent and full. After short silence then
And summons read, the great consult began.

BOOK II

The Argument

The consultation begun, Satan debates whether another battle be to be hazarded for the recovery of Heaven: some advise it, others dissuade: a third proposal is preferred, mentioned before by Satan, to search the truth of that prophecy or tradition in Heaven concerning another world, and another kind of creature equal or not much inferior to themselves, about this time to be created: their doubt who shall be sent on this difficult search: Satan their chief undertakes alone the voyage, is honoured and applauded. The council thus ended, the rest betake them several ways and to several employments, as their inclinations lead them, to entertain the time till Satan return. He passes on his journey to Hell gates, finds them shut, and who sat there to guard them, by whom at length they are opened, and discover to him the great gulf between Hell and Heaven; with what difficulty he passes through, directed by Chaos, the power of that place, to the sight of this new world which he sought.

High on a throne of royal state, which far
Outshone the wealth of Ormus and of Ind,
Or where the gorgeous East with richest hand
Show'rs on her kings barbaric pearl and gold,
Satan exalted sat, by merit raised
To that bad eminence; and from despair
Thus high uplifted beyond hope, aspires
Beyond thus high, insatiate to pursue
Vain war with Heav'n, and by success untaught
His proud imaginations thus displayed.
  Powers and Dominions, deities of Heaven,
For since no deep within her gulf can hold
Immortal vigour, though oppressed and fall'n,

I give not Heav'n for lost. From this descent
15   Celestial Virtues rising, will appear
More glorious and more dread than from no fall,
And trust themselves to fear no second fate:
Me though just right, and the fixed laws of Heav'n
Did first create your leader, next, free choice,
20   With what besides, in counsel or in fight,
Hath been achieved of merit, yet this loss
Thus far at least recovered, hath much more
Established in a safe unenvied throne
Yielded with full consent. The happier state
25   In Heav'n, which follows dignity, might draw
Envy from each inferior; but who here
Will envy whom the highest place exposes
Foremost to stand against the Thunderer's aim
Your bulwark, and condemns to greatest share
30   Of endless pain? Where there is then no good
For which to strive, no strife can grow up there
From faction; for none sure will claim in Hell
Precédence, none, whose portion is so small
Of present pain, that with ambitious mind
35   Will covet more. With this advantage then
To union, and firm faith, and firm accord,
More than can be in Heav'n, we now return
To claim our just inheritance of old,
Surer to prosper than prosperity
40   Could have assured us; and by what best way,
Whether of open war or covert guile,
We now debate; who can advise, may speak.
    He ceased, and next him Moloch, sceptred king
Stood up, the strongest and the fiercest Spirit
45   That fought in Heav'n; now fiercer by despair:
His trust was with th' Eternal to be deemed
Equal in strength, and rather than be less
Cared not to be at all; with that care lost
Went all his fear: of God, or Hell, or worse
50   He recked not, and these words thereafter spake.
    My sentence is for open war: of wiles,
More unexpért, I boast not: them let those

Contrive who need, or when they need, not now.
For while they sit contriving, shall the rest,
55   Millions that stand in arms, and longing wait
The signal to ascend, sit ling'ring here
Heav'n's fugitives, and for their dwelling place
Accept this dark opprobrious den of shame,
The prison of his tyranny who reigns
60   By our delay? No, let us rather choose
Armed with Hell flames and fury all at once
O'er Heav'n's high tow'rs to force resistless way,
Turning our tortures into horrid arms
Against the Torturer; when to meet the noise
65   Of his almighty engine he shall hear
Infernal thunder, and for lightning see
Black fire and horror shot with equal rage
Among his angels; and his throne itself
Mixed with Tartarean sulphur, and strange fire,
70   His own invented torments. But perhaps
The way seems difficult and steep to scale
With upright wing against a higher foe.
Let such bethink them, if the sleepy drench
Of that forgetful lake benumb not still,
75   That in our proper motion we ascend
Up to our native seat: descent and fall
To us is adverse. Who but felt of late
When the fierce foe hung on our broken rear
Insulting, and pursued us through the deep,
80   With what compulsion and laborious flight
We sunk thus low? Th' ascent is easy then;
Th' event is feared; should we again provoke
Our stronger, some worse way his wrath may find
To our destruction: if there be in Hell
85   Fear to be worse destroyed: what can be worse
Than to dwell here, driv'n out from bliss, condemned
In this abhorrèd deep to utter woe;
Where pain of unextinguishable fire
Must exercise us without hope of end
90   The vassals of his anger, when the scourge
Inexorably, and the torturing hour

Calls us to penance? More destroyed than thus
We should be quite abolished and expire.
What fear we then? What doubt we to incense
95   His utmost ire? Which to the heighth enraged,
Will either quite consume us, and reduce
To nothing this essential, happier far
Than miserable to have eternal being:
Or if our substance be indeed divine,
100 And cannot cease to be, we are at worst
On this side nothing; and by proof we feel
Our power sufficient to disturb his Heav'n,
And with perpetual inroads to alarm,
Though inaccessible, his fatal throne:
105 Which if not victory is yet revenge.
    He ended frowning, and his look denounced
Desperate revenge, and battle dangerous
To less than gods. On th' other side up rose
Belial, in act more graceful and humane:
110 A fairer person lost not Heav'n; he seemed
For dignity composed and high explóit:
But all was false and hollow; though his tongue
Dropped manna, and could make the worse appear
The better reason, to perplex and dash
115 Maturest counsels: for his thoughts were low;
To vice industrious, but to nobler deeds
Timorous and slothful: yet he pleased the ear,
And with persuasive accent thus began.
    I should be much for open war, O Peers,
120 As not behind in hate; if what was urged
Main reason to persuade immediate war,
Did not dissuade me most, and seem to cast
Ominous conjecture on the whole success:
When he most excels in fact of arms,
125 In what he counsels and in what excels
Mistrustful, grounds his courage on despair
And utter dissolution, as the scope
Of all his aim, after some dire revenge.
First, what revenge? The tow'rs of Heav'n are filled
130 With armèd watch, that render all accéss

Impregnable; oft on the bordering deep
Encamp their legions, or with óbscure wing
Scout far and wide into the realm of Night,
Scorning surprise. Or could we break our way
135   By force, and at our heels all Hell should rise
With blackest insurrection, to confound
Heav'n's purest light, yet our great Enemy
All incorruptible would on his throne
Sit unpolluted, and th' ethereal mould
140   Incapable of stain would soon expel
Her mischief, and purge off the baser fire
Victorious. Thus repulsed, our final hope
Is flat despair: we must exasperate
Th' Almighty Victor to spend all his rage,
145   And that must end us, that must be our cure,
To be no more; sad cure; for who would lose,
Though full of pain, this intellectual being,
Those thoughts that wander through eternity,
To perish rather, swallowed up and lost
150   In the wide womb of uncreated Night,
Devoid of sense and motion? And who knows,
Let this be good, whether our angry Foe
Can give it, or will ever? How he can
Is doubtful; that he never will is sure.
155   Will he, so wise, let loose at once his ire,
Belike through impotence, or unaware,
To give his enemies their wish, and end
Them in his anger, whom his anger saves
To punish endless? Wherefore cease we then?
160   Say they who counsel war, we are decreed,
Reserved and destined to eternal woe;
Whatever doing, what can we suffer more,
What can we suffer worse? Is this then worst,
Thus sitting, thus consulting, thus in arms?
165   What when we fled amain, pursued and strook
With Heav'n's afflicting thunder, and besought
The deep to shelter us? This Hell then seemed
A refuge from those wounds: or when we lay
Chained on the burning lake? That sure was worse.

170 What if the breath that kindled those grim fires
Awaked should blow them into sevenfold rage
And plunge us in the flames? Or from above
Should intermitted vengeance arm again
His red right hand to plague us? What if all
175 Her stores were opened, and this firmament
Of Hell should spout her cataracts of fire,
Impendent horrors, threatening hideous fall
One day upon our heads; while we perhaps
Designing or exhorting glorious war,
180 Caught in a fiery tempest shall be hurled
Each on his rock transfixed, the sport and prey
Of racking whirlwinds, or for ever sunk
Under yon boiling ocean, wrapped in chains;
There to converse with everlasting groans,
185 Unrespited, unpitied, unreprieved,
Ages of hopeless end; this would be worse.
War therefore, open or concealed, alike
My voice dissuades; for what can force or guile
With him, or who deceive his mind, whose eye
190 Views all things at one view? He from Heav'n's heighth
All these our motions vain, sees and derides;
Not more Almighty to resist our might
Than wise to frustrate all our plots and wiles.
Shall we then live thus vile, the race of Heav'n
195 Thus trampled, thus expelled to suffer here
Chains and these torments? Better these than worse
By my advice: since Fate inevitable
Subdues us, and omnipotent decree,
The Victor's will. To suffer, as to do,
200 Our strength is equal, nor the law unjust
That so ordains: this was at first resolved,
If we were wise, against so great a foe
Contending, and so doubtful what might fall.
I laugh, when those who at the spear are bold
205 And vent'rous, if that fail them, shrink and fear
What yet they know must follow, to endure
Exile, or ignominy, or bonds, or pain,
The sentence of their Conqueror: this is now

Our doom; which if we can sustain and bear,
210 Our súpreme Foe in time may much remit
His anger, and perhaps thus far removed
Not mind us not offending, satisfied
With what is punished; whence these raging fires
Will slacken, if his breath stir not their flames.
215 Our purer essence then will overcome
Their noxious vapour, or inured not feel,
Or changed at length, and to the place conformed
In temper and in nature, will receive
Familiar the fierce heat, and void of pain;
220 This horror will grow mild, this darkness light,
Besides what hope the never-ending flight
Of future days may bring, what chance, what change
Worth waiting, since our present lot appears
For happy though but ill, for ill not worst,
225 If we procure not to ourselves more woe.
    Thus Belial with words clothed in reason's garb
Counselled ignoble ease and peaceful sloth,
Not peace: and after him thus Mammon spake.
    Either to disenthrone the King of Heav'n
230 We war, if war be best, or to regain
Our own right lost: him to unthrone we then
May hope when everlasting Fate shall yield
To fickle Chance, and Chaos judge the strife:
The former vain to hope argues as vain
235 The latter: for what place can be for us
Within Heav'n's bound, unless Heav'n's Lord supreme
We overpower? Suppose he should relent
And publish grace to all, on promise made
Of new subjection; with what eyes could we
240 Stand in his presence humble, and receive
Strict laws imposed, to celebrate his throne
With warbled hymns, and to his Godhead sing
Forced hallelujahs; while he lordly sits
Our envied sov'reign, and his altar breathes
245 Ambrosial odours and ambrosial flowers,
Our servile offerings. This must be our task
In Heav'n, this our delight: how wearisome

Eternity so spent in worship paid
To whom we hate. Let us not then pursue
250   By force impossible, by leave obtained
Unácceptáble, though in Heav'n, our state
Of splendid vassalage, but rather seek
Our own good from ourselves, and from our own
Live to ourselves, though in this vast recess,
255   Free, and to none accountable, preferring
Hard liberty before the easy yoke
Of servile pomp. Our greatness will appear
Then most conspicuous, when great things of small,
Useful of hurtful, prosperous of adverse,
260   We can create, and in what place soe'er
Thrive under evil, and work ease out of pain
Through labour and endurance. This deep world
Of darkness do we dread? How oft amidst
Thick clouds and dark doth Heav'n's all-ruling Sire
265   Choose to reside, his glory unobscured,
And with the majesty of darkness round
Covers his throne; from whence deep thunders roar
Must'ring their rage, and Heav'n resembles Hell?
As he our darkness, cannot we his light
270   Imitate when we please? This desert soil
Wants not her hidden lustre, gems and gold;
Nor want we skill or art, from whence to raise
Magnificence; and what can Heav'n show more?
Our torments also may in length of time
275   Become our elements, these piercing fires
As soft as now severe, our temper changed
Into their temper; which must needs remove
The sensible of pain. All things invite
To peaceful counsels, and the settled state
280   Of order, how in safety best we may
Compose our present evils, with regard
Of what we are and where, dismissing quite
All thoughts of war: ye have what I advise.
      He scarce had finished, when such murmur filled
285   Th' assembly, as when hollow rocks retain
The sound of blust'ring winds, which all night long

Had roused the sea, now with hoarse cadence lull
Seafaring men o'erwatched, whose bark by chance
Or pinnace anchors in a craggy bay
290   After the tempest: such applause was heard
As Mammon ended, and his sentence pleased,
Advising peace: for such another field
They dreaded worse than Hell: so much the fear
Of thunder and the sword of Michaël
295   Wrought still within them; and no less desire
To found this nether empire, which might rise
By policy, and long procéss of time,
In emulation opposite to Heav'n.
Which when Beëlzebub perceived, than whom,
300   Satan except, none higher sat, with grave
Aspéct he rose, and in his rising seemed
A pillar of state; deep on his front engraven
Deliberation sat and public care;
And princely counsel in his face yet shone,
305   Majestic though in ruin: sage he stood
With Atlantéan shoulders fit to bear
The weight of mightiest monarchies; his look
·Drew·audience and attention still as night
Or summer's noontide air, while thus he spake.
310   Thrones and imperial Powers, offspring of Heav'n
Ethereal Virtues; or these titles now
Must we renounce, and changing style be called
Princes of Hell? For so the popular vote
Inclines, here to continue, and build up here
315   A growing empire; doubtless; while we dream,
And know not that the King of Heav'n hath doomed
This place our dungeon, not our safe retreat
Beyond his potent arm, to live exempt
From Heav'n's high jurisdiction, in new league
320   Banded against his throne, but to remain
In strictest bondage, though thus far removed,
Under th' inevitable curb, reserved
His captive multitude: for he, be sure
In heighth or depth, still first and last will reign
325   Sole King, and of his kingdom lose no part

By our revolt, but over Hell extend
His empire, and with iron sceptre rule
Us here, as with his golden those in Heav'n.
What sit we then projecting peace and war?
330 War hath determined us, and foiled with loss
Irreparable; terms of peace yet none
Vouchsafed or sought; for what peace will be giv'n
To us enslaved, but custody severe,
And stripes, and arbitrary punishment
335 Inflicted? and what peace can we return,
But to our power hostility and hate,
Untamed reluctance, and revenge though slow,
Yet ever plotting how the Conqueror least
May reap his conquest, and may least rejoice
340 In doing what we most in suffering feel?
Nor will occasion want, nor shall we need
With dangerous expedition to invade
Heav'n, whose high walls fear no assault or siege
Or ambush from the deep. What if we find
345 Some easier enterprise? There is a place
(If ancient and prophetic fame in Heav'n
Err not) another world, the happy seat
Of some new race called *Man*, about this time
To be created like to us, though less
350 In power and excellence, but favoured more
Of him who rules above; so was his will
Pronounced among the gods, and by an oath,
That shook Heav'n's whole circumference, confirmed.
Thither let us bend all our thoughts, to learn
355 What creatures there inhabit, of what mould,
Or substance, how endued, and what their power,
And where their weakness, how attempted best,
By force or subtlety: though Heav'n be shut,
And Heav'n's high Arbitrator sit secure
360 In his own strength, this place may lie exposed
The utmost border of his kingdom, left
To their defence who hold it: here perhaps
Some advantageous act may be achieved
By sudden onset, either with Hell fire

365 To waste his whole Creation, or possess
All as our own, and drive as we were driven,
The puny habitants, or if not drive,
Seduce them to our party, that their God
May prove their foe, and with repenting hand
370 Abolish his own works. This would surpass
Common revenge, and interrupt his joy
In our confusion, and our joy upraise
In his disturbance, when his darling sons
Hurled headlong to partake with us, shall curse
375 Their frail original, and faded bliss,
Faded so soon. Advise if this be worth
Attempting, or to sit in darkness here
Hatching vain empires. Thus Beëlzebub
Ended his devilish counsel, first devised
380 By Satan, and in part proposed: for whence,
But from the author of all ill could spring
So deep a malice, to confound the race
Of mankind in one root, and earth with Hell
To mingle and involve, done all to spite
385 The great Creator? But their spite still serves
His glory to augment. The bold design
Pleased highly those infernal States, and joy
Sparkled in all their eyes; with full assent
They vote: whereat his speech he thus renews.
390   Well have ye judged, well ended long debate,
Synod of gods, and like to what ye are,
Great things resolved, which from the lowest deep
Will once more lift us up, in spite of Fate,
Nearer our ancient seat; perhaps in view
395 Of those bright confines, whence with neighbouring arms
And opportune excursion we may chance
Re-enter Heav'n; or else in some mild zone
Dwell not unvisited of Heav'n's fair light
Secure, and at the bright'ning orient beam
400 Purge off this gloom; the soft delicious air,
To heal the scar of these corrosive fires
Shall breathe her balm. But first whom shall we send
In search of this new world, whom shall we find

Sufficient? Who shall tempt with wand'ring feet
405 The dark unbottomed infinite abyss
And through the palpable obscure find out
His uncouth way, or spread his airy flight
Upborne with indefatigable wings
Over the vast abrupt, ere he arrive
410 The happy isle; what strength, what art can then
Suffice, or what evasion bear him safe
Through the strict senteries and stations thick
Of angels watching round? Here he had need
All circumspection, and we now no less
415 Choice in our suffrage; for on whom we send,
The weight of all and our last hope relies.
    This said, he sat; and expectation held
His look suspense, awaiting who appeared
To second, or oppose, or undertake
420 The perilous attempt: but all sat mute,
Pondering the danger with deep thoughts; and each
In other's count'nance read his own dismay
Astonished: none among the choice and prime
Of those Heav'n-warring champions could be found
425 So hardy as to proffer or accept
Alone the dreadful voyage; till at last
Satan, whom now transcendent glory raised
Above his fellows, with monarchal pride
Conscious of highest worth, unmoved thus spake.
430   O progeny of Heav'n, empyreal Thrones,
With reason hath deep silence and demur
Seized us, though undismayed: long is the way
And hard, that out of Hell leads up to light;
Our prison strong, this huge convéx of fire,
435 Outrageous to devour, immures us round
Ninefold, and gates of burning adamant
Barred over us prohibit all egress.
These past, if any pass, the void profound
Of unessential Night receives him next
440 Wide gaping, and with utter loss of being
Threatens him, plunged in that abortive gulf.
If thence he 'scape into whatever world,

Or unknown region, what remains him less
Than unknown dangers and as hard escape.
445   But I should ill become this throne, O Peers,
And this imperial sov'reignty, adorned
With splendour, armed with power, if aught proposed
And judged of public moment, in the shape
Of difficulty or danger could deter
450   Me from attempting. Wherefore do I assume
These royalties, and not refuse to reign,
Refusing to accept as great a share
Of hazard as of honour, due alike
To him who reigns, and so much to him due
455   Of hazard more, as he above the rest
High honoured sits? Go therefore mighty Powers,
Terror of Heav'n, though fall'n; intend at home,
While here shall be our home, what best may ease
The present misery, and render Hell
460   More tolerable; if there be cure or charm
To respite or deceive, or slack the pain
Of this ill mansion: intermit no watch
Against a wakeful Foe, while I abroad
Through all the coasts of dark destruction seek
465   Deliverance for us all: this enterprise
None shall partake with me. Thus saying rose
The monarch, and prevented all reply,
Prudent, lest from his resolution raised
Others among the chief might offer now
470   (Certain to be refused) what erst they feared;
And so refused might in opinion stand
His rivals, winning cheap the high repute
Which he through hazard huge must earn. But they
Dreaded not more th' adventure than his voice
475   Forbidding; and at once with him they rose;
Their rising all at once was as the sound
Of thunder heard remote. Towards him they bend
With awful reverence prone; and as a god
Extol him equal to the highest in Heav'n.
480   Nor failed they to express how much they praised,
That for the general safety he despised

His own: for neither do the Spirits damned
Lose all their virtue; lest bad men should boast
Their specious deeds on earth, which glory excites,
485 Or close ambition varnished o'er with zeal.
Thus they their doubtful consultations dark
Ended rejoicing in their matchless chief:
As when from mountain tops the dusky clouds
Ascending, while the north wind sleeps, o'erspread
490 Heav'n's cheerful face, the louring element
Scowls o'er the darkened landscape snow, or show'r;
If chance the radiant sun with farewell sweet
Extend his ev'ning beam, the fields revive,
The birds their notes renew, and bleating herds
495 Attest their joy, that hill and valley rings.
O shame to men! Devil with devil damned
Firm concord holds, men only disagree
Of creatures rational, though under hope
Of Heav'nly grace: and God proclaiming peace,
500 Yet live in hatred, enmity, and strife
Among themselves, and levy cruel wars,
Wasting the earth, each other to destroy:
As if (which might induce us to accord)
Man had not Hellish foes enow besides,
505 That day and night for his destruction wait.
    The Stygian Council thus dissolved; and forth
In order came the grand infernal Peers:
Midst came their mighty Paramount, and seemed
Alone th' Antagonist of Heav'n, nor less
510 Than Hell's dread Emperor with pomp supreme,
And God-like imitated state; him round
A globe of fiery Seraphim enclosed
With bright emblazonry, and horrent arms.
Then of their session ended they bid cry
515 With trumpets' regal sound the great result:
Toward the four winds four speedy Cherubim
Put to their mouths the sounding alchemy
By herald's voice explained: the hollow abyss
Heard far and wide, and all the host of Hell
520 With deaf'ning shout, returned them loud acclaim.

Thence more at ease their minds and somewhat raised
By false presumptuous hope, the rangèd powers
Disband, and wand'ring, each his several way
Pursues, as inclination or sad choice
525   Leads him perplexed, where he may likeliest find
Truce to his restless thoughts, and entertain
The irksome hours, till his great chief return.
Part on the plain, or in the air sublime
Upon the wing, or in swift race contend,
530   As at th' Olympian games or Pythian fields;
Part curb their fiery steeds, or shun the goal
With rapid wheels, or fronted brígades form.
As when to warn proud cities war appears
Waged in the troubled sky, and armies rush
535   To battle in the clouds, before each van
Prick forth the airy knights, and couch their spears
Till thickest legions close; with feats of arms
From either end of heav'n the welkin burns.
Others with vast Typhoean rage more fell
540   Rend up both rocks and hills, and ride the air
In whirlwind; Hell scarce holds the wild uproar.
As when Alcides from Oechalia crowned
With conquest, felt th' envenomed robe, and tore
Through pain up by the roots Thessalian pines,
545   And Lichas from the top of Oeta threw
Into th' Euboic Sea. Others more mild,
Retreated in a silent valley, sing
With notes angelical to many a harp
Their own heroic deeds and hapless fall
550   By doom of battle; and complain that Fate
Free virtue should enthrall to Force or Chance.
Their song was partial, but the harmony
(What could it less when Spirits immortal sing?)
Suspended Hell, and took with ravishment
555   The thronging audience. In discourse more sweet
(For eloquence the soul, song charms the sense,)
Others apart sat on a hill retired,
In thoughts more elevate, and reasoned high
Of Providence, Foreknowledge, Will and Fate,

560 Fixed Fate, Free Will, Foreknowledge absolute,
And found no end, in wand'ring mazes lost.
Of good and evil much they argued then,
Of happiness and final misery,
Passion and apathy, and glory and shame,
565 Vain wisdom all, and false philosophy:
Yet with a pleasing sorcery could charm
Pain for a while or anguish, and excite
Fallacious hope, or arm th' obdurèd breast
With stubborn patience as with triple steel.
570 Another part in squadrons and gross bands,
On bold adventure to discover wide
That dismal world, if any clime perhaps
Might yield them easier habitation, bend
Four ways their flying march, along the banks
575 Of four infernal rivers that disgorge
Into the burning lake their baleful streams;
Abhorrèd Styx the flood of deadly hate,
Sad Acheron of sorrow, black and deep;
Cocytus, named of lamentation loud
580 Heard on the rueful stream; fierce Phlegethon
Whose waves of torrent fire inflame with rage.
Far off from these a slow and silent stream,
Lethe the river of oblivion rolls
Her wat'ry labyrinth, whereof who drinks,
585 Forthwith his former state and being forgets,
Forgets both joy and grief, pleasure and pain.
Beyond this flood a frozen continent
Lies dark and wild, beat with perpetual storms
Of whirlwind and dire hail, which on firm land
590 Thaws not, but gathers heap and ruin seems
Of ancient pile; all else deep snow and ice,
A gulf profound as that Serbonian bog
Betwixt Damiata and Mount Casius old,
Where armies whole have sunk: the parching air
595 Burns frore, and cold performs th' effect of fire.
Thither by Harpy-footed Furies haled,
At certain revolutions all the damned
Are brought: and feel by turns the bitter change

Of fierce extremes, extremes by change more fierce,
600 From beds of raging fire to starve in ice
Their soft ethereal warmth, and there to pine
Immovable, infixed, and frozen round,
Periods of time, thence hurried back to fire.
They ferry over this Lethean sound
605 Both to and fro, their sorrow to augment,
And wish and struggle, as they pass, to reach
The tempting stream, with one small drop to lose
In sweet forgetfulness all pain and woe.
All in one moment, and so near the brink;
610 But Fate withstands, and to oppose th' attempt
Medusa with Gorgonian terror guards
The ford, and of itself the water flies
All taste of living wight, as once it fled
The lip of Tantalus. Thus roving on
615 In cónfused march forlorn, th' adventurous bands
With shudd'ring horror pale, and eyes aghast
Viewed first their lamentable lot, and found
No rest: through many a dark and dreary vale
They passed, and many a region dolorous,
620 O'er many a frozen, many a fiery alp,
Rocks, caves, lakes, fens, bogs, dens, and shades of death,
A universe of death, which God by curse
Created evil, for evil only good,
Where all life dies, death lives, and nature breeds,
625 Perverse, all monstrous, all prodigious things,
Abominable, unutterable, and worse
Than fables yet have feigned, or fear conceived,
Gorgons, and Hydras, and Chimeras dire.
     Meanwhile the Adversary of God and man,
630 Satan with thoughts inflamed of highest design,
Puts on swift wings, and toward the gates of Hell
Explores his solitary flight; sometimes
He scours the right-hand coast, sometimes the left,
Now shaves with level wing the deep, then soars
635 Up to the fiery concave tow'ring high.
As when far off at sea a fleet descried
Hangs in the clouds, by equinoctial winds

Close sailing from Bengala, or the isles
Of Ternate and Tidore, whence merchants bring
640 Their spicy drugs: they on the trading flood
Through the wide Ethiopian to the Cape
Ply stemming nightly toward the pole. So seemed
Far off the flying Fiend: at last appear
Hell bounds high reaching to the horrid roof,
645 And thrice threefold the gates; three folds were brass,
Three iron, three of adamantine rock,
Impenetrable, impaled with circling fire,
Yet unconsumed. Before the gates there sat
On either side a formidable shape;
650 The one seemed woman to the waist, and fair,
But ended foul in many a scaly fold
Voluminous and vast, a serpent armed
With mortal sting: about her middle round
A cry of Hell-hounds never ceasing barked
655 With wide Cerberean mouths full loud, and rung
A hideous peal: yet, when they list, would creep,
If aught disturbed their noise, into her womb,
And kennel there, yet there still barked and howled
Within unseen. Far less abhorred than these
660 Vexed Scylla bathing in the sea that parts
Calabria from the hoarse Trinacrian shore:
Nor uglier follow the night-hag, when called
In secret, riding through the air she comes
Lured with the smell of infant blood, to dance
665 With Lapland witches, while the labouring moon
Eclipses at their charms. The other shape,
If shape it might be called that shape had none
Distinguishable in member, joint, or limb,
Or substance might be called that shadow seemed,
670 For each seemed either; black it stood as Night,
Fierce as ten Furies, terrible as Hell,
And shook a dreadful dart; what seemed his head
The likeness of a kingly crown had on.
Satan was now at hand, and from his seat
675 The monster moving onward came as fast,
With horrid strides, Hell trembled as he strode.

Th' undaunted Fiend what this might be admired,
Admired, not feared; God and his Son except,
Created thing naught valued he nor shunned;
680   And with disdainful look thus first began.
        Whence and what art thou, execrable shape,
That dar'st though grim and terrible, advance
Thy miscreated front athwart my way
To yonder gates? Through them I mean to pass,
685   That be assured, without leave asked of thee:
Retire, or taste thy folly, and learn by proof,
Hell-born, not to contend with Spirits of Heav'n.
        To whom the goblin full of wrath replied,
Art thou that traitor angel, art thou he,
690   Who first broke peace in Heav'n and faith, till then
Unbroken, and in proud rebellious arms
Drew after him the third part of Heav'n's sons
Conjured against the Highest, for which both thou
And they outcást from God, are here condemned
695   To waste eternal days in woe and pain?
And reckon'st thou thyself with Spirits of Heav'n,
Hell-doomed, and breath'st defiance here and scorn,
Where I reign king, and to enrage thee more,
Thy king and lord? Back to thy punishment,
700   False fugitive, and to thy speed add wings,
Lest with a whip of scorpions I pursue
Thy ling'ring, or with one stroke of this dart
Strange horror seize thee, and pangs unfelt before.
        So spake the grisly terror, and in shape,
705   So speaking and so threat'ning, grew tenfold
More dreadful and deform: on th' other side
Incensed with indignation Satan stood
Unterrified, and like a comet burned,
That fires the length of Ophiucus huge
710   In th' Arctic sky, and from his horrid hair
Shakes pestilence and war. Each at the head
Levelled his deadly aim; their fatal hands
No second stroke intend, and such a frown
Each cast at th' other, as when two black clouds
715   With heav'n's artillery fraught, come rattling on

Over the Caspian, then stand front to front
Hov'ring a space, till winds the signal blow
To join their dark encounter in mid air:
So frowned the mighty combatants, that Hell
720 Grew darker at their frown, so matched they stood;
For never but once more was either like
To meet so great a foe: and now great deeds
Had been achieved, whereof all Hell had rung,
Had not the snaky sorceress that sat
725 Fast by Hell gate, and kept the fatal key,
Ris'n, and with hideous outcry rushed between.
      O father, what intends thy hand, she cried,
Against thy only son? What fury O son,
Possesses thee to bend that mortal dart
730 Against thy father's head? and know'st for whom;
For him who sits above and laughs the while
At thee ordained his drudge, to execute
Whate'er his wrath, which he calls justice, bids,
His wrath which one day will destroy ye both.
735   She spake, and at her words the Hellish pest
Forbore, then these to her Satan returned:
      So strange thy outcry, and thy words so strange
Thou interposest, that my sudden hand
Prevented spares to tell thee yet by deeds
740 What it intends; till first I know of thee,
What thing thou art, thus double-formed, and why
In this infernal vale first met thou call'st
Me father, and that phantasm call'st my son?
I know thee not, nor ever saw till now
745 Sight more detestable than him and thee.
      T' whom thus the portress of Hell gate replied;
Hast thou forgot me then, and do I seem
Now in thine eye so foul, once deemed so fair
In Heav'n, when at th' assembly, and in sight
750 Of all the Seraphim with thee combined
In bold conspiracy against Heav'n's King,
All on a sudden miserable pain
Surprised thee, dim thine eyes, and dizzy swum
In darkness, while thy head flames thick and fast

755 Threw forth, till on the left side op'ning wide,
Likest to thee in shape and count'nance bright,
Then shining Heav'nly fair, a goddess armed
Out of thy head I sprung: amazement seized
All th' host of Heav'n; back they recoiled afraid
760 At first, and called me *Sin*, and for a Sign
Portentous held me; but familiar grown,
I pleased, and with attractive graces won
The most averse, thee chiefly, who full oft
Thyself in me thy perfect image viewing
765 Becam'st enamoured, and such joy thou took'st
With me in secret, that my womb conceived
A growing burden. Meanwhile war arose,
And fields were fought in Heav'n; wherein remained
(For what could else) to our Almighty Foe
770 Clear victory, to our part loss and rout
Through all the Empyrean: down they fell
Driv'n headlong from the pitch of Heaven, down
Into this deep, and in the general fall
I also; at which time this powerful key
775 Into my hand was giv'n, with charge to keep
These gates for ever shut, which none can pass
Without my op'ning. Pensive here I sat
Alone, but long I sat not, till my womb
Pregnant by thee, and now excessive grown
780 Prodigious motion felt and rueful throes.
At last this odious offspring whom thou seest
Thine own begotten, breaking violent way
Tore through my entrails, that with fear and pain
Distorted, all my nether shape thus grew
785 Transformed: but he my inbred enemy
Forth issued, brandishing his fatal dart
Made to destroy: I fled, and cried out *Death*;
Hell trembled at the hideous name, and sighed
Through all her caves, and back resounded *Death*.
790 I fled, but he pursued (though more, it seems,
Inflamed with lust than rage) and swifter far,
Me overtook his mother all dismayed,
And in embraces forcible and foul

Engend'ring with me, of that rape begot
795 These yelling monsters that with ceaseless cry
Surround me, as thou saw'st, hourly conceived
And hourly born, with sorrow infinite
To me, for when they list into the womb
That bred them they return, and howl and gnaw
800 My bowels, their repast; then bursting forth
Afresh with conscious terrors vex me round,
That rest or intermission none I find.
Before mine eyes in opposition sits
Grim Death my son and foe, who sets them on,
805 And me his parent would full soon devour
For want of other prey, but that he knows
His end with mine involved; and knows that I
Should prove a bitter morsel, and his bane,
Whenever that shall be; so Fate pronounced.
810 But thou O father, I forewarn thee, shun
His deadly arrow; neither vainly hope
To be invulnerable in those bright arms,
Though tempered Heav'nly, for that mortal dint,
Save he who reigns above, none can resist.
815   She finished, and the subtle Fiend his lore
Soon learned, now milder, and thus answered smooth.
Dear daughter, since thou claim'st me for thy sire,
And my fair son here show'st me, the dear pledge
Of dalliance had with thee in Heav'n, and joys
820 Then sweet, now sad to mention, through dire change
Befall'n us unforeseen, unthought of, know
I come no enemy, but to set free
From out this dark and dismal house of pain,
Both him and thee, and all the Heav'nly host
825 Of Spirits that in our just pretenses armed
Fell with us from on high: from them I go
This uncouth errand sole, and one for all
Myself expose, with lonely steps to tread
Th' unfounded deep, and through the void immense
830 To search with wand'ring quest a place foretold
Should be, and, by concurring signs, ere now
Created vast and round, a place of bliss

In the purlieus of Heav'n, and therein placed
A race of upstart creatures, to supply
835 Perhaps our vacant room, though more removed,
Lest Heav'n surcharged with potent multitude
Might hap to move new broils: be this or aught
Than this more secret now designed, I haste
To know, and this once known, will soon return,
840 And bring ye to the place where thou and Death
Shall dwell at ease, and up and down unseen
Wing silently the buxom air, embalmed
With odours; there ye shall be fed and filled
Immeasurably, all things shall be your prey.
845 He ceased, for both seemed highly pleased, and Death
Grinned horrible a ghastly smile, to hear
His famine should be filled, and blest his maw
Destined to that good hour: no less rejoiced
His mother bad, and thus bespake her sire.
850   The key of this infernal pit by due,
And by command of Heav'n's all-powerful King
I keep, by him forbidden to unlock
These adamantine gates: against all force
Death ready stands to interpose his dart,
855 Fearless to be o'ermatched by living might.
But what owe I to his commands above
Who hates me, and hath hither thrust me down
Into this gloom of Tartarus profound,
To sit in hateful office here confined,
860 Inhabitant of Heav'n, and Heav'nly-born,
Here in perpetual agony and pain,
With terrors and with clamours compassed round
Of mine own brood, that on my bowels feed:
Thou art my father, thou my author, thou
865 My being gav'st me; whom should I obey
But thee, whom follow? thou wilt bring me soon
To that new world of light and bliss, among
The gods who live at ease, where I shall reign
At thy right hand voluptuous, as beseems
870 Thy daughter and thy darling, without end.
    Thus saying, from her side the fatal key,

Sad instrument of all our woe, she took;
And towards the gate rolling her bestial train,
Forthwith the huge portcullis high up drew,
875 Which but herself not all the Stygian powers
Could once have moved; then in the key-hole turns
Th' intricate wards, and every bolt and bar
Of massy iron or solid rock with ease
Unfastens: on a sudden open fly
880 With impetuous recoil and jarring sound
Th' infernal doors, and on their hinges grate
Harsh thunder, that the lowest bottom shook
Of Erebus. She opened, but to shut
Excelled her power; the gates wide open stood,
885 That with extended wings a bannered host
Under spread ensigns marching might pass through
With horse and chariots ranked in loose array;
So wide they stood, and like a furnace mouth
Cast forth redounding smoke and ruddy flame.
890 Before their eyes in sudden view appear
The secrets of the hoary deep, a dark
Illimitable Ocean without bound,
Without dimension, where length, breadth, and heighth,
And time and place are lost; where eldest Night
895 And Chaos, ancestors of Nature, hold
Eternal anarchy, amidst the noise
Of endless wars, and by confusion stand.
For Hot, Cold, Moist, and Dry, four champions fierce
Strive here for mast'ry, and to battle bring
900 Their embryon atoms; they around the flag
Of each his faction, in their several clans,
Light-armed or heavy, sharp, smooth, swift or slow,
Swarm populous, unnumbered as the sands
Of Barca or Cyrene's torrid soil,
905 Levied to side with warring winds, and poise
Their lighter wings. To whom these most adhere,
He rules a moment; Chaos umpire sits,
And by decision more embroils the fray
By which he reigns: next him high arbiter
910 Chance governs all. Into this wild abyss,

The womb of Nature and perhaps her grave,
Of neither sea, nor shore, nor air, nor fire,
But all these in their pregnant causes mixed
Confus'dly, and which thus must ever fight,
915   Unless th' Almighty Maker them ordain
His dark materials to create more worlds,
Into this wild abyss the wary Fiend
Stood on the brink of Hell and looked a while,
Pondering his voyage; for no narrow frith
920   He had to cross. Nor was his ear less pealed
With noises loud and ruinous (to compare
Great things with small) than when Bellona storms,
With all her battering engines bent to raze
Some capital city; or less than if this frame
925   Of heav'n were falling, and these elements
In mutiny had from her axle torn
The steadfast earth. At last his sail-broad vans
He spreads for flight, and in the surging smoke
Uplifted spurns the ground, thence many a league
930   As in a cloudy chair ascending rides
Audacious, but that seat soon failing, meets
A vast vacuity: all unawares
Flutt'ring his pennons vain plumb down he drops
Ten thousand fathom deep, and to this hour
935   Down had been falling, had not by ill chance
The strong rebuff of some tumultuous cloud
Instínct with fire and nitre hurried him
As many miles aloft: that fury stayed,
Quenched in a boggy Syrtis, neither sea,
940   Nor good dry land: nigh foundered on he fares,
Treading the crude consistence, half on foot,
Half flying; behooves him now both oar and sail.
As when a gryphon through the wilderness
With wingèd course o'er hill or moory dale,
945   Pursues the Arimaspian, who by stealth
Had from his wakeful custody purloined
The guarded gold: so eagerly the Fiend
O'er bog or steep, through strait, rough, dense, or rare,
With head, hands, wings, or feet pursues his way,

950 And swims or sinks, or wades, or creeps, or flies:
    At length a universal hubbub wild
    Of stunning sounds and voices all confused
    Borne through the hollow dark assaults his ear
    With loudest vehemence: thither he plies,
955 Undaunted to meet there whatever Power
    Or Spirit of the nethermost abyss
    Might in that noise reside, of whom to ask
    Which way the nearest coast of darkness lies
    Bordering on light; when straight behold the throne
960 Of Chaos, and his dark pavilion spread
    Wide on the wasteful deep; with him enthroned
    Sat sable-vested Night, eldest of things,
    The consort of his reign; and by them stood
    Orcus and Ades, and the dreaded name
965 Of Demogorgon; Rumour next and Chance,
    And Tumult and Confusion all embroiled,
    And Discord with a thousand various mouths.
        T' whom Satan turning boldly, thus. Ye Powers
    And Spirits of this nethermost abyss,
970 Chaos and ancient Night, I come no spy,
    With purpose to explore or to disturb
    The secrets of your realm, but by constraint
    Wand'ring this darksome desert, as my way
    Lies through your spacious empire up to light,
975 Alone, and without guide, half lost, I seek
    What readiest path leads where your gloomy bounds
    Confine with Heav'n; or if some other place
    From your dominion won, th' Ethereal King
    Possesses lately, thither to arrive
980 I travel this profound, direct my course;
    Directed, no mean recompense it brings
    To your behoof, if I that region lost,
    All usurpation thence expelled, reduce
    To her original darkness and your sway
985 (Which is my present journey) and once more
    Erect the standard there of ancient Night;
    Yours be th' advantage all, mine the revenge.
        Thus Satan; and him thus the Anarch old

With falt'ring speech and visage incomposed
990   Answered. I know thee, stranger, who thou art,
That mighty leading angel, who of late
Made head against Heav'n's King, though overthrown.
I saw and heard, for such a numerous host
Fled not in silence through the frighted deep
995   With ruin upon ruin, rout on rout,
Confusion worse confounded; and Heav'n gates
Poured out by millions her victorious bands
Pursuing. I upon my frontiers here
Keep residence; if all I can will serve,
1000   That little which is left so to defend,
Encroached on still through [y]our intestine broils
Weak'ning the sceptre of old Night: first Hell
Your dungeon stretching far and wide beneath;
Now lately heav'n and earth, another world
1005   Hung o'er my realm, linked in a golden chain
To that side Heav'n from whence your legions fell:
If that way be your walk, you have not far;
So much the nearer danger; go and speed;
Havoc and spoil and ruin are my gain.
1010   He ceased; and Satan stayed not to reply,
But glad that now his sea should find a shore,
With fresh alacrity and force renewed
Springs upward like a pyramid of fire
Into the wide expanse, and through the shock
1015   Of fighting elements, on all sides round
Environed wins his way; harder beset
And more endangered, than when Argo passed
Through Bosporus betwixt the justling rocks:
Or when Ulysses on the larboard shunned
1020   Charybdis, and by th' other whirlpool steered.
So he with difficulty and labour hard
Moved on, with difficulty and labour he;
But he once passed, soon after when man fell,
Strange alteration! Sin and Death amain
1025   Following his track, such was the will of Heav'n,
Paved after him a broad and beaten way
Over the dark abyss, whose boiling gulf

Tamely endured a bridge of wondrous length
From Hell continued reaching th' utmost orb
1030 Of this frail world; by which the Spirits perverse
With easy intercourse pass to and fro
To tempt or punish mortals, except whom
God and good angels guard by special grace.
But now at last the sacred influence
1035 Of light appears, and from the walls of Heav'n
Shoots far into the bosom of dim Night
A glimmering dawn; here Nature first begins
Her farthest verge, and Chaos to retire
As from her outmost works a broken foe
1040 With tumult less and with less hostile din,
That Satan with less toil, and now with ease
Wafts on the calmer wave by dubious light
And like a weather-beaten vessel holds
Gladly the port, though shrouds and tackle torn;
1045 Or in the emptier waste, resembling air,
Weighs his spread wings, at leisure to behold
Far off th' empyreal Heav'n, extended wide
In circuit, undetermined square or round,
With opal tow'rs and battlements adorned
1050 Of living sapphire, once his native seat;
And fast by hanging in a golden chain
This pendent world, in bigness as a star
Of smallest magnitude close by the moon.
Thither full fraught with mischievous revenge,
1055 Accurst, and in a cursèd hour he hies.

BOOK III

The Argument

God sitting on his throne sees Satan flying towards this world, then newly created; shows him to the Son who sat at his right hand; foretells the success of Satan in perverting mankind; clears his own justice and wisdom from all imputation, having created man free and able enough to have withstood his temptation; yet declares his purpose of grace towards him, in regard he fell not of his own malice, as did Satan, but by him seduced. The Son of God renders praises to his Father for the manifestation of his gracious purpose towards man; but God again declares, that grace cannot be extended towards man without the satisfaction of divine justice; man hath offended the majesty of God by aspiring to Godhead, and therefore with all his progeny devoted to death must die, unless someone can be found sufficient to answer for his offence, and undergo his punishment. The Son of God freely offers himself a ransom for man: the Father accepts him, ordains his Incarnation, pronounces his Exaltation above all names in Heaven and earth; commands all the angels to adore him; they obey, and hymning to their harps in full choir, celebrate the Father and the Son. Meanwhile Satan alights upon the bare convex of this world's outermost orb; where wandering he first finds a place since called the Limbo of Vanity; what persons and things fly up thither; thence comes to the gate of Heaven, described ascending by stairs, and the waters above the firmament that flow about it: his passage thence to the orb of the sun; he finds there Uriel the regent of that orb, but first changes himself into the shape of a meaner angel; and pretending a zealous desire to behold the new Creation and man whom God had placed here, inquires of him the place of his habitation, and is directed; alights first on Mount Niphates.

Hail holy Light, offspring of Heav'n first-born,
Or of th' Eternal co-eternal beam
May I express thee unblamed? Since God is light,
And never but in unapproachèd light
5   Dwelt from eternity, dwelt then in thee,
Bright effluence of bright essence increate.
Or hear'st thou rather pure ethereal stream,
Whose fountain who shall tell? Before the sun,
Before the heavens thou wert, and at the voice
10   Of God, as with a mantle didst invest
The rising world of waters dark and deep,
Won from the void and formless infinite.
Thee I revisit now with bolder wing,
Escaped the Stygian pool, though long detained
15   In that obscure sojóurn, while in my flight
Through utter and through middle darkness borne
With other notes than to th' Orphéan lyre
I sung of Chaos and eternal Night,
Taught by the Heav'nly Muse to venture down
20   The dark descent, and up to reascend,
Though hard and rare: thee I revisit safe,
And feel thy sov'reign vital lamp; but thou
Revisit'st not these eyes, that roll in vain
To find thy piercing ray, and find no dawn;
25   So thick a drop serene hath quenched their orbs,
Or dim suffusion veiled. Yet not the more
Cease I to wander where the Muses haunt
Clear spring, or shady grove, or sunny hill,
Smit with the love of sacred song; but chief
30   Thee Sion and the flow'ry brooks beneath
That wash thy hallowed feet, and warbling flow,
Nightly I visit: nor sometimes forget
Those other two equalled with me in fate,
So were I equalled with them in renown,
35   Blind Thamyris and blind Maeonides,
And Tiresias and Phineus prophets old.
Then feed on thoughts, that voluntary move
Harmonious numbers; as the wakeful bird

Sings darkling, and in shadiest covert hid
40 Tunes her nocturnal note. Thus with the year
Seasons return, but not to me returns
Day, or the sweet approach of ev'n or morn,
Or sight of vernal bloom, or summer's rose,
Or flocks, or herds, or human face divine;
45 But cloud instead, and ever-during dark
Surrounds me, from the cheerful ways of men
Cut off, and for the Book of Knowledge fair
Presented with a universal blank
Of Nature's works to me expunged and razed,
50 And wisdom at one entrance quite shut out.
So much the rather thou celestial Light
Shine inward, and the mind through all her powers
Irradiate, there plant eyes, all mist from thence
Purge and dispense, that I may see and tell
55 Of things invisible to mortal sight.
    Now had th' Almighty Father from above,
From the pure Empyrean where he sits
High throned above all heighth, bent down his eye,
His own works and their works at once to view:
60 About him all the sanctities of Heaven
Stood thick as stars, and from his sight received
Beatitude past utterance; on his right
The radiant image of his glory sat,
His only Son; on earth he first beheld
65 Our two first parents, yet the only two
Of mankind, in the happy garden placed,
Reaping immortal fruits of joy and love,
Uninterrupted joy, unrivalled love
In blissful solitude; he then surveyed
70 Hell and the gulf between, and Satan there
Coasting the wall of Heav'n on this side Night
In the dun air sublime, and ready now
To stoop with wearied wings, and willing feet
On the bare outside of this world, that seemed
75 Firm land imbosomed without firmament,
Uncertain which, in ocean or in air.
Him God beholding from his prospect high,

Wherein past, present, future he beholds,
Thus to his only Son foreseeing spake.
80   Only begotten Son, seest thou what rage
Transports our Adversary, whom no bounds
Prescribed, no bars of Hell, nor all the chains
Heaped on him there, nor yet the main abyss
Wide interrupt can hold; so bent he seems
85   On desperate revenge, that shall redound
Upon his own rebellious head. And now
Through all restraint broke loose he wings his way
Not far off Heav'n, in the precincts of light,
Directly towards the new created world,
90   And man there placed, with purpose to assay
If him by force he can destroy, or worse,
By some false guile pervert; and shall pervert;
For man will hearken to his glozing lies,
And easily transgress the sole command,
95   Sole pledge of his obedience: so will fall
He and his faithless progeny: whose fault?
Whose but his own? Ingrate, he had of me
All he could have; I made him just and right,
Sufficient to have stood, though free to fall.
100   Such I created all th' ethereal Powers
And Spirits, both them who stood and them who failed;
Freely they stood who stood, and fell who fell.
Not free, what proof could they have giv'n sincere
Of true allegiance, constant faith or love,
105   Where only what they needs must do, appeared,
Not what they would? What praise could they receive?
What pleasure I from such obedience paid,
When will and reason (reason also is choice)
Useless and vain, of freedom both despoiled,
110   Made passive both, had served necessity,
Not me. They therefore as to right belonged,
So were created, nor can justly accuse
Their Maker, or their making, or their fate,
As if predestination overruled
115   Their will, disposed by absolute decree
Or high foreknowledge; they themselves decreed

Their own revolt, not I: if I foreknew,
Foreknowledge had no influence on their fault,
Which had no less proved certain unforeknown.
120   So without least impúlse or shadow of Fate,
Or aught by me immutably foreseen,
They trespass, authors to themselves in all
Both what they judge and what they choose; for so
I formed them free, and free they must remain,
125   Till they enthrall themselves: I else must change
Their nature, and revoke the high decree
Unchangeable, eternal, which ordained
Their freedom; they themselves ordained their Fall.
The first sort by their own suggestion fell,
130   Self-tempted, self-depraved: man falls deceived
By the other first: man therefore shall find grace;
The other none: in mercy and justice both,
Through Heav'n and earth, so shall my glory excel,
But mercy first and last shall brightest shine.
135   Thus while God spake, ambrosial fragrance filled
All Heav'n, and in the blessèd Spirits elect
Sense of new joy ineffable diffused:
Beyond compare the Son of God was seen
Most glorious, in him all his Father shone
140   Substantially expressed, and in his face
Divine compassion visibly appeared,
Love without end, and without measure grace,
Which uttering thus he to his Father spake.
    O Father, gracious was that word which closed
145   Thy sov'reign sentence, that man should find grace;
For which both Heav'n and earth shall high extol
Thy praises, with th' innumerable sound
Of hymns and sacred songs, wherewith thy throne
Encompassed shall resound thee ever blest.
150   For should man finally be lost, should man
Thy creature late so loved, thy youngest son
Fall circumvented thus by fraud, though joined
With his own folly? That be from thee far,
That far be from thee, Father, who art judge
155   Of all things made, and judgest only right.

Or shall the Adversary thus obtain
His end, and frustrate thine, shall he fulfil
His malice, and thy goodness bring to naught,
Or proud return though to his heavier doom,
160   Yet with revenge accomplished and to Hell
Draw after him the whole race of mankind,
By him corrupted? Or wilt thou thyself
Abolish thy creation, and unmake,
For him, what for thy glory thou hast made?
165   So should thy goodness and thy greatness both
Be questioned and blasphemed without defence.
     To whom the great Creator thus replied.
O Son, in whom my soul hath chief delight,
Son of my bosom, Son who art alone
170   My Word, my wisdom, and effectual might,
All hast thou spoken as my thoughts are, all
As my eternal purpose hath decreed:
Man shall not quite be lost, but saved who will,
Yet not of will in him, but grace in me
175   Freely vouchsafed; once more I will renew
His lapsèd powers, though forfeit and enthralled
By sin to foul exorbitant desires;
Upheld by me, yet once more he shall stand
On even ground against his mortal foe,
180   By me upheld, that he may know how frail
His fall'n condition is, and to me owe
All his deliverance, and to none but me.
Some I have chosen of peculiar grace
Elect above the rest; so is my will:
185   The rest shall hear me call, and oft be warned
Their sinful state, and to appease betimes
Th' incensèd Deity, while offered grace
Invites; for I will clear their senses dark,
What may suffice, and soften stony hearts
190   To pray, repent, and bring obedience due.
To prayer, repentance, and obedience due,
Though but endeavoured with sincere intent,
Mine ear shall not be slow, mine eye not shut.
And I will place within them as a guide

195 My umpire conscience, whom if they will hear,
Light after light well-used they shall attain,
And to the end persisting, safe arrive.
This my long sufferance and my day of grace
They who neglect and scorn, shall never taste;
200 But hard be hardened, blind be blinded more,
That they may stumble on, and deeper fall;
And none but such from mercy I exclude.
But yet all is not done; man disobeying,
Disloyal breaks his fealty, and sins
205 Against the high supremacy of Heav'n,
Affecting Godhead, and so losing all,
To expiate his treason hath naught left,
But to destruction sacred and devote,
He with his whole posterity must die,
210 Die he or Justice must; unless for him
Some other able, and as willing, pay
The rigid satisfaction, death for death.
Say Heav'nly Powers, where shall we find such love,
Which of ye will be mortal to redeem
215 Man's mortal crime, and just th' unjust to save,
Dwells in all Heaven charity so dear?
    He asked, but all the Heav'nly choir stood mute,
And silence was in Heav'n: on man's behalf
Patron or intercessor none appeared,
220 Much less that durst upon his own head draw
The deadly forfeiture, and ransom set.
And now without redemption all mankind
Must have been lost, adjudged to death and Hell
By doom severe, had not the Son of God,
225 In whom the fulness dwells of love divine,
His dearest mediation thus renewed.
    Father, thy word is past, man shall find grace;
And shall grace not find means, that finds her way,
The speediest of thy wingèd messengers,
230 To visit all thy creatures, and to all
Comes unprevented, unimplored, unsought,
Happy for man, so coming; he her aid
Can never seek, once dead in sins and lost;

Atonement for himself or offering meet,
235 Indebted and undone, hath none to bring:
Behold me then, me for him, life for life
I offer, on me let thine anger fall;
Account me man; I for his sake will leave
Thy bosom, and this glory next to thee
240 Freely put off, and for him lastly die
Well pleased, on me let Death wreck all his rage;
Under his gloomy power I shall not long
Lie vanquished; thou hast given me to possess
Life in myself for ever, by thee I live,
245 Though now to Death I yield, and am his due
All of me that can die, yet that debt paid,
Thou wilt not leave me in the loathsome grave
His prey, nor suffer my unspotted soul
For ever with corruption there to dwell;
250 But I shall rise victorious, and subdue
My vanquisher, spoiled of his vaunted spoil;
Death his death's wound shall then receive, and stoop
Inglorious, of his mortal sting disarmed.
I through the ample air in triumph high
255 Shall lead Hell captive maugre Hell, and show
The powers of darkness bound. Thou at the sight
Pleased, out of Heaven shalt look down and smile,
While by thee raised I ruin all my foes,
Death last, and with his carcass glut the grave:
260 Then with the multitude of my redeemed
Shall enter Heaven long absent, and return,
Father, to see thy face, wherein no cloud
Of anger shall remain, but peace assured,
And reconcilement; wrath shall be no more
265 Thenceforth, but in thy presence joy entire.
    His words here ended, but his meek aspéct
Silent yet spake, and breathed immortal love
To mortal men, above which only shone
Filial obedience: as a sacrifice
270 Glad to be offered, he attends the will
Of his great Father. Admiration seized
All Heav'n, what this might mean, and whither tend

Wond'ring; but soon th' Almighty thus replied:
　O thou in Heav'n and earth the only peace
275　Found out for mankind under wrath, O thou
　My sole complacence! Well thou know'st how dear
　To me are all my works, nor man the least
　Though last created, that for him I spare
　Thee from my bosom and right hand, to save,
280　By losing thee a while, the whole race lost.
　Thou therefore whom thou only canst redeem,
　Their nature also to thy nature join;
　And be thyself man among men on earth,
　Made flesh, when time shall be, of virgin seed,
285　By wondrous birth: be thou in Adam's room
　The head of all mankind, though Adam's son.
　As in him perish all men, so in thee
　As from a second root shall be restored,
　As many as are restored, without thee none.
290　His crime makes guilty all his sons; thy merit
　Imputed shall absolve them who renounce
　Their own both righteous and unrighteous deeds,
　And live in thee transplanted, and from thee
　Receive new life. So man, as is most just,
295　Shall satisfy for man, be judged and die,
　And dying rise, and rising with him raise
　His brethren, ransomed with his own dear life.
　So Heav'nly love shall outdo Hellish hate,
　Giving to death, and dying to redeem,
300　So dearly to redeem what Hellish hate
　So easily destroyed, and still destroys
　In those who, when they may, accept not grace.
　Nor shalt thou by descending to assume
　Man's nature, lessen or degrade thine own.
305　Because thou hast, though throned in highest bliss
　Equal to God, and equally enjoying
　God-like fruition, quitted all to save
　A world from utter loss, and hast been found
　By merit more than birthright Son of God,
310　Found worthiest to be so by being good,
　Far more than great or high; because in thee

Love hath abounded more than glory abounds,
Therefore thy humiliation shall exalt
With thee thy manhood also to this throne;
315 Here shalt thou sit incarnate, here shalt reign
Both God and man, Son both of God and man,
Anointed universal King; all power
I give thee, reign for ever, and assume
Thy merits; under thee as Head Supreme
320 Thrones, Princedoms, Powers, Dominions I reduce:
All knees to thee shall bow, of them that bide
In Heaven, or earth, or under earth in Hell;
When thou attended gloriously from Heav'n
Shalt in the sky appear, and from thee send
325 The summoning Archangels to proclaim
Thy dread tribunal: forthwith from all winds
The living, and forthwith the cited dead
Of all past ages to the general doom
Shall hasten, such a peal shall rouse their sleep.
330 Then all thy saints assembled, thou shalt judge
Bad men and angels, they arraigned shall sink
Beneath thy sentence; Hell, her numbers full,
Thenceforth shall be for ever shut. Meanwhile
The world shall burn, and from her ashes spring
335 New heav'n and earth, wherein the just shall dwell,
And after all their tribulations long
See golden days, fruitful of golden deeds,
With joy and love triúmphing, and fair truth.
Then thou thy regal sceptre shalt lay by,
340 For regal sceptre then no more shall need,
God shall be All in All. But all ye gods,
Adore him, who to compass all this dies,
Adore the Son, and honour him as me.
    No sooner had th' Almighty ceased, but all
345 The multitude of angels with a shout
Loud as from numbers without number, sweet
As from blest voices, uttering joy, Heav'n rung
With jubilee, and loud hosannas filled
Th' eternal regions: lowly reverent
350 Towards either throne they bow, and to the ground

With solemn adoration down they cast
Their crowns inwove with amarant and gold,
Immortal amarant, a flow'r which once
In Paradise, fast by the Tree of Life
355   Began to bloom, but soon for man's offence
To Heav'n removed where first it grew, there grows,
And flow'rs aloft shading the Fount of Life,
And where the river of bliss through midst of Heav'n
Rolls o'er Elysian flow'rs her amber stream;
360   With these that never fade the Spirits elect
Bind their resplendent locks inwreathed with beams;
Now in loose garlands thick thrown off, the bright
Pavement that like a sea of jasper shone
Impurpled with celestial roses smiled.
365   Then crowned again their golden harps they took,
Harps ever tuned, that glittering by their side
Like quivers hung, and with preamble sweet
Of charming symphony they introduce
Their sacred song, and waken raptures high;
370   No voice exempt, no voice but well could join
Melodious part, such concord is in Heav'n.
    Thee Father first they sung omnipotent,
Immutable, immortal, infinite,
Eternal King; thee Author of all being,
375   Fountain of light, thyself invisible
Amidst the glorious brightness where thou sitt'st
Throned inaccessible, but when thou shad'st
The full blaze of thy beams, and through a cloud
Drawn round about thee like a radiant shrine,
380   Dark with excessive bright thy skirts appear,
Yet dazzle Heav'n, that brightest Seraphim
Approach not, but with both wings veil their eyes.
Thee next they sang of all Creation first,
Begotten Son, Divine Similitude,
385   In whose conspicuous count'nance, without cloud
Made visible, th' Almighty Father shines,
Whom else no creature can behold; on thee
Impressed th' effulgence of his glory abides,
Transfused on thee his ample Spirit rests.

390 He Heav'n of Heav'ns and all the Powers therein
By thee created, and by thee threw down
Th' aspiring Dominations: thou that day
Thy Father's dreadful thunder didst not spare,
Nor stop thy flaming chariot wheels, that shook
395 Heav'n's everlasting frame, while o'er the necks
Thou drov'st of warring angels disarrayed.
Back from pursuit thy Powers with loud acclaim
Thee only extolled, Son of thy Father's might,
To execute fierce vengeance on his foes,
400 Not so on man; him through their malice fall'n,
Father of mercy and grace, thou didst not doom
So strictly, but much more to pity incline:
No sooner did thy dear and only Son
Perceive thee purposed not to doom frail man
405 So strictly, but much more to pity inclined,
He to appease thy wrath, and end the strife
Of mercy and justice in thy face discerned,
Regardless of the bliss in which he sat
Second to thee, offered himself to die
410 For man's offence. O unexampled love,
Love nowhere to be found less than divine!
Hail Son of God, Saviour of men, thy name
Shall be the copious matter of my song
Henceforth, and never shall my harp thy praise
415 Forget, nor from thy Father's praise disjoin.
    Thus they in Heav'n, above the starry sphere,
Their happy hours in joy and hymning spent.
Meanwhile upon the firm opacous globe
Of this round world, whose first convéx divides
420 The luminous inferior orbs, enclosed
From Chaos and th' inroad of Darkness old,
Satan alighted walks: a globe far off
It seemed, now seems a boundless continent
Dark, waste, and wild, under the frown of Night
425 Starless exposed, and ever-threat'ning storms
Of Chaos blust'ring round, inclement sky;
Save on that side which from the wall of Heav'n
Though distant far some small reflection gains

Of glimmering air less vexed with tempest loud:
430 Here walked the Fiend at large in spacious field.
As when a vulture on Imaus bred,
Whose snowy ridge the roving Tartar bounds,
Dislodging from a region scarce of prey
To gorge the flesh of lambs or yeanling kids
435 On hills where flocks are fed, flies toward the springs
Of Ganges or Hydaspes, Indian streams;
But in his way lights on the barren plains
Of Sericana, where Chineses drive
With sails and wind their cany wagons light:
440 So on this windy sea of land, the Fiend
Walked up and down alone bent on his prey,
Alone, for other creature in this place
Living or lifeless to be found was none,
None yet, but store hereafter from the earth
445 Up hither like aërial vapours flew
Of all things transitory and vain, when sin
With vanity had filled the works of men:
Both all things vain, and all who in vain things
Built their fond hopes of glory or lasting fame,
450 Or happiness in this or th' other life;
All who have their reward on earth, the fruits
Of painful superstition and blind zeal,
Naught seeking but the praise of men, here find
Fit retribution, empty as their deeds;
455 All th' unaccomplished works of Nature's hand,
Abortive, monstrous, or unkindly mixed,
Dissolved on earth, fleet hither, and in vain,
Till final dissolution, wander here,
Not in the neighbouring moon, as some have dreamed;
460 Those argent fields more likely habitants,
Translated saints, or middle Spirits hold
Betwixt th' angelical and human kind:
Hither of ill-joined sons and daughters born
First from the ancient world those Giants came
465 With many a vain explóit, though then renowned:
The builders next of Babel on the plain
Of Sennaär, and still with vain design

New Babels, had they wherewithal, would build:
Others came single; he who to be deemed
470   A god, leaped fondly into Etna flames,
Empedocles, and he who to enjoy
Plato's Elysium, leaped into the sea,
Cleombrotus, and many more too long,
Embryos and idiots, eremites and friars
475   White, black and grey, with all their trumpery.
Here pilgrims roam, that strayed so far to seek
In Golgotha him dead, who lives in Heav'n;
And they who to be sure of Paradise
Dying put on the weeds of Dominic,
480   Or in Franciscan think to pass disguised;
They pass the planets seven, and pass the fixed,
And that crystálline sphere whose balance weighs
The trepidation talked, and that first moved;
And now Saint Peter at Heav'n's wicket seems
485   To wait them with his keys, and now at foot
Of Heav'n's ascent they lift their feet, when lo
A violent crosswind from either coast
Blows them transverse ten thousand leagues awry
Into the devious air; then might ye see
490   Cowls, hoods and habits with their wearers tossed
And fluttered into rags; then relics, beads,
Indulgences, dispenses, pardons, bulls,
The sport of winds: all these upwhirled aloft
Fly o'er the backside of the world far off
495   Into a Limbo large and broad, since called
The Paradise of Fools, to few unknown
Long after, now unpeopled, and untrod;
All this dark globe the Fiend found as he passed,
And long he wandered, till at last a gleam
500   Of dawning light turned thitherward in haste
His travelled steps; far distant he descries
Ascending by degrees magnificent
Up to the wall of Heaven a structure high,
At top whereof, but far more rich appeared
505   The work as of a kingly palace gate
With frontispiece of diamond and gold

Embellished; thick with sparkling orient gems
The portal shone, inimitable on earth
By model, or by shading pencil drawn.
510   The stairs were such as whereon Jacob saw
Angels ascending and descending, bands
Of guardians bright, when he from Esau fled
To Padan-Aram, in the field of Luz
Dreaming by night under the open sky,
515   And waking cried, *This is the gate of Heav'n.*
Each stair mysteriously was meant, nor stood
There always, but drawn up to Heav'n sometimes
Viewless, and underneath a bright sea flowed
Of jasper, or of liquid pearl, whereon
520   Who after came from earth, sailing arrived,
Wafted by angels, or flew o'er the lake
Rapt in a chariot drawn by fiery steeds.
The stairs were then let down, whether to dare
The Fiend by easy ascent, or aggravate
525   His sad exclusion from the doors of bliss.
Direct against which opened from beneath,
Just o'er the blissful seat of Paradise,
A passage down to th' earth, a passage wide,
Wider by far than that of aftertimes
530   Over Mount Sion, and, though that were large,
Over the Promised Land to God so dear,
By which to visit oft those happy tribes,
On high behests his angels to and fro
Passed frequent, and his eye with choice regard
535   From Paneas the fount of Jordan's flood
To Beërsaba, where the Holy Land
Borders on Egypt and the Arabian shore;
So wide the op'ning seemed, where bounds were set
To darkness, such as bound the ocean wave.
540   Satan from hence now on the lower stair
That scaled by steps of gold to Heaven gate
Looks down with wonder at the sudden view
Of all this world at once. As when a scout
Through dark and desert ways with peril gone
545   All night; at last by break of cheerful dawn

Obtains the brow of some high-climbing hill,
Which to his eye discovers unaware
The goodly prospect of some foreign land
First seen, or some renowned metropolis
550 With glistering spires and pinnacles adorned,
Which now the rising sun gilds with his beams.
Such wonder seized, though after Heaven seen,
The Spirit malign, but much more envy seized
At sight of all this world beheld so fair.
555 Round he surveys, and well might, where he stood
So high above the circling canopy
Of night's extended shade; from eastern point
Of Libra to the fleecy star that bears
Andromeda far off Atlantic seas
560 Beyond th' horizon; then from pole to pole
He views in breadth, and without longer pause
Down right into the world's first region throws
His flight precipitant, and winds with ease
Through the pure marble air his óblique way
565 Amongst innumerable stars, that shone
Stars distant, but nigh hand seemed other worlds;
Or other worlds they seemed, or happy isles,
Like those Hesperian gardens famed of old,
Fortunate fields, and groves and flow'ry vales,
570 Thrice happy isles, but who dwelt happy there
He stayed not to inquire: above them all
The golden sun in splendour likest Heaven
Allured his eye: thither his course he bends
Through the calm firmament; but up or down
575 By centre or eccentric, hard to tell,
Or longitude, where the great luminary
Aloof the vulgar constellations thick,
That from his lordly eye keep distance due,
Dispenses light from far; they as they move
580 Their starry dance in numbers that compute
Days, months, and years, towards his all-cheering lamp
Turn swift their various motions, or are turned
By his magnetic beam, that gently warms
The universe, and to each inward part

585   With gentle penetration, though unseen,
       Shoots invisible virtue even to the deep:
       So wondrously was set his station bright.
       There lands the Fiend, a spot like which perhaps
       Astronomer in the sun's lucent orb
590   Through his glazed optic tube yet never saw.
       The place he found beyond expression bright,
       Compared with aught on earth, metal or stone;
       Not all parts like, but all alike informed
       With radiant light, as glowing iron with fire;
595   If metal, part seemed gold, part silver clear;
       If stone, carbuncle most or chrysolite,
       Ruby or topaz, to the twelve that shone
       In Aaron's breastplate, and a stone besides
       Imagined rather oft than elsewhere seen,
600   That stone, or like to that which here below
       Philosophers in vain so long have sought,
       In vain, though by their powerful art they bind
       Volátile Hermes, and call up unbound
       In various shapes old Proteus from the sea,
605   Drained through a limbeck to his native form.
       What wonder then if fields and regions here
       Breathe forth elixir pure, and rivers run
       Potable gold, when with one virtuous touch
       Th' arch-chemic sun so far from us remote
610   Produces with terrestrial humour mixed
       Here in the dark so many precious things
       Of colour glorious and effect so rare?
       Here matter new to gaze the Devil met
       Undazzled; far and wide his eye commands,
615   For sight no obstacle found here, nor shade,
       But all sunshine, as when his beams at noon
       Culminate from th' equator, as they now
       Shot upward still direct, whence no way round
       Shadow from body opaque can fall, and the air,
620   Nowhere so clear, sharpened his visual ray
       To objects distant far, whereby he soon
       Saw within ken a glorious angel stand,
       The same whom John saw also in the sun:

His back was turned, but not his brightness hid;
625   Of beaming sunny rays, a golden tiar
Circled his head, nor less his locks behind
Illustrious on his shoulders fledge with wings
Lay waving round; on some great charge employed
He seemed, or fixed in cogitation deep.
630   Glad was the Spirit impure; as now in hope
To find who might direct his wand'ring flight
To Paradise the happy seat of man,
His journey's end and our beginning woe.
But first he casts to change his proper shape,
635   Which else might work him danger or delay:
And now a stripling Cherub he appears,
Not of the prime, yet such as in his face
Youth smiled celestial, and to every limb
Suitable grace diffused, so well he feigned;
640   Under a coronet his flowing hair
In curls on either cheek played, wings he wore
Of many a coloured plume sprinkled with gold,
His habit fit for speed succinct, and held
Before his decent steps a silver wand.
645   He drew not nigh unheard, the angel bright,
Ere he drew nigh, his radiant visage turned,
Admonished by his ear, and straight was known
Th' Archangel Uriel, one of the seven
Who in God's presence, nearest to his throne
650   Stand ready at command, and are his eyes
That run through all the heavens, or down to the earth
Bear his swift errands over moist and dry,
O'er sea and land: him Satan thus accosts.
Uriel, for thou of those sev'n Spirits that stand
655   In sight of God's high throne, gloriously bright,
The first art wont his great authentic will
Interpreter through highest Heav'n to bring,
Where all his sons thy embassy attend;
And here art likeliest by supreme decree
660   Like honour to obtain, and as his eye
To visit oft this new Creation round;
Unspeakable desire to see, and know

All these his wondrous works, but chiefly man,
His chief delight and favour, him for whom
665 All these bright works so wondrous he ordained,
Hath brought me from the choirs of Cherubim
Alone thus wand'ring. Brightest Seraph tell
In which of all these shining orbs hath man
His fixèd seat, or fixèd seat hath none,
670 But all these shining orbs his choice to dwell;
That I may find him, and with secret gaze,
Or open admiration him behold
On whom the great Creator hath bestowed
Worlds, and on whom hath all these graces poured;
675 That both in him and all things, as is meet,
The Universal Maker we may praise;
Who justly hath driv'n out his rebel foes
To deepest Hell, and to repair that loss
Created this new happy race of men
680 To serve him better: wise are all his ways.
      So spake the false dissembler unperceived;
For neither man nor angel can discern
Hypocrisy, the only evil that walks
Invisible, except to God alone,
685 By his permissive will, through Heav'n and earth:
And oft though wisdom wake, suspicion sleeps
At wisdom's gate, and to simplicity
Resigns her charge, while goodness thinks no ill
Where no ill seems: which now for once beguiled
690 Uriel, though regent of the sun, and held
The sharpest sighted Spirit of all in Heav'n;
Who to the fraudulent impostor foul
In his uprightness answer thus returned.
Fair angel, thy desire which tends to know
695 The works of God, thereby to glorify
The great Work-Master, leads to no excess
That reaches blame, but rather merits praise
The more it seems excess, that led thee hither
From thy empyreal mansion thus alone,
700 To witness with thine eyes what some perhaps

Contented with report hear only in Heav'n:
For wonderful indeed are all his works,
Pleasant to know, and worthiest to be all
Had in remembrance always with delight;
705   But what created mind can comprehend
Their number, or the wisdom infinite
That brought them forth, but hid their causes deep.
I saw when at his word the formless mass,
This world's material mould, came to a heap:
710   Confusion heard his voice, and wild uproar
Stood ruled, stood vast infinitude confined;
Till at his second bidding darkness fled,
Light shone, and order from disorder sprung:
Swift to their several quarters hasted then
715   The cumbrous elements, earth, flood, air, fire
And this ethereal quintessence of heav'n
Flew upward, spirited with various forms,
That rolled orbicular, and turned to stars
Numberless, as thou seest, and how they move;
720   Each had his place appointed, each his course,
The rest in circuit walls this universe.
Look downward on that globe whose hither side
With light from hence, though but reflected, shines;
That place is earth the seat of man, that light
725   His day, which else as th' other hemisphere
Night would invade, but there the neighbouring moon
(So call that opposite fair star) her aid
Timely interposes, and her monthly round
Still ending, still renewing, through mid heav'n,
730   With borrowed light her countenance triform
Hence fills and empties to enlighten th' earth,
And in her pale dominion checks the night.
That spot to which I point is Paradise,
Adam's abode, those lofty shades his bower.
735   Thy way thou canst not miss, me mine requires.
    Thus said, he turned, and Satan bowing low,
As to superior Spirits is wont in Heav'n,
Where honour due and reverence none neglects,

Took leave, and toward the coast of earth beneath,
740 Down from th' ecliptic, sped with hoped success,
Throws his steep flight in many an airy wheel,
Nor stayed, till on Niphates' top he lights.

BOOK IV

The Argument

Satan now in prospect of Eden, and nigh the place where he must now attempt the bold enterprise which he undertook alone against God and man, falls into many doubts with himself, and many passions, fear, envy, and despair; but at length confirms himself in evil, journeys on to Paradise, whose outward prospect and situation is described, overleaps the bounds, sits in the shape of a cormorant on the Tree of Life, as highest in the garden to look about him. The garden described; Satan's first sight of Adam and Eve; his wonder at their excellent form and happy state, but with resolution to work their Fall; overhears their discourse, thence gathers that the Tree of Knowledge was forbidden them to eat of, under penalty of death; and thereon intends to found his Temptation, by seducing them to transgress: then leaves them a while, to know further of their state by some other means. Meanwhile Uriel descending on a sunbeam warns Gabriel, who had in charge the gate of Paradise, that some evil Spirit had escaped the deep, and passed at noon by his sphere in the shape of a good angel down to Paradise, discovered after by his furious gestures in the mount. Night coming on, Adam and Eve, discourse of going to their rest: their bower described; their evening worship. Gabriel drawing forth his bands of night-watch to walk the round of Paradise, appoints two strong angels to Adam's bower, lest the evil spirit should be there doing some harm to Adam or Eve sleeping; there they find him at the ear of Eve, tempting her in a dream, and bring him, though unwilling, to Gabriel; by whom questioned, he scornfully answers, prepares resistance, but hindered by a sign from Heaven, flies out of Paradise.

O for that warning voice, which he who saw
Th' Apocalypse, heard cry in Heav'n aloud,
Then when the Dragon, put to second rout,
Came furious down to be revenged on men,

5   *Woe to the inhabitants on earth!* that now,
While time was, our first parents had been warned
The coming of their secret foe, and 'scaped
Haply so 'scaped his mortal snare; for now
Satan, now first inflamed with rage, came down,

10   The Tempter ere th' Accuser of mankind,
To wreck on innocent frail man his loss
Of that first battle, and his flight to Hell:
Yet not rejoicing in his speed, though bold,
Far off and fearless, nor with cause to boast,

15   Begins his dire attempt, which nigh the birth
Now rolling, boils in his tumultuous breast,
And like a devilish engine back recoils
Upon himself; horror and doubt distract
His troubled thoughts, and from the bottom stir

20   The Hell within him, for within him Hell
He brings, and round about him, nor from Hell
One step no more than from himself can fly
By change of place: now conscience wakes despair
That slumbered, wakes the bitter memory

25   Of what he was, what is, and what must be
Worse; of worse deeds worse sufferings must ensue.
Sometimes towards Eden which now in his view
Lay pleasant, his grieved look he fixes sad,
Sometimes towards heav'n and the full-blazing sun,

30   Which now sat high in his meridian tower:
Then much revolving, thus in sighs began.
     O thou that with surpassing glory crowned,
Look'st from thy sole dominion like the God
Of this new world; at whose sight all the stars

35   Hide their diminished heads; to thee I call,
But with no friendly voice, and add thy name
O sun, to tell thee how I hate thy beams
That bring to my remembrance from what state
I fell, how glorious once above thy sphere;

40 Till pride and worse ambition threw me down
Warring in Heav'n against Heav'n's matchless King:
Ah wherefore! he deserved no such return
From me, whom he created what I was
In that bright eminence, and with his good
45 Upbraided none; nor was his service hard.
What could be less than to afford him praise,
The easiest recompense, and pay him thanks,
How due! Yet all his good proved ill in me,
And wrought but malice; lifted up so high
50 I 'sdained subjection, and thought one step higher
Would set me highest, and in a moment quit
The debt immense of endless gratitude,
So burdensome, still paying, still to owe;
Forgetful what from him I still received,
55 And understood not that a grateful mind
By owing owes not, but still pays, at once
Indebted and discharged; what burden then?
O had his powerful destiny ordained
Me some inferior angel, I had stood
60 Then happy; no unbounded hope had raised
Ambition. Yet why not? Some other Power
As great might have aspired, and me though mean
Drawn to his part; but other Powers as great
Fell not, but stand unshaken, from within
65 Or from without, to all temptations armed.
Hadst thou the same free will and power to stand?
Thou hadst: whom hast thou then or what to accuse,
But Heav'n's free love dealt equally to all?
Be then his love accurst, since love or hate,
70 To me alike, it deals eternal woe.
Nay cursed be thou; since against his thy will
Chose freely what it now so justly rues.
Me miserable! Which way shall I fly
Infinite wrath, and infinite despair?
75 Which way I fly is Hell; myself am Hell;
And in the lowest deep a lower deep
Still threat'ning to devour me opens wide,
To which the Hell I suffer seems a Heav'n.

O then at last relent: is there no place
80   Left for repentance, none for pardon left?
None left but by submission; and that word
Disdain forbids me, and my dread of shame
Among the Spirits beneath, whom I seduced
With other promises and other vaunts
85   Than to submit, boasting I could subdue
Th' Omnipotent. Ay me, they little know
How dearly I abide that boast so vain,
Under what torments inwardly I groan;
While they adore me on the throne of Hell,
90   With diadem and sceptre high advanced
The lower still I fall, only supreme
In misery; such joy ambition finds.
But say I could repent and could obtain
By act of grace my former state; how soon
95   Would heighth recall high thoughts, how soon unsay
What feigned submission swore: ease would recant
Vows made in pain, as violent and void.
For never can true reconcilement grow
Where wounds of deadly hate have pierced so deep:
100   Which would but lead me to a worse relapse
And heavier fall: so should I purchase dear
Short intermission bought with double smart.
This knows my punisher; therefore as far
From granting he, as I from begging peace:
105   All hope excluded thus, behold instead
Of us outcást, exíled, his new delight,
Mankind created, and for him this world.
So farewell hope, and with hope farewell fear,
Farewell remorse: all good to me is lost;
110   Evil be thou my good; by thee at least
Divided empire with Heav'n's King I hold
By thee, and more than half perhaps will reign;
As man ere long, and this new world shall know.
     Thus while he spake, each passion dimmed his face
115   Thrice changed with pale, ire, envy and despair,
Which marred his borrowed visage, and betrayed
Him counterfeit, if any eye beheld.

For Heav'nly minds from such distempers foul
Are ever clear. Whereof he soon aware,
120   Each perturbation smoothed with outward calm,
Artificer of fraud; and was the first
That practised falsehood under saintly show,
Deep malice to conceal, couched with revenge:
Yet not enough had practised to deceive
125   Uriel once warned; whose eye pursued him down
The way he went, and on th' Assyrian mount
Saw him disfigured, more than could befall
Spirit of happy sort: his gestures fierce
He marked and mad demeanour, then alone,
130   As he supposed, all unobserved, unseen.
So on he fares, and to the border comes
Of Eden, where delicious Paradise,
Now nearer, crowns with her enclosure green,
As with a rural mound the champaign head
135   Of a steep wilderness, whose hairy sides
With thicket overgrown, grotesque and wild,
Access denied; and overhead up grew
Insuperable heighth of loftiest shade,
Cedar, and pine, and fir, and branching palm,
140   A sylvan scene, and as the ranks ascend
Shade above shade, a woody theatre
Of stateliest view. Yet higher than their tops
The verdurous wall of Paradise up sprung:
Which to our general sire gave prospect large
145   Into his nether empire neighbouring round.
And higher than that wall a circling row
Of goodliest trees loaden with fairest fruit,
Blossoms and fruits at once of golden hue
Appeared, with gay enamelled colours mixed:
150   On which the sun more glad impressed his beams
Than in fair evening cloud, or humid bow,
When God hath show'red the earth; so lovely seemed
That landscape: and of pure now purer air
Meets his approach, and to the heart inspires
155   Vernal delight and joy, able to drive
All sadness but despair: now gentle gales

Fanning their odoriferous wings dispense
Native perfumes and whisper whence they stole
Those balmy spoils. As when to them who sail
160   Beyond the Cape of Hope, and now are passed
Mozámbique, off at sea northeast winds blow
Sabéan odours from the spicy shore
Of Araby the blest, with such delay
Well pleased they slack their course, and many a league
165   Cheered with the grateful smell old Ocean smiles.
So entertained those odorous sweets the Fiend
Who came their bane, though with them better pleased
Than Asmodéus with the fishy fume,
That drove him, though enamoured, from the spouse
170   Of Tobit's son, and with a vengeance sent
From Media post to Egypt, there fast bound.
     Now to th' ascent of that steep savage hill
Satan had journeyed on, pensive and slow;
But further way found none, so thick entwined,
175   As one continued brake, the undergrowth
Of shrubs and tangling bushes had perplexed
All path of man or beast that passed that way:
One gate there only was, and that looked east
On th' other side: which when th' Arch-felon saw
180   Due entrance he disdained, and in contempt,
At one slight bound high overleaped all bound
Of hill or highest wall, and sheer within
Lights on his feet. As when a prowling wolf,
Whom hunger drives to seek new haunt for prey,
185   Watching where shepherds pen their flocks at eve
In hurdled cotes amid the field secure,
Leaps o'er the fence with ease into the fold:
Or as a thief bent to unhoard the cash
Of some rich burgher, whose substantial doors,
190   Cross-barred and bolted fast, fear no assault,
In at the window climbs, or o'er the tiles;
So clomb this first grand thief into God's fold:
So since into his Church lewd hirelings climb.
Thence up he flew, and on the Tree of Life,
195   The middle tree and highest there that grew,

Sat like a cormorant; yet not true life
Thereby regained, but sat devising death
To them who lived; nor on the virtue thought
Of that life-giving plant, but only used
200   For prospect, what well used had been the pledge
Of immortality. So little knows
Any, but God alone, to value right
The good before him, but perverts best things
To worst abuse, or to their meanest use.
205   Beneath him with new wonder now he views
To all delight of human sense exposed
In narrow room Nature's whole wealth, yea more,
A Heav'n on earth, for blissful Paradise
Of God the garden was, by him in the east
210   Of Eden planted; Eden stretched her line
From Auran eastward to the royal towers
Of great Seleucia, built by Grecian kings,
Or where the sons of Eden long before
Dwelt in Telassar: in this pleasant soil
215   His far more pleasant garden God ordained;
Out of this fertile ground he caused to grow
All trees of noblest kind for sight, smell, taste;
And all amid them stood the Tree of Life,
High eminent, blooming ambrosial fruit
220   Of vegetable gold; and next to life
Our death the Tree of Knowledge grew fast by,
Knowledge of Good bought dear by knowing ill.
Southward through Eden went a river large,
Nor changed his course, but through the shaggy hill
225   Passed underneath ingulfed, for God had thrown
That mountain as his garden mould high raised
Upon the rapid current, which through veins
Of porous earth with kindly thirst up drawn,
Rose a fresh fountain, and with many a rill
230   Watered the garden; thence united fell
Down the steep glade, and met the nether flood,
Which from his darksome passage now appears,
And now divided into four main streams,
Runs diverse, wand'ring many a famous realm

235 And country whereof here needs no account,
But rather to tell how, if art could tell,
How from that sapphire fount the crispèd brooks,
Rolling on orient pearl and sands of gold,
With mazy error under pendent shades

240 Ran nectar, visiting each plant, and fed
Flow'rs worthy of Paradise which not nice art
In beds and curious knots, but Nature boon
Poured forth profuse on hill and dale and plain,
Both where the morning sun first warmly smote

245 The open field, and where the unpierced shade
Embrowned the noontide bowers: thus was this place,
A happy rural seat of various view;
Groves whose rich trees wept odorous gums and balm,
Others whose fruit burnished with golden rind

250 Hung amiable, Hesperian fables true,
If true, here only, and of delicious taste:
Betwixt them lawns, or level downs, and flocks
Grazing the tender herb, were interposed,
Or palmy hillock, or the flow'ry lap

255 Of some irriguous valley spread her store,
Flow'rs of all hue, and without thorn the rose:
Another side, umbrageous grots and caves
Of cool recess, o'er which the mantling vine
Lays forth her purple grape, and gently creeps

260 Luxuriant; meanwhile murmuring waters fall
Down the slope hills, dispersed, or in a lake,
That to the fringèd bank with myrtle crowned,
Her crystal mirror holds, unite their streams.
The birds their choir apply; airs, vernal airs,

265 Breathing the smell of field and grove, attune
The trembling leaves, while universal Pan
Knit with the Graces and the Hours in dance
Led on th' eternal spring. Not that fair field
Of Enna, where Prosérpine gath'ring flow'rs

270 Herself a fairer flow'r by gloomy Dis
Was gathered, which cost Ceres all that pain
To seek her through the world; nor that sweet grove
Of Daphne by Orontes, and th' inspired

Castalian spring, might with this Paradise
275 Of Eden strive; nor that Nyseian isle
Girt with the river Triton, where old Cham,
Whom Gentiles Ammon call and Libyan Jove,
Hid Amalthea and her florid son
Young Bacchus from his stepdame Rhea's eye;
280 Nor where Abássin kings their issue guard,
Mount Amara, though this by some supposed
True Paradise under the Ethiop line
By Nilus' head, enclosed with shining rock,
A whole day's journey high, but wide remote
285 From this Assyrian garden, where the Fiend
Saw undelighted all delight, all kind
Of living creatures new to sight and strange:
Two of far nobler shape erect and tall,
Godlike erect, with native honour clad
290 In naked majesty seemed lords of all,
And worthy seemed, for in their looks divine
The image of their glorious Maker shone,
Truth, wisdom, sanctitude severe and pure,
Severe, but in true filial freedom placed;
295 Whence true authority in men; though both
Not equal, as their sex not equal seemed;
For contemplation he and valour formed,
For softness she and sweet attractive grace,
He for God only, she for God in him:
300 His fair large front and eye sublime declared
Absolute rule; and hyacinthine locks
Round from his parted forelock manly hung
Clust'ring, but not beneath his shoulders broad:
She as a veil down to the slender waist
305 Her unadornèd golden tresses wore
Dishevelled, but in wanton ringlets waved
As the vine curls her tendrils, which implied
Subjection, but required with gentle sway,
And by her yielded, by him best received,
310 Yielded with coy submission, modest pride,
And sweet reluctant amorous delay.
Nor those mysterious parts were then concealed;

Then was not guilty shame, dishonest shame
Of nature's works, honour dishonourable,
315   Sin-bred, how have ye troubled all mankind
With shows instead, mere shows of seeming pure,
And banished from man's life his happiest life,
Simplicity and spotless innocence.
So passed they naked on, nor shunned the sight
320   Of God or angel, for they thought no ill:
So hand in hand they passed, the loveliest pair
That ever since in love's embraces met,
Adam the goodliest man of men since born
His sons, the fairest of her daughters Eve.
325   Under a tuft of shade that on a green
Stood whispering soft, by a fresh fountain side
They sat them down, and after no more toil
Of their sweet gard'ning labour than sufficed
To recommend cool Zephyr, and made ease
330   More easy, wholesome thirst and appetite
More grateful, to their supper fruits they fell,
Nectarine fruits which the compliant boughs
Yielded them, sidelong as they sat recline
On the soft downy bank damasked with flow'rs:
335   The savoury pulp they chew, and in the rind
Still as they thirsted scoop the brimming stream;
Nor gentle purpose, nor endearing smiles
Wanted, nor youthful dalliance as beseems
Fair couple, linked in happy nuptial league,
340   Alone as they. About them frisking played
All beasts of th' earth, since wild, and of all chase
In wood or wilderness, forest or den;
Sporting the lion ramped, and in his paw
Dandled the kid; bears, tigers, ounces, pards
345   Gambolled before them, th' unwieldy elephant
To make them mirth used all his might, and wreathed
His lithe proboscis; close the serpent sly
Insinuating, wove with Gordian twine
His braided train, and of his fatal guile
350   Gave proof unheeded; others on the grass
Couched, and now filled with pasture gazing sat,

Or bedward ruminating: for the sun
Declined was hasting now with prone career
To th' Ocean Isles, and in th' ascending Scale
355   Of Heav'n the stars that usher evening rose:
When Satan still in gaze, as first he stood,
Scarce thus at length failed speech recovered sad.
    O Hell! What do mine eyes with grief behold,
Into our room of bliss thus high advanced
360   Creatures of other mould, earth-born perhaps,
Not Spirits, yet to Heav'nly Spirits bright
Little inferior; whom my thoughts pursue
With wonder, and could love, so lively shines
In them divine resemblance, and such grace
365   The hand that formed them on their shape hath poured.
Ah gentle pair, ye little think how nigh
Your change approaches, when all these delights
Will vanish and deliver ye to woe,
More woe, the more your taste is now of joy;
370   Happy, but for so happy ill secured
Long to continue, and this high seat your Heav'n
Ill fenced for Heav'n to keep out such a foe
As now is entered; yet no purposed foe
To you whom I could pity thus forlorn
375   Though I unpitied: league with you I seek,
And mutual amity so strait, so close,
That I with you must dwell, or you with me
Henceforth; my dwelling haply may not please
Like this fair Paradise, your sense, yet such
380   Accept your Maker's work; he gave it me,
Which I as freely give; Hell shall unfold,
To entertain you two, her widest gates,
And send forth all her kings; there will be room,
Not like these narrow limits, to receive
385   Your numerous offspring; if no better place,
Thank him who puts me loath to this revenge
On you who wrong me not for him who wronged.
And should I at your harmless innocence
Melt, as I do, yet public reason just,
390   Honour and empire with revenge enlarged,

By conquering this new world, compels me now
To do what else though damned I should abhor.
    So spake the Fiend, and with necessity,
The tyrant's plea, excused his devilish deeds.
395   Then from his lofty stand on that high tree
Down he alights among the sportful herd
Of those four-footed kinds, himself now one,
Now other, as their shape served best his end
Nearer to view his prey, and unespied
400   To mark what of their state he more might learn
By word or action marked: about them round
A lion now he stalks with fiery glare,
Then as a tiger, who by chance hath spied
In some purlieu two gentle fawns at play,
405   Straight couches close, then rising changes oft
His couchant watch, as one who chose his ground
Whence rushing he might surest seize them both
Gripped in each paw: when Adam first of men
To first of women Eve thus moving speech,
410   Turned him all ear to hear new utterance flow.
    Sole partner and sole part of all these joys,
Dearer thyself than all; needs must the power
That made us, and for us this ample world
Be infinitely good, and of his good
415   As liberal and free as infinite,
That raised us from the dust and placed us here
In all this happiness, who at his hand
Have nothing merited, nor can perform
Aught whereof he hath need, he who requires
420   From us no other service than to keep
This one, this easy charge, of all the trees
In Paradise that bear delicious fruit
So various, not to taste that only Tree
Of Knowledge, planted by the Tree of Life,
425   So near grows death to life, whate'er death is,
Some dreadful thing no doubt; for well thou know'st
God hath pronounced it death to taste that Tree,
The only sign of our obedience left
Among so many signs of power and rule

430 Conferred upon us, and dominion giv'n
Over all other creatures that possess
Earth, air, and sea. Then let us not think hard
One easy prohibition, who enjoy
Free leave so large to all things else, and choice
435 Unlimited of manifold delights:
But let us ever praise him, and extol
His bounty, following our delightful task
To prune these growing plants, and tend these flow'rs,
Which were it toilsome, yet with thee were sweet.
440   To whom thus Eve replied. O thou for whom
And from whom I was formed flesh of my flesh,
And without whom am to no end, my guide
And head, what thou hast said is just and right.
For we to him indeed all praises owe,
445 And daily thanks, I chiefly who enjoy
So far the happier lot, enjoying thee
Pre-eminent by so much odds, while thou
Like consort to thyself canst nowhere find.
That day I oft remember, when from sleep
450 I first awaked, and found myself reposed
Under a shade of flow'rs, much wond'ring where
And what I was, whence thither brought, and how.
Not distant far from thence a murmuring sound
Of waters issued from a cave and spread
455 Into a liquid plain, then stood unmoved
Pure as th' expanse of heav'n; I thither went
With unexperienced thought, and laid me down
On the green bank, to look into the clear
Smooth lake, that to me seemed another sky.
460 As I bent down to look, just opposite,
A shape within the wat'ry gleam appeared
Bending to look on me: I started back,
It started back, but pleased I soon returned,
Pleased it returned as soon with answering looks
465 Of sympathy and love; there I had fixed
Mine eyes till now, and pined with vain desire,
Had not a voice thus warned me, What thou seest,
What there thou seest fair creature is thyself,

With thee it came and goes: but follow me,
470 And I will bring thee where no shadow stays
Thy coming, and thy soft embraces, he
Whose image thou art, him thou shall enjoy
Inseparably thine, to him shalt bear
Multitudes like thyself, and thence be called
475 Mother of human race: what could I do,
But follow straight, invisibly thus led?
Till I espied thee, fair indeed and tall,
Under a platan, yet methought less fair,
Less winning soft, less amiably mild,
480 Than that smooth wat'ry image; back I turned,
Thou following cried'st aloud, Return, fair Eve;
Whom fli'st thou? Whom thou fli'st, of him thou art,
His flesh, his bone; to give thee being I lent
Out of my side to thee, nearest my heart
485 Substantial life, to have thee by my side
Henceforth an individual solace dear;
Part of my soul I seek thee, and thee claim
My other half: with that thy gentle hand
Seized mine, I yielded, and from that time see
490 How beauty is excelled by manly grace
And wisdom, which alone is truly fair.
    So spake our general mother, and with eyes
Of conjugal attraction unreproved,
And meek surrender, half embracing leaned
495 On our first father; half her swelling breast
Naked met his under the flowing gold
Of her loose tresses hid: he in delight
Both of her beauty and submissive charms
Smiled with superior love, as Jupiter
500 On Juno smiles, when he impregns the clouds
That shed May flowers; and pressed her matron lip
With kisses pure: aside the Devil turned
For envy, yet with jealous leer malign
Eyed them askance, and to himself thus plained.
505   Sight hateful, sight tormenting! Thus these two
Imparadised in one another's arms
The happier Eden, shall enjoy their fill

Of bliss on bliss, while I to Hell am thrust,
Where neither joy nor love, but fierce desire,
510   Among our other torments not the least,
Still unfulfilled with pain of longing pines;
Yet let me not forget what I have gained
From their own mouths; all is not theirs it seems:
One fatal Tree there stands of Knowledge called,
515   Forbidden them to taste: knowledge forbidd'n?
Suspicious, reasonless. Why should their Lord
Envy them that? Can it be sin to know,
Can it be death? And do they only stand
By ignorance, is that their happy state,
520   The proof of their obedience and their faith?
O fair foundation laid whereon to build
Their ruin! Hence I will excite their minds
With more desire to know, and to reject
Envious commands, invented with design
525   To keep them low whom knowledge might exalt
Equal with gods; aspiring to be such,
They taste and die: what likelier can ensue?
But first with narrow search I must walk round
This garden, and no corner leave unspied;
530   A chance but chance may lead where I may meet
Some wand'ring Spirit of Heav'n, by fountain side,
Or in thick shade retired, from him to draw
What further would be learnt. Live while ye may,
Yet happy pair; enjoy, till I return,
535   Short pleasures, for long woes are to succeed.
    So saying, his proud step he scornful turned,
But with sly circumspection, and began
Through wood, through waste, o'er hill, o'er dale his roam.
Meanwhile in utmost longitude, where heav'n
540   With earth and Ocean meets, the setting sun
Slowly descended, and with right aspéct
Against the eastern gate of Paradise
Levelled his evening rays: it was a rock
Of alabaster, piled up to the clouds,
545   Conspicuous far, winding with one ascent
Accessible from earth, one entrance high;

The rest was craggy cliff, that overhung
Still as it rose, impossible to climb.
Betwixt these rocky pillars Gabriel sat
550 Chief of th' angelic guards, awaiting night;
About him exercised heroic games
Th' unarmèd youth of Heav'n, but nigh at hand
Celestial armoury, shields, helms, and spears,
Hung high with diamond flaming, and with gold.
555 Thither came Uriel, gliding through the even
On a sunbeam, swift as a shooting star
In autumn thwarts the night, when vapours fired
Impress the air, and shows the mariner
From what point of his compass to beware
560 Impetuous winds: he thus began in haste.
      Gabriel, to thee thy course by lot hath giv'n
Charge and strict watch that to this happy place
No evil thing approach or enter in;
This day at heighth of noon came to my sphere
565 A Spirit, zealous, as he seemed, to know
More of th' Almighty's works, and chiefly man
God's latest image: I described his way
Bent on all speed, and marked his airy gait;
But in the mount that lies from Eden north,
570 Where he first lighted, soon discerned his looks
Alien from Heav'n, with passions foul obscured:
Mine eye pursued him still, but under shade
Lost sight of him; one of the banished crew
I fear, hath ventured from the deep, to raise
575 New troubles; him thy care must be to find.
      To whom the wingèd warrior thus returned:
Uriel, no wonder if thy perfect sight,
Amid the sun's bright circle where thou sitt'st,
See far and wide: in at this gate none pass
580 The vigilance here placed, but such as come
Well known from Heav'n; and since meridian hour
No creature thence: if Spirit of other sort,
So minded, have o'erleaped these earthy bounds
On purpose, hard thou know'st it to exclude
585 Spiritual substance with corporeal bar.

But if within the circuit of these walks,
In whatsoever shape he lurk, of whom
Thou tell'st, by morrow dawning I shall know.
      So promised he, and Uriel to his charge
590 Returned on that bright beam, whose point now raised
Bore him slope downward to the sun now fall'n
Beneath the Azores; whether the prime orb,
Incredible how swift, had thither rolled
Diurnal, or this less volúble earth
595 By shorter flight to th' east, had left him there
Arraying with reflected purple and gold
The clouds that on his western throne attend:
Now came still ev'ning on, and twilight grey
Had in her sober livery all things clad;
600 Silence accompanied, for beast and bird,
They to their grassy couch, these to their nests
Were slunk, all but the wakeful nightingale;
She all night long her amorous descant sung;
Silence was pleased: now glowed the firmament
605 With living sapphires: Hesperus that led
The starry host, rode brightest, till the moon
Rising in clouded majesty, at length
Apparent queen unveiled her peerless light,
And o'er the dark her silver mantle threw.
610   When Adam thus to Eve: Fair consort, th' hour
Of night, and all things now retired to rest
Mind us of like repose, since God hath set
Labour and rest, as day and night to men
Successive, and the timely dew of sleep
615 Now falling with soft slumb'rous weight inclines
Our eye-lids; other creatures all day long
Rove idle unemployed, and less need rest;
Man hath his daily work of body or mind
Appointed, which declares his dignity,
620 And the regard of Heav'n on all his ways;
While other animals unactive range,
And of their doings God takes no account.
Tomorrow ere fresh morning streak the east
With first approach of light, we must be ris'n,

625 And at our pleasant labour, to reform
Yon flow'ry arbours, yonder alleys green,
Our walk at noon, with branches overgrown,
That mock our scant manuring, and require
More hands than ours to lop their wanton growth:
630 Those blossoms also, and those dropping gums,
That lie bestrewn unsightly and unsmooth,
Ask riddance, if we mean to tread with ease;
Meanwhile, as nature wills, night bids us rest.
     To whom thus Eve with perfect beauty adorned.
635 My author and disposer, what thou bidd'st
Unargued I obey; so God ordains,
God is thy law, thou mine: to know no more
Is woman's happiest knowledge and her praise.
With thee conversing I forget all time,
640 All seasons and their change, all please alike.
Sweet is the breath of morn, her rising sweet,
With charm of earliest birds; pleasant the sun
When first on this delightful land he spreads
His orient beams, on herb, tree, fruit, and flow'r,
645 Glist'ring with dew; fragrant the fertile earth
After soft showers; and sweet the coming on
Of grateful ev'ning mild, then silent night
With this her solemn bird and this fair moon,
And these the gems of heav'n, her starry train:
650 But neither breath of morn when she ascends
With charm of earliest birds, nor rising sun
On this delightful land, nor herb, fruit, flow'r,
Glist'ring with dew, nor fragrance after showers,
Nor grateful ev'ning mild, nor silent night
655 With this her solemn bird, nor walk by moon,
Or glittering starlight without thee is sweet.
But wherefore all night long shine these, for whom
This glorious sight, when sleep hath shut all eyes?
     To whom our general ancestor replied.
660 Daughter of God and man, accomplished Eve,
Those have their course to finish, round the earth,
By morrow ev'ning, and from land to land
In order, though to nations yet unborn,

Minist'ring light prepared, they set and rise;
665 Lest total darkness should by night regain
Her old possession, and extinguish life
In nature and all things, which these soft fires
Not only enlighten, but with kindly heat
Of various influence foment and warm,
670 Temper or nourish, or in part shed down
Their stellar virtue on all kinds that grow
On earth, made hereby apter to receive
Perfection from the sun's more potent ray.
These then, though unbeheld in deep of night,
675 Shine not in vain, nor think, though men were none,
That heav'n would want spectators, God want praise;
Millions of spiritual creatures walk the earth
Unseen, both when we wake, and when we sleep:
All these with ceaseless praise his works behold
680 Both day and night: how often from the steep
Of echoing hill or thicket have we heard
Celestial voices to the midnight air,
Sole, or responsive each to other's note
Singing their great Creator: oft in bands
685 While they keep watch, or nightly rounding walk
With Heav'nly touch of instrumental sounds
In full harmonic number joined, their songs
Divide the night, and lift our thoughts to Heaven.
    Thus talking hand in hand alone they passed
690 On to their blissful bower; it was a place
Chos'n by the sov'reign Planter, when he framed
All things to man's delightful use; the roof
Of thickest covert was inwoven shade
Laurel and myrtle, and what higher grew
695 Of firm and fragrant leaf; on either side
Acanthus, and each odorous bushy shrub
Fenced up the verdant wall; each beauteous flow'r,
Iris all hues, roses, and jessamine
Reared high their flourished heads between, and wrought
700 Mosaic; underfoot the violet,
Crocus, and hyacinth with rich inlay
Broidered the ground, more coloured than with stone

Of costliest emblem: other creature here
Beast, bird, insect, or worm durst enter none;
705　Such was their awe of man. In shadier bower
More sacred and sequestered, though but feigned,
Pan or Silvanus never slept, nor nymph,
Nor Faunus haunted. Here in close recess
With flowers, garlands, and sweet-smelling herbs
710　Espousèd Eve decked first her nuptial bed,
And Heav'nly choirs the hymenean sung,
What day the genial angel to our sire
Brought her in naked beauty more adorned,
More lovely than Pandora, whom the gods
715　Endowed with all their gifts, and O too like
In sad event, when to th' unwiser son
Of Japhet brought by Hermes, she ensnared
Mankind with her fair looks, to be avenged
On him who had stole Jove's authentic fire.
720　　Thus at their shady lodge arrived, both stood,
Both turned, and under open sky adored
The God who made both sky, air, earth and heav'n
Which they beheld, the moon's resplendent globe
And starry pole: Thou also mad'st the night,
725　Maker omnipotent, and thou the day,
Which we in our appointed work employed
Have finished happy in our mutual help
And mutual love, the crown of all our bliss
Ordained by thee, and this delicious place
730　For us too large, where thy abundance wants
Partakers, and uncropped falls to the ground.
But thou hast promised from us two a race
To fill the earth, who shall with us extol
Thy goodness infinite, both when we wake,
735　And when we seek, as now, thy gift of sleep.
　　This said unanimous, and other rites
Observing none, but adoration pure
Which God likes best, into their inmost bower
Handed they went; and eased the putting off
740　These troublesome disguises which we wear,
Straight side by side were laid, nor turned I ween

Adam from his fair spouse, nor Eve the rites
Mysterious of connubial love refused:
Whatever hypocrites austerely talk
745 Of purity and place and innocence,
Defaming as impure what God declares
Pure, and commands to some, leaves free to all.
Our Maker bids increase, who bids abstain
But our destroyer, foe to God and man?
750 Hail wedded love, mysterious law, true source
Of human offspring, sole propriety,
In Paradise of all things common else.
By thee adulterous lust was driv'n from men
Among the bestial herds to range, by thee
755 Founded in reason, loyal, just, and pure,
Relations dear, and all the charities
Of father, son, and brother first were known.
Far be it, that I should write thee sin or blame,
Or think thee unbefitting holiest place,
760 Perpetual fountain of domestic sweets,
Whose bed is undefiled and chaste pronounced,
Present, or past, as saints and patriarchs used.
Here Love his golden shafts employs, here lights
His constant lamp, and waves his purple wings,
765 Reigns here and revels; not in the bought smile
Of harlots, loveless, joyless, unendeared,
Casual fruition, nor in court amours
Mixed dance, or wanton masque, or midnight ball,
Or serenade, which the starved lover sings
770 To his proud fair, best quitted with disdain.
These lulled by nightingales embracing slept,
And on their naked limbs the flow'ry roof
Show'red roses, which the morn repaired. Sleep on,
Blest pair; and O yet happiest if ye seek
775 No happier state, and know to know no more.
    Now had night measured with her shadowy cone
Half way up hill this vast sublunar vault,
And from their ivory port the Cherubim
Forth issuing at th' accustomed hour stood armed
780 To their night watches in warlike parade,

When Gabriel to his next in power thus spake.
   Uzziel, half these draw off, and coast the south
With strictest watch; these other wheel the north,
Our circuit meets full west. As flame they part
785   Half wheeling to the shield, half to the spear.
From these, two strong and subtle Spirits he called
That near him stood, and gave them thus in charge.
   Ithuriel and Zephon, with winged speed
Search through this garden, leave unsearched no nook,
790   But chiefly where those two fair creatures lodge,
Now laid perhaps asleep secure of harm.
This ev'ning from the sun's decline arrived
Who tells of some infernal Spirit seen
Hitherward bent (who could have thought?) escaped
795   The bars of Hell, on errand bad no doubt:
Such where ye find, seize fast, and hither bring.
   So saying, on he led his radiant files,
Dazzling the moon; these to the bower direct
In search of whom they sought: him there they found
800   Squat like a toad, close at the ear of Eve;
Assaying by his devilish art to reach
The organs of her Fancy, and with them forge
Illusions as he list, phantasms and dreams,
Or if, inspiring venom, he might taint
805   Th' animal spirits that from pure blood arise
Like gentle breaths from rivers pure, thence raise
At least distempered, discontented thoughts,
Vain hopes, vain aims, inordinate desires
Blown up with high conceits engend'ring pride.
810   Him thus intent Ithuriel with his spear
Touched lightly; for no falsehood can endure
Touch of celestial temper, but returns
Of force to its own likeness: up he starts
Discovered and surprised. As when a spark
815   Lights on a heap of nitrous powder, laid
Fit for the tun some magazine to store
Against a rumoured war, the smutty grain
With sudden blaze diffused, inflames the air:
So started up in his own shape the Fiend.

820 Back stepped those two fair angels half amazed
     So sudden to behold the grisly King;
     Yet thus, unmoved with fear, accost him soon.
        Which of those rebel Spirits adjudged to Hell
     Com'st thou, escaped thy prison, and transformed,
825 Why sat'st thou like an enemy in wait
     Here watching at the head of these that sleep?
        Know ye not then said Satan, filled with scorn,
     Know ye not me? Ye knew me once no mate
     For you, there sitting where ye durst not soar;
830 Not to know me argues yourselves unknown,
     The lowest of your throng; or if ye know,
     Why ask ye, and superfluous begin
     Your message, like to end as much in vain?
     To whom thus Zephon, answering scorn with scorn.
835 Think not, revolted Spirit, thy shape the same,
     Or undiminished brightness, to be known
     As when thou stood'st in Heav'n upright and pure;
     That glory then, when thou no more wast good,
     Departed from thee, and thou resemblest now
840 Thy sin and place of doom obscure and foul.
     But come, for thou, be sure, shalt give account
     To him who sent us, whose charge is to keep
     This place inviolable, and these from harm.
        So spake the Cherub, and his grave rebuke
845 Severe in youthful beauty, added grace
     Invincible: abashed the Devil stood,
     And felt how awful goodness is, and saw
     Virtue in her shape how lovely, saw, and pined
     His loss; but chiefly to find here observed
850 His lustre visibly impaired; yet seemed
     Undaunted. If I must contend, said he,
     Best with the best, the sender not the sent,
     Or all at once; more glory will be won,
     Or less be lost. Thy fear, said Zephon bold,
855 Will save us trial what the least can do
     Single against thee wicked, and thence weak.
        The Fiend replied not, overcome with rage;
     But like a proud steed reined, went haughty on,

Champing his iron curb: to strive or fly
860   He held it vain; awe from above had quelled
His heart, not else dismayed. Now drew they nigh
The western point, where those half-rounding guards
Just met, and closing stood in squadron joined
Awaiting next command. To whom their chief
865   Gabriel from the front thus called aloud.
      O friends, I hear the tread of nimble feet
Hasting this way, and now by glimpse discern
Ithuriel and Zephon through the shade,
And with them comes a third of regal port,
870   But faded splendour wan; who by his gait
And fierce demeanour seems the Prince of Hell,
Not likely to part hence without contést;
Stand firm, for in his look defiance lours.
      He scarce had ended, when those two approached
875   And brief related whom they brought, where found,
How busied, in what form and posture couched.
      To whom with stern regard thus Gabriel spake.
Why hast thou, Satan, broke the bounds prescribed
To thy transgressions, and disturbed the charge
880   Of others, who approve not to transgress
By thy example, but have power and right
To question thy bold entrance on this place;
Employed it seems to violate sleep, and those
Whose dwelling God hath planted here in bliss?
885   To whom thus Satan with contemptuous brow.
Gabriel, thou hadst in Heav'n th' esteem of wise,
And such I held thee; but this question asked
Puts me in doubt. Lives there who loves his pain?
Who would not, finding way, break loose from Hell,
890   Though thither doomed? Thou wouldst thyself, no doubt,
And boldly venture to whatever place
Farthest from pain, where thou might'st hope to change
Torment with ease, and soonest recompense
Dole with delight, which in this place I sought;
895   To thee no reason; who know'st only good,
But evil hast not tried: and wilt object

His will who bound us? Let him surer bar
His iron gates, if he intends our stay
In that dark durance: thus much what was asked.
900 The rest is true, they found me where they say;
But that implies not violence or harm.
     Thus he in scorn. The warlike angel moved,
Disdainfully half smiling thus replied.
O loss of one in Heav'n to judge of wise,
905 Since Satan fell, whom folly overthrew,
And now returns him from his prison 'scaped,
Gravely in doubt whether to hold them wise
Or not, who ask what boldness brought him hither
Unlicensed from his bounds in Hell prescribed;
910 So wise he judges it to fly from pain
However, and to 'scape his punishment.
So judge thou still, presumptuous, till the wrath,
Which thou incurr'st by flying, meet thy flight
Sevenfold, and scourge that wisdom back to Hell,
915 Which taught thee yet no better, that no pain
Can equal anger infinite provoked.
But wherefore thou alone? Wherefore with thee
Came not all Hell broke loose? Is pain to them
Less pain, less to be fled, or thou than they
920 Less hardy to endure? Courageous chief,
The first in flight from pain, hadst thou alleged
To thy deserted host this cause of flight,
Thou surely hadst not come sole fugitive.
     To which the Fiend thus answered frowning stern.
925 Not that I less endure, or shrink from pain,
Insulting angel, well thou know'st I stood
Thy fiercest, when in battle to thy aid
The blasting volleyed thunder made all speed
And seconded thy else not dreaded spear.
930 But still thy words at random, as before,
Argue thy inexperience what behooves
From hard assays and ill successes past
A faithful leader, not to hazard all
Through ways of danger by himself untried,

935   I therefore, I alone first undertook
     To wing the desolate abyss, and spy
     This new-created world, whereof in Hell
     Fame is not silent, here in hope to find
     Better abode, and my afflicted powers
940   To settle here on earth, or in mid air;
     Though for possession put to try once more
     What thou and thy gay legions dare against;
     Whose easier business were to serve their Lord
     High up in Heav'n, with songs to hymn his throne,
945   And practised distances to cringe, not fight.
        To whom the warrior angel soon replied.
     To say and straight unsay, pretending first
     Wise to fly pain, professing next the spy,
     Argues no leader but a liar traced,
950   Satan, and couldst thou faithful add? O name,
     O sacred name of faithfulness profaned!
     Faithful to whom? To thy rebellious crew?
     Army of fiends, fit body to fit head;
     Was this your discipline and faith engaged,
955   Your military obedience, to dissolve
     Allegiance to th' acknowledged Power Supreme?
     And thou sly hypocrite, who now wouldst seem
     Patron of liberty, who more than thou
     Once fawned, and cringed, and servilely adored
960   Heav'n's awful Monarch? Wherefore but in hope
     To dispossess him, and thyself to reign?
     But mark what I aread thee now, avaunt;
     Fly hither whence thou fledd'st: if from this hour
     Within these hallowed limits thou appear,
965   Back to th' infernal pit I drag thee chained,
     And seal thee so, as henceforth not to scorn
     The facile gates of Hell too slightly barred.
        So threatened he, but Satan to no threats
     Gave heed, but waxing more in rage replied.
970   Then when I am thy captive talk of chains,
     Proud limitary Cherub, but ere then
     'Far heavier load thyself expect to feel

From my prevailing arm, though Heaven's King
Ride on thy wings, and thou with thy compeers,
975   Used to the yoke, draw'st his triumphant wheels
In progress through the road of Heav'n star-paved.
     While thus he spake, th' angelic squadron bright
Turned fiery red, sharp'ning in moonèd horns
Their phalanx, and began to hem him round
980   With ported spears, as thick as when a field
Of Ceres ripe for harvest waving bends
Her bearded grove of ears, which way the wind
Sways them; the careful ploughman doubting stands
Lest on the threshing floor his hopeful sheaves
985   Prove chaff. On th' other side Satan alarmed
Collecting all his might dilated stood,
Like Teneriffe or Atlas unremoved:
His stature reached the sky, and on his crest
Sat Horror plumed; nor wanted in his grasp
990   What seemed both spear and shield: now dreadful deeds
Might have ensued, nor only Paradise
In this commotion, but the starry cope
Of heav'n perhaps, or all the elements
At least had gone to wrack, disturbed and torn
995   With violence of this conflict, had not soon
Th' Eternal to prevent such horrid fray
Hung forth in heav'n his golden Scales, yet seen
Betwixt Astraea and the Scorpion sign,
Wherein all things created first he weighed,
1000 The pendulous round earth with balanced air
In counterpoise, now ponders all events,
Battles and realms: in these he put two weights
The sequel each of parting and of fight;
The latter quick up flew, and kicked the beam;
1005 Which Gabriel spying, thus bespake the Fiend.
     Satan, I know thy strength, and thou know'st mine,
Neither our own but giv'n; what folly then
To boast what arms can do, since thine no more
Than Heav'n permits, nor mine, though doubled now
1010 To trample thee as mire: for proof look up,

And read thy lot in yon celestial sign
Where thou art weighed, and shown how light, how weak,
If thou resist. The Fiend looked up and knew
His mounted scale aloft: nor more; but fled
1015 Murmuring, and with him fled the shades of night.

BOOK V

The Argument

Morning approached, Eve relates to Adam her troublesome dream; he likes it not, yet comforts her: they come forth to their day labours: their morning hymn at the door of the bower. God to render man inexcusable sends Raphael to admonish him of his obedience, of his free estate, of his enemy near at hand; who he is, and why his enemy, and whatever else may avail Adam to know. Raphael comes down to Paradise, his appearance described, his coming discerned by Adam afar off sitting at the door of his bower; he goes out to meet him, brings him to his lodge, entertains him with choicest fruits of Paradise got together by Eve; their discourse at table: Raphael performs his message, minds Adam of his state and of his enemy; relates at Adam's request who that enemy is, and how he came to be so, beginning from his first revolt in Heaven and the occasion thereof; how he drew his legions after him to the parts of the North, and there incited them to rebel with him, persuading all but only Abdiel a Seraph, who in argument dissuades and opposes him, then forsakes him.

Now Morn her rosy steps in th' eastern clime
Advancing, sowed the earth with orient pearl,
When Adam waked, so customed, for his sleep
Was airy light, from pure digestion bred,
And temperate vapours bland, which th' only sound
Of leaves and fuming rills, Aurora's fan,
Lightly dispersed, and the shrill matin song
Of birds on every bough; so much the more
His wonder was to find unwakened Eve
With tresses discomposed, and glowing cheek,
As through unquiet rest: he on his side

Leaning half-raised, with looks of cordial love
Hung over her enamoured, and beheld
Beauty, which whether waking or asleep,
15   Shot forth peculiar graces; then with voice
Mild, as when Zephyrus on Flora breathes,
Her hand soft touching, whispered thus. Awake
My fairest, my espoused, my latest found,
Heav'n's last best gift, my ever new delight,
20   Awake, the morning shines, and the fresh field
Calls us; we lose the prime, to mark how spring
Our tended plants, how blows the citron grove,
What drops the myrrh, and what the balmy reed,
How Nature paints her colours, how the bee
25   Sits on the bloom extracting liquid sweet.
      Such whispering waked her, but with startled eye
On Adam, whom embracing, thus she spake.
      O sole in whom my thoughts find all repose,
My glory, my perfection, glad I see
30   Thy face, and morn returned, for I this night,
Such night till this I never passed, have dreamed,
If dreamed, not as I oft am wont, of thee,
Works of day past, or morrow's next design,
But of offence and trouble, which my mind
35   Knew never till this irksome night; methought
Close at mine ear one called me forth to walk
With gentle voice, I thought it thine; it said,
Why sleep'st thou Eve? Now is the pleasant time,
The cool, the silent, save where silence yields
40   To the night-warbling bird, that now awake
Tunes sweetest his love-laboured song; now reigns
Full orbed the moon, and with more pleasing light
Shadowy sets off the face of things; in vain,
If none regard; heav'n wakes with all his eyes,
45   Whom to behold but thee, Nature's desire,
In whose sight all things joy, with ravishment
Attracted by thy beauty still to gaze.
I rose as at thy call, but found thee not;
To find thee I directed then my walk;
50   And on methought, alone I passed through ways

That brought me on a sudden to the Tree
Of interdicted Knowledge: fair it seemed,
Much fairer to my Fancy than by day:
And as I wond'ring looked, beside it stood
55   One shaped and winged like one of those from Heav'n
By us oft seen; his dewy locks distilled
Ambrosia; on that tree he also gazed;
And O fair plant, said he, with fruit surcharged,
Deigns none to ease thy load and taste thy sweet,
60   Nor god, nor man; is knowledge so despised?
Or envy, or what reserve forbids to taste?
Forbid who will, none shall from me withhold
Longer thy offered good, why else set here?
This said he paused not, but with vent'rous arm
65   He plucked, he tasted; me damp horror chilled
At such bold words vouched with a deed so bold:
But he thus overjoyed, O fruit divine,
Sweet of thyself, but much more sweet thus cropped,
Forbidden here, it seems, as only fit
70   For gods, yet able to make gods of men:
And why not gods of men, since good, the more
Communicated, more abundant grows,
The Author not impaired, but honoured more?
Here, happy creature, fair angelic Eve,
75   Partake thou also; happy though thou art,
Happier thou may'st be, worthier canst not be:
Taste this, and be henceforth among the gods
Thyself a goddess, not to earth confined,
But sometimes in the air, as we, sometimes
80   Ascend to Heav'n, by merit thine, and see
What life the gods live there, and such live thou.
So saying, he drew nigh, and to me held,
Even to my mouth of that same fruit held part
Which he had plucked; the pleasant savoury smell
85   So quickened appetite, that I, methought,
Could not but taste. Forthwith up to the clouds
With him I flew, and underneath beheld
The earth outstretched immense, a prospect wide
And various: wond'ring at my flight and change

90   To this high exaltation; suddenly
     My guide was gone, and I, methought, sunk down,
     And fell asleep; but O how glad I waked
     To find this but a dream! Thus Eve her night
     Related, and thus Adam answered sad.

95   Best image of myself and dearer half,
     The trouble of thy thoughts this night in sleep
     Affects me equally; nor can I like
     This uncouth dream, of evil sprung I fear;
     Yet evil whence? In thee can harbour none,

100 Created pure. But know that in the soul
     Are many lesser faculties that serve
     Reason as chief; among these Fancy next
     Her office holds; of all external things,
     Which the five watchful senses represent,

105 She forms imaginations, airy shapes,
     Which Reason joining or disjoining, frames
     All what we affirm or what deny, and call
     Our knowledge or opinion; then retires
     Into her private cell when nature rests.

110 Oft in her absence mimic Fancy wakes
     To imitate her; but misjoining shapes,
     Wild work produces oft, and most in dreams,
     Ill matching words and deeds long past or late.
     Some such resemblances methinks I find

115 Of our last ev'ning's talk, in this thy dream,
     But with addition strange; yet be not sad.
     Evil into the mind of god or man
     May come and go, so unapproved, and leave
     No spot or blame behind: which gives me hope

120 That what in sleep thou didst abhor to dream,
     Waking thou never wilt consent to do.
     Be not disheartened then, nor cloud those looks
     That wont to be more cheerful and serene
     Than when fair morning first smiles on the world,

125 And let us to our fresh employments rise
     Among the groves, the fountains, and the flow'rs
     That open now their choicest bosomed smells
     Reserved from night, and kept for thee in store.

So cheered he his fair spouse, and she was cheered,
130   But silently a gentle tear let fall
From either eye, and wiped them with her hair;
Two other precious drops that ready stood,
Each in their crystal sluice, he ere they fell
Kissed as the gracious signs of sweet remorse
135   And pious awe, that feared to have offended.
So all was cleared, and to the field they haste.
But first from under shady arborous roof,
Soon as they forth were come to open sight
Of day-spring, and the sun, who scarce up risen
140   With wheels yet hov'ring o'er the ocean brim,
Shot parallel to the earth his dewy ray,
Discovering in wide landscape all the east
Of Paradise and Eden's happy plains,
Lowly they bowed adoring, and began
145   Their orisons, each morning duly paid
In various style, for neither various style
Nor holy rapture wanted they to praise
Their Maker, in fit strains pronounced or sung
Unmeditated, such prompt eloquence
150   Flowed from their lips, in prose or numerous verse,
More tuneable than needed lute or harp
To add more sweetness, and they thus began.
These are thy glorious works, Parent of good,
Almighty, thine this universal frame,
155   Thus wondrous fair; thyself how wondrous then!
Unspeakable, who sitt'st above these heavens
To us invisible or dimly seen
In these thy lowest works, yet these declare
Thy goodness beyond thought, and power divine:
160   Speak ye who best can tell, ye sons of light,
Angels, for ye behold him, and with songs
And choral symphonies, day without night,
Circle his throne rejoicing, ye in Heav'n,
On earth join all ye creatures to extol
165   Him first, him last, him midst, and without end.
Fairest of stars, last in the train of night,
If better thou belong not to the dawn,

Sure pledge of day, that crown'st the smiling morn
With thy bright circlet, praise him in thy sphere
170 While day arises, that sweet hour of prime.
Thou sun, of this great world both eye and soul,
Acknowledge him thy greater, sound his praise
In thy eternal course, both when thou climb'st,
And when high noon hast gained, and when thou fall'st.
175 Moon, that now meet'st the orient sun, now fli'st
With the fixed stars, fixed in their orb that flies,
And ye five other wand'ring fires that move
In mystic dance not without song, resound
His praise who out of darkness called up light.
180 Air, and ye elements the eldest birth
Of Nature's womb, that in quaternion run
Perpetual circle multiform; and mix
And nourish all things, let your ceaseless change
Vary to our great Maker still new praise.
185 Ye mists and exhalations that now rise
From hill or steaming lake, dusky or grey,
Till the sun paint your fleecy skirts with gold,
In honour to the world's great Author rise,
Whether to deck with clouds the uncoloured sky,
190 Or wet the thirsty earth with falling showers,
Rising or falling still advance his praise.
His praise ye winds, that from four quarters blow,
Breathe soft or loud; and wave your tops, ye pines,
With every plant, in sign of worship wave.
195 Fountains and ye, that warble, as ye flow,
Melodious murmurs, warbling tune his praise.
Join voices all ye living souls, ye birds,
That singing up to heaven gate ascend,
Bear on your wings and in your notes his praise;
200 Ye that in waters glide, and ye that walk
The earth, and stately tread, or lowly creep;
Witness if I be silent, morn or even,
To hill, or valley, fountain, or fresh shade
Made vocal by my song, and taught his praise.
205 Hail universal Lord, be bounteous still
To give us only good; and if the night

Have gathered aught of evil or concealed,
Disperse it, as now light dispels the dark.
 So prayed they innocent, and to their thoughts
210 Firm peace recovered soon and wonted calm.
On to their morning's rural work they haste
Among sweet dews and flow'rs; where any row
Of fruit-trees overwoody reached too far
Their pampered boughs, and needed hands to check
215 Fruitless embraces: or they led the vine
To wed her elm; she spoused about him twines
Her marriageable arms, and with her brings
Her dow'r th' adopted clusters, to adorn
His barren leaves. Them thus employed beheld
220 With pity Heav'n's high King, and to him called
Raphael, the sociable Spirit, that deigned
To travel with Tobias, and secured
His marriage with the seven-times-wedded maid.
 Raphael, said he, thou hear'st what stir on earth
225 Satan from Hell 'scaped through the darksome gulf
Hath raised in Paradise, and how disturbed
This night the human pair, how he designs
In them at once to ruin all mankind.
Go therefore, half this day as friend with friend
230 Converse with Adam, in what bow'r or shade
Thou find'st him from the heat of noon retired,
To respite his day-labour with repast,
Or with repose; and such discourse bring on,
As may advise him of his happy state,
235 Happiness in his power left free to will,
Left to his own free will, his will though free,
Yet mutable; whence warn him to beware
He swerve not too secure: tell him withal
His danger, and from whom, what enemy
240 Late fall'n himself from Heav'n, is plotting now
The fall of others from like state of bliss;
By violence, no, for that shall be withstood,
But by deceit and lies; this let him know,
Lest wilfully transgressing he pretend
245 Surprisal, unadmonished, unforewarned.

So spake th' Eternal Father, and fulfilled
All justice: nor delayed the wingèd saint
After his charge received; but from among
Thousand celestial ardours, where he stood
250　Veiled with his gorgeous wings, up springing light
Flew through the midst of Heav'n; th' angelic choirs
On each hand parting, to his speed gave way
Through all th' empyreal road; till at the gate
Of Heav'n arrived, the gate self-opened wide
255　On golden hinges turning, as by work
Divine the sov'reign Architect had framed.
From hence, no cloud, or, to obstruct his sight,
Star interposed, however small he sees,
Not unconform to other shining globes,
260　Earth and the gard'n of God, with cedars crowned
Above all hills. As when by night the glass
Of Galileo, less assured, observes
Imagined lands and regions in the moon:
Or pilot from amidst the Cyclades
265　Delos or Samos first appearing kens
A cloudy spot. Down thither prone in flight
He speeds, and through the vast ethereal sky
Sails between worlds and worlds, with steady wing
Now on the polar winds, then with quick fan
270　Winnows the buxom air; till within soar
Of tow'ring eagles, to all the fowls he seems
A phoenix, gazed by all, as that sole bird
When to enshrine his relics in the sun's
Bright temple, to Egyptian Thebes he flies.
275　At once on th' eastern cliff of Paradise
He lights, and to his proper shape returns
A Seraph winged; six wings he wore, to shade
His lineaments divine; the pair that clad
Each shoulder broad, came mantling o'er his breast
280　With regal ornament; the middle pair
Girt like a starry zone his waist, and round
Skirted his loins and thighs with downy gold
And colours dipped in Heav'n; the third his feet
Shadowed from either heel with feathered mail

285   Sky-tinctured grain. Like Maia's son he stood,
And shook his plumes, that Heav'nly fragrance filled
The circuit wide. Straight knew him all the bands
Of angels under watch; and to his state,
And to his message high in honour rise;
290   For on some message high they guessed him bound.
Their glittering tents he passed, and now is come
Into the blissful field, through groves of myrrh,
And flow'ring odours, cassia, nard, and balm;
A wilderness of sweets; for Nature here
295   Wantoned as in her prime, and played at will
Her virgin fancies, pouring forth more sweet,
Wild above rule or art; enormous bliss.
Him through the spicy forest onward come
Adam discerned, as in the door he sat
300   Of his cool bow'r, while now the mounted sun
Shot down direct his fervid rays to warm
Earth's inmost womb, more warmth than Adam needs;
And Eve within, due at her hour prepared
For dinner savoury fruits, of taste to please
305   True appetite, and not disrelish thirst
Of nectarous draughts between, from milky stream,
Berry or grape: to whom thus Adam called.
    Haste hither Eve, and worth thy sight behold
Eastward among those trees, what glorious shape
310   Comes this way moving; seems another morn
Ris'n on mid-noon; some great behest from Heav'n
To us perhaps he brings, and will vouchsafe
This day to be our guest. But go with speed,
And what thy stores contain, bring forth and pour
315   Abundance, fit to honour and receive
Our Heav'nly stranger; well we may afford
Our givers their own gifts, and large bestow
From large bestowed, where Nature multiplies
Her fertile growth, and by disburd'ning grows
320   More fruitful, which instructs us not to spare.
    To whom thus Eve, Adam, earth's hallowed mould,
Of God inspired, small store will serve, where store,
All seasons, ripe for use hangs on the stalk;

Save what by frugal storing firmness gains
325 To nourish, and superfluous moist consumes:
But I will haste and from each bough and brake,
Each plant and juiciest gourd will pluck such choice
To entertain our angel guest, as he
Beholding shall confess that here on earth
330 God hath dispensed his bounties as in Heav'n.
    So saying, with dispatchful looks in haste
She turns, on hospitable thoughts intent
What choice to choose for delicacy best,
What order, so contrived as not to mix
335 Tastes, not well joined, inelegant, but bring
Taste after taste upheld with kindliest change;
Bestirs her then, and from each tender stalk
Whatever Earth all-bearing Mother yields
In India east or west, or middle shore
340 In Pontus or the Punic coast, or where
Alcinous reigned, fruit of all kinds, in coat,
Rough, or smooth rined, or bearded husk, or shell
She gathers, tribute large, and on the board
Heaps with unsparing hand; for drink the grape
345 She crushes, inoffensive must, and meaths
From many a berry, and from sweet kernels pressed
She tempers dulcet creams, nor these to hold
Wants her fit vessels pure, then strews the ground
With rose and odours from the shrub unfumed.
350 Meanwhile our primitive great sire, to meet
His god-like guest, walks forth, without more train
Accompanied than with his own complete
Perfections; in himself was all his state,
More solemn than the tedious pomp that waits
355 On princes, when their rich retínue long
Of horses led, and grooms besmeared with gold
Dazzles the crowd, and sets them all agape.
Nearer his presence Adam though not awed,
Yet with submiss approach and reverence meek,
360 As to a superior nature, bowing low,
    Thus said. Native of Heav'n, for other place
None can than Heav'n such glorious shape contain;

Since by descending from the thrones above,
Those happy places thou hast deigned a while
365   To want, and honour these, vouchsafe with us
Two only, who yet by sov'reign gift possess
This spacious ground, in yonder shady bow'r
To rest, and what the garden choicest bears
To sit and taste, till this meridian heat
370   Be over, and the sun more cool decline.
    Whom thus the angelic Virtue answered mild.
Adam, I therefore came, nor art thou such
Created, or such place hast here to dwell,
As may not oft invite, though Spirits of Heav'n
375   To visit thee; lead on then where thy bow'r
O'ershades; for these mid-hours, till ev'ning rise
I have at will. So to the sylvan lodge
They came, that like Pomona's arbour smiled
With flow'rets decked and fragrant smells; but Eve
380   Undecked, save with herself more lovely fair
Than wood-nymph, or the fairest goddess feigned
Of three that in Mount Ida naked strove,
Stood to entertain her guest from Heav'n; no veil
She needed, virtue-proof, no thought infirm
385   Altered her cheek. On whom the angel Hail
Bestowed, the holy salutation used
Long after to blest Mary, second Eve.
    Hail mother of mankind, whose fruitful womb
Shall fill the world more numerous with thy sons
390   Than with these various fruits the trees of God
Have heaped this table. Raised of grassy turf
Their table was, and mossy seats had round,
And on her ample square from side to side
All autumn piled, though spring and autumn here
395   Danced hand in hand. A while discourse they hold;
No fear lest dinner cool; when thus began
Our author. Heav'nly stranger, please to taste
These bounties which our Nourisher, from whom
All perfect good unmeasured out, descends,
400   To us for food and for delight hath caused
The earth to yield; unsavoury food perhaps

To spiritual natures; only this I know,
That one celestial Father gives to all.
　　To whom the angel. Therefore what he gives
405　(Whose praise be ever sung) to man in part
Spiritual, may of purest Spirits be found
No ingrateful food: and food alike those pure
Intelligential substances require
As doth your rational; and both contain
410　Within them every lower faculty
Of sense, whereby they hear, see, smell, touch, taste,
Tasting concoct, digest, assimilate,
And corporeal to incorporeal turn.
For know, whatever was created, needs
415　To be sustained and fed; of elements
The grosser feeds the purer, earth the sea,
Earth and the sea feed air, the air those fires
Ethereal, and as lowest first the moon;
Whence in her visage round those spots, unpurged
420　Vapours not yet into her substance turned.
Nor doth the moon no nourishment exhale
From her moist continent to higher orbs.
The sun that light imparts to all, receives
From all his alimental recompense
425　In humid exhalations, and at even
Sups with the ocean: though in Heav'n the trees
Of life ambrosial fruitage bear, and vines
Yield nectar, though from off the boughs each morn
We brush mellifluous dews, and find the ground
430　Covered with pearly grain: yet God hath here
Varied his bounty so with new delights,
As may compare with Heaven; and to taste
Think not I shall be nice. So down they sat,
And to their viands fell, nor seemingly
435　The angel, nor in mist, the common gloss
Of theologians, but with keen dispatch
Of real hunger, and concoctive heat
To transubstantiate; what redounds, transpires
Through Spirits with ease; nor wonder; if by fire
440　Of sooty coal th' empiric alchemist

Can turn, or holds it possible to turn
Metals of drossiest ore to perfect gold
As from the mine. Meanwhile at table Eve
Ministered naked, and their flowing cups
445 With pleasant liquors crowned: O innocence
Deserving Paradise! if ever, then,
Then had the sons of God excuse to have been
Enamoured at that sight; but in those hearts
Love unlibidinous reigned, nor jealousy
450 Was understood, the injured lover's Hell.
Thus when with meats and drinks they had sufficed,
Not burdened nature, sudden mind arose
In Adam, not to let th' occasion pass
Given him by this great conference to know
455 Of things above his world, and of their being
Who dwell in Heav'n, whose excellence he saw
Transcend his own so far, whose radiant forms
Divine effulgence, whose high power so far
Exceeded human, and his wary speech
460 Thus to th' empyreal minister he framed.
    Inhabitant with God, now know I well
Thy favour, in this honour done to man,
Under whose lowly roof thou hast vouchsafed
To enter, and these earthly fruits to taste,
465 Food not of angels, yet accepted so,
As that more willingly thou couldst not seem
At Heav'n's high feasts to have fed: yet what compare?
    To whom the wingèd hierarch replied.
O Adam, one Almighty is, from whom
470 All things proceed, and up to him return,
If not depraved from good, created all
Such to perfection, one first matter all,
Endued with various forms, various degrees
Of substance, and in things that live, of life;
475 But more refined, more spiritous, and pure,
As nearer to him placed or nearer tending
Each in their several active spheres assigned,
Till body up to spirit work, in bounds
Proportioned to each kind. So from the root

480 Springs lighter the green stalk, from thence the leaves
More airy, last the bright consummate flow'r
Spirits odórous breathes: flow'rs and their fruit
Man's nourishment, by gradual scale sublimed
To vital spirits aspire, to animal,
485 To intellectual, give both life and sense,
Fancy and understanding, whence the soul
Reason receives, and reason is her being,
Discursive, or intuitive; discourse
Is oftest yours, the latter most is ours,
490 Differing but in degree, of kind the same.
Wonder not then, what God for you saw good
If I refuse not, but convert, as you,
To proper substance; time may come when men
With angels may participate, and find
495 No inconvenient diet, nor too light fare:
And from these corporal nutriments perhaps
Your bodies may at last turn all to Spirit,
Improved by tract of time, and winged ascend
Ethereal, as we, or may at choice
500 Here or in Heav'nly Paradises dwell;
If ye be found obedient, and retain
Unalterably firm his love entire
Whose progeny you are. Meanwhile enjoy
Your fill what happiness this happy state
505 Can comprehend, incapable of more.
    To whom the patriarch of mankind replied.
O favourable Spirit, propitious guest,
Well hast thou taught the way that might direct
Our knowledge, and the scale of Nature set
510 From centre to circumference, whereon
In contemplation of created things
By steps we may ascend to God. But say,
What meant that caution joined, *if ye be found
Obedient?* can we want obedience then
515 To him, or possibly his love desert
Who formed us from the dust, and placed us here
Full to the utmost measure of what bliss
Human desires can seek or apprehend?

To whom the angel. Son of Heav'n and earth,
520 Attend: that thou art happy, owe to God;
That thou continuest such, owe to thyself,
That is, to thy obedience; therein stand.
This was that caution giv'n thee; be advised.
God made thee perfect, not immutable;
525 And good he made thee, but to persevere
He left it in thy power, ordained thy will
By nature free, not overruled by Fate
Inextricable, or strict necessity;
Our voluntary service he requires,
530 Not our necessitated, such with him
Finds no acceptance, nor can find, for how
Can hearts, not free, be tried whether they serve
Willing or no, who will but what they must
By destiny, and can no other choose?
535 Myself and all th' angelic host that stand
In sight of God enthroned, our happy state
Hold, as you yours, while our obedience holds;
On other surety none; freely we serve,
Because we freely love, as in our will
540 To love or not; in this we stand or fall:
And some are fall'n, to disobedience fall'n,
And so from Heav'n to deepest Hell; O fall
From what high state of bliss into what woe!
To whom our great progenitor. Thy words
545 Attentive, and with more delighted ear,
Divine instructor, I have heard, than when
Cherubic songs by night from neighbouring hills
Aërial music send: nor knew I not
To be both will and deed created free;
550 Yet that we never shall forget to love
Our Maker, and obey him whose command
Single, is yet so just, my constant thoughts
Assured me, and still assure: though what thou tell'st
Hath passed in Heav'n, some doubt within me move,
555 But more desire to hear, if thou consent,
The full relation, which must needs be strange,
Worthy of sacred silence to be heard;

And we have yet large day, for scarce the sun
Hath finished half his journey, and scarce begins
His other half in the great zone of heav'n.
    Thus Adam made request, and Raphael
After short pause assenting, thus began.
    High matter thou enjoin'st me, O prime of men,
Sad task and hard, for how shall I relate
To human sense th' invisible explóits
Of warring Spirits; how without remorse
The ruin of so many glorious once
And perfect while they stood; how last unfold
The secrets of another world, perhaps
Not lawful to reveal? yet for thy good
This is dispensed, and what surmounts the reach
Of human sense, I shall delineate so,
By lik'ning spiritual to corporal forms,
As may express them best, though what if earth
Be but the shadow of Heav'n, and things therein
Each to other like, more than on earth is thought?
    As yet this world was not, and Chaos wild
Reigned where these heav'ns now roll, where earth now
        rests
Upon her centre poised, when on a day
(For time, though in eternity, applied
To motion, measures all things durable
By present, past, and future) on such day
As Heav'n's Great Year brings forth, th' empyreal host
Of angels by imperial summons called,
Innumerable before th' Almighty's throne
Forthwith from all the ends of Heav'n appeared
Under their hierarchs in orders bright:
Ten thousand thousand ensigns high advanced,
Standards, and gonfalons 'twixt van and rear
Stream in the air, and for distinction serve
Of hierarchies, of orders, and degrees;
Or in their glittering tissues bear imblazed
Holy memorials, acts of zeal and love
Recorded eminent. Thus when in orbs
Of circuit inexpressible they stood,

Orb within orb, the Father infinite,
By whom in bliss embosomed sat the Son,
Amidst as from a flaming Mount, whose top
Brightness had made invisible, thus spake.
600   Hear all ye angels, progeny of Light,
Thrones, Dominations, Princedoms, Virtues, Powers,
Hear my decree, which unrevoked shall stand.
This day I have begot whom I declare
My only Son, and on this holy hill
605 Him have anointed, whom ye now behold
At my right hand; your head I him appoint;
And by myself have sworn to him shall bow
All knees in Heav'n, and shall confess him Lord:
Under his great vicegerent reign abide
610 United as one individual soul
For ever happy: him who disobeys
Me disobeys, breaks union, and that day
Cast out from God and blessèd vision, falls
Into utter darkness, deep engulfed, his place
615 Ordained without redemption, without end.
      So spake th' Omnipotent, and with his words
All seemed well pleased; all seemed, but were not all.
That day, as other solemn days, they spent
In song and dance about the sacred hill,
620 Mystical dance, which yonder starry sphere
Of planets and of fixed in all her wheels
Resembles nearest, mazes intricate,
Eccentric, intervolved, yet regular
Then most, when most irregular they seem,
625 And in their motions harmony divine
So smooths her charming tones, that God's own ear
Listens delighted. Ev'ning now approached
(For we have also our ev'ning and our morn,
We ours for change delectable, not need);
630 Forthwith from dance to sweet repast they turn
Desirous; all in circles as they stood,
Tables are set, and on a sudden piled
With angels' food, and rubied nectar flows
In pearl, in diamond, and massy gold,

635   Fruit of delicious vines, the growth of Heav'n.
       On flow'rs reposed, and with fresh flow'rets crowned,
       They eat, they drink, and in communion sweet
       Quaff immortality and joy, secure
       Of surfeit where full measure only bounds
640   Excess, before th' all bounteous King, who show'red
       With copious hand, rejoicing in their joy.
       Now when ambrosial night with clouds exhaled
       From that high Mount of God, whence light and shade
       Spring both, the face of brightest Heav'n had changed
645   To grateful twilight (for night comes not there
       In darker veil) and roseate dews disposed
       All but the unsleeping eyes of God to rest,
       Wide over all the plain, and wider far
       Than all this globous earth in plain outspread,
650   (Such are the courts of God) th' angelic throng
       Dispersed in bands and files their camp extend
       By living streams among the Trees of Life,
       Pavilions numberless, and sudden reared,
       Celestial tabernacles, where they slept
655   Fanned with cool winds, save those who in their course
       Melodious hymns about the sov'reign throne
       Alternate all night long: but not so waked
       Satan, so call him now, his former name
       Is heard no more in Heav'n; he of the first,
660   If not the first Archangel, great in power,
       In favour and pre-eminence, yet fraught
       With envy against the Son of God, that day
       Honoured by his great Father, and proclaimed
       Messiah King anointed, could not bear
665   Through pride that sight, and thought himself impaired.
       Deep malice thence conceiving and disdain,
       Soon as midnight brought on the dusky hour
       Friendliest to sleep and silence, he resolved
       With all his legions to dislodge, and leave
670   Unworshipped, unobeyed the throne supreme
       Contemptuous, and his next subordinate
       Awak'ning, thus to him in secret spake.
           Sleep'st thou companion dear, what sleep can close

Thy eye-lids? and remember'st what decree
675 Of yesterday, so late hath passed the lips
Of Heav'n's Almighty. Thou to me thy thoughts
Wast wont, I mine to thee was wont to impart;
Both waking we were one; how then can now
Thy sleep dissent? New laws thou seest imposed;
680 New laws from him who reigns, new minds may raise
In us who serve, new counsels, to debate
What doubtful may ensue; more in this place
To utter is not safe. Assemble thou
Of all those myriads which we lead the chief;
685 Tell them that by command, ere yet dim night
Her shadowy cloud withdraws, I am to haste,
And all who under me their banners wave,
Homeward with flying march where we possess
The quarters of the North, there to prepare
690 Fit entertainment to receive our King
The great Messiah, and his new commands,
Who speedily through all the hierarchies
Intends to pass triumphant, and give laws.
    So spake the false Archangel, and infused
695 Bad influence into th' unwary breast
Of his associate; he together calls,
Or several one by one, the regent Powers,
Under him regent, tells, as he was taught,
That the Most High commanding, now ere night,
700 Now ere dim night had disencumbered Heav'n,
The great hierarchal standard was to move;
Tells the suggested cause, and casts between
Ambiguous words and jealousies, to sound
Or taint integrity; but all obeyed
705 The wonted signal, and superior voice
Of their great Potentate; for great indeed
His name, and high was his degree in Heav'n;
His count'nance, as the morning star that guides
The starry flock, allured them, and with lies
710 Drew after him the third part of Heav'n's host:
Meanwhile th' Eternal eye, whose sight discerns
Abstrusest thoughts, from forth his holy Mount

And from within the golden lamps that burn
Nightly before him, saw without their light
715 Rebellion rising, saw in whom, how spread
Among the sons of morn, what multitudes
Were banded to oppose his high decree;
And smiling to his only Son thus said.
　　Son, thou in whom my glory I behold
720 In full resplendence, heir of all my might,
Nearly it now concerns us to be sure
Of our omnipotence, and with what arms
We mean to hold what anciently we claim
Of deity or empire, such a foe
725 Is rising, who intends to erect his throne
Equal to ours, throughout the spacious North;
Nor so content, hath in his thought to try
In battle what our power is, or our right.
Let us advise, and to this hazard draw
730 With speed what force is left, and all employ
In our defence, lest unawares we lose
This our high place, our sanctuary, our hill.
　　To whom the Son with calm aspéct and clear
Light'ning divine, ineffable, serene,
735 Made answer. Mighty Father, thou thy foes
Justly hast in derision, and secure
Laugh'st at their vain designs and tumults vain,
Matter to me of glory, whom their hate
Illústrates, when they see all regal power
740 Giv'n me to quell their pride, and in event
Know whether I be dextrous to subdue
Thy rebels, or be found the worst in Heav'n.
　　So spake the Son, but Satan with his powers
Far was advanced on wingèd speed, an host
745 Innumerable as the stars of night,
Or stars of morning, dew-drops, which the sun
Impearls on every leaf and every flow'r.
Regions they passed, the mighty regencies
Of Seraphim and Potentates and Thrones
750 In their triple degrees, regions to which
All thy dominion, Adam, is no more

Than what this garden is to all the earth,
And all the sea, from one entire globose
Stretched into longitude; which having passed
755   At length into the limits of the North
They came, and Satan to his royal seat
High on a hill, far blazing, as a mount
Raised on a mount, with pyramids and tow'rs
From diamond quarries hewn, and rocks of gold,
760   The palace of great Lucifer, (so call
That structure in the dialect of men
Interpreted) which not long after, he
Affecting all equality with God,
In imitation of that Mount whereon
765   Messiah was declared in sight of Heav'n,
The Mountain of the Congregation called;
For thither he assembled all his train,
Pretending so commanded to consult
About the great reception of their King,
770   Thither to come, and with calumnious art
Of counterfeited truth thus held their ears.
　　　Thrones, Dominations, Princedoms, Virtues, Powers,
If these magnific titles yet remain
Not merely titular, since by decree
775   Another now hath to himself engrossed
All power, and us eclipsed under the name
Of King anointed, for whom all this haste
Of midnight march, and hurried meeting here,
This only to consult how we may best
780   With what may be devised of honours new
Receive him coming to receive from us
Knee-tribute yet unpaid, prostration vile,
Too much to one, but double how endured,
To one and to his image now proclaimed?
785   But what if better counsels might erect
Our minds and teach us to cast off this yoke?
Will ye submit your necks, and choose to bend
The supple knee? ye will not, if I trust
To know ye right, or if ye know yourselves
790   Natives and sons of Heav'n possessed before

By none, and if not equal all, yet free,
Equally free; for orders and degrees
Jar not with liberty, but well consist.
Who can in reason then or right assume
795   Monarchy over such as live by right
His equals, if in power and splendour less,
In freedom equal? or can introduce
Law and edíct on us, who without law
Err not, much less for this to be our Lord,
800   And look for adoration to th' abuse
Of those imperial titles which assert
Our being ordained to govern, not to serve?
    Thus far his bold discourse without control
Had audience, when among the Seraphim
805   Abdiel, than whom none with more zeal adored
The Deity, and divine commands obeyed,
Stood up, and in a flame of zeal severe
The current of his fury thus opposed.
    O argument blasphémous, false and proud!
810   Words which no ear ever to hear in Heav'n
Expected, least of all from thee, ingrate
In place thyself so high above thy peers.
Canst thou with impious obloquy condemn
The just decree of God, pronounced and sworn,
815   That to his only Son by right endued
With regal sceptre, every soul in Heav'n
Shall bend the knee, and in that honour due
Confess him rightful King? unjust thou say'st
Flatly unjust, to bind with laws the free,
820   And equal over equals to let reign,
One over all with unsucceeded power.
Shalt thou give law to God, shalt thou dispute
With him the points of liberty, who made
Thee what thou art, and formed the Powers of Heav'n
825   Such as he pleased, and circumscribed their being?
Yet by experience taught we know how good,
And of our good, and of our dignity
How provident he is, how far from thought
To make us less, bent rather to exalt

830   Our happy state under one head more near
       United. But to grant it thee unjust,
       That equal over equals monarch reign:
       Thyself though great and glorious dost thou count,
       Or all angelic nature joined in one,
835   Equal to him begotten Son, by whom
       As by his Word the mighty Father made
       All things, ev'n thee, and all the Spirits of Heav'n
       By him created in their bright degrees,
       Crowned them with glory, and to their glory named
840   Thrones, Dominations, Princedoms, Virtues, Powers,
       Essential Powers, nor by his reign obscured,
       But more illustrious made, since he the head
       One of our number thus reduced becomes,
       His laws our laws, all honour to him done
845   Returns our own. Cease then this impious rage,
       And tempt not these; but hasten to appease
       Th' incensèd Father, and th' incensèd Son,
       While pardon may be found in time besought.
           So spake the fervent angel, but his zeal
850   None seconded, as out of season judged,
       Or singular and rash, whereat rejoiced
       Th' Apostate, and more haughty thus replied.
       That we were formed then say'st thou? and the work
       Of secondary hands, by task transferred
855   From Father to his Son? strange point and new!
       Doctrine which we would know whence learnt: who saw
       When this creation was? remember'st thou
       Thy making, while the Maker gave thee being?
       We know no time when we were not as now;
860   Know none before us, self-begot, self-raised
       By our own quick'ning power, when fatal course
       Had circled his full orb, the birth mature
       Of this our native Heav'n, ethereal sons.
       Our puissance is our own, our own right hand
865   Shall teach us highest deeds, by proof to try
       Who is our equal: then thou shalt behold
       Whether by supplication we intend
       Address, and to begirt th' Almighty throne

Beseeching or besieging. This report,
870   These tidings carry to th' anointed King;
And fly, ere evil intercept thy flight.
      He said, and as the sound of waters deep
Hoarse murmur echoed to his words applause
Through the infinite host, nor less for that
875   The flaming Seraph fearless, though alone
Encompassed round with foes, thus answered bold.
      O alienate from God, O Spirit accurst,
Forsaken of all good; I see thy fall
Determined, and thy hapless crew involved
880   In this perfidious fraud, contagion spread
Both of thy crime and punishment: henceforth
No more be troubled how to quit the yoke
Of God's Messiah; those indulgent laws
Will not now be vouchsafed, other decrees
885   Against thee are gone forth without recall;
That golden sceptre which thou didst reject
Is now an iron rod to bruise and break
Thy disobedience. Well thou didst advise,
Yet not for thy advice or threats I fly
890   These wicked tents devoted, lest the wrath
Impendent, raging into sudden flame
Distinguish not: for soon expect to feel
His thunder on thy head, devouring fire.
Then who created thee lamenting learn,
895   When who can uncreate thee thou shalt know.
      So spake the Seraph Abdiel faithful found,
Among the faithless, faithful only he;
Among innumerable false, unmoved,
Unshaken, unseduced, unterrified,
900   His loyalty he kept, his love, his zeal;
Nor number, nor example with him wrought
To swerve from truth, or change his constant mind
Though single. From amidst them forth he passed,
Long way through hostile scorn, which he sustained
905   Superior, nor of violence feared aught;
And with retorted scorn his back he turned
On those proud tow'rs to swift destruction doomed.

BOOK VI

The Argument

Raphael continues to relate how Michael and Gabriel were
sent forth to battle against Satan and his angels. The first
fight described: Satan and his powers retire under night: he
calls a council, invents devilish engines, which in the second
5   day's fight put Michael and his angels to some disorder; but
they at length pulling up mountains overwhelmed both the
forces and machines of Satan: yet the tumult not so ending,
God on the third day sends Messiah his Son, for whom he
had reserved the glory of that victory: he in the power of his
10 Father coming to the place, and causing all his legions to
stand still on either side, with his chariot and thunder driving
into the midst of his enemies, pursues them unable to resist
towards the wall of Heaven; which opening, they leap down
with horror and confusion into the place of punishment pre-
15 pared for them in the deep: Messiah returns with triumph to
his Father.

All night the dreadless angel unpursued
Through Heav'n's wide champaign held his way, till Morn,
Waked by the circling Hours, with rosy hand
Unbarred the gates of light. There is a cave
5 Within the Mount of God, fast by his throne,
Where light and darkness in perpetual round
Lodge and dislodge by turns, which makes through Heav'n
Grateful vicissitude, like day and night;
Light issues forth, and at the other door
10 Obsequious darkness enters, till her hour
To veil the Heav'n, though darkness there might well
Seem twilight here; and now went forth the Morn
Such as in highest Heav'n, arrayed in gold
Empyreal; from before her vanished night,

15   Shot through with orient beams: when all the plain
Covered with thick embattled squadrons bright,
Chariots and flaming arms, and fiery steeds
Reflecting blaze on blaze, first met his view:
War he perceived, war in procinct, and found
20   Already known what he for news had thought
To have reported: gladly then he mixed
Among those friendly Powers who him received
With joy and acclamations loud, that one
That of so many myriads fall'n, yet one
25   Returned not lost: on to the sacred hill
They led him high applauded, and present
Before the seat supreme; from whence a voice
From midst a golden cloud thus mild was heard.
      Servant of God, well done, well hast thou fought
30   The better fight, who single hast maintained
Against revolted multitudes the cause
Of truth, in word mightier than they in arms;
And for the testimony of truth hast borne
Universal reproach, far worse to bear
35   Than violence: for this was all thy care
To stand approved in sight of God, though worlds
Judged thee perverse: the easier conquest now
Remains thee, aided by this host of friends,
Back on thy foes more glorious to return
40   Than scorned thou didst depart, and to subdue
By force, who reason for their law refuse,
Right reason for their law, and for their King
Messiah, who by right of merit reigns.
Go Michael of celestial armies prince,
45   And thou in military prowess next,
Gabriel, lead forth to battle these my sons
Invincible, lead forth my armèd saints
By thousands and by millions ranged for fight;
Equal in number to that Godless crew
50   Rebellious, them with fire and hostile arms
Fearless assault, and to the brow of Heav'n
Pursuing drive them out from God and bliss,
Into their place of punishment, the gulf

Of Tartarus, which ready opens wide
55   His fiery Chaos to receive their fall.
      So spake the sov'reign voice, and clouds began
To darken all the hill, and smoke to roll
In dusky wreaths, reluctant flames, the sign
Of wrath awaked: nor with less dread the loud
60   Ethereal trumpet from on high gan blow:
At which command the powers militant,
That stood for Heav'n, in mighty quadrate joined
Of union irresistible, moved on
In silence their bright legions, to the sound
65   Of instrumental harmony that breathed
Heroic ardour to advent'rous deeds
Under their godlike leaders, in the cause
Of God and his Messiah. On they move
Indíssolúbly firm; nor obvious hill,
70   Nor strait'ning vale, nor wood, nor stream divides
Their perfect ranks; for high above the ground
Their march was, and the passive air upbore
Their nimble tread; as when the total kind
Of birds in orderly array on wing
75   Came summoned over Eden to receive
Their names of thee; so over many a tract
Of Heav'n they marched, and many a province wide
Tenfold the length of this terrene: at last
Far in th' horizon to the North appeared
80   From skirt to skirt a fiery region, stretched
In battailous aspéct, and nearer view
Bristled with upright beams innumerable
Of rigid spears, and helmets thronged, and shields
Various, with boastful argument portrayed,
85   The banded powers of Satan hasting on
With furious expedition; for they weened
That selfsame day by fight, or by surprise
To win the Mount of God, and on his throne
To set the envier of his state, the proud
90   Aspirer, but their thoughts proved fond and vain
In the mid way: though strange to us it seemed
At first, that angel should with angel war,

And in fierce hosting meet, who wont to meet
So oft in festivals of joy and love
95 Unanimous, as sons of one great Sire,
Hymning th' Eternal Father: but the shout
Of battle now began, and rushing sound
Of onset ended soon each milder thought.
High in the midst exalted as a god
100 Th' Apostate in his sun-bright chariot sat
Idol of majesty divine, enclosed
With flaming Cherubim, and golden shields;
Then lighted from his gorgeous throne, for now
'Twixt host and host but narrow space was left,
105 A dreadful interval, and front to front
Presented stood in terrible array
Of hideous length: before the cloudy van,
On the rough edge of battle ere it joined
Satan with vast and haughty strides advanced,
110 Came tow'ring, armed in adamant and gold;
Abdiel that sight endured not, where he stood
Among the mightiest, bent on highest deeds,
And thus his own undaunted heart explores.
  O Heav'n! that such resemblance of the Highest
115 Should yet remain, where faith and realty
Remain not; wherefore should not strength and might
There fail where virtue fails, or weakest prove
Where boldest; though to sight unconquerable?
His puissance, trusting in th' Almighty's aid,
120 I mean to try, whose reason I have tried
Unsound and false; nor is it aught but just,
That he who in debate of truth hath won,
Should win in arms, in both disputes alike
Victor; though brutish that contést and foul,
125 When reason hath to deal with force, yet so
Most reason is that reason overcome.
  So pondering, and from his arméd peers
Forth stepping opposite, half way he met
His daring foe, at this prevention more
130 Incensed, and thus securely him defied.
  Proud, art thou met? thy hope was to have reached

The heighth of thy aspiring unopposed,
The throne of God unguarded, and his side
Abandoned at the terror of thy power
135   Or potent tongue; fool, not to think how vain
Against th' Omnipotent to rise in arms;
Who out of smallest things could without end.
Have raised incessant armies to defeat
Thy folly; or with solitary hand
140   Reaching beyond all limit, at one blow
Unaided could have finished thee, and whelmed
Thy legions under darkness; but thou seest
All are not of thy train; there be who faith
Prefer, and piety to God, though then
145   To thee not visible, when I alone
Seemed in thy world erroneous to dissent
From all: my sect thou seest, now learn too late
How few sometimes may know, when thousands err.
    Whom the grand Foe with scornful eye askance
150   Thus answered. Ill for thee, but in wished hour
Of my revenge, first sought for thou return'st
From flight, seditious angel, to receive
Thy merited reward, the first assay
Of this right hand provoked, since first that tongue
155   Inspired with contradiction durst oppose
A third part of the gods, in synod met
Their deities to assert, who while they feel
Vigour divine within them, can allow
Omnipotence to none. But well thou com'st
160   Before thy fellows, ambitious to win
From me some plume, that thy success may show
Destruction to the rest: this pause between
(Unanswered lest thou boast) to let thee know;
At first I thought that liberty and Heav'n
165   To Heav'nly souls had been all one; but now
I see that most through sloth had rather serve,
Minist'ring Spirits, trained up in feast and song;
Such hast thou armed, the minstrelsy of Heav'n,
Servility with freedom to contend,
170   As both their deeds compared this day shall prove.

To whom in brief thus Abdiel stern replied.
Apostate, still thou err'st, nor end wilt find
Of erring, from the path of truth remote:
Unjustly thou deprav'st it with the name
175 Of servitude to serve whom God ordains,
Or Nature; God and Nature bid the same,
When he who rules is worthiest, and excels
Them whom he governs. This is servitude,
To serve th' unwise, or him who hath rebelled
180 Against his worthier, as thine now serve thee,
Thyself not free, but to thyself enthralled;
Yet lewdly dar'st our minist'ring upbraid.
Reign thou in Hell thy Kingdom, let me serve
In Heav'n God ever blest, and his divine
185 Behests obey, worthiest to be obeyed;
Yet chains in Hell, not realms expect: meanwhile
From me returned, as erst thou saidst, from flight,
This greeting on thy impious crest receive.
So saying, a noble stroke he lifted high,
190 Which hung not, but so swift with tempest fell
On the proud crest of Satan, that no sight,
Nor motion of swift thought, less could his shield
Such ruin intercept: ten paces huge
He back recoiled; the tenth on bended knee
195 His massy spear upstayed; as if on earth
Winds under ground or waters forcing way
Sidelong, had pushed a mountain from his seat
Half sunk with all his pines. Amazement seized
The rebel Thrones, but greater rage to see
200 Thus foiled their mightiest; ours joy filled, and shout,
Presage of victory and fierce desire
Of battle: whereat Michaël bid sound
Th' Archangel trumpet; through the vast of Heav'n
It sounded, and the faithful armies rung
205 Hosanna to the Highest: nor stood at gaze
The adverse legions, nor less hideous joined
The horrid shock: now storming fury rose,
And clamour such as heard in Heav'n till now
Was never; arms on armour clashing brayed

210   Horrible discord, and the madding wheels
       Of brazen chariots raged; dire was the noise
       Of conflict; overhead the dismal hiss
       Of fiery darts in flaming volleys flew,
       And flying vaulted either host with fire.
215   So under fiery cope together rushed
       Both battles main, with ruinous assault
       And inextinguishable rage; all Heav'n
       Resounded, and had earth been then, all earth
       Had to her centre shook. What wonder? when
220   Millions of fierce encount'ring angels fought
       On either side, the least of whom could wield
       These elements, and arm him with the force
       Of all their regions: how much more of power
       Army against army numberless to raise
225   Dreadful combustion warring, and disturb,
       Though not destroy, their happy native seat;
       Had not th' Eternal King Omnipotent
       From his stronghold of Heav'n high overruled
       And limited their might; though numbered such
230   As each divided legion might have seemed
       A numerous host, in strength each armèd hand
       A legion; led in fight, yet leader seemed
       Each warrior single as in chief, expért
       When to advance, or stand, or turn the sway
235   Of battle, open when, and when to close
       The ridges of grim war; no thought of flight,
       None of retreat, no unbecoming deed
       That argued fear; each on himself relied,
       As only in his arm the moment lay
240   Of victory; deeds of eternal fame
       Were done, but infinite: for wide was spread
       That war and various; sometimes on firm ground
       A standing fight, then soaring on main wing
       Tormented all the air; all air seemed then
245   Conflicting fire: long time in even scale
       The battle hung; till Satan, who that day
       Prodigious power had shown, and met in arms
       No equal, ranging through the dire attack

Of fighting Seraphim confused, at length
250 Saw where the sword of Michael smote, and felled
Squadrons at once, with huge two-handed sway
Brandished aloft the horrid edge came down
Wide wasting; such destruction to withstand
He hasted, and opposed the rocky orb
255 Of tenfold adamant, his ample shield
A vast circumference: at his approach
The great Archangel from his warlike toil
Surceased, and glad as hoping here to end
Intestine war in Heav'n, the Arch-foe subdued
260 Or captive dragged in chains, with hostile frown
And visage all inflamed first thus began.
    Author of evil, unknown till thy revolt,
Unnamed in Heav'n, now plenteous, as thou seest
These acts of hateful strife, hateful to all,
265 Though heaviest by just measure on thyself
And thy adherents: how hast thou disturbed
Heav'n's blessèd peace, and into Nature brought
Misery, uncreated till the crime
Of thy rebellion? how hast thou instilled
270 Thy malice into thousands, once upright
And faithful, now proved false. But think not here
To trouble holy rest; Heav'n casts thee out
From all her confines. Heav'n the seat of bliss
Brooks not the works of violence and war.
275 Hence then, and evil go with thee along
Thy offspring, to the place of evil, Hell,
Thou and thy wicked crew; there mingle broils,
Ere this avenging sword begin thy doom,
Or some more sudden vengeance winged from God
280 Precipitate thee with augmented pain.
    So spake the Prince of angels; to whom thus
The Adversary. Nor think thou with wind
Of airy threats to awe whom yet with deeds
Thou canst not. Hast thou turned the least of these
285 To flight, or if to fall, but that they rise
Unvanquished, easier to transact with me
That thou shouldst hope, imperious, and with threats

To chase me hence? err not that so shall end
The strife which thou call'st evil, but we style
290   The strife of glory: which we mean to win,
Or turn this Heav'n itself into the Hell
Thou fablest; here however to dwell free,
If not to reign: meanwhile thy utmost force,
And join him named Almighty to thy aid,
295   I fly not, but have sought thee far and nigh.
    They ended parle, and both addressed for fight
Unspeakable; for who, though with the tongue
Of angels, can relate, or to what things
Liken on earth conspicuous, that may lift
300   Human imagination to such heighth
Of godlike power: for likest gods they seemed,
Stood they or moved, in stature, motion, arms
Fit to decide the empire of great Heav'n.
Now waved their fiery swords, and in the air
305   Made horrid circles; two broad suns their shields
Blazed opposite, while Expectation stood
In horror; from each hand with speed retired
Where erst was thickest fight, th' angelic throng,
And left large field, unsafe within the wind
310   Of such commotion, such as to set forth
Great things by small, if Nature's concord broke,
Among the constellations war were sprung,
Two planets rushing from aspéct malign
Of fiercest opposition in mid sky,
315   Should combat, and their jarring spheres confound.
Together both with next to Almighty arm,
Uplifted imminent one stroke they aimed
That might determine, and not need repeat,
As not of power, at once; nor odds appeared
320   In might or swift prevention; but the sword
Of Michael from the armoury of God
Was giv'n him tempered so, that neither keen
Nor solid might resist that edge: it met
The sword of Satan with steep force to smite
325   Descending, and in half cut sheer, nor stayed,
But with swift wheel reverse, deep ent'ring shared

All his right side; then Satan first knew pain,
And writhed him to and fro convolved; so sore
The griding sword with discontinuous wound
330   Passed through him, but th' ethereal substance closed
Not long divisible, and from the gash
A stream of nectarous humour issuing flowed
Sanguine, such as celestial Spirits may bleed,
And all his armour stained erewhile so bright.
335   Forthwith on all sides to his aid was run
By angels many and strong, who interposed
Defence, while others bore him on their shields
Back to his chariot, where it stood retired
From off the files of war; there they him laid
340   Gnashing for anguish and despite and shame
To find himself not matchless, and his pride
Humbled by such rebuke, so far beneath
His confidence to equal God in power.
Yet soon he healed; for Spirits that live throughout
345   Vital in every part, not as frail man
In entrails, heart or head, liver or reins,
Cannot but by annihilating die;
Nor in their liquid texture mortal wound
Receive, no more than can the fluid air:
350   All heart they live, all head, all eye, all ear,
All intellect, all sense, and as they please,
They limb themselves, and colour, shape or size
Assume, as likes them best, condense or rare.
    Meanwhile in other parts like deeds deserved
355   Memorial, where the might of Gabriel fought,
And with fierce ensigns pierced the deep array
Of Moloch furious king, who him defied,
And at his chariot wheels to drag him bound
Threatened, nor from the Holy One of Heav'n
360   Refrained his tongue blasphémous; but anon
Down cloven to the waist, with shattered arms
And uncouth pain fled bellowing. On each wing
Uriel and Raphaël his vaunting foe,
Though huge, and in a rock of diamond armed,
365   Vanquished Adramelech, and Asmadai,

Two potent Thrones, that to be less than gods
Disdained, but meaner thoughts learned in their flight,
Mangled with ghastly wounds through plate and mail.
Nor stood unmindful Abdiel to annoy
370 The atheist crew, but with redoubled blow
Ariel and Arioch, and the violence
Of Ramiel scorched and blasted overthrew.
I might relate of thousands, and their names
Eternize here on earth; but those elect
375 Angels contented with their fame in Heav'n
Seek not the praise of men: the other sort
In might though wondrous and in acts of war,
Nor of renown less eager, yet by doom
Cancelled from Heav'n and sacred memory,
380 Nameless in dark oblivion let them dwell.
For strength from Truth divided and from Just,
Illaudable, naught merits but dispraise
And ignominy, yet to glory aspires
Vainglorious, and through infamy seeks fame:
385 Therefore eternal silence be their doom.
    And now their mightiest quelled, the battle swerved,
With many an inroad gored; deformèd rout
Entered, and foul disorder; all the ground
With shivered armour strewn, and on a heap
390 Chariot and charioteer lay overturned
And fiery foaming steeds; what stood, recoiled
O'er-wearied, through the faint Satanic host
Defensive scarce, or with pale fear surprised,
Then first with fear surprised and sense of pain,
395 Fled ignominious, to such evil brought
By sin of disobedience, till that hour
Not liable to fear or flight or pain.
Far otherwise th' inviolable saints
In cubic phalanx firm advanced entire,
400 Invulnerable, impenetrably armed:
Such high advantages their innocence
Gave them above their foes, not to have sinned,
Not to have disobeyed; in fight they stood
Unwearied, unobnoxious to be pained

405   By wound, though from their place by violence moved.
     Now night her course began, and over Heav'n
   Inducing darkness, grateful truce imposed,
   And silence on the odious din of war:
   Under her cloudy covert both retired,
410   Victor and vanquished: on the foughten field
   Michaël and his angels prevalent
   Encamping, placed in guard their watches round,
   Cherubic waving fires: on th' other part
   Satan with his rebellious disappeared,
415   Far in the dark dislodged, and void of rest,
   His Potentates to council called by night;
   And in the midst thus undismayed began.
     O now in danger tried, now known in arms
   Not to be overpowered, companions dear,
420   Found worthy not of liberty alone,
   Too mean pretence, but what we more affect,
   Honour, dominion, glory, and renown,
   Who have sustained one day in doubtful fight
   (And if one day, why not eternal days?)
425   What Heaven's Lord had powerfullest to send
   Against us from about his throne, and judged
   Sufficient to subdue us to his will,
   But proves not so: then fallible, it seems,
   Of future we may deem him, though till now
430   Omniscient thought. True is, less firmly armed,
   Some disadvantage we endured and pain,
   Till now not known, but known as soon contemned,
   Since now we find this our empyreal form
   Incapable of mortal injury
435   Imperishable, and though pierced with wound,
   Soon closing, and by native vigour healed.
   Of evil then so small as easy think
   The remedy; perhaps more valid arms,
   Weapons more violent, when next we meet,
440   May serve to better us, and worse our foes,
   Or equal what between us made the odds,
   In nature none: if other hidden cause
   Left them superior, while we can preserve

Unhurt our minds, and understanding sound,
445 Due search and consultation will disclose.
  He sat; and in th' assembly next upstood
Nisroch, of Principalities the prime;
As one he stood escaped from cruel fight,
Sore toiled, his riven arms to havoc hewn,
450 And cloudy in aspéct thus answering spake.
Deliverer from new Lords, leader to free
Enjoyment of our right as gods; yet hard
For gods, and too unequal work we find
Against unequal arms to fight in pain,
455 Against unpained, impassive; from which evil
Ruin must needs ensue; for what avails
Valour or strength, though matchless, quelled with pain
Which all subdues, and makes remiss the hands
Of mightiest. Sense of pleasure we may well
460 Spare out of life perhaps, and not repine,
But live content, which is the calmest life:
But pain is perfect misery, the worst
Of evils, and excessive, overturns
All patience. He who therefore can invent
465 With what more forcible we may offend
Our yet unwounded enemies, or arm
Ourselves with like defence, to me deserves
No less than for deliverance what we owe.
  Whereto with look composed Satan replied.
470 Not uninvented that, which thou aright
Believ'st so main to our success, I bring;
Which of us who beholds the bright surfáce
Of this ethereous mould whereon we stand,
This continent of spacious Heav'n, adorned
475 With plant, fruit, flow'r ambrosial, gems and gold,
Whose eye so superficially surveys
These things, as not to mind from whence they grow
Deep under ground, materials dark and crude,
Of spiritous and fiery spume, till touched
480 With Heav'n's ray, and tempered they shoot forth
So beauteous, op'ning to the ambient light.
These in their dark nativity the deep

Shall yield us, pregnant with infernal flame,
Which into hollow engines long and round
485   Thick-rammed, at th' other bore with touch of fire
Dilated and infuriate shall send forth
From far with thund'ring noise among our foes
Such implements of mischief as shall dash
To pieces, and o'erwhelm whatever stands
490   Adverse, that they shall fear we have disarmed
The Thunderer of his only dreaded bolt.
Nor long shall be our labour, yet ere dawn,
Effect shall end our wish. Meanwhile revive;
Abandon fear; to strength and counsel joined
495   Think nothing hard, much less to be despaired.
He ended, and his words their drooping cheer
Enlightened, and their languished hope revived.
Th' invention all admired, and each, how he
To be th' inventor missed, so easy it seemed
500   Once found, which yet unfound most would have thought
Impossible: yet haply of thy race
In future days, if malice should abound,
Someone intent on mischief, or inspired
With dev'lish machination might devise
505   Like instrument to plague the sons of men
For sin, on war and mutual slaughter bent.
Forthwith from council to the work they flew,
None arguing stood, innumerable hands
Were ready; in a moment up they turned
510   Wide the celestial soil, and saw beneath
Th' originals of nature in their crude
Conception; sulphurous and nitrous foam
They found, they mingled, and with subtle art,
Concocted and adusted they reduced
515   To blackest grain, and into store conveyed:
Part hidden veins digged up (nor hath this earth
Entrails unlike) of mineral and stone,
Whereof to found their engines and their balls
Of missive ruin; part incentive reed
520   Provide, pernicious with one touch to fire.
So all ere day-spring, under conscious night

Secret they finished, and in order set,
With silent circumspection unespied.
Now when fair morn orient in Heav'n appeared
525 Up rose the victor angels, and to arms
The matin trumpet sung: in arms they stood
Of golden panoply, refulgent host,
Soon banded; others from the dawning hills
Looked round, and scouts each coast light-armèd scour,
530 Each quarter, to descry the distant foe,
Where lodged, or whither fled, or if for fight,
In motion or in halt: him soon they met
Under spread ensigns moving nigh, in slow
But firm battalion; back with speediest sail
535 Zophiel, of Cherubim the swiftest wing,
Came flying, and in mid air aloud thus cried.
  Arm, warriors, arm for fight, the foe at hand,
Whom fled we thought, will save us long pursuit
This day, fear not his flight; so thick a cloud
540 He comes, and settled in his face I see
Sad resolution and secure: let each
His adamantine coat gird well, and each
Fit well his helm, grip fast his orbèd shield,
Borne ev'n or high, for this day will pour down,
545 If I conjecture aught, no drizzling show'r,
But rattling storm of arrows barbed with fire.
So warned he them aware themselves, and soon
In order, quit of all impediment;
Instant without disturb they took alarm,
550 And onward move embattled; when behold
Not distant far with heavy pace the foe
Approaching gross and huge; in hollow cube
Training his devilish enginery, impaled
On every side with shadowing squadrons deep,
555 To hide the fraud. At interview both stood
A while, but suddenly at head appeared
Satan: and thus was heard commanding loud.
  Vanguard, to right and left the front unfold;
That all may see who hate us, how we seek
560 Peace and composure, and with open breast

Stand ready to receive them, if they like
Our overture, and turn not back perverse;
But that I doubt; however witness Heaven,
Heav'n witness thou anon, while we discharge
565 Freely our part; ye who appointed stand
Do as ye have in charge, and briefly touch
What we propound, and loud that all may hear.
      So scoffing in ambiguous words, he scarce
Had ended; when to right and left the front
570 Divided, and to either flank retired.
Which to our eyes discovered new and strange,
A triple-mounted row of pillars laid
On wheels (for like to pillars most they seemed
Or hollowed bodies made of oak or fir
575 With branches lopped, in wood or mountain felled),
Brass, iron, stony mould, had not their mouths
With hideous orifice gaped on us wide,
Portending hollow truce; at each behind
A Seraph stood, and in his hand a reed
580 Stood waving tipped with fire; while we suspense,
Collected stood within our thoughts amused,
Not long, for sudden all at once their reeds
Put forth, and to a narrow vent applied
With nicest touch. Immediate in a flame,
585 But soon obscured with smoke, all Heav'n appeared,
From those deep-throated engines belched, whose roar
Embowelled with outrageous noise the air,
And all her entrails tore, disgorging foul
Their devilish glut, chained thunderbolts and hail
590 Of iron globes, which on the victor host
Levelled, with such impetuous fury smote,
That whom they hit, none on their feet might stand,
Though standing else as rocks, but down they fell
By thousands, Angel on Archangel rolled,
595 The sooner for their arms; unarmed they might
Have easily as Spirits evaded swift
By quick contraction or remove; but now
Foul dissipation followed and forced rout;
Nor served it to relax their serried files.

600   What should they do? if on they rushed, repulse
        Repeated, and indecent overthrow
        Doubled, would render them yet more despised,
        And to their foes a laughter; for in view
        Stood ranked of Seraphim another row
605   In posture to displode their second tire
        Of thunder: back defeated to return
        They worse abhorred. Satan beheld their plight,
        And to his mates thus in derision called.
           O friends, why come not on these victors proud?
610   Erewhile they fierce were coming, and when we,
        To entertain them fair with open front
        And breast, (what could we more?) propounded terms
        Of composition, straight they changed their minds,
        Flew off, and into strange vagáries fell,
615   As they would dance, yet for a dance they seemed
        Somewhat extravagant and wild, perhaps
        For joy of offered peace: but I suppose
        If our proposals once again were heard
        We should compel them to a quick result.
620   To whom thus Belial in like gamesome mood.
        Leader, the terms we sent were terms of weight,
        Of hard conténts, and full of force urged home,
        Such as we might perceive amused them all,
        And stumbled many; who receives them right,
625   Had need from head to foot well understand;
        Not understood, this gift they have besides,
        They show us when our foes walk not upright.
           So they among themselves in pleasant vein
        Stood scoffing, heighthened in their thoughts beyond
630   All doubt of victory; eternal might
        To match with their inventions they presumed
        So easy, and of his thunder made a scorn,
        And all his host derided, while they stood
        Awhile in trouble; but they stood not long,
635   Rage prompted them at length, and found them arms
        Against such Hellish mischief fit to oppose.
        Forthwith (behold the excellence, the power
        Which God hath in his mighty angels placed)

Their arms away they threw, and to the hills
640 (For earth hath this variety from Heav'n
        Of pleasure situate in hill and dale)
        Light as the lightning glimpse they ran, they flew,
        From their foundations loos'ning to and fro
        They plucked the seated hills with all their load,
645 Rocks, waters, woods, and by the shaggy tops
        Uplifting bore them in their hands: amaze,
        Be sure, and terror seized the rebel host,
        When coming towards them so dread they saw
        The bottom of the mountains upward turned,
650 Till on those cursèd engines' triple-row
        They saw them whelmed, and all their confidence
        Under the weight of mountains buried deep,
        Themselves invaded next, and on their heads
        Main promontories flung, which in the air
655 Came shadowing, and oppressed whole legions armed;
        Their armour helped their harm, crushed in and bruised
        Into their substance pent, which wrought them pain
        Implacable, and many a dolorous groan,
        Long struggling underneath, ere they could wind
660 Out of such prison, though Spirits of purest light,
        Purest at first, now gross by sinning grown.
        The rest in imitation to like arms
        Betook them, and the neighbouring hills uptore;
        So hills amid the air encountered hills
665 Hurled to and fro with jaculation dire,
        That under ground they fought in dismal shade;
        Infernal noise; war seemed a civil game
        To this uproar; horrid confusion heaped
        Upon confusion rose: and now all Heav'n
670 Had gone to wrack, with ruin overspread,
        Had not th' Almighty Father where he sits
        Shrined in his sanctuary of Heav'n secure,
        Consulting on the sum of things, foreseen
        This tumult, and permitted all, advised:
675 That his great purpose he might so fulfil,
        To honour his Anointed Son avenged
        Upon his enemies, and to declare

All power on him transferred: whence to his Son
Th' Assessor of his throne he thus began.
680   Effulgence of my Glory, Son beloved,
Son in whose face invisible is beheld
Visibly, what by Deity I am,
And in whose hand what by decree I do,
Second Omnipotence, two days are passed,
685   Two days, as we compute the days of Heav'n,
Since Michael and his powers went forth to tame
These disobedient; sore hath been their fight,
As likeliest was, when two such foes met armed;
For to themselves I left them, and thou know'st,
690   Equal in their creation they were formed,
Save what sin hath impaired, which yet hath wrought
Insensibly, for I suspend their doom;
Whence in perpetual fight they needs must last
Endless, and no solution will be found:
695   War wearied hath performed what war can do,
And to disordered rage let loose the reins,
With mountains as with weapons armed, which makes
Wild work in Heav'n, and dangerous to the main.
Two days are therefore passed, the third is thine;
700   For thee I have ordained it, and thus far
Have suffered, that the glory may be thine
Of ending this great war, since none but thou
Can end it. Into thee such virtue and grace
Immense I have transfused, that all may know
705   In Heav'n and Hell thy power above compare,
And this perverse commotion governed thus,
To manifest thee worthiest to be heir
Of all things, to be heir and to be King
By sacred unction, thy deservèd right.
710   Go then thou Mightiest in thy Father's might,
Ascend my chariot, guide the rapid wheels
That shake Heav'n's basis, bring forth all my war,
My bow and thunder, my almighty arms
Gird on, and sword upon thy puissant thigh;
715   Pursue these sons of darkness, drive them out
From all Heav'n's bounds into the utter deep:

There let them learn, as likes them, to despise
God and Messiah his anointed King.
    He said, and on his Son with rays direct
720   Shone full; he all his Father full expressed
Ineffably into his face received,
And thus the filial Godhead answering spake.
    O Father, O Supreme of Heav'nly thrones,
First, highest, holiest, best, thou always seek'st
725   To glorify thy Son, I always thee,
As is most just; this I my glory account,
My exaltation, and my whole delight,
That thou in me well pleased, declar'st thy will
Fulfilled, which to fulfil is all my bliss.
730   Sceptre and power, thy giving, I assume,
And gladlier shall resign, when in the end
Thou shalt be All in All, and I in thee
For ever, and in me all whom thou lov'st:
But whom thou hat'st, I hate, and can put on
735   Thy terrors, as I put thy mildness on,
Image of thee in all things; and shall soon,
Armed with thy might, rid Heav'n of these rebelled,
To their prepared ill mansion driven down
To chains of darkness, and th' undying worm,
740   That from thy just obedience could revolt,
Whom to obey is happiness entire.
Then shall thy saints unmixed, and from th' impure
Far separate, circling thy holy Mount
Unfeignèd hallelujahs to thee sing,
745   Hymns of high praise, and I among them chief.
So said, he o'er his sceptre bowing, rose
From the right hand of Glory where he sat,
And the third sacred morn began to shine
Dawning through Heav'n: forth rushed with whirlwind
        sound
750   The chariot of Paternal Deity,
Flashing thick flames, wheel within wheel undrawn,
Itself instínct with Spirit, but convóyed
By four Cherubic shapes; four faces each
Had wondrous; as with stars their bodies all

755   And wings were set with eyes, with eyes the wheels
       Of beryl, and careering fires between;
       Over their heads a crystal firmament,
       Whereon a sapphire throne, inlaid with pure
       Amber, and colours of the show'ry arch.
760   He in celestial panoply all armed
       Of radiant urim, work divinely wrought,
       Ascended, at his right hand Victory
       Sat eagle-winged, beside him hung his bow
       And quiver with three-bolted thunder stored,
765   And from about him fierce effusion rolled
       Of smoke and bickering flame, and sparkles dire;
       Attended with ten thousand thousand saints,
       He onward came, far off his coming shone,
       And twenty thousand (I their number heard)
770   Chariots of God, half on each hand were seen:
       He on the wings of Cherub rode sublime
       On the crystálline sky, in sapphire throned.
       Illustrious far and wide, but by his own
       First seen; them unexpected joy surprised,
775   When the great ensign of Messiah blazed
       Aloft by angels borne, his sign in Heav'n:
       Under whose conduct Michael soon reduced
       His army, circumfused on either wing,
       Under their Head embodied all in one.
780   Before him Power Divine his way prepared;
       At his command the uprooted hills retired
       Each to his place, they heard his voice and went
       Obsequious; Heav'n his wonted face renewed,
       And with fresh flow'rets hill and valley smiled.
785   This saw his hapless foes but stood obdured,
       And to rebellious fight rallied their powers
       Insensate, hope conceiving from despair.
       In Heav'nly Spirits could such perverseness dwell?
       But to convince the proud what signs avail,
790   Or wonders move th' obdúrate to relent?
       They hardened more by what might most reclaim,
       Grieving to see his glory, at the sight
       Took envy, and aspiring to his heighth,

Stood re-embattled fierce, by force or fraud
795   Weening to prosper, and at length prevail
Against God and Messiah, or to fall
In universal ruin last, and now
To final battle drew, disdaining flight,
Or faint retreat; when the great Son of God
800   To all his host on either hand thus spake.
     Stand still in bright array ye saints, here stand
Ye angels armed, this day from battle rest;
Faithful hath been your warfare, and of God
Accepted, fearless in his righteous cause,
805   And as ye have received, so have ye done
Invincibly; but of this cursèd crew
The punishment to other hand belongs;
Vengeance is his, or whose he sole appoints;
Number to this day's work is not ordained
810   Nor multitude; stand only and behold
God's indignation on these Godless poured
By me; not you but me they have despised,
Yet envied; against me is all their rage,
Because the Father, t' whom in Heav'n supreme
815   Kingdom and power and glory appertains,
Hath honoured me according to his will.
Therefore to me their doom he hath assigned;
That they may have their wish, to try with me
In battle which the stronger proves, they all,
820   Or I alone against them, since by strength
They measure all, of other excellence
Not emulous, nor care who them excels;
Nor other strife with them do I vouchsafe.
    So spake the Son, and into terror changed
825   His count'nance too severe to be beheld
And full of wrath bent on his enemies.
At once the Four spread out their starry wings
With dreadful shade contiguous, and the orbs
Of his fierce chariot rolled, as with the sound
830   Of torrent floods, or of a numerous host.
He on his impious foes right onward drove,

Gloomy as Night; under his burning wheels
The steadfast Empyrean shook throughout,
All but the throne itself of God. Full soon
835   Among them he arrived; in his right hand
Grasping ten thousand thunders, which he sent
Before him, such as in their souls infixed
Plagues; they astonished all resistance lost,
All courage; down their idle weapons dropped;
840   O'er shields and helms, and helmèd heads he rode
Of Thrones and mighty Seraphim prostrate,
That wished the mountains now might be again
Thrown on them as a shelter from his ire.
Nor less on either side tempestuous fell
845   His arrows, from the fourfold-visaged four,
Distinct with eyes, and from the living wheels,
Distinct alike with multitude of eyes;
One spirit in them ruled, and every eye
Glared lightning, and shot forth pernicious fire
850   Among th' accurst, that withered all their strength,
And of their wonted vigour left them drained,
Exhausted, spiritless, afflicted, fall'n.
Yet half his strength he put not forth, but checked
His thunder in mid volley, for he meant
855   Not to destroy, but root them out of Heav'n:
The overthrown he raised, and as a herd
Of goats or timorous flock together thronged
Drove them before him thunderstruck, pursued
With terrors and with furies to the bounds
860   And crystal wall of Heav'n, which op'ning wide,
Rolled inward, and a spacious gap disclosed
Into the wasteful deep; the monstrous sight
Strook them with horror backward, but far worse
Urged them behind; headlong themselves they threw
865   Down from the verge of Heav'n; eternal wrath
Burnt after them to the bottomless pit.
    Hell heard th' unsufferable noise, Hell saw
Heav'n ruining from Heav'n and would have fled
Affrighted; but strict Fate had cast too deep

870   Her dark foundations, and too fast had bound.
        Nine days they fell; confounded Chaos roared,
        And felt tenfold confusion in their fall
        Through his wide anarchy, so huge a rout
        Encumbered him with ruin: Hell at last
875   Yawning received them whole, and on them closed,
        Hell their fit habitation fraught with fire
        Unquenchable, the house of woe and pain.
        Disburdened Heav'n rejoiced, and soon repaired
        Her mural breach, returning whence it rolled.
880   Sole Victor from th' expulsion of his foes
        Messiah his triumphal chariot turned:
        To meet him all his saints, who silent stood
        Eye witnesses of his almighty acts,
        With jubilee advanced; and as they went,
885   Shaded with branching palm, each order bright,
        Sung triumph, and him sung victorious King,
        Son, heir, and Lord, to him dominion giv'n,
        Worthiest to reign: he celebrated rode
        Triumphant through mid Heav'n, into the courts
890   And temple of his mighty Father throned
        On high; who into glory him received,
        Where now he sits at the right hand of bliss.
            Thus measuring things in Heav'n by things on earth
        At thy request, and that thou may'st beware
895   By what is past, to thee I have revealed
        What might have else to human race been hid;
        The discord which befell, and war in Heav'n
        Among th' angelic Powers, and the deep fall
        Of those too high aspiring, who rebelled
900   With Satan, he who envies now thy state,
        Who now is plotting how he may seduce
        Thee also from obedience, that with him
        Bereaved of happiness thou may'st partake
        His punishment, eternal misery;
905   Which would be all his solace and revenge,
        As a despite done against the Most High,
        Thee once to gain companion of his woe.

But listen not to his temptations, warn
Thy weaker; let it profit thee to have heard
910   By terrible example the reward
Of disobedience; firm they might have stood,
Yet fell; remember, and fear to transgress.

BOOK VII

The Argument

Raphael at the request of Adam relates how and wherefore
this world was first created; that God, after the expelling of
Satan and his angels out of Heaven, declared his pleasure to
create another world and other creatures to dwell therein;
sends his Son with glory and attendance of angels to perform
the work of Creation in six days: the angels celebrate with
hymns the performance thereof, and his reascension into
Heaven.

Descend from Heav'n Urania, by that name
If rightly thou art called, whose voice divine
Following, above th' Olympian hill I soar,
Above the flight of Pegasean wing.
The meaning, not the name I call: for thou
Nor of the Muses nine, nor on the top
Of old Olympus dwell'st, but Heav'nly born,
Before the hills appeared, or fountain flowed
Thou with eternal Wisdom didst converse,
Wisdom thy sister, and with her didst play
In presence of th' Almighty Father, pleased
With thy celestial song. Up led by thee
Into the Heav'n of Heav'ns I have presumed,
An earthly guest, and drawn empyreal air,
Thy temp'ring; with like safety guided down
Return me to my native element:
Lest from this flying steed unreined, (as once
Bellerophon, though from a lower clime)
Dismounted, on th' Aleian field I fall
Erroneous there to wander and forlorn.
Half yet remains unsung but narrower bound
Within the visible diurnal sphere;

Standing on earth, not rapt above the pole,
More safe I sing with mortal voice, unchanged
25   To hoarse or mute, though fall'n on evil days,
On evil days though fall'n, and evil tongues;
In darkness, and with dangers compassed round,
And solitude; yet not alone, while thou
Visit'st my slumbers nightly, or when Morn
30   Purples the east: still govern thou my song,
Urania, and fit audience find, though few.
But drive far off the barbarous dissonance
Of Bacchus and his revellers, the race
Of that wild rout that tore the Thracian bard
35   In Rhodope, where woods and rocks had ears
To rapture, till the savage clamour drowned
Both harp and voice; nor could the Muse defend
Her son. So fail not thou, who thee implores:
For thou art Heav'nly, she an empty dream.
40   Say Goddess, what ensued when Raphael,
The affable Archangel, had forewarned
Adam by dire example to beware
Apostasy, by what befell in Heaven
To those apostates, lest the like befall
45   In Paradise to Adam or his race,
Charged not to touch the interdicted Tree,
If they transgress, and slight that sole command,
So easily obeyed amid the choice
Of all tastes else to please their appetite,
50   Though wand'ring. He with his consorted Eve
The story heard attentive, and was filled
With admiration, and deep muse to hear
Of things so high and strange, things to their thought
So unimaginable as hate in Heav'n,
55   And war so near the peace of God in bliss
With such confusion: but the evil soon
Driv'n back redounded as a flood on those
From whom it sprung, impossible to mix
With blessedness. Whence Adam soon repealed
60   The doubts that in his heart arose: and now
Led on, yet sinless, with desire to know

What nearer might concern him, how this world
Of heav'n and earth conspicuous first began,
When, and whereof created, for what cause,
65 What within Eden or without was done
Before his memory, as one whose drouth
Yet scarce allayed still eyes the current stream,
Whose liquid murmur heard new thirst excites,
Proceeded thus to ask his Heav'nly guest.
70   Great things and full of wonder in our ears,
Far differing from this world, thou hast revealed
Divine interpreter, by favour sent
Down from the Empyrean to forewarn
Us timely of what might else have been our loss,
75 Unknown, which human knowledge could not reach:
For which to the infinitely Good we owe
Immortal thanks, and his admonishment
Receive with solemn purpose to observe
Immutably his sov'reign will, the end
80 Of what we are. But since thou hast vouchsafed
Gently for our instruction to impart
Things above earthly thought, which yet concerned
Our knowing, as to highest Wisdom seemed,
Deign to descend now lower, and relate
85 What may no less perhaps avail us known,
How first began this heav'n which we behold
Distant so high, with moving fires adorned
Innumerable, and that which yields or fills
All space, the ambient air wide interfused
90 Embracing round this florid earth; what cause
Moved the Creator in his holy rest
Through all eternity so late to build
In Chaos, and the work begun, how soon
Absolved, if unforbid thou may'st unfold
95 What we, not to explore the secrets ask
Of his eternal empire, but the more
To magnify his works, the more we know.
And the great light of day yet wants to run
Much of his race though steep, suspense in heav'n
100 Held by thy voice, thy potent voice he hears,

And longer will delay to hear thee tell
His generation, and the rising birth
Of Nature from the unapparent deep:
Or if the star of ev'ning and the moon
105   Haste to thy audience, night with her will bring
Silence, and sleep list'ning to thee will watch,
Or we can bid his absence, till thy song
End, and dismiss thee ere the morning shine.
     Thus Adam his illustrious guest besought:
110   And thus the godlike angel answered mild.
This also thy request with caution asked
Obtain: though to recount Almighty works
What words or tongue of Seraph can suffice,
Or heart of man suffice to comprehend?
115   Yet what thou canst attain, which best may serve
To glorify the Maker, and infer
Thee also happier, shall not be withheld
Thy hearing, such commission from above
I have received, to answer thy desire
120   Of knowledge within bounds; beyond abstain
To ask, nor let thine own inventions hope
Things not revealed, which th' invisible King,
Only omniscient, hath suppressed in night,
To none communicable in earth or Heaven:
125   Enough is left besides to search and know.
But knowledge is as food, and needs no less
Her temperance over appetite, to know
In measure what the mind may well contain,
Oppresses else with surfeit, and soon turns
130   Wisdom to folly, as nourishment to wind.
     Know then, that after Lucifer from Heav'n
(So call him, brighter once amidst the host
Of angels, than that star the stars among)
Fell with his flaming legions through the deep
135   Into his place, and the great Son returned
Victorious with his saints, th' Omnipotent
Eternal Father from his throne beheld
Their multitude, and to his Son thus spake.
     At least our envious Foe hath failed, who thought

140 All like himself rebellious, by whose aid
 This inaccessible high strength, the seat
 Of Deity supreme, us dispossessed,
 He trusted to have seized, and into fraud
 Drew many, who their place knows here no more;
145 Yet far the greater part have kept, I see,
 Their station, Heav'n yet populous retains
 Number sufficient to possess her realms
 Though wide, and this high temple to frequent
 With ministeries due and solemn rites:
150 But lest his heart exalt him in the harm
 Already done, to have dispeopled Heav'n,
 My damage fondly deemed, I can repair
 That detriment, if such it be to lose
 Self-lost, and in a moment will create
155 Another world, out of one man a race
 Of men innumerable, there to dwell,
 Not here, till by degrees of merit raised
 They open to themselves at length the way
 Up hither, under long obedience tried,
160 And earth be changed to Heav'n, and Heav'n to earth,
 One Kingdom, joy and union without end.
 Meanwhile inhabit lax, ye Powers of Heav'n,
 And thou my Word, begotten Son, by thee
 This I perform, speak thou, and be it done:
165 My overshadowing Spirit and might with thee
 I send along, ride forth, and bid the deep
 Within appointed bounds be heav'n and earth;
 Boundless the deep, because I am who fill
 Infinitude, nor vacuous the space.
170 Though I uncircumscribed myself retire,
 And put not forth my goodness, which is free
 To act or not; Necessity and Chance
 Approach not me, and what I will is Fate.
  So spake th' Almighty, and to what he spake
175 His Word, the filial Godhead, gave effect.
 Immediate are the acts of God, more swift
 Than time or motion, but to human ears
 Cannot without procéss of speech be told,

So told as earthly notion can receive.
180   Great triumph and rejoicing was in Heav'n
When such was heard declared the Almighty's will;
Glory was sung to the Most High, good will
To future men, and in their dwellings peace:
Glory to him whose just avenging ire
185   Had driven out th' ungodly from his sight
And th' habitations of the just; to him
Glory and praise, whose wisdom had ordained
Good out of evil to create, instead
Of Spirits malign a better race to bring
190   Into their vacant room, and thence diffuse
His good to worlds and ages infinite.
So sang the hierarchies: meanwhile the Son
On his great expedition now appeared,
Girt with omnipotence, with radiance crowned
195   Of majesty divine, sapience and love
Immense, and all his Father in him shone.
About his chariot numberless were poured
Cherub and Seraph, Potentates and Thrones,
And Virtues, wingèd Spirits, and chariots winged,
200   From the armoury of God, where stand of old
Myriads between two brazen mountains lodged
Against a solemn day, harnessed at hand,
Celestial equipage; and now came forth
Spontaneous, for within them Spirit lived,
205   Attendant on their Lord: Heav'n opened wide
Her ever-during gates, harmonious sound
On golden hinges moving, to let forth
The King of Glory in his powerful Word
And Spirit coming to create more worlds.
210   On Heav'nly ground they stood, and from the shore
They viewed the vast immeasurable abyss
Outrageous as a sea, dark, wasteful, wild,
Up from the bottom turned by furious winds
And surging waves, as mountains to assault
215   Heav'n's heighth, and with the centre mix the pole.
        Silence, ye troubled waves, and thou deep, peace
Said then th' omnific Word, your discord end:

Nor stayed, but on the wings of Cherubim
Uplifted, in paternal glory rode
220 Far into Chaos, and the world unborn;
For Chaos heard his voice: him all his train
Followed in bright procession to behold
Creation, and the wonders of his might.
Then stayed the fervid wheels, and in his hand
225 He took the golden compasses, prepared
In God's eternal store, to circumscribe
This universe and all created things:
One foot he centred, and the other turned
Round through the vast profundity obscure,
230 And said, Thus far extend, thus far thy bounds,
This be thy just circumference, O world.
Thus God the heav'n created, thus the earth,
Matter unformed and void: darkness profound
Covered th' abyss: but on the wat'ry calm
235 His brooding wings the Spirit of God outspread,
And vital virtue infused, and vital warmth
Throughout the fluid mass, but downward purged
The black tartareous cold infernal dregs
Adverse to life: then founded, then conglobed
240 Like things to like, the rest to several place
Disparted, and between spun out the air,
And earth self-balanced on her centre hung.
    Let there be light, said God, and forthwith light
Ethereal, first of things, quintessence pure
245 Sprung from the deep, and from her native east
To journey through the airy gloom began,
Sphered in a radiant cloud, for yet the sun
Was not; she in a cloudy tabernacle
Sojourned the while. God saw the light was good;
250 And light from darkness by the hemisphere
Divided: light the day, and darkness night
He named. Thus was the first day ev'n and morn:
Nor passed uncelebrated, nor unsung
By the celestial choirs, when orient light
255 Exhaling first from darkness they beheld;
Birthday of heav'n and earth; with joy and shout

The hollow universal orb they filled,
And touched their golden harps, and hymning praised
God and his works; Creator him they sung,
260   Both when first ev'ning was, and when first morn.
    Again, God said, let there be firmament
Amid the waters, and let it divide
The waters from the waters: and God made
The firmament, expanse of liquid, pure,
265   Transparent, elemental air, diffused
In circuit to the uttermost convéx
Of this great round: partition firm and sure,
The waters underneath from those above
Dividing: for as the earth, so he the world
270   Built on circumfluous waters calm, in wide
Crystálline ocean, and the loud misrule
Of Chaos far removed, lest fierce extremes
Contiguous might distemper the whole frame:
And heav'n he named the firmament: so ev'n
275   And morning chorus sung the second day.
    The earth was formed, but in the womb as yet
Of waters, embryon immature involved,
Appeared not: over all the face of earth
Main ocean flowed, not idle, but with warm
280   Prolific humour soft'ning all her globe,
Fermented the Great Mother to conceive,
Satiate with genial moisture, when God said
Be gathered now ye waters under heav'n
Into one place, and let dry land appear.
285   Immediately the mountains huge appear
Emergent, and their broad bare backs upheave
Into the clouds, their tops ascend the sky:
So high as heaved the tumid hills, so low
Down sunk a hollow bottom broad and deep,
290   Capacious bed of waters: thither they
Hasted with glad precipitance, uprolled
As drops on dust conglobing from the dry;
Part rise in crystal wall, or ridge direct,
For haste; such flight the great command impressed
295   On the swift floods: as armies at the call

Of trumpet (for of armies thou hast heard)
Troop to their standard, so the wat'ry throng,
Wave rolling after wave, where way they found,
If steep, with torrent rapture, if through plain,
300 Soft-ebbing; nor withstood them rock or hill,
But they, or under ground, or circuit wide
With serpent error wand'ring, found their way,
And on the washy ooze deep channels wore;
Easy, ere God had bid the ground be dry.
305 All but within those banks, where rivers now
Stream, and perpetual draw their humid train.
The dry land, earth, and the great receptacle
Of congregated waters he called seas:
And saw that it was good, and said, Let th' earth
310 Put forth the verdant grass, herb yielding seed,
And fruit tree yielding fruit after her kind;
Whose seed is in herself upon the earth.
He scarce had said, when the bare earth, till then
Desert and bare, unsightly, unadorned,
315 Brought forth the tender grass, whose verdure clad
Her universal face with pleasant green,
Then herbs of every leaf, that sudden flow'red
Op'ning their various colours, and made gay
Her bosom smelling sweet: and these scarce blown,
320 Forth flourished thick the clust'ring vine, forth crept
The swelling gourd, up stood the corny reed
Embattled in her field: and the humble shrub,
And bush with frizzled hair implicit: last
Rose as in dance the stately trees, and spread
325 Their branches hung with copious fruit; or gemmed
Their blossoms: with high woods the hills were crowned,
With tufts the valleys and each fountain side,
With borders long the rivers. That earth now
Seemed like to Heav'n, a seat where gods might dwell,
330 Or wander with delight, and love to haunt
Her sacred shades: though God had not yet rained
Upon the earth, and man to till the ground
None was, but from the earth a dewy mist
Went up and watered all the ground, and each

335 Plant of the field, which ere it was in the earth
     God made, and every herb, before it grew
     On the green stem; God saw that it was good:
     So ev'n and morn recorded the third day.
           Again th' Almighty spake: Let there be lights
340 High in th' expanse of heaven to divide
     The day from night; and let them be for signs,
     For seasons, and for days, and circling years,
     And let them be for lights as I ordain
     Their office in the firmament of heav'n
345 To give light on the earth; and it was so.
     And God made two great lights, great for their use
     To man, the greater to have rule by day,
     The less by night altern: and made the stars,
     And set them in the firmament of heav'n
350 To illuminate the earth, and rule the day
     In their vicissitude, and rule the night,
     And light from darkness to divide. God saw,
     Surveying his great work, that it was good:
     For of celestial bodies first the sun
355 A mighty sphere he framed, unlightsome first,
     Though of ethereal mould: then formed the moon
     Globose, and every magnitude of stars,
     And sowed with stars the heaven thick as a field:
     Of light by far the greater part he took,
360 Transplanted from her cloudy shrine, and placed
     In the sun's orb, made porous to receive
     And drink the liquid light, firm to retain
     Her gathered beams, great palace now of light.
     Hither as to their fountain other stars
365 Repairing, in their golden urns draw light,
     And hence the morning planet gilds his horns;
     By tincture or reflection they augment
     Their small peculiar, though from human sight
     So far remote, with diminution seen.
370 First in his east the glorious lamp was seen,
     Regent of day, and all th' horizon round
     Invested with bright rays, jocund to run
     His longitude through heav'n's high road: the grey

Dawn, and Pleiades before him danced
375   Shedding sweet influence: less bright the moon,
But opposite in levelled west was set
His mirror, with full face borrowing her light
From him, for other light she needed none
In that aspéct, and still that distance keeps
380   Till night, then in the east her turn she shines,
Revolved on heaven's great axle, and her reign
With thousand lesser lights dividual holds,
With thousand thousand stars, that then appeared
Spangling the hemisphere: then first adorned
385   With their bright luminaries that set and rose,
Glad ev'ning and glad morn crowned the fourth day.
    And God said, Let the waters generate
Reptile with spawn abundant, living soul:
And let fowl fly about the earth, with wings
390   Displayed on the op'n firmament of heav'n.
And God created the great whales, and each
Soul living, each that crept, which plenteously
The waters generated by their kinds,
And every bird of wing after his kind;
395   And saw that it was good, and blessed them, saying,
Be fruitful, multiply, and in the seas
And lakes and running streams the waters fill;
And let the fowl be multiplied on the earth.
Forthwith the sounds and seas, each creek and bay
400   With fry innumerable swarm, and shoals
Of fish that with their fins and shining scales
Glide under the green wave, in schools that oft
Bank the mid sea: part single or with mate
Graze the sea-weed their pasture, and through groves
405   Of coral stray, or sporting with quick glance
Show to the sun their waved coats dropped with gold,
Or in their pearly shells at ease, attend
Moist nutriment, or under rocks their food
In jointed armour watch: on smooth the seal,
410   And bended dolphins play: part huge of bulk
Wallowing unwieldy, enormous in their gait
Tempest the ocean: there Leviathan

Hugest of living creatures, on the deep
Stretched like a promontory sleeps or swims,
415   And seems a moving land, and at his gills
Draws in, and at his trunk spouts out a sea.
Meanwhile the tepid caves, and fens and shores
Their brood as numerous hatch, from the egg that soon
Bursting with kindly rupture forth disclosed
420   Their callow young, but feathered soon and fledge
They summed their pens, and soaring th' air sublime
With clang despised the ground, under a cloud
In prospect; there the eagle and the stork
On cliffs and cedar tops their eyries build:
425   Part loosely wing the region, part more wise
In common, ranged in figure wedge their way,
Intelligent of seasons, and set forth
Their airy caravan high over seas
Flying, and over lands with mutual wing
430   Easing their flight; so steers the prudent crane
Her annual voyage, borne on winds; the air
Floats, as they pass, fanned with unnumbered plumes:
From branch to branch the smaller birds with song
Solaced the woods, and spread their painted wings
435   Till ev'n, nor then the solemn nightingale
Ceased warbling, but all night tuned her soft lays:
Others on silver lakes and rivers bathed
Their downy breast; the swan with archèd neck
Between her white wings mantling proudly, rows
440   Her state with oary feet: yet oft they quit
The dank, and rising on stiff pennons, tow'r
The mid aërial sky: others on ground
Walked firm; the crested cock whose clarion sounds
The silent hours, and th' other whose gay train
445   Adorns him, coloured with the florid hue
Of rainbows and starry eyes. The waters thus
With fish replenished, and the air with fowl,
Ev'ning and morn solémnized the fifth day.
    The sixth, and of Creation last arose
450   With ev'ning harps and matin, when God said,
Let the earth bring forth soul living in her kind,

Cattle and creeping things, and beast of the earth,
Each in their kind. The earth obeyed, and straight
Op'ning her fertile womb teemed at a birth
455 Innumerous living creatures, perfect forms,
Limbed and full-grown: out of the ground uprose
As from his lair the wild beast where he wons
In forest wild, in thicket, brake, or den;
Among the trees in pairs they rose, they walked:
460 The cattle in the fields and meadows green:
Those rare and solitary, these in flocks
Pasturing at once, and in broad herds upsprung.
The grassy clods now calved, now half appeared
The tawny lion, pawing to get free
465 His hinder parts, then springs as broke from bonds,
And rampant shakes his brinded mane; the ounce,
The libbard and the tiger, as the mole
Rising, the crumbled earth above them threw
In hillocks; the swift stag from under ground
470 Bore up his branching head: scarce from his mould
Behemoth biggest born of earth upheaved
His vastness: fleeced the flocks and bleating rose,
As plants: ambiguous between sea and land
The river horse and scaly crocodile.
475 At once came forth whatever creeps the ground,
Insect or worm; those waved their limber fans
For wings, and smallest lineaments exact
In all the liveries decked of summer's pride
With spots of gold and purple, azure and green:
480 These as a line their long dimension drew,
Streaking the ground with sinuous trace; not all
Minims of nature; some of serpent kind
Wondrous in length and corpulence involved
Their snaky folds, and added wings. First crept
485 The parsimonious emmet, provident
Of future, in small room large heart enclosed,
Pattern of just equality perhaps
Hereafter, joined in her popular tribes
Of commonalty: swarming next appeared
490 The female bee that feeds her husband drone

Deliciously, and builds her waxen cells
With honey stored: the rest are numberless,
And thou their natures know'st, and gav'st them names,
Needless to thee repeated; nor unknown
495   The serpent subtlest beast of all the field,
Of huge extent sometimes, with brazen eyes
And hairy mane terrific, though to thee
Not noxious, but obedient at thy call.
Now heav'n in all her glory shone, and rolled
500   Her motions, as the great First Mover's hand
First wheeled their course; earth in her rich attire
Consummate lovely smiled; air, water, earth,
By fowl, fish, beast, was flown, was swum, was walked
Frequent; and of the sixth day yet remained;
505   There wanted yet the master work, the end
Of all yet done; a creature who not prone
And brute as other creatures, but endued
With sanctity of reason, might erect
His stature, and upright with front serene
510   Govern the rest, self-knowing, and from thence
Magnanimous to correspond with Heav'n,
But grateful to acknowledge whence his good
Descends, thither with heart and voice and eyes
Directed in devotion, to adore
515   And worship God supreme, who made him chief
Of all his works: therefore the Omnipotent
Eternal Father (for where is not he
Present) thus to his Son audibly spake.
   Let us make now man in our image, man
520   In our similitude, and let them rule
Over the fish and fowl of sea and air,
Beast of the field, and over all the earth,
And every creeping thing that creeps the ground.
This said, he formed thee, Adam, thee O man
525   Dust of the ground, and in thy nostrils breathed
The breath of life; in his image he
Created thee, in the image of God
Express, and thou becam'st a living soul.
Male he created thee, but thy consort

530 Female for race; then blessed mankind, and said,
Be fruitful, multiply, and fill the earth,
Subdue it, and throughout dominion hold
Over fish of the sea, and fowl of the air,
And every living thing that moves on the earth.

535 Wherever thus created, for no place
Is yet distinct by name, thence, as thou know'st
He brought thee into this delicious grove,
This garden, planted with the trees of God,
Delectable both to behold and taste;

540 And freely all their pleasant fruit for food
Gave thee, all sorts are here that all th' earth yields,
Variety without end; but of the Tree
Which tasted works Knowledge of Good and Evil,
Thou may'st not; in the day thou eat'st, thou diest;

545 Death is the penalty imposed, beware,
And govern well thy appetite, lest Sin
Surprise thee, and her black attendant Death.
Here finished he, and all that he had made
Viewed, and behold all was entirely good;

550 So ev'n and morn accomplished the sixth day:
Yet not till the Creator from his work
Desisting, though unwearied, up returned
Up to the Heav'n of Heav'ns his high abode,
Thence to behold this new created world

555 Th' addition of his empire, how it showed
In prospect from his throne, how good, how fair,
Answering his great Idea. Up he rode
Followed with acclamation and the sound
Symphonious of ten thousand harps that tuned

560 Angelic harmonies: the earth, the air
Resounded, (thou remember'st, for thou heard'st)
The heav'ns and all the constellations rung,
The planets in their stations list'ning stood,
While the bright pomp ascended jubilant.

565 Open, ye everlasting gates, they sung,
Open, ye Heav'ns, your living doors; let in
The great Creator from his work returned
Magnificent, his six days' work, a world;

Open, and henceforth oft; for God will deign
570 To visit oft the dwellings of just men
Delighted, and with frequent intercourse
Thither will send his wingèd messengers
On errands of supernal grace. So sung
The glorious train ascending: he through Heav'n,
575 That opened wide her blazing portals, led
To God's eternal house direct the way,
A broad and ample road, whose dust is gold
And pavement stars, as stars to thee appear,
Seen in the Galaxy, that Milky Way
580 Which nightly as a circling zone thou seest
Powdered with stars. And now on earth the seventh
Ev'ning arose in Eden, for the sun
Was set, and twilight from the east came on,
Forerunning night; when at the holy Mount
585 Of Heav'n's high-seated top, th' imperial throne
Of Godhead, fixed for ever firm and sure,
The Filial Power arrived, and sat him down
With his great Father (for he also went
Invisible, yet stayed: such privilege
590 Hath Omnipresence) and the work ordained,
Author and end of all things, and from work
Now resting, blessed and hallowed the seventh day,
As resting on that day from all his work,
But not in silence holy kept; the harp
595 Had work and rested not, the solemn pipe,
And dulcimer, and organs of sweet stop,
All sounds on fret by string or golden wire
Tempered soft tunings, intermixed with voice
Choral or unison: of incense clouds
600 Fuming from golden censers hid the Mount.
Creation and the six days' acts they sung,
Great are thy works, Jehovah, infinite
Thy power; what thought can measure thee or tongue
Relate thee; greater now in thy return
605 Than from the Giant angels; thee that day
Thy thunders magnified; but to create
Is greater than created to destroy.

Who can impair thee, mighty King, or bound
Thy empire? easily the proud attempt
610 Of Spirits apostate and their counsels vain
Thou hast repelled, while impiously they thought
Thee to diminish, and from thee withdraw
The number of thy worshippers. Who seeks
To lessen thee, against his purpose serves
615 To manifest the more thy might: his evil
Thou usest, and from thence creat'st more good.
Witness this new-made world, another Heav'n
From Heaven gate not far, founded in view
On the clear hyaline, the glassy sea;
620 Of amplitude almost immense, with stars
Numerous, and every star perhaps a world
Of destined habitation; but thou know'st
Their seasons: among these the seat of men,
Earth with her nether Ocean circumfused,
625 Their pleasant dwelling place. Thrice happy men,
And sons of men, whom God hath thus advanced,
Created in his image, there to dwell
And worship him, and in reward to rule
Over his works, on earth, in sea, or air,
630 And multiply a race of worshippers
Holy and just: thrice happy if they know
Their happiness, and persevere upright.
    So sung they, and the Empyrean rung,
With hallelujahs: thus was the Sabbath kept.
635 And thy request think now fulfilled, that asked
How first this world and face of things began,
And what before thy memory was done
From the beginning, that posterity
Informed by thee might know; if else thou seek'st
640 Aught, not surpassing human measure, say.

BOOK VIII

The Argument

Adam inquires concerning celestial motions, is doubtfully answered, and exhorted to search rather things more worthy of knowledge: Adam assents, and still desirous to detain Raphael, relates to him what he remembered since his own
5 creation, his placing in Paradise, his talk with God concerning solitude and fit society, his first meeting and nuptials with Eve, his discourse with the angel thereupon; who after admonitions repeated departs.

The angel ended, and in Adam's ear
So charming left his voice, that he a while
Thought him still speaking, still stood fixed to hear;
Then as new waked thus gratefully replied.
5 What thanks sufficient, or what recompense
Equal have I to render thee, divine
Historian, who thus largely hast allayed
The thirst I had of knowledge, and vouchsafed
This friendly condescension to relate
10 Things else by me unsearchable, now heard
With wonder, but delight, and, as is due,
With glory áttribúted to the high
Creator; something yet of doubt remains,
Which only thy solution can resolve.
15 When I behold this goodly frame, this world
Of heav'n and earth consisting, and compute
Their magnitudes, this earth a spot, a grain,
An atom, with the firmament compared
And all her numbered stars, that seem to roll
20 Spaces incomprehensible (for such
Their distance argues and their swift return
Diurnal) merely to officiate light

Round this opacous earth, this punctual spot,
One day and night; in all their vast survéy
25   Useless besides, reasoning I oft admire,
How Nature wise and frugal could commit
Such disproportions, with superfluous hand
So many nobler bodies to create,
Greater so manifold, to this one use,
30   For aught appears, and on their orbs impose
Such restless revolution day by day
Repeated, while the sedentary earth,
That better might with far less compass move,
Served by more noble than herself, attains
35   Her end without least motion, and receives,
As tribute such a sumless journey brought
Of incorporeal speed, her warmth and light;
Speed, to describe whose swiftness number fails.
      So spake our sire, and by his count'nance seemed
40   Ent'ring on studious thoughts abstruse, which Eve
Perceiving where she sat retired in sight,
With lowliness majestic from her seat,
And grace that won who saw to wish her stay,
Rose, and went forth among her fruits and flow'rs,
45   To visit how they prospered, bud and bloom,
Her nursery; they at her coming sprung
And touched by her fair tendance gladlier grew.
Yet went she not, as not with such discourse
Delighted, or not capable her ear
50   Of what was high: such pleasure she reserved,
Adam relating, she sole auditress;
Her husband the relater she preferred
Before the angel, and of him to ask
Chose rather; he, she knew would intermix
55   Grateful digressions, and solve high dispute
With conjugal caresses; from his lip
Not words alone pleased her. O when meet now
Such pairs, in love and mutual honour joined?
With goddess-like demeanour forth she went;
60   Not unattended, for on her as queen
A pomp of winning Graces waited still,

And from about her shot darts of desire
Into all eyes to wish her still in sight.
And Raphael now to Adam's doubt proposed
65   Benevolent and facile thus replied.
    To ask or search I blame thee not, for heav'n
Is as the Book of God before thee set,
Wherein to read his wondrous works, and learn
His seasons, hours, or days, or months, or years:
70   This to attain, whether heav'n move or earth,
Imports not, if thou reckon right; the rest
From man or angel the great Architect
Did wisely to conceal, and not divulge
His secrets to be scanned by them who ought
75   Rather admire; or if they list to try
Conjecture, he his fabric of the heav'ns
Hath left to their disputes, perhaps to move
His laughter at their quaint opinions wide
Hereafter, when they come to model heav'n
80   And calculate the stars, how they will wield
The mighty frame, how build, unbuild, contrive
To save appearances, how gird the sphere
With centric and eccentric scribbled o'er,
Cycle and epicycle, orb in orb:
85   Already by thy reasoning this I guess,
Who art to lead thy offspring, and supposest
That bodies bright and greater should not serve
The less not bright, nor heav'n such journeys run,
Earth sitting still, when she alone receives
90   The benefit: consider first, that great
Or bright infers not excellence; the earth
Though, in comparison of heav'n, so small,
Nor glistering, may of solid good contain
More plenty than the sun that barren shines,
95   Whose virtue on itself works no effect,
But in the fruitful earth; there first received
His beams, unactive else, their vigour find.
Yet not to earth are those bright luminaries
Officious, but to thee earth's habitant.
100   And for heav'n's wide circuit, let it speak

The Maker's high magnificence, who built
So spacious, and his line stretched out so far;
That man may know he dwells not in his own;
An edifice too large for him to fill,
105   Lodged in a small partition, and the rest
Ordained for uses to his Lord best known.
The swiftness of those circles áttribúte,
Though numberless, to his Omnipotence,
That to corporeal substances could add
110   Speed almost spiritual; me thou think'st not slow,
Who since the morning hour set out from Heav'n
Where God resides, and ere mid-day arrived
In Eden, distance inexpressible
By numbers that have name. But this I urge,
115   Admitting motion in the heav'ns, to show
Invalid that which thee to doubt it moved;
Not that I so affirm, though so it seem
To thee who hast thy dwelling here on earth.
God to remove his ways from human sense,
120   Placed heav'n from earth so far, that earthly sight,
If it presume, might err in things too high,
And no advantage gain. What if the sun
Be centre to the world, and other stars
By his attractive virtue and their own
125   Incited, dance about him various rounds?
Their wand'ring course now high, now low, then hid,
Progressive, retrograde, or standing still,
In six thou seest, and what if seventh to these
The planet earth, so steadfast though she seem,
130   Insensibly three different motions move?
Which else to several spheres thou must ascribe,
Moved contrary with thwart obliquities,
Or save the sun his labour, and that swift
Nocturnal and diurnal rhomb supposed,
135   Invisible else above all stars, the wheel
Of day and night; which needs not thy belief,
If earth industrious of herself fetch day
Travelling east, and with her part averse
From the sun's beam meet night, her other part

140 Still luminous by his ray. What if that light
  Sent from her through the wide transpicuous air,
  To the terrestrial moon be as a star
  Enlight'ning her by day, as she by night
  This earth? reciprocal, if land be there,
145 Fields and inhabitants: her spots thou seest
  As clouds, and clouds may rain, and rain produce
  Fruits in her softened soil, for some to eat
  Allotted there; and other suns perhaps
  With their attendant moons thou wilt descry
150 Communicating male and female light,
  Which two great sexes animate the world,
  Stored in each orb perhaps with some that live.
  For such vast room in Nature unpossessed
  By living soul, desért and desolate,
155 Only to shine, yet scarce to cóntribute
  Each orb a glimpse of light, conveyed so far
  Down to this habitable, which returns
  Light back to them, is obvious to dispute.
  But whether thus these things, or whether not,
160 Whether the sun predominant in heav'n
  Rise on the earth, or earth rise on the sun,
  He from the east his flaming road begin,
  Or she from west her silent course advance
  With inoffensive pace that spinning sleeps
165 On her soft axle, while she paces ev'n,
  And bears thee soft with the smooth air along,
  Solicit not thy thoughts with matters hid,
  Leave them to God above, him serve and fear;
  Of other creatures, as him pleases best,
170 Wherever placed, let him dispose: joy thou
  In what he gives to thee, this Paradise
  And thy fair Eve; heav'n is too high
  To know what passes there; be lowly wise:
  Think only what concerns thee and thy being;
175 Dream not of other worlds, what creatures there
  Live, in what state, condition or degree,
  Contented that thus far hath been revealed
  Not of earth only but of highest Heav'n.

To whom thus Adam cleared of doubt, replied.
180   How fully hast thou satisfied me, pure
Intelligence of Heav'n, angel serene,
And freed from intricacies, taught to live,
The easiest way, nor with perplexing thoughts
To interrupt the sweet of life, from which
185   God hath bid dwell far off all anxious cares,
And not molest us, unless we ourselves
Seek them with wand'ring thoughts, and notions vain.
But apt the mind or fancy is to rove
Unchecked, and of her roving is no end;
190   Till warned, or by experience taught, she learn,
That not to know at large of things remote
From use, obscure and subtle, but to know
That which before us lies in daily life,
Is the prime wisdom; what is more, is fume,
195   Or emptiness, or fond impertinence,
And renders us in things that most concern
Unpractised, unprepared, and still to seek.
Therefore from this high pitch let us descend
A lower flight, and speak of things at hand
200   Useful, whence haply mention may arise
Of something not unseasonable to ask
By sufferance, and thy wonted favour deigned.
Thee I have heard relating what was done
Ere my remembrance: now hear me relate
205   My story, which perhaps thou hast not heard;
And day is yet not spent; till then thou seest
How subtly to detain thee I devise,
Inviting thee to hear while I relate,
Fond, were it not in hope of thy reply:
210   For while I sit with thee, I seem in Heav'n,
And sweeter thy discourse is to my ear
Than fruits of palm-tree pleasantest to thirst
And hunger both, from labour, at the hour
Of sweet repast; they satiate, and soon fill,
215   Though pleasant, but thy words with grace divine
Imbued, bring to their sweetness no satiety.
To whom thus Raphael answered Heav'nly meek.

Nor are thy lips ungraceful, sire of men,
Nor tongue ineloquent; for God on thee
220 Abundantly his gifts hath also poured
Inward and outward both, his image fair:
Speaking or mute all comeliness and grace
Attends thee, and each word, each motion forms.
Nor less think we in Heav'n of thee on earth
225 Than of our fellow servant, and inquire
Gladly into the ways of God with man:
For God we see hath honoured thee, and set
On man his equal love: say therefore on;
For I that day was absent, as befell,
230 Bound on a voyage uncouth and obscure,
Far on excursion toward the gates of Hell;
Squared in full legion (such command we had)
To see that none thence issued forth a spy,
Or enemy, while God was in his work,
235 Lest he incensed at such eruption bold,
Destruction with Creation might have mixed.
Not that they durst without his leave attempt,
But us he sends upon his high behests
For state, as sov'reign King, and to inure
240 Our prompt obedience. Fast we found, fast shut
The dismal gates, and barricadoed strong;
But long ere our approaching heard within
Noise, other than the sound of dance or song,
Torment, and loud lament, and furious rage.
245 Glad we returned up to the coasts of light
Ere sabbath ev'ning: so we had in charge.
But thy relation now; for I attend,
Pleased with thy words no less than thou with mine.
    So spake the Godlike Power, and thus our sire.
250 For man to tell how human life began
Is hard; for who himself beginning knew?
Desire with thee still longer to converse
Induced me. As new waked from soundest sleep
Soft on the flow'ry herb I found me laid
255 In balmy sweat, which with his beams the sun
Soon dried, and on the reeking moisture fed.

Straight toward heav'n my wond'ring eyes I turned,
And gazed a while the ample sky, till raised
By quick instinctive motion up I sprung,
260 As thitherward endeavouring, and upright
Stood on my feet; about me round I saw
Hill, dale, and shady woods, and sunny plains,
And liquid lapse of murmuring streams; by these,
Creatures that lived, and moved, and walked, or flew,
265 Birds on the branches warbling; all things smiled,
With fragrance and with joy my heart o'erflowed.
Myself I then perused, and limb by limb
Surveyed, and sometimes went, and sometimes ran
With supple joints, as lively vigour led:
270 But who I was, or where, or from what cause,
Knew not; to speak I tried, and forthwith spake,
My tongue obeyed and readily could name
Whate'er I saw. Thou sun, said I, fair light,
And thou enlightened earth, so fresh and gay,
275 Ye hills and dales, ye rivers, woods, and plains,
And ye that live and move, fair creatures, tell,
Tell, if ye saw, how came I thus, how here?
Not of myself; by some great Maker then,
In goodness and in power pre-eminent;
280 Tell me, how may I know him, how adore,
From whom I have that thus I move and live,
And feel that I am happier than I know.
While thus I called, and strayed I knew not whither,
From where I first drew air, and first beheld
285 This happy light, when answer none returned,
On a green shady bank profuse of flow'rs
Pensive I sat me down; there gentle sleep
First found me, and with soft oppression seized
My drowsèd sense, untroubled, though I thought
290 I then was passing to my former state
Insensible, and forthwith to dissolve:
When suddenly stood at my head a dream,
Whose inward apparition gently moved
My fancy to believe I yet had being,
295 And lived: one came, methought, of shape divine,

And said, thy mansion wants thee, Adam, rise,
First man, of men innumerable ordained
First father, called by thee I come thy guide
To the garden of bliss, thy seat prepared.
300   So saying, by the hand he took me raised,
And over fields and waters, as in air
Smooth sliding without step, last led me up
A woody mountain; whose high top was plain,
A circuit wide, enclosed, with goodliest trees
305   Planted, with walks, and bowers, that what I saw
Of earth before scarce pleasant seemed. Each tree
Loaden with fairest fruit that hung to the eye
Tempting, stirred in me sudden appetite
To pluck and eat; whereat I waked, and found
310   Before mine eyes all real, as the dream
Had lively shadowed: here had new begun
My wand'ring, had not he who was my guide
Up hither, from among the trees appeared
Presence divine. Rejoicing, but with awe
315   In adoration at his feet I fell
Submiss: he reared me, and Whom thou sought'st I am,
Said mildly, Author of all this thou seest
Above, or round about thee or beneath.
This Paradise I give thee, count it thine
320   To till and keep, and of the fruit to eat:
Of every tree that in the garden grows
Eat freely with glad heart; fear here no dearth:
But of the tree whose operation brings
Knowledge of good and ill, which I have set
325   The pledge of thy obedience and thy faith,
Amid the garden by the Tree of Life,
Remember what I warn thee, shun to taste,
And shun the bitter consequence: for know,
The day thou eat'st thereof, my sole command
330   Transgressed, inevitably thou shalt die;
From that day mortal, and this happy state
Shalt lose, expelled from hence into a world
Of woe and sorrow. Sternly he pronounced
The rigid interdiction, which resounds

335 Yet dreadful in mine ear, though in my choice
Not to incur; but soon his clear aspéct
Returned and gracious purpose thus renewed.
Not only these fair bounds, but all the earth
To thee and to thy race I give; as lords
340 Possess it, and all things that therein live,
Or live in sea, or air, beast, fish, and fowl.
In sign whereof each bird and beast behold
After their kinds; I bring them to receive
From thee their names, and pay thee fealty
345 With low subjection; understand the same
Of fish within their wat'ry residence,
Not hither summoned, since they cannot change
Their element to draw the thinner air.
As thus he spake, each bird and beast behold
350 Approaching two and two, these cow'ring low
With blandishment, each bird stooped on his wing.
I named them, as they passed, and understood
Their nature, with such knowledge God endued
My sudden apprehension: but in these
355 I found not what methought I wanted still;
And to the Heav'nly vision thus presumed.
　　O by what name, for thou above all these,
Above mankind, or aught than mankind higher,
Surpassest far my naming, how may I
360 Adore thee, Author of this universe,
And all this good to man, for whose well-being
So amply, and with hands so liberal
Thou hast provided all things: but with me
I see not who partakes. In solitude
365 What happiness, who can enjoy alone,
Or all enjoying, what contentment find?
Thus I presumptuous; and the vision bright,
As with a smile more brightened, thus replied.
　　What call'st thou solitude, is not the earth
370 With various living creatures, and the air
Replenished, and all these at thy command
To come and play before thee? Know'st thou not
Their language and their ways? They also know,

And reason not contemptibly; with these
375 Find pastime, and bear rule; thy realm is large.
So spake the Universal Lord, and seemed
So ordering. I with leave of speech implored,
And humble deprecation thus replied.
    Let not my words offend thee, Heav'nly Power,
380 My Maker, be propitious while I speak.
Hast thou not made me here thy substitute,
And these inferior far beneath me set?
Among unequals what society
Can sort, what harmony or true delight?
385 Which must be mutual, in proportion due
Giv'n and received; but in disparity
The one intense, the other still remiss
Cannot well suit with either, but soon prove
Tedious alike: of fellowship I speak
390 Such as I seek, fit to participate
All rational delight, wherein the brute
Cannot be human consort; they rejoice
Each with their kind, lion with lioness;
So fitly them in pairs thou hast combined;
395 Much less can bird with beast, or fish with fowl
So well converse, nor with the ox the ape;
Worse then can man with beast, and least of all.
Whereto th' Almighty answered, not displeased.
A nice and subtle happiness I see
400 Thou to thyself proposest, in the choice
Of thy associates, Adam, and wilt taste
No pleasure, though in pleasure, solitary.
What think'st thou then of me, and this my state?
Seem I to thee sufficiently possessed
405 Of happiness, or not? who am alone
From all eternity, for none I know
Second to me or like, equal much less.
How have I then with whom to hold converse
Save with the creatures which I made, and those
410 To me inferior, infinite descents
Beneath what other creatures are to thee?
    He ceased, I lowly answered. To attain

The heighth and depth of thy eternal ways
All human thoughts come short, supreme of things;
415 .   Thou in thy self art perfect, and in thee
Is no deficience found; not so is man,
But in degree, the cause of his desire
By conversation with his like to help,
Or solace his defects. No need that thou
420   Shouldst propagate, already infinite;
And through all numbers absolute though One;
But man by number is to manifest
His single imperfection, and beget
Like of his like, his image multiplied,
425   In unity defective, which requires
Collateral love, and dearest amity.
Thou in thy secrecy although alone,
Best with thyself accompanied, seek'st not
Social communication, yet so pleased,
430   Canst raise thy creature to what heighth thou wilt
Of union or communion, deified;
I by conversing cannot these erect
From prone, nor in their ways complacence find.
Thus I emboldened spake, and freedom used
435   Permissive, and acceptance found, which gained
This answer from the gracious voice divine.

    Thus far to try thee, Adam, I was pleased,
And find thee knowing not of beasts alone,
Which thou hast rightly named, but of thyself,
440   Expressing well the spirit within thee free,
My image, not imparted to the brute,
Whose fellowship therefore unmeet for thee
Good reason was thou freely shouldst dislike,
And be so minded still; I, ere thou spak'st,
445   Knew it not good for man to be alone,
And no such company as then thou saw'st
Intended thee, for trial only brought,
To see how thou could'st judge of fit and meet:
What next I bring shall please thee, be assured,
450   Thy likeness, thy fit help, thy other self,
Thy wish exactly to thy heart's desire.

He ended, or I heard no more, for now
My earthly by his Heav'nly overpowered,
Which it had long stood under, strained to the heighth
455   In that celestial colloquy sublime,
As with an object that excels the sense,
Dazzled and spent, sunk down, and sought repair
Of sleep, which instantly fell on me, called
By nature as in aid, and closed mine eyes.
460   Mine eyes he closed, but open left the cell
Of Fancy my internal sight, by which
Abstráct as in a trance methought I saw,
Though sleeping, where I lay, and saw the shape
Still glorious before whom awake I stood,
465   Who stooping opened my left side, and took
From thence a rib, with cordial spirits warm,
And life-blood streaming fresh; wide was the wound,
But suddenly with flesh filled up and healed:
The rib he formed and fashioned with his hands;
470   Under his forming hands a creature grew,
Manlike, but different sex, so lovely fair,
That what seemed fair in all the world, seemed now
Mean, or in her summed up, in her contained
And in her looks, which from that time infused
475   Sweetness into my heart, unfelt before,
And into all things from her air inspired
The spirit of love and amorous delight.
She disappeared, and left me dark, I waked
To find her, or for ever to deplore
480   Her loss, and other pleasures all abjure:
When out of hope, behold her, not far off,
Such as I saw her in my dream, adorned
With what all earth or Heaven could bestow
To make her amiable: on she came,
485   Led by her Heav'nly Maker, though unseen,
And guided by his voice, nor uninformed
Of nuptial sanctity and marriage rites:
Grace was in all her steps, Heav'n in her eye,
In every gesture dignity and love.
490   I overjoyed could not forbear aloud.

This turn hath made amends; thou hast fulfilled
Thy words, Creator bounteous and benign,
Giver of all things fair, but fairest this
Of all thy gifts, nor enviest. I now see
495   Bone of my bone, flesh of my flesh, my self
Before me; woman is her name, of man
Extracted; for this cause he shall forgo
Father and mother, and to his wife adhere;
And they shall be one flesh, one heart, one soul.

500   She heard me thus, and though divinely brought,
Yet innocence and virgin modesty,
Her virtue and the conscience of her worth,
That would be wooed, and not unsought be won,
Not obvious, not obtrusive, but retired,
505   The more desirable, or to say all,
Nature herself, though pure of sinful thought,
Wrought in her so, that seeing me, she turned;
I followed her, she what was honour knew,
And with obsequious majesty approved
510   My pleaded reason. To the nuptial bow'r
I led her blushing like the Morn: all Heav'n,
And happy constellations on that hour
Shed their selectest influence; the earth
Gave sign of gratulation, and each hill;
515   Joyous the birds, fresh gales and gentle airs
Whispered it to the woods, and from their wings
Flung rose, flung odours from the spicy shrub,
Disporting, till the amorous bird of night
Sung spousal, and bid haste the ev'ning star
520   On his hill top, to light the bridal lamp.
Thus have I told thee all my state, and brought
My story to the sum of earthly bliss
Which I enjoy, and must confess to find
In all things else delight indeed, but such
525   As used or not, works in the mind no change,
Nor vehement desire, these delicacies
I mean of taste, sight, smell, herbs, fruits and flow'rs,
Walks, and the melody of birds; but here
Far otherwise, transported I behold,

530   Transported touch; here passion first I felt,
       Commotion strange, in all enjoyments else
       Superior and unmoved, here only weak
       Against the charm of beauty's powerful glance.
       Or Nature failed in me, and left some part
535   Not proof enough such object to sustain,
       Or from my side subducting, took perhaps
       More than enough; at least on her bestowed
       Too much of ornament, in outward show
       Elaborate, of inward less exact.
540   For well I understand in the prime end
       Of Nature her th' inferior, in the mind
       And inward faculties, which most excel,
       In outward also her resembling less
       His image who made both, and less expressing
545   The character of that dominion giv'n
       O'er other creatures; yet when I approach
       Her loveliness, so absolute she seems
       And in herself complete, so well to know
       Her own, that what she wills to do or say,
550   Seems wisest, virtuousest, discreetest, best;
       All higher knowledge in her presence falls
       Degraded, wisdom in discourse with her
       Looses discount'nanced and like folly shows;
       Authority and reason on her wait,
555   As one intended first, not after made
       Occasionally; and to consúmmate all,
       Greatness of mind and nobleness their seat
       Build in her loveliest, and create an awe
       About her, as a guard angelic placed.
560   To whom the angel with contracted brow.
           Accuse not Nature, she hath done her part;
       Do thou but thine, and be not diffident
       Of Wisdom; she deserts thee not, if thou
       Dismiss not her, when most thou need'st her nigh,
565   By áttribúting overmuch to things
       Less excellent, as thou thyself perceiv'st.
       For what admir'st thou, what transports thee so,
       An outside? fair no doubt, and worthy well

Thy cherishing, thy honouring, and thy love,
570 Not thy subjection: weigh with her thyself;
Then value: oft times nothing profits more
Than self-esteem, grounded on just and right
Well managed; of that skill the more thou know'st,
The more she will acknowledge thee her head,
575 And to realities yield all her shows:
Made so adorn for thy delight the more,
So awful, that with honour thou may'st love
Thy mate, who sees when thou art seen least wise.
But if the sense of touch whereby mankind
580 Is propagated seem such dear delight
Beyond all other, think the same vouchsafed
To cattle and each beast; which would not be
To them made common and divulged, if aught
Therein enjoyed were worthy to subdue
585 The soul of man, or passion in him move.
What higher in her society thou find'st
Attractive, human, rational, love still;
In loving thou dost well, in passion not,
Wherein true love consists not; love refines
590 The thoughts, and heart enlarges, hath his seat
In reason, and is judicious, is the scale
By which to Heav'nly love thou may'st ascend,
Not sunk in carnal pleasure, for which cause
Among the beasts no mate for thee was found.
595   To whom thus half abashed Adam replied.
Neither her outside formed so fair, nor aught
In procreation common to all kinds
(Though higher of the genial bed by far,
And with mysterious reverence I deem)
600 So much delights me as those graceful acts,
Those thousand decencies that daily flow
From all her words and actions, mixed with love
And sweet compliance, which declare unfeigned
Union of mind, or in us both one soul;
605 Harmony to behold in wedded pair
More grateful than harmonious sound to the ear.
Yet these subject not; I to thee disclose

What inward thence I feel, not therefore foiled,
Who meet with various objects, from the sense
610   Variously representing; yet still free
Approve the best, and follow what I approve.
To love thou blam'st me not, for love thou say'st
Leads up to Heav'n. Is both the way and guide;
Bear with me then, if lawful what I ask;
615   Love not the Heav'nly Spirits, and how their love
Express they, by looks only, or do they mix
Irradiance, virtual or immediate touch?
    To whom the angel with a smile that glowed
Celestial rosy red, love's proper hue,
620   Answered. Let it suffice thee that thou know'st
Us happy, and without love no happiness.
Whatever pure thou in the body enjoy'st
(And pure thou wert created) we enjoy
In eminence, and obstacle find none
625   Of membrane, joint, or limb, exclusive bars:
Easier than air with air, if Spirits embrace,
Total they mix, union of pure with pure
Desiring; nor restrained conveyance need
As flesh to mix with flesh, or soul with soul.
630   But I can now no more; the parting sun
Beyond the earth's green cape and verdant isles
Hesperian sets, my signal to depart.
Be strong, live happy, and love, but first of all
Him whom to love is to obey, and keep
635   His great command; take heed lest passion sway
Thy judgement to do aught, which else free will
Would not admit; thine and of all thy sons
The weal or woe in thee is placed; beware.
I in thy persevering shall rejoice,
640   And all the blest: stand fast; to stand or fall
Free in thine own arbitrament it lies.
Perfect within, no outward aid require;
And all temptation to transgress repel.
    So saying, he arose; whom Adam thus
645   Followed with benediction. Since to part,
Go Heavenly guest, ethereal messenger,

Sent from whose sov'reign goodness I adore.
Gentle to me and affable hath been
Thy condescension, and shall be honoured ever
650   With grateful memory: thou to mankind
Be good and friendly still, and oft return.
    So parted they, the angel up to Heav'n
From the thick shade, and Adam to his bow'r.

BOOK IX

The Argument

Satan having compassed the earth, with meditated guile
returns as a mist by night into Paradise, enters into the serpent
sleeping. Adam and Eve in the morning go forth to their
labours, which Eve proposes to divide in several places, each
labouring apart: Adam consents not, alleging the danger, lest
that Enemy, of whom they were forewarned, should attempt
her found alone: Eve loath to be thought not circumspect or
firm enough, urges her going apart, the rather desirous to
make trial of her strength; Adam at last yields: the serpent
finds her alone; his subtle approach, first gazing, then speaking,
with much flattery extolling Eve above all other creatures.
Eve wondering to hear the serpent speak, asks how he attained
to human speech and such understanding not till now; the
serpent answers, that by tasting of a certain tree in the garden
he attained both to speech and reason, till then void of both:
Eve requires him to bring her to that tree, and finds it to be
the Tree of Knowledge forbidden: the serpent now grown
bolder, with many wiles and arguments induces her at length
to eat; she pleased with the taste deliberates a while whether
to impart thereof to Adam or not, at last brings him of the
fruit, relates what persuaded her to eat thereof: Adam at first
amazed, but perceiving her lost, resolves through vehemence
of love to perish with her; and extenuating the trespass eats
also of the fruit: the effects thereof in them both; they seek
to cover their nakedness; then fall to variance and accusation
of one another.

No more of talk where God or angel guest
With man, as with his friend, familiar used
To sit indulgent, and with him partake
Rural repast, permitting him the while

5   Venial discourse unblamed: I now must change
       Those notes to tragic; foul distrust, and breach
       Disloyal on the part of man, revolt,
       And disobedience: on the part of Heav'n
       Now alienated, distance and distaste,
10   Anger and just rebuke, and judgement giv'n,
       That brought into this world a world of woe,
       Sin and her shadow Death, and misery
       Death's harbinger: sad task, yet argument
       Not less but more heroic than the wrath
15   Of stern Achilles on his foe pursued
       Thrice fugitive about Troy wall; or rage
       Of Turnus for Lavinia disespoused,
       Or Neptune's ire or Juno's, that so long
       Perplexed the Greek and Cytherea's son;
20   If answerable style I can obtain
       Of my celestial patroness, who deigns
       Her nightly visitation unimplored,
       And díctates to me slumb'ring, or inspires
       Easy my unpremeditated verse:
25   Since first this subject for heroic song
       Pleased me long choosing, and beginning late;
       Not sedulous by nature to indite
       Wars, hitherto the only argument
       Heroic deemed, chief mast'ry to dissect
30   With long and tedious havoc fabled knights
       In battles feigned; the better fortitude
       Of patience and heroic martyrdom
       Unsung; or to describe races and games,
       Or tilting furniture, emblazoned shields,
35   Impreses quaint, caparisons and steeds;
       Bases and tinsel trappings, gorgeous knights
       At joust and tournament; then marshalled feast
       Served up in hall with sewers, and seneschals;
       The skill of artifice or office mean,
40   Not that which justly gives heroic name
       To person or to poem. Me of these
       Nor skilled nor studious, higher argument
       Remains, sufficient of itself to raise

That name, unless an age too late, or cold
45   Climate, or years damp my intended wing
Depressed, and much they may, if all be mine,
Not hers who brings it nightly to my ear.
       The sun was sunk, and after him the star
Of Hesperus, whose office is to bring
50   Twilight upon the earth, short arbiter
'Twixt day and night, and now from end to end
Night's hemisphere had veiled the horizon round:
When Satan who late fled before the threats
Of Gabriel out of Eden, now improved
55   In meditated fraud and malice, bent
On man's destruction, maugre what might hap
Of heavier on himself, fearless returned.
By night he fled, and at midnight returned
From compassing the earth, cautious of day,
60   Since Uriel regent of the sun descried
His entrance, and forewarned the Cherubim
That kept their watch; thence full of anguish driv'n,
The space of seven continued nights he rode
With darkness, thrice the equinoctial line
65   He circled, four times crossed the car of Night
From pole to pole, traversing each colure;
On the eighth returned, and on the coast averse
From entrance or Cherubic watch, by stealth
Found unsuspected way. There was a place,
70   Now not, though sin, not time, first wrought the change,
Where Tigris at the foot of Paradise
Into a gulf shot underground, till part
Rose up a fountain by the Tree of Life;
In with the river sunk, and with it rose
75   Satan involved in rising mist, then sought
Where to lie hid; sea he had searched and land
From Eden over Pontus, and the pool
Maeotis, up beyond the river Ob;
Downward as far Antarctic; and in length
80   West from Orontes to the ocean barred
At Darien, thence to the land where flows
Ganges and Indus: thus the orb he roamed

With narrow search; and with inspection deep
Considered every creature, which of all
85   Most opportune might serve his wiles, and found
The serpent subtlest beast of all the field.
Him after long debate, irresolute
Of thoughts revolved, his final sentence chose
Fit vessel, fittest imp of fraud, in whom
90   To enter, and his dark suggestions hide
From sharpest sight: for in the wily snake,
. Whatever sleights none would suspicious mark,
As from his wit and native subtlety
Proceeding, which in other beasts observed
95   Doubt might beget of diabolic pow'r
Active within beyond the sense of brute.
Thus he resolved, but first from inward grief
His bursting passion into plaints thus poured.
      O earth, how like to Heav'n, if not preferred
100   More justly, seat worthier of gods, as built
With second thoughts, reforming what was old!
For what god after better worse would build?
Terrestrial Heav'n, danced round by other heav'ns
That shine, yet bear their bright officious lamps,
105   Light above light, for thee alone, as seems,
In thee concentring all their precious beams
Of sacred influence: as God in Heav'n
Is centre, yet extends to all, so thou
Centring receiv'st from all those orbs; in thee,
110   Not in themselves, all their known virtue appears
Productive in herb, plant, and nobler birth
Of creatures animate with gradual life
Of growth, sense, reason, all summed up in man.
With what delight could I have walked thee round,
115   If I could joy in aught, sweet interchange
Of hill and valley, rivers, woods and plains,
Now land, now sea, and shores with forest crowned,
Rocks, dens, and caves; but I in none of these
Find place or refuge; and the more I see
120   Pleasures about me, so much more I feel
Torment within me, as from the hateful siege

Of contraries; all good to me becomes
Bane, and in Heav'n much worse would be my state.
But neither here seek I, no nor in Heav'n
125 To dwell, unless by mast'ring Heav'n's Supreme;
Nor hope to be myself less miserable
By what I seek, but others to make such
As I, though thereby worse to me redound:
For only in destroying I find ease
130 To my relentless thoughts; and him destroyed,
Or won to what may work his utter loss,
For whom all this was made, all this will soon
Follow, as to him linked in weal or woe;
In woe then; that destruction wide may range:
135 To me shall be the glory sole among
The infernal Powers, in one day to have marred
What he Almighty styled, six nights and days
Continued making, and who knows how long
Before had been contriving, though perhaps
140 Not longer than since I in one night freed
From servitude inglorious well nigh half
Th' angelic name, and thinner left the throng
Of his adorers: he to be avenged,
And to repair his numbers thus impaired,
145 Whether such virtue spent of old now failed
More angels to create, if they at least
Are his created, or to spite us more,
Determined to advance into our room
A creature formed of earth, and him endow,
150 Exalted from so base original,
With Heav'nly spoils, our spoils: what he decreed
He effected; man he made, and for him built
Magnificent this world, and earth his seat,
Him lord pronounced, and, O indignity!
155 Subjected to his service angel wings,
And flaming ministers to watch and tend
Their earthy charge: of these the vigilance
I dread, and to elude, thus wrapped in mist
Of midnight vapour glide obscure, and pry
160 In every bush and brake, where hap may find

The serpent sleeping, in whose mazy folds
To hide me, and the dark intent I bring.
O foul descent! that I who erst contended
With Gods to sit the highest, am now constrained
165   Into a beast, and mixed with bestial slime,
This essence to incarnate and imbrute,
That to the heighth of Deity aspired;
But what will not ambition and revenge
Descend to? who aspires must down as low
170   As high he soared, obnoxious first or last
To basest things. Revenge, at first though sweet,
Bitter ere long back on itself recoils;
Let it; I reck not, so it light well aimed,
Since higher I fall short, on him who next
175   Provokes my envy, this new favourite
Of Heav'n, this man of clay, son of despite,
Whom us the more to spite his Maker raised
From dust: spite then with spite is best repaid.
    So saying, through each thicket dank or dry,
180   Like a black mist low creeping, he held on
His midnight search, where soonest he might find
The serpent: him fast sleeping soon he found
In labyrinth of many a round self-rolled,
His head the midst, well stored with subtle wiles:
185   Not yet in horrid shade or dismal den,
Nor nocent yet, but on the grassy herb
Fearless unfeared he slept: in at his mouth
The Devil entered, and his brutal sense,
In heart or head, possessing soon inspired
190   With act intelligential; but his sleep
Disturbed not, waiting close th' approach of morn.
Now when as sacred light began to dawn
In Eden on the humid flow'rs, that breathed
Their morning incense, when all things that breathe,
195   From th' earth's great altar send up silent praise
To the Creator, and his nostrils fill
With grateful smell, forth came the human pair
And joined their vocal worship to the choir
Of creatures wanting voice; that done, partake

200 The season, prime for sweetest scents and airs:
     Then cómmune how that day they best may ply
     Their growing work: for much their work outgrew
     The hands' dispatch of two gard'ning so wide.
     And Eve first to her husband thus began.
205   Adam, well may we labour still to dress
     This garden, still to tend plant, herb and flow'r,
     Our pleasant task enjoined, but till more hands
     Aid us, the work under our labour grows,
     Luxurious by restraint; what we by day
210 Lop overgrown, or prune, or prop, or bind,
     One night or two with wanton growth derides
     Tending to wild. Thou therefore now advise
     Or hear what to my mind first thoughts present;
     Let us divide our labours, thou where choice
215 Leads thee, or where most needs, whether to wind
     The woodbine round this arbour, or direct
     The clasping ivy where to climb, while I
     In yonder spring of roses intermixed
     With myrtle, find what to redress till noon:
220 For while so near each other thus all day
     Our task we choose, what wonder if so near
     Looks intervene and smiles, or object new
     Casual discourse draw on, which intermits
     Our day's work brought to little, though begun
225 Early, and th' hour of supper comes unearned.
         To whom mild answer Adam thus returned.
     Sole Eve, associate sole, to me beyond
     Compare above all living creatures dear,
     Well hast thou motioned, well thy thoughts employed
230 How we might best fulfil the work which here
     God hath assigned us, nor of me shalt pass
     Unpraised: for nothing lovelier can be found
     In woman, than to study household good,
     And good works in her husband to promote.
235 Yet not so strictly hath our Lord imposed
     Labour, as to debar us when we need
     Refreshment, whether food, or talk between,
     Food of the mind, or this sweet intercourse

Of looks and smiles, for smiles from reason flow,
240 To brute denied, and are of love the food,
Love not the lowest end of human life.
For not to irksome toil, but to delight
He made us, and delight to reason joined.
These paths and bowers doubt not but our joint hands
245 Will keep from wilderness with ease, as wide
As we need walk, till younger hands ere long
Assist us: but if much convérse perhaps
Thee satiate, to short absence I could yield.
For solitude sometimes is best society,
250 And short retirement urges sweet return.
But other doubt possesses me, lest harm
Befall thee severed from me; for thou know'st
What hath been warned us, what malicious Foe
Envying our happiness, and of his own
255 Despairing, seeks to work us woe and shame
By sly assault; and somewhere nigh at hand
Watches, no doubt, with greedy hope to find
His wish and best advantage, us asunder,
Hopeless to circumvent us joined, where each
260 To other speedy aid might lend at need;
Whether his first design be to withdraw
Our fealty from God, or to disturb
Conjugal love, than which perhaps no bliss
Enjoyed by us excites his envy more;
265 Or this, or worse, leave not the faithful side
That gave thee being, still shades thee and protects.
The wife, where danger or dishonour lurks,
Safest and seemliest by her husband stays,
Who guards her, or with her the worst endures.
270   To whom the virgin majesty of Eve,
As one who loves, and some unkindness meets,
With sweet austere composure thus replied.
Offspring of Heav'n and earth, and all earth's lord,
That such an Enemy we have, who seeks
275 Our ruin, both by thee informed I learn,
-   And from the parting angel overheard
As in a shady nook I stood behind,

Just then returned at shut of evening flow'rs.
But that thou shouldst my firmness therefore doubt
280   To God or thee, because we have a foe
May tempt it, I expected not to hear.
His violence thou fear'st not, being such,
As we, not capable of death or pain,
Can either not receive, or can repel.
285   His fraud is then thy fear, which plain infers
Thy equal fear that my firm faith and love
Can by his fraud be shaken or seduced;
Thoughts, which how found they harbour in thy breast,
Adam, misthought of her to thee so dear?
290   To whom with healing words Adam replied.
Daughter of God and man, immortal Eve,
For such thou art, from sin and blame entire:
Not diffident of thee do I dissuade
Thy absence from my sight, but to avoid
295   Th' attempt itself, intended by our Foe.
For he who tempts, though in vain, at least asperses
The tempted with dishonour foul, supposed
Not incorruptible of faith, not proof
Against temptation: thou thyself with scorn
300   And anger wouldst resent the offered wrong,
Though ineffectual found: misdeem not then,
If such affront I labour to avert
From thee alone, which on us both at once
The Enemy, though bold, will hardly dare,
305   Or daring, first on me th' assault shall light.
Nor thou his malice and false guile contemn;
Subtle he needs must be, who could seduce
Angels, nor think superfluous others' aid.
I from the influence of thy looks receive
310   Accéss in every virtue, in thy sight
More wise, more watchful, stronger, if need were
Of outward strength; while shame, thou looking on,
Shame to be overcome or over-reached
Would utmost vigour raise, and raised unite.
315   Why shouldst not thou like sense within thee feel
When I am present, and thy trial choose

With me, best witness of thy virtue tried.
   So spake domestic Adam in his care
And matrimonial love; but Eve, who thought
320   Less áttribúted to her faith sincere,
Thus her reply with accent sweet renewed.
   If this be our condition, thus to dwell
In narrow circuit straitened by a Foe,
Subtle or violent, we not endued
325   Single with like defence, wherever met,
How are we happy, still in fear of harm?
But harm precedes not sin: only our Foe
Tempting affronts us with his foul esteem
Of our integrity: his foul esteem
330   Sticks no dishonour on our front, but turns
Foul on himself; then wherefore shunned or feared
By us? Who rather double honour gain
From his surmise proved false, find peace within,
Favour from Heav'n, our witness from th' event.
335   And what is faith, love, virtue unassayed
Alone, without exterior help sustained?
Let us not then suspect our happy state
Left so imperfect by the Maker wise,
As not secure to single or combined.
340   Frail is our happiness, if this be so,
And Eden were no Eden thus exposed.
   To whom thus Adam fervently replied.
O woman, best are all things as the will
Of God ordained them; his creating hand
345   Nothing imperfect or deficient left
Of all that he created, much less man,
Or aught that might his happy state secure,
Secure from outward force; within himself
The danger lies, yet lies within his power:
350   Against his will he can receive no harm.
But God left free the will, for what obeys
Reason, is free, and reason he made right,
But bid her well beware, and still erect,
Lest by some fair appearing good surprised
355   She díctate false, and misinform the will

To do what God expressly hath forbid.
Not then mistrust, but tender love enjoins,
That I should mind thee oft, and mind thou me.
Firm we subsist, yet possible to swerve,
360 Since reason not impossibly may meet
Some specious object by the Foe suborned,
And fall into deception unaware,
Not keeping strictest watch, as she was warned.
Seek not temptation then, which to avoid
365 Were better, and most likely if from me
Thou sever not: trial will come unsought.
Wouldst thou approve thy constancy, approve
First thy obedience; th' other who can know,
Not seeing thee attempted, who attest?
370 But if thou think, trial unsought may find
Us both securer than thus warned thou seem'st,
Go; for thy stay, not free, absents thee more;
Go in thy native innocence, rely
On what thou hast of virtue, summon all,
375 For God towards thee hath done his part, do thine.
      So spake the patriarch of mankind, but Eve
Persisted, yet submiss, though last, replied.
      With thy permission, then, and thus forewarned
Chiefly by what thy own last reasoning words
380 Touched only, that our trial, when least sought,
May find us both perhaps far less prepared,
The willinger I go, nor much expect
A Foe so proud will first the weaker seek;
So bent, the more shall shame him his repulse.
385 Thus saying, from her husband's hand her hand
Soft she withdrew, and like a wood-nymph light
Oread or Dryad, or of Delia's train,
Betook her to the groves, but Delia's self
In gait surpassed and goddess-like deport,
390 Though not as she with bow and quiver armed,
But with such gard'ning tools as art yet rude,
Guiltless of fire had formed, or angels brought.
To Pales, or Pomona thus adorned,
Likeliest she seemed, Pomona when she fled

395   Vertumnus, or to Ceres in her prime,
       Yet virgin of Proserpina from Jove.
       Her long with ardent look his eye pursued
       Delighted, but desiring more her stay.
       Oft he to her his charge of quick return
400   Repeated, she to him as oft engaged
       To be returned by noon amid the bow'r,
       And all things in best order to invite
       Noontide repast, or afternoon's repose.
       O much deceived, much failing, hapless Eve,
405   Of thy presumed return! event perverse!
       Thou never from that hour in Paradise
       Found'st either sweet repast, or sound repose;
       Such ambush hid among sweet flow'rs and shades
       Waited with Hellish rancour imminent
410   To intercept thy way, or send thee back
       Despoiled of innocence, of faith, of bliss.
       For now, and since first break of dawn the Fiend,
       Mere serpent in appearance, forth was come,
       And on his quest, where likeliest he might find
415   The only two of mankind, but in them
       The whole intended race, his purposed prey.
       In bow'r and field he sought, where any tuft
       Of grove or garden-plot more pleasant lay,
       Their tendance or plantation for delight;
420   By fountain or by shady rivulet
       He sought them both, but wished his hap might find
       Eve separate; he wished, but not with hope
       Of what so seldom chanced, when to his wish,
       Beyond his hope, Eve separate he spies,
425   Veiled in a cloud of fragrance, where she stood,
       Half spied, so thick the roses bushing round
       About her glowed, oft stooping to support
       Each flow'r of slender stalk, whose head though gay
       Carnation, purple, azure, or specked with gold,
430   Hung drooping unsustained; them she upstays
       Gently with myrtle band, mindless the while,
       Herself, though fairest unsupported flow'r,
       From her best prop so far, and storm so nigh.

Nearer he drew, and many a walk traversed
435   Of stateliest covert, cedar, pine, or palm,
Then voluble and bold, now hid, now seen
Among thick-woven arborets and flow'rs
Embordered on each bank, the hand of Eve:
Spot more delicious than those gardens feigned
440   Or of revived Adonis, or renowned
Alcinous, host of old Laertes' son,
Or that, not mystic, where the sapient king
Held dalliance with his fair Egyptian spouse.
Much he the place admired, the person more.
445   As one who long in populous city pent,
Where houses thick and sewers annoy the air,
Forth issuing on a summer's morn to breathe
Among the pleasant villages and farms
Adjoined, from each thing met conceives delight,
450   The smell of grain, or tedded grass, or kine,
Or dairy, each rural sight, each rural sound;
If chance with nymph-like step fair virgin pass,
What pleasing seemed, for her now pleases more,
She most, and in her look sums all delight.
455   Such pleasure took the serpent to behold
This flow'ry plat, the sweet recess of Eve
Thus early, thus alone; her Heav'nly form
Angelic, but more soft, and feminine,
Her graceful innocence, her every air
460   Of gesture or least action overawed
His malice, and with rapine sweet bereaved
His fierceness of the fierce intent it brought:
That space the Evil One abstracted stood
From his own evil, and for the time remained
465   Stupidly good, of enmity disarmed,
Of guile, of hate, of envy, of revenge;
But the hot Hell that always in him burns,
Though in mid-Heav'n, soon ended his delight,
And tortures him now more, the more he sees
470   Of pleasure not for him ordained: then soon
Fierce hate he recollects, and all his thoughts
Of mischief, gratulating, thus excites.

Thoughts, whither have ye led me, with what sweet
Compulsion thus transported to forget
475   What hither brought us, hate, not love, nor hope
Of Paradise for Hell, hope here to taste
Of pleasure, but all pleasure to destroy,
Save what is in destroying; other joy
To me is lost. Then let me not let pass
480   Occasion which now smiles; behold alone
The woman, opportune to all attempts,
Her husband, for I view far round, not nigh,
Whose higher intellectual more I shun,
And strength, of courage haughty, and of limb
485   Heroic built, though of terrestrial mould,
Foe not informidable, exempt from wound,
I not; so much hath Hell debased, and pain
Enfeebled me, to what I was in Heav'n.
She fair, divinely fair, fit love for gods,
490   Not terrible, though terror be in love
And beauty, not approached by stronger hate,
Hate stronger, under show of love well-feigned,
The way which to her ruin now I tend.
So spake the Enemy of mankind, enclosed
495   In serpent, inmate bad, and toward Eve
Addressed his way, not with indented wave,
Prone on the ground, as since, but on his rear,
Circular base of rising folds, that tow'red
Fold above fold, a surging maze, his head
500   Crested aloft, and carbuncle his eyes;
With burnished neck of verdant gold, erect
Amidst his circling spires, that on the grass
Floated redundant: pleasing was his shape,
And lovely, never since of serpent kind
505   Lovelier, not those that in Illyria changed
Hermione and Cadmus, or the god
In Epidaurus; nor to which transformed
Ammonian Jove, or Capitoline was seen,
He with Olympias, this with her who bore
510   Scipio the heighth of Rome. With tract oblique
At first, as one who sought accéss, but feared

To interrupt, sidelong he works his way.
As when a ship by skilful steersman wrought
Nigh river's mouth or foreland, where the wind
Veers oft, as oft so steers, and shifts her sail;
So varied he, and of his tortuous train
Curled many a wanton wreath in sight of Eve,
To lure her eye; she busied heard the sound
Of rustling leaves, but minded not, as used
To such disport before her through the field,
From every beast, more duteous at her call,
Than at Circean call the herd disguised.
He bolder now, uncalled before her stood;
But as in gaze admiring: oft he bowed
His turret crest, and sleek enamelled neck,
Fawning, and licked the ground whereon she trod.
His gentle dumb expression turned at length
The eye of Eve to mark his play; he glad
Of her attention gained, with serpent tongue
Organic, or impúlse of vocal air,
His fraudulent temptation thus began.
        Wonder not, sov'reign mistress, if perhaps
Thou canst, who art sole wonder, much less arm
Thy looks, the Heav'n of mildness, with disdain,
Displeased that I approach thee thus, and gaze
Insatiate, I thus single, nor have feared
Thy awful brow, more awful thus retired.
Fairest resemblance of thy Maker fair,
Thee all things living gaze on, all things thine
By gift, and thy celestial beauty adore
With ravishment beheld, there best beheld
Where universally admired; but here
In this enclosure wild, these beasts among,
Beholders rude, and shallow to discern
Half what in thee is fair, one man except,
Who sees thee? (and what is one?) who shouldst be seen
A goddess among gods, adored and served
By angels numberless, thy daily train.
        So glozed the Tempter, and his proem tuned;
Into the heart of Eve his words made way,

Though at the voice much marvelling; at length
Not unamazed she thus in answer spake.
What may this mean? Language of man pronounced
By tongue of brute, and human sense expressed?
555 The first at least of these I thought denied
To beasts, whom God on their Creation-day
Created mute to all articulate sound;
The latter I demur, for in their looks
Much reason, and in their actions oft appears.
560 Thee, serpent, subtlest beast of all the field
I knew, but not with human voice endued;
Redouble then this miracle, and say,
How cam'st thou speakable of mute, and how
To me so friendly grown above the rest
565 Of brutal kind, that daily are in sight?
Say, for such wonder claims attention due.
       To whom the guileful Tempter thus replied.
Empress of this fair world, resplendent Eve,
Easy to me it is to tell thee all
570 What thou command'st, and right thou shouldst be obeyed:
I was at first as other beasts that graze
The trodden herb, of abject thoughts and low,
As was my food, nor aught but food discerned
Or sex, and apprehended nothing high:
575 Till on a day roving the field, I chanced
A goodly tree far distant to behold
Loaden with fruit of fairest colours mixed,
Ruddy and gold: I nearer drew to gaze;
When from the boughs a savoury odour blown,
580 Grateful to appetite, more pleased my sense
Than smell of sweetest fennel, or the teats
Of ewe or goat dropping with milk at ev'n,
Unsucked of lamb or kid, that tend their play.
To satisfy the sharp desire I had
585 Of tasting those fair apples, I resolved
Not to defer; hunger and thirst at once,
Powerful persuaders, quickened at the scent
Of that alluring fruit, urged me so keen.
About the mossy trunk I wound me soon,

590   For high from ground the branches would require
      Thy utmost reach or Adam's: round the tree
      All other beasts that saw, with like desire
      Longing and envying stood, but could not reach.
      Amid the tree now got, where plenty hung
595   Tempting so nigh, to pluck and eat my fill
      I spared not, for such pleasure till that hour
      At feed or fountain never had I found.
      Sated at length, ere long I might perceive
      Strange alteration in me, to degree
600   Of reason in my inward powers, and speech
      Wanted not long, though to this shape retained.
      Thenceforth to speculations high or deep
      I turned my thoughts, and with capacious mind
      Considered all things visible in heav'n,
605   Or earth, or middle, all things fair and good;
      But all that fair and good in thy divine
      Semblance, and in thy beauty's Heav'nly ray
      United I beheld; no fair to thine
      Equivalent or second, which compelled
610   Me thus, though importune perhaps, to come
      And gaze, and worship thee of right declared
      Sov'reign of creatures, universal dame.
          So talked the spirited sly snake; and Eve
      Yet more amazed unwary thus replied.
615   Serpent, thy overpraising leaves in doubt
      The virtue of that fruit, in thee first proved:
      But say, where grows the tree, from hence how far?
      For many are the trees of God that grow
      In Paradise, and various, yet unknown
620   To us, in such abundance lies our choice,
      As leaves a greater store of fruit untouched,
      Still hanging incorruptible, till men
      Grow up to their provision, and more hands
      Help to disburden Nature of her bearth.
625   To whom the wily adder, blithe and glad.
      Empress, the way is ready, and not long,
      Beyond a row of myrtles, on a flat,
      Fast by a fountain, one small thicket past

Of blowing myrrh and balm; if thou accept
630   My conduct, I can bring thee thither soon.
        Lead then, said Eve. He leading swiftly rolled
In tangles, and made intricate seem straight,
To mischief swift. Hope elevates, and joy
Brightens his crest, as when a wand'ring fire,
635   Compact of unctuous vapour, which the night
Condenses, and the cold environs round,
Kindled through agitation to a flame,
Which oft, they say, some evil Spirit attends
Hovering and blazing with delusive light,
640   Misleads th' amazed night-wanderer from his way
To bogs and mires, and oft through pond or pool,
There swallowed up and lost, from succour far.
So glistered the dire snake, and into fraud
Led Eve our credulous mother, to the tree
645   Of prohibition, root of all our woe;
Which when she saw, thus to her guide she spake.
        Serpent, we might have spared our coming hither,
Fruitless to me, though fruit be here to excess,
The credit of whose virtue rest with thee,
650   Wondrous indeed, if cause of such effects.
But of this tree we may not taste nor touch;
God so commanded, and left that command
Sole daughter of his voice; the rest, we live
Law to ourselves, our reason is our law.
655   To whom the Tempter guilefully replied.
Indeed? hath God then said that of the fruit
Of all these garden trees ye shall not eat,
Yet lords declared of all in earth or air?
        To whom thus Eve yet sinless. Of the fruit
660   Of each tree in the garden we may eat,
But of the fruit of this fair tree amidst
The garden, God hath said, Ye shall not eat
Thereof, nor shall ye touch it, lest ye die.
        She scarce had said, though brief, when now more bold
665   The Tempter, but with show of zeal and love
To man, and indignation at his wrong,
New part puts on, and as to passion moved,

Fluctuates disturbed, yet comely, and in act
Raised, as of some great matter to begin.
670 As when of old some orator renowned
In Athens or free Rome, where eloquence
Flourished, since mute, to some great cause addressed,
Stood in himself collected, while each part,
Motion, each act won audience ere the tongue,
675 Sometimes in heighth began, as no delay
Of preface brooking through his zeal of right.
So standing, moving, or to heighth upgrown
The Tempter all impassioned thus began.
      O sacred, wise, and wisdom-giving plant,
680 Mother of science, now I feel thy power
Within me clear, not only to discern
Things in their causes, but to trace the ways
Of highest agents, deemed however wise.
Queen of this universe, do not believe
685 Those rigid threats of death; ye shall not die:
How should ye? by the fruit? it gives you life
To knowledge. By the Threat'ner? look on me,
Me who have touched and tasted, yet both live,
And life more perfect have attained than Fate
690 Meant me, by vent'ring higher than my lot.
Shall that be shut to man, which to the beast
Is open? or will God incense his ire
For such a petty trespass, and not praise
Rather your dauntless virtue, whom the pain
695 Of death denounced, whatever thing death be,
Deterred not from achieving what might lead
To happier life, knowledge of good and evil;
Of good, how just? of evil, if what is evil
Be real, why not known, since easier shunned?
700 God therefore cannot hurt ye, and be just;
Not just, not God; not feared then, nor obeyed:
Your fear itself of death removes the fear.
Why then was this forbid? Why but to awe,
Why but to keep ye low and ignorant,
705 His worshippers; he knows that in the day
Ye eat thereof, your eyes that seem so clear,

Yet are but dim, shall perfectly be then
Opened and cleared, and ye shall be as gods,
Knowing both good and evil as they know.
710 That ye should be as gods, since I as man,
Internal man, is but proportion meet,
I of brute human, ye of human gods.
So ye shall die perhaps, by putting off
Human, to put on gods, death to be wished,
715 Though threatened, which no worse than this can bring.
And what are gods that man may not become
As they, participating god-like food?
The gods are first, and that advantage use
On our belief, that all from them proceeds;
720 I question it, for this fair earth I see,
Warmed by the sun, producing every kind,
Them nothing: if they all things, who enclosed
Knowledge of good and evil in this tree,
That whoso eats thereof, forthwith attains
725 Wisdom without their leave? and wherein lies
Th' offence, that man should thus attain to know?
What can your knowledge hurt him, or this tree
Impart against his will if all be his?
Or is it envy, and can envy dwell
730 In Heav'nly breasts? these, these and many more
Causes import your need of this fair fruit.
Goddess humane, reach then, and freely taste.
     He ended, and his words replete with guile
Into her heart too easy entrance won:
735 Fixed on the fruit she gazed, which to behold
Might tempt alone, and in her ears the sound
Yet rung of his persuasive words, impregned
With reason, to her seeming, and with truth;
Meanwhile the hour of noon drew on, and waked
740 An eager appetite, raised by the smell
So savoury of that fruit, which with desire,
Inclinable now grown to touch or taste,
Solicited her longing eye; yet first
Pausing a while, thus to herself she mused.
745   Great are thy virtues, doubtless, best of fruits,

Though kept from man, and worthy to be admired,
Whose taste, too long forborne, at first assay
Gave elocution to the mute, and taught
The tongue not made for speech to speak thy praise:
750   Thy praise he also who forbids thy use,
Conceals not from us, naming thee the Tree
Of Knowledge, knowledge both of good and evil;
Forbids us then to taste, but his forbidding
Commends thee more, while it infers the good
755   By thee communicated, and our want:
For good unknown, sure is not had, or had
And yet unknown, is as not had at all.
In plain then, what forbids he but to know,
Forbids us good, forbids us to be wise?
760   Such prohibitions bind not. But if death
Bind us with after-bands, what profits then
Our inward freedom? In the day we eat
Of this fair fruit, our doom is, we shall die.
How dies the serpent? he hath eat'n and lives,
765   And knows, and speaks, and reasons, and discerns,
Irrational till then. For us alone
Was death invented? or to us denied
This intellectual food, for beasts reserved?
For beasts it seems: yet that one beast which first
770   Hath tasted, envies not, but brings with joy
The good befall'n him, author unsuspect,
Friendly to man, far from deceit or guile.
What fear I then, rather what know to fear
Under this ignorance of good and evil,
775   Of God or death, of law or penalty?
Here grows the cure of all, this fruit divine,
Fair to the eye, inviting to the taste,
Of virtue to make wise: what hinders then
To reach, and feed at once both body and mind?
780   So saying, her rash hand in evil hour
Forth reaching to the fruit, she plucked, she ate:
Earth felt the wound, and Nature from her seat
Sighing through all her works gave signs of woe,
That all was lost. Back to the thicket slunk

785 The guilty serpent, and well might, for Eve
Intent now wholly on her taste, naught else
Regarded, such delight till then, as seemed,
In fruit she never tasted, whether true
Or fancied so, through expectation high
790 Of knowledge, nor was Godhead from her thought.
Greedily she engorged without restraint,
And knew not eating death: satiate at length,
And heightened as with wine, jocund and boon,
Thus to herself she pleasingly began.
795   O sov'reign, virtuous, precious of all trees
In Paradise, of operation blest
To sapience, hitherto obscured, infamed,
And thy fair fruit let hang, as to no end
Created; but henceforth my early care,
800 Not without song, each morning, and due praise
Shall tend thee, and the fertile burden ease
Of thy full branches offered free to all;
Till dieted by thee I grow mature
In knowledge, as the gods who all things know;
805 Though others envy what they cannot give;
For had the gift been theirs, it had not here
Thus grown. Experience, next to thee I owe,
Best guide; not following thee, I had remained
In ignorance, thou open'st wisdom's way,
810 And giv'st accéss, though secret she retire.
And I perhaps am secret; Heav'n is high,
High and remote to see from thence distinct
Each thing on earth; and other care perhaps
May have diverted from continual watch
815 Our great Forbidder, safe with all his spies
About him. But to Adam in what sort
Shall I appear? shall I to him make known
As yet my change, and give him to partake
Full happiness with me, or rather not,
820 But keep the odds of knowledge in my power
Without copartner? so to add what wants
In female sex, the more to draw his love,
And render me more equal, and perhaps,

A thing not undesirable, sometime
825   Superior; for inferior who is free?
This may be well: but what if God have seen,
And death ensue? then I shall be no more,
And Adam wedded to another Eve,
Shall live with her enjoying, I extinct;
830   A death to think. Confirmed then I resolve,
Adam shall share with me in bliss or woe:
So dear I love him, that with him all deaths
I could endure, without him live no life.
     So saying, from the tree her step she turned,
835   But first low reverence done, as to the power
That dwelt within, whose presence had infused
Into the plant sciential sap, derived
From nectar, drink of gods. Adam the while
Waiting desirous her return, had wove
840   Of choicest flow'rs a garland to adorn
Her tresses, and her rural labours crown,
As reapers oft are wont their harvest queen.
Great joy he promised to his thoughts, and new
Solace in her return, so long delayed;
845   Yet oft his heart, divine of something ill,
Misgave him; he the falt'ring measure felt;
And forth to meet her went, the way she took
That morn when first they parted; by the Tree
Of Knowledge he must pass, there he her met,
850   Scarce from the tree returning; in her hand
A bough of fairest fruit that downy smiled,
New gathered, and ambrosial smell diffused.
To him she hasted, in her face excuse
Came prologue, and apology to prompt,
855   Which with bland words at will she thus addressed.
     Hast thou not wondered, Adam, at my stay?
Thee I have missed, and thought it long, deprived
Thy presence, agony of love till now
Not felt, nor shall be twice, for never more
860   Mean I to try, what rash untried I sought,
The pain of absence from thy sight. But strange
Hath been the cause, and wonderful to hear:

This tree is not as we are told, a tree
Of danger tasted, nor to evil unknown
865   Op'ning the way, but of divine effect
To open eyes, and make them gods who taste;
And hath been tasted such: the serpent wise,
Or not restrained as we, or not obeying,
Hath eaten of the fruit, and is become,
870   Not dead, as we are threatened, but thenceforth
Endued with human voice and human sense,
Reasoning to admiration, and with me
Persuasively hath so prevailed, that I
Have also tasted, and have also found
875   Th' effects to correspond, opener mine eyes,
Dim erst, dilated spirits, ampler heart,
And growing up to godhead; which for thee
Chiefly I sought, without thee can despise.
For bliss, as thou hast part, to me is bliss,
880   Tedious, unshared with thee, and odious soon.
Thou therefore also taste, that equal lot
May join us, equal joy, as equal love;
Lest thou not tasting, different degree
Disjoin us, and I then too late renounce
885   Deity for thee, when Fate will not permit.
      Thus Eve with count'nance blithe her story told;
But in her cheek distemper flushing glowed.
On th' other side, Adam, soon as he heard
The fatal trespass done by Eve, amazed,
890   Astonied stood and blank, while horror chill
Ran through his veins, and all his joints relaxed;
From his slack hand the garland wreathed for Eve
Down dropped, and all the faded roses shed:
Speechless he stood and pale, till thus at length
895   First to himself he inward silence broke.
      O fairest of Creation, last and best
Of all God's works, creature in whom excelled
Whatever can to sight or thought be formed,
Holy, divine, good, amiable or sweet!
900   How art thou lost, how on a sudden lost,
Defaced, deflow'red, and now to death devote?

Rather how hast thou yielded to transgress
The strict forbiddance, how to violate
The sacred fruit forbidd'n! Some cursèd fraud
905 Of Enemy hath beguiled thee, yet unknown,
And me with thee hath ruined, for with thee
Certain my resolution is to die;
How can I live without thee, how forgo
Thy sweet convérse and love so dearly joined,
910 To live again in these wild woods forlorn?
Should God create another Eve, and I
Another rib afford, yet loss of thee
Would never from my heart; no no, I feel
The link of nature draw me: flesh of flesh,
915 Bone of my bone thou art, and from thy state
Mine never shall be parted, bliss or woe.
  So having said, as one from sad dismay
Recomforted, and after thoughts disturbed
Submitting to what seemed remédiless,
920 Thus in calm mood his words to Eve he turned.
Bold deed thou hast presumed, advent'rous Eve,
And peril great provoked, who thus hath dared
Had it been only coveting to eye
That sacred fruit, sacred to abstinence,
925 Much more to taste it under ban to touch.
But past who can recall, or done undo?
Not God omnipotent, nor Fate, yet so
Perhaps thou shalt not die, perhaps the fact
Is not so heinous now, foretasted fruit,
930 Profaned first by the serpent, by him first
Made common and unhallowed ere our taste;
Nor yet on him found deadly; he yet lives,
Lives, as thou saidst, and gains to live as man
Higher degree of life, inducement strong
935 To us, as likely tasting to attain
Proportional ascent, which cannot be
But to be gods, or angels demi-gods.
Nor can I think that God, Creator wise,
Though threat'ning, will in earnest so destroy
940 Us his prime creatures, dignified so high,

Set over all his works, which in our Fall,
For us created, needs with us must fail,
Dependent made; so God shall uncreate,
Be frustrate, do, undo, and labour lose,
945   Not well conceived of God, who though his power
Creation could repeat, yet would be loath
Us to abolish, lest the Adversary
Triumph and say; Fickle their state whom God
Most favours, who can please him long? Me first
950   He ruined, now mankind; whom will he next?
Matter of scorn, not to be given the Foe.
However I with thee have fixed my lot,
Certain to undergo like doom; if death
Consort with thee, death is to me as life;
955   So forcible within my heart I feel
The bond of nature draw me to my own,
My own in thee, for what thou art is mine;
Our state cannot be severed, we are one,
One flesh; to lose thee were to lose myself.
960   So Adam, and thus Eve to him replied.
O glorious trial of exceeding love,
Illustrious evidence, example high!
Engaging me to emulate, but short
Of thy perfection, how shall I attain,
965   Adam, from whose side I boast me sprung,
And gladly of our union hear thee speak,
One heart, one soul in both; whereof good proof
This day affords, declaring thee resolved,
Rather than death or aught than death more dread
970   Shall separate us, linked in love so dear,
To undergo with me one guilt, one crime,
If any be, of tasting this fair fruit,
Whose virtue, for of good still good proceeds,
Direct, or by occasion hath presented
975   This happy trial of thy love, which else
So eminently never had been known.
Were it that I thought death menaced would ensue
This my attempt, I would sustain alone
The worst, and not persuade thee, rather die

980   Deserted, than oblige thee with a fact
       Pernicious to thy peace, chiefly assured
       Remarkably so late of thy so true,
       So faithful love unequalled; but I feel
       Far otherwise th' event, not death, but life
985   Augmented, opened eyes, new hopes, new joys,
       Taste so divine, that what of sweet before
       Hath touched my sense, flat seems to this, and harsh.
       On my experience, Adam, freely taste,
       And fear of death deliver to the winds.
990   So saying, she embraced him, and for joy
       Tenderly wept, much won that he his love
       Had so ennobled, as of choice to incur
       Divine displeasure for her sake, or death.
       In recompense (for such compliance bad
995   Such recompense best merits) from the bough
       She gave him of that fair enticing fruit
       With liberal hand: he scrupled not to eat
       Against his better knowledge, not deceived,
       But fondly overcome with female charm.
1000   Earth trembled from her entrails, as again
       In pangs, and Nature gave a second groan;
       Sky loured, and muttering thunder, some sad drops
       Wept at completing of the mortal sin
       Original; while Adam took no thought,
1005   Eating his fill, nor Eve to iterate
       Her former trespass feared, the more to soothe
       Him with her loved society, that now
       As with new wine intoxicated both
       They swim in mirth, and fancy that they feel
1010   Divinity within them breeding wings
       Wherewith to scorn the earth: but that false fruit
       Far other operation first displayed,
       Carnal desire inflaming; he on Eve
       Began to cast lascivious eyes, she him
1015   As wantonly repaid; in lust they burn:
       Till Adam thus gan Eve to dalliance move.
           Eve, now I see thou art exact of taste,
       And elegant, of sapience no small part,

Since to each meaning savour we apply,
1020 And palate call judicious; I the praise
Yield thee, so well this day thou hast purveyed.
Much pleasure we have lost, while we abstained
From this delightful fruit, nor known till now
True relish, tasting; if such pleasure be
1025 In things to us forbidden, it might be wished,
For this one tree had been forbidden ten.
But come, so well refreshed, now let us play,
As meet is, after such delicious fare;
For never did thy beauty since the day
1030 I saw thee first and wedded thee, adorned
With all perfections so inflame my sense
With ardour to enjoy thee, fairer now
Than ever, bounty of this virtuous tree.
      So said he, and forbore not glance or toy
1035 Of amorous intent, well understood
Of Eve, whose eye darted contagious fire.
Her hand he seized, and to a shady bank,
Thick overhead with verdant roof embow'red
He led her nothing loath; flow'rs were the couch,
1040 Pansies, and violets, and asphodel,
And hyacinth, earth's freshest softest lap.
There they their fill of love and love's disport
Took largely, of their mutual guilt the seal,
The solace of their sin, till dewy sleep
1045 Oppressed them, wearied with their amorous play.
Soon as the force of that fallacious fruit,
That with exhilarating vapour bland
About their spirits had played, and inmost powers
Made err, was now exhaled, and grosser sleep
1050 Bred of unkindly fumes, with conscious dreams
Encumbered, now had left them, up they rose
As from unrest, and each the other viewing,
Soon found their eyes how opened, and their minds
How darkened; innocence, that as a veil
1055 Had shadowed them from knowing ill, was gone;
Just confidence, and native righteousness
And honour from about them, naked left

To guilty Shame: he covered, but his robe
Uncovered more. So rose the Danite strong
1060 Herculean Samson from the harlot-lap
Of Phílistéan Dálila, and waked
Shorn of his strength, they destitute and bare
Of all their virtue: silent, and in face
Confounded long they sat, as strucken mute,
1065 Till Adam, though not less than Eve abashed,
At length gave utterance to these words constrained.
　　O Eve, in evil hour thou didst give ear
To that false worm, of whomsoever taught
To counterfeit man's voice, true in our Fall,
1070 False in our promised rising; since our eyes
Opened we find indeed, and find we know
Both good and evil, good lost, and evil got,
Bad fruit of knowledge, if this be to know,
Which leaves us naked thus, of honour void,
1075 Of innocence, of faith, of purity,
Our wonted ornaments now soiled and stained,
And in our faces evident the signs
Of foul concupiscence; whence evil store;
Even shame, the last of evils; of the first
1080 Be sure then. How shall I behold the face
Henceforth of God or angel, erst with joy
And rapture so oft beheld? those Heav'nly shapes
Will dazzle now this earthly, with their blaze
Insufferably bright. O might I here
1085 In solitude live savage, in some glade
Obscured, where highest woods impenetrable
To star or sunlight, spread their umbrage broad
And brown as evening: cover me ye pines,
Ye cedars, with innumerable boughs
1090 Hide me, where I may never see them more.
But let us now, as in bad plight, devise
What best may for the present serve to hide
The parts of each from other, that seem most
To shame obnoxious, and unseemliest seen;
1095 Some tree whose broad smooth leaves together sewed,
And girded on our loins, may cover round

Those middle parts, that this new comer, Shame,
There sit not, and reproach us as unclean.
   So counselled he, and both together went
1100 Into the thickest wood, there soon they chose
The fig-tree, not that kind for fruit renowned,
But such as at this day to Indians known
In Malabar or Deccan spreads her arms
Branching so broad and long, that in the ground
1105 The bended twigs take root, and daughters grow
About the mother tree, a pillared shade
High overarched, and echoing walks between;
There oft the Indian herdsman shunning heat
Shelters in cool, and tends his pasturing herds
1110 At loopholes cut through thickest shade: those leaves
They gathered, broad as Amazonian targe,
And with what skill they had, together sewed,
To gird their waist, vain covering if to hide
Their guilt and dreaded shame; O how unlike
1115 To that first naked glory. Such of late
Columbus found th' American so girt
With feathered cincture, naked else and wild
Among the trees on isles and woody shores.
Thus fenced, and as they thought, their shame in part
1120 Covered, but not at rest or ease of mind,
They sat them down to weep, nor only tears
Rained at their eyes, but high winds worse within
Began to rise, high passions, anger, hate,
Mistrust, suspicion, discord, and shook sore
1125 Their inward state of mind, calm region once
And full of peace, now tossed and turbulent:
For understanding ruled not, and the will
Heard not her lore, both in subjection now
To sensual appetite, who from beneath
1130 Usurping over sov'reign reason claimed
Superior sway: from thus distempered breast,
Adam, estranged in look and altered style,
Speech intermitted thus to Eve renewed.
   Would thou hadst hearkened to my words, and stayed
1135 With me, as I besought thee, when that strange

Desire of wand'ring this unhappy morn,
I know not whence possessed thee; we had then
Remained still happy, not as now, despoiled
Of all our good, shamed, naked, miserable.
1140 Let none henceforth seek needless cause to approve
The faith they owe; when earnestly they seek
Such proof, conclude, they then begin to fail.
    To whom soon moved with touch of blame thus Eve.
What words have passed thy lips, Adam severe,
1145 Imput'st thou that to my default, or will
Of wand'ring, as thou call'st it, which who knows
But might as ill have happened thou being by,
Or to thyself perhaps: hadst thou been there,
Or here th' attempt, thou couldst not have discerned
1150 Fraud in the serpent, speaking as he spake;
No ground of enmity between us known,
Why he should mean me ill, or seek to harm.
Was I to have never parted from thy side?
As good have grown there still a lifeless rib.
1155 Being as I am, why didst not thou the head
Command me absolutely not to go,
Going into such danger as thou saidst?
Too facile then thou didst not much gainsay,
Nay, didst permit, approve, and fair dismiss.
1160 Hadst thou been firm and fixed in thy dissent,
Neither had I transgressed, nor thou with me.
    To whom then first incensed Adam replied.
Is this the love, is this the recompense
Of mine to thee, ingrateful Eve, expressed
1165 Immutable when thou wert lost, not I,
Who might have lived and joyed immortal bliss,
Yet willingly chose rather death with thee:
And am I now upbraided, as the cause
Of thy transgressions? not enough severe,
1170 It seems, in thy restraint: what could I more?
I warned thee, I admonished thee, foretold
The danger, and the lurking Enemy
That lay in wait; beyond this had been force,
And force upon free will hath here no place.

1175 But confidence then bore thee on, secure
Either to meet no danger, or to find
Matter of glorious trial, and perhaps
I also erred in overmuch admiring
What seemed in thee so perfect, that I thought
1180 No. evil durst attempt thee, but I rue
That error now, which is become my crime,
And thou th' accuser. Thus it shall befall
Him who to worth in women overtrusting
Lets her will rule; restraint she will not brook,
1185 And left to herself, if evil thence ensue,
She first his weak indulgence will accuse.
      Thus they in mutual accusation spent
The fruitless hours, but neither self-condemning,
And of their vain contést appeared no end.

BOOK X

The Argument

Man's transgression known, the guardian angels forsake Paradise, and return up to Heaven to approve their vigilance, and are approved, God declaring that the entrance of Satan could not be by them prevented. He sends his Son to judge the transgressors, who descends and gives sentence accordingly; then in pity clothes them both, and reascends. Sin and Death sitting till then at the gates of Hell, by wondrous sympathy feeling the success of Satan in this new world, and the sin by man there committed, resolve to sit no longer confined in Hell, but to follow Satan their sire up to the place of man: to make the way easier from Hell to and fro, they pave a broad highway or bridge over Chaos, according to the track that Satan first made; then preparing for earth, they meet him proud of his success returning to Hell; their mutual gratulation. Satan arrives at Pandaemonium, in full assembly relates with boasting his success against man; instead of applause is entertained with a general hiss by all his audience, transformed with himself also suddenly into serpents, according to his doom given in Paradise; then deluded by a show of the Forbidden Tree springing up before them, they greedily reaching to take of the fruit, chew dust and bitter ashes. The proceedings of Sin and Death; God foretells the final victory of his Son over them, and the renewing of all things; but for the present commands his angels to make several alterations in the heavens and elements. Adam more and more perceiving his fallen condition heavily bewails, rejects the condolement of Eve; she persists and at length appeases him: then to evade the curse likely to fall on their offspring, proposes to Adam violent ways which he approves not, but conceiving better hope, puts her in mind of the late promise made them, that her seed should be revenged on the serpent, and exhorts her with him to seek peace of the offended Deity, by repentance and supplication.

Meanwhile the heinous and despiteful act
Of Satan done in Paradise, and how
He in the serpent had perverted Eve,
Her husband she, to taste the fatal fruit,
5 Was known in Heav'n; for what can 'scape the eye
Of God all-seeing, or deceive his heart
Omniscient, who in all things wise and just,
Hindered not Satan to attempt the mind
Of man, with strength entire, and free will armed,
10 Complete to have discovered and repulsed
Whatever wiles of foe or seeming friend.
For still they knew, and ought to have still remembered
The high injunction not to taste that fruit,
Whoever tempted; which they not obeying,
15 Incurred, what could they less, the penalty,
And manifold in sin, deserved to fall.
Up into Heav'n from Paradise in haste
Th' angelic guards ascended, mute and sad
For man, for of his state by this they knew,
20 Much wond'ring how the subtle Fiend had stol'n
Entrance unseen. Soon as th' unwelcome news
From earth arrived at Heaven gate, displeased
All were who heard, dim sadness did not spare
That time celestial visages, yet mixed
25 With pity, violated not their bliss.
About the new-arrived, in multitudes
Th' ethereal people ran, to hear and know
How all befell: they towards the throne supreme
Accountable made haste to make appear
30 With righteous plea, their utmost vigilance,
And easily approved; when the Most High
Eternal Father from his secret cloud,
Amidst in thunder uttered thus his voice.
    Assembled angels, and ye Powers returned
35 From unsuccessful charge, be not dismayed,

Nor troubled at these tidings from the earth,
Which your sincerest care could not prevent,
Foretold so lately what would come to pass,
When first this Tempter crossed the gulf from Hell.
40 I told ye then he should prevail and speed
On his bad errand, man should be seduced
And flattered out of all, believing lies
Against his Maker; no decree of mine
Concurring to necessitate his Fall,
45 Or touch with lightest moment of impúlse
His free will, to her own inclining left
In even scale. But fall'n he is, and now
What rests but that the mortal sentence pass
On his transgression, death denounced that day,
50 Which he presumes already vain and void,
Because not yet inflicted, as he feared,
By some immediate stroke; but soon shall find
Forbearance no acquittance ere day end.
Justice shall not return as bounty scorned.
55 But whom send I to judge them? whom but thee
Vicegerent Son, to thee I have transferred
All judgement, whether in Heav'n, or earth, or Hell.
Easy it might be seen that I intend
Mercy colléague with justice, sending thee
60 Man's friend, his Mediator, his designed
Both ransom and Redeemer voluntary,
And destined man himself to judge man fall'n.
    So spake the Father, and unfolding bright
Toward the right hand his glory, on the Son
65 Blazed forth unclouded deity; he full
Resplendent all his Father manifest
Expressed, and thus divinely answered mild.
    Father Eternal, thine is to decree,
Mine both in Heav'n and earth to do thy will
70 Supreme, that thou in me thy Son beloved
May'st ever rest well pleased. I go to judge
On earth these thy transgressors, but thou know'st,
Whoever judged, the worst on me must light,
When time shall be, for so I undertook

75   Before thee; and not repenting, this obtain
Of right, that I may mitigate their doom
On me derived; yet I shall temper so
Justice with mercy, as may illústrate most
Them fully satisfied, and thee appease.
80   Attendance none shall need, nor train, where none
Are to behold the judgement, but the judged,
Those two; the third best absent is condemned,
Convict by flight, and rebel to all law;
Conviction to the serpent none belongs.
85   Thus saying, from his radiant seat he rose
Of high collateral glory: him Thrones and Powers,
Princedoms, and Dominations ministrant
Accompanied to Heaven gate, from whence
Eden and all the coast in prospect lay.
90   Down he descended straight; the speed of Gods
Time counts not, though with swiftest minutes winged.
Now was the sun in western cadence low
From noon, and gentle airs due at their hour
To fan the earth now waked, and usher in
95   The ev'ning cool when he from wrath more cool
Came the mild Judge and Intercessor both
To sentence man: the voice of God they heard
Now walking in the garden, by soft winds
Brought to their ears, while day declined; they heard
100   And from his presence hid themselves among
The thickest trees, both man and wife, till God
Approaching, thus to Adam called aloud.
    Where art thou Adam, wont with joy to meet
My coming seen far off? I miss thee here,
105   Not pleased, thus entertained with solitude,
Where obvious duty erewhile appeared unsought:
Or come I less conspicuous, or what change
Absents thee, or what chance detains? Come forth.
He came, and with him Eve, more loath, though first
110   To offend, discount'nanced both, and discomposed;
Love was not in their looks, either to God
Or to each other, but apparent guilt,
And shame, and perturbation, and despair,

Anger, and obstinacy, and hate, and guile.
115   Whence Adam falt'ring long, thus answered brief.
     I heard thee in the garden, and of thy voice
Afraid, being naked, hid myself. To whom
The gracious Judge without revile replied.
     My voice thou oft hast heard, and hast not feared,
120   But still rejoiced, how is it now become
So dreadful to thee? that thou art naked, who
Hath told thee? hast thou eaten of the tree
Whereof I gave thee charge thou shouldst not eat?
     To whom thus Adam sore beset replied.
125   O Heav'n! in evil strait this day I stand
Before my Judge, either to undergo
Myself the total crime, or to accuse
My other self, the partner of my life;
Whose failing, while her faith to me remains,
130   I should conceal, and not expose to blame
By my complaint; but strict necessity
Subdues me, and calamitous constraint,
Lest on my head both sin and punishment,
However insupportable, be all
135   Devolved; though should I hold my peace, yet thou
Wouldst easily detect what I conceal.
This woman whom thou mad'st to be my help,
And gav'st me as thy perfect gift, so good,
So fit, so ácceptáble, so divine,
140   That from her hand I could suspect no ill,
And what she did, whatever in itself,
Her doing seemed to justify the deed;
She gave me of the tree, and I did eat.
     To whom the sov'reign Presence thus replied.
145   Was she thy God, that her thou didst obey
Before his voice, or was she made thy guide,
Superior, or but equal, that to her
Thou didst resign thy manhood, and the place
Wherein God set thee above her made of thee,
150   And for thee, whose perfection far excelled
Hers in all real dignity: adorned
She was indeed, and lovely to attract

Thy love, not thy subjection, and her gifts
Were such as under government well seemed,
155 Unseemly to bear rule, which was thy part
And person, hadst thou known thyself aright.
     So having said, he thus to Eve in few:
Say woman, what is this which thou hast done?
     To whom sad Eve with shame nigh overwhelmed,
160 Confessing soon, yet not before her Judge
Bold or loquacious, thus abashed replied.
The serpent me beguiled and I did eat.
     Which when the Lord God heard, without delay
To judgement he proceeded on th' accused
165 Serpent though brute, unable to transfer
The guilt on him who made him instrument
Of mischief, and polluted from the end
Of his creation; justly then accurst,
As vitiated in nature: more to know
170 Concerned not man (since he no further knew)
Nor altered his offence; yet God at last
To Satan first in sin his doom applied,
Though in mysterious terms, judged as then best:
And on the serpent thus his curse let fall.
175   Because thou hast done this, thou art accurst
Above all cattle, each beast of the field;
Upon thy belly grovelling thou shalt go,
And dust shalt eat all the days of thy life.
Between thee and the woman I will put
180 Enmity, and between thine and her seed;
Her seed shall bruise thy head, thou bruise his heel.
     So spake this oracle, then verified
When Jesus son of Mary second Eve,
Saw Satan fall like lightning down from Heav'n,
185 Prince of the Air; then rising from his grave
Spoiled Principalities and Powers, triumphed
In open show, and with ascension bright
Captivity led captive through the air,
The realm itself of Satan long usurped,
190 Whom he shall tread at last under our feet;
Ev'n he who now foretold his fatal bruise,

And to the woman thus his sentence turned.
   Thy sorrow I will greatly multiply
By thy conception; children thou shalt bring
195   In sorrow forth, and to thy husband's will
Thine shall submit, he over thee shall rule.
   On Adam last thus judgement he pronounced.
Because thou hast hearkened to the voice of thy wife,
And eaten of the tree concerning which
200   I charged thee, saying: Thou shalt not eat thereof,
Cursed is the ground for thy sake, thou in sorrow
Shalt eat thereof all the days of thy life;
Thorns also and thistles it shall bring thee forth
Unbid, and thou shalt eat the herb of the field,
205   In the sweat of thy face shalt thou eat bread,
Till thou return unto the ground, for thou
Out of the ground wast taken; know thy birth,
For dust thou art, and shalt to dust return.
   So judged he man, both Judge and Saviour sent,
210   And th' instant stroke of death denounced that day
Removed far off; then pitying how they stood
Before him naked to the air, that now
Must suffer change, disdained not to begin
Thenceforth the form of servant to assume,
215   As when he washed his servants' feet, so now
As father of his family he clad
Their nakedness with skins of beasts, or slain,
Or as the snake with youthful coat repaid;
And thought not much to clothe his enemies:
220   Nor he their outward only with the skins
Of beasts, but inward nakedness, much more
Opprobrious, with his robe of righteousness,
Arraying covered from his Father's sight.
To him with swift ascent he up returned,
225   Into his blissful bosom reassumed
In glory as of old, to him appeased,
All, though all-knowing, what had passed with man
Recounted, mixing intercession sweet.
   Meanwhile ere thus was sinned and judged on earth,
230   Within the gates of Hell sat Sin and Death,

In counterview within the gates, that now
Stood open wide, belching outrageous flame
Far into Chaos, since the Fiend passed through,
Sin opening, who thus now to Death began.
235   O Son, why sit we here each other viewing
Idly, while Satan our great author thrives
In other worlds, and happier seat provides
For us his offspring dear? It cannot be
But that success attends him; if mishap,
240   Ere this he had returned, with fury driv'n
By his avengers, since no place like this
Can fit his punishment, or their revenge.
Methinks I feel new strength within me rise,
Wings growing, and dominion giv'n me large
245   Beyond this deep; whatever draws me on,
Or sympathy, or some connatural force
Powerful at greatest distance to unite
With secret amity things of like kind
By secretest conveyance. Thou my shade
250   Inseparable must with me along:
For Death from Sin no power can separate.
But lest the difficulty of passing back
Stay his return perhaps over this gulf
Impassable, impervious, let us try
255   Advent'rous work, yet to thy power and mine
Not unagreeable, to found a path
Over this main from Hell to that new world
Where Satan now prevails, a monument
Of merit high to all th' infernal host,
260   Easing their passage hence, for intercourse,
Or transmigration, as their lot shall lead.
Nor can I miss the way, so strongly drawn
By this new felt attraction and instínct.
       Whom thus the meagre Shadow answered soon.
265   Go whither Fate and inclination strong
Leads thee, I shall not lag behind, nor err
The way, thou leading, such a scent I draw
Of carnage, prey innumerable, and taste
The savour of death from all things there that live:

270   Nor shall I to the work thou enterprisest
       Be wanting, but afford thee equal aid.
         So saying, with delight he snuffed the smell
       Of mortal change on earth. As when a flock
       Of ravenous fowl, though many a league remote,
275   Against the day of battle, to a field,
       Where armies lie encamped, come flying, lured
       By the scent of living carcasses designed
       For death, the following day, in bloody fight.
       So scented the grim feature, and upturned
280   His nostril wide into the murky air,
       Sagacious of his quarry from so far.
       Then both from out Hell gates into the waste
       Wide anarchy of Chaos damp and dark
       Flew diverse, and with power (their power was great)
285   Hovering upon the waters; what they met
       Solid or slimy, as in raging sea
       Tossed up and down, together crowded drove
       From each side shoaling towards the mouth of Hell.
       As when two polar winds blowing adverse
290   Upon the Cronian Sea, together drive
       Mountains of ice, that stop th' imagined way
       Beyond Petsora eastward, to the rich
       Cathayan coast. The aggregated soil
       Death with his mace petrific, cold and dry,
295   As with a trident smote, and fixed as firm
       As Delos floating once; the rest his look
       Bound with Gorgonian rigor not to move,
       And with asphaltic slime; broad as the gate,
       Deep to the roots of Hell the gathered beach
300   They fastened, and the mole immense wrought on
       Over the foaming deep high arched, a bridge
       Of length prodigious joining to the wall
       Immovable of this now fenceless world
       Forfeit to Death; from hence a passage broad,
305   Smooth, easy, inoffensive down to Hell.
       So, if great things to small may be compared,
       Xerxes, the liberty of Greece to yoke,
       From Susa his Memnonian palace high

Came to the sea, and over Hellespont
310   Bridging his way, Europe with Asia joined,
And scourged with many a stroke th' indignant waves.
Now had they brought the work by wondrous art
Pontifical, a ridge of pendent rock
Over the vexed abyss, following the track
315   Of Satan, to the selfsame place where he
First lighted from his wing, and landed safe
From out of Chaos to the outside bare
Of this round world: with pins of adamant
And chains they made all fast, too fast they made
320   And durable; and now in little space
The confines met of empyrean Heav'n
And of this world, and on the left hand Hell
With long reach interposed; three several ways
In sight, to each of these three places led.
325   And now their way to earth they had descried,
To Paradise first tending, when behold
Satan in likeness of an angel bright
Betwixt the Centaur and the Scorpion steering
His zenith, while the sun in Aries rose:
330   Disguised he came, but those his children dear
Their parent soon discerned, though in disguise.
He, after Eve seduced, unminded slunk
Into the wood fast by, and changing shape
To observe the sequel, saw his guileful act
335   By Eve, though all unweeting, seconded
Upon her husband, saw their shame that sought
Vain covertures; but when he saw descend
The Son of God to judge them, terrified
He fled, not hoping to escape, but shun
340   The present, fearing guilty what his wrath
Might suddenly inflict; that past, returned
By night, and list'ning where the hapless pair
Sat in their sad discourse, and various plaint,
Thence gathered his own doom, which understood
345   Not instant, but of future time. With joy
And tidings fraught, to Hell he now returned,
And at the brink of Chaos, near the foot

Of this new wondrous pontifice, unhoped
Met who to meet him came, his offspring dear.
350   Great joy was at their meeting, and at sight
Of that stupendious bridge his joy increased.
Long he admiring stood, till Sin, his fair
Enchanting daughter, thus the silence broke.
    O parent, these are thy magnific deeds,
355   Thy trophies, which thou view'st as not thine own;
Thou art their author and prime architect:
For I no sooner in my heart divined,
My heart, which by a secret harmony
Still moves with thine, joined in connection sweet,
360   That thou on earth hadst prospered, which thy looks
Now also evidence, but straight I felt
Though distant from thee worlds between, yet felt
That I must after thee with this thy son;
Such fatal consequence unites us three:
365   Hell could no longer hold us in her bounds,
Nor this unvoyageable gulf obscure
Detain from following thy illustrious track.
Thou hast achieved our liberty, confined
Within Hell gates till now, thou us empow'red
370   To fortify thus far, and overlay
With this portentous bridge the dark abyss.
Thine now is all this world, thy virtue hath won
What thy hands builded not, thy wisdom gained
With odds what war hath lost, and fully avenged
375   Our foil in Heav'n; here thou shalt monarch reign,
There didst not; there let him still victor sway,
As battle hath adjudged, from this new world
Retiring, by his own doom alienated,
And henceforth monarchy with thee divide
380   Of all things parted by th' empyreal bounds,
His quadrature, from thy orbicular world,
Or try thee now more dang'rous to his throne.
    Whom thus the Prince of Darkness answered glad.
Fair daughter, and thou son and grandchild both,
385   High proof ye now have giv'n to be the race
Of Satan (for I glory in the name,

Antagonist of Heav'n's Almighty King)
Amply have merited of me, of all
Th' infernal empire, that so near Heav'n's door
390   Triumphal with triumphal act have met,
Mine with this glorious work, and made one realm
Hell and this world, one realm, one continent
Of easy thoroughfare. Therefore while I
Descend through darkness, on your road with ease
395   To my associate Powers, them to acquaint
With these successes, and with them rejoice,
You two this way, among these numerous orbs
All yours, right down to Paradise descend;
There dwell and reign in bliss; thence on the earth
400   Dominion exercise and in the air,
Chiefly on man, sole lord of all declared;
Him first make sure your thrall, and lastly kill.
My substitutes I send ye, and create
Plenipotent on earth, of matchless might
405   Issuing from me: on your joint vigour now
My hold of this new kingdom all depends,
Through Sin to Death exposed by my exploit.
If your joint power prevail, th' affairs of Hell
No detriment need fear; go and be strong.
410   So saying he dismissed them, they with speed
Their course through thickest constellations held
Spreading their bane; the blasted stars looked wan,
And planets, planet-strook, real eclipse
Then suffered. Th' other way Satan went down
415   The causey to Hell gate; on either side
Disparted Chaos overbuilt exclaimed,
And with resounding surge the bars assailed,
That scorned his indignation: through the gate,
Wide open and unguarded, Satan passed,
420   And all about found desolate; for those
Appointed to sit there, had left their charge,
Flown to the upper world; the rest were all
Far to the inland retired, about the walls
Of Pandaemonium, city and proud seat
425   Of Lucifer, so by allusion called,

Of that bright star to Satan paragoned.
There kept their watch the legions, while the grand
In council sat, solicitous what chance
Might intercept their Emperor sent; so he
430 Departing gave command, and they observed.
As when the Tartar from his Russian foe
By Astrakhan over the snowy plains
Retires, or Bactrian Sophy from the horns
Of Turkish crescent, leaves all waste beyond
435 The realm of Aladule, in his retreat
To Tauris or Casbeen. So these the late
Heav'n-banished host, left desert utmost Hell
Many a dark league, reduced in careful watch
Round their metropolis, and now expecting
440 Each hour their great adventurer from the search
Of foreign worlds: he through the midst unmarked,
In show plebeian angel militant
Of lowest order, passed; and from the door
Of that Plutonian hall, invisible
445 Ascended his high throne, which under state
Of richest texture spread, at th' upper end
Was placed in regal lustre. Down a while
He sat, and round about him saw unseen:
At last as from a cloud his fulgent head
450 And shape star-bright appeared, or brighter, clad
With what permissive glory since his Fall
Was left him, or false glitter: all amazed
At that so sudden blaze the Stygian throng
Bent their aspéct, and whom they wished beheld,
455 Their mighty chief returned: loud was th' acclaim:
Forth rushed in haste the great consulting Peers,
Raised from their dark Divan, and with like joy
Congratulant approached him, who with hand
Silence, and with these words attention won.
460   Thrones, Dominations, Princedoms, Virtues, Powers,
For in possession such, not only of right,
I call ye and declare ye now, returned
Successful beyond hope, to lead ye forth
Triumphant out of this infernal pit

465 Abominable, accurst, the house of woe,
  And dungeon of our Tyrant. Now possess,
  As lords, a spacious world, to our native Heaven
  Little inferior, by my adventure hard
  With peril great achieved. Long were to tell
470 What I have done, what suffered, with what pain
  Voyaged th' unreal, vast, unbounded deep
  Of horrible confusion, over which
  By Sin and Death a broad way now is paved
  To expedite your glorious march; but I
475 Toiled out my uncouth passage, forced to ride
  Th' untractable abyss, plunged in the womb
  Of unoriginal Night and Chaos wild,
  That jealous of their secrets fiercely opposed
  My journey strange, with clamorous uproar
480 Protesting Fate supreme; thence how I found
  The new created world, which fame in Heav'n
  Long had foretold, a fabric wonderful
  Of absolute perfection, therein man
  Placed in a Paradise, by our exíle
485 Made happy: him by fraud I have seduced
  From his Creator, and the more to increase
  Your wonder, with an apple; he thereat
  Offended, worth your laughter, hath giv'n up
  Both his beloved man and all his world,
490 To Sin and Death a prey, and so to us,
  Without our hazard, labour, or alarm,
  To range in, and to dwell, and over man
  To rule, as over all he should have ruled.
  True is, me also he hath judged, or rather
495 Me not, but the brute serpent in whose shape
  Man I deceived: that which to me belongs,
  Is enmity, which he will put between
  Me and mankind; I am to bruise his heel;
  His seed, when is not set, shall bruise my head:
500 A world who would not purchase with a bruise,
  Or much more grievous pain? Ye have th' account
  Of my performance: what remains, ye gods,
  But up and enter now into full bliss.

So having said, a while he stood, expecting
505   Their universal shout and high applause
To fill his ear, when contrary he hears
On all sides, from innumerable tongues
A dismal universal hiss, the sound
Of public scorn; he wondered, but not long
510   Had leisure, wond'ring at himself now more;
His visage drawn he felt to sharp and spare,
His arms clung to his ribs, his legs entwining
Each other, till supplanted down he fell
A monstrous serpent on his belly prone,
515   Reluctant, but in vain; a greater power
Now ruled him, punished in the shape he sinned,
According to his doom: he would have spoke,
But hiss for hiss returned with forkèd tongue
To forkèd tongue, for now were all transformed
520   Alike, to serpents all as áccessóries
To his bold riot: dreadful was the din
Of hissing through the hall, thick swarming now
With complicated monsters, head and tail,
Scorpion and asp, and amphisbaena dire,
525   Cerastes horned, hydrus, and ellops drear,
And dipsas (not so thick swarmed once the soil
Bedropped with blood of Gorgon, or the isle
Ophiusa); but still greatest he the midst,
Now dragon grown, larger than whom the sun
530   Engendered in the Pythian vale on slime,
Huge Python, and his power no less he seemed
Above the rest still to retain; they all
Him followed issuing forth to th' open field,
Where all yet left of that revolted rout
535   Heav'n-fall'n, in station stood or just array,
Sublime with expectation when to see
In triumph issuing forth their glorious chief;
They saw, but other sight instead, a crowd
Of ugly serpents; horror on them fell,
540   And horrid sympathy; for what they saw,
They felt themselves now changing; down their arms,
Down fell both spear and shield, down they as fast,

And the dire hiss renewed, and the dire form
Catched by contagion, like in punishment,
545 As in their crime. Thus was th' applause they meant,
Turned to exploding hiss, triumph to shame
Cast on themselves from their own mouths. There stood
A grove hard by, sprung up with this their change,
His will who reigns above, to aggravate
550 Their penance, laden with fair fruit like that
Which grew in Paradise, the bait of Eve
Used by the Tempter: on that prospect strange
Their earnest eyes they fixed, imagining
For one forbidden tree a multitude
555 Now ris'n, to work them further woe or shame;
Yet parched with scalding thirst and hunger fierce,
Though to delude them sent, could not abstain,
But on they rolled in heaps, and up the trees
Climbing, sat thicker than the snaky locks
560 That curled Megaera: greedily they plucked
The fruitage fair to sight, like that which grew
Near that bituminous lake where Sodom flamed;
This more delusive, not the touch, but taste
Deceived; they fondly thinking to allay
565 Their appetite with gust, instead of fruit
Chewed bitter ashes, which th' offended taste
With spattering noise rejected: oft they assayed,
Hunger and thirst constraining, drugged as oft,
With hatefullest disrelish writhed their jaws
570 With soot and cinder filled; so oft they fell
Into the same illusion, not as man
Whom they triúmphed once lapsed. Thus were they
              plagued
And worn with famine, long and ceaseless hiss,
Till their lost shape, permitted, they resumed,
575 Yearly enjoined, some say, to undergo
This annual humbling certain numbered days,
To dash their pride, and joy for man seduced.
However some tradition they dispersed
Among the heathen of their purchase got,
580 And fabled how the serpent, whom they called

Ophion with Eurynome, the wide-
Encroaching Eve perhaps, had first the rule
Of high Olympus, thence by Saturn driv'n
And Ops, ere yet Dictaean Jove was born.
585   Meanwhile in Paradise the hellish pair
Too soon arrived, Sin there in power before,
Once actual, now in body, and to dwell
Habitual habitant; behind her Death
Close following pace for pace, not mounted yet
590   On his pale horse: to whom Sin thus began.
         Second of Satan sprung, all conquering Death,
What think'st thou of our empire now, though earned
With travail difficult, not better far
Than still at Hell's dark threshold to have sat watch,
595   Unnamed, undreaded, and thyself half-starved?
         Whom thus the Sin-born monster answered soon.
To me, who with eternal famine pine,
Alike is Hell, or Paradise, or Heaven,
There best, where most with ravin I may meet;
600   Which here, though plenteous, all too little seems
To stuff this maw, this vast unhidebound corpse.
         To whom th' incestuous mother thus replied.
Thou therefore on these herbs, and fruits, and flow'rs
Feed first, on each beast next, and fish, and fowl,
605   No homely morsels, and whatever thing
The scythe of Time mows down, devour unspared,
Till I in man residing through the race,
His thoughts, his looks, words, actions all infect,
And season him thy last and sweetest prey.
610   This said, they both betook them several ways,
Both to destroy, or unimmortal make
All kinds, and for destruction to mature
Sooner or later; which th' Almighty seeing,
From his transcendent seat the saints among,
615   To those bright orders uttered thus his voice.
         See with what heat these dogs of Hell advance
To waste and havoc yonder world, which I
So fair and good created, and had still
Kept in that state, had not the folly of man

620   Let in these wasteful Furies, who impute
       Folly to me, so doth the Prince of Hell
       And his adherents, that with so much ease
       I suffer them to enter and possess
       A place so Heav'nly, and conniving seem
625   To gratify my scornful enemies,
       That laugh, as if transported with some fit
       Of passion, I to them had quitted all,
       At random yielded up to their misrule;
       And know not that I called and drew them thither
630   My Hell-hounds, to lick up the draff and filth
       Which man's polluting sin with taint hath shed
       On what was pure, till crammed and gorged, nigh burst
       With sucked and glutted offal, at one sling
       Of thy victorious arm, well-pleasing Son,
635   Both Sin, and Death, and yawning grave at last
       Through Chaos hurled, obstruct the mouth of Hell
       For ever, and seal up his ravenous jaws.
       Then heav'n and earth renewed shall be made pure
       To sanctity that shall receive no stain:
640   Till then the curse pronounced on both precedes.
          He ended, and the Heav'nly audience loud
       Sung hallelujah, as the sound of seas,
       Through multitude that sung: Just are thy ways,
       Righteous are thy decrees on all thy works;
645   Who can extenuate thee? Next, to the Son,
       Destined restorer of mankind, by whom
       New heav'n and earth shall to the ages rise,
       Or down from Heav'n descend. Such was their song,
       While the Creator calling forth by name
650   His mighty angels gave them several charge,
       As sorted best with present things. The sun
       Had first his precept so to move, so shine,
       As might affect the earth with cold and heat
       Scarce tolerable, and from the north to call
655   Decrepit winter, from the south to bring
       Solstitial summer's heat. To the blank moon
       Her office they prescribed, to th' other five
       Their planetary motions and aspécts

In sextile, square, and trine, and opposite,
660 Of noxious efficacy, and when to join
In synod unbenign, and taught the fixed
Their influence malignant when to show'r,
Which of them rising with the sun, or falling,
Should prove tempestuous: to the winds they set
665 Their corners, when with bluster to confound
Sea, air, and shore, the thunder when to roll
With terror through the dark aërial hall.
Some say he bid his angels turn askance
The poles of earth twice ten degrees and more
670 From the sun's axle; they with labour pushed
Oblique the centric globe: some say the sun
Was bid turn reins from th' equinoctial road
Like distant breadth to Taurus with the sev'n
Atlantic Sisters, and the Spartan Twins
675 Up to the Tropic Crab; thence down amain
By Leo and the Virgin and the Scales,
As deep as Capricorn, to bring in change
Of seasons to each clime; else had the spring
Perpetual smiled on earth with vernant flow'rs,
680 Equal in days and nights, except to those
Beyond the polar circles; to them day
Had unbenighted shone, while the low sun
To recompense his distance, in their sight
Had rounded still th' horizon, and not known
685 Or east or west, which had forbid the snow
From cold Estotiland, and south as far
Beneath Magellan. At that tasted fruit
The sun, as from Thyestean banquet, turned
His course intended; else how had the world
690 Inhabited, though sinless, more than now,
Avoided pinching cold and scorching heat?
These changes in the heav'ns, though slow, produced
Like change on sea and land, sideral blast,
Vapour, and mist, and exhalation hot,
695 Corrupt and pestilent: now from the north
Of Norumbega, and the Samoed shore
Bursting their brazen dungeon, armed with ice

And snow and hail and stormy gust and flaw,
Boreas and Caecias and Argestes loud
700 And Thrascias rend the woods and seas upturn;
With adverse blast upturns them from the south
Notus and Afer black with thund'rous clouds
From Serraliona; thwart of these as fierce
Forth rush the levant and the ponent winds
705 Eurus and Zephyr, with their lateral noise,
Sirocco, and Libecchio. Thus began
Outrage from lifeless things; but Discord first
Daughter of Sin, among th' irrational,
Death introduced through fierce antipathy:
710 Beast now with beast gan war, and fowl with fowl,
And fish with fish; to graze the herb all leaving,
Devoured each other; nor stood much in awe
Of man, but fled him, or with count'nance grim
Glared on him passing: these were from without
715 The growing miseries, which Adam saw
Already in part, though hid in gloomiest shade,
To sorrow abandoned, but worse felt within,
And in a troubled sea of passion tossed,
Thus to disburden sought with sad complaint.
720   O miserable of happy! is this the end
Of this new glorious world, and me so late
The glory of that glory? who now, become
Accurst of blessèd, hide me from the face
Of God, whom to behold was then my heighth
725 Of happiness: yet well, if here would end
The misery; I deserved it, and would bear
My own deservings; but this will not serve;
All that I eat or drink, or shall beget,
Is propagated curse. O voice once heard
730 Delightfully, *Increase and multiply*,
Now death to hear! for what can I increase
Or multiply, but curses on my head?
Who of all ages to succeed, but feeling
The evil on him brought by me, will curse
735 My head, Ill fare our ancestor impure,
For this we may thank Adam; but his thanks

Shall be the execration; so besides
Mine own that bide upon me, all from me
Shall with a fierce reflux on me redound,
740 On me as on their natural centre light
Heavy, though in their place. O fleeting joys
Of Paradise, dear bought with lasting woes!
Did I request thee, Maker, from my clay
To mould me man, did I solicit thee
745 From darkness to promote me, or here place
In this delicious garden? as my will
Concurred not to my being, it were but right
And equal to reduce me to my dust,
Desirous to resign, and render back
750 All I received, unable to perform
Thy terms too hard, by which I was to hold
The good I sought not. To the loss of that,
Sufficient penalty, why hast thou added
The sense of endless woes? inexplicable
755 Thy justice seems; yet to say truth, too late,
I thus contest; then should have been refused
Those terms whatever, when they were proposed:
Thou didst accept them; wilt thou enjoy the good,
Then cavil the conditions? and though God
760 Made thee without thy leave, what if thy son
Prove disobedient, and reproved, retort,
Wherefore didst thou beget me? I sought it not:
Wouldst thou admit for his contempt of thee
That proud excuse? yet him not thy election,
765 But natural necessity begot.
God made thee of choice his own, and of his own
To serve him; thy reward was of his grace;
Thy punishment then justly is at his will.
Be it so, for I submit, his doom is fair,
770 That dust I am, and shall to dust return:
O welcome hour whenever! why delays
His hand to execute what his decree
Fixed on this day? why do I overlive,
Why am I mocked with death, and lengthened out
775 To deathless pain? how gladly would I meet

Mortality my sentence, and be earth
Insensible, how glad would lay me down
As in my mother's lap! there I should rest
And sleep secure; his dreadful voice no more
780   Would thunder in my ears, no fear of worse
To me and to my offspring would torment me
With cruel expectation. Yet one doubt
Pursues me still, lest all I cannot die,
Lest that pure breath of life, the spirit of man
785   Which God inspired, cannot together perish
With this corporeal clod; then in the grave,
Or in some other dismal place, who knows
But I shall die a living death? O thought
Horrid, if true! yet why? it was but breath
790   Of life that sinned; what dies but what had life
And sin? the body properly hath neither.
All of me then shall die: let this appease
The doubt, since human reach no further knows.
For though the Lord of all be infinite,
795   Is his wrath also? be it, man is not so,
But mortal doomed. How can he exercise
Wrath without end on man whom death must end?
Can he make deathless death? that were to make
Strange contradiction, which to God himself
800   Impossible is held, as argument
Of weakness, not of power. Will he draw out,
For anger's sake, finite to infinite
In punished man, to satisfy his rigour
Satisfied never; that were to extend
805   His sentence beyond dust and Nature's law,
By which all causes else according still
To the reception of their matter act,
Not to th' extent of their own sphere. But say
That death be not one stroke, as I supposed,
810   Bereaving sense, but endless misery
From this day onward, which I feel begun
Both in me, and without me, and so last
To perpetuity; ay me, that fear
Comes thund'ring back with dreadful revolution

815   On my defenceless head; both Death and I
      Am found eternal, and incorporate both,
      Nor I on my part single; in me all
      Posterity stands cursed. Fair patrimony
      That I must leave ye, sons; O were I able
820   To waste it all myself, and leave ye none!
      So disinherited how would ye bless
      Me now your curse! Ah, why should all mankind
      For one man's fault thus guiltless be condemned,
      If guiltless? But from me what can proceed,
825   But all corrupt, both mind and will depraved,
      Not to do only, but to will the same
      With me? how can they then acquitted stand
      In sight of God? Him after all disputes
      Forced I absolve: all my evasions vain
830   And reasonings, though through mazes, lead me still
      But to my own conviction: first and last
      On me, me only, as the source and spring
      Of all corruption, all the blame lights due,
      So might the wrath. Fond wish! couldst thou support
835   That burden heavier than the earth to bear,
      Than all the world much heavier, though divided
      With that bad woman? Thus what thou desir'st,
      And what thou fear'st, alike destroys all hope
      Of refuge, and concludes thee miserable
840   Beyond all past example and future,
      To Satan only like both crime and doom.
      O conscience, into what abyss of fears
      And horrors hast thou driv'n me; out of which
      I find no way, from deep to deeper plunged!
845   Thus Adam to himself lamented loud
      Through the still night, not now, as ere man fell,
      Wholesome and cool, and mild, but with black air
      Accompanied, with damps and dreadful gloom,
      Which to his evil conscience represented
850   All things with double terror: on the ground
      Outstretched he lay, on the cold ground, and oft
      Cursed his creation, Death as oft accused
      Of tardy execution, since denounced

The day of his offence. Why comes not Death,
855   Said he, with one thrice accéptáble stroke
To end me? Shall Truth fail to keep her word,
Justice divine not hasten to be just?
But Death comes not at call, Justice divine
Mends not her slowest pace for prayers or cries.
860   O woods, O fountains, hillocks, dales and bow'rs,
With other echo late I taught your shades
To answer, and resound far other song.
Whom thus afflicted when sad Eve beheld,
Desolate where she sat, approaching nigh,
865   Soft words to his fierce passion she assayed:
But her with stern regard he thus repelled.
      Out of my sight, thou serpent, that name best
Befits thee with him leagued, thyself as false
And hateful; nothing wants, but that thy shape,
870   Like his, and colour serpentine may show
Thy inward fraud, to warn all creatures from thee
Henceforth; lest that too Heav'nly form, pretended
To Hellish falsehood, snare them. But for thee
I had persisted happy, had not thy pride
875   And wand'ring vanity, when least was safe,
Rejected my forewarning, and disdained
Not to be trusted, longing to be seen
Though by the Devil himself, him overweening
To overreach, but with the serpent meeting
880   Fooled and beguiled; by him thou, I by thee,
To trust thee from my side, imagined wise,
Constant, mature, proof against all assaults,
And understood not all was but a show
Rather than solid virtue, all but a rib
885   Crookèd by nature, bent, as now appears,
More to the part siníster from me drawn,
Well if thrown out, as supernumerary
To my just number found. O why did God,
Creator wise, that peopled highest Heav'n
890   With Spirits masculine, create at last
This novelty on earth, this fair defect
Of nature, and not fill the world at once

With men as angels without feminine,
Or find some other way to generate

895   Mankind? this mischief had not then befall'n,
And more that shall befall, innumerable
Disturbances on earth through female snares,
And strait conjunction with this sex: for either
He never shall find out fit mate, but such

900   As some misfortune brings him, or mistake,
Or whom he wishes most shall seldom gain
Through her perverseness, but shall see her gained
By a far worse, or if she love, withheld
By parents, or his happiest choice too late

905   Shall meet, already linked and wedlock-bound
To a fell adversary, his hate or shame:
Which infinite calamity shall cause
To human life, and household peace confound.
      He added not, and from her turned, but Eve

910   Not so repulsed, with tears that ceased not flowing,
And tresses all disordered, at his feet
Fell humble, and embracing them, besought
His peace, and thus proceeded in her plaint.
      Forsake me not thus, Adam, witness Heav'n

915   What love sincere, and reverence in my heart
I bear thee, and unweeting have offended,
Unhappily deceived; thy suppliant
I beg, and clasp thy knees; bereave me not,
Whereon I live, thy gentle looks, thy aid,

920   Thy counsel in this uttermost distress,
My only strength and stay: forlorn of thee,
Whither shall I betake me, where subsist?
While yet we live, scarce one short hour perhaps,
Between us two let there be peace, both joining,

925   As joined in injuries, one enmity
Against a foe by doom express assigned us,
That cruel serpent: on me exercise not
Thy hatred for this misery befall'n,
On me already lost, me than thyself

930   More miserable; both have sinned, but thou
Against God only, I against God and thee,

And to the place of judgement will return,
There with my cries importune Heaven, that all
The sentence from thy head removed may light
935 On me, sole cause to thee of all this woe,
Me me only just object of his ire.
    She ended weeping, and her lowly plight,
Immovable till peace obtained from fault
Acknowledged and deplored, in Adam wrought
940 Commiseration; soon his heart relented
Towards her, his life so late and sole delight,
Now at his feet submissive in distress,
Creature so fair his reconcilement seeking,
His counsel whom she had displeased, his aid;
945 As one disarmed, his anger all he lost,
And thus with peaceful words upraised her soon.
    Unwary, and too desirous, as before,
So now of what thou know'st not, who desir'st
The punishment all on thyself; alas,
950 Bear thine own first, ill able to sustain
His full wrath whose thou feel'st as yet least part,
And my displeasure bear'st so ill. If prayers
Could alter high decrees, I to that place
Would speed before thee, and be louder heard,
955 That on my head all might be visited,
Thy frailty and infirmer sex forgiv'n,
To me committed and by me exposed.
But rise, let us no more contend, nor blame
Each other, blamed enough elsewhere, but strive
960 In offices of love, how we may light'n
Each other's burden in our share of woe;
Since this day's death denounced, if aught I see,
Will prove no sudden, but a slow-paced evil,
A long day's dying to augment our pain,
965 And to our seed (O hapless seed!) derived.
    To whom thus Eve, recovering heart, replied.
Adam, by sad experiment I know
How little weight my words with thee can find,
Found so erroneous, thence by just event
970 Found so unfortunate; nevertheless,

Restored by thee, vile as I am, to place
Of new acceptance, hopeful to regain
Thy love, the sole contentment of my heart,
Living or dying, from thee I will not hide
975   What thoughts in my unquiet breast are ris'n,
Tending to some relief of our extremes,
Or end, though sharp and sad, yet tolerable,
As in our evils, and of easier choice.
If care of our descent perplex us most,
980   Which must be born to certain woe, devoured
By Death at last, and miserable it is
To be to others cause of misery,
Our own begotten, and of our loins to bring
Into this cursèd world a woeful race,
985   That after wretched life must be at last
Food for so foul a monster, in thy power
It lies, yet ere conception to prevent
The race unblest, to being yet unbegot.
Childless thou art, childless remain:
990   So Death shall be deceived his glut, and with us two
Be forced to satisfy his rav'nous maw.
But if thou judge it hard and difficult,
Conversing, looking, loving, to abstain
From love's due rites, nuptial embraces sweet,
995   And with desire to languish without hope,
Before the present object languishing
With like desire, which would be misery
And torment less than none of what we dread,
Then both ourselves and seed at once to free
1000   From what we fear for both, let us make short,
Let us seek Death, or he not found, supply
With our own hands his office on ourselves;
Why stand we longer shivering under fears,
That show no end but death, and have the power,
1005   Of many ways to die the shortest choosing,
Destruction with destruction to destroy.
    She ended here, or vehement despair
Broke off the rest; so much of death her thoughts
Had entertained, as dyed her cheeks with pale.

1010   But Adam with such counsel nothing swayed,
To better hopes his more attentive mind
Labouring had raised, and thus to Eve replied.
    Eve, thy contempt of life and pleasure seems
To argue in thee something more sublime
1015 And excellent than what thy mind contemns;
But self-destruction therefore sought, refutes
That excellence thought in thee, and implies,
Not thy contempt, but anguish and regret
For loss of life and pleasure overloved.
1020 Or if thou covet death, as utmost end
Of misery, so thinking to evade
The penalty pronounced, doubt not but God
Hath wiselier armed his vengeful ire than so
To be forestalled; much more I fear lest death
1025 So snatched will not exempt us from the pain
We are by doom to pay; rather such acts
Of cóntumácy will provoke the Highest
To make death in us live: then let us seek
Some safer resolution, which methinks
1030 I have in view, calling to mind with heed
Part of our sentence, that thy seed shall bruise
The serpent's head; piteous amends, unless
Be meant, whom I conjecture, our grand Foe
Satan, who in the serpent hath contrived
1035 Against us this deceit: to crush his head
Would be revenge indeed; which will be lost
By death brought on our selves, or childless days
Resolved, as thou proposest; so our Foe
Shall 'scape his punishment ordained, and we
1040 Instead shall double ours upon our heads.
No more be mentioned then of violence
Against ourselves, and wilful barrenness,
That cuts us off from hope, and savours only
Rancour and pride, impatience and despite,
1045 Reluctance against God and his just yoke
Laid on our necks. Remember with what mild
And gracious temper he both heard and judged
Without wrath or reviling; we expected

Immediate dissolution, which we thought
1050 Was meant by death that day, when lo, to thee
Pains only in child-bearing were foretold,
And bringing forth, soon recompensed with joy,
Fruit of thy womb: on me the curse aslope
Glanced on the ground; with labour I must earn
1055 My bread; what harm? Idleness had been worse;
My labour will sustain me; and lest cold
Or heat should injure us, his timely care
Hath unbesought provided, and his hands
Clothed us unworthy, pitying while he judged;
1060 How much more, if we pray him, will his ear
Be open, and his heart to pity incline,
And teach us further by what means to shun
Th' inclement seasons, rain, ice, hail and snow,
Which now the sky with various face begins
1065 To show us in this mountain, while the winds
Blow moist and keen, shattering the graceful locks
Of these fair spreading trees; which bids us seek
Some better shroud, some better warmth to cherish
Our limbs benumbed, ere this diurnal star
1070 Leave cold the night, how we his gathered beams
Reflected, may with matter sere foment,
Or by collision of two bodies grind
The air attrite to fire, as late the clouds
Justling or pushed with winds rude in their shock
1075 Tine the slant lightning, whose thwart flame driv'n down
Kindles the gummy bark of fir or pine,
And sends a comfortable heat from far,
Which might supply the sun: such fire to use,
And what may else be remedy or cure
1080 To evils which our own misdeeds have wrought,
He will instruct us praying, and of grace
Beseeching him, so as we need not fear
To pass commodiously this life, sustained
By him with many comforts, till we end
1085 In dust, our final rest and native home.
What better can we do, than to the place
Repairing where he judged us, prostrate fall

Before him reverent, and there confess
Humbly our faults, and pardon beg, with tears
1090   Watering the ground, and with our sighs the air
Frequenting, sent from hearts contrite, in sign
Of sorrow unfeigned, and humiliation meek.
Undoubtedly he will relent and turn
From his displeasure; in whose look serene,
1095   When angry most he seemed and most severe,
What else but favour, grace, and mercy shone?
   So spake our father penitent, nor Eve
Felt less remorse: they forthwith to the place
Repairing where he judged them prostrate fell
1100   Before him reverent, and both confessed
Humbly their faults, and pardon begged, with tears
Watering the ground, and with their sighs the air
Frequenting, sent from hearts contrite, in sign
Of sorrow unfeigned, and humiliation meek.

BOOK XI

The Argument

The Son of God presents to his Father the prayers of our
first parents now repenting, and intercedes for them: God
accepts them, but declares that they must no longer abide in
Paradise; sends Michael with a band of Cherubim to dispossess
5 them; but first to reveal to Adam future things: Michael's
coming down. Adam shows to Eve certain ominous signs; he
discerns Michael's approach, goes out to meet him: the angel
denounces their departure. Eve's lamentation. Adam pleads,
but submits: the angel leads him up to a high hill, sets before
10 him in vision what shall happen till the Flood.

Thus they in lowliest plight repentant stood
Praying, for from the mercy-seat above
Prevenient grace descending had removed
The stony from their hearts, and made new flesh
5 Regenerate grow instead, that sighs now breathed
Unutterable, which the spirit of prayer
Inspired, and winged for Heav'n with speedier flight
Than loudest oratory: yet their port
Not of mean suitors, nor important less
10 Seemed their petition, than when th' ancient pair
In fables old, less ancient yet than these,
Deucalion and chaste Pyrrha to restore
The race of mankind drowned, before the shrine
Of Themis stood devout. To Heav'n their prayers
15 Flew up, nor missed the way, by envious winds
Blown vagabond or frustrate: in they passed
Dimensionless through Heav'nly doors; then clad
With incense, where the golden altar fumed,
By their great Intercessor, came in sight
20 Before the Father's throne: them the glad Son

Presenting, thus to intercede began.
     See Father, what first fruits on earth are sprung
From thy implanted grace in man, these sighs
And prayers, which in this golden censer, mixed
25   With incense, I thy priest before thee bring.
Fruits of more pleasing savour from thy seed
Sown with contrition in his heart, than those
Which his own hand manuring all the trees
Of Paradise could have produced, ere fall'n
30   From innocence. Now therefore bend thine ear
To supplication, hear his sighs though mute;
Unskilful with what words to pray, let me
Interpret for him, me his advocate
And propitiation, all his works on me
35   Good or not good ingraft; my merit those
Shall perfect, and for these my death shall pay.
Accept me, and in me from these receive
The smell of peace toward mankind, let him live
Before thee reconciled, at least his days
40   Numbered, though sad, till death, his doom (which I
To mitigate thus plead, not to reverse)
To better life shall yield him, where with me
All my redeemed may dwell in joy and bliss,
Made one with me as I with thee am one.
45   To whom the Father, without cloud, serene.
All thy request for man, accepted Son,
Obtain, all thy request was my decree:
But longer in this Paradise to dwell,
The law I gave to Nature him forbids:
50   Those pure immortal elements that know
No gross, no unharmonious mixture foul,
Eject him tainted now, and purge him off
As a distemper, gross to air as gross,
And mortal food, as may dispose him best
55   For dissolution wrought by sin, that first
Distempered all things, and of incorrupt
Corrupted. I at first with two fair gifts
Created him endowed, with happiness
And immortality: that fondly lost,

60   This other served but to eternize woe;
        Till I provided death; so death becomes
        His final remedy, and after life
        Tried in sharp tribulation, and refined
        By faith and faithful works, to second life,
65   Waked in the renovation of the just,
        Resigns him up with heav'n and earth renewed.
        But let us call to synod all the blest
        Through Heav'n's wide bounds; from them I will not hide
        My judgements, how with mankind I proceed,
70   As with the peccant angels late they saw;
        And in their state, though firm, stood more confirmed.
            He ended, and the Son gave signal high
        To the bright minister that watched; he blew
        His trumpet, heard in Oreb since perhaps
75   When God descended, and perhaps once more
        To sound at general doom. Th' angelic blast
        Filled all the regions: from their blissful bow'rs
        Of amarantine shade, fountain or spring,
        By the waters of life, where'er they sat
80   In fellowships of joy: the sons of light
        Hasted, resorting to the summons high,
        And took their seats; till from his throne supreme
        Th' Almighty thus pronounced his sov'reign will.
            O sons, like one of us man is become
85   To know both good and evil, since his taste
        Of that defended fruit; but let him boast
        His knowledge of good lost, and evil got,
        Happier, had it sufficed him to have known
        Good by itself, and evil not at all.
90   He sorrows now, repents, and prays contrite,
        My motions in him; longer than they move,
        His heart I know, how variable and vain
        Self-left. Lest therefore his now bolder hand
        Reach also of the Tree of Life, and eat,
95   And live for ever, dream at least to live
        For ever, to remove him I decree,
        And send him from the garden forth to till
        The ground whence he was taken, fitter soil.

Michael, this my behest have thou in charge,
100 Take to thee from among the Cherubim
Thy choice of flaming warriors, lest the Fiend
Or in behalf of man, or to invade
Vacant possession some new trouble raise:
Haste thee, and from the Paradise of God
105 Without remorse drive out the sinful pair,
From hallowed ground th' unholy, and denounce
To them and to their progeny from thence
Perpetual banishment. Yet lest they faint
At the sad sentence rigorously urged,
110 For I behold them softened and with tears
Bewailing their excess, all terror hide.
If patiently thy bidding they obey,
Dismiss them not disconsolate; reveal
To Adam what shall come in future days,
115 As I shall thee enlighten; intermix
My cov'nant in the woman's seed renewed;
So send them forth, though sorrowing, yet in peace:
And on the east side of the garden place,
Where entrance up from Eden easiest climbs,
120 Cherubic watch, and of a sword the flame
Wide waving, all approach far off to fright,
And guard all passage to the Tree of Life:
Lest Paradise a réceptácle prove
To Spirits foul, and all my trees their prey,
125 With whose stol'n fruit man once more to delude.
He ceased; and th' Archangelic Power prepared
For swift descent, with him the cohort bright
Of watchful Cherubim; four faces each
Had, like a double Janus, all their shape
130 Spangled with eyes more numerous than those
Of Argus, and more wakeful than to drowse,
Charmed with Arcadian pipe, the pastoral reed
Of Hermes, or his opiate rod. Meanwhile
To resalute the world with sacred light
135 Leucothea waked, and with fresh dews embalmed
The earth, when Adam and first matron Eve
Had ended now their orisons, and found

Strength added from above, new hope to spring
Out of despair, joy, but with fear yet linked;
140   Which thus to Eve his welcome words renewed.
     Eve, easily may faith admit, that all
The good which we enjoy from Heav'n descends;
But that from us aught should ascend to Heav'n
So prevalent as to concern the mind
145   Of God high-blest, or to incline his will,
Hard to belief may seem; yet this will prayer,
Or one short sigh of human breath upborne
Ev'n to the seat of God. For since I sought
By prayer th' offended Deity to appease,
150   Kneeled and before him humbled all my heart,
Methought I saw him placable and mild,
Bending his ear; persuasion in me grew
That I was heard with favour; peace returned
Home to my breast, and to my memory
155   His promise, that thy seed shall bruise our Foe;
Which then not minded in dismay, yet now
Assures me that the bitterness of death
Is past, and we shall live. Whence hail to thee,
Eve rightly called, mother of all mankind,
160   Mother of all things living, since by thee
Man is to live, and all things live for man.
     To whom thus Eve with sad demeanour meek.
Ill worthy I such title should belong
To me transgressor, who for thee ordained
165   A help, became thy snare; to me reproach
Rather belongs, distrust and all dispraise:
But infinite in pardon was my Judge,
That I who first brought death on all, am graced
The source of life; next favourable thou,
170   Who highly thus to entitle me vouchsaf'st,
Far other name deserving. But the field
To labour calls us now with sweat imposed,
Though after sleepless night; for see the Morn,
All unconcerned with our unrest, begins
175   Her rosy progress smiling; let us forth,
I never from thy side henceforth to stray,

Where'er our day's work lies, though now enjoined
Laborious, till day droop; while here we dwell,
What can be toilsome in these pleasant walks?
180   Here let us live, though in fall'n state, content.
　　So spake, so wished much-humbled Eve, but Fate
Subscribed not; Nature first gave signs, impressed
On bird, beast, air, air suddenly eclipsed
After short blush of morn; nigh in her sight
185   The bird of Jove, stooped from his airy tow'r,
Two birds of gayest plume before him drove:
Down from a hill the beast that reigns in woods,
First hunter then, pursued a gentle brace,
Goodliest of all the forest, hart and hind;
190   Direct to th' eastern gate was bent their flight.
Adam observed, and with his eye the chase
Pursuing, not unmoved to Eve thus spake.
　　O Eve, some further change awaits us nigh,
Which Heav'n by these mute signs in Nature shows
195   Forerunners of his purpose, or to warn
Us haply too secure of our discharge
From penalty, because from death released
Some days; how long, and what till then our life,
Who knows, or more than this, that we are dust,
200   And thither must return and be no more.
Why else this double object in our sight
Of flight pursued in th' air and o'er the ground
One way the self-same hour? Why in the east
Darkness ere day's mid-course, and morning light
205   More orient in yon western cloud that draws
O'er the blue firmament a radiant white,
And slow descends, with something Heav'nly fraught.
　　He erred not, for by this the Heav'nly bands
Down from a sky of jasper lighted now
210   In Paradise, and on a hill made halt,
A glorious apparition, had not doubt
And carnal fear that day dimmed Adam's eye.
Not that more glorious, when the angels met
Jacob in Mahanaim, where he saw
215   The field pavilioned with his guardians bright;

Nor that which on the flaming mount appeared
In Dothan, covered with a camp of fire,
Against the Syrian king, who to surprise
One man, assassin-like had levied war,
220   War unproclaimed. The princely hierarch
In their bright stand, there left his powers to seize
Possession of the garden; he alone,
To find where Adam sheltered, took his way,
Not unperceived of Adam, who to Eve,
225   While the great visitant approached, thus spake.
      Eve, now expect great tidings, which perhaps
Of us will soon determine, or impose
New laws to be observed; for I descry
From yonder blazing cloud that veils the hill
230   One of the Heav'nly host, and by his gait
None of the meanest, some great Potentate
Or of the Thrones above, such majesty
Invests him coming; yet not terrible,
·That I should fear, nor sociably mild,
235   As Raphael, that I should much confide,
But solemn and sublime, whom not to offend,
With reverence I must meet, and thou retire.
He ended; and th' Archangel soon drew nigh,
Not in his shape celestial, but as man
240   Clad to meet man; over his lucid arms
A military vest of purple flowed
Livelier than Meliboean, or the grain
Of Sarra, worn by kings and heroes old
In time of truce; Iris had dipped the woof;
245   His starry helm unbuckled showed him prime
In manhood where youth ended; by his side
As in a glittering zodiac hung the sword,
Satan's dire dread, and in his hand the spear.
Adam bowed low; he kingly from his state
250   Inclined not, but his coming thus declared.
      Adam, Heav'n's high behest no preface needs:
Sufficient that thy prayers are heard, and Death,
Then due by sentence when thou didst transgress,
Defeated of his seizure many days

255   Giv'n thee of grace, wherein thou may'st repent,
      And one bad act with many deeds well done
      May'st cover: well may then thy Lord appeased
      Redeem thee quite from Death's rapacious claim;
      But longer in this Paradise to dwell
260   Permits not; to remove thee I am come,
      And send thee from the garden forth to till
      The ground whence thou wast taken, fitter soil.
          He added not, for Adam at the news
      Heart-strook with chilling gripe of sorrow stood,
265   That all his senses bound; Eve, who unseen
      Yet all had heard, with audible lament
      Discovered soon the place of her retire.
          O unexpected stroke, worse than of Death!
      Must I thus leave thee Paradise? thus leave
270   Thee native soil, these happy walks and shades,
      Fit haunt of gods? where I had hope to spend,
      Quiet though sad, the respite of that day
      That must be mortal to us both. O flow'rs,
      That never will in other climate grow,
275   My early visitation, and my last
      At ev'n, which I bred up with tender hand
      From the first op'ning bud, and gave ye names,
      Who now shall rear ye to the sun, or rank
      Your tribes, and water from th' ambrosial fount?
280   Thee lastly nuptial bower, by me adorned
      With what to sight or smell was sweet; from thee
      How shall I part, and whither wander down
      Into a lower world, to this obscure
      And wild, how shall we breathe in other air
285   Less pure, accustomed to immortal fruits?
          Whom thus the angel interrupted mild.
      Lament not Eve, but patiently resign
      What justly thou hast lost; nor set thy heart,
      Thus over-fond, on that which is not thine;
290   Thy going is not lonely, with thee goes
      Thy husband, him to follow thou art bound;
      Where he abides, think there thy native soil.
          Adam by this from the cold sudden damp

Recovering, and his scattered spirits returned,
295 To Michael thus his humble words addressed.
　　Celestial, whether among the Thrones, or named
Of them the highest, for such of shape may seem
Prince among princes, gently hast thou told
Thy message, which might else in telling wound,
300 And in performing end us; what besides
Of sorrow and dejection and despair
Our frailty can sustain, thy tidings bring,
Departure from this happy place, our sweet
Recess, and only consolation left
305 Familiar to our eyes, all places else
Inhospitable appear and desolate,
Nor knowing us nor known: and if by prayer
Incessant I could hope to change the will
Of him who all things can, I would not cease
310 To weary him with my assiduous cries:
But prayer against his absolute decree
No more avails than breath against the wind,
Blown stifling back on him that breathes it forth:
Therefore to his great bidding I submit.
315 This most afflicts me, that departing hence,
As from his face I shall be hid, deprived
His blessèd count'nance; here I could frequent,
With worship, place by place where he vouchsafed
Presence divine, and to my sons relate;
320 On this mount he appeared, under this tree
Stood visible, among these pines his voice
I heard, here with him at this fountain talked:
So many grateful altars I would rear
Of grassy turf, and pile up every stone
325 Of lustre from the brook, in memory,
Or monument to ages, and thereon
Offer sweet smelling gums and fruits and flow'rs:
In yonder nether world where shall I seek
His bright appearances, or footstep trace?
330 For though I fled him angry, yet recalled
To life prolonged and promised race, I now
Gladly behold though but his utmost skirts

Of glory, and far off his steps adore.
　　To whom thus Michael with regard benign.
335　Adam, thou know'st Heav'n his, and all the earth,
Not this rock only; his omnipresence fills
Land, sea, and air, and every kind that lives,
Fomented by his virtual power and warmed:
All th' earth he gave thee to possess and rule,
340　No déspicáble gift; surmise not then
His presence to these narrow bounds confined
Of Paradise or Eden: this had been
Perhaps thy capital seat, from whence had spread
All generations, and had hither come
345　From all the ends of th' earth, to celebrate
And reverence thee their great progenitor.
But this pre-eminence thou hast lost, brought down
To dwell on even ground now with thy sons:
Yet doubt not but in valley and in plain
350　God is as here, and will be found alike
Present, and of his presence many a sign
Still following thee, still compassing thee round
With goodness and paternal love, his face
Express, and of his steps the track divine.
355　Which that thou may'st believe, and be confirmed
Ere thou from hence depart, know I am sent
To show thee what shall come in future days
To thee and to thy offspring; good with bad
Expect to hear, supernal grace contending
360　With sinfulness of men; thereby to learn
True patience, and to temper joy with fear
And pious sorrow, equally inured
By moderation either state to bear,
Prosperous or adverse: so shalt thou lead
365　Safest thy life, and best prepared endure
Thy mortal passage when it comes. Ascend
This hill; let Eve (for I have drenched her eyes)
Here sleep below while thou to foresight wak'st,
As once thou slept'st, while she to life was formed.
370　　To whom thus Adam gratefully replied.
Ascend, I follow thee, safe guide, the path

Thou lead'st me, and to the hand of Heav'n submit,
However chast'ning, to the evil turn
My obvious breast, arming to overcome
375   By suffering, and earn rest from labour won,
If so I may attain. So both ascend
In the visions of God; it was a hill
Of Paradise the highest, from whose top
The hemisphere of earth in clearest ken
380   Stretched out to the amplest reach of prospect lay.
Not higher that hill nor wider looking round,
Whereon for different cause the Tempter set
Our second Adam in the wilderness,
To show him all earth's kingdoms and their glory.
385   His eye might there command whatever stood
City of old or modern fame, the seat
Of mightiest empire, from the destined walls
Of Cambalu, seat of Cathayan Khan
And Samarkand by Oxus, Temir's throne,
390   To Paquin of Sinaean kings, and thence
To Agra and Lahore of Great Mogul
Down to the golden Chersonese, or where
The Persian in Ecbatan sat, or since
In Hispahan, or where the Russian Czar
395   In Moscow, or the Sultan in Bizance,
Turkéstan-born; nor could his eye not ken
Th' empire of Negus to his utmost port
Ercoco and the less marítime kings
Mombaza, and Quiloa, and Melind,
400   And Sofala thought Ophir, to the realm
Of Congo, and Angola farthest south;
Or thence from Niger flood to Atlas mount
The kingdoms of Almansor, Fez and Sus,
Morocco and Algiers, and Tremisen;
405   On Europe thence, and where Rome was to sway
The world: in spirit perhaps he also saw
Rich Mexico the seat of Motezume,
And Cusco in Peru, the richer seat
Of Atabalipa, and yet unspoiled
410   Guiana, whose great city Geryon's sons

Call El Dorado: but to nobler sights
Michael from Adam's eyes the film removed
Which that false fruit that promised clearer sight
Had bred; then purged with euphrasy and rue
415 The visual nerve, for he had much to see;
And from the Well of Life three drops instilled.
So deep the power of these ingredients pierced,
Even to the inmost seat of mental sight,
That Adam now enforced to close his eyes,
420 Sunk down and all his spirits became entranced:
But him the gentle angel by the hand
Soon raised, and his attention thus recalled.
     Adam, now ope thine eyes, and first behold
Th' effects which thy original crime hath wrought
425 In some to spring from thee, who never touched
Th' excepted tree, nor with the snake conspired,
Nor sinned thy sin, yet from that sin derive
Corruption to bring forth more violent deeds.
     His eyes he opened, and beheld a field,
430 Part arable and tilth, whereon were sheaves
New reaped, the other part sheep-walks and folds;
I' th' midst an altar as the landmark stood
Rustic, of grassy sward; thither anon
A sweaty reaper from his tillage brought
435 First fruits, the green ear, and the yellow sheaf,
Unculled, as came to hand; a shepherd next
More meek came with the firstlings of his flock
Choicest and best; then sacrificing, laid
The innards and their fat, with incense strewed,
440 On the cleft wood, and all due rites performed.
His off'ring soon propitious fire from heav'n
Consumed with nimble glance, and grateful steam;
The other's not, for his was not sincere;
Whereat he inly raged, and as they talked,
445 Smote him into the midriff with a stone
That beat out life; he fell, and deadly pale
Groaned out his soul with gushing blood effused.
Much at that sight was Adam in his heart
Dismayed, and thus in haste to th' angel cried.

450   O teacher, some great mischief hath befall'n
To that meek man, who well had sacrificed;
Is piety thus and pure devotion paid?
    T' whom Michael thus, he also moved, replied.
These two are brethren, Adam, and to come
455 Out of thy loins; th' unjust the just hath slain,
For envy that his brother's offering found
From Heav'n acceptance; but the bloody fact
Will be avenged, and th' other's faith approved
Lose no reward, though here thou see him die,
460 Rolling in dust and gore. To which our sire.
    Alas, both for the deed and for the cause!
But have I now seen death? Is this the way
I must return to native dust? O sight
Of terror, foul and ugly to behold,
465 Horrid to think, how horrible to feel!
    To whom thus Michaël. Death thou hast seen
In his first shape on man; but many shapes
Of death, and many are the ways that lead
To his grim cave, all dismal; yet to sense
470 More terrible at th' entrance than within.
Some, as thou saw'st, by violent stroke shall die,
By fire, flood, famine; by intemperance more
In meats and drinks, which on the earth shall bring
Diseases dire, of which a monstrous crew
475 Before thee shall appear; that thou may'st know
What misery th' inabstinence of Eve
Shall bring on men. Immediately a place
Before his eyes appeared, sad, noisome, dark;
A lazar-house it seemed, wherein were laid
480 Numbers of all diseased, all maladies
Of ghastly spasm, or racking torture, qualms
Of heart-sick agony, all feverous kinds,
Convulsions, epilepsies, fierce catarrhs,
Intestine stone and ulcer, colic pangs,
485 Demoniac frenzy, moping melancholy
And moon-struck madness, pining atrophy,
Marasmus, and wide-wasting pestilence,
Dropsies, and asthmas, and joint-racking rheums.

Dire was the tossing, deep the groans; Despair
490   Tended the sick busiest from couch to couch;
And over them triumphant Death his dart
Shook, but delayed to strike, though oft invoked
With vows, as their chief good, and final hope.
Sight so deform what heart of rock could long
495   Dry-eyed behold? Adam could not, but wept
Though not of woman born; compassion quelled
His best of man, and gave him up to tears
A space, till firmer thoughts restrained excess,
And scarce recovering words his plaint renewed.
500   O miserable mankind, to what fall
Degraded, to what wretched state reserved!
Better end here unborn. Why is life giv'n
To be thus wrested from us? rather why
Obtruded on us thus? who if we knew
505   What we receive, would either not accept
Life offered, or soon beg to lay it down,
Glad to be so dismissed in peace. Can thus
Th' image of God in man created once
So goodly and erect, though faulty since,
510   To such unsightly sufferings be debased
Under inhuman pains? Why should not man,
Retaining still divine similitude
In part, from such deformities be free,
And for his Maker's image sake exempt?
515   Their Maker's image, answered Michael, then
Forsook them, when themselves they vilified
To serve ungoverned appetite, and took
His image whom they served, a brutish vice,
Inductive mainly to the sin of Eve.
520   Therefore so abject is their punishment,
Disfiguring not God's likeness, but their own,
Or if his likeness, by themselves defaced
While they pervert pure Nature's healthful rules
To loathsome sickness, worthily, since they
525   God's image did not reverence in themselves.
      I yield it just, said Adam, and submit.
But is there yet no other way, besides

These painful passages, how we may come
To death, and mix with our connatural dust?
530   There is, said Michael, if thou well observe
The rule of *Not too much*, by temperance taught
In what thou eat'st and drink'st, seeking from thence
Due nourishment, not gluttonous delight,
Till many years over thy head return:
535 So may'st thou live, till like ripe fruit thou drop
Into thy mother's lap, or be with ease
Gathered, not harshly plucked, for death mature:
This is old age; but then thou must outlive
Thy youth, thy strength, thy beauty, which will change
540 To withered weak and grey; thy senses then
Obtuse, all taste of pleasure must forgo,
To what thou hast, and for the air of youth
Hopeful and cheerful, in thy blood will reign
A melancholy damp of cold and dry
545 To weigh thy spirits down, and last consume
The balm of life. To whom our ancestor.
    Henceforth I fly not death, nor would prolong
Life much, bent rather how I may be quit
Fairest and easiest of this cumbrous charge,
550 Which I must keep till my appointed day
Of rend'ring up, and patiently attend
My dissolution. Michaël replied,
    Nor love thy life, nor hate; but what thou liv'st
Live well, how long or short permit to Heav'n:
555 And now prepare thee for another sight.
    He looked and saw a spacious plain, whereon
Were tents of various hue; by some were herds
Of cattle grazing: others, whence the sound
Of instruments that made melodious chime
560 Was heard, of harp and organ; and who moved
Their stops and chords was seen: his volant touch
Instinct through all proportions low and high
Fled and pursued transverse the resonant fugue.
In other part stood one who at the forge
565 Labouring, two massy clods of iron and brass
Had melted (whether found where casual fire

Had wasted woods on mountain or in vale,
Down to the veins of earth, there gliding hot
To some cave's mouth, or whether washed by stream
570   From underground); the liquid ore he drained
Into fit moulds prepared; from which he formed
First his own tools; then, what might else be wrought
Fusile or grav'n in metal. After these,
But on the hither side a different sort
575   From the high neighbouring hills, which was their seat,
Down to the plain descended: by their guise
Just men they seemed, and all their study bent
To worship God aright, and know his works
Not hid, nor those things last which might preserve
580   Freedom and peace to men: they on the plain
Long had not walked, when from the tents behold
A bevy of fair women, richly gay
In gems and wanton dress; to the harp they sung
Soft amorous ditties, and in dance came on:
585   The men though grave, eyed them, and let their eyes
Rove without rein, till in the amorous net
Fast caught, they liked, and each his liking chose;
And now of love they treat till th' ev'ning star
Love's harbinger appeared; and all in heat
590   They light the nuptial torch, and bid invoke
Hymen, then first to marriage rites invoked;
With feast and music all the tents resound.
Such happy interview and fair event
Of love and youth not lost, songs, garlands, flow'rs,
595   And charming symphonies attached the heart
Of Adam, soon inclined to admit delight,
The bent of nature; which he thus expressed.
    True opener of mine eyes, prime angel blest,
Much better seems this vision, and more hope
600   Of peaceful days portends, than those two past;
Those were of hate and death, or pain much worse,
Here nature seems fulfilled in all her ends.
    To whom thus Michael. Judge not what is best
By pleasure, though to nature seeming meet,
605   Created, as thou art, to nobler end

Holy and pure, conformity divine.
Those tents thou saw'st so pleasant, were the tents
Of wickedness, wherein shall dwell his race
Who slew his brother; studious they appear
610   Of arts that polish life, inventors rare,
Unmindful of their Maker, though his Spirit
Taught them, but they his gifts acknowledged none.
Yet they a beauteous offspring shall beget;
For that fair female troop thou saw'st, that seemed
615   Of goddesses, so blithe, so smooth, so gay,
Yet empty of all good wherein consists
Woman's domestic honour and chief praise;
Bred only and completed to the taste
Of lustful appetence, to sing, to dance,
620   To dress, and troll the tongue, and roll the eye.
To these that sober race of men whose lives
Religious titled them the sons of God,
Shall yield up all their virtue, all their fame
Ignobly, to the trains and to the smiles
625   Of these fair atheists, and now swim in joy,
(Erelong to swim at large) and laugh; for which
The world erelong a world of tears must weep.
     To whom thus Adam of short joy bereft.
O pity and shame, that they who to live well
630   Entered so fair, should turn aside to tread
Paths indirect, or in the mid-way faint!
But still I see the tenor of man's woe
Holds on the same, from woman to begin.
     From man's effeminate slackness it begins,
635   Said th' angel, who should better hold his place
By wisdom, and superior gifts received.
But now prepare thee for another scene.
     He looked and saw wide territory spread
Before him, towns, and rural works between,
640   Cities of men with lofty gates and tow'rs,
Concourse in arms, fierce faces threat'ning war,
Giants of mighty bone, and bold emprise;
Part wield their arms, part curb the foaming steed,
Single or in array of battle ranged

645 Both horse and foot, nor idly must'ring stood;
One way a band select from forage drives
A herd of beeves, fair oxen and fair kine
From a fair meadow ground; or fleecy flock,
Ewes and their bleating lambs over the plain,
650 Their booty; scarce with life the shepherds fly,
But call in aid, which makes a bloody fray;
With cruel tournament the squadrons join;
Where cattle pastured late, now scattered lies
With carcasses and arms th' ensanguined field
655 Deserted: others to a city strong
Lay siege, encamped; by battery, scale, and mine,
Assaulting; others from the wall defend
With dart and jav'lin, stones and sulphurous fire;
On each hand slaughter and gigantic deeds.
660 In other part the sceptred heralds call
To council in the city gates: anon
Grey-headed men and grave, with warriors mixed,
Assemble, and harangues are heard, but soon
In factious opposition, till at last
665 Of middle age one rising, eminent
In wise deport, spake much of right and wrong,
Of justice, of religion, truth and peace,
And judgement from above: him old and young
Exploded, and had seized with violent hands,
670 Had not a cloud descending snatched him thence
Unseen among the throng: so violence
Proceeded, and oppression, and sword-law
Through all the plain, and refuge none was found.
Adam was all in tears, and to his guide
675 Lamenting turned full sad; O what are these,
Death's ministers, not men, who thus deal death
Inhumanly to men, and multiply
Ten thousandfold the sin of him who slew
His brother; for of whom such massacre
680 Make they but of their brethren, men of men?
But who was that just man, whom had not Heav'n
Rescued, had in his righteousness been lost?
  To whom thus Michael. These are the product

Of those ill-mated marriages thou saw'st:
685 Where good with bad were matched, who of themselves
Abhor to join; and by imprudence mixed,
Produce prodigious births of body or mind.
Such were these giants, men of high renown;
For in those days might only shall be admired,
690 And valour and heroic virtue called;
To overcome in battle, and subdue
Nations, and bring home spoils with infinite
Manslaughter, shall be held the highest pitch
Of human glory, and for glory done
695 Of triumph, to be styled great conquerors,
Patrons of mankind, gods, and sons of gods,
Destroyers rightlier called and plagues of men.
Thus fame shall be achieved, renown on earth,
And what most merits fame in silence hid.
700 But he the seventh from thee, whom thou beheld'st
The only righteous in a world perverse,
And therefore hated, therefore so beset
With foes for daring single to be just,
And utter odious truth, that God would come
705 To judge them with his saints: him the Most High
Rapt in a balmy cloud with wingèd steeds
Did, as thou saw'st, receive to walk with God
High in salvation and the climes of bliss,
Exempt from death, to show thee what reward
710 Awaits the good, the rest what punishment;
Which now direct thine eyes and soon behold.
    He looked, and saw the face of things quite changed;
The brazen throat of war had ceased to roar,
All now was turned to jollity and game,
715 To luxury and riot, feast and dance,
Marrying or prostituting, as befell,
Rape or adultery, where passing fair
Allured them; thence from cups to civil broils.
At length a reverend sire among them came,
720 And of their doings great dislike declared,
And testified against their ways; he oft
Frequented their assemblies, whereso met,

Triumphs or festivals, and to them preached
Conversion and repentance, as to souls
725   In prison under judgements imminent:
But all in vain: which when he saw, he ceased
Contending, and removed his tents far off;
Then from the mountain hewing timber tall,
Began to build a vessel of huge bulk,
730   Measured by cubit, length, and breadth, and heighth,
Smeared round with pitch, and in the side a door
Contrived, and of provisions laid in large
For man and beast: when lo a wonder strange!
Of every beast, and bird, and insect small
735   Came sevens, and pairs, and entered in, as taught
Their order: last the sire, and his three sons
With their four wives; and God made fast the door.
Meanwhile the south wind rose, and with black wings
Wide hovering, all the clouds together drove
740   From under heav'n; the hills to their supply
Vapour, and exhalation dusk and moist,
Sent up amain; and now the thickened sky
Like a dark ceiling stood; down rushed the rain
Impetuous, and continued till the earth
745   No more was seen; the floating vessel swum
Uplifted; and secure with beakèd prow
Rode tilting o'er the waves, all dwellings else
Flood overwhelmed, and them with all their pomp
Deep under water rolled; sea covered sea,
750   Sea without shore; and in their palaces
Where luxury late reigned, sea-monsters whelped
And stabled; of mankind, so numerous late,
All left, in one small bottom swum embarked.
How didst thou grieve then, Adam, to behold
755   The end of all thy offspring, end so sad,
Depopulation; thee another flood,
Of tears and sorrow a flood thee also drowned,
And sunk thee as thy sons; till gently reared
By th' angel, on thy feet thou stood'st at last,
760   Though comfortless, as when a father mourns
His children, all in view destroyed at once;

And scarce to th' angel utter'dst thus thy plaint.
  O visions ill foreseen! better had I
Lived ignorant of future, so had borne
765   My part of evil only, each day's lot
Enough to bear; those now, that were dispensed
The burd'n of many ages, on me light
At once, by my foreknowledge gaining birth
Abortive, to torment me ere their being,
770   With thought that they must be. Let no man seek
Henceforth to be foretold what shall befall
Him or his children, evil he may be sure,
Which neither his foreknowing can prevent,
And he the future evil shall no less
775   In apprehension than in substance feel
Grievous to bear: but that care now is past,
Man is not whom to warn: those few escaped
Famine and anguish will at last consume
Wand'ring that wat'ry desert: I had hope
780   When violence was ceased, and war on earth,
All would have gone well, peace would have crowned
With length of happy days the race of man;
But I was far deceived; for now I see
Peace to corrupt no less than war to waste.
785   How comes it thus? unfold, celestial guide,
And whether here the race of man will end.
To whom thus Michael. Those whom last thou saw'st
In triumph and luxurious wealth, are they
First seen in acts of prowess imminent
790   And great explóits, but of true virtue void;
Who having spilt much blood, and done much waste
Subduing nations, and achieved thereby
Fame in the world, high titles, and rich prey,
Shall change their course to pleasure, ease, and sloth,
795   Surfeit, and lust, till wantonness and pride
Raise out of friendship hostile deeds in peace.
The conquered also, and enslaved by war
Shall with their freedom lost all virtue lose
And fear of God, from whom their piety feigned
800   In sharp contést of battle found no aid

Against invaders; therefore cold in zeal
Thenceforth shall practise how to live secure,
Worldly or dissolute, on what their lords
Shall leave them to enjoy; for th' earth shall bear
805   More than enough, that temperance may be tried:
So all shall turn degenerate, all depraved,
Justice and temperance, truth and faith forgot;
One man except, the only son of light
In a dark age, against example good,
810   Against allurement, custom, and a world
Offended; fearless of reproach and scorn,
Or violence, he of their wicked ways
Shall them admonish, and before them set
The paths of righteousness, how much more safe,
815   And full of peace, denouncing wrath to come
On their impenitence; and shall return
Of them derided, but of God observed
The one just man alive; by his command
Shall build a wondrous ark, as thou beheld'st,
820   To save himself and household from amidst
A world devote to universal wrack.
No sooner he with them of man and beast
Select for life shall in the ark be lodged,
And sheltered round, but all the cataracts
825   Of heav'n set open on the earth shall pour
Rain day and night, all fountains of the deep
Broke up, shall heave the ocean to usurp
Beyond all bounds, till inundation rise
Above the highest hills: then shall this mount
830   Of Paradise by might of waves be moved
Out of his place, pushed by the hornèd flood,
With all his verdure spoiled, and trees adrift
Down the great river to the op'ning gulf,
And there take root an island salt and bare,
835   The haunt of seals and orcs, and sea-mews' clang.
To teach thee that God áttribútes to place
No sanctity, if none be thither brought
By men who there frequent, or therein dwell.
And now what further shall ensue, behold.

840   He looked, and saw the ark hull on the flood,
      Which now abated, for the clouds were fled,
      Driv'n by a keen north wind, that blowing dry
      Wrinkled the face of deluge, as decayed;
      And the clear sun on his wide wat'ry glass
845   Gazed hot, and of the fresh wave largely drew,
      As after thirst, which made their flowing shrink
      From standing lake to tripping ebb, that stole
      With soft foot towards the deep, who now had stopped
      His sluices, as the heav'n his windows shut.
850   The ark no more now floats, but seems on ground
      Fast on the top of some high mountain fixed.
      And now the tops of hills as rocks appear;
      With clamour thence the rapid currents drive
      Towards the retreating sea their furious tide.
855   Forthwith from out the ark a raven flies,
      And after him, the surer messenger,
      A dove sent forth once and again to spy
      Green tree or ground whereon his foot may light;
      The second time returning, in his bill
860   An olive leaf he brings, pacific sign:
      Anon dry land appears, and from his ark
      The ancient sire descends with all his train;
      Then with uplifted hands, and eyes devout,
      Grateful to Heav'n, over his head beholds
865   A dewy cloud, and in the cloud a bow
      Conspicuous with three listed colours gay,
      Betok'ning peace from God, and cov'nant new.
      Whereat the heart of Adam erst so sad
      Greatly rejoiced, and thus his joy broke forth.
870   O thou who future things canst represent
      As present, Heav'nly instructor, I revive
      At this last sight, assured that man shall live
      With all the creatures, and their seed preserve.
      Far less I now lament for one whole world
875   Of wicked sons destroyed, than I rejoice
      For one man found so perfect and so just,
      That God vouchsafes to raise another world
      From him, and all his anger to forget.

But say, what mean those coloured streaks in heav'n,
880   Distended as the brow of God appeased,
Or serve they as a flow'ry verge to bind
The fluid skirts of that same wat'ry cloud,
Lest it again dissolve and show'r the earth?
　　To whom th' Archangel. Dextrously thou aim'st;
885   So willingly doth God remit his ire,
Though late repenting him of man depraved,
Grieved at his heart, when looking down he saw
The whole earth filled with violence, and all flesh
Corrupting each their way; yet those removed,
890   Such grace shall one just man find in his sight,
That he relents, not to blot out mankind,
And makes a covenant never to destroy
The earth again by flood, nor let the sea
Surpass his bounds, nor rain to drown the world
895   With man therein or beast; but when he brings
Over the earth a cloud, will therein set
His triple-coloured bow, whereon to look
And call to mind his cov'nant: day and night,
Seed time and harvest, heat and hoary frost
900   Shall hold their course, till fire purge all things new,
Both heav'n and earth, wherein the just shall dwell.

BOOK XII

The Argument

The angel Michael continues from the Flood to relate what
shall succeed; then, in the mention of Abraham, comes by
degrees to explain, who that Seed of the Woman shall be,
which was promised Adam and Eve in the Fall; his Incarnation,
5   Death, Resurrection, and Ascension; the state of the Church
till his second coming. Adam, greatly satisfied and recomforted
by these relations and promises descends the hill with Michael;
wakens Eve, who all this while had slept, but with gentle
dreams composed to quietness of mind and submission.
10 Michael in either hand leads them out of Paradise, the fiery
sword waving behind them, and the Cherubim taking their
stations to guard the place.

As one who in his journey baits at noon,
Though bent on speed, so here the Archangel paused
Betwixt the world destroyed and world restored,
If Adam aught perhaps might interpose;
5   Then with transition sweet new speech resumes.
    Thus thou hast seen one world begin and end;
And man as from a second stock proceed.
Much thou hast yet to see, but I perceive
Thy mortal sight to fail; objects divine
10 Must needs impair and weary human sense:
Henceforth what is to come I will relate;
Thou therefore give due audience, and attend.
This second source of men, while yet but few,
And while the dread of judgement past remains
15 Fresh in their minds, fearing the Deity,
With some regard to what is just and right
Shall lead their lives, and multiply apace,
Labouring the soil, and reaping plenteous crop,

Corn wine and oil; and from the herd or flock,
20   Oft sacrificing bullock, lamb, or kid,
With large wine-offerings poured, and sacred feast,
Shall spend their days in joy unblamed, and dwell
Long time in peace by families and tribes
Under paternal rule; till one shall rise
25   Of proud ambitious heart, who not content
With fair equality, fraternal state,
Will arrogate dominion undeserved
Over his brethren, and quite dispossess
Concord and law of Nature from the earth,
30   Hunting (and men not beasts shall be his game)
With war and hostile snare such as refuse
Subjection to his empire tyrannous:
A mighty hunter thence he shall be styled
Before the Lord, as in despite of Heav'n,
35   Or from Heav'n claiming second sov'reignty;
And from rebellion shall derive his name,
Though of rebellion others he accuse.
He with a crew, whom like ambition joins
With him or under him to tyrannize,
40   Marching from Eden towards the west, shall find
The plain, wherein a black bituminous gurge
Boils out from underground, the mouth of Hell;
Of brick, and of that stuff they cast to build
A city and tow'r, whose top may reach to Heav'n;
45   And get themselves a name, lest far dispersed
In foreign lands their memory be lost,
Regardless whether good or evil fame.
But God who oft descends to visit men
Unseen, and through their habitations walks
50   To mark their doings, them beholding soon,
Comes down to see their city, ere the tower
Obstruct Heav'n's tow'rs, and in derision sets
Upon their tongues a various spirit to raze
Quite out their native language, and instead
55   To sow a jangling noise of words unknown:
Forthwith a hideous gabble rises loud
Among the builders; each to other calls

Not understood, till hoarse, and all in rage,
As mocked they storm; great laughter was in Heav'n
60   And looking down, to see the hubbub strange
And hear the din; thus was the building left
Ridiculous, and the work Confusion named.
    Whereto thus Adam fatherly displeased.
O execrable son so to aspire
65   Above his brethren, to himself assuming
Authority usurped, from God not giv'n:
He gave us only over beast, fish, fowl
Dominion absolute; that right we hold
By his donation; but man over men
70   He made not lord; such title to himself
Reserving, human left from human free.
But this usurper his encroachment proud
Stays not on man; to God his tower intends
Siege and defiance: wretched man! what food
75   Will he convey up thither to sustain
Himself and his rash army, where thin air
Above the clouds will pine his entrails gross,
And famish him of breath, if not of bread?
    To whom thus Michael. Justly thou abhorr'st
80   That son, who on the quiet state of men
Such trouble brought, affecting to subdue
Rational liberty; yet know withal,
Since thy original lapse, true liberty
Is lost, which always with right reason dwells
85   Twinned, and from her hath no dividual being:
Reason in man obscured, or not obeyed,
Immediately inordinate desires
And upstart passions catch the government
From reason, and to servitude reduce
90   Man till then free. Therefore since he permits
Within himself unworthy powers to reign
Over free reason, God in judgement just
Subjects him from without to violent lords;
Who oft as undeservedly enthrall
95   His outward freedom: tyranny must be,
Though to the tyrant thereby no excuse,

Yet sometimes nations will decline so low
From virtue, which is reason, that no wrong,
But justice, and some fatal curse annexed
100   Deprives them of their outward liberty,
Their inward lost: witness th' irreverent son
Of him who built the ark, who for the shame
Done to his father, heard this heavy curse,
Servant of servants, on his vicious race.
105   Thus will the latter, as the former world,
Still tend from bad to worse, till God at last
Wearied from their iniquities, withdraw
His presence from among them, and avert
His holy eyes; resolving from thenceforth
110   To leave them to their own polluted ways;
And one peculiar nation to select
From all the rest, of whom to be invoked,
A nation from one faithful man to spring:
Him on this side Euphrates yet residing,
115   Bred up in idol-worship; O that men
(Canst thou believe?) should be so stupid grown,
While yet the patriarch lived, who 'scaped the Flood,
As to forsake the living God, and fall
To worship their own work in wood and stone
120   For gods! Yet him God the Most High vouchsafes
To call by vision from his father's house,
His kindred and false gods, into a land
Which he will show him, and from him will raise
A mighty nation, and upon him show'r
125   His benediction so, that in his seed
All nations shall be blest; he straight obeys,
Not knowing to what land, yet firm believes:
I see him, but thou canst not, with what faith
He leaves his gods, his friends, and native soil
130   Ur of Chaldea, passing now the ford
To Haran, after him a cumbrous train
Of herds and flocks, and numerous servitude;
Not wand'ring poor, but trusting all his wealth
With God, who called him, in a land unknown.
135   Canaan he now attains, I see his tents

Pitched about Sechem, and the neighbouring plain
Of Moreh; there by promise he receives
Gift to his progeny of all that land;
From Hamath northward to the desert south
140 (Things by their names I call, though yet unnamed)
From Hermon east to the great western sea,
Mount Hermon, yonder sea, each place behold
In prospect, as I point them; on the shore
Mount Carmel; here the double-founted stream
145 Jordan, true limit eastward; but his sons
Shall dwell to Senir, that long ridge of hills.
This ponder, that all nations of the earth
Shall in his Seed be blessèd; by that Seed
Is meant thy great Deliverer, who shall bruise
150 The Scrpcnt's head; whereof to thee anon
Plainlier shall be revealed. This patriarch blest,
Whom *faithful Abraham* due time shall call,
A son, and of his son a grandchild leaves,
Like him in faith, in wisdom, and renown;
155 The grandchild with twelve sons increased, departs
From Canaan, to a land hereafter called
Egypt, divided by the river Nile;
See where it flows, disgorging at seven mouths
Into the sea: to sojourn in that land
160 He comes invited by a younger son
In time of dearth, a son whose worthy deeds
Raise him to be the second in that realm
Of Pharaoh: there he dies, and leaves his race
Growing into a nation, and now grown
165 Suspected to a sequent king, who seeks
To stop their overgrowth, as inmate guests
Too numcrous; whence of guests he makes them slaves
Inhospitably, and kills their infant males:
Till by two brethren (those two brethren call
170 Moses and Aaron) sent from God to claim
His people from enthralment, they return
With glory and spoil back to their promised land.
But first the lawless tyrant, who denies
To know their God, or message to regard,

175 Must be compelled by signs and judgements dire;
To blood unshed the rivers must be turned,
Frogs, lice, and flies must all his palace fill
With loathed intrusion, and fill all the land;
His cattle must of rot and murrain die,
180 Botches and blains must all his flesh emboss,
And all his people; thunder mixed with hail,
Hail mixed with fire must rend th' Egyptian sky
And wheel on th' earth, devouring where it rolls;
What it devours not, herb, or fruit, or grain,
185 A darksome cloud of locusts swarming down
Must eat, and on the ground leave nothing green:
Darkness must overshadow all his bounds,
Palpable darkness, and blot out three days;
Last with one midnight stroke all the first-born
190 Of Egypt must lie dead. Thus with ten wounds
The river-dragon tamed at length submits
To let his sojourners depart, and oft
Humbles his stubborn heart, but still as ice
More hardened after thaw, till in his rage
195 Pursuing whom he late dismissed, the sea
Swallows him with his host, but them lets pass
As on dry land between two crystal walls,
Awed by the rod of Moses so to stand
Divided, till his rescued gain their shore:
200 Such wondrous power God to his saint will lend,
Though present in his angel, who shall go
Before them in a cloud, and pillar of fire,
By day a cloud, by night a pillar of fire,
To guide them in their journey, and remove
205 Behind them, while th' obdúrate king pursues:
All night he will pursue, but his approach
Darkness defends between till morning watch;
Then through the fiery pillar and the cloud
God looking forth will trouble all his host
210 And craze their chariot wheels: when by command
Moses once more his potent rod extends
Over the sea; the sea his rod obeys;
On their embattled ranks the waves return,

And overwhelm their war: the race elect
215   Safe towards Canaan from the shore advance
Through the wild desert, not the readiest way,
Lest ent'ring on the Canaanite alarmed
War terrify them inexpért, and fear
Return them back to Egypt, choosing rather
220   Inglorious life with servitude; for life
To noble and ignoble is more sweet
Untrained in arms, where rashness leads not on.
This also shall they gain by their delay
In the wide wilderness, there they shall found
225   Their government, and their great senate choose
Through the twelve tribes, to rule by laws ordained:
God from the mount of Sinai, whose grey top
Shall tremble, he descending, will himself
In thunder lightning and loud trumpet's sound
230   Ordain them laws; part such as appertain
To civil justice, part religious rites
Of sacrifice, informing them, by types
And shadows, of that destined Seed to bruise
The Serpent, by what means he shall achieve
235   Mankind's deliverance. But the voice of God
To mortal ear is dreadful; they beseech
That Moses might report to them his will,
And terror cease; he grants what they besought
Instructed that to God is no accéss
240   Without mediator, whose high office now
Moses in figure bears, to introduce
One greater, of whose day he shall foretell,
And all the prophets in their age the times
Of great Messiah shall sing. Thus laws and rites
245   Established, such delight hath God in men
Obedient to his will, that he vouchsafes
Among them to set up his tabernacle,
The Holy One with mortal men to dwell:
By his prescrípt a sanctuary is framed
250   Of cedar, overlaid with gold, therein
An ark, and in the ark his testimony,
The records of his Cov'nant; over these

A mercy-seat of gold between the wings
Of two bright Cherubim; before him burn
255 Seven lamps as in a zodiac representing
The Heav'nly fires; over the tent a cloud
Shall rest by day, a fiery gleam by night,
Save when they journey, and at length they come,
Conducted by his angel to the land
260 Promised to Abraham and his seed: the rest
Were long to tell, how many battles fought,
How many kings destroyed, and kingdoms won,
Or how the sun shall in mid heav'n stand still
A day entire, and night's due course adjourn,
265 Man's voice commanding, Sun in Gibeon stand,
And thou moon in the vale of Aialon,
Till Israel overcome; so call the third
From Abraham, son of Isaac, and from him
His whole descent, who thus shall Canaan win.
270   Here Adam interposed. O sent from Heav'n,
Enlight'ner of my darkness, gracious things
Thou hast revealed, those chiefly which concern
Just Abraham and his seed: now first I find
Mine eyes true op'ning, and my heart much eased,
275 Erewhile perplexed with thoughts what would become
Of me and all mankind; but now I see
His day, in whom all nations shall be blest,
Favour unmerited by me, who sought
Forbidden knowledge by forbidden means.
280 This yet I apprehend not, why to those
Among whom God will deign to dwell on earth
So many and so various laws are giv'n;
So many laws argue so many sins
Among them; how can God with such reside?
285   To whom thus Michael. Doubt not but that sin
Will reign among them, as of thee begot;
And therefore was law given them to evince
Their natural pravity, by stirring up
Sin against law to fight; that when they see
290 Law can discover sin, but not remove,
Save by those shadowy expiations weak,

The blood of bulls and goats, they may conclude
Some blood more precious must be paid for man,
Just for unjust, that in such righteousness
295 To them by faith imputed, they may find
Justification towards God, and peace
Of conscience, which the law by ceremonies
Cannot appease, nor man the moral part
Perform, and not performing cannot live.
300 So law appears imperfect, and but giv'n
With purpose to resign them in full time
Up to a better cov'nant, disciplined
From shadowy types to truth, from flesh to spirit,
From imposition of strict laws, to free
305 Acceptance of large grace, from servile fear
To filial, works of law to works of faith.
And therefore shall not Moses, though of God
Highly beloved, being but the minister
Of law, his people into Canaan lead;
310 But Joshua whom the Gentiles Jesus call,
His name and office bearing, who shall quell
The adversary Serpent, and bring back
Through the world's wilderness long wandered man
Safe to eternal Paradise of rest.
315 Meanwhile they in their earthly Canaan placed
Long time shall dwell and prosper, but when sins
National interrupt their public peace,
Provoking God to raise them enemies:
From whom as oft he saves them penitent
320 By judges first, then under kings; of whom
The second, both for piety renowned
And puissant deeds, a promise shall receive
Irrevocable, that his regal throne
For ever shall endure; the like shall sing
325 All prophecy, that of the royal stock
Of David (so I name this king) shall rise
A son, the Woman's Seed to thee foretold,
Foretold to Abraham, as in whom shall trust
All nations, and to kings foretold, of kings
330 The last, for of his reign shall be no end.

But first a long succession must ensue,
And his next son for wealth and wisdom famed,
The clouded ark of God till then in tents
Wand'ring, shall in a glorious temple enshrine.
335 Such follow him, as shall be registered
Part good, part bad, of bad the longer scroll,
Whose foul idolatries, and other faults
Heaped to the popular sum, will so incense
God, as to leave them, and expose their land,
340 Their city, his temple, and his holy ark
With all his sacred things, a scorn and prey
To that proud city, whose high walls thou saw'st
Left in confusion, Babylon thence called.
There in captivity he lets them dwell
345 The space of seventy years, then brings them back,
Rememb'ring mercy, and his Cov'nant sworn
To David, 'stablished as the days of Heav'n.
Returned from Babylon by leave of kings
Their lords, whom God disposed, the house of God
350 They first re-edify, and for a while
In mean estate live moderate, till grown
In wealth and multitude, factious they grow;
But first among the priests dissension springs,
Men who attend the altar, and should most
355 Endeavour peace: their strife pollution brings
Upon the temple itself: at last they seize
The sceptre, and regard not David's sons,
Then lose it to a stranger, that the true
Anointed King Messiah might be born
360 Barred of his right; yet at his birth a star
Unseen before in heav'n proclaims him come,
And guides the eastern sages, who inquire
His place, to offer incense, myrrh, and gold;
His place of birth a solemn angel tells
365 To simple shepherds, keeping watch by night;
They gladly thither haste, and by a choir
Of squadroned angels hear his carol sung.
A virgin is his mother, but his sire
The power of the Most High; he shall ascend

370 The throne hereditary, and bound his reign
With earth's wide bounds, his glory with the Heav'ns.
    He ceased, discerning Adam with such joy
Surcharged, as had like grief been dewed in tears,
Without the vent of words, which these he breathed.
375   O prophet of glad tidings, finisher
Of utmost hope! now clear I understand
What oft my steadiest thoughts have searched in vain,
Why our great expectation should be called
The Seed of Woman: virgin mother, hail,
380 High in the love of Heav'n, yet from my loins
Thou shalt proceed, and from thy womb the Son
Of God Most High; so God with man unites.
Needs must the Serpent now his capital bruise
Expect with mortal pain: say where and when
385 Their fight, what stroke shall bruise the Victor's heel.
    To whom thus Michael. Dream not of their fight,
As of a duel, or the local wounds
Of head or heel: not therefore joins the Son
Manhood to Godhead, with more strength to foil
390 Thy enemy; nor so is overcome
Satan, whose fall from Heav'n, a deadlier bruise,
Disabled not to give thee thy death's wound:
Which he, who comes thy Saviour, shall recure,
Not by destroying Satan, but his works
395 In thee and in thy seed: nor can this be,
But by fulfilling that which thou didst want,
Obedience to the law of God, imposed
On penalty of death, and suffering death,
The penalty to thy transgression due,
400 And due to theirs which out of thine will grow:
So only can high justice rest apaid.
The law of God exact he shall fulfil
Both by obedience and by love, though love
Alone fulfil the law; thy punishment
405 He shall endure by coming in the flesh
To a reproachful life and cursèd death,
Proclaiming life to all who shall believe
In his redemption, and that his obedience

Imputed becomes theirs by faith, his merits
410 To save them, not their own, though legal works.
For this he shall live hated, be blasphemed,
Seized on by force, judged, and to death condemned
A shameful and accurst, nailed to the cross
By his own nation, slain for bringing life;
415 But to the cross he nails thy enemies,
The law that is against thee, and the sins
Of all mankind, with him there crucified,
Never to hurt them more who rightly trust
In this his satisfaction; so he dies,
420 But soon revives, death over him no power
Shall long usurp; ere the third dawning light
Return, the stars of morn shall see him rise
Out of his grave, fresh as the dawning light,
Thy ransom paid, which man from death redeems,
425 His death for man, as many as offered life
Neglect not, and the benefit embrace
By faith not void of works: this Godlike act
Annuls thy doom, the death thou shouldst have died,
In sin for ever lost from life; this act
430 Shall bruise the head of Satan, crush his strength
Defeating Sin and Death, his two main arms,
And fix far deeper in his head their stings
Than temporal death shall bruise the Victor's heel,
Or theirs whom he redeems, a death like sleep,
435 A gentle wafting to immortal life.
Nor after resurrection shall he stay
Longer on earth than certain times to appear
To his disciples, men who in his life
Still followed him; to them shall leave in charge
440 To teach all nations what of him they learned
And his salvation, them who shall believe
Baptizing in the profluent stream, the sign
Of washing them from guilt of sin to life
Pure, and in mind prepared, if so befall,
445 For death, like that which the Redeemer died.
All nations they shall teach; for from that day
Not only to the sons of Abraham's loins

Salvation shall be preached, but to the sons
Of Abraham's faith wherever through the world;
450 So in his seed all nations shall be blest.
Then to the Heav'n of Heav'ns he shall ascend
With victory, triúmphing through the air
Over his foes and thine; there shall surprise
The Serpent, prince of air, and drag in chains
455 Through all his realm, and there confounded leave;
Then enter into glory, and resume
His seat at God's right hand, exalted high
Above all names in Heav'n; and thence shall come,
When this world's dissolution shall be ripe,
460 With glory and power to judge both quick and dead,
To judge th' unfaithful dead, but to reward
His faithful, and receive them into bliss,
Whether in Heav'n or earth, for then the earth
Shall all be Paradise, far happier place
465 Than this of Eden, and far happier days.
    So spake the angel Michaël, then paused,
As at the world's great period; and our sire
Replete with joy and wonder thus replied.
    O goodness infinite, goodness immense!
470 That all this good of evil shall produce,
And evil turn to good; more wonderful
Than that which by creation first brought forth
Light out of darkness! full of doubt I stand,
Whether I should repent me now of sin
475 By me done and occasioned, or rejoice
Much more, that much more good thereof shall spring,
To God more glory, more good will to men
From God, and over wrath grace shall abound.
But say, if our Deliverer up to Heav'n
480 Must reascend, what will betide the few
His faithful, left among th' unfaithful herd,
The enemies of truth; who then shall guide
His people, who defend? will they not deal
Worse with his followers than with him they dealt?
485   Be sure they will, said th' angel; but from Heav'n
He to his own a Comforter will send,

    The promise of his Father, who shall dwell
    His Spirit within them, and the law of faith
    Working through love, upon their hearts shall write,
490   To guide them all in truth, and also arm
    With spiritual armour, able to resist
    Satan's assaults, and quench his fiery darts,
    What man can do against them, not afraid,
    Though to the death, against such cruelties
495   With inward consolations recompensed,
    And oft supported so as shall amaze
    Their proudest persecutors: for the Spirit
    Poured first on his apostles, whom he sends
    To evangelize the nations, then on all
500   Baptized, shall them with wondrous gifts endue
    To speak all tongues, and do all miracles,
    As did their Lord before them. Thus they win
    Great numbers of each nation to receive
    With joy the tidings brought from Heav'n: at length
505   Their ministry performed, and race well run,
    Their doctrine and their story written left,
    They die; but in their room, as they forewarn,
    Wolves shall succeed for teachers, grievous wolves,
    Who all the sacred mysteries of Heav'n
510   To their own vile advantages shall turn
    Of lucre and ambition, and the truth
    With superstitions and traditions taint,
    Left only in those written records pure,
    Though not but by the Spirit understood.
515   Then shall they seek to avail themselves of names,
    Places and titles, and with these to join
    Secular power, though feigning still to act
    By spiritual, to themselves appropriating
    The Spirit of God, promised alike and giv'n
520   To all believers; and from that pretence,
    Spiritual laws by carnal power shall force
    On every conscience; laws which none shall find
    Left them enrolled, or what the Spirit within
    Shall on the heart engrave. What will they then
525   But force the Spirit of grace itself, and bind

His consort Liberty; what, but unbuild
His living temples, built by faith to stand,
Their own faith not another's: for on earth
Who against faith and conscience can be heard
530   Infallible? yet many will presume:
Whence heavy persecution shall arise
On all who in the worship persevere
Of spirit and truth; the rest, far greater part,
Will deem in outward rites and specious forms
535   Religion satisfied; truth shall retire
Bestuck with sland'rous darts, and works of faith
Rarely be found: so shall the world go on,
To good malignant, to bad men benign,
Under her own weight groaning, till the day
540   Appear of respiration to the just,
And vengeance to the wicked, at return
Of him so lately promised to thy aid,
The Woman's Seed, obscurely then foretold,
Now amplier known thy Saviour and thy Lord,
545   Last in the clouds from Heav'n to be revealed
In glory of the Father, to dissolve
Satan with his perverted world, then raise
From the conflagrant mass, purged and refined,
New heav'ns, new earth, ages of endless date
550   Founded in righteousness and peace and love,
To bring forth fruits joy and eternal bliss.
        He ended; and thus Adam last replied.
How soon hath thy prediction, seer blest,
Measured this transient world, the race of time,
555   Till time stand fixed: beyond is all abyss,
Eternity, whose end no eye can reach.
Greatly instructed I shall thence depart,
Greatly in peace of thought, and have my fill
Of knowledge, what this vessel can contain;
560   Beyond which was my folly to aspire.
Henceforth I learn, that to obey is best,
And love with fear the only God, to walk
As in his presence, ever to observe
His Providence, and on him sole depend,

565   Merciful over all his works, with good
       Still overcoming evil, and by small
       Accomplishing great things, by things deemed weak
       Subverting worldly strong, and worldly wise
       By simply meek; that suffering for truth's sake
570   Is fortitude to highest victory,
       And to the faithful death the gate of life;
       Taught this by his example whom I now
       Acknowledge my Redeemer ever blest.
           To whom thus also th' angel last replied:
575   This having learnt, thou hast attained the sum
       Of wisdom; hope no higher, though all the stars
       Thou knew'st by name, and all th' ethereal Powers,
       All secrets of the deep, all Nature's works,
       Or works of God in Heav'n, air, earth, or sea,
580   And all the riches of this world enjoy'dst,
       And all the rule, one empire; only add
       Deeds to thy knowledge answerable, add faith,
       Add virtue, patience, temperance, add love,
       By name to come called charity, the soul
585   Of all the rest: then wilt thou not be loath
       To leave this Paradise, but shalt possess
       A paradise within thee, happier far.
       Let us descend now therefore from this top
       Of speculation; for the hour precise
590   Exacts our parting hence; and see the guards,
       By me encamped on yonder hill, expect
       Their motion, at whose front a flaming sword,
       In signal of remove, waves fiercely round;
       We may no longer stay: go, waken Eve;
595   Her also I with gentle dreams have calmed
       Portending good, and all her spirits composed
       To meek submission: thou at season fit
       Let her with thee partake what thou hast heard,
       Chiefly what may concern her faith to know,
600   The great deliverance by her Seed to come
       (For by the Woman's Seed) on all mankind,
       That ye may live, which will be many days,
       Both in one faith unanimous though sad,

With cause for evils past, yet much more cheered
605 With meditation on the happy end.
    He ended, and they both descend the hill;
Descended, Adam to the bow'r where Eve
Lay sleeping ran before, but found her waked;
And thus with words not sad she him received.
610   Whence thou return'st, and whither went'st, I know;
For God is also in sleep, and dreams advise,
Which he hath sent propitious, some great good
Presaging, since with sorrow and heart's distress
Wearied I fell asleep: but now lead on;
615 In me is no delay; with thee to go,
Is to stay here; without thee here to stay,
Is to go hence unwilling; thou to me
Art all things under Heav'n, all places thou,
Who for my wilful crime art banished hence.
620 This further consolation yet secure
I carry hence; though all by me is lost,
Such favour I unworthy am vouchsafed,
By me the promised Seed shall all restore.
    So spake our mother Eve, and Adam heard
625 Well pleased, but answered not; for now too nigh
Th' Archangel stood, and from the other hill
To their fixed station, all in bright array
The Cherubim descended; on the ground
Gliding meteorous, as ev'ning mist
630 Ris'n from a river o'er the marish glides,
And gathers ground fast at the labourer's heel
Homeward returning. High in front advanced,
The brandished sword of God before them blazed
Fierce as a comet; which with torrid heat,
635 And vapour as the Libyan air adust,
Began to parch that temperate clime; whereat
In either hand the hast'ning angel caught
Our ling'ring parents, and to th' eastern gate
Led them direct, and down the cliff as fast
640 To the subjected plain; then disappeared.
They looking back, all th' eastern side beheld
Of Paradise, so late their happy seat,

Waved over by that flaming brand, the gate
With dreadful faces thronged and fiery arms:
645   Some natural tears they dropped, but wiped them soon;
The world was all before them, where to choose
Their place of rest, and Providence their guide:
They hand in hand with wand'ring steps and slow,
Through Eden took their solitary way.

PARADISE REGAINED

THE FIRST BOOK

I who erewhile the happy garden sung,
By one man's disobedience lost, now sing
Recovered Paradise to all mankind,
By one man's firm obedience fully tried
5 Through all temptation, and the Tempter foiled
In all his wiles, defeated and repulsed,
And Eden raised in the waste wilderness.
    Thou Spirit who led'st this glorious eremite
Into the desert, his victorious field
10 Against the spiritual Foe, and brought'st him thence
By proof th' undoubted Son of God, inspire,
As thou art wont, my prompted song else mute,
And bear through heighth or depth of nature's bounds
With prosperous wing full-summed, to tell of deeds
15 Above heroic, though in secret done,
And unrecorded left through many an age,
Worthy t' have not remained so long unsung.
    Now had the great proclaimer with a voice
More awful than the sound of trumpet, cried
20 Repentance, and Heaven's Kingdom nigh at hand
To all baptized: to his great baptism flocked
With awe the regions round, and with them came
From Nazareth the son of Joseph deemed
To the flood Jordan, came as then obscure,
25 Unmarked, unknown; but him the Baptist soon
Descried, divinely warned, and witness bore
As to his worthier, and would have resigned
To him his Heavenly office, nor was long
His witness unconfirmed: on him baptized
30 Heaven opened, and in likeness of a dove

The Spirit descended, while the Father's voice
From Heav'n pronounced him his beloved Son.
That heard the Adversary, who roving still
About the world, at that assembly famed
35   Would not be last, and with the voice divine
Nigh thunder-struck, th' exalted man, to whom
Such high attest was giv'n, a while surveyed
With wonder, then with envy fraught and rage
Flies to his place, nor rests, but in mid air
40   To Council summons all his mighty peers,
Within thick clouds and dark ten-fold involved,
A gloomy cónsistory; and them amidst
With looks aghast and sad he thus bespake.
        O ancient Powers of air and this wide world,
45   For much more willingly I mention air,
This our old conquest, than remember Hell
Our hated habitation; well ye know
How many ages, as the years of men,
This universe we have possessed, and ruled
50   In manner at our will th' affairs of earth,
Since Adam and his facile consort Eve
Lost Paradise deceived by me, though since
With dread attending when that fatal wound
Shall be inflicted by the Seed of Eve
55   Upon my head; long the decrees of Heav'n
Delay, for longest time to him is short;
And now too soon for us the circling hours
This dreaded time have compassed, wherein we
Must bide the stroke of that long-threatened wound,
60   At least if so we can, and by the head
Broken be not intended all our power
To be infringed, our freedom and our being
In this fair empire won of earth and air;
For this ill news I bring: the Woman's Seed
65   Destined to this, is late of woman born;
His birth to our just fear gave no small cause,
But his growth now to youth's full flow'r, displaying
All virtue, grace and wisdom to achieve
Things highest, greatest, multiplies my fear.

70   Before him a great prophet, to proclaim
His coming, is sent harbinger, who all
Invites, and in the consecrated stream
Pretends to wash off sin, and fit them so
Purified to receive him pure, or rather
75   To do him honour as their King; all come,
And he himself among them was baptized,
Not thence to be more pure, but to receive
The testimony of Heaven, that who he is
Thenceforth the nations may not doubt; I saw
80   The prophet do him reverence, on him rising
Out of the water, Heav'n above the clouds
Unfold her crystal doors, thence on his head
A perfect dove descend, whate'er it meant,
And out of Heav'n the sov'reign voice I heard,
85   This is my Son belov'd, in him am pleased.
His mother then is mortal, but his Sire
He who obtains the monarchy of Heav'n,
And what will he not do to advance his Son?
His first-begot we know, and sore have felt,
90   When his fierce thunder drove us to the deep;
Who this is we must learn, for man he seems
In all his lineaments, though in his face
The glimpses of his Father's glory shine.
Ye see our danger on the utmost edge
95   Of hazard, which admits no long debate,
But must with something sudden be opposed,
Not force, but well-couched fraud, well-woven snares,
Ere in the head of nations he appear
Their King, their leader, and supreme on earth.
100   I, when no other durst, sole undertook
The dismal expedition to find out
And ruin Adam, and the expóit performed
Successfully; a calmer voyage now
Will waft me; and the way found prosperous once
105   Induces best to hope of like success.
      He ended, and his words impression left
Of much amazement to th' infernal crew,
Distracted and surprised with deep dismay

At these sad tidings; but no time was then
110   For long indulgence to their fears or grief:
Unanimous they all commit the care
And management of this main enterprise
To him their great dictator, whose attempt
At first against mankind so well had thrived
115   In Adam's overthrow, and led their march
From Hell's deep-vaulted den to dwell in light,
Regents and potentates, and kings, yea gods
Of many a pleasant realm and province wide.
So to the coast of Jordan he directs
120   His easy steps; girded with snaky wiles,
Where he might likeliest find this new-declared,
This man of men, attested Son of God,
Temptation and all guile on him to try;
So to subvert whom he suspected raised
125   To end his reign on earth so long enjoyed:
But contrary unweeting he fulfilled
The purposed counsel preordained and fixed
Of the Most High, who in full frequence bright
Of angels, thus to Gabriel smiling spake.
130   Gabriel this day by proof thou shalt behold,
Thou and all angels cónversant on earth
With man or men's affairs, how I begin
To verify that solemn message late,
On which I sent thee to the virgin pure
135   In Galilee, that she should bear a son
Great in renown, and called the Son of God;
Then told'st her doubting how these things could be
To her a virgin, that on her should come
The Holy Ghost, and the power of the Highest
140   O'ershadow her: this man born and now upgrown,
To show him worthy of his birth divine
And high prediction, henceforth I expose
To Satan; let him tempt and now assay
His utmost subtlety, because he boasts
145   And vaunts of his great cunning to the throng
Of his apostasy; he might have learnt
Less overweening, since he failed in Job,

Whose constant perseverance overcame
Whate'er his cruel malice could invent.
150 He now shall know I can produce a man
Of female seed, far abler to resist
All his solicitations, and at length
All his vast force, and drive him back to Hell,
Winning by conquest what the first man lost
155 By fallacy surprised. But first I mean
To exercise him in the wilderness;
There he shall first lay down the rudiments
Of his great warfare, ere I send him forth
To conquer Sin and Death the two grand foes,
160 By humiliation and strong sufferance:
His weakness shall o'ercome Satanic strength
And all the world, and mass of sinful flesh;
That all the angels and ethereal powers,
They now, and men hereafter may discern,
165 From what consummate virtue I have chose
This perfect man, by merit called my Son,
To earn Salvation for the sons of men.
    So spake the Eternal Father, and all Heaven
Admiring stood a space, then into hymns
170 Burst forth, and in celestial measures moved,
Circling the throne and singing, while the hand
Sung with the voice, and this the argument.
    Victory and triumph to the Son of God
Now ent'ring his great duel, not of arms,
175 But to vanquish by wisdom Hellish wiles.
The Father knows the Son; therefore secure
Ventures his filial virtue, though untried,
Against whate'er may tempt, whate'er seduce,
Allure, or terrify, or undermine.
180 Be frustrate all ye strategems of Hell,
And devilish machinations come to nought.
    So they in Heav'n their odes and vigils tuned:
Meanwhile the Son of God, who yet some days
Lodged in Bethabara where John baptized,
185 Musing and much revolving in his breast,
How best the mighty work he might begin

Of Saviour to mankind, and which way first
Publish his Godlike office now mature,
One day forth walked alone, the Spirit leading;
190 And his deep thoughts, the better to converse
With solitude, till far from track of men,
Thought following thought, and step by step led on,
He entered now the bordering desert wild,
And with dark shades and rocks environed round,
195 His holy meditations thus pursued.
    O what a multitude of thoughts at once
Awakened in me swarm, while I consider
What from within I feel myself, and hear
What from without comes often to my ears,
200 Ill sorting with my present state compared.
When I was yet a child, no childish play
To me was pleasing, all my mind was set
Serious to learn and know, and thence to do
What might be public good; myself I thought
205 Born to that end, born to promote all truth,
All righteous things: therefore above my years,
The Law of God I read, and found it sweet,
Made it my whole delight, and in it grew
To such perfection, that ere yet my age
210 Had measured twice six years, at our great feast
I went into the Temple, there to hear
The teachers of our Law, and to propose
What might improve my knowledge or their own;
And was admired by all; yet this not all
215 To which my spirit aspired; victorious deeds
Flamed in my heart, heroic acts, one while
To rescue Israel from the Roman yoke,
Then to subdue and quell o'er all the earth
Brute violence and proud tyrannic pow'r,
220 Till truth were freed, and equity restored:
Yet held it more humane, more Heavenly, first
By winning words to conquer willing hearts,
And make persuasion do the work of fear;
At least to try, and teach the erring soul
225 Not wilfully misdoing, but unware

Misled; the stubborn only to subdue.
These growing thoughts my mother soon perceiving
By words at times cast forth inly rejoiced,
And said to me apart, high are thy thoughts
230 O Son, but nourish them and let them soar
To what heighth sacred virtue and true worth
Can raise them, though above example high;
By matchless deeds express thy matchless Sire.
For know, thou art no son of mortal man,
235 Though men esteem thee low of parentage,
Thy Father is the Eternal King, who rules
All Heaven and earth, angels and sons of men.
A messenger from God foretold thy birth
Conceived in me a virgin; he foretold
240 Thou shouldst be great and sit in David's throne,
And of thy kingdom there should be no end.
At thy nativity a glorious choir
Of angels in the fields of Bethlehem sung
To shepherds watching at their folds by night,
245 And told them the Messiah now was born,
Where they might see him, and to thee they came;
Directed to the manger where thou lay'st,
For in the inn was left no better room:
A star, not seen before in heaven appearing
250 Guided the wise men thither from the east,
To honour thee with incense, myrrh, and gold,
By whose bright course led on they found the place,
Affirming it thy star new-grav'n in heaven,
By which they knew thee King of Israel born.
255 Just Simeon and prophetic Anna, warned
By vision, found thee in the Temple, and spake
Before the altar and the vested priest,
Like things of thee to all that present stood.
This having heard, straight I again revolved
260 The Law and Prophets, searching what was writ
Concerning the Messiah, to our scribes
Known partly, and soon found of whom they spake
I am; this chiefly, that my way must lie
Through many a hard assay even to the death,

265 Ere I the promised Kingdom can attain,
Or work Redemption for mankind, whose sins'
Full weight must be transferred upon my head.
Yet neither thus disheartened or dismayed,
The time prefixed I waited, when behold
270 The Baptist (of whose birth I oft had heard,
Not knew by sight) now come, who was to come
Before Messiah and his way prepare.
I as all others to his baptism came,
Which I believed was from above; but he
275 Straight knew me, and with loudest voice proclaimed
Me him (for it was shown him so from Heaven)
Me him whose harbinger he was; and first
Refused on me his baptism to confer,
As much his greater, and was hardly won;
280 But as I rose out of the laving stream,
Heaven opened her eternal doors, from whence
The Spirit descended on me like a dove,
And last the sum of all, my Father's voice,
Audibly heard from Heav'n, pronounced me his,
285 Me his beloved Son, in whom alone
He was well-pleased; by which I knew the time
Now full, that I no more should live obscure,
But openly begin, as best becomes
The authority which I derived from Heaven.
290 And now by some strong motion I am led
Into this wilderness, to what intent
I learn not yet, perhaps I need not know;
For what concerns my knowledge God reveals.
    So spake our Morning Star then in his rise,
295 And looking round on every side beheld
A pathless desert, dusk with horrid shades;
The way he came not having marked, return
Was difficult, by human steps untrod;
And he still on was led, but with such thoughts
300 Accompanied of things past and to come
Lodged in his breast, as well might recommend
Such solitude before choicest society.
Full forty days he passed, whether on hill

Sometimes, anon in shady vale, each night
305　Under the covert of some ancient oak,
Or cedar, to defend him from the dew,
Or harboured in one cave, is not revealed;
Nor tasted human food, nor hunger felt
Till those days ended, hungered then at last
310　Among wild beasts: they at his sight grew mild,
Nor sleeping him nor waking harmed, his walk
The fiery serpent fled, and noxious worm,
The lion and fierce tiger glared aloof.
But now an aged man in rural weeds,
315　Following, as seemed, the quest of some stray ewe,
Or withered sticks to gather; which might serve
Against a winter's day when winds blow keen,
To warm him wet returned from field at eve,
He saw approach, who first with curious eye
320　Perused him, then with words thus uttered spake.
　　Sir, what ill chance hath brought thee to this place
So far from path or road of men, who pass
In troop or caravan? For single none
Durst ever, who returned, and dropped not here
325　His carcass, pined with hunger and with drouth.
I ask thee rather, and the more admire,
For that to me thou seem'st the man, whom late
Our new baptizing Prophet at the ford
Of Jordan honoured so, and called thee Son
330　Of God; I saw and heard, for we sometimes
Who dwell this wild, constrained by want, come forth
To town or village nigh (nighest is far)
Where aught we hear, and curious are to hear,
What happens new; fame also finds us out.
335　　To whom the Son of God. Who brought me hither
Will bring me hence, no other guide I seek.
　　By miracle he may, replied the swain,
What other way I see not, for we here
Live on rough roots and stubs, to thirst inured
340　More than the camel, and to drink go far,
Men to much misery and hardship born;
But if thou be the Son of God, command

That out of these hard stones be made thee bread;
So shalt thou save thyself and us relieve
345   With food, whereof we wretched seldom taste.
       He ended, and the Son of God replied.
Think'st thou such force in bread? Is it not written
(For I discern thee other than thou seem'st)
Man lives not by bread only, but each word
350   Proceeding from the mouth of God; who fed
Our fathers here with manna; in the mount
Moses was forty days, nor ate nor drank,
And forty days Elijah without food
Wandered this barren waste, the same I now:
355   Why dost thou then suggest to me distrust,
Knowing who I am, as I know who thou art?
       Whom thus answered th' Arch-Fiend now undisguised.
'Tis true, I am that Spirit unfortunate,
Who leagued with millions more in rash revolt
360   Kept not my happy station, but was driv'n
With them from bliss to the bottomless deep,
Yet to that hideous place not so confined
By rigour unconniving, but that oft
Leaving my dolorous prison I enjoy
365   Large liberty to round this globe of earth,
Or range in th' air, nor from the Heav'n of Heav'ns
Hath he excluded my resort sometimes.
I came among the sons of God, when he
Gave up into my hands Uzzéan Job
370   To prove him, and illústrate his high worth;
And when to all his angels he proposed
To draw the proud King Ahab into fraud
That he might fall in Ramoth, they demurring,
I undertook that office, and the tongues
375   Of all his flattering prophets glibbed with lies
To his destruction, as I had in charge.
For what he bids I do; though I have lost
Much lustre of my native brightness, lost
To be beloved of God, I have not lost
380   To love, at least contémplate and admire
What I see excellent in good, or fair,

Or virtuous; I should so have lost all sense.
What can be then less in me than desire
To see thee and approach thee, whom I know
385 Declared the Son of God, to hear attent
Thy wisdom, and behold thy Godlike deeds?
Men generally think me much a foe
To all mankind: why should I? they to me
Never did wrong or violence, by them
390 I lost not what I lost, rather by them
I gained what I have gained, and with them dwell
Copartner in these regions of the world,
If not disposer; lend them oft my aid,
Oft my advice by presages and signs,
395 And answers, oracles, portents and dreams,
Whereby they may direct their future life.
Envy they say excites me, thus to gain
Companions of my misery and woe.
At first it may be; but long since with woe
400 Nearer acquainted, now I feel by proof,
That fellowship in pain divides not smart,
Nor lightens aught each man's peculiar load.
Small consolation then, were man adjoined:
This wounds me most (what can it less) that man,
405 Man fall'n shall be restored, I never more.
   To whom our Saviour sternly thus replied.
Deservedly thou griev'st, composed of lies
From the beginning, and in lies wilt end;
Who boast'st release from Hell, and leave to come
410 Into the Heav'n of Heavens; thou com'st indeed,
As a poor miserable captive thrall
Comes to the place where he before had sat
Among the prime in splendour, now deposed,
Ejected, emptied, gazed, unpitied, shunned,
415 A spectacle of ruin or of scorn
To all the host of Heaven; the happy place
Imports to thee no happiness, no joy,
Rather inflames thy torment, representing
Lost bliss, to thee no more communicable,
420 So never more in Hell than when in Heaven.

But thou art serviceable to Heaven's King.
Wilt thou impute to obedience what thy fear
Extorts, or pleasure to do ill excites?
What but thy malice moved thee to misdeem
425 Of righteous Job, then cruelly to afflict him
With all inflictions? But his patience won.
The other service was thy chosen task,
To be a liar in four hundred mouths;
For lying is thy sustenance, thy food.
430 Yet thou pretend'st to truth; all oracles
By thee are giv'n, and what confessed more true
Among the nations? That hath been thy craft,
By mixing somewhat true to vent more lies.
But what have been thy answers, what but dark
435 Ambiguous and with double sense deluding,
Which they who asked have seldom understood,
And not well understood as good not known?
Whoever by consulting at thy shrine
Returned the wiser, or the more instruct
440 To fly or follow what concerned him most,
And run not sooner to his fatal snare?
For God hath justly giv'n the nations up
To thy delusions; justly, since they fell
Idolatrous; but when his purpose is
445 Among them to declare his Providence
To thee not known, whence hast thou then thy truth,
But from him or his angels president
In every province, who themselves disdaining
To approach thy temples, give thee in command
450 What to the smallest tittle thou shalt say
To thy adorers; thou with trembling fear,
Or like a fawning parasite obey'st;
Then to thyself ascrib'st the truth foretold.
But this thy glory shall be soon retrenched;
455 No more shalt thou by oracling abuse
The Gentiles; henceforth oracles are ceased,
And thou no more with pomp and sacrifice
Shalt be inquired at Delphos or elsewhere,
At least in vain, for they shall find thee mute.

460 God hath now sent his living Oracle
Into the world, to teach his final will,
And sends his Spirit of Truth henceforth to dwell
In pious hearts, an inward oracle
To all truth requisite for men to know.
465   So spake our Saviour; but the subtle Fiend,
Though inly stung with anger and disdain,
Dissembled, and this answer smooth returned.
    Sharply thou hast insisted on rebuke,
And urged me hard with doings, which not will
470 But misery hath wrested from me; where
Easily canst thou find one miserable,
And not enforced oft-times to part from truth,
If it may stand him more in stead to lie,
Say and unsay, feign, flatter, or abjure?
475 But thou art placed above me, thou art Lord;
From thee I can and must submiss endure
Check or reproof, and glad to 'scape so quit.
Hard are the ways of truth, and rough to walk,
Smooth on the tongue discoursed, pleasing to th' ear,
480 And tuneable as sylvan pipe or song;
What wonder then if I delight to hear
Her dictates from thy mouth? Most men admire
Virtue, who follow not her lore: permit me
To hear thee when I come (since no man comes)
485 And talk at least, though I despair to attain.
Thy Father, who is holy, wise and pure,
Suffers the hypocrite or atheous priest
To tread his sacred courts, and minister
About his altar, handling holy things,
490 Praying or vowing, and vouchsafed his voice
To Balaam reprobate, a prophet yet
Inspired; disdain not such access to me.
    To whom our Saviour with unaltered brow.
Thy coming hither, though I know thy scope,
495 I bid not or forbid; do as thou find'st
Permission from above; thou canst not more.
    He added not; and Satan bowing low
His grey dissimulation, disappeared

Into thin air diffused: for now began
500   Night with her sullen wing to double-shade
The desert, fowls in their clay nests were couched;
And now wild beasts came forth the woods to roam.

Meanwhile the new-baptized, who yet remained
At Jordan with the Baptist, and had seen
Him whom they heard so late expressly called
Jesus Messiah, Son of God declared,
5 And on that high authority had believed,
And with him talked, and with him lodged, I mean
Andrew and Simon, famous after known
With others though in Holy Writ not named,
Now missing him their joy so lately found,
10 So lately found, and so abruptly gone,
Began to doubt, and doubted many days,
And as the days increased, increased their doubt:
Sometimes they thought he might be only shown,
And for a time caught up to God, as once
15 Moses was in the Mount, and missing long;
And the great Thisbite who on fiery wheels
Rode up to Heaven, yet once again to come.
Therefore as those young prophets then with care
Sought lost Elijah, so in each place these
20 Nigh to Bethabara; in Jericho
The city of palms, Aenon, and Salem old,
Machaerus and each town or city walled
On this side the broad lake Genezaret,
Or in Perea, but returned in vain.
25 Then on the bank of Jordan, by a creek
Where winds with reeds, and osiers whisp'ring play,
Plain fishermen, no greater men them call,
Close in a cottage low together got
Their unexpected loss and plaints outbreathed.
30   Alas, from what high hope to what relapse
Unlooked for are we fall'n! Our eyes beheld
Messiah certainly now come, so long

Expected of our fathers; we have heard
His words, his wisdom full of grace and truth;
35   Now, now, for sure, deliverance is at hand,
The kingdom shall to Israel be restored:
Thus we rejoiced, but soon our joy is turned
Into perplexity and new amaze:
For whither is he gone, what accident
40   Hath rapt him from us? will he now retire
After appearance, and again prolong
Our expectation? God of Israel,
Send thy Messiah forth, the time is come;
Behold the kings of the earth how they oppress
45   Thy chosen, to what heighth their power unjust
They have exalted, and behind them cast
All fear of thee; arise and vindicate
Thy glory, free thy people from their yoke;
But let us wait; thus far he hath performed,
50   Sent his Anointed, and to us revealed him,
By his great Prophet, pointed at and shown,
In public, and with him we have conversed;
Let us be glad of this, and all our fears
Lay on his Providence; he will not fail
55   Nor will withdraw him now, nor will recall,
Mock us with his blest sight, then snatch him hence;
Soon we shall see our hope, our joy return.
    Thus they out of their plaints new hope resume
To find whom at the first they found unsought:
60   But to his mother Mary, when she saw
Others returned from baptism, not her son,
Nor left at Jordan, tidings of him none;
Within her breast, though calm; her breast though pure,
Motherly cares and fears got head, and raised
65   Some troubled thoughts, which she in sighs thus clad.
    O what avails me now that honour high
To have conceived of God, or that salute
Hail highly favoured, among women blest;
While I to sorrows am no less advanced,
70   And fears as eminent, above the lot
Of other women, by the birth I bore,

In such a season born when scarce a shed
Could be obtained to shelter him or me
From the bleak air; a stable was our warmth,
75   A manger his, yet soon enforced to fly
Thence into Egypt, till the murd'rous king
Were dead, who sought his life, and missing filled
With infant blood the streets of Bethlehem;
From Egypt home returned, in Nazareth
80   Hath been our dwelling many years; his life
Private, unactive, calm, contemplative,
Little suspicious to any king; but now
Full grown to man, acknowledged, as I hear,
By John the Baptist, and in public shown,
85   Son owned from Heaven by his Father's voice;
I looked for some great change; to honour? no,
But trouble, as old Simeon plain foretold,
That to the fall and rising he should be
Of many in Israel, and to a sign
90   Spoken against, that through my very soul
A sword shall pierce; this is my favoured lot,
My exaltation to afflictions high;
Afflicted I may be, it seems, and blest;
I will not argue that, nor will repine.
95   But where delays he now? some great intent
Conceals him: when twelve years he scarce had seen,
I lost him, but so found, as well I saw
He could not lose himself; but went about
His Father's business; what he meant I mused,
100   Since understand; much more his absence now
Thus long to some great purpose he obscures.
But I to wait with patience am inured;
My heart hath been a storehouse long of things
And sayings laid up, portending strange events.
105   Thus Mary pondering oft, and oft to mind
Recalling what remarkably had passed
Since first her salutation heard, with thoughts
Meekly composed awaited the fulfilling:
The while her son tracing the desert wild,
110   Sole but with holiest meditations fed,

Into himself descended, and at once
All his great work to come before him set;
How to begin, how to accomplish best
His end of being on earth, and mission high:
115   For Satan with sly preface to return
Had left him vacant, and with speed was gone
Up to the middle region of thick air,
Where all his Potentates in council sat;
There without sign of boast, or sign of joy,
120   Solicitous and blank he thus began.
      Princes, Heaven's ancient sons, ethereal Thrones,
Demonian Spirits now, from the element
Each of his reign allotted, rightlier called,
Powers of fire, air, water, and earth beneath,
125   So may we hold our place and these mild seats
Without new trouble; such an enemy
Is risen to invade us, who no less
Threatens than our expulsion down to Hell;
I, as I undertook, and with the vote
130   Consenting in full frequence was empower'd,
Have found him, viewed him, tasted him, but find
Far other labour to be undergone
Than when I dealt with Adam first of men,
Though Adam by his wife's allurement fell,
135   However to this man inferior far,
If he be man by his mother's side at least,
With more than human gifts from Heaven adorned,
Perfections absolute, graces divine,
And amplitude of mind to greatest deeds.
140   Therefore I am returned, lest confidence
Of my success with Eve in Paradise
Deceive ye to persuasion oversure
Of like succeeding here; I summon all
Rather to be in readiness, with hand
145   Or counsel to assist; lest I who erst
Thought none my equal, now be overmatched.
      So spake the old Serpent doubting, and from all
With clamour was assured their utmost aid
At his command; when from amidst them rose

150 Belial the dissolutest Spirit that fell,
The sensualest, and after Asmodai
The fleshliest incubus, and thus advised.
      Set women in his eye and in his walk,
Among daughters of men the fairest found;
155 Many are in each region passing fair
As the noon sky; more like to goddesses
Than mortal creatures, graceful and discreet,
Expért in amorous arts, enchanting tongues
Persuasive, virgin majesty with mild
160 And sweet allayed, yet terrible to approach,
Skilled to retire, and in retiring draw
Hearts after them tangled in amorous nets.
Such object hath the power to soft'n and tame
Severest temper, smooth the rugged'st brow,
165 Enerve, and with voluptuous hope dissolve,
Draw out with credulous desire, and lead
At will the manliest, resolutest breast,
As the magnetic hardest iron draws.
Women, when nothing else, beguiled the heart
170 Of wisest Solomon, and made him build,
And made him bow to the gods of his wives.
      To whom quick answer Satan thus returned.
Belial, in much uneven scale thou weigh'st
All others by thyself; because of old
175 Thou thyself dot'st on womankind, admiring
Their shape, their colour, and attractive grace,
None are, thou think'st, but taken with such toys.
Before the Flood thou with thy lusty crew,
False-titled sons of God, roaming the earth
180 Cast wanton eyes on the daughters of men,
And coupled with them, and begot a race.
Have we not seen, or by relation heard,
In courts and regal chambers how thou lurk'st,
In wood or grove by mossy fountain side,
185 In valley or green meadow to waylay
Some beauty rare, Callisto, Clymene,
Daphne, or Semele, Antiopa,
Or Amymone, Syrinx, many more

Too long, then lay'st thy scapes on names adored,
190   Apollo, Neptune, Jupiter, or Pan,
Satyr, or Faun, or Sylvan? But these haunts
Delight not all; among the sons of men,
How many have with a smile made small account
Of beauty and her lures, easily scorned
195   All her assaults, on worthier things intent?
Remember that Pelléan conqueror,
A youth, how all the beauties of the East
He slightly viewed, and slightly overpassed;
How he surnamed of Africa dismissed
200   In his prime youth the fair Iberian maid.
For Solomon he lived at ease, and full
Of honour, wealth, high fare, aimed not beyond
Higher design than to enjoy his state;
Thence to the bait of women lay exposed;
205   But he whom we attempt is wiser far
Than Solomon, of more exalted mind,
Made and set wholly on the accomplishment
Of greatest things; what woman will you find,
Though of this age the wonder and the fame,
210   On whom his leisure will vouchsafe an eye
Of fond desire? or should she confident,
As sitting queen adored on Beauty's throne,
Descend with all her winning charms begirt
To enamour, as the zone of Venus once
215   Wrought that effect on Jove, so fables tell;
How would one look from his majestic brow
Seated as on the top of Virtue's hill,
Discount'nance her despised, and put to rout
All her array; her female pride deject,
220   Or turn to reverent awe? For Beauty stands
In the admiration only of weak minds
Led captive; cease to admire, and all her plumes
Fall flat and shrink into a trivial toy,
At every sudden slighting quite abashed:
225   Therefore with manlier objects we must try
His constancy, with such as have more show
Of worth, of honour, glory, and popular praise;

Rocks whereon greatest men have oftest wrecked;
Or that which only seems to satisfy
230   Lawful desires of nature, not beyond;
And now I know he hungers where no food
Is to be found, in the wide wilderness;
The rest commit to me, I shall let pass
No advantage, and his strength as oft assay.

235   He ceased, and heard their grant in loud acclaim;
Then forthwith to him takes a chosen band
Of Spirits likest to himself in guile
To be at hand, and at his beck appear,
If cause were to unfold some active scene
240   Of various persons each to know his part;
Then to the desert takes with these his flight;
Where still from shade to shade the Son of God
After forty days' fasting had remained,
Now hung'ring first, and to himself thus said.

245   Where will this end? four times ten days I have passed
Wand'ring this woody maze, and human food
Nor tasted, nor had appetite; that fast
To virtue I impute not, or count part
Of what I suffer here; if nature need not,
250   Or God support nature without repast
Though needing, what praise is it to endure?
But now I feel I hunger, which declares,
Nature hath need of what she asks; yet God
Can satisfy that need some other way,
255   Though hunger still remain: so it remain
Without this body's wasting, I content me,
And from the sting of famine fear no harm,
Nor mind it, fed with better thoughts that feed
Me hung'ring more to do my Father's will.

260   It was the hour of night, when thus the Son
Communed in silent walk, then laid him down
Under the hospitable covert nigh
Of trees thick interwoven; there he slept,
And dreamed, as appetite is wont to dream,
265   Of meats and drinks, nature's refreshment sweet;
Him thought he by the brook of Cherith stood

And saw the ravens with their horny beaks
Food to Elijah bringing even and morn,
Though ravenous, taught to abstain from what they
       brought:
270   He saw the Prophet also how he fled
Into the desert, and how there he slept
Under a juniper; then how awaked,
He found his supper on the coals prepared,
And by the angel was bid rise and eat,
275   And eat the second time after repose,
The strength whereof sufficed him forty days;
Sometimes that with Elijah he partook,
Or as a guest with Daniel at his pulse.
Thus wore out night, and now the herald lark
280   Left his ground-nest, high tow'ring to descry
The morn's approach, and greet her with his song:
As lightly from his grassy couch up rose
Our Saviour, and found all was but a dream;
Fasting he went to sleep, and fasting waked.
285   Up to a hill anon his steps he reared,
From whose high top to ken the prospect round,
If cottage were in view, sheep-cote or herd;
But cottage, herd or sheep-cote none he saw,
Only in a bottom saw a pleasant grove,
290   With chant of tuneful birds resounding loud;
Thither he bent his way, determined there
To rest at noon, and entered soon the shade
High-roofed and walks beneath, and alleys brown
That opened in the midst a woody scene,
295   Nature's own work it seemed (Nature taught Art)
And to a superstitious eye the haunt
Of wood-gods and wood-nymphs; he viewed it round,
When suddenly a man before him stood,
Not rustic as before, but seemlier clad,
300   As one in city, or court, or palace bred,
And with fair speech these words to him addressed.
    With granted leave officious I return,
But much more wonder that the Son of God
In this wild solitude so long should bide

305 Of all things destitute, and well I know,
    Not without hunger. Others of some note,
    As story tells, have trod this wilderness;
    The fugitive bondwoman with her son,
    Outcast Nebaioth, yet found he relief
310 By a providing angel; all the race
    Of Israel here had famished, had not God
    Rained from Heaven manna; and that Prophet bold
    Native of Thebèz wand'ring here was fed
    Twice by a voice inviting him to eat.
315 Of thee these forty days none hath regard,
    Forty and more deserted here indeed.
        To whom thus Jesus; what conclud'st thou hence?
    They all had need, I as thou seest have none.
        How hast thou hunger then? Satan replied,
320 Tell me if food were now before thee set,
    Wouldst thou not eat? Thereafter as I like
    The giver, answered Jesus. Why should that
    Cause thy refusal, said the subtle Fiend,
    Hast thou not right to all created things,
325 Owe not all creatures by just right to thee
    Duty and service, nor to stay till bid,
    But tender all their power? nor mention I
    Meats by the law unclean, or offered first
    To idols – those young Daniel could refuse;
330 Nor proffered by an enemy, though who
    Would scruple that, with want oppressed? behold
    Nature ashamed, or better to express,
    Troubled that thou shouldst hunger, hath purveyed
    From all the elements her choicest store
335 To treat thee as beseems, and as her Lord
    With honour; only deign to sit and eat.
        He spake no dream, for as his words had end,
    Our Saviour lifting up his eyes beheld
    In ample space under the broadest shade
340 A table richly spread, in regal mode,
    With dishes piled, and meats of noblest sort
    And savour, beasts of chase, or fowl of game,
    In pastry built, or from the spit, or boiled,

Grisamber-steamed; all fish from sea or shore,
345 Freshet, or purling brook, or shell or fin,
And exquisitest name, for which was drained
Pontus and Lucrine bay, and Afric coast.
Alas how simple, to these cates compared,
Was that crude apple that diverted Eve!
350 And at a stately sideboard, by the wine
That fragrant smell diffused, in order stood
Tall stripling youths rich-clad, of fairer hue
Than Ganymede or Hylas; distant more
Under the trees now tripped, now solemn stood
355 Nymphs of Diana's train, and Naiades
With fruits and flowers from Amalthea's horn,
And ladies of th' Hesperides, that seemed
Fairer than feigned of old, or fabled since
Of fairy damsels met in forest wide
360 By knights of Logres, or of Lyonesse,
Lancelot or Pelleas, or Pellenore;
And all the while harmonious airs were heard
Of chiming strings, or charming pipes, and winds
Of gentlest gale Arabian odours fanned
365 From their soft wings, and Flora's earliest smells.
Such was the splendour, and the Tempter now
His invitation earnestly renewed.
     What doubts the Son of God to sit and eat?
These are not fruits forbidden; no interdict
370 Defends the touching of these viands pure;
Their taste no knowledge works, at least of evil,
But life preserves, destroys life's enemy,
Hunger, with sweet restorative delight.
All these are Spirits of air, and woods, and springs,
375 Thy gentle ministers, who come to pay
Thee homage, and acknowledge thee their Lord:
What doubt'st thou Son of God? sit down and eat.
     To whom thus Jesus temperately replied:
Said'st thou not that to all things I had right?
380 And who withholds my pow'r that right to use?
Shall I receive by gift what of my own,
When and where likes me best, I can command?

I can at will, doubt not, as soon as thou,
Command a table in this wilderness,
385   And call swift flights of angels ministrant
Arrayed in glory on my cup to attend:
Why shouldst thou then obtrude this diligence,
In vain, where no acceptance it can find,
And with my hunger what hast thou to do?
390   Thy pompous delicacies I contemn,
And count thy specious gifts no gifts but guiles.
    To whom thus answered Satan malcontent:
That I have also power to give thou seest;
If of that pow'r I bring thee voluntary
395   What I might have bestowed on whom I pleased,
And rather opportunely in this place
Chose to impart to thy apparent need,
Why shouldst thou not accept it? but I see
What I can do or offer is suspéct;
400   Of these things others quickly will dispose
Whose pains have earned the far-fet spoil. With that
Both table and provision vanished quite
With sound of Harpies' wings, and talons heard;
Only the impórtune Tempter still remained,
405   And with these words his temptation pursued.
    By hunger, that each other creature tames,
Thou art not to be harmed, therefore not moved;
Thy temperance invincible besides,
For no allurement yields to appetite,
410   And all thy heart is set on high designs,
High actions; but wherewith to be achieved?
Great acts require great means of enterprise;
Thou art unknown, unfriended, low of birth,
A carpenter thy father known, thyself
415   Bred up in poverty and straits at home;
Lost in a desert here and hunger-bit:
Which way or from what hope dost thou aspire
To greatness? whence authority deriv'st,
What followers, what retínue canst thou gain,
420   Or at thy heels the dizzy multitude,
Longer than thou canst feed them on thy cost?

Money brings honour, friends, conquest, and realms;
What raised Antipater the Edomite,
And his son Herod placed on Judah's throne
425 (Thy throne) but gold that got him puissant friends?
Therefore, if at great things thou wouldst arrive,
Get riches first, get wealth, and treasure heap,
Not difficult, if thou hearken to me,
Riches are mine, fortune is in my hand;
430 They whom I favour thrive in wealth amain,
While virtue, valour, wisdom sit in want.
    To whom thus Jesus patiently replied;
Yet wealth without these three is impotent,
To gain dominion or to keep it gained.
435 Witness those ancient empires of the earth,
In heighth of all their flowing wealth dissolved:
But men endued with these have oft attained
In lowest poverty to highest deeds;
Gideon and Jephtha, and the shepherd lad,
440 Whose offspring on the throne of Judah sat
So many ages, and shall yet regain
That seat, and reign in Israel without end.
Among the heathen, (for throughout the world
To me is not unknown what hath been done
445 Worthy of memorial) canst thou not remember
Quintius, Fabricius, Curius, Regulus?
For I esteem those names of men so poor
Who could do mighty things, and could contemn
Riches though offered from the hand of kings.
450 And what in me seems wanting, but that I
May also in this poverty as soon
Accomplish what they did, perhaps and more?
Extol not riches then, the toil of fools,
The wise man's cumbrance if not snare, more apt
455 To slacken virtue, and abate her edge,
Than prompt her to do aught may merit praise.
What if with like aversion I reject
Riches and realms; yet not for that a crown,
Golden in show, is but a wreath of thorns,
460 Brings dangers, troubles, cares, and sleepless nights

To him who wears the regal diadem,
When on his shoulders each man's burden lies;
For therein stands the office of a king,
His honour, virtue, merit and chief praise,
465   That for the public all this weight he bears.
Yet he who reigns within himself, and rules
Passions, desires, and fears, is more a king;
Which every wise and virtuous man attains:
And who attains not, ill aspires to rule
470   Cities of men, or headstrong multitudes,
Subject himself to anarchy within,
Or lawless passions in him which he serves.
But to guide nations in the way of truth
By saving doctrine, and from error lead
475   To know, and knowing worship God aright,
Is yet more kingly; this attracts the soul,
Governs the inner man, the nobler part,
That other o'er the body only reigns,
And oft by force, which to a generous mind
480   So reigning can be no sincere delight.
Besides to give a kingdom hath been thought
Greater and nobler done, and to lay down
Far more magnanimous, than to assume.
Riches are needless then, both for themselves,
485   And for thy reason why they should be sought,
To gain a sceptre, oftest better missed.

THE THIRD BOOK

So spake the Son of God, and Satan stood
A while as mute, confounded what to say,
What to reply, confuted and convinced
Of his weak arguing, and fallacious drift;
5   At length collecting all his Serpent wiles,
With soothing words renewed, him thus accosts.
    I see thou know'st what is of use to know,
What best to say canst say, to do canst do;
Thy actions to thy words accord, thy words
10 To thy large heart give utterance due, thy heart
Contains of good, wise, just, the perfect shape.
Should kings and nations from thy mouth consult,
Thy counsel would be as the oracle
Urim and Thummim, those oraculous gems
15 On Aaron's breast: or tongue of seers old
Infallible; or wert thou sought to deeds
That might require th' array of war, thy skill
Of conduct would be such, that all the world
Could not sustain thy prowess, or subsist
20 In battle, though against thy few in arms.
These godlike virtues wherefore dost thou hide?
Affecting private life, or more obscure
In savage wilderness, wherefore deprive
All earth her wonder at thy acts, thyself
25 The fame and glory, glory the reward
That sole excites to high attempts the flame
Of most erected spirits, most tempered pure
Ethereal, who all pleasures else despise,
All treasures and all gain esteem as dross,
30 And dignities and powers, all but the highest?
Thy years are ripe, and over-ripe; the son
Of Macedonian Philip had ere these

Won Asia and the throne of Cyrus held
At his dispose, young Scipio had brought down
35   The Carthaginian pride, young Pompey quelled
The Pontic king and in triúmph had rode.
Yet years, and to ripe years judgement mature,
Quench not the thirst of glory, but augment.
Great Julius, whom now all the world admires
40   The more he grew in years, the more inflamed
With glory, wept that he had lived so long
Inglorious: but thou yet art not too late.
        To whom our Saviour calmly thus replied.
Thou neither dost persuade me to seek wealth
45   For empire's sake, nor empire to affect
For glory's sake by all thy argument.
For what is glory but the blaze of fame,
The people's praise, if always praise unmixed?
And what the people but a herd confused,
50   A miscellaneous rabble, who extol
Things vulgar, and well weighed, scarce worth the praise?
They praise and they admire they know not what;
And know not whom, but as one leads the other;
And what delight to be by such extolled,
55   To live upon their tongues and be their talk,
Of whom to be dispraised were no small praise?
His lot who dares be singularly good.
Th' intelligent among them and the wise
Are few, and glory scarce of few is raised.
60   This is true glory and renown, when God
Looking on the earth, with approbation marks
The just man, and divulges him through Heaven
To all his angels, who with true applause
Recount his praises; thus he did to Job,
65   When to extend his fame through Heaven and earth,
As thou to thy reproach may'st well remember,
He asked thee, hast thou seen my servant Job?
Famous he was in Heaven, on earth less known;
Where glory is false glory, áttribúted
70   To things not glorious, men not worthy of fame.
They err who count it glorious to subdue

By conquest far and wide, to overrun
Large countries, and in field great battles win,
Great cities by assault: what do these worthies,
75 But rob and spoil, burn, slaughter, and enslave
Peaceable nations, neighbouring, or remote,
Made captive, yet deserving freedom more
Than those their conquerors, who leave behind
Nothing but ruin wheresoe'er they rove,
80 And all the flourishing works of peace destroy,
Then swell with pride, and must be titled gods,
Great benefactors of mankind, deliverers,
Worshipped with temple, priest and sacrifice;
One is the son of Jove, of Mars the other,
85 Till conqueror Death discover them scarce men,
Rolling in brutish vices, and deformed,
Violent or shameful death their due reward.
But if there be in glory aught of good,
It may by means far different be attained
90 Without ambition, war, or violence;
By deeds of peace, by wisdom eminent,
By patience, temperance; I mention still
Him whom thy wrongs with saintly patience borne,
Made famous in a land and times obscure;
95 Who names not now with honour patient Job?
Poor Socrates (who next more memorable?)
By what he taught and suffered for so doing,
For truth's sake suffering death unjust, lives now
Equal in fame to proudest conquerors.
100 Yet if for fame and glory aught be done,
Aught suffered; if young African for fame
His wasted country freed from Punic rage,
The deed becomes unpraised, the man at least,
And loses, though but verbal, his reward.
105 Shall I seek glory then, as vain men seek
Oft not deserved? I seek not mine, but his
Who sent me, and thereby witness whence I am.
    To whom the Tempter murmuring thus replied.
Think not so slight of glory; therein least
110 Resembling thy great Father: he seeks glory,

And for his glory all things made, all things
Orders and governs, nor content in Heaven
By all his angels glorified, requires
Glory from men, from all men good or bad,
115 Wise or unwise, no difference, no exemption;
Above all sacrifice, or hallowed gift
Glory he requires, and glory he receives
Promiscuous from all nations, Jew, or Greek,
Or barbarous, nor exception hath declared;
120 From us his foes pronounced glory he exacts.
    To whom our Saviour fervently replied.
And reason; since his word all things produced,
Though chiefly not for glory as prime end,
But to show forth his goodness, and impart
125 His good communicable to every soul
Freely; of whom what could he less expect
Than glory and benediction, that is thanks,
The slightest, easiest, readiest recompense
From them who could return him nothing else,
130 And not returning that would likeliest render
Contempt instead, dishonour, obloquy?
Hard recompense, unsuitable return
For so much good, so much beneficence.
But why should man seek glory? who of his own
135 Hath nothing, and to whom nothing belongs
But condemnation, ignominy, and shame?
Who for so many benefits received
Turned recreant to God, ingrate and false,
And so of all true good himself despoiled,
140 Yet, sacrilegious, to himself would take
That which to God alone of right belongs;
Yet so much bounty is in God, such grace,
That who advance his glory, not their own,
Them he himself to glory will advance.
145   So spake the Son of God; and here again
Satan had not to answer, but stood struck
With guilt of his own sin, for he himself
Insatiable of glory had lost all,
Yet of another plea bethought him soon.

150   Of glory as thou wilt, said he, so deem,
        Worth or not worth the seeking, let it pass:
        But to a kingdom thou art born, ordained
        To sit upon thy father David's throne;
        By mother's side thy father, though thy right
155   Be now in powerful hands, that will not part
        Easily from possession won with arms;
        Judaea now and all the promised land
        Reduced a province under Roman yoke,
        Obeys Tiberius; nor is always ruled
160   With temperate sway; oft have they violated
        The Temple, oft the Law with foul affronts,
        Abominations rather, as did once
        Antiochus: and think'st thou to regain
        Thy right by sitting still or thus retiring?
165   So did not Maccabeus: he indeed
        Retired into the desert, but with arms;
        And o'er a mighty king so oft prevailed,
        That by strong hand his family obtained,
        Though priests, the crown, and David's throne usurped,
170   With Modin and her suburbs once content.
        If kingdom move thee not, let move thee zeal,
        And duty; zeal and duty are not slow;
        But on Occasion's forelock watchful wait.
        They themselves rather are occasion best,
175   Zeal of thy father's house, duty to free
        Thy country from her heathen servitude;
        So shalt thou best fulfil, best verify
        The Prophets old, who sung thy endless reign,
        The happier reign the sooner it begins;
180   Reign then; what canst thou better do the while?
            To whom our Saviour answer thus returned.
        All things are best fulfilled in their due time,
        And time there is for all things, Truth hath said;
        If of my reign prophetic writ hath told,
185   That it shall never end, so when begin
        The Father in his purpose hath decreed,
        He in whose hand all times and seasons roll.
        What if he hath decreed that I shall first

Be tried in humble state, and things adverse,
190 By tribulations, injuries, insults,
Contempts, and scorns, and snares, and violence,
Suffering, abstaining, quietly expecting
Without distrust or doubt, that he may know
What I can suffer, how obey? who best
195 Can suffer, best can do; best reign, who first
Well hath obeyed; just trial ere I merit
My exaltation without change or end.
But what concerns it thee when I begin
My everlasting kingdom, why art thou
200 Solicitous, what moves thy inquisition?
Know'st thou not that my rising is thy fall,
And my promotion will be thy destruction?
     To whom the Tempter inly racked replied.
Let that come when it comes; all hope is lost
205 Of my reception into grace; what worse?
For where no hope is left, is left no fear;
If there be worse, the expectation more
Of worse torments me than the feeling can.
I would be at the worst; worst is my port,
210 My harbour and my ultimate repose,
The end I would attain, my final good.
My error was my error, and my crime
My crime; whatever for itself condemned,
And will alike be punished; whether thou
215 Reign or reign not; though to that gentle brow
Willingly I could fly, and hope thy reign,
From that placíd aspéct and meek regard,
Rather than aggravate my evil state,
Would stand between me and thy Father's ire,
220 (Whose ire I dread more than the fire of Hell)
A shelter and a kind of shading cool
Interposition, as a summer's cloud.
If I then to the worst that can be haste,
Why move thy feet so slow to what is best,
225 Happiest both to thyself and all the world,
That thou who worthiest art shouldst be their king?
Perhaps thou linger'st in deep thoughts detained

Of the enterprise so hazardous and high;
No wonder, for though in thee be únited
230   What of perfection can in man be found,
Or human nature can receive, consider
Thy life hath yet been private, most part spent
At home, scarce viewed the Galilean towns,
And once a year Jerusalem, few days'
235   Short sojourn; and what thence couldst thou observe?
The world thou hast not seen, much less her glory,
Empires, and monarchs, and their radiant courts,
Best school of best experience, quickest in sight
In all things that to greatest actions lead.
240   The wisest, unexperienced, will be ever
Timorous and loath, with novice modesty,
(As he who seeking asses found a kingdom)
Irresolute, unhardy, unadvent'rous:
But I will bring thee where thou soon shalt quit
245   Those rudiments, and see before thine eyes
The monarchies of the earth, their pomp and state,
Sufficient introduction to inform
Thee, of thyself so apt, in regal arts,
And regal mysteries; that thou may'st know
250   How best their opposition to withstand.
      With that (such power was giv'n him then) he took
The Son of God up to a mountain high.
It was a mountain at whose verdant feet
A spacious plain outstretched in circuit wide
255   Lay pleasant; from his side two rivers flowed,
Th' one winding, the other straight, and left between
Fair champaign with less rivers interveined,
Then meeting joined their tribute to the sea:
Fertile of corn the glebe, of oil and wine,
260   With herds the pastures thronged, with flocks the hills;
Huge cities and high-towered, that well might seem
The seats of mightiest monarchs, and so large
The prospect was, that here and there was room
For barren desert fountainless and dry.
265   To this high mountain top the Tempter brought
Our Saviour, and new train of words began.

Well have we speeded, and o'er hill and dale,
Forest and field, and flood, temples and towers
Cut shorter many a league; here thou behold'st
270   Assyria and her empire's ancient bounds,
Araxes and the Caspian lake, thence on
As far as Indus east, Euphrates west,
And oft beyond; to south the Persian bay,
And inaccessible the Arabian drouth:
275   Here Nineveh, of length within her wall
Several days' journey, built by Ninus old,
Of that first golden monarchy the seat,
And seat of Salmanassar, whose success
Israel in long captivity still mourns;
280   There Babylon the wonder of all tongues,
As ancient, but rebuilt by him who twice
Judah and all thy father David's house
Led captive, and Jerusalem laid waste,
Till Cyrus set them free; Persepolis
285   His city there thou seest, and Bactra there;
Ecbatana her structure vast there shows,
And Hecatompylos her hundred gates,
There Susa by Choaspes, amber stream,
The drink of none but kings; of later fame
290   Built by Emathian, or by Parthian hands,
The great Seleucia, Nisibis, and there
Artaxata, Teredon, Ctesiphon,
Turning with easy eye thou may'st behold.
All these the Parthian, now some ages past,
295   By great Arsaccs led, who founded first
That empire, under his dominion holds,
From the luxurious kings of Antioch won.
And just in time thou com'st to have a view
Of his great power; for now the Parthian king
300   In Ctesiphon hath gathered all his host
Against the Scythian, whose incursions wild
Have wasted Sogdiana; to her aid
He marches now in haste; see, though from far,
His thousands, in what martial equipage
305   They issue forth, steel bows, and shafts their arms

Of equal dread in flight, or in pursuit;
All horsemen, in which fight they most excel;
See how in warlike muster they appear,
In rhombs and wedges, and half moons, and wings.
310   He looked and saw what numbers numberless
The city gates outpoured, light-armèd troops
In coats of mail and military pride;
In mail their horses clad, yet fleet and strong,
Prancing their riders bore, the flower and choice
315   Of many provinces from bound to bound;
From Arachosia, from Candaor east,
And Margiana to the Hyrcanian cliffs
Of Caucasus, and dark Iberian dales,
From Atropatia and the neighbouring plains
320   Of Adiabéne, Media, and the south
Of Susiana to Balsara's hav'n.
He saw them in their forms of battle ranged,
How quick they wheeled, and flying behind them shot
Sharp sleet of arrowy showers against the face
325   Of their pursuers, and overcame by flight;
The field all iron cast a gleaming brown,
Nor wanted clouds of foot, nor on each horn,
Cuirassiers all in steel for standing fight;
Chariots or elephants endorsed with towers
330   Of archers, nor of labouring pioneers
A multitude with spades and axes armed
To lay hills plain, fell woods, or valleys fill,
Or where plain was raise hill, or overlay
With bridges rivers proud, as with a yoke;
335   Mules after these, camels and dromedaries,
And waggons fraught with útensils of war.
Such forces met not, nor so wide a camp,
When Agrican with all his northern powers
Besieged Albracca, as romances tell;
340   The city of Gallaphrone, from thence to win
The fairest of her sex Angelica
His daughter, sought by many prowest knights,
Both paynim, and the peers of Charlemagne.
Such and so numerous was their chivalry;

345 At sight whereof the Fiend yet more presumed,
And to our Saviour thus his words renewed.
     That thou may'st know I seek not to engage
Thy virtue, and not every way secure
On no slight grounds thy safety; hear, and mark
350 To what end I have brought thee hither and shown
All this fair sight; thy kingdom though foretold
By Prophet or by angel, unless thou
Endeavour, as thy father David did,
Thou never shalt obtain; prediction still
355 In all things, and all men, supposes means;
Without means used, what it predicts revokes.
But say thou wert possessed of David's throne
By free consent of all, none opposite,
Samaritan or Jew; how couldst thou hope
360 Long to enjoy it quiet and secure,
Between two such enclosing enemies
Roman and Parthian? therefore one of these
Thou must make sure thy own; the Parthian first
By my advice, as nearer and of late
365 Found able by invasion to annoy
Thy country, and captive lead away her kings
Antigonus, and old Hyrcanus bound,
Maugre the Roman: it shall be my task
To render thee the Parthian at dispose;
370 Choose which thou wilt by conquest or by league.
By him thou shalt regain, without him not,
That which alone can truly reinstall thee
To David's royal seat, his true successor,
Deliverance of thy brethren, those ten tribes
375 Whose offspring in his territory yet serve
In Habor, and among the Medes dispersed;
Ten sons of Jacob, two of Joseph lost
Thus long from Israel; serving as of old
Their fathers in the land of Egypt served,
380 This offer sets before thee to deliver.
These if from servitude thou shalt restore
To their inheritance, then, nor till then,
Thou on the throne of David in full glory,

From Egypt to Euphrates and beyond
385   Shalt reign, and Rome or Caesar not need fear.
To whom our Saviour answered thus unmoved.
Much ostentation vain of fleshly arm,
And fragile arms, much instrument of war
Long in preparing, soon to nothing brought,
390   Before mine eyes thou hast set; and in my ear
Vented much policy, and projects deep
Of enemies, of aids, battles and leagues,
Plausible to the world, to me worth naught.
Means I must use thou say'st, prediction else
395   Will unpredict and fail me of the throne:
My time I told thee, (and that time for thee
Were better farthest off) is not yet come;
When that comes think not thou to find me slack
On my part aught endeavouring, or to need
400   Thy politic maxims, or that cumbersome
Luggage of war there shown me, argument
Of human weakness rather than of strength.
My brethren, as thou call'st them, those ten tribes,
I must deliver, if I mean to reign
405   David's true heir, and his full sceptre sway
To just extent over all Israel's sons;
But whence to thee this zeal, where was it then
For Israel, or for David, or his throne,
When thou stood'st up his tempter to the pride
410   Of numb'ring Israel, which cost the lives
Of three score and ten thousand Israelites
By three days' pestilence? such was thy zeal
To Israel then, the same that now to me.
As for those captive tribes, themselves were they
415   Who wrought their own captivity, fell off
From God to worship calves, the deities
Of Egypt, Baal next and Ashtaroth,
And all the idolatries of heathen round,
Besides their other worse than heathenish crimes;
420   Nor in the land of their captivity
Humbled themselves, or penitent besought
The God of their forefathers; but so died

Impenitent, and left a race behind
Like to themselves, distinguishable scarce
425   From Gentiles, but by circumcision vain,
And God with idols in their worship joined.
Should I of these the liberty regard,
Who freed, as to their ancient patrimony,
Unhumbled, unrepentant, unreformed,
430   Headlong would follow, and to their gods perhaps
Of Bethel and of Dan? no, let them serve
Their enemies, who serve idols with God.
Yet he at length, time to himself best known,
Rememb'ring Abraham by some wondrous call
435   May bring them back repentant and sincere,
And at their passing cleave the Assyrian flood,
While to their native land with joy they haste,
As the Red Sea and Jordan once he cleft,
When to the promised land their fathers passed;
440   To his due time and providence I leave them.
       So spake Israel's true King, and to the Fiend
Made answer meet, that made void all his wiles.
So fares it when with truth falsehood contends.

Perplexed and troubled at his bad success
The Tempter stood, nor had what to reply,
Discovered in his fraud, thrown from his hope,
So oft, and the persuasive rhetoric
5   That sleeked his tongue, and won so much on Eve,
So little here, nay lost; but Eve was Eve,
This far his over-match, who self-deceived
And rash, beforehand had no better weighed
The strength he was to cope with, or his own:
10 But as a man who had been matchless held
In cunning, overreached where least he thought,
To salve his credit, and for very spite
Still will be tempting him who foils him still,
And never cease, though to his shame the more;
15 Or as a swarm of flies in vintage-time,
About the wine-press where sweet must is poured,
Beat off, returns as oft with humming sound;
Or surging waves against a solid rock,
Though all to shivers dashed, the assault renew,
20 Vain battery, and in froth or bubbles end;
So Satan, whom repulse upon repulse
Met ever; and to shameful silence brought,
Yet gives not o'er though desperate of success,
And his vain importunity pursues.
25 He brought our Saviour to the western side
Of that high mountain, whence he might behold
Another plain, long but in breadth not wide;
Washed by the southern sea, and on the north
To equal length backed with a ridge of hills
30 That screened the fruits of the earth and seats of men
From cold Septentrion blasts; thence in the midst
Divided by a river, of whose banks

On each side an imperial city stood,
With towers and temples proudly elevate
35 On seven small hills, with palaces adorned,
Porches and theatres, baths, aqueducts,
Statues and trophies, and triumphal arcs,
Gardens and groves presented to his eyes,
Above the heighth of mountains interposed.
40 By what strange parallax or optic skill
Of vision multiplied through air, or glass
Of telescope, were curious to inquire:
And now the Tempter thus his silence broke.
    The city which thou seest no other deem
45 Than great and glorious Rome, queen of the earth
So far renowned, and with the spoils enriched
Of nations; there the Capitol thou seest
Above the rest lifting his stately head
On the Tarpeian rock, her citadel
50 Impregnable, and there Mount Palatine
The imperial palace, compass huge, and high
The structure, skill of noblest architects,
With gilded battlements, conspicuous far,
Turrets and terraces, and glittering spires.
55 Many a fair edifice besides, more like
Houses of gods (so well I have disposed
My airy microscope) thou may'st behold
Outside and inside both, pillars and roofs
Carved work, the hand of famed artificers
60 In cedar, marble, ivory or gold.
Thence to the gates cast round thine eye, and see
What conflux issuing forth, or ent'ring in,
Praetors, proconsuls to their provinces
Hasting or on return, in robes of state;
65 Lictors and rods the ensigns of their power;
Legions and cohorts, turms of horse and wings:
Or embassies from regions far remote
In various habits on the Appian road,
Or on the Aemilian, some from furthest south,
70 Syene, and where the shadow both way falls,
Meroë Nilotic isle, and more to west,

The realm of Bocchus to the Blackmoor sea;
From the Asian kings and Parthian among these,
From India and the golden Chersoness,
75   And utmost Indian isle Tapróbanè,
Dusk faces with white silken turbans wreathed:
From Gallia, Gades, and the British west,
Germans and Scythians, and Sarmatians north
Beyond Danubius to the Tauric pool.
80   All nations now to Rome obedience pay,
To Rome's great Emperor, whose wide domain
In ample territory, wealth and power,
Civility of manners, arts, and arms,
And long renown thou justly may'st prefer
85   Before the Parthian; these two thrones except,
The rest are barbarous, and scarce worth the sight,
Shared among petty kings too far removed;
These having shown thee, I have shown thee all
The kingdoms of the world, and all their glory.
90   This Emperor hath no son, and now is old,
Old, and lascivious, and from Rome retired
To Capreae an island small but strong
On the Campanian shore, with purpose there
His horrid lusts in private to enjoy,
95   Committing to a wicked favourite
All public cares, and yet of him suspicious,
Hated of all, and hating; with what ease,
Endued with regal virtues as thou art,
Appearing, and beginning noble deeds,
100   Might'st thou expel this monster from his throne
Now made a sty, and in his place ascending,
A victor-people free from servile yoke!
And with my help thou may'st; to me the power
Is given, and by that right I give it thee.
105   Aim therefore at no less than all the world,
Aim at the highest, without the highest attained
Will be for thee no sitting, or not long
On David's throne, be prophesied what will.
      To whom the Son of God unmoved replied.
110   Nor doth this grandeur and majestic show

Of luxury, though called magnificence,
More than of arms before, allure mine eye,
Much less my mind; though thou shouldst add to tell
Their sumptuous gluttonies, and gorgeous feasts
115 On citron tables or Atlantic stone;
(For I have also heard, perhaps have read)
Their wines of Setia, Cales, and Falerne,
Chios and Crete, and how they quaff in gold,
Crystal and myrrhine cups embossed with gems
120 And studs of pearl, to me shouldst tell who thirst
And hunger still: then embassies thou show'st
From nations far and nigh; what honour that,
But tedious waste of time to sit and hear
So many hollow compliments and lies,
125 Outlandish flatteries? then proceed'st to talk
Of the emperor, how easily subdued,
How gloriously; I shall, thou say'st, expel
A brutish monster: what if I withal
Expel a devil who first made him such?
130 Let his tormentor Conscience find him out;
For him I was not sent, nor yet to free
That people victor once, now vile and base,
Deservedly made vassal, who once just,
Frugal, and mild, and temperate, conquered well,
135 But govern ill the nations under yoke,
Peeling their provinces, exhausted all
By lust and rapine; first ambitious grown
Of triumph, that insulting vanity;
Then cruel, by the sports to blood inured
140 Of fighting beasts, and men to beasts exposed;
Luxurious by their wealth, and greedier still,
And from the daily scene effeminate.
What wise and valiant man would seek to free
These thus degenerate, by themselves enslaved,
145 Or could of inward slaves make outward free?
Know therefore when my season comes to sit
On David's throne, it shall be like a tree
Spreading and overshadowing all the earth,
Or as a stone that shall to pieces dash

150   All monarchies besides throughout the world,
       And of my kingdom there shall be no end:
       Means there shall be to this, but what the means,
       Is not for thee to know, nor me to tell.
          To whom the Tempter impudent replied.
155   I see all offers made by me how slight
       Thou valu'st, because offered, and reject'st:
       Nothing will please the difficult and nice,
       Or nothing more than still to contradict:
       On the other side know also thou, that I
160   On what I offer set as high esteem,
       Nor what I part with mean to give for naught;
       All these which in a moment thou behold'st,
       The kingdoms of the world to thee I give;
       For giv'n to me, I give to whom I please,
165   No trifle; yet with this reserve, not else,
       On this condition, if thou wilt fall down,
       And worship me as thy superior lord,
       Easily done, and hold them all of me;
       For what can else so great a gift deserve?
170   Whom thus our Saviour answered with disdain.
       I never liked thy talk, thy offers less,
       Now both abhor, since thou hast dared to utter
       The abominable terms, impious condition;
       But I endure the time, till which expired,
175   Thou hast permission on me. It is written
       The first of all commandments, Thou shalt worship
       The Lord thy God, and only him shalt serve;
       And dar'st thou to the Son of God propound
       To worship thee accurst, now more accurst
180   For this attempt bolder than that on Eve,
       And more blasphémous? which expect to rue.
       The kingdoms of the world to thee were giv'n,
       Permitted rather, and by thee usurped;
       Other donation none thou canst produce:
185   If given, by whom but by the King of kings,
       God over all supreme? If given to thee,
       By thee how fairly is the Giver now
       Repaid? But gratitude to thee is lost

Long since. Wert thou so void of fear or shame,
190 As offer them to me the Son of God,
To me my own, on such abhorrèd pact,
That I fall down and worship thee as God?
Get thee behind me; plain thou now appear'st
That Evil One, Satan for ever damned.

195   To whom the Fiend with fear abashed replied.
Be not so sore offended, Son of God;
Though Sons of God both angels are and men,
If I to try whether in higher sort
Than these thou bear'st that title, have proposed
200 What both from men and angels I receive,
Tetrarchs of fire, air, flood, and on the earth
Nations besides from all the quartered winds,
God of this world invoked and world beneath;
Who then thou art, whose coming is foretold
205 To me is fatal, me it most concerns.
The trial hath endamaged thee no way,
Rather more honour left and more esteem;
Me naught advantaged, missing what I aimed.
Therefore let pass, as they are transitory,
210 The kingdoms of this world; I shall no more
Advise thee; gain them as thou canst, or not.
And thou thyself seem'st otherwise inclined
Than to a worldly crown, addicted more
To contemplation and profound dispute,
215 As by that early action may be judged,
When slipping from thy mother's eye thou went'st
Alone into the Temple; there wast found
Among the gravest Rabbis disputant
On points and questions fitting Moses' chair,
220 Teaching not taught; the childhood shows the man,
As morning shows the day. Be famous then
By wisdom; as thy empire must extend,
So let thy mind o'er all the world,
In knowledge, all things in it comprehend;
225 All knowledge is not couched in Moses' law,
The Pentateuch or what the Prophets wrote;
The Gentiles also know, and write, and teach

To admiration, led by Nature's light;
And with the Gentiles much thou must converse,
230   Ruling them by persuasion as thou mean'st;
Without their learning how wilt thou with them,
Or they with thee hold conversation meet?
How wilt thou reason with them, how refute
Their idolisms, traditions, paradoxes?
235   Error by his own arms is best evinced.
Look once more ere we leave this specular mount
Westward, much nearer by southwest, behold
Where on the Áegean shore a city stands
Built nobly, pure the air, and light the soil,
240   Athens the eye of Greece, mother of arts
And eloquence, native to famous wits
Or hospitable, in her sweet recess,
City or suburban, studious walks and shades;
See there the olive grove of Academe,
245   Plato's retirement, where the Attic bird
Trills her thick-warbled notes the summer long;
There flow'ry hill Hymettus with the sound
Of bees' industrious murmur oft invites
To studious musing; there Ilissus rolls
250   His whispering stream; within the walls then view
The schools of ancient sages; his who bred
Great Alexander to subdue the world,
Lyceum there, and painted Stoa next:
There thou shalt hear and learn the secret power
255   Of harmony in tones and numbers hit
By voice or hand, and various-measured verse,
Aeolian charms and Dorian lyric odes,
And his who gave them breath, but higher sung,
Blind Melesigenes thence Homer called,
260   Whose poem Phoebus challenged for his own.
Thence what the lofty grave tragedians taught
In chorus or iambic, teachers best
Of moral prudence, with delight received
In brief sententious precepts, while they treat
265   Of fate, and chance, and change in human life;
High actions, and high passions best describing:

Thence to the famous orators repair,
Those ancient, whose resistless eloquence
Wielded at will that fierce democracy,
270   Shook the Arsenal and fulmined over Greece,
To Macedon, and Artaxerxes' throne;
To sage philosophy next lend thine ear,
From heaven descended to the low-roofed house
Of Socrates, see there his tenement,
275   Whom well-inspired the oracle pronounced
Wisest of men; from whose mouth issued forth
Mellifluous streams that watered all the schools
Of Academics old and new, with those
Surnamed Peripatetics, and the sect
280   Epicurean, and the Stoic severe;
These here revolve, or, as thou lik'st, at home,
Till time mature thee to a kingdom's weight;
These rules will render thee a king complete
Within thyself, much more with empire joined.
285   To whom our Saviour sagely thus replied.
Think not but that I know these things, or think
I know them not; not therefore am I short
Of knowing what I ought: he who receives
Light from above, from the fountain of light,
290   No other doctrine needs, though granted true;
But these are false, or little else but dreams,
Conjectures, fancies, built on nothing firm.
The first and wisest of them all professed
To know this only, that he nothing knew;
295   The next to fabling fell and smooth conceits,
A third sort doubted all things, though plain sense;
Others in virtue placed felicity,
But virtue joined with riches and long life;
In corporal pleasure he, and careless ease;
300   The Stoic last in philosophic pride,
By him called virtue; and his virtuous man,
Wise, perfect in himself, and all possessing
Equal to God, oft shames not to prefer,
As fearing God nor man, contemning all
305   Wealth, pleasure, pain or torment, death and life,

Which when he lists, he leaves, or boasts he can,
For all his tedious talk is but vain boast,
Or subtle shifts conviction to evade.
Alas what can they teach, and not mislead;
310 Ignorant of themselves, of God much more,
And how the world began, and how man fell
Degraded by himself, on grace depending?
Much of the soul they talk, but all awry,
And in themselves seek virtue, and to themselves
315 All glory arrogate, to God give none;
Rather accuse him under usual names,
Fortune and Fate, as one regardless quite
Of mortal things. Who therefore seeks in these
True wisdom, finds her not, or by delusion
320 Far worse, her false resemblance only meets,
An empty cloud. However, many books,
Wise men have said, are wearisome; who reads
Incessantly, and to his reading brings not
A spirit and judgement equal or superior,
325 (And what he brings, what needs he elsewhere seek)
Uncertain and unsettled still remains,
Deep versed in books and shallow in himself,
Crude or intoxicate, collecting toys,
And trifles for choice matters, worth a sponge;
330 As children gathering pebbles on the shore.
Or if I would delight my private hours
With music or with poem, where so soon
As in our native language can I find
That solace? All our Law and story strewed
335 With hymns, our Psalms with artful terms inscribed,
Our Hebrew songs and harps in Babylon,
That pleased so well our victors' ear, declare
That rather Greece from us these arts derived;
Ill imitated, while they loudest sing
340 The vices of their deities, and their own
In fable, hymn, or song, so personating
Their gods ridiculous, and themselves past shame.
Remove their swelling epithets, thick-laid
As varnish on a harlot's cheek, the rest,

345   Thin-sown with aught of profit or delight,
Will far be found unworthy to compare
With Sion's songs, to all true tastes excelling,
Where God is praised aright, and Godlike men,
The Holiest of Holies, and his saints;
350   Such are from God inspired, not such from thee;
Unless where moral virtue is expressed
By light of Nature not in all quite lost.
Their orators thou then extoll'st, as those
The top of eloquence, statists indeed,
355   And lovers of their country, as may seem;
But herein to our Prophets far beneath,
As men divinely taught, and better teaching
The solid rules of civil government
In their majestic unaffected style
360   Than all the oratory of Greece and Rome.
In them is plainest taught, and easiest learnt,
What makes a nation happy, and keeps it so,
What ruins kingdoms, and lays cities flat;
These only with our Law best form a king.

365   So spake the Son of God; but Satan now
Quite at a loss, for all his darts were spent,
Thus to our Saviour with stern brow replied.

   Since neither wealth, nor honour, arms nor arts,
Kingdom nor empire pleases thee, nor aught
370   By me proposed in life contemplative,
Or active, tended on by glory, or fame,
What dost thou in this world? The wilderness
For thee is fittest place; I found thee there,
And thither will return thee; yet remember
375   What I foretell thee; soon thou shalt have cause
To wish thou never hadst rejected thus
Nicely or cautiously my offered aid,
Which would have set thee in short time with ease
On David's throne; or throne of all the world,
380   Now at full age, fulness of time, thy season,
When prophecies of thee are best fulfilled.
Now contrary, if I read aught in heaven,
Or heaven write aught of Fate, by what the stars

Voluminous, or single characters,
385 In their conjunction met, give me to spell,
Sorrows, and labours, opposition, hate,
Attends thee, scorns, reproaches, injuries,
Violence and stripes, and lastly cruel death;
A kingdom they portend thee, but what kingdom,
390 Real or allegoric I discern not,
Nor when; eternal sure, as without end,
Without beginning; for no date prefixed
Directs me in the starry rubric set.
     So saying he took (for still he knew his power
395 Not yet expired) and to the wilderness
Brought back the Son of God, and left him there,
Feigning to disappear. Darkness now rose,
As daylight sunk, and brought in louring night,
Her shadowy offspring, unsubstantial both,
400 Privation mere of light and absent day.
Our Saviour meek and with untroubled mind
After his airy jaunt, though hurried sore,
Hungry and cold betook him to his rest,
Wherever, under some concóurse of shades
405 Whose branching arms thick intertwined might shield
From dews and damps of night his sheltered head,
But sheltered slept in vain, for at his head
The Tempter watched, and soon with ugly dreams
Disturbed his sleep; and either tropic now
410 Gan thunder, and both ends of heav'n; the clouds
From many a horrid rift abortive poured
Fierce rain with lightning mixed, water with fire
In ruin reconciled: nor slept the winds
Within their stony caves, but rushed abroad
415 From the four hinges of the world, and fell
On the vexed wilderness, whose tallest pines,
Though rooted deep as high, and sturdiest oaks
Bowed their stiff necks, loaden with stormy blasts,
Or torn up sheer: ill wast thou shrouded then,
420 O patient Son of God, yet only stood'st
Unshaken; not yet stayed the terror there;
Infernal ghosts, and Hellish Furies, round

Environed thee; some howled, some yelled, some shrieked,
Some bent at thee their fiery darts, while thou
425   Sat'st unappalled in calm and sinless peace.
Thus passed the night so foul till morning fair
Came forth with pilgrim steps in amice grey;
Who with her radiant finger stilled the roar
Of thunder, chased the clouds, and laid the winds,
430   And grisly spectres, which the Fiend had raised
To tempt the Son of God with terrors dire.
And now the sun with more effectual beams
Had cheered the face of earth, and dried the wet
From drooping plant, or dropping tree; the birds
435   Who all things now behold more fresh and green,
After a night of storm so ruinous,
Cleared up their choicest notes in bush and spray
To gratulate the sweet return of morn;
Nor yet amidst this joy and brightest morn
440   Was absent, after all his mischief done,
The Prince of Darkness; glad would also seem
Of this fair change, and to our Saviour came,
Yet with no new device, they were all spent;
Rather by this his last affront resolved,
445   Desperate of better course, to vent his rage
And mad despite to be so oft repelled.
Him walking on a sunny hill he found,
Backed on the north and west by a thick wood;
Out of the wood he starts in wonted shape;
450   And in a careless mood thus to him said.
    Fair morning yet betides thee Son of God,
After a dismal night; I heard the rack
As earth and sky would mingle; but myself
Was distant; and these flaws, though mortals fear them
455   As dangerous to the pillared frame of heaven,
Or to the earth's dark basis underneath,
Are to the main as inconsiderable,
And harmless, if not wholesome, as a sneeze
To man's less universe, and soon are gone;
460   Yet as being ofttimes noxious where they light
On man, beast, plant, wasteful and turbulent,

Like turbulencies in the affairs of men,
Over whose heads they roar, and seem to point,
They oft fore-signify and threaten ill:
465   This tempest at this desert most was bent;
Of men at thee, for only thou here dwell'st.
Did I not tell thee, if thou didst reject
The perfect season offered with my aid
To win thy destined seat, but wilt prolong
470   All to the push of Fate, pursue thy way
Of gaining David's throne no man knows when,
For both the when and how is nowhere told,
Thou shalt be what thou art ordained, no doubt;
For angels have proclaimed it, but concealing
475   The time and means: each act is rightliest done,
Not when it must, but when it may be best.
If thou observe not this, be sure to find,
What I foretold thee, many a hard assay
Of dangers, and adversities and pains,
480   Ere thou of Israel's sceptre get fast hold;
Whereof this ominous night that closed thee round,
So many terrors, voices, prodigies
May warn thee, as a sure foregoing sign.
    So talked he, while the Son of God went on
485   And stayed not, but in brief him answered thus.
    Me worse than wet thou find'st not; other harm
Those terrors which thou speak'st of, did me none;
I never feared they could, though noising loud
And threatening nigh; what they can do as signs
490   Betok'ning, or ill boding, I contemn
As false portents, not sent from God, but thee;
Who knowing I shall reign past thy preventing,
Obtrud'st thy offered aid, that I accepting
At least might seem to hold all power of thee,
495   Ambitious Spirit, and wouldst be thought my God,
And storm'st refused, thinking to terrify
Me to thy will; desist, thou art discerned
And toil'st in vain, nor me in vain molest.
    To whom the Fiend now swoll'n with rage replied:
500   Then hear, O Son of David, virgin-born,

For Son of God to me is yet in doubt;
Of the Messiah I have heard foretold
By all the Prophets; of thy birth at length
Announced by Gabriel with the first I knew,
505 And of the angelic song in Bethlehem field,
On thy birth-night, that sung thee Saviour born.
From that time seldom have I ceased to eye
Thy infancy, thy childhood, and thy youth,
Thy manhood last, though yet in private bred;
510 Till at the ford of Jordan whither all
Flocked to the Baptist, I among the rest,
Though not to be baptized, by voice from Heav'n
Heard thee pronounced the Son of God beloved.
Thenceforth I thought thee worth my nearer view
515 And narrower scrutiny, that I might learn
In what degree or meaning thou art called
The Son of God, which bears no single sense;
The Son of God I also am, or was,
And if I was, I am; relation stands;
520 All men are Sons of God; yet thee I thought
In some respect far higher so declared.
Therefore I watched thy footsteps from that hour,
And followed thee still on to this waste wild;
Where by all best conjectures I collect
525 Thou art to be my fatal enemy.
Good reason then, if I beforehand seek
To understand my adversary, who
And what he is; his wisdom, power, intent,
By parle, or composition, truce, or league
530 To win him, or win from him what I can.
And opportunity I here have had
To try thee, sift thee, and confess have found thee
Proof against all temptation as a rock
Of adamant, and as a centre, firm
535 To the utmost of mere man both wise and good,
Not more; for honours, riches, kingdoms, glory
Have been before contemned, and may again:
Therefore to know what more thou art than man,
Worth naming Son of God by voice from Heav'n,

540 Another method I must now begin.
　　　So saying he caught him up, and without wing
Of hippogriff bore through the air sublime
Over the wilderness and o'er the plain;
Till underneath them fair Jerusalem,
545 The holy city lifted high her towers,
And higher yet the glorious Temple reared
Her pile, far off appearing like a mount
Of alabaster, topped with golden spires:
There on the highest pinnacle he set
550 The Son of God; and added thus in scorn:
　　　There stand, if thou wilt stand; to stand upright
Will ask thee skill; I to thy Father's house
Have brought thee, and highest placed; highest is best;
Now show thy progeny; if not to stand,
555 Cast thyself down; safely if Son of God:
For it is written, He will give command
Concerning thee to his angels, in their hands
They shall uplift thee, lest at any time
Thou chance to dash thy foot against a stone.
560 　　　To whom thus Jesus: Also it is written,
Tempt not the Lord thy God, he said and stood.
But Satan smitten with amazement fell
As when Earth's son Antaeus (to compare
Small things with greatest) in Irassa strove
565 With Jove's Alcides and oft foiled still rose,
Receiving from his mother Earth new strength,
Fresh from his fall, and fiercer grapple joined,
Throttled at length in the air, expired and fell;
So after many a foil the Tempter proud,
570 Renewing fresh assaults, amidst his pride
Fell whence he stood to see his victor fall.
And as that Theban monster that proposed
Her riddle, and him, who solved it not, devoured;
That once found out and solved, for grief and spite
575 Cast herself headlong from th' Ismenian steep,
So struck with dread and anguish fell the Fiend,
And to his crew, that sat consulting, brought
Joyless triumphals of his hoped success,

Ruin, and desperation, and dismay,
580   Who durst so proudly tempt the Son of God.
So Satan fell and straight a fiery globe
Of angels on full sail of wing flew nigh,
Who on their plumy vans received him soft
From his uneasy station, and upbore
585   As on a floating couch through the blithe air,
Then in a flow'ry valley set him down
On a green bank, and set before him spread
A table of celestial food, divine,
Ambrosial, fruits fetched from the Tree of Life,
590   And from the Fount of Life ambrosial drink,
That soon refreshed him wearied, and repaired
What hunger, if aught hunger had impaired,
Or thirst; and as he fed, angelic choirs
Sung Heavenly anthems of his victory
595   Over temptation, and the Tempter proud.
      True image of the Father whether throned
In the bosom of bliss, and light of light
Conceiving, or remote from Heaven, enshrined
In fleshly tabernacle, and human form,
600   Wand'ring the wilderness, whatever place,
Habit, or state, or motion, still expressing
The Son of God, with Godlike force endued
Against the attempter of thy Father's throne,
And thief of Paradise; him long of old
605   Thou didst debel, and down from Heav'n cast
With all his army; now thou hast avenged
Supplanted Adam, and by vanquishing
Temptation, hast regained lost Paradise,
And frústrated the conquest fraudulent:
610   He never more henceforth will dare set foot
In Paradise to tempt; his snares are broke:
For though that seat of earthly bliss be failed,
A fairer Paradise is founded now
For Adam and his chosen sons, whom thou
615   A Saviour art come down to re-install.
Where they shall dwell secure, when time shall be
Of Tempter and temptation without fear.

But thou, Infernal Serpent, shalt not long
Rule in the clouds; like an autumnal star
620   Or lightning thou shalt fall from heav'n trod down
Under his feet: for proof, ere this thou feel'st
Thy wound, yet not thy last and deadliest wound
By this repulse received, and hold'st in Hell
No triumph; in all her gates Abaddon rues
625   Thy bold attempt; hereafter learn with awe
To dread the Son of God: he all unarmed
Shall chase thee with the terror of his voice
From thy demoniac holds, possession foul,
Thee and thy legions; yelling they shall fly,
630   And beg to hide them in a herd of swine,
Lest he command them down into the deep
Bound, and to torment sent before their time.
Hail Son of the Most High, heir of both worlds,
Queller of Satan, on thy glorious work
635   Now enter, and begin to save mankind.
      Thus they the Son of God our Saviour meek
Sung victor, and from Heavenly feast refreshed
Brought on his way with joy; he unobserved
Home to his mother's house private returned.

SAMSON AGONISTES

OF THAT SORT OF DRAMATIC POEM WHICH IS CALLED TRAGEDY

Tragedy, as it was anciently composed, hath been ever held the gravest, moralest, and most profitable of all other poems: therefore said by Aristotle to be of power by raising pity and fear, or terror, to purge the mind of those and such like

5   passions, that is to temper and reduce them to just measure with a kind of delight, stirred up by reading or seeing those passions well-imitated. Nor is nature wanting in her own effects to make good his assertion: for so in physic things of melancholic hue and quality are used against melancholy, sour

10 against sour, salt to remove salt humours. Hence philosophers and other gravest writers, as Cicero, Plutarch, and others, frequently cite out of tragic poets, both to adorn and illustrate their discourse. The Apostle Paul himself thought it not unworthy to insert a verse of Euripides into the text of Holy

15 Scripture, I Cor. 15. 33, and Paraeus commenting on the *Revelation*, divides the whole book as a tragedy, into acts, distinguished each by a chorus of Heavenly harpings and song between. Heretofore men in highest dignity have laboured not a little to be thought able to compose a tragedy. Of that

20 honour Dionysius the elder was no less ambitious, than before of his attaining to the tyranny. Augustus Caesar also had begun his *Ajax*, but unable to please his own judgement with what he had begun, left it unfinished. Seneca the philosopher is by some thought the author of those tragedies (at least the

25 best of them) that go under that name. Gregory Nazianzen, a Father of the Church, thought it not unbeseeming the sanctity of his person to write a tragedy, which he entitled *Christ Suffering*. This is mentioned to vindicate tragedy from the small esteem, or rather infamy, which in the account of

30 many it undergoes at this day with other common interludes; happening through the poet's error of intermixing comic stuff

with tragic sadness and gravity; or introducing trivial and vulgar persons, which by all judicious hath been counted absurd; and brought in without discretion, corruptly to gratify
35   the people. And though ancient tragedy use no prologue, yet using sometimes, in case of self-defence, or explanation, that which Martial calls an epistle; in behalf of this tragedy, coming forth after the ancient manner, much different from what among us passes for best, thus much beforehand may be
40   epistled: that chorus is here introduced after the Greek manner, not ancient only but modern, and still in use among the Italians. In the modelling therefore of this poem, with good reason, the ancients and Italians are rather followed, as of much more authority and fame. The measure of verse used
45   in the chorus is of all sorts, called by the Greeks *monostrophic*, or rather *apolelymenon*, without regard had to *strophe, antistrophe*, or *epode*, which were a kind of stanzas framed only for the music, then used with the chorus that sung; not essential to the poem, and therefore not material; or being
50   divided into stanzas or pauses, they may be called *alloeostropha*. Division into act and scene referring chiefly to the stage (to which this work was never intended) is here omitted.

It suffices if the whole drama be found not produced beyond the fifth act. Of the style and uniformity, and that commonly
55   called the plot, whether intricate or explicit, which is nothing indeed but such economy, or disposition of the fable as may stand best with verisimilitude and decorum; they only will best judge who are not unacquainted with Aeschylus, Sophocles, and Euripides, the three tragic poets unequalled
60   yet by any, and the best rule to all who endeavour to write tragedy. The circumscription of time wherein the whole drama begins and ends, is according to ancient rule, and best example, within the space of twenty-four hours.

The Argument

Samson made captive, blind, and now in the prison at Gaza, there to labour as in a common workhouse, on a festival day, in the general cessation from labour, comes forth into the open air, to a place nigh, somewhat retired there to sit a while and bemoan his condition. Where he happens at length to be visited by certain friends and equals of his tribe, which make the chorus, who seek to comfort him what they can; then by his old father Manoa, who endeavours the like, and withal tells him his purpose to procure his liberty by ransom; lastly, that this feast was proclaimed by the Philistines as a day of thanksgiving for their deliverance from the hands of Samson, which yet more troubles him. Manoa then departs to prosecute his endeavour with the Philistian lords for Samson's redemption; who in the meanwhile is visited by other persons; and lastly by a public officer to require his coming to the feast before the lords and people, to play or show his strength in their presence; he at first refuses, dismissing the public officer with absolute denial to come; at length persuaded inwardly that this was from God, he yields to go along with him, who came now the second time with great threatenings to fetch him; the chorus yet remaining in the place, Manoa returns full of joyful hope, to procure ere long his son's deliverance: in the midst of which discourse an Hebrew comes in haste confusedly at first; and afterward more distinctly relating the catastrophe, what Samson had done to the Philistines, and by accident to himself; wherewith the tragedy ends.

The Persons

Samson
Manoa, the father of Samson
Dalila his wife
Harapha of Gath
Public Officer
Messenger
Chorus of Danites

The Scene before the Prison in Gaza

Samson. A little onward lend thy guiding hand
To these dark steps, a little further on;
For yonder bank hath choice of sun or shade;
There I am wont to sit, when any chance
5   Relieves me from my task of servile toil,
Daily in the common prison else enjoined me,
Where I a prisoner chained, scarce freely draw
The air imprisoned also, close and damp,
Unwholesome draught: but here I feel amends,
10   The breath of heav'n fresh-blowing pure and sweet,
With day-spring born; here leave me to respire.
This day a solemn feast the people hold
To Dagon their sea-idol, and forbid
Laborious works; unwillingly this rest
15   Their superstition yields me; hence with leave
Retiring from the popular noise, I seek
This unfrequented place to find some ease;
Ease to the body some, none to the mind
From restless thoughts, that like a deadly swarm
20   Of hornets armed, no sooner found alone,
But rush upon me thronging, and present
Times past, what once I was, and what am now.
O wherefore was my birth from Heaven foretold
Twice by an angel, who at last in sight
25   Of both my parents all in flames ascended
From off the altar, where an off'ring burned,
As in a fiery column charioting
His godlike presence, and from some great act
Or benefit revealed to Abraham's race?
30   Why was my breeding ordered and prescribed
As of a person separate to God,
Designed for great explóits; if I must die
Betrayed, captíved, and both my eyes put out,
Made of my enemies the scorn and gaze;
35   To grind in brazen fetters under task
With this Heav'n-gifted strength? O glorious strength
Put to the labour of a beast, debased

Lower than bondslave! Promise was that I
Should Israel from Philistian yoke deliver;
40   Ask for this great deliverer now, and find him
Eyeless in Gaza at the mill with slaves,
Himself in bonds under Philistian yoke;
Yet stay, let me not rashly call in doubt
Divine prediction; what if all foretold
45   Had been fulfilled but through mine own default,
Whom have I to complain of but myself?
Who this high gift of strength committed to me,
In what part lodged, how easily bereft me,
Under the seal of silence could not keep,
50   But weakly to a woman must reveal it,
O'ercome with importunity and tears.
O impotence of mind, in body strong!
But what is strength without a double share
Of wisdom? Vast, unwieldy, burdensome,
55   Proudly secure, yet liable to fall
By weakest subtleties; not made to rule,
But to subserve where wisdom bears command.
God, when he gave me strength, to show withal
How slight the gift was, hung it in my hair.
60   But peace, I must not quarrel with the will
Of highest dispensation, which herein
Haply had ends above my reach to know:
Suffices that to me strength is my bane,
And proves the source of all my miseries;
65   So many, and so huge, that each apart
Would ask a life to wail, but chief of all,
O loss of sight, of thee I most complain!
Blind among enemies, O worse than chains,
Dungeon, or beggary, or decrepit age!
70   Light the prime work of God to me is extinct,
And all her various objects of delight
Annulled, which might in part my grief have eased;
Inferior to the vilest now become
Of man or worm; the vilest here excel me,
75   They creep, yet see; I dark in light exposed
To daily fraud, contempt, abuse and wrong,

Within doors, or without, still as a fool,
In power of others, never in my own;
Scarce half I seem to live, dead more than half.
80 O dark, dark, dark, amid the blaze of noon,
Irrecoverably dark, total eclipse
Without all hope of day!
O first-created beam, and thou great word,
Let there be light, and light was over all;
85 Why am I thus bereaved thy prime decree?
The sun to me is dark
And silent as the moon,
When she deserts the night
Hid in her vacant interlunar cave.
90 Since light so necessary is to life,
And almost life itself, if it be true
That light is in the soul,
She all in every part, why was the sight
To such a tender ball as th' eye confined?
95 So obvious and so easy to be quenched,
And not, as feeling, through all parts diffused,
That she might look at will through every pore?
Then had I not been thus exiled from light;
As in the land of darkness yet in light,
100 To live a life half dead, a living death,
And buried; but O yet more miserable!
Myself my sepulchre, a moving grave,
Buried, yet not exempt
By privilege of death and burial
105 From worst of other evils, pains and wrongs,
But made hereby obnoxious more
To all the miseries of life,
Life in captivity
Among inhuman foes.
110 But who are these? For with joint pace I hear
The tread of many feet steering this way;
Perhaps my enemies who come to stare
At my affliction, and perhaps to insult,
Their daily practice to afflict me more.
115 *Chorus.* This, this is he; softly a while,

Let us not break in upon him;
O change beyond report, thought, or belief!
See how he lies at random, carelessly diffused,
With languished head unpropped,
120 As one past hope, abandoned,
And by himself given over;
In slavish habit, ill-fitted weeds
O'erworn and soiled;
Or do my eyes misrepresent? Can this be he,
125 That heroic, that renowned,
Irresistible Samson? whom unarmed
No strength of man, or fiercest wild beast could withstand;
Who tore the lion, as the lion tears the kid,
Ran on embattled armies clad in iron,
130 And weaponless himself,
Made arms ridiculous, useless the forgery
Of brazen shield and spear, the hammered cuirass,
Chalybean tempered steel, and frock of mail
Adamantean proof;
135 But safest he who stood aloof,
When insupportably his foot advanced;
In scorn of their proud arms and warlike tools,
Spurned them to death by troops. The bold Ascalonite
Fled from his lion ramp, old warriors turned
140 Their plated backs under his heel;
Or grovelling soiled their crested helms in the dust.
Then with what trivial weapon came to hand,
The jaw of a dead ass, his sword of bone,
A thousand foreskins fell, the flower of Palestine
145 In Ramath-lechi famous to this day:
Then by main force pulled up, and on his shoulders bore
The gates of Azza, post, and massy bar
Up to the hill by Hebron, seat of giants old,
No journey of a sabbath day, and loaded so,
150 Like whom the Gentiles feign to bear up heaven.
Which shall I first bewail,
Thy bondage or lost sight,
Prison within prison
Inseparably dark?

155 Thou art become (O worst imprisonment!)
The dungeon of thyself; thy soul
(Which men enjoying sight oft without cause complain)
Imprisoned now indeed,
In real darkness of the body dwells,
160 Shut up from outward light
To incorporate with gloomy night;
For inward light alas
Puts forth no visual beam.
O mirror of our fickle state,
165 Since man on earth unparalleled!
The rarer thy example stands,
By how much from the top of wondrous glory,
Strongest of mortal men,
To lowest pitch of abject fortune thou art fall'n.
170 For him I reckon not in high estate
Whom long descent of birth
Or the sphere of fortune raises;
But thee whose strength, while virtue was her mate,
Might have subdued the earth,
175 Universally crowned with highest praises.
Samson. I hear the sound of words, their sense the air
Dissolves unjointed ere it reach my ear.
Chorus. He speaks, let us draw nigh. Matchless in might,
The glory late of Israel, now the grief;
180 We come thy friends and neighbours not unknown
From Eshtaol and Zora's fruitful vale
To visit or bewail thee, or if better,
Counsel or consolation we may bring,
Salve to thy sores; apt words have power to swage
185 The tumours of a troubled mind,
And are as balm to festered wounds.
Samson. Your coming, friends, revives me, for I learn
Now of my own experience, not by talk,
How counterfeit a coin they are who friends
190 Bear in their superscription (of the most
I would be understood); in prosperous days
They swarm, but in adverse withdraw their head
Not to be found, though sought. Ye see, O friends,

How many evils have enclosed me round;
195   Yet that which was the worst now least afflicts me,
Blindness; for had I sight, confused with shame,
How could I once look up, or heave the head,
Who like a foolish pilot have shipwrecked
My vessel trusted to me from above,
200   Gloriously rigged; and for a word, a tear,
Fool, have divulged the secret gift of God
To a deceitful woman: tell me friends,
Am I not sung and proverbed for a fool
In every street, do they not say, how well
205   Are come upon him his deserts? yet why?
Immeasurable strength they might behold
In me, of wisdom nothing more than mean;
This with the other should, at least, have paired,
These two proportioned ill drove me transverse.
210   *Chorus.* Tax not divine disposal; wisest men
Have erred, and by bad women been deceived;
And shall again, pretend they ne'er so wise.
Deject not then so overmuch thyself,
Who hast of sorrow thy full load besides;
215   Yet truth to say, I oft have heard men wonder
Why thou shouldst wed Philistian women rather
Than of thine own tribe fairer, or as fair,
At least of thy own nation, and as noble.
Samson. The first I saw at Timna, and she pleased
220   Me, not my parents, that I sought to wed,
The daughter of an infidel: they knew not
That what I motioned was of God; I knew
From intimate impúlse, and therefore urged
The marriage on; that by occasion hence
225   I might begin Israel's deliverance,
The work to which I was divinely called;
She proving false, the next I took to wife
(O that I never had! fond wish too late)
Was in the vale of Sorec, Dálila,
230   That specious monster, my accomplished snare.
I thought it lawful from my former act,
And the same end; still watching to oppress

Israel's oppressors: of what now I suffer
She was not the prime cause, but I myself,
235 . Who vanquished with a peal of words (O weakness!)
Gave up my fort of silence to a woman.
Chorus. In seeking just occasion to provoke
The Philistine, thy country's enemy,
Thou never wast remiss. I bear thee witness:
240 Yet Israel still serves with all his sons.
Samson. That fault I take not on me, but transfer
On Israel's governors and heads of tribes,
Who, seeing those great acts which God had done
Singly by me against their conquerors,
245 Acknowledged not, or not at all considered,
Deliverance offered: I on th' other side
Used no ambition to commend my deeds;
The deeds themselves, though mute, spoke loud the doer;
But they persisted deaf, and would not seem
250 To count them things worth notice, till at length
Their lords the Philistines with gathered powers
Entered Judea seeking me, who then
Safe to the rock of Etham was retired,
Not flying, but forecasting in what place
255 To set upon them, what advantaged best;
Meanwhile the men of Judah to prevent
The harass of their land, beset me round;
I willingly on some conditions came
Into their hands, and they as gladly yield me
260 To the uncircumcised a welcome prey,
Bound with two cords; but cords to me were threads
Touched with the flame: on their whole host I flew
Unarmed, and with a trivial weapon felled
Their choicest youth; they only lived who fled.
265 Had Judah that day joined, or one whole tribe,
They had by this possessed the towers of Gath,
And lorded over them whom now they serve;
But what more oft in nations grown corrupt,
And by their vices brought to servitude,
270 Than to love bondage more than liberty,
Bondage with ease than strenuous liberty;

And to despise, or envy, or suspect
Whom God hath of his special favour raised
As their deliverer; if he aught begin,
275   How frequent to desert him, and at last
To heap ingratitude on worthiest deeds?
Chorus. Thy words to my remembrance bring
How Succoth and the fort of Penuel
Their great deliverer contemned,
280   The matchless Gideon in pursuit
Of Madian and her vanquished kings:
And how ingrateful Ephraim
Had dealt with Jephtha, who by argument,
Not worse than by his shield and spear
285   Defended Israel from the Ammonite,
Had not his prowess quelled their pride
In that sore battle when so many died
Without reprieve adjudged to death,
For want of well pronouncing *shibboleth.*
290   *Samson.* Of such examples add me to the roll;
Me easily indeed mine may neglect,
But God's proposed deliverance not so.
Chorus. Just are the ways of God,
And justifiable to men;
295   Unless there be who think not God at all;
If any be, they walk obscure;
For of such doctrine never was there school,
But the heart of the fool,
And no man therein doctor but himself.
300   Yet more there be who doubt his ways not just,
As to his own edícts, found contradicting,
Then give the reins to wand'ring thought,
Regardless of his glory's diminution;
Till by their own perplexities involved
305   They ravel more, still less resolved,
But never find self-satisfying solution.
As if they would confine th' interminable,
And tie him to his own prescript,
Who made our laws to bind us, not himself,
310   And hath full right to exempt

Whom so it pleases him by choice
From national obstriction, without taint
Of sin, or legal debt;
For with his own laws he can best dispense.
315   He would not else who never wanted means,
Nor in respect of th' enemy just cause
To set his people free,
Have prompted this heroic Nazarite,
Against his vow of strictest purity,
320   To seek in marriage that fallacious bride,
Unclean, unchaste.
        Down Reason then, at least vain reasonings down,
Though Reason here aver
That moral verdict quits her of unclean:
325   Unchaste was subsequent, her stain not his.
        But see here comes thy reverend sire
With careful step, locks white as down,
Old Mánoa: advise
Forthwith how thou ought'st to receive him.
330   *Samson.* Ay me, another inward grief awaked,
With mention of that name renews th' assault.
Manoa. Brethren and men of Dan, for such ye seem,
Though in this uncouth place; if old respect,
As I suppose, towards your once gloried friend,
335   My son now captive, hither hath informed
Your younger feet, while mine cast back with age
Came lagging after; say if he be here.
Samson. As signal now in low dejected state,
As erst in highest, behold him where he lies.
340   *Manoa.* O miserable change! is this the man,
That invincible Samson, far renowned,
The dread of Israel's foes, who with a strength
Equivalent to angels walked their streets,
None offering fight; who single combatant
345   Duelled their armies ranked in proud array,
Himself an army, now unequal match
To save himself against a coward armed
At one spear's length. O ever-failing trust
In mortal strength! and O what not in man

350   Deceivable and vain! Nay what thing good
       Prayed for, but often proves our woe, our bane?
       I prayed for children, and thought barrenness
       In wedlock a reproach; I gained a son,
       And such a son as all men hailed me happy;
355   Who would be now a father in my stead?
       O wherefore did God grant me my request,
       And as a blessing with such pomp adorned?
       Why are his gifts desirable, to tempt
       Our earnest prayers, then giv'n with solemn hand
360   As graces, draw a scorpion's tail behind?
       For this did the angel twice descend? for this
       Ordained thy nurture holy, as of a plant;
       Select, and sacred, glorious for a while,
       The miracle of men: then in an hour
365   Ensnared, assaulted, overcome, led bound,
       Thy foes' derision, captive, poor, and blind
       Into a dungeon thrust, to work with slaves?
       Alas methinks whom God hath chosen once
       To worthiest deeds, if he through frailty err,
370   He should not so o'erwhelm, and as a thrall
       Subject him to so foul indignities,
       Be it but for honour's sake of former deeds.
       Samson. Appoint not Heavenly disposition, father,
       Nothing of all these evils hath befall'n me
375   But justly; I myself have brought them on,
       Sole author I, sole cause: if aught seem vile,
       As vile hath been my folly, who have profaned
       The mystery of God giv'n me under pledge
       Of vow, and have betrayed it to a woman,
380   A Canaanite, my faithless enemy.
       This well I knew, nor was at all surprised,
       But warned by oft experience: did not she
       Of Timna first betray me, and reveal
       The secret wrested from me in her heighth
385   Of nuptial love professed, carrying it straight
       To them who had corrupted her, my spies,
       And rivals? In this other was there found
       More faith? who also in her prime of love,

Spousal embraces, vitiated with gold,
390   Though offered only, by the scent conceived
Her spurious first-born; treason against me?
Thrice she assayed with flattering prayers and sighs,
And amorous reproaches to win from me
My capital secret, in what part my strength
395   Lay stored, in what part summed, that she might know:
Thrice I deluded her, and turned to sport
Her importunity, each time perceiving
How openly, and with what impudence
She purposed to betray me, and (which was worse
400   Than undissembled hate) with what contempt
She sought to make me traitor to myself;
Yet the fourth time, when must'ring all her wiles,
With blandished parleys, feminine assaults,
Tongue-batteries, she surceased not day nor night
405   To storm me over-watched, and wearied out.
At times when men seek most repose and rest,
I yielded, and unlocked her all my heart,
Who with a grain of manhood well resolved
Might easily have shook off all her snares:
410   But foul effeminacy held me yoked
Her bond-slave; O indignity, O blot
To honour and religion! servile mind
Rewarded well with servile punishment!
The base degree to which I now am fall'n,
415   These rags, this grinding, is not yet so base
As was my former servitude, ignoble,
Unmanly, ignominious, infamous,
True slavery, and that blindness worse than this,
That saw not how degenerately I served.
420   *Manoa.* I cannot praise thy marriage choices, son,
Rather approved them not; but thou didst plead
Divine impulsion prompting how thou might'st
Find some occasion to infest our foes.
I state not that; this I am sure; our foes
425   Found soon occasion thereby to make thee
Their captive, and their triumph; thou the sooner
Temptation found'st, or over-potent charms

To violate the sacred trust of silence
Deposited within thee; which to have kept
430 Tacit, was in thy power; true; and thou bear'st
Enough, and more the burden of that fault;
Bitterly hast thou paid, and still art paying
That rigid score. A worse thing yet remains:
This day the Philistines a popular feast
435 Here celebrate in Gaza; and proclaim
Great pomp, and sacrifice, and praises loud
To Dagon, as their god who hath delivered
Thee Samson bound and blind into their hands,
Them out of thine, who slew'st them many a slain.
440 So Dagon shall be magnified, and God,
Besides whom is no God, compared with idols,
Disglorified, blasphemed, and had in scorn
By th' idolatrous rout amidst their wine;
Which to have come to pass by means of thee,
445 Samson, of all thy sufferings think the heaviest,
Of all reproach the most with shame that ever
Could have befall'n thee and thy father's house.
Samson. Father, I do acknowledge and confess
That I this honour, I this pomp have brought
450 To Dagon, and advanced his praises high
Among the heathen round; to God have brought
Dishonour, obloquy, and oped the mouths
Of idolists, and atheists; have brought scandal
To Israel, diffidence of God, and doubt
455 In feeble hearts, propense enough before
To waver, or fall off and join with idols;
Which is my chief affliction, shame and sorrow,
The anguish of my soul, that suffers not
Mine eye to harbour sleep, or thoughts to rest.
460 This only hope relieves me, that the strife
With me hath end; all the contést is now
'Twixt God and Dagon; Dagon hath presumed,
Me overthrown, to enter lists with God,
His deity comparing and preferring
465 Before the God of Abraham. He, be sure,
Will not connive, or linger, thus provoked,

But will arise and his great name assert:
Dagon must stoop, and shall ere long receive
Such a discomfit, as shall quite despoil him
470   Of all these boasted trophies won on me,
And with confusion blank his worshippers.
Manoa. With cause this hope relieves thee, and these words
I as a prophecy receive: for God,
Nothing more certain, will not long defer
475   To vindicate the glory of his name
Against all competition, nor will long
Endure it, doubtful whether God be Lord,
Or Dagon. But for thee what shall be done?
Thou must not in the meanwhile here forgot
480   Lie in this miserable loathsome plight
Neglected. I already have made way
To some Philistian lords, with whom to treat
About thy ransom: well they may by this
Have satisfied their utmost of revenge
485   By pains and slaveries, worse than death inflicted
On thee, who now no more canst do them harm.
Samson. Spare that proposal, father, spare the trouble
Of that solicitation; let me here,
As I deserve, pay on my punishment;
490   And expiate, if possible, my crime,
Shameful garrulity. To have revealed
Secrets of men, the secrets of a friend,
How heinous had the fact been, how deserving
Contempt, and scorn of all, to be excluded
495   All friendship, and avoided as a blab,
The mark of fool set on his front?
But I God's counsel have not kept, his holy secret
Presumptuously have published, impiously,
Weakly at least, and shamefully: a sin
500   That Gentiles in their parables condemn
To their abyss and horrid pains confined.
Manoa. Be penitent and for thy fault contrite,
But act not in thy own affliction, son;
Repent the sin, but if the punishment
505   Thou canst avoid, self-preservation bids;

Or th' execution leave to high disposal,
And let another hand, not thine, exact
Thy penal forfeit from thyself; perhaps
God will relent, and quit thee all his debt;
510 Who evermore approves and more accepts
(Best pleased with humble and filial submission)
Him who imploring mercy sues for life,
Than who self-rigorous chooses death as due;
Which argues over-just, and self-displeased
515 For self-offence, more than for God offended.
Reject not then what offered means, who knows
But God hath set before us, to return thee
Home to thy country and his sacred house,
Where thou may'st bring thy off'rings, to avert
520 His further ire, with prayers and vows renewed.
Samson. His pardon I implore; but as for life,
To what end should I seek it? when in strength
All mortals I excelled, and great in hopes
With youthful courage and magnanimous thoughts
525 Of birth from Heav'n foretold and high explóits,
Full of divine instínct, after some proof
Of acts indeed heroic, far beyond
The sons of Anak, famous now and blazed,
Fearless of danger, like a petty god
530 I walked about admired of all and dreaded
On hostile ground, none daring my affront.
Then swoll'n with pride into the snare I fell
Of fair fallacious looks, venereal trains,
Softened with pleasure and voluptuous life;
535 At length to lay my head and hallowed pledge
Of all my strength in the lascivious lap
Of a deceitful concubine who shore me
Like a tame wether, all my precious fleece,
Then turned me out ridiculous, despoiled,
540 Shav'n, and disarmed among my enemies.
Chorus. Desire of wine and all delicious drinks,
Which many a famous warrior overturns,
Thou couldst repress, nor did the dancing ruby
Sparkling, outpoured, the flavour, or the smell,

545   Or taste that cheers the heart of gods and men,
       Allure thee from the cool crystálline stream.
       Samson. Wherever fountain or fresh current flowed
       Against the eastern ray, translucent, pure
       With touch ethereal of heaven's fiery rod
550   I drank, from the clear milky juice allaying
       Thirst, and refreshed; nor envied them the grape
       Whose heads that turbulent liquor fills with fumes.
       Chorus. O madness, to think use of strongest wines
       And strongest drinks our chief support of health,
555   When God with these forbidd'n made choice to rear
       His mighty champion, strong above compare,
       Whose drink was only from the liquid brook.
       Samson. But what availed this temperance, not complete
       Against another object more enticing?
560   What boots it at one gate to make defence,
       And at another to let in the foe
       Effeminately vanquished? by which means,
       Now blind, disheartened, shamed, dishonoured, quelled,
       To what can I be useful, wherein serve
565   My nation, and the work from Heav'n imposed,
       But to sit idle on the household hearth,
       A burdenous drone; to visitants a gaze,
       Or pitied object, these redundant locks
       Robustious to no purpose clust'ring down,
570   Vain monument of strength; till length of years
       And sedentary numbness craze my limbs
       To a contemptible old age obscure.
       Here rather let me drudge and earn my bread,
       Till vermin or the draff of servile food
575   Consume me, and oft-invocated death
       Hasten the welcome end of all my pains.
       Manoa. Wilt thou then serve the Philistines with that gift
       Which was expressly giv'n thee to annoy them?
       Better at home lie bed-rid, not only idle,
580   Inglorious, unemployed, with age outworn.
       But God who caused a fountain at thy prayer
       From the dry ground to spring, thy thirst to allay
       After the brunt of battle, can as easy

Cause light again within thy eyes to spring,
585   Wherewith to serve him better than thou hast;
And I persuade me so; why else this strength
Miraculous yet remaining in those locks?
His might continues in thee not for naught,
Nor shall his wondrous gifts be frustrate thus.
590   *Samson.* All otherwise to me my thoughts portend,
That these dark orbs no more shall treat with light,
Nor th' other light of life continue long,
But yield to double darkness nigh at hand:
So much I feel my genial spirits droop,
595   My hopes all flat, nature within me seems
In all her functions weary of herself;
My race of glory run, and race of shame,
And I shall shortly be with them that rest.
Manoa. Believe not these suggestions which proceed
600   From anguish of the mind and humours black,
That mingle with thy fancy. I however
Must not omit a father's timely care
To prosecute the means of thy deliverance
By ransom or how else: meanwhile be calm,
605   And healing words from these thy friends admit.
Samson. O that torment should not be confined
To the body's wounds and sores
With maladies innumerable
In heart, head, breast, and reins;
610   But must secret passage find
To th' inmost mind,
There exercise all his fierce accidents,
And on her purest spirits prey,
As on entrails, joints, and limbs,
615   With answerable pains, but more intense,
Though void of corporal sense.
    My griefs not only pain me
As a ling'ring disease,
But finding no redress, ferment and rage,
620   Nor less than wounds immedicable
Rankle, and fester, and gangrene,
To black mortification.

Thoughts my tormentors armed with deadly stings
Mangle my apprehensive tenderest parts,
625 Exasperate, exulcerate, and raise
Dire inflammation which no cooling herb
Or med'cinal liquor can assuage,
Nor breath of vernal air from snowy alp.
Sleep hath forsook and giv'n me o'er
630 To death's benumbing opium as my only cure.
Thence faintings, swoonings of despair,
And sense of Heav'n's desertion.
　　I was his nursling once and choice delight,
His destined from the womb,
635 Promised by Heavenly message twice descending.
Under his special eye
Abstemious I grew up and thrived amain;
He led me on to mightiest deeds
Above the nerve of mortal arm
640 Against the uncircumcised, our enemies.
But now hath cast me off as never known,
And to those cruel enemies,
Whom I by his appointment had provoked,
Left me all helpless with th' irreparable loss
645 Of sight, reserved alive to be repeated
The subject of their cruelty, or scorn.
Nor am I in the list of them that hope;
Hopeless are all my evils, all remédiless;
This one prayer yet remains, might I be heard,
650 No long petition, speedy death,
The close of all my miseries, and the balm.
Chorus. Many are the sayings of the wise
In ancient and in modern books enrolled;
Extolling patience as the truest fortitude;
655 And to the bearing well of all calamities,
All chances incident to man's frail life;
Consolatories writ
With studied argument, and much persuasion sought,
Lenient of grief and anxious thought;
660 But with th' afflicted in his pangs their sound
Little prevails, or rather seems a tune,

Harsh, and of dissonant mood from his complaint,
Unless he feel within
Some source of consolation from above;
665 Secret refreshings, that repair his strength,
And fainting spirits uphold.
     God of our fathers, what is man!
That thou towards him with hand so various,
Or might I say contrarious,
670 Temper'st thy providence through his short course,
Not evenly, as thou rul'st
The angelic orders and inferior creatures mute,
Irrational and brute.
Nor do I name of men the common rout,
675 That wand'ring loose about
Grow up and perish, as the summer fly,
Heads without name, no more remembered;
But such as thou hast solemnly elected,
With gifts and graces eminently adorned
680 To some great work, thy glory,
And people's safety, which in part they effect:
Yet toward these thus dignified, thou oft
Amidst their heighth of noon,
Changest thy countenance, and thy hand with no regard
685 Of highest favours past
From thee on them, or them to thee of service.
     Nor only dost degrade them, or remit
To life obscured, which were a fair dismission,
But throw'st them lower than thou didst exalt them high,
690 Unseemly falls in human eye,
Too grievous for the trespass or omission;
Oft leav'st them to the hostile sword
Of heathen and profane, their carcasses
To dogs and fowls a prey, or else captíved:
695 Or to th' unjust tribunals, under change of times,
And condemnation of the ingrateful multitude.
If these they 'scape, perhaps in poverty
With sickness and disease thou bow'st them down,
Painful diseases and deformed,
700 In crude old age;

Though not disordinate, yet causeless suff 'ring
The punishment of dissolute days; in fine,
Just or unjust, alike seem miserable,
For oft alike, both come to evil end.

705   So deal not with this once thy glorious champion,
The image of thy strength, and mighty minister.
What do I beg? how hast thou dealt already?
Behold him in this state calamitous, and turn
His labours, for thou canst, to peaceful end.

710   But who is this, what thing of sea or land?
Female of sex it seems,
That so bedecked, ornate, and gay,
Comes this way sailing
Like a stately ship

715 Of Tarsus, bound for th' isles
Of Javan or Gadier
With all her bravery on, and tackle trim,
Sails filled, and streamers waving,
Courted by all the winds that hold them play,

720 An amber scent of odorous perfume
Her harbinger, a damsel train behind;
Some rich Philistian matron she may seem,
And now at nearer view, no other certain
Than Dálila thy wife.

725 *Samson.* My wife, my traitress, let her not come near me.
Chorus. Yet on she moves, now stands and eyes thee fixed,
About t' have spoke, but now, with head declined
Like a fair flower surcharged with dew, she weeps
And words addressed seem into tears dissolved,

730 Wetting the borders of her silken veil:
But now again she makes address to speak.
Dalila. With doubtful feet and wavering resolution
I came, still dreading thy displeasure, Samson,
Which to have merited, without excuse,

735 I cannot but acknowledge; yet if tears
May expiate (though the fact more evil drew
In the perverse event than I foresaw),
My penance hath not slackened, though my pardon
No way assured. But conjugal affection

740   Prevailing over fear, and timorous doubt
      Hath led me on desirous to behold
      Once more thy face, and know of thy estate.
      If aught in my ability may serve
      To lighten what thou suffer'st, and appease
745   Thy mind with what amends is in my power,
      Though late, yet in some part to recompense
      My rash but more unfortunate misdeed.
      Samson. Out, out hyena; these are thy wonted arts,
      And arts of every woman false like thee,
750   To break all faith, all vows, deceive, betray,
      Then as repentant to submit, beseech,
      And reconcilement move with feigned remorse,
      Confess, and promise wonders in her change,
      Not truly penitent, but chief to try
755   Her husband, how far urged his patience bears,
      His virtue or weakness which way to assail:
      Then with more cautious and instructed skill
      Again transgresses, and again submits;
      That wisest and best men, full oft beguiled,
760   With goodness principled not to reject
      The penitent, but ever to forgive,
      Are drawn to wear out miserable days,
      Entangled with a poisonous bosom snake,
      If not by quick destruction soon cut off
765   As I by thee, to ages an example.
      Dalila. Yet hear me Samson; not that I endeavour
      To lessen or extenuate my offence,
      But that on th' other side if it be weighed
      By itself, with aggravations not surcharged,
770   Or else with just allowance counterpoised,
      I may, if possible, thy pardon find
      The easier towards me, or thy hatred less.
      First granting, as I do, it was a weakness
      In me, but incident to all our sex,
775   Curiosity, inquisitive, importune
      Of secrets, then with like infirmity
      To publish them, both common female faults;
      Was it not weakness also to make known

For importunity, that is for naught,
780 Wherein consisted all thy strength and safety?
To what I did thou show'dst me first the way.
But I to enemies revealed, and should not.
Nor shouldst thou have trusted that to woman's frailty:
Ere I to thee, thou to thyself wast cruel.
785 Let weakness then with weakness come to parle,
So near related, or the same of kind;
Thine forgive mine, that men may censure thine
The gentler, if severely thou exact not
More strength from me, than in thyself was found.
790 And what if love, which thou interpret'st hate,
The jealousy of love, powerful of sway
In human hearts, nor less in mine towards thee,
Caused what I did? I saw thee mutable
Of fancy, feared lest one day thou wouldst leave me
795 As her at Timna, sought by all means therefore
How to endear, and hold thee to me firmest:
No better way I saw than by importuning
To learn thy secrets, get into my power
Thy key of strength and safety: thou wilt say,
800 Why then revealed? I was assured by those
Who tempted me, that nothing was designed
Against thee but safe custody, and hold:
That made for me; I knew that liberty
Would draw thee forth to perilous enterprises,
805 While I at home sat full of cares and fears
Wailing thy absence in my widowed bed;
Here I should still enjoy thee day and night
Mine and love's prisoner, not the Philistines',
Whole to myself, unhazarded abroad,
810 Fearless at home of partners in my love.
These reasons in love's law have passed for good,
Though fond and reasonless to some perhaps;
And love hath oft, well meaning, wrought much woe,
Yet always pity or pardon hath obtained.
815 Be not unlike all others, not austere
As thou art strong, inflexible as steel.
If thou in strength all mortals dost exceed,

In uncompassionate anger do not so.
Samson. How cunningly the sorceress displays
820   Her own transgressions, to upbraid me mine!
That malice not repentance brought thee hither,
By this appears: I gave, thou say'st, th' example,
I led the way; bitter reproach, but true,
I to myself was false ere thou to me;
825   Such pardon therefore as I give my folly,
Take to thy wicked deed: which when thou seest
Impartial, self-severe, inexorable,
Thou wilt renounce thy seeking, and much rather
Confess it feigned; weakness is thy excuse,
830   And I believe it, weakness to resist
Philistian gold: if weakness may excuse,
What murderer, what traitor, parricide,
Incestuous, sacrilegious, but may plead it?
All wickedness is weakness: that plea therefore
835   With God or man will gain thee no remission.
But love constrained thee; call it furious rage
To satisfy thy lust: love seeks to have love;
My love how couldst thou hope, who took'st the way
To raise in me inexpiable hate,
840   Knowing, as needs I must, by thee betrayed?
In vain thou striv'st to cover shame with shame,
Or by evasions thy crime uncover'st more.
Dalila. Since thou determin'st weakness for no plea
In man or woman, though to thy own condemning,
845   Hear what assaults I had, what snares besides,
What sieges girt me round, ere I consented;
Which might have awed the best resolved of men,
The constantest to have yielded without blame.
It was not gold, as to my charge thou lay'st,
850   That wrought with me: thou know'st the magistrates
And princes of my country came in person,
Solicited, commanded, threatened, urged,
Adjured by all the bonds of civil duty
And of religion, pressed how just it was,
855   How honourable, how glorious to entrap
A common enemy, who had destroyed

Such numbers of our nation: and the priest
Was not behind, but ever at my ear,
Preaching how meritorious with the gods
860   It would be to ensnare an irreligious
Dishonourer of Dagon: what had I
To oppose against such powerful arguments?
Only my love of thee held long debate;
And combated in silence all these reasons
865   With hard contést: at length that grounded maxim
So rife and celebrated in the mouths
Of wisest men; that to the public good
Private respects must yield; with grave authority
Took full possession of me and prevailed;
870   Virtue, as I thought, truth, duty so enjoining.
    Samson. I thought where all thy circling wiles would end;
In feigned religion, smooth hypocrisy.
But had thy love, still odiously pretended,
Been, as it ought, sincere, it would have taught thee
875   Far other reasonings, brought far other deeds.
I before all the daughters of my tribe
And of my nation chose thee from among
My enemies, loved thee, as too well thou knew'st,
Too well; unbosomed all my secrets to thee,
880   Not out of levity, but overpow'red
By thy request, who could deny thee nothing;
Yet now am judged an enemy. Why then
Didst thou at first receive me for thy husband?
Then, as since then, thy country's foe professed:
885   Being once a wife, for me thou wast to leave
Parents and country; nor was I their subject,
Nor under their protection but my own;
Thou mine, not theirs: if aught against my life
Thy country sought of thee, it sought unjustly,
890   Against the law of nature, law of nations,
No more thy country, but an impious crew
Of men conspiring to uphold their state
By worse than hostile deeds, violating the ends
For which our country is a name so dear;
895   Not therefore to be obeyed. But zeal moved thee;

To please thy gods thou didst it; gods unable
To acquit themselves and prosecute their foes
But by ungodly deeds, the contradiction
Of their own deity, gods cannot be:
900 Less therefore to be pleased, obeyed, or feared;
These false pretéxts and varnished colours failing,
Bare in thy guilt how foul must thou appear?
Dalila. In argument with men a woman ever
Goes by the worse, whatever be her cause.
905 *Samson.* For want of words no doubt, or lack of breath;
Witness when I was worried with thy peals.
Dalila. I was a fool, too rash, and quite mistaken
In what I thought would have succeeded best.
Let me obtain forgiveness of thee, Samson,
910 Afford me place to show what recompense
Towards thee I intend for what I have misdone,
Misguided; only what remains past cure
Bear not too sensibly, nor still insist
To afflict thyself in vain: though sight be lost,
915 Life hath yet many solaces, enjoyed
Where other senses want not their delights
At home in leisure and domestic ease,
Exempt from many a care and chance to which
Eyesight exposes daily men abroad.
920 I to the lords will intercede, not doubting
Their favourable ear, that I may fetch thee
From forth this loathsome prison-house, to abide
With me, where my redoubled love and care
With nursing diligence, to me glad office,
925 May ever tend about thee to old age
With all things grateful cheered, and so supplied,
That what by me thou hast lost thou least may miss.
Samson. No, no, of my condition take no care;
It fits not; thou and I long since are twain;
930 Nor think me so unwary or accurst
To bring my feet again into the snare
Where once I have been caught; I know thy trains
Though dearly to my cost, thy gins, and toils;
Thy fair enchanted cup, and warbling charms

935   No more on me have power, their force is nulled,
         So much of adder's wisdom I have learnt
         To fence my ear against thy sorceries.
         If in my flower of youth and strength, when all men
         Loved, honoured, feared me, thou alone could hate me
940   Thy husband, slight me, sell me, and forgo me;
         How wouldst thou use me now, blind, and thereby
         Deceivable, in most things as a child
         Helpless, thence easily contemned, and scorned,
         And last neglected? How wouldst thou insult
945   When I must live uxorious to thy will
         In perfect thraldom, how again betray me,
         Bearing my words and doings to the lords
         To gloss upon, and censuring, frown or smile?
         This gaol I count the house of liberty
950   To thine whose doors my feet shall never enter.
         Dalila. Let me approach at least, and touch thy hand.
         Samson. Not for thy life, lest fierce remembrance wake
         My sudden rage to tear thee joint by joint.
         At distance I forgive thee, go with that;
955   Bewail thy falsehood, and the pious works
         It hath brought forth to make thee memorable
         Among illustrious women, faithful wives:
         Cherish thy hastened widowhood with the gold
         Of matrimonial treason: so farewell.
960   *Dalila.* I see thou art implacable, more deaf
         To prayers, than winds and seas; yet winds to seas
         Are reconciled at length, and sea to shore:
         Thy anger, unappeasable, still rages,
         Eternal tempest never to be calmed.
965   Why do I humble thus myself, and suing
         For peace, reap nothing but repulse and hate?
         Bid go with evil omen and the brand
         Of infamy upon my name denounced?
         To mix with thy concernments I desist
970   Henceforth, nor too much disapprove my own.
         Fame if not double-faced is double-mouthed,
         And with contráry blast proclaims most deeds;
         On both his wings, one black, th' other white,

Bears greatest names in his wild airy flight.
975 My name perhaps among the circumcised
In Dan, in Judah, and the bordering tribes,
To all posterity may stand defamed,
With malediction mentioned, and the blot
Of falsehood most unconjugal traduced.
980 But in my country where I most desire,
In Ecron, Gaza, Asdod, and in Gath
I shall be named among the famousest
Of women, sung at solemn festivals,
Living and dead recorded, who to save
985 Her country from a fierce destroyer, chose
Above the faith of wedlock bands; my tomb
With odours visited and annual flowers.
Not less renowned than in Mount Ephraim,
Jael, who with inhospitable guile
990 Smote Sisera sleeping through the temples nailed.
Nor shall I count it heinous to enjoy
The public marks of honour and reward
Conferred upon me, for the piety
Which to my country I was judged to have shown.
995 At this whoever envies or repines
I leave him to his lot, and like my own.
Chorus. She's gone, a manifest serpent by her sting
Discovered in the end, till now concealed.
Samson. So let her go, God sent her to debase me,
1000 And aggravate my folly who committed
To such a viper his most sacred trust
Of secrecy, my safety, and my life.
Chorus. Yet beauty, though injurious, hath strange power,
After offence returning, to regain
1005 Love once possessed, nor can be easily
Repulsed, without much inward passion felt
And secret sting of amorous remorse.
Samson. Love-quarrels oft in pleasing concord end,
Not wedlock-treachery endangering life.
1010 *Chorus.* It is not virtue, wisdom, valour, wit,
Strength, comeliness of shape, or amplest merit
That woman's love can win or long inherit;

But what it is, hard is to say,
Harder to hit,
1015 (Which way soever men refer it)
Much like thy riddle, Samson, in one day
Or seven, though one should musing sit;
      If any of these or all, the Timnian bride
Had not so soon preferred
1020 Thy paranymph, worthless to thee compared,
Successor in thy bed,
Nor both so loosely disallied
Their nuptials, nor this last so treacherously
Had shorn the fatal harvest of thy head.
1025 Is it for that such outward ornament
Was lavished on their sex, that inward gifts
Were left for haste unfinished, judgement scant,
Capacity not raised to apprehend
Or value what is best
1030 In choice, but oftest to affect the wrong?
Or was too much of self-love mixed,
Of constancy no root infixed,
That either they love nothing, or not long?
      Whate'er it be, to wisest men and best
1035 Seeming at first all Heavenly under virgin veil,
Soft, modest, meek, demure,
Once joined, the contrary she proves, a thorn
Intestine, far within defensive arms
A cleaving mischief, in his way to virtue
1040 Adverse and turbulent; or by her charms
Draws him awry enslaved
With dotage, and his sense depraved
To folly and shameful deeds which ruin ends.
What pilot so expért but needs must wreck
1045 Embarked with such a steers-mate at the helm?
      Favoured of Heav'n who finds
One virtuous rarely found,
That in domestic good combines:
Happy that house! his way to peace is smooth:
1050 But virtue which breaks through all opposition,
And all temptation can remove,

Most shines and most is ácceptáble above.
   Therefore God's universal law
Gave to the man despotic power
1055 Over his female in due awe,
Nor from that right to part an hour,
Smile she or lour:
So shall he least confusion draw
On his whole life, not swayed
1060 By female usurpation, nor dismayed.
   But had we best retire? I see a storm.
Samson. Fair days have oft contracted wind and rain.
Chorus. But this another kind of tempest brings.
Samson. Be less abstruse, my riddling days are past.
1065 *Chorus.* Look now for no enchanting voice, nor fear
The bait of honeyed words; a rougher tongue
Draws hitherward, I know him by his stride,
The giant Hárapha of Gath, his look
Haughty as is his pile high-built and proud.
1070 Comes he in peace? what wind hath blown him hither
I less conjecture than when first I saw
The sumptuous Dálila floating this way:
His habit carries peace, his brow defiance.
Samson. Or peace or not, alike to me he comes.
1075 *Chorus.* His fraught we soon shall know, he now arrives.
Harapha. I come not Samson, to condole thy chance,
As these perhaps, yet wish it had not been,
Though for no friendly intent. I am of Gath,
Men call me Hárapha, of stock rénowned
1080 As Og or Anak and the Emims old
That Kiriathaim held; thou know'st me now,
If thou at all art known. Much I have heard
Of thy prodigious might and feats performed
Incredible to me, in this displeased,
1085 That I was never present on the place
Of those encounters, where we might have tried
Each other's force in camp or listed field:
And now am come to see of whom such noise
Hath walked about, and each limb to survey,
1090 If thy appearance answer loud report.

Samson. The way to know were not to see but taste.
Harapha. Dost thou already single me; I thought
Gyves and the mill had tamed thee? O that fortune
Had brought me to the field where thou art famed
1095 To have wrought such wonders with an ass's jaw;
I should have forced thee soon with other arms,
Or left thy carcass where the ass lay thrown:
So had the glory of prowess been recovered
To Palestine, won by a Philistine
1100 From the unforeskinned race, of whom thou bear'st
The highest name for valiant acts; that honour
Certain to have won by mortal duel from thee,
I lose, prevented by thy eyes put out.
Samson. Boast not of what thou wouldst have done, but do
1105 What then thou wouldst; thou seest it in thy hand.
Harapha. To combat with a blind man I disdain,
And thou hast need much washing to be touched.
Samson. Such usage as your honourable lords
Afford me assassinated and betrayed,
1110 Who durst not with their whole united powers
In fight withstand me single and unarmed,
Nor in the house with chamber ambushes
Close-banded durst attack me, no, not sleeping,
Till they had hired a woman with their gold
1115 Breaking her marriage faith to circumvent me.
Therefore without feigned shifts let be assigned
Some narrow place enclosed, where sight may give thee,
Or rather flight, no great advantage on me;
Then put on all thy gorgeous arms, thy helmet
1120 And brigandine of brass, thy broad habergeon,
Vant-brace and greaves, and gauntlet, add thy spear
A weaver's beam, and seven-times-folded shield;
I only with an oaken staff will meet thee,
And raise such outcries on thy clattered iron,
1125 Which long shall not withhold me from thy head,
That in a little time while breath remains thee,
Thou oft shalt wish thyself at Gath to boast
Again in safety what thou wouldst have done
To Samson, but shalt never see Gath more.

1130 *Harapha*. Thou durst not thus disparage glorious arms
Which greatest heroes have in battle worn,
Their ornament and finery, had not spells
And black enchantments, some magician's art
Armed thee or charmed thee strong, which thou from
      Heaven
1135 Feign'dst at thy birth was giv'n thee in thy hair,
Where strength can least abide, though all thy hairs
Were bristles ranged like those that ridge the back
Of chafed wild boars, or ruffled porcupines.
Samson. I know no spells, use no forbidden arts;
1140 My trust is in the living God who gave me
At my nativity this strength, diffused
No less through all my sinews, joints and bones,
Than thine, while I preserved these locks unshorn,
The pledge of my unviolated vow.
1145 For proof hereof, if Dagon be thy god,
Go to his temple, invocate his aid
With solemnest devotion, spread before him
How highly it concerns his glory now
To frustrate and dissolve these magic spells,
1150 Which I to be the power of Israel's God
Avow, and challenge Dagon to the test,
Offering to combat thee his champion bold,
With th' utmost of his godhead seconded:
Then thou shalt see, or rather to thy sorrow
1155 Soon feel, whose God is strongest, thine or mine.
Harapha. Presume not on thy God; whate'er he be,
Thee he regards not, owns not, hath cut off
Quite from his people, and delivered up
Into thy enemies' hand, permitted them
1160 To put out both thine eyes, and fettered send thee
Into the common prison, there to grind
Among the slaves and asses thy comrádes,
As good for nothing else; no better service
With those thy boist'rous locks, no worthy match
1165 For valour to assail, nor by the sword
Of noble warrior, so to stain his honour,
But by the barber's razor best subdued.

Samson. All these indignities, for such they are
From thine, these evils I deserve and more,
1170   Acknowledge them from God inflicted on me
Justly, yet despair not of his final pardon
Whose ear is ever open; and his eye
Gracious to re-admit the suppliant;
In confidence whereof I once again
1175   Defy thee to the trial of mortal fight,
By combat to decide whose god is God,
Thine or whom I with Israel's sons adore.
Harapha. Fair honour that thou dost thy God, in trusting
He will accept thee to defend his cause,
1180   A murderer, a revolter, and a robber.
Samson. Tongue-doughty giant, how dost thou prove me
      these?
Harapha. Is not thy nation subject to our lords?
Their magistrates confessed it, when they took thee
As a league-breaker and delivered bound
1185   Into our hands: for hadst thou not committed
Notorious murder on those thirty men
At Ascalon, who never did thee harm,
Then like a robber stripp'dst them of their robes?
The Philistines, when thou hadst broke the league,
1190   Went up with armèd powers thee only seeking,
To others did no violence nor spoil.
Samson. Among the daughters of the Philistines
I chose a wife, which argued me no foe;
And in your city held my nuptial feast:
1195   But your ill-meaning politician lords,
Under pretence of bridal friends and guests,
Appointed to await me thirty spies,
Who threat'ning cruel death constrained the bride
To wring from me and tell to them my secret,
1200   That solved the riddle which I had proposed.
When I perceived all set on enmity,
As on my enemies, wherever chanced,
I used hostility, and took their spoil
To pay my underminers in their coin.
1205   My nation was subjected to your lords.

It was the force of conquest; force with force
Is well ejected when the conquered can.
But I a private person, whom my country
As a league-breaker gave up bound, presumed
1210 Single rebellion and did hostile acts.
I was no private but a person raised
With strength sufficient and command from Heav'n
To free my country; if their servile minds
Me their deliverer sent would not receive,
1215 But to their masters gave me up for naught,
Th' unworthier they; whence to this day they serve.
I was to do my part from Heav'n assigned,
And had performed it if my known offence
Had not disabled me, not all your force:
1220 These shifts refuted, answer thy appellant,
Though by his blindness maimed for high attempts,
Who now defies thee thrice to single fight,
As a petty enterprise of small enforce.
Harapha. With thee a man condemned, a slave enrolled,
1225 Due by the law to capital punishment?
To fight with thee no man of arms will deign.
Samson. Cam'st thou for this, vain boaster, to survey me,
To descant on my strength, and give thy verdict?
Come nearer, part not hence so slight informed;
1230 But take good heed my hand survey not thee.
Harapha. O Baäl-zebub! can my ears unused
Hear these dishonours, and not render death?
Samson. No man withholds thee, nothing from thy hand
Fear I incurable; bring up thy van,
1235 My heels are fettered, but my fist is free.
Harapha. This insolence other kind of answer fits.
Samson. Go baffled coward, lest I run upon thee,
Though in these chains, bulk without spirit vast,
And with one buffet lay thy structure low,
1240 Or swing thee in the air, then dash thee down
To the hazard of thy brains and shattered sides.
Harapha. By Astaroth ere long thou shalt lament
These braveries in irons loaden on thee.
Chorus. His giantship is gone somewhat crestfall'n,

1245 Stalking with less unconscionable strides,
And lower looks, but in a sultry chafe.
Samson. I dread him not, nor all his giant brood,
Though fame divulge him father of five sons
All of gigantic size, Goliah chief.

1250 *Chorus.* He will directly to the lords, I fear,
And with malicious counsel stir them up
Some way or other yet further to afflict thee.
Samson. He must allege some cause, and offered fight
Will not dare mention, lest a question rise

1255 Whether he durst accept the offer or not,
And that he durst not plain enough appeared.
Much more affliction than already felt
They cannot well impose, nor I sustain;
If they intend advantage of my labours

1260 The work of many hands, which earns my keeping
With no small profit daily to my owners.
But come what will, my deadliest foe will prove
My speediest friend, by death to rid me hence,
The worst that he can give, to me the best.

1265 Yet so it may fall out, because their end
Is hate, not help to me, it may with mine
Draw their own ruin who attempt the deed.
Chorus. O how comely it is and how reviving
To the spirits of just men long oppressed!

1270 When God into the hands of their deliverer
Puts invincible might
To quell the mighty of the earth, th' oppressor,
The brute and boist'rous force of violent men
Hardy and industrious to support

1275 Tyrannic power, but raging to pursue
The righteous and all such as honour truth;
He all their ammunition
And feats of war defeats
With plain heroic magnitude of mind

1280 And celestial vigour armed;
Their armouries and magazines contemns,
Renders them useless, while
With winged expedition

Swift as the lightning glance he executes
1285 His errand on the wicked, who surprised
Lose their defence distracted and amazed.
    But patience is more oft the exercise
Of saints, the trial of their fortitude,
Making them each his own deliverer,
1290 And victor over all
That tyranny or fortune can inflict;
Either of these is in thy lot,
Samson, with might endued
Above the sons of men; but sight bereaved
1295 May chance to number thee with those
Whom patience finally must crown.
This idol's day hath been to thee no day of rest,
   Labouring thy mind
More than the working day thy hands,
1300 And yet perhaps more trouble is behind.
For I descry this way
Some other tending, in his hand
A sceptre or quaint staff he bears,
Comes on amain, speed in his look.
1305 By his habit I discern him now
A public officer, and now at hand.
His message will be short and voluble.
Officer. Hebrews, the pris'ner Samson here I seek.
Chorus. His manacles remark him, there he sits.
1310 *Officer.* Samson, to thee our lords thus bid me say;
This day to Dagon is a solemn feast,
With sacrifices, triumph, pomp, and games;
Thy strength they know surpassing human rate,
And now some public proof thereof require
1315 To honour this great feast, and great assembly;
Rise therefore with all speed and come along,
Where I will see thee heartened and fresh clad,
To appear as fit before th' illustrious lords.
Samson. Thou know'st I am an Hebrew, therefore tell
    them,
1320 Our Law forbids at their religious rites
My presence; for that cause I cannot come.

Officer. This answer, be assured, will not content them.
Samson. Have they not sword-players, and every sort
Of gymnic artists, wrestlers, riders, runners,
1325   Jugglers and dancers, antics, mummers, mimics,
But they must pick me out with shackles tired,
And over-laboured at their public mill,
To make them sport with blind activity?
Do they not seek occasion of new quarrels
1330   On my refusal to distress me more,
Or make a game of my calamities?
Return the way thou cam'st, I will not come.
Officer. Regard thyself, this will offend them highly.
Samson. Myself? my conscience and internal peace.
1335   Can they think me so broken, so debased
With corporal servitude, that my mind ever
Will condescend to such absurd commands?
Although their drudge, to be their fool or jester,
And in my midst of sorrow and heart-grief
1340   To show them feats, and play before their god,
The worst of all indignities, yet on me
Joined with extreme contempt? I will not come.
Officer. My message was imposed on me with speed,
Brooks no delay: is this thy resolution?
1345   *Samson.* So take it with what speed thy message needs.
Officer. I am sorry what this stoutness will produce.
Samson. Perhaps thou shalt have cause to sorrow indeed.
Chorus. Consider, Samson; matters now are strained
Up to the heighth, whether to hold or break;
1350   He's gone, and who knows how he may report
Thy words by adding fuel to the flame?
Expect another message more imperious,
More lordly thund'ring than thou well wilt bear.
Samson. Shall I abuse this consecrated gift
1355   Of strength, again returning with my hair
After my great transgression, so requite
Favour renewed, and add a greater sin
By prostituting holy things to idols;
A Nazarite in place abominable
1360   Vaunting my strength in honour to their Dagon?

Besides, how vile, contemptible, ridiculous,
What act more execrably unclean, profane?
Chorus. Yet with this strength thou serv'st the Philistines,
Idolatrous, uncircumcised, unclean.
1365 *Samson.* Not in their idol-worship, but by labour
Honest and lawful to deserve my food
Of those who have me in their civil power.
Chorus. Where the heart joins not, outward acts defile not.
Samson. Where outward force constrains, the sentence
holds;
1370 But who constrains me to the temple of Dagon,
Not dragging? the Philistian lords command.
Commands are no constraints. If I obey them,
I do it freely; venturing to displease
God for the fear of man, and man prefer,
1375 Set God behind: which in his jealousy
Shall never, unrepented, find forgiveness.
Yet that he may dispense with me or thee
Present in temples at idolatrous rites
For some important cause, thou need'st not doubt.
1380 *Chorus.* How thou wilt here come off surmounts my reach.
Samson. Be of good courage, I begin to feel
Some rousing motions in me which dispose
To something extraordinary my thoughts.
I with this messenger will go along,
1385 Nothing to do, be sure, that may dishonour
Our Law, or stain my vow of Nazarite.
If there be aught of presage in the mind,
This day will be remarkable in my life
By some great act, or of my days the last.
1390 *Chorus.* In time thou hast resolved, the man returns.
Officer. Samson, this second message from our lords
To thee I am bid say. Art thou our slave,
Our captive, at the public mill our drudge,
And dar'st thou at our sending and command
1395 Dispute thy coming? Come without delay;
Or we shall find such engines to assail
And hamper thee, as thou shalt come of force,
Though thou wert firmlier fastened than a rock.

Samson. I could be well content to try their art,
1400   Which to no few of them would prove pernicious.
Yet knowing their advantages too many,
Because they shall not trail me through their streets
Like a wild beast, I am content to go.
Masters' commands come with a power resistless
1405   To such as owe them absolute subjection;
And for a life who will not change his purpose?
(So mutable are all the ways of men)
Yet this be sure, in nothing to comply
Scandalous or forbidden in our Law.
1410   *Officer.* I praise thy resolution; doff these links:
By this compliance thou wilt win the lords
To favour, and perhaps to set thee free.
Samson. Brethren farewell, your company along
I will not wish, lest it perhaps offend them
1415   To see me girt with friends; and how the sight
Of me as of a common enemy,
So dreaded once, may now exasperate them
I know not. Lords are lordliest in their wine;
And the well-feasted priest then soonest fired
1420   With zeal, if aught religion seem concerned:
No less the people on their holy-days
Impetuous, insolent, unquenchable;
Happen what may, of me expect to hear
Nothing dishonourable, impure, unworthy
1425   Our God, our Law, my nation, or myself;
The last of me or no I cannot warrant.
Chorus. Go, and the Holy One
Of Israel be thy guide
To what may serve his glory best, and spread his name
1430   Great among the heathen round:
Send thee the angel of thy birth, to stand
Fast by thy side, who from thy father's field
Rode up in flames after his message told
Of thy conception, and be now a shield
1435   Of fire; that Spirit that first rushed on thee
In the camp of Dan
Be efficacious in thee now at need.

For never was from Heaven imparted
Measure of strength so great to mortal seed,
1440   As in thy wond'rous actions hath been seen.
But wherefore comes old Mánoa in such haste
With youthful steps? much livelier than erewhile
He seems: supposing here to find his son,
Or of him bringing to us some glad news?
1445   *Manoa.* Peace with you brethren; my inducement hither
Was not at present here to find my son,
By order of the lords new parted hence
To come and play before them at their feast.
I heard all as I came; the city rings,
1450   And numbers thither flock; I had no will,
Lest I should see him forced to things unseemly.
But that which moved my coming now, was chiefly
To give ye part with me what hope I have
With good success to work his liberty.
1455   *Chorus.* That hope would much rejoice us to partake
With thee; say reverend sire, we thirst to hear.
Manoa. I have attempted one by one the lords
Either at home, or through the street passing,
With supplication prone and father's tears
1460   To accept of ransom for my son their prisoner;
Some much averse I found and wondrous harsh,
Contemptuous, proud, set on revenge and spite;
That part most reverenced Dagon and his priests;
Others more moderate seeming, but their aim
1465   Private reward, for which both God and state
They easily would set to sale; a third
More generous far and civil, who confessed
They had enough revenged, having reduced
Their foe to misery beneath their fears,
1470   The rest was magnanimity to remit,
If some convenient ransom were proposed.
What noise or shout was that? it tore the sky.
Chorus. Doubtless the people shouting to behold
Their once great dread, captive, and blind before them,
1475   Or at some proof of strength before them shown.
Manoa. His ransom, if my whole inheritance

May compass it, shall willingly be paid
And numbered down: much rather I shall choose
To live the poorest in my tribe, than richest,
1480 And he in that calamitous prison left.
No, I am fixed not to part hence without him.
For his redemption all my patrimony,
If need be, I am ready to forgo
And quit: not wanting him, I shall want nothing.
1485 *Chorus.* Fathers are wont to lay up for their sons,
Thou for thy son art bent to lay out all;
Sons wont to nurse their parents in old age,
Thou in old age car'st how to nurse thy son.
Made older than thy age through eyesight lost.
1490 *Manoa.* It shall be my delight to tend his eyes,
And view him sitting in the house, ennobled
With all those high explóits by him achieved,
And on his shoulders waving down those locks,
That of a nation armed the strength contained:
1495 And I persuade me God had not permitted
His strength again to grow up with his hair
Garrisoned round about him like a camp
Of faithful soldiery, were not his purpose
To use him further yet in some great service,
1500 Not to sit idle with so great a gift
Useless, and thence ridiculous about him.
And since his strength with eyesight was not lost,
God will restore him eyesight to his strength.
Chorus. Thy hopes are not ill-founded nor seem vain
1505 Of his delivery, and thy joy thereon
Conceived, agreeable to a father's love,
In both which we, as next, participate.
Manoa. I know your friendly minds and – O what noise!
Mercy of Heav'n what hideous noise was that!
1510 Horribly loud unlike the former shout.
Chorus. Noise call you it or universal groan
As if the whole inhabitation perished;
Blood, death, and dreadful deeds are in that noise,
Ruin, destruction at the utmost point.
1515 *Manoa.* Of ruin indeed methought I heard the noise,

O it continues, they have slain my son.
Chorus. Thy son is rather slaying them; that outcry
From slaughter of one foe could not ascend.
Manoa. Some dismal accident it needs must be;
1520   What shall we do, stay here or run and see?
Chorus. Best keep together here, lest running thither
We unawares run into danger's mouth.
This evil on the Philistines is fall'n,
From whom could else a general cry be heard?
1525   The sufferers then will scarce molest us here;
From other hands we need not much to fear.
What if his eyesight (for to Israel's God
Nothing is hard) by miracle restored,
He now be dealing dole among his foes,
1530   And over heaps of slaughtered walk his way?
Manoa. That were a joy presumptuous to be thought.
Chorus. Yet God hath wrought things as incredible
For his people of old; what hinders now?
Manoa. He can I know, but doubt to think he will;
1535   Yet hope would fain subscribe, and tempts belief.
A little stay will bring some notice hither.
Chorus. Of good or bad so great, of bad the sooner;
For evil news rides post, while good news baits.
And to our wish I see one hither speeding,
1540   An Hebrew, as I guess, and of our tribe.
Messenger. O whither shall I run, or which way fly
The sight of this so horrid spectacle
Which erst my eyes beheld and yet behold;
For dire imagination still pursues me.
1545   But providence or instinct of nature seems,
Or reason though disturbed, and scarce consulted,
To have guided me aright, I know not how,
To thee first reverend Mánoa, and to these
My countrymen, whom here I knew remaining,
1550   As at some distance from the place of horror,
So in the sad event too much concerned.
Manoa. The accident was loud, and here before thee
With rueful cry, yet what it was we hear not;
No preface needs, thou seest we long to know.

1555   *Messenger.* It would burst forth, but I recover breath
       And sense distract, to know well what I utter.
       Manoa. Tell us the sum, the circumstance defer.
       Messenger. Gaza yet stands, but all her sons are fall'n,
       All in a moment overwhelmed and fall'n.
1560   *Manoa.* Sad, but thou know'st to Israelites not saddest
       The desolation of a hostile city.
       Messenger. Feed on that first, there may in grief be surfeit.
       Manoa. Relate by whom.
       Messenger.   By Samson.
       Manoa.   That still lessens
       The sorrow, and converts it nigh to joy.
1565   *Messenger.* Ah Mánoa I refrain, too suddenly
       To utter what will come at last too soon;
       Lest evil tidings with too rude irruption
       Hitting thy agèd ear should pierce too deep.
       Manoa. Suspense in news is torture, speak them out.
1570   *Messenger.* Then take the worst in brief, Samson is dead.
       Manoa. The worst indeed, O all my hope's defeated
       To free him hence! but death who sets all free
       Hath paid his ransom now and full discharge.
       What windy joy this day had I conceived
1575   Hopeful of his delivery, which now proves
       Abortive as the first-born bloom of spring
       Nipped with the lagging rear of winter's frost.
       Yet ere I give the reins to grief, say first,
       How died he? death to life is crown or shame.
1580   All by him fell thou say'st; by whom fell he,
       What glorious hand gave Samson his death's wound?
       Messenger. Unwounded of his enemies he fell.
       Manoa. Wearied with slaughter then or how? explain.
       Messenger. By his own hands.
       Manoa.   Self-violence? what cause
1585   Brought him so soon at variance with himself
       Among his foes?
       Messenger.   Inevitable cause
       At once both to destroy and be destroyed;
       The edifice where all were met to see him
       Upon their heads and on his own he pulled.

1590 *Manoa.* O lastly overstrong against thyself!
      A dreadful way thou took'st to thy revenge.
      More than enough we know; but while things yet
      Are in confusion, give us if thou canst,
      Eye-witness of what first or last was done,
1595 Relation more particular and distinct.
      Messenger. Occasions drew me early to this city,
      And as the gates I entered with sun-rise,
      The morning trumpets festival proclaimed
      Through each high street; little I had dispatched
1600 When all abroad was rumoured that this day
      Samson should be brought forth to show the people
      Proof of his mighty strength in feats and games;
      I sorrowed at his captive state, but minded
      Not to be absent at that spectacle.
1605 The building was a spacious theatre
      Half round on two main pillars vaulted high,
      With seats where all the lords and each degree
      Of sort, might sit in order to behold;
      The other side was open, where the throng
1610 On banks and scaffolds under sky might stand;
      I among these aloof obscurely stood.
      The feast and noon grew high, and sacrifice
      Had filled their hearts with mirth, high cheer, and wine,
      When to their sports they turned. Immediately
1615 Was Samson as a public servant brought,
      In their state livery clad; before him pipes
      And timbrels; on each side went armèd guards,
      Both horse and foot before him and behind,
      Archers, and slingers, cataphracts and spears.
1620 At sight of him the people with a shout
      Rifted the air clamouring their god with praise,
      Who had made their dreadful enemy their thrall.
      He patient but undaunted where they led him,
      Came to the place, and what was set before him
1625 Which without help of eye might be assayed,
      To heave, pull, draw, or break, he still performed
      All with incredible, stupendious force,
      None daring to appear antagonist.

At length for intermission sake they led him
1630 Between the pillars; he his guide requested
(For so from such as nearer stood we heard)
As over-tired to let him lean a while
With both his arms on those two massy pillars
That to the archèd roof gave main support.
1635 He unsuspicious led him; which when Samson
Felt in his arms, with head a while inclined,
And eyes fast fixed he stood, as one who prayed,
Or some great matter in his mind revolved.
At last with head erect thus cried aloud,
1640 Hitherto, lords, what your commands imposed
I have performed, as reason was, obeying,
Not without wonder or delight beheld.
Now of my own accord such other trial
I mean to show you of my strength, yet greater;
1645 As with amaze shall strike all who behold.
This uttered, straining all his nerves he bowed;
As with the force of winds and waters pent,
When mountains tremble, those two massy pillars
With horrible convulsion to and fro,
1650 He tugged, he shook, till down they came and drew
The whole roof after them, with burst of thunder
Upon the heads of all who sat beneath,
Lords, ladies, captains, counsellors, or priests,
Their choice nobility and flower, not only
1655 Of this but each Philistian city round
Met from all parts to solemnize this feast.
Samson with these immixed, inevitably
Pulled down the same destruction on himself;
The vulgar only 'scaped who stood without.
1660 *Chorus.* O dearly-bought revenge, yet glorious!
Living or dying thou hast fulfilled
The work for which thou wast foretold
To Israel, and now li'st victorious
Among thy slain self-killed,
1665 Not willingly, but tangled in the fold
Of dire Necessity, whose law in death conjoined
Thee with thy slaughtered foes in number more

Than all thy life had slain before.
Semichorus. While their hearts were jocund and sublime,
1670 Drunk with idolatry, drunk with wine,
And fat regorged of bulls and goats,
Chanting their idol, and preferring
Before our living Dread who dwells
In Silo his bright sanctuary:
1675 Among them he a spirit of frenzy sent,
Who hurt their minds,
And urged them on with mad desire
To call in haste for their destroyer;
They only set on sport and play
1680 Unweetingly importuned
Their own destruction to come speedily upon them.
So fond are mortal men
Fall'n into wrath divine,
As their own ruin on themselves to invite,
1685 Insensate left, or to sense reprobate,
And with blindness internal struck.
Semichorus. But he though blind of sight,
Despised and thought extinguished quite,
With inward eyes illuminated,
1690 His fiery virtue roused
From under ashes into sudden flame,
And as an evening dragon came,
Assailant on the perchèd roosts,
And nests in order ranged
1695 Of tame villatic fowl; but as an eagle
His cloudless thunder bolted on their heads.
So virtue giv'n for lost,
Depressed, and overthrown, as seemed,
Like that self-begotten bird
1700 In the Arabian woods embossed,
That no second knows nor third,
And lay erewhile a holocaust,
From out her ashy womb now teemed,
Revives, reflourishes, then vigorous most
1705 When most unactive deemed,
And though her body die, her fame survives,

A secular bird ages of lives.
Manoa. Come, come, no time for lamentation now,
Nor much more cause; Samson hath quit himself
1710 Like Samson, and heroically hath finished
A life heroic, on his enemies
Fully revenged, hath left them years of mourning,
And lamentation to the sons of Caphtor
Through all Philistian bounds. To Israel
1715 Honour hath left, and freedom, let but them
Find courage to lay hold on this occasion;
To himself and father's house eternal fame;
And which is best and happiest yet, all this
With God not parted from him, as was feared,
1720 But favouring and assisting to the end.
Nothing is here for tears, nothing to wail
Or knock the breast, no weakness, no contempt,
Dispraise, or blame, nothing but well and fair
And what may quiet us in a death so noble.
1725 Let us go find the body where it lies
Soaked in his enemies' blood, and from the stream
With lavers pure and cleansing herbs wash off
The clotted gore. I with what speed the while
(Gaza is not in plight to say us nay)
1730 Will send for all my kindred, all my friends,
To fetch him hence and solemnly attend
With silent obsequy and funeral train
Home to his father's house: there will I build him
A monument, and plant it round with shade
1735 Of laurel ever green, and branching palm,
With all his trophies hung, and acts enrolled
In copious legend, or sweet lyric song.
Thither shall all the valiant youth resort,
And from his memory inflame their breasts
1740 To matchless valour, and adventures high:
The virgins also shall on feastful days
Visit his tomb with flowers, only bewailing
His lot unfortunate in nuptial choice,
From whence captivity and loss of eyes.
1745 *Chorus.* All is best, though we oft doubt,

What th' unsearchable dispose
Of highest wisdom brings about,
And ever best found in the close.
Oft he seems to hide his face,
1750   But unexpectedly returns
And to his faithful champion hath in place
Bore witness gloriously; whence Gaza mourns
And all that band them to resist
His uncontrollable intent;
1755   His servants he with new acquist
Of true experience from this great event
With peace and consolation hath dismissed,
And calm of mind all passion spent.

THE LATIN AND GREEK POEMS

ELEGIARUM LIBER

Elegia Prima ad Carolum Diodatum

Tandem, care, tuae mihi pervenere tabellae,
    Pertulit et voces nuntia charta tuas,
Pertulit occidua Devae Cestrensis ab ora
    Vergivium prono qua petit amne salum.
5 Multum, crede, iuvat terras aluisse remotas
    Pectus amans nostri, tamque fidele caput,
Quodque mihi lepidum tellus longinqua sodalem
    Debet, at unde brevi reddere iussa velit.
Me tenet urbs reflua quam Thamesis alluit unda,
10   Meque nec invitum patria dulcis habet.
Iam nec arundiferum mihi cura revisere Camum,
    Nec dudum vetiti me laris angit amor.
Nuda nec arva placent, umbrasque negantia molles;
    Quam male Phoebicolis convenit ille locus!
15 Nec duri libet usque minas perferre magistri
    Caeteraque ingenio non subeunda meo.
Si sit hoc exilium, patrios adiisse penates,
    Et vacuum curis otia grata sequi,
Non ego vel profugi nomen sortemve recuso,
20   Laetus et exilii conditione fruor.
O utinam vates nunquam graviora tulisset
    Ille Tomitano flebilis exul agro;
Non tunc Ionio quicquam cessisset Homero
    Neve foret victo laus tibi prima Maro.
25 Tempora nam licet hic placidis dare libera Musis,
    Et totum rapiunt me mea vita libri.
Excipit hinc fessum sinuosi pompa theatri,
    Et vocat ad plausus garrula scena suos.

Seu catus auditur senior, seu prodigus haeres,
30   Seu procus, aut posita casside miles adest,
Sive decennali fecundus lite patronus
    Detonat inculto barbara verba foro,
Saepe vafer gnato succurrit servus amanti,
    Et nasum rigidi fallit ubique patris;
35 Saepe novos illic virgo mirata calores
    Quid sit amor nescit, dum quoque nescit, amat.
Sive cruentatum furiosa Tragoedia sceptrum
    Quassat, et effusis crinibus ora rotat;
Et dolet, et specto, iuvat et spectasse dolendo;
40   Interdum et lacrimis dulcis amaror inest:
Seu puer infelix indelibata reliquit
    Gaudia, et abrupto flendus amore cadit;
Seu ferus e tenebris iterat Styga criminis ultor,
    Conscia funereo pectora torre movens;
45 Seu maeret Pelopeia domus, seu nobilis Ili,
    Aut luit incestos aula Creontis avos.
Sed neque sub tecto semper nec in urbe latemus,
    Irrita nec nobis tempora veris eunt.
Nos quoque lucus habet vicina consitus ulmo
50   Atque suburbani nobilis umbra loci.
Saepius hic blandas spirantia sidera flammas
    Virgineos videas praeteriisse choros.
Ah quoties dignae stupui miracula formae
    Quae possit senium vel reparare Iovis;
55 Ah quoties vidi superantia lumina gemmas,
    Atque faces quotquot volvit uterque polus;
Collaque bis vivi Pelopis quae brachia vincant,
    Quaeque fluit puro nectare tincta via,
Et decus eximium frontis, tremulosque capillos,
60   Aurea quae fallax retia tendit Amor;
Pellacesque genas, ad quas hyacinthina sordet
    Purpura, et ipse tui floris, Adoni, rubor.
Cedite laudatae toties Heroides olim,
    Et quaecunque vagum cepit amica Iovem.
65 Cedite Achaemeniae turrita fronte puellae,
    Et quot Susa colunt, Memnoniamque Ninon.
Vos etiam Danaae fasces submittite Nymphae,

Et vos Iliacae, Romuleaeque nurus;
Nec Pompeianas Tarpeia Musa columnas
70   Iactet, et Ausoniis plena theatra stolis.
Gloria virginibus debetur prima Britannis;
      Extera sat tibi sit femina posse sequi.
Tuque urbs Dardaniis Londinum structa colonis
      Turrigerum late conspicienda caput,
75   Tu nimium felix intra tua moenia claudis
      Quicquid formosi pendulus orbis habet.
Non tibi tot caelo scintillant astra sereno
      Endymioneae turba ministra deae,
Quot tibi conspicuae formaque auroque puellae
80   Per medias radiant turba videnda vias.
Creditur huc geminis venisse invecta columbis
      Alma pharetrigero milite cincta Venus,
Huic Cnidon, et riguas Simoentis flumine valles,
      Huic Paphon, et roseam posthabitura Cypron.
85   Ast ego, dum pueri sinit indulgentia caeci,
      Moenia quam subito linquere fausta paro;
Et vitare procul malefidae infamia Circes
      Atria, divini Molyos usus ope.
Stat quoque iuncosas Cami remeare paludes,
90   Atque iterum raucae murmur adire Scholae.
Interea fidi parvum cape munus amici,
      Paucaque in alternos verba coacta modos.

Elegy I

TO CHARLES DIODATI

At last, dear friend, your letter has reached me. The paper messenger has carried your words from the western bank of Chester's river Dee, where it rushes down to the Vergivian Sea.⁴ I am delighted, believe me, that distant lands have bred a heart so loving towards me, and a mind so true, and that a remote region owes me a charming companion, and is ready to repay the debt soon, at my bidding.

I am now in the city washed by the tides of the Thames, staying, not unwillingly, in my delightful birthplace. At present I do not care to revisit the reedy Cam; I do not yearn for my rooms, recently forbidden to me. Bare fields devoid of pleasant shade do not please me. How ill that place suits the votaries of Phoebus!¹⁴ Nor is it pleasing constantly to have to put up with the threats of a stern tutor,[15] and other things besides that my spirit cannot bear. If this be exile – to have returned to my father's home, where I am free of care and can enjoy delightful leisure – then I reject neither the name nor the lot of an outlaw, but gladly accept the terms of my banishment. Ah, if only that poet[21] who was a sad exile in the land of Tomis had had no worse sufferings than this to bear! Then he would have yielded nothing to Ionian Homer,[23] and you, O vanquished Maro,[24] would have been stripped of the prime glory.

For here I am permitted to devote my spare hours to the gentle Muses, and books (which are my whole life) completely carry me away. When I am tired, the splendour of the round theatre[27] draws me out, and the babbling stage invites my applause. Sometimes I listen to a crafty old man, sometimes a spendthrift heir; sometimes a suitor appears, or a soldier with doffed helm. Sometimes a lawyer, grown rich on a ten-year-old case, thunders out his barbarous jargon to an uncouth court. Often a cunning slave comes to the aid of a love-struck son, and cheats the stern father at every turn – right under his nose. There, often, a virgin girl, marvelling at the strange fire within her, does not know what love is, and loves without knowing it.

Sometimes raging Tragedy brandishes her bloodstained sceptre,[37] with dishevelled hair and rolling eyes. The sight pains me, but I look, and there is pleasure in the pain. Sometimes there is a sweet bitterness even in tears: as when an unfortunate youth leaves joys untasted, and is torn from his love to perish and be mourned; or when a cruel avenger of crime returns from the shades across the Styx, tormenting guilty souls with a deadly torch; or when the house of Pelops or of noble Ilus[45] mourns, or Creon's palace atones for incestuous forebears.[46]

But I am not always confined under a roof, or in the city. Springtime does not pass me by in vain. I also frequent a dense grove of elms nearby, and a glorious shady spot just outside the city. Here you may often see groups of maidens passing by – stars breathing out seductive flames. Ah, how often have I been stunned by the miraculous grace of a figure that might rejuvenate the feeble old age of Jove himself! Ah, how often have I seen eyes brighter than jewels or all the heavenly fires that wheel about the celestial poles; necks which outshine the shoulders of twice-living Pelops[57] or that [Milky] Way steeped in pure nectar; a brow of surpassing loveliness, and flowing tresses (golden nets spread by deceitful Cupid), and alluring cheeks beside which the crimson hyacinth, and even your rosy flower,[62] Adonis, seem paltry. Give way, you heroines[63] so often praised of old, and every mistress who captivated inconstant Jove. Give way, you Achaemenian[65] girls with turreted foreheads, and all who dwell in Susa or Memnonian Nineveh.[66] You also, Danaan[67] nymphs, and you of Troy and Rome, submit. Let not the Tarpeian Muse[69] boast of Pompey's colonnade, or the theatre thronged with Ausonian[70] robes. The prime glory belongs to British maidens; it is enough for you foreign women that you may follow after. And you, London, city built by Dardanian[73] colonists, conspicuous on all sides with your towered head, you (happy beyond measure) enclose within your walls whatever beauty the pendulous globe of the earth contains. The stars that shine from a clear sky – that multitude of handmaidens about Endymion's goddess[78] – are not so numerous as the shining girls that are seen in your streets, radiant with beauty and with gold. It is said that bountiful Venus came here, drawn by her twin doves and attended by her quiver-bearing troops, preferring this place to Cnidos and the valleys watered by Simois, to Paphos and rosy Cyprus.[84]

But as for me, I intend to leave these fortunate walls as soon as possible, while the blind boy's[85] indulgence permits, and with the help of divine Moly[88] to fly far from the infamous halls of faithless Circe. It is also decided that I shall go back to the reedy fens of the Cam, back to the hoarse roar of the University. Meanwhile, accept the small gift of a loyal friend, these few words constrained into alternate measures.[92]

Elegia Secunda

Anno aetatis 17

IN OBITUM PRAECONIS ACADEMICI CANTABRIGIENSIS

Te, qui conspicuus baculo fulgente solebas
   Palladium toties ore ciere gregem,
Ultima praeconum praeconem te quoque saeva
   Mors rapit, officio nec favet ipsa suo.
5 Candidiora licet fuerint tibi tempora plumis
   Sub quibus accipimus delituisse Iovem,
O dignus tamen Haemonio iuvenescere succo,
   Dignus in Aesonios vivere posse dies,
Dignus quem Stygiis medica revocaret ab undis
10   Arte Coronides, saepe rogante dea.
Tu si iussus eras acies accire togatas,
   Et celer a Phoebo nuntius ire tuo,
Talis in Iliaca stabat Cyllenius aula
   Alipes, aetherea missus ab arce patris.
15 Talis et Eurybates ante ora furentis Achillei
   Rettulit Atridae iussa severa ducis.
Magna sepulcrorum regina, satelles Averni
   Saeva nimis Musis, Palladi saeva nimis,
Quin illos rapias qui pondus inutile terrae?
20   Turba quidem est telis ista petenda tuis.
Vestibus hunc igitur pullis Academia luge,
   Et madeant lacrimis nigra feretra tuis.
Fundat et ipsa modos querebunda Elegeia tristes,
   Personet et totis naenia moesta scholis.

Elegy II
At the Age of Seventeen
ON THE DEATH OF THE CAMBRIDGE UNIVERSITY BEADLE
Conspicuous with your shining mace,[1] you were wont to summon
the flock of Pallas[2] with your call; but (beadle though you were)
fierce Death, the last beadle, has seized you, showing no favour to
her own office. Although your brows were whiter than the plumage

in which Jove is fabled to have disguised himself,[6] yet you deserved
to be made young again with Haemonian drugs,[7] deserved to relive
your life, like Aeson; you deserved to be called back from the waters
of the Styx by the healing art of Coronides,[10] at the persistent bidding
of the goddess. If your Phoebus[12] commanded you to go as a swift
messenger and summon the gowned battalions, you were like wing-
footed Cyllenius,[13] when he was sent from the heavenly heights of
his father, and stood in the palace of Troy. You were like Eurybates[15]
when in the face of furious Achilles he delivered the stern command
of his lord, Atrides.

Great queen[17] of sepulchres, companion of Avernus, too cruel to
the Muses, too cruel to Pallas, why don't you carry off those who
are a useless burden on the earth? That is the crowd at which to aim
your darts. Mourn this man, therefore, O dark-robed University.
May his black hearse be wet with your tears. May wailing Elegy
herself pour forth sad measures, and the melancholy dirge resound
through all the schools.

Elegia Tertia

Anno aetatis 17

IN OBITUM PRAESULIS WINTONIENSIS

Moestus eram, et tacitus nullo comitante sedebam,
    Haerebantque animo tristia plura meo,
Protinus en subiit funestae cladis imago
    Fecit in Angliaco quam Libitina solo;
5 Dum procerum ingressa est splendentes marmore turres
    Dira sepulcrali mors metuenda face;
Pulsavitque auro gravidos et iaspide muros,
    Nec metuit satrapum sternere falce greges.
Tunc memini clarique ducis, fratrisque verendi
10 Intempestivis ossa cremata rogis.
Et memini heroum quos vidit ad aethera raptos,
    Flevit et amissos Belgia tota duces.
At te praecipue luxi, dignissime praesul,

Wintoniaeque olim gloria magna tuae;
15 Delicui fletu, et tristi sic ore querebar,
      Mors fera, Tartareo diva secunda Iovi,
Nonne satis quod silva tuas persentiat iras,
      Et quod in herbosos ius tibi detur agros,
Quodque afflata tuo marcescant lilia tabo,
20   Et crocus, et pulchrae Cypridi sacra rosa?
Nec sinis ut semper fluvio contermina quercus
      Miretur lapsus praetereuntis aquae.
Et tibi succumbit liquido quae plurima caelo
      Evehitur pennis quamlibet augur avis,
25 Et quae mille nigris errant animalia silvis,
      Et quod alunt mutum Proteos antra pecus.
Invida, tanta tibi cum sit concessa potestas,
      Quid iuvat humana tingere caede manus?
Nobileque in pectus certas acuisse sagittas,
30   Semideamque animam sede fugasse sua?
Talia dum lacrimans alto sub pectore volvo,
      Roscidus occiduis Hesperus exit aquis,
Et Tartessiaco submerserat aequore currum
      Phoebus, ab eöo littore mensus iter.
35 Nec mora, membra cavo posui refovenda cubili;
      Condiderant oculos noxque soporque meos,
Cum mihi visus eram lato spatiarier agro;
      Heu nequit ingenium visa referre meum.
Illic punicea radiabant omnia luce,
40   Ut matutino cum iuga sole rubent.
Ac veluti cum pandit opes Thaumantia proles,
      Vestitu nituit multicolore solum.
Non dea tam variis ornavit floribus hortos
      Alcinoi, Zephyro Chloris amata levi.
45 Flumina vernantes lambunt argentea campos,
      Ditior Hesperio flavet arena Tago.
Serpit odoriferas per opes levis aura Favoni,
      Aura sub innumeris humida nata rosis.
Talis in extremis terrae Gangetidis oris
50   Luciferi regis fingitur esse domus.
Ipse racemiferis dum densas vitibus umbras
      Et pellucentes miror ubique locos,

Ecce mihi subito praesul Wintonius astat,
    Sidereum nitido fulsit in ore iubar;
55 Vestis ad auratos defluxit candida talos,
    Infula divinum cinxerat alba caput.
Dumque senex tali incedit venerandus amictu,
    Intremuit laeto florea terra sono.
Agmina gemmatis plaudunt caelestia pennis,
60   Pura triumphali personat aethra tuba.
Quisque novum amplexu comitem cantuque salutat,
    Hosque aliquis placido misit ab ore sonos:
Nate veni, et patrii felix cape gaudia regni;
    Semper ab hinc duro, nate, labore vaca.
65 Dixit, et aligerae tetigerunt nablia turmae,
    At mihi cum tenebris aurea pulsa quies.
Flebam turbatos Cephaleia pellice somnos;
    Talia contingant somnia saepe mihi.

Elegy III
At the Age of Seventeen
ON THE DEATH OF THE BISHOP OF WINCHESTER

Full of grief, I sat silent and alone, my mind gripped by many
sorrows, when lo! a vision suddenly arose of the deadly pestilence
that Libitina[4] brought to English soil, while grim Death – fearful
with her sepulchral torch – entered the gleaming marble palaces of
the nobility, beat upon massive walls of gold and jasper, and did not
shrink from mowing down troops of nobles with her scythe. Then
I remembered that famous leader and his revered brother,[9] whose
bones were burned on untimely fires; and I remembered the heroes
whom all Belgia[12] saw carried off to Heaven, the lost leaders whom
she mourned. But above all I mourned for you, most worthy Bishop,
once the great glory of your Winchester. I melted with tears, and
thus complained with sad speech: 'Fierce Death, goddess second to
Tartarean Jove,[16] is it not enough that the forest feels your rage, and
that you are given power over the grassy fields, and that the lily, the
crocus, and the rose sacred to beautiful Cypris[20] all wither before
your putrid breath? Is it not enough that you forbid the oak on the
river-bank to look forever on the water flowing by it? The multitude
of birds that glide on their wings through the bright air submit to
you, despite their gift of prophecy, and so do the thousand beasts

that wander in dark forests, and the silent herd that feeds in the caves of Proteus.[26] Envious goddess, when so much power has been granted to you, what pleasure can there be in staining your hands with human blood? What pleasure is there in sharpening arrows to pierce a noble breast, and driving a half-divine soul from its home?'

As I wept and pondered these things deep in my heart, dewy Hesperus[32] arose from the western waves. Phoebus, having completed his journey from the eastern shore, had sunk his chariot in the Tartessian sea.[33] I promptly lay down on my hollow bed to find repose. Night and sleep had closed my eyes, when it seemed to me that I was walking in a broad field. Alas! I lack the skill to report what I saw. There everything glowed with a reddish light, as when mountain tops blush in the morning sun. The earth shone, attired with many colours, as when the daughter of Thaumas[41] displays her riches. Chloris,[44] the goddess loved by mild Zephyrus, did not adorn the gardens of Alcinous with flowers so various. Silver streams washed the verdant meadows, and their sands gleamed a richer gold than those of Hesperian Tagus.[46] A gentle breeze of Favonius[47] stole through the fragrant opulence: a dewy breath born under innumerable roses. Such is the fabled home of royal Lucifer[50] on the furthest shores of the land of the Ganges. As I marvelled at the dense shadows under the clustering vines and the shining spaces all around me, lo! the Bishop of Winchester suddenly stood beside me. A starry radiance beamed from his shining face,[54] a white robe flowed down to his golden feet, and a white fillet encircled his divine head. While the revered old man stepped forward, dressed in this way, the flowery earth trembled with a joyful sound. The celestial multitude clapped their jewelled wings and the clear air resounded to the blast of a triumphal trumpet. All greeted their new companion with singing and an embrace, and one spoke these words with gentle lips: 'Come, my son, receive in joy the blessings of your Father's kingdom and henceforth rest forever from your hard labours.'[64] He spoke, and the winged squadrons touched their harps. But my golden rest was driven away with the darkness, and I wept for the sleep which Cephalus' paramour[67] had broken. May such dreams often befall me![68]

Elegia Quarta

Anno aetatis 18

AD THOMAM IUNIUM, PRAECEPTOREM SUUM, APUD
MERCATORES ANGLICOS HAMBURGAE AGENTES, PASTORIS
MUNERE FUNGENTEM

Curre per immensum subito mea littera pontum;
    I, pete Teutonicos laeve per aequor agros;
Segnes rumpe moras, et nil, precor, obstet eunti,
    Et festinantis nil remoretur iter.
5 Ipse ego Sicanio frenantem carcere ventos
    Aeolon, et virides sollicitabo deos,
Caeruleamque suis comitatam Dorida nymphis,
    Ut tibi dent placidam per sua regna viam.
At tu, si poteris, celeres tibi sume iugales,
10 Vecta quibus Colchis fugit ab ore viri;
Aut queis Triptolemus Scythicas devenit in oras,
    Gratus Eleusina missus ab urbe puer.
Atque ubi Germanas flavere videbis arenas,
    Ditis ad Hamburgae moenia flecte gradum,
15 Dicitur occiso quae ducere nomen ab Hama,
    Cimbrica quem fertur clava dedisse neci.
Vivit ibi antiquae clarus pietatis honore
    Praesul Christicolas pascere doctus oves;
Ille quidem est animae plusquam pars altera nostrae,
20 Dimidio vitae vivere cogor ego.
Hei mihi quot pelagi, quot montes interiecti
    Me faciunt alia parte carere mei!
Charior ille mihi quam tu doctissime Graium
    Cliniadi, pronepos qui Telamonis erat;
25 Quamque Stagirites generoso magnus alumno,
    Quem peperit Libyco Chaonis alma Iovi.
Qualis Amyntorides, qualis Philyreius heros
    Myrmidonum regi, talis et ille mihi.
Primus ego Aonios illo praeeunte recessus
30 Lustrabam, et bifidi sacra vireta iugi;

Pieriosque hausi latices, Clioque favente,
    Castalio sparsi laeta ter ora mero.
Flammeus at signum ter viderat arietis Aethon,
    Induxitque auro lanea terga novo,
35 Bisque novo terram sparsisti Chlori senilem
    Gramine, bisque tuas abstulit Auster opes:
Necdum eius licuit mihi lumina pascere vultu,
    Aut linguae dulces aure bibisse sonos.
Vade igitur, cursuque Eurum praeverte sonorum;
40   Quam sit opus monitis res docet, ipsa vides.
Invenies dulci cum coniuge forte sedentem,
    Mulcentem gremio pignora chara suo,
Forsitan aut veterum praelarga volumina patrum
    Versantem, aut veri biblia sacra Dei;
45 Caelestive animas saturantem rore tenellas,
    Grande salutiferae religionis opus.
Utque solet, multam sit dicere cura salutem,
    Dicere quam decuit, si modo adesset, herum.
Haec quoque paulum oculos in humum defixa modestos,
50   Verba verecundo sis memor ore loqui:
Haec tibi, si teneris vacat inter praelia Musis
    Mittit ab Angliaco littore fida manus.
Accipe sinceram, quamvis sit sera, salutem;
    Fiat et hoc ipso gratior illa tibi.
55 Sera quidem, sed vera fuit, quam casta recepit
    Icaris a lento Penelopeia viro.
Ast ego quid volui manifestum tollere crimen,
    Ipse quod ex omni parte levare nequit?
Arguitur tardus merito, noxamque fatetur,
60   Et pudet officium deseruisse suum.
Tu modo da veniam fasso, veniamque roganti;
    Crimina diminui, quae patuere, solent.
Non ferus in pavidos rictus diducit hiantes,
    Vulnifico pronos nec rapit ungue leo.
65 Saepe sarissiferi crudelia pectora Thracis
    Supplicis ad moestas delicuere preces.
Extensaeque manus avertunt fulminis ictus,
    Placat et iratos hostia parva deos.
Iamque diu scripsisse tibi fuit impetus illi,

70   Neve moras ultra ducere passus Amor.
        Nam vaga Fama refert, heu nuntia vera malorum!
            In tibi finitimis bella tumere locis,
        Teque tuamque urbem truculento milite cingi,
            Et iam Saxonicos arma parasse duces.
75   Te circum late campos populatur Enyo,
            Et sata carne virum iam cruor arva rigat.
        Germanisque suum concessit Thracia Martem;
            Illuc Odrysios Mars pater egit equos.
        Perpetuoque comans iam deflorescit oliva,
80   Fugit et aerisonam diva perosa tubam,
        Fugit io terris, et iam non ultima virgo
            Creditur ad superas iusta volasse domos.
        Te tamen interea belli circumsonat horror,
            Vivis et ignoto solus inopsque solo;
85   Et, tibi quam patrii non exhibuere penates,
            Sede peregrina quaeris egenus opem.
        Patria, dura parens, et saxis saevior albis
            Spumea quae pulsat littoris unda tui,
        Siccine te decet innocuos exponere foetus,
90   Siccine in externam ferrea cogis humum,
        Et sinis ut terris quaerant alimenta remotis
            Quos tibi prospiciens miserat ipse Deus,
        Et qui laeta ferunt de caelo nuntia, quique
            Quae via post cineres ducat ad astra, docent?
95   Digna quidem Stygiis quae vivas clausa tenebris,
            Aeternaque animae digna perire fame!
        Haud aliter vates terrae Thesbitidis olim
            Pressit inassueto devia tesqua pede,
        Desertasque Arabum salebras, dum regis Achabi
100   Effugit atque tuas, Sidoni dira, manus.
        Talis et horrisono laceratus membra flagello,
            Paulus ab Aemathia pellitur urbe Cilix;
        Piscosaeque ipsum Gergessae civis Iesum
            Finibus ingratus iussit abire suis.
105   At tu sume animos, nec spes cadat anxia curis
            Nec tua concutiat decolor ossa metus.
        Sis etenim quamvis fulgentibus obsitus armis,
            Intententque tibi millia tela necem,

At nullis vel inerme latus violabitur armis,
110   Deque tuo cuspis nulla cruore bibet.
Namque eris ipse Dei radiante sub aegide tutus;
    Ille tibi custos, et pugil ille tibi;
Ille Sionaeae qui tot sub moenibus arcis
    Assyrios fudit nocte silente viros;
115 Inque fugam vertit quos in Samaritidas oras
    Misit ab antiquis prisca Damascus agris,
Terruit et densas pavido cum rege cohortes,
    Aere dum vacuo buccina clara sonat,
Cornea pulvereum dum verberat ungula campum,
120   Currus arenosam dum quatit actus humum,
Auditurque hinnitus equorum ad bella ruentum,
    Et strepitus ferri, murmuraque alta virum.
Et tu (quod superest miseris) sperare memento,
    Et tua magnanimo pectore vince mala.
125 Nec dubites quandoque frui melioribus annis,
    Atque iterum patrios posse videre lares.

Elegy IV
At the Age of Eighteen
TO THOMAS YOUNG, HIS TUTOR, NOW PERFORMING THE OFFICE
OF CHAPLAIN AMONG THE ENGLISH MERCHANTS IN HAMBURG
Run swiftly across the boundless deep, my letter.[1] Go, seek the
Teutonic lands over the smooth surface of the sea. Break off sluggish
delays and let nothing, I entreat you, stand in the way of your going,
nothing detain the speed of your journey. I myself shall implore
Aeolus, who restrains the winds in his Sicilian prison, and the
sea-green gods, and sea-blue Doris[7] with her retinue of nymphs, to
give you peaceful passage through their realms. And you, if you can,
get hold of that swift team that the Colchian[10] drove when she fled
from her husband's face, or that with which young Triptolemus[11]
reached the shores of Scythia, a welcome messenger from the city
of Eleusis. And when you see Germany's golden sands, turn your
steps to the walls of prosperous Hamburg, which is said to derive
its name from Hama,[15] who was slain (so they say) with a Danish
club. A pastor lives there, renowned for his veneration of the primitive
faith, and well-instructed in the art of feeding Christ's sheep. Truly
that man is more than the other half of my soul,[19] and without him

I am forced to live a life divided in two. Alas, how many seas, how many mountains are thrust between us to deprive me of my other self! He is dearer to me than you, O wisest of the Greeks,[23] were to Cliniades, scion of Telamon; dearer than the great Stagirite[25] was to his noble pupil, whom the bountiful woman of Chaonia[26] bore to Libyan Jove. What the son of Amyntor and what Philyra's heroic son were to the king of the Myrmidons,[28] such is this man to me. Guided by him, I first wandered the Aonian retreats and the sacred glades of the twin-peaked mountain.[30] There I drank of the Pierian waters and, favoured by Clio,[31] I thrice wet my joyful lips with Castalian wine. But flaming Aethon[33] has thrice looked upon the sign of the Ram, arraying his fleecy back with fresh gold, and you, Chloris, have twice strewn the old earth with new grass, and Auster[36] has twice carried your wealth away, since last my eyes were permitted to feast upon his countenance, or my ears to drink in the sweet strains of his voice.

Go, then, and outstrip howling Eurus[39] in your journey. Circumstances declare, and you yourself can see, how necessary it is for me to urge you on. You will find him sitting perhaps with his sweet wife, fondling on his lap the pledges of their love; or perhaps turning over the copious volumes of the old Fathers, or the Holy Bible of the true God, or feeding delicate souls with heavenly dew – which is the great work of healing religion. Be sure to give him a warm greeting, as the custom is, and to speak as would befit your master, if only he could be there. Then, fixing your bashful eyes on the ground, remember to speak these words with respectful lips: 'These verses a faithful hand sends to you from the shores of England – if there is leisure for the gentle Muses in the midst of battles.[51] Accept this sincere greeting, though it be late, and let it be the more welcome to you for that very reason. Late indeed, but true, was that greeting that chaste Penelope, Icarius' daughter, received from her tardy husband.[56] But why should I wish to deny a manifest fault, which the offender himself can in no way mitigate? He is justly accused of tardiness, he confesses his crime, and he is ashamed to have failed in his duty. Only grant pardon to one who confesses and asks your forgiveness; for offences frankly acknowledged are wont to be lessened. The wild beast does not open gaping jaws upon terrified prey; the lion does not rend the fallen with death-dealing claw. The merciless heart of the pike-bearing Thracian has often melted at a suppliant's tearful entreaties. Outstretched hands avert the thunder-bolt, and a small sacrifice placates the angry gods.

He has long felt the urge to write to you, and now Love has not suffered any further delays. For wandering Rumour – a truthful messenger of evils, alas! – reports that wars are about to burst out in lands bordering upon you, that you and your city are surrounded by ferocious soldiers, and that the Saxon leaders[74] have already prepared their munitions of war. All around you Enyo[75] is laying the land to waste, and blood is watering fields sown with human flesh. Thrace has given up her Mars to the Germans; thither father Mars has driven his Odrysian[78] horses. The ever-flourishing olive now withers, and the goddess[80] who abhors the brazen trumpet has fled – look! she has fled from the earth – and it is believed that the virgin of Justice[82] was not the last to fly to a home in the heavens. But you, meanwhile, live alone and helpless in an alien land, where the horror of war sounds all around you. Impoverished, you seek in foreign parts the sustenance that your ancestral homeland denied you. O native land, stern parent, harder than the white cliffs beaten by the foaming waves of your shore, does it become you to expose your innocent children in this way? O heart of iron, do you thus drive them onto alien soil, and do you suffer them to seek their sustenance in foreign lands – men sent to you by God himself in his Providence, men who bring you glad tidings from Heaven, and who teach you the way that leads beyond death to the stars? You indeed deserve to live shut up in Stygian darkness and to perish by everlasting hunger of the soul! In just this way the Tishbite prophet[97] with unaccustomed foot once trod remote wastelands and the rugged deserts of Arabia, when he fled King Ahab's hands, and your hands, vile woman of Sidon. In this way Cilician Paul was driven out from the Emathian city, his flesh torn by the hissing scourge;[102] and the ungrateful people of fishy Gergessa commanded Jesus himself to depart out of their coasts.[104]

But take courage. Do not let anxious hope succumb to care and do not let pale fear send a shudder through your bones. For although you are surrounded by gleaming weapons, and a thousand missiles threaten you with death, yet no weapon shall wound your defenceless side, no spear shall drink your blood. For you shall be safe under the bright shield of God. He will be your defender, he will be your champion – he who in the silent night vanquished so many Assyrian soldiers under the walls of Zion's citadel;[114] who turned to flight those whom old Damascus sent from her ancient domain against the borders of Samaria. He terrified their close-packed cohorts and their trembling king, when the clear trumpet sounded in empty air, the horny hoof beat the dusty plain, the hard-driven chariot shook the sandy earth, and there was heard the neighing of horses charging into battle, the clashing of steel, and the loud roar of men.[122]

And you, remember to hope. Hope remains yet for the wretched. Vanquish misfortune with your great-souled spirit. Doubt not that some day you will enjoy better years and will again be able to see your native land.'

Elegia Quinta

Anno aetatis 20

IN ADVENTUM VERIS

In se perpetuo Tempus revolubile gyro
    Iam revocat Zephyros vere tepente, novos.
Induiturque brevem Tellus reparata iuventam,
    Iamque soluta gelu dulce virescit humus.
5 Fallor? an et nobis redeunt in carmina vires,
    Ingeniumque mihi munere veris adest?
Munere veris adest, iterumque vigescit ab illo
    (Quis putet?) atque aliquod iam sibi poscit opus.
Castalis ante oculos, bifidumque cacumen oberrat,
10 Et mihi Pirenen somnia nocte ferunt.
Concitaque arcano fervent mihi pectora motu,
    Et furor, et sonitus me sacer intus agit.
Delius ipse venit, video Peneide lauro
    Implicitos crines, Delius ipse venit.
15 Iam mihi mens liquidi raptatur in ardua coeli,
    Perque vagas nubes corpore liber eo.
Perque umbras, perque antra feror, penetralia vatum,
    Et mihi fana patent interiora deum.
Intuiturque animus toto quid agatur Olympo,

20   Nec fugiunt oculos Tartara caeca meos.
      Quid tam grande sonat distento spiritus ore?
        Quid parit haec rabies, quid sacer iste furor?
      Ver mihi, quod dedit ingenium, cantabitur illo;
        Profuerint isto reddita dona modo.
25   Iam, Philomela, tuos foliis adoperta novellis
        Instituis modulos, dum silet omne nemus.
      Urbe ego, tu silva, simul incipiamus utrique,
        Et simul adventum veris uterque canat.
      Veris io rediere vices; celebremus honores
30   Veris, et hoc subeat Musa perennis opus.
      Iam sol Aethiopas fugiens Tithoniaque arva,
        Flectit ad Arctoas aurea lora plagas.
      Est breve noctis iter, brevis est mora noctis opacae,
        Horrida cum tenebris exulat illa suis.
35   Iamque Lycaonius plaustrum caeleste Boötes
        Non longa sequitur fessus ut ante via;
      Nunc etiam solitas circum Iovis atria toto
        Excubias agitant sidera rara polo.
      Nam dolus, et caedes, et vis cum nocte recessit,
40   Neve Giganteum dii timuere scelus.
      Forte aliquis scopuli recubans in vertice pastor,
        Roscida cum primo sole rubescit humus,
      Hac, ait, hac certe caruisti nocte puella
        Phoebe tua, celeres quae retineret equos.
45   Laeta suas repetit silvas, pharetramque resumit
        Cynthia, Luciferas ut videt alta rotas,
      Et tenues ponens radios gaudere videtur
        Officium fieri tam breve fratris ope.
      Desere, Phoebus ait, thalamos Aurora seniles;
50   Quid iuvat effoeto procubuisse toro?
      Te manet Aeolides viridi venator in herba,
        Surge, tuos ignes altus Hymettus habet.
      Flava verecundo dea crimen in ore fatetur,
        Et matutinos ocius urget equos.
55   Exuit invisam Tellus rediviva senectam,
        Et cupit amplexus Phoebe subire tuos;
      Et cupit, et digna est, quid enim formosius illa,
        Pandit ut omniferos luxuriosa sinus,

Atque Arabum spirat messes, et ab ore venusto
60   Mitia cum Paphiis fundit amoma rosis.
Ecce coronatur sacro frons ardua luco,
        Cingit ut Idaeam pinea turris Opim;
Et vario madidos intexit flore capillos,
        Floribus et visa est posse placere suis.
65   Floribus effusos ut erat redimita capillos,
        Taenario placuit diva Sicana deo.
Aspice Phoebe tibi faciles hortantur amores,
        Mellitasque movent flamina verna preces.
Cinnamea Zephyrus leve plaudit odorifer ala,
70   Blanditiasque tibi ferre videntur aves.
Nec sine dote tuos temeraria quaerit amores
        Terra, nec optatos poscit egena toros;
Alma salutiferum medicos tibi gramen in usus
        Praebet, et hinc titulos adiuvat ipsa tuos.
75   Quod si te pretium, si te fulgentia tangunt
        Munera (muneribus saepe coemptus Amor)
Illa tibi ostentat quascunque sub aequore vasto,
        Et superiniectis montibus abdit opes.
Ah quoties cum tu clivoso fessus Olympo
80   In vespertinas praecipitaris aquas,
Cur te, inquit, cursu languentem Phoebe diurno
        Hesperiis recipit caerula mater aquis?
Quid tibi cum Tethy? Quid cum Tartesside lympha?
        Dia quid immundo perluis ora salo?
85   Frigora Phoebe mea melius captabis in umbra;
        Huc ades, ardentes imbue rore comas.
Mollior egelida veniet tibi somnus in herba;
        Huc ades, et gremio lumina pone meo.
Quaque iaces circum mulcebit lene susurrans
90   Aura per humentes corpora fusa rosas.
Nec me (crede mihi) terrent Semeleia fata,
        Nec Phaetonteo fumidus axis equo;
Cum tu Phoebe tuo sapientius uteris igni,
        Huc ades, et gremio lumina pone meo.
95   Sic Tellus lasciva suos suspirat amores;
        Matris in exemplum caetera turba ruunt.
Nunc etenim toto currit vagus orbe Cupido,

Languentesque fovet solis ab igne faces.
Insonuere novis lethalia cornua nervis,
100   Triste micant ferro tela corusca novo.
Iamque vel invictam tentat superasse Dianam,
Quaeque sedet sacro Vesta pudica foco.
Ipsa senescentem reparat Venus annua formam,
Atque iterum tepido creditur orta mari.
105   Marmoreas iuvenes clamant *Hymenaee* per urbes;
Litus *io Hymen*, et cava saxa sonant.
Cultior ille venit tunicaque decentior apta;
Puniceum redolet vestis odora crocum.
Egrediturque frequens ad amoeni gaudia veris
110   Virgineos auro cincta puella sinus.
Votum est cuique suum, votum est tamen omnibus unum,
Ut sibi quem cupiat det Cytherea virum.
Nunc quoque septena modulatur arundine pastor,
Et sua quae iungat carmina Phyllis habet.
115   Navita nocturno placat sua sidera cantu,
Delphinasque leves ad vada summa vocat.
Iupiter ipse alto cum coniuge ludit Olympo,
Convocat et famulos ad sua festa deos.
Nunc etiam Satyri, cum sera crepuscula surgunt,
120   Pervolitant celeri florea rura choro,
Sylvanusque sua cyparissi fronde revinctus,
Semicaperque deus, semideusque caper.
Quaeque sub arboribus Dryades latucre vetustis
Per iuga, per solos expatiantur agros.
125   Per sata luxuriat fruticetaque Maenalius Pan,
Vix Cybcle mater, vix sibi tuta Ceres;
Atque aliquam cupidus praedatur Oreada Faunus,
Consulit in trepidos dum sibi nympha pedes,
Iamque latet, latitansque cupit male tecta videri,
130   Et fugit, et fugiens pervelit ipsa capi.
Dii quoque non dubitant caelo praeponere silvas,
Et sua quisque sibi numina lucus habet.
Et sua quisque diu sibi numina lucus habeto,
Nec vos arborea dii precor ite domo.
135   Te referant miseris te Iupiter aurea terris
Saecla! Quid ad nimbos aspera tela redis?

Tu saltem lente rapidos age Phoebe iugales
   Qua potes, et sensim tempora veris eant.
Brumaque productas tarde ferat hispida noctes,
140   Ingruat et nostro serior umbra polo.

Elegy V
At the Age of Twenty
ON THE COMING OF SPRING

Now, as spring grows warm, Time, revolving in its never-ending cycle, calls back the fresh zephyrs. Earth, revived, decks herself in her brief youth, and the soil, released from icy coldness, turns delightfully green. Am I deceived, or are my powers of song also returning, and has inspiration come to me as a gift of the spring? As a gift of the spring it has come, and again it begins to bloom (who would have thought it?) and now it demands some task for itself. The Castalian spring and the twin-peaked mountain[9] hover before my eyes, and by night dreams bring Pirene[10] to me. My heart burns, stirred by a secret impulse, and I am driven on by inspired frenzy and the divine sound within me. The Delian himself is coming – I see his hair garlanded with Daphne's laurel[13] – the Delian himself is coming. Now my mind is rapt to the heights of the clear, transparent sky and, free of the body, I pass through the wandering clouds. Through shadows I am borne, and through caves, the secret places of the poets, and the still more secret sanctuaries of the gods lie open before me. My spirit perceives all that is done on Olympus, and the secret things of Tartarus do not flee from my sight. What sublime song does my spirit pour forth from parted lips? What is this madness, this divine frenzy, bringing to birth? Spring, which gave me inspiration, shall be praised by the song she inspired; so shall the gifts bring profit to the giver.

Now, Philomela,[25] hidden among newly-opened leaves, you begin your melodious song, while all the grove is still. I in the city, you in the forest, let us both begin together, and both together sing the coming of spring. Look! Springtime is here again! Let us sing the praises of spring, and let the Muse take up her perennial[30] task. Now the sun, fleeing from the Ethiopians and Tithonus' fields,[31] turns his golden reins to northern regions. Short is night's journey, short her dark lingering; frightful night is banished with her gloom. And now Lycaonian[35] Boötes does not follow a long and weary course behind the celestial Wain, as he once did. Now even the stars are sparsely scattered throughout the heavens as they hold their accustomed vigil around the halls of Jove. For fraud, murder, and violence vanish with the night, and the gods fear no evil deed from the Giants.[40] Perhaps some shepherd, reclining on a craggy summit while the dewy earth grows red beneath the first rays of the sun, says: 'This night, Phoebus, this night you surely must have gone without a girl to delay your swift horses!' When from on high Cynthia[46] sees the Lightbringer's chariot, she joyfully returns to her woods, takes up her quiver and, laying her pale beams aside, seems to be glad that her brother's help has shortened her own task. 'Aurora,' Phoebus exclaims, 'leave that old man's bedchamber. What joy is it to lie in a bed of impotence?[50] The hunter Aeolides[51] is waiting for you on the green grass. Get up! Your flame awaits you on lofty Hymettus.' With blushing face, the golden-haired goddess acknowledges her fault, and urges the horses of the dawn into a gallop.

Earth, reviving, casts off her hated old age, and yearns, Phoebus, to be received in your embraces. She yearns for them, and she is worthy of them, for what is more beautiful than she when she voluptuously bares her all-sustaining breasts, breathes out Arabian spice-harvests, and pours balsam and Paphian[60] roses from her lovely lips? Look, her lofty brow is crowned with a sacred grove, as Idaean Ops is garlanded with a turret of pines.[62] She binds her dewy locks with many-coloured flowers and, with her flowers, seems fit to attract her lover as when the Sicanian goddess,[66] her flowing hair garlanded with flowers, attracted the Taenarian god. Look, Phoebus, willing loves call to you, and spring breezes inspire honey-sweet entreaties. Fragrant Zephyrus gently fans his cinnamon-scented wings and the birds seem to offer you their blandishments. Earth is not so rash as to seek your love without offering you a dowry, and it is not as a pauper that she begs the longed-for nuptials. She bountifully provides you with health-giving herbs for medicine and so contributes to your renown. If a reward, if glittering gifts can touch your heart (love is often bought with gifts), she spreads before you all the wealth that she keeps hidden away under the vast deep and beneath the piled mountains. Ah, how often when you plunge into western waters, wearied in your descent from the steep heavens, she cries: 'Why, Phoebus, when you are fatigued after your daily journey, should the azure mother receive you in her Hesperian waves? What have you to do with Tethys?[83] What is the Tartessian flood to you? Why do you bathe your divine face in putrid brine? You will do better to seek coolness in my shade, Phoebus; come here and douse your fiery locks in dew. A sweeter sleep will come over you in the cool grass; come here and lay your glories in my lap. Around where you lie, a gently whispering breeze will caress our bodies, stretched out on dewy roses. Believe me, I am not afraid of Semele's fate,[91] or of the smoking axle of Phaethon's chariot.[92] You will use your fires more wisely, Phoebus, when you come here and lay your glories in my lap.'

Thus lascivious Earth sighs out her passionate longing, and the throng of other creatures rush to follow the Mother's example. For wandering Cupid now runs over the whole world, and rekindles his dying torch in the sun's fire. His lethal bow resounds with new strings, and his glittering arrows, tipped with new steel, have a threatening gleam. And now he tries to conquer even unconquerable Diana,[101] and chaste Vesta,[102] who sits by the sacred hearth. Venus herself restores her ageing beauty with the yearly cycle, and looks as if she has risen anew from the warm sea.[104] Young men cry *Hymenaee* through marble cities; *io Hymen*[106] echoes from the shore and hollow rocks. Hymen himself appears in splendid attire, becomingly dressed in the appropriate tunic; his fragrant robe exhales the scent of crimson saffron. Troops of maidens, their virgin breasts girdled with gold, come forth to enjoy the delights of spring. Each has her own prayer, but the prayers are all the same: that Cytherea[112] may grant her the husband of her desire.

Now the shepherd plays on his seven-reed pipe, and Phyllis[114] accompanies his music with her singing. The sailor propitiates the stars with his nightly song and summons nimble dolphins to the surface of the sea.[116] Jupiter himself dallies with his wife on high Olympus and calls even the menial gods to his feast. And now, as evening twilight comes on, a troop of dancing Satyrs flits through the flowery meadows, and with them comes Sylvanus, crowned with his chaplet of cypress leaves, a god half-goat, a goat half-god.[122] The Dryads who hide beneath ancient trees now wander abroad over mountains and the deserted, open country. Maenalian Pan[125] runs riot over sown fields and thickets; mother Cybele and Ceres[126] are hardly safe from him. Lustful Faunus[127] seizes one of the Oreads, while the Nymph seeks safety on trembling feet. Now she hides, but hiding, ill-concealed, she wishes to be seen; she flees, but fleeing yearns to be caught. The gods themselves unhesitatingly prefer the woods to heaven, and each grove has its own deity.

And long may each grove have its own deity! I entreat you, gods, do not forsake your home among the trees. May the Golden Age draw you back to the wretched earth, Jupiter! Why go back to your cruel weapons in the clouds? You, Phoebus, at least drive your swift team as lazily as you can, and let springtime pass slowly. May hideous winter be slow in bringing back its prolonged nights, and may it be later in the day when darkness invades our sky.

Elegia Sexta

AD CAROLUM DIODATUM, RURI COMMORANTEM

Qui cum idibus Decemb. scripsisset, et sua carmina excusari postulasset si solito minus essent bona, quod inter lautitias quibus erat ab amicis exceptus, haud satis felicem operam Musis dare se posse affirmabat, hunc habuit responsum.

Mitto tibi sanam non pleno ventre salutem,
    Qua tu distento forte carere potes.
At tua quid nostram prolectat Musa Camenam,
    Nec sinit optatas posse sequi tenebras?
5 Carmine scire velis quam te redamemque colamque,
    Crede mihi vix hoc carmine scire queas,
Nam neque noster amor modulis includitur arctis,
    Nec venit ad claudos integer ipse pedes.
Quam bene solennes epulas, hilaremque Decembrim,
10   Festaque coelifugam quae coluere Deum,
Deliciasque refers, hiberni gaudia ruris,
    Haustaque per lepidos Gallica musta focos.
Quid quereris refugam vino dapibusque poesin?
    Carmen amat Bacchum, carmina Bacchus amat.
15 Nec puduit Phoebum virides gestasse corymbos,
    Atque hederam lauro praeposuisse suae.
Saepius Aoniis clamavit collibus *Euoe*

Mista Thyoneo turba novena choro.
Naso Corallaeis mala carmina misit ab agris;
20   Non illic epulae non sata vitis erat.
Quid nisi vina, rosasque racemiferumque Lyaeum
     Cantavit brevibus Teia Musa modis?
Pindaricosque inflat numeros Teumesius Euan,
     Et redolet sumptum pagina quaeque merum;
25 Dum gravis everso currus crepat axe supinus,
     Et volat Eleo pulvere fuscus eques.
Quadrimoque madens lyricen Romanus Iaccho
     Dulce canit Glyceran, flavicomamque Chloen.
Iam quoque lauta tibi generoso mensa paratu,
30 ·   Mentis alit vires, ingeniumque fovet.
Massica fecundam despumant pocula venam,
     Fundis et ex ipso condita metra cado.
Addimus his artes, fusumque per intima Phoebum
     Corda; favent uni Bacchus, Apollo, Ceres.
35 Scilicet haud mirum tam dulcia carmina per te
     Numine composito tres peperisse deos.
Nunc quoque Thressa tibi caelato barbitos auro
     Insonat arguta molliter icta manu;
Auditurque chelys suspensa tapetia circum,
40   Virgineos tremula quae regat arte pedes.
Illa tuas saltem teneant spectacula Musas,
     Et revocent, quantum crapula pellit iners.
Crede mihi dum psallit ebur comitataque plectrum
     Implet odoratos festa chorea tholos,
45 Percipies tacitum per pectora serpere Phoebum,
     Quale repentinus permeat ossa calor;
Perque puellares oculos digitumque sonantem
     Irruet in totos lapsa Thalia sinus.
Namque elegia levis multorum cura deorum est,
50   Et vocat ad numeros quemlibet illa suos;
Liber adest elegis, Eratoque, Ceresque, Venusque,
     Et cum purpurea matre tenellus Amor.
Talibus inde licent convivia larga poetis,
     Saepius et veteri commaduisse mero.
55 At qui bella refert, et adulto sub Iove caelum,
     Heroasque pios, semideosque duces,

Et nunc sancta canit superum consulta deorum,
    Nunc latrata fero regna profunda cane,
Ille quidem parce Samii pro more magistri
60   Vivat, et innocuos praebeat herba cibos;
Stet prope fagineo pellucida lympha catillo,
    Sobriaque e puro pocula fonte bibat.
Additur huic scelerisque vacans et casta iuventus,
    Et rigidi mores, et sine labe manus.
65 Qualis veste nitens sacra et lustralibus undis
    Surgis ad infensos augur iture deos.
Hoc ritu vixisse ferunt post rapta sagacem
    Lumina Tiresian, Ogygiumque Linon,
Et lare devoto profugum Calchanta, senemque
70   Orpheon edomitis sola per antra feris;
Sic dapis exiguus, sic rivi potor Homerus
    Dulichium vexit per freta longa virum,
Et per monstrificam Perseiae Phoebados aulam,
    Et vada femineis insidiosa sonis,
75 Perque tuas, rex ime, domos, ubi sanguine nigro
    Dicitur umbrarum detinuisse greges.
Diis etenim sacer est vates, divumque sacerdos,
    Spirat et occultum pectus, et ora Iovem.
At tu si quid agam scitabere (si modo saltem
80   Esse putas tanti noscere siquid agam)
Paciferum canimus caelesti semine regem,
    Faustaque sacratis saecula pacta libris,
Vagitumque Dei, et stabulantem paupere tecto
    Qui suprema suo cum patre regna colit.
85 Stelliparumque polum, modulantesque aethere turmas,
    Et subito elisos ad sua fana deos.
Dona quidem dedimus Christi natalibus illa;
    Illa sub auroram lux mihi prima tulit.
Te quoque pressa manent patriis meditata cicutis;
90   Tu mihi, cui recitem, iudicis instar eris.

Elegy VI

TO CHARLES DIODATI, STAYING IN THE COUNTRY

Diodati had written on 13 December and asked that his poems be excused if they were less good than usual. Owing to the lavish entertainment his friends had given him, he could not, he said, pay proper service to the Muses. This was the answer he received.

I, who have no full stomach, wish you the good health that you, with your stuffed one, might need. But why does your Muse entice my one out, and not permit her to seek the obscurity she desires? It may be that you wish to learn from a poem how much I return your love, and cherish you. Believe me, you can hardly learn that from a poem, for my love cannot be confined in close-fitting metres and is too sound to come to you on the limping feet[8] of elegy.

How well you describe the seasonal feasts, the merriment of December, the festal days that do reverence to the heaven-descended God, the charms and delights of winter in the countryside, and the quaffing of French wines by the welcoming fireside. But why do you complain that poetry flees from wine and banqueting? Song loves Bacchus, and Bacchus loves song. Phoebus was not ashamed to wear green clusters and to set the ivy above his own laurel. Often the chorus of the Nine, mingled with Thyoneus' throng,[18] has raised the cry *Euoe* on the Aonian hills. The verses that Ovid sent from the land of the Coralli were bad because they had no banquets there, and did not cultivate the vine.[20] Of what but wine, roses, and cluster-bearing Lyaeus,[21] did the Teian poet[22] sing in his short verses? Teumesian Euan[23] inspired Pindar's odes, and every page diffuses the fragrance of the unmixed wine he has been drinking, as the heavy chariot crashes and is thrown backwards, axle overturned, and the driver speeds on, blackened with Olympian dust. The Roman lyrist[27] was drunk with four-year-old wine when he sang sweetly of Glycera and golden-haired Chloe. Now the sumptuous table with its rich fare strengthens *your* mind and warms *your* genius. Your goblets of Massic[31] wine foam with abundant genius, and from the wine-jar itself you pour out the carefully stored verses. To these we may add the arts, and Apollo's presence in your innermost heart; Bacchus, Apollo and Ceres are as one in showing favour to you. It is small wonder, to be sure, that the united divinity of three gods should have brought forth such sweet songs through you. Now the gold-chased Thracian lyre[37] is also sounding for you, under the gentle touch of a skilled hand; in tapestried halls you hear the lyre that with its trembling strings directs the maidens' dancing feet. Let these scenes, at any rate, hold your Muse's attention, and call back whatever powers sluggish inebriation drives away. Believe me, when the ivory key[43] resounds, and the dancing festive company pours into the perfumed halls, you will feel Apollo stealing silently into your heart like a sudden heat permeating the bones, and from the girls' eyes and music-making fingers Thalia[48] will flow into your whole breast.

For light elegy is cared for by many gods, and she calls whoever she wants to her measures; Bacchus attends elegy, and so do Erato[51] and Ceres, and Venus, and tender Cupid with his rosy mother. For such poets, then, lavish banquets are permissible and they may often get drunk on vintage wine. But the poet who sings of wars, of heaven ruled by mature Jove, of pious heroes and semi-divine princes, who sings now of the sacred councils of the high gods, now of the infernal realm and its fierce barking dog[58] – such a poet must indeed live frugally, after the fashion of the Samian master,[59] and herbs must supply his harmless diet. Let crystal-clear water stand beside him in a beechen bowl, and let him drink sober draughts from the pure spring. In addition, his youth must be chaste and free from wickedness, his morals strict and his hand without stain. He must be like you, augur-priest, when shining in your sacred vestments and holy water, you rise to go into the presence of the angry gods. By this rule, so they say, the wise Tiresias[68] lived after the loss of his sight, and Ogygian Linus, and Calchas, after he had fled his doomed home,[69] and aged Orpheus when he tamed the wild beasts in their lonely caves.[70] Thus sparing of food, thus drinking of the stream, Homer[71] conveyed Dulichian[72] Odysseus over wide seas – through the palace where the daughter of Phoebus and Perseis[73] turned men into monsters, past the shallows made treacherous by the Sirens' song, and through your courts, infernal king, where he is said to have detained troops of shades with an offering of black blood.[76] For the poet is sacred to the gods; he is their priest, and his innermost heart and his lips breathe out Jove.

But if you would know what I am doing (if indeed you think it worthwhile to know whether I am doing anything), I am singing the King born of heavenly seed, the bringer of peace, and the blessed

ages promised in the sacred books, the cries of the infant God, and
the stabling under a poor roof of him who dwells with his Father in
the realms above. I am singing the star-bearing sky, the hosts that
sang in the upper air, and the pagan gods suddenly shattered in their
own shrines. These are my birthday-gifts to Christ; the first light of
dawn brought them to me. For you too[89] these strains composed on
my native pipes are waiting; and you, when I recite them to you,
shall be the judge of their worth.

Elegia Septima

Anno aetatis undevigesimo

Nondum blanda tuas leges Amathusia noram,
    Et Paphio vacuum pectus ab igne fuit.
Saepe cupidineas, puerilia tela, sagittas,
    Atque tuum sprevi maxime numen, Amor.
5 Tu puer imbelles dixi transfige columbas;
    Conveniunt tenero mollia bella duci:
Aut de passeribus tumidos age, parve, triumphos;
    Haec sunt militiae digna trophaea tuae.
In genus humanum quid inania dirigis arma?
10 Non valet in fortes ista pharetra viros.
Non tulit hoc Cyprius (neque enim deus ullus ad iras
    Promptior) et duplici iam ferus igne calet.
Ver erat, et summae radians per culmina villae
    Attulerat primam lux tibi Maie diem:
15 At mihi adhuc refugam quaerebant lumina noctem,
    Nec matutinum sustinuere iubar.
Astat Amor lecto, pictis Amor impiger alis;
    Prodidit astantem mota pharetra deum;
Prodidit et facies, et dulce minantis ocelli,
20   Et quicquid puero dignum et Amore fuit.
Talis in aeterno iuvenis Sigeius Olympo
    Miscet amatori pocula plena Iovi;
Aut qui formosas pellexit ad oscula nymphas
    Thiodamantaeus naiade raptus Hylas;

25   Addideratque iras, sed et has decuisse putares,
          Addideratque truces, nec sine felle minas.
      Et miser exemplo sapuisses tutius, inquit;
          Nunc mea quid possit dextera testis eris.
      Inter et expertos vires numerabere nostras,
30   Et faciam vero per tua damna fidem.
      Ipso ego si nescis strato Pythone superbum
          Edomui Phoebum, cessit et ille mihi;
      Et quoties meminit Peneidos, ipse fatetur
          Certius et gravius tela nocere mea.
35   Me nequit adductum curvare peritius arcum,
          Qui post terga solet vincere Parthus eques.
      Cydoniusque mihi cedit venator, et ille
          Inscius uxori qui necis author erat.
      Est etiam nobis ingens quoque victus Orion,
40   Herculeaeque manus, Herculeusque comes.
      Iupiter ipse licet sua fulmina torqueat in me,
          Haerebunt lateri spicula nostra Iovis.
      Caetera quae dubitas melius mea tela docebunt,
          Et tua non leviter corda petenda mihi.
45   Nec te stulte tuae poterunt defendere Musae,
          Nec tibi Phoebaeus porriget anguis opem.
      Dixit, et aurato quatiens mucrone sagittam,
          Evolat in tepidos Cypridos ille sinus.
      At mihi risuro tonuit ferus ore minaci,
50   Et mihi de puero non metus ullus erat.
      Et modo qua nostri spatiantur in urbe Quirites,
          Et modo villarum proxima rura placent.
      Turba frequens, facieque simillima turba dearum,
          Splendida per medias itque reditque vias.
55   Auctaque luce dies gemino fulgore coruscat.
          Fallor? an et radios hinc quoque Phoebus habet?
      Haec ego non fugi spectacula grata severus,
          Impetus et quo me fert iuvenilis agor.
      Lumina luminibus male providus obvia misi,
60   Neve oculos potui continuisse meos.
      Unam forte aliis supereminuisse notabam;
          Principium nostri lux erat illa mali.
      Sic Venus optaret mortalibus ipsa videri,

Sic regina deum conspicienda fuit.
65 Hanc memor obiecit nobis malus ille Cupido
Solus et hos nobis texuit ante dolos.
Nec procul ipse vafer latuit, multaeque sagittae,
Et facis a tergo grande pependit onus.
Nec mora; nunc ciliis haesit, nunc virginis ori,
70 Insilit hinc labiis, insidet inde genis;
Et quascunque agilis partes iaculator oberrat,
Hei mihi, mille locis pectus inerme ferit.
Protinus insoliti subierunt corda furores;
Uror amans intus, flammaque totus eram.
75 Interea misero quae iam mihi sola placebat
Ablata est, oculis non reditura meis.
Ast ego progredior tacite querebundus, et excors,
Et dubius volui saepe referre pedem.
Findor; et haec remanet, sequitur pars altera votum;
80 Raptaque tam subito gaudia flere iuvat.
Sic dolet amissum proles Iunonia coelum,
Inter Lemniacos praecipitata focos.
Talis et abreptum solem respexit, ad Orcum
Vectus ab attonitis Amphiaraus equis.
85 Quid faciam infelix, et luctu victus? Amores
Nec licet inceptos ponere, neve sequi.
O utinam spectare semel mihi detur amatos
Vultus, et coram tristia verba loqui!
Forsitan et duro non est adamante creata,
90 Forte nec ad nostras surdeat illa preces.
Crede mihi nullus sic infeliciter arsit;
Ponar in exemplo primus et unus ego.
Parce precor teneri cum sis deus ales amoris;
Pugnent officio nec tua facta tuo.
95 Iam tuus O certe est mihi formidabilis arcus,
Nate dea, iaculis nec minus igne potens:
Et tua fumabunt nostris altaria donis,
Solus et in superis tu mihi summus eris.
Deme meos tandem, verum nec deme furores;
100 Nescio cur, miser est suaviter omnis amans:
Tu modo da facilis, posthaec mea siqua futura est,
Cuspis amaturos figat ut una duos.

Haec ego mente olim laeva, studioque supino
  Nequitiae posui vana trophaea meae.
Scilicet abreptum sic me malus impulit error,
  Indocilisque aetas prava magistra fuit.
5 Donec Socraticos umbrosa Academia rivos
  Praebuit, admissum dedocuitque iugum.
Protinus extinctis ex illo tempore flammis,
  Cincta rigent multo pectora nostra gelu.
Unde suis frigus metuit puer ipse sagittis,
10 Et Diomedeam vim timet ipsa Venus.

Elegy VII
At the Age of 19 [18?]

I was not yet acquainted with your laws, lovely Amathusia,[1] and my heart was free from Paphian[2] fire. Often I scorned Cupid's arrows as childish weapons, and most of all, Love, I scorned your divinity. 'Boy,' I said, 'go and shoot the unwarlike doves. Soft battles befit the tender warrior. Or go and win high triumphs over the sparrows, little lad. These are the trophies your martial spirit deserves. Why aim your feeble weapons at mankind? That quiver of yours has no power against strong men.' The Cyprian lad[11] could not suffer this (for no god is swifter to anger), and now the fierce boy burned with double fire.

It was spring, and the first light of dawn, shining over the high gables of the farmhouse had ushered in May Day. But my eyes still sought the retreating night, and could not endure the brilliance of dawn. Love stood beside my bed, unwearied Love with painted wings; his swinging quiver betrayed the standing god. His face betrayed him too, and his sweetly threatening eyes, and everything else befitting the boy Love. Thus the Sigeian youth[21] appears when he mixes brimming cups for amorous Jove on eternal Olympus; thus appeared Hylas,[24] Theodamas' son, who drew the lovely nymphs to his kisses and was carried off by a naiad. Cupid was angry (but you would have thought his anger only made him more becoming), and he uttered stern threats, full of bitterness.

'Wretch,' he said, 'you might have learned wisdom more safely from the example of others. Now you will witness for yourself what

my right hand can do. You shall be numbered among those who
have felt my strength, and by your punishment I shall assuredly
make men believe in me. It was I (in case you don't know) who
vanquished proud Phoebus after he had killed the Python.[31] Even
he yielded to me. And as often as he remembers Daphne, he confesses
that my arrows wound more surely and more gravely than his own.
The Parthian horseman,[36] who conquers by turning his back, cannot
bend the taut bow more skilfully than I. The Cydonian[37] hunter
yields first place to me, and so does he who unwittingly killed his
wife.[38] Huge Orion was conquered by me;[39] so were the hands of
Hercules,[40] and Hercules' companion too. Jove himself may hurl his
thunderbolts at me, but my darts will stick in Jove's side. As for the
rest of your doubts, they will be better taught by my arrows and by
your own heart, at which I must aim no gentle stroke. Fool! Your
Muses will not be able to protect you, nor will Phoebus' serpent[46]
offer you any cure.' Thus he spake and, shaking a golden-tipped
arrow,[47] flew away to the warm breast of his Cyprian mother. But I
was inclined to laugh at the threats that the fierce boy thundered at
me; I had no fear of him at all.

Sometimes I took my pleasure in the city, where our citizens walk
abroad, and sometimes in the country, with its outlying farmhouses.
A great crowd, a radiant crowd with faces just like goddesses, come
and go along the walks. The day shines doubly bright, augmented
with their splendour. Am I deceived, or does Phoebus also derive
his rays from them? I did not turn austerely aside from these pleasing
sights; I was carried along by the impulse of youth. Not foreseeing
the danger, I sent my eyes to meet their eyes; I was powerless to
hold back my gaze. By chance I caught sight of one who surpassed
all the others; that was the beginning of my woe. In such a form
Venus herself might choose to appear to mortals; in such a form the
queen of the gods[64] must have shown herself. Vengeful Cupid,
remembering his threat, threw her in my path; he alone wove these
nets for me. Not far off the cunning boy himself was lurking, with
many arrows and his huge torch weighing down on his back. Without
delay he fixed himself now in the maiden's eyelids, now in her face;
then he sprang upon her lips, then settled upon her cheeks. Wherever
the nimble archer flitted, alas for me, he hit my defenceless breast
in a thousand places. At once strange passions stole into my heart;
I burned inwardly with love, I was all one flame.

Meanwhile, she who alone could bring me happiness was swept away, never to be seen by me again. But I went on, silently lamenting, senseless and in doubt, often yearning to retrace my steps. I am torn in two: one half of me stays here, the other half follows my desire. There is pleasure in weeping for joys so suddenly snatched away. So Juno's son,[81] hurled down among the hearths of Lemnos, mourned for the heaven he had lost. So Amphiaraus[84] looked back at the vanishing sun when his horses, terrified by thunder, bore him down to hell. Wretched and grief-stricken, what should I do? I can neither subdue nor pursue this new feeling of love. O that I might be granted to look but once on those beloved features and to speak of my sorrows in her presence! Perhaps she is not made of unyielding adamant, perhaps she will not be deaf to my prayers. No one, surely, has ever suffered the fires of love so unhappily; I may be cited as the first and only example. Be merciful, I pray, since you are the winged god of tender love. Do not let your actions be at variance with your office. O son of the goddess, whose arrows are as potent as fire, now you may be sure that I dread your bow. Your altars will smoke with my offerings, and you alone will be supreme to me among the gods. Take away my madness, then – yet do not take it away. I know not why, but every lover finds his pain sweet. Only be gracious enough to grant, if any maiden is ever to be mine in the future, that one arrow may pierce us both, making us lovers.

————

[Epilogue to the Elegies]

These vain trophies of my wantonness I once set up with foolish purpose and lazy endeavour. It is clear that mischievous error led me astray and ignorant youth was a perverse teacher. Until at length the shady Academy[5] offered its Socratic streams, and taught me how to escape from the yoke to which I had submitted. From that moment the flames were extinguished, and thenceforward my heart has been rigid, surrounded with thick ice. Whence even the boy-god fears a frost for his arrows, and Venus herself dreads my Diomedean[10] strength.

In Proditionem Bombardicam

Cum simul in regem nuper satrapasque Britannos
   Ausus es infandum perfide Fauxe nefas,
Fallor? an et mitis voluisti ex parte videri,
   Et pensare mala cum pietate scelus?
5 Scilicet hos alti missurus ad atria caeli,
   Sulphureo curru flammivolisque rotis.
Qualiter ille feris caput inviolabile Parcis
   Liquit Iordanios turbine raptus agros.

On the Gunpowder Plot

Perfidious Fawkes, when, in recent years, you dared that unspeakable crime against the king and the British lords, did you – or am I deceived? – wish to appear merciful, in a way, and make recompense for your wickedness with evil piety? Clearly you wanted to send them to the courts of high heaven, in a sulphurous chariot with flaming wheels. In just this way, he[7] whose life the fierce Parcae could not cut was swept up from the fields of the Jordan in a whirlwind.

In eandem

Siccine tentasti caelo donasse Iacobum
   Quae septemgemino Belua monte lates?
Ni meliora tuum poterit dare munera numen,
   Parce precor donis insidiosa tuis.
5 Ille quidem sine te consortia serus adivit
   Astra, nec inferni pulveris usus ope.
Sic potius foedos in caelum pelle cucullos,
   Et quot habet brutos Roma profana deos,
Namque hac aut alia nisi quemque adiuveris arte,
10   Crede mihi caeli vix bene scandet iter.

On the same

So was this the way you tried to send James to heaven, you lurking Beast[2] on the seven hills? Unless your godhead can give better gifts, please spare us your deceitful presents. He has indeed now joined the fellowship of the stars, at a ripe old age, without your help and without use of hellish gunpowder.[6] So use it instead to hurl your filthy friars to heaven,[7] and all the immovable gods of profane Rome; for, believe me, unless you help them in this or some other way, they will scarcely succeed in climbing the heavenly road.

In eandem

Purgatorem animae derisit Iacobus ignem,
    Et sine quo superum non adeunda domus.
Frenduit hoc trina monstrum Latiale corona
    Movit et horrificum cornua dena minax.
5 Et nec inultus ait temnes mea sacra Britanne,
    Supplicium spreta relligione dabis.
Et si stelligeras unquam penetraveris arces,
    Non nisi per flammas triste patebit iter.
O quam funesto cecinisti proxima vero,
10   Verbaque ponderibus vix caritura suis!
Nam prope Tartareo sublime rotatus ab igni
    Ibat ad aethereas umbra perusta plagas.

On the same

James scoffed at the purgatorial fire,[1] without which the soul cannot reach its home above. At this the triple-crowned monster of Latium[3] gnashed its teeth and shook its ten horns[4] with horrifying menace. 'Briton,' it said, 'your scorn for that which is sacred to me will not go unpunished. You will pay the penalty for despising religion, and you will never win your way through to the starry citadels unless a painful road opens to you through the flames.' O how near your prophecy came to deadly truth, how little your words fell short of being fulfilled! For he was almost whirled up to the heavenly regions by Tartarean fire, a burnt-up shade.

In eandem

Quem modo Roma suis devoverat impia diris,
  Et Styge damnarat Taenarioque sinu,
Hunc vice mutata iam tollere gestit ad astra,
  Et cupit ad superos evehere usque deos.

On the same
Impious Rome once cursed this man with dire imprecations,[1] condemned him to the Styx and the Taenarian abyss.[2] Now, reversing her aims, she longs to elevate him to the stars and desires to convey him up even to the gods above.

In Inventorem Bombardae

Iapetionidem laudavit caeca vetustas,
  Qui tulit aetheream solis ab axe facem;
At mihi maior erit, qui lurida creditur arma,
  Et trifidum fulmen surripuisse Iovi.

On the Inventor of Gunpowder
Blind antiquity praised the son of Iapetus[1] who brought down heavenly fire from the sun's chariot; but to my mind, a greater man is he who is thought to have stolen from Jove his ghastly arms and three-forked thunderbolt.

Ad Leonoram Romae Canentem

Angelus unicuique suus (sic credite gentes)
  Obtigit aethereis ales ab ordinibus.
Quid mirum, Leonora tibi si gloria maior?
  Nam tua praesentem vox sonat ipsa Deum.
5   Aut Deus, aut vacui certe mens tertia coeli
  Per tua secreto guttura serpit agens;

Serpit agens, facilisque docet mortalia corda
　　Sensim immortali assuescere posse sono.
Quod si cuncta quidem Deus est, per cunctaque fusus,
10　　In te una loquitur, caetera mutus habet.

To Leonora singing at Rome
A winged angel from the heavenly hierarchies – believe me, you
nations – hovers over each particular individual. What wonder,
Leonora, if you have a greater glory? For your very voice pours forth
the presence of God. Either God or at least the third mind,[5] quitting
heaven, moves imperceptibly through your throat with secret power;
with power he moves, and graciously teaches mortal hearts how they
can insensibly become accustomed to immortal sound. If God is all
things, and poured through all things, in you alone he speaks, in
silence holds all else.

Ad eandem

Altera Torquatum cepit Leonora poetam,
　　Cuius ab insano cessit amore furens.
Ah miser ille tuo quanto felicius aevo
　　Perditus, et propter te Leonora foret!
5　Et te Pieria sensisset voce canentem
　　Aurea maternae fila movere lyrae,
Quamvis Dircaeo torsisset lumina Pentheo
　　Saevior, aut totus desipuisset iners,
Tu tamen errantes caeca vertigine sensus
10　　Voce eadem poteras composuisse tua;
Et poteras aegro spirans sub corde quietem
　　Flexanimo cantu restituisse sibi.

To the same
Another Leonora captivated the poet Torquato,[1] who went mad with
raging love for her. Ah, poor man, how much more blissfully might
he have been brought to ruin in your time and for your sake, Leonora!
He would have heard you singing with Picrian[5] voice as you touched
the strings of your mother's[6] lyre. Even if he had rolled his eyes

more fiercely than Dircaean Pentheus,[7] or was so completely mad
that he was incapable of doing anything, your voice could have
composed his wits wandering in their blind giddiness. Breathing
peace into his troubled heart with your heart-moving song, you
might have restored him to himself.

Ad eandem

Credula quid liquidam Sirena Neapoli iactas,
    Claraque Parthenopes fana Acheloiados,
Littoreamque tua defunctam naiada ripa
    Corpora Chalcidico sacra dedisse rogo?
5   Illa quidem vivitque, et amoena Tibridis unda
    Mutavit rauci murmura Pausilipi.
Illic Romulidum studiis ornata secundis,
    Atque homines cantu detinet atque deos.

To the same
Why, credulous Naples, do you boast of your clear-voiced Siren,
and of the famous shrine of Achelous' daughter, Parthenope?[2] Why
do you boast that when she, a naiad of the shore, perished on your
coast, you burned her sacred body on a Chalcidian[4] pyre? In truth,
she lives, and has exchanged the roar of hoarse Posillipo[6] for the
Tiber's delightful waves. There she is honoured by the eager applause
of the sons of Romulus, and she holds gods and men spellbound
with her song.

SILVARUM LIBER

In Obitum Procancellarii Medici

Anno aetatis 16 [17]

Parere fati discite legibus,
Manusque Parcae iam date supplices,
   Qui pendulum telluris orbem
      Iapeti colitis nepotes.
5 Vos si relicto mors vaga Taenaro
Semel vocarit flebilis, heu morae
   Tentantur incassum dolique;
      Per tenebras Stygis ire certum est.
Si destinatam pellere dextera
10 Mortem valeret, non ferus Hercules
   Nessi venenatus cruore
      Aemathia iacuisset Oeta.
Nec fraude turpi Palladis invidae
Vidisset occisum Ilion Hectora, aut
15 Quem larva Pelidis peremit
      Ense Locro, Iove lacrimante.
Si triste fatum verba Hecateia
Fugare possint, Telegoni parens
   Vixisset infamis, potentique
20   Aegiali soror usa virga.
Numenque trinum fallere si queant
Artes medentum, ignotaque gramina,
   Non gnarus herbarum Machaon
      Eurypyli cecidisset hasta.
25 Laesisset et nec te Philyreie
Sagitta echidnae perlita sanguine,
   Nec tela te fulmenque avitum
      Caese puer genitricis alvo.
Tuque O alumno maior Apolline,
30 Gentis togatae cui regimen datum,

Frondosa quem nunc Cirrha luget,
　　Et mediis Helicon in undis,
Iam praefuisses Palladio gregi
Laetus, superstes, nec sine gloria,
35　　Nec puppe lustrasses Charontis
　　　Horribiles barathri recessus.
At fila rupit Persephone tua
Irata, cum te viderit artibus
　　Succoque pollenti tot atris
40　　　Faucibus eripuisse mortis.
Colende praeses, membra precor tua
Molli quiescant cespite, et ex tuo
　　Crescant rosae, calthaeque busto,
　　　Purpureoque hyacinthus ore.
45 Sit mite de te iudicium Aeaci,
Subrideatque Aetnaea Proserpina,
　　Interque felices perennis
　　　Elysio spatiere campo.

On the death of the Vice-Chancellor, a Physician
At the Age of 16 [17]

Learn to obey the laws of Fate, and now raise suppliant hands to
the goddess of destiny,[2] you descendants of Iapetus[4] who inhabit the
pendulous globe of the earth.[3] If Death, the mournful wanderer from
Taenarus,[5] once calls you, alas, it is useless to try delays and tricks;
your journey through Stygian darkness is inescapable. If man's right
hand had the strength to drive back destined death, fierce Hercules
would not have been laid low by Nessus' poisoned blood on Emathian
Oeta;[12] nor would Troy have seen Hector slain by malicious Pallas'
base deceit,[14] nor Sarpedon slain with a Locrian sword by the man
disguised as Achilles, while Jove wept.[16] If Hecate's spells could
banish miserable fate, Telegonus' mother[18] would have lived on in
her infamy, and Aegialeus' sister[20] would have survived to use her
powerful wand. If medical arts and mysterious drugs could cheat
the three goddesses, then Machaon, who knew all medicinal herbs,
would not have fallen to Eurypylus' spear;[24] nor would the arrow
smeared with Hydra's blood have afflicted you, son of Philyra;[25] nor
would you, boy[28] cut from your mother's womb, have been struck
by your grandfather's bolts and thunder.

And you, who are greater than your pupil Apollo, you who were given rule over the gowned tribe, you whom leafy Cirrha[31] now mourns, and Helicon amidst its streams, you would now be presiding over Pallas' flock,[33] joyful, still living, and not without glory; you would not have crossed over the horrid deeps of the abyss in Charon's[35] boat. But Persephone[37] broke the thread of your life, angry when she saw that by your arts and powerful potions you had snatched so many from the dark jaws of death. Reverend Chancellor, may your limbs rest peacefully in the soft turf, and from your grave may roses and marigolds and the purple-lipped hyacinth grow. May Aeacus[45] judge you mildly, may Sicilian[46] Proserpine smile, and may you walk for ever among the blessed in the Elysian fields.

In Quintum Novembris

Anno aetatis 17

Iam pius extrema veniens Iacobus ab arcto
Teucrigenas populos, lateque patentia regna
Albionum tenuit, iamque inviolabile foedus
Sceptra Caledoniis coniunxerat Anglica Scotis:
5   Pacificusque novo felix divesque sedebat
In solio, occultique doli securus et hostis:
Cum ferus ignifluo regnans Acheronte tyrannus,
Eumenidum pater, aethereo vagus exul Olympo,
Forte per immensum terrarum erraverat orbem,
10 Dinumerans sceleris socios, vernasque fideles,
Participes regni post funera moesta futuros;
Hic tempestates medio ciet aere diras,
Illic unanimes odium struit inter amicos,
Armat et invictas in mutua viscera gentes;
15 Regnaque olivifera vertit florentia pace,
Et quoscunque videt purae virtutis amantes,
Hos cupit adiicere imperio, fraudumque magister
Tentat inaccessum sceleri corrumpere pectus,
Insidiasque locat tacitas, cassesque latentes
20 Tendit, ut incautos rapiat, ceu Caspia tigris

Insequitur trepidam deserta per avia praedam
Nocte sub illuni, et somno nictantibus astris.
Talibus infestat populos Summanus et urbes
Cinctus caeruleae fumanti turbine flammae.
25 Iamque fluentisonis albentia rupibus arva
Apparent, et terra Deo dilecta marino,
Cui nomen dederat quondam Neptunia proles
Amphitryoniaden qui non dubitavit atrocem
Aequore tranato furiali poscere bello,
30 Ante expugnatae crudelia saecula Troiae.
    At simul hanc opibusque et festa pace beatam
Aspicit, et pingues donis Cerealibus agros,
Quodque magis doluit, venerantem numina veri
Sancta Dei populum, tandem suspiria rupit
35 Tartareos ignes et luridum olentia sulphur.
Qualia Trinacria trux ab Iove clausus in Aetna
Efflat tabifico monstrosus ab ore Typhoeus.
Ignescunt oculi, stridetque adamantinus ordo
Dentis, ut armorum fragor, ictaque cuspide cuspis.
40 Atque pererrato solum hoc lacrimabile mundo
Inveni, dixit, gens haec mihi sola rebellis,
Contemtrixque iugi, nostraque potentior arte.
Illa tamen, mea si quicquam tentamina possunt,
Non feret hoc impune diu, non ibit inulta.
45 Hactenus, et piceis liquido natat aere pennis;
Qua volat, adversi praecursant agmine venti,
Densantur nubes, et crebra tonitrua fulgent.
    Iamque pruinosas velox superaverat Alpes,
Et tenet Ausoniae fines, a parte sinistra
50 Nimbifer Appenninus erat, priscique Sabini,
Dextra veneficiis infamis Hetruria, nec non
Te furtiva Tibris Thetidi videt oscula dantem;
Hinc Mavortigenae consistit in arce Quirini.
Reddiderant dubiam iam sera crepuscula lucem,
55 Cum circumgreditur totam Tricoronifer urbem,
Panificosque deos portat, scapulisque virorum
Evehitur, praeeunt summisso poplite reges,
Et mendicantum series longissima fratrum;
Cereaque in manibus gestant funalia caeci,

60   Cimmeriis nati in tenebris, vitamque trahentes.
Templa dein multis subeunt lucentia taedis
(Vesper erat sacer iste Petro) fremitusque canentum
Saepe tholos implet vacuos, et inane locorum.
Qualiter exululat Bromius, Bromiique caterva,

65   Orgia cantantes in Echionio Aracyntho,
Dum tremit attonitus vitreis Asopus in undis,
Et procul ipse cava responsat rupe Cithaeron.
   His igitur tandem solenni more peractis,
Nox senis amplexus Erebi taciturna reliquit,

70   Praecipitesque impellit equos stimulante flagello,
Captum oculis Typhlonta, Melanchaetemque ferocem,
Atque Acherontaeo prognatam patre Siopen
Torpidam, et hirsutis horrentem Phrica capillis.
Interea regum domitor, Phlegetontius haeres

75   Ingreditur thalamos (neque enim secretus adulter
Producit steriles molli sine pellice noctes);
At vix compositos somnus claudebat ocellos,
Cum niger umbrarum dominus, rectorque silentum,
Praedatorque hominum falsa sub imagine tectus

80   Astitit. Assumptis micuerunt tempora canis,
Barba sinus promissa tegit, cineracea longo
Syrmate verrit humum vestis, pendetque cucullus
Vertice de raso, et ne quicquam desit ad artes,
Cannabeo lumbos constrinxit fune salaces,

85   Tarda fenestratis figens vestigia calceis.
Talis, uti fama est, vasta Franciscus eremo
Tetra vagabatur solus per lustra ferarum,
Silvestrique tulit genti pia verba salutis
Impius, atque lupos domuit, Libycosque leones.

90   Subdolus at tali Serpens velatus amictu
Solvit in has fallax ora execrantia voces;
Dormis nate? Etiamne tuos sopor opprimit artus?
Immemor O fidei, pecorumque oblite tuorum,
Dum cathedram venerande tuam, diademaque triplex

95   Ridet Hyperboreo gens barbara nata sub axe,
Dumque pharetrati spernunt tua iura Britanni;
Surge, age, surge piger, Latius quem Caesar adorat,
Cui reserata patet convexi ianua caeli,

Turgentes animos, et fastus frange procaces,
100   Sacrilegique sciant, tua quid maledictio possit,
Et quid Apostolicae possit custodia clavis;
Et memor Hesperiae disiectam ulciscere classem,
Mersaque Iberorum lato vexilla profundo,
Sanctorumque cruci tot corpora fixa probrosae,
105   Thermodoontea nuper regnante puella.
At tu si tenero mavis torpescere lecto
Crescentesque negas hosti contundere vires,
Tyrrhenum implebit numeroso milite Pontum,
Signaque Aventino ponet fulgentia colle:
110   Relliquias veterum franget, flammisque cremabit,
Sacraque calcabit pedibus tua colla profanis,
Cuius gaudebant soleis dare basia reges.
Nec tamen hunc bellis et aperto Marte lacesses,
Irritus ille labor; tu callidus utere fraude,
115   Quaelibet haereticis disponere retia fas est;
Iamque ad consilium extremis rex magnus ab oris
Patricios vocat, et procerum de stirpe creatos,
Grandaevosque patres trabea, canisque verendos;
Hos tu membratim poteris conspergere in auras,
120   Atque dare in cineres, nitrati pulveris igne
Aedibus iniecto, qua convenere, sub imis.
Protinus ipse igitur quoscumque habet Anglia fidos
Propositi, factique mone, quisquamne tuorum
Audebit summi non iussa facessere Papae?
125   Perculsosque metu subito, casumque stupentes
Invadat vel Gallus atrox, vel saevus Iberus.
Saecula sic illic tandem Mariana redibunt,
Tuque in belligeros iterum dominaberis Anglos.
Et nequid timeas, divos divasque secundas
130   Accipe, quotque tuis celebrantur numina fastis.
Dixit et adscitos ponens malefidus amictus
Fugit ad infandam, regnum illaetabile, Lethen.
    Iam rosea Eoas pandens Tithonia portas
Vestit inauratas redeunti lumine terras;
135   Maestaque adhuc nigri deplorans funera nati
Irrigat ambrosiis montana cacumina guttis;
Cum somnos pepulit stellatae ianitor aulae

Nocturnos visus, et somnia grata revolvens.
　　Est locus aeterna septus caligine noctis
140　Vasta ruinosi quondam fundamina tecti,
Nunc torvi spelunca Phoni, Prodotaeque bilinguis
Effera quos uno peperit Discordia partu.
Hic inter caementa iacent praeruptaque saxa,
Ossa inhumata virum, et traiecta cadavera ferro;
145　Hic Dolus intortis semper sedet ater ocellis,
Iurgiaque, et stimulis armata Calumnia fauces,
Et Furor, atque viae moriendi mille videntur,
Et Timor, exanguisque locum circumvolat Horror,
Perpetuoque leves per muta silentia Manes,
150　Exululat tellus et sanguine conscia stagnat.
Ipsi etiam pavidi latitant penetralibus antri
Et Phonos, et Prodotes, nulloque sequente per antrum,
Antrum horrens, scopulosum, atrum feralibus umbris,
Diffugiunt sontes, et retro lumina vortunt;
155　Hos pugiles Romae per saecula longa fideles
Evocat antistes Babylonius, atque ita fatur.
Finibus occiduis circumfusum incolit aequor
Gens exosa mihi, prudens Natura negavit
Indignam penitus nostro coniungere mundo;
160　Illuc, sic iubeo, celeri contendite gressu,
Tartareoque leves difflentur pulvere in auras
Et rex et pariter satrapae, scelerata propago;
Et quotquot fidei caluere cupidine verae
Consilii socios adhibete, operisque ministros.
165　Finierat, rigidi cupide paruere gemelli.
　　Interea longo flectens curvamine coelos
Despicit aetherea dominus qui fulgurat arce,
Vanaque perversae ridet conamina turbae,
Atque sui causam populi volet ipse tueri.
170　　Esse ferunt spatium, qua distat ab Aside terra
Fertilis Europe, et spectat Mareotidas undas;
Hic turris posita est Titanidos ardua Famae
Aerea, lata, sonans, rutilis vicinior astris
Quam superimpositum vel Athos vel Pelion Ossae.
175　Mille fores aditusque patent, totidemque fenestrae,
Amplaque per tenues translucent atria muros;

Excitat hic varios plebs agglomerata susurros;
Qualiter instrepitant circum mulctralia bombis
Agmina muscarum, aut texto per ovilia iunco,
180 Dum Canis aestivum coeli petit ardua culmen.
Ipsa quidem summa sedet ultrix matris in arce,
Auribus innumeris cinctum caput eminet olli,
Queis sonitum exiguum trahit, atque levissima captat
Murmura, ab extremis patuli confinibus orbis.
185 Nec tot Aristoride servator inique iuvencae
Isidos, immiti volvebas lumina vultu,
Lumina non unquam tacito nutantia somno,
Lumina subiectas late spectantia terras.
Istis illa solet loca luce carentia saepe
190 Perlustrare, etiam radianti impervia soli.
Millenisque loquax auditaque visaque linguis
Cuilibet effundit temeraria; veraque mendax
Nunc minuit, modo confictis sermonibus auget.
Sed tamen a nostro meruisti carmine laudes
195 Fama, bonum quo non aliud veracius ullum,
Nobis digna cani, nec te memorasse pigebit
Carmine tam longo; servati scilicet Angli
Officiis vaga diva tuis, tibi reddimus aequa.
Te Deus aeternos motu qui temperat ignes,
200 Fulmine praemisso alloquitur, terraque tremente:
Fama siles? an te latet impia Papistarum
Coniurata cohors in meque meosque Britannos,
Et nova sceptrigero caedes meditata Iacobo?
Nec plura, illa statim sensit mandata Tonantis,
205 Et satis ante fugax stridentes induit alas,
Induit et variis exilia corpora plumis;
Dextra tubam gestat Temesaeo ex aere sonaram.
Nec mora iam pennis cedentes remigat auras,
Atque parum est cursu celeres praevertere nubes,
210 Iam ventos, iam solis equos post terga reliquit:
Et primo Angliacas solito de more per urbes
Ambiguas voces, incertaque murmura spargit,
Mox arguta dolos, et detestabile vulgat
Proditionis opus, nec non facta horrida dictu,
215 Authoresque addit sceleris, nec garrula caecis

Inisidiis loca structa silet; stupuere relatis,
Et pariter iuvenes, pariter tremuere puellae,
Effetique senes pariter, tantaeque ruinae
Sensus ad aetatem subito penetraverat omnem.
220   Attamen interea populi miserescit ab alto
Aethereus Pater, et crudelibus obstitit ausis
Papicolum; capti poenas raptantur ad acres;
At pia thura Deo, et grati solvuntur honores;
Compita laeta focis genialibus omnia fumant,
225   Turba choros iuvenilis agit: Quintoque Novembris
Nulla dies toto occurrit celebratior anno.

On the Fifth of November
At the Age of 17

Now the devout James, coming from the far north, began his reign
over the Troy-descended people[2] and the wide realm of Albion, and
now an inviolable league had united the sceptres of the English and
the Caledonian Scots. Happy and wealthy, the bringer of peace was
sitting on his new throne, fearing no enemy or secret plot, when the
fierce tyrant who rules Acheron's fiery waves,[7] the father of the
Furies, the wandering exile from heavenly Olympus, had chanced
to be roaming the earth's vast globe, counting his companions in
crime, his faithful slaves by birth,[10] who were destined to share his
kingdom after their miserable deaths. Here he stirs up wild storms
in the middle air;[12] there he instigates hatred between loving friends.
He arms invincible nations for a death-struggle, and overturns king-
doms that were flourishing under the olive of peace. Wherever he
sees lovers of pure virtue, he seeks to add them to his empire. A
master of fraud, he seeks to corrupt the heart that is closed to
wickedness. Silently he sets his traps, and stretches hidden nets to
catch the unwary, as when a Caspian tigress pursues its trembling
prey through a pathless desert, under a moonless night, while the
stars wink drowsily. With such horrors, and girt with a smoking
whirlwind of blue flame, Summanus[23] infests cities and people. And
now appear the white cliffs and wave-resounding rocks of the land
loved by the sea-god and named of old after Neptune's son,[27] who
did not fear to cross the sea and challenge Amphitryon's terrible
son[28] to furious battle, before the cruel days of the sack of Troy.

But as soon as he caught sight of this land, blessed with prosperity and joyful peace, its fields rich with Ceres' gifts, and – what grieved him more – its people worshipping the sacred divinity of the true God, he broke into sighs that stank of Tartarean fire and yellow sulphur; such sighs as the ferocious monster Typhoeus, imprisoned by Jove under Trinacrian Etna, breathes from his infectious mouth.[37] His eyes flash fire, and he gnashes his rows of steel-hard teeth so they make a din like clashing weapons, like the grating of spear against spear. 'I have wandered over the whole world,' he said, 'and have found only one cause for tears: this nation alone rebels against me, is scornful of my yoke, and stronger than my wiles. Yet if my efforts are of any avail, these people will not carry on with impunity, will not go unpunished.' This said, he swam through the liquid air on pitch-black wings. Wherever he flies, a multitude of warring winds rush before him, clouds gather, and countless thunderbolts flash.

And now he had swiftly crossed the snowy Alps and reached the borders of Italy. To his left were the cloud-capped Apennines and the ancient land of the Sabines; to his right, Etruria, infamous for witchcraft. Nor did he fail to see you, Tiber, giving furtive kisses to Thetis.[52] Thence he alighted in the citadel of Quirinus,[53] son of Mars. Now, when evening dusk brought dubious twilight, the wearer of the triple crown[55] makes a circuit of the whole city, carrying his gods made of bread,[56] and he himself is carried on men's shoulders. Before him go kings on bended knee, and a long line of mendicant friars. They carry wax candles in their hands, for they are blind. They were born in Cimmerian[60] darkness, and in darkness they still lead their lives. They enter temples gleaming with many torches (it was the eve[62] sacred to St Peter), and their cacophonous chanting repeatedly fills the hollow cupolas and empty spaces. They sound just like Bromius[64] and his rout, when they raise their Bacchanalian cries on Echionian Aracynthus,[65] while astonished Asopus[66] trembles beneath his glassy waves, and distant Cithaeron[67] itself echoes from its hollow cliff.

When these rites had at last been performed according to custom, Night silently quit the embrace of old Erebus,[69] and drove her swift steeds with the goading whip: blind Typhlon, fierce Melanchaetes, torpid Siope, born of a hellish sire, and shaggy Phrix with bristling mane.[73]

Meanwhile, the tamer of kings,[74] the heir of Phlegethon, enters his bridal-bed (for the secret adulterer never passes a barren night without a sweet whore). But sleep had hardly closed his eyes in peaceful rest, when the dark lord of shadows, the ruler of the silent shades, the predator of men, stood beside him, under cover of a false shape. His temples gleamed with white hair, assumed for his disguise; a long beard covered his chest, his ash-coloured robe swept the ground with its long train, a hood dangled from his tonsured head; and, to complete his wiles, he had bound his lecherous loins with a hempen rope, and fastened latticed sandals to his slow feet.[85] In such garb, so legend has it, Francis would wander the waste wilderness, alone among the horrid haunts of wild beasts, and (impious himself) brought the pious word of salvation to the forest folk,[88] and tamed wolves and Libyan lions.

Cloaked in this disguise, the sly Serpent uttered these sly words from his foul lips: 'Are you sleeping,[92] my son? Does slumber weigh down your limbs? O, unmindful of the faith, forgetful of your flocks – you, who ought to be revered – while a barbarous nation, born under the Hyperborean[95] sky, laughs at your throne and triple diadem, and the British archers despise your laws. Sluggard, awake, arise! You to whom the Holy Roman Emperor bows down, you for whom the gate of vaulted heaven lies open and unlocked. Break their lofty spirits and haughty impudence! Let the sacrilegious know the power of your malediction and the power of your custodianship of the Apostolic key![101] Avenge the scattered Hesperian fleet,[102] the Iberian standards sunk in the wide deep, and the bodies of so many saints fixed on the shameful cross in the Amazonian virgin's[105] recent reign. Remember! But if you would rather lie torpid on your soft bed, and shrink from crushing your enemy's growing strength, he will fill the Tyrrhenian Sea[108] with a numerous host and plant his glittering standards on the Aventine hill.[109] He will smash your relics of the ancients and burn them in the flames; he will tread your sacred neck under his profane feet – you, whose shoes kings have rejoiced to kiss. Yet do not challenge him with arms and open war. That would be a wasted effort. Be prudent and use covert guile. It is lawful to spread any kind of net for heretics. Even now their great king is summoning to Parliament, from the furthest corners of their land, the patricians, the men of high descent,[117] and the venerable fathers,[118] gowned and grey-haired. These you might scatter in the air – tear them limb from limb, and burn them to cinders – if you ignite nitrous powder under the halls where they will assemble. At once, therefore, give notice of the proposed action to however many of the faithful are still left in England. Will any of your followers hear the sovereign Pope's commands and not eagerly perform them? While the people are panic-stricken and stunned by the unexpected catastrophe, let the fierce Frenchman or savage Spaniard invade them. In this way the Marian age[127] will at last return to that land, and you will once again hold the warlike English under your sway. And (lest you should fear) know that all the gods and goddesses support you – all those deities you worship on your feast days.' So the deceiver spake, and putting off his disguise, fled to unspeakable Lethe,[132] his joyless kingdom.

Now the rosy wife of Tithonus,[133] throwing open the gates of dawn, dresses the gilded earth with returning light and, still mourning the sad death of her black son,[135] she sprinkles the mountain summits with ambrosial drops. Then the janitor[137] of the starry courts shook off his slumbers, and turned over in his mind his nocturnal visions and delightful dreams.

There is a place,[139] enveloped in eternal darkness and night, which was of old the vast foundation of a ruined edifice. Now it has become the cavernous den of savage Murder and double-tongued Treason, twins whom fierce Discord bore at one birth. Here, amid rubble and jagged[143] rocks, lie the unburied bones of men, and corpses pierced by iron. Here dark Guile, with eyes twisted askance, forever sits; here are Strife, and Calumny, her jaws armed with fangs, and Fury. Here a thousand ways of dying are seen, and Fear, and bloodless Horror flying about the place, and insubstantial ghosts forever flitting through the dead silences. The conscious[150] earth wails and rots with blood. Murder and Treason themselves lurk trembling in the depths of the cave, and though no one pursues them through the cave (a horrible cave, with a projecting outcrop of rock, and black with deadly shadows) they flee guiltily with backward glances. The Babylonian[156] high-priest summons these champions of Rome, faithful to her for long ages, and says: 'In the western limits of the world, surrounded by the sea, there dwells a nation that is odious to me. Prudent Nature refused to join it up with our continent, finding it unworthy. Thither turn your steps with all speed – such is my command. Let the king and all his nobles – the whole wicked brood – be blown into thin air with Tartarean powder. Bring into the plot as comrades and abettors of the deed all those who are fired with zeal for the true faith.' He ended, and the pitiless pair zealously obeyed him.

Meanwhile the Lord, who turns the heavens in their wide vault, and hurls the lightning from his ethereal citadel, looks down and laughs[168] at the vain exertions of the wicked crew, and himself undertakes to defend the cause of his people.

Men say[170] there is an expanse, facing Lake Mareotis,[171] which divides fertile Europe from Asia. Here Rumour, daughter of the Titaness,[172] has her lofty tower – brazen, broad, full of noise, and closer to the glimmering stars than Athos or Pelion piled upon Ossa.[174] A thousand doors and entrances, and as many windows, gape wide, and the spacious courts inside shine through the thin walls. Here a swarming crowd of people start various whispers, as when swarms of flies hum and buzz about the milk-pails or through the wattled sheepfolds,[179] when the Dog Star attains the summit of the summer skies. Rumour herself, her mother's avenger,[181] sits on the topmost pinnacle, and lifts her head girt with innumerable ears. With these, she can catch the smallest sound and apprehend the slightest murmur from the uttermost ends of the wide globe. Not even you, Arestor's son,[185] cruel guard of the heifer Isis, rolled so many eyes in your inexorable face as she – eyes that never succumb to silent sleep, eyes that gaze far and wide over the lower lands. With these she often peers into places devoid of light, places inaccessible even to the sun's rays. With her thousand tongues, the imprudent blab then pours out everything she has heard or seen to anyone who cares to listen. Now she dilutes the truth with lies, now she embellishes it with made-up speeches.

But you nevertheless deserve to be praised in my song, Rumour, for one good report, than which none was ever more honest. You are worthy of my song, nor shall I ever regret having commemorated you at such length in my poem. We English, who were plainly saved by your good offices,[198] inconstant goddess, render you your just reward. God, who guides the eternal fires in their motion, hurled down a thunderbolt, and thus addressed you, while the earth trembled: 'Are you silent, Rumour? Can't you see that an impious crew of Papists is conspiring against me and my Britons, and plotting a new kind of murder against sceptre-bearing James?' He spoke no more, but she at once responded to the Thunderer's commands and, swift enough before, she now put on whistling wings, and covered her slender body with varied plumage; in her right hand she took a shrill trumpet of Temesan[207] brass. Without delay, she beat the yielding air with her wings. Not content to outstrip the swift clouds in her flight, she now leaves behind the winds and the horses of the sun. As is her wont, she first spread ambiguous words and uncertain whispers through the English cities; anon, with a clear voice, she divulges the plots and the detestable work of treason. She does not conceal the unutterable crime, and she adds the names of its wicked authors. Nor is her garrulous tongue silent about the places prepared for the secret treachery. Her news amazes all hearers. Young men, maidens, and feeble old men alike tremble, and people of all ages are struck to the heart by the sense of so great a catastrophe. But meanwhile the heavenly Father from on high took pity on his people and frustrated the cruel deed dared by the Papists. They are captured and carried away to harsh punishments; pious incense and grateful prayers are offered to God; the joyful crossroads smoke with festive bonfires, and crowds of young people dance. In all the year no day is more celebrated than the fifth of November.

In Obitum Praesulis Eliensis

Anno aetatis 17

Adhuc madentes rore squalebant genae,
    Et sicca nondum lumina;
Adhuc liquentis imbre turgebant salis
    Quem nuper effudi pius,
5 Dum maesta caro iusta persolvi rogo
    Wintoniensis praesulis,
Cum centilinguis Fama (proh semper mali
    Cladisque vera nuntia)
Spargit per urbes divitis Britanniae,
10   Populosque Neptuno satos,
Cessisse morti, et ferreis sororibus
    Te generis humani decus,
Qui rex sacrorum illa fuisti in insula
    Quae nomen Anguillae tenet.

15   Tunc inquietum pectus ira protinus
      Ebulliebat fervida,
   Tumulis potentem saepe devovens deam:
      Nec vota Naso in Ibida
   Concepit alto diriora pectore,
20   Graiusque vates parcius
   Turpem Lycambis execratus est dolum,
      Sponsamque Neobolen suam.
   At ecce diras ipse dum fundo graves,
      Et imprecor neci necem,
25   Audisse tales videor attonitus sonos
      Leni, sub aura, flamine:
   Caecos furores pone, pone vitream
      Bilemque et irritas minas.
   Quid temere violas non nocenda numina,
30   Subitoque ad iras percita?
   Non est, ut arbitraris elusus miser,
      Mors atra Noctis filia,
   Erebove patre creta, sive Erinnye,
      Vastove nata sub Chao:
35   Ast illa caelo missa stellato, Dei
      Messes ubique colligit;
   Animasque mole carnea reconditas
      In lucem et auras evocat:
   Ut cum fugaces excitant Horae diem
40   Themidos Iovisque filiae;
   Et sempiterni ducit ad vultus patris;
      At iusta raptat impios
   Sub regna furvi luctuosa Tartari
      Sedesque subterraneas.
45   Hanc ut vocantem lactus audivi, cito
      Foedum reliqui carcerem,
   Volatilesque faustus inter milites
      Ad astra sublimis feror:
   Vates ut olim raptus ad coelum senex
50   Auriga currus ignei.
   Non me Bootis terruere lucidi
      Sarraca tarda frigore, aut
   Formidolosi Scorpionis brachia,

Non ensis Orion tuus.
55   Praetervolavi fulgidi solis globum,
      Longeque sub pedibus deam
Vidi triformem, dum coercebat suos
      Frenis dracones aureis.
Erraticorum siderum per ordines,
60   Per lacteas vehor plagas,
Velocitatem saepe miratus novam,
      Donec nitentes ad fores
Ventum est Olympi, et regiam crystallinam, et
      Stratum smaragdis atrium.
65   Sed hic tacebo, nam quis effari queat
      Oriundus humano patre
Amoenitates illius loci? mihi
      Sat est in aeternum frui.

On the death of the Bishop of Ely
At the Age of 17

My cheeks were still wet and drenched with tears, and my eyes, not
yet dry, were still swollen with the shower of salt water that I had
recently poured forth in dutiful and sorrowful tribute to the Bishop
of Winchester,[6] when hundred-tongued Rumour (always, alas, a true
messenger of evil and disaster) spread through Britain's prosperous
cities and the nation sprung from Neptune[10] the news that you had
succumbed to death and the cruel sisters[11] – you, the ornament of
mankind, who were the prince of the saints in that island that bears
the name 'Eel'.[14] Then my seething breast at once boiled with hot
rage. I often cursed the goddess[17] who holds sway over the grave.
No fiercer curses did Ovid conceive against Ibis[18] in the depths of
his heart; more restrained than I was the Greek poet[20] who poured
execrations on the base trickery of Lycambes, and upon Neobule,
his promised bride. But lo, while I was pouring out these grievous
curses, and calling down death upon Death, it seemed, to my astonish-
ment, that I could hear these words breathed gently on the breeze:
'Put aside your blind rage, put aside your gleaming bile[28] and empty
threats. Why do you recklessly assail deities who cannot be harmed
and are quickly roused to anger? Death is not, as you, poor wretch,
imagine, the dark daughter of Night.[32] She is not the daughter of
Erebus, or of a Fury, nor was she born of vast Chaos. But, sent from

starry heaven, she gathers from all places the harvest of God. She
summons into the light and air souls that had been hidden under a
mound of flesh, as when the flying Hours,[39] daughters of Jove and
Themis, rouse the day; and she leads them before the face of the
eternal Father. But the wicked she justly carries down to the doleful
realms of dark Tartarus, the infernal mansion. When I heard her
calling, I was joyful; I quickly left my foul prison, and was carried
up to the stars, favoured highly among the winged hosts, as once
that old prophet[49] was snatched up to heaven, driving a chariot of
fire. I was not terrified by bright Boötes and his Wain, sluggish in
the cold, or by the claws of the terrible Scorpion, or by your sword,
Orion. I flew by the sun's fiery globe, and far below my feet I saw
the triform goddess,[56] checking her dragon-team with golden reins.
Through the series of planets, through the Milky Way, I was carried,
often marvelling at my incredible speed, until I came to the glittering
gates of Olympus, the crystalline court, and the entrance-hall paved
with emeralds. But here I fall silent, for what son of a mortal father
can describe the bliss of that place? For me it is enough to enjoy it
for all eternity.'

Naturam non pati senium

Heu quam perpetuis erroribus acta fatiscit
Avia mens hominum, tenebrisque immersa profundis
Oedipodioniam volvit sub pectore noctem!
Quae vesana suis metiri facta deorum
5   Audet, et incisas leges adamante perenni
Assimilare suis, nulloque solubile saeclo
Consilium fati perituris alligat horis.
   Ergone marcescet sulcantibus obsita rugis
Naturae facies, et rerum publica mater
10   Omniparum contracta uterum sterilescet ab aevo?
Et se fassa senem male certis passibus ibit
Sidereum tremebunda caput? num tetra vetustas
Annorumque aeterna fames, squalorque situsque
Sidera vexabunt? An et insatiabile Tempus
15   Esuriet Caelum, rapietque in viscera patrem?

Heu, potuitne suas imprudens Iupiter arces
Hoc contra munisse nefas, et Temporis isto
Exemisse malo, gyrosque dedisse perennes?
Ergo erit ut quandoque sono dilapsa tremendo
20   Convexi tabulata ruant, atque obvius ictu
Stridat uterque polus, superaque ut Olympius aula
Decidat, horribilisque retecta Gorgone Pallas.
Qualis in Aegaeam proles Iunonia Lemnon
Deturbata sacro cecidit de limine caeli.
25   Tu quoque Phoebe tui casus imitabere nati
Praecipiti curru, subitaque ferere ruina
Pronus, et extincta fumabit lampade Nereus,
Et dabit attonito feralia sibila ponto.
Tunc etiam aerei divulsis sedibus Haemi
30   Dissultabit apex, imoque allisa barathro
Terrebunt Stygium deiecta Ceraunia Ditem
In superos quibus usus erat, fraternaque bella.
    At Pater omnipotens fundatis fortius astris
Consuluit rerum summae, certoque peregit
35   Pondere fatorum lances, atque ordine summo
Singula perpetuum iussit servare tenorem.
Volvitur hinc lapsu mundi rota prima diurno,
Raptat, et ambitos socia vertigine caelos.
Tardior haud solito Saturnus, et acer ut olim
40   Fulmineum rutilat cristata casside Mavors.
Floridus aeternum Phoebus iuvenile coruscat,
Nec fovet effetas loca per declivia terras
Devexo temone deus; sed semper amica
Luce potens eadem currit per signa rotarum.
45   Surgit odoratis pariter formosus ab Indis
Aethereum pecus albenti qui cogit Olympo
Mane vocans, et serus agens in pascua coeli;
Temporis et gemino dispertit regna colore.
Fulget, obitque vices alterno Delia cornu,
50   Caeruleumque ignem paribus complectitur ulnis.
Nec variant elementa fidem, solitoque fragore
Lurida perculsas iaculantur fulmina rupes.
Nec per inane furit leviori murmure Corus,
Stringit et armiferos aequali horrore Gelonos

55   Trux Aquilo, spiratque hiemem, nimbosque volutat.
      Utque solet, Siculi diverberat ima Pelori
      Rex maris, et rauca circumstrepit aequora concha
      Oceani tubicen, nec vasta mole minorem
      Aegaeona ferunt dorso Balearica cete.
60   Sed neque Terra tibi saecli vigor ille vetusti
      Priscus abest; servatque suum Narcissus odorem,
      Et puer ille suum tenet et puer ille decorem
      Phoebe tuusque et Cypri tuus, nec ditior olim
      Terra datum sceleri celavit montibus aurum
65   Conscia, vel sub aquis gemmas. Sic denique in aevum
      Ibit cunctarum series iustissima rerum,
      Donec flamma orbem populabitur ultima, late
      Circumplexa polos, et vasti culmina caeli,
      Ingentique rogo flagrabit machina mundi.

That Nature does not suffer from old age

Alas! How persistent are the errors which drive man's straying mind to exhaustion. How profound the darkness that swallows him when he broods in his heart over Oedipean night.[3] In his madness he dares to measure the gods' deeds by his own, and to liken his own laws to those carved in everlasting adamant. He binds to his own perishing hours the decree of Fate that cannot be undone by passing ages.

Will then the face of Nature wither and be furrowed with wrinkles? Will our common mother[9] contract her all-producing womb and become barren with age? Will she confess herself old and move along with uncertain steps, her starry head doddering? Will the stars be vexed by loathsome old age, the eternal hunger of the years, squalor, and decay? Will insatiable Time devour Heaven, cramming his own father into his stomach?[15] Alas, was Jupiter so improvident? Could he not fortify his citadels against such calamity, exempting them from Time's evils? Could he not have given them perpetual revolutions? Some day, then, the floors of vaulted heaven will fall with a tremendous crash,[19] and both poles will groan with the jarring shock; the Olympian will plummet from his heavenly hall, and Pallas with him, her ghastly Gorgon[22] shield uncovered. So Juno's son[23] fell on Aegean Lemnos, thrown down from heaven's sacred threshold. You too, Phoebus, will fall in your careering chariot like your son[25] before you, suddenly pitched headlong in your ruin; Nereus[27] will steam with the quenching of your lamp, and his astonished waters will send up a fearful hiss. The pinnacle of lofty Haemus,[29] its foundations rent asunder, will then fly to pieces, and the Ceraunian mountains, once used against gods in fratricidal wars,[32] will be thrown down into the lowest chasm of hell where they will terrify Stygian Dis.

But the omnipotent Father has consulted on the sum of things,[34] and founded the stars more strongly. He has poised the scales of Fate with a sure balance, and commanded each thing to keep its course for ever in the great order. Thus the prime wheel[37] of the universe turns its daily rotation and, by imparting its whirling motion, carries with it the circling heavens. Saturn is no slower now than in the past, and Mars, as fierce as he ever was, darts red lightning from his crested helmet. Phoebus shines with the bloom of eternal youth; he does not steer his chariot down declining slopes to warm an exhausted earth, but forever strong with friendly light drives his wheels through the same signs of the zodiac.[44] As beautiful as ever, from the spicy Indies arises the star that gathers the heavenly flock, calling them when the sky whitens at morning, and driving them back into the heavenly pastures at evening; thus it divides the realms of time with double beauty.[48] Delia[49] waxes and wanes with alternating horns, and clasps the fire of heaven with unchanged arms. The elements faithfully adhere to their kind, and in their usual way lurid lightning-bolts strike and shatter the rocks with a crash. Corus[53] rages through empty space with a roar no gentler than of old, and wild Aquilo[55] afflicts the armed Scythians with as much shivering as ever, as he blows winter on them and rolls the clouds along. The king of the sea shakes the base of Sicilian Pelorus[56] as he was wont to do, and the ocean's trumpeter[58] blows his hoarse conch over the level deep. The Balearic whales bear on their backs an Aegaeon[59] of no less monstrous size. Nor, Earth, have you lost that primeval vigour which you had in ancient times. Narcissus[61] still keeps his fragrance, and your beloved boy, Phoebus, and yours, Cypris, still retain their beauty.[63] The earth was no richer in days of yore, when she guiltily concealed gold – the source of crime – beneath the mountains, and gems beneath the seas.

So, in fact, the perfect sequence of the entire universe will continue for all time, until the final conflagration will destroy the world, enveloping everything from pole to pole, and the summits of vast heaven, and the frame of the world burns in a mighty funeral pyre.[69]

De Idea Platonica quemadmodum Aristoteles intellexit

Dicite sacrorum praesides nemorum deae,
Tuque O noveni perbeata numinis
Memoria mater, quaeque in immenso procul
Antro recumbis otiosa Aeternitas,
5   Monumenta servans, et ratas leges Iovis,
Caelique fastos atque ephemeridas deum,
Quis ille primus cuius ex imagine
Natura sollers finxit humanum genus,
Aeternus, incorruptus, aequaevus polo,
10   Unusque et universus, exemplar Dei?
Haud ille Palladis gemellus innubae
Interna proles insidet menti Iovis;
Sed quamlibet natura sit communior,
Tamen seorsus extat ad morem unius,
15   Et, mira, certo stringitur spatio loci;
Seu sempiternus ille siderum comes
Caeli pererrat ordines decemplicis,
Citimumve terris incolit lunae globum:
Sive inter animas corpus adituras sedens
20   Obliviosas torpet ad Lethes aquas:
Sive in remota forte terrarum plaga
Incedit ingens hominis archetypus gigas,
Et diis tremendus erigit celsum caput
Atlante maior portitore siderum.
25   Non cui profundum caecitas lumen dedit
Dircaeus augur vidit hunc alto sinu;
Non hunc silenti nocte Pleiones nepos
Vatum sagaci praepes ostendit choro;
Non hunc sacerdos novit Assyrius, licet
30   Longos vetusti commemoret atavos Nini,
Priscumque Belon, inclytumque Osiridem.
Non ille trino gloriosus nomine
Ter magnus Hermes (ut sit arcani sciens)
Talem reliquit Isidis cultoribus.
35   At tu perenne ruris Academi decus
(Haec monstra si tu primus induxti scholis)

Iam iam poetas urbis exules tuae
Revocabis, ipse fabulator maximus,
Aut institutor ipse migrabis foras.

On the Platonic form as Aristotle understood it
Say, goddesses[1] who preside over the sacred groves, and you,
Memory,[3] blessed mother of the ninefold deity,[2] and you, Eternity,
who recline at ease in some vast and distant cavern, preserving the
records and unalterable laws of Jove, the calendars of heaven and
the journals of the gods,[6] say who was that first being – eternal,
incorruptible, coeval with the heavens, single yet universal, the image
of God – in whose likeness ingenious Nature formed the human
race? He is not the twin brother of the virgin Athene, lurking unborn
in the mind of Jove.[12] Although all men participate in his nature, he
has a separate existence like an ordinary individual and – strange to
tell – is confined to definite spatial limits. Perhaps that eternal
companion of the stars wanders at will through the ten celestial
spheres, or perhaps he inhabits the moon's globe, close to our earth.
Perhaps he sits in a torpor beside Lethe, river of oblivion, among
the souls waiting to enter a body[20] – or perhaps this archetype of
man is a huge giant who strides along in some remote region of the
earth, terrifying the gods as he rears his lofty head higher than
star-bearing Atlas.[24] The Dircean seer,[26] whose blindness brought
profound vision, never saw this man in the depths of his innermost
mind; nor did Pleione's swift-winged grandson[27] reveal him to the
wise band of prophets in the silent night. The Assyrian priest[29] did
not know him, though he could recount the long lineage of ancient
Ninus,[30] primeval Belus,[31] and renowned Osiris. Nor did thrice-great
Hermes,[33] glorious with his triple name, bequeath any such tradition
to the worshippers of Isis[34] – though he was versed in arcane know-
ledge. But you, the everlasting glory of the grove of the Academy,[35] if
you were the first to introduce such monstrosities into the philosophic
schools, you must now recall the poets whom you exiled from your
city, for you yourself are the greatest fabler of all – either that, or
you, the founder, must yourself suffer exile.

Ad Patrem

Nunc mea Pierios cupiam per pectora fontes
Irriguas torquere vias, totumque per ora
Volvere laxatum gemino de vertice rivum;
Ut tenues oblita sonos audacibus alis
5   Surgat in officium venerandi Musa parentis.
Hoc utcunque tibi gratum pater optime carmen
Exiguum meditatur opus, nec novimus ipsi
Aptius a nobis quae possint munera donis
Respondere tuis, quamvis nec maxima possint
10   Respondere tuis, nedum ut par gratia donis
Esse queat, vacuis quae redditur arida verbis.
Sed tamen haec nostros ostendit pagina census,
Et quod habemus opum charta numeravimus ista,
Quae mihi sunt nullae, nisi quas dedit aurea Clio
15   Quas mihi semoto somni peperere sub antro,
Et nemoris laureta sacri Parnassides umbrae.
   Nec tu vatis opus divinum despice carmen,
Quo nihil aethereos ortus, et semina caeli,
Nil magis humanam commendat origine mentem,
20   Sancta Prometheae retinens vestigia flammae.
Carmen amant superi, tremebundaque Tartara carmen
Ima ciere valet, divosque ligare profundos,
Et triplici duros Manes adamante coercet.
Carmine sepositi retegunt arcana futuri
25   Phoebades, et tremulae pallentes ora Sibyllae;
Carmina sacrificus sollennes pangit ad aras,
Aurea seu sternit motantem cornua taurum;
Seu cum fata sagax fumantibus abdita fibris
Consulit, et tepidis Parcam scrutatur in extis.
30   Nos etiam patrium tunc cum repetemus Olympum,
Aeternaeque morae stabunt immobilis aevi,
Ibimus auratis per caeli templa coronis,
Dulcia suaviloquo sociantes carmina plectro,
Astra quibus, geminique poli convexa sonabunt.
35   Spiritus et rapidos qui circinat igneus orbes
Nunc quoque sidereis intercinit ipse choreis

Immortale melos, et inenarrabile carmen;
Torrida dum rutilus compescit sibila Serpens,
Demissoque ferox gladio mansuescit Orion;
40   Stellarum nec sentit onus Maurusius Atlas.
Carmina regales epulas ornare solebant,
Cum nondum luxus, vastaeque immensa vorago
Nota gulae, et modico spumabat coena Lyaeo.
Tum de more sedens festa ad convivia vates,
45   Aesculea intonsos redimitus ab arbore crines,
Heroumque actus, imitandaque gesta canebat,
Et Chaos, et positi late fundamina mundi,
Reptantesque deos, et alentes numina glandes,
Et nondum Aetnaeo quaesitum fulmen ab antro.
50   Denique quid vocis modulamen inane iuvabit,
Verborum sensusque vacans, numerique loquacis?
Silvestres decet iste choros, non Orphea, cantus,
Qui tenuit fluvios et quercubus addidit aures
Carmine, non cithara, simulacraque functa canendo
55   Compulit in lacrimas: habet has a carmine laudes.
      Nec tu perge precor sacras contemnere Musas,
Nec vanas inopesque puta, quarum ipse peritus
Munere, mille sonos numeros componis ad aptos,
Millibus et vocem modulis variare canoram
60   Doctus, Arionii merito sis nominis haeres.
Nunc tibi quid mirum, si me genuisse poetam
Contigerit, caro si tam prope sanguine iuncti
Cognatas artes, studiumque affine sequamur:
Ipse volens Phoebus se dispertire duobus,
65   Altera dona mihi, dedit altera dona parenti,
Dividuumque deum genitorque puerque tenemus.
      Tu tamen ut simules teneras odisse Camenas,
Non odisse reor, neque enim, pater, ire iubebas
Qua via lata patet, qua pronior area lucri,
70   Certaque condendi fulget spes aurea nummi;
Nec rapis ad leges, male custoditaque gentis
Iura, nec insulsis damnas clamoribus aures.
Sed magis excultam cupiens ditescere mentem,
Me procul urbano strepitu, secessibus altis
75   Abductum Aoniae iucunda per otia ripae,

Phoebaeo lateri comitem sinis ire beatum.
Officium cari taceo commune parentis,
Me poscunt maiora; tuo pater optime sumptu
Cum mihi Romuleae patuit facundia linguae,
80 Et Latii veneres, et quae Iovis ora decebant
Grandia magniloquis elata vocabula Graiis,
Addere suasisti quos iactat Gallia flores,
Et quam degeneri novus Italus ore loquelam
Fundit, barbaricos testatus voce tumultus,
85 Quaeque Palaestinus loquitur mysteria vates.
Denique quicquid habet caelum, subiectaque coelo
Terra parens, terraeque et coelo interfluus aer,
Quicquid et unda tegit, pontique agitabile marmor,
Per te nosse licet, per te, si nosse libebit.
90 Dimotaque venit spectanda scientia nube,
Nudaque conspicuos inclinat ad oscula vultus,
Ni fugisse velim, ni sit libasse molestum.
    I nunc, confer opes quisquis malesanus avitas
Austriaci gazas, Peruanaque regna praeoptas.
95 Quae potuit maiora pater tribuisse, vel ipse
Iupiter, excepto, donasset ut omnia, coelo?
Non potiora dedit, quamvis et tuta fuissent,
Publica qui iuveni commisit lumina nato
Atque Hyperionios currus, et frena diei,
100 Et circum undantem radiata luce tiaram.
Ergo ego iam doctae pars quamlibet ima catervae
Victrices hederas inter laurosque sedebo;
Iamque nec obscurus populo miscebor inerti,
Vitabuntque oculos vestigia nostra profanos.
105 Este procul vigiles curae, procul este querelae,
Invidiaeque acies transverso tortilis hirquo;
Saeva nec anguiferos extende Calumnia rictus;
In me triste nihil foedissima turba potestis,
Nec vestri sum iuris ego; securaque tutus
110 Pectora, vipereo gradiar sublimis ab ictu.
    At tibi, care pater, postquam non aequa merenti
Posse referre datur, nec dona rependere factis,
Sit memorasse satis, repetitaque munera grato
Percensere animo, fidaeque reponere menti.

115   Et vos, O nostri, iuvenilia carmina, lusus,
       Si modo perpetuos sperare audebitis annos,
       Et domini superesse rogo, lucemque tueri,
       Nec spisso rapient oblivia nigra sub Orco,
       Forsitan has laudes, decantatumque parentis
120   Nomen, ad exemplum, sero servabitis aevo.

To his Father

Now I wish that the Pierian fountains[1] would divert their refreshing channels through my breast, and that the whole stream pouring from the twin peaks[3] would flow from my lips, so that my Muse, forgetting trivial songs, might rise on bold wings to do her duty and honour my father. The poem that she is meditating is a feeble composition, best of fathers, and perhaps not pleasing to you, but I do not know what gifts of mine could more appropriately repay your gifts to me, though my greatest gifts could never repay yours – for your gifts can never be matched by the barren gratitude of empty words. Nevertheless, this page shows all my possessions, and I have counted out on this paper all the wealth that I own, for I own nothing but what golden Clio[14] has given me – the fruit of dreams in a distant cavern, fruit of laurel groves in a sacred wood, the shades of Parnassus.

Do not despise divine song, the poet's work. Nothing provides clearer evidence of our divine source, our heavenly seed; nothing better graces by its origin the human mind, for poetry retains some holy sparks of the Promethean fire.[20] The high gods love poetry, and poetry has power to shake the trembling depths of Tartarus and bind the gods below; it chains the unyielding ghosts with triple adamant. With poetry Apollo's priestesses and the trembling, pallid Sibyls reveal secrets of the future.[25] The sacrificial priest composes verses at ceremonial altars, both when he smites the bull that tosses its horns and when he consults secret destiny in the smoking flesh and, sagacious of the future, discerns fate in the warm entrails. We too, when we return to our native Olympus, and the never-ending ages stand fixed in changeless eternity, shall walk through the temples of heaven wearing crowns of gold, blending our sweet songs with the soft harp, so that the stars and the twin poles of heaven's vault will echo.[33] Even now, the fiery spirit[35] who circles the swift spheres is itself singing, in harmony with the starry choirs, an immortal melody, an inexpressible song.[37] Meanwhile the shining Serpent[38] restrains his hot hissing, and fierce Orion, grown mild, lowers his sword, and Mauretanian Atlas no longer feels the weight of the stars.

Songs were the customary adornments of royal feasts in the days when luxury and the bottomless gulf of insatiable gluttony were not yet known, and wine sparkled at the table only in moderation. The custom then was that the poet would sit at the festal banquet, his unshorn hair garlanded with oak leaves, and he would sing of the deeds of heroes, of their exemplary exploits, of Chaos and the broad foundations of the world. He would sing of crawling gods and deities nourished by acorns,[48] of the thunderbolt not yet brought from the chasm of Etna.[49] In short, what use is the inane modulation of the voice without words, meaning, and rhythm of speech? That kind of song suits the woodland choristers, but not Orpheus, who held back rivers and gave ears to the oak trees by his song, not his lyre, and by his singing drew tears from lifeless ghosts.[55] That fame he owes to song.

Desist then, I implore you, from despising the sacred Muses; don't think them worthless or unprofitable. It is by their gift that you yourself have the skill to match a thousand notes to fit rhythms, and the expertise to vary the singer's voice through a thousand modulations – may you deservedly inherit Arion's fame.[60] Now, since it has been my lot to be born a poet, why should you think it so strange that we, who are so closely joined by blood, should pursue sister arts and kindred interests? Phoebus[64] himself, wishing to divide himself between us two, gave some gifts to me and others to my father; and, father and son, we share the divided god. But though you pretend to hate the delicate Muses, I do not believe that you really hate them. For, father, you did not bid me go where the broad way stretches open, where it is easier to reap a harvest of lucre, and where the golden hope of piling up money shines bright and sure. You do not drive me into the law, and our country's ill-guarded statutes; you do not condemn my ears to that ridiculous clamour. But, wishing rather to enrich the mind that you have cultivated, you have led me far away from the din of the city, into deep seclusion and delightful leisure by the Aonian[75] stream, and you allow me to walk by Apollo's side as his blessed companion.

I say nothing of a dear father's usual kindness, for I must speak of greater things. When, at your expense, dear father, I had acquired fluency in the tongue of Romulus, the beauties of Latin, and the lofty speech of the sublime Greeks, fit for Jove's own lips, you persuaded me to add the flowers that are the boast of France, the language that the modern Italian pours from his decadent lips (his utterance testifying to the barbarian invasions), and those sacred mysteries uttered by the Hebrew prophets. In short, all that heaven contains, and mother earth below the sky, and the air that flows between earth and sky, and whatever the water conceals, and the bright, tossing surface of the sea – all this, thanks to you, I am able to know, if I choose to learn about it. Knowledge comes into view from behind a parting cloud. Naked, she visibly bends her face to my kisses – if I choose not to run away, if I do not find her irksome.

Go now and pile up riches, whoever has an insane preference for the ancient treasures of Austria or the realms of Peru.[94] What greater gift could a father have given – or Jove himself – though he had given all things except heaven? He gave no greater gifts (even had they proved safe) who gave to his young son[98] the universal light, the chariot of Hyperion,[99] the reins of day, and the tiara that radiates waves of light. Therefore, I who now have a place, albeit a low one, among the ranks of the learned, shall one day sit among those who are crowned with the victor's ivy and laurel.[102] I shall not mingle unknown with the uncultivated throng, and my steps will shun the sight of profane eyes. Begone, wakeful cares; begone, complaints, and the goatish, sidelong glance of squint-eyed Envy. Spiteful Calumny, do not gape with serpent jaws. You cannot harm me, detestable band; I am not under your power. I shall walk high above your viper's sting, with a safe, untroubled breast.

But for you, dear father, since I cannot repay you as you deserve, or do anything to repay your gifts, let it suffice that I have recorded them, and that I count over your repeated favours with a grateful mind, and cherish them in a loyal heart.[114]

And you, my youthful poems and amusements, if only you dare hope to live for ever, to survive your master's pyre and see the light, and if dark oblivion does not carry you down to crowded Orcus,[118] then perhaps these praises, and the name of the father celebrated in them, will be preserved as an example for future ages.

Psalm CXIV

Ἰσραὴλ ὅτε παῖδες, ὅτ' ἀγλαὰ φῦλ' Ἰακώβου
Αἰγύπτιον λίπε δῆμον, ἀπεχθέα, βαρβαρόφωνον,
Δὴ τότε μοῦνον ἔην ὅσιον γένος υἷες Ἰούδα.
Ἐν δὲ θεὸς λαοῖσι μέγα κρείων βαϲίλευεν.

5   Εἶδε καὶ ἐντροπάδην φύγαδ' ἐρρώησε θάλασσα,
Κύματι εἰλυμένη ῥοθίῳ, ὁ δ' ἄρ' ἐστυφελίχθη
Ἱρὸς Ἰορδάνης ποτὶ ἀργυροειδέα πηγήν.
Ἐκ δ' ὄρεα σκαρθμοῖσιν ἀπειρέσια κλονέοντο,
Ὡς κριοὶ σφριγόωντες ἐϋτραφερῷ ἐν ἀλωῇ.

10   Βαιότεραι δ' ἄμα πᾶσαι ἀνασκίρτησαν ἐρίπναι,
Οἷα παραὶ σύριγγι φίλῃ ὑπὸ μητέρι ἄρνες.
Τίπτε σύ γ' αἰνὰ θάλασσα πέλωρ φυγάδ' ἐρρώησας;
Κύματι εἰλυμένη ῥοθίῳ; τί δ' ἄρ' ἐστυφελίχθης
Ἱρὸς Ἰορδάνη ποτὶ ἀργυροειδέα πηγήν;

15   Τίπτ' ὄρεα σκαρθμοῖσιν ἀπειρέσια κλονέεσθε
Ὡς κριοὶ σφριγόωντες ἐϋτραφερῷ ἐν ἀλωῇ;
Βαιότεραι τί δ' ἄρ' ὕμμες ἀνασκιρτήσατ' ἐρίπναι,
Οἷα παραὶ σύριγγι φίλῃ ὑπὸ μητέρι ἄρνες;
Σείεο γαῖα τρέουσα θεὸν μεγάλ' ἐκτυπέοντα

20   Γαῖα θεὸν τρείουϲ' ὕπατον σέβας Ἰσϲακίδαο
Ὅς τε καὶ ἐκ σπιλάδων ποταμοὺς χέε μορμύροντας,
Κρήνην τ' ἀέναον πέτρης ἀπὸ δακρυοέσσης.

Psalm 114

When the children of Israel, when the glorious tribes of Jacob left
the land of Egypt, a hateful land of barbarous speech, then indeed
were the sons of Judah the one devout race, and among these peoples
Almighty God was king. The sea saw this, and fled in reverence,
coiled in roaring waves. Sacred Jordan was thrust back to its silver
source. The immense mountains leapt and tumbled like lusty rams
in a rich meadow. At the same time all the smaller crags skipped
like lambs about their dear mother at the sound of the pipe. Why,
monstrous and terrible sea, did you rush in flight, coiled in roaring
waves? Why, sacred Jordan, were you thrust back to your silver
source? Why, immense mountains, did you leap and tumble like
lusty rams in a rich meadow? Why, smaller crags, did you skip like

lambs about their dear mother at the sound of the pipe? Shake, earth, in fear of God who thunders mightily; earth, fear God, the highest majesty of Isaac's seed, who pours forth roaring torrents from the crags, and an everlasting spring from the weeping rock.

Philosophus ad Regem

Philosophus ad regem quendam qui eum ignotum et insontem inter reos forte captum inscius damnaverat, τὴν ἐπὶ θανάτῳ πορευόμενος, ηαεγ συβιτο μισιτ.

Ὦ ἄνα εἰ ὀλέσῃς με τὸν ἔννομον, οὐδέ τιν' ἀνδρῶν
Δεινὸν ὅλως δράσαντα, σοφώτατον ἴσθι κάρηνον
Ῥηϊδίως ἀφέλοιο, τὸ δ'ὕστερον αὖθι νοήσεις,
Μαψιδίως δ' ἄρ' ἔπειτα τεὸν πρὸς θυμὸν ὀδύρῃ,
5 Τοιόνδ' ἐκ πόλεως περιώνυμον ἄλκαρ ὀλέσσας.

A Philosopher to a King
These impromptu verses were sent to a king by a philosopher who was being taken to his death because the king had unwittingly condemned him – unrecognized and innocent – when he happened to be arrested along with some criminals.

If, O King, you destroy me, a law-abiding man who has done no harm to anybody, know that you may easily destroy a very wise head, but later you will see what you have done, and you will lament in vain to your heart[4] that you have destroyed so famous a guardian of the city.

Ad Salsillum poetam Romanum aegrotantem. Scazontes.

O Musa gressum quae volens trahis claudum,
Vulcanioque tarda gaudes incessu,
Nec sentis illud in loco minus gratum

Quam cum decentes flava Deiope suras
5   Alternat aureum ante Iunonis lectum,
Adesdum et haec s'is verba pauca Salsillo
Refer, Camena nostra cui tantum est cordi,
Quamque ille magnis praetulit immerito divis.
Haec ergo alumnus ille Londini Milto,
10   Diebus hisce qui suum linquens nidum
Polique tractum (pessimus ubi ventorum,
Insanientis impotensque pulmonis
Pernix anhela sub Iove exercet flabra)
Venit feraces Itali soli ad glebas,
15   Visum superba cognitas urbes fama
Virosque doctaeque indolem iuventutis,
Tibi optat idem hic fausta multa Salsille,
Habitumque fesso corpori penitus sanum;
Cui nunc profunda bilis infestat renes,
20   Praecordiisque fixa damnosum spirat.
Nec id pepercit impia quod tu Romano
Tam cultus ore Lesbium condis melos.
O dulce divum munus, O Salus Hebes
Germana! Tuque Phoebe morborum terror
25   Pythone caeso, sive tu magis Paean
Libenter audis, hic tuus sacerdos est.
Querceta Fauni, vosque rore vinoso
Colles benigni, mitis Evandri sedes,
Siquid salubre vallibus frondet vestris,
30   Levamen aegro ferte certatim vati.
Sic ille caris redditus rursum Musis
Vicina dulci prata mulcebit cantu.
Ipse inter atros emirabitur lucos
Numa, ubi beatum degit otium aeternum,
35   Suam reclivis semper Aegeriam spectans.
Tumidusque et ipse Tibris hinc delinitus
Spei favebit annuae colonorum;
Nec in sepulcris ibit obsessum reges
Nimium sinistro laxus irruens loro;
40   Sed frena melius temperabit undarum,
Adusque curvi salsa regna Portumni.

To Salzilli, the Roman poet, when he was ill. Scazons.

O Muse, who willingly drags a lame[1] foot, and enjoys Vulcan's halting gait,[2] and finds it no less pleasing, in its place, than the graceful ankles of fair-haired Deiopea[4] when she dances before Juno's golden couch, come now, if you please, and carry these few words to Salzilli, who is so fond of my poetry that he ranks it undeservedly above that of the great, divine poets. These lines therefore come to you, Salzilli, from Milton, a nursling of London who has lately left his nest and his own quarter of the sky (where the worst of winds, with wildly raging lungs, swiftly drives the furious gusts under the heavens), and has come to Italy's fruitful soil to see her cities, renowned by proud fame, her men, and the learning and genius of her youth. That same Milton wishes you many blessings, Salzilli, and sound health for your exhausted body, whose kidneys suffer from an excess of bile, which spreads disease from its fixed seat in your entrails. This cursed disease has shown you no mercy, though you are a cultured poet and have framed Roman lips to the poetry of Lesbos.[22]

O sweet gift of the gods, Health, sister of Hebe![23] And you, Phoebus (or Paean,[25] if you prefer to be called by that name), the terror of all diseases since you slew the Python – this man Salzilli is your own priest. Oak groves of Faunus,[27] and you hills rich with the dewy grape, mild Evander's home,[28] if any healing plant grows in your valleys, eagerly bring it to cure the sick poet. Then, restored to his dear Muses, he will delight the surrounding meadows with his sweet song. Numa[34] himself will marvel, lying in the dark groves where he spends eternity in blessed leisure, gazing forever upon his Egeria. The swollen Tiber himself, charmed by the song, will favour the farmers' annual hopes; he will not, with his left rein loose, rush on to invest kings in their tombs,[39] but will better bridle his waves, as far as the briny realms of curving Portumnus.[41]

Mansus

Ioannes Baptista Mansus Marchio Villensis vir ingenii laude, tum literarum studio, nec non et bellica virtute apud Italos clarus in primis est. Ad quem Torquati Tassi dialogus extat de Amicitia scriptus; erat enim Tassi amicissimus; ab quo etiam inter Campaniae principes celebratur, in illo poemate cui titulus *Gerusalemme Conquistata*, lib. 20.

> Fra cavalier magnanimi, è cortesi
> Risplende il Manso . . .

Is authorem Neapoli commorantem summa benevolentia prosecutus est, multaque ei detulit humanitatis officia. Ad hunc itaquc hospes ille antequam ab ea urbe discederet, ut ne ingratum se ostenderet, hoc carmen misit.

Haec quoque Manse tuae meditantur carmina laudi
Pierides, tibi Manse choro notissime Phoebi,
Quandoquidem ille alium haud aequo est dignatus honore,
Post Galli cineres, et Mecaenatis Hetrusci.
5   Tu quoque si nostrae tantum valet aura Camenae,
Victrices hederas inter, laurosque sedebis.
Te pridem magno felix concordia Tasso
Iunxit, et aeternis inscripsit nomina chartis.
Mox tibi dulciloquum non inscia Musa Marinum
10 Tradidit; ille tuum dici se gaudet alumnum,
Dum canit Assyrios divum prolixus amores;
Mollis et Ausonias stupefecit carmine nymphas.
Ille itidem moriens tibi soli debita vates
Ossa, tibi soli supremaque vota reliquit.
15 Nec manes pietas tua cara fefellit amici;
Vidimus arridentem operoso ex aere poetam.
Nec satis hoc visum est in utrumque, et nec pia cessant
Officia in tumulo; cupis integros rapere Orco,
Qua potes, atque avidas Parcarum eludere leges:
20 Amborum genus, et varia sub sorte peractam
Describis vitam, moresquc, et dona Minervae;
Aemulus illius Mycalen qui natus ad altam

Rettulit Aeolii vitam facundus Homeri.
Ergo ego te Clius et magni nomine Phoebi
25   Manse pater, iubeo longum salvere per aevum
Missus Hyperboreo iuvenis peregrinus ab axe.
Nec tu longinquam bonus aspernabere Musam,
Quae nuper gelida vix enutrita sub Arcto
Imprudens Italas ausa est volitare per urbes.
30   Nos etiam in nostro modulantes flumine cygnos
Credimus obscuras noctis sensisse per umbras,
Qua Thamesis late puris argenteus urnis
Oceani glaucos perfundit gurgite crines.
Quin et in has quondam pervenit Tityrus oras.
35   Sed neque nos genus incultum, nec inutile Phoebo,
Qua plaga septeno mundi sulcata Trione
Brumalem patitur longa sub nocte Booten.
Nos etiam colimus Phoebum, nos munera Phoebo
Flaventes spicas, et lutea mala canistris,
40   Halantemque crocum (perhibet nisi vana vetustas)
Misimus, et lectas Druidum de gente choreas.
(Gens Druides antiqua sacris operata deorum
Heroum laudes imitandaque gesta canebant.)
Hinc quoties festo cingunt altaria cantu
45   Delo in herbosa Graiae de more puellae
Carminibus laetis memorant Corineida Loxo,
Fatidicamque Upin, cum flavicoma Hecaerge,
Nuda Caledonio variatas pectora fuco.
Fortunate senex, ergo quacunque per orbem
50   Torquati decus, et nomen celebrabitur ingens,
Claraque perpetui succrescet fama Marini,
Tu quoque in ora frequens venies plausumque virorum,
Et parili carpes iter immortale volatu.
Dicetur tum sponte tuos habitasse penates
55   Cynthius, et famulas venisse ad limina Musas.
At non sponte domum tamen idem, et regis adivit
Rura Pheretiadae caelo fugitivus Apollo;
Ille licet magnum Alciden susceperat hospes;
Tantum ubi clamosos placuit vitare bubulcos,
60   Nobile mansueti cessit Chironis in antrum,
Irriguos inter saltus frondosaque tecta

Peneium prope rivum: ibi saepe sub ilice nigra
Ad citharae strepitum blanda prece victus amici
Exilii duros lenibat voce labores.

65 Tum neque ripa suo, barathro nec fixa sub imo
Saxa stetere loco; nutat Trachinia rupes,
Nec sentit solitas, immania pondera, silvas;
Emotaeque suis properant de collibus orni,
Mulcenturque novo maculosi carmine lynces.

70 Diis dilecte senex, te Iupiter aequus oportet
Nascentem, et miti lustrarit lumine Phoebus,
Atlantisque nepos; neque enim nisi carus ab ortu
Diis superis poterit magno favisse poetae.
Hinc longaeva tibi lento sub flore senectus

75 Vernat, et Aesonios lucratur vivida fusos,
Nondum deciduos servans tibi frontis honores,
Ingeniumque vigens, et adultum mentis acumen.
O mihi si mea sors talem concedat amicum,
Phoebaeos decorasse viros qui tam bene norit,

80 Si quando indigenas revocabo in carmina reges,
Arturumque etiam sub terris bella moventem;
Aut dicam invictae sociali foedere mensae,
Magnanimos heroas, et (O modo spiritus adsit)
Frangam Saxonicas Britonum sub Marte phalanges.

85 Tandem ubi non tacitae permensus tempora vitae,
Annorumque satur cineri sua iura relinquam,
Ille mihi lecto madidis astaret ocellis,
Astanti sat erit si dicam sim tibi curae;
Ille meos artus, liventi morte solutos,

90 Curaret parva componi molliter urna.
Forsitan et nostros ducat de marmore vultus,
Nectens aut Paphia myrti aut Parnasside lauri
Fronde comas, at ego secura pace quiescam.
Tum quoque, si qua fides, si praemia certa bonorum,

95 Ipse ego caelicolum semotus in aethera divum,
Quo labor et mens pura vehunt, atque ignea virtus,
Secreti haec aliqua mundi de parte videbo
(Quantum fata sinunt), et tota mente serenum
Ridens purpureo suffundar lumine vultus,

100 Et simul aethereo plaudam mihi laetus Olympo.

Manso

Giovanni Battista Manso, Marquis of Villa, is one of the most renowned gentlemen in Italy, not only for his famous intellect and literary interests, but also for his military prowess. There is extant a dialogue *On Friendship* which Torquato Tasso dedicated to him, for he was a close friend of Tasso, who praised him among the Campanian nobles in that poem entitled *Jerusalem Conquered*, Book XX:

> Among magnanimous and courteous knights
> Manso shines . . .

When the present author was staying in Naples, the Marquis treated him with the greatest kindness, and showed him many courteous attentions. Before he left the city, therefore, his guest sent him this poem, so as not to seem ungrateful.

These verses too,[1] Manso, the Pierides[2] sing in your praise; in praise of you, Manso, so well known to Phoebus' choir, for the god has deemed hardly anyone worthy of equal honour since the death of Gallus and Etruscan Maecenas.[4] You also, if the breath of my Muse has power, will sit among victorious ivy and laurels.[6]

You were once joined to the great Tasso in a glad friendship that has written your names in the records of eternity. Soon afterwards the Muse – knowing what she did – entrusted the sweet-tongued Marino[9] to your care. He delighted to be called your foster-son while he wrote at length of the gods' Assyrian loves;[11] his sweet song entranced the young women of Italy. Dying, this poet left his bones, as was right, to you alone; to you alone he entrusted his last wishes. Nor has your loving devotion failed your friend's spirit; we have seen him smiling from his sculptured bronze.[16] But to you this did not seem sufficient for either poet, and your loyal services did not cease at the tomb. You wished, so far as you could, to snatch them from Orcus[18] unharmed and so cheat the voracious laws of the Fates; so you wrote an account of their lineage, the varying fortune of their lives, their characters, and their gifts from Minerva.[21] Thus you rival him born on lofty Mycale[22] – that eloquent biographer of Aeolian Homer.[23] Therefore, father Manso, in the name of Clio[24] and of great Phoebus, I, a youthful traveller sent from Hyperborean[26] skies, wish you a long and healthy life. You, in your benevolence, will not scorn a remote Muse who, though sparely nourished under the frozen Bear, has recently been rash enough to venture a flight through the cities of Italy. I believe that in the dark shades of night I too have heard swans[30] singing on my river, where the silver Thames with pure urns lets her shimmering locks flow in the ocean's wide flood. Indeed, our Tityrus[31] once visited these shores.

But we are no uncultured race, useless to Phoebus, we who suffer long nights under wintry Boötes[37] in that region of the world furrowed by the seven-starred Wain. We also worship Phoebus,[38] and have sent him our gifts – golden ears of grain, baskets of rosy apples, the fragrant crocus (unless antiquity reports falsely) and choirs selected from the clan of the Druids. The ancient clan of the Druids was well versed in the rites of the gods, and would sing the praises of heroes and their exemplary deeds.[43] So now, whenever Greek girls circle the altars of grassy Delos with festive chants, as is their custom, their joyful songs commemorate Loxo, daughter of Corineus,[46] prophetic Upis, and flaxen-haired Hecaërge, damsels whose bare breasts were painted with Caledonian woad.

Fortunate old man! For wherever Torquato's glory and great name will be honoured throughout the world, and wherever immortal Marino's brilliant fame will spread, your name and fame will also be constantly on men's lips, and you will enjoy an equal flight in your way to immortality. Men will then say that Cynthius[55] was a willing guest in your house, and that the Muses came like maid-servants to your door. For Apollo came unwillingly, a fugitive from heaven, to the house and fields of Pheretiades,[57] even though that king had received great Alcides as his guest.[58] When Apollo wished, as much as possible, to get away from the noisy ploughmen, he would retire to gentle Chiron's[60] famous cave, beside the river Peneus, amid well-watered forest pastures and leafy canopies. There, under the dark oak, yielding to his friend's flattering entreaty, he often lightened the hard labours of exile by singing to the music of his lyre. Then neither the river banks nor the rocks fixed in the lowest chasm would stay in their places; the Trachinian cliff[66] swayed to and fro and no longer felt its great, familiar burden of forests; the mountain ashes, uprooted, hastened from their hills, and spotted lynxes were tamed by the marvellous song.[69]

Aged man, beloved by the gods, Jupiter must have been favourable to you at birth, and Phoebus and the grandson of Atlas[72] must have shed their kindly light on you, for no one could have befriended so great a poet unless he was dear to the gods from birth. That is why your old age is green with lingering blossoms and is still vigorous, with a life-thread as long as Aeson's;[75] your brow preserves its honours[76] unwithered, your spirit is strong, and your mind as sharp as it is mature. O may Fate grant me such a friend, who knows so well how to honour the votaries of Phoebus – if ever I shall call back into song the kings of my native land, and Arthur waging war even under the earth,[81] or tell of the great-hearted heroes of the Table, made invincible by their fellowship; and (if only I have the inspiration) I shall shatter the Saxon shield-wall[84] with British arms! At last, when I have measured out a life in which poetry had not been silent, and when, full of years, I pay my last debt to the grave, that friend would stand by my bedside, with tears in his eyes, and it would be enough for me to say to him, as he stood there, 'Take care of me.' He would see to it that my limbs, relaxed in livid death, were gently laid in a small urn. Perhaps he might have my face copied in marble, binding my hair with leaves of Paphian myrtle[92] or Parnassian laurel, and I should rest in tranquil peace. Then, if faith has any meaning, if rewards are assured for the righteous, I myself, having been transported to the celestial realms of the heavenly gods, where labour, a pure mind, and ardent virtue lead, shall see these events (so far as the Fates allow) from some part of that secret world, and with a wholly serene mind and my smiling face suffused with rosy light, I shall joyfully clap my hands on heavenly Olympus.

Epitaphium Damonis

Argumentum

Thyrsis et Damon eiusdem viciniae pastores, eadem studia sequuti a pueritia amici erant, ut qui plurimum. Thyrsis animi causa profectus peregre de obitu Damonis nuntium accepit. Domum postea reversus, et rem ita esse comperto, se, suamque solitudinem hoc carmine deplorat. Damonis autem sub persona hic intelligitur Carolus Deodatus ex urbe Hetruriae

Luca paterno genere oriundus, caetera Anglus; ingenio, doc-
trina, clarissimisque caeteris virtutibus, dum viveret, iuvenis
egregius.

Himerides nymphae (nam vos et Daphnin et Hylan,
Et plorata diu meministis fata Bionis)
Dicite Sicelicum Thamesina per oppida carmen:
Quas miser effudit voces, quae murmura Thyrsis,
5   Et quibus assiduis exercuit antra querelis
Fluminaque, fontesque vagos, nemorumque recessus,
Dum sibi praereptum queritur Damona, neque altam
Luctibus exemit noctem loca sola pererrans.
Et iam bis viridi surgebat culmus arista,
10   Et totidem flavas numerabant horrea messes,
Ex quo summa dies tulerat Damona sub umbras,
Nec dum aderat Thyrsis; pastorem scilicet illum
Dulcis amor Musae Thusca retinebat in urbe.
Ast ubi mens expleta domum pecorisque relicti
15   Cura vocat, simul assueta seditque sub ulmo,
Tum vero amissum tum denique sentit amicum,
Coepit et immensum sic exonerare dolorem.
    Ite domum impasti, domino iam non vacat, agni.
Hei mihi! quae terris, quae dicam numina coelo,
20   Postquam te immiti rapuerunt funere Damon;
Siccine nos linquis, tua sic sine nomine virtus
Ibit, et obscuris numero sociabitur umbris?
At non ille animas virga qui dividit aurea,
Ista velit, dignumque tui te ducat in agmen,
25   Ignavumque procul pecus arceat omne silentum.
    Ite domum impasti, domino iam non vacat, agni.
Quicquid erit, certe, nisi me lupus ante videbit,
Indeplorato non comminuere sepulcro,
Constabitque tuus tibi honos, longumque vigebit
30   Inter pastores: illi tibi vota secundo
Solvere post Daphnin, post Daphnin dicere laudes
Gaudebunt, dum rura Pales, dum Faunus amabit:
Si quid id est, priscamque fidem coluisse, piumque,
Palladiasque artes, sociumque habuisse canorum.
35   Ite domum impasti, domino iam non vacat, agni.

Haec tibi certa manent, tibi erunt haec praemia Damon.
At mihi quid tandem fiet modo? quis mihi fidus
Haerebit lateri comes, ut tu saepe solebas
Frigoribus duris, et per loca foeta pruinis,
40   Aut rapido sub sole, siti morientibus herbis,
Sive opus in magnos fuit eminus ire leones,
Aut avidos terrere lupos praesepibus altis?
Quis fando sopire diem cantuque solebit?
    Ite domum impasti, domino iam non vacat, agni.
45   Pectora cui credam? quis me lenire docebit
Mordaces curas, quis longam fallere noctem
Dulcibis alloquiis, grato cum sibilat igni
Molle pirum, et nucibus strepitat focus, at malus Auster
Miscet cuncta foris, et desuper intonat ulmo.
50   Ite domum impasti, domino iam non vacat, agni.
Aut aestate, dies medio dum vertitur axe,
Cum Pan aesculea somnum capit abditus umbra,
Et repetunt sub aquis sibi nota sedilia nymphae,
Pastoresque latent, stertit sub sepe colonus,
55   Quis mihi blanditiasque tuas, quis tum mihi risus,
Cecropiosque sales referet, cultosque lepores?
    Ite domum impasti, domino iam non vacat, agni.
At iam solus agros, iam pascua solus oberro,
Sicubi ramosae densantur vallibus umbrae,
60   Hic serum expecto; supra caput imber et Eurus
Triste sonant, fractaeque agitata crepuscula silvae.
    Ite domum impasti, domino iam non vacat, agni.
Heu quam culta mihi prius arva procacibus herbis
Involvuntur, et ipsa situ seges alta fatiscit!
65   Innuba neglecto marcescit et uva racemo,
Nec myrteta iuvant; ovium quoque taedet, at illae
Moerent, inque suum convertunt ora magistrum.
    Ite domum impasti, domino iam non vacat, agni.
Tityrus ad corylos vocat, Alphesiboeus ad ornos,
70   Ad salices Aegon, ad flumina pulcher Amyntas,
Hic gelidi fontes, hic illita gramina musco,
Hic Zephyri, hic placidas interstrepit arbutus undas;
Ista canunt surdo, frutices ego nactus abibam.
    Ite domum impasti, domino iam non vacat, agni.

75 Mopsus ad haec, nam me redeuntem forte notarat
(Et callebat avium linguas, et sidera Mopsus)
Thyrsi quid hoc? dixit, quae te coquit improba bilis?
Aut te perdit amor, aut te male fascinat astrum,
Saturni grave saepe fuit pastoribus astrum;
80 Intimaque obliquo figit praecordia plumbo.
    Ite domum impasti, domino iam non vacat, agni.
Mirantur nymphae, et quid te Thyrsi futurum est?
Quid tibi vis? aiunt, non haec solet esse iuventae
Nubila frons, oculique truces, vultusque severi;
85 Illa choros, lususque leves, et semper amorem
Iure petit; bis ille miser qui serus amavit.
    Ite domum impasti, domino iam non vacat, agni.
Venit Hyas, Dryopeque, et filia Baucidis Aegle
Docta modos, citharaeque sciens, sed perdita fastu,
90 Venit Idumanii Chloris vicina fluenti;
Nil me blanditiae, nil me solantia verba,
Nil me, si quid adest, movet, aut spes ulla futuri.
    Ite domum impasti, domino iam non vacat, agni.
Hei mihi quam similes ludunt per prata iuvenci,
95 Omnes unanimi secum sibi lege sodales,
Nec magis hunc alio quisquam secernit amicum
De grege; sic densi veniunt ad pabula thoes,
Inque vicem hirsuti paribus iunguntur onagri;
Lex eadem pelagi, deserto in littore Proteus
100 Agmina phocarum numerat, vilisque volucrum
Passer habet semper quicum sit, et omnia circum
Farra libens volitet, sero sua tecta revisens;
Quem si fors letho obiecit, seu milvus adunco
Fata tulit rostro, seu stravit arundine fossor,
105 Protinus ille alium socio petit inde volatu.
Nos durum genus, et diris exercita fatis
Gens homines aliena animis, et pectore discors;
Vix sibi quisque parem de millibus invenit unum,
Aut si sors dederit tandem non aspera votis,
110 Illum inopina dies qua non speraveris hora
Surripit, aeternum linquens in saecula damnum.
    Ite domum impasti, domino iam non vacat, agni.
Heu quis me ignotas traxit vagus error in oras

Ire per aereas rupes, Alpemque nivosam!
115 Ecquid erat tanti Romam vidisse sepultam,
Quamvis illa foret, qualem dum viseret olim,
Tityrus ipse suas et oves et rura reliquit;
Ut te tam dulci possem caruisse sodale,
Possem tot maria alta, tot interponere montes,
120 Tot silvas, tot saxa tibi, fluviosque sonantes?
Ah certe extremum licuisset tangere dextram,
Et bene compositos placide morientis ocellos,
Et dixisse vale, nostri memor ibis ad astra.
         Ite domum impasti, domino iam non vacat, agni.
125 Quamquam etiam vestri nunquam meminisse pigebit
Pastores Thusci, Musis operata iuventus,
Hic charis, atque lepos; et Thuscus tu quoque Damon,
Antiqua genus unde petis Lucumonis ab urbe.
O ego quantus eram, gelidi cum stratus ad Arni
130 Murmura, populeumque nemus, qua mollior herba,
Carpere nunc violas, nunc summas carpere myrtos,
Et potui Lycidae certantem audire Menalcam.
Ipse etiam tentare ausus sum, nec puto multum
Displicui, nam sunt et apud me munera vestra
135 Fiscellae, calathique et cerea vincla cicutae;
Quin et nostra suas docuerunt nomina fagos
Et Datis, et Francinus, erant et vocibus ambo
Et studiis noti, Lydorum sanguinis ambo.
         Ite domum impasti, domino iam non vacat, agni.
140 Haec mihi tum laeto dictabat roscida luna,
Dum solus teneros claudebam cratibus hoedos.
Ah quoties dixi, cum te cinis ater habebat,
Nunc canit, aut lepori nunc tendit retia Damon,
Vimina nunc texit, varios sibi quod sit in usus;
145 Et quae tum facili sperabam mente futura
Arripui voto levis, et praesentia finxi.
Heus bone numquid agis? nisi te quid forte retardat,
Imus? et arguta paulum recubamus in umbra,
Aut ad aquas Colni, aut ubi iugera Cassibelauni?
150 Tu mihi percurres medicos, tua gramina, succos,
Helleborumque, humilesque crocos, foliumque hyacinthi,
Quasque habet ista palus herbas, artesque medentum.

Ah pereant herbae, pereant artesque medentum
Gramina, postquam ipsi nil profecere magistro.
155 Ipse etiam, nam nescio quid mihi grande sonabat
Fistula, ab undecima iam lux est altera nocte,
Et tum forte novis admoram labra cicutis,
Dissiluere tamen rupta compage, nec ultra
Ferre graves potuere sonos; dubito quoque ne sim
160 Turgidulus, tamen et referam, vos cedite silvae.
     Ite domum impasti, domino iam non vacat, agni.
Ipse ego Dardanias Rutupina per aequora puppes
Dicam, et Pandrasidos regnum vetus Inogeniae,
Brennumque Arviragumque duces, priscumque Belinum,
165 Et tandem Armoricos Britonum sub lege colonos;
Tum gravidam Arturo fatali fraude Iogernen,
Mendaces vultus, assumptaque Gorlois arma,
Merlini dolus. O mihi tum si vita supersit,
Tu procul annosa pendebis fistula pinu
170 Multum oblita mihi, aut patriis mutata Camenis
Brittonicum strides, quid enim? omnia non licet uni
Non sperasse uni licet omnia; mi satis ampla
Merces, et mihi grande decus (sim ignotus in aevum
Tum licet, externo penitusque inglorius orbi)
175 Si me flava comas legat Usa, et potor Alauni,
Vorticibusque frequens Abra, et nemus omne Treantae,
Et Thamesis meus ante omnes, et fusca metallis
Tamara, et extremis me discant Orcades undis.
     Ite domum impasti, domino iam non vacat, agni.
180 Haec tibi servabam lenta sub cortice lauri,
Haec, et plura simul; tum quae mihi pocula Mansus,
Mansus Chalcidicae non ultima gloria ripae,
Bina dedit, mirum artis opus, mirandus et ipse,
Et circum gemino caelaverat argumento:
185 In medio rubri maris unda, et odoriferum ver,
Littora longa Arabum, et sudantes balsama silvae;
Has inter Phoenix divina avis, unica terris,
Caeruleum fulgens diversicoloribus alis,
Auroram vitreis surgentem respicit undis.
190 Parte alia polus omnipatens, et magnus Olympus,
Quis putet? hic quoque Amor, pictaeque in nube pharetrae,

Arma corusca, faces, et spicula tincta pyropo;
Nec tenues animas, pectusque ignobile vulgi
Hinc ferit, at circum flammantia lumina torquens,
195   Semper in erectum spargit sua tela per orbes
Impiger, et pronos nunquam collimat ad ictus;
Hinc mentes ardere sacrae, formaeque deorum.
    Tu quoque in his, nec me fallit spes lubrica Damon,
Tu quoque in his certe es, nam quo tua dulcis abiret
200   Sanctaque simplicitas, nam quo tua candida virtus?
Nec te Lethaeo fas quaesivisse sub Orco,
Nec tibi conveniunt lacrimae, nec flebimus ultra;
Ite procul lacrimae, purum colit aethera Damon,
Aethera purus habet, pluvium pede reppulit arcum;
205   Heroumque animas inter, divosque perennes,
Aethereos haurit latices et gaudia potat
Ore sacro. Quin tu coeli post iura recepta
Dexter ades, placidusque fave quicunque vocaris,
Seu tu noster eris Damon, sive aequior audis
210   Diodotus, quo te divino nomine cuncti
Coelicolae norint, silvisque vocabere Damon.
Quod tibi purpureus pudor, et sine labe iuventus
Grata fuit, quod nulla tori libata voluptas,
En etiam tibi virginei servantur honores;
215   Ipse caput nitidum cinctus rutilante corona,
Laetaque frondentis gestans umbracula palmae
Aeternum perages immortales hymenaeos;
Cantus ubi, choreisque furit lyra mista beatis,
Festa Sionaeo bacchantur et Orgia thyrso.

Damon's Elegy
Argument

Thyrsis and Damon, shepherds of the same neighbourhood, had
from childhood pursued the same interests and been the closest
friends. Thyrsis, who had gone abroad for the improvement of his
mind, received news of Damon's death. Having returned home, and
found the news to be true, he bewailed himself and his loneliness
in this poem. 'Damon' here represents Charles Diodati, who was
descended on his father's side from the Tuscan city of Lucca, but
was English in all other respects. While he lived, he was a young

man of outstanding talents, learning and other most illustrious virtues.

Nymphs of Himera[1] (for you remember Daphnis and Hylas, and the long-lamented fate of Bion),[2] sing a Sicilian song through the cities of the Thames. Tell what cries, what moans, unhappy Thyrsis[4] poured forth; his ceaseless laments that disturbed the caves, the rivers, the straying brooks, and the deep woods, while he mourned for Damon,[7] carried off before his time. Wandering through lonely places, he filled deep night with his grief. And now the green-eared stalk had twice[9] sprung up, and as many times the granaries had gathered in the yellow harvests, since Damon's last day had carried him down to the shades – and still Thyrsis was not there; love of the sweet Muse detained that shepherd in a Tuscan city. But when he had filled his mind with foreign sights, and care for the flock he had left behind called him home, he sat down under his accustomed elm, and then – in that moment – then indeed the loss of his friend truly came home to him, and he tried to lighten his huge load of sorrow with these words:

'Go home unfed, my lambs, your master has no time for you now.[18] Ah me, what deities can I invoke in earth or heaven, Damon, now that they have carried you off to cruel death? Is this the way you leave me? Must your virtue vanish without a name, and be numbered among the unknown shades? But no, he[23] who marshals the souls with his golden wand would not want that; he would lead you into a company that is worthy of you, and drive far off all the base rabble of the silent dead.

'Go home unfed, my lambs, your master has no time for you now. Whatever happens, unless a wolf sees me first,[27] you can be sure that you will not moulder in the grave unwept. Your fame will survive you, and long flourish among shepherds. They will rejoice to pay their vows to you, next after Daphnis,[31] and to sing praises of you, next after Daphnis, so long as Pales[32] and Faunus love the fields – if it means anything that you cherished ancient faith and piety, and the arts of Pallas,[34] and had a poet as your friend.

'Go home unfed, my lambs, your master has no time for you now. These rewards are certain to be yours, Damon; you will enjoy them. But what will now become of me? What faithful companion will stay by my side, as you used to do, in the bitter cold when frost covered everything, or when under the hot sun green things perished in the drought, whether our task was to go within a spear's cast of great lions, or to chase ravenous wolves from the high sheepfolds? Who now will lull my day to rest with talk and song?

'Go home unfed, my lambs, your master has no time for you now. To whom shall I open my heart? Who will teach me to soothe gnawing cares and beguile the long night with delightful conversation, while the ripe pear hisses before the cheerful fire, nuts crack open on the hearth, and the cruel south wind wreaks havoc outside, roaring through the crown of the elm.

'Go home unfed, my lambs, your master has no time for you now. Or in summer, when the sun is in the mid heavens, and Pan takes his sleep, hidden under a shady oak, and the nymphs seek their familiar haunts under the water, and the shepherds seek cover, and the ploughman snores under the hedge, who then will bring back to me your charm, your laughter, your Attic wit,[56] and your refined sense of humour?

'Go home unfed, my lambs, your master has no time for you now. But now I wander alone through the fields, alone through the pastures, waiting for evening in valleys where shady branches grow thick. Overhead rain and the south-east wind sound mournfully through the troubled twilight of the windswept forest.

'Go home unfed, my lambs, your master has no time for you now. Alas, how my once well-tilled fields are overgrown with wanton weeds; even the tall grain rots with mould! The unwedded grapes[65] wither on the neglected vine, and the myrtle groves[66] bring no joy; I am weary even of my sheep, and they turn to their master with mournful eyes.

'Go home unfed, my lambs, your master has no time for you now. Tityrus[69] calls me to the hazels, Alphesiboeus[69] to the ash trees, Aegon[70] to the willows, beautiful Amyntas[70] to the rivers: "Here are cool springs, here are mossy lawns, here are soft breezes, here the wild strawberry whispers among quiet streams." They sing to deaf ears. I reach the bushes and slip away from them.

'Go home unfed, my lambs, your master has no time for you now. Then Mopsus[75] came – by chance he had happened to see me returning – Mopsus, who was expert in the language of the birds and in the stars. "What's the matter, Thyrsis?" he said. "What melancholy is tormenting you? You must either be pining with love

or bewitched by an evil star; Saturn's[79] star has often been malignant
to shepherds; his slanting leaden shaft pierces to the inmost heart."

'Go home unfed, my lambs, your master has no time for you now.
The nymphs are astonished and cry: "What will become of you,
Thyrsis? What do you want? Youth is not accustomed to have a
clouded brow, wild eyes, or a stern face; youth rightly seeks dances,
cheerful games, and love, always love. Twice wretched is he who
loves too late."

'Go home unfed, my lambs, your master has no time for you now.
Along came Hyas[88] and Dryope, and Aegle, daughter of Baucis (an
excellent musician, skilled on the harp, but spoiled through pride),
along came Chloris, who lives by the Idumanian river.[90] No charms,
no comforting words can move me, and nothing in the present; nor
is there any hope for the future.

'Go home unfed, my lambs, your master has no time for you now.
Ah me, how like one another are the young bulls frisking in the
meadows, all companions together, of one mind, bound each to each
by law; no one of them singles out another as a particular friend
from the herd. Wolves also hunt in packs, and the shaggy wild asses
mate together by turn. The same law holds for the sea; on the
deserted shore Proteus[99] counts his herds of seals. Even the lowest
of birds, the sparrow,[101] always has a mate with whom he happily
flits around the stacks of grain, and returns late to his nest. If by
chance death carries off his mate, whether by the kite's hooked beak
or the common labourer's arrow, he immediately seeks another
companion for his flight. But we men are a hard race, a race vexed
by the cruel Fates, with minds unfriendly to one another, and hearts
at discord. It is hard to find one kindred spirit among a thousand,
and if destiny, at last softening to our prayers, does grant one, an
unexpected day and an unlooked-for hour snatch him away, leaving
a pain that lasts for ever.

'Go home unfed, my lambs, your master has no time for you now.
Alas, what desire of wandering enticed me to foreign shores, over
the towering peaks of the snowy Alps? Was it so important to see
buried Rome – even if it had appeared as in ancient times, when
Tityrus[117] left his fields and his sheep to see it – that I could allow
myself to be deprived of so dear a companion, that I could put so
many seas, so many mountains, so many forests, so many rocks, and
so many roaring rivers between us? Ah, I might at least have held

his right hand at the end and closed his eyes in peaceful death, and said: "Farewell! Remember me as you ascend to the stars."

'Go home unfed, my lambs, your master has no time for you now. And yet I shall never regret my memory of you, Tuscan shepherds, young men devoted to the Muses, for grace and charm are with you; and you too, Damon, were a Tuscan, tracing your descent from the ancient city of Lucca. Ah, how grand I was when I lay beside the cool, murmuring Arno,[129] on the soft grass by a poplar grove, plucking now violets, now sprays of myrtle, and could listen to Menalcas and Lycidas contending in song.[132] I too was bold enough to try, and I do not think I displeased you too much, for I still have your gifts,[134] rush baskets, and wicker baskets, and pipes fastened with wax; indeed, Dati and Francini,[137] both renowned poets and scholars, and both of Lydian blood,[138] taught their beech trees my name.

'Go home unfed, my lambs, your master has no time for you now. When, happy and unaccompanied, I would shut the young kids in their wattled folds, the dewy moon would often tell me things. Ah, how often (when death's black ashes already held you) would I say: "Now Damon is singing, or stretching nets for the hare; now he is weaving willow baskets for his various uses." What my eager mind then hoped for the future, I lightly seized on with my wishes, and imagined it to be really present. "Ho there, friend, what are you doing? Shall we go – unless you have something better to do? Shall we lie for a while in the murmuring shade – either by the waters of Colne, or in the acres of Cassivelaunus?[149] You can tell me all about your medicinal herbs and potions – hellebore, the humble crocus, the hyacinth leaf, all the plants of the marsh – and the arts of the physician."[152]

'Ah, let the herbs and potions perish, and the arts of the physician, since they were of no use to their master. For my part, my pipe was sounding I know not what lofty strain[155] – it is now eleven nights and a day since then – and I had casually set my lips to new pipes, but they burst asunder, broken at the fastening, no longer able to bear the grand notes. I fear that I may seem conceited, but I will tell of it. Give place, woodlands.[160]

'Go home unfed, my lambs, your master has no time for you now. I would tell of Trojan ships in the Rutupian Sea,[162] and of the ancient realm of Inogen, daughter of Pandrasus,[163] and of the chieftains Brennus and Arviragus, and old Belinus,[164] and the Armorican colonists[165] who came at length under British law; then of Igraine, pregnant with Arthur by a fatal deception – the counterfeit face and dissembled arms of Gorlois, Merlin's trick.[168] Then, my pastoral pipe, if life remains to me, you will hang on an old pine tree, far off and forgotten by me – or else, changed by my native Muses, you will sound forth a British strain, and why not? One man cannot do everything, or hope to do everything. For me it would be sufficient reward and ample honour (though I remain forever unknown and utterly inglorious throughout the rest of the world) if only fair-haired Ouse[175] would read me, and he who drinks of the Alne, and Humber full of eddies, and every wood along the Trent, and before all my Thames, and the Tamar, discoloured by metallic ore, and if the Orkneys among their remote waves would learn my song.

'Go home unfed, my lambs, your master has no time for you now. I was keeping these things for you in pliant laurel bark,[180] these and more besides. I was saving the two cups that Manso[181] gave me – Manso, not the least glory of the Chalcidian[182] shore. They are a marvellous work of art, and he himself is a marvel. Around them runs an engraving with a double subject. In the middle are the waves of the Red Sea, the fragrant spring, the long shores of Arabia, and forests dripping with balsam; among these the phoenix,[187] that divine bird, unique on earth, gleaming blue with many-coloured wings, watching Aurora rise above the glassy waves. In another part are the infinite sky and great Olympus – who would have thought it? Here too is Cupid,[191] with his brightly coloured quiver in a cloud, his glittering weapons, his torches, and his arrows tipped with fiery bronze. From that height he does not strike shallow spirits and the base hearts of the rabble but, looking around him with flaming eyes, he tirelessly shoots his arrows aloft in a ceaseless shower through the heavenly spheres, and never aims a downward shot; hence he kindles holy minds and the essences of the gods.

'You too are among them, Damon – no elusive hope deceives me – assuredly you too are among them, for where else could your sweet and holy simplicity and your radiant white virtue have gone? It would be improper to look for you in Lethean Orcus. Nothing is here for tears. I shall weep no more. Begone, my tears. Damon dwells now in the pure aether; being pure himself, the aether is where he dwells, and he spurns the rainbow with his foot. Among the souls of heroes and the everlasting gods he drinks heavenly draughts and quaffs joys with his holy lips. Now that you have received the rights of heaven, stand by my side and gently favour me, by whatever name you are called,[208] whether you are my Damon, or whether you prefer to be called Diodati – the divine name[210] by which the inhabitants of heaven will know you, though the woods still call you Damon.

'Because the rosy blush of modesty and a youth without stain were dear to you, because you never tasted the pleasure of the bed,[213] look! virginal honours[214] are reserved for you. Your radiant head circled with a gleaming crown, the shady fronds of joyous palm[216] in your hands, you shall perform the immortal marriage-rite[217] for ever and ever; singing is heard there, and the ecstatic sound of the lyre mingles with the blessed dances, and secret, festal rites rave in Bacchic delight under the thyrsus[219] of Zion.'

GREEK AND LATIN POEMS
ADDED IN 1673

Apologus de Rustico et Hero

Rusticus ex malo sapidissima poma quotannis
    Legit, et urbano lecta dedit domino:
Hic incredibili fructus dulcedine captus
    Malum ipsam in proprias transtulit areolas.
5   Hactenus illa ferax, sed longo debilis aevo,
    Mota solo assueto, protinus aret iners.
Quod tandem ut patuit domino, spe lusus inani,
    Damnavit celeres in sua damna manus.
Atque ait, Heu quanto satius fuit illa coloni
10   (Parva licet) grato dona tulisse animo!
Possem ego avaritiam frenare, gulamque voracem:
    Nunc periere mihi et foetus et ipsa parens.

A Fable of a Peasant and his Landlord

Every year a peasant gathered the most savoury apples from his tree
and gave the pick of the crop to his landlord, who lived in the city.
The landlord, delighted by the incredible sweetness of the fruit,
transplanted the tree into his own gardens. Until now, it had been
productive, but it was weakened by old age, and once moved from
its accustomed soil it promptly withered and became barren. When,
at length, this came to the landlord's attention, and he saw that he
had been deluded by a vain hope, he cursed his hands for being so
swift in causing his own loss: 'Alas,' he cried, 'how much better it
was to accept my tenant's gifts with a grateful heart, small though
they were! If only I had bridled my avarice and voracious gluttony!
Now I have lost both fruit and tree.'

In Effigiei eius Sculptorem

'Αμαθεῖ γεγράφθαι χειρὶ τήνδε μὲν εἰκόνα
Φαίης τάχ' ἄν, πρὸς εἶδος αὐτοφυὲς βλέπων·
Τὸν δ' ἐκτυπωτὸν οὐκ ἐπιγνόντες φίλοι
Γελᾶτε φαύλου δυσμίμημα ζωγράφου.

On the Engraver of his Portrait

Were you to look at the original, you would perhaps say that this
likeness was made by an incompetent hand. Friends, since you cannot
recognize the man depicted, laugh at the rotten picture of a rotten
artist.

Ad Ioannem Rousium Oxoniensis Academiae Bibliothecarium

Jan. 23 1646 [1647]

De libro Poematum amisso, quem ille sibi denuo mitti postula-
bat, ut cum aliis nostris in Bibliotheca publica reponeret, Ode.

Strophe I
Gemelle cultu simplici gaudens liber,
Fronde licet gemina,
Munditieque nitens non operosa,
Quam manus attulit
5   Iuvenilis olim,
Sedula tamen haud nimii poetae;
Dum vagus Ausonias nunc per umbras
Nunc Britannica per vireta lusit,
Insons populi, barbitoque devius
10   Indulsit patrio, mox itidem pectine Daunio
Longinquum intonuit melos
Vicinis, et humum vix tetigit pede;

Antistrophe

Quis te, parve liber, quis te fratribus
Subduxit reliquis dolo,
15 Cum tu missus ab urbe,
Docto iugiter obsecrante amico,
Illustre tendebas iter
Thamesis ad incunabula
Caerulei patris,
20 Fontes ubi limpidi
Aonidum, thyasusque sacer
Orbi notus per immensos
Temporum lapsus redeunte coelo,
Celeberque futurus in aevum?

Strophe 2

25 Modo quis deus, aut editus deo
Pristinam gentis miseratus indolem
(Si satis noxas luimus priores
Mollique luxu degener otium)
Tollat nefandos civium tumultus,
30 Almaque revocet studia sanctus
Et relegatas sine sede Musas
Iam pene totis finibus Angligenum;
Immundasque volucres
Unguibus imminentes
35 Figat Apollinea pharetra,
Phineamque abigat pestem procul amne Pegaseo?

Antistrophe

Quin tu, libelle, nuntii licet mala
Fide, vel oscitantia
Semel erraveris agmine fratrum,
40 Seu quis te teneat specus,
Seu qua te latebra, forsan unde vili
Callo tereris institoris insulsi,
Laetare felix; en iterum tibi
Spes nova fulget posse profundam
45 Fugere Lethen, vehique superam
In Iovis aulam remige penna;

Strophe 3
Nam te Rousius sui
Optat peculi, numeroque iusto
Sibi pollicitum queritur abesse,
50   Rogatque venias ille cuius inclyta
Sunt data virum monumenta curae:
Teque adytis etiam sacris
Voluit reponi quibus et ipse praesidet
Aeternorum operum custos fidelis,
55   Quaestorque gazae nobilioris
Quam cui praefuit Ion,
Clarus Erechtheides,
Opulenta dei per templa parentis
Fulvosque tripodas, donaque Delphica
60   Ion Actaea genitus Creusa.

Antistrophe
Ergo tu visere lucos
Musarum ibis amoenos,
Diamque Phoebi rursus ibis in domum
Oxonia quam valle colit
65   Delo posthabita,
Bifidoque Parnassi iugo:
Ibis honestus,
Postquam egregiam tu quoque sortem
Nactus abis, dextri prece sollicitatus amici.
70   Illic legeris inter alta nomina
Authorum, Graiae simul et Latinae
Antiqua gentis lumina, et verum decus.

Epodos
Vos tandem haud vacui mei labores,
Quicquid hoc sterile fudit ingenium;
75   Iam sero placidam sperare iubeo
Perfunctam invidia requiem, sedesque beatas
Quas bonus Hermes
Et tutela dabit solers Rousi,
Quo neque lingua procax vulgi penetrabit, atque longe
80   Turba legentum prava facesset;

At ultimi nepotes,
Et cordatior aetas
Iudicia rebus aequiora forsitan
Adhibebit integro sinu.
85 Tum livore sepulto,
Si quid meremur sana posteritas sciet
Rousio favente.

Ode tribus constat Strophis, totidemque Antistrophis una demum epodo clausis, quas, tametsi omnes nec versuum numero, nec certis ubique colis exacte respondeant, ita tamen secuimus, commode legendi potius, quam ad antiquos concinendi modos rationem spectantes. Alioquin hoc genus rectius fortasse dici monostrophicum debuerat. Metra partim sunt κατὰ σχέσιν, partim ἀπολελυμένα. Phaleucia quae sunt, spondaeum tertio loco bis admittunt, quod idem in secundo loco Catullus ad libitum fecit.

To John Rous, Librarian of Oxford University
Jan. 23 1646 [1647]
An ode about a lost book of my poems, which he asked me to replace with a second copy, so that he might place it in the public library with my other books.

Strophe I
Twin-born book,[1] rejoicing in a single cover but with a double title-page, shining with an unlaboured elegance that a youthful hand once gave you – an eager, but not too poetic hand – while he sported about, wandering now through the forest-shades of Italy, now through the green fields of England, aloof from the throng, off the beaten track, giving himself up to his native lute; then presently sounding a foreign air to his neighbours with a Daunian[10] lyre, his feet scarcely touching the ground.

Antistrophe
Who was it, little book, who craftily stole you, leaving your brothers behind, when you had been sent from the city at my learned friend's urgent request, and were making your illustrious journey to the cradle of blue father Thames,[18] where the clear springs of the

Muses[22] are, and the sacred Bacchic dance,[21] which has been world-famous through all the vast ages that have elapsed under the turning heaven, and will be famous for ever?

Strophe 2

But what god or demi-god[25] will take pity on the ancient genius of our nation (if we have atoned sufficiently for our past sins, our degenerate idleness and soft luxury) and will put an end to this abominable Civil War,[29] and with his sacred power restore our bountiful studies and recall the banished Muses, who have been left with scarcely any refuge in all of England? Who with Apollo's arrows will transfix the filthy birds with menacing claws, and drive the plague of Phineus far from the stream of Pegasus?[36]

Antistrophe

And yet, little book, although you have in this one instance, because of a messenger's dishonesty or negligence, wandered from your brothers' company – and may now be lying in a ditch, or else in a robber's hideout, where perhaps some boorish pedlar is rubbing you to bits with grubby, calloused hands – you may rejoice in your good fortune. Look, there is a new gleam of hope that you might be able to escape the depths of Lethe[45] and be carried on soaring wing to the high court of Jove.

Strophe 3

For Rous wishes to add you to his store. He complains that you are missing from the full number promised to him, and asks that you come to him – Rous, to whose care are entrusted the glorious records of men. He even wants to place you in those hallowed innermost sanctuaries over which he himself presides, the faithful custodian of immortal works, the guardian of a treasure more renowned than that which Ion,[56] Erectheus' illustrious grandson, presided over in his divine father's magnificent temple, with its golden tripods and Delphic offerings – Ion the son of Actaean[60] Creusa.

Antistrophe

Therefore you will go to see the delightful groves of the Muses, and you will go again to the divine home of Phoebus, where he dwells in the valley of Oxford, which he prefers to Delos[65] or the twin peaks of Parnassus. You will go with honour, since you leave my side assured of a glorious destiny, and at the request of a well-wishing friend. There you will be read among the lofty names of authors who were the ancient luminaries and the true glory of the Greek and Latin peoples.

Epode

You have not been in vain then, my labours – whatever my barren genius has brought forth. Now at last I bid you hope for rest, beyond the reach of malice, and for the blessed abode provided by kind Hermes[77] and Rous's watchful care. The insolent clamour of the crowd will not penetrate there, and the vulgar rabble of readers will be far away. But our remote descendants in a more judicious age will perhaps judge things more fairly with a more honest heart. Then, when spite is buried, a sane posterity will know, thanks to Rous, what my deserts are.

This ode has three strophes, three antistrophes, and a concluding epode. Although these units do not all have the same number of lines and do not strictly correspond in all particulars, I have divided them in this way with a view for ease of reading rather than conformity to ancient rules of versification. In other respects a poem of this kind should perhaps more accurately be called monostrophic. The meters are partly in regular patterns, partly free. In two Phaleucian lines I have admitted a spondee in the third foot, a practice that Catullus freely followed in the second foot.

LATIN POEMS FROM
THE PROSE WORKS

Epigram from Pro Populo Anglicano Defensio

Quis expedivit Salmasio suam Hundredam,
Picamque *docuit nostra verba conari?*
Magister artis venter, et Iacobei
Centum, exulantis viscera marsupii regis.
5   *Quod si dolosi spes refulserit nummi*,
Ipse Antichristi qui modo primatum Papae
Minatus uno est dissipare sufflatu,
Cantabit ultro Cardinalitium *melos*.

Epigram from Pro Populo Anglicano Defensio
Who inspired Salmasius with his 'hundred' and taught the magpie
to attempt our words? His teacher was his belly and a hundred
Jacobuses[3] (the vitals of the exiled king's purse). If ever the hope
shines of making a dishonest bit of cash, this same fellow (who lately
threatened with one puff to overthrow the supremacy of the Pope,[6]
the Antichrist) will gleefully warble a Cardinal's tune.

Epigram from Defensio Secunda

Gaudete scombri, et quicquid est piscium salo,
Qui frigida hieme incolitis algentes freta;
Vestrum misertus ille Salmasius eques
Bonus amicire nuditatem cogitat;
5   Chartaeque largus apparat papyrinos
Vobis cucullos praeferentes Claudii
Insignia nomenque et decus Salmasii,

Gestetis ut per omne cetarium forum
Equitis clientes, scriniis mungentium
10   Cubito virorum, et capsulis gratissimos.

Epigram from Defensio Secunda

Rejoice, you mackerels and all briny fish who spend your winters freezing in the cold sea! The good knight Salmasius,[3] pitying you, plans to clothe your nakedness. Lavish with his stationery, he is making paper cowls[6] for you. They bear the insignia, name and rank of Claudius Salmasius, so you may wear them proudly as the knight's retainers through the whole fish-market and be most welcome to the chests and boxes of the men who wipe their noses on their elbows.[10]

UNPUBLISHED LATIN POEMS

Carmina Elegiaca

Surge, age, surge, leves, iam convenit, excute somnos,
    Lux oritur, tepidi fulcra relinque tori.
Iam canit excubitor gallus, praenuntius ales
    Solis, et invigilans ad sua quemque vocat.
5 Flammiger Eois Titan caput exerit undis
    Et spargit nitidum laeta per arva iubar.
Daulias argutum modulatur ab ilice carmen
    Edit et excultos mitis alauda modos.
Iam rosa fragrantes spirat silvestris odores,
10   Iam redolent violae luxuriatque seges.
Ecce novo campos Zephyritis gramine vestit
    Fertilis, et vitreo rore madescit humus.
Segnes invenias molli vix talia lecto
    Cum premat imbellis lumina fessa sopor.
15 Illic languentes abrumpunt somnia somnos
    Et turbant animum tristia multa tuum;
Illic tabifici generantur semina morbi.
    Qui pote torpentem posse valere virum?
Surge, age, surge, leves, iam convenit, excute somnos
20   Lux oritur, tepidi fulcra relinque tori.

Elegiac Verses

Get up, come on, get up! It's time. Shake off useless slumbers. Dawn is rising; leave the posts of that warm bed. Now crows the sentinel cock, the harbinger bird of sunrise, vigilant to call everyone to work. Flaming Titan[5] lifts his head above the eastern waves and scatters radiant sunshine over the joyful fields. The Daulian bird[7] sings a piercing song from her oak, and the gentle lark pours forth her well-trilled song. Now the wild rose breathes out sweet perfumes; now violets emit their scent, and the corn is flourishing. Look! Zephyr's fertile consort[11] clothes the fields with fresh grass, and the ground is moist with glassy dew. Lazybones, you will hardly find delights like these in your soft bed, where feeble lethargy weighs down your tired eyes. There dreams interrupt your languid slumbers and many griefs disturb your mind. The seeds of wasting disease are bred there. How can a lazy man have the strength to do anything? Get up, come on, get up! It's time. Shake off useless slumbers. Dawn is rising; leave the posts of that warm bed.

[Asclepiads]

Ignavus satrapam dedecet inclytum
Somnus qui populo multifido praeest.
Dum Dauni veteris filius armiger
Stratus purpureo procubuit [toro]
5   Audax Euryalus, Nisus et impiger
Invasere cati nocte sub horrida
Torpentes Rutilos castraque Volscia:
Hinc caedes oritur clamor et absonus.

Asclepiads

Idle slumber ill becomes a famous governor who has charge over a populous nation. While old Daunus's warlike son[3] lay stretched out on his crimson bed,[4] bold Euryalus and energetic Nisus cunningly attacked the drowsy Rutulians and the Volscian camp under cover of dreadful night. Hence arose slaughter and discordant clamour.

NOTES

Abbreviations

In these notes references to critics are usually by surname only. For bibliographical details see Further Reading. The abbreviation *Var.* refers to the *Variorum Commentary on the Poems of John Milton* (6 vols., 1970–). I have used the following abbreviations of specific manuscripts and editions of Milton's works:

BMS	Bridgewater Manuscript of *A Masque*
Ed I	*Paradise Lost.* First edition (1667)
Ed II	*Paradise Lost.* Second edition (1674)
MS	The Manuscript of *Paradise Lost* i
TMS	The Trinity Manuscript
1637	*A Maske Presented at Ludlow Castle* (1637)
1638	*Justa Edouardo King naufrago* (1638)
1645	*Poems of Mr. John Milton* (1645)
1671	*Paradise Regain'd. A Poem in IV Books. To which is added Samson Agonistes* (1671)
1673	*Poems, &c. Upon Several Occasions* (1673)

The following abbreviations are used for titles of works by Milton.

CD	*Christian Doctrine (De Doctrina Christiana)*
DDD	*Doctrine and Discipline of Divorce*
Ep. Dam.	*Epitaphium Damonis*
Nativity	*On the Morning of Christ's Nativity*
PL	*Paradise Lost*
PR	*Paradise Regained*
Q Nov	*In Quintum Novembris*
RCG	*Reason of Church Government*
REW	*Ready and Easy Way*
SA	*Samson Agonistes*
TKM	*Tenure of Kings and Magistrates*
YP	*The Complete Prose Works of John Milton*, edited by Don M. Wolfe *et al.*, 8 vols. (New Haven, 1953–82)

The following abbreviations are of works by other authors:

Ariosto, *Orl. Fur.*	*Orlando Furioso*
Boiardo, *Orl. Inn.*	*Orlando Innamorato*
Claudian, *De Rapt. Pros.*	*De Raptu Proserpinae*
Dante, *Inf.*, *Purg.*, *Par.*	*Inferno, Purgatorio, Paradiso*
Fletcher, *CV*	*Christs Victorie, and Triumph*
Hesiod, *Theog.*, *WD*	*Theogony, Works and Days*
Homer, *Il.*, *Od.*	*Iliad, Odyssey*
Lucretius, *De Rerum Nat.*	*De Rerum Natura*
Ovid, *Her.*, *Met.*	*Heroides, Metamorphoses*
Spenser, *FQ*, *Shep. Cal.*	*Faerie Queene, Shepheardes Calender*
Sylvester, *DWW*	Joshuah Sylvester, *The Divine Weeks and Works of Guillaume de Saluste, Sieur du Bartas*
Tasso, *Gerus. Lib.*	*Gerusalemme Liberata*
Virgil, *Aen.*, *Ecl.*, *Georg.*	*Aeneid, Eclogues, Georgics*

Unless otherwise stated, all biblical citations are from the Authorized Version (A.V.). LXX refers to the Septuagint (the Greek version of the Old Testament (O.T.)) and Junius-Tremellius refers to *Testamenti Veteris Biblia Sacra* (1581), the Protestant Latin version of the O.T. by Franciscus Junius and Immanuel Tremellius.

Abbreviations of academic journals used are:

CLS	*Comparative Literature Studies*
EC	*Essays in Criticism*
ELH	*A Journal of English Literary History*
ELR	*English Literary Renaissance*
JEGP	*Journal of English and Germanic Philology*
JHI	*Journal of the History of Ideas*
MLN	*Modern Language Notes*
MLR	*Modern Language Review*
MQ	*Milton Quarterly*
MS	*Milton Studies*
N&Q	*Notes and Queries*
PMLA	*Publications of the Modern Language Association of America*
RES	*Review of English Studies*
SEL	*Studies in English Literature*
SP	*Studies in Philology*
UTQ	*University of Toronto Quarterly*

An asterisk signifies that the word or sense so marked is the earliest recorded instance in the *Oxford English Dictionary*. See Preface, pp. xii–xiii.

POEMS 1645

On the Morning of Christ's Nativity. Composed 1629.

M. in *Elegia VI* 88 says that he began this poem before dawn on Christmas Day. His first great (though not his earliest) poem, it is placed first in both *1645* and *1673*.

1. *this the happy morn* Cp. W. Drummond, *Phoebus arise* 15: 'This is that happie Morne'.

5. *holy sages* Hebrew prophets. See e.g. Isa. 9. 6.

6. *deadly* entailing spiritual death (*OED* 5).
   forfeit crime (*OED* 1) and penalty (*OED* 4).
   release remit a sin (*OED* 3b) and revoke a sentence (*OED* 1).

8. *unsufferable* unendurable.

10. *wont* was wont (the past participle used as a preterite).

11. *trinal unity* the Holy Trinity.

13. *everlasting day* Cp. Rev. 21. 25 (and 22. 5): 'there shall be no night there'.

14. *house of mortal clay* Cp. Marston, *Scourge of Villainy* (1598) III viii 194: 'smoakie house of mortall clay'.

15. *Heav'nly Muse* Urania, the Muse of Christian poetry. See *PL* vii 1*n*.
   vein poetic style and personal disposition.

16. *Afford* manage to give.

19. *team* horses of the sun's chariot.

21. *spangled . . . bright* The stars above London in 1629 become the stars and angels that overlooked Christ's birth.

23. *star-led wizards* the Magi.
   odours spices.

24. *prevent* anticipate.

25. *blessèd feet* Cp. Shakespeare, *1 Henry IV* I i 25–7: 'Those blessed feet / Which fourteen hundred years ago were nailed / For our advantage to the bitter cross'.

28. *From . . . fire* In Isa. 6. 6–7 a Seraph touches Isaiah's lips with a burning coal taken from God's altar. In *RCG* (1642), M. says that the Christian poet must pray to 'that eternall Spirit . . . who sends out his Seraphim with the hallow'd fire of his Altar to touch and purify the lips of whom he pleases' (*YP* 1. 821).
   secret set apart.

33. *doffed her gaudy trim* 'removed her gay clothing (of leaves and flowers)'.

34. *sympathize* be in accord with.

35. *season* both 'time of the year' and 'fit occasion' (*OED* 14).

36. *wanton* sport amorously. Cp. the earth's lust for the sun in *Elegia V* 55–95.

paramour lover.

38. *woos* both 'entreats' and 'solicits alluringly'.

39–40. *To hide ... naked shame* Cp. Adam and Eve's shame after their Fall (Gen. 3. 7–10, *PL* ix 1079–98). Man's sin makes Nature *guilty* (cp. *PL* x 649f.).

39. *front* face (*OED* 1).

41. *Pollute* polluted.

43. *Confounded* ashamed (*OED* 3).

45. *cease* The transitive usage was idiomatic (*OED* 5).

46–60. *Peace* prevailed over the Roman world at the time of Christ's birth. Church Fathers (e.g. Augustine, *City of God* xviii 46) saw this as a fulfilment of O.T. prophecies. See also Dante, *Par.* vi 55–7 and Tasso, *Canzone* 58f.

47. *olive* an emblem of peace.

48. *turning sphere* the firmament (outermost of the Ptolemaic spheres), which revolved daily around the earth.

49. *harbinger* forerunner (*OED* 3). The other sense, 'one sent before a lord to commandeer a lodging' (*OED* 2), is also relevant to the Lord who found no room at the inn. 'Harbinger' is cognate with French *auberge*.

50. *turtle* turtle dove. Cp. Jonson's 'turtle-footed peace' (*Every Man Out of His Humour* Ep. 27–8).

amorous loving (towards Peace).

51. *myrtle* an attribute of Venus, goddess of love. The *wand* also suggests a harbinger's wand of office.

53. *No war, or battle's sound* Cp. Spenser on Saturn's reign (*FQ* V, proem 9): 'No warre was knowne, no dreadfull trompets sound'.

56. *hookèd* armed with scythes. Cp. *FQ* V viii 28: 'a charret hye, / With yron wheeles and hookes arm'd dreadfully'.

59. *awful* filled with awe, reverential.

64. *whist* hushed, still.

68. *birds of calm* halcyons (kingfishers). Classical writers believed that the sea remained calm during the few days around the winter solstice when halcyons laid their eggs and sat *brooding* on their floating nests.

71. *influence* an ethereal fluid streaming from stars and planets and acting on the character and destiny of men. Cp. *PL* iv 667–73, vii 375, viii 513, ix 105–6, x 662, etc.

74. *Lucifer* the morning star, Venus. This Lucifer dutifully dismisses the stars, but 'Lucifer' was also a name for Satan, who would wish 'that stars and men pay as little attention to the great event as possible' (Brooks and Hardy 98). Cp. Lucifer-Satan leading his stellar angels from God's throne (*PL* v 704–10, 755–60).

75. *orbs* the concentric hollow spheres which carried stars and planets around the earth in the Ptolemaic cosmology.

76. *bespake* spoke out, perhaps 'with some notion of objection or remonstrance' (*OED* 2). Cp. *Lycidas* 112.

77. *gloom* *darkness (*OED* sb¹ 2).

79–83. *sun . . . greater Sun* Cp. the Nativity scene in Fletcher, *CV* (1610) i 78: 'heav'n awaked with all his eyes, / To see another Sunne, at midnight rise'. Cp. also the sun's awe of Elizabeth in Spenser, *Shep. Cal.* April 77: 'He blusht to see another Sunne belowe'. M.'s pun on 'Son' has a biblical source in Malachi 4. 2. Cp. *PL* iv 37.

81. *As* as if.

84. *axle-tree* axle of the sun's chariot. Cp. the sun's 'burning axle-tree' in George Chapman, *Bussy D'Ambois* (1607) V iii 151–2.

85. *lawn* open space between woods.

86. *Or ere* Both words mean 'before'.

88. *then*] than *1645, 1673*. 'Than' and 'then' were originally the same word. M. here means 'then' but spells 'than' for the sake of rhyme.

89. *Pan* the Greek god of shepherds – in the Renaissance a symbol of Christ. See E.K.'s gloss to Spenser, *Shep. Cal.* May 54: 'Great pan) is Christ, the very God of all shepheards, which calleth himselfe the greate and good shepherd.' In lines 181–3 M. alludes to a rival tradition which saw Pan as a devil (see 183*n* below).

90. *kindly* both 'lovingly' and 'as one of their kind'. 'Kind' could mean 'birth', 'offspring' or 'Nature in general' (*OED* 1a, 11, 4).

92. *silly* simple, rustic, lowly.

96. *warbled* *melodiously sung (*OED* 1).

97. *noise* melodious sound (*OED* 5a).

98. *rapture* *ecstasy (*OED* 5a), with overtones of 'seizing and carrying off' (*OED* 1). Cp. *PL* vii 36.

  took captivated.

100. *close* conclusion of a musical phrase; a cadence.

102–3. *hollow round . . . seat* the sphere of the moon *(Cynthia* being the moon-goddess Diana). The moon marked a great boundary between *Nature* below and the heavens above. Nature (the realm of the four elements) was subject to change and decay; the heavens (formed of *aether* and the quintessence) were pure and unchanging. The Music of the Spheres (see below, 125–32*n*) was meant to be audible only above the moon; hence Nature's dismay at hearing it.

103. *airy region* the division of the universe (*OED* 'region' 3a) between the earth and the moon.

  thrilling piercing (*OED* 4), delighting (*OED* 5).

104. *won* persuaded (*OED* 9), with overtones of 'delivered, redeemed' (*OED* 8), alluding to the Fall.

110. *globe* troop (Latin *globus*) and sphere (notice *circular*). Cp. *PL* ii 512 and *PR* iv 581–2.

111. *shame-faced* modest (*OED* 1).

   arrayed *adorned (*OED* 9b), with a play on 'ray' ('beam').

112–13. *Cherubim . . . Seraphim* According to Pseudo-Dionysius, Seraphim rank highest, and Cherubim second highest, among the nine orders of angels. Seraphim were angels of love, Cherubim were angels of comtemplation and knowledge.

114. *wings displayed* Each angel unfolds his wings, and the whole host is deployed (*OED* 'display' 1b) like the wings of an army. Notice *ranks* and cp. *PL* vi 778.

115. *choir* There may be a pun on *'order of angels' (*OED* 4, earliest instance 1642). Cp. *PL* iii 666.

116. *unexpressive* inexpressible; coined by Shakespeare in *As You Like It* III ii 10. Cp. *Lycidas* 176.

119–23. *sons of morning . . . foundations* Cp. God's question at Job 38. 4– 7: 'Where wast thou when I laid the foundations of the earth . . . When the morning stars sang together, and all the sons of God shouted for joy?' Cp. also Ps. 102. 25: 'Of old hast thou laid the foundation of the earth', and Isa. 14. 12: 'Lucifer, son of the morning'.

122. *hinges* the two poles making the earth's axis (*OED* 3). Cp. Spenser, *FQ* I xi 21: 'To move the world from off his steadfast henge'. Cp. also Job 26. 7: 'He . . . hangeth the earth upon nothing'. 'Hinge' derives from 'hang'.

124. *welt'ring* rolling.

125–32. *Ring . . . symphony* the Pythagorean notion of the Music of the Spheres. Each sphere of the universe was thought to produce a note as it revolved around the earth. The resulting music was inaudible on earth (since the Fall), but a sinless soul might hear it. Cp. *Arcades* 62–73, *Solemn Music* 19–24, *A Masque* 1020–21, *PL* v 178, M.'s prose *Prolusion* ii (*YP* 1. 234–9); also Plato, *Republic* x 616–17 and Shakespeare, *The Merchant of Venice* V i 60–65.

126. *Once* only.

130. *the base* the earth as base of the universe; with a play on 'ground bass'. The seventeenth-century *organ* (a traditional image for universal harmony) played 'ground bass' beneath the varied harmony of other instruments. The earth will play 'ground bass' under the spheres.

131. *ninefold harmony* Cp. *Arcades* 64 ('nine infolded spheres'). Plato has eight spheres (*Republic* x 617–18); M. in *PL* iii 481–3 has ten. Dante has nine and relates them to the nine angelic orders (*Par.* xxviii 25–78). Here the *ninefold harmony* may consist of eight spheres plus the earth, whose bass note is needed if our universe is to *Make up full consort to* the nine angelic orders.

132. *consort* accord or harmony of several voices or instruments playing or singing in tune (*OED* 3a), company of musicians (*OED* 4), fellowship (*OED* 1).

135. *age of gold* Cp. Virgil's famous prophecy of the birth of a boy who will restore the Golden Age (*Ecl.* iv 6–10). Early Christians (e.g. Augustine, *City of God* x 27) read this 'Messianic' eclogue as a prophecy of Christ. Lactantius also speaks of Christ as restoring the Golden Age (*Divine Institutes* V vii).

136. *speckled* spotted (perhaps suggesting the plague).

138. *lep'rous Sin* Cp. Sylvester, *DWW* (1592–1608), *The Fathers* (1605): 'The Leprosie of our contagious sinne' (518).

mould the whole earth and the clay from which man was made. Cp. *A Masque* 17, *Arcades* 73.

140. **peering* *OED*'s earliest participial instance, meaning both 'looking narrowly' and 'just appearing'. Hell shrinks from daylight in Homer, *Il.* xx 61–4 and Virgil, *Aen.* viii 243–6. Cp. also *A Masque* 732–6.

141–4. *Truth . . . Mercy* Cp. Ps. 85. 10: 'Mercy and truth are met together, righteousness and peace have kissed each other'. The 'righteousness' of the A.V. is *justitia* in the Vulgate. A medieval and Renaissance allegorical tradition made *Truth, Justice* and *Mercy* three of the four daughters of God. The fourth daughter was Peace (see line 46).

142. *down return* Astraea, goddess of Justice, lived among men during the Golden Age, but later fled the earth (Ovid, *Met.* i 150). Virgil announces her *return* in his 'Messianic' eclogue (iv 6). Lactantius says that Astraea returned with the coming of Christ (*Divine Institutes* V v-vii).

143–4. *Orbed . . . between*] *1673*; Th' enamelled arras of the rainbow wearing, / And Mercy set between *1645*. Cp. Rev. 4. 3: 'there was a rainbow round about the throne', and Gen. 9. 13.

enamelled arras brightly coloured fabric.

146. *tissued* woven with gold or silver thread (*OED* 1).

149. *Fate* that which God has willed or spoken (Latin *fari*, 'to speak'). Cp. *PL* vii 131.

151. *infancy* Brooks and Hardy (100) note the play on Latin *infans*, 'unspeaking', and cite a sermon by Lancelot Andrewes (Christmas 1618): '*An infant; Verbum infans*, the *Word* without a word, the *aeternall Word* not able to speak a word'. Cp. also Fletcher, *CV* (1610) i 79.

152. *bitter cross* See above, 25*n*.

155. *ychained* Spenserian archaism.

sleep death.

156. *wakeful* *rousing (*OED* 6, sole instance).

trump trumpet.

doom Judgement. Cp. Matt. 24. 31, I Cor. 15. 51–2.

157. *clang* sound of a trumpet (Latin, *clangor*).

158. *As on Mount Sinai* Exod. 19. 16–18.

164. *middle air* Christ was expected to appear in the clouds (Dan. 7. 13, Matt. 24. 30, I Thess. 4. 17), which occupied the second of three 'regions' of the air.

166. *perfect* including 'complete' (*OED* 3).

168. *Th' old Dragon* Cp. Rev. 20. 2: 'the dragon, that old serpent, which is the Devil, and Satan'.

169. *straiter* narrower.

170. *casts* extends, throws (like a net).

172. *Swinges* lashes. Pronounce with a soft 'g' as in 'hinges'.

173–228. See *PL* i 373*n* for the patristic belief (still current in 1629) that pagan gods were fallen angels. Tuve (62–72) rejects that identification here. She argues that the hymn's false gods are not devils, but fictions, which 'is why some of them are lovely'. But fictions would not be a *damnèd crew* (228), or *dread* Christ (222) or flee to Hell.

173. *The oracles are dumb* Cp. Fletcher, *CV* (1610) i 82: 'The cursed Oracles were strucken dumb'. An ancient tradition held that pagan oracles ceased with the coming of Christ. Cp. *PR* i 456–64 and see Eusebius, *Praeparatio Evangelica* v 16. Lines 173–80 share many details with Prudentius's poem *Apotheosis* 402–43.

175. *words deceiving* The Delphic oracle was notorious for its treacherous ambiguity. See *PR* i 430–41.

178. *Delphos* Delphi.

179–80. *breathèd . . . Inspires* The Romans thought that Apollo's priestess at Delphi had breathed in (was literally *inspired* by) intoxicating vapours rising from the earth.

180. *cell* the innermost part of a temple, where the god's idol stood (Latin *cella*).

181. *lonely* *unfrequented, desolate (*OED* 3).

183. *A voice of weeping* Cp. Matt. 2. 18 (the slaughter of the innocents): 'In Rama was there a voice heard, lamentation and weeping'. Cp. also Plutarch's story of a ship's pilot sailing past the isle of Paxi. A voice from Paxi told the pilot to proclaim 'great Pan is dead' when he reached Pelodes. He did so, and at once heard many voices weeping (*De Defectu Oraculorum* xvii). Eusebius cites Plutarch in *Praeparatio Evangelica* v 17, and notes that the event occurred when Christ was banishing devils. He identifies Pan as a devil. Others identified Pan as the crucified Christ (see above, 89*n*). M. had identified Pan with Christ in line 89, but now implies that he was a devil.

185. *poplar pale* white-leaved poplar.

186. *Genius* a local deity. Cp. *Lycidas* 183.

188. *The nymphs . . . mourn* Cp. Fairfax's translation of Tasso iii 75, where Godfrey fells an enchanted wood to make siege engines for his army and 'The weeping Nymphes fled from their bowres exilde'.

191. *lars* lares, Roman gods of the household.

lemures Roman spirits of the dead (hence *urns*).

193. *drear* horrid, doleful (*OED* 'dreary' 2, 3).

194. *flamens* an order of Roman priests.

quaint elaborate.

195. *marble . . . sweat* The sweating of marble statues was a bad omen. Cp. Virgil, *Georg.* i 480.

196. *While . . . seat* So Virgil describes the gods of Troy abandoning their shrines and altars (*Aen.* ii 351–2).

197. *Peor* Baal-Peor, a Canaanite sun-god (Num. 25. 3–5). Cp. *PL* i 406–14.

Baälim the plural of 'Baal', referring to such gods as Baal-Zebub and Baal-Berith. Cp. *PL* i 422.

199. *twice-battered god* Dagon, the Philistine god whose idol was twice thrown down when the ark of the Covenant was placed beside it. See I Sam. 5. 2–4 and *PL* i 457–63.

200. *Ashtaroth* Ashtoreth, the Phoenician moon-goddess (see *PL* i 438–9n). As at *PR* iii 417, M. uses the plural form.

201. *Heav'n's queen* Astarte is 'queen of heaven' at Jer. 7. 44. Roman Catholics used the title of Mary, and M. might be satirical at their expense (notice *tapers*).

203. *Libyc Hammon* Ammon, an Egyptian (and Libyan) god depicted as a ram.

shrinks draws in.

204. *Tyrian* Phoenician (from Tyre).

Thammuz the Phoenician Adonis, a beautiful youth loved by Astarte and killed by a boar. Cp. *PL* i 446–57.

205. *sullen* *baleful (*OED* 1d) and dull in colour (*OED* 4a, notice *blackest hue*).

Moloch an Ammonite fire-god. Children were sacrificed to him while the sound of *cymbals* drowned their cries. Cp. *PL* i 392–403.

209. *the grisly king* M. uses the phrase of Satan at *PL* iv 821. *Moloch* means 'king' in Hebrew (cp. *PL* i 392).

210. *dismal* sinister (*OED* 2), dire (*OED* 4).

211–28. Cp. Isaiah's prophecy of the destruction of Egypt's gods (Isa. 19. 1–3).

211. *brutish* in animal form. Cp. *PL* i 478–82.

215. **unshow'red* Egypt is almost rainless.

lowings Osiris was worshipped in the form of the sacred bull Apis.

216–20. *Nor . . . ark* Set tricked his brother Osiris into entering a *chest*, which Set cast adrift on the Nile. Isis (Osiris's wife) recovered the chest, but Set dismembered Osiris's body and scattered the pieces over the earth. Isis then gathered the pieces and restored life to the body.

218. *shroud* winding sheet (*OED* 2a) and place of shelter (*OED* 3).

219. **timbrelled* accompanied by tambourines.

220. *sable-stolèd* black-robed. There may be a play on 'stole' as the ecclesiastical vestment worn by Jesuits and other priests when engaged in exorcism or conjuration (*OED* 2b).

ark chest (*OED* 1). The priests of Osiris carried his image in a little gold-plated wooden casket (Herodotus ii 63).

221. *from Judah's land* Cp. Isa. 19. 17: 'the land of Judah shall be a terror unto Egypt'.

223. *eyn* eyes (archaic plural).

226. *Typhon* Set (see above, 216–20n) was anciently conflated with the Greek Typhon, a hundred-headed serpent (hence *snaky twine*) who so terrified the gods that they fled to Egypt disguised as animals. See *PL* i 481n.

227–8. *Our babe . . . crew* alluding to the infant Hercules, who strangled two snakes sent by Juno to kill him in his cradle. Hercules was a common 'type' of Christ. Cp. *The Passion* 13–14 and *PR* iv 563–71.

231. **Pillows* *OED*'s earliest instance of the verb.

orient both 'eastern' and 'bright'.

233–4. *Troop . . . grave* Cp. Shakespeare, *A Midsummer Night's Dream* III ii 382–3: 'ghosts wandering here and there / Troop home to churchyards'; also *Hamlet* I i 140–46.

234. *fettered* bound to the body. Cp. *A Masque* 463–73.

236. *Night-steeds* horses drawing Night's chariot.

moon-loved maze fairy rings. Cp. Shakespeare, *A Midsummer Night's Dream* II i 99: 'the quaint mazes in the wanton green'.

239. *our tedious song* Cp. Phineas Fletcher, *The Purple Island* viii 58 (concluding a long catalogue of personified sins): 'But if I all this rout and foul aray / Should muster up, and place in battell ray, / Too long your selves & flocks my tedious song would stay'. *The Purple Island* was published in 1633, but there are so many possible echoes of it in M.'s early poems that it is reasonable to assume that M. had seen a MS, perhaps at Cambridge, where Fletcher had studied, and where *The Purple Island* was eventually published. For other likely echoes prior to 1633 see *L'Allegro* 31–2n, *Psalm 136* 22n, *Song. On May Morning* 5–6n.

240. *youngest teemèd* latest born. Theologians had debated whether the *star* of Matt. 2. 2 was a new creation.

241. *fixed* Cp. Matt. 2. 9: 'the star, which they saw in the east, went before them, till it came and stood over where the young child was'.

polished car gleaming chariot.

244. *Bright-harnessed* bright-armoured.

A Paraphrase on Psalm 114

Headnote. at fifteen years old This and the following psalm may have been school exercises based on Latin or Greek versions of the Bible. They are M.'s earliest English poems.

1. *Terah's faithful son* Abraham (an exemplar of faith in Heb. 11. 8–9). Terah was an idolater (Josh. 24. 2; cp. *PL* xii 113–15).

3. *Pharian fields* Egypt (from Pharos, an island near Alexandria). Sylvester had coined the adjective in *DWW* I i (1605): 'the high *Pharian-Tower*' (489).

10. *foil* defeat.

Psalm 136

Date: 1624 (see previous headnote).

10. (also 13, 17, 21, 25). *That] 1645*; Who *1673*.

18. *painted* adorned with bright or varied colours (*OED* 3).
    state splendour, majesty.

22. *wat'ry plain* Cp. *PL* i 397, iv 455. The phrase is found in Spenser, *FQ* IV xi 24, Drayton, *Polyolbion* (1612–22) xv 110, and Phineas Fletcher, *The Purple Island* (1633) iii 28. M. might have seen Fletcher's MS. See *Nativity* 239*n*.

41. *fell* cruel.

45–6. *ruddy waves . . . Erythraean main* the Red Sea (from Greek *erythros*, red). Cp. Sylvester, *Bethulian's Rescue* (1614) ii 232: 'the Erythraean ruddy Billowes'.

49. *walls of glass* The Red Sea divides into 'Two Walls of Glasse' in Sylvester, *DWW* (1592–1608), *The Lawe* (1606) 697. Cp. *PL* xii 197.

54. *tawny king* Cp. Fairfax's translation of Tasso, *Gerus. Lib*. iii 38: 'Affrikes tawnie kings'.

65. *Seon* Sihon, king of the Amorites (Num. 21. 21–32).

66. *Amorean* Amorite.

69. *Og* the giant King of Bashan, killed by Moses (Num. 21. 33–5, Deut. 3. 11, Josh. 13. 12). Cp. *SA* 1080.

73. *his servant Israël* Jacob (Gen. 35. 10–12).

The Passion

Date: March 1630? The opening lines allude to *On the Morning of Christ's Nativity*, so this poem was probably written the following Easter. Good Friday fell on 26 March.

1. *ethereal* heavenly.
   mirth religious joy.

4. *divide* both 'divide into two choirs' and 'perform musical "divisions" (elaborate variations on a theme)'. Cp. *PL* iv 688.

6. *In wintry . . . light* 'like daylight shortened at the winter solstice'.

13–14. *hero . . . labours* alluding to Hercules as a 'type' of Christ. Cp. *Nativity* 227–8.
   wight living being.

15. *priest* Christ is called 'high priest' at Heb. 2. 17.

16. *dropped . . . oil* 'Christ' and 'Messiah' mean 'anointed' in Greek and Hebrew. Jesus was anointed at Matt. 26. 7 (cp. Heb. 1. 9). High priests were also anointed (Exod. 29. 7), as were kings (notice *regal*).

17. *tabernacle* human body (cp. II Cor. 5. 1). Christ's body replaces the tabernacle which contained the Jewish Law (Heb. 9. 1–14). Cp. *PR* iv 599.

18. *front* forehead.

21. *brethren's* Christ frequently referred to mankind as his 'brethren'. See e.g. Matt. 12. 47–50.

22. *latter*] *1645*; latest *1673*.

23. *Phoebus* Apollo as god of poetry, and as sun-god, bound for the *horizon*.
   bound both 'directing [his] course' and 'confined, restricted'.

26. *Cremona's trump* Marco Girolamo Vida's *Christiad*, a Latin epic published in Cremona in 1535.

28. *still* quiet.

30. *the pole* the sky (*OED* 4).

31. *flattered* beguiled, charmed (*OED* 6).

34–5. *The leaves . . . white* Cp. William Browne, *Britannia's Pastorals* (1613–16) I v 75–8, where the poet's tears are said to mix with his ink so as to turn his 'late white paper to a weed of mourning'. Some seventeenth-century funeral elegies were printed in white letters on black paper.

37. *the prophet* Ezekiel. He had a vision of God's *chariot* when he was by the river *Chebar* (Ezek. 1 and 10).

39. *Salem* Jerusalem.

42. **ecstatic* standing outside the body (coined from 'ecstatical').

43. *sepulchral rock* the Holy Sepulchre was 'hewn out of a rock' (Mark 15. 46).

44. *casket* treasure-chest. The context suggests 'coffin', but *OED* cites that sense only from 1870.

store treasure.

47. *lively* vividly (*OED* 4) and feelingly (*OED* 3b), as in 'making him . . . lively to lament' (1625).

49. *characters* both 'letters' and 'engraved signs'.

50. *viewless* invisible.

51. *weeping on the mountains wild* Cp. Jer. 9. 10: 'For the mountains will I take up a weeping'.

56. *pregnant cloud* alluding to Ixion, the would-be ravisher of Hera. Ixion *got* (begot) the *race* of centaurs on a cloud that Zeus put in Hera's place (Pindar, *Pythian Odes* ii 21–48). Cp. M.'s veiled allusions to the same myth in *PL* iv 499–500 and *PR* iv 318–21.

On Time

Date: unknown (usually dated 1633). In *TMS* M. wrote (and later deleted) the subtitle: 'to be set on a clock case'.

1. *Fly* pass rapidly and flee.

envious malicious, spiteful.

till . . . race Cp. Rev. 10. 6 ('there should be time no longer') and *PL* xii 554–6: 'the race of time, / Till time stand fixed: beyond is all abyss, / Eternity, whose end no eye can reach'.

2–3. *leaden-stepping . . . plummet's pace* The plummet was a lead weight (not a pendulum) whose slow descent impelled a clock. The leaden-stepping hours are thus a measure of clock-time, though M. also glances at the 'Hours' (*Horae*) – goddesses of the seasons whom Theocritus (xv 102–4) calls 'soft-footed' and 'slowest of the blessed'.

4. *womb* stomach (*OED* 1), suggesting the ancient identification of Chronos (Time) with Cronos (Saturn), who devoured his own children. Cp. also *PL* ii 911, where Chaos is 'The womb of Nature and perhaps her grave'.

9. *when as* when.

10. *self consumed* Cp. *A Masque* 596, where the Elder Brother promises that 'evil' will be 'Self-fed, and self-consumed'.

12. *individual* inseparable (*OED* 2), hence 'everlasting'. But the modern sense 'peculiar to a particular person' existed, and M. may play upon it to affirm personal immortality and repudiate the Averroistic doctrine of the absorption of individual souls. Cp. *PL* iv 486, v 610.

14. *sincerely* wholly (*OED* 4b). Cp. Latin *sincerus*, 'pure'.

18. *happy-making sight* the 'beatific vision'. Cp. *PL* i 684, iii 61–2, v 613.

20. *quit* having left behind.

21. *Attired* crowned. Cp. Rev. 12. 1: 'upon her head a crown of twelve stars'. 'Attire' was fancifully connected with 'tiara' (*OED* sb 4).

Upon the Circumcision

Date: unknown (usually dated 1633). The Feast of the Circumcision falls on 1 January. The opening lines again recall *Nativity* (cp. *The Passion* 1–4). The poem regards the circumcision as a 'type' of the Crucifixion.

1. *Powers* one of nine angelic orders (here a synecdoche for all angels). *wingèd warriors* Cp. Tasso, *Gerus. Lib.* ix 60: *guerrieri alati*. Gabriel is a 'wingèd warrior' in *PL* 576.
2. *erst* formerly.
6–9. *if . . . sorrow* 'if your fiery nature prevents you from sharing our sorrow by weeping tears, then fan your flames with sighs and draw up vapour from the seas of our tears (as the sun draws vapour from the sea)'. Angelologists supposed that angels, being made of fire, could not weep. Angels do weep in *PL* i 620 and x 23–4.
10. *heraldry* *heraldic pomp (*OED* 4).
  whilere a while ago.
14. *seize* including the legal sense 'take possession of' (*OED* 5b). Christ submits to the Mosaic Law in submitting to circumcision.
17. *doom* Judgement.
19. *secret* removed from the resort of men (*OED* 1b). Cp. *PL* i 6, viii 427.
20. *Emptied his glory* Cp. Phil. 2. 7: 'made himself of no reputation'. The Greek says that Christ 'emptied himself'.
21. *cov'nant* the Mosaic Law. Cp. Matt. 5. 17.
24. *excess* violation of law (*OED* 4). Cp. *PL* xi 111.
28. *pierce . . . heart* referring to the spear that pierced Christ's side (John 19. 34). Cp. also 'the circumcision of the heart' (Deut. 10. 16, Rom. 2. 28–9, etc.).

At a Solemn Music

Date: unknown (usually dated 1633, but conjectures range from 1631 to 1637). *TMS* has two preliminary drafts of the whole poem, a separate draft of ll.17–28, and a fair copy. The modern equivalent of the title would be 'At a Sacred Concert'.

1. *Sirens* Plato attributes the Music of the Spheres to the singing of eight celestial Sirens (*Republic* x 616–17). M. alludes to these in *Arcades* 63–4.
pledges offspring (*OED* 2d) and assurances.

2. *Sphere-borne*] *TMS* (all three versions); Sphere-born *1645, 1673. Born* is supported by *pledges* and *A Masque* 241 (where Echo is 'daughter of the sphere'), but *borne* points more clearly to Plato's Sirens (who are carried by the spheres). The two spellings were not always distinguished.

4. *Dead . . . pierce* So Orpheus' songs moved woods and rocks to ecstasy (Ovid, *Met.* xi 1–4).

*inbreathed including 'inspired'.

pierce touch or move deeply (*OED* 5).

6. *concent* harmony, both of sounds (*OED* 1) and hearts (*OED* 2). *1645* reads 'content', but *1673* and *TMS* (all versions) have 'concent', and a Bodleian copy of *1645* has been so corrected, perhaps in M.'s hand.

7. *Ay* forever.

sapphire-coloured God's throne resembles 'a sapphire stone' in Ezek. 1. 26.

9. *solemn jubilee* sacred rejoicing. The Hebrew Jubilee was a ritual emancipation of slaves occurring every fifty years. It was a 'type' of the Atonement. See *PL* iii 348*n*.

10. *burning* The word *Seraphim* was associated with the Hebrew root *saraph*, to burn. Cp. *PL* ii 512 and Spenser, *Hymn to Heavenly Beauty*, 94f.: 'Those eternal burning Seraphins'.

12. **Cherubic* 'Cherub' is found in Old English, but this is *OED*'s earliest instance of the adjective. 'Seraphic' is cited from 1632.

14. *just* righteous in the sight of God; justified (*OED* 1).

palms Cp. Rev. 7. 9: 'a great multitude, which no man could number, of all nations . . . stood before the throne, and before the Lamb, clothed with white robes, and palms in their hands'.

17. *That* so that.

*undiscording.

18. *noise* melodious sound (*OED* 5a). Cp. *Nativity* 97.

19–24. *As once . . . good* The comparison of Edenic existence to a music broken by Adam's sin was commonplace. Cp. Sylvester, *DWW* (1592–1608), *The Furies* (1598) 43f.:

> This mightie World did seeme an Instrument
> Trew-strung, well-tunde, and handled excellent,
> Whose symphonie resounded sweetly-shrill,
> Th' Almighties praise, who plaid upon it still . . .
> But Adam, beeing cheefe of all the stringes
> Of this large Lute, ore-retched, quickly brings
> All out of tune.

19. *disproportioned* disharmonious.

20–21. *Nature's chime . . . all creatures* Cp. Jonson, *Underwoods* (1640) lxxv

26–7: 'The month of youth, which calls all creatures forth / To do their offices in Nature's chime'. Jonson's poem was written in 1632.

22. *whose love* both God's love for his creatures and theirs for him.

motion both 'activity' (of *all creatures*) and 'a working of God in the soul' (*OED* 9b). There might also be a play on *'musical movement' (*OED* 12), which *OED* cites from 1674.

swayed ruled (*OED* 9). The sequence *motion swayed . . . stood* also suggests the precariousness of innocence. Cp. *PL* viii 635.

23. *diapason* complete concord (*OED* 2), including concord of the octave (*OED* 1), associated with Pythagoras and the Music of the Spheres.

27. *consort* harmony of voices, company of musicians (*OED* sb¹ 3, 4) and spouse (*OED* sb¹ 3). The last sense refers to the Church as bride of Christ (Rev. 19).

An Epitaph on the Marchioness of Winchester

Jane Paulet, wife of the Catholic (and subsequently Royalist) Marquis of Winchester, died on 15 April 1631, after giving birth to a stillborn son. The cause of death was an infected abscess in her cheek. She was twenty-three. Numerous tributes survive, including eulogies by Jonson and Davenant. The Marchioness was a Catholic, but a newsletter of 21 April 1631 states that she was 'inclining to become a Protestant' (*Court and Times of Charles I*, ed. T. Birch, 1894, ii 106). Lines 53–60 may indicate that the poem was intended for a volume of Cambridge elegies. No evidence of a personal connection between M. and the Marchioness's family is known to have survived.

1. *marble* tomb.

3. *viscount* Thomas, Viscount Savage.

earl's heir through her mother Elizabeth, daughter of Thomas Darcy, Earl Rivers.

7. *Summers . . . one* Horace gives his age as 'four times eleven Decembers' in *Epistulae* I xx 27.

8. *told* counted.

11–14. *had . . . life* 'Had her life-span been as complete as her praise, her death would have seemed natural.'

16. *Quickly . . . lover* She married John Paulet in 1622, when she was fourteen.

17. *virgin choir* bridesmaids.

request invoke.

18. *god* Hymen, the god of marriage.

20. *scarce-well-lighted flame* The sputtering of Hymen's torch foreboded death at the wedding of Orpheus and Eurydice (Ovid, *Met.* x 6–7). Contrast *L'Allegro* 125–6.

22. *cypress* an emblem of funerals. Hymen's *garland* was composed of roses and marjoram.

23. *matrons* midwives (*OED* 2).

24. *greet her of* congratulate her on.

   son Charles, born 1629, later sixth Marquis and Duke of Bolton.

26. *Lucina* Juno Lucina, the Roman goddess of childbirth.

27. *blame* fault.

28. *Atropos* one of the three Fates or *Parcae*. She cut the thread of life which Clotho spun and Lachesis measured. As Atropos Morta she presided over stillbirth.

35. *slip* cutting taken from a plant. In M.'s simile the *slip* is Jane, the *flower* is her son, and the *swain* is death. The swain means to pluck only the flower, but takes the cutting. Homer (*Il.* viii 306–8) and Virgil (*Aen.* ix 433–6) liken dying warriors to flowers cut by the plough or weighed down by a *vernal shower* (39).

43–6. *pearls . . . funeral* The *sad morn* is imagined to have foreseen the blossom's destruction and so wept *tears* of *dew*. Aurora, goddess of the dawn, wept dew for her son Memnon, slain by Achilles.

49. *travail* labour, including 'pain of childbirth' (*OED* 4).

50. *seize* establish in a place of dignity (*OED* 1): a legal term (notice *lease*). *1645* and *1673* have the spelling *sease*, and Brooks and Hardy (121–2) hear a play on 'cease' meaning 'bring to rest' (*OED* 7).

56. *Helicon* a mountain in Boeotia, sacred to the Muses.

57. *bays* sprigs of laurel, emblematic of poetry.

59. *Came* the river Cam, hence Cambridge. Cp. *Lycidas* 103.

63. *Syrian shepherdess* Rachel. See Gen. 30. 22–4 for her bearing Joseph *after years of barrenness,* and Gen. 35. 16–20 for her death in giving birth to Benjamin.

66. *him* Jacob. He *served* Rachel's father Laban for fourteen years so as to win Rachel (Gen. 29. 18–27).

   Song. On May Morning

Dated variously between 1629 and 1631. The similarities to M.'s Latin *Elegia V*, composed in the spring of 1629, suggest 1 May 1629 as a likely date. Brooks and Hardy (123) note that 'May is not merely . . . the month, but a girl in a May-day dance', led in by another dancer, Venus 'the goddess of love and fertility'. May is implicitly the May Queen presiding over a fertility rite. Cp. Spenser, *Shep. Cal.* May 1–36.

1. *morning star* Venus.

harbinger forerunner. Cp. Shakespeare, *A Midsummer Night's Dream* III ii 380: 'yonder shines Aurora's harbinger', and Sandys's Ovid, xv 189–91: '*Lucifer* . . . the Harbinger of Day'.

2–4. *dancing . . . pale primrose* Cp. Phineas Fletcher, *The Apollyonists* (1627) v 27: 'The lovely Spring / Comes dancing on; the Primrose strewes her way'.

3. *green lap* Cp. Spenser, *FQ* VII vii 34, where May, 'the fayrest mayd on ground', throws 'flowres out of her lap'. Cp. also Shakespeare, *Richard II* V ii 46: 'the green lap of the new-come spring'.

5–6. *inspire . . . warm desire* Cp. Phineas Fletcher, *The Purple Island* xii 82: 'Those springing thoughts in winter hearts inspire, / Inspiriting dead souls, and quickning warm desire'. Fletcher is describing the eyes of Christ's bride, the Church, which he likens to 'May-time stars'. *The Purple Island* was published in 1633, but M. might have seen a MS before then. See *Nativity* 239n.

On Shakespeare. 1630

M.'s first published English poem; it appeared anonymously in the Second Folio of Shakespeare (1632) as *An Epitaph on the admirable Dramatic Poet, W. Shakespeare*. It reappeared (with M.'s initials) in *Poems: Written by Wil. Shakespeare, Gent.* (1640). The present title is used in *1645* and *1673*.

1–8. *What needs . . . monument* echoing the anonymous epitaph on Sir Edward Stanley, which was attributed to Shakespeare:

> Not monumental stones preserves our fame;
> Nor sky-aspiring pyramids our name;
> The memory of him for whom this stands
> Shall outlive marble and defacers' hands . . .

Cp. also Horace, *Odes* iii 30, Propertius III ii 19, Shakespeare, *Sonnet* LV, William Browne, *Britannia's Pastorals* (1613–16) II i 1016–17, and line 22 of Jonson's tribute in Shakespeare's First Folio: 'Thou art a monument without a tomb'.

1 (and 6). *What* why.

4. **ypointing* *OED*'s earliest participial instance of 'pointing'. The prefix 'y-' is a Spenserian archaism, here used inaccurately. The ME 'y-' was a prefix of the past, not the present, participle.

5. *son of Memory* M. implies that Shakespeare was brother to the Muses (daughters of Memory). Browne calls the English poets 'sons of Memory' (*Britannia's Pastorals* II i 1027). Cp. *Lycidas* 19.

6. *weak*] *1640, 1645, 1673*; dull *1632*.

8. *live-long* *enduring (*OED* 2, sole instance). Brooks and Hardy (126) hear a secondary suggestion that the *monument* is 'alive', because built of 'human stone' (Shakespeare's readers). See below, **14***n*. *1632* has 'lasting'.

10. *easy numbers* inspired verse. Cp. Heminge and Condell's preface to the First Folio (1623): 'His mind and hand went together; And what he thought, he uttered with that easinesse, that wee have scarse received from him a blot in his papers'. Contrast Jonson's praise of Shakespeare's 'art' (*To the Memory of . . . Mr. William Shakespeare* 55–64).

11. *unvalued* invaluable (*OED* 1).

12. *Delphic* Apollo, god of poetry, had his oracle at Delphi.

13. *itself*] *1645, 1673*; herself *1632*; ourself *1640*.

14. *Dost make us marble* Cp. *Il Penseroso* 42: 'Forget thyself to marble'. Here the conceit implies that Shakespeare's readers will become the *monument* spoken of in line 8.

    conceiving becoming possessed with emotion (*OED* 6).

On the University Carrier

Thomas Hobson died, aged eighty-six, on 1 January 1631. He had been a familiar Cambridge figure for over sixty years, driving a weekly coach to London and hiring out horses. His insistence that customers take the horse nearest the door gave rise to the phrase 'Hobson's choice'. His death occasioned many affectionate, semi-comic verses. M.'s first Hobson poem appeared anonymously, with a few inferior variants, in *Wit Restored* (1658).

1. *girt* girth: a leather belt securing the saddle to a horse.

5. *'Twas* The use of 'it' for 'he' (*OED* 2d) was not insulting. Cp. Shakespeare, *Macbeth* I iv 58: 'It is a peerless kinsman'.

    shifter trickster (*OED* 3), with puns on 'transfer from one place to another', 'change lodgings', 'provide for one's own safety', 'make a living', 'elude' (*OED* 'shift' 12, 15, 7, 5, 17), and 'put off, defer' (*OED* 17c), as in 'death nae langer wad be shifted' (1721).

8. *Dodged* *used shifts or changes of position so as to baffle or catch him (*OED* 1b).

    the Bull the Bull Inn, Bishopsgate (Hobson's London terminus).

10. *Had not . . . failed* The plague closed the university in 1630, and so put an end to Hobson's journeys.

    carriage both 'conveyance' and 'habitual behaviour' (*OED* 15).

13. *ta'en . . . inn* taken a room in his last inn.

14. *chamberlain* attendant at an inn in charge of the bedchambers.

Another on the Same

See previous headnote. Incomplete versions of this poem were published in *A Banquet of Jests* (1640) and *Wit Restored* (1658).

4. *jog . . . trot* A 'jog-trot' is a slow, monotonous pace. *OED* cites this sense only from 1709, but Hobson was famous for his advice to impatient travellers: 'You will get to London time enough, if you don't ride too fast.'

5. *sphere-metal* the indestructible material of the celestial spheres, which were in perpetual motion.

7. *Time numbers motion* Plato and Aristotle call time a measure of motion (see *PL* v 579–82*n*).

9. *engine* machine, here a clock.

10. *principles* *motive forces in a machine (*OED* 9) and rules adopted as a guide to action (*OED* 7).

12. *breathing* rest, breathing space.

14. *vacation* freedom from business (*OED* 1).

   term cessation (*OED* 1b), with obvious puns on the university calendar.

15. *drive away* banish (with an obvious pun).

16. *quickened* restored to life and hurried up (see above, 4*n*).

18. *carry . . . fetched* A play on 'fetch and carry' and on 'fetch' meaning 'restore to consciousness' (*OED* 2d).

19. *cross* opposed (to Hobson's travels).

   doctors of the university.

20. *put down* deposed from office (*OED* v¹ 41c) and killed (*OED* 41g).
bearers porters (*OED* 1) and pall-bearers (*OED* 1c).

22. *heaviness* grief (with an obvious pun).

26. *pressed to death* Felons who refused to plead were placed under a board and crushed with weights. M. plays on that sense and 'ready for action' (*OED* 'prest' 1), as in 'prest and ready for any service' (1632).

   more weight There might be a pun on 'wait' (though Hobson is tired of waiting). The felon's cry was a plea for immediate death.

29–31. *Obedient . . . seas* i.e. he went back and forth like the tides.

32. *wain* wagon, with a pun on 'wane' suggesting tides (*OED* v 1c) and the declining period of a person's life (*OED* sb¹ 6).

   increase growth in wealth (*OED* 4) and rising of the tide (*OED* 1b).

34. *superscription* address on a letter and inscription on a grave.

L'Allegro

The date of the companion poems *L'Allegro* and *Il Penseroso* is unknown. They may have been written during M.'s last long vacation from Cambridge (summer 1631), or when he was in Hammersmith (1632–5) or Horton (1635–8). *L'Allegro* is Italian for 'the cheerful man'. *Il Penseroso* is Italian for 'the contemplative man'.

1. *Melancholy* in Galenic medicine, a physiological condition caused by an excess of black bile. It could lead to madness or depression. Aristotelian medicine recognized another kind of melancholy, which (in moderate degrees) was suited to poetic or prophetic inspiration. Thus the *melancholy* banished here might not be the 'divinest Melancholy' of *Il Penseroso*. See Robert Burton, *Anatomy of Melancholy* (1621).

2. *Of . . . born* The genealogy is M.'s invention. *Cerberus* was the hound of Hades. M. substitutes him for Night's consort, Erebus. H. Neville Davies (*MQ* 23, March 1989, 1–7) hears a play between *Cerberus* and 'Erebus' and between 'heart-eating' and 'heart-easing' (13). *Cerberus* means 'heart-eating'. Cp. 'eating cares' (135).

3. *Stygian cave* Cerberus lived in a cave on the banks of the Styx. Aeneas heard *shrieks* of dead children as he passed the cave (Virgil, *Aen.* vi 426–7).

5. *uncouth* desolate.

cell den of a wild beast (*OED* 3c).

6. *brooding* *hovering over (*OED* 6, earliest instance 1697) and *meditating moodily (*OED* 7, earliest instance 1751).

7. *night-raven* a name given to a nocturnal bird whose cry was a bad omen; perhaps an owl.

8. *shades* trees.

*low-browed of rocks: beetling (*OED* 2).

10. *Cimmerian* Homer's Cimmerians live on the edge of the world in a land of perpetual darkness (*Od.* xi 13–19).

11. *fair and free* a common phrase in which *free* means 'of gentle birth and breeding'. Cp. Chaucer, *Romance of the Rose* 633: 'Mirthe, that is so fair and free'.

12. *yclept* named (Spenserian archaism).

Euphrosyne 'Mirth', one of the three *Graces*. Her sisters were Aglaia ('Brilliance') and Thalia ('Bloom'). One tradition made *Venus* and *Bacchus* their parents.

17. *as some sager sing* The genealogy is M.'s invention, but Jonson pairs *Zephyr* (the west wind) with *Aurora* (the dawn) in his *Entertainment at Highgate* (1616). Like M., Jonson rhymes 'a-Maying' with 'playing' (93–

4). M.'s *playing* includes 'have sexual intercourse' (*OED* 10c, cp. *PL* ix 1027).

20. *a-Maying* celebrating the rites of May Day (an ancient fertility rite associated with sexual licence).

21. *beds of violets* Adam and Eve make love on a bed of violets after their Fall (*PL* ix 1034–45). Cp. also Hera's seduction of Zeus in Homer, *Il.* xiv 346–51.

22. *roses washed in dew* Cp. Shakespeare, *The Taming of the Shrew* II i 174: 'morning roses newly washed with dew'.

24. *buxom, blithe, and debonair* a common concatenation, as in Thomas Randolph, *Aristippus* (1630), 18: 'A Bowle of wine is wondrous boone cheere / To make one blith, buxome, and deboneere'.

    buxom bright, lively.

    debonair affable, courteous. Davies (see above, 2*n*) hears a play on *de bon air* alluding to Euphrosyne's father, the wind-god Zephyrus.

27. *Quips* witty sayings.

    Cranks verbal tricks.

    wanton carefree (*OED* 3).

    Wiles playful tricks.

28. *Becks* upward nods, 'come-ons'. Cp. Burton, *Anatomy of Melancholy* III ii II iv: 'With becks and nods he first began / To try the wench's mind, / With becks and nods and smiles again / An answer he did find'.

29. *Hebe* goddess of youth.

31–2. *Sport . . . sides* Cp. Phineas Fletcher, *The Purple Island* iv 13: 'Here sportfull Laughter dwells, here ever sitting, / Defies all lumpish griefs, and wrinkled care'. *The Purple Island* was published in 1633 but M. might have seen a MS before then. See *Nativity* 239*n*.

33. *trip it* dance.

    ye] *1645*; you *1673*.

34. *fantastic* *making elaborate movements (*OED* 6b). Cp. 'light fantastic round' (*A Masque* 144) and Drayton, *Nimphidia* (1627) 29: 'light fantastick mayde'.

40. *unreprovèd* irreproachable. A Latin use of the past participle.

45–6. *to come . . . good morrow* Opinion is divided as to whether it is L'Allegro or the lark who comes to L'Allegro's window. The syntax favours L'Allegro, but editors prior to Masson (1874) assumed it was the lark.

45. *in spite of sorrow* in defiance of sorrow (not 'despite an existing sorrow').

50. *Scatters the rear* a military metaphor. Cp. *PL* vi 12–18.

52. *Stoutly struts* Cp. the peacock in Sylvester, *DWW* (1592–1608) I iv (1605): 'To woo his Mistresse, strowting stately by-her' (188).

55. *hoar* grey from lack of foliage (*OED* 4) or from mist.

57. *not unseen* Contrast Il Penseroso, who walks 'unseen' (65).

60. *state* stately progress, as of a monarch.

62. *dight* arrayed.

67. *tells his tale* either 'numbers his flock' (as in William Browne, *The Shepherd's Pipe* v 7–10) or 'tells his story' (as in Browne's *Britannia's Pastorals* I iii 355–6).

71. *Russet lawns* *untilled land (*OED* 'lawn' 1b) scorched reddish-brown by the sun.

   fallows ploughed land (*OED* 1).

72. *nibbling flocks* Cp. Shakespeare, *The Tempest* IV i 62: 'nibbling sheep'.

74. *labouring* moving slowly with painful exertion (*OED* 14, hence *rest*).

75. *pied* variegated. Cp. Shakespeare, *Love's Labour's Lost* V ii 882: 'daisies pied'.

78. *tufted* growing in clusters.

79. *lies* lodges.

80. *Cynosure* the Pole Star, hence 'centre of attraction' (*OED* 2b). Cp. *A Masque* 342n.

83–88. *Corydon* and *Thyrsis* are men, *Phyllis* and *Thestylis* women. These are stock pastoral names, but cp. Virgil, *Ecl.* vii (Corydon meeting Thyrsis) and *Ecl.* ii 10–11 (Thestylis preparing *herbs* and *messes*).

86. *neat-handed dexterous (*OED*), implying 'elegant in cookery' (*OED* 'neat' 8b).

90. *tanned* sun-dried.

   haycock conical heap of hay.

91. *secure* carefree (*OED* 1).

94. *rebecks* three-stringed fiddles.

96. *chequered shade* Cp. Shakespeare, *Titus Andronicus* II iii 14–15: 'the green leaves . . . make a chequered shadow on the ground'.

98. *holiday* The word answers a question that has exercised cultural materialists: 'Why isn't anyone in *L'Allegro* doing any work?' In fact the poem does describe work. Phyllis and Thestylis are burdened with chores even while their men enjoy a rare day off (86–8).

102. *Mab* queen of the fairies. Cp. Shakespeare, *Romeo and Juliet* I iv 54–95 and Jonson, *Entertainment at Althorp* (1616) 47–54, where Mab 'pinches countrey wenches' and robs 'cream-bowles'.

   junkets cream cheeses or other cream dishes.

   ate] eat *1645, 1673*; pronounced 'et'. Cp. *PL* ix 781.

103. *She* the maid telling the story.

104. *And he by*] *1645*; And by the *1673*.

   friar's lantern the Jack o' Lantern or Will o' the Wisp: a delusive light which misled travellers. Cp. *A Masque* 432–7, *PL* ix 634–42, and Shakespeare, *A Midsummer Night's Dream* II i 39, III i 106–11.

105. *drudging goblin* Hobgoblin (also called Robin Goodfellow and Puck). Most familiar from Shakespeare's *A Midsummer Night's Dream*, he appears in Jonson's *Love Restored* (1616), where he 'sweeps the hearth for the country maids' and 'does all their other drudgery' (54–5).

106. *cream-bowl* Robin's traditional reward. See Burton, *Anatomy of Melancholy* I ii I ii: 'A bigger kind there is . . . called with us hobgoblins and Robin Goodfellows, that would in those superstitious times grind corn for a mess of milk, cut wood, or do any manner of drudgery work.'

109. *end* put (corn) into a barn (*OED* v²). Robin threshes more corn in one night than ten men could stack in a day.

110. *lubber fiend beneficent goblin, 'Lob-lie-by-the-fire'. *Lubber* plays on 'big, idle lout' (*OED* 1a) and 'drudge' (*OED* 1c).

111. *chimney* fireplace. These were large, so the goblin is of at least human size. Lob-lie-by-the-fire is a 'Giant' in Beaumont and Fletcher's *Knight of the Burning Pestle* (1613) III iv.

113. *crop-full filled to repletion (*OED* 2).

flings rushes.

120. *weeds of peace* courtly raiment. Cp. Shakespeare, *Troilus and Cressida* III iii 239: 'great Hector in his weeds of peace'.

triumphs pageants, tournaments (*OED* 4).

121. *store of* many.

122. *Rain influence* The ladies' eyes are imagined as stars, affecting human destiny by raining etherial fluid down on mankind. See *Nativity* 71*n*.

125. *Hymen* the god of marriage. The *saffron robe* and *taper* (torch) are his usual attributes.

126. *clear* bright (*OED* 4b). A blazing hymeneal torch was a good omen. Contrast the smoky torch that presaged doom at the wedding of Orpheus and Eurydice (Ovid, *Met.* x 1–7). Sandys's 1632 comment describes that torch as burning 'not clearly'. See below, 145–50*n* and *Epitaph on the Marchioness of Winchester* 20.

127. *revelry* including 'the revels', dances concluding a *masque*.

128. *antique* either 'ancient' (implying serious, allegorical pageantry) or 'grotesque'. Cp. *Il Penseroso* 158. An 'antic' was a 'grotesque pageant' (*OED* 3).

131. *anon* at once, instantly (*OED* 4).

132. *sock* the low-heeled slipper of the Greek comic actor; here, a metonymy for comedy. Cp. *Il Penseroso* 102.

133. *Fancy's child* Cp. Shakespeare, *Love's Labour's Lost* I i 171: 'child of fancy'.

135. *eating cares* translating Horace, *Odes* II xi 18: *curas edaces*.

136. *Lydian airs* Plato preferred the Dorian to the Lydian mode of music, which he condemned for its moral laxity (*Republic* iii 398–9). But a minority tradition saw the Lydian mode as relaxing and delightful. See Horace, *Odes* IV xv 30–32, and M.'s ironic remark in *Areopagitica*: 'No musick must be heard, no song be set or sung, but what is grave and *Dorick*' (*YP* 2. 523).

137. *Married* Cp. the marriage of 'Voice' and 'Verse' in *Solemn Music* 2–3.

138. *meeting* coming forward in welcome (*OED* ppl. a. 2).

139. *bout* circuit (*OED* 1).

142. *melting* delicately modulated (*OED* ppl. a. 1c).

143. *tie* including 'connect notes by a tie or ligature' (*OED* 3c).

145–50. *That Orpheus'* . . . *Eurydice* Eurydice was killed by a snake on her wedding day. Her husband Orpheus sought her in Hades, and so moved Proserpine and Pluto that they permitted Eurydice to return – on condition that Orpheus should not look back at her. He did so, and lost her again. See Virgil, *Georg.* iv 453–527, Ovid, *Met.* x 1–85 and cp. *Il Penseroso* 105–8n.

147. *Elysian* Orpheus was reunited with Eurydice in Elysium after his death (Ovid, *Met.* xi 61–6). See *Lycidas* 58–63 and *PL* vii 32–9 for Orpheus' murder by the Maenads.

150–51. *These delights* . . . *live* echoing the ending of Marlowe's 'The Passionate Shepherd to his Love' (1599): 'If these delights thy mind may move, / Then live with me, and be my love'.

Il Penseroso

See headnote to *L'Allegro*.

1–4. *Hence* . . . *joys* Cp. the song praising melancholy ('Hence all ye vain delights') in John Fletcher's *The Nice Valour* (printed 1647, but in MS collections from about 1620). Cp. also Sylvester, *Henry the Great* (1621) 333–4: 'Hence, hence false Pleasures, momentary Joyes; / Mock us no more with your illuding Toyes'.

3. *bestead* help.

4. *toys* idle fancies (*OED* 4).

6. *fond* foolish.

possess *occupy the thoughts of (*OED* 1d).

8–10. *gay motes* . . . *Morpheus' train* Cp. the Cave of Sleep in Sylvester, *DWW* (1592–1608), *The Vocation* (1606) 540–62. *Morpheus,* the god of dreams, is surrounded by 'Fantastike swarmes of *Dreames'* resembling 'Th' unnumbred Moats which in the Sunne doo play' (554–60).

10. *pensioners* military retainers (*OED* 2b), with a possible pun on the Cambridge sense: 'undergraduate student who is not a Scholar on the foundation of a college' (*OED* 6). A sly dig at soporific Cambridge students would be typical of M.

13–16. *too bright* . . . *hue* Cp. *PL* iii 377–82: 'Dark with excessive bright'.

14. *hit* suit, be agreeable to (*OED* 15).

17. *Black, but* Cp. Song of Sol. 1. 5: 'I am black but comely, O ye daughters of Jerusalem'.

18. *Memnon's sister* Memnon was a black Ethiopian king who fought for Troy. Homer calls him the 'handsomest of men' (*Od.* xi 522). Later writers gave him a beautiful sister, Himera. See e.g. John Lydgate, *Troy Book* v 2887–906 and Guido de Columnis, *Historia Destructionis Troiae* xxxiii.

19. *starred* *stellified (*OED* 5).

   queen Cassiopeia, wife of the Ethiopian King Cephalus. She was changed into a constellation because she claimed to be more beautiful than the Nereids (Hyginus, *Astronomica* II x). Ovid (*Her.* xv 36) depicts her daughter Andromeda as a beautiful black woman.

23. *Vesta* Roman goddess of the hearth, Saturn's daughter, vowed to virginity. M. invents the story of her motherhood.

24. *solitary Saturn* Saturn was associated with melancholic, 'saturnine' humours through astrology. The god Saturn had reigned in the Golden Age (Ovid, *Met.* i 89–112), a time of sexual licence (Propertius III xiii 25–46, Tibullus II iii 69–74). M. blends the traditions, placing Saturn and Vesta in *secret shades* even though incest was not yet a sin. Contrast the open-air love-making of Zephyr and Aurora (*L'Allegro* 17–23).

29–30. *Ida's . . . Jove* Saturn reigned on Mount Ida in Crete, and Jove was born there. Jove ended the Golden Age by usurping Saturn's throne. Cp. *PL* i 512–16.

31. *nun* pagan priestess (*OED* 1b).

33. *grain* dye.

35. *stole* long robe (*OED* 1).

   cypress lawn fine black linen.

36. *decent* including 'comely' (*OED* 2). Cp. *PL* viii 601.

38. *wonted state* accustomed dignity (*OED* 'state' 19).

39. *commercing* communicating.

42. *Forget thyself to marble* 'become so entranced that you are as still as a statue'. Cp. *On Shakespeare* 13–14 and Thomas Tomkins, *Albumazar* (1615) I iv 4: 'Marvel thyself to marble'.

43. *sad* grave, dignified (*OED* 4b).

   leaden Saturn was associated with lead. *cast* glance, expression (*OED* 6).

44. *fast* fixedly.

48. *Ay* continually. Cp. the *Muses* singing around *Jove's* altar in Hesiod, *Theog.* 1–10, and M.'s *Prolusion ii* (*YP* 1. 237).

53. *fiery-wheelèd throne* Ezekiel's chariot. See Ezek. 1 and 10 and cp. *The Passion* 36–40.

54. *Cherub Contemplation* Cherubim were angels of knowledge and lived in contemplation of God. See *Nativity* 111–12n.

55. *hist* *summon silently (*OED* 1).

56. *Philomel* the nightingale. See *A Masque* 234n.

57. *plight* state of mind (*OED* sb² 6), with possible reference to the other Philomela's plight after she had been raped by Tereus. See *A Masque* 234*n*.

58. *Smoothing the rugged brow of Night* Cp. *PR* ii 164 ('smooth the rugged'st brow') and *A Masque* 251–2 ('smoothing the raven down / Of darkness').

59. *Cynthia* Diana, goddess of the moon. She was sometimes identified with Hecate, whose chariot was drawn by dragons.

63. *chantress* songstress.

64. *even-song* Cp. the cock's 'matin' in *L'Allegro* 114.

65. *unseen* Cp. 'not unseen' in *L'Allegro* 57.

66. *smooth-shaven green* Cp. Sylvester, *DWW* (1592–1608), *The Tropheis* (1607) 940: 'new-shav'n Fields'.

73. *plat* patch, plot.

74. *curfew* bell rung at eight or nine p.m. as a sign to extinguish fires.

76. *sullen* of a deep or mournful tone (*OED* 3b).

77. *air* weather, climate (*OED* 4).

83. *bellman* nightwatchman calling the hours.
    charm exorcizing incantation.

84. *bless* protect (*OED* v¹ 3).

87. *outwatch the Bear* both 'outdo Ursa Major in staying awake' and 'watch Ursa Major until it disappears'. Ursa Major never sets. Jonson had coined 'outwatch' in *The Fortunate Isles* (1625) 35, where the 'melancholic student' Merefool says that he has 'outwatched' ghosts in the hope of summoning a planetary Intelligence. Merefool later tries to summon Plato and Hermes Trismegistus (141–55).

88. *thrice-great Hermes* Hermes Trismegistus, supposed author of the *Corpus Hermeticum* (mystical writings now thought to date from the first to the third centuries AD). Neo-Platonic doctrine made Hermes the father of all knowledge. *With thrice-great Hermes* means 'reading Hermetic philosophy', but also implies that Hermes (like Plato) has been 'unsphered' and is now literally present in Il Penseroso's tower, from which he observes Ursa Major (a Hermetic symbol of perfection).
    unsphere *summon from his celestial sphere. Cp. *A Masque* 3.

90. *regions* divisions of the universe (*OED* 3a).

92. *nook* remote part of the world (*OED* 4).

93. *daemons* spirits (not necessarily evil) presiding over the four elements and inhabiting every part of the universe in Hermetic lore. See esp. the Hermetic *Definitions of Asclepius to King Amon* xiii–xiv. Cp. *PR* ii 122.

95. *consent* harmony, accord (*OED* 4).

98. *pall* the tragic actor's mantle (Latin *palla*) and a royal robe (*OED* 6b). Carey notes that *pall* and *sceptre* occur together in Ovid's description of tragedy (*Amores* III i 11–13).

99. *Thebes* the city of Oedipus, and the scene of tragedies by Aeschylus, Sophocles and Euripides.

Pelops' line   Pelops's descendants Atreus, Thyestes, Agamemnon, Orestes, Electra, and Iphigeneia appear in tragedies by Aeschylus, Sophocles, Euripides, and Seneca.

100. *Troy*   the scene of tragedies by Sophocles and Euripides. The epithet *divine* is Homeric (*Od.* xi 86, xvii 293).

102. *buskined*   The 'buskin' was the high boot of the Greek tragic actor. Cp. the comic 'sock' in *L'Allegro* 132.

104. *Musaeus*   a mythical Greek poet and priest said to have been the son or pupil of Orpheus.

105–8. *Or bid . . . seek*   See *L'Allegro* 145–50*n* for the story of Orpheus and Eurydice. M. now omits any mention of the unhappy ending. There were versions in which Orpheus recovered Eurydice.

107. *iron tears*   suggesting Pluto's unyielding, 'stony' heart (*OED* 'iron' 3d). Cp. Spenser, *FQ* V x 28: 'yron eyes'.

109. *him*   Chaucer, whose *Squire's Tale* is unfinished.

112. *who had Canace to wife*   echoing Spenser's continuation of Chaucer: 'Triamond had Canacee to wife' (*FQ* IV iii 52).

113. *virtuous*   magical.

120. **more than meets the ear*   *OED*'s earliest instance of the phrase (*OED* 'meet' 2e). M. is referring to Spenser, and perhaps to Ariosto and Tasso (whose epics had been allegorized).

121. *pale career*   moonlit course.

122. *civil-suited*   soberly dressed. Cp. Shakespeare, *Romeo and Juliet* III ii 10–11: 'Come, civil night, / Thou sober-suited matron'.

123. *tricked and frounced*   adorned and curly-haired.

124. *Attic boy*   Cephalus, an Athenian prince and hunter loved by Aurora (Ovid, *Met.* vii 690–865).

127. *still*   gentle.

130. *minute*   small. Most editors adopt Warton's 1791 note: 'drops falling at intervals of a minute'. Warton was presumably thinking of minute guns or bells, fired or tolled at intervals of a minute 'as a sign of mourning' (*OED* 'minute' IV 7). Neither existed in M.'s time.

132. *flaring beams*   echoing Marlowe, *Hero and Leander* ii 332.

134. *Sylvan*   Silvanus, the Roman wood-god.

141. *Day's garish eye*   Cp. Shakespeare, *Romeo and Juliet* II ii 25: 'the garish sun'.

145. *consort*   musical harmony.

147–9. *And . . . displayed*   'And let some strange, mysterious dream hover around Sleep's wings, displaying itself in a stream of life-like mental images'.

148. *his*   Sleep's.

airy stream   Cp. Night's address to Fant'sy in Jonson, *The Vision of Delight* 41–6: 'Create of airy forms a stream . . . / And though it be a waking dream, / Yet let it like an odour rise . . . / And fall like sleep upon their eyes'. *The Vision of Delight* was performed in 1617 and printed in 1640.

151–2. *sweet music . . . underneath* Cp. Shakespeare, *The Tempest* I ii 390: 'Where should this music be? i' th' air or th' earth?'

153. *to mortals good* Cp. *Lycidas* 183–5: 'Henceforth thou art the Genius of the shore / . . . and shalt be good / To all that wander in that perilous flood'.

154. *Genius* protective local deity.

155. *due* dutiful, obedient.

156. *pale* enclosure (perhaps the court of a Cambridge college).

157. *embowèd roof* vaulted roof of a chapel.

158. *antique* venerable; many editors modernize to *antic* (an architectural term meaning 'fantastic, grotesque').

  massy proof massive, tested strength.

159. *storied* ornamented with stained glass.

  dight decorated.

161. **pealing* earliest instance of the sense 'sound forth' (*OED* 'peal' v³ 1).

163. *service* musical setting of the canticles in the Anglican Church.

170–71. *spell / Of* *engage in study of (*OED* 6b), with overtones of magical spells (cp. lines 85–96).

175–6. *These pleasures . . . live* See *L'Allegro* 151–2n.

  Sonnet I ('O nightingale')

Usually dated *c.* 1628–30. Like *On May Morning*, it is a poem of spring, and may have been composed at the same time.

1–2. *O . . . still* Cp. *Elegia* V 25–6. Many Italian sonnets begin with an address to a nightingale.

2. *still* quiet.

4. *jolly* showy, finely dressed (*OED* 8, 9) and amorous, good-looking (*OED* 7, 10).

  Hours the Horae, goddesses of the seasons.

5–7. *liquid notes . . . success in love* A medieval fancy held that it was a good omen for a lover to hear the nightingale before the cuckoo in May. M.'s source may be *The Cuckoo and the Nightingale*, now attributed to Sir Thomas Clanvowe, but then attributed to Chaucer.

6. *shallow* shrill, thin (*OED* 4).

9. *rude* unmusical (*OED* 7).

  bird of hate the cuckoo (which was associated with cuckoldry).

THE ITALIAN POEMS

M.'s five Italian sonnets and the *canzone* '*Ridonsi donne*' were once thought to date from his Italian journey (1638–9), but are now usually dated *c.* 1629–30. They are love poems in the tradition of Petrarch, addressed to (or describing) a lady called Emilia.

Sonnet II ('*Donna leggiadra*')

1. M. reveals his lady's name by alluding to the Italian province of 'Emilia', through which the *Reno* flows. Smart (121–7) decodes the allusion and cites Italian precedents.
2. *nobil varco* [*famous ford*] The Rubicon (made famous when Julius Caesar forded it) also runs through Emilia.
8. *Là* [*there*] in her eyes.
10. A comparison of the lady to Orpheus (Ovid, *Met.* xi 45–6).
11. A comparison to Homer's Sirens. Cp. *Sonnet IV* 14.

Sonnet III ('*Qual in colle aspro*')

10. *Arno* the river of Florence (here a figure for the Tuscan dialect, as the *Thames* represents English). Cp. *Canzone* 7.

Canzone

A *canzone* is an Italian lyric consisting of several long stanzas, with lines of irregular length, and a short concluding stanza. Its structure influenced Spenser's *Epithalamion* and M.'s *Lycidas*. The present poem consists of only one stanza and an envoy.

1. The youths and maidens who tease M. for writing in Italian are English and in England.
7–12. Rivers again represent languages (cp. *Sonnet III* 10). The *altri rivi* ('other streams') are English and Latin. Cp. *Lycidas* 174–5, where the 'other groves and other streams' are those of Heaven. That meaning might be implicit here, but the 'immortal guerdon of unfading leaves' (*L'immortal guiderdon d'eterne frondi*) is primarily poetic fame on earth (cp. the 'fair guerdon' of *Lycidas* 73). Since the youths and maidens are teasing M., there may be an ironic allusion to Ariosto's Limbo of Vanity, where Astolfo

saw 'other lakes and rivers, other rills / From ours down here on earth' (*Orl. Fur.* xxxiv 72).

13. It was common practice for a poet to address his own *canzone* in the envoy. Cp. Spenser, *Epithalamion* 426–32.

Sonnet IV ('Diodati, e te'l dirò')

1. *Diodati* Charles Diodati, the closest friend of M.'s youth. M. addressed his first and sixth Latin elegies to him, and commemorated his early death in *Epitaphium Damonis*. Diodati died while M. was in Italy, so *Sonnet IV* must antedate M.'s Italian journey.

6. *idea* including the Platonic sense.

12. *faticosa* suffering eclipse. Cp. *PL* ii 665.

14. Odysseus put wax in the ears of his crew so that they would not be allured by the song of the Sirens (Homer, *Od.* xii). Cp. *Sonnet II* 11–12.

Sonnet V ('Per certo i bei vostr' occhi')

6. *quel lato* ['that side']. i.e. the left, where his heart is.

Sonnet VII ('How soon hath Time')

Date: either 9 December 1631 (M.'s twenty-third birthday) or, as Parker (784–7) argues, 9 December 1632 (when M. ceased being twenty-three). Parker's revised date has been widely, but not universally, accepted. In December 1631 M. was in the middle of his last year at Cambridge; one year later he was pursuing solitary studies at his father's house. In 1633 he enclosed the sonnet in a letter 'To a Friend'. The friend (perhaps M.'s old tutor, Thomas Young) had warned M. against excessive study and had urged him to join the ministry. M.'s reply acknowledges 'a certaine belatednesse', but cites the parables of the vineyard and the talents to justify his 'not taking thought of beeing late so it give advantage to be more fit' (*YP* 1. 320). Hunter (179–83) points out that twenty-three was the earliest age for being ordained as deacon, and that many of M.'s classmates had already been ordained by 9 December 1632. It may be that the *more timely-happy spirits* of line 8 are these classmates, and not rival poets (as has often been assumed). But M.'s poetic calling is not irrelevant to *Sonnet VII*. Line 4 implies poetic productivity, and the poetic and priestly vocations were closely associated in M.'s mind.

2. *Stol'n on his wing* including the intransitive sense 'steal (himself) away'. Cp. Kyd, *The Spanish Tragedy* (1592) III xi 46: 'Then time steales on, And steales, and steales'.

3. *hasting* *speeding (*OED* 1), with wry overtones of the older sense 'ripening early' (*OED* 2).

full career full speed (with a play on the active life M. is not leading).

4. *bud or blossom* a common metaphor for poetry (from Latin *flos*). Cp. *Lycidas* 1–5.

5. *semblance* outward appearance.

deceive misrepresent.

8. *timely-* seasonable (*OED* 2) and ripening early (*OED* 1).

endu'th *is inherent in (*OED* 9b), with overtones of 'endow with dignities' (*OED* V) and 'clothe or cover' (*OED* IV) playing against *inward*.

9. *it* inward ripeness (7).

9–12. *Yet . . . Heaven* Cp. Pindar, *Nemean Odes* iv 41–3: 'But, whatsoever excellence Lord Destiny assigned me, well I know that the lapse of time will bring it to its appointed perfection.'

10. *still* always.

strictest *most precise (*OED* 8a).

even / To both 'level with, neither higher nor lower' (*OED* a 5a) and 'fully' (*OED* adv. 7) as in 'even to the edge of doom' (Shakespeare, *Sonnet* CXVI). Cp. Latin *usque ad*.

13–14. *All . . . eye* 'All my inward ripeness is ever under the eyes of God, if I have grace to use it in that way'. Some critics prefer: 'All that matters is whether I have grace to use my abilities in accordance with God's will, as one ever in his sight'.

14. *task-master* Cp. the parable of the vineyard (Matt. 20. 1–16). Those who began to labour late received the same reward as those who had worked throughout the day.

Sonnet VIII ('Captain or colonel')

Date: November ? 1642. The Civil War had begun on 22 August 1642. After the battle of Edgehill (23 October 1642), the Parliamentarian army retreated, leaving the road to London undefended. The Royalist forces advanced, causing panic in the city. The London trained bands were hastily assembled, and marched out to face Charles's army on Turnham Green, just a few miles from M.'s house on Aldersgate Street. Battle was averted when Charles ordered a retreat (13 November). The sonnet is untitled in *1645* and *1673*, but in *TMS* there is a fair copy in the hand of an amanuensis entitled 'On his door when the City expected an assault'. This is erased, and 'When the assault was intended to the City' substituted in M.'s hand (with the date '1642', later crossed through).

1. *colonel* Three syllables, pronounced 'coronel'. See the account in *OED* (which states that the accent in seventeenth-century verse was often on the last syllable).

2. *defenceless doors* M.'s house lay outside the city walls.

3. *If deed of honour did thee ever please*] *1673;* if ever deed of honour did thee please *TMS, 1645.*

5. *charms* both 'songs' and 'magic spells' (Latin *carmina*).

6. *gentle* noble, courteous.

10. *Emathian conqueror* Alexander the Great. M. is alluding to the sack of Thebes in 335 BC, when Alexander spared only the house where Pindar had lived (Plutarch, *Alexander* 11, Pliny vii 29). 'Emathia' is a district of Macedon.

12. *repeated air* the reciting of the chorus (Latin idiom).

13. *Electra's poet* Euripides. After Sparta defeated Athens in the Peloponnesian War, the Spartan general Lysander called a council to decide the conquered city's fate (404 BC). The Theban envoy proposed that Athens be destroyed and its people enslaved. A man from Phocis then sang the first chorus from Euripides' *Electra*. The whole council melted with compassion and could not destroy a city which had produced such great men (Plutarch, *Lysander* 15).

14. *walls* Warton objected that the walls of Athens were not saved, but torn down to the sound of flutes. Modern critics therefore take *walls* to mean 'houses'. But M. is more accurate than his critics. The Spartans razed the Long Walls and the Piraeus circuit, but spared the Athenian city wall (Plutarch, *Lysander* 14, Xenophon, *Hellenica* II ii 20, Diodorus Siculus XIII cvii 4).

Sonnet IX ('Lady that in the prime')

Date: *c.* 1642–45. The poem follows *Sonnet VIII* in *TMS*, which suggests that it was written after 1642. The lady's identity is unknown.

1. *prime* the 'springtime' of human life (*OED* 8).

2. *the broad way* Cp. Matt. 7. 13: 'Broad is the way, that leadeth to destruction, and many there be that go in thereat.'

and the green Cp. Job 8. 12–13 on the 'greenness' of 'the paths of all that forget God'. Cp. also Samuel Daniel, *Delia* 6: 'green paths of youth and love'.

3–4. *those few . . . Truth* Cp. Matt. 7. 14: 'narrow is the way, which leadeth unto life, and few there be that find it'. The hill of truth was a commonplace.

Cp. Hesiod, *WD* 287–92, Plato, *Republic* ii 364, Donne, *Satire III* 79f.

5. *better part*   See Luke 10. 39–42.

Mary, Martha's sister, sat at Jesus's feet while Martha was burdened with chores. When Martha complained, Jesus said: 'one thing is needful; and Mary hath chosen that good part'.

Ruth   Unlike Orpah, Ruth chose to abandon her home in Moab and live with Naomi, her Hebrew mother-in-law (Ruth 1. 16).

6. *overween*   are presumptuous.

7. *fret their spleen*   consume themselves with spite.

9–14. *Thy . . . pure*   alluding to the parable of the wise and foolish virgins (Matt. 25. 1–13). The wise ones took oil for their lamps and so were admitted to the marriage feast.

11. *hope that reaps not shame*   Cp. Rom. 5. 5 ('hope maketh not ashamed') and Gal. 6. 7 ('whatsoever a man soweth, that shall he also reap').

12. *feastful*   festive.

Sonnet X ('Daughter to that good Earl')

Date: *c.* 1642–5. The fair copy in *TMS* is entitled 'To the Lady Margaret Ley'. Lady Margaret was the daughter of James Ley (1550–1629), Earl of Marlborough from 1626. After a distinguished career as lawyer and judge (he was made Lord Chief Justice in 1622), Ley retired from the Bench in 1624 to become Lord High Treasurer. But proving less useful in this position than Charles had wished, he resigned his post in 1628 to assume the less important office of Lord President of the Council. He died on 14 March 1629.

Most of the Earl's family supported the King in the Civil War, but Lady Margaret's husband, John Hobson, fought for Parliament. Edward Phillips, M.'s nephew and biographer, reports that Lady Margaret and her husband were M.'s near neighbours and close friends in the 1640s after his wife had left him.

1–10. M. follows the Horatian tradition of beginning a poem of praise by referring to the addressee's descent. Cp. *Sonnet XVII* ('Lawrence of virtuous father') and *Sonnet XVIII* ('Cyriack, whose grandsire').

3. *fee*   bribe (*OED* sb² 10c). M. may imply a contrast with Bacon, at whose trial for corruption the Earl had presided (1621). Honigmann and Carey cite some gossip about the Earl's own shady dealings, but M.'s praise is echoed by Thomas Fuller, who in *The Worthies of England* (1662) describes the Earl as 'a person of great gravity, ability, and integrity'.

4. *left them both*   Ley retired as Lord President of the Council on 14

December 1628. Clarendon says that he 'was removed under pretence of his age and disability for the work'.

5–6. *sad breaking . . . Broke him* Parliament was dissolved on 10 March 1629 amidst much tumult (the Speaker was forcibly held down in his chair while the Commons passed resolutions condemning the King's policies). The Earl died four days later, aged seventy-nine. Charles ruled without Parliament for the next eleven years. *Breaking* came to be a technical term for dissolving Parliament, but the earliest instance is from 1715 (*OED* 'break' 2f).

6. *dishonest* shameful (*OED* 1).

7. *Chaeronea* where King Philip II of Macedon conquered the Thebans and Athenians in 338 BC.

8. *old man eloquent* the Athenian orator Isocrates, aged ninety-eight in 338 BC. M. probably errs in thinking that he mourned the battle's outcome. Isocrates had urged Philip to unite the Greeks, and (if *Letter* 3 is genuine) he did so again after Chaeronea. Patterson (40) detects some sinister motive in M.'s inaccuracy, but M. is true to his (then respectable) source, Dionysius of Halicarnassus, who reports that Isocrates starved himself after Chaeronea so as not to outlive the good of Athens (*Isocrates* 1).

9. *later born, than to* born too late to. The Earl was about sixty when M. and Margaret were born.

Arcades

This 'entertainment' (also called 'a masque' in *TMS*) was performed at an unknown date early in the 1630s for Alice, Dowager Countess of Derby, then aged about seventy. She had long been associated with poets. Spenser had dedicated poems to her, Marston had composed a masque in her honour (1607), and she had participated in Jonson's *Masque of Blackness* (1605) and *Masque of Beauty* (1607). Her first husband (to whom she owed her title) was Ferdinando Stanley, Earl of Derby (d. 1594). In 1600 she married Sir Thomas Egerton (d. 1617), and her daughter married his son, Sir John. John Egerton became Earl of Bridgewater in 1617, and M.'s *A Masque* (*Comus*) was performed in his honour (1634). The 'noble persons' of the Countess's family in *Arcades* may have included some of the Earl's children who acted in *A Masque*. M.'s friend Henry Lawes, who composed the music for *A Masque*, had been music tutor to the Earl's children since 1626, and so probably managed both performances.

The 'Arcades' of the title are inhabitants of Arcadia, a mountainous area in Greece associated with pastoral poetry in Virgil's *Eclogues* and Renaissance pastoral fictions.

[stage direction] *seat of state* the chair in which the Countess sat as principal spectator.

5 (and 17). *This this is she* Cp. Jonson, *Entertainment at Althorp* (1616) 113–14 ('This is she / This is she') and *Pleasure Reconciled to Virtue* (1618) 308: 'She, she it is'.

8. *raise* *laud, extol (*OED* 18d).

9. *erst* formerly (referring to previous poetic tributes to the Countess, such as those of Spenser and Marston).

12. *Less than half* Cp. I Kings 10. 7 (the Queen of Sheba's words to Solomon): 'I believed not the words, until I came . . . and behold, the half was not told me: thy wisdom and prosperity exceedeth the fame which I heard'.

14. *state* canopy over a throne (*OED* 20b).

20. *Latona* mother of Apollo and Diana.

21. *Cybele* a Phrygian goddess, identified with Rhea (Jove's mother). Virgil (*Aen.* vi 784–7) refers to her turreted crown (hence *towered*) and describes her as holding a hundred of her grandchildren.

23. *give her odds* compete with her on equal terms.

24. *this clime* See *PL* ix 44–5*n* for the theory that northern climates were unfavourable to creative genius.

[stage direction] *Genius* protective local deity. Cp. *Il Penseroso* 154 and *Lycidas* 183.

26. *gentle swains* well-born servants (an oxymoron).

28. *Arcady* Arcadia.

30. *secret sluice* hidden channel (translating *occultas . . . vias*, Virgil, *Aen.* iii 695).

31. *Arethuse* one of Diana's nymphs. She excited the passion of the Arcadian river-god *Alpheus* when she bathed naked in his waters. He pursued her, but Diana turned her into a river and cleft the ground beneath her feet. Still pursued by Alpheus, Arethusa flowed under the earth and rose as a fountain on the isle of Ortygia, just off Sicily (Ovid, *Met.* v 574–61, Virgil, *Aen.* iii 694–6).

32. *breathing roses* both 'roses emitting fragrance' and 'human roses'.

33. *silver-buskined* wearing high silver boots.

34. *free* noble, generous (*OED* 4a).

37. *reverence* bow (*OED* 2).

39. *solemnity* festival, occasion of ceremony (*OED* 2).

41. *shallow-searching* looking superficially.
    Fame rumour.

42. *shades* trees.

44. *lot* divinely appointed destiny.
    pow'r deity.

47. *ringlets* *curled locks (*OED* 3). M. likens the leaves to intricate (*quaint*)

and sportive (*wanton*) human hair. Cp. Eve's 'wanton ringlets' (*PL* iv 306). The echo of 'quaint mazes in the wanton green' (Shakespeare, *A Midsummer Night's Dream* II i 99) also suggests 'fairy ring' (*OED* 'ringlet' 2).

49. *noisome* injurious.

blasting withering.

50. *evil dew* mildew. Cp. Shakespeare, *The Tempest* I ii 321: 'As wicked dew as e'er my mother brushed'.

51. *thwarting thunder blue* lightning cutting across the sky. Cp. Shakespeare, *Julius Caesar* I iii 50: 'the cross blue lightning'. Blue fire was associated with ghosts and devils (*OED* 1c).

52. *cross* adverse, thwarting.

planet Saturn, the planet of malign astrological aspect (hence *dire-looking*).

53. *cankered* *venomous (*OED* 4).

worm the cankerworm (a caterpillar that destroys buds and leaves). Cp. *Lycidas* 45.

54. *fetch my round* walk my circuit.

57. *tasselled horn* hunting horn. Cp. *L'Allegro* 53-6.

59. *Number my ranks* count my rows (of trees), like an officer inspecting the ranks. Cp. *PL* i 567-71.

60. *puissant . . . murmurs* magic charms. Cp. *A Masque* 526.

63. *celestial Sirens' harmony* the Music of the Spheres. The allusion is not to Homer's Sirens, but to those in Plato's myth of Er (*Republic* x 616-17). Plato depicts the universe as eight concentric whorls threaded on a spindle of adamant. *Necessity* holds the spindle on her knees, while her *daughters* (the Fates Lachesis, Clotho and Atropos) rotate the whorls. On the rim of each whorl stands a Siren, who sings a single note as she is borne around. Together, the eight Sirens produce a harmony. M. has nine Sirens to accord with the nine Ptolemaic spheres. Cp. *Solemn Music* 1-2, *Nativity* 131.

64. *enfolded* concentric.

65. *those who hold . . . shears* the Fates. Strictly speaking, Atropos alone held the shears that cut the thread of life.

vital fatal to life (*OED* 6).

71. *measured* *having a marked rhythm (*OED* 3b).

72-3. *none . . . unpurgèd ear* Pythagorean doctrine held that our physical nature made it impossible for us to hear the Music of the Spheres. See *Nativity* 125n and cp. Shakespeare, *The Merchant of Venice* V i 64-5: 'But whilst this muddy vesture of decay / Doth grossly close it in, we cannot hear it'.

73. *mould* earth as the material of the human body (*OED* 4).

74. *blaze* proclaim as with a trumpet (*OED* v² 2), with a hint of 'shine, be conspicuous' (*OED* v¹ 6); notice *lustre* (76).

77. *hit* imitate exactly (*OED* 14).

81. *state* chair of state (*OED* 20). The Countess would have been sitting

opposite the stage. The masquers now move towards her, as was customary at the conclusion of a masque.

82. *stem* stock, descent.

84. *enamelled* beautified with various colours (*OED* 3), thus 'full of flowers'. Cp. *Lycidas* 139.

89. *star-proof* proof against malignant astral influences (see line 52).

94. *Queen* The Countess was a Queen (of the Isle of Man), but here the title might be hyperbole (cp. *deity*). I owe this point to Jeremy Maule.

97. *Ladon* a river in Arcadia. Ovid speaks of its sandy banks (*Met.* i 702).

98–102. *Lyncaeus* . . . *Cyllene* . . . *Erymanth* . . . *Maenalus* Arcadian mountains associated with Pan.

98. *hoar* ancient and white with snow. Cp. *L'Allegro* 55.

99. *Trip* dance.

ranks rows (of trees and dancers).

106. *Syrinx* an Arcadian nymph pursued by Pan. She was changed into reeds when she reached the river Ladon (Ovid, *Met.* i 689–712).

Lycidas

On 10 August 1637 Edward King, a Fellow of Christ's College, Cambridge, and a former classmate of M.'s, drowned in the Irish Sea. His body was not recovered. *Lycidas* is dated November 1637 in *TMS*. It was first published as the last English poem in a commemorative volume, *Justa Edouardo King naufrago* (1638), a collection of Latin, Greek, and English poems by King's Cambridge contemporaries. The present text follows *1645*, but freely draws on the punctuation of *1638* in places where it is clearly superior.

M.'s poem is a pastoral elegy, a form established in the third century BC when Theocritus composed his lament for Daphnis (*Idyll* I). Other classical poems in the genre include Bion's *Lament for Adonis*, Moschus's *Lament for Bion*, and Virgil's *Eclogue* X. M.'s poem includes many traditional features, such as the procession of mourners and the lament of nature, but he omits the refrain, which was prominent in ancient examples of the form. In pastoral elegy the poet and his subject are described as shepherds. Christian poets of the Middle Ages and Renaissance were therefore able to combine classical decorum with allusions to the bad shepherds of Ezekiel 34, John 10 and other scriptural passages. Thus the pastoral elegy became a vehicle for anti-ecclesiastical satire. Examples include the *Eclogues* of Petrarch (VI and VII) and Mantuan (IX). M.'s poem stands firmly in this tradition – most obviously in St Peter's 'digression' (108–31), though political references may be found throughout the poem. The Laudian censorship was still strong in 1637, so M. had to word his criticisms carefully. On 30 June 1637 Bastwick, Burton and Prynne had had their ears cropped and been sentenced to life imprisonment for publishing anti-prelatical pamphlets. Burton and Prynne were in prison-ships on the Irish Sea when M. wrote *Lycidas*. M. signed the poem 'J.M.' in *1638*.

Headnote. M. added the headnote in *1645* when the Anglican censorship had fallen. *1638* has no headnote. *TMS* has only the first sentence.

monody a mournful ode, often a funeral song, sung by a single voice.

1. *Yet once more* Cp. Heb. 12. 26–7: 'Yet once more I shake not the earth only, but also heaven. And this word, Yet once more, signifieth the removing of those things that are shaken, as of things that are made, that those things which cannot be shaken may remain'.

laurels an emblem of poetry, sacred to Apollo.

2. *myrtles* an emblem of love, sacred to Venus.

ivy an emblem of frenzy, immortality, poetry, or learning, sacred to Bacchus. Horace calls ivy 'the reward of poets' brows' (*Odes* I i 29). Petrarch was crowned with laurel, myrtle and ivy in 1341.

never sere never withered (i.e. evergreen).

3. *crude* unripe (*OED* 4). Cp. *Sonnet VII* 7: 'inward ripeness doth much less appear'.

4. *rude* unskilled.

5. *Shatter* both 'scatter' (*OED* 1) and 'destroy'.

*mellowing OED's earliest participial instance.

6. *dear* heartfelt (*OED* a¹ 7a) and dire (*OED* a² 2).

8. *ere his prime* Edward King drowned at the age of twenty-five.

8–9. *Lycidas . . . Young Lycidas* The repetition of a name for pathetic effect is common in pastoral. Cp. Virgil, *Ecl.* v 50–53, Castiglione, *Alcon* 24–6, Spenser, *Astrophel* 7–8, Phineas Fletcher, *The Purple Island* ix 3, and M.'s *Fair Infant* 25–6.

10. *Who would not sing for Lycidas?* Cp. Virgil, *Ecl.* x 3: *neget quis carmina Gallo?* ('Who would not sing for Gallus?').

10–11. *he knew . . . Himself* 'he himself knew how'. Cp. also the Delphic maxim 'know thyself' (Plato, *Protagoras* 343B).

11. *to . . . rhyme* King had written encomiastic Latin verses.

13. *welter* of a dead body: to be tossed on the waves (*OED* 3b).

parching drying (impossible in water).

14. *meed* recompense.

tear elegy. A common metonymy, as in Spenser's *The Teares of the Muses*.

15. *Begin then* Cp. the refrains urging the Muses to 'begin' in Theocritus i, Moschus, *Lament for Bion*, and Virgil, *Ecl.* viii.

well the Muses' fountain (either Aganippe on Mount Helicon or the Pierian spring at the foot of Mount Olympus).

17. *somewhat loudly* Cp. Virgil, *Ecl.* iv 1: 'Sicilian Muses, let us sing a somewhat loftier strain' (*paulo maiora canamus*).

18. *coy* shyly reserved (*OED* 2).

19. *Muse* poet under the guidance of a Muse (*OED* 2c).

20. *lucky* well-omened.

22. *sable* black.

23. *self-same hill* M. and King were students at Christ's College, Cambridge.

25. *lawns* forest glades (*OED* 1).

26. *opening eye-lids of the morn* Cp. Job 41. 18: 'the eye-lids of the morning', and Middleton, *A Game at Chess* (*1624*) I i 79: 'the opening eyelids of the morn'. *TMS 1st reading* and *1638* have 'glimmering eyelids'.

28. *What time* when (*OED* 10a), not a Latinism.

winds blows.

sultry *characterized by sweltering heat (*OED* 2a), and so suggesting the insect hum of midday.

29. *Battening* fattening. Sheep fed on *dews* (wet grass) would not grow fat, and would even suffer from 'rank mist' (126). E. F. Daniels therefore takes *battening* to mean 'enclosing in pens' (*Explicator* 21, 1962–3, item 43). But sheep eat dew in Virgil (*Ecl.* viii 15) and Phineas Fletcher (*The Purple Island* vi 77). John Creaser (*Essays and Studies*, 1981, 123–47) takes *dews* to be an allegory of the manna of the Gospel (135).

30. *star* Venus as Hesperus, the evening star. *1638* retains *TMS 1st reading*: 'Oft till the ev'n star bright'.

31. *westering] *TMS*, *1645*, *1673*; burnished *TMS 1st reading*, *1638*.

33. *flute*,] *1645*, *1673*; flute: *1638*. The *1638* pointing is clearer, but it removes an attractive syntactical ambiguity and a pun. The lighter pointing of the later editions allows *Tempered* to modify *satyrs* as well as *ditties*, and so mean 'restrained within bounds' (*OED* 8) as well as 'attuned' (*OED* 16).

oaten made from oat straw.

34. *satyrs* horse-tailed (or goat-legged) attendants of Dionysus. Notoriously boisterous and lecherous, they might be Cambridge undergraduates. Virgil depicts *fauns* dancing 'in measured time' to a pastoral song (*Ecl.* vi 27).

36. *Damoetas* a conventional pastoral name (see Theocritus vi, Virgil, *Ecl.* ii, iii, v). M. might be referring to a specific Cambridge tutor, perhaps the quasi-anagrammatic Joseph Mead.

39–41. *Thee . . . mourn* Cp. Ovid, *Met.* xi 44–6: 'Thee, Orpheus, thee the sorrowful birds, the throng of beasts, the flinty rocks, and trees which oft had followed thy songs, did mourn'. Cp. also Moschus, *Lament for Bion* 1–7, 27–35.

40. *gadding* straggling.

45. *canker* the cankerworm (caterpillar).

46. *taint-worm* an intestinal parasite fatal to newly-weaned calves.

weanling *recently weaned (*OED* B).

48. *whitethorn* hawthorn.

50. *Where were ye nymphs* Cp. Theocritus i 66–9 ('where were ye, nymphs, when Daphnis died in pain?'); also Virgil, *Ecl.* x 9–12.

51. *loved*] *TMS, 1645, 1673*; lord *1638*.

52. *steep* variously identified as Holyhead, Penmaenmawr, or Bardsey. Bardsey was associated with *Bards*, and holy men were buried there, but it lies fifty miles south of King's route. Philemon Holland's translation of Camden's *Britannia* may have misled M. about Bardsey's location (see A. L. Owen, *The Famous Druids*, 1962, 53).

53. *Bards* are connected with *Druids* by Diodorus Siculus (V xxxi 2–5), Strabo (iv 4 4), and Julius Caesar (*Gallic War* vi 14). M. typically identifies the poetic and priestly vocations. Cp. *Mansus* 42–3.

54. *Mona* Anglesey. It was not *shaggy* (wooded) in M.'s day, but Drayton in *Polyolbion* (1598–1622) tells how it had once been dark with sacred oaks (ix 425–9).

55. *Deva* the Dee (a *wizard stream* because it was credited with powers of divination). See Drayton, *Polyolbion* x 186–210. Drayton makes the same claim for the Weaver, which he calls a 'Wizard River' (xi 71).

56. *Ay me*] *TMS, 1645, 1673*; Ah me *1638*.

fondly foolishly.

58–63. *What could . . . shore* After his second loss of Eurydice (see *L'Allegro* 145–50n), Orpheus shunned the love of other women. Enraged by his rejection, the Maenads (female followers of Bacchus) tore him to pieces, their *hideous roar* drowning out his lyre. All nature mourned as Orpheus' severed head floated down the *Hebrus* (Ovid, *Met.* xi 1–66, Virgil, *Georg.* iv 485–527). These lines are much revised in *TMS*. Cp. *PL* vii 32–9.

58. *the Muse* Calliope. Carey cites *Greek Anthology* vii 8: 'Thy mother Calliope . . . bewailed thee. Why sigh we for our dead sons, when not even the gods have power to protect their children from death?'

64. *boots* avails.

65. *homely* unsophisticated (*OED* 4). Cp. *Animadversions* (1641): 'is Christian piety so homely . . . that none will study and teach her, but for lucre and preferment!' (*YP* 1. 719). The *shepherd's trade* is both poetry and the ministry.

66. *meditate . . . Muse* *compose poetry (*OED* 1c). The usage imitates Virgil (*Ecl.* i 2, vi 8).

67. *use*] *TMS, 1645, 1673*; do *1638*.

68–9. *To sport . . . hair Amaryllis* and *Neaera* are stock names for shepherd-esses or nymphs, employed by Theocritus, Virgil, Horace, Ariosto, George Buchanan, and John Fletcher, among others.

69. *Or with*] *TMS, 1645, 1673*; Hid in *TMS 1st reading, 1638. 1638* invites the fantasy of sporting with both women at once (cp. Spenser, *FQ* II xii 66–8).

70. *Fame is the spur* Cp. Spenser, *Teares of the Muses* 454: 'Due praise, that is the spur of doing well'.

clear noble (Latin *clarus*) and pure (*OED* 14).

73. *guerdon* reward.

74. *blaze* brilliant display (*OED* 5b).

75. *blind Fury* Atropos, the Fate who severs the thread of life (here a *Fury* to emphasize her fierceness, and *blind* to show that she acts indiscriminately). Cp. 'Blind mouths' (119).

77. *trembling ears* Cp. Virgil, *Ecl.* vi 3–4, where Apollo (*Phoebus*) plucks the poet's ear as a warning. The rhyme of *shears* and *ears* might also make a topical allusion to the infamous mutilation of Bastwick, Burton, and Prynne (see headnote). Cp. M.'s use of the same rhyme in reference to ear-cropping in *On the New Forcers* 16–17. Cp. also *Of Reformation* (*YP* 1. 606), where M. complains that bishops have 'made our eares tender, and startling'.

76. *slits* severs (*OED* 1b) – a rare usage. Elsewhere M. uses 'slit' of mutilation. In *An Apology for Smectymnuus* (1642) he blames bishops for 'slitting noses' (*YP* 1. 894) and in *The History of Britain* (1670) he speaks of 'slit Noses' and 'Ears cropt' (*YP* 5. 349).

*thin-spun drawn out in spinning to a slender thread.

79. *glistering foil* a thin leaf of metal placed under a gem to enhance (*set off*) its brilliancy.

81. *those pure eyes* Cp. Hab. 1. 13: 'Thou art of purer eyes than to behold evil'.

85. *Arethuse* a famous Sicilian spring, here representing Greek pastoral poetry. Theocritus (i 117) and Virgil (*Ecl.* x 1) invoke Arethuse. See also below, 132*n*.

86. *Mincius* a river in Mantua (Virgil's birthplace), here representing Latin pastoral poetry. Virgil celebrates Mincius's *reeds* and slow windings in *Georg.* iii 14–15.

87. *mood* musical mode.

88. *oat* the oaten flute of pastoral song.

89–131. The procession of mourners is a topos in pastoral elegy. See Theocritus i 77f., Spenser, *Shep. Cal.* November 142–51 and cp. Virgil, *Ecl.* x 19f. and M.'s *Ep. Dam.* 69–90.

89. *herald* Triton, Neptune's son.

90. *in Neptune's plea* Triton comes either to gather evidence for Neptune's court (*OED* 'plea' 1), or to plead Neptune's innocence.

91. *felon* savage, wild (*OED* 1b), criminal.

93. *rugged* stormy, tempestuous (*OED* 4a).

96. *Hippotades* Aeolus, guardian of the winds, which he kept in a large *dungeon* (Homer, *Od.* x 1–79, Virgil *Aen.* i 50f., Ovid, *Met.* iv 663).

99. *Panope* one of the fifty Nereids (sea-nymphs). They calmed the seas (hence *sleek*).

100. *perfidious bark* In Protestant iconography a ship symbolized the Church of Antichrist. See David Berkeley, *Inwrought with Figures Dim* (1974), 132.

101. *eclipse* a portent of disaster (cp. *PL* i 596-9) and (for Puritans) a symbol of spiritual darkness in the Church.

102. *sacred* inviolable (*OED* 5b); perhaps also 'accursed' (*OED* 6). Notice *curses* (101).

103. *Camus* the river Cam, representing Cambridge University.

footing slow The Cam is slow-moving, but there may be a pun on 'pedant' as J. M. Morse suggests (*N&Q* 5, 1958, 211).

104. *mantle hairy* the Cam's reeds and the fur of the academic gown.

sedge formed of reeds.

105. *Inwrought having (a pattern) worked in.

106. *sanguine flower* the hyacinth, *inscribed* AI AI ('alas, alas') by Apollo in grief for the youth Hyacinthus, whom he had accidentally killed (Ovid, *Met.* x 215). See *Fair Infant* 23-7n. The hyacinth appears in many pastoral elegies.

107. *pledge* child, viewed as a hostage to fortune (*OED* 2d).

109. *pilot* St Peter, who was a *Galilean* fisherman when Christ called him (Luke 5. 3-11). Peter denounces false teachers in II Pet. 2, in Dante, *Par.* xxvii 19-66, and Petrarch, *Ecl.* vi.

110. *Two massy keys* Cp. Phineas Fletcher, *The Purple Island* (1633) vii 61: 'two keyes he bore, / Heav'ns doores and hells to shut, and open wide: / But late his keyes are marr'd, or broken quite'. Fletcher is describing the Pope as impostor. Cp. Fletcher's *The Apollyonists* (1627) iii 16. M.'s St Peter retains authority over the keys Christ gave him at Matt. 16. 19.

111. *amain* with full force, once and for all.

112. *mitred* wearing the mitre (a bishop's head-dress). Critics infer that M. was not opposed to all bishops in 1637 (as he was to be in 1642, when he described the mitre as 'that *Turbant* of pride', *YP* 1. 953). But St Peter might be a 'bishop' and still condemn prelacy (see below, 119n, 120n).

bespake spoke out, remonstrated (*OED* 2).

113. *for* instead of.

swain shepherd, rustic (*OED* 4).

114. *Enow*] *1645, 1673*; enough *TMS, 1638*. 'Enow' is the plural.

114-29. Numerous biblical passages describe the shepherd's true office and its abuses. See esp. John 10. 1-28 and Ezek. 34. See also Dante, *Par.* xxvii 55-7, xxix 103f., Petrarch, *Ecl.* vi, vii, and Spenser, *Shep. Cal.* May, September.

115. *Creep . . . intrude . . . climb* Cp. John 10. 1: 'He that entereth not by the door into the sheepfold, but climbeth up some other way, the same is a thief and a robber'. Cp. *PL* iv 183-93 and Spenser, *FQ* I iii 17.

116. *reck'ning* both 'rendering an account of oneself to God' (*OED* 4c) and 'computation of the sum due to one' (*OED* 3a).

117. *shearers' feast* festive supper for the sheep-shearers (hence, material rewards of the ministerial office).

118. *worthy bidden guest* Cp. Matt. 22. 8 (the parable of the marriage supper): 'The wedding is ready, but they which were bidden were not worthy'.

119. *Blind mouths* Ruskin comments: 'A "Bishop" means "a person who sees". A "Pastor" means "a person who feeds". The most unbishoply character a man can have is therefore to be blind. The most unpastoral is, instead of feeding, to want to be fed – to be a Mouth' (*Sesame and Lilies* i 22). M. often distinguishes true 'bishops' from prelates. Cp. *Of Reformation* (*YP* 1. 606): 'were it not that the Tyranny of Prelates under the name of *Bishops* hath made our eares tender, and startling, we might call every good Minister a *Bishop*'. Cp. also the title of William Prynne's *Lord Bishops, None of the Lord's Bishops* (1640).

120. *sheep-hook* The crosier is a sign of episcopal office, but its presence here need not be a concession to prelacy. In *Of Reformation* M. associates 'the Pastorly *Rod*, and Sheep-hooke of CHRIST' with Presbyterianism (*YP* 1. 605).

122. *What recks it them* 'What do they care?' (*OED* 'reck' v 8). The echo of *reck'ning* (116) hints at their true cares.

sped provided for (*OED* 6d).

123. *list* choose (to play pipes) and listen (to the noise).

lean and flashy meagre and trifling. In *An Apology for Smectymnuus* M. describes the Anglican liturgy as 'in conception leane and dry, of affections empty and unmoving' (*YP* 1. 939).

124. *Grate . . . straw* Cp. Virgil, *Ecl.* iii 27: 'to murder a rotten tune on a grating straw'.

scrannel thin, unmelodious.

126. *swoll'n with wind* Petrarch makes sheep-rot an allegory of Church corruption in *Ecl.* vi 21–31 and vii 19–27. Cp. also Dante on Florentine preaching: 'the sheep, who know nothing, return from pasture fed with wind' (*Par.* xxix 106–7).

draw inhale.

128. *grim Wolf* the Church of Rome, particularly the Jesuits, who were notorious for *privy* conversions. Two wolves appeared in the heraldic arms of their founder. Cp. Spenser, *Shep. Cal.* September 148–60.

129. *nothing said*] *TMS 1st reading, 1645, 1673*; little said *TMS, 1638*. Editors conjecture that M. changed 'nothing' to 'little' in recognition of Laud's protest against the Queen's papal agent in October 1637. More likely, he feared Laud's censors. He restored 'nothing' as soon as he could.

130. *two-handed engine* a famous crux. *At the door* means 'at hand'. In

Matt. 24. 33 the Last Judgment is 'even at the doors'. Cp. *Animadversions*: 'thy Kingdome is now at hand, and thou standing at the dore' (*YP* 1. 707). Christ the Judge will 'set the sheep on his right hand, but the goats on the left' (Matt. 25. 33), so *two-handed* may mean 'leading in two directions (right hand and left hand)' (*OED* 'two-hand' 3). Christ would then be the 'agent' (*OED* 'engine' 10a) of Judgment (H. F. Rollins, *RES* 5, 1954, 25–36). Others take the 'engine' to be a weapon 'wielded with both hands' (*OED* 'two-handed' 1). Cp. 'the Axe of Gods reformation' in *Of Reformation* (*YP* 1. 582).

131. *smite . . . no more* I Sam. 26. 8.

132. *Alpheus* a river in Arcadia, fabled to pass unmixed through the sea before mingling its waters with the 'fountain Arethuse' in Sicily (85). See *Arcades* 30–31.

135. *bells* bell-shaped flowers.

136. *use* haunt, frequent (*OED* 17a).

137. *wanton* sportive, unrestrained.

138. *swart star* Sirius, the dog-star, associated with the heat of summer. *Swart* (blackened by heat) is a transferred epithet.

139. *quaint* curiously patterned.

enamelled adorned with various colours (*OED* 3).

140. *suck the honied showers* Cp. Shakespeare, *Hamlet* III i 157: 'sucked the honey of his music vows'.

141. *purple* make purple (i.e. any dazzling colour). 'Purple' was a colour of ecclesiastical mourning (*OED* 2c).

142–51. *Bring . . . lies* Floral catalogues are a pastoral topos. Cp. Theocritus i 132–3, Moschus, *Lament for Bion* 5–7 and Spenser, *Shep. Cal.* April 60–63, 136–44. M.'s catalogue is much revised in *TMS*. One cancelled version includes the lines: 'Bring the rathe primrose that unwedded dies / Colouring the pale cheek of unenjoyed love'. Evans (84) cites this as evidence of M.'s commitment to lifelong celibacy, but the pathos of 'unwedded' is that Lycidas died young, before he could wed. Cp. Shakespeare, *The Winter's Tale* IV iv 122–5: 'pale primroses, / That die unmarried, ere they can behold / Bright Phoebus in his strength (a malady / Most incident to maids)'.

142. *rathe* early in the year (*OED* 3b).

143. *tufted* *growing in clusters.

crow-toe hyacinth, wild hyacinth, or buttercup.

pale jessamine white jasmine.

144. *pink* dianthus.

*freaked streaked (*OED* 1).

146. *woodbine* honeysuckle.

147. *wan* pale (*OED* 4e), as in 'the wan and yellow colour of Golde' (1567). The *cowslip* was also known as 'St Peter's keys'.

148. *sad* including 'dark-coloured' (*OED* 8b).

149. *amaranthus* Greek 'unfading'. The name was used both of the English 'love-lies-bleeding' and an immortal flower of Heaven (see *PL* iii 353*n*). The latter did not *shed* its flowers – but it might do so for Lycidas.

150. *daffadillies* a poetic (and dialect) form of 'daffodil' used by Spenser (*Shep. Cal.* April 60) and Drayton (*Ecl.* iii 81).

151. *laureate* decked with laurel, emblem of poetry.

hearse bier (*OED* 5) or an elaborate structure on which friends of the deceased would pin poetic epitaphs (*OED* 2c).

157. *whelming*] *1645, 1673*; humming *TMS, 1638*. Cp. Shakespeare, *Pericles* III i 63–4: 'humming water must o'erwhelm thy corpse'.

158. *monstrous* *abounding in monsters (*OED* 3b) or immense.

159. *moist vows* tearful prayers (Latin *votum*).

160. *fable of* fabled abode of.

Bellerus an eponymous giant or hero invented by M. to explain 'Bellerium' (the Latin name for Land's End). In *TMS* M. first wrote 'Corineus' – the name of the legendary hero for whom Cornwall was named.

161. *vision . . . mount* St Michael was said to have appeared to fishermen on St Michael's Mount in Cornwall in 495.

162. *Namancos* Nemancos, a region in north-west Spain.

Bayona a Spanish fortress about fifty miles south of Cape Finisterre. The two names represent the threat of Catholicism against which St Michael guards England.

163. *angel* St Michael. He is asked to turn his gaze away from Spain and melt with pity at the sight of Lycidas's body.

164. *waft* convey safely to land (*OED* v¹ 2). *Dolphins* (who are friendly to man) were thought to waft living or dead humans. They rescued the poets Arion and Icadius, and wafted the dead bodies of Hesiod and the drowned child Melicertes. The latter was resurrected as Palaemon, a 'Genius of the shore' (185). Dolphins were a symbol of Christian resurrection. See John Creaser, *RES* n.s. 36, no. 142 (May 1985), 235–43.

168. *day-star* either the sun or Lucifer, the morning star. Both were symbols of resurrection. W. Hall (another contributor to *1638*) likens the drowned Edward King to the sun that sinks in Ocean 'Till with new beams from seas he seems to rise'. Cp. Fletcher, *CV* (1610) iv 12, on Christ's Resurrection: 'So fairest Phosphor the bright Morning starre, / But neewely washt in the green element, / Before the drouzie Night is halfe aware, / Shooting his flaming locks with deaw besprent, / Springs lively up into the orient'. Cp. also Virgil, *Aen.* viii 589–91.

169. *repairs* including 'adorns' (*OED* 1).

170. *tricks* adorns, trims (*OED* 5, 6).

ore *gold. *OED* cites the sense 'precious metal' from 1639.

171. *forehead of the morning sky*   Cp. Shakespeare, *Coriolanus* II i 57: 'forehead of the morning'.

173. *him*   Christ (see Matt. 14. 25–31).

174. *groves . . . streams*   Cp. Rev. 22. 1–2 on the 'pure river of water of life' and the 'tree of life, which bare twelve manner of fruits'.

175. *nectar*   the drink of the gods, sometimes used to protect corpses from decay. See *A Masque* 838*n*.

oozy locks   hair moist from the sea. Cp. Shakespeare, *Pericles* III i 61: 'scarcely coffined, in the ooze'.

176. *unexpressive*   inexpressible. The *nuptial song* is the Lamb's marriage-song, sung by all his servants, 'both small and great' (Rev. 19. 5). Critics often say that Lycidas joins an exclusive choir of 144,000 male virgins who were 'not defiled with women' (Rev. 14. 1–4). But notice *all the saints* (178).

177. *In . . . love*   This line is not in *1638*.

178. *entertain*   receive (*OED* 12).

saints   the blessed dead in Heaven (*OED* B 1) and the angels (*OED* 3b, cp. *PL* vi 46).

181. *wipe . . . eyes*   Cp. Rev. 21. 4: 'And God shall wipe away all tears from their eyes'; also Isa. 25. 8, Rev. 7. 17.

183. *Genius*   local guardian spirit. Cp. the Genius of the Wood in *Arcades*. Carey notes that 'in Virgil, *Ecl.* v 64–5, the dead Daphnis is imagined as a god, being good to his worshippers'. *Be good* (184) echoes Virgil's *sis bonus*.

186–93. M.'s epilogue forms a stanza of *ottava rima*.

186. *uncouth*   both 'unskilled' and 'unknown'. M. in *1638* signed *Lycidas* only with the initials 'J.M.'.

188. *tender*   responsive.

stops   finger-holes.

quills   pastoral pipes.

189. *eager thought*   Contrast the reluctant beginning (4–7).

Doric   Theocritus, Moschus and Bion wrote in the Doric dialect. There was also a Doric mode of music.

190. *stretched . . . hills*   The setting sun elongates the hills' shadows. Cp. Virgil, *Ecl.* i 83, ii 67.

192. *twitched*   pulled up around his shoulders.

mantle blue   R. C. Fox, *Explicator* ix (1951) 54 notes that blue was the colour of hope. Shepherds usually wear grey in pastoral.

193. *pastures new*   Cp. Phineas Fletcher, *The Purple Island* (1633) vi 77: 'Tomorrow shall ye feast in pastures new'.

A Masque presented at Ludlow Castle

Popularly known as *Comus* since the late seventeenth century, *A Masque* was performed on 29 September at Ludlow Castle in Shropshire to celebrate the Earl of Bridgewater's appointment as Lord President of Wales. The Earl's three children were among the performers: Lady Alice Egerton, aged fifteen, played the Lady, and her brothers John, Viscount Brackley, aged eleven, and Lord Thomas Egerton, aged nine, played the two brothers. Henry Lawes, who was the children's music tutor, composed the music for the songs and played the part of the Attendant Spirit. It was probably Lawes who invited M. to compose the text. Lawes published the poem in 1637.

The text survives in various versions reflecting several stages of composition. *TMS* has many corrections and revisions, some added after the performance. Other versions are the Bridgewater manuscript (*BMS*), the first printed edition (issued anonymously in 1637), the printed text of *1645* (followed here), and that of 1673, which differs significantly from *1645* in only one passage (lines 166–9).

[Stage direction] *Attendant Spirit*] *1637, 1645, 1673*; a guardian spirit, or daemon *TMS, BMS*.

2. *mansion* dwelling place (*OED* 2), with overtones of John 14. 2 ('in my Father's house are many mansions'), though the Spirit comes from before Jove's *threshold*, not from Heaven.

3. *insphered* placed in a celestial sphere. Cp. *Il Penseroso* 88–9: 'unsphere / The spirit of Plato'.

4. *sérene air* the bright, cloudless aether above earth's atmosphere.

5. *smoke and stir* of earth's atmosphere and earth's bustling inhabitants.

5–6. *dim spot . . . Which men call earth* See Plato, *Phaedo* 109–11. What we call 'the earth' is but a cloudy hollow in the surface of the true earth, which lies far above us.

7. *pestered* crowded together (*OED* 3) and plagued (*OED* 4), as in: 'pestred with infectious or obnoxious ayres' (1625).

pinfold cattle pen, hence 'place of confinement' (*OED* 2).

8. *frail* including 'transient' (*OED* 1b).

feverish *restless (*OED* 2) and apt to cause fever (*OED* 4).

9. *crown that Virtue gives* I Cor. 9. 24–5.

10. *mortal change* both 'changeful life' and 'death'. Cp. 'quick immortal change' (841).

11. *sainted seats* Cp. Rev. 4. 4: 'And round about the throne were four and twenty seats: and upon the seats I saw four and twenty elders sitting, clothed in white raiment; and they had on their heads crowns of gold'. Cp.

also Fletcher, *CV* (1610) iii 53: 'ye glad Spirits, that now sainted sit / On your coelestiall thrones'.

13. *golden key* Cp. Matt. 16. 19: 'I will give unto thee the keys of the kingdom of heaven'. Jonson in *Hymenaei* (1606) equips Truth with 'a curious bunch of golden kayes, / With which heaven gates she locketh, and displayes' (897-8). Cp. *Lycidas* 111.

16. *ambrosial* *belonging to Paradise (*OED* 1b).
    weeds the 'sky-robes' of line 83.

17. *this sin-worn mould* either 'this terrestrial earth [*OED* "mould" sb¹ 6] worn out by sin' or 'this earthy body [*OED* "mould" sb¹ 4] which sinners wear as a garment'.

18. *But to my task* Cp. John Fletcher, *The Faithful Shepherdess* (c. 1609) III i 180-81: 'But to my charge: heere must I stay, / To see what mortalls loose their way'. The speaker is a Satyr, sent by Pan to protect virgins wandering in the wood.

18-21. *Neptune... rule* After vanquishing the Titans, *Jove* and his brothers Pluto and *Neptune* divided the universe between them by drawing lots. Jove took the sky, Neptune the sea, and Pluto the underworld (Homer, *Il.* xv 187-93).

20. *nether Jove* Pluto. Cp. Homer, *Il.* ix 457 ('Zeus of the underworld') and Virgil, *Aen.* iv 638 ('Stygian Jove').

21. *sea-girt isles* Jonson calls Britain 'This sea-girt isle' in *Underwoods* lxvii 33. Cp. also M.'s translation of Geoffrey of Monmouth in *The History of Britain:* 'Beyond the realm of Gaul, a land there lies, / Sea-girt it lies'.

22-3. *gems... the deep* Cp. Shakespeare, *Richard II* II i 46: 'This precious stone set in the silver sea'.

23. *unadornèd without other ornaments.

24. *tributary* paying tribute (as 'tributary' rivers).

25. *By course* in due order.
    several separate.

27. *this isle* mainland Britain.

28. *the main* the high sea.

29. *quarters* divides into parts. These may be 'fewer or more than four' (*OED* 2), but Britain did have a fourfold government (the Lord Presidency of Wales being one).

30. *tract... sun* Wales and the Marches. Cp. Aeschylus, *Suppliants* 254-5: 'I rule all the region facing the setting sun'.

31. *peer* the Earl of Bridgewater.
    mickle great.

32. *tempered awe* temperately used authority.

33. *haughty* of exalted courage (*OED* 2).
    nation Wales.

proud in arms Cp. Virgil, *Aen.* i 21: 'a people proud in war' (*populum . . . belloque superbum*).

35. *state* throne (*OED* 20), pomp befitting high rank (*OED* 17).

37. *pérplexed* entangled.

wood a common symbol for human life. Cp. Dante, *Inf.* i 1–3, Spenser, *FQ* I i 7–10.

38. *horror* including the Latin sense 'bristling'.

39. *passenger* wayfarer.

48. *After . . . transformed* 'After the Tuscan sailors had been transformed'. Bacchus turned the pirates who had kidnapped him into dolphins. See Homeric Hymn *To Dionysus*, and Ovid, *Met.* iii 582–691.

49. *Tyrrhene shore* the west coast of Italy, opposite Corsica and Sardinia. *listed* wished.

50–51. *Circe's island . . . daughter of the Sun* Cp. Homer, *Od.* x 135–8: 'We came to the island of Aiaia. There lived fair-haired Circe . . . fathered by Helios'. Cp. also Browne, *Inner Temple Masque* (performed 1615, printed 1772): 'mighty Circe daughter to the Sun' (32).

50. *who knows not Circe* Cp. Spenser, *Shep. Cal.* August 141: 'Roselend (who knows not Roselend?)', and *FQ* VI x 16: 'Poore Colin Clout, (who knows not Colin Clout?)'.

51. *charmèd cup* Circe offered a cup, but used her wand to turn men into beasts (*Od.* x 233–9, *Met.* xiv 277–80). M. here omits the wand and so emphasizes the drinker's moral choice. (In his *Inner Temple Masque* Browne omits the cup.) When Comus enters (92) he holds both cup and wand and so is equipped for temptation or coercion. The whore of Babylon had 'a golden cup in her hand full of abominations and filthiness of her fornication' (Rev. 17. 4). M. in *An Apology for Smectymnuus* distinguishes between the 'charming cup' of chaste love and the 'thick intoxicating potion' of lust (*YP* 1. 891–2).

54. *nymph* Homer's Circe is a goddess.

54–5. *gazed . . . youth* Cp. Homeric Hymn vii 1f.: 'I will tell of Dionysus, the son of glorious Semele, how he appeared on a jutting headland by the shore of the fruitless sea, seeming like a stripling in the first flush of manhood: his rich dark hair was waving about him'.

58. *Comus* The name is a Latinization of Greek *komos*, 'revelry'. Philostratus (*Imagines* i 2) describes Comus as an effeminate youth, crowned with roses, and carrying a torch. He stands outside a marriage chamber, falling into a drunken sleep. Jonson associates Comus with Bacchus and Priapus in *Poetaster* (1602) III iv 114–16, and makes him a belly-god in *Pleasure Reconciled to Virtue* (performed 1618, printed 1640).

59. *frolic of* sportive in.

60. *Celtic, and Iberian* French and Spanish.

65. *orient* shining.

66. *drouth of Phoebus* thirst caused by the hot sun.

67. *fond* foolish.

68–77. *Soon as . . . sty* Comus's magic differs in many ways from that of Homer's Circe. Comus uses his cup to transform people into any kind of animal; Circe uses her wand to turn men into pigs. Comus changes the head alone; Circe changes both head and body. Comus's victims do not see their disfigurement; Circe's want to be men again. Comus's victims forget their *native home;* Circe's forget 'their own country' while drinking, but Circe restores their minds when she transforms them (*Od.* x 236–40).

69. *Th' express resemblance* Cp. Heb. 1. 3: 'the express image of his person', and Gen. 1. 27.

71. *ounce* lynx.

73. *perfect* complete.

   misery despicable condition (*OED* 5).

74. **disfigurement.*

75. *boast themselves more comely* Plutarch has a dialogue in which Grillus, one of Odysseus's men, would rather be a pig than a man (*Moralia* 985D–992E). Cp. Spenser, *FQ* II xii 86–7 and Browne, *Inner Temple Masque* 193–216.

79. *advent'rous* perilous (*OED* 2).

83. *Iris' woof* rainbow-coloured thread. Cp. *PL* xi 244.

84. *weeds* clothes.

   swain shepherd, attendant (*OED* 4, 2).

86–8. A compliment to Henry Lawes, who wrote the music for *A Masque* and played the part of the Attendant Spirit.

88. *nor of less faith* and no less trustworthy (than talented).

90. *Likeliest* best fitted (to give *aid*).

   present immediate.

92. *hateful steps*] virgin steps *TMS 1st reading.* The cancelled version is presumably a slip made in anticipation of lines 145–50.

   viewless invisible.

93. *star . . . fold* The evening star's appearance was a signal for shepherds to pen their sheep. Cp. Virgil, *Ecl.* vi 85–6.

95. *gilded car of day* the sun's chariot.

96. *allay* cool down.

97. *steep* fast-flowing (*OED* 3e).

   Atlantic stream the river Ocean. See *PL* i 202n.

98. *slope* setting. Cp. *Lycidas* 31.

99. *pole* the sky (*OED* sb² 4).

101. *chamber* Cp. Ps. 19. 4–5: 'the sun, which is as a bridegroom coming out of his chamber'.

105. *rosy twine* crown of roses. See above, 58*n*.

107. *Rigour . . . bed* Cp. Shakespeare, Falstaff: 'What doth gravity out of his bed at midnight?' (Shakespeare, *1 Henry IV,* II iv 284).

110. *saws* maxims.

111. *purer fire* the celestial fire of the stars. Comus claims to be *of* this fire, but he can only *imitate* it. Cp. Thomas Randolph, 'Eclogue to Master Jonson' (written *c.* 1632, printed 1638): 'But we, whose souls are made of purer fire' (98).

112. *choir* *a band of dancers (*OED* 5a).

113. *watchful spheres* Cp. Gen. 1. 14: 'let them be for signs, and for seasons, and for days, and years'. Plato says that heavenly bodies were created to guard the numbers of time (*Timaeus* 38c). Comus also plays on *watchful* as 'wakeful'.

115. *sounds* straits.

116. *morris* Puritans deplored morris dances, which the Stuart kings James I and Charles I defended in *The Book of Sports* (repr. 1633). M. celebrates such pastimes in *L'Allegro,* but is contemptuous of 'morrice' and 'May pole' in his political prose (*YP* 1. 931, 3. 358).

117. *shelves* sandbanks.

118. *Trip* dance.

  pert sprightly.

  dapper neat, trim.

121. *wakes* nocturnal revels (*OED* 4c).

123. *sweets to prove* pleasures to taste.

129. *Cotytto* a Thracian earth-goddess worshipped with loud music and nocturnal torchlit orgies. Juvenal associates her rites with male transvestites (*Satires* II 91f.).

130. *mysterious* versed in occult arts (*OED* 2).

131–5. *dragon . . . Hecat'* Hecate rode a chariot drawn by dragons (Ovid, *Met.* vii 218–19). Here the *dragon womb* is *darkness,* which *spits* gloom from itself. Cp. Chaos as a 'womb' at *PL* ii 150, 911.

132. *Stygian* hellish (from the black river Styx).

134. *chair* chariot (*OED* 'char' 1).

135. *Hecat'* Hecate, goddess of witchcraft.

138–41. *blabbing . . . tell-tale* sun Cp. Phineas Fletcher, *Britain's Ida* (1628) ii 3, on day as a revealer of adultery: 'The thick-locked boughs shut out the tell-tale sun, / (For Venus hated his all-blabbing light, / Since her known fault)'. Cp. also Shakespeare, *The Rape of Lucrece* 806: 'the tell-tale Day'.

138. *scout* a 'sneak' (*OED* 4a) and one sent ahead.

139. *nice* shy (*OED* 5) and *morally strict (*OED* 7d).

  Indian steep the Himalayas. Cp. Shakespeare, *A Midsummer Night's Dream* II i 69: 'the furthest steep of India'.

140. *cabined loophole* tiny window.

141. *descry* reveal (*OED* 2). Cp. John Fletcher, *The Faithful Shepherdess* (*c.* 1609) III i 150–51: 'lye by me, the sooner we begin, / The longer ere day descry our sin'.

142. *solemnity* ceremony (*OED* 1).

144. *fantastic* grotesque (*OED* 6).

round ring-dance.

[Stage direction] *Measure* dance (*OED* 20).

antic grotesque gesture or posture (*OED* 2). The full, informative stage direction is from *TMS* and *BMS* (*1637, 1645* and *1673* print only 'The Measure').

145–6. *different . . . footing* Martz (24) hears 'a metrical pun' as Comus shifts from tetrameter couplets to blank verse.

147. *shrouds* hiding-places.

151. *trains* wiles (*OED* 1b) and bait to lure an animal into a trap (*OED* 3). Cp. *course* (159) *Baited* (161) and *snares* (164).

154. *dazzling spells* Comus here threw sparkling powder into the air. *TMS* at first read 'powdered spells'. Cp. 'this magic dust' (165).

spongy absorbent.

155. *blear* *dim, misty (*OED* 2). In earlier usage the word was applied only to eyes, not the object of vision.

156. *presentments* appearances.

157. *quaint habits* unfamiliar or foppish clothes.

159. *course* including 'hunt' (*OED* 7).

161. *glozing* flattering, deceiving.

163. *Wind me* insinuate myself (suggesting a constrictor snake; notice *hug*, 164).

*easy-hearted easily moved to trust.

165. *virtue* power, efficacy.

166. *I shall appear some harmless villager* Comus does not exit until line 329 and so cannot change costume. Magic alone causes the Lady to see a 'shepherd' (270). Contrast the Attendant Spirit, who enters *habited like a shepherd* (489).

166–9. *I . . . here* In *1673* this passage reads: 'I shall appear some harmless villager / And hearken, if I may, her business here, / But here she comes, I fairly step aside'. The list of errata emends 'business here' to 'business hear'. Opinion is divided as to whether M., his editor, or a printer was responsible for the changes.

167. *gear* doings, 'goings on' (*OED* 11b).

168. *fairly* quietly, softly (*OED* 5).

172. *riot* wanton revelry (*OED* 2).

174. *loose unlettered hinds* lewd illiterate farmworkers. Cp. Marlowe, *Hero and Leander* (1598) ii 218: 'vicious, harebrained, and illit'rate hinds'.

175. *teeming* breeding.

granges granaries.

176. *Pan* the Greek god of shepherds, associated with sexual licence. But the Lady might mean God, whom the merrymakers praise amiss. See *Nativity* 89*n*.

178. **swilled* inebriated (*OED*'s sole instance).

179. **wassailers* revellers (*OED*), coined from the drinking salutation 'wassail' (OE *was hal*).

180. *inform* *direct, guide (*OED* 4d).

189. *sad* grave, serious (*OED* 4).

votarist a person bound by a vow.

in palmer's weed dressed like a pilgrim.

190. *Phoebus' wain* the sun's chariot.

193. *engaged* exposed to risk (*OED* v 2).

194. *envious* malicious (*OED* 2).

195. *Had stole*] *1645, 1673*; Had stol'n *TMS, BMS, 1637*.

197. **dark lantern* a lantern with a shutter by which the light can be concealed. Highwaymen used them (hence *thievish* and *felonious*). *OED*'s earliest instance is from 1650, but the Lady speaks as if dark lanterns were familiar objects.

198–9. *filled their lamps / With everlasting oil* Cp. Fletcher, *CV* (1610) iii 36: 'the pale starres . . . Quenched their everlasting lamps in night'.

203. *rife* *loud-sounding (*OED* 4c).

perfect heard distinctly.

204. *single* absolute (*OED* 4).

205–9. *A thousand . . . wildernesses* M. recalls tales of spirits in the Gobi desert. Travellers who lag behind the caravan will hear familiar voices calling them by name, but if they follow the call they will perish (Marco Polo, *Travels* i 36). In John Fletcher's *The Faithful Shepherdess* (*c*. 1609), the virgin Clorin claims to be magically protected from 'voices calling me in dead of night, / To make me followe, and so tole me on, / Through mires and standing pooles' (I i 118–20). Cp. 432–7*n* and *PL* ix 631–42.

205. *fantasies* hallucinations, phantoms (*OED* 3, 2).

207. **calling . . . *beck'ning OED*'s earliest participial instances.

208. *airy tongues* Cp. Echo's 'airy tongue' in Shakespeare, *Romeo and Juliet* II ii 162. The Lady will soon invoke Echo (230f.).

210. *astound* *amaze (*OED* 2), stupefy (*OED* 1).

212. **siding* taking the side of a person (*OED* 1, earliest participial instance).

214. *hovering*] flittering *TMS 1st reading* (retained in *1637*).

215. *Chastity* The Lady substitutes chastity for charity, which traditionally follows *Faith* and *Hope* (I Cor. 13. 13).

unblemished] unspotted *TMS 1st reading*. See below, 1009*n*.

216. *I see ye visibly* In Plato's *Phaedrus* (250) Socrates says that if we could see the ideal Forms (as we did before we were born), the sight would be ravishing.

219. *guardian*] cherub *TMS 1st reading*.

221−4. *Was I deceived . . . night* Cp. Ovid, *Fasti* v 549: 'Am I deceived, or is that a clash of arms? I am not deceived, there was a clash of arms.' Ovid is describing the descent of Mars, Rome's *glist'ring guardian*.

221−2. **cloud . . . silver lining OED* 's earliest instance of the proverb ('lining' 2b).

226. *I cannot hallo* Cp. *The Two Noble Kinsmen* III ii 8−9: 'What if I hallooed for him? / I cannot hallo.' The speaker is the jailer's daughter, benighted in a wood.

230. *Echo* a talkative nymph condemned by Juno to repeat the last phrases of whatever she heard. She fell in love with *Narcissus* (237) and pined when he spurned her (Ovid, *Met.* iii 351−401). Echo sings in Jonson, *Cynthia's Revels* (1601) I ii and Browne, *Inner Temple Masque* (performed 1615) 267−79. Carey notes that 'the Lady's loneliness is enhanced because, unusually, no echo replies'. But Martz (24) finds it 'hard to believe that Lawes would have passed up a chance to perform this song with echoes'. The Lady says that Echo did reply (275).

231. *airy shell* vault of the air.

232. *Meander* a river in Phrygia.

margent bank, margin.

234. **love-lorn* not 'pining from love' (as *OED*) but 'ruined [*OED* "lorn" 1] through another's love'. The allusion is to Philomela, who became a nightingale after her brother-in-law Tereus raped her in a forest (Ovid, *Met.* vi 424−674). See below, 566*n*.

241. *parley* speech.

241−3. Echo is *daughter of the sphere* because she lives in the *airy shell* (231) below the moon. Were she to help the Lady, Echo might be elevated to a higher level where she could answer the Music of the Spheres.

242. *translated* conveyed to heaven (*OED* 1b).

243. *give resounding grace*] hold a counterpoint *TMS 1st reading, BMS*. There may be a play on *grace* meaning 'additional notes not essential to the harmony' (*OED* 3). Line 243 is an alexandrine 'mimicking the lengthening of heaven's song by echo' (Carey).

244. *mould* earth as the material of the human body (*OED* 4).

248. *his* its (the *something holy* of line 246).

251. *fall* cadence.

252. *it smiled*] *1645, 1673*; she smiled *TMS, BMS, 1637*.

253. *Sirens* sea-nymphs who drew sailors to destruction by their alluring songs (Homer, *Od.* xii 37−72, 167−200). Homer's Circe warns Odysseus about the Sirens, but does not sing with them. Sirens attend Circe in Browne's *Inner Temple Masque* (1−96).

254. **kirtled* wearing a skirt.

Naiades freshwater nymphs attendant on Homer's Circe (*Od.* x 348–51).

255. *potent herbs* Circe transforms men with powerful drugs (*potentibus herbis*) in Virgil (*Aen.* vii 19).

256. *take the prisoned soul* either 'take the soul prisoner' or 'release the soul from its bodily prison'.

257. *Scylla* a once beautiful nymph transformed into a monster by Circe (Ovid, *Met.* xiv 8–74). Even Scylla, who had most cause to hate Circe, is enraptured by her singing. Cp. Silius Italicus (xiv 476) on Daphnis's pipe-playing: 'Scylla's dogs fell silent; black Charybdis stood still'. Cp. also Shakespeare, *A Midsummer Night's Dream* II i 149–52: 'once I sat upon a promontory, / And heard a mermaid on a dolphin's back / Uttering such dulcet and harmonious breath / That the rude sea grew civil at her song'.

258. *barking waves* Cp. Virgil, *Aen.* vii 588: *latrantibus undis,* and Fletcher, *CV* (1610) iii 23: 'barking surges'. M.'s 'barking' suggests Scylla's dogs.

259. *Charybdis* a whirlpool opposite Scylla. See *PL* ii 1019–20n.

262.**home-felt* felt in one's heart (*OED*). Cp. 'native home' (76).

265. *Hail foreign wonder* Cp. Ferdinand's first words to Miranda in Shakespeare, *The Tempest* I ii 422–7: 'Most sure, the goddess / On whom these airs attend! . . . O you wonder!'

267. *Unless the* 'Unless (you are) the'.

268. *Sylvan* Sylvanus, a Roman wood-god.

269. *unkindly* unnatural.

272. **unattending* inattentive (sole instance in *OED*).

273. *éxtreme shift* last resource (*OED* 'shift' 5d).

277–90. M. uses dialogue in single lines (*stichomythia*), common in Greek drama.

278. *Dim darkness* 'Dim darkness' covers the earth in Shakespeare's *The Rape of Lucrece* (118), when Lucrece greets Tarquin, not knowing that he plans to rape her.

286. *hit* guess.

287. *Imports their loss* 'Does their loss matter?'

290. *Hebe* goddess of youth.

*unrazored.

291–2. *what time . . . came* i.e. at evening: the time for unyoking oxen (Homer, *Il.* xvi 779, Virgil, *Ecl.* ii 66).

292. *traces* straps securing a draught animal (*OED* sb² 1).

293. **swinked* wearied (from *swink*, labour; the normal past-participle was *swonk*).

hedger workman who trims hedges.

294. *mantling* **spreading, covering (*OED* 2).

297. *port* bearing.

more than human Cp. Euripides, *Iphigenia in Tauris* 260–74, where a herdsman mistakes Orestes and Pylades for gods.

299. *element* sky, atmosphere (*OED* 10).

301. *plighted* contracted into folds.

*awe-strook.

312. *Dingle* wooded hollow.

313. *bosky bourn* bushy stream.

315. *attendance* attendants.

316. *shroud* seek shelter (*OED* v¹ 2c).

317. *low-roosted* Larks build their nests on the ground.

318. *thatched pallet* straw nest.

if otherwise if you prefer.

322–5. *courtesy ... princes* Cp. Ariosto, *Orl. Fur.* xiv 62 and Harington's translation (1591) xiv 52: 'curtesie oftimes in simple bowres / Is found as great as in the stately towres'. Cp. also Aeschylus, *Agamemnon* 772f.: 'Justice shines in smoky hovels ... she turns her eyes from proud halls', and contrast Marlowe, *Hero and Leander* (1598) i 394–5: 'lofty Pride that dwells / In towered courts is oft in shepherds' cells'.

325. *first was named* 'Courtesy' derives from 'court'. Cp. Spenser, *FQ* VI i 1: 'Of Court it seemes, men Courtesie doe call'.

326. *yet is most pretended* ambiguous. If *yet* means 'still' and *pretended* means 'aspired to' (*OED* 9), the courtiers still genuinely aspire to the *courtesy* that was named for them. If *yet* means 'nevertheless' and *pretended* means 'feigned', the courtiers merely pretend to be courteous.

327. *warranted* protected from danger (*OED* v 1).

329. *Eye me* 'Keep your (protective) watch over me'.

square adapt.

trial ordeal and test.

331. *Unmuffle* *remove a muffling (*OED*'s earliest intransitive use). Cp. Shakespeare, *Romeo and Juliet* V iii 21: 'Muffle me, night'.

332. *wont'st* are used to.

benison blessing.

333. *Stoop* *bow the head (*OED* 8a).

334. *disinherit Chaos* dispossess primeval darkness. Moonlight in John Fletcher's *The Faithful Shepherdess* (*c.* 1609) gives 'day / Again from Chaos' (II ii 59–60).

335. *shades* trees.

336. *influence* light flowing like astral influences (*Nativity* 71n).

338. *rush candle* candle made by dipping a rush in tallow (which gave a weak light).

wicker hole window filled with wicker-work (instead of glass).

339. *clay habitation* wattle hut plastered with clay.

340. *rule* *shaft of light (*OED* 18c).

341. *star of Arcady* Arcturus (in Boötes) by which Greek navigators steered. Boötes was a stellification of the Arcadian prince Arcas. See Ovid, *Fasti* ii 153–92.

342. *Cynosure* the North Star, in Ursa Minor. The Phoenicians steered by it (hence *Tyrian*).

344. *wattled cotes* sheepfolds made of plaited branches.

345. *pastoral reed* shepherd's pipe.

stops finger-holes.

349. *close* confined (*OED* 3), enclosed with darkness (*OED* 5).

355. **unpillowed.*

356. *amazement* stupefaction, frenzy (*OED* 1).

357–65. *Or while . . . delusion* These lines are not in *TMS* or *BMS*, which instead have the following three lines (deleted in *TMS*): 'So fares as did forsaken Proserpine / When the big rolling flakes of pitchy clouds / And darkness wound her in'. See *PL* iv 268–71 on Pluto's rape of Proserpine.

358. *savage hunger* hunger of wild beasts.

savage heat lust of cruel men. Centaurs pursue nymphs 'with savage heat' in Marlowe, *Hero and Leander* (1598) i 115.

359. **over-exquisite* over-precise (not in *OED*).

360. *cast* forecast (*OED* 41).

361. *be so* 'be as you imagine them' (i.e. *evils*).

362. *forestall* *think of before the proper time; 'to meet (misfortune etc.) halfway' (*OED* 7).

365. **self-delusïon.*

366. *so to seek* so deficient.

367. **unprincipled* not instructed (*OED* 1).

368. *bosoms* carries in its bosom (*OED* 4).

369. *single* mere.

370. *trust*] *TMS, 1637, 1645, 1673*; hope *BMS*.

372. *misbecoming* unbecoming.

373–4. *Virtue . . . light* Cp. Jonson, *Pleasure Reconciled to Virtue* (performed 1618, printed 1640) 339–42: '[Virtue] still herself refines, / By her owne light'. Spenser's Redcrosse Knight is also confident that 'Vertue gives her selfe light', but in Errour's den his armour makes only 'A litle glooming light, much like a shade' (*FQ* I i 12–14).

375. *flat* including 'lifeless, dull'.

376. *seeks* resorts.

377–8. *Contemplation . . . wings* Cp. Plato on the soul's 'wings' (*Phaedrus* 249). Cp. also Marvell, *The Garden* 52–6.

378. *plumes* *preens (*OED* 6, first recorded instance 1821). Cp. 'Letter 8' (to Charles Diodati): 'What am I doing? Growing my wings and practising flight' (*YP* 1. 327).

380. *to-ruffled* ruffled up (*to-* is an intensive prefix).

382. *th' centre* of the earth.

384–5. *Benighted . . . dungeon TMS* first had (and *BMS* retains): 'Walks in black vapours, though the noontide brand / Blaze in the summer solstice'.

385. *Himself is his own dungeon* Cp. *SA* 155–6.

386. *affects* is drawn to (*OED* 2).

387. *secrecy* retirement, seclusion (*OED* 2b).

389. *senate-house* implying the protection of the law as well as the safety of a public place.

390. *weeds* clothing.

391. *beads* rosary.

maple dish wooden bowl.

393. *Hesperian tree* a tree bearing golden apples. Ge (Earth) gave it as a wedding-present to Hera, who planted it in the Garden of the Hesperides and set a dragon to guard it. Heracles killed the dragon and stole the apples. The tree is associated with female beauty by Marlowe (*Hero and Leander* ii 297–300), Shakespeare (*Pericles* I i 20–30), John Fletcher (*The Faithful Shepherdess* II iv 30–32), and Jonson (*Every Man in his Humour* III i 16–23).

395. **unenchanted* Heracles put the dragon to sleep.

398. *unsunned* hidden. Cp. Spenser's Mammon 'Sunning his threasure' (*FQ* II vii Arg.).

401. *Danger* power to do injury (*OED* 1b).

wink on overlook.

403. **surrounding OED*'s earliest participial instance.

404. *it recks me not* I am not concerned.

406. **ill-greeting* that greets with evil intent.

touch a euphemism for sexual contact (*OED* 1b).

attempt try to ravish (*OED* 9c).

407. *unownèd* *lost (*OED*'s sole instance of this figurative sense).

408. *Infer* draw a conclusion.

409. *or controversy*] *1637, 1645, 1673*; or question, no *TMS, BMS*.

410. *equal poise* equilibrium. The metaphor is of a balance.

411. *arbitrate th' event* decide the outcome.

413. *squint suspicïon* Cp. Francis Quarles, *Feast for Worms* (1620) 1482: 'squint-eyed Suspition'.

421. *in cómplete steel* fully armed. 'Complete armour' was a common term, but *cómplete steel* recalls the ghost in Shakespeare's *Hamlet* (I iv 52). The Elder Brother sees chastity as armour against ghosts and evil things that walk by night (432–7).

422. **quivered nymph* a nymph whose arrows mark her as one of Diana's attendants (see 441–6). The Elder Brother is overconfident. Diana's nymphs were not immune to assault. Daphne and Syrinx escaped ravishment only by being metamorphosed, and Callisto did not escape. Syrinx's and Callisto's arrows only added to Pan's and Jupiter's lust (Ovid, *Met.* i 695–8, ii 409–16), and Callisto almost forgot to pick up her quiver after Jove raped her (*Met.* ii 439–40).

423. *trace* traverse.

unharboured *affording no shelter.

426. *mountaineer* mountain savage. Shakespeare coined the word and always used it of criminals. Cp. Sandys' Ovid, i 512, where Apollo assures the fleeing Daphne that he is 'No Mountainere'.

429. *shagged* *covered with scrub (*OED* 2b).

horrid bristling.

430. *unblenched* undismayed (*OED* 1).

431. *Be it not* 'So long as it is not'.

432–7. *Some say . . . true virginity* Cp. John Fletcher, *The Faithful Shepherdess* I i 111–17: 'Yet I have heard (my mother told it me) / And now I do believe it, if I keepe / My virgin flower uncropt, pure, chaste, and faire, / No Goblin, Wood-god, Faiery, Elfe, or Fiend, / Satyr or other power that haunts the groaves / Shall hurt my body, or by vaine illusion / Draw me to wander after idle fiers'. Cp. also Browne, *Britannia's Pastorals* (1613–16) I ii 29–38, and Shakespeare, *Hamlet* I i 120–23: 'Some say . . . no spirit dare stir abroad'.

433. *fire* the will-o'-the-wisp.

moorish marshy.

434. *Blue* *the colour of things hurtful (*OED* a 8).

hag evil spirit (*OED* 1), or witch.

unlaid by exorcism.

435. *curfew* the evening bell, rung at nine o'clock.

436. *swart* black (*OED* 1), malignant (*OED* 3).

439. *schools of Greece* Greek philosophers.

440. *arms of chastity* The Elder Brother's beliefs suit an idealistic eleven-year-old, but the twenty-five-year-old M. knew of one famous occasion when Diana's *bow* (441) and Minerva's *shield* (447) failed to save a virgin. Pluto prevailed over both weapons when he seized Proserpine (Claudian, *De Rapt. Pros.* ii 204–32). M. had likened the Lady to Proserpine in an earlier version of 357–65 (see note).

442. *silver-shafted* both 'armed with silver arrows' and 'shining like the moon'.

443. *brinded* tawny.

444. *pard* panther or leopard.

445. *bolt* arrow.

447. *Gorgon shield* The virgin goddess Minerva wore on her shield the head of the Gorgon Medusa, with which she froze her enemies to stone. The Elder Brother takes comfort in Minerva's shield, but Medusa's own story is not comforting. Minerva had turned Medusa into a Gorgon to

punish her for being raped by Neptune in Minerva's temple (Ovid, *Met.* iv 798–803). The Elder Brother also takes comfort in Minerva's power to *freeze* her *foes,* but in the event it is Comus who will freeze the Lady (658–61, 817–18).

452. *blank* *prostrating the whole faculties (*OED* 6).

454. *sincerely* in a pure or perfect degree (*OED* 4).

455. **liveried* wearing the uniform of (Heaven's) servants.

458. *no gross ear can hear* Cp. *Arcades* 72–3.

459. *oft converse* frequent communion.

461. *temple of the mind* John 2. 21 and I Cor. 3. 16.

462. *turns it . . . soul's essence* The conversion of body to soul was a Neo-Platonic rather than a Platonic doctrine. See Fallon (82) and cp. M.'s monism at *PL* v 469–503.

465. *lavish* licentious.

465–75. *But most . . . state* The argument follows Plato's *Phaedo* 81: virtuous souls are liberated at death, but souls who have lived only for the body are 'dragged down again into the visible world', where they are seen 'prowling about tombs and sepulchres', still 'craving after the corporeal'.

466. *the inward parts* Cp. Ps. 51. 6: 'Thou desirest truth in the inward parts'.

468. *Embodies* *takes on a sensual character (*OED* 2).
   *imbrutes sinks to the level of a brute.

472. *Lingering*] *1645, 1673*; Hovering *TMS, BMS, 1637.*

474. *sensualty*] *TMS, 1645*; sensuality *BMS, 1637, 1673.*

478. *musical as is Apollo's lute* Cp. Shakespeare, *Love's Labour's Lost* IV iii 339–40, where love (not philosophy) is 'sweet and musical / As bright Apollo's lute'.

479. *nectared* sweet and heavenly (the food of the gods).

480. *crude* indigestible (*OED* 3).

483. *night-foundered* engulfed in night.

491. *iron stakes* swords.

493. *father's*] *TMS, BMS*; father *1637, 1645, 1673.*

494. *Thyrsis* a common name in pastoral poetry, where it is used of shepherd singers (Theocritus i, Virgil, *Ecl.* vii).

495. *huddling* *hurrying in disorder (*OED* v 7, earliest instance 1646). *Madrigal* Lawes composed madrigals (part-songs for three or more voices), but here M. means 'song' (*OED* 2b), with a play on the pastoral etymology (Italian *mandra*, 'a flock').

495–512. The shift to couplets signals a shift to the pastoral mood of such dramas as John Fletcher's *The Faithful Shepherdess* and Jonson's *Sad Shepherd.*

497. *swain*] *1637, 1645, 1673*; shepherd *TMS, BMS.*

499. *wether* castrated ram.

501. *next* nearest.

502. *toy* trifle.

506. *To this* compared with this.

509. *sadly* gravely, in earnest (*OED* 7).

513. *vain* devoid of significance.

fabulous mere fables.

517. *Chimeras* fire-breathing monsters with a lion's head, goat's body and dragon's tail (Homer, *Il.* vi 179–82).

520. *navel* centre.

530. *Charáctered* engraved like a face on a coin (notice *mintage*), with overtones of 'face or features as betokening moral qualities' (*OED* sb 10).

531. *crofts* enclosed ground used for tillage or pasture (*OED* 1).

532. **brow* be on the brow of (*OED* 1), hence 'overlook'.

534. **stabled wolves* either 'wolves in their lairs' (cp. *PL* xi 752) or 'wolves in the fold'. Cp. Virgil, *Ecl.* iii 80: *Triste lupus stabilis* ('The wolf is a bane to the fold').

535. *Hecate* goddess of witchcraft (see line 135).

538. *inveigle* beguile, entice, entrap.

invite try to attract.

539. *unweeting* unsuspecting.

540. *by then* by the time that.

*chewing ruminating. *OED*'s earliest participial instance.

542. *knot-grass* any plant with a knotty stem (*OED* 2).

dew-besprent sprinkled with dew.

545. *flaunting* waving gaily like a plume or banner (*OED* 1).

546. *melancholy* the reflective mood invoked in *Il Penseroso*.

547. *meditate* practise (see *Lycidas* 66n).

548. *close* conclusion of a musical phrase (*OED* 2).

550. *barbarous dissonance* M. uses the same phrase of 'Bacchus and his revellers' at *PL* vii 32.

552. *stop of sudden silence* ordered by Comus at line 145.

553. *drowsy-frighted*] *1637, 1645, 1673, BMS*; drowsy-flighted *TMS*. Either version is possible. The horses have been frighted out of their drowsiness and they have also been flying drowsily. Cp. the 'drowsy, slow, and flagging wings' of Night's horses in Shakespeare, *2 Henry VI* IV i 5.

554. *litter* a curtained vehicle containing a couch (*OED* 2a).

close-curtained Sleep Cp. Shakespeare, *Macbeth* II i 51, 'curtained sleep'.

555. *sound* the Lady's song (230–43).

556. *steam*] *TMS, BMS, 1637, 1645*; stream *1673*.

558. *took* charmed, captivated.

560. *Still* silent and always. Denying her nature, Silence wishes to be silent no more (*never more / Still*) and to be always replaced by song. Cp. *PL* iv 604.

566. *hapless nightingale* Cp. the Lady's reference to Philomela, the 'love-lorn nightingale' (234). The Spirit now tactfully turns the allusion back upon the Lady, and so implies that her danger is real.

568. *lawns* open spaces between woods.

585. *period* sentence.

586. *for me* so far as I'm concerned.

589–90. *Virtue . . . enthralled* The Elder Brother now admits (what he would not admit at 420–31) that virgins can be *Surprised* (captured, seized) by *force*. His word *assailed* also contradicts the Lady's claim that heaven would keep her 'honour unassailed' (220). Physical assault cannot remove *Virtue*, but virtue cannot prevent assault.

594. *at last* at the Last Judgment. Cp. *PL* x 190, 635.

598. *pillared firmament* Cp. Job 26. 11: 'the pillars of heaven'.

599. *stubble* the short stalks of grain left after reaping. The Bible associates stubble with a poor foundation (I Cor. 3. 12) and the burning of the damned (Mal. 4. 1).

604. *sooty flag* Cp. Phineas Fletcher, *The Apollyonists* (1627) ii 39: 'All hell run out, and sooty flags display'.
Acheron one of the rivers of Hell.

605. *Harpies* taloned bird-women at Hell's gate (Virgil, *Aen.* vi 289).
Hydras fifty-headed serpents guarding Tartarus (*Aen.* vi 576).
forms] *1645, 1673*; bugs *TMS, BMS, 1637*.

606. *Ind* India.

607. *purchase* booty, plunder (*OED* 8a).

608–9. *to a foul death, / Cursed as his life*] *1645, 1673*; and cleave his scalp / Down to the hips *TMS, BMS, 1637*.

610. *emprise* chivalric enterprise.

611. *stead* service.

615. *sinews* including 'strength, energy' (*OED* 3).

619–21. *shepherd . . . healing herb* Commentators have identified the *shepherd lad* as M. himself, M.'s close friend Charles Diodati (a medical student interested in herbs, *Ep. Dam.* 150–52), or some other friend. See further 638*n*, below.

620. *to see to* to look at.

621. *virtuous* potent, efficacious.

626. *scrip* a small bag carried by a shepherd (*OED* sb 1).

627. *simples* medicinal herbs.

631–3. *The leaf . . . soil* Cp. Marvell's description in *Upon Appleton House* (*c.* 1650) of 'Conscience' as a 'plant': 'A prickling leaf it bears . . . But flowers eternal, and divine, / That in the crowns of saints do shine' (357–60).

632. *another country* probably Heaven (as opposed to earth, *this soil*). But some see *this soil* as England and the other country as Greece (or Italy). See below, 638*n*.

635. *clouted shoon* either 'patched shoes' or 'shoes studded with nails' (*OED* 'clout-shoe'). Cp. Shakespeare, *2 Henry VI*, IV ii 182 and Phineas Fletcher, *The Purple Island* (1633) viii 26.

636. *Moly* a mythical herb (with a black root and a white flower) given by *Hermes* to Odysseus to protect him from Circe's magic (Homer, *Od.* x 287–303, Ovid, *Met.* xiv 291–2). Sandys allegorizes Moly as 'temperance' (*Ovid's Metamorphosis*, 1632, 480).

638. **haemony* Various derivations have been proposed, including Haemonia (Thessaly) and Greek *haimonios*, 'blood-red' (thus suggesting Christ's blood). Charlotte F. Otten (*ELR* 5, 1975, 81–95) notes that *androsaemon* ('man's blood') was a real herb, famous as a demonifuge. It fits M.'s description, and Henry Lawes had exorcized a ghost with it.

640. *blast* infection.

damp noxious vapour.

646. *lime-twigs* twigs smeared with a sticky substance to catch birds. Cp. 'gums of glutinous heat' (917).

647. *came off* *escaped (*OED* 'come' 65g).

650. **hardihood.*

651. *brandished blade* Cp. Hermes' instruction that Odysseus rush on Circe with drawn sword (Homer, *Od.* x 294–5).

651–2. *break . . . ground* So Spenser's Guyon broke the cup offered him by Excess, 'And with the liquor stained all the lond' (*FQ* II xii 57). Guyon also overthrew Genius's bowl and 'broke his staffe' (*FQ* II xii 49).

655. *sons of Vulcan vomit smoke* Cacus (a son of Vulcan) 'vomited smoke' while fighting Hercules (Virgil, *Aen.* viii 252–3).

[Stage direction] *puts by* refuses.

goes about attempts.

660. *nerves* sinews (the supposed source of bodily strength).

661. *Daphne* a virgin nymph chased by *Apollo.* Her father rescued her by turning her into a laurel (Ovid, *Met.* i 547–52). Comus inverts the story so that metamorphosis becomes a weapon against chastity.

663. *Thou canst not touch the freedom of my mind* Cp. Augustine on the chastity of rape victims: 'there will be no pollution, if the lust is another's . . . purity is a virtue of the mind' (*City of God* i 18). See also Marcus (318).

664. *corporal rind* bodily shell.

665. **immanacled* At line 853 the Attendant Spirit distinguishes Comus's 'clasping charm' from his 'numbing spell'. The Lady is now immanacled by the 'clasping charm', which prevents her from rising, though it does not paralyse her (stage direction 658). The 'numbing spell' (described in lines 659–62) will completely freeze her.

669. *fancy* including 'amorous inclination' (*OED* 8b). 'Fancy' is the first

masquer in Spenser's masque of Cupid, where he is the father of 'Desyre' (*FQ* III xii 7–9).

beget In *TMS* this suggestive word is deleted, replaced with 'invent', then restored.

670. *returns* revives.

672–705. *And . . . appetite* These lines are inserted in *TMS* on a pasted leaf.

672. *cordial* stimulating (*OED* 2).

julep sweet drink (*OED* 1) and something to assuage the heat of passion (*OED* 2).

673. *his* its.

crystal bounds glass goblet.

674. *balm* aromatic fragrance (*OED* 4).

675–6. *Nepenthes . . . Helena* Returning from Troy, Menelaus and Helen were entertained in Egypt by Thone and his wife Polydamna. Polydamna gave Helen the drug *Nepenthes*, which could banish all sorrows from the mind (Homer, *Od.* iv 219–32). Nepenthes was not an aphrodisiac, but Comus's mention of the adulteress Helen is suggestive.

681. *usage* active use, with a play on 'usury' (notice *lent, cov'nants, trust, borrower*). Shakespeare *(Sonnets* IV and VI) and Marlowe (*Hero and Leander* i 232–6) associate procreation with usury.

delicacy pampering indulgence (*OED* 2) and voluptuousness (*OED* 1).

682. *cov'nants* clauses of a legal agreement (*OED* 4b).

trust (Nature's) confidence in (the Lady's) intention to pay (*OED* 3).

685. **unexempt condition* condition to which there can be no exceptions.

687. *Refreshment . . . pain* echoing Spenser's tempter Despair: 'Sleepe after toyle, port after stormie seas, / Ease after warre, death after life does greatly please' (*FQ* I ix 40).

688. *That have* You who have.

694. *aspécts* faces and looks.

696. **brewed* *OED*'s earliest participial instance.

698. *vizored* masked.

forgery deceit.

700. *lickerish* tempting to the palate (*OED* 1) and lustful (*OED* 3).

701–3. *Were it . . . good things* Juno was the goddess of marriage, so *a draught for Juno* might hint at chaste marriage as one of the Lady's lawful options. The Lady would reject even a decent (let alone an indecent) proposal from Comus, but marriage is still one of the *good things* that *good men* might give. This hint is stronger in a cancelled passage in *TMS* (755f.): 'thou man of lies and fraud, if thou give me it / I throw it on the ground, were it a draft for Juno / I should reject thy hand's treasonous offer, none / But such as are good men can give good things'.

701. *banquets* A 'banquet' might be a 'light repast between meals' (*OED*

2) rather than a feast, so Juno could banquet and still be *well-governed* in her *appetite*.

702–3. *none . . . things* Cp. Euripides, *Medea* 618: 'There is no benefit in the gifts of a bad man'. Cp. *PR* ii 321–2.

707. **budge* pompous, formal (*OED* a 1), with a pun on budge as the lamb's wool *fur* on academic gowns (*OED* sb¹ 1).

Stoic The Stoic school of philosophy (founded by Zeno in *c.* 300 BC) despised luxury and regarded the body as the prison of the soul. Later Stoics included Seneca, Epictetus and Marcus Aurelius. Cp. *PR* iv 300–308.

708. *Cynic* The Cynic school (founded by Antisthenes, a pupil of Socrates) despised riches as a distraction from self-knowledge. Diogenes the Cynic lived in a *tub*.

711. **unwithdrawing* not holding anything back, bountiful.

714. *sate* satisfy and glut.

 curious fastidious.

716. *green shops* mulberry trees (the silkworms' workshops).

719. *hutched* stored in a coffer (*OED* 1).

720. *store* furnish.

721. *pulse* legume seeds such as beans or lentils. Cp. Daniel 1. 12–16: 'give us pulse to eat, and water to drink'.

722. *frieze* coarse woollen cloth.

728. *surcharged* overburdened (*OED* 3) and overstocked (*OED* 2).

732–6. *th' unsought . . . brows* The *forehead of the deep* is the earth's crust as seen from its core. *They below* are dwellers in the underworld, for whom this diamond-studded crust is a star-studded sky. Gems were thought to grow and shine under the earth, so *unsought* gems would eventually illumine Hell. *They below* (the inhabitants of the underworld) would then *grow inured to light* and invade the surface. *TMS* at first read: 'Would so bestud the centre with their starlight'.

733. **emblaze* illuminate (*OED* v¹ 1).

736. *shameless brows* Cp. Shakespeare, *A Midsummer Night's Dream* III ii 382–5: 'Damned spirits all . . . to their wormy beds are gone, / For fear lest day should look their shames upon'.

737. *coy* shy, reserved.

 cozened duped.

737–55. *List . . . young yet*] *BMS* omits these lines. Perhaps they were felt to be too sexually explicit for the Ludlow performance.

738. *that . . . name Virginity* Cp. Marlowe, *Hero and Leander* (1598) i 269: 'This idol which you term virginity', and John Fletcher, *The Faithful Shepherdess* (*c.* 1609) I i 124–5: 'Sure there is a power / In that great name of virgin'.

739–40. *Beauty . . . current* The economic imagery (*coin, hoarded*) recalls lines 680–85, but Comus no longer speaks of repaying Nature's debt by procreating. He simply urges the Lady to *be current* ('be in circulation'). Cp. Marlowe, *Hero and Leander* i 265–6: 'Base bullion for the stamp's sake we allow, / Even so for men's impression do we you'.

741. *mutual* including 'intimate' (*OED* 3), 'responsive' (*OED* 5).

partaken including the now obsolete sense 'share with others' (*OED* 'partake' 2).

743–4. *If you . . . head* Cp. Shakespeare, *A Midsummer Night's Dream* I i 76–8: 'But earthlier happy is the rose distilled / Than that which, withering on the virgin thorn, / Grows, lives, and dies in single blessedness'.

745. *brag* display and boast.

746. *solemnities* festivals.

748. *homely* plain.

750. *sorry grain* poor colour.

ply work at.

751. *sampler* specimen of embroidery.

tease comb in preparation for spinning. *huswife's* Pronounce 'hussif's'.

752. *vermeil* vermilion.

756–61. *I . . . pride* These lines may have been spoken aside.

757. *juggler* sorcerer (*OED* 2), trickster (*OED* 3). Cp. Plato's identification of the Sophist as a 'juggler' (*Sophist* 235b).

759. *rules* maxims.

pranked dressed up.

760. *bolt* either 'utter hastily' (*OED* v² 5) or 'sift' (*OED* v¹ 1), hence 'argue selectively'.

764. **cateress* OED cites 'caterer' from 1592.

770. *lewdly-pampered* wickedly overfed, with overtones of lasciviousness. Cp. Gloucester's 'lust-dieted man' (Shakespeare, *King Lear* IV i 70).

773. *unsuperflous even proportion* Editors cite Shakespeare, *King Lear* III iv 28–35 and IV i 73–4. Cp. also Guyon's reply to Mammon in *FQ* II vii 15: 'through fowle intemperaunce / Frayle men are oft captiv'd to covetise: / But would they thinke, with how small allowaunce / Untroubled Nature doth her selfe suffise, / Such superfluities they would despise'.

778. *besotted* *morally stupefied (*OED* 2).

779–806. These lines are not in *TMS* or *BMS*. They first appear in *1637* and so were written after the Ludlow performance.

782. *sun-clad* Cp. Rev. 12. 1: 'a woman clothed with the sun'.

785. *mystery* a religious truth known only from divine revelation (*OED* 2). Cp. *An Apology for Smectymnuus*, where M. writes of 'those chaste and high mysteries . . . that *the body is for the Lord and the Lord for the body*' (*YP* 1. 892). St Paul calls marriage 'a great mystery' (Eph. 5. 32).

786–7. *sage / And serious* Cp. 'our sage and serious Poet *Spencer*' (*YP* 2. 516).

787. *Virginity* The fifteen-year-old Lady is a virgin, but she need not be advocating lifelong celibacy. 'Virginity' in Reformed doctrine could include chaste marriage. See Calvin, *Institutes* IV xii 28: *species secunda virginitatis, est matrimonii casta dilectio* ('the second kind of virginity is the chaste love of marriage'). Phillip Stubbes in *The Anatomie of Abuses* (1583) describes marriage as 'pure virginitie' (sig. G8ᵛ). Eve in *PL* has 'virgin majesty' even after consummating her marriage (ix 270). See also *Ep. Dam.* 214n.

790. *gay* showy (*OED* 3) and specious, plausible (*OED* 5).

791. *fence* fencing skill (*OED*'s earliest figurative instance).

793. *uncontrollèd* indisputable, irrepressible.

797. *brute earth . . . shake* So in Horace, *Odes* I xxxiv 9–12, Jove's thunderbolt shakes the earth, confirming the gods' existence.

nerves sinews.

803. *Dips* *suffuses with moisture (*OED* 4a).

804. *Speaks* utters (*thunder*) and pronounces sentence (*chains*).

Erebus primeval darkness; here, the underworld.

805. *Saturn's crew* the Titans and Giants who made war on Jove. See *PL* i 198–9n.

808. *canon laws* rules; with a glance at 'Canon Law' (laws established by an ecclesiastical council). Cp. Comus as priest (125–37).

foundation any institution such as a college or monastery.

809. *suffer* tolerate.

809–10. *lees . . . blood* The melancholic humour was thought to settle in the blood like the *lees* (dregs) of wine, causing madness or depression.

816. *rod reversed* Circe freed Ulysses' men with her 'reversed wand' (Ovid, *Met.* xiv 300). Sandys (481) sees the wand as 'perswasions of pleasure', and its reversal as 'discipline'.

817. *backward mutters of dissevering power* charms spoken backwards so as to release the Lady. Spenser's Britomart releases Amoret by forcing Busyrane 'his charmes back to reverse' (*FQ* III xii 36).

mutters muttered spells.

822. *Meliboeus* perhaps Spenser (who tells Sabrina's story in *FQ* II x 14–19). 'Meliboe' is a wise old shepherd in *FQ* VI ix–xi. Cp. Virgil, *Ecl.* i and vii.

823. *soothest* most truthful.

826. *Sabrina* the nymph of the river Severn. M.'s version of her legend emphasizes her virginity and obscures the fact that she was born from the adulterous union of *Locrine* and Estrildis. Locrine's queen *Guendolen* raised an army, killed Locrine, and drowned Estrildis and Sabrina in the Severn (named for Sabrina). See Geoffrey of Monmouth, *Historia Regum Britanniae* II i–v, and Drayton, *Polyolbion* vi 130–78. Spenser's Sabrina is a 'sad virgin innocent of all', but her death is still caused by 'disloyall love' and she does

not become a goddess (*FQ* II x 19). Drayton makes her a goddess and associates her with *Nereus* (*Polyolbion* v 1–30).

827. *Whilom* formerly.

828. *Brute* Brutus, great-grandson of Aeneas and the founder of Britain.

831. *Commended* entrusted. Most sources say that Sabrina was thrown into the river. She drowns herself in the tragedy *Locrine* (1595).

835. *Nereus* 'the old man of the sea' (Homer, *Il.* xviii 141), a benign sea-deity, father of the fifty Nereids.

836. *lank* *drooping, languid (*OED* 3).

838. *nectared lavers* basins of nectar. Nereids pour 'soueraine balme, and Nectar good' into Marinell's wound (Spenser, *FQ* III iv 40), and the Nereid Thetis protects Patroclus' corpse with nectar (Homer, *Il.* xix 38). Cp. *Lycidas* 175.

asphodel immortal flower of Elysium (Homer, *Od.* xi 539).

840. *ambrosial oils* Aphrodite protects Hector's corpse with ambrosial oil in Homer, *Il.* xxiii 186–7.

841. *quick* swift and living.

immortal change change to an immortal. The phrase may hint that Sabrina never died. Cp. 'this mortal change' (10) and see *PL* xi 700–710.

844–57. Sabrina's healing powers, her care for cattle, and her special concern for virgins recall Fletcher's Clorin. Cp. *The Faithful Shepherdess* (c. 1609) I i 39–40, V iii 74–5.

845. *Helping* remedying.

urchin blasts infections breathed by goblins.

ill-luck signs Elves brought disease or bad luck to animals and humans by firing 'elf-shot' (neolithic flint arrows) and tying 'elf-locks' (matted animal or human hair). Cp. Shakespeare, *Romeo and Juliet* I iv 88–91.

846. *shrewd* mischievous (*OED* 1), as in 'that shrewd and knavish sprite / Called Robin Goodfellow' (Shakespeare, *A Midsummer Night's Dream* II i 33–4).

849. *Carol* *celebrate in song (*OED* 3b).

852. *old swain* Meliboeus (see line 822).

853. *clasping charm* the spell with which Comus has held the Lady in his chair since line 659.

numbing spell the spell now paralysing the Lady. Stronger than the 'clasping charm', it deprives its victim of speech and movement. Comus must have cast the spell before exiting (Thyrsis and Sabrina both attribute it to his magic). See 815–19, 905–7, 916–17 and cp. Comus's description of the 'numbing spell' at 659–62.

854. *warbled melodiously sung (*OED* 1), performed with trills (*OED* v 2a).

856. *To aid a virgin* In Fletcher's *The Faithful Shepherdess* (c. 1609) a river-god rises to heal the virgin Amoret who has been stabbed and cast in his spring. See esp. III ii 149–50: 'If thou bee'st a virgin pure, / I can give a present cure'.

858. *adjuring* OED's sole participial instance. OED suggests 'exorcising', but M. probably means 'entreating'.

862. *knitting* plaiting (OED 3).

863. *amber-* ambergris, an aromatic substance found floating in tropical seas. It was used as a perfume and in cooking, even though it was (rightly) suspected to be sperm whale dung. Thomas Browne comments on its source in *Pseudodoxia Epidemica* (1658 edn., III xxvi): 'Ordure makes the best Musk, and from the most fetid substances may be drawn the most odoriferous Essences' (Robbins i 274). Other seventeenth-century authors thought that ambergris might be whale's sperm (see OED 'amber' 1a, 1693 citation). Cp. *PR* ii 344, *SA* 720. See also 917n, below.

864. *honour's* chastity's.

865. *lake* Virgil calls the Tiber a *lacus* (*Aen.* viii 74).

868. *Oceanus* the Titan, father of earth's rivers.

869. *earth-shaking* Homer's epithet for Poseidon, god of the sea and earthquakes.

   mace trident (OED 1b).

870. *Tethys* wife of Oceanus and mother of the rivers.

871. *Nereus* see above, 835n.

872. *Carpathian wizard* Proteus, the shepherd (hence *hook*) of Poseidon's seals. Virgil and Ovid call him a 'Carpathian seer' because he lived in the Carpathian Sea, between Rhodes and Crete (Virgil, *Georg.* iv 387, Ovid, *Met.* xi 249).

873. *Triton* Neptune's herald, with his conch-shell.

   winding twisting and trumpeting.

874. *Glaucus* a Boeotian fisherman who became an oracular sea-god after eating a magical herb (Ovid, *Met.* xiii 917–68).

875. *Leucothea* Greek, 'white goddess'. Neptune transformed the mortal woman Ino into this marine deity after she leapt from a cliff to escape persecution by Juno (Ovid, *Met.* iv 512–42). The Romans identified her with Matuta, goddess of the dawn (cp. *PL* xi 135).

876. *her son* Melicertes. Ino was holding him when she leapt into the sea. Neptune transformed him into Palaemon, god of harbours.

877. *Thetis* a Nereid, Achilles' mother. She has *tinsel-slippered feet* because Homer calls her 'silver-footed' (*Il.* xviii 127).

878. *Sirens* The Attendant Spirit has so far invoked benign marine deities. Now he calls on the singers who accompany Circe and lure men to destruction (see above, 253n).

879–82. *By dead . . . locks* These lines are deleted in *TMS*.

879. *Parthenope* one of the Sirens. Enraged by Odysseus's escape, she threw herself off her rock, drowning herself. Her *tomb* was near Naples (Strabo I ii 13).

880. *Ligea* another Siren (according to the twelfth-century Homeric commentator, Eustathius). Virgil makes her a river nymph with shining hair (*Georg.* iv 336).

884. *wily* full of wile 'in a lighter sense: an amorous or playful trick' (*OED* 1c).

886. **-paven* paved.

893. **azurn* azure (cp. Italian *azzurino*).

894. *turkis* turquoise.

897. *printless feet* Cp. Shakespeare's elves, treading 'on the sand with printless foot' (Shakespeare, *The Tempest* V i 34).

904. *charmèd band* magic bonds.

907. *unblest* unhallowed, wicked (*OED* 3).

912. *Drops . . . fountain pure* A river-god revives a virgin with a pure 'drop' of water in William Browne, *Britannia's Pastorals* (1613–16) I i 747–52, and in John Fletcher, *The Faithful Shepherdess* (*c.* 1609) III ii 149–64.

917. *gums of glutinous heat* Glue was made from horses' hoofs, which had to be heated to liquefy (hence *heat*). Some see a sexual significance in Comus's hot, sticky *gums*. Kerrigan (47–8) infers that 'the Lady is guilty'; Marcus (317) argues that the Lady 'is brought into involuntary association with a pollution she despises'.

921. *Amphitrite* a Nereid, wife of Neptune.

923. *Anchises* ancestor of Brutus, Locrine and Sabrina (see 828*n*, above).

924–37. *May thy . . . cinnamon* River gods who have rescued virgins are blessed in octosyllabic couplets in John Fletcher (*The Faithful Shepherdess* III ii 229–40) and Browne (*Britannia's Pastorals* I ii 266–86).

928. *singèd* scorching.

930. *torrent* *torrential (*OED* B cites no adjectival usage before *PL* ii 581, 'torrent fire').

934. *head* source of a river (*OED* 16), with a glance at the goddess Cybele, whose head was *crowned / With many a tower*.

937. *TMS* and *BMS* have the note *Song ends* after this line. *1637* and *1645* have a space. No music has survived for lines 922–37.

941. *device* cunning trick.

942. *waste* unnecessary.

949. *gratulate* give thanks for (*OED* 4), welcome.

959. *sunshine holiday* Cp. *L'Allegro* 98.

960. *duck or nod* curtsy or bow.

961. *trippings* dances.

962. *court guise* courtly deportment.

963. *Mercury . . . devise* Mercury introduces the final dances in Jonson's *Pleasure Reconciled to Virtue* (performed 1618, printed 1640) after 'the voluptuous Comus' is 'Beat from his grove' (146–7). Jonson associates Mercury with dancing Dryads in *Pan's Anniversary* (performed 1620, printed 1640) 176–8.

964. *mincing* 'a dancing term that meant doubling the time to make twice as many steps to a musical measure' (J. Demaray, *Milton and the Masque Tradition*, 1968, 119).

Dryades woodland nymphs.

965. *lawns . . . leas* glades . . . meadows.

969. *three fair branches* Cp. Spenser on the brothers Priamond, Diamond and Triamond (*FQ* IV ii 43): 'Like three faire branches'.

970. *timely* early (*OED* 1).

971. *patience* enduring of suffering (*OED* 1).

972. *assays* trials (*OED* 1), tribulations (*OED* 2).

976. *Ocean* Plato's river Ocean flows on the outer surface of the True Earth, above our atmosphere (*Phaedo* 112E).

978. *Where day never shuts his eye* Night was thought to be the earth's shadow. The sky above this shadow was bright blue and all the stars were visible. See *PL* iii 556–7n and C. S. Lewis, *The Discarded Image* (1964) 112.

979. *broad fields of the sky* Cp. Lucretius, *De Rerum Nat.* v 553: 'the broad pastures of the sky'.

980. *liquid* clear, bright (*OED* 2).

982–3. *Hesperus . . . tree* See above, 393n. The garden of the Hesperides was on the edge of Ocean, far to the west. M. (following Plato) locates Ocean above our atmosphere, so the garden of the Hesperides is in the heavens. Cp. *PL* iii 568.

984. *crispèd shades* trees with curled leaves.

985. *spruce* lively.

986. *Graces* three naked goddesses (Euphrosyne, Aglaia and Thalia) who attended Venus and presided over the joys of domestic life. Cp. *L'Allegro* 12–16.

Hours three goddesses who presided over the seasons. They opened heaven's gate (*PL* vi 3) and yoked Phoebus's horses at morning (hence *rosy-bosomed*). The Graces dance with the Hours at *PL* iv 267.

988. *That* so that. The *1673* errata say 'leave out *that*', but it is included in *1637*, *1645* and the revised *TMS*.

990. **cedarn* composed of cedars (cp. *azurn*, 893).

991. *Nard . . . cassia* aromatic plants. See *PL* v 293n.

992. *Iris* goddess of the rainbow and messenger of Juno.

993. *blow* cause to bloom.

995. *purfled* variegated.

996. *Elysian* of Elysium, the classical abode of the blessed dead.

997. *(List . . . true)* a warning that what follows is allegory.

999. *Adonis* a hunter loved by Venus (*th' Assyrian queen*). He was killed by a boar, but restored to life in the Garden of Adonis. Cp. *PL* ix 440 and Spenser, *FQ* III vi 46–8. Spenser's Garden of Adonis is on this earth, and Venus and Adonis make love there; M.'s Adonis sleeps in a paradise above our earth.

1003. *spangled sheen* Cp. Shakespeare, *A Midsummer Night's Dream* II i 29: 'spangled starlight sheen'.

1004–8. *Cupid . . . bride* See Apuleius, *The Golden Ass* iv 28–vi 24. *Cupid* loved the mortal woman *Psyche*, whom he visited in darkness. He fled when Psyche discovered his identity. Psyche (Greek, 'soul') endured many trials until Jove allowed her to marry Cupid in heaven. Boccaccio in *De Genealogiis Deorum* v 22 allegorizes the story, taking Psyche to be the soul and Cupid to be pure Love. M.'s *Celestial Cupid* may be Christ as Bridegroom of the soul (Matt. 25. 1–13).

1004. *advanced* elevated, raised on high.

1009. *unspotted* Cp. Eph. 5. 25–8: 'Husbands, love your wives, even as Christ also loved the church, and gave himself for it . . . that he might present it to himself a glorious church, not having spot, or wrinkle, or any such thing'.

1010–11. *twins . . . Youth and joy* Spenser and Apuleius give Cupid and Psyche one child, *Voluptas* or 'Pleasure' (*FQ* III vi 50). Plato calls wisdom and virtue the twin progeny of the soul (*Symposium* 209A). Cp. M.'s *An Apology for Smectymnuus* (1642): 'the first and chiefest office of love, begins and ends in the soule, producing those happy twins of her divine generation knowledge and vertue' (*YP* 1. 892).

1015. *bowed welkin* arch of the sky.

1017. *corners of the moon* the moon's horns (Latin *cornu*). Cp. Shakespeare, *Macbeth* III v 24: 'Upon the corner of the moon'.

1021. *Higher . . . chime* above the Music of the Spheres, hence to Heaven.

1022–3. *Or if . . . stoop to her* M. wrote these lines in the guest book of the Cerdogni family in Geneva on 10 June 1639. Cp. Marlowe, *Hero and Leander* i 365–6: 'hands so pure, so innocent, nay such / As might have made heaven stoop to have a touch'.

ENGLISH POEMS ADDED IN 1673

On the Death of a Fair Infant Dying of a Cough

Date: M.'s caption *Anno aetatis 17* means 'at the age of seventeen' (not 'in his seventeenth year'). Cp. M.'s use of the same caption in *Elegia II* and *Elegia III* (which were certainly written when M. was seventeen). M.'s caption would therefore place the date of composition between 9 December 1625 and 8 December 1626; however, Edward Phillips, M.'s nephew, wrote in 1694 that the poem was occasioned by 'the Death of one of his Sister's Children (a Daughter), who died in her Infancy' (Darbishire 62). W. R. Parker has identified this daughter as Anne Phillips (12 January 1626–22 January 1628), and so argued for 1628 as the date of composition. M. might have misdated the poem (as he misdated *In Obitum Procancellarii medici*).

1–2. *O fairest . . . fading* Cp. *The Passionate Pilgrim* (1599) x 1–4: 'Sweet rose, fair flower, untimely pluckd, soon vaded, / Plucked in the bud and vaded in the spring!'

1. *blown* in bloom.

blasted balefully breathed upon.

2. *primrose* a symbol of swiftly-fading beauty. Cp. *Lycidas* 142.

**timelessly* unseasonably.

6–7. *thought to kiss / But killed* a common conceit. See e.g. Shakespeare, *Venus and Adonis* 1110.

8. *Aquilo* Boreas, the north wind. He wooed the Athenian princess Orithyia in vain, then carried her off in storm and darkness (Ovid, *Met.* vi 682–710). M. makes him the driver of Winter's chariot.

9. *boist'rous* savagely violent (*OED* 9a) and rough in weather (*OED* 8).

13. *eld* old age.

15. *icy-pearlèd car* chariot covered with hailstones. Cp. hail as 'Ice-pearls' in Sylvester, *DWW, The Vocation* (1608) 293.

16. *middle empire of the freezing air* the cold middle layer of the earth's atmosphere. Cp. *PL* i 516, *PR* i 39f.

19. *chair* chariot (*OED* sb²).

20. *cold-kind* both 'cold by nature' and 'kind in intention, but cold in effect'.

23–7. *Apollo . . . flower* Apollo accidentally killed his beloved Hyacinthus, a Spartan prince, when his discus bounced and struck the boy. The hyacinth flower sprang from Hyacinthus's blood. See Ovid, *Met.* x 162–216 and cp. *Lycidas* 160. Other versions state that Zephyrus or Boreas diverted Apollo's discus.

23. *unweeting* unwitting.

25–6. *Young Hyacinth . . . Young Hyacinth* Cp. Spenser, *Astrophel* 7–8: 'Young Astrophel, the pride of shepheards praise, / Young Astrophel, the rustick lasses love', and *FQ* III vi 45: 'Sad *Amaranthus*, made a flowre but late, / Sad *Amaranthus*, in whose purple gore / Me seemes I see *Amintas* wretched fate'. See also *Lycidas* 8–9n.

25. *Eurotas* a river in Laconia, flowing by Sparta.

31. *wormy bed* Cp. Shakespeare, *A Midsummer Night's Dream* III ii 384: 'wormy beds'.

39. *first-moving sphere* the *primum mobile*, the outermost sphere of the Ptolemaic universe, which communicated movement to the lower spheres. Cp. *PL* iii 482–3, viii 133–6.

40. *Elysian fields* abode of the blessed dead, which Homer placed in the western Ocean (*Od.* iv 561–9) and Plato placed above the earth (*Phaedo* 112E).

45. *behoof* benefit, advantage (*OED* 1).

47. *Earth's sons* the Giants, who warred against the gods, causing them to flee to the earth, where they adopted various disguises (Ovid, *Met.* v 321–31).

48. **sheeny* having a shiny surface.

50. *that just maid* Astraea (Justice). See *Nativity* 142n.

53. The line is short a foot, presumably due to a printer's error. Suggestions for the missing disyllable include: 'Mercy', 'Virtue', 'Peace in', and 'Temp'rance'.

54. *white-robèd* the traditional garb of *Truth*. See e.g. Cesare Ripa, *Iconologia* (1611) 530.

57. *golden-wingèd host* the angels.

58. *weed* our 'garment' of flesh (*OED* sb^2 3).

59. *prefixèd* preordained.

62. *set . . . on fire* perhaps playing on 'Seraph', which was associated with Hebrew *saraph*, 'to burn'. Cp. *PL* ii 512.

66. *his* God's.

68. *pestilence* The plague had broken out in London in 1625. Carey therefore concludes that the poem was written in 1625–6, and that Anne Phillips cannot be its subject. But M. might be anticipating a future plague (such as came in 1630 and 1637). Anne's birth in January 1626 might be said to have 'driven away' the plague of 1625. See Parker (738).

75. *render* give back (*OED* 3).

76. *will an offspring give* Cp. Isa. 56. 5: 'unto them will I give in mine house and within my walls a place and a name better than of sons and daughters: I will give them an everlasting name, that shall not be cut off'.

At a Vacation Exercise

Date: July 1628. M. had been chosen to preside as 'Father' or 'Dictator' at the College assembly set near the beginning of the long vacation (July – early October). M.'s poem accords with the festive tone of the occasion. It was delivered as a public oration, immediately following M.'s sixth Latin *Prolusion* (which had argued that sportive exercises are sometimes not inconsistent with philosophical studies).

1. *Hail native language* When M. spoke these words, he had just ended *Prolusion vi* by announcing (in Latin) that he will now 'overleap the University Statutes as if they were the wall of Romulus and run off from Latin into English'.

4. *infant* including 'unspeaking' (Latin *infans*).

8. *latter task* the present English poem (as distinct from the preceding Latin oration).

12. *thither* into the preceding Latin.

16. *neglect* of placing English after Latin.

19. *toys* fancies, conceits (*OED* 4).

trimming slight sparse adornment.

20. *late fantastics* those recently given to wild or fanciful notions (*OED* 'fantastic' sb 1). M. might be thinking of bad metaphysical poets who prefer wit to the *richest robes* of Spenser's decorative style.

27. *suspect* suspicion.

29–52. *Yet had ... captivity* These lines are a digression from the task in hand (see below, 54*n*). In them M. confides to his audience his high poetic vocation.

32. *fancy* imagination.

33. *deep* high (Latin *altus*).

34. *wheeling poles* axes of the rotating Ptolemaic universe, above which was the unmoving empyreal Heaven. Cp. *PL* vii 23: 'rapt above the pole'.

36. *thunderous throne* of Jove.

37. *unshorn* a common classical epithet for Apollo.

38. *Hebe* goddess of youth.

40. *spheres of watchful fire* spheres of the stars and planets keeping perpetual watch in the universe. Cp. *Nativity* 21: 'all the spangled host keep watch in squadrons bright'.

42. *lofts* both 'upper floors of a warehouse' (*OED* 5a) and 'upper regions of the sky' (*OED* 1). The image is of clouds used as a storage space for Jove's thunderbolts.

piled both 'laid in piles' and 'armed with pointed heads' (*OED* a¹ 2).

46. *beldam* grandmother, aged woman.

48. *Demodocus* the bard at the court of King Alcinous. His songs about the Trojan war moved Odysseus to tears (Homer, *Od.* viii 487–543).

53. *But fie . . . stray* So Horace turns from a high epic subject in *Odes* III iii 70: *qua, Musa, tendis? desine pervicax / referre sermones deorum* ('Muse, where are you going? Cease wilfully reporting the debates of the gods').

54. *another way* M. (as 'Father' and Ens) must now return to his task of introducing his ten 'sons', the Aristotelian 'categories'.

56. *Predicament* one of ten Aristotelian categories 'predicated' of any particular entity. M. also puns on his own 'predicament' of having to talk about them. Aristotle's categories were 'Substance' and its nine 'Accidents'. Four of these (Substance, Quantity, Quality, and Relation) are represented in the portion of the performance M. has preserved. M. played the part of 'Father' and ten fellow students played the 'sons'.

65. *still* always.

66. *invisible* As an abstraction, Substance is perceived only through accidental attributes (quantity, quality, etc.).

69. *Sibyl* prophetess.

71. *prospective glass* magic crystal for seeing the future.

74. *Accident* both 'one of the nine categories after Substance' and 'mishap'.

76–8. *underling . . . under* playing on the etymology of 'substance' as that which 'stands under' things.

90. *loose this Gordian knot* resolve the paradoxes of Aristotle's theory. An oracle proclaimed that whoever untied the Gordian knot would rule all Asia. Alexander (who had been Aristotle's pupil) cut it with his sword. [Stage direction] *spake in prose*. The speeches have not survived.

91. *Rivers arise.* Two brothers named Rivers had been admitted to Christ's College on 10 May 1628. One of them played the part of Relation. M.'s catalogue of rivers parodies those in Spenser, *FQ* IV xi 24–47 and throughout Drayton's *Polyolbion* (1612–22).

92. *gulfy* full of eddies.
   Dun the Don, in Yorkshire.

95. *sullen* flowing sluggishly (*OED* 5).

96. *maiden's* Sabrina's. See *A Masque* 824f.

98. *hallowed Dee* echoing Drayton, *Polyolbion* x 215. Drayton explains that changes in the Dee's course were deemed to be prophetic. Cp. *Lycidas* 55.

99. *Humber . . . Scythian's name* The river Humber was said to have taken its name from a Scythian invader who drowned in it, after Locrine defeated him.

Sonnet XI ('A book was writ of late')

Date: late 1645 or early 1646. This and the next sonnet are a response to
the attacks M. suffered after the publication of his four divorce tracts, *The
Doctrine and Discipline of Divorce* (1643, 1644), *The Judgement of Martin
Bucer* (1644), *Tetrachordon* and *Colasterion* (both 1645). M.'s liberal views
on divorce earned him the hostility of the Presbyterians, his old allies
against prelacy (see headnote to *Sonnet XII*). *Sonnet XI* follows *Sonnet XII*
in *TMS*, and it is widely agreed that *Sonnet XII* was written first. The title
On the detraction which followed upon my writing certain treatises appears only
in *TMS*, where it covers both sonnets. *Sonnet XI* is more cool and detached
than *Sonnet XII*, using colloquialisms and comic rhymes to express con-
tempt for an unlearned age.

1–4. *Tetrachordon . . . pored on* M.'s rhyme perhaps mocks Wither's *Prince
Henry's Obsequies* (1612), *Elegy V*: 'Who was himself a book for kings to
pore on: / And might have been thy *Basilikon Doron*'.
1. *Tetrachordon* Greek, 'four-stringed'. A 'tetrachord' was a four-stringed
instrument (*OED* 1) or a four-note scale (*OED* 2a). The tract's title refers
to four key biblical passages on marriage and divorce (Gen. 1. 27–8, 2. 18,
23–4; Deut. 24. 1–2; Matt. 5. 31–2, 19. 3–11; I Cor. 7. 10–16) which M.
tries to 'harmonize' with each other and with his argument for divorce on
the grounds of incompatibility.
3. *it walked the town* Horace (*Epistulae* I xx) addresses his book as if it were
a prostitute walking the streets. But conceits treating books as living things
are not uncommon. Cp. M.'s *Areopagitica*: 'books are not absolutely dead
things, but do contain a potency of life in them'.
4. *Numb'ring* *comprising (as its readers) and determining the number of
(*OED* 7, 2c).
5. *stall-reader* reader at booksellers' stalls. These were mainly in St Paul's
Churchyard.
7. *spelling false* both 'misspelling the title' and 'failing to understand the
argument' (*OED* 'spell' v^2 2b = 'understand').
   Mile-End Green the eastern limit of London, a mile beyond Aldgate.
8–9. *Gordon . . . Galasp* M.'s contempt is less for the bearers of these
Scottish names than for the English who accept them, yet balk at *Tetra-
chordon*. The names are nevertheless calculated to evoke anti-Scottish
feeling harmful to M.'s Presbyterian critics. *Galasp* is George Gillespie, a
Covenanter and member of the Westminster Assembly. *Gordon, Macdonnel*
(Macdonald), and *Colkitto* (a nickname for Coll Keitache) were officers in
Montrose's Royalist army. By naming a Presbyterian in the same breath as
three Royalists, M. implies that there is little to choose between them.

10. *rugged* harsh.

like equally harsh.

sleek easy.

11. *Quintilian* Roman teacher of rhetoric (late first century AD). His *Instituto Oratoria* I v 8 condemns the use of foreign words.

12. *Sir John Cheke* an English humanist (1514–57). He was the first Professor of Greek at Cambridge and King Edward VI's tutor. The meaning of lines 12–14 has been much debated. Masson (iii 283) took *like ours* to mean 'your age, in contrast to our age, did not hate learning'. Smart (73–4) infers the opposite sense: Cheke's age and M.'s are alike in that they '*hated not learning worse than toad or asp,* – but as much as they hated either'. In support of this strained reading, Smart cites Cheke's testimony that his age was hostile to the study of Greek. But M. in *Tetrachordon* praises Cheke's age as 'the purest and sincerest that ever shon yet on the reformation of this Iland' (*YP* 2. 716).

Sonnet XII ('I did but prompt the age')

Date: see previous headnote. M. in 1641–2 had allied himself with the Presbyterians against the bishops, so the Presbyterian hostility to his divorce tracts came as a shock. William Prynne, Herbert Palmer, Daniel Featley, Thomas Edwards and Robert Baillie all called for the suppression of M.'s divorce tracts, and M. was summoned to the House of Lords for examination (see below, 8n). Despite this hostility, some have doubted whether *Sonnet XII* is aimed at the Presbyterians. N. H. Henry, *MLN* 66 (1951) 509–13, thinks that the *owls* and other animals of line 4 are the radicals who embraced M.'s doctrines all too eagerly (e.g. Mrs Attaway, who cited M. when she left her husband). M. may have been embarrassed by this enthusiasm, but his sonnet is aimed against those who *Railed* (6) against him. The *TMS* title *On the detraction which followed upon my writing certain treatises* also tells for the traditional interpretation. Some have thought that M.'s main attack is against the Presbyterians, but that lines 9–11 extend the attack 'from those who ignorantly rejected his doctrine to those who, with equal ignorance, accepted and misapplied it as a sanction of licence' (*Var.* 2. 2. 396). But *licence* (11) and *revolt* (10) are puns aimed at the Presbyterians.

1. *quit their clogs* rid themselves of their encumbrances. A 'clog' was a heavy piece of wood attached to a prisoner's leg or neck to prevent escape (*OED* 2).

2. *known rules of ancient liberty* the Mosaic divorce law; also the natural law of right reason, which M. believed to be 'of more antiquity' than 'marriage it selfe' (*YP* 2. 237).

4. *owls* a symbol of benighted ignorance. In *Areopagitica* (1644) M. likens England to an eagle gazing at the sun, while those 'timorous' birds 'that love the twilight, flutter about, amazed at what she means, and in their envious gabble would prognosticate a year of sects and schisms' (*YP* 2. 558).

cuckoos a symbol of ingratitude.

asses a symbol of obstinate stupidity.

apes a symbol of empty mockery.

dogs a symbol of quarrelsomeness.

6. *Latona's twin-born progeny* Apollo and Diana. Fleeing Juno, and suffering from thirst, Latona tried to drink from a pool, but some peasants (*hinds*) prevented her by muddying the water. She turned them into frogs (Ovid, *Met.* vi 317–81). *Twin-born* glances at M.'s tracts *Tetrachordon* and *Colasterion*, which were published on the same day, 4 March 1645 (Parker 897, n118).

7. *fee* absolute and rightful possession (*OED* 2b).

8. *casting pearl to hogs* Cp. Matt. 7. 6: 'Give not that which is holy unto the dogs, neither cast ye your pearls before swine'. Honigmann (117) thinks that *hogs* may also play on the name 'Bacon'. A Judge Bacon examined M. in December 1644, and another Bacon, a member of the Commons, helped prepare an ordinance against heresy in 1646.

10. *And still revolt when truth would set them free*] *TMS, 1673*; And hate the truth whereby they should be free; *TMS 1st reading*. Cp. John 8. 32: 'And the truth shall make you free'. *still* continually.

revolt draw back from a course of action, return to one's allegiance (*OED* 2b). M.'s Presbyterian detractors 'revolt' by backsliding into conservative traditions. M. also plays on the other sense of 'revolt' to imply that the Presbyterians are rebels against *Truth*. He employs the same pun in his prose, always at the Presbyterians' expense. See John Leonard, 'Revolting as Backsliding in Milton's Sonnet XII', *N&Q* 241, n.s. 43 (September 1996), 269–73.

11. *Licence* licentiousness and licence to print (recalling the Licensing Order of 14 June 1643). The pun is very common in M.'s prose.

12. *For who ... good* Cp. *TKM:* 'None can love freedom heartilie, but good men; the rest love not freedom, but licence; which never hath more scope or indulgence then under Tyrants' (*YP* 3. 190).

13. *mark* target.

rove shoot (with arrows) away from a mark; hence, wander from the point (*OED* v¹ 2).

14. *For all* in spite of. Some editors take *For* to mean 'from', but M. is not condemning the Civil War. He is blaming the Presbyterians for making it futile.

Sonnet XIII. To Mr. H. Lawes, on his Airs

There are three drafts of the sonnet in *TMS*, the first being dated 9 February 1645 (i.e. 1646). M. had long been a friend of Henry Lawes, who had written the music for *A Masque* and played the part of the Attendant Spirit. Lawes may also have collaborated with M. in producing *Arcades*. The two friends had opposing political views. Lawes had been a member of the King's Music, and remained a Royalist. M.'s sonnet was first published in Lawes's *Choice Psalmes* (1648), which was dedicated to Charles I (then a prisoner) and commemorated Henry's brother William who had died fighting for the King. Henry Lawes died in 1662.

1. *well-measured* composed in good measure or rhythm (*OED* 1).

2–3. *First . . . accent* 'First taught our English musicians how to give each word its proper measure of length and stress'. Lawes was not original in this regard, but he was famous for the degree to which he subordinated the music to the words. Cp. Waller's 'To Mr. Henry Lawes, Who Had Then Newly Set a Song of Mine, in the Year 1635' (printed 1686): 'But you alone may truly boast / That not a syllable is lost, / The writer's and the setter's skill / At once the ravished ears do fill' (21–4).

2. *span* measure (*OED* 2b).

3. *accent* a technical term in prosody and music: the 'rhythm or measure of the verse' (*OED* 6) and 'the marks placed over words to show the various notes or turns of phrases to which they were sung' (*OED* 7). Lawes respects both kinds of accent.

scan both 'pass judgement' (*OED* 2b) and 'determine the number and nature of poetic feet'.

4. *Midas' ears* King Midas was given ass's ears when he preferred Pan's pipe to Apollo's lyre (Ovid, *Met*. xi 146–79). Cp. Phineas Fletcher, *The Purple Island* i 17: 'Our *Midas* eares'.

committing short and long matching a long syllable with a short note, or a short syllable with a long note. 'Commit' means *place in a state of hostility or incongruity' (*OED* 9b).

5. *exempts* singles out.

6. *wan* healthily pale.

8. *air* melody.

humour fit, suit (*OED* 2).

10. *Phoebus' choir* the Muses (i.e. the poets whose verses Lawes set to music).

11. *story* 'The story of Ariadne set by him in music' (marginal note in *Choice Psalmes*, 1648). William Cartwright's *Complaint of Ariadne* was set by Lawes in his *Ayres and Dialogues* (1653).

12–14. *Dante . . . Purgatory* In *Purg.* ii 76–117, Dante meets the shade of his friend *Casella* the musician, and asks him to sing. Casella responds by singing one of Dante's *canzoni,* that he had set to music in life.

14. *milder shades* Dante met Casella on the threshold of Purgatory, which was less dark than Purgatory itself.

Sonnet XIV ('When Faith and Love which parted from thee never')

Date: December 1646. There are three drafts of the poem in *TMS*. One, struck through, is titled 'On the religious memory of Mrs Catharine Thomason my Christian friend deceased 16 December 1646'. Mrs Thomason was the wife of M.'s friend George Thomason, a London bookseller and collector of contemporary pamphlets. The Thomason tracts (now in the British Library) number over 22,000, and include several of M.'s pamphlets, inscribed *Ex dono authoris.* Mrs Thomason also loved to read. George Thomason's will bequeaths books from 'my late dear wife's library' (Smart 70).

4. *Of death, called life* Cp. John 12. 25: 'he that hateth his life in this world shall keep it unto life eternal'.

8. *Followed thee up* Cp. Rev. 14. 13: 'Blessed are the dead which die in the Lord . . . their works do follow them'. In *CD* i 13 M. argues that the soul dies with the body and is resurrected with it. Either he was not yet a mortalist in 1646, or he chose not to obtrude his views into this sonnet.

9. *knew them best* best knew them to be.

12. *spake*] *TMS* (all three drafts); speak *1673*.

on glorious themes] *1673* and *TMS* fair copy; in glorious themes *TMS* first two drafts. H. J. C. Grierson, in TLS (15 January 1925) 40, prefers 'in' to 'on' and argues that *themes* has the musical sense 'strains'. Most editors follow him. There may be a musical pun, but M. has *spake* (not 'sang'). Since the speakers are Catharine Thomason's good works, M. may pun on *theme* as 'a subject treated by action (instead of by discourse)' (*OED* 1b).

14. *And drink . . . streams* Ps. 36. 8–9, Rev. 22. 1 and 17.

Sonnet XV. On the Late Massacre in Piedmont

Date: May? 1655. The sect known as the Vaudois or Waldensians had been persecuted since its foundation in the twelfth century. Protestants in M.'s time believed that the sect was even older, and that it retained Apostolic purity. The Vaudois lived in Alpine villages in France and Italy. On the

Italian side they lived in the territories of the Duke of Savoy. In 1561 the Duke had granted them the right to dwell in the valleys of the Pellice and the Angrogna, in Piedmont, but they had spread to other villages excluded by the treaty. In April 1655 an army was sent to expel the encroaching Vaudois, who fled to the hills. The army pursued, razing villages in the tolerated area. On 24 April the Duke's Piedmontese, French and Irish troops massacred the villagers and committed such atrocities as hurling women and children from precipices. Over 1,700 Vaudois were killed. Protestant Europe was outraged and Cromwell contemplated a military expedition. This became unnecessary when the Vaudois defeated their oppressors in July, and the Duke reaffirmed the 1561 treaty (18 August). As Cromwell's Secretary, M. composed several letters in which Cromwell voiced his protest and urged other Protestant powers to intervene. The only text of the sonnet is that of *1673*.

1. *Avenge* Cp. Rev. 6. 9–10: 'the souls of them that were slain for the word of God . . . cried with a loud voice, saying, How long, O Lord, holy and true, dost thou not judge and avenge our blood?' Cp. also Luke 18. 17: 'shall not God avenge his own elect?'

saints true believers.

1–2. *bones / Lie scattered* Cp. Ps. 141. 7: 'Our bones are scattered at the grave's mouth'.

3. *kept . . . of old* So in *Likeliest Means* M. praises 'those ancientest reformed churches of the *Waldenses,* if they rather continu'd not pure since the apostles' (*YP* 7. 291).

4. *stocks and stones* gods of wood and stone. Cp. Jer. 2. 27 and 3. 29 (but the phrase had long been proverbial, *OED* 'stock' sb¹ 1d).

5. *thy book* Cp. Rev. 20. 12: 'the dead were judged out of those things which were written in the books, according to their works'.

6. *thy sheep* Cp. Rom. 8. 35–6 (citing Ps. 44. 22): 'Who shall separate us from the love of Christ? shall tribulation, or distress, or persecution . . . or peril, or sword? As it is written, For thy sake we are killed all the day long; We are accounted as sheep for the slaughter'.

7–8. *rolled / Mother with infant* Sir Samuel Morland, who carried Cromwell's protest to the Duke of Savoy, confirms the atrocity in his *History of the Evangelical Churches of the Valleys of Piedmont* (1658) 363, 368, 374.

10. *martyred blood . . . sow* Cp. Tertullian's famous maxim that 'the blood of the martyrs is the seed of the Church'. The *hundredfold* (13) crop also recalls the parable of the sower, some of whose seeds fell onto good soil and brought forth fruit 'an hundredfold' (Matt. 13. 3). Editors also see an allusion to Cadmus, who sowed dragons' teeth from which grew armed men.

11. *sway* implying 'tyranny *and* instability' (Hill 209).

12. *triple Tyrant* the Pope with his three-tiered crown.
14. *Early* *before it is too late (*OED* 5a).

Babylonian woe Protestants commonly identified the Babylon of Revelation with papal Rome. Jay Ruud (*MQ* 26, October 1992, 80–81) compares Ps. 137. 8–9: 'O daughter of Babylon, who art to be destroyed; / Happy shall he be, that rewardeth thee / As thou hast served us. / Happy shall he be, that taketh and dasheth thy little ones / Against the stones'. Ruud infers that M. is advocating 'appropriate "eye for an eye" justice' (see lines 7–8) 'rather than a universal Armageddon'. The allusion does imply counter-atrocities, but M. does not say who should inflict them. He counsels the Vaudois to *fly*, not fight. Cp. Rom. 12. 19: 'Dearly beloved, avenge not yourselves, but rather give place unto wrath: for it is written, Vengeance is mine; I will repay, saith the Lord'.

Sonnet XVI ('When I consider how my light is spent')

Date: much debated, but M. obviously wrote the sonnet after he had lost his sight in 1652. The only text is that of *1673*.

1. *When I consider* a common sonnet opening. Cp. Henry Lok's 'When I consider of the holy band', and Shakespeare, Sonnet XV: 'When I consider every thing that grows'.
   light eyesight (*OED* 4).
   spent extinguished.
2. *Ere half my days* M. was forty-three in 1652 – more than halfway through the biblical lifespan of seventy years. Critics have suggested that *days* means 'working days', or conjectured that M. may have expected to live as long as his father, who had been eighty-four when he died in 1647.
3. *that one talent* literary talent, with a punning allusion to the parable of the talents (Matt. 25. 14–30). M. modestly claims only one talent, not five or two. The man who received one talent hid it, and was cast into 'outer darkness'.
4. *useless* including a pun on 'usury'. Cp. the Lord's rebuke of the man who hid his talent: 'I should have received mine own with usury' (Matt. 25. 27).
7. *light* both 'eyesight' and 'daylight'. Notice *day-labour* and cp. John 9. 4: 'I must work the works of him that sent me, while it is day: the night cometh, when no man can work'. Jesus spoke these words just before curing a blind man. Cp. also the parable of the vineyard (Matt. 20. 1–16). Some day-labourers worked for a full day, others for only part of the day, yet all received the same wages.
8. *fondly* foolishly.

prevent forestall (*OED* 5).

9. *murmur* complaint (*OED* 2).

11. *mild yoke* Cp. Matt. 11. 30: 'my yoke is easy'.

state splendour befitting high rank (*OED* 17b).

12-14. *Thousands . . . wait* Cp. Spenser's angels in *A Hymne of Heavenly Love*: 'There they in their trinall triplicities / About him wait, and on his wit depend, / Either with nimble wings to cut the skies, / When he them on his messages doth send, / Or on his owne dread presence to attend' (64-8). Medieval angelologists distinguished between higher angels, who never leave God's presence, and lower ones who execute his will. Protestants recognized no such distinction. In *PL* even the greatest angels carry God's messages.

14. *wait* including 'be in readiness to receive orders' (*OED* 9a) and 'place one's hope in God' (*OED* 14h).

Sonnet XVII ('Lawrence of virtuous father virtuous son')

On 17 December 1651 M. moved from Scotland Yard to a new house in Petty France, Westminster. There, says his nephew and biographer Edward Phillips, he frequently received visitors, including 'young *Laurence* (the Son of him that was President of *Oliver's* Council) to whom there is a Sonnet among the rest, in his Printed Poems' (Darbishire 74). Edward Lawrence (1633-57) was the elder son of Henry Lawrence (1600-1664), who became President of Cromwell's Council of State in 1654. M. praises Henry Lawrence in *Defensio Secunda*. His studious son became an MP in November 1656 and died the following year, aged twenty-four. M.'s sonnet could have been written in any winter between 1651-2 and 1656-7. The only text is that of *1673*.

1. *of virtuous father virtuous son* Cp. Horace, *Odes* I xvi 1: *O matre pulchra ilia pulchrior* ('O lovelier daughter of a lovely mother').

4. *waste* both 'spend time', referring to *day*, and 'diminish one's store of', referring to *what may be won* (both *OED* 8).

5. *season* winter.

gaining advancing.

6. *Favonius* Zephyrus, the west wind. Horace invokes Favonius and the delights of spring in *Odes* I iv. In *Odes* IV xii he describes spring in a poem of invitation.

re-inspire including 'breathe upon once more'.

8. *lily . . . spun* Cp. Matt. 6. 28-9: 'Consider the lilies of the field, how they grow; they toil not, neither do they spin: and yet I say unto you, That even Solomon in all his glory was not arrayed like one of these'.

9. *neat* elegant, tasteful, simple.

10. *Of Attic taste* such as the Athenians, with their simple and refined tastes, would have enjoyed.

12. *Tuscan air* Italian song.

13–14. *spare / To interpose them oft* a famous crux. Some take *spare* to mean 'forbear' (*OED* 6c), and so infer that M. is advising Lawrence to enjoy himself, but not too often. Others take *spare* to mean 'spare time for' (*OED* 8c), and so infer that M. is advocating frequent delights. Yet others see deliberate ambiguity. Niall Rudd (*Hermathena* 158, 1995, 109–15) makes a strong case for 'forbear' when he points out that no one has ever produced a parallel case of 'spare' meaning 'spare time for', with the infinitive and without a noun like 'time'. Rudd sees 'a *judicious* invitation' (111), modelled on the last two lines of Horace, *Odes* IV xii, which advise Virgil to relax from his serious concerns for 'a brief moment' as 'an occasional holiday'.

Sonnet XVIII ('Cyriack, whose grandsire on the Royal Bench')

Date: 1655? Cyriack Skinner (1627–1700) may have been one of M.'s pupils in the 1640s (Aubrey refers to him in his life of Harrington as a 'scolar to John Milton'). He was certainly M.'s close friend in the 1650s. Edward Phillips singles him out 'above all' others that visited M.'s house in Petty France (Darbishire 74). Skinner was prominent in the Rota, a republican debating club set up in 1659. His political views accorded with M.'s. The only complete text of the sonnet is from *1673*, but a scribal copy of lines 5–14 survives in *TMS*. Peter Beal has identified the handwriting as Skinner's own. Beal also identifies Skinner as the author of the anonymous early life of M. that Darbishire attributed to John Phillips. See *Index of English Literary Manuscripts* II ii (1993) 85–6.

1. *grandsire* Skinner's maternal grandfather was Sir Edward Coke (1552–1664), the most celebrated lawyer of his age, and Chief Justice of the King's Bench from 1613 to 1616, when he was removed from office for opposing the royal prerogative. Coke was famed for defending Parliament's privileges against kings and archbishops.

2. *Themis* Greek goddess of justice.

3. *volumes* Coke's legal works included the *Reports* and *Institutes of the Laws of England*.

4. *others* other judges.

5. *resolve* an imperative ('Today resolve to drench deep thoughts with me'). *drench* drown (*OED* 2), with wine.

6. *that after no repenting draws* that doesn't entail any regrets.

7. *Let . . . pause* 'put aside, for the moment, your studies of mathematics and physics'.

8. *what . . . the French* referring to Skinner's political interests. *The Swede* is probably Charles X, who invaded Poland in 1655. (The mode of designation was idiomatic, as in 'Hamlet the Dane'.) *The French* alludes to the war between France and Spain, and perhaps to the Treaty of Westminster (24 October 1655), by which Cromwell established friendly relations with France. Editors compare Horace, *Odes* II xi 1–4. Cp. also Horace's advice to Maecenas in III xxix 25–9: 'concerned for the City, you fear / what the Seres may do next, or Bactra / (once ruled by Cyrus), or the dissident Don'.

intend] *1673*; intends *TMS*. *1673*'s subjunctive is more suggestive of Coffee House conjectures.

9. *betimes* while there is yet time.

11. *a time ordains* Cp. Eccles. 3. 1: 'To every thing there is a season, and a time to every purpose under the heaven'.

Sonnet XIX ('Methought I saw')

Date: 1658? Modern critics have debated the identity of the wife described in this sonnet. The traditional view (unquestioned until 1945) holds that the sonnet is about M.'s second wife, Katherine Woodcock, who died in February 1658 after giving birth in October 1657 to a daughter Katherine (who died six weeks after her mother). Some critics think that the subject is Mary Powell, M.'s first wife, who died in May 1652, three days after giving birth to her third daughter, Deborah. The reference to ritual purification (5–6) can support either identification. Only Katherine lived long enough to be purified, but M.'s simile might be a dream-reversal of fact. A likely pun on 'Katherine' (see 9*n*) supports the traditional identification. M.'s second marriage was happy. His first marriage was unhappy, at least in its beginnings. Those who see Mary as the sonnet's subject assume that she and M. were reconciled.

1. *Methought I saw* Cp. Ralegh's sonnet on Spenser's *Faerie Queene*, 'Methought I saw the grave where Laura lay' (1590), and William Smith's 'Methought I saw the nymph I would embrace' (*Chloris*, 1596, no. 13). Cp. also Adam's dream of Eve beginning 'methought I saw' (*PL* viii 462f.), and see below 13–14*n*.

late espousèd either 'recently married' or 'recently deceased wife', or both. The first meaning could not apply to Mary Powell.

2. *Alcestis* In Euripides' *Alcestis*, Admetus is permitted to escape death if he can persuade someone else to die for him. His wife Alcestis volunteers,

on condition that Admetus never remarry. While the palace mourns, Heracles (*Jove's great son*) arrives as a guest. Admetus hides his loss and plays host. Heracles discovers the truth, wrestles with Death, and rescues Alcestis. He then restores her, veiled, to Admetus, who receives her, not knowing who she is. Admetus is overjoyed when he lifts the veil, but Alcestis must remain silent until she is ritually cleansed.

5. *as whom* as one whom.

6. *old Law* See Lev. 12. 4–8. After the birth of a daughter, a woman was deemed to be unclean for eighty days. She could not enter the Temple during that period.

did save The Mosaic ritual included 'atonement' (Lev. 12. 7), but M. plays on the higher sense of Christian salvation.

7. *yet once more* See *Lycidas* 1 n.

9. *all in white* Cp. the Church as bride of Christ: 'to her was granted that she should be arrayed in fine linen, clean and white: for the fine linen is the righteousness of saints'.

pure as her mind E. S. Le Comte (*N&Q* 1, 1954, 245–6) hears a pun on 'Katherine' (Greek *katharos*, 'pure').

10. *Her face was veiled* like that of Alcestis; but M. (unlike Admetus) recognizes his wife in spite of the veil. M. was blind throughout his second marriage, so a veil would have special poignancy if Katherine were the poem's subject. M. had seen her only with *fancied sight* (Smart).

13–14. *But O . . . she fled* M.'s failed *embrace* has numerous epic precedents, the closest being Aeneas's three attempts to embrace the shade of his wife Creusa (Virgil, *Aen.* ii 789–95) and Achilles' one attempt to embrace the shade of Patroclus, who appears to him in a dream (Homer, *Il.* xxiii 99–107). Cp. also *Od.* xi 204–9 (Odysseus and his mother), *Aen.* vi 700–702 (Aeneas and Anchises), and *Purg.* ii 80–81 (Dante and Casella). Cp. also *PL* viii 478, where Eve 'disappeared, and left [Adam] dark'. Adam wakes expecting to be alone, 'When out of hope, behold her, not far off, / Such as I saw her in my dream' (481–2).

14. *day brought back my night* night and day are reversed for a blind man who sees only in his dreams.

The Fifth Ode of Horace

Date: guesses range from 1629 to 1655. Critics also disagree about the poem's quality. Some find it stiff, but Martindale (42–6) sees signs of M.'s mature mastery. The only text is that of *1673*.

1. *odours* perfumes (*OED* 2).

8. *admire* wonder at.

9. *credulous, all gold* credulously believing that you are all gold (all beauty and virtue).

10. *vacant* without other lovers (modifying *thee*).

11. *flattering* of the weather: delusively encouraging hope (*OED* 2b).

gales winds, possibly breezes (cp. *PL* iv 156).

13–14. *vowed / Picture* votive tablet, containing the poet's image, and hung as a thanks-offering on the wall of Neptune's temple. The poet is grateful for having survived the shipwreck of his love for Pyrrha.

15. *weeds* clothing.

On the New Forcers of Conscience under the Long Parliament

Date: spring or summer 1646? In 1643 the Long Parliament had decided to replace episcopacy with a new form of Church government. Parliament established the Westminster Assembly of Divines to reorganize the Church. A large majority of the Assembly were Presbyterians. The Independent minority pleaded for the rights of the individual conscience, but the majority refused to grant liberty of dissent. The issue was debated from 1644 to 1646, both in the Assembly and in pamphlets. On 28 August 1646 Parliament established the ordination of ministers by Classical Presbyteries. M.'s poem was probably written in anticipation of that event, rather than as a response to it (see below, 15*n*).

The poem is a *sonetto caudato* ('tailed sonnet'), M.'s only example of the form. M.'s sonnet has two 'tails', each consisting of a half-line and a couplet. Italian poets used tailed sonnets for humorous or satirical subjects. Texts: *1673* and *TMS*.

Title. The *TMS* title is 'On the Forcers of Conscience'.

1. *thrown off* Episcopacy was not formally abolished until 9 October 1646, but Parliament had resolved to abolish it in 1643, declaring that government by archbishops and bishops 'is evil' and shall 'be taken away'.

lord Honigmann (197) hears a pun on 'Laud', referring to Archbishop William Laud.

2. *renounced his liturgy* The Assembly forbade use of the Book of Common Prayer in 1645.

3. *widowed whore plurality* Pluralism was the practice of securing income from more than one benefice at a time. Presbyterians had condemned Anglican ministers for the abuse, but were quick to practise it themselves.

4. *abhorred* playing on *whore*.

5. *adjure* entreat, with overtones of 'impose an oath upon another' (*OED* 1). *civil sword* authority of the state.

7. *ride* tyrannize over.

classic referring to the *classis* or presbytery, a body of elders acting as a disciplinary court in the Presbyterian system. Presbyterians had called episcopacy 'the hierarchy', so *classic hierarchy* implies that there is little to choose between the two systems.

8. *A.S.* Adam Stewart, a Scottish Presbyterian resident in London in the 1640s. He signed his pamphlets with his initials.

Rutherford Samuel Rutherford, one of four Scottish members on the Assembly of Divines.

11. *named* declared to be (*OED* 2c).

12. *shallow*] *1673*; 'hare-brained' corr. to 'shallow' *TMS*.

Edwards Thomas Edwards, an English Presbyterian. He attacked M.'s divorce pamphlets in *Gangraena* (1646).

Scotch What-d'ye-call often identified (without evidence) as Robert Baillie, a Scottish Commissioner on the Assembly who had attacked M.'s divorce pamphlets in *Dissuasive from the Errors of the Time* (1645).

14. *packings*] *TMS*; packing *1673*. M. may mean packed votes or more general 'fraudulent dealings' (*OED* sb² 1).

Trent the Council of Trent (1545–63), notorious among all Protestants.

15. *Parliament* The Presbyterians in Parliament had lost ground to the Independents between August 1645 and May 1646, so in the spring of 1646 M. had some cause to hope that Parliament might *succour our just fears* (18), even though Parliament had established the Westminster Assembly. On 21 April 1646 the Commons rebuked the Assembly and resolved that Parliament alone could grant or withhold toleration. M. may have hoped for more, but the Presbyterians began to recover their domination after 5 May 1646, when the King took refuge with the Scots. The Westminster Assembly was eventually abolished by the Rump Parliament on 22 February 1649.

17. *Clip your . . . ears*] *TMS* at first had: 'Crop ye as close as marginal P—'s ears', thus clearly alluding to William Prynne, whose ears had twice been cropped (most recently, in 1637 for attacking the bishops). M. had once admired Prynne, but he became disillusioned when Prynne opposed toleration and M.'s divorce pamphlets (*YP* 2. 722–3).

phylacteries small boxes containing sacred scriptures, worn on the forehead by pious Jews; here (as in Matt. 23. 5) a metaphor for self-righteous ostentation.

balk pass over. Lines 15–17 mean: 'so that Parliament will put an end to your pharisaical hypocrisy, though they won't cut your ears off (as Laud would have done)'.

19. *they* Parliament. *TMS* at first had 'you'.

20. *writ large written out in full (*OED* 'large' adv. 4). Etymologically, *priest* is a contracted form of *Presbyter*.

PSALM PARAPHRASES ADDED IN 1673

Psalms I–VIII

Date: 1653. M. translated these psalms from the Hebrew in 1653, when he had been blind for a year and a half. His blindness clearly influenced his rendering of *Psalm VI* 14, where he says his eye 'is waxen old and dark'. No other versifier of this psalm uses the word 'dark'. A.V. has 'Mine eye is consumed'. The *Terzetti* of Psalm II are *terza rima*.

Psalms LXXX–LXXXVIII

M. translated these psalms in April 1648, when there was much controversy over the metrical psalter. M.'s marginal notes supply the literal Hebrew, or a translation of it, at points where his own translation paraphrases. The following notes attempt to elucidate M.'s notes.

Psalm LXXX

11. *Awake   Gnorera* means 'arouse'.
19. *smoking wrath   Gnashanta* means 'you are smoking'.
23. *largely   Shalish* means 'third of a measure'.
27–8. *laugh . . . throw   Jilgnagu* means 'mock'.

Psalm LXXXI

29. *in thunder deep   Besether ragnam* means 'in the secret place of thunder'.

Psalm LXXXII

1. *great assembly   Bagnadath–el* means 'assembly of God'.
3. *Among . . . hands   Bekerev* means 'in the midst of'.
5–6. *pervert . . . wrong   Tishphetu gnavel* means 'judge falsely'.
9–10. *regard . . . cause   Shiphtu-dal* means 'judge the poor'.
19–20. *moved . . . out of order gone   Jimmotu* means 'moved'.
25–6. *judge . . . redress   Shophta* means 'judge'.

Psalm LXXXIII

5-6. *swell . . . storm outrageously Jehemajun* means 'are in tumult'.

9-10. *contrive . . . plots and counsels Jagnarimu Sod* means 'deliberate cunningly'.

11. *Them to ensnare Jithjagnatsu gnal* means 'conspire against'.

12. *Whom . . . hide and keep Tsephuneca* means 'your hidden things'.

17. *with all their might Lev jachdau* means 'together with one heart'.

47-8. *God's houses . . . stately palaces* M.'s note (*Neoth Elohim bears both*) means that the Hebrew phrase can be rendered by either English phrase. This is true of *Elohim,* which means 'God', and can also be used as a superlative. *Neoth,* however, means 'pastures' (as in Ps. 23).

Psalm LXXXVIII

31-2. *Thou break'st . . . break me* M.'s note (*The* Heb. *bears both*) claims that either line 31 or line 32 would be a correct translation. Only line 31 is correct.

59. *shake* The meaning of the Hebrew word is disputed. M.'s Latin note (*Prae Concussione*) translates his own English text. The Hebrew word can be taken to mean 'youth', as in A.V. 'from my youth up'.

UNCOLLECTED ENGLISH POEMS

The four sonnets included here express republican views and so may have been unpublishable in *1673*. All four appear in *TMS* (the text followed here). They were published (in a mangled form) after M.'s death in *Letters of State* (1694), edited by Edward Phillips. I have noted the *1694* variants only when they would significantly alter the meaning.

On the Lord General Fairfax at the Siege of Colchester

Date: July–August 1648. Sir Thomas Fairfax won many victories for Parliament in the Civil War. After commanding the right wing at Marston Moor (July 1644), he was made Commander-in-Chief of the New Model Army (January 1645). He crushed the King's forces at Naseby (June 1645), capturing a Royalist standard with his own hands. In 1648 several concerted

Royalist risings initiated the Second Civil War. Fairfax drove the Royalists out of Kent, and laid siege to Colchester (13 June). The town fell on 27 August. M.'s sonnet was evidently written after the Scots invaded England (8 July) and probably before news came of their defeat by Cromwell at Preston (17 August). Fairfax's star waned in later months. Though a commissioner for the King's trial, he disapproved of his execution, and resigned as Commander-in-Chief when he was ordered to lead the army against Charles II in 1650.

3. *jealous* including 'suspicious, fearful' (*OED* 5).

5. *virtue*] *TMS*; valour *1694*. 'Virtue' here includes 'courage, valour' (*OED* 7).

6. *though*] *TMS*; while *1694*.

6-7. *rebellions . . . Hydra heads* The Hydra was a many-headed serpent killed by Hercules. When one head was cut off, two more grew in its place. *displays* spreads out as a banner or like a dragon's *wings*. Cp. Spenser, *FQ* I xi 10.

7-8. *false North . . . broken league* The Scots (who had been Parliament's allies) invaded England in support of the King on 8 July 1648. The invasion violated the Solemn League and Covenant (1643). The proximity of *North* to *serpent* associates Scotland with Satan, whose throne was in the North (Isa. 14. 13; cp. *PL* v 689, 726).

8. *imp . . . wings* engraft feathers onto a bird's wing so as to improve its powers of flight (*OED* 'imp' 4). Hydras were not winged, but a controverted word in Euripides' *Ion* 195 may have suggested that they were.

their] *TMS*; her *1694*.

10. *war, but endless*] *TMS*; war, but acts of *1694*.

still continually.

11. *truth, and right*] *TMS*; injured truth *1694*.

12. *public faith* Honigmann shows that the phrase referred to a much-resented 'form of National Debt'. Parliament had borrowed money from private creditors 'on the public faith', and used the same catch-phrase to fob off the army, whose pay was in arrears. M. condemns Parliament's abuse of '*The Publick Faith*' in his *Character of the Long Parliament* (*YP* 5. 444).

To the Lord General Cromwell, May 1652

The sonnet addresses Cromwell as a member of the Committee for the Propagation of the Gospel (hence the full *TMS* title, followed in this edition). The Committee had been appointed on 10 February 1652 to settle the state of religion in England. On 18 February John Owen and other

Independents on the Committee proposed to set up an Established Church, with a paid clergy, and with certain limits to liberty of dissent. M. urges Cromwell to defend religious liberty, and to make no provision for a stipendiary clergy.

1. *who through a cloud*] *TMS*; that through a crowd *1694*. M.'s *cloud* recalls Aeneas enduring a 'war-cloud' (*nubem belli*) of javelins (Virgil, *Aen.* x 809). Cp. also Marvell, 'An Horatian Ode' (1650), which describes Cromwell as lightning 'Breaking the clouds where it was nursed' (14).

2. *detractions*] *TMS*; distractions *1694*. Cromwell was a target for slanders, but M. might also be punning on the now obsolete sense of 'detractions' as 'delays' (*OED* 3). Cromwell had forced the King's execution through Parliament.

4. *peace and truth* The words 'Truth and Peace' appeared on a coin issued by Parliament to honour Cromwell's victories at Preston, Dunbar and Worcester (Hughes). They were a catch-phrase among the Parliamentarians (Honigmann 146–7).

5. *neck of crownèd Fortune* alluding to the execution of Charles I. Cp. Josh. 10. 24: 'Come near, put your feet upon the necks of these kings'. Phillips wisely omitted the line from *1694*.

6. *reared God's trophies* alluding to the ancient Greek custom of raising monuments of victory on a battlefield.

7. *Darwen* a small stream near Preston, where Cromwell routed the Scottish Covenanters under the Duke of Hamilton (17–19 August 1648).

　imbrued stained with blood.

8. *Dunbar* where Cromwell defeated the Covenanters under Leslie (3 September 1650).

9. *Worcester's laureate wreath* Cromwell crushed the Covenanters under Charles II at Worcester on 3 September 1651. He described the battle as his 'crowning mercy'.

12. *secular chains* alluding to the proposals that Parliament should enforce the limits of religious toleration.

14. *hireling* The proposals of 1652 provided for a stipendiary clergy, paid by the government. M. believed that ministers should support themselves. Cp. John 10. 13: 'The hireling fleeth, because he is an hireling, and careth not for the sheep'.

　wolves Matt. 7. 15, Acts 20. 29. Cp. *PL* iv 183–93, xii 508–11.

　maw belly, appetite. Cp. Phil. 3. 19: 'whose God is their belly'.

To Sir Henry Vane the Younger

Date: June–July 1652. The sonnet was first published in George Sikes's *Life and Death of Sir Henry Vane* (1662) 93–4, where it is introduced by the words: 'The Character of this deceased Statesman . . . I shall exhibite to you in a paper of Verses, composed by a learned Gentleman, and sent him, *July* 3. 1652'. The sonnet also appears in *TMS*, in the hand of an amanuensis, and with the present title (crossed through). Phillips's text (*1694*) is very poor.

Sir Henry Vane (1613–62) was called 'the Younger' to distinguish him from his father, who lived until 1655. Vane had been Governor of Massachusetts (1635–7) and Treasurer of the Navy (1639–50). His good services in the latter capacity prepared the way for Blake's victories over the Dutch. In Parliament, Vane always championed the Puritan cause, and as a lay member of the Assembly of Divines (from 1643) he advocated religious toleration. He disapproved of the King's execution, but joined the Council of State soon afterwards. He finally broke with Cromwell in 1653 when Cromwell dissolved the Long Parliament. He was executed in 1662 after the King's Restoration.

1. *young . . . counsel old* Cp. Sylvester, *DWW*, *The Fathers* (1608) 109: '*Isaac*, in yeares young, but in wisedome growne'. Vane was nearly forty in 1652; M. was forty-three.

2. *senator* from Latin *senex*, 'old', playing against *young* (Honigmann).

3. *helm* of the ship of state.

   gowns togas worn by Roman senators. The phrase *gowns not arms* alludes to the ancient maxim *cedant arma togae* ('let arms yield to the toga'), quoted by Cicero in *De Officiis* I xxii 77.

4. *fierce Epirot* Pyrrhus, King of Epirus, invaded Italy in 280 BC. He often defeated the Romans, but could not break their spirit. M. in *Defensio Secunda* says that Appius Claudius 'delivered Italy from Pyrrhus' by opposing his peace proposals with a stirring speech in the Senate (*YP* 4. 585).

   the African Hannibal invaded Italy in 219 BC and inflicted numerous defeats on the Romans. M. praises the Senate's spirit of resistance in *Areopagitica* (*YP* 2. 557).

6. *drift* scheme, plot (*OED* 5).

   hollow insincere, false (*OED* 5), with a pun on 'Holland' (as *states* puns on 'States-General'). Shots had been exchanged between the English and Dutch fleets in May 1652, but the Dutch ambassadors remained in London until 30 June, claiming to want peace. Many suspected them of espionage.

   spelled discovered by close observation (*OED* v² 2a).

7. *upheld* once assented to (*OED* 4), with overtones of 'kept from sinking'

(*OED* 1). *Move* and *equipage* carry on the image of war as a launched ship. Vane had prepared the navy.

8. *nerves* sinews (thought to be the source of strength).

iron and gold M. in his Commonplace Book twice noted Machiavelli's dictum (*Discorsi* ii 10) that iron, not gold, is the sinew (*il nervo*) of war (*YP* 1. 414–15, 498). M. might also be referring to a defiant utterance by one of the Dutch ambassadors on 30 June 1652: 'The English are about to attack a mountain of gold; we are about to attack a mountain of iron' (Honigmann).

9. *equipage* apparatus of war, tackle of a ship (*OED* 3).

12. *either sword* the civil and the spiritual power. In *Observations on the Articles of Peace* M. identifies the spiritual sword as 'the Word of God' (*YP* 3. 324).

To Mr Cyriack Skinner upon his Blindness

Date: early 1655 or late 1654 (see lines 1–3). On Skinner, see headnote to *Sonnet XVIII* ('Cyriack, whose grandsire'). The present edition follows *TMS* except for the title, which is found only in *1694*. The *TMS* copy is in a hand that Peter Beal has identified as Skinner's own. See headnote to *Sonnet XVIII*.

1. *this three years' day* for the past three years (*OED* 'day' 11). The idiom does not imply an anniversary of the day when M. lost his sight.

1–2. *clear . . . spot* M. took pride in his personal appearance. In *Defensio Secunda* (*YP* 4. 583) he insists that blindness had not disfigured him – an opinion confirmed by Skinner in what is now known to be his biography of M. (Darbishire 32).

3. *light* eyesight (*OED* 4).

4. *orbs* eyes (*OED* 10). In earlier usage, the word implied a Petrarchan conceit of eyes as stars, as in 'her bright Eyes (the Orbes which Beauty move)' (Drummond). M.'s *idle orbs* are implicitly contrasted with *sun or moon or star* (5).

doth sight appear] *TMS*; doth day appear *1694*. Cp. *PL* iii 41–2: 'but not to me returns / Day'.

7. *bate a jot*] *TMS*; bate one jot *1694*. lessen the least part. Cp. Shakespeare, *Coriolanus* II ii 144–5: 'neither will they bate / One jot of ceremony'.

8. *bear up* uphold principles (*OED* 21a), *keep up courage (*OED* 21c, earliest instance 1656). The context (*steer / Right onward*) also invites a play on the nautical sense 'bring the helm "up" so as to sail against the wind' (*OED* 37).

9. *Right onward*] Uphillward *TMS* 1st reading.

10. *conscience* including 'inward knowledge' (*OED* 1a).

*overplied overworked, with a pun on 'ply' in the nautical sense 'beat up against the wind' (*OED* v² 6).

11. *In liberty's defence* In *Defensio Secunda* M. reports that his physicians had warned him that he would lose his sight if he answered Salmasius's *Defensio Regia*. M. chose to do his duty, even though it would cost him his sight (*YP* 4. 588).

12. *all Europe talks*] *TMS*; all Europe rings *1694*. John Aubrey reports that 'the only inducement of severall foreigners that came over into England, was chiefly to see O. Protector & Mr. J. Milton, . . . he was much more admired abrode then at home' (Darbishire 7).

13. *masque* masquerade, false show, with overtones of Royalist court masques.

14. *had I no better guide* implying that M. does have a better guide, in Heaven. *1694* reads 'other guide'.

'Fix Here . . .'

Date: April 1638? M. wrote this curious little poem of two lines on the back of a brief letter sent him by Henry Lawes. The letter contained M.'s exit visa and was therefore probably written just before M. went abroad in April 1638. The letter was discovered with M.'s Commonplace Book and was first published in 1876.

1. **overdated OED*'s earliest instance is from *Of Reformation* (1641), where M. expresses his contempt for 'overdated Ceremonies'. 'Overdated' there means 'out of date' or 'gone on too long'.

TRANSLATIONS FROM THE PROSE WORKS

From Of Reformation *(1641)*

All three translations allude to the Donation of Constantine, by which the Emperor Constantine was believed to have endowed Pope Sylvester I with the western part of his empire. M. believed that Constantine's gift had 'marr'd all in the Church' (*YP* 1. 558). He cites Dante, Petrarch and Ariosto as Roman Catholic poets who shared his view.

From The Reason of Church Government *(1641)*

The line translates a favourite saying of the Emperor Tiberius. Several ancient sources report the saying, and Jonson quotes it in *Sejanus* II 330. The ultimate source may be Euripides' lost play, *Bellerophon.* M. in his prose tract attributes Tiberius's cruel selfishness to the bishops, who would drag down the monarchy with them 'in a generall ruine' (*YP* 1. 770).

From An Apology for Smectymnuus *(1642)*

M. cites Horace and Sophocles to justify his satirical and harsh treatment of the bishops (*YP* 1. 904–5).

(v) 3. *junkets* sweetmeats. *knacks* choice dishes.

From the title-page of Areopagitica *(1644)*

M.'s version of Euripides is not quite so embracing of freedom as is the original Greek. Where Euripides extends free speech to anyone who 'wishes' to advise the city, M. speaks of those who 'can, and will' offer advice. M.'s 'can' is potentially restrictive for it implies that there are some who are unable (and so, perhaps, unfit) to 'advise the public', even if they want to do so.

From Tetrachordon *(1645)*

M. cites Horace in his divorce pamphlet because he wants to expose the hypocrisy of those who 'care only to live by the outward constraint of law', when they ought to follow 'the inward and uncompell'd actions of vertue' (*YP* 2. 639).

From The Tenure of Kings and Magistrates *(1649)*

M.'s pamphlet appeared on 13 February 1649, a fortnight after King Charles's execution, which it defended. Seneca's lines are spoken by Hercules after he has killed the tyrant Lycus.

From The History of Britain *(1670)*

The first four books of M.'s *History* were written in 1649. Passages (xi) and (xii) are translations of Geoffrey of Monmouth, *Historia Regum Britanniae* I xi. In (xi) Brutus prays to Diana; in (xii) Diana replies. Brutus is the mythical Trojan founder of Britain.

Passage (xiii) is taken from the medieval chronicle, *Flores Historiarum*. The murder of the child-king Kenelm is related in the account of AD 821. A dove miraculously appeared above the altar of St Peter's in Rome, and dropped a note revealing the location of Kenelm's body. M.'s lines translate a Latin version of the note. M. himself dismisses the story with contempt (*YP* 5. 252).

PARADISE LOST

M.'s great epic is the culmination of two ambitions. Since his youth M. had wanted to write an epic. He refers to the hope in *Elegia VI, Mansus, Epitaphium Damonis* and elsewhere – but his plan had been to write an Arthuriad. He had also planned to write a tragedy about the Fall of Man. Edward Phillips reports that part of Satan's address to the sun (iv 32–41) was shown to him 'several Years before the Poem was begun', when it was intended to be 'the very beginning' of a tragedy (Darbishire 72). Aubrey reports that M. began writing *PL* in earnest in about 1658 and finished in about 1663 (Darbishire 13). The invocation to book vii was clearly written after the Restoration.

When first published in 1667, *PL* was a poem of ten books. Critics often see this ten-book scheme as a vestige of M.'s original dramatic design, a double five-act structure. An alternative model is Tasso's twenty-book epic *Gerusalemme Liberata*, to which M. often alludes in *PL*. For the second edition of 1674, M. split books vii and x into two, thus creating a twelve-book epic. His model here is Virgil's twelve-book *Aeneid*. Homer's *Iliad* and *Odyssey* each have twenty-four books, so the second edition of *PL* has the same relation to them as the first edition had had to *Jerusalem Delivered*.

The Verse, line 4. *invention of a barbarous age* Latin poets first began to use rhyme in Christian hymns of the fifth and sixth centuries.
line 14. *apt numbers* appropriate rhythm.
   quantity number.
line 21. *the first in English* An exaggeration. The Earl of Surrey, who

introduced blank verse into England, had used it in his translation of selections of Virgil's *Aeneid* (an *heroic poem*).

BOOK I

The Argument, line **9**. *centre* (centre of) the earth.

line **10**. *yet not made* Our universe was created after Satan fell from Heaven (vii 131–5), but before he escaped from Hell (ii 830–32, 1004–6).

line **11**. *utter* utter and outer.

line **23**. *angels . . . Fathers* Cp. *CD* i 7: 'many of the Greek Fathers, and some of the Latin, were of the opinion that angels . . . existed long before this world' (trans. Carey, *YP* 6. 313). Fathers who shared M.'s view included Jerome, Origen, Gregory of Nazianzen, Basil, and Chrysostom.

1. *man's* mankind's and Adam's (*Adam* in Hebrew means 'man').

   fruit including 'consequences'.

4. *one greater man* Christ, the Second Adam (Romans 5. 19). Homer (*Od.* i 1) and Virgil (*Aen.* i 1) had sung of one 'man'; M. will sing of two.

6–16. The identity of M.'s *Muse* remains a mystery, despite attempts to see her as Father, Son, or Holy Spirit. M.'s widow identified her as 'God's grace, and the Holy Spirit' (Newton lvi). See below, 17*n*. See also iii 19*n*, vii 1–12, and ix 21–4.

8. *That shepherd* Moses, the supposed author of Genesis. He was tending sheep on Mount Horeb (*Oreb*), when God called him (Exod. 3. 1). He later received the Law on Horeb, or Sinai, one of Horeb's spurs (Exod. 19. 20).

10. *out of Chaos* M. believed that God created the universe out of unformed matter, not out of nothing. See *CD* i 7.

   Sion hill Mount Zion, the site of Solomon's Temple.

11. *Siloa's brook* a spring near the Temple. Jesus cured a blind man with its waters (John 9. 7).

12. *oracle* the sanctuary housing the ark of the Covenant in Solomon's Temple (I Kings 6. 19).

15. *Aonian mount* Helicon, sacred to the Muses. Porter (45–7) sees a specific allusion to Hesiod, whom the Muses visited while he tended his flocks on Helicon. Hesiod sang how 'from the beginning', 'heaven and earth and all things rose out of Chaos' (*Theog.* 115–16).

16. *Things . . . rhyme* translating Ariosto, *Orl. Fur.* i 2: *Cosa non detta in prosa mai, né in rima.* Cp. also Horace, *Odes* III i 2–3: 'songs never heard before'.

17. *Spirit* the Holy Spirit, despite M.'s insistence in *CD* i 6 that the Holy Spirit is never invoked in the Bible (*YP* 6. 295). *Dove-like* (21) points to the doves of Mark 1. 10, Luke 3. 22 and John 1. 32, which even *CD* identifies with 'the actual person of the Holy Spirit, or its symbol' (trans. Carey, *YP* 6. 285). If *chiefly* refers to *thou*, Spirit and Muse are distinct; if to *Instruct* (19), they are identical.

19. *Instruct* Latin *instruere*, 'to build', linking *temples* and *heart*.

21-2. *brooding* Cp. Gen. 1. 2. M. follows Junius-Tremellius (*incubabat*) rather than A.V. ('moved') and so preserves the image of a brooding dove.

24. *argument* subject-matter (*OED* 6).

25. *assert* defend, take the part of (*OED* 2).

26. *justify* both 'justify to men' and 'ways of God to men'.

28. *what cause* echoing Virgil, *Aen.* i 8: *Musa mihi causas memor* ('tell me the cause, O Muse').

29. *grand* pre-eminent (*OED* 3a) and all-inclusive (*OED* 6), as in 'grand total'.

30. *fall off* of friends: to become estranged. Of subjects: to revolt, withdraw from allegiance (*OED* 'fall' 92e), with overtones of 'the Fall'.

33. *Who first seduced them* Cp. Homer's question as to who sowed discord among the Greeks (*Il.* i 8).

34. *infernal Serpent* Cp. Rev. 12. 9: 'that old serpent, called the Devil, and Satan'.

35-6. *deceived / The mother of mankind* There may be a pun on 'dis-Eved'. See Gen. 3. 20: 'Adam called his wife's name Eve; because she was the mother of all living'. 'Eve' meant 'life', and M. relates the name to prelapsarian immortality (xi 161-171). Cp. *PR* i 51-2.

36. *what time* when (*OED* 10a), not a Latinism.

38-49. *aspiring . . . arms* echoing several biblical accounts of Satan's fall. Cp. Isa. 14. 12-15, Luke 10. 18, II Pet. 2. 4, Jude 6, Rev. 20. 1-2.

43. *impious war* Latin *bellum impium*, 'civil war'.

46. *ruin* falling from a height (*OED* 1b), Latin *ruina*.
  combustion confusion, tumult (*OED* 5b) and conflagration.

48. *adamantine chains* Satan was bound with 'chains of darkness' (Jude 6, II Pet. 2. 4) or 'a great chain' (Rev. 20. 1-2). Cp. also Phineas Fletcher, *The Purple Island* (1633) xii 64: 'the Dragon . . . bound in adamantine chain'. Adamant was a mythical substance of impenetrable hardness.

50. *space* extent of time (*OED* 3) and linear distance (*OED* 5a). The devils *Lay* for *Nine* days after their fall, which also lasted nine days (vi 871). Hesiod's Titans fell for nine days and nights from heaven to earth and nine more from earth to Tartarus (*Theog.* 720-25).

52. *fiery gulf* Satan is chained on a fiery lake. See lines 184 and 210, and cp. Rev. 19. 20: 'a lake of fire burning with brimstone'.

56. *round he throws his baleful eyes* Cp. Ariosto's description of the Saracen Rodomonte: *Rivolge gli occhi orribili* (*Orl. Fur.* xviii 18).

57. *witnessed* bore witness to (his own *affliction*) and beheld (his followers').

59. *angels' ken* angels' range of sight. The early texts do not use apostrophes, so *ken* might be a verb.

66. *hope never comes* recalling the inscription over Dante's Hell: *Lasciate ogne speranza, voi ch' intrate* (*Inf.* iii. 9); 'Abandon every hope, you who enter'. Cp. also Euripides, *Troades* 681.

68. *Still* always.

71. *those*] *Ed I, Ed II*; *these MS*.

72. *utter* utter and outer (cp. Matthew 25. 30).

74. *the centre* the earth (*OED* 2b).

pole celestial pole. M. here measures the distance from Heaven to Hell as thrice the radius of the universe. At ii 1051–3 our whole universe is a speck in Chaos. Homer and Hesiod place Hades as far below earth as heaven is above it (*Il.* viii 16, *Theog.* 722–25). Virgil places Tartarus 'twice' as far below (*Aen.* vi 577).

81. *Beëlzebub* Hebrew 'Lord of the Flies', one of many forms of the Philistine sun-god Baal ('prince of the devils' in Matt. 12. 24). Notice that Beëlzebub will not get that name until *long after* (80). See below, i 361–5*n*.

82. *Satan* Hebrew 'Enemy'. This is Satan's name *in Heav'n*, not Hell. The devils see God, not Satan, as the 'great Enemy' (ii 137). Satan lost his 'former name' when he rebelled (v 658). He acknowledges his new name only at x 386.

84. *how fall'n! how changed* Cp. Isa. 14. 12 ('How art thou fallen . . . O Lucifer') and Virgil, *Aen* ii. 274–5 (*quantum mutatus ab illo / Hectore*). Satan is unable to put any name to his companion. Cp. Dryden's revision in *The State of Innocence* (1721): 'Ho, *Asmaday*, awake, / If thou art he: But, ah! how chang'd from him!' (20).

93. *He with his thunder* The devils repeatedly avoid naming 'God'. See e.g. i 122, 161–2, ii 59, etc. Contrast iii 695, where Uriel at once names God.

102. *me preferring* liking me better and putting me forward.

105–6. *What . . . lost* Cp. Satan's boast in Fairfax's translation (1600) of Tasso, *Gerus. Lib.* iv 15: 'We lost the field, yet lost we not our heart'.

107. *study of* effort to achieve.

109. *And . . . overcome* 'What else does "not being overcome" mean?'

114. *Doubted* feared for.

116. *Fate* imagined by Satan to be an independent force, but cp.*CD* i 2: 'fate or *fatum* is only what is *fatum*, spoken, by some almighty power' (trans. Carey, *YP* 6. 131).

gods angels. Even God calls angels 'gods' (iii 341).

117. *empyreal* of the highest Heaven.

123. *triúmphs* prevails, exults, rides in pomp (as in a Roman triumph).

126. *racked*] *Ed I, Ed II*; wracked *MS*. Satan is wrecked, ruined (*OED* 'wrack' 2, 3), but *In pain* gives priority to *racked*.

128. *Powers*] *MS*; Powers, *Ed I, Ed II*. Richardson (who was unaware of *MS*) noted in 1734: 'the Comma after Powers, as in all Editions we have Noted, perplexes the Sense. 'twas not *Satan*, but Those Powers that led the *Seraphim* to War under His Conduct. One of these Powers is This Bold Companion who Here under a Compliment he makes to *Satan* Proudly Insinuates his Own Merit.' *Powers* and *Seraphim* (129) are two of nine angelic orders, the others being Cherubim, Thrones, Dominations, Virtues, Principalities, Archangels, Angels.

134. *event* outcome.

139. *perish* including 'incur spiritual death' (*OED* 1b).

141. *glory* effulgence, bliss of heaven, halo (*OED* 6, 7a, 9).
extinct extinguished.

144. *Of force* perforce and due to the force.

146. *entire* unimpaired, undiminished (*OED* 4c).

147. *support* endure, undergo, esp. with fortitude or without giving way (*OED* 1b).

148. *suffice* satisfy.

152. *deep* Chaos (the usual meaning in *PL*).

153–5. *What . . . punishment?* 'What can it avail us that our strength is undiminished, and that our being is eternal, if our punishment is also eternal?'

156. **Arch-Fiend* coined on the analogy of 'Archangel'.

158. *Doing or suffering* acting or enduring. Satan anticipates the famous words of Mutius Scaevola as he thrust his hand into a flaming brazier as a demonstration of Roman courage. See ii 199*n* and cp. *PR* iii 194–5.

159–68. *To do aught good . . . aim* contrast God's power to bring good out of evil (xii 470–8).

166. *succeed* ensue (with *evil* as subject).

167. *if I fail not* unless I am mistaken. *Fail* means 'err' (*OED* 11), but the sequence *succeed . . . fail* also hints at Satan's ultimate failure.
disturb forcibly divert.

168. *destined* intended (*OED* 2) – but the sense of 'destiny' tells against Satan's boast.

173. *The fiery*] *Ed I, Ed II*; This fiery *MS*.

178. *slip* let slip.

180. *dreary* **dismal, gloomy (*OED* 4), dire, horrid, (*OED* 2).

182. *livid* of a bluish leaden colour (*OED* 1). Virgil (*Aen.* vi 320) and Statius (*Thebaid* i 54) describe the rivers of Hades as *livida*.

183–91. The rhymes signal a change of scene (as in a blank verse drama) and create an impression of order emerging from destruction.

185. *There rest, if any rest* Cp. Shakespeare, *Richard II* V i 5–6: 'Here let us rest, if this rebellious earth / Hath any resting for her true king's queen'.

186. *afflicted powers* routed armies.

187. *offend* strike so as to hurt (*OED* 6).

196. *rood* either a linear measure (6–8 yards) or a measure of land (about a quarter of an acre).

198–9. *Titanian . . . Typhon* Titans and Giants were *Earth-born* monsters who rebelled against *Jove* and were confined in Tartarus, the classical hell. In Homer and Hesiod, the hundred-armed *Briareos* is Zeus's ally, but Virgil makes him a Titan (*Aen.* vi 287, x 565). *Typhon* (Typhoeus) was a Giant with a hundred serpent-heads. At first the gods fled his attack (see i 481*n*), but Jove crushed him under Mount Etna (Ovid, *Met.* v 346–53). M. often compares these rebellions to Satan's (see i 50, 480–81, 510, 576, 778, ii 539, vii 605).

201. *Leviathan* a whale, but the name was also associated with Satan. Cp. Isa. 27. 1: 'the Lord . . . shall punish leviathan the piercing serpent, even leviathan the crooked serpent; and he shall slay the dragon that is in the sea'. The story of the illusory island was a commonplace often applied to Satan. See J. H. Pitman, 'Milton and the Physiologus', *MLN* 40 (1925) 439. Contrast the undeceptive Leviathan at vii 412–16. Boiardo and Ariosto tell how the paladin Astolfo mistook a whale for an island and was carried off (*Orl. Inn.* II xiv 3, *Orl. Fur.* VI 37–43).

202. *Océan stream* the river Ocean, described by Homer as encircling the world. Homer locates such strange and wonderful creatures as the Pygmies and the Cimmerians 'by the stream of Ocean'. See e.g. *Il.* i 423, *Od.* iv 567.

204. *night-foundered* engulfed in night. (The vessel is also about to founder.)

207. *lee* shelter (from wind) given by neighbouring object.

208. *Invests* wraps, covers.

224. *horrid* dreadful and bristling (with *spires*).

226. *incumbent* pressing with his weight upon (*OED* 1a).

227. *unusual weight* Cp. Spenser's dragon, whose flight 'did forcibly divide / The yielding aire, which nigh too feeble found / Her flitting partes, and element unsound, / To beare so great a weight' (*FQ* I xi 18).

228. *lights* alights, with overtones of 'lessens the weight' (*OED* v¹ 1).

229–30. *MS* pointing. *Ed I* and *Ed II* (semicolon after *fire*, comma after *hue*) focus the simile exclusively on *hue*. *MS* likens the flying Satan to a flying *hill*.

230–37. *force . . . smoke* Cp. the descriptions of *Etna* in Virgil, (*Aen.* iii 570–82), Ovid (*Met.* v. 346–58), and Tasso (*Gerus. Lib.* iii 8). The Giant Encaladus was buried under Etna after the Giants' revolt. See above, 198–9*n*. M. combines imagery of birth (*conceiving*) and excretion (*wind, entrails, bottom, stench*).

231. *subterranean wind* the cause of earthquakes in classical and Renaissance seismology. Cp. Ovid, *Met.* xv 296–305.

232. *Pelorus* Cape Faro, near Mount Etna in Sicily.

235. *Sublimed* converted directly from solid to vapour by volcanic heat.

236. *involved* enveloped, wreathed.

239. *Stygian* black as the river Styx.

244. *change for* take in exchange for.

254–6. *The mind . . . the same* Amalric of Bena's heresy that Heaven and Hell are states of mind had been condemned in 1204, but continued to attract seventeenth-century sects. Satan's boast takes an ironic twist at iv 75.

257. *all but less than* eliding the idioms 'all but equal to' and 'only less than'.

263. *Better to reign in Hell, than serve in Heav'n* The thought was proverbial (as was its opposite). See e.g. Ps. 84. 10, Homer, *Od.* xi 488, Aeschylus, *Promethus Bound* 965. M.'s version is close to Phineas Fletcher, *The Apollyonists* (1627) i 20: 'To be in heaven the second he disdaines: / So now the first in hell, and flames he raignes'. Cp. *The Purple Island* (1633) vii 10.

265. *associates* companions in arms (*OED* B 2). *Copartners*, *loss* and *share* also evoke the image of a failed business venture.

266. *astonished* including 'thunderstruck' (Latin *extonare*).

oblivious causing oblivion.

276. *edge* critical moment (*OED* 6b), line of battle (*OED* 5a). Cp. Latin *acies* and 'rough edge of battle' (vi 108).

282. *pernicious* destructive, ruinous.

284–7. *shield . . . moon* Cp. Achilles' shield, from which 'the light glimmered far, as from the moon' (Homer, *Il.* xix 574).

285. *Ethereal temper* tempered in Heaven and tempered in celestial fire (Greek *aithein*, 'to burn').

288. *Tuscan artist* Galileo. He studied the moon with a telescope (*optic glass*). M. had visited him in Florence in 1638 or 1639. He is the only one of M.'s contemporaries to be named in *PL*. Cp. iii 588–90, v 261–3. *Fesole* (Fiesole) overlooks *Valdarno* (the valley of the Arno).

292–4. *spear . . . wand* Cp. Homer's simile likening Polyphemus's club to the mast of a 'black ship of twenty oars' (*Od.* ix 322). M. implies relative magnitudes ('spear is to pine as pine is to wand'), but also evokes an image of Satan hobbling on a light walking-stick or twig (*OED* 'wand' 1c, 2a). See Fish (159).

294. *ammiral* flagship. M.'s spelling 'gives the true etymology, from *emir* . . . not from *admire*' (Ricks). Cp. Satan as 'Sultan' (i 348).

296. *marl* soil.

299. *Nathless* nevertheless.

302. *autumnal leaves* Similes comparing the passing generations (or numberless dead) to falling leaves are frequent in epic. Cp. Homer, *Il.* vi 146, Virgil, *Aen.* vi 309–10, Dante, *Inf.* iii 112–15, Ariosto, *Orl. Fur.* xvi 75.

The image is especially apt to fallen angels. Cp. Isa. 34. 4: 'all the host of heaven . . . shall fall down, as the leaf falleth off from the vine'.

303. *Vallombrosa* a wooded valley in Tuscany (Etruria), which M. may have visited. The name ('valley of shadows') evokes 'valley of the shadow of death' (Ps. 23).

304. *overarched* M. repeats the neologism at ix 1107.

sedge seaweed. Cp. Isa. 57. 20: 'The wicked are like the troubled sea, when it cannot rest, whose waters cast up mire and dirt'. Homer likens the routed Achaians to seaweed cast up by a storm (*Il.* ix 5–9).

305. *Orion* The constellation (representing an armed giant) was associated with stormy weather (see Amos 5. 8, Virgil, *Aen.* i 535 and vii 719, Apollonius Rhodius, *Argonautica* i 1202).

306. *vexed* disturbed.

307. *Busiris* a mythical Pharaoh who sacrificed strangers. He was commonly identified with the Pharaoh of Exod. 1. M. identifies him with the Pharaoh of Exod. 14 who pursued the Israelites (*sojourners of Goshen*) through the Red Sea.

312. *Abject* cast down (literal and metaphorical).

314. *deep*] *Ed I, Ed II*; deeps *MS*.

315. *Princes, Potentates* suggesting 'Principalities' and 'Powers' (see above, 128*n*).

320. *virtue* strength. M. pointedly withholds the title of the angelic order of 'Virtues'. See ii 310–13, v 772–4, x 460–62 for further examples of such taunting with titles.

324. *Seraph* M. coined the singular on the analogy of *Cherub* and *Cherubim* (*OED*).

328–9. *thunderbolts / Transfix us* Cp. Virgil, *Aen.* i 44, where Oilean Ajax is pierced through the chest (*transfixo pectore*) by a thunderbolt which impales him to a rock.

339. *Amram's son* Moses, who summoned a plague of locusts with his *rod* (Exod. 10. 12–15).

340–41. *pitchy cloud / Of locusts* echoing Sylvester, *DWW* (1592–1608), *The Lawe* (1606): 'a sable Clowde / Of horned *Locusts*' (533–4).

341. *warping* rising, swarming, whirling through the air (*OED*).

345. *cope* vault or canopy like that of the sky (*OED* 7d).

348. *Sultan* the title of the Ottoman emperors. The word carried a smear of despotism in M.'s time.

351–5. *the populous North . . . sands* refers to the Goths, Huns, and Vandals who inundated the Roman Empire and plunged Europe into the Dark Ages. For Satan's association with the North, see v 689*n*.

353. *Rhene, Danaw* Rhine, Danube.

361–5. *their names . . . new names* Contrast Rev. 3. 12, where it is the righteous who get a 'new name'. Here the *new names* are those of future devils. The *blotted* angelic names never appear in *PL*. Cp. i 80–81, v 658, vi 373–85. For God's blotting of names, see Exod. 32. 33 and Rev. 3. 5: 'He that overcometh . . . I will not blot out his name out of the book of life'. M. has *Books* (not 'Book') to suggest the great number of angels. 'Blot out' implies 'annihilate, destroy' (*OED* 5), as in xi 891: 'to blot out mankind'.

366. *sufferance* divine permission (*OED* 6c).

372. *gay* showy, specious, immoral (*OED* 3, 5, 2).

religions rites (*OED* 3a).

373. *devils to adore for deities* Cp. Deut. 32. 17: 'They sacrificed unto devils, not to God'. Justin Martyr, Tertullian, Origen, Lactantius, and Augustine had argued that pagan gods were fallen angels, and the belief continued uninterrupted until the Renaissance. Cp. *Nativity* 173ff. and see C. A. Patrides, 'The Cessation of the Oracles: The History of a Legend' (*MLR* 60, 1965, 500–507).

376. *who first, who last* Cp. Homer, *Il.* v 703 ('who then was the first and who the last that they slaughtered?') and Virgil, *Aen.* xi 664 ('whom first, whom last, fierce maid, did you strike down with your dart?'). Catalogues of warriors are frequent in epic. Cp. Homer, *Il.* ii 484–877, Virgil, *Aen.* vii 641–817, Ariosto, *Orl. Fur.* xiv.

380. *promiscuous* indiscriminate.

386. *Thund'ring out of Sion* Joel 3. 16 and Amos 1. 2 prophesy how God 'shall roar out of Zion'.

387. *Between the Cherubim* a common phrase in the O.T. (see e.g. M.'s translation of Psalm 80. 1). There were images of Cherubim on the ark of the Covenant and more Cherubim flanked the ark in the Holy of Holies (Exod. 25. 18–21, I Kings 6. 23, 8. 6–7).

391. *affront* insult and face in defiance.

392. *Moloch* Hebrew 'king'. A god of the Ammonites, whose capital was *Rabba*, 'city of waters' (II Samuel 12. 27). Hollow brass idols depicted Moloch enthroned, with arms outstretched, wearing a crown on his calf's head. Children were sacrificed by being placed in his red-hot arms.

395. *passed through fire* Cp. II Kings 23. 10: 'that no man might make his son or daughter to pass through the fire to Molech'. A marginal comment in the Geneva Bible explains that Moloch's worshippers 'smote on the tabret [timbrel] while their children were burning, that their crye shulde not be heard'. See also Lev. 18. 21.

403. *opprobrious hill* the Mount of Olives. See below, 416*n*.

grove Groves are associated with idolatry throughout the O.T. See Deut. 16. 21: 'Thou shalt not plant thee a grove of any trees near unto the altar of the Lord thy God'. Cp. I Kings 14. 23, I Kings 16. 33, I Kings 18. 19, II Kings 21. 7, II Kings 23. 4, and see *PR* ii 289 and note.

404. *Hinnom* a valley adjacent to Jerusalem. Patrick Hume, the earliest editor of *PL* (1695), derived the name from a Hebrew verb meaning 'cry out through excessive torment'.

Tophet from Hebrew *toph*, 'a timbrel'. See lines 394–5.

405. *Gehenna* Greek, 'valley of Hinnom', translated in the A.V. (e.g. at Matt. 5. 29) as 'Hell'.

Type symbol (*OED* 1).

406. *Chemos* Moabite fertility-god, identified by Jerome with the phallic god Priapus. See Num. 25 for Israel's *wanton rites* (414) and the plague (*woe*) that followed.

407–11. *Aroer, Hesebon, Sibma* and *Elealè* were northern Moabite towns. *Nebo* was in the *Abarim* mountains in the south.

409. *Seon* the Amorite King Sihon, conqueror of Moab, conquered in his turn by Moses (Num. 21. 21–30).

411. *Asphaltic pool* the Dead Sea, which has deposits of bitumen.

416. *hill of scandal* the Mount of Olives, where Solomon built temples for Chemos and Moloch (I Kings 11. 7).

417. *lust hard by hate* The context invites a priapic pun.

418. *Josiah* a reforming King of Judah. He destroyed the groves and idols of Moloch and Chemos (II Kings 23. 10–14).

422. *Baälim and Ashtaroth* plural forms of 'Baal' and 'Ashtoreth'. 'Baal' means 'lord' and is prefixed to proper names (e.g. Baal-Peor, Baal-Zebub). Cp. Judges 10. 6: 'the children of Israel . . . served Baalim and Ashtaroth'.

425. *uncompounded* undifferentiated into members. Cp. vi 350–53.

429. *Dilated* enlarged. Cp. iv 986.

432. *these*] MS; those *Ed I, Ed II*. MS is supported by line 437.

438–9. *Astoreth . . . Astarte* the Phoenician (*Sidonian*) original of Aphrodite, called *queen of Heav'n* at Jer. 44. 19. She had a bull's head above her own head, from which sprang lunar *crescent horns* (cp. *Nativity* 200).

443. *offensive mountain* the Mount of Olives, where the *uxorious king* Solomon built a temple for Astoreth to please his wives (II Kings 23. 13, I Kings 11. 4–5).

444. *heart . . . large* intellect . . . capacious. Cp. I Kings 4. 29: 'God gave Solomon . . . largeness of heart'. The Hebrew word translated as 'heart' in A.V. means 'intellect' (*OED* 'large' 3c).

446–52. *Thammuz . . . wounded* Thammuz follows Astarte because they were lovers (identified with Venus and Adonis). Here *Adonis* is a river in Lebanon, discoloured every July with reddish mud (supposedly Thammuz's blood). This *annual wound* was the occasion of a religious festival. See *Nativity* 204.

452–7. *love-tale . . . Judah* Cp. Ezek. 8. 14: 'Then he brought me to the door of the gate of the Lord's house which was toward the north; and, behold, there sat women weeping for Thammuz'.

457–61. *Next . . . fell flat* The Philistines placed the ark of the Covenant (which they had captured) in Dagon's temple. When they entered the temple the next morning, 'behold, Dagon was fallen upon his face to the ground before the ark of the Lord: and the head of Dagon and both the palms of his hands were cut off upon the threshold; only the stump of Dagon was left to him' (I Sam. 5. 4).

460. *grunsel* groundsel, threshold.

462-3. *upward . . . fish* John Selden had derived Dagon's name from Hebrew *dag*, 'fish' (*De Dis Syris* ii 3).

464-6. The five main Philistine cities were *Azotus* (or Asdod), *Gath*, *Ascalon*, *Accaron* (or Ecron), and *Gaza* (or Azza). M. employs the variant forms in *SA*.

467. *Rimmon* the chief Syrian god.

471. *A leper once he lost* Elisha told the Syrian general Naaman he would be cured of leprosy if he washed in the Jordan. At first Naaman scoffed ('Are not Abana and Pharpar, rivers of Damascus, better than all the waters of Israel?'), but he obeyed, was healed, and renounced Rimmon for God (II Kings 5. 8-19).

gained a king King Ahaz of Judah defeated Syria, then converted to Rimmon's cult (II Kings 16. 7-17).

472. *sottish* foolish.

478. *Osiris, Isis, Orus* Egyptian gods represented with the heads of beasts (respectively a bull, a cow, and a falcon).

479. *abused* deceived (*OED* 4a).

481. *disguised in brutish forms* Ovid tells how the Olympian gods fled from Typhon into Egypt, hiding in bestial forms that the Egyptians later worshipped (*Met.* v 319-31). See above, 198-9n. Cp. also Virgil, *Aen.* viii 698, where Egypt's 'monstrous gods' fight for Antony at Actium.

484. *calf in Oreb* Aaron made the 'calf in Horeb' (Ps. 106. 19) while Moses was receiving the Law (Exod. 32). The gold had been *borrowed* from Egypt (Exod. 12. 35), and the calf was traditionally identified with the Egyptian Apis.

rebel king Jeroboam, who led ten tribes of Israel in revolt against Solomon's son Rehoboam (I Kings 12. 12-23). The oxymoron implies that kingship is a kind of rebellion. Cp. vi 199, xii 36. In *Defensio* (1651) M. denies that Jeroboam was a rebel (*YP* 4. 406).

485. *Doubled* repeated (*OED* 3) and made twice as many (*OED* 1). Jeroboam set up two calves, 'the one in Bethel, and the other . . . in Dan' (I Kings 12. 29).

486. *Lik'ning . . . ox* Cp. Ps. 106. 20: 'they changed their glory into the similitude of an ox that eateth grass'.

487-9. *Jehovah . . . gods* God smote the Egyptian firstborn, 'both man and beast', at the passover (Exod. 12. 12).

490. *Belial* Hebrew 'worthlessness'. The word is not a name, and 'Belial' was never worshipped as a god. But the biblical phrase 'sons of Belial', common in the O.T., encouraged personification, as in II Cor. 6. 15. M.'s Belial is a coward. He comes *last*, in contrast to soldier Moloch, who came 'First' (392).

495. *Eli's sons* Cp. I. Sam. 2. 12: 'the sons of Eli were sons of Belial'. Although priests, they 'lay with the women that assembled at the door of the tabernacle' (I Sam. 2. 22).

498. *luxurious* given to luxury, and lascivious, unchaste (*OED* 1).

499. *riot* wanton revel (*OED* 2), debauchery (*OED* 1).

500. *injury* including 'offensive speech, reviling' (*OED* 2).

   outrage including 'violent clamour, outcry' (*OED* 2b).

502. *flown* swollen, in flood (*OED* 'flow' 11b), often used figuratively of persons, as in Spenser, *FQ* II ii 36: 'In wine and meats she flowd above the bancke'.

504–5. *when . . . rape* following *Ed II*. *MS* and *Ed I* read 'when hospitable doors / Yielded their matrons to prevent [*MS* avoid] worse rape'. Both versions allude to Gen. 19 and Judges 19, but *Ed II* gives priority to Judges. At Gen. 19. 8 Lot begs the Sodomites to rape his daughters rather than his angel guests. No rape took place and the angels destroyed Sodom. At *Gibeah* a Levite escaped *worse* (homosexual) *rape* by surrendering his concubine to 'certain sons of Belial'. The woman's fate could not have been worse. She was abused 'all the night' and died the next morning – possibly at the Levite's hands (Judges 19. 28–9). The change from 'Yielded' to *Exposed* might imply a moral judgement. Cp. Adam's 'To me committed and by me exposed' (x 957).

508. *Javan* Noah's grandson, ancestor of the Ionian Greeks (Gen. 10. 1–5).

509. *Heav'n and Earth* Uranus and Gaea, progenitors of the gods.

510. **boasted* *OED*'s earliest participial instance.

510–13. *Titan . . . found* The Christian Lactantius (*Divine Institutes* I xiv) tells how *Titan*, the eldest son of Uranus and Gaea (*Heav'n and Earth*), was deposed by his brother *Saturn*, who was in turn deposed by his son *Jove*.

513. *measure* retribution (*OED* 15).

514–15. *Crete . . . Ida* Jove (Zeus) was born and secretly raised in a cave on Mount Ida in Crete.

516. *middle air* the second of three supposed layers of the atmosphere, extending only to the mountain-tops. Satan was associated with this region, on account of his title 'prince of the power of the air' (Eph. 2. 2). See *PR* i 39–47.

517. *Delphian cliff* the site of Apollo's oracle.

518. *Dodona* the site of Zeus's oracle, in northern Greece.

519. *Doric land* Greece.

519-21. *Saturn . . . isles* Following his defeat by Jove, Saturn fled over *Adria* (the Adriatic) to *th' Hesperian fields* (Italy), and thence to *the Celtic* fields (France) and *the utmost isles* (Britain).

523. *damp* dazed, stupefied (*OED* 2).

525. *found themselves not lost* Cp. Matt. 10. 39: 'He that findeth his life shall lose it'. The angels' newly-found selves are not the ones they have lost (see i 361-5n).

527. *doubtful* both 'full of apprehension' (*OED* 5) and 'giving cause for apprehensions' (*OED* 4).

528. *recollecting* remembering and pulling (himself) together.

530. *fainting*] Ed II; fainted *MS*, *Ed I*.

532. *clarions* shrill trumpets used in war.

534. *Azazel* Hebrew 'God strengthens'. Cabbalistic lore made him one of four standard-bearers in Satan's army. 'Azazel' was sometimes thought to be his original name (see Bernard Bamberger, *Fallen Angels*, 1952, 278), but M.'s rebels have lost their angelic names. See i 80-81, 361-3, v 658 and cp. vi 371-85. In the Hebrew version of Lev. 16. 8, the word translated as 'scapegoat' means 'goat for Azazel', a wicked spirit.

536. *advanced* raised, elevated (*OED* 4).

541. **upsent* Cp. the neologisms 'upwhirled' (iii 493) and 'upgrown' (ix 677).

542. *concave* vault.

543. *reign* realm (*OED* 2).

546. *orient* lustrous and rising.

548. **serried* pressed close together, shoulder to shoulder.

550. *phalanx* Greek and Macedonian battle formation consisting of heavy infantry presenting an impenetrable thicket of spears. Greek phalanxes were usually eight ranks deep; Satan's is *Of depth immeasurable* (549).

550-59. *Dorian . . . minds* Cp. Plutarch's description of Spartans marching to *flutes*: 'it was a sight at once solemn and terrifying to see them marching in step to the pipes, creating no gap in the phalanx nor suffering any disturbance of spirit, but approaching the confrontation calmly and happily in time to the music' (*Lycurgus* 22). Plato describes the *Dorian mood* (mode) as 'the note or accent which a brave man utters in the hour of danger and stern resolve, or when his cause is falling, and he is going to wounds or death' (*Republic* iii 399, trans. Jowett).

556. *swage* assuage, relieve.

560-61. *Breathing . . . silence* Cp. Homer's Achaians marching 'silently, breathing valour, / stubbornly minded each in his heart to stand by the others' (*Il.* iii 8). *Breathing* also suggests wind instruments such as *flutes*. Cp. vi 63-8.

563. *horrid* bristling (Latin *horridus*) with spears.

568. *traverse* across the ranks (having looked down the *files*).

573. *since created man* since man was created (Latin idiom).

575. *small infantry* Pygmies. On the war of Pygmies and cranes see Homer, *Il.* iii 3–6. Notice the pun on *infantry*.

577. *Phlegra* The war between the gods and the Giants began at Phlegra in Macedonia and ended at Phlegra in Italy.

579. *auxiliar* assisting, with a mocking pun on *auxilia* (foreign, low-paid troops in the Roman army).

580. *Uther's son* King Arthur, some of whose knights were Breton (*Armoric*).

583. *Aspramont* 'the dark mountain': a mountain in Calabria. Romantic epics tell how Charlemagne defeated a Saracen army there. See Andrea da Barbarino's *Aspromonte* and Ariosto, *Orl. Fur.* i 30, xvii 14, xxvii 54. *Montalban* 'the white mountain': the home of the paladin Rinaldo.

584. *Damasco* Damascus. Christians and Saracens joust there in Ariosto, *Orl. Fur.* xvii.

Trebizond a Byzantine city on the Black Sea, famous for tournaments.

585. *Biserta* Bizerte, a port in Tunisia, from which Boiardo's Troiano leads a Muslim invasion of Spain (*Orl. Inn.* ii).

586–7. *Charlemagne ... Fontarabbia* There is no known source for Charlemagne's *fall* at *Fontarabbia* (Fuenterrabia, on the Spanish coast), though Charlemagne's paladin Roland made a famous last stand at Roncesvalles, some forty miles away. M. may be alluding to the events of August 1659, when Charles II visited Fuenterrabia in an attempt to muster French and Spanish support (Fowler).

588. *observed* including 'reverenced, honoured' (*OED* 4b). The syntax allows either Satan or his troops to be the observer.

594. *glory* see above, i 141*n*.

594–9. *sun ... monarchs* Charles II's censor objected to these lines – and with reason. An eclipse had provoked *fear of change* on the day of Charles's birth, 29 May 1630. Royalists officially claimed the event as a good omen (see e.g. Dryden, *Astraea Redux*, 288–91), but M.'s nephew, Edward Phillips, remembered it as a portent of the Interregnum. See *Chronicle of the Kings of England* (1665), 498. See also Edward Chamberlayne, *Anglia Notitiae* (1669), 127: 'the Sun suffered an Eclipse, a sad presage as some then divined, that this Prince's Power should for some time be eclipsed, as it hath been'. Cp. Tasso's comparison of Argantes to a comet that 'tidings sad of death and mischief brings / To mighty lords, to monarchs, and to kings' (*Gerus. Lib.* vii 52).

595. *horizontal* on the horizon.

597. *disastrous* ill-starred (Latin *dis* + *astrum*), with a hint that 'Lucifer' has been 'dis-starred'. See v 708, vii 131, x 425.

599. *Perplexes* puzzles and torments.

601. *intrenched* wounded (*OED* 'entrench' 3), *furrowed (*OED* 'intrench' 1, earliest instance 1754).

603. *courage*] *Ed I, Ed II*; valour *MS*.

considerate prudent, deliberate (*OED* 2), as in 'the willing and considerate murderer' (1597); from Latin *considerare*, 'to watch the stars'.

609. *amerced / Of* *deprived of (*OED* 2d). 'Amerce' meant 'fine' and one was amerced 'in' or 'with' (not 'of') a sum. M.'s usage puns on the root *amercié*, 'at the mercy of'.

615. *blasted heath* echoing Shakespeare, *Macbeth* I iii 77.

620. *Tears such as angels weep* Angels were usually thought to be incapable of weeping, but cp. Shakespeare, *Measure for Measure* II ii 121–2, where 'proud man' is said to play 'such fantastic tricks before high heaven / As makes the angels weep'. M.'s good angels eat (v 434–5), make love (viii 620–29), and maybe weep (xi 23–5), so Satan's tears need not reveal a coarsened nature, though they might express a tyrant's sentimentality. Newton in 1749 saw an allusion to the Persian King Xerxes, who wept while reviewing his 'vast army, and reflecting that they were mortal, at the time that he was hast'ning them to their fate, and to the intended destruction of the greatest people in the world, to gratify his own vain glory'. Cp. x 307–11n.

624. *event* outcome.

632. *puissant* powerful.

636. *different* perhaps 'deferent', in the sense 'protracted, lingering' (*OED* 'defer' 4b).

646. *work* plan (*OED* 11).

close design secret scheming.

650. *Space* *stellar depths (*OED* 8), but even this sense is too small. Satan is referring to Chaos (not just our universe), and *worlds* here means 'universes'. Cp. ii 916, 1004, 1052, iii 74, vii 191, 209, etc. Nicholas of Cusa and Giordano Bruno had argued for an infinite universe with many habitable worlds. The theory had neo-Platonic and Epicurean sources, but it was still a 'a fringe belief' in M.'s time (Marjara 77). Cp. Lucretius, *De Rerum Nat.* ii 1048–89.

651. *fame* rumour. See ii 346–52, 830, x 481–2 for the rumour of man's creation, and see vii 150–56n for God's motives in creating us.

654. *favour equal* Raphael later speaks of God's 'equal love' for men and angels (viii 228). Beëlzebub will soon claim that man is 'favoured more' (ii 350).

656. *eruption* breaking out (suggesting Hell's volcanoes).

662. *Open or understood* overt or covert. Cp. Belial's 'open or concealed' (ii 187). Belial wants to escape God's notice; Satan wants God to know his enemy.

666–7. *highly* haughtily (*OED* 5) and loudly (*OED* 3c). The paronomasia (*highly . . . Highest*) is typical of M. Cp. i 642, iv 181, v 869, ix 11, etc.

672. *scurf* sulphurous deposit (suggesting also a diseased body).

673. *his womb* 'the perverted body-landscape of Hell' (Ricks) – but this nuance might have been weaker in M.'s time, when *his* served for *its*. M. uses 'its' only three times in his poetry.

676. *pioneers* military engineers.

678. *Mammon* an Aramaic word for 'riches', personified at Matt. 6. 24 and Luke 16. 13. Medieval tradition identified Mammon with Plutus, the god of wealth, and so with Pluto, god of the underworld. Burton made him prince of the lowest order of devils (*Anatomy of Melancholy* I ii I 2).

679. *erected* high-souled (*OED* 2) and upright (in posture).

684. *vision beatific* mystical experience of seeing God.

685. *suggestion* devilish temptation (*OED* 1).

686. *centre* (centre of) the earth.

686–8. *impious . . . hid* Cp. Ovid's description of men rifling earth's bowels (*viscera terrae*) in search of riches (*Met.* i 137–40); also Spenser, *FQ* II vii 17, where 'a cursed hand' seeking 'hid treasures' wounds the 'wombe / Of his great Grandmother'; also Phineas Fletcher, *The Apollyonists* (1627) v 4: 'The earth (their Grandame Earth) they fierce invade, / And all her bowels search, and rent, and tear'. The oxymoron *precious bane* (692) recalls Giles Fletcher, *CV* (1610) ii 54, where men wound 'their mothers side' while searching for 'pretious perills'.

690. *ribs* veins of ore (technical term). Pearce in 1733 compared viii 465–9 where God opens Adam's side and extracts 'a rib . . . wide was the wound'. *admire* marvel.

694. *Babel* the Tower of Babel (xii 38–62).
　works of Memphian kings the Egyptian pyramids.

703. *founded*] *MS, Ed I*; found out *Ed II*. The devils had found the ore in lines 688–90. Now they melt it.

704. *bullion dross* boiling dregs.

711. *Rose like an exhalation* Exhalations were thought to cause comets, meteors (both bad omens), and pestilence. See ix 180*n*, x 692–4.

712. *dulcet symphonies and voices sweet* Pandaemonium, like Troy and Thebes, arises to the sound of music.

713. *pilasters* square columns or pillars.

714. *overlaid* surmounted.

715. *architrave* the lowest member of the entablature in a classical temple: the main beam that rests on the columns.

716. *Cornice* the uppermost member of the entablature, surmounting the frieze.
　bossy carved in relief.

717. *fretted* adorned with carved or wrought patterns.

718. *Alcairo* Cairo (ancient Memphis).

720. *Belus* a Babylonian god. Herodotus describes his temple as a series of eight towers placed one on top of another (i 181).

Serapis a god of Ptolemaic Egypt (composite of Osiris and Apis).

728. *cressets* iron baskets hung from the ceiling.

729. *naphtha and asphaltus* oil and pitch, to be placed in *lamps* and *cressets* respectively.

731. *Admiring* marvelling.

732–5. *architect . . . residence* Cp. the gods' palaces built by Hephaestos (Homer, *Il.* i 605–8) and Mulciber (Ovid, *Met.* ii 1–4).

738. *his name* Hephaestos (in *Greece*), or *Mulciber* (or Vulcan) in Italy (*Ausonian land*). His angelic name has been blotted out and M. never speaks it.

740–46. *how he fell . . . isle* Cp. the daylong fall of Homer's Hephaestos (*Il.* i 591–5): '[Zeus] caught me by the foot and threw me from the magic threshold, / and all day long I dropped helpless, and about sunset / I landed in Lemnos'.

745. *zenith* highest point of the celestial sphere (*OED* 1, referring to Mulciber's fall) and culminating point of a heavenly body (*OED* 2, referring to *sun*).

746. *Aégean* For accent cp. *PR* iv 238 and Fairfax's Tasso (i 61): 'O'er Aegean Seas by many a Greekish hold'.

750. *engines* plots (*OED* 3) and machines used in warfare (*OED* 5).

756. **Pandaemonium* Greek 'seat of all demons (or *daimones*)'. The original spelling allows the devils to see themselves as classical *daimones* rather than demons (though *daimones* still suggests demons through N.T. usage). Cp. *PR* ii 122.

capital] *Ed I*, *Ed II*; 'Capitoll' corr. to 'Capitall' (in a different hand) *MS*.

757. *peers* nobles. Pandaemonium has a King and House of Lords, but no Commons (see below, i 792*n*). Cp. ii 507 ('grand infernal Peers') and contrast i 39 and v 812, where 'peers' means 'equals'. Satan exploits the ambiguity at ii 445.

759. *place* rank, official position.

choice promotion or election from the ranks.

764. *Wont* were wont to.

Soldan's Sultan's.

765. *paynim* pagan.

768–75. *bees . . . affairs* Homer's Achaians marching to a council (*Il.* ii 87–90), Virgil's busy Carthaginians (*Aen.* i 430–35) and Virgil's dead awaiting reincarnation (*Aen.* vi 707–9) are all likened to bees. Seventeenth-century apiarists would kill off a swarm by lowering the hive into a flaming sulphur pit. This fiery end could serve as a warning to those who praised the swarm's Royalist politics (see John Simons, *MQ* 21. 1, March 1987, 21–2). Virgil (*Aen.* xii 583–92) and Apollonius Rhodius (*Argonautica* ii

130–34) liken panic-stricken defenders of a city to bees whose hive is filled with smoke. See also Virgil, *Georg.* iv 149–227.

769. *Taurus* the zodiacal sign of the Bull (hence *rides*).

774. *expatiate* both 'wander at will' and 'speak at length'. The word adds mock grandeur to the devils.

780. *that Pygméan race* See above, 575n. The Pygmies were supposed to live beyond the Himalayas (*the Indian mount*).

781–8. *faery elves . . . rebounds* Encounters with elves are frequent in folklore. Aubrey tells of a shepherd who came across dancing elves: 'He sayd the ground opened, and he was brought into strange places under ground where they used musicall Instruments, violls, and Lutes.' Such encounters bring *joy* at the time, but 'never any afterwards enjoy themselves' (*Remaines*, 1686–7, 204). A medieval tradition held that the less sinful fallen angels were allowed to haunt earth's forests, where they were known as 'elves'.

782. *midnight revels* Cp. Shakespeare, *A Midsummer Night's Dream*, II i 141 ('moonlight revels'), but M.'s elves are quite un-Shakespearean.

783–4. *sees, / Or dreams he sees* Cp. Virgil, *Aen.* vi 751–4, where Aeneas glimpses Dido's shade 'as one who sees . . . or thinks to have seen, the moon / Rising through cloud'.

785. *arbitress* witness (lit. 'one who goes to see', *ad + bito*).

790. *at large* free, uncramped – with a play on the other sense of 'large'. Ricks remarks that 'nothing could more effectively belittle the devils' than this 'superbly contemptuous pun' (*Milton's Grand Style*, 15).

792. *Court* The royal connotation is ominous. Parliament was also a 'court', but there is no House of Commons in Pandaemonium, where Satan sits enthroned amidst *Lords*.

795. *close recess* secret and secluded place.

   conclave secret assembly (*OED* 4), suggesting 'the assembly of Cardinals met for the election of a Pope' (*OED* 3). In Phineas Fletcher's *The Apollyonists* (1627) jesuitical devils conceive the Gunpowder Plot after meeting in 'deepe Conclave' (i 17).

797. *Frequent* crowded.

798. *consult* a secret meeting for purposes of sedition (*OED* 2).

BOOK II

1–6. *High . . . eminence* Cp. the bright throne of Spenser's Lucifera (*FQ* I iv 8); also M.'s description in *Defensio* of Charles I enthroned (*YP* 4. 506).

2. *Ormus* Hormuz, an island town in the Persian Gulf, famous for jewels.

5. *merit* desert of either good or evil (*OED* 2a).

7. *high uplifted beyond hope* both 'lifted high above (his) hope' and 'lifted high in a place so low as to be beyond all hope'. Cp. i 66, iv 160.

9. *success* outcome (with a wry pun on the modern sense).

11. *Powers and Dominions* angelic orders (Col. 1. 16).

10. *imaginations* schemes, plots (*OED* 2a).

15. *Virtues* the angelic order, with overtones of 'manliness, valour' (*OED* 'virtue' 7).

24-40. *The happier . . . assured us* Lewis (98) calls Satan's argument 'nonsense', since its corollary is that 'every approach to victory must take away the grounds on which victory is hoped'. Waldock (69-70) replies that Satan's speech is rhetoric, not logic, and should be judged 'by its effect'.

41. *open war or covert guile* Cp. Tasso's Satan urging 'open force, or secret guile' (*Gerus. Lib.* iv 16, trans. Fairfax). Notice that Satan asks the devils to debate how (not whether) to return.

43. *Moloch* As at i 392, Moloch is first on his feet. The contrast between the bellicose Moloch and the eloquent coward Belial has epic precedent in the contrasts between Virgil's Turnus and Drances (*Aen.* xi 336f.) and Tasso's Argantes and Orcanes (*Gerus. Lib.* x 35f.). See below, 109n.

50. *recked* cared.

thereafter accordingly.

51. *sentence* judgement.

52. *More unexpért* less experienced.

63. *horrid* horrifying and bristling (with *flames*).

65. *engine* machine of war (God's thunder).

69. *Tartarean* of Tartarus, the classical hell.

strange fire Cp. Lev. 10. 1-2: 'the sons of Aaron . . . offered strange fire before the Lord, which he commanded them not. And there went out fire from the Lord, and devoured them, and they died'.

73. *drench* soporific potion (*OED* 2) and *act of drenching (*OED* 4, earliest instance 1808, but the verb had existed since medieval times).

74. *forgetful* causing oblivion.

75. *in our proper motion we ascend* Moloch is proved wrong when Satan encounters a 'vast vacuity' in Chaos and plummets downward (ii 932-5). The devils may have lost their angelic buoyancy, but Marjara (148-9) sees M. as confirming the New Philosophy of Galileo and debunking Aristotelian physics.

79. *Insulting* making assaults (*OED* 3) and exulting.

81. *ascent is easy* Contrast Virgil, *Aen.* vi 126-9: 'the descent to Avernus is easy . . . but to retrace one's steps and escape to the upper air, this is the task, this is the toil'. See also ii 432-3, iii 19-21, 524.

82. *event* outcome.

89. *exercise* vex, afflict (*OED* 4b).

90. *vassals of his anger* Cp. Spenser, *Tears of the Muses* 126: 'vassals of

Gods wrath, and slaves of sin'; also Romans 9. 22: 'vessels of wrath fitted to destruction'. In *The Hierarchie of the Blessed Angels* (1635), Thomas Heywood had identified 'vessels of wrath' as a demonic order commanded by Belial (436). Moloch's pun might therefore be a jibe at Belial, who styles himself 'vessel', but is really a 'vassal'.

92. *penance* punishment (*OED* 5), suggesting Roman Catholic mortification of the flesh (notice *scourge*).

94. *What doubt we* Why do we hesitate.

97. *essential* essence (adj. for noun).

99–101. *if . . . nothing* 'if we are indeed indestructible, we are already in the worst possible state, which is not annihilation'.

104. *fatal* upheld by Fate and deadly.

106. *denounced* portended.

109. *Belial* See i 490n. M.'s cowardly orator resembles Tasso's Orcanes, who makes a disguised plea for capitulation in the Saracen council (*Gerus. Lib.* x 48). Cp. also Virgil's Drances, who in council was 'valiant of tongue, though his hand was cold for battle' (*Aen.* xi 337–8).

110. *person* person of rank (*OED* 2c) and mask (Latin *persona*). Notice *false and hollow*.

114. *reason* argument.

116. *To vice industrious* Cp. Sylvester, *DWW* (1592–1608), *Eden* (1598) 304: 'To vertue dull, to vice ingenious'.

123. *success* outcome (with a wry pun on the modern sense).

124. *fact* feat of valour (*OED* 1b).

127. *scope* target.

139. *ethereal mould* that which is fashioned of pure fire (in contrast to Moloch's *baser fire*).

148. *thoughts . . . eternity* Cp. Lucretius, *De Rerum Nat.* ii 1044–7: 'the mind seeks to discover what exists out there in the infinity of space beyond the walls of the world, where the intellect longs to peer, and the mind flies free by its own projection'.

wander a recurrent word in *PL*, where it has 'almost always a pejorative, or melancholy connotation' (MacCaffrey 188). See e.g., i 365, ii 561, iii 667, vii 50, ix 1136, and Fish (130–41).

150. *wide womb of uncreated Night* Cp. Spenser, *FQ* III vi 36: 'in the wide wombe of the world there lyes, / In hatefull darkenesse and in deepe horrore, / An huge eternall *Chaos*'.

151. *Devoid of sense and motion* Cp. Claudio's dread of death that ends 'This sensible warm motion' (Shakespeare, *Measure for Measure* III i 120).

152. *Let this be good* 'supposing this were desirable'.

156. *Belike* in all likelihood.

impotence lack of self-restraint (*OED* 3), sarcastically contrasted with God's omnipotence.

159-63. *Wherefore . . . worse* Referring to Moloch's question 'what can be worse / Than to dwell here?' (85-6).

160. *they who* Belial avoids naming Moloch, who is in any case nameless (see i 361-5). The 'courteously impersonal form' (Fowler) is appropriate to Parliamentary debate, where names were (and still are) prohibited.

165. *amain* at full speed.

170-74. *What if . . . What if* The coward's question. Cp. Tasso's Orcanes: 'But what if that appointed day they [the pagan reinforcements] miss? / Or else, ere we expect, what if they came?' (*Gerus. Lib.* x 44, trans. Fairfax).

170. *breath that kindled* Cp. Isa. 30. 33: 'the pile [of Hell] is fire and much wood; the breath of the Lord, like a stream of brimstone, doth kindle it'.

170-71. *fires . . . sevenfold* Cp. the fiery furnace into which Nebuchadnezzar cast Shadrach, Meshach, and Abed-nego. The furnace was heated 'seven times more than it was wont to be heated' (Dan. 3. 19).

174. *red right hand* Cp. Horace's image of Jove exciting civil war in Rome by hurling thunderbolts with a 'red right hand', *rubente dextera* (*Odes* I ii 1-4).

176. *cataracts* flood-gates (Latin, *cataractae*). At Gen. 7. 11, the Vulgate and Junius-Tremellius describe Noah's Flood as coming from *cataractae*. See xi 824n. Our *firmament* rained water, Hell rains fire.

182. *racking* both 'torturing' and 'driving'.

184. *converse with* both 'talk by means of' and 'dwell with'.

185. *Unrespited, unpitied, unreprieved* M. is fond of triple collocations of the prefix 'un-'. See e.g. iii 231, v 899.

187. *open or concealed* Cp. 'open or understood' (i 662) and 'open war or covert guile' (ii 41).

188-9. *what can . . . With him* How can force or guile hurt him?

191. *motions* proposals.

199. *To suffer, as to do* echoing the famous words spoken by Mutius Scaevola, when he burned his hand so as to give the Etruscan Porsenna a demonstration of Roman fortitude: *Et facere et pati fortia Romanum est* (Livy ii 12). Belial manages to sound like Scaevola, but his whole purpose is to avoid *the flames* (172). Cp. i 158 and *PR* iii 195.

212. *mind* be concerned about (*OED* 8), be aware of (*OED* 4). The latter sense casts doubt on God's omniscience.

214. *his breath . . . flames* See above, 170n.

215-19. *Our . . . pain* Belial considers three possibilities: (1) the angels' *purer essence* will prevail over Hell's flames and so remove pain at its source, (2) the angels will get used to Hell, though neither they nor it will change, (3) Hell's flames will cause the angels' *purer essence* to change, and so deprive the angels of their ability to feel pain. Belial prefers a comfortable life to his angelic essence, but at least he is concerned for his essence. Mammon is indifferent about it at ii 276–7, where he welcomes Belial's (3) as the angels' best hope.

216. *inured* accustomed, but M.'s voice behind Belial may play on 'burn in' (*OED* 'inure' v²) as in 'He . . . inures the Marke of the Beast, the Devills Flesh-brand, upon one or other part of the body' (1646). Belial's *purer essence* will also be 'burned away' (Latin *inurere*, 'remove by burning').

218. *temper* physiological temperament (the mixture of humours determining one's physical and mental constitution).

220. *light* both 'lightly borne' and 'luminous'.

224. *For happy* as for happiness.

233. *strife* between *Fate* and *Chance* (Bentley), or God and the devils (Pearce). 'There may also be an allusion to the Empedoclean notion of a universal Strife' (Fowler).

243. *Forced* both 'compulsory' and 'produced with effort'.

hallelujahs an imperative (Hebrew 'praise Jah'). Cp. 'unfeignèd halleluijahs' (vi 744).

lordly both 'haughty' and 'as Lord'.

245. **Ambrosial* divinely fragrant (*OED* 1c).

250. *by leave obtained* if God were to grant us permission.

256. *easy yoke* Cp. Matt. 11. 28–30: 'Come unto me . . . For my yoke is easy'. Cp. also Samson's contempt for those who prefer 'Bondage with ease' to 'strenuous liberty' (*SA* 271).

263–7. *How oft . . . throne* Cp. Ps. 18. 11: 'He made darkness his secret place; his pavilion round about him were dark waters and thick clouds of the skies'. See also II Chron. 6. 1: 'The Lord hath said that he would dwell in thick darkness'.

275. *our elements* both 'elements composing our bodies' and 'our places of abode' (*OED* 'element' 12). Demons were thought to dwell in the four elements (see *Il Penseroso* 93–4). Augustine had denied that devils could assume bodies of Hell-fire (*City of God* xxi 10), but M. allows more to Mammon's hopes. The irony lies in Mammon's shameful readiness to relinquish his *purer essence* (see above, 215–19n).

277. *temper* proportionate mixture of elements (*OED* 1), bodily constitution (*OED* 8).

278. *The sensible* *the element (in a spiritual being) that is capable of feeling (*OED* B 3, sole instance). Cp. M.'s use of 'speakable' in the active sense 'able to speak' (ix 563).

281. *Compose* set in order (*OED* 15).

282. *where*] *Ed I*; *were Ed II*.

285. *hollow rocks* imitating *cava saxa*, a stock phrase in Latin verse (cp. Virgil, *Aen.* iii 566, Lucan, *Pharsalia* iv 455). M.'s simile also recalls Tasso's description of the Christian army at prayer: 'Such noise their passions

make, as when one hears / The hoarse sea waves roar, hollow rocks betwixt' (*Gerus. Lib.* iii 6, trans. Fairfax). See also *Gerus. Lib.* ix 22.

288. *o'erwatched* worn out with watching (*OED* 3).

297. *policy* statecraft, including the bad sense 'crafty device, stratagem' (*OED* 4b).

302. *front* forehead or face (*OED* 1, 2).

306. **Atlantéan* Poets often likened statesmen to the Titan Atlas, whom Jove condemned to bear the heavens on his shoulders. See e.g. Spenser's Sonnet to Lord Burleigh prefaced to *FQ.*

312. *style* ceremonial title. Cp. Satan's preoccupation with titles at v 772–7, x 460–2, and *PR* ii 121–5.

324. *first and last* Cp. Rev. 22. 13: 'I am Alpha and Omega, the beginning and the end, the first and last'.

327. *iron sceptre* Cp. Rev. 19. 15 ('he shall rule them with a rod of iron') and M.'s translation of Ps. 2 (line 20): 'With iron sceptre bruised'. Cp. also Abdiel's distinction between God's 'golden sceptre' and 'iron rod' (v 886–7). God's *golden* (328) and *iron* sceptres symbolized Mercy and Justice. Cp. Fletcher, *CV* (1610) i 75, where Mercy begs the Father not to use the 'yron scepter' of Justice against man.

329. *What* Why.

330. *determined us* put an end to us (*OED* 1) and decided our course (*OED* 16).

336. *to* to the limit of.

337. *reluctance* struggling (*OED* 1).

349–50. *less / In power* Cp. Ps. 8. 5: 'thou hast made him a little lower than the angels, and hast crowned him with glory and honour'.

350. *favoured more* Beëlzebub's *more* might be petulant. Satan and Raphael both say that men and angels are 'equal' in God's favour (i 654, viii 228). Flannagan suggests that *favoured more* might mean 'resembling his father more, as in the idiom "He favored his father" '. M. never says that angels were made in God's image, but iv 567 implies that they were.

352–3. *oath . . . shook* Cp. Isa. 13. 12–13: 'I will make a man more precious than fine gold; even a man than the golden wedge of Ophir. Therefore I will shake the heavens'. Cp. also Heb. 6. 17 and 12. 26, Homer, *Il.* i 530, Virgil, *Aen.* ix 106.

355. *mould* bodily form (*OED* sb³ 10b), with overtones of 'earth regarded as the material of the human body' (*OED* sb¹ 4).

357. *attempted* both 'try with temptations' (*OED* 'attempt' II 5) and 'try with violence, make an attack upon' (*OED* III).

367. *puny* including 'born since us' (French *puis né*).

368. *their God* not 'our God' or 'God'. This is the first time in *PL* that any devil has spoken the name.

369–70. *repenting . . . Abolish* Cp. Gen. 6. 7: 'And the Lord said, I will destroy man . . . for it repenteth me that I have made them'. Cp. iii 162–6 and ix 945–51.

374. *partake with us* both 'share our fate' and 'take our side'.

375. *original*] *Ed II*; originals *Ed I*. Some editors prefer 'originals' because it more obviously refers to both Adam and Eve. But 'original' could mean 'derivation, parentage' (*OED* sb 1) as well as 'progenitor' (*OED* sb 2), and it might also mean 'pattern, archetype' (*OED* sb 3), and so imply a sneer at God as the original of man's image.

376. *Advise* consider, ponder (*OED* 3).

377. *sit in darkness* Cp. Ps. 107. 10–11: 'Such as sit in darkness and in the shadow of death, being bound in affliction and iron; Because they rebelled against the words of God'.

378. *Hatching vain empires* Cp. God's Spirit *brooding* on the abyss (i 20–22, vii 233–40).

383. *one root* Adam and Eve (root of our family tree) and the forbidden Tree, 'root of all our woe' (ix 645).

387. *States* dignitaries, nobles (*OED* 24). Editors infer a reference to the three Estates of the Realm (Lords, Clergy, Commons), but Pandaemonium has no Commons. See i 792*n*.

391. *Synod* assembly (usually of clergy, so *Synod of gods* is satirical, cp. vi 156).

404. *tempt* attempt (Satan will also 'tempt' God by testing how far he can go).

405. *abyss* Greek, 'bottomless'.

406. *obscure* *darkness (*OED* B 1, adj. as noun). *Palpable obscure* recalls Exod. 10. 21: 'darkness which may be felt' (Junius-Tremellius: *palpare possit tenebras*).

407. *uncouth* unknown.

409. *abrupt* *precipice (*OED* B, earliest instance of the adj. used as a noun). Corns (88) sees these coinages as reflecting the 'abortive gulf' (ii 441) of Chaos: 'readers too are left groping for some familiar substantive to fix upon: we find instead the shaky premise of a new noun'.

410. *happy isle* The first of a series of 'metaphors and similes in which Satan is a voyager or trader, and earth an island' (Fowler). Cp. ii 636–42, 1043–4, iv 159–65, ix 513–16. The phrase also hints at the Fortunate Isles of Greek myth (cp. iii 568–70 and note).

412. *senteries* sentries.

415. *Choice in our suffrage* care in our vote (which never takes place).

418. *suspense* attentive, in suspense, hanging (*OED* a 1, 2, 4).

420. *all sat mute* So 'all stood mute' when God called for a volunteer to die for man (iii 217). Most critics see Satan's heroic offer (ii 426–66) as a parody of the Son's (iii 222–65). Cp. Homer, *Il.* vii 92–3, where Hector challenges any Greek to single combat, and all sat 'silent, / ashamed to refuse him, and afraid to accept his challenge'.

425. *proffer* volunteer (oneself) and offer (the *voyage*) to someone else (and so be seen to decline it).

432-3. *long . . . light* Another echo of the Sibyl's warning to Aeneas (see above, 81*n*). Cp. also Dante, *Inf.* xxxiv 95 ('long is the way, and arduous the road').

435. *Outrageous to devour* violently destructive.

436. *gates . . . adamant* Cp. the adamantine gates of Virgil's Tartarus (*Aen.* vi 552). On adamant, see i 48*n*.

439. *unessential* *possessing no essence (*OED* 1). Cp. 'uncreated Night' (ii 150) and 'unsubstantial' night in *PR* iv 399.

441. *abortive* Chaos is a 'womb' (ii 150, 911, x 476) containing *embryon atoms* (ii 900) and *pregnant causes* (913). Satan may also think of Chaos 'as a miscarrying womb . . . from which the traveller may never be born, or which may render him as if unborn' (Fowler).

444. *escape.*] *Ed I, Ed II, Ed III*; escape? *Ed IV*. The earlier pointing admits no doubt about the magnitude of the dangers Satan is facing.

445. *Peers* nobles (cp. i 757, ii 507), but with overtones of 'companions', 'equals' (*OED* 3, 1). Satan had 'set himself in glory above his peers' (i 39), so he is naturally evasive as to whether Hell's Peers are equal to each other or to him. M. and Salmasius had debated the precise meaning of 'Peer' (Latin, *parem*). See *Defensio* (*YP* 4. 463).

450-56. *Wherefore . . . honoured sits?* Cp. the heroic speech of Homer's Sarpedon: 'Glaukos, why is it you and I are honoured before all others / with pride of place, the choice meats and the filled wine cups / in Lykia . . . ? Therefore it is our duty in the forefront of the Lykians / to take our stand, and bear our part in the blazing of battle' (*Il.* xii 310-16).

452. *Refusing* 'if I refuse'.

457. *intend* occupy yourselves with (*OED* 12). *Go* invites a pun on 'start on a journey' (*OED* 'intend' 6b), contrasting Satan's heroic voyage with the passive adventurism of those who *intend at home*.

461. *deceive* wile away (*OED* 5).

467. *prevented* pre-empted.

468. *raised* made bold.

478. *reverence* bow (*OED* 2).

prone bending forward and downward (*OED* 1). Fowler understands 'grovelling' (*OED* 4), and contrasts the good angels' obeisance (iii 349). But *Towards him they bend* need not imply prostration. Even good angels bow 'low' to 'superior Spirits' (iii 736-8).

485. *close* secret.

varnished speciously tricked out.

488-95. *As when . . . rings* Cp. Ariosto's lovely simile likening Olimpia's tearful face to sunlight after a shower, when birds sing in 'beams of light' (*Orl. Fur.* xi 65).

490. *louring element* threatening sky.

496–7. *Devil with devil damned / Firm concord holds* Cp. Matt. 12. 25–6: 'Every kingdom divided against itself is brought to desolation . . . if Satan cast out Satan, he is divided against himself; how shall then his kingdom stand?'

504. *enow* enough.

507. *Peers* nobles, Peers of the Realm.

508. *Paramount* Lord paramount, supreme ruler.

509. *Antagonist* translating 'Satan', which means 'enemy', 'adversary' or 'antagonist'. Cp. x 386–7.

512. *globe* body of soldiers (Latin *globus*). Flying angels might also adopt a spherical formation. Cp. vi 399, *PR* iv 581, and Fletcher, *CV* (1610) iv 13: 'A globe of winged Angels'.

fiery Seraphim Seraphs were associated with fire on account of Hebrew *saraph*, 'to burn'. Cp. v 807.

513. **emblazonry* heraldic devices.

*horrent bristling.

515. *result* outcome of deliberations (*OED* 3a).

517. *alchemy* brass (trumpets).

520. **acclaim* shout of applause (coined from the verb).

521. *raised* encouraged.

522. *rangèd powers* armies drawn up in ranks.

526. *entertain* while away (*OED* 9b).

527. *his*] *Ed I*; this *Ed II*.

528–55. *Part . . . audience* Athletic games and musical contests are frequent in classical epic. Cp. Homer, *Il.* ii 774–9, xxiii 262ff., *Od.* viii 100ff., Virgil, *Aen.* v 104ff., Apollonius Rhodius, *Argonautica* ii 1ff., Statius, *Thebaid* vi 255ff. M.'s infernal games most closely resemble *Aen.* vi 642–59.

528. *sublime* raised aloft (*OED* 1) and elated (*OED* 3b).

530. *Pythian fields* The Pythian games (supposedly instituted by Apollo after he had killed the serpent Python) took place at Delphi.

531. *shun the goal* swing tight around the turning-pole in a chariot race. Cp. Homer, *Il.* xxiii 318–41.

532. *fronted* confronting each other (in mock battle).

533–8. *to warn . . . burns* Armies appeared in the sky above Jerusalem before it fell to Antiochus (II Macc. 5. 1–4), and again before it fell to the Romans (Josephus, *De Bellis* VI v 3). Armies were also seen fighting in England's skies in 1640, 1643, 1648, 1659, 1660 and 1661. M.'s nephew, Edward Phillips, recalled that the Civil War had been portended by battles 'in the Ayre'. Radical pamphlets saw such battles as a warning against the Restoration. *Mirabilis Annus* (1661) likens airy battles over London to those preceding Jerusalem's fall. Patrick Hume in 1695 recognized that M. was alluding to 'our Civil Wars'. See John Leonard, ' "To Warn Proud Cities": a Topical Reference in Milton's Airy Knights Simile', *Renaissance and Reformation* 19 (1995) 63−71.

536. *Prick* spur.

couch lower to the attack position.

538. *welkin* sky.

539. **Typhoean* See i 197−200n. Typhoeus's name was associated with 'typhoon' and meant *whirlwind* (541).

540. *ride the air* torment the air (cp. vi 244) by riding on whirlwinds. Cp. Ps. 18. 10 and Shakespeare, *Macbeth*, 'Cherubins, hors'd / Upon the sightless couriers of the air' (I vii 22−3).

542−6. *Alcides . . . Euboic Sea* Hercules (*Alcides*) had killed the centaur Nessus by shooting him with an arrow dipped in the Hydra's poisonous blood. Mortally wounded, Nessus told Hercules' wife, Deianeira, that she should soak a robe in his blood. The robe, he said, would revive Hercules' love. Not suspecting treachery, Deianeira soaked a robe in the now *envenomed* blood, and presented it to Hercules after he returned from another victory at *Oechalia*. Tormented by the robe's corrosive touch, Hercules threw his friend *Lichas* (who had innocently brought the robe) from the top of Mount *Oeta* in Thessaly into the Euboean Sea. See Ovid, *Met.* ix 134f., Sophocles, *Trachiniae*, and Seneca, *Hercules Furens*.

550. *complain* compose a musical lament (*OED* 1b) and grumble.

552. *partial* both 'polyphonic' and 'prejudiced'.

554. *Suspended* riveted the attention of (*OED* 5a) and deferred. The parenthesis 'suspends as it were the event' (Newton).

took captivated, charmed.

557. *retired* 'in Thought, as well as from the Company' (Richardson).

561. *in wand'ring mazes lost* echoing Virgil, *Aen.* v 590 (on the Cretan labyrinth) and Ariosto, *Orl. Fur.* xiii 50 (on the maze palace of Atlante). Mazes are a recurrent image in *PL*. Cp. iv 239, v 620−24, ix 499, x 830.

564. *apathy* the Stoic virtue of freedom from passion.

568. *obdurèd* hardened, especially 'in wickedness or sin' (*OED* 1). Cp. vi 785.

570. *gross* massed.

575−81. The epithet attached to each river translates its Greek name.

591. *pile* massive building.

592. *Serbonian bog* Lake Serbonis, on the Egyptian coast. Diodorus Siculus tells how 'whole armies' had been engulfed in its quicksands, 'for as the sand is walked upon it gives way but gradually, deceiving with a kind of malevolent cunning those who advance upon it' (I xxx 5−7). Apollonius Rhodius tells how the monster Typhon was whelmed beneath Serbonis after warring against Zeus (*Argonautica* ii 1210–15). For other bog similes, see ii 939 and ix 634–45.

594. *parching* withering with cold (*OED* 'parch' 2b).

595. *frore* frozen. Hell's icy torments were traditional. Cp. Dante, *Inf.* xxxii.

596. *Harpy-footed* taloned. Harpies (monsters with women's faces) carried souls off to the avenging *Furies* (Homer, *Od.* xx 77, Virgil, *Aen.* iii 211f.). *haled*] hailed *Ed I*, *Ed II*. This is a region of *hail* (589), so the early spelling may be a pun.

600. *starve* die by freezing.

604. *Lethean sound* Lethe, river of forgetfulness. Virgil's dead, after suffering for a thousand years, are permitted to drink from Lethe before being reincarnated (*Aen.* vi 748–51). M.'s devils have no second chance.

611. *Medusa* the snaky-haired Gorgon whose look turned men to stone.

613. *wight* person.

614. *Tantalus* was 'tantalized' in Hades by being set in a pool from which he could not drink, and under trees whose fruit he could not eat (Homer, *Od.* xi 582–92). Cp. x 556–77.

628. *Gorgons, Hydras . . . Chimeras* The Hydra was a venomous serpent with nine heads, the Chimera a fire-breathing monster. For Gorgons, see above, 611*n*. Aeneas is threatened by the shades of Gorgons and the Chimera in Virgil's hell (*Aen.* vi 288–9).

631. *toward*] *Ed I*; towards *Ed II*.

632. *Explores* makes proof of (a Latinism).

634. *shaves* barely escapes touching.

637. *Hangs in the clouds* Ships seen in a mirage appear to fly. The simile suits the master of illusions who burdens the air with 'unusual weight' (i 227).

equinoctial at the equator.

638. *Close sailing* sailing close to the wind.

Bengala Bengal. The ships are sailing south and west from India around the Cape of Good Hope (641). At iv 159–65 Satan is likened to ships sailing in the opposite direction.

639. *Ternate and Tidore* Spice Islands in the Moluccas.

640. *spicy drugs* any spice or medicinal substance.

641. *Ethiopian* Indian Ocean.

642. *Ply* beat up against the wind (*OED* v² II 6).

stemming holding course (*OED* v³ 1e).

645. *thrice threefold* overgoing the 'threefold' bronze wall encircling Hesiod's Tartarus (*Theog.* 726–33).

647. *impaled* fenced in.

650–9. *seemed woman . . . unseen* Phineas Fletcher in *The Apollyonists* (1627) depicts 'Sin' (Satan's daughter by Eve) as half woman, half serpent, and makes her 'Porter to th' infernall gate' (i 10–12). Cp. also Phineas Fletcher's Hamartia in *The Purple Island* (1633) xii 27–31, Virgil's Scylla (*Aen.* iii 424–8), Ovid's Scylla (*Met.* xiv 59–67), and Spenser's Errour (*FQ* I i 14f.). M. does not name Sin until line 760.

652. *Voluminous,* consisting of many coils (*OED* 1).

654. *cry* pack.

655. *Cerberean* From Cerberus, the many-headed watchdog of hell.

660. *Scylla* a once beautiful nymph, whose lower parts were changed into a ring of barking dogs when Circe poured poison into the bay where she bathed (Ovid, *Met.* xiv 50–74). Scylla then preyed on sailors (see below, ii 1019*n*). Chrysostom had likened Sin to Scylla in *Homily on I Corinthians* ix 9. See M. J. Edwards, *N&Q* n.s. 42 (December 1995) 448–50.

661. *Trinacrian* Sicilian.

662. *night-hag* Hecate, Scylla's mother and goddess of witchcraft. Her approach was signalled by howling dogs.

Lapland famous for witchcraft.

665. *labouring* eclipsed (*OED* 3b), but suggesting also pains of childbirth (*womb, infant*). Lucan (*Pharsalia* vi 499–506, 554–8) describes witches causing lunar eclipses (*labores*) and drinking *infant blood*.

677. *admired* wondered.

679. *Created thing* The heretical implication that God and his Son were creatures shocked Bentley, but M. did believe the Son was created. See *CD* i 5 (esp. *YP* 6. 211).

683. *miscreated front* misshapen face. Cp. the 'miscreated mould' of Spenser's monster Disdayne (*FQ* II vii 42). Guyon is about to fight Disdayne, when Mammon 'did his hasty hand withhold, / And counseld him abstaine from perilous fight: / For nothing might abash the villein bold'. Sin offers similar advice to Satan (810–14).

686. *taste* know.

proof experience.

688. *goblin* evil spirit.

692. *Drew . . . the third part* Cp. Rev. 12. 4: '[the dragon's] tail drew the third part of the stars of heaven, and did cast them to the earth'. Cp. v 710.

693. *Conjured* sworn together (*OED* 1), constrained by oath (*OED* 3), bewitched (*OED* 7).

694. *God* Death's readiness to name God sets him apart from the devils, who call God anything but 'God' (see i 93*n*). Death has not yet committed himself to Satan, but his own claim to rule Hell (698) implicitly defies God (see ii 327).

701. *whip of scorpions* Cp. Rehoboam's threat to Israel: 'my father hath chastised you with whips, but I will chastise you with scorpions' (I Kings 12. 11). A 'scorpion' was thought to be a studded whip.

708–11. *comet . . . war* Cp. Tasso's simile likening Argantes to a comet that brings death 'To mighty lords, to monarchs, and to kings' (*Gerus. Lib.* vii 52, trans. Fairfax). Cp. also Virgil, *Aen.* x 272–5 and Spenser, *FQ* III i 16, where Aeneas's plumed helmet and Florimell's hair are likened to comets. Comets were bad omens. One appearing in Ophiucus in 1618 was thought to have presaged the Thirty Years War (Fowler).

709. *Ophiucus* The constellation of the Serpent Bearer in the northern sky. Cp. Satan as 'Infernal Serpent' raising rebellion in the North (i 34, v 689).

710. *horrid* bristling (Latin *horridus*).

hair playing on the etymology of 'comet' (Greek κομήτης, 'long-haired').

714–16. *two black clouds . . . Caspian* Boiardo likens Orlando and Agricane to clashing thunderclouds (*Orl. Inn.* I xvi 10). Tasso likens Argantes to thunderclouds over the *Caspian* (*Gerus. Lib.* vi 38).

722. *foe* the Son of God (see Heb. 2. 14 and I Cor. 15. 26).

735. *pest* plague.

752–61. *All . . . me* Sin's birth from Satan's head is modelled on Athene's birth from the head of Zeus, which theologians had compared to God's generation of the Son.

755. *left side* Eve was created from Adam's left (or 'sinister') side (viii 465, x 886).

758–9. *amazement seized / All th' host of Heav'n* echoing Hesiod, *Theog.* (588), where 'amazement seized' men and gods as they beheld the first woman, whom Hephaestos had made to punish men for stealing fire. Cp. Eve as Pandora (iv 714).

760. *Sign* portent (*OED* 9) and mere semblance (*OED* 8b). The paronomasia suggests that *Sin* received her name because she was a portentous *sign*.

772. *pitch* summit.

778–87. *my womb . . . Death* Cp. James 1. 15: 'Then when lust hath conceived, it bringeth forth sin: and sin, when it is finished, bringeth forth death'.

809. *so Fate pronounced* Cp. *CD* i 2: 'fate or *fatum* is only what is *fatum*, spoken, by some almighty power' (trans. Carey, *YP* 6. 131).

813. *dint* blow from a weapon.

825. *pretences* claims (*OED* 1), with overtones of the modern sense (cp. vi 421).

829. *unfounded* bottomless.

833. *purlieus* outskirts (*OED* 3).

836. *surcharged* overpopulated (*OED* 5c).

842. *buxom* yielding (*OED* 2). The phrase *the buxom air* echoes Spenser. Spenser's dragon, wounded by Redcrosse, whips 'the buxome aire' with his tail (*FQ* I xi 37), and Spenser's Jove, disguised as an eagle, spreads 'wide wings to beat the buxome ayre' (III xi 34).

embalmed balmy, fragrant (with ominous overtones of death and decay).

850. *due* just title.

869–70. *right hand . . . without end* Sin parodies the Nicene creed: 'We believe in . . . Jesus Christ . . . who sitteth on the right hand of the Father, and . . . of whose kingdom there shall be no end'.

875. *powers* armies.

877. *wards* the ridges inside a lock and the incisions on a key corresponding to them.

883. *Erebus* hell.

885. **bannered.*

889. *redounding* billowing.

890–1039. In *CD* i 7 M. argues that God created the universe out of primal matter (not nothing). This matter 'was good, and it contained the seeds of all subsequent good' (trans. Carey, *YP* 6. 308). Many critics have nevertheless doubted whether Chaos is good in *PL*. Schwartz (22–4) sees 'Hell and Chaos' as 'allied' against God. Adams (76) sees Chaos as the common enemy of God and Satan. M.'s Chaos seems hostile partly because it continues to exist after the Creation (ii 911, iii 418–26). Contrast Ovid, *Met.* i 19f., where Chaos is all used up. See A. B. Chambers, 'Chaos in *Paradise Lost*', *JHI* 24 (1963) 55–84 (p. 83). See further, v 472*n*.

891. *secrets* secret places (*OED* B 5), with a hint of 'secret parts', sexual organs (*OED* B 6). Chaos is a 'womb' (ii 150, 911).

hoary ancient (*OED* 1c) and hory ('foul, filthy'). At Job 41. 32, Leviathan surges through the sea so that 'one would think the deep to be hoary' (greyish white).

898. *Hot, Cold, Moist, and Dry* The four contraries. In the universe they combine to form the four elements, while in the human body they form the four humours. The union of hot and dry produces fire and choler; that of hot and moist, air and blood; of cold and moist, water and phlegm; of cold and dry, earth and melancholy. In the universe, we encounter the contraries only in their combined forms. Satan meets them raw.

900. *embryon atoms* indivisible units of matter that are the seeds of everything. Cp. *pregnant causes* (913). Atomist philosophers held that the universe was formed of an infinite number of atoms that had collided with each other while falling through infinite space. Atoms were of various shapes and sizes: hooked (*sharp*) ones formed solids, while round (*smooth*) ones formed fluids. There was no Creator, and all was brought together by Chance (Lucretius, *De Rerum Nat.* ii). Marjara (93) sees M. as confining the atoms to Chaos, since 'Chaos is the only place where such atomies could exist'.

903–6. *unnumbered . . . wings* The *sands* correspond to atoms and the *winds* to the four contraries. Ariosto uses the same simile as an image for Fortune (*Orl. Fur.* xxxiii 50).

904. *Barca . . . Cyrene* cities in the Libyan desert.

905. *Levied* lifted up (on the wind) and enlisted as troops.

poise add weight to (*OED* 4a).

909. *arbiter* judge, with an overtone of capricious arbitration.

910. *Chance governs all* 'The only important school of philosophy which attributed chance to nature was atomism' (Marjara 92).

910–18. *Into . . . Stood* Bentley in 1732 objected to Satan's standing *Into this wild abyss*. Strictly, Satan stands and looks. But M.'s syntax, and the absence of the expected verb of motion, mime Satan's hesitation.

910. *abyss* The literal meaning ('bottomless') suggests that Satan is looking down even though he means to ascend. Vertigo is to be expected in Chaos (see 893–4).

911. *The womb . . . grave* translating Lucretius, *De Rerum Nat.* v 259. Lucretius is speaking of the earth, not Chaos.

916. *more worlds* other universes. See i 650*n*.

919. *frith* firth, estuary.

921. *ruinous* falling, crashing (as of towers).

921–2. *to compare / Great things with small* a Virgilian formula (*Ecl.* i 24, *Georg.* iv 176), but Virgil's 'small things' really are small (puppies, bees). M.'s *small* things (the sacking of a city, the distintegration of the universe) would be great in any other poem. Cp. vi 310, x 306, and *PR* iv 563–4.

922. *Bellona* Roman goddess of war.

927. *vans* *wings (*OED* sb¹ 3).

932. *vast vacuity* Porter (58) compares Hesiod's 'great chasm' in Tartarus, through which a man might fall for a year, buffeted by whirlwinds (*Theog.* 740–43). Satan might fall for thousands of years (*to this hour*).

933. *pennons* *wings (from Latin *pennae* or English 'pinion').

936. *rebuff* *repelling blast (*OED* 2), with a play on 'snub'. Even Chaos rejects Satan.

937. *instinct* *impelled, inflamed (*OED* 2). Thunder and lightning were thought to arise when earth's hot sulphurous vapours mixed with cold nitrous vapours in the atmosphere. Chaos 'spontaneously forms gunpowder' (Schwartz 27).

939. *boggy Syrtis* The Syrtes were two shifting sandbanks off the north coast of Africa between Cyrene and Carthage. Lucan (*Pharsalia* ix 303f.) describes Cato of Utica's heroic journey through the greater Syrtis, which Nature had left 'ambiguous between sea and land'. Tasso (*Gerus. Lib.* xv 18) names Syrtis alongside Mount Casius and Damietta (the site of M.'s Serbonian bog, ii 592–3). Apollonius Rhodius describes Syrtis as a misty wasteland (*Argonautica* iv 1235f.). The Trojan fleet encounters the Syrtes in Virgil, *Aen.* i 111.

943–7. *gryphon . . . gold* Gryphons (or griffins) were monsters (part lion, part eagle) that guarded the gold of Scythia against the one-eyed Arimaspians (Herodotus iii 116).

944. *moory* marshy.

945. *Arimaspian* Earlier authors used the form 'Arimasp'.

948-50. *O'er bog . . . flies* The monosyllables, which 'cannot be pronounced but slowly, and with many pauses' (Newton), mime the difficulty of Satan's voyage.

952. *stunning* deafening. *OED*'s earliest participial instance.

954. *vehemence* including 'mindlessness' (Latin *vehe-mens*).

964. *Orcus and Ades* variant names for Pluto (Hades).

965. *Demogorgon* Lucan (*Pharsalia* vi 744-9) and Statius (*Thebaid* iv 516) depict the gods of the underworld as dreading a mysterious being whose name causes the earth to shake. A medieval scribe supplied the name 'Demogorgon', perhaps in error for *Demiourgos* (the Creator in Platonic philosophy). Demogorgon passed into literature through Boccaccio's *De Genealogiis Deorum*. See e.g. Spenser, *FQ* I i 37 and IV ii 47. In *Prolusion i* M. identifies Demogorgon 'with the Chaos of the ancients' (*YP* 1. 222).

971-2. *disturb / The secrets* Bentley wanted to emend *disturb* to 'disclose', but *secrets* means 'secret places' (*OED* 5) and Satan is hinting at his own disruptive powers, which even Chaos might notice.

977. *Confine with* border on.

980. *I travel this profound, direct my course* The comma (common to all seventeenth-century editions) allows *direct* to act as both adjective and verb and so permits Satan to be evasive as to whether he is asking for directions. Satan is reluctant to admit that he is more than *half lost* (975).

982. *behoof* advantage.

988. *Anarch* Chaos, ruler of anarchy (and so no ruler).

989. *incomposed* agitated and disarranged.

990. *I know thee, stranger, who thou art* Cp. Mark 1. 24 and Luke 4. 34, where a devil addresses Christ: 'I know thee who thou art, the Holy One of God'.

999. *serve* suffice.

1000. *so* in this way (by residing on the frontiers).

1001. *[y]our*] our *Ed I*, *Ed II*. Zachary Pearce proposed the emendation in 1733. Chaos does have *intestine broils* (civil wars), but these cannot *weaken* him, for they are the means 'By which he reigns' (908-9). Heaven's civil war has *encroached* on Chaos by bringing Hell and our universe into being (1002-5). *Intestine broils* echoes Marlowe, *Hero and Leander* (1598) i 252: 'And with intestine broils the world destroy'.

1004. *heaven* the universe surrounding our earth, as distinct from *Heaven* (1006), the abode of God.

1005. *golden chain* see below, 1051n.

1007. *walk* Satan 'swims or sinks, or wades, or creeps, or flies' through Chaos, but he never takes a *walk*. Empson (118) hears Chaos as jeering, but the understatement also implies a haughty compliment.

1008. *speed* both 'meet with success' and 'make haste'; perhaps also 'destroy, kill' (*OED* 9c).

1013. *pyramid* spire, flame-shape (supposedly derived from Greek *pyr*, 'fire').

1018. *justling rocks* the Symplegades ('clashing ones') – rocks through which the Argonauts passed in search of the golden fleece (Apollonius Rhodius, *Argonautica* ii 552–611).

1019–20. *Ulysses . . . steered* The monsters Scylla and Charybdis threatened any sailor passing through the Straits of Messina between Italy and Sicily. On Circe's advice, Odysseus chose the lesser evil of Scylla in preference to the *whirlpool* of *Charybdis*. Scylla devoured six of his men as he passed under her rock (*Od.* xii 234–59). Homer does not place Scylla in a *whirlpool*.

1019. *larboard* port (opposite of starboard).

1024–8. *Sin and Death . . . a bridge* See x 293–305.

1024. *amain* with main force and at full speed.

1034. *influence* astral influence (see *Nativity* 71*n*), here applied metaphorically to Heaven's influence on Chaos.

1039. *works* fortifications (*her* refers to *Nature*).

1043. *holds* holds a course for.

1044. *shrouds* the standing rigging of a ship (*OED* sb² 1).

tackle torn Cp. Shakespeare, *Coriolanus* IV v 67–8 (Aufidius addressing the disguised Coriolanus): 'Though thy tackle's torn, / Thou show'st a noble vessel.' 'Tackle' is the running rigging used to work a ship's sails (*OED* 2a).

1046. *Weighs* keeps steady.

1048. *undetermined . . . round* Heaven is so *wide*, that Satan can only guess at its shape.

1050. *living* native, unhewn.

1051. *golden chain* The golden chain with which Zeus threatens to pull gods, earth and sea (Homer, *Il.* viii 18–27) was from ancient times interpreted as an allegory of universal concord. See e.g. Plato (*Theaetetus* 153D), Chaucer (*The Knight's Tale* I (A) 2987–93), Spenser (*FQ* II vii 46), and M.'s *Prolusion ii* (*YP* 1. 236). From this tradition Fowler concludes that M.'s image has the effect of 'binding and ordering' the turmoil of Chaos. Ricks, noting the proximity of *chain* to *pendent*, draws the opposite inference that 'the universe is like a beautiful jewel or "pendent", liable to be stolen'.

1052. *pendent world* The whole universe, hanging in space. Cp. Shakespeare, *Measure for Measure* III i 124–5: 'blown with restless violence round about / The pendent world'.

1053. *magnitude* one of the classes into which astronomers ranked the fixed stars according to brilliancy. The simile makes the universe appear much smaller than it had seemed at i 74 or ii 999–1006.

1054. *fraught with* big with the menace of (*OED* ppl. a 3b). Cp.the nautical imagery in 1043–4).

1055. *he hies* he makes haste. M. opens book iii with the same alliteration.

BOOK III

1. *Light* physical light alone (Kelley 91–4, Bauman 214–32) or a metaphor for the Son of God (Hunter[2] 149–56). Either light could be *first-born* (see Gen. 1. 3 and Col. 1. 15).

2–3. *Or . . . unblamed* 'Or may I, without committing blasphemy, describe you as being co-eternal with God?' M. in *CD* i 5 denies that the Son is co-eternal with the Father.

3. *God is light* I John 1. 5.

4. **unapproachèd* inaccessible (see ix 5n). God dwells 'in the light which no man can approach unto' (I Tim. 6. 16).

6. *effluence* emanation.

7. *hear'st thou rather* 'Would you rather be called'. Cp. the cautious addressing of divine beings in vii 1–2 and *Ep. Dam.* 208.

   ethereal consisting of ether, the subtlest element. See vii 244n.

7–8. *stream . . . fountain* Cp. Lactantius, *Divine Institutes* IV xxix: 'the [Father] is as it were an overflowing fountain, the [Son] as a stream flowing forth from it: the former as the sun, the latter as it were a ray extended from the sun' (*cit.* Hunter[2] 150). See also iii 375.

10. *invest* cover.

11. *world of waters dark and deep* Cp. Spenser, *FQ* I i 39: 'the world of waters wide and deepe'.

12–16. The *void and formless infinite* and *middle darkness* are Chaos; the *Stygian pool* and *utter* darkness are Hell.

17. *Orphéan lyre* Orpheus descended to Hades in search of his wife Eurydice (see *L'Allegro* 145–50n). M. sings with *other notes* because his song was never intended to charm the ears of Hell. Orpheus was also the supposed author of the Orphic *Hymn to Night*, which sees Night as a beneficent deity. M.'s Night is malevolent. See A. B. Chambers, 'Chaos in *Paradise Lost*', *JHI* 24 (1963), 55–84 (p. 75).

19. *Taught by the Heav'nly Muse* M. 'speaks *to* the light *about* the Muse', so the Light is not the Muse (Bauman 230).

20–21. *The dark descent . . . hard and rare* another echo of the Sibyl's warning to Aeneas. See ii 432–3n.

25. *quenched* *destroyed the sight of the eye (*OED* 1c). Eyes were thought to emit beams and M. imagines these as having been extinguished.

25–6. *drop serene . . . suffusion* translating *gutta serena* and *suffusio nigra*, medical terms for ocular diseases.

29. *Smit with the love of sacred song* Cp. Lucretius, *De Rerum Nat.*, i 922–5: 'high hope of renown has . . . struck into my heart sweet love of the Muses . . . I love to approach virgin springs'. Cp. also Virgil, *Georg.* ii 475–7.

30. *Sion* the sacred mountain (as opposed to Helicon or Parnassus). Cp. i 10–12.

32. *nor sometimes forget* often remember.

34. *So were I* Would that I were.

35. *Thamyris* a legendary Thracian poet, punished with blindness for boasting that he could outsing the Muses (Homer, *Il.* ii 594–600).

Maeonides Homer.

36. *Tiresias* the blind Theban prophet. Cp. Marvell's 'On Mr Milton's *Paradise Lost*': 'Just heaven thee, like Tiresias, to requite, / Rewards with prophecy thy loss of sight' (43–4).

Phineus a Thracian prophet, blinded by the gods.

37. *voluntary* freely (as in a musical 'voluntary', chosen by the performer). *move* put forth, utter (*OED* 4).

38. *numbers* verses.

wakeful bird nightingale.

39. *darkling* in the dark.

47. *Book of Knowledge* the Book of Nature, God's revelation in his creatures.

48. *blank* void (*OED* 7), but *expunged* and *razed* also suggest a blank page in Nature's book. The Romans *expunged* writing on waxed tablets by covering it with little pricks, or *razed* it by shaving the tablets clean.

60. *sanctities* angels.

61. *his sight* seeing him, and being seen by him.

62. *his right* Heb. 1. 2–3: 'His Son . . . sat down on the right hand of the Majesty on high'.

67. *fruits* playing on Latin *fruitio*, 'enjoyment'.

71. *this side Night* that part of Chaos between Heaven and the universe.

72. *dun* dusky.

sublime aloft.

73. *stoop* descend from a height (*OED* 5a) and descend swiftly on prey (*OED* 6, hawking term).

74. *world* universe. The *bare outside* is a hard outer shell.

75. *without* both 'on the outside of' and 'not having'. The *land* on the *outside* of our *firmament* is unsheltered by any firmament. The oxymoron *imbosomed without* implies the vulnerability of a universe imbosomed in nothing but itself.

76. *Uncertain . . . air* Satan cannot tell whether the universe is surrounded by ocean or air.

81. *Transports* both 'conveys' and 'carries away' (with hate).

Adversary the literal meaning of *Satan* (see i 82n).

83. *main* vast, uninterrupted. Cp. 'Main ocean' (vii 279).

84. *Wide interrupt* forming a wide breach.

93. *glozing* flattering.

119. *unforeknown M. in *CD* i 3 argues that future events are certain for no other reason than that God foreknows them (*YP* 6. 164–5). In his anxiety to acquit his *foreknowledge*, God now says that the Fall would have been *certain* even if he had not foreknown it. This statement can only damage God's (and M.'s) theodicy, for it inadvertently concedes that the certainty (not just the possibility) of the Fall is grounded in something other than divine foreknowledge.

120. *impúlse* instigation, esp. a strong suggestion supposed to come from a good or evil spirit (*OED* 3).

129. *first sort* fallen angels.

suggestion prompting from within (*OED* 1b), devilish temptation (*OED* 1a). See v 702*n*.

136. *Spirits elect* unfallen angels. Cp. I Tim. 5. 21: 'the elect angels'.

140. *Substantially* M. in *CD* i 5 argues that God imparted to the Son his 'divine substance', but not his 'total essence' (trans. Carey, *YP* 6. 211–12).

153–4. *That be . . . from thee* Cp. Abraham's plea for the Sodomites: 'That be far from thee to do after this manner, to slay the righteous with the wicked: and that the righteous should be as the wicked, that be far from thee' (Gen. 18. 25).

158. *naught* nothing, nought (*OED* 1) and wickedness (*OED* 2).

166. *blasphemed* reviled, defamed.

169. *Son of my bosom* Cp. John 1. 18: 'the only begotten Son, which is in the bosom of the Father'.

170. *my . . . effectual might* Cp. I Cor. 1. 24: 'Christ the power of God'. Cp. also Venus's words to Cupid at *Aen.* i 664: 'Son, who art alone my strength, my mighty power'. Patristic tradition had applied Virgil's line to Christ.

177. *exorbitant* forsaking the right path (*OED* 3), immoderate (*OED* 4a), abnormal (*OED* 2c).

178. *yet once more* See *Lycidas* 1*n*.

180. *know how frail* Cp. Ps. 39. 4: 'That I may know how frail I am'.

183. *peculiar grace* M. rejects Calvinist predestination in *CD* i 4 (*YP* 6. 181), but here God implies that some are predestined to be saved. Danielson (82–3) compares Richard Baxter's *Catholick Theologie* (1675), which distinguishes between 'sufficient Grace' (offered to everyone) and 'efficient Grace' (given to a few). Thus no one is predestined to damnation but some are predestined to salvation.

186. *betimes* in time.

189. *stony hearts* 'I will take the stony heart out of their flesh, and will give them an heart of flesh' (Ezek. 11. 19).

200. *hard be hardened* M. in *CD* i 8 says that 'hardening of the heart . . . is usually the last punishment' inflicted on sinners 'in this life' (trans. Carey, *YP* 6. 336–7).

206. *Affecting* aspiring to.

208. *sacred* *set apart (*OED* 2b), accursed (*OED* 6).

devote consigned to destruction (*OED* 'devoted' 3).

211. *Some other able* Immortal angels are presumably *able* to redeem man by choosing to *be mortal* (214). But see below, 281*n*.

212. *rigid* strict (also suggesting *rigor mortis*).

satisfaction the theological term for Christ's sacrifice.

215. *just th' unjust to save* Cp. I Pet. 3. 18: 'the just for the unjust'.

217. *stood mute* Cp. ii 418–29, where the devils 'sat mute' until Satan volunteered to undertake the voyage to earth.

219. *Patron* advocate.

224. *doom* Judgement.

225. *fulness dwells* Cp. Col. 2. 9: 'For in him dwelleth all the fulness of the Godhead bodily'.

231. *unprevented* before being prayed for. Cp. 'Prevenient grace' (xi 3).

233. *dead in sins* Cp. Eph. 2. 4: 'when we were dead in sins'.

234. *meet* fitting, adequate.

241. *wreck* wreak, give vent to (*OED* v² 2), but suggesting too that the Son is a rock on which Death's rage will wreck itself. Cp. iv 11 ('wreck on innocent frail man').

244. *Life in myself forever* Cp. John 5. 26: 'For as the Father hath life in himself; so hath he given to the Son to have life in himself'.

247–9. *Thou wilt not . . . corruption* Cp. Ps. 16. 10: 'Thou will not leave my soul in hell; neither wilt thou suffer thine Holy One to see corruption'.

250. *I shall rise* The Son's confidence might not emerge from easy foreknowledge. In *CD* i 5 M. denies omniscience to the Son (*YP* 6. 265–6).

251–4. *spoiled . . . triumph* Cp. Col. 2. 15: 'And having spoiled principalities and powers, he made a shew of them openly, triumphing over them'.

251. *spoil* prey (*OED* 4), with overtones of 'spoils of war'. Human nature, exalted by the Resurrection, 'was very often referred to as "spoil"' (Fowler, ix 147–51*n*).

252–3. *Death . . . sting* Cp. I Cor. 15. 55: 'O death, where is thy sting?'

255. *lead Hell captive* Cp. Eph. 4. 8: 'he led captivity captive'.

maugre in spite of.

258. *ruin* hurl to the ground and destroy.

259. *Death last* Cp. I Cor. 15. 26: 'The last enemy that shall be destroyed is death'.

261. *long absent* The Son seems to imagine a longer absence than thirty-three years. See Empson (127–9).

271. *Admiration* astonishment and veneration.

276. *complacence* pleasure, delight (*OED* 2).

281–2. *Thou . . . join* 'Therefore join to thy nature the nature of those whom thou alone canst redeem'.

281. *thou only canst redeem* At line 211 God had implied that angels were 'able' to redeem us. Are we now to infer that God was then deliberately misleading the angels (as he does at vi 44–55)?

286. *The head* Cp. I Cor. 11. 3: 'The head of every man is Christ'.

287–8. *As in him . . . restored* Cp. I Cor. 15. 22: 'as in Adam all die, even so in Christ shall all be made alive'.

291. *Imputed* attributed vicariously (*OED* 2, theological term).

293. *transplanted* continuing the horticultural image begun in *seed* and *root* (284, 288). Cp. *CD* i 21, 'Of Ingrafting in Christ', where M. defines ingrafting as 'the process by which God the Father plants believers in Christ. That is to say, he makes them sharers in Christ, and renders them fit to join, eventually, in one body with Christ' (trans. Carey, *YP* 6. 477).

299. *Giving* submitting.

300. *dearly* lovingly and at great cost.

307. *fruition* pleasurable possession (*OED* 1). 'Christ is ready to renounce *God-like fruition* for man, but man will not renounce the fruit that makes him Godlike' (Fowler).

   quitted renounced (*OED* 6b), left (*OED* 7), redeemed, set free (*OED* 1a), remitted a debt (*OED* 4).

309. *By merit* Cp. Satan 'by merit raised' (ii 5).

317–18. *all power / I give thee* Cp. Matt. 28. 18: 'All power is given unto me'.

320. *Thrones . . . Dominions* The four angelic orders named at Col. 1. 16 (with *Princedoms* for 'principalities').

321–2. *All knees . . . earth* Cp. Phil. 2. 10: 'at the name of Jesus every knee should bow, of things in heaven, and things in earth, and things under the earth'.

324–9. *Shalt in the sky appear . . . rouse their sleep* See Revelation, Matt. 24. 30–31, and I Cor 15. 51–2.

327. *cited* summoned, roused.

330. *saints* all the elect.

331. *arraigned* accused.

334. *The world shall burn* See II Peter 3. 10–13.

340. *need* be needed.

341. *God shall be All in All* Empson (130) takes God to mean that he is 'going to abdicate', but see I Cor. 15. 28: 'then shall the Son also himself be subject unto him that put all things under him, that God may be all in all'. Cp. vi 730–33.

342–3. *Adore him . . . as me* Cp. John 5. 23: 'All men should honour the Son, even as they honour the Father'.

347. *rung* probably a transitive verb, with *multitude of angels* (345) the subject, and *Heav'n* the object.

348. *jubilee* jubilation. Fowler hears a play on the Hebrew Jubilee – a ritual celebration occurring every fifty years, when slaves were freed. It was a 'type' of the Atonement.

hosannas Hebrew 'save now' or 'saṽe, pray'.

351–2. *down . . . crowns* Cp. Rev. 4. 10, where the twenty-four elders 'cast their crowns before the throne'.

353. *amarant* Greek 'unfading': a legendary immortal flower. The crown of glory 'that fadeth not away' (I Pet. 1. 4) is in the Greek said to be *amarantinon*. Clement of Alexandria says that the righteous will be awarded crowns of amarant in Heaven (*Paedagogus* II viii 78). Cp. *Lycidas* 149.

363. *sea of jasper* Cp. Rev. 4. 6: 'before the throne there was a sea of glass like unto crystal'. See also iii 518–19.

367. **preamble* musical prelude.

370. *exempt* excluded.

373. *Immutable, immortal, infinite,* a direct lift from Sylvester, *DWW* (1592–1608), I i 45. M. often uses triple negatives. See e.g. ii 185, iii 231, *PR* iii 429.

375. *Fountain of light* see above, iii 7–8*n*.

377. *but* except.

378–80. *cloud . . . dark* At the dedication of the Temple 'the house was filled with a cloud, even the house of the Lord; for the glory of the Lord had filled the house of God. Then said Solomon, The Lord hath said that he would dwell in thick darkness' (II Chron. 5. 13 – 6. 1). Cp. ii 263–7.

381. *that* so that.

382. *veil their eyes* Isa. 6. 2.

383. *of all Creation first* Cp. Col. 1. 15: 'the firstborn of every creature'.

385. *without cloud* Contrast the Father, who appears *through a cloud* (378).

387. *Whom else no creature can behold* Cp. John 1. 18: 'No man hath seen God at any time; the only begotten Son, which is in the bosom of the Father, he hath declared him'.

388. **effulgence* coined from Latin *effulgens*.

392. *Dominations* an angelic order ('Dominions' at iii 320 and Col. 1. 16).

405. *much more to pity inclined* The clause could refer either to the Father (402) or the Son.

412–15. *Hail . . . disjoin* echoing many pagan hymns, which end with a hailing of the god and a promise to resume his praises. Cp. the Homeric hymn to Delian Apollo.

412. *thy name* The name 'Christ' never appears in *PL*.

413. *my song* Bentley wanted to emend to 'our songs', but the shift to the first person allows M. to refer to his own poem.

418. *opacous* opaque.

419. *first convéx* the outer shell encompassing the universe.

422. *alighted* both 'landed' and 'illumined' (*OED* 'alight' v³ 1). Satan and the shell on which he walks are dimly lit by the reflected light of Heaven (427 30).

429. *vexed* tossed about.

431. *Imaus* mountains extending from the Himalayas to the Arctic Ocean.

432. *roving Tartar* Nomadic Mongols had ravaged Asia and Europe under Genghis Khan and Tamerlane. Ricks hears a pun on Tartarus (*Milton's Grand Style*, 126). Martindale (128) finds the pun 'far-fetched', but it had been a commonplace since 1237, when Friar Julian of Hungary referred to Mongol Tatars as *Tartari*, 'people of hell'. *Tartar* was also a variant of 'Tartarus' (*OED* 'Tartar' sb⁴).

434. *yeanling* newborn. Fowler associates the *lambs* and *kids* with the sheep and goats separated at the Last Judgement (Matt. 25. 32–3).

436. *Hydaspes* now the river Jhelum, which rises in Kashmir.

438. *Sericana* China. Travellers' reports of *cany wagons* reached a wide audience through Mendoza's *Historie of the Great and Mightie Kingdome of China* (trans. Parke, 1588).

   *cany made of cane or bamboo.

441. *Walked up and down* Cp. Job 1. 7: 'Whence comest thou? Then Satan answered the Lord, and said, From going to and fro in the earth, and from walking up and down in it'.

444–97. M.'s *Paradise of Fools* is indebted to Ariosto's Limbo of Vanity on the moon (*Orl. Fur.* xxxiv 73ff.). Ariosto's Limbo is less satirical than M.'s, but it includes one anti-ecclesiastical stanza (on the Constantine Donation) that M. translated. See *Ah Constantine* in this volume.

444. *store* plenty (*OED* 4b) and a body of persons (*OED* 3).

446. *vain* empty, foolish (*OED* 2, 3).

449. *fond* infatuated and foolish.

452. *painful* painstaking.

456. *Abortive* prematurely born (see line 474) and failing of the intended effect.

   unkindly unnaturally.

457. *fleet* glide away, flit, vanish (*OED* 10). Of the soul: to pass away from the body (*OED* 10b).

459. *some* Ariosto. See above, 444–97n.

461. *Translated saints* holy men removed from earth by God. Such were Enoch (Gen. 5. 24) and Elijah (II Kings 2. 11). Cp. xi 705–10. Although M. scorns Ariosto's notion of the moon's inhabitants, M.'s own speculation is indebted to *Orl. Fur.* xxxiv 58–68, where Astolfo ascends to the moon in Elijah's chariot.

461–2. *middle . . . kind* M.'s contemporaries were excited by the possibility of extraterrestrial life. See e.g. John Wilkins, *The Discovery of a World in the Moone* (1638). Wilkins paraphrases Nicholas of Cusa: 'the inhabiters of the Sunne are like the nature of that Planet, more cleare and bright, more intellectual and spirituall than those in the Moone, . . . and those of the earth . . . more grosse and materiall than either, so that these intellectuall natures in the Sun, are more forme than matter, those in the earth more matter than forme, and those in the Moone betwixt both' (194). There was much curiosity as to whether aliens would be infected by Adam's sin (Wilkins 189–90). M. hints strongly that they would not (iii 568–71, viii 144–58).

463–4. *ill-joined . . . Giants* Gen. 6. 4 describes how the Sons of God begot a race of Giants on the daughters of men. M. returns to the story in xi 573–627 and (with a different interpretation) in *PR* ii 178–81.

467. *Sennaär* the LXX and Vulgate form of 'Shinar' (Gen. 11. 2). M. returns to the Babel story in xii 38–62.

470. *fondly* foolishly.

471. *Empedocles* a pre-Socratic philosopher who threw himself into Etna so as to conceal his mortality. His plan was frustrated when the volcano threw up one of his sandals.

473. *Cleombrotus* a youth who drowned himself so as to enjoy the immortality promised in Plato's *Phaedo*.

474. *Embryos and idiots* were consigned by Franciscan theologians to a limbo above the earth. M. satirizes this doctrine by placing the *friars* in their own limbo.

474. *eremites* hermits.

475. *White, black and grey* Carmelites, Dominicans, Franciscans.
  trumpery religious ornaments (*OED* 2c), imposture (*OED* 1).

477. *Golgotha* Calvary, where Christ was crucified and buried. Cp. Luke 24. 5–6: 'Why seek ye the living among the dead? He is not here but is risen'.

479. *weeds* robes.

481–3. *They . . . moved* Moving outward through the Ptolemaic system, the traveller from earth would pass the seven planetary spheres, the *fixed* stars, the ninth (*crystálline*) sphere, and the *primum mobile* (*first moved*). The *trepidation* (oscillation) of the eighth sphere had been added to Ptolemy's system so as to account for the precession of the equinoxes; it was much debated (*talked*) in M.'s time. *Balance* and *weighs* allude punningly to Libra, the Scales: a point of reference for measuring the trepidation or 'libration' (Fowler).

484. *wicket* not the *palace gate* of line 505, but 'a small door made in, or placed beside, a large one, for ingress and egress when the large one is closed' (*OED* 1). The image implies that Roman superstition seeks clandestine ingress.

485. *keys* Matt. 16. 19 (cp. *Lycidas* 110).

489. *devious* off the main road (*OED* 1), erring, straying (*OED* 3); also a transferred epithet implying the Friars' deviousness.

491. *beads* rosaries.

492. *dispenses* dispensations.

bulls papal decrees.

493. **upwhirled* Cp. the neologisms 'upsent' (i 541) and 'upgrown' (ix 677).

494. *backside* lower hemisphere of the universe – with a scatological pun (notice *winds*).

496. *Paradise of Fools* The phrase 'fool's paradise' had long been proverbial.

501. *travelled* including travailed, wearied.

502. *degrees* steps or rungs of a stairway or ladder (*OED* 1a). Since *each stair mysteriously was meant* (516), there is also a play on degrees of dignity or rank. See below, 516*n*.

506. *frontispiece* pediment over a door (*OED* 2).

507. *orient* lustrous, sparkling.

510-15. *Jacob . . . gate of Heav'n* Jacob fled to Padan-Aram (in Syria) after cheating his brother Esau out of their father's blessing. While sleeping in Luz, he had a dream of angels ascending and descending a ladder reaching to Heaven (Gen. 28. 10-17). Fowler sees a parallel between Jacob and Satan, who has 'fled retribution and is at a parting of the ways where he could still repent'. But God has said that the devils will not find grace (iii 129-32) and the ladder confronts Satan with his *exclusion* (525).

513. The *Ed I* and *Ed II* pointing (comma after *Luz*, not *Padan-Aram*) creates the false impression that Padan-Aram is in the field of Luz. Luz is in the Judaean hills, not Syria.

516. *mysteriously* allegorically. D. C. Allen (*MLN* 68, 1953, 360) shows that Jacob's ladder was sometimes identified with Zeus's golden chain (see ii 1051*n*) and interpreted as a symbol of the Chain of Being. M.'s stairway may be the 'golden chain' of ii 1051, but here it is retractable.

518. *Viewless* invisible.

sea the waters that flow 'above the firmament' (Gen. 1. 7). H. F. Robins (*PMLA* 69, 1954, 903-14) argues that this sea envelops the whole *primum mobile*, even though Satan had walked on 'firm land' at iii 75 and 418. But the sea flows only *underneath* the stairway, 'about' its foot (Argument to book iii).

519. *liquid* including 'clear, transparent, bright' (*OED* 2).

521. *Wafted by angels* refers to Lazarus, who was 'carried by the angels into Abraham's bosom' (Luke 16. 22).

522. *Rapt . . . fiery steeds* Elijah ascended to Heaven in a *chariot* drawn by 'horses of fire' (II Kings 2. 11).

524. *easy ascent* Cp. 'Th' ascent is easy' (ii 81) and contrast Virgil, *Aen.* vi 126 ('the descent . . . is easy . . . but to retrace one's steps . . . this is the task'). See ii 432–3, iii 19–21.

528. *A passage down to th' earth* Since the passage opens *just o'er* Paradise, and Satan views the universe in *breadth* from *pole to pole* (561–2), Satan is standing at some point on the celestial equator, not at a celestial pole. The *primum mobile* is constantly rotating, so one of two conclusions must follow: (1) the passage is also rotating and just happens to be below the stairway when Satan reaches it, or (2) the shell on which Satan stands is a motionless sphere exterior to the *primum mobile*. In either case, the universe 'is lying, as it were, on its side' (Fowler), with earth's axis parallel to Heaven's floor.

534. *and* and so did.

   choice careful in choosing (*OED* 3a).

535. *Paneas* Greek name for the city of Dan, the northernmost city of Canaan.

536. *Beërsaba* Beersheba, the southernmost city of Canaan. The phrase 'from Dan even to Beersheba' is common in the O.T.

543. *scout* The military sense suggests that Satan has come to conquer the cosmic *metropolis*.

546. *Obtains* reaches (*OED* 5) and occupies (*OED* 6).

547. *discovers* reveals.

552. *though after Heaven seen* though he had seen Heaven.

556–7. *circling . . . shade* the earth's shadow rotating around the universe. It does not extend beyond the sphere of the moon, and beyond it the sky is blue, with stars, sun, and planets clearly visible.

556. *canopy* Canopies over beds or thrones were often conical in shape.

558. *fleecy star* Aries, the Ram.

559. *Andromeda* a constellation adjacent to Aries. In Greek myth Andromeda was a beautiful princess menaced by a dragon.

562. *world's first region* the vast space between the universe's outer shell and the earth's atmosphere.

563. *precipitant* rushing headlong.

564. *marble* gleaming, sparkling (Greek *marmareos*).

567. *happy isles* alluding to the Fortunate Isles, or Islands of the Blest, in Greek mythology. Cp. ii 410, where the devils speak of man's 'happy isle'. Here the plural implies that inhabitants of *other worlds* may have escaped man's Fall.

568. *Hesperian gardens* Editors detect a foreshadowing of the Fall in this allusion to the stolen apples of the Hesperides (see *A Masque* 393n), but M. might be implying that extraterrestrials have their own, perhaps uneaten, forbidden fruit. See above, 461–2n.

571. *above them* Fowler notes that the sun is above the stars *in splendour* (572), but below them in space. Since Satan does not know whether he is moving *up or down*, M. might intend both senses of *above*.

575. *By centre or eccentric* by a centric or eccentric orbit. A centric orbit has the earth (or sun) at its centre; an eccentric orbit does not. M. avoids choosing between the Ptolemaic and Copernican systems. Cp. viii 83.

576. *longitude* the distance he flew (measured by degrees of arc) along the ecliptic.

578. *distance due* Cp. Satan's contemptuous reference to the courtier angels' 'practised distances' about God's throne (iv 945).

580. *numbers that compute* rhythms that measure.

581. *Days . . . years* Cp. Gen. I. 14: 'Let there be lights in the firmament of the heaven to divide the day from the night; and let them be for signs, and for seasons, and for days, and years'. See also Plato, *Timaeus* (38–40).

582–3. *turned / By his magnetic beam* Kepler's theory that the sun's magnetism was responsible for planetary motions was popular in M.'s time. See Marjara (123–7).

588–90. *a spot . . . saw* Galileo had observed sun-spots through his telescope (*optic tube*) in 1610.

592. *metal*] medal *Ed I, Ed II*. The case for emending is clinched by the repetition of *metal* and *stone* in lines 595–6.

596. *carbuncle* any red gem, including 'a mythical gem said to emit a light in the dark' (*OED* 1).

chrysolite any green gem.

597. *to the twelve* 'up to and including all the twelve'. See Exod. 28. 17–20 for the jewels in *Aaron's breastplate*. See also *PR* iii 14*n*.

598. *a stone* the Philosopher's Stone. Alchemists had identified it with the *urim* on Aaron's breastplate (Exod. 28. 30). The stone allegedly had the power to heal all diseases and restore Paradise, as well as transmute base metals into gold. See Lyndy Abraham, *Marvell and Alchemy* (1990) 16.

599. *Imagined . . . seen* 'elsewhere imagined more often than seen'.

601. *Philosophers* magicians, alchemists (*OED* 2).

603. *volátile* able to fly (*OED* 2a) and evaporating rapidly (*OED* 3a).

Hermes the winged god and the element mercury. Hermes Trismegistus (see *Il Penseroso* 88*n*) was the reputed father of alchemy. Alchemists would *bind* mercury by sealing it in a *limbeck* (alembic) and solidifying it.

604. *Proteus* the shape-shifting sea-god (from ancient times a symbol of matter). Alchemists can dissolve matter into its *native form*, but they cannot recompose the four contraries of this primal matter (see ii 898) into the Philosopher's Stone. The allusion to shape-shifting prepares for Satan's first metamorphosis (634).

606. *here* in the sun.

607. *elixir* the liquid form of the Philosopher's Stone, capable of curing all diseases and prolonging life.

608. *Potable* drinkable.

virtuous energizing.

609. *arch-chemic* chief of the alchemists. The sun's rays were thought to penetrate the earth and generate precious metals and stones. Cp. *A Masque* 732–6.

610. *humour* moisture.

617. *equator* the celestial equator, where (before the Fall) the sun would *culminate* or reach its highest point. After the Fall, *direct* (and therefore shadowless) beams occur only at the points where ecliptic and equator coincide.

620. *visual ray* The eye was thought to emit a beam onto the object perceived.

622. *ken* range of vision.

623. *The same whom John saw* Cp. Rev. 19. 17: 'I saw an angel standing in the sun'.

625. **beaming* *OED*'s earliest instance of the participial adjective.

tiar crown.

627. *Illustrious* lustrous, gleaming.

634. *casts* schemes (*OED* 43) and casts off (his present shape).

636–9. *Cherub . . . feigned* Cp. II Cor. 11. 14: 'Satan himself is transformed into an angel of light'.

637. *prime* prime rank, with overtones of 'prime of life'.

643. *succinct* *scant, close-fitting (*OED* 3a).

644. *decent* comely (*OED* 2).

648. *Uriel* Hebrew 'Light (or fire) of God'. The name is not biblical, but it appears as the name of an angel in the apocryphal II Esdras (4. 1) and the pseudepigraphal I Enoch (22. 2). Uriel is also prominent in cabbalistic lore.

one of the seven See Rev. 1. 5, 8. 2, and Tob. 12. 15 for the seven angels before God's throne. The Bible does not name them, but I Enoch lists them as Uriel, Raphael, Raguel, Michael, Zerachiel, Gabriel, Remiel. Other lists exist, but this is the only one to place Uriel *first* (656).

650. *are his eyes* Cp. Zech. 4. 10: 'those seven . . . are the eyes of the Lord which run to and fro through the whole earth'.

655. *God* The disguised Satan now speaks the name for the first time.

656. *authentic* authoritative (*OED* 1).

Interpreter one who makes known the will of another; a title of Mercury as messenger of the gods (*OED* 3). Cp. vii 72.

664. *favour* favourite (*OED* 1d), perhaps also 'resemblance'. See ii 350*n*.

667. *wand'ring* See ii 148*n*.

671–2. *That I may . . . behold* Cp. Herod's question to the Magi concerning the Second Adam: 'when ye have found him, bring me word again, that I may come and worship him also' (Matt. 2. 8).

694. *tends* inclines.

709. *mould* substance.

716. *quintessence* the fifth element, of which the heavenly bodies were made.

717. *spirited with various forms* presided over by various angelic spirits or Intelligences. Cp. Plato, *Timaeus* 41E.

718. *rolled orbicular* referring both to the spherical shape of the newly-created stars and the orbits that they follow.

726. *Night* earth's night (but with a glance at Chaos and Night, who *would invade* the universe).

730. *triform* alluding to the moon's phases; but ancient poets called the lunar goddess *triformis* because of her triple nature (Luna in heaven, Diana on earth, and Hecate or Proserpina in hell). Virgil associates 'threefold Hecate' with Chaos (*Aen.* iv 510–11).

731. *Hence* from here (the sun).

fills and empties M. often imagines light as a liquid. Cp. iii 7–8 and vii 359–65.

732. *checks the night* holds night in check. Ricks hears a pun on ' "chequers, variegates with its rays" as in Robert Greene: "checkt the night with golden rays" (1590, *OED*)'.

738. *reverence* including 'obeisance, bow' (*OED* 2).

740. *ecliptic* the sun's orbit around the earth.

sped including 'prospered' (*hoped success*).

742. *Niphates* a mountain on the border of Armenia and Assyria.

BOOK IV

3. *second rout* St John prophesies a second battle in Heaven at Rev. 12. 3–12.

5. *Woe . . . earth* Cp. Rev. 12. 12: 'Woe to the inhabiters of the earth and of the sea! for the devil is come down unto you, having great wrath, because he knoweth that he hath but a short time'.

10. *Accuser* translating Greek *diabolos*. Cp. Rev. 12. 10: 'the accuser of our brethren is cast down, which accused them before our God day and night'.

11. *wreck* wreak, avenge (*OED* v² 3) and ruin (*OED* v¹ 4). Wreaking vengeance, Satan will ruin both man and himself. Cp. iii 241.

17. *engine* cannon and plot. Cp. i 750, ix 172–4.

18. *distract* drive mad (*OED* 6), draw in different directions (*OED* 1).

20. *Hell within him* Contrast Satan's boast at i 254–5, and cp. the words of Marlowe's Mephostophilis in *Doctor Faustus* I iii 76: 'Why, this is hell, nor am I out of it'. Cp. also II i 121–2: 'where we are is hell, / And where hell is, there must we ever be'.

27. *Eden* Hebrew 'delight' (contrasting with *grieved, sad*).

31. *revolving* pondering.

32–113. *O thou . . . know* M.'s nephew and biographer Edward Phillips reports that this soliloquy (at least lines 32–41) was written 'several Years before the Poem was begun', and was intended to begin a tragedy on the Fall (Darbishire 72). Cp. the opening addresses to the sun in Aeschylus, *Prometheus Bound*, and Euripides, *Phoenissae*.

33. *Look'st* both 'survey' and 'seem to be'.

   sole unique (and suggesting *sol*, 'the sun').

36–7. *thy name / O sun* See *Nativity* 83n for the pun on 'Son'. This is the nearest Satan comes, after his expulsion from Heaven, to naming the Son or even acknowledging his existence.

37. *hate thy beams* Cp. John 3. 20: 'Every one that doeth evil hateth the light'.

43. *he created what I was* Satan had claimed to be 'self-begot' (v 860). He might have been lying, or he might now be suddenly convinced of his creatureliness. See Empson, 64–5.

45. *Upbraided none* Cp. James 1. 5: 'God, that giveth to all men liberally, and upbraideth not'.

50. *'sdained* disdained.

51. *quit* requite, pay.

53. *still . . . still* continually . . . continually (but in line 56 *still* includes 'nevertheless').

56. *By owing owes not* The first 'owe' means 'acknowledge as belonging to oneself' (*OED* 1c). Thus a *grateful mind*, simply by acknowledging a debt, ceases to owe it. Fowler traces the idea to Cicero, *Pro Plancio* xxviii 68. See also *Ad Patrem* 111–14.

61. *Power* celestial being (*OED* 7).

66, 67, 71. *thou* Satan himself.

75. *myself am Hell* See above, 20n.

79. *O then at last relent* The Church Father Origen had thought that Satan might be saved through *repentance* (80), but M.'s God excludes the rebel angels from grace at iii 129–32 and v 615. Cp. Matt. 25. 41, Rev. 20. 10.

79–80. *is there no place / Left for repentance* Cp. Heb. 12. 17: 'when he [Esau] would have inherited the blessing, he was rejected: for he found no place of repentance, though he sought it carefully with tears'.

81. *that word* 'submission'.

87. *abide* pay the penalty for (erroneous form of 'abye') and abide by, remain true to.

94. *grace* unmerited favour of God. *Act of grace* was also a legal term

meaning 'formal pardon, *spec.* a free and general pardon, granted by an Act of Parliament' (*OED* 15b).

97. *violent* not free or voluntary (*OED* 5b).

110. *Evil be thou my good* Cp. Isa. 5. 20: 'Woe unto them that call evil good, and good evil'. Satan need not be pledging himself to evil as an absolute. Stephen Fallon compares the moral relativism of Hobbes in *Leviathan* (1651) 24: 'these words of Good, Evil, and Contemptible, are ever used with relation to the person that useth them: There being nothing simply and absolutely so; nor any common Rule of Good and Evill, to be taken from the nature of the objects themselves'. For Satan, 'good' is 'the arbitrarily imposed "good" of God, who first gave names to things' (Fallon 219).

112. *reign* govern.

115. *pale* pallor.

116. *borrowed* assumed, counterfeit (*OED* 2a).

118. *distempers* disorders arising from an imbalance of the four humours. Cp. ii 218, 276-7.

122-4. *practised . . . practised* plotted evil (*OED* 9b) . . . become proficient.

123. *couched* lying hidden.

125. *warned* summoned to duty (*OED* 7a), a military term.

126. *Assyrian mount* Niphates (iii 742).

132. *delicious Paradise* 'Paradise of delights', translating the Vulgate's *in Paradiso deliciarum* (Gen. 2. 15), which the A.V. renders as 'the garden of Eden'.

134. *champaign head* treeless plateau.

135. *hairy sides* 'The Freudian idea that the happy garden is an image of the human body would not have frightened Milton in the least' (Lewis 47). *Mound* (134) even suggests the *mons veneris*. A myrtle-clad mount in Spenser's Garden of Adonis has precisely this significance (*FQ* III vi 43).

136. *grotesque* *of landscape: romantic, picturesque (*OED* B 2b), from 'grotto'.

140. *sylvan scene* echoing Virgil, *Aen.* i 164 (*silvis scaena*).

141. *woody theatre* Cp. Spenser, *FQ* III v 39: 'And mighty woods, which did the valley shade, / And like a stately Theatre it made'.

149. *enamelled* bright and variegated in colour.

151. *humid bow* rainbow.

153. *of* out of (both Satan's emergence and the transformation of *pure* into *purer air*).

154. *inspires* infuses (*joy*) and breathes in (*air*).

156. *gentle gales* breezes.

158-9. *stole / Those balmy spoils* Cp. Ariosto's earthly Paradise: 'From flowers, fruit and grass the breezes stole / The varied perfumes' (*Orl. Fur.* xxxiv 51).

159–65. *As . . . smiles* Cp. Diodorus Siculus's description of the fragrant breezes of Arabia Felix wafting out to sea (III xlvi 4); also Ariosto's account of spice-laden breezes delighting 'sailors out at sea' (*Orl. Fur.* xviii 138, xv 16).

160. *Hope* Good Hope (contrasting with Satan's *despair*).

162. *Sabéan* of Saba (the biblical Sheba).

163. *Araby the blest* Arabia Felix (modern Yemen).

165. *grateful* pleasing.

old Ocean the Titan Oceanus.

167. *bane* destroyer, murderer.

168–71. *Asmodéus . . . bound* In the apocryphal Book of Tobit, Tobias (*Tobit's son*) travelled to Media and married Sarah, whose previous seven husbands had been killed on their wedding night by the demon Asmodeus. Instructed by the angel Raphael, Tobias burned the heart and liver of a fish. Smelling the *fishy fume*, Asmodeus 'fled into the utmost parts of Egypt, and the angel bound him' (Tob. 8. 3). Tobias later cured his father's blindness with the fish's gall (Tob. 11. 8). Cp. v 221–3.

170. *with a vengeance* with great violence (*OED* 4b) and with a curse (*OED* 4a).

172. *savage* wild, wooded.

175. *brake* thicket.

176. *had perplexed* would have entangled.

181. *bound . . . bound* The contemptuous pun looks back to *fast bound* (171).

182. *sheer* entirely and perpendicularly.

183–7. *wolf . . . fold* Cp. John 10. 1: 'He that entereth not by the door into the sheepfold, but climbeth up some other way, the same is a thief and a robber'. Cp. also Ariosto's Saracen Rodomonte leaping the moat of Paris 'with one bound' like a hunting dog (*Orl. Fur.* xiv 130, xvi 20). Once in the city, he slaughters Christians like a wolf among sheep (*Orl. Fur.* xvi 23). Cp. also Virgil, *Aen.* ix 59–64, 563–5.

186. *hurdled cotes* sheep-pens of wattled fences.

secure overconfident (*OED* 1), with a wry pun on 'safe'.

191. *In at the window climbs* Cp. Spenser's Kirkrapine, a 'sturdie thiefe / Wont to robbe Churches' who 'in at the window crept' (I iii 17). Spenser and M. both echo Joel 2. 9, where the *thief* is an avenging army: 'they shall climb up upon the houses; they shall enter in at the windows like a thief'. The army turns 'the garden of Eden' into 'a desolate wilderness' (2. 3).

188. **unhoard* take out of a hoard.

192. *clomb* archaic past tense of 'climb'.

193. *lewd* unprincipled (*OED* 5), with a play on 'not in holy orders' (*OED* 1). Thus *lewd hirelings* implies that a paid clergy is not a real clergy. M. thought that ministers should support themselves. See his *Considerations*

Touching the Likeliest Means to Remove Hirelings Out of the Church (1659) and his condemnation of 'hireling wolves' in his sonnet *To the Lord General Cromwell* (14).

196. *cormorant* a seabird noted for gluttony, hence a symbol for human rapaciousness (*OED* 2). At Isa. 34. 11 the cormorant is associated with the day of God's vengeance when Edom will lie waste: 'The cormorant and the bittern shall possess it'. Contrast Raphael as phoenix, v 272.

198. *virtue* power, efficacy. M. is elsewhere evasive as to whether the Tree of Life was truly *life-giving*. See iv 219-20, xi 93-8 and notes.

200. *well used* i.e. by Adam and Eve. Satan *only used* the Tree of Life *for prospect* (lookout); Adam and Eve might have used it as a *pledge*.

211. *Auran* the province of Hauran on the eastern border of Israel (Ezek. 47. 18).

212. *great Seleucia* a city on the Tigris, built by Alexander's general Seleucus Nicator (called *great* to distinguish it from other cities of the same name). See *PR* iii 291.

213-14. *sons of Eden . . . Telassar* Cp. II Kings 19. 11 and Isa. 37. 12, where the Assyrians destroy 'the children of Eden which were in Telassar'.

219. **ambrosial* divinely fragrant (*OED* 1c). The etymology (Greek *ambrotos*, 'immortal') suggests that the Tree of Life might bestow immortality, but see xi 93-6.

220. *vegetable gold* Fowler hears an echo of 'potable gold' (see iii 680*n*) and 'vegetable stone' – both forms of the elixir of life or Philosopher's Stone. Cp. also Virgil's description of the golden bough (*Aen.* vi 143-4).

222. *Knowledge . . . ill* Cp. *CD* i 10: 'It was called the tree of knowledge of good and evil because of what happened afterwards: for since it was tasted, not only do we know evil, but also we do not even know good except through evil' (trans. Carey, *YP* 6. 352). Cp. ix 1070-73, xi 84-9.

223. *a river* the Tigris (identified at ix 71).

228. *kindly* natural.

233. **main streams* Cp. Gen. 2. 10: 'And a river went out of Eden . . . and became into four heads'.

237. *crispèd* rippling.

239. *error* wandering; 'the evil meaning is consciously and ominously excluded' (Stein 66). Cp. vii 302.

241. *nice* fastidious.

242. *knots* flower-beds laid out in intricate designs (*OED* 7).
boon bountiful.

246. **Embrowned* darkened (*OED* 1).

248. *odorous gums* Cp. Spenser's Garden of Adonis, where a grove of myrtles dropped 'sweet gum' and 'Threw forth most dainty odours' (*FQ* III vi 43). Spenser's grove symbolizes the *mons veneris* (see above, 135*n*).

250. *amiable* desirable.

Hesperian fables See iii 568n and *A Masque* 393n. Ralegh in *The History of the World* (1614) notes that the dragon guarding the apples of the Hesperides was 'taken from the Serpent, which tempted Evah' (86).

255. *irriguous* well-watered.

256. *without thorn* a traditional inference from Gen. 3. 18.

257. *umbrageous* shady.

258. *mantling* enveloping (*OED* 2).

262–3. *Myrtle* and *mirror* are attributes of Venus, goddess of love and gardens.

264. *airs* breezes and melodies.

266. *universal Pan* A spurious etymology (Greek πᾶν, 'all') encouraged the notion that the wood-god Pan was a symbol of universal nature. See also *Nativity* 89n.

267. *Graces, Hours* See *A Masque* 986n.

268. *eternal spring* There are no seasons until earth is tilted on its axis, after the Fall (x 651–91). Ovid, *Met.* v 391, describes *Enna*, where *Proserpine* was ravished, as a land of *perpetuum ver*, 'eternall Spring' (trans. Sandys).

269–72. *Enna . . . world* Ovid tells how *Dis* (Pluto, Hades) snatched *Proserpine*, daughter of the grain-goddess *Ceres*, from the Sicilian meadow of *Enna*. The earth grew barren while Ceres searched for her daughter. Jove promised that Proserpine should be restored if she had eaten no food in Hades, but she had eaten seven pomegranate seeds and so had to stay in Hades half the year (*Met.* v 385ff., *Fasti* iv 420ff.). Sandys notes that Proserpine's pomegranate 'is held to have a relation' to the apple that 'thrust *Evah* out of Paradice'. See George Sandys, *Ovid's Metamorphosis* (1632), 195.

270. *Herself a fairer flow'r* Cp. ix 432: 'Herself, though fairest unsupported flow'r'; also Ovid, *Met.* v 398–401, where Proserpine's gathered flowers (*collecti flores*) fall from her robe, and she grieves for them even as she herself is abducted. M. often alludes to Proserpine's abduction in *PL*. See 381–5n below, ix 396, 838–42n.

273–4. *Daphne* a grove of laurels on the river *Orontes* in Syria. It had a *Castalian spring* named for that of the Muses on Mount Parnassus, and an oracle of Apollo (hence *inspired*).

275–9. *Nyseian . . . eye* Diodorus Siculus (III lxvii–lxx) tells how King *Ammon* of Libya had a son, *Bacchus*, by the nymph *Amalthea*. Fearing his jealous wife *Rhea*, Ammon hid Amalthea and Bacchus on Nysa, an island in *the river Triton* near modern Tunis. Christian commentators identified Jupiter-Ammon with Noah's son Ham (*Cham*).

278. *florid* ruddy (Bacchus was the god of wine).

281. *Amara* a mountain-top fastness where Abyssinian kings raised their sons (*issue*) among secluded gardens and palaces. Peter Heylyn in his *Cosmographie* (1652) says it was 'a dayes journey high', adding 'some have taken (but mistaken) it for the place of *Paradise*' (iv 64).

282. *Ethiop line* equator.

286. **undelighted all delight* 'Eden' means 'delight'.

291. *worthy* here probably an adverb (*OED* B) signifying that Adam and Eve really were what they *seemed* to be.

293. *severe* austerely plain ('like a severe style in music or architecture', Lewis 118). Cp. xi 1144, 1169.

295. *Whence* from God's image.

296. *their sex not equal seemed* Joseph Wittreich in *Feminist Milton* (1987) 86 argues valiantly but unpersuasively that Adam and Eve *seem* unequal only because we are seeing them through Satan's eyes. Raphael and the Son both insist upon Adam's headship (viii 561-78, x 145-56), as does M. in his prose (*YP* 2. 589-90, 6. 355).

299. *He . . . him* Cp. I Cor. 11. 3: 'the head of every man is Christ; and the head of the woman is the man; and the head of Christ is God'.

300. *front* forehead.

sublime of lofty aspect.

301. *hyacinthine* Cp. Odysseus's hair that 'hung down like hyacinthine petals', shining like 'gold on silver' (Homer, *Od.* vi 231-2).

301-8. *locks . . . sway* Cp. I Cor. 11. 14-15: 'Doth not even nature itself teach you, that, if a man have long hair, it is a shame unto him? But if a woman have long hair, it is a glory to her: for her hair is given her for a covering'. The A.V. marginal gloss explains that the woman's 'covering' is a 'sign that she is under the power of her husband'.

306. *wanton* sportive, luxuriant (*OED* 3, 7a), but with proleptic overtones of the pejorative sense, which M. often uses elsewhere (e.g., i 414, 454, iv 768, ix 1015).

310. *coy* shyly reserved (*OED* 2), not 'coquettish'.

312. *mysterious* secret, awe-inspiring (as in a religious rite). See 743*n* below. The etymology (Greek *muein*, 'to close lips or eyes') is paradoxical when nothing is hidden. Contrast Donne, 'Elegy 19': '[women] are mystic books, which only we . . . May see revealed' (41-3).

313. *dishonest* including 'dishonourable', 'unchaste' and 'unseemly to the sight' (*OED* 1, 2, 3).

321. *hand in hand* a recurrent motif. Cp. iv 488-9, 689, 739, ix 385-6, 1037, xii 648.

323. *goodliest* most handsome and well-proportioned.

323-4. *since . . . sons* The syntax was not unidiomatic. Bush cites Browne, *Pseudodoxia* I i: 'he [Adam] was the wisest of all men since'.

329. *recommend cool Zephyr* 'make a cool breeze welcome' (Zephyr was god of the west wind).

332. *Nectarine* sweet as nectar (*OED*), though the nectarine peach was also known.

compliant including ***'pliant' (*OED* 2).

333. *recline* recumbent (sole instance in *OED*).

334. *damasked* woven with rich designs, variegated (*OED* 1, 3).

336. *brimming* *OED*'s earliest participial instance.

337. *purpose* conversation (*OED* 4b).

endearing *OED*'s earliest participial instance.

338. *Wanted* were lacking.

dalliance caressing (*OED* 2).

341. *chase* unenclosed parkland (*OED* 3) and (ominously, since there were no carnivores) hunted animals (*OED* 4a).

343. *ramped* stood on his hind legs – 'a threatening posture' (*OED* 'ramp' 3a), but here benign. Cp. vii 466.

344. *Dandled the kid* Cp. Isa. 11. 6: 'the leopard shall lie down with the kid; and the calf and the young lion and the fatling together'.

ounces lynxes.

pards leopards.

348. *Insinuating* winding (Latin *insinuare*), with a proleptic hint of 'dark suggestions' (ix 90).

Gordian twine coils as convoluted as the Gordian knot, which only Alexander could disentangle (by cutting it with his sword).

352. *ruminating* chewing the cud.

353. *prone career* descending course and headlong gallop (the chariot of the sun).

354. *Ocean Isles* the Azores (identified in line 592).

ascending Scale The sun is in Aries (x 329), so the stars 'rise in Libra, the Scales, the portion of the sky exactly opposite' (Fowler).

358–62. *What ... Little inferior* Cp. Ps. 8. 4–5 (and Heb. 2. 6–7): 'What is man, that thou art mindful of him ... / For thou hast made him a little lower than the angels, / And hast crowned him with glory and honour'.

359. *room* place. Cp. 'vacant room' (vii 190).

360. *mould* bodily form (*OED* sb³ 10b) and earth regarded as the material of the human body (*OED* sb¹ 4). Cp. ii 355.

370. *so happy* such happiness.

376. *strait* intimate (*OED* 14) and strict, severe (*OED* 6).

381. *freely give* Satan parodies Matt. 10. 8: 'freely ye have received, freely give'.

381–3. *Hell ... kings* Cp. Isaiah's prophecy of the fall of Babylon: 'Hell from beneath is moved for thee to meet thee at thy coming: it stirreth up the dead for thee, even all the chief ones of the earth; it hath raised up from their thrones all the kings of the nations' (Isa. 14. 9). This analogue suggests that Satan is gloating, but cp. also Claudian, *De Rapt. Pros.* ii 276–306, where Pluto genuinely tries to console the abducted Proserpine by telling her that Hades is spacious. He concludes: 'kings in purple robes will kneel at your feet' (300). Cp. iv 269, ix 432, and ix 838–42.

382. *entertain*   an ambiguous word, which could mean 'treat in (any) specified manner' (*OED* 8), even torture, as in 'entertained with all variety of persecution' (1611). Satan plays on 'receive', 'show hospitality to' (*OED* 12, 13), but Hell's *gates* will also 'admit and contain' mankind (*OED* 11). Cp. Satan's offer to prepare 'Fit entertainment' for the Messiah (v 690).

387. *for*   in place of.

393-4. *necessity,* / *The tyrant's plea*   Cp. M.'s contempt in *Eikonoklastes* for Royalist appeals to 'the necessity of the times' (*YP* 3. 373). But 'necessity' was really Cromwell's word. Legend later had it that he had stood over the body of King Charles and muttered 'Cruel necessity!' He pleaded 'accident and necessity' against the Levellers, 'providence and necessity' when trying the King, and *la necessité* when dissolving the Rump. M. approved of these acts, but he may have had misgivings when Cromwell 'saw it was necessary' to dissolve the Barebones Parliament (as they were debating tithes) and become Lord Protector, assuming regal pomp 'of necessity'. See Antonia Fraser, *Cromwell: Our Chief of Men* (1973), 210, 229, 274, 293, 423, 447, 449, 462-3.

402. *A lion now he stalks*   Cp. I Pet. 5. 8: 'your adversary the devil, as a roaring lion, walketh about, seeking whom he may devour'. Contrast the playful lion of line 343.

404. *purlieu*   outskirts of a forest (*OED* 1).

410. *Turned him all ear*   Adam's words turned Satan all ear. Fowler thinks that *all ear* might be M.'s coinage, but Drummond had used the phrase in his Sonnet XXV. Cp. also *A Masque* 560.

411. *Sole . . . sole*   only . . . chief (with a pun on 'soul').

423-4. *Tree* / *Of Knowledge*   In accordance with Gen. 2. 16-17, the name 'Tree of Knowledge of Good and Evil' antedates the Fall (cp. viii 323-33). Some biblical commentators had thought that so deceptive a name must be Satan's invention. Cp. ix 1070-73 and see Arnold Williams, *The Common Expositor* (1948) 105-7.

425. *whate'er death is*   Adam and Eve as yet barely grasp the notion of annihilation (cp. ix 695, 775). After the Fall they have difficulty in thinking of death as anything else (see ix 826-33, x 770-816).

427. *pronounced*   both 'passed sentence' and 'uttered a vocal sound'. *Death* is as yet an empty word in Paradise. Contrast ii 788 where 'Hell trembled at the hideous name'.

447. *odds*   the amount by which one thing exceeds another (*OED* 1b). Eve means that Adam is superior, but her syntax allows herself to be *Pre-eminent* in enjoying him.

451. *of*]   *Ed II*; on *Ed I*.

459. *lake*   not a 'pool', though critics repeatedly write of 'Eve at the pool'. Eve's *liquid plain* (455) is a genuine geographical feature (260-63), far grander than the small woodland pool in which Narcissus lost himself (*Met.*

iii 407–12). Sandys uses 'liquid plain' to translate Ovid's *campoque* . . .
aquae (*Met.* i 41–2): a description of earth's primeval ocean. See further,
McColley (77).

460–68. *As* . . . *thyself* The allusion to Ovid's proud Narcissus (*Met.* iii
402–510) need not convict Eve of sinful pride. Eve did not know that the
beautiful face was her own, and (unlike Narcissus) she turned from her
reflection when she learned the truth. Bush cites a tradition that 'some of
the newly created angels looked up to God, others fell in love with them-
selves'. But cp. also the Self-love of Spenser's 'High Eternal Power': 'It
loved itself because itself was fair; / (For fair is loved)' (*An Hymn of
Heavenly Love* 29–30).

466. *vain* futile. There may be overtones of 'indulging in personal vanity',
but *OED* does not cite that sense before 1692. Cp. Spenser's Britomart
gazing into Merlin's 'glassie globe': 'Her selfe a while therein she vewd in
vaine' (*FQ* III ii 22).

467. *a voice* belonging to God (viii 485–6) or possibly an angel (iv 712).

470. *stays* awaits (*OED* 14) and hinders. The former sense refers to Adam,
the latter to Eve's reflection.

472. *shall* So all early editions. Many editors emend to 'shalt', and so make
thou the sole subject of *enjoy*. But *shall enjoy* could be governed by *he* (with
thy soft embraces as object). See Adams (90).

474–5. *thence be called* / *Mother of human race* Cp. Gen. 3. 20: 'And Adam
called his wife's name Eve; because she was the mother of all living'. 'Eve'
means 'life'. In Genesis, Adam names 'Eve' only after the Fall, when he
and she are subject to death. Some commentators thought that Adam chose
the name in defiance of God. Others associated it with misery and sin. M.
rejects this misogynistic tradition by giving 'Eve' prelapsarian status. Adam
bestows the name in line 481. Cp. v 385–8, xi 156–71.

476–91. Cp. Adam's recollection of these events at viii 481–520.

478. *platan* plane tree.

486. *individual* both 'inseparable' (*OED* A 2) and 'distinguished by attributes
of [her] own' (*OED* A 4).

488. *other half* Cp. Plato, *Symposium* 189d–193e.

493. *unreproved* irreproachable. See ix 5*n*.

499–500. *Jupiter* . . . *clouds* Jupiter was god of the sky and Juno goddess
of the air, and their union was sometimes allegorized as the marriage of
Aether and Aer. See e.g. Natale Conti, *Mythologiae* (1567) II iv. Conti cites
Iliad xiv 346–51, where Zeus and Hera make love under a cloud. Notice,
however, that M.'s Jupiter *impregns the clouds*, not Juno. The substitution
of clouds for Juno is troubling because it recalls Ixion, who fathered the
centaurs on a cloud that he mistook for Juno. M. compares Eve with Ixion's
cloud in *Tetrachordon* (*YP* 2. 597–8).

507. *happier Eden* See 27*n* above.

511. *pines* torments.

515. *knowledge forbidd'n* Satan speaks here as if he believed the fruit really could give knowledge. Contrast x 485-7.

522. *ruin* fall (Latin *ruina*), but *foundation* and *build* also suggest the paradox of building ruins.

530. *A chance but chance* 'An opportunity, even if only a fortuitous one'.

538. **roam* act of wandering (coined from the verb).

539. *utmost longitude* uttermost west.

541. *with right aspéct* directly.

548. *Still* continually.

549. *Gabriel* Hebrew 'Strength of God'. Muslim and cabbalistic lore made Gabriel a 'warrior' (576); M. might also have known a tradition (embodied in I Enoch 20. 7) which gave Gabriel charge of Paradise and the Cherubim.

552. *unarmèd* Cp. the devils' more warlike games (ii 532-8).

555-6. *gliding . . . star* Cp. Tasso, *Gerus. Lib.* ix 62, where an angel descends to earth as 'in the stillness of a moonshine even / A falling star so glideth down from Heaven' (trans. Fairfax); also Homer, *Il.* iv 75-9.

555. *even* both 'evening' and 'nearly *even* sunbeam' (Empson[2] 157). See below, 590*n*.

557. *thwarts* both 'traverses' (*OED* 1) and 'frustrates'. Cp. 'checks the night' (iii 732).

vapours fired ignited exhalations (thought to cause shooting stars).

567. *God's latest image* God's first image was the Son. M. neither denies nor explicitly states that angels bear God's image.

described traced (*OED* 5) with the eye. Uriel had given Satan directions (iii 722-35), but he is here referring to what he saw, not what he said. Adams therefore urges modernizing editors to print 'descried'. He points out that 'descry' and 'describe' were often confused in the seventeenth century. No editor has followed Adams's advice, though most agree that Uriel means 'descried'. I retain *described* because it suggests that Uriel never took his eye off Satan, whom he closely *marked*. 'Descry' would imply that Uriel merely caught sight of Satan.

568. *gait* journey (*OED* 'gate' sb[2] 6) and manner of flying.

572. *shade* trees.

580. *vigilance* vigilant guards.

590. *beam* sunbeam and balance beam (*now raised* because the sun has set, allowing Uriel to slide *downward*).

592-5. *whether . . . there* As at iii 573-6, M. does not commit himself to either the Ptolemaic or the Copernican system. *Ed I* and *Ed II* spell 'whither' thus admitting a pun.

592. *prime orb* either the sun or the *primum mobile* (both move with *incredible* speed in the Ptolemaic system).

594. *Diurnal* in the space of one day.

volúble moving rapidly (*OED* 3) and capable of ready rotation on its axis (*OED* 2).

600. *accompanied* both 'joined their company' and 'played a musical accompaniment'.

603. *descant* warbled song, melodious strain (*OED* 3).

605. *Hesperus* Venus, the evening star.

608. *Apparent* plainly seen (*OED* 1), with a play on 'heir apparent' (notice *queen*). Cp. Ariosto's erotic description of the moon breaking through clouds: 'The moon at this petition parts the cloud . . . As fair as when she offered herself nude / To Endymion' (*Orl. Fur.* xviii 185).

617. *unemployed* *idle (*OED* 2a). *OED*'s earliest instance modifying sentient creatures.

620. *regard* observant attention and esteem.

627. *walk*] *Ed II*; walks *Ed I*.

628. *manuring* cultivating of plants (*OED* 2b) and inhabiting (*OED* 1b) of Paradise.

632. *Ask riddance* need to be cleared.

635. *author* one who gives existence (*OED* 1) and one who has authority (*OED* 5).

   disposer ruler (*OED* 2).

640. *seasons* times of day.

641–56. *Sweet . . . sweet* Many critics liken Eve's embedded lyric to a sonnet, but M.'s rhetorical figure has a closer analogue in Hector's farewell to Andromache (Homer, *Il.* vi 447–55). Like Eve, Hector lists the things that are dear to him, then he repeats his list with negatives, before directly addressing his spouse in the second person. In both cases it is the direct address that turns the preceding double *enumeratio* into a declaration of love.

642. *charm* the blended singing of many birds (*OED*).

648. *solemn bird* the nightingale (see line 602).

660. *accomplished* complete, perfect.

661. *Those* Perhaps a misprint for 'these' (as editors since Newton have conjectured), but Adam might well prefer to look at Eve than at the stars.

664. *light prepared* Ps. 74. 16 (see below, 724–5n).

668. *kindly* natural and benign.

669. *influence* see *Nativity* 71n.

   foment cherish with heat.

670. *Temper* heal or refresh by restoring the proper 'temper' of elements or humours (see ii 276–7).

674. *unbeheld*.

676. *want . . . want* lack . . . lack.

685. *rounding* walking the rounds (see line 862) and singing 'rounds' (*responsive each to other's note*).

688. *Divide the night* both 'divide the night into watches' and 'perform with musical "divisions"' (*OED* 11a). Cp. *Passion* 4.

690. *blissful bower* recalling Spenser's Bower of Bliss (*FQ* II xii), but cp. also Venus's 'blisfull bowre of joy above' (*FQ* III vi 95).

691. *Planter* Cp. Gen. 2. 8: 'God planted a garden'. God is also the planter of a new world colony. Cp. i 650–53 and see J. M. Evans, *Milton's Imperial Epic* (1996) 4: 'God . . . is "the sovran Planter", a periphrasis that links him with the royal patron of England's first transatlantic colony'.

694. *Laurel and myrtle* emblems of Apollo and Venus.

698. *jessamine* jasmine.

699. *flourished* luxuriant, adorned with flowers.

701. *Crocus, and hyacinth* The same plants spontaneously arise when Hera seduces Zeus on Mount Ida (Homer, *Il.* xiv 347–9).

703. *emblem* ornament of inlaid work (*OED* 1), with a play on the emblematic properties of the flowers: 'the humility of the *violet*, prudence of the *hyacinth*, amiability of the *jessamine*' (Fowler).

705. *shadier*] *Ed I*; shady *Ed II*.

707–8. *Pan or Silvanus . . . Faunus* wood-gods represented as half man, half goat. All were fertility gods and Silvanus was also associated with gardens and limits.

708. *close* secret.

711. *hymenean* wedding hymn. Hymen was the ancient god of marriage. Cp. *L'Allegro* 125 and *Elegia V* 105–8.

712. *genial* presiding over marriage and generation. At viii 484–7 Eve is led by her Maker, not an *angel*.

714. *Pandora* Greek 'all gifts', the first woman, created at Jove's command. Prometheus ('Forethought') and Epimetheus ('Afterthought') were sons of Iapetus (*Japhet*). Prometheus stole Jove's fire for man. Jove, *to be avenged*, sent Hermes to Epimetheus with Pandora as a gift. She came with a sealed jar containing the world's ills. In Renaissance versions, Epimetheus opened the jar, but Hesiod credits Pandora with the act (*WD* 93). In *Theog.* he dispenses with the jar, as if woman were punishment enough. M.'s simile is compatible with any of these versions.

717. *Japhet* Noah's son (Gen. 9–10). His identification with the Titan Iapetus was traditional.

719. *authentic* belonging to himself (*OED* 7), original (*OED* 4).

724. *pole* sky.

Thou also mad'st Eighteenth-century critics applauded the 'masterly transition' whereby the poet's voice 'passes into' that of Adam and Eve (Addison, *Spectator*, no. 231). The effect is lost when quotation marks are placed before *Thou*.

724–5. *the night . . . the day* Cp. Ps. 74. 16: 'The day is thine, the night also is thine: thou hast prepared the light and the sun'.

730. *wants* lacks.

735. *gift of sleep* Ps. 127. 2, Homer, *Il.* ix 712–13, Virgil, *Aen.* ii 268–9.

739. *Handed* *joined hand in hand (*OED* 3), a sense coined by M. in *DDD*: 'if any two be but once handed in the Church'.

741. *ween* surmise.

743. *Mysterious* awe-inspiring, sacred. St Paul calls the union of husband and wife 'a great mystery' (Eph. 5. 32), dignified by Christ's marriage to his Church. Cp. also the 'mysterious rites' of marriage in Jonson, *Hymenaei* 137.

744–9. *hypocrites . . . foe* Cp. I Tim. 4. 1–3: 'in the latter times some shall depart from the faith, giving heed to seducing spirits, and doctrines of devils; speaking lies in hypocrisy; having their conscience seared with a hot iron; forbidding to marry'. M. dignifies sex by having Adam and Eve make love before the Fall.

747. *commands to some* I. Cor. 7. 1.

748. *Our Maker bids increase* Gen. 1. 28.

751. *propriety* right of possession or use (*OED* 1a). Before the Fall, monogamous marriage was the only property right.

756. *charities* *feelings or acts of affection (*OED* 2b).

761. *bed is undefiled* Cp. Heb. 13. 4: 'Marriage is honourable in all, and the bed undefiled'.

762. *patriarchs* By including them in his hymn to wedded love, M. might be hinting at polygamy, which they had practised and he defended in *CD*. See A. Rudrum, 'Polygamy in *Paradise Lost*', *EC* 20 (1970), 18–23.

763. *Love* Cupid, whose golden arrows (*shafts*) kindled love.

764. *purple* brilliant and imperial (notice *Reigns*).

766. *unendeared* both 'devoid of affection' and 'lacking value'. 'Endear' could mean 'enhance the value of' (*OED* 2), as in 'love endeareth the meanest things' (1594).

768. *masque* masquerade, masked ball.

769. *starved* perished with cold (*OED* 4), from standing outside the mistress's door. See e.g. Ovid, *Amores* i 6, 9; iii 11a. Serenades were sung at night, in the open air (*in sereno*).

773. *repaired* replaced (with new roses).

774. *Blest pair* Cp. Virgil, *Aen.* ix 446, on the intimate friends Nisus and Euryalus: *Fortunati ambo!*

776. *shadowy cone* earth's shadow rotating around the earth (see iii 556–7). When the shadow is *Half way* between the horizon and the zenith it is nine o'clock.

777. *sublunar* beneath the moon.

778. *ivory port* ivory gate – the source of false dreams in Homer (*Od.* xix 562f.) and Virgil (*Aen.* vi 893f.). True dreams issued from a gate of horn. Fowler notes that M.'s Cherubim use the ivory gate because they 'are to interrupt a false dream'. Others might feel that the allusion implies that the good angels will fail. Homer says that dreams issuing from the ivory gate are ineffectual, 'their message is never accomplished' (*Od.* xix 565).

782. *Uzziel* Hebrew 'My strength is God'. A man at Exod. 6. 18, but cabbalistic tradition attributed the name to one of seven angels before God's throne (West 154).

785. *shield . . . spear* left . . . right.

788. *Ithuriel* Hebrew 'Discovery of God'. The name is not biblical. R. H. West (*SP* 47, 1950, 211–23) conjectures that M. may have made 'this one up' (219), but Ithuriel is an angel in Moses Cordovero's *Pardes Rimmonim* (Cracow, 1592) and other sixteenth-century tracts. See Gustav Davidson, *A Dictionary of Angels* (1967) 152. M. did not coin angels.

Zephon Hebrew 'a looking out'. Zephon is a man at Num. 26. 15, and a devil in Selden's *De Dis Syris* (1617), I iii 43. He may yet emerge as an angel.

791. *secure* free from anxiety (*OED* 1).

793. *Who* one who.

802. *Fancy* the faculty of forming mental images. Were Satan able to reach Eve's Fancy, he would enjoy greater freedom to form *illusions* than if he just had access to her *spirits*, which produce more abstract *hopes* and *desires*.

805. *animal spirits* the highest of three kinds of fine vapours produced in the human body. The liver and heart produced natural and vital spirits, which rose to the brain to become animal spirits (Latin *anima*, 'soul'). These then imparted motion to the body and conveyed sense data to the reason. At v 485 Raphael speaks of still higher 'intellectual' spirits, which may be M.'s invention. Hunter (46–55) cites many sources to show that Satan has no direct access to Eve's reason.

807. *distempered* vexed (by an imbalance of the four 'humours').

809. *conceits* notions (*OED* 1), with overtones of *pride*. The context (*Blown up, engend'ring*) also suggests a sexual impregnation. Satan might be parodying the immaculate conception, which was thought to have taken place through Mary's *ear* (800).

812. *celestial temper* both the weapon, 'tempered Heav'nly' (ii 813), and Ithuriel's angelic 'temperament' (ii 218, 277).

815. *Lights* alights and kindles.

nitrous powder gunpowder.

816. *tun* barrel.

magazine storehouse for explosives.

817. *Against* in preparation for.

*rumoured OED's earliest participial instance.

smutty black. Smut is a fungous disease that turns cereal grains into a black powder.

821. *grisly King* Moloch's epithet at *Nativity* 209.

828. *Know ye not me* Satan does not know himself, for he appeals to an identity that is no longer his. *There sitting* recalls the unfallen Lucifer, who aspired to 'sit also on the mount of the congregation' (Isa. 14. 13). Satan will not acknowledge the name 'Satan' until x 386.

840. *obscure* lowly (answering *unknown*, *lowest*) and gloomy.

848. *pined* mourned.

856. *Single* in single combat (*OED* 15) and simple, honest, sincere (*OED* 14).

868. *shade* trees.

869. *port* bearing.

870. *wan* gloomy, sad, sickly.

873. *lours* scowls.

879. *transgressions* including 'crossing the bounds' (*OED* 1b).

charge both the responsibility and those whom Gabriel is responsible for (Adam and Eve).

880. *approve* test by experience (*OED* 8) and commend. The former sense draws Satan's contempt (see line 895).

886. *esteem of wise* reputation for wisdom.

892–3. *change . . . with* exchange . . . for.

893–4. *recompense / Dole with delight* 'replace grief with joy'. But Satan also hints punningly at his true purpose, which is 'delightfully to deal out death'. *Recompense* includes 'mete out in requital' (*OED* 3) and *dole* includes 'distribution of gifts' (*OED* sb² 5), including 'death' (*OED* sb² 5b). Cp. Samson 'dealing dole among his foes' (*SA* 1529).

895. *To thee no reason* Since Gabriel has never experienced pain, he cannot understand the need to escape it.

896. *object* put forward as an objection.

899. *durance* imprisonment.

thus much what So much in answer to what.

904. *O . . . wise* 'O what a loss to Heaven to lose such a judge of wisdom as you!'

911. *However* in any way he can.

918. *all Hell broke loose* already proverbial (*OED* 'hell' 10).

926. *stood* withstood.

928. *The*] Ed I; Thy *Ed II*.

929. *seconded* both 'assisted' and 'taken the place of a defeated combatant' (*OED* 2c).

930. *at random* wide of the mark. A military metaphor: guns fired 'at random' when firing at long range (*OED* 5b).

932. *assays* afflictions, efforts, attacks (*OED* 2, 14, 15).

939. *afflicted powers* downcast armies (cp. i 186).

940. *mid air* Satan will become 'prince of the power of the air' (Eph. 2. 2).

942. *gay* brilliantly good (used ironically, *OED* 6b), showily dressed (*OED* 4).

945. *practised distances* Satan contemptuously draws a parallel between the good angels' court etiquette (which prescribes various *distances* from the *throne*) and their keeping at a safe distance in battle. *Distances* also plays on 'musical intervals' (*OED* 5c) kept in *songs*.

959. *fawned . . . adored* Waldock (81) dismisses Gabriel's 'unsupported calumny'; Empson (111) takes it as proof that Heaven was 'unattractive' even 'before Satan fell'. But Satan *servilely adored* God on the day of the Son's exaltation, when he 'seemed well-pleased' (v 617).

962. *aread* advise.

avaunt begone.

965. *drag thee chained* Cp. Rev. 20. 1–3: 'an angel . . . having . . . a great chain in his hand . . . laid hold on the dragon . . . and bound him a thousand years, and cast him into the bottomless pit'.

967. *facile* easily moved.

969. *waxing more in rage* both 'growing more angry' and 'growing bigger in his anger' (*OED* 'more' 1). See lines 985–8.

971. *limitary* both 'stationed on the boundary' (*OED* 2) and 'subject to limits' (*OED* 1).

976. *road of Heav'n* not the Milky Way (as editors claim) but a *star-paved* road in Heaven that Raphael likens to the Milky Way at vii 577–81. A *progress* is a state procession.

978. *moonèd horns* crescent formation (for *phalanx* see i 550*n*).

980. *ported spears* not as in 'port arms', but 'With their Spears borne pointed towards him' (Hume, 1695). Cp. Randle Holme, *The Academy of Armory* (1688): 'Port your pike, is in three motions to . . . beare it forward aloft' (III xix 147). The blades therefore face Satan, whose *stature reached the sky* (988).

980–85. *field . . . chaff* Empson[2] (172) claims that the simile 'makes the good angels look weak', and epic precedent supports his view. Homer (*Il.* ii 147–50), Tasso (*Gerus. Lib.* xx 60), Apollonius Rhodius (*Argonautica* iii 1386f.) and Ariosto (*Orl. Fur.* xvi 68) compare demoralized armies to a wind-tossed cornfield. Cp. also Phineas Fletcher's simile likening devils escaped from Hell to a tempest descending on corn: 'the Plowmans hopes new-eard / Swimme on the playne' (*The Apollyonists* ii 40). In Ps. 1. 4 it is the ungodly who are 'like the chaff which the wind driveth away'.

981. *Ceres* corn (Ceres being goddess of agriculture).

983. *careful* anxious.

985. *alarmed* called to arms.

987. *Teneriffe or Atlas* mountains in the Canary Islands and Morocco. Atlas was also a rebel Titan (see ii 306*n*). Cp. Tasso's Solimano, who resists a Christian assault as a mountain assailed with storms 'Doth unremovèd, steadfast, still withstand / Storm, thunder, lightning, tempest, wind and tide' (*Gerus. Lib.* ix 31, trans. Fairfax).

unremoved unremovable (see ix 5*n*).

989. *Horror* from Latin *horrere*, to bristle.

992. *cope* vault.

997. *Scales* the constellation Libra. M. also alludes to Zeus weighing the fates of pagan epic combatants (Homer, *Il.* viii 68–77, xxii 208–13, Virgil, *Aen.* xii 725–7). In pagan epics the loser's fate sinks downward; Gabriel declares Satan to be *light* (1012). Cp. Dan. 5. 27: 'TEKEL; Thou art weighed in the balances, and found wanting'.

998. *Astraea* goddess of justice. She lived on earth during the Golden Age, but human wickedness drove her to the heavens, where she was stellified as Virgo (Ovid, *Met.* i 149f.). Cp. *Nativity* 141–3.

999–1000. *he weighed . . . air* God uses a balance in Creation at Job 28. 24 and Isa. 40. 12.

1001. *ponders* weighs in the scales (*OED* 1) and considers.

BOOK V

2. *orient* sparkling (*OED* 2) and eastern.

5. *bland* *gentle, balmy, soothing (*OED* 2). Contrast the 'exhilarating vapour bland' produced by the forbidden fruit (ix 1047).

only mere.

6. *Aurora's fan* leaves stirred by the morning breeze. Aurora was goddess of morning.

12. *cordial* heartfelt.

15. *peculiar graces* charms all her own. An echo of iii 183 ('chosen of peculiar grace') might imply that Eve's grace 'is out of the ordinary, excessive, and, as in Calvin's scheme, irresistible. It is grace out of proportion to merit' (Rumrich[2] 140).

16. *Zephyrus on Flora* the west wind over flowers. The flower-goddess Flora is Zephyr's consort in Ovid, *Fasti* v 197.

17–25. *Awake . . . sweet* Cp. Song of Sol. 2. 10–12: 'Rise up, my love, my fair one, and come away . . . . The flowers appear on the earth; The time of the singing of birds is come'. Like Solomon, Adam wakens his love with an aubade. Contrast Satan's serenade (v 38–47), which is a parody of Song of Sol.

21. *prime* first hour of the day, beginning at six o'clock.

22. *tended* *OED*'s earliest participial instance.

blows blooms.

23. *balmy reed* balsam.

34. *offence* including 'occasion of unbelief or doubt' (*OED* 2).

38. *Why sleep'st thou* See below, 673*n*.

44. *heav'n wakes with all his eyes* Cp. Giles Fletcher on the Nativity, *CV* (1610) i 78: 'heav'n awaked all his eyes, / To see another Sunne, at midnight rise'. The *eyes* are stars.

47. *still* continually.

56-7. *dewy . . . Ambrosia* Cp. Virgil's Venus: 'her ambrosial hair exhaled divine perfume' (*Aen.* i 403-4).

60. *god* angel. Some modernizing editors retain the early editions' 'God'. Cp. v 117.

61. *reserve* restriction (*OED* 6), self-restraint (*OED* 9), knowledge withheld from one person by another (*OED* 10).

66. *vouched with* backed by.

72. *Communicated* shared (*OED* 4). The context (*divine, gods, Taste*) also suggests 'partake of the Holy Communion' (*OED* 6b). Cp. ix 755.

79. *as we* Zachary Pearce noted in 1733 how these words are placed so as to refer either to *Ascend to Heaven* or to *in the air*. Empson[2] (163) sees 'a natural embarrassment' in Satan's implied doubt 'as to whether he could go to Heaven himself'. Contrast Raphael's unequivocal 'as we' (v 499), and see i 516*n* for Satan's confinement to the air.

84. *savoury* appetizing, but the word derives from Latin *sapere* meaning both 'taste' and 'know'. The noun 'savour' could still mean 'perception, understanding' (*OED* 5). In biblical usage (e.g., Gen. 8. 21), 'savour' was used of sacrifices that God found pleasing (*OED* 2c), so Eve's dream implies that God wants her to eat the apple.

86. *Could not . . . Forthwith* Eve dreams of the consequences of eating, but the crucial act is absent from her dream – perhaps because Satan cannot 'make her go through the motions of disobedience, even in her fancy' (Fish 222).

94. *sad* grave, serious (*OED* 4a).

98. *uncouth* strange (*OED* 3) and distasteful (*OED* 4).

99. *harbour* lodge; often with some notion of lurking or concealment (*OED* 7). Evil may *come and go*, but cannot reside, in unfallen minds (117).

102. *Fancy* the mental faculty which produces images. See iv 802*n*.

104. *represent* bring clearly before the mind (*OED* 2a).

106. *frames* directs to a certain purpose (*OED* 5c).

109. *cell* compartment of the brain.

115. *our last evening's talk* either the discussion about the prohibition (iv 421ff.) or Eve's question about the stars (iv 657-8), to which her dream has offered a flattering answer (v 44-7). Satan did not overhear Eve's question (he exited at iv 535), so the dream-answer (v 44-5) might not be his. Eve's own *Fancy* may have played a part, as Adam surmises.

117. *god* probably 'angel' (see above, 60*n*), but maybe God, whose omniscience extends to evil.

118. *so* so long as it remains.

unapproved *not sanctioned (*OED* 3) and not put to the proof (*OED* 'approve' 8).

123. *wont* are accustomed.

131. *wiped them with her hair* echoing Luke 7. 38, where Mary Magdalene washes Jesus's feet with her tears and 'did wipe them with the hairs of her head'. See also x 910–12.

136. *cleared* including 'freed from the imputation of guilt'.

137. *arborous.

142. *Discovering* revealing.

145. *orisons* prayers.

146–7. *various style . . . holy rapture* formal elaboration . . . extempore effusion. Anglicans preferred the former, Puritans the latter. Adam and Eve have both.

147. *wanted* lacked.

150. *numerous* rhythmic, harmonious (*OED* 5).

151. *tuneable* melodious, sweet-sounding (*OED* 1).

153–208. The morning hymn imitates Ps. 148 and the Song of the Three Holy Children (35–66), an apocryphal song set for Matins in the 1549 Book of Common Prayer as the Canticle *Benedicite*.

158–9. *these declare / Thy goodness* Cp. Ps. 19. 1: 'The heavens declare the glory of God'.

165. *Him . . . end* Cp. Rev. 22. 13 ('I am Alpha and Omega, the beginning and end') and Jonson, 'To Heaven' 10 ('First, midst, and last, converted one and three').

166. *Fairest of stars* Venus or Lucifer, the morning star.

last in the train of night Lucifer is the last star to disappear in the morning, and (as Hesperus) the first to appear in the evening.

174. *fall'st* The setting sun was commonly said to 'fall' (*OED* 7e), but here the word is proleptic.

178. *song* the Music of the Spheres, audible to unfallen man (see *Nativity* 125–8, *Arcades* 63–73).

181. *quaternion* group of four.

198. *singing up to heaven gate* Cp. Shakespeare, *Sonnet* XXIX (11–12) and *Cymbeline* II iii 20.

205. *still* always.

213. *overwoody* having too many branches.

214. *pampered* overloaded – with a pun on French *pampre*, 'vine-branch'.

215–19. *vine . . . leaves* The *elm* traditionally 'wedded' the *vine* in an emblem of 'masculine strength' and 'feminine softness' (Fowler). Cp. ix 217 and Horace, *Odes* II xv 4, IV v 30, but notice also the matriarchal possibilities in *adopted* (218).

221. *Raphael* Hebrew 'Health of God'. The angel Raphael appears in the

apocryphal Book of Tobit, to which M. alludes in lines 222-3. Raphael helped Tobit's son Tobias win a wife (see iv 168-71n) and he told Tobias how to cure Tobit's blindness (Tob. 11. 7-14). As in *PL*, God sends Raphael to earth in answer to a prayer: 'The prayer of both was heard in the presence of . . . God' (Tob. 3. 16).

229. *friend with friend* So God spoke to Moses, 'face to face, as a man speaketh unto his friend' (Exod. 33. 11).

238. *secure* overconfident (*OED* 1).

244. *pretend* plead, offer as an excuse.

249. *ardours* bright angels (from Latin *ardere*, 'to burn').

250. *Veiled . . . wings* Cp. iii 382 and Isa. 6. 2.

261-2. *glass / Of Galileo* telescope. Galileo is the only contemporary of M. to be named in *PL*.

262-3. *less assured . . . Imagined lands* Cp. i 288-91, where M. has more faith in Galileo's observations of lunar 'lands, / Rivers, or mountains'. Philosophers since Plutarch had conjectured that the moon's spots were seas or mountains; Galileo claimed that the telescope revealed them more clearly.

264. *Cyclades* an archipelago in the south Aegean. *Delos* was the traditional centre, but here appears as a *spot* to a *pilot* sailing from *amidst* the group. Since Delos is compared to the earth (260), this displacement from centre to periphery might hint at a Copernican universe: Delos was famous for having floated adrift (see x 296). *Samos* lies outside the Cyclades, off the coast of Asia Minor.

265. *kens* discerns.

266-76. *Down . . . lights* Raphael's descent to earth is modelled on the earthward descents of Virgil's Mercury (*Aen*. iv 238-58) and Tasso's Michael (*Gerus. Lib*. ix 60-62). Cp. also Satan's descent at iii 562-90.

266. *prone* bent forward.

269-70. Having sailed through interstellar space with *steady wing*, Raphael now beats earth's yielding (*buxom*) atmosphere with *quick fan*.

272. *phoenix* a mythical bird that existed one at a time (hence *sole*). It was consumed by fire every 500 years, but would rise from its ashes (*relics*), which it then carried to the temple of the sun at Heliopolis in Egypt (Ovid, *Met*. xv 391-407). The phoenix symbolized friendship, marriage, and resurrection. Cp. *SA* 1699-1707. Virgil's Mercury, alighting in Libya, is likened to a seabird (*Aen*. iv 254).

277. *six wings* like the Seraphim in Isa. 6. 2.

279. *mantling* covering as with a mantle. Raphael is naked but for his *wings*.

281. *zone* belt.

282. *Skirted* bordered.

284. *mail* plumage (*OED* 5), suggesting also scale-armour (*OED* 2).

285. *grain* dye.

Maia's son Mercury, messenger of the gods.

286. *shook . . . fragrance* So, in Fairfax's Tasso, Gabriel descending 'shook his wings with rory [dewy] May dews wet' (*Gerus. Lib.* i 14).

288. *state* rank and stateliness of bearing.

289. *message* mission, errand.

293. *odours* aromatic substances.

cassia a cinnamon-like spice.

nard spikenard, source of an aromatic ointment.

balm balsam.

295. *Wantoned . . . prime* Cp. Shakespeare, *Sonnet* XCVII: 'Bearing the wanton burthen of the prime' (7). *Wantoned* means 'revelled', but the pejorative sense has appeared often enough (e.g. i 414, iv 768) for its exclusion to be ominous.

played at will both 'freely acted out' and 'sported amorously with carnal desire' (*OED* 'play' 10c, 'will' 2).

297. *enormous* both 'immense' and 'unfettered by rules' (*OED* 1), with proleptic overtones of 'wicked, outrageous' (*OED* 2).

299. *in the door* Cp. Gen. 18. 1–2: '[Abraham] sat in the tent door in the heat of the day; and he lift up his eyes and looked, and, lo, three men stood by him'. Adam's entertainment of Raphael is modelled on Abraham's entertainment of the three angels.

300–302. *mounted . . . womb* The sexual metaphor is probably intended. Cp. Earth's erotic invitation to Phoebus in *Elegia V* 81f. The sun's rays were thought to penetrate the earth (see iii 609*n*).

306. **nectarous*.

milky often applied to the fruit juices (*OED* 1b), and here modifying *Berry* and *grape* as well as *stream*.

321. *mould* model, pattern (*OED* sb³ 5) and earth regarded as the material of the human body (*OED* sb¹ 4).

Adam (Hebrew, 'red') was thought to have been named for the red earth (Hebrew *adamah*) from which he was made (Gen. 2. 7).

322. *inspired* given the breath of life.

store . . . store reserve . . . abundance.

324. *frugal* economical (from Latin *fruges*, 'fruits').

327. *gourd* any fruit of the melon family.

335. *inelegant* *wanting in aesthetic refinement (*OED* 2) and ill-chosen (from Latin *eligere*, to select). Cp. ix 1017.

336. *upheld* sustained, continued.

kindliest most natural.

338. *Earth all-bearing Mother* translates the Greek and Latin titles Παμμήτορ γῆ, Magna Mater and Omniparens.

339. *India* Indies.

339–41. *middle shore* includes *Pontus*, the south coast of the Black Sea (abundant in grain, fruit and nuts) and the *Punic* (Carthaginian) coast of the Mediterranean, famous for figs.

341. *Alcinous* King of the Phaeacians on the mythical island of Scheria. His gardens contained trees that never failed to bear fruit, winter or summer (Homer, *Od.* vii 112-32).

342. *rined* rinded ('rine' was a variant form of 'rind').

345. *must* unfermented grape-juice.

meaths (non-alcoholic) mead.

348. *Wants* lacks.

349. **unfumed* naturally scented, not burned for incense.

350. *primitive* original (*OED* 1), as in 'Adam in his primitive estate' (1630).

353. *state* stateliness of bearing (*OED* 18a), bodily form (*OED* 9a), imposing display (*OED* 17a).

354-7. *tedious . . . *agape* M. contrasts Adam's naked majesty with the kind of pomp that accompanied Charles II's entry into London on 29 May 1660. From his hiding-place in Bartholomew Close, M. would have heard what John Evelyn saw: 'a Triumph of above 20,000 horse & foote, brandishing their swords and shouting with unexpressable joy: The wayes straw'd with flowers, the bells ringing, the streetes hung with Tapissry, fountaines running with wine: The Major [Mayor], Aldermen, all the Companies in their liver[ie]s, Chaines of Gold, banners; Lords & nobles, Cloth of Silver, gold & vellvet every body clad in, the windos & balconies all set with Ladys, Trumpets, Musick, & myriads of people flocking the streetes & ways as far as *Rochester*, so as they were 7 houres in passing the Citty'.

354. *solemn* awe-inspiring (*OED* 7).

360. *bowing low* Abraham 'bowed himself toward the ground' before angels (Gen. 18. 2), but when St John fell at an angel's feet 'to worship him', the angel said: 'See thou do it not: I am thy fellow servant' (Rev. 19. 10). Cp. ii 478*n*.

365. *want* miss, be parted from.

371. *Virtue* Raphael was a 'Seraph' at line 277 and will be an 'Archangel' at vii 41. M. uses these titles freely, in accordance with Protestant tradition.

378. *Pomona* Roman goddess of fruit-trees. Cp. ix 393-4.

381-2. *fairest . . . strove* alluding to the judgement of Paris, who chose Venus over Juno and Minerva as the most beautiful goddess. Venus's prize was the apple of discord. Cp. Marlowe, *Hero and Leander* (1598): 'Where Venus in her naked glory strove' (i 12).

384. *virtue-proof* armoured in virtue, but the counter-inference 'proof *against* virtue' also suggests itself. Fowler hears a further nuance: 'proof against Raphael, *the angelic virtue* (line 371)'. Raphael and Eve are both naked (see above, 279*n*), so Eve is to be doubly commended for not needing a *veil*.

no thought infirm Cp. Spenser, *Epithalamion*: 'That suffers not one looke to glaunce awry, / Which may let in a little thought unsownd' (236–7).

385–7. *Hail . . . second Eve* Cp. Luke 1. 28: 'Hail, thou that art highly favoured, the Lord is with thee: blessed art thou among women'. A Roman Catholic tradition derived *Ave* from *Eva* (inverted because Mary restored what Eve lost). M. celebrates Eve's nature, by placing her *un*inverted name alongside the word that had supposedly inverted it. Cp. Adam's hailing of Eve at xi 158.

388. *mother of mankind* Cp. Gen. 3. 20: 'Adam called his wife's name Eve; because she was the mother of all living'.

396. *No fear lest dinner cool* Fire was discovered only after the Fall (cp. ix 392, x 1070–78). M.'s vegetarian joke might also make a political point. John Simon, in *N&Q* n.s. 31 (September 1984), 326–7, hears an allusion to Shakespeare's *Timon of Athens* III vi 67–8: 'Make not a city feast of it, to let the meat cool ere we can agree upon the first place'. Simon notes: 'another consequence of the Fall was the jockeying for place and preferment to be found in courts'. Cp. M.'s contempt for marshalled (carefully ranked) feasts in ix 37.

397. *author* ancestor (*OED* 2a).

406. *of* by.

407. *No ingrateful* pleasant (with a hint that God's gifts should be gratefully accepted).

408. *Intelligential substances* angels. Cp. viii 181.

412. *concoct, digest, assimilate* Three stages of digestion.

417. *fires* heavenly bodies, of which the *moon* is *lowest*.

419–20. *spots . . . turned* Contrast i 287–91, where M. follows Galileo's theory that lunar spots are landscape features.

424. *alimental* nourishing.

429. *mellifluous* honey-flowing.

430. *pearly grain* manna. Cp. Exod. 16. 14.

433. *nice* difficult to please.

434. *nor seemingly* not just in appearance. In insisting that Raphael really did eat, M. follows Gen. 18. 8 and 19. 3 ('they did eat') rather than Tob. 12. 19, where Raphael says: 'I did neither eat nor drink, but ye did see a vision'. Most Reformers shared M.'s interpretation of Genesis, but not his materialist view that angels need food (414).

435. *in mist* both 'mystically' (*OED* 'mist' sb²) and 'in vapour'. Orthodox *theologians* saw angels as immaterial beings that took bodies of air. See e.g. Donne, 'Air and Angels'.

gloss both 'deceptive appearance' (*OED* sb² 1b) and 'comment inserted in the margin' (*OED* sb¹ 1).

437. *concoctive* digestive (*OED* 1), with overtones of the alchemical sense 'bring to a perfect or mature state by heat' (*OED* 'concoct' 2).

438. *transubstantiate* convert from one substance into another (*OED* 1). By using the word of digestion M. mocks the doctrine of 'transubstantiation' and the *real* (437) presence championed by Catholic *theologians*.

redounds remains undigested.

transpires passes out as vapour through the pores (*OED* 3a).

440. *empiric* experimental (*OED* 1b), with overtones of the pejorative sense 'impostor, charlatan' (*OED* 2b).

445. *crowned* filled to the brim (a classical metaphor, see e.g. Homer, *Il.* i 470).

446–8. *if ever . . . sight* Gen. 6. 2 tells how the 'sons of God saw the daughters of men that they were fair; and they took them wives of all which they chose'. The *sons of God* were usually identified as human sons of Seth (see xi 622*n*), but M. here follows a patristic tradition identifying them with angels (see *PR* i 179–81 and note).

449. **unlibidinous* not given to lust (sole instance in *OED*).

467. *yet what compare?* 'yet how can one begin to compare them?'

468. *hierarch* *commander of a celestial hierarchy (*OED* 2).

472. *one first matter* M.'s universe was created out of Chaos (ii 916, vii 233), not out of nothing. In *CD* i 7 M. argues that the primal matter was good and had its origin in God: 'it was good, and it contained the seeds of all subsequent good. It was a substance, and could only have been derived from the source of all substance. It was in a confused and disordered state at first, but afterwards God made it ordered and beautiful' (trans. Carey, *YP* 6. 308). Many critics have nevertheless doubted whether the Chaos of *PL* is good. See ii 890–1039*n*. M. in *CD* does not call the primal matter 'Chaos', and in *PL* he does not say that Chaos came from God. He describes Chaos as 'eternal' and 'unoriginal' (ii 896, iii 19, x 477).

478. *bounds* both 'limits' and 'leaps'. Notice *Springs* (480). M.'s universe is both hierarchical and dynamic.

479–83. The *root*, *stalk*, *leaves*, *flow'r* and *fruit* are literal and metaphorical, providing an image for the universe and one illustration of its dynamism. Raphael is also justifying his eating of *fruit*.

481. *consummate* complete, perfect.

483. *gradual scale* The etymologies (Latin *gradus*, 'step', *scala*, 'ladder') point to the *scala naturae* or cosmic ladder. See lines 509–12 and cp. iii 501–25.

sublimed elevated (*OED* 2a), refined (*OED* 2b). The word had alchemical overtones.

484. *spirits* See iv 805*n*. The usual hierarchy (in ascending order) was natural, *vital* and *animal* spirits, with the immaterial soul distinct from all three. Stephen Fallon (104) notes that M. omits natural spirits and adds *intellectual* spirits, which are 'his own invention'. Since the soul receives *her being* from the spirits (487), M. implies that the soul is material.

488. *Discursive, or intuitive* Aquinas had distinguished angelic intuition (the immediate apprehension of truth) from human reason (the arguing from premisses to conclusions). M. acknowledges that this distinction holds *most* of the time, but his angels sometimes reason (see e.g. v 831f.), while Adam and Eve sometimes intuit (see viii 354, xii 610–13).

493. *proper* my own.

497–500. *Your bodies . . . dwell* a clear indication that God did not intend the prohibition to last for ever. Adam and Eve are on probation in the Garden until they have proved their worthiness to *ascend*. Cp. vii 157–61 and see Lewis (68), Danielson (178).

498. *tract* duration, lapse.

499. *as we* See v 79 and note. Unlike the dream-angel, Raphael is clear that he can ascend to Heaven.

502. *entire* including 'wholly devoted', 'sincere' (*OED* 3c, 10).

505. *incapable* unable to contain (*OED* 1).

509. *scale of Nature* the *scala naturae* (ladder of Nature) or 'Chain of Being', extending from God down to the lowest dregs of the universe (see e.g. Macrobius, *In Somnium Scipionis* I xiv 15). It was often identified with Jacob's ladder and M. makes this connection at iii 510–18.

518. *apprehend* feel emotionally (*OED* 7).

525. *persevere* including 'continue in a state of grace' (*OED* 1e).

538. *surety* ground of certainty or safety (*OED* 6).

547. *Cherubic songs* See iv 680–88.

552. *yet* in addition, besides (*OED* 1a).

557. *Worthy of sacred silence* translating Horace, *Odes* II xiii 29–32: *sacro digna silentio*. Horace describes Alcaeus and Sappho singing in Hades. Alcaeus sang of war and the expulsion of tyrants. M. cites Horace's lines approvingly in his *Defensio* (*YP* 4. 441).

558. *large day* most of the day.

566. *remorse* pity, compassion (*OED* 3a).

571. *dispensed* permitted (*OED* 5b).

574–6. *earth . . . like* The doctrine that our world is but a *shadow* of the divine is from Plato, *Republic* x. M. stresses the likeness of the two worlds, not their differences.

578–9. *earth . . . poised* echoing Sandys's Ovid (*Met.* i 12): 'the self-poiz'd Earth'.

580–82. *For time . . . future* M.'s belief that time existed before the creation of our universe runs counter to a long philosophical tradition. Plato (*Timaeus* 37–8), Aristotle (*Physics* iv 11–12), and Augustine (*City of God* xi 5–6) all argue that time began with the universe. In *CD* i 7 M. conjectures that Satan fell before 'the first beginnings of this world. There is certainly no reason why we should conform to the popular belief that motion and time, which is the measure of motion, could not, according to our concepts of "before" and "after", have existed before this world was made' (trans. Carey, *YP* 6. 313–14).

583. *Great Year* the cycle completed by the heavenly bodies when they have returned to their original positions (Plato, *Timaeus* 39D). A common estimate was 36,000 years.

583–4. *empyreal . . . imperial* Raphael's pun carefully preserves imperial authority for God. Contrast Beëlzebub's 'imperial Powers' (ii 310).

588. *Ten thousand thousand* Cp. Dan. 7. 10: 'ten thousand times ten thousand stood before him'.

589. *gonfalons* banners hanging from cross-bars, often used in ecclesiastical processions.

598. *flaming Mount* Exod. 19. 19.

599. *Brightness . . . invisible* Cp. 'darkness visible' (i 63).

600. *progeny of Light* The angels were created by the Son (v 835– 7), so *Light* probably refers to him. Cp. iii 1–8.

603. *This day I have begot* echoing Ps. 2. 7 ('Thou art my Son; this day have I begotten thee') and Heb. 1. 5 ('For unto which of the angels said he at any time, Thou art my Son, This day have I begotten thee?'). M. in *CD* i 5 takes these verses to mean that 'God begot the Son in the sense of making him a king'. Thus the 'begetting' is metaphorical and refers to the Son's 'exaltation above the angels' (trans. Carey, *YP* 6. 207). Many have thought that M.'s interpretation is strained, but it has biblical precedent in Acts 13. 33 and Heb. 5. 5. M. believed that the Son was created before the angels, whom he created (see v 835–40 and note).

605. *anointed* Cp. M.'s *Brief Notes Upon a Late Sermon* (1660): 'who is [God's] *Anointed*, not every King, but they only who were anointed or made Kings by his special command' (*YP* 7. 475).

606. *head* Cp. Col. 2. 9: 'ye are complete in him, which is the head of all principality and power'.

607. *by myself have sworn* Cp. Gen. 22. 16: 'By myself have I sworn, saith the Lord'.

607–8. *bow / All knees* Cp. Phil. 2. 9–11: 'at the name of Jesus every knee should bow, of things in heaven, and things in earth, and things under the earth'.

609. *vicegerent* exercising God's authority (*OED* 2).

610. *individual* indivisible (*OED* 1).

611. *him who disobeys* 'whoever disobeys him'.

614. *utter* outer and total.

618. *solemn* of days or seasons: set apart for religious ceremonies (*OED* 2).

621. *fixed* the fixed stars.

622. *mazes intricate* Cp. Virgil's *Aen.* v 575f., where Iulus leads the Trojan boys in a mazelike ride on horseback, 'interweaving circle with alternate

circle', tracing a course like the Cretan labyrinth. Heaven's mazes have their counterpart in the 'wand'ring mazes' of Hell (ii 561).

623. *Eccentric* an off-centre planetary orbit (see viii 83n).

intervolved intertwined.

625. *their* refers both to angels and planets and so associates angelic singing with the Music of the Spheres. Cp. Job 38. 7: 'the morning stars sang together, and all the sons of God shouted for joy'.

627. *now* Added in *Ed II*.

637–40. *They . . . show'red*] *Ed I* reads: 'They eat, they drink, and with refection sweet / Are filled, before th' all bounteous King, who show'red'.

637. *communion* fellowship, esp. 'an organic union of persons united by common religious faith' (*OED* 4).

639. *full measure only bounds* only full measure bounds.

642. *ambrosial night* Cp. Homer, *Il.* ii 57: 'a divine dream came to me through the ambrosial night'. The allusion is ominous, since Agamemnon's dream lured him into a disastrous attack. See below, 673n.

645. *night comes not there* Cp. Rev. 21. 25: 'There shall be no night there'.

646. *roseate* *rose-scented (*OED* 3), with a pun on Latin *ros*, 'dew'.

652. *living streams . . . Trees of Life* Cp. Rev. 22. 2: 'On either side of the river, was there the tree of life'.

657–8. *but not so waked / Satan* Cp. Virgil's description of Dido's sleeplessness (*Aen.* iv 529). It was night, and all other creatures were sleeping, 'but not the soul-wracked Phoenician queen' (*at non infelix animi Phoenissa*).

658. *former name* Patristic tradition took Isa. 14. 12 to mean that Satan's original name was 'Lucifer'. Raphael likens Satan to Lucifer the morning star (v 708, 762, vii 131), but he never says that Satan was named 'Lucifer'. Satan's former name has been blotted from the books of life (i 361–5) and so is *heard no more*.

659–60. *of the first, / If not the first* Raphael's ambiguous wording leaves open the question of Satan's precise rank.

664. *Messiah* Hebrew 'anointed'.

669. *dislodge* leave a place of encampment (*OED* 2b) and drive a foe out of his position (*OED* 1c). The latter sense has God's *throne* (670) as object.

671. *subordinate* Raphael never names him. He lost his original name when he rebelled (i 361–5), and he will not be known as 'Beëlzebub' until 'long after' man's Fall (i 81).

673. *Sleep'st thou* echoing many previous epics, where heroes and villains are roused from sleep by a voice which lures them into rash or adventurous acts. Cp. Dream waking Agamemnon (Homer, *Il.* ii 23), Mercury waking Aeneas (Virgil, *Aen.* iv 560), Allecto waking Turnus (*Aen.* vii 421), Ismeno waking Solimano (Tasso, *Gerus. Lib.* x 8) and Satan waking the Pope in

M.'s *Q Nov* 92. Cp. also above, 38*n*, where Eve (unusually) does not wake when Satan asks 'Why sleep'st thou?'

680. *minds* purposes, intentions (*OED* II), esp. 'the way in which one person is affected towards another' (*OED* II 15b).

681. *debate* both 'discuss' and 'contend, fight for' (*OED* 2).

685. *Tell them that by command* Satan has received no command and he does not clearly say that he has. His own command (*Tell them*) arrogates the commanding voice of God. See below, 699*n*.

689. *North* the traditional site of Lucifer's throne (Isa. 14. 13).

690. *Fit entertainment* a Satanic ambiguity, since 'entertain' could have the military sense 'engage an enemy's forces' (*OED* 9c), as in: 'Porus had prepared an Army to entertain [Alexander]' (1654). Cp. iv 382, vi 611.

695. *Bad influence* malignant astral 'influences'. See *Nativity* 71*n*. Satan was associated with Lucifer, the morning star.

699. *the Most High* God, but also Satan, who is *commanding*. Cp. Lucifer's words at Isa. 14. 14: 'I shall be like the most High'.

702. *suggested* falsely imputed (*OED* 2) and insinuated (*OED* 4). The former sense refers to God's supposed command, which Satan pretends to be obeying (v 768–9); the latter sense refers to Satan's real motive of rebellion. The angels fall at 'their own suggestion' (iii 129) because they are free to hear the *Ambiguous words* (703) either as a genuine proposal to welcome the Messiah or as a call to rebellion. Abdiel hears only the innocent sense (v 883). See Leonard (149–59). 'Suggest' implies 'seduce, tempt away' (*OED* 2).

703. *jealousies* including 'suspicions, apprehensions of evil' (*OED* 5).

sound make trial of (*OED* v² 6b) and convey an impression of (*OED* v¹ 4). The subordinate conveys a false impression of his own *integrity* while sounding out others. *Sound* also implies 'healthy, untainted'. Cp. II Tim. 1. 13: 'hold fast the form of sound words which thou hast heard of me'.

704. *integrity* including 'innocence, sinlessness' (*OED* 3), as in 'Adam in his integritie should have wrought, but without wearinesse' (1622).

706. *Potentate* ruler, with overtones of angelic 'Potentates' or 'Powers' (Latin *potestates*). Cp. v 749.

707. *name* fame (*OED* 6), but suggesting also Satan's 'former name' (658).

708. *count'nance* including 'feigned appearance' (*OED* 2b), 'show of feeling towards another' (*OED* 7), 'repute in the world' (*OED* 9), 'position, standing, dignity' (*OED* 10).

morning star 'Lucifer, son of the morning' (Isa. 14. 12). Virgil likens Pallas to Lucifer the morning star in *Aen.* viii 589.

710. *Drew after him* Marching in the van of his host, Satan acts like the evening star, not the *morning star*, which appears 'last in the train of night' (v 166). Bentley wanted to emend to 'evening star', but (as Empson² 185 notes) 'the inversion acts as part of the conflict of feeling'. Lucifer-Satan leads his stellar angels 'only towards night'. Cp. *Nativity* 74.

third part Cp. Rev. 12. 4: 'And his tail drew the third part of the stars of heaven, and did cast them to the earth'. Cp. ii 692.

712. *Abstrusest* most secret.

713. *golden lamps* Cp. Rev. 4. 5: 'There were seven lamps of fire burning before the throne, which are the seven Spirits of God'. These lamps are perhaps identical with the seven angels of iii 648 or the seven planetary Intelligences (Empson² 184).

716. *sons of morn* angels. Cp. Job 38. 7: 'when the morning stars sang together, And all the sons of God shouted for joy'.

721. *Nearly* closely, particularly.

724–5. *foe / Is rising* 'Satan' means 'foe' (see i 82*n*).

725–6. *erect his throne . . . North* Cp. Isa. 14. 12–13: 'How art thou fallen from heaven, O Lucifer . . . ! For thou hast said in thine heart, I will . . . exalt my throne above the stars of God: I will sit also upon the mount of the congregation, in the sides of the north'.

736–7. *derision . . . Laugh'st* Cp. Ps. 2. 4: 'He that sitteth in the heavens shall laugh: / The Lord shall have them in derision'.

739. *Illústrates* renders illustrious (*OED* 4).

740. *in event* by the outcome.

741. *dextrous* including 'situated on the right side' (*OED* 1), alluding to the Son's position at God's 'right hand' (iii 279, v 606, vi 892). Cp. ii 174 ('His red right hand').

743. *powers* armies (*OED* 9) or angelic 'Powers', here standing for all angelic orders. Cp. vi 898.

745–6. *stars . . . dew-drops* Cp. Rev. 12. 3–4, where Satan as dragon cast a third of 'the stars of heaven' to earth. Cp. also Hos. 6. 4: 'O Judah . . . your goodness is as a morning cloud, and as the early dew it goeth away'. Cp. also Marvell, 'On a Drop of Dew' (printed 1681).

748. *regencies* *districts under the control of a regent (*OED* 4).

750. *triple degrees* 'Dionysius the Areopagite' had distinguished nine orders in three groups of three: Seraphim, Cherubim, Thrones; Dominions, Virtues, Powers; Principalities, Archangels, Angels. M. uses these titles, but follows Protestant tradition in rejecting Dionysius's strict hierarchy. Many of M.'s highest angels (including Michael and Satan) are 'Archangels', and some angels have more than one title.

to in comparison with which.

753–4. *globose . . . longitude* globe projected onto a flat plane.

758. *pyramids* Cp. M.'s description of the 'pyramidal figure' of prelacy in *RCG*: 'her pyramid aspires and sharpens to ambition . . . it is the most dividing, and schismaticall forme that Geometricians know of' (*YP* 1. 790).

760. *Lucifer* the morning star. Raphael is not naming Satan's 'former

namc', but using a metaphor to *interpret* it. See above, 658*n*, and cp. vii 131–3, x 425.

761. *dialect of men*   Homer also distinguishes human from divine names (*Il.* xiv 291, xx 74), but where Homer confidently names both ('Xanthus to the gods, to men Scamander'), M. declines to intrude upon God's mysteries.

763. *Affecting*   aspiring to (*OED* 1) and assuming a false appearance of (*OED* 6a).

764. *that Mount*   the 'flaming mount' of line 598.

766. *Mountain of the Congregation*   Cp. Lucifer's boast at Isa. 14. 13: 'I will sit also upon the mount of the congregation'. Isaiah's Lucifer aspires to God's own mountain; Satan claims the name.

773. *magnific titles*   Titles like 'Power' and 'Domination' might seem to support Satan's argument, but Protestants understood angelic titles to refer to essences, not offices. See e.g. Thomas Heywood, *The Hierarchie of the Blessed Angels* (1635) 210. Satan therefore errs in inferring *power* from *Powers*.

775. *engrossed*   monopolized (*OED* 4).

776. *eclipsed*   Cp. i 597 and vii 364–8.

778. **hurried*   *OED*'s earliest participial instance.

786. *yoke*   Cp. Matt. 11. 29–30: 'Take my yoke upon you, and learn of me; for I am meek and . . . my yoke is easy'.

799. *much less for this to be our Lord*   Satan's contemptuous *this* pointedly withholds the name 'Messiah'. Cp. Luke 19. 14: 'We will not have this man to reign over us'.

805. *Abdiel*   Hebrew 'Servant of God'. Abdiel is an angel in the *Sepher Raziel* (West 154).

821. **unsucceeded*   with no successor.

835–40. *by whom . . . Powers*   Cp. Col. 1. 16–17: 'By him [Christ] were all things created . . . whether they be thrones, or dominions, or principalities, or powers: all things were created by him, and for him: And he is before all things'. M. believed that God created the Son, who then created the angels. See above, 603*n*.

839. *Crowned . . . glory*   Cp. Ps. 8. 5: 'Thou hast . . . crowned him [man] with glory'. This verse was taken as a prophecy of the Incarnation, so Abdiel might hint at an angelic Incarnation (*One of our number*). See Danielson (219–24).

860. **self-begot*   Satan at iv 43 had admitted that God created him, but that speech is subsequent to this one in time, so we cannot conclude that Satan is now lying. Satan might genuinely doubt God's claims until the Son expels him from Heaven. See Empson (64–5). Satan claims to be his own creator in Prudentius, *Hamartigenia* 171–2 (Evans 113).

864. *Our puissance is our own* Cp. Ps. 12. 4: 'Our lips are our own: who is lord over us?'

864–5. *right hand / Shall teach* Cp. Ps. 45. 4: 'Thy right hand shall teach thee terrible things'. Cp. also Virgil's blasphemous Mezentius, whose only deity is his own right hand, *dextra mihi* (*Aen.* x 773).

868. *Address* both 'dutiful approach' (*OED* 9) and (military) 'skill, dexterity' (*OED* 4), as in 'His Royal Highness employs all his Address in alarming the enemy' (1710).

875. *flaming Seraph* Hebrew *saraph*, 'to burn'.

883. *indulgent laws* the laws of line 693 (which the Messiah has never threatened or promised).

886–7. *golden sceptre . . . iron rod* See ii 327*n*.

890. *wicked tents* So Moses warns the Israelites not to join Korah's rebellion: 'Depart, I pray you, from the tents of these wicked men . . . lest ye be consumed' (Num. 16. 26). Cp. also Ps. 84. 10: 'I had rather be a doorkeeper in the house of my God, than to dwell in the tents of wickedness'.

devoted doomed (*OED* 3), but the other sense 'faithful, loyal' attaches itself to *I* (889).

903. *single* including 'simple, honest' (*OED* 14).

906. *retorted* flung back (scorn) – with a play on Latin *retortus*, 'turned back' (*his back he turned*).

907. *swift destruction* Cp. II Pet. 2. 1: 'there shall be false teachers among you, who privily shall bring in damnable heresies, even denying the Lord that bought them, and bring upon themselves swift destruction'.

BOOK VI

1. *dreadless angel* Abdiel.

2. *champaign* plain.

3. *Hours* the Horae, goddesses of the seasons and gatekeepers of heaven (Homer, *Il.* v 749, Spenser, *FQ* VII vii 45).

rosy hand the Homeric 'rosy-fingered' (*Il.* i 477).

4. *Unbarred the gates of light* Cp. Ovid, *Met.* ii 112–14: 'Aurora . . . opened wide her purple gates'. The allusion is proleptic of Satan's defeat, for Ovid continues: 'the stars all flee away, and Lucifer closes their ranks as, last of all, he departs from his watchtower in the sky' (114–15).

4–8. *There is a cave . . . day and night* Cp. Hesiod's abysm where Day and Night hold alternate residence: 'Night and Day approach and greet each other as they pass in and out over the great bronze threshold' (*Theog.* 744–54). M. inverts Hesiod by placing the cave in Heaven, not Hell, and by describing it before, not after, the celestial battle. See Porter (60).

8. *Grateful vicissitude* delightful change.

10. *Obsequious* following dutifully.

12. *twilight* Cp. Rev. 21. 25: 'there shall be no night there'.

15. *Shot through* variegated in colour; the military context also suggests 'pierced'.

    orient resplendent.

16. *embattled* set in battle array.

19. *in procinct* ready for battle (Latin *in procinctu*). Cp. also Chapman's Homer, *Il.* xi 89: 'in all procinct of warre'.

24. *of so many myriads . . . one* Cp. Ovid's Deucalion and Pyrrha, survivors of the Greek flood (*Met.* i 325–6): 'Jove saw that of so many thousands, one man was left; and of so many thousands, one woman'.

29. *Servant of God, well done* echoing the parable of the talents: 'Well done, thou good and faithful servant' (Matt. 25. 21). 'Abdiel' means 'servant of God'.

29–30. *fought . . . fight* Cp. I Tim. 6. 12: 'fight the good fight'.

33–4. *borne . . . reproach* Cp. Ps. 69. 7: 'for thy sake I have borne reproach'.

42. *Right reason* conscience, planted by God in all men.

44. *Michael* Hebrew 'Who is like God?' See Rev. 12.7f. for Michael's role in the war (and cp. Dan. 10. 13 and 12. 1). Following Jewish and patristic tradition, M. makes Michael prince of angels. Most Protestants identified him with Christ.

49. *Equal* perhaps 'at least equal' (*OED* 1a). Only a third of the angels rebelled (ii 692, v 710), so Michael's army might outnumber Satan's two to one. Cp. Satan's words at vi 166 ('I see that most . . . had rather serve') and see Empson (41).

54. *Tartarus* hell.

56–7. *clouds . . . smoke* Mount Sinai was covered with clouds and 'altogether on a smoke' when God issued the Ten Commandments (Exod. 19. 18).

58. *reluctant* *writhing (*OED* 1). There may be a play on the modern sense, which M. also coined (*OED* 2b).

60. *gan* began to.

62. *quadrate* square formation.

64–5. *In silence . . . breathed* Cp. the fallen angels marching silently to Dorian flute music (i 550–59). Both angelic armies are adapted from Plutarch's Spartans (*Lycurgus* 22) and Homer's Achaians (*Il.* iii 8). See i 550–59*n*, i 560–61*n*.

69. *obvious* in the way.

70. *strait'ning* hemming in.

73–6. *as when . . . of thee* Similes comparing armies to birds are common in epic (see e.g. Homer, *Il.* ii 459f., Virgil, *Aen.* vii 699f.), but Raphael chooses similes that fit Adam's experience. See Gen. 2. 20: 'And Adam gave names to all cattle and to the fowl of the air, and to every beast of the field'. Cp. also viii 349–54.

78. *terrene* *the earth (*OED* 5a).

80. *fiery region* Cp. Homer, *Il.* ii 455–8: 'As obliterating fire lights up a vast forest / along the crests of a mountain, and the flare shows far off, / so as they marched, from the magnificent bronze the gleam went / dazzling all about through the upper air to the heaven'.

81. *battailous* warlike.

82. *beams* The initial sense 'rays of light' changes to 'shafts of spears'. Satan promises a new morning, but brings only war. (*OED* has no instance of 'beam' meaning 'spear', but cp. Spenser, *FQ* III vii 40 and I Sam. 17. 7.)

84. *argument* heraldic devices.

86. *expedition* warlike enterprise (*OED* 2a) and speed (*OED* 5).

90. *fond* foolish.

93. *hosting* hostile encounter (*OED*) and entertaining as guests (*OED* 'host' v² 1). *Fierce hosting* is an oxymoron when war is *strange*. Cp. 'Fit entertainment' (v 690).

  wont were accustomed.

96. *Hymning OED's earliest instance of the verb. The noun dates from Anglo-Saxon times.

101–2. *enclosed / With flaming Cherubim* Satan enthroned is an *Idol* of the Father (see i 387*n*).

107. *cloudy* gloomy, frowning (*OED* 6).

108. *edge* line of battle (*OED* 5a). Cp. i 276*n*.

115. *realty* sincerity, honesty (*OED* 2).

118. *to sight* seemingly.

120. *tried* proved by trial.

129. *prevention* obstruction (*OED* 4).

130. *securely* confidently.

137–9. *out of smallest things . . . armies* echoing Matt. 3. 9 ('God is able of these stones to raise up children unto Abraham') and Matt. 26. 53. Cp. also Cromwell's assurance at Naseby 'that GOD would do great things, by small means; and by things that are not, bring to nought things that are' (Joshua Sprigge, *Anglia Rediviva* (1647) 43).

141. **Unaided.*

147. *sect* a politically charged word in M.'s time, when it was used to smear Puritan schismatics. Like Abdiel, M. is proud of the designation. See *Eikonoklastes* (1649): 'I never knew that time in *England*, when men of truest Religion were not counted Sectaries' (*YP* 3. 348).

153. *assay* attack, assault (*OED* 15).

156. *synod* assembly (usually ecclesiastical, so a synod of *gods* is absurd). Cp. ii 391.

161. *success* fortune (i.e. ill – but Abdiel will be more 'successful' than Satan expects).

163. *Unanswered . . . boast* 'Lest you boast I was unable to answer you'.

165. *all one* one and the same (*OED* 'all' 5b).

167–8. *Minist'ring . . . minstrelsy* Satan's contemptuous pun brings out the common etymology: *ministerium*, 'office, service'. Cp. Heb. 1. 14: 'Are they not all ministering spirits?'

169. *Servility* both 'obsequiousness' and 'the condition of being in bondage' (*OED* 1). Abdiel's word *servitude* (175) ignores the charge of obsequiousness.

174. *deprav'st* pervert the meaning of (*OED* 3), vilify (*OED* 4).

182. *lewdly* wickedly (*OED* 2), ignorantly (*OED* 1).

183–4. *Reign . . . Heav'n* Contrast Satan's words at i 263: 'Better to reign in Hell, than serve in Heav'n'.

193. *ruin* including 'swift descent'.

196. *Winds under ground* the supposed cause of earthquakes (cp. i 230–37).

197. *pushed a mountain from his seat* Contrast Satan as an irremovable mountain at iv 985–7. Cp. also vi 643f.

199. *Thrones* a synecdoche for all angelic orders. The oxymoron *rebel Thrones* is also politically suggestive. Cp. 'rebel king' (i 484) and Michael's revelation that the first king derived his name from 'Rebellion' (xii 36).

209. *brayed* made a loud harsh jarring sound (*OED* 3).

210. *madding* furiously whirling.

215. *cope* sky (*OED* sb¹ 7) and shock of combat (*OED* sb²).

216. *battles main* the main bodies of the armies (as distinct from van and wings).

222. *These elements* the earth and its atmosphere, realm of the four elements.

223. *regions* divisions of the universe (*OED* 3a).

225. *combustion* confusion, tumult (*OED* 5b).

232–3. *yet . . . chief* 'yet each single warrior seemed like a commander-in-chief'.

234. *sway* force bearing its object in a certain direction (*OED* 3), as in 'Push'd and yielding to superior sway . . . the Spartan ranks gave way' (1757).

236. *ridges of grim war* Probably 'ranks' (*when to close*), but cp. the Homeric phrase πολέμοιο γέφυραι (*Il.* iv 371, xi 160, etc.), which might refer to the space between two battle lines.

239. *moment* moment of a balance (*OED* 5), hence 'deciding factor'. Notice *sway* (234) and *even scale* (245).

243. *main* strong, vigorous.

244. *Tormented* agitated (*OED* 3).

248. **attack* OED's earliest instance of the noun.

254. *orb* circle (*OED* 1).

255. *adamant* a mythical substance of impenetrable hardness, usually identified with diamond or steel. M. here imagines it to be a metal folded back on itself ten times (*tenfold*).

259. *Intestine war* civil war.

262–3. *evil . . . Unnamed* Contrast Adam's statement that 'Evil into the mind of god or man / May come and go' (v 117–19). Michael speaks as one who has been a complete stranger to evil.

272. *casts* throws and vomits (*OED* 25).

274. *Brooks* endures, 'stomachs' (*OED* 3).

282. *Adversary* translates 'Satan'.

284–8. *Hast . . . hence* 'Have you turned the weakest of my host to flight, or to fall, but that they rise unconquered? And do you think that I am easier to deal (*transact*) with than they are? Are you so imperious as to try to chase me away with threats?'

288. *Err not* Don't imagine.

296. *parle* parley.

addressed made ready (*OED* 3a).

305. *two broad suns* Cp. Euripides, *The Bacchae* 918 and Virgil, *Aen.* iv 470. When Pentheus denied Dionysus's divinity, he was maddened and lured to his destruction by a vision of two suns blazing in the heavens.

306. *Expectation* personifying the other angels' apprehension. Cp. Shakespeare, *Troilus and Cressida* Prol., and *Henry V* II Prol.: 'now sits Expectation in the air'.

311. *Great things by small* See ii 921–2n.

broke broken.

313–14. *aspéct . . . opposition* astrological terms denoting the relative position of the heavenly bodies. Two *planets* were in 'opposition' when they occupied opposite signs. Their influence on men was then *malign*.

315. *jarring spheres confound* refers both to physically colliding *planets* (313) and discordant celestial music. *Jarring* means 'striking' and 'out of tune', *spheres* means 'planets' (*OED* 10b) and 'music of the spheres' (*OED* 2b), *confound* means 'smash' (*OED* 1d) and 'throw into confusion'. Cp. x 412–14.

318. *determine* decide the matter.

need repeat need to be repeated.

319. *As not of power* since it would be impossible to repeat such a blow.

at once refers back to *determine*.

320. *prevention* anticipation.

321. *armoury of God* Cp. Jer. 50. 25: 'The Lord hath opened his armoury, and hath brought forth the weapons of his indignation'.

325. *in half cut sheer* 'Overgoing Virgil: Turnus' sword merely shatters in fragments' (Fowler). See *Aen.* xii 741.

326. *shared* cut into parts, cut off (*OED*).

328. *convolved* *contorted (*OED* 3). The older sense 'coiled' (*OED* 2) anticipates Satan's serpent metamorphosis (x 504f.).

329. *griding cutting keenly (earliest participial instance).

*discontinuous gaping (*OED* 1).

332. *nectarous humour* Cp. the divine ichor that flows from Aphrodite's hand when Diomedes wounds her. Homer explains that the gods have no blood, for they do not eat food or drink wine (*Il.* v 339–42). M.'s angels (who drink nectar) bleed *nectarous* fluid (*humour*). *Sanguine* means 'blood-red' (*OED* 1), but also suggests the sanguine *humour* which in Renaissance physiology gave rise to courage. Thus Satan's loss of this humour implies a loss of morale.

344. *Yet soon he healed* Cp. Pope's parody: 'But airy substance soon unites again' (*The Rape of the Lock* iii 152).

346. *reins* kidneys.

352. *limb provide themselves with limbs (*OED* v 2, sole instance).

353. *likes* pleases.

condense or rare dense or airy.

355. *the might of Gabriel* the mighty Gabriel (Homeric diction); *Gabriel* means 'Strength of God'.

356. *ensigns* either 'standard bearers' (*OED* 7) or 'companies serving under one standard' (*OED* 6). As many as 500 men might serve in an 'ensign'.

357. *Moloch* The name is not supposed to exist until after man's Fall (see i 364–5). Raphael might foreknow the names of future devils (cp. xii 140), but to name them here implies the failure of his mission. He had withheld 'Beëlzebub' from book v (see v 671*n*), but now allows many devils' names to infiltrate book vi. See below, 371–85*n*.

359–60. *Holy One . . . blasphémous* Cp. II Kings 19. 22: 'Whom hast thou reproached and blasphemed . . . ? the Holy One of Israel'.

360. *Refrained* from Latin *refrenare*, 'to bridle'. The early spelling 'refreined' (*Ed I, Ed II*) might pun on 'reins'. Notice *chariot* (358). Moloch's tongue runs away with him.

362. *uncouth* unfamiliar (*OED* 2), unpleasant (*OED* 4).

bellowing Cp. Ares bellowing when Diomedes wounds him (Homer, *Il.* v 860). Moloch's bellowing is also 'typical of a bull god' (Flannagan).

365. *Adramelech* 'King of fire', a Sepharvite god worshipped at Samaria with human sacrifice (II Kings 17. 31).

Asmadai Asmodeus ('creature of judgement'), a Persian god who will encounter Raphael again (see iv 167–71).

369. *annoy* injure.

370. *atheist* *impious (*OED* B).

371–85. *Ariel* ('lion of God'), *Arioch* ('lion-like'), and *Ramiel* ('thunder of God') are devils, but Raphael might be naming their *Cancelled* angelic names. All three names had been used of good as well as bad angels in pseudepigraphal, rabbinical and demonological texts. See Harris Fletcher, *Milton's Rabbinical Readings* (1930) 268–79 and R. H. West, *SP* 47 (1950) 211–23 (pp. 215–17). The names are troubling however we take them. Raphael should not name *Cancelled* angelic names (see i 362, v 659), but he cannot name devils without presupposing man's Fall (see above, 357*n*).

379. *Cancelled* blotted out (*OED* 3a). Cp. i 362, v 658.

382. *Illaudable* unworthy of praise.

383. *ignominy* including 'namelessness' (Latin *in*, 'not' + *nomen*, 'name').

386. *battle* army (*OED* 8).

swerved gave way (*OED* 4).

391. *what stood* those who resisted.

392. **Satanic.*

393. *Defensive scarce* scarcely able to defend themselves.

399. *cubic phalanx* See i 550*n*. Angels might fly in a cube formation. The cube symbolized 'virtue and stability' (Fowler). Contrast the rebels' 'hollow cube' (vi 552).

entire unwearied (*OED* 4e), with unbroken ranks (*OED* 5b), honest, upright (*OED* 9).

404. *unobnoxious* not liable (*OED* 1).

407. *Inducing* drawing, overspreading (*OED* 7).

411. *prevalent* victorious.

413. *Cherubic . . . fires* overgoing Homer (*Il.* viii 553f.), where the victorious Trojans merely attend camp-fires.

415. *dislodged* shifted his quarters (*OED* 1b, military term).

416. *Potentates* either 'leaders' or a synecdoche for all angelic orders.

416. *council called by night* Nocturnal councils in which a defeated army recovers its morale are frequent in epic. See e.g. Homer, *Il.* ix *passim*, xix 243–314, and Virgil, *Aen.* ix 224–313.

421. *mean pretence . . . affect* modest ambition . . . aspire to. But M.'s voice behind Satan plays on 'base pretext . . . assume a false appearance of'.

429. *Of future* In the future.

430. *Omniscient* 'Omnipotent' would better suit the context, but Satan is mocking God. A God who knows about Satan's plans might still be powerless to thwart them.

432. *known as soon contemned* no sooner known than despised.

438. *valid* strong, powerful (*OED* 3).

440. *worse* injure (*OED* 2) and worst, get the better of.

444. *sound* unaffected by injury (*OED* a 2) and search into.

447. *Nisroch* an Assyrian god (II Kings 19. 37). According to Stephanus's *Dictionary* (1621), the Hebrew name means 'Flight' or 'Delicate temptation'. See Dewitt T. Starnes and Ernest William Talbert, *Classical Myth and Legend in Renaissance Dictionaries* (1955), 268.

455. *impassive* not feeling pain (*OED* 1), from the theological term 'impassible'.

456-7. *avails / Valour* Both words are from Latin *valere*, 'to be worth, or strong', so Nisroch 'sharply implies that valour ceases to be itself when . . .' (Ricks).

458. *remiss* slack, weak.

464. *He who* whoever (hinting that Nisroch might seek a new leader).

invent Nisroch means 'plan' (*OED* 2a), as in 'a plot invented . . . by Cacodaemons' (1641), but the technological sense existed and Satan plays upon it in line 470 when he announces his invention of gunpowder.

465. *offend* attack (*OED* 5), injure (*OED* 6).

467. *to me* in my opinion.

471. *main* highly important.

472-81. *Which . . . light* The sun was thought to generate precious metals and gems within the earth. Cp. iii 608-12 and *A Masque* 732-6.

473. *ethereous* 'a new word for a new way of looking at matter as instinct not with heavenly spirit but with chemical power' – James Mengert in *MS* 14 (1980), 95-115 (108). The usual word is 'ethereal'.

477. *mind* give heed to.

478. *crude* raw, unripe.

479. *spiritous* refined (*OED* 1).

spume frothy matter produced in the refining of metals.

479-81. *touched . . . light* Svendsen (119) notes how the images (*touched, tempered, shoot, opening*) anticipate the invention of gunpowder.

483. *infernal flame* Satan means 'fire from underground', but M.'s voice behind him anticipates Hell-fire.

484. *engines* machines of war (*OED* 5a). The diabolic invention of gunpowder has many epic precedents. Cp. Ariosto, *Orl. Fur.* ix 28f., ix 91, xi 21-8, Spenser, *FQ* I vii 13, Daniel, *Civil Wars* (1609) vi 26-7. Erasmo di Valvasone had introduced the invention of artillery into his angelic war in *L'Angeleida* (1590). See Kirkconnell (81). Notice that Raphael never names Satan's weapons as 'cannon'. Cp. *Orl. Fur.* ix 28-9, where the innocent Olimpia describes 'a strange new weapon' without naming it. Ariosto in his own voice later names many kinds of artillery (*Orl. Fur.* xi 24-5). Our perspective is that of Ariosto; Adam's is that of Olimpia.

485. *other bore* the touch-hole.

touch contact (with *fire*) and touch-powder (gunpowder over the touch-hole). The same pun recurs at vi 520, 566, 584.

486. *infuriate* raging.

488. *implements* playing on Latin *implementum*, 'a filling up'.

489. *To pieces* to confusion (*OED* 1c) and 'to smithereens'.

491. *only* unique, peerless (*OED* 5).

496. *cheer* mood, spirits.

498. *admired* marvelled at.

504. *machination* both 'plotting' and 'mechanical appliance for war' (*OED* 4).

511. *originals* original elements (*OED* 6a).

512. *nitrous foam* saltpetre (an ingredient in gunpowder).

514. *Concocted and adusted* heated and dried up (alchemical terms).

518. *found* cast (in a foundry).

519. *missive* missile (adj.).

    incentive reed kindling match.

520. *pernicious* destructive (*OED* a¹, from Latin *perniciosus*) and swift (*OED* a², from Latin *pernix*).

521. *conscious* privy to (*OED* 2) and guilty (*OED* 4b). Night is personified as an accomplice.

535. *Zophiel* Hebrew 'Spy of God'. The name is not biblical, but it appears in *The Zohar* where Zophiel is one of two angelic chieftains under Michael (Numbers 154a).

536. *in mid air earliest instance of 'mid air' and 'in mid air' (*OED*). Cp. ii 718, iv 940.

541. *Sad* steadfast, firm (*OED* 2).

    secure confident.

545. *conjecture* prognosticate, gather from signs (*OED* 1).

548. *impediment* military baggage (*OED* 3).

549. *Instant without disturb* urgent without panic.

    took alarm took up arms.

550. *embattled* drawn up in battle formation.

553. *Training* hauling.

    enginery artillery.

    impaled surrounded for defence (*OED* 1c, military term).

555. *At interview* in mutual view (*OED* 2).

560. *composure* settlement of disputes (*OED* 4) and constructing (*OED* 1) of weapons. See also 613*n*, below.

    breast heart (*OED* 5a) and broad front of a moving company (*OED* 7). *Peace* might contain a pun on 'piece' meaning 'cannon' (*OED* 11).

562. *overture* opening of negotiations (*OED* 3) and aperture, hole (*OED* 1) – the cannons' 'hideous orifice' (577). There may be a further pun on 'overthrow' (*OED* 8) referring both to the previous day's defeat and the expected victory.

    perverse peevish (*OED* 3), with a pun on Latin *perversus*, 'turned the wrong way' (*turn not back*).

564–6. *discharge . . . charge* 'perform our duty' and 'discharge our explosives'.

567. *propound* There may be a pun on 'pound' meaning 'fire heavy shot

(*OED* v¹ 4a), but *OED* has no instance before 1815. 'Crush by beating, pulverize' (*OED* 1) was current.

568. *ambiguous words* Satan's puns may cause us to groan, but they are not at first obvious to the good angels who have never heard of artillery.

572. *triple-mounted* either 'arranged in three rows' (see 605, 650) or 'having three barrels mounted on one stock'. M. may be thinking of the kind of ordnance called 'organs' or *orgues*, which could fire several barrels at once.

576. *mould* moulded out of (*Brass*, etc.).

578. *hollow* insincere – with a pun on *hollowed* cannon (574).

580. *suspense* cautious (*OED* 3), in suspense.

581. *amused* including the military sense: 'divert the attention of the enemy from one's real designs' (*OED* 5).

586-9. *deep-throated . . . disgorging* Cp. the scatological body-landscape of Hell (eg: i 230-37, 670-74).

587. *Embowelled* disembowelled (*OED* 2), or filled the bowels (*OED* 3) to breaking point (*entrails tore*).

589. *chained* The devils are using chain-shot, linked cannonballs capable of felling whole ranks.

594. *Angel on Archangel rolled* Angels are the lowest, and Archangels the second lowest, order in Pseudo-Dionysius's hierarchy. M. uses such titles freely, but the present line does imply some kind of hierarchy.

597. *quick contraction or remove* See i 777–80 and iv 810–19 for the angels' ability to change size.

598. *dissipation* scattering, dispersal (*OED* 1).

599. **serried* pressed together, in close order.

601. *indecent* shameful.

605. *posture* position of a weapon in drill or warfare (*OED* 2b).
   *displode fire, discharge.
   tire volley (*OED* 3).

611. *entertain* punning on the military sense 'engage an enemy' (*OED* 9c). Cp. v 690.
   open front candid face (*OED* 'open' 16, 'front' 3a) and divided front rank (*OED* 'front' 5a). See vi 569–70: 'the front / Divided'. *With open front* implies 'with open arms', but also the now obsolete phrase 'with open face' meaning 'brazenly' (*OED* 'open' 5b), as in: 'with open face . . . vent Blasphemies' (1650).

613. *composition* truce (*OED* 23b), with a possible pun on 'chemical composition' (gunpowder).

614. *vagáries* frolics (*OED* 3a) and rambling from the subject under discussion (*OED* 2).

615. *As they would dance* Cp. Aeneas's taunt to Meriones in Homer, *Il.* xvi 617.

619. *result* outcome of deliberations (*OED* 3a) and action of springing back to a former position (*OED* 1).

620–27. Belial's puns are obvious except for *amused* (see above, 581*n*), *stumbled* ('nonplussed' and 'tripped up'), and *understand* ('comprehend' and 'prop up' *OED* 9).

635. *Rage prompted them* Cp. *Aen.* i 150: *furor arma ministrat*, 'rage supplies them with arms'. The allusion prepares for the Messiah's entry, for Virgil is describing rioters who hurl stones until a noble man pacifies them.

644–6. The hurling of *hills* as missiles recalls the war between the gods and Giants, which M. has already likened to the War in Heaven (cp. i 50, 197–200, 230–37). See esp. Claudian, *Gigantomachia* 70f.: 'One giant brandishes Thessalian Oeta in his mighty hand, another gathers all his strength and hurls Pangaeus at the foe, Athos with his snows arms another; this one roots up Ossa, that tears out Rhodope . . .' Cp. also Hesiod, *Theog.* 713–20 and Ovid, *Met.* i 151–62.

646. *amaze* astonishment, panic (*OED* 3).

654. *Main* of great bulk (*OED* 3), formed of solid rock (*OED* 4b).

655. *oppressed* crushed in battle (*OED* 1a).

657. *pent* closely confined.

664. *hills . . . hills* Cp. Tasso, *Gerus. Lib.* xvi 5: 'hill gainst hill, and mount gainst mountaine smote' (trans. Fairfax); also Virgil's simile describing the ships at Actium (*Aen.* viii 692): *montis concurrere montibus altos* ('high mountains clashed with mountains').

665. *jaculation* throwing.

667. *civil* orderly, humane, refined, non-military (*OED*), with a pun on 'Civil War'.

668. *To* compared with.

668–9. *confusion . . . confusion* Cp. ii 996: 'Confusion worse confounded'. The war threatens to reduce Heaven to Chaos.

671–3. *Almighty Father . . . sum of things* echoing Ovid, *Met.* ii 300, where Earth begs Jove, the *pater omnnipotens*, to place the public interest first (*rerum consule summae*) and kill Phaethon so as to save the world from conflagration.

674. *advised* having considered (*OED* 1).

677. *declare* manifest, show forth.

679. *Assessor* *one who sits beside (*OED* 1).

680. *Effulgence radiance.

681–2. *invisible . . . Visibly* Cp. Col. 1. 15: 'the image of the invisible God'.

684. *Second omnipotence* Cp. John 5. 19: 'The Son can do nothing of himself, but what he seeth the Father do'. M. in *CD* i 5 cites this verse to show that the Son derives his power from the Father (*YP* 6. 266).

692. *Insensibly* imperceptibly.

698. *main* whole continent of Heaven.

701. *suffered* permitted.

709. *unction* anointing (iii 317, v 605).

712. *war* *instruments of war (*OED* 6a).

714. *Gird . . . thigh* Cp. Ps. 45. 3: 'Gird thy sword upon thy thigh, O most mighty'.

728. *well pleased* Cp. Matt. 3. 17: 'my beloved Son, in whom I am well pleased'.

731–2. *resign . . . All in All* See iii 341*n*.

734. *whom thou hat'st, I hate* Cp. Ps. 139. 21: 'Do not I hate them, O Lord, that hate thee?'

738. *prepared ill mansion* Hell. Contrast John 14. 2: 'In my Father's house are many mansions . . . I go to prepare a place for you'.

739. *th' undying worm* Mark 9. 44.

744. *Unfeignèd hallelujahs* Cp. 'forced hallelujahs' (ii 243).

748. *sacred morn* Cp. Homer, *Il.* xi 84.

749–59. The Messiah's living chariot, with its four-faced Cherubim, is taken from Ezekiel 1 and 10.

752. *instinct* *impelled, moved, animated (*OED* 2).

753. *four faces* of man, lion, ox and eagle (Ezek. 1. 10) or cherub, man, lion and eagle (Ezek. 10. 14).

759. *show'ry arch* rainbow. See Ezek. 1. 28.

761. *urim* Hebrew 'lights': gems worn by Aaron in his breastplate (Exod. 28. 30). Cp. iii 598 and *PR* iii 13–15.

762. *Victory* M.'s personification is modelled on Nike, the winged Greek goddess.

763–4. The *eagle* was Jupiter's bird and *thunder* his weapon.

765. *effusion* copious emission of smoke (*OED* 1c).

766. *bickering* *coruscating, quivering (*OED* 3) and skirmishing with arrows (*OED* 'bicker' 1b). Messiah's chariot shoots 'arrows' of 'fire' (see vi 845–50 and Ezek. 1. 13).

769–70. *twenty thousand . . . Chariots* Cp. Ps. 68. 17: 'The chariots of God are twenty thousand'.

771. *on wings of Cherub* Cp. Ps. 18. 10: 'He rode upon a cherub, and did fly'.

sublime lifted up.

773. *Illustrious* shining.

776. *his sign* anticipating the Second Coming: 'And then shall appear the sign of the Son of man in heaven' (Matt. 24. 30).

777. *reduced* led back (*OED* 2b).

778. *circumfused* spread around.

785. *obdured* obdurate, hardened in sin. See iii 200*n*.

788. *In . . . dwell* Cp. *Aen.* i 11 (Virgil's wonder at Juno's malice): 'Can such anger dwell in heavenly hearts?' Satan will echo the same line when tempting Eve (ix 729–30).

789–91. *what signs . . . hardened* Cp. God's hardening of Pharaoh's heart to all his *signs* (Exod. 14. 4–8).

794. **re-embattled* drawn up again in battle array.

801–2. *Stand still . . . this day* echoing Moses' words when God destroyed the Egyptians in the Red Sea: 'Fear ye not, stand still, and see the salvation of the Lord which he will shew to you this day' (Exod. 14. 13).

808. *Vengeance is his* a biblical commonplace. See e.g. Rom. 12. 19: 'Vengeance is mine; I will repay'.

809. *Number . . . not ordained* Messiah will defeat the rebels unaided. M. may also be alluding to the numerological commonplace that One is not a number (Fowler).

815. *Kingdom . . . glory* Cp. the Lord's Prayer (Matt. 6. 13).

827. *the Four* the 'four Cherubic shapes' of line 753.

832. *Gloomy as Night* So Hector, shining in bronze, breached the Achaians' rampart 'with dark face like sudden night' (Homer, *Il.* xii 462). Heaven's night is not gloomy (v 645, vi 11–12), so the Son must be dark as Chaos – but even Chaos pales before him (vi 862–6).

833. *steadfast Empyrean shook* So Olympus shook when Zeus went out to fight Typhoeus (Hesiod, *Theog.* 842–3). Cp. also Isa. 13. 12: 'I will shake the heavens'. God's throne remains unshaken (834), so Satan was lying when he said that he 'shook his throne' (i 105).

838. *Plagues* blows, wounds (*OED* 1), divine punishments, often with reference to 'the ten plagues' of Egypt (*OED* 2). Cp. the allusions to Pharaoh in lines 789–91 and 801–2. The Great Plague of 1665 killed 60,000 Londoners.

840. *O'er . . . rode* Cp. M.'s description in *An Apology* of Zeal ascending 'his fiery Chariot' drawn by beasts that resemble 'those four' seen by Ezekiel: 'with these the invincible warriour Zeale shaking loosely the slack reins drives over the heads of Scarlet Prelats . . . brusing their stiffe necks under his flaming wheels' (*YP* 1. 900).

842–3. *mountains . . . shelter* Cp. Rev. 6. 16, where the damned cry 'to the mountains and rocks, Fall on us, and hide us from the face of him that sitteth on the throne, and from the wrath of the Lamb'. See also Luke 23. 30, Hos. 10. 8.

846. *Distinct* adorned (*OED* 4).

849. *pernicious* destructive and swift.

853. *half his strength* Contrast Hesiod's Zeus, who 'no longer checked his might', but 'put forth all his strength' to quell the Titans (*Theog.* 685–7).

857. *goats or timorous flock* Cp. Homer's comparison of fleeing Trojans to 'fawns' (*Il.* xxii 1). Cp. also the parable of the sheep and goats (Matt. 25.

33). The goats were sent 'into everlasting fire, prepared for the devil and his angels' (25. 41).

859. *furies* with overtones of 'Furies' – the avenging goddesses of Greek myth (see ii 596*n*).

861. *Rolled inward* Cp. Rev. 6. 14 on the Last Judgement: 'And the heaven departed as a scroll when it is rolled together'.

862. *wasteful* desolate, uninhabited, void (*OED* 3) and laying waste (*OED* 1).

868. *ruining* falling headlong.

871. *Nine days they fell* Hesiod's Titans fall for nine days from heaven to earth and for a further nine days from earth to Tartarus (*Theog.* 720–25). The angels' nine-day fall precedes their nine-day stupor in Hell (i 50).

873. *rout* uproar, disreputable crowd, defeated army.

874. *Encumbered* blocked up (*OED* 6), harassed, pressed hardly upon (*OED* 3b), burdened.

874–5. *Hell . . . Yawning . . . closed* Cp. Isa. 5. 14: 'hell hath enlarged herself, and opened her mouth without measure: and their glory, and their multitude, and their pomp, and he that rejoiceth, shall descend into it'.

884. *jubilee* joyful shouting (*OED* 5b).

885. *palm* an emblem of victory presaging apocalyptic triumphs (Rev. 7. 9).

892. *right hand* '[The Son] sat down on the right hand of the Majesty on high' (Heb. 1. 3).

898. *powers* armies (*OED* 9) or 'Powers', standing for all angelic orders. Cp. v 743.

909. *Thy weaker* Eve (the 'weaker vessel' of I Pet. 3. 7). It is odd that Raphael should speak about her as if she were absent. M. will soon tell us that she has been 'attentive' to the whole story (vii 50–51). Raphael might be ignoring Eve in compliance with God's instruction that he 'Converse with Adam' (v 230), or (as Jean Gagen suggests) M. might be inconsistent as to how much Eve hears. See ix 275–6*n*.

BOOK VII

1–50. M.'s third invocation in *PL*. The first two were at i 1–49 and iii 1–55. Most critics see ix 1–47 as a fourth invocation, but M. does not address his Muse after book vii. See ix 1–47*n*.

1. *Descend from Heav'n* echoing Horace's invocation of the Muse Calliope: *Descende caelo* (*Odes* III iv 1).

Urania one of the nine Muses (the Muse of astronomy in late Roman times). The name means 'heavenly'. Du Bartas in *L'Uranie* had made

Urania the Muse of Christian poetry. M. invokes *the meaning, not the name* (5) because he invokes a truly heavenly source of inspiration.

2. *If rightly thou art called* Cp. the cautious addressing of divine beings in iii 7 and *Ep. Dam.* 208.

3. *Olympian hill* M. diminishes pagan epic by calling Mount Olympus 'a mere hill' (Fowler). The distinction between hill and mountain was well established (see *OED* 'hill' 1a).

4. *Pegasean* The winged horse Pegasus was a symbol for inspired poetry. He had created the Muses' spring, Hippocrene ('horse spring'), with a stamp of his hoof. He was also associated with Bellerophon (see below, 18–20*n*).

8–12. *Before . . . song* Cp. Prov. 8. 24–31, where *Wisdom* tells of her origins before Creation: 'When there were no depths, I was brought forth; when there were no fountains abounding with water. Before the mountains were settled, before the hills was I brought forth . . . Then I was by him, as one brought up with him; was daily his delight, rejoicing always before him'. Wisdom was often identified as the Son, but M. in *CD* i 7 takes her to be a personification of the Father's wisdom.

9. *converse* keep company (*OED* 2).

10. *play* M. follows the Vulgate (*ludens*) rather than A.V. ('rejoicing') or Junius-Tremellius (*laetificans*). There may be a musical pun on *play*, suggesting that Wisdom and Urania play instruments to accompany their *song* (12).

15. *Thy temp'ring* 'the air tempered (made suitable) by you'; also implying that the Muse has 'guided' and 'attuned' M. himself (*OED* 'temper' 7, 15).

18–20. *Bellerophon . . . forlorn* Bellerophon killed the Chimera (see ii 628) and defeated the Solymi and Amazons, but he incurred the gods' anger when he tried to fly to heaven upon Pegasus. Zeus sent an insect to sting the horse, and Bellerophon fell down to the *Aleian field* ('plain of wandering'). Cp. Homer, *Il.* vi 200–202. Natale Conti, in *Mythologiae* (1567) IX iv, says that Bellerophon was blinded in his fall.

18. *clime* region, atmosphere; with a pun on 'climb'.

20. *Erroneous* straying (physical and moral).

22. *diurnal sphere* the visible universe, which appears to rotate daily.

23. *rapt* transported, enraptured.

  pole celestial pole.

24–5. *unchanged / To hoarse or mute* M. would be *hoarse* if he were to become a turncoat, and *mute* if he were censored.

25–7. *evil days . . . dangers* M. probably wrote these lines shortly after the Restoration, when he was in *danger* of being dismembered like Orpheus (32–8). Several of his old republican colleagues, including Sir Henry Vane, were hanged, drawn and quartered. M. was spared that fate by the Act of Oblivion (August 1660). See Lieb[2] 70–80.

27. *darkness* M. had been totally blind since 1652.

29. *Visit'st . . . nightly* Cp. Ps. 17. 3: 'thou hast visited me in the night'. M.'s early biographers report that he composed at night or in the early hours of the morning. See Darbishire (33) and cp. iii 32 and ix 22.

32. *barbarous dissonance* The same phrase occurs in *A Masque* (550), again in the context of Bacchic revelry. Here *Bacchus and his revellers* are probably the Royalists, whom M. in *REW* calls 'these tigers of Bacchus' (*YP* 7. 452).

34. *Thracian bard* Orpheus. See *Lycidas* 58–63n for the story of his dismemberment by the Bacchantes.

35. *Rhodope* a mountain range in Thrace.

36. *rapture* ecstasy (a sense coined by M. in *Nativity* 98), with overtones of 'seizing and carrying off as prey' (*OED* 1).

37. *the Muse* Calliope, the Muse of epic poetry.

46. *touch* Cp. Gen. 3. 3: 'neither shall ye touch it, lest ye die'.

50. *wand'ring* innocent meandering – but the hint of moral aberration is strong after *Erroneous there to wander* (20). Cp. vii 302.

   consorted both 'accompanied' and 'wedded'.

50–51. *Eve . . . heard* M. here insists that Eve heard the whole story of Satan's rebellion, but Eve later speaks as if she had been absent. See ix 275–8 and note.

52. *admiration* astonishment.

   muse meditation (*OED* sb²).

57. *redounded* flowed back (*OED* 4), from Latin *unda*, 'a wave'. Cp. the allusion to the whelming of Pharaoh in vi 800.

59. *repealed* abandoned (*OED* 2). For Adam's *doubts* see v 554.

63. *conspicuous* visible (in contrast to the invisible Heaven).

66. *drouth* thirst. Cp. Dante, *Purg.* xviii 4, where Dante thirsts for more of Virgil's discourse.

67. *current* running.

72. *Divine interpreter* echoing Mercury's title as messenger of the gods, *interpres divum* (Virgil, *Aen.* iv 378).

79. *end* final purpose.

83. *seemed* seemed good (*OED* 7e).

88. *yields or fills / All space* 'The air *yields* to solid bodies or *fills* the space they leave vacant' (Fowler). *Space* might also refer to 'outer space', before which *the ambient air* (earth's atmosphere) *yields* or gives way.

90. *florid* flowery, resplendent, flourishing (*OED* 1, 4, 6).

90–91. *what cause / Moved* Cp. i 28–30: 'what cause / Moved our grand parents . . . to fall off?'

92. *late* recently (*OED* 4); perhaps also 'at a late date' – but Milton in *CD* i 7 says only a fool would ask 'what God did before the creation of the world' (trans. Carey, *YP* 6. 299).

94. *Absolved* completed (*OED* 2).

unforbid unforbidden.

97. *magnify* glorify. Cp. Job 36. 24: 'magnify his work'.

98–100. *And . . . hears* Appeals to continue a narrative are common in epic. See esp. Homer, *Od.* xi 372–6, where Alcinous asks Odysseus to go on speaking until the dawn.

99. *suspense* attentive (*OED* 1), hanging (*OED* 4), *held back (*OED* 5).

102. *His generation* 'how he was created'.

103. *unapparent deep* invisible Chaos.

106. *watch* stay awake (*OED* 1).

109. *illustrious* including 'bright, shining' (*OED* 1).

116. *infer* *make, render (*OED* 1c, sole instance).

121. *inventions* speculations.

hope hope for, aspire to.

126–30. *knowledge . . . wind* Cp. Davenant, *Gondibert* (1651) II viii 22: 'If knowledg, early got, self vallew breeds, / By false digestion it is turn'd to winde'.

131. *Lucifer* the morning star, substituting for Satan's 'former name', which is now 'heard no more' (v 659). Notice that Satan was *brighter* among the angels than Lucifer among the stars (not merely 'as bright as Lucifer' or even 'as bright relative to the angels as Lucifer is to the stars'). Cp. v 760, x 425.

142. *us dispossessed* 'once he had dispossessed us'.

143. *fraud* *the state of being defrauded (*OED* 5) – a passive usage unique to M., from Latin *fraus*. Cp. ix 643, *PR* i 372.

144. *place . . . more* Cp. Job 7. 10: 'He [that dies] shall return no more to his house, neither shall his place know him any more'.

150–56. *But . . . innumerable* Empson (56) infers that God 'creates us to spite the devils' – a view Satan shares (ix 147–9). Whatever God's motive for creating us, he does not make the number of men tally with that of the rebel angels. Notice *men innumerable* (156) and cp. Augustine, *City of God*, xxii 1: 'God is gathering a people so numerous that from them he may fill the places of the fallen angels and repair their number. Thus that beloved Heavenly City will not be deprived of its full number of citizens, and might even rejoice in a still more numerous population'. Cp. iii 289.

152. *fondly* foolishly.

154. *in a moment* See below, 176n.

159. *long obedience* God did not intend the prohibition to last for ever. Adam and Eve and their descendants might have worked their way up to Heaven. See v 493–500.

162. *inhabit lax* spread out, occupy the now vacant territories.

165. *overshadowing* Cp. Gabriel's words to Mary: 'the power of the Highest shall overshadow thee' (Luke 1. 35).

Spirit Editors cite *CD* i 7 as proof that M. must mean 'God's power' not 'the Holy Spirit'. But even *CD* allows the Spirit of Gen. 1. 2 to be a 'person' – provided it remain 'subordinate' to the Father (*YP* 6. 304). Cp. i 17*n*.

169. *nor vacuous* M.'s God creates out of Chaos, not out of nothing (see ii 890–1039*n* and v 472*n*). Chaos is infinite because God fills it, but God withholds his *goodness* (171) from Chaos until he uses it for Creation.

170. *uncircumscribed* Dante celebrates God as *non circunscritto* in *Purg.* xi 2. Nicholas of Cusa had described God as a circle whose centre is everywhere and whose circumference is nowhere. Cp. ix 107–8.

172. *Necessity and Chance* 'Necessity' was especially associated with Aristotle's notion of creation, which M. saw as a limit on God's omnipotence (see *CD* i 2). The atomist philosophers Democritus and Empedocles made 'Chance' the cause of all things. M. limits Chance to the uncreated atoms of Chaos. See ii 895–910 and Marjara (93).

173. *what I will is Fate* In *CD* i 2 M. points out that 'Fate' means 'that which is spoken' (from Latin *fari*, 'to speak'). See i 116*n* and cp. *PR* iv 316–17.

176. *Immediate are the acts of God* Augustine had argued for an immediate Creation (*De Genesi* i 1–3). The literal-minded Satan sneers at God for requiring six days (ix 136–9).

179. *earthly notion* human understanding.

182–3. *Glory . . . men* Luke 2. 14.

191. *worlds* ages (*OED* 5) or universes (*OED* 9), of which God might create an *infinite* number. Cp. i 650, ii 916, vii 209, x 362.

199–201. *chariots . . . brazen mountains* Cp. Zech. 6. 1: 'there came four chariots out from between two . . . mountains of brass'.

200. *armoury of God* Cp. Jer. 50. 25: 'The Lord hath opened his armoury'.

204. *within . . . lived* Cp. the animated chariot of vi 845–50.

205–6. *Heav'n opened . . . gates* Cp. the self-opening gates of Ps. 24. 7 (cit. below, 565–7*n*).

212. *Outrageous* enormous (*OED* 1) and violent (*OED* 2).
  wasteful desolate (*OED* 3) and devastating (*OED* 1).

217. **omnific* all-creating.

221. *him* the Son.

224. *fervid* burning.

225. *compasses* Cp. Prov. 8. 27: 'he set a compass upon the face of the depth'. See also Dante, *Par.* xix 40: 'He that turned His compass round the limit of the world'.

230. *Thus . . . bounds* Cp. Job 38. 11: 'Hitherto shalt thou come, but no further: and here shall thy proud waves be stayed'.

231. *just* exact (*OED* 9), suitable (*OED* 7).
  world universe.

233. *Matter unformed and void* Cp. Gen. 1. 2: 'the earth was without form, and void'. Cp. also Plato's account of Creation from formless matter (*Timaeus* 50).

235. *brooding* See i 21–2*n*.

236. *vital virtue* life-giving power.

237–42. *downward . . . hung* Cp. the differentiation of the four elements in Ovid, *Met.* i 21–31, Lucretius, *De Rerum Nat.* v 432ff., and Claudian, *De Rapt. Pros.* i 248–53. According to these poets, heavy elements sank to the centre to form the earth. M.'s *cold infernal dregs* sink beneath the universe rather than to its heart. Thus M.'s universe is wholly good (no part is *Adverse to life*), but Chaos still threatens it from outside. See ii 890–1039*n*.

238. *tartareous* crusty, gritty (*OED* a² 2), with a play on Tartarus, hell.

239. *founded* attached (*OED* v² 5).

conglobed gathered into (concentric) spherical regions.

242. *earth . . . hung* Cp. Ovid, *Met.* i 12–13: *pendebat in aere tellus / ponderibus librata suis* ('the earth hangs poised by her own weight in the air'). Cp. also Job 26. 7: 'He . . . hangeth the earth upon nothing'.

244. *Ethereal* Ancient cosmologists thought of ether as a fifth element (*quintessence*). It filled all space beyond the sphere of the moon, and stars and planets were composed of it. See iii 7 ('pure ethereal stream') and iii 716.

248. *she* light (see line 360).

tabernacle Cp. Ps. 19. 4: 'he set a tabernacle for the sun'.

254. *orient* eastern, shining, rising like the dawn.

255. *Exhaling* rising as vapour (*OED* 2).

256. *joy and shout* Cp. Job 38. 7, where the angels 'shouted for joy' as they witnessed Creation.

261–3. *firmament . . . Waters* Cp. Gen. 1. 6: 'And God said, Let there be a firmament in the midst of the waters, and let it divide the waters from the waters'. M. identifies the 'firmament' with the space between the earth and the universe's outer shell. Others identified it with the shell itself. The waters below the firmament are earth's seas. The waters above the firmament form an *ocean* (271) on the universe's shell. See below, 271*n*.

264. **expanse* from Latin *expansum*, which correctly translates the Hebrew word rendered as 'firmament' in A.V.

liquid clear, bright, transparent (*OED* 2).

266–7. *convéx . . . round* vault . . . universe.

269. *world* universe.

271. *Crystálline ocean* not the crystalline sphere of iii 482, but the jasper sea of iii 518–19, that flows about the foot of the stair leading to Heaven. See iii 518*n*.

273. *distemper* disturb the due proportion of elements (*OED* 1), and so reduce them to their raw 'contraries' (see ii 898*n*).

277. *embryon* embryo. Earth is both *the Great Mother* about to *conceive* (281), and the foetus enveloped (*involved*) in protective *waters*. *Magna Mater* was a title of Cybele, mother of the gods (cp. v 338).

279. *Main* uninterrupted.

280. *Prolific humour* generative liquid. Earth's seas now act as penetrating seed as well as nursing fluid. Cp. i 21–2n.

281. *Fermented* (from Latin *fervere*, 'to boil') has alchemical overtones (*OED* 1b), as in: '*Ferments* . . . Seminal sparks hidden in matter . . . put into motion, and by the variety of that motion producing the variety of bodies' (1677).

282. *genial* generative.

288. *tumid* swollen.

291. **precipitance* headlong fall (*OED* 1).

292. *conglobing* gathering into spheres. At lines 239–40 the entire universe 'conglobed'. As above, so below. Cp. Marvell, 'On a Drop of Dew', 5–8.

293. *crystal wall* anticipating the parting of the Red Sea. See xii 197: 'two crystal walls'.

ridge direct surge forward in waves.

296. *of armies thou hast heard* Raphael again chooses a simile to fit Adam's understanding. Cp. vi 73–6.

299. *rapture* force of movement (*OED* 2) and joy.

302. *serpent error wand'ring* All three words evoke the Fall for the fallen reader, but Adam and Eve hear only the innocent meaning. Thus *error* implies 'moral trangression' (*OED* 5) but means 'winding course' (*OED* 1). *Serpent* might be nothing more than a present participle (from Latin *serpere*, 'to creep'). See Stein (66), Ricks (110), Fish (130–41).

308. *congregated* echoing the Junius-Tremellius version of Gen. 1. 10: *congregationem vero aquarum vocavit maria*.

321. *swelling*] smelling *Ed I*, *Ed II*. Bentley's emendation has been widely accepted.

322. *and*] *Ed II*; add *Ed I*.

humble low-growing.

323. *implicit* entangled (*OED* 1).

325. *gemmed* put forth blossoms (*OED* 1a), from Latin *gemmare*, but suggesting also 'adorned with gems'.

331–3. *not yet rained . . . mist* Gen. 2. 5–6.

332. *till the ground* Cp. Gen. 2. 5: 'there was not a man to till the ground'. 'Till' might include any kind of cultivation (*OED* 4). Ploughing was unknown before the Fall.

338. *recorded* bore witness to (*OED* 10).

348. *altern* **in turns (*OED* 4).

351. *vicissitude* reciprocal succession (*OED* 4).

356. *of ethereal mould* fashioned from ether, which is naturally luminous (iii 7, vii 244).

357. *every magnitude* every class of brightness into which the stars are ranked by astronomers.

360. *cloudy shrine* the 'cloudy tabernacle' of line 248.

362–4. *liquid light . . . fountain* Cp. Lucretius, *De Rerum Nat.* v 281: *liquidi fons luminis, aetherius sol* ('the ethereal sun, fountain of liquid light'). *Liquid* includes 'clear, bright, transparent' (*OED* 2).

364. *other stars* Raphael's first hint that our sun might be one of many stars. He will develop the idea in viii 148–58.

366. *his*] *Ed I*; her *Ed II*. 'His' points to 'Lucifer', 'her' to 'Venus'. Fowler prefers 'her' since 'his' introduces an 'inappropriate association' with Satan. But book vii is full of such prolepses (see eg. 302, 412, 427–31, 494–8). Raphael had explicitly named the *morning planet* as 'Lucifer' at vii 131 (cp. v 760, x 425). He never names 'Venus'. Lucifer has *horns* in accordance with Galileo's observations.

367. *tincture* active principle emanating from afar (*OED* 6b), with overtones of the alchemical 'universal tincture', the elixir (*OED* 6a). See iii 600–612 for the sun's alchemical powers. The context (*fountain, urns*) also evokes the etymology, from Latin *tingere*, 'to dip'.

368. *small peculiar* own small light. Kepler and Boyle shared M.'s belief that stars and planets shone with their own light as well as with the reflected light of the sun (Marjara 66–7). See further viii 150n.

370. *First in his east the* Flannagan emends to 'First in the east his', but the *Ed I* and *Ed II* phrasing suggests the freshness of Creation. The new sun does not just arise 'in the east': it defines the east by arising there for the first time.

372. *jocund to run* Cp. Ps. 19. 4–5: 'he set a tabernacle for the sun. Which is as a bridegroom coming out of his chamber, and rejoiceth as a strong man to run a race'.

374–5. *Pleiades . . . sweet influence* Cp. Job 38. 31: 'Canst thou bind the sweet influences of the Pleiades?'

379. *In that aspéct* i.e. when full.

382. *dividual* *shared (*OED* 3).

388. *Reptile* creeping animal (*OED* 1), translating Junius-Tremellius, *reptilia animantia* (Gen. 1. 20). A.V. has 'moving creature'.

403. *Bank the mid sea* The fish are so numerous as to form living banks – shelving elevations in the sea where fish gather.

406–10. *Show . . . play* Fowler notes that *waved, coats, dropped,* and *bended* are heraldic terms. Cp. the 'mantling' swan (439) and 'rampant' lion (466) and contrast the haughty impreses of vi 84 and ix 34–7.

406. *waved* both 'glimpsed through the waves' and 'striped with "wavy" heraldic markings' (*OED* 1c).

dropped spotted.

407. *attend* watch for.

409. *smooth* a stretch of calm water (*OED* 1c, nautical term).

410. *bended* suggesting the dolphin's curved shape as it leaps, but playing also on the heraldic term 'bendy' (i.e. divided into diagonal lines).

411. M.'s eighteenth-century editors noted how the scansion ('Wállowing / unwíeld/y, enór/mous in/ their gáit') is mimetically unwieldy.

412. *Leviathan* Cp. the Satanic Leviathan of i 200–208. It is surprising to re-encounter the simile 'amidst the joyful numbering of God's created' (Fish 150), but this Leviathan is not treacherous, for he resembles a *moving land*, not an 'island' (i 205).

419. *kindly* natural.

420. *callow* unfledged.

fledge fledged.

421. *summed their pens* brought their feathers to full growth.

422. *clang* harsh cry (Latin *clangor*).

despised looked down upon.

422–3. *under . . . prospect* The ground seemed to be under a cloud (of birds).

425. *loosely* separately.

region sky.

426. *wedge* *fly in a wedge formation (*OED* 4c).

427. *Intelligent of seasons* There are no seasons until x 651–707, when God sends his angels to tilt the earth on its axis. Do the *prudent* (430) birds sense the imminent Fall? Cp. Jer. 8. 7: 'the stork in the heaven knoweth her appointed times; and the turtle and the crane and the swallow observe the time of their coming; but my people know not the judgment of the Lord'.

429. *mutual wing* Birds flying in formation were thought to support each other with their wings (Svendsen 158).

432. *Floats* undulates.

434. *Solaced* *made cheerful.

439. *mantling* forming a mantle.

439–40. *rows / Her state* The swan is monarch, royal barge, and rowers all in one.

441. *dank* pool, mere (*OED* 2).

tow'r soar aloft into (*OED* 5).

444. *other* peacock.

451. *soul*] foul *Ed I* and *Ed II*. Bentley's emendation has been widely accepted ('fowl' were created on the previous day).

452. *Cattle* domestic livestock (not just bovine animals).

454. *teemed* gave birth to (*OED* 1).

456. *full-grown No hyphen in *Ed I* or *Ed II*.

457. *wons* dwells.

461. *Those . . . these* wild beasts . . . cattle. Future carnivores are already distinguished from their prey. The former rise in *pairs* (459), the latter in *flocks* or *herds* (461–2).

rare spread out at wide intervals (*OED* 3a).

466. *brinded* tawny with streaks (*OED*).

ounce lynx.

467. *libbard* leopard.

470. *mould* earth and pattern by which something is shaped.

471. *Behemoth* a huge biblical beast (Job 40. 15), identified with the elephant. A marginal note in the Geneva Bible also identifies him with the Devil (Hughes).

474. *river horse* translating the Greek 'hippopotamus'.

475. *creeps* *creeps along (*OED* 5a).

476. *worm* any creeping animal, including serpents.

482. *Minims* smallest forms of animal life (*OED* 4).

483. *involved* coiled.

484. *wings* Cp. Isa. 30. 6: 'fiery flying serpent'.

485. *parsimonious emmet* thrifty ant. M. in *REW* celebrates the ant as an example 'of a frugal and self-governing democratie or Commonwealth; safer and more thriving in the joint providence and counsel of many industrious equals, then under the single domination of one imperious Lord' (*YP* 7. 427). Cp. i 768–75, where the monarchical beehive is associated with Hell.

486. *large heart* capacious intellect. See i 444*n*. Cp. also Virgil's description of bees as having *ingentis animos angusto in pectore*, 'huge souls in tiny breasts' (*Georg.* iv 83).

488. *popular* populous (*OED* 3) and plebeian (*OED* 2b).

489. *commonalty* common people, with overtones of 'a self-governing commonwealth, a republic' (*OED* 1b).

493. *gav'st them names* See viii 342–54 and Gen. 2. 19–20.

494–8. *Needless . . . call* Fish (156) comments: 'with every other reader I am condemned to see in this praise of the serpent an ominousness that is simply not there'.

497. *hairy mane* Cp. the maned sea-serpents that emerge from the sea to devour Laocoon and his sons and so ensure Troy's fall (Virgil, *Aen.* ii 203–7).

terrific terrifying.

502. *Consummate* complete, perfect.

504. *Frequent* in throngs.

505–10. *There wanted yet . . . Govern the rest* Cp. Ovid, *Met.* i 76–7: 'The nobler Creature, with a mind possest, / Was wanting yet, that should command the rest' (trans. Sandys, 1632). Ovid also celebrates man's erect stature (i 84–6).

505. *end* completion and purpose.

508–9. *erect / His stature* both 'stand upright' and 'elevate his condition' (*OED* 'erect' 2, 'stature' 4), as in 'Erect my spirite into thy blisse' (1589). Man's erect stance is a sign that he was created for Heaven. See viii 259–61, and contrast Mammon, 'the least erected Spirit' (i 679).

509. *front* brow or face.

510. **self-knowing* Cp. the Platonic and Delphic maxim 'Know thyself'. See xi 531*n*.

511. *Magnanimous* great-souled, nobly ambitious, lofty of purpose.
   correspond both 'be in harmony' and 'hold communication'.

528. *Express* exact, truly depicted (*OED* 1a), well-framed (*OED* 1b). Cp. Heb. 1. 3, where the Son is made in 'the express image' of God. Cp. also Shakespeare, *Hamlet* II ii 286f.: 'What a piece of work is a man . . . how express and admirable, in action how like an angel, in apprehension how like a god!'

536. *thence* both 'from there' (the world outside Paradise) and 'for that cause' (to subdue the earth).

537. *delicious* delightful. See iv 132*n*.

544. *Thou may'st not* 'Taste' is understood, the abrupt omission being mimetic of restraint.

547. *Surprise* **betray into doing something not intended (*OED* 4b), overpower the will (*OED* 1b), catch in the act (*OED* 3). Cp. the dictionary definition given by Edward Phillips (M.'s nephew): 'to lead a man into an Error, by causing him to do a thing over hastily' (1696).

557. *Idea* Platonic Form (the sole occurrence of the word in M.'s English poetry).

559. *Symphonious* harmonious.
   tuned performed.

563. *stations*] *Ed I*; station *Ed II*. The singular limits the meaning to 'appointed place'; the plural plays on 'station' as 'the apparent standing still of a planet' (*OED* 5). Cp. vii 98–102, where Adam says the sun will 'delay' to hear of its Creation.

564. *pomp* triumphal procession (*OED* 2).
   *jubilant from Latin *jubilare*, 'to shout with joy'. There may be overtones of the Hebrew 'Jubilee' (see iii 348*n*), with which *jubilare* was associated. Cp. vi 884.

565. *Open, ye everlasting gates* Cp. Ps. 24. 7: 'Lift up your heads, O ye gates; and be ye lift up, ye everlasting doors; and the King of glory shall come in'. Cp. also Fletcher, *CV* (1610) iv 15: 'Tosse up your heads ye everlasting gates, / And let the Prince of glorie enter in'.

575. *blazing portals* Fowler identifies these with the signs of Capricorn and Cancer, but the Messiah has now left our universe. Raphael likens Heaven's *road* to our *Milky Way* in a simile (577–9). Thus M. overgoes Ovid,

Met. i 168–71, where the Milky Way is the gods' highway to Jove's hall.

578. *pavement stars* Cp. iv 976: 'the road of Heav'n star-paved'.

580. *zone* *belt of the sky (*OED* 5).

588–90. *(for . . . Omnipresence]* *Ed I* and *Ed II* have two opening brackets (before *for* and *such*). Most editors remove the first, and so identify the *Father* as *Author and end.* Fowler removes the second and cites Heb. 12. 2 ('author and finisher') as evidence that the Son is *Author and end.* All editors assume that there can be only one opening bracket, but it is just possible that M. is breaking the rules of punctuation to suggest God's omnipresence and to imply that both Father and Son are Author and end.

596. *dulcimer* the bagpipe of Dan. 3. 5, rendered as 'dulcimer' in A.V.

597. *fret* bar on the finger-board of a stringed instrument.

598. *Tempered* brought into harmony.

599. *Choral or unison* in parts or in unison.

605. *Giant angels* The allusion to the Giants' revolt against Jove implies that the Greek myth is a garbled memory of the angels' rebellion. Cp. i 50, 199–200, 230–37, vi 643–66.

619. *hyaline* transliterating the Greek word for 'glassy', used in Rev. 4. 6 ('a sea of glass like unto crystal'). Cp. 'sea of jasper' (iii 518–19) and 'crystálline ocean' (vii 271).

620. *immense* immeasurable.

621. *Numerous* both 'of great number' and 'that can be numbered' (*OED* 4). Cp. Ps. 147. 4: 'He telleth the number of the stars; he calleth them all by their names'.

622. *destined habitation* See iii 667–70 and v 500 for further hints that men might colonize other worlds. At iii 566–72 and viii 146–8 M. conjectures that other worlds might already be inhabited.

623. *seasons* Cp. Acts 1. 7: 'it is not for you to know the times or the seasons, which the Father hath put in his own power'.

624. *nether Ocean* the earth's seas, or 'waters below the firmament', as distinct from the 'clear hyaline', or 'waters above the firmament'.

631–2. *thrice happy if they know / Their happiness* Cp. Virgil on the happiness of simple peasants: 'O, happy, if he knew his happy state' (*Georg.* ii 457, trans. Dryden). Elsewhere M. implies that Adam and Eve lost their happiness by knowing it. See viii 282, ix 1072, xi 89 and esp. iv 774–5: 'O yet happiest if ye seek / No happier state, and know to know no more'.

632. *persevere* including the theological sense: 'continuance in a state of grace until it is succeeded by a state of glory' (*OED* 'perseverance' 2).

634. *hallelujahs* Hebrew, 'praise the Lord'.

636. *face of things* echoing v 43: 'Shadowy sets off the face of things'.

BOOK VIII

1–4. *The . . . replied* These lines were added in *Ed II*, when M. divided the original book vii into the present books vii and viii. *Ed I* vii 641 reads: 'To whom thus Adam gratefully replied'.

2. *charming* spellbinding.

3. *still stood fixed* So in Apollonius Rhodius, *Argonautica* i 512–16, Orpheus holds his audience spellbound while he sings of Creation. Cp. also Homer, *Od.* xiii 1–2.

7. *Historian* including 'storyteller' (*OED* 2).

9. *condescension* consent (*OED* 4), courteous disregard of rank (*OED* 1). 'A beautiful word, which we have spoiled' (Lewis 79).

14. *solution* explanation (*OED* 1b).

15–38. *When I behold . . . fails* Cp. Eve's question about the stars (iv 657–8). Adam is now dissatisfied with the answer he had given Eve (iv 660–88).

15. *this goodly frame* the universe (echoing Shakespeare, *Hamlet* II ii 310).

17–18. *spot . . . atom* Astronomers since antiquity had been aware that the earth was a mere speck in the universe.

19. *numbered* numerous and reckoned by number. Cp. Ps. 147. 4: 'He telleth the number of the stars; he calleth them all by their names'.

22. *officiate* minister, supply (*OED* 4a).

23. *opacous* dark.

punctual point-like (*OED* 3a), but the modern sense existed and prepares for the idea that the earth has timely motions (128–40).

25. *admire* marvel.

30. *For aught appears* so far as can be seen.

32. *sedentary* *motionless (*OED* 3b), slothful (*OED* 2b).

33. *compass* circular course (*OED* 11a).

36. *sumless* incalculable.

45. *visit* inspect (*OED* 9).

46. *nursery* nursery-garden and the activity of tending it.

51. *auditress The *OED* cites 'auditor' from the fourteenth century.

52–8. *Her husband . . . joined* The emphasis on Eve's choice (*preferred*, *chose*) softens, but does not remove, the hierarchical implication from I Cor. 14. 35: 'if they will learn any thing, let them ask their husbands at home: for it is a shame for women to speak in the church'.

61. *pomp* procession, train. The *Graces* attended Venus.

still continually.

65. *facile* affable, courteous (*OED* 4).

67. *Book of God* a traditional metaphor for the heavens.

74. *scanned* discussed minutely (*OED* 3a), with a play on Latin *scandere*, 'to climb'.

75. *admire* marvel.

78. *quaint* ingenious (*OED* 1a).
wide wide of the mark.

80. *calculate* predict the motions of (*OED* 2), frame (*OED* 5).
wield direct, guide, hold in check (*OED* 4).

82. *save appearances* reconcile hypotheses with observed facts. To 'save (or salve) the appearances' was a scholastic term, borrowed from the Greeks. It need not be pejorative. See *OED* 'salve' v² 1, 'save' 12a.

83. *centric and eccentric* orbits with the earth (or sun) at the centre or off-centre respectively.

84. *epicycle* a smaller orbit whose centre corresponds to a fixed point on the circumference of the main orbit. A planet had a forward motion when on the outer part of the epicycle, and a retrograde motion when on the inner part. Both the Ptolemaic and Copernican systems had epicycles.

91. *infers* implies (*OED* 4).

99. *officious* attentive, dutiful (*OED* 1, 2a).

100. *speak* bespeak (but cp. Ps. 19. 1: 'The heavens declare the glory of God').

102. *line ... far* Cp. Job 38. 5, where God asks, about the earth: 'Who hath laid the measures thereof, if thou knowest? or who hath stretched the line upon it?'

108. *numberless* incalculable (*swiftness*) and innumerable (*circles*, stellar orbits).

110. *Speed almost spiritual* the speed of angelic Intelligences (cp. 'the speed of thought').

122. *advantage* including 'place of vantage, elevation' (*OED* 3).

123. *world* universe.
other stars another hint (cp. vii 364) that the sun might be one of many stars. Raphael develops the idea in lines 148–58.

124. *attractive virtue* power of attraction. Kepler had theorized that the sun attracted the planets by magnetism. See iii 582–3*n*.

125. *rounds* circles and circular dances.

126. *wand'ring* 'Planet' is derived from Greek πλανήτης, 'wanderer'.

127. *retrograde* See above, 84*n*.

128. *six* Mercury, Venus, Mars, Jupiter, Saturn, and the moon. In Ptolemaic astronomy, the seventh planet is the sun; in Copernican, the earth.

130. *three different motions* The first two are daily and yearly. Editors disagree about the third. If Raphael refers to the precession of the equinoxes, he does so proleptically, for there was no precession before the Fall (see x 668f.). Fowler therefore identifies the third motion with Copernicus's

'motion in declination', whereby the earth's axis was thought to swivel so as to point always in the same direction.

131. *several spheres* Even with his epicycles, Ptolemy was obliged to posit a ninth sphere beyond the fixed stars. Aristotle had imagined fifty-six spheres.

132. *thwart obliquities* oblique paths that cross each other. There may be a pun on 'obliquity of the ecliptic' (*OED* 1), referring to the inclination of the equator to the ecliptic. The pun would have to be proleptic, for equator and ecliptic coincided before the Fall.

134. *rhomb* Greek 'wheel' or 'spinning top'. Raphael is referring to the *primum mobile*, which revolved around the universe in twenty-four hours, carrying the lower spheres with it. Copernicus dispensed with this first-moved sphere.

142. *terrestrial moon* both 'earth's moon' and 'earth-like moon'.

144–8. *if land . . . there* Cp. i 290–91, iii 460–62 and v 418–22.

148. *other suns* Nicholas of Cusa had conjectured that the fixed stars were suns with planetary systems, and that suns, planets, and moons were inhabited. Kepler rejected the idea, but Bruno and Descartes were among those who accepted it. M. imagines that stars might be inhabited at iii 566–71, 606–12, vii 621–5. See also i 650 and note.

149. *moons* any satellites (including planets) *attendant* on a sun. Cp. Wilkins, *The Discovery of a World in the Moon* (1638) Proposition xi: 'as their world is our Moone, so our world is their Moone'.

150. *male and female* original and reflected. Raphael associates gender with *light*, not specific heavenly bodies, so it is misleading to speak of 'male suns and female moons' or to invoke Apollo and Diana. *Moons* (planets) exchange female light reciprocally (140–44), and they also have some 'peculiar' light of their own (vii 368). Even *suns* might borrow some female light from their stellar neighbours (vii 364–9). See vii 368*n*.

151. *animate the world* endow the universe with life (by sustaining life on neighbouring heavenly bodies).

152. *Stored* including 'provide for the continuance of a race or breed' (*OED* 'store' 2a).

157. *this habitable* imitating a phrase used by the Greeks to distinguish their world from barbarian lands. Since it occurs in the context of what is *obvious* (open) *to dispute*, Raphael might hint that other worlds are civilized.

164. *inoffensive* unobstructed (Latin *inoffensus*) and harmless (*OED* 1).

sleeps *spins with imperceptible motion (*OED* 3c, used of spinning tops, earliest instance 1854).

167. *Solicit* disturb, disquiet (*OED* 1), with an etymological play on 'put the whole in motion' (Latin *sollus, ciere*).

168. *Leave . . . fear* 'Fear God, and keep his commandments: for this is the whole duty of man' (Eccles. 12. 13).

181. *Intelligence* angelic spirit.

187. *wand'ring thoughts* Cp. Belial's 'thoughts that wander through eternity' (ii 148).

194. *fume* something unsubstantial, transient, imaginary (*OED* 5), something which goes to the head and clouds the reason (*OED* 6). Cp. ix 1050.

195. *fond impertinence* foolish irrelevance.

197. *still to seek* always searching.

198. *pitch* summit.

202. *sufferance* (divine) permission.

209. *Fond* foolish.

218. *Nor are thy lips ungraceful* Cp. Ps. 45. 2: 'Grace is poured into thy lips: Therefore God hath blessed thee'.

   *ungraceful The *OED* also credits M.'s nephew, Edward Phillips, with the earliest instance of 'ungracefulness'.

225. *fellow servant* When St John tried to worship an angel, the angel said: 'I am thy fellow servant' (Rev. 22. 9).

228. *equal love* Contrast Beëlzebub's jealous claim that men are 'favoured more' than angels (ii 350). Cp. also i 651.

229–40. *For . . . obedience* Raphael's explanation does not reflect well on God. A God who would mar Creation in a fit of temper or go out of his way to disappoint his angels seems neither omnipotent nor good. See Empson (110).

230. *uncouth* strange, desolate, unpleasant.

239. *state* ceremony.

   inure strengthen by exercise.

243–4. *Noise . . . rage* Cp. Aeneas outside the gate of Tartarus, hearing cries of torment (Virgil, *Aen.* vi 557–9); also Astolfo listening to the howls of the damned (Ariosto, *Orl. Fur.* xxxiv 4).

246. *sabbath ev'ning* the evening that began the seventh day. Following Hebrew custom, Milton reckons days from sunset to sunset.

251. *who himself beginning knew* Cp. v 859–63. Like Satan, Adam cannot remember his origins, but where Satan takes this as proof that he was not created, Adam infers the existence of a *Maker* (278).

256. *reeking* steaming (*OED* 2), without unpleasant associations. *OED*'s earliest instance of the sense 'smell unpleasantly' is from 1710 (*OED* 3).

263. *lapse* *gliding flow (*OED* 6), with proleptic overtones of 'the Fall' (*OED* 2b), as in 'thy original lapse' (xii 83).

268. *went* walked.

269. *as*] Ed I; and Ed II.

272. *readily could name* Adam's ability to intuit true names indicates his native wisdom (see below, 352–3*n*).

276. *live and move* Cp. Acts 17. 28: 'For in him we live, and move, and have our being'.

282. *happier than I know* Cp. iv 774–5: 'O yet happiest if ye seek / No happier state, and know to know no more'. Both statements imply that to know one's happiness is to lose it. Cp. also ix 1070–73, and contrast vii 631–2: 'thrice happy if they know / Their happiness'.

288. *oppression* weighing down.

292. *stood at my head a dream* Homer's Oneiros ('Dream') stands at Agamemnon's head while falsely promising speedy victory (*Il.* ii 20). M. had earlier associated Dream with Satan (see v 38, 642, 673 and notes). Cp. *PR* iv 407.

296. *mansion* dwelling-place. Gen. 2. 8 and 2. 15 make clear that Adam was created outside Paradise, which he received as a gift, not a birthright.

300–314. *by the hand . . . divine* Cp. Eve's dream of flying (v 86–93). Adam's flight is *real* (310) and his *guide* (312) does not abandon him. Contrast v 91: 'My guide was gone'.

311. *lively* vividly (*OED* 4).

316. *Whom . . . I am* Cp. God's reply when Moses asks for his name: 'I AM that I AM. . . . Thus shalt thou say unto the children of Israel, I AM hath sent me unto you' (Exod. 3. 14).

320. *till and keep* In the A.V. Adam's task was to 'dress' the garden (Gen. 2. 15). God commands him to 'till the ground' (Gen. 3. 23) after the Fall. M. follows the Hebrew, Greek (LXX) and Latin versions, which dignify work by using the same word in both verses.

324. *Knowledge . . . ill* M. follows Gen. 2. 17 in making God, not Satan, author of the Tree's name. See iv 423–4*n*, ix 1072*n*.

331. *From that day mortal* a traditional solution to Gen. 2. 17, where God tells Adam that he will die on 'the day' he eats. (Adam lived to be 930.)

332. *lose* Fowler and Campbell retain the *Ed I* and *Ed II* spelling 'loose' because it indicates 'violate' (*OED* 8) or 'break up, do away with' (*OED* 7a) as well as 'lose'. But 'lose' must be dominant when God warns Adam about the loss of Paradise in a poem called *Paradise Lost*. 'Lose' could in any case include 'destroy, be the ruin of' (*OED* 2a). Cp. viii 553, ix 959.

334. *interdiction* prohibition.

337. *purpose* conversation (*OED* 4).

350. *two and two* The animals had been created in 'broad herds' (vii 462). Now as Adam names them they shrink to more manageable proportions. Cp. Gen. 7. 9 ('two and two unto Noah into the ark').

351. *stooped* bowed to a superior authority (*OED* 2a).

350. *cow'ring* the quivering of young hawks, who shake their wings, in sign of obedience to the old ones (*OED* 1b).

352–3. *named . . . nature* Cp. *Tetrachordon* (1645): 'Adam who had the wisdom giv'n him to know all creatures, and to name them according to their properties, no doubt but had the gift to discern perfectly' (*YP* 2. 602); also *CD* i 7: 'he could not have given names to the animals in that extempore way, without great intelligence' (trans. Carey, *YP* 6. 324). The idea that Adam had named things 'rightly' (439) was supported by Gen. 2. 19 ('whatsoever Adam called every living creature, that was the name thereof') and by Plato's *Cratylus*. Cp. also Bacon, *Of the Interpretation of Nature*: 'when man shall be able to call the creatures by their true names he shall again command them'.

354. *sudden* extempore (*OED* 7), of mental faculties: quick, sharp (*OED* 4b).

355. *found not* Cp. Gen. 2. 20: 'for Adam there was not found an help meet'. M. takes Genesis to mean that Adam (not God) failed to find what he was looking for.

357. *O by what name* Cp. Moses' question at Exod. 3. 13 ('What is his name?') and God's reply (cit. above, 316*n*). Cp. also Prov. 30. 4: 'What is his name, and what is his son's name, if thou canst tell?' Lieb (172) cites *CD* i 5: 'the giving of a name is always acknowledged to be the function of a superior, whether father or lord' (trans. Carey, *YP* 6. 261).

371. *Replenished* abundantly stocked (*OED* 1).

373. *Their language* Hughes and Fowler cite the pseudepigraphal Book of Jubilees, which states that animals spoke in Paradise (3. 28). But M.'s animals were created 'mute to all articulate sound' (ix 557). *Language* here means 'inarticulate sounds used by the lower animals' (*OED* 1c). God is testing Adam's appreciation of human language, which was made for rational conversation. Adam would not deserve Eve if he were to be content with animals' language.

379–80. *Let . . . speak* Cp. Abraham's plea at Gen. 18. 30: 'Oh let not the Lord be angry, and I will speak'.

383–4. *Among unequals what . . . delight* Adam requests an equal, and God promises to give him his 'wish exactly' (viii 451). But Raphael, the Son, and M. himself (both in *PL* and in his prose) deny that Eve was Adam's equal. See iv 296*n*.

384. *sort* suit, fit, be in harmony (*OED* 18).

387. *intense . . . remiss* taut . . . slack. The image is of strings in a musical instrument. Man's string is too taut and that of the animals too slack for there to be *harmony* between them.

390. *participate* share with others (*OED* 2).

392. *consort* both 'spouse' and 'harmonious music' (*OED* sb² 3b).

396. *converse* associate familiarly (*OED* 2) and have sexual intercourse (*OED* 2b). Adam has not yet asked for the 'meet and happy conversation' that M. saw as the 'noblest end of mariage' (*DDD*, *YP* 2. 246), and God will not grant his request until he does so. The entire episode is a test of Adam's ability to give 'conversation' its fully human meaning. See lines 412, 418, 432.

399. *nice* fastidious, with overtones of 'lascivious' (*OED* 2).

402. *in pleasure* including 'in Eden' (*Eden* being Hebrew for 'pleasure').

406-7. *none . . . less* Cp. Horace's Jove, who 'has created nothing greater than himself, nor alike, nor second' (*Odes* I xii 17-18). M. substitutes *equal* for 'greater'.

417. *But in degree* except relatively (Adam is a *perfect* man, but does not have God's *absolute* perfection).

419. *solace* *alleviate, assuage (*OED* 1c).

421. *through all numbers absolute* perfect in all parts (*OED* 'absolute' 4, Latin *numerus*) and complete in all numbers (*OED* 'absolute' 5b). 'The divine monad contains all other numbers' (Fowler). Critics disagree as to whether Adam is conversing with the Father or the Son. The present line implies that the distinction is unimportant for unfallen man. Contrast x 55-6.

423. *single imperfection* imperfection of being single.

426. *Collateral* mutual (lit. 'side by side'). Cp. iv 741: 'Straight side by side were laid'.

427. *secrecy* retirement, seclusion (*OED* 2b).

427-8. *alone . . . accompanied* echoing Cicero's famous description of Scipio Africanus: *Numquam minus solum, quam cum solus* ('never less alone than when alone'), *De Officiis* III i 1.

433. *complacence* pleasure, delight, satisfaction (*OED* 2).

435. *Permissive* allowed.

445. *Knew . . . alone* Cp. Gen. 2. 18: 'And the Lord God said, It is not good that the man should be alone'.

450. *thy fit help, thy other self* M. expands Gen. 2. 18 ('an help meet for him') in accordance with his own gloss in *Tetrachordon*: 'The originall here is more expressive then other languages word for word can render it . . . God as it were not satisfy'd with the naming of a help, goes on describing *another self, a second self, a very self it self*' (*YP* 2. 600). *Other self* translates Greek and Latin terms for intimate friends.

453. *earthly* earthly nature. Cp. Dan. 10. 17: 'For how can the servant of this my lord talk with this my lord? for as for me, straightway there remained no strength in me, neither is there breath left in me'.

454. *stood under* been exposed to (*OED* 77b).

460. *Mine eyes he closed* Contrast the open-eyed *trance* at Num. 24. 4: 'He . . . saw the vision of the Almighty, falling into a trance, but having his eyes open'.

461. *Fancy* Cp. Adam's account of Fancy's role in dreams (v 102-9).

462. *Abstráct* withdrawn, removed (*OED* 2).

462-82. *methought . . . dream* alluding to M.'s own *Sonnet XIX* ('Methought I saw my late espousèd Saint'), in which the blind poet awakens to *dark, loss*, and despair ('I waked, she fled, and day brought back my night'). Adam wakes to behold Eve *Such as I saw her in my dream*.

465. *left side* The Bible does not specify from which side Eve was taken (Gen. 2. 21), but the left was a traditional inference, since that was the side nearest Adam's heart (cp. iv 484). See ii 755 and x 884–8 for the 'sinister' implications.

466. *cordial spirits* vital spirits from the heart.

471–3. *so lovely . . . summed up* Fowler hears an ominous echo of Marino's description of Helen: 'So well does beauty's aggregate / In that fair face summed up unite, / Whatever is fair in all the world / Flowers in her' (*L'Adone* ii 173).

476. *air* mien, look (*OED* 14a), breath (*OED* 9), inspiration (*OED* 10), as in 'a kind of divine ayre informing men of their truth' (1660).

476–7. *inspired / The spirit* including 'breathed the breath'.

481–520. See iv 440–491 for Eve's version of these events.

481. *When out of hope* when I had given up hope.

484. *amiable* lovely.

494. *enviest* give reluctantly (*OED* v 3).

495–9. *Bone . . . soul* Cp. Gen. 2. 23–4: 'And Adam said, This is now bone of my bones, and flesh of my flesh: she shall be called Woman because she was taken out of Man. Therefore shall a man leave his father and his mother, and shall cleave unto his wife: and they shall be one flesh'. M. adds *one heart, one soul* in accordance with his view that marriage is more than a fleshly union. Cp. *Tetrachordon*, *YP* 2. 605–14.

502. *conscience* internal conviction (*OED* 1a).

504. *obvious* bold, forward (*OED* 2).

　obtrusive forward, unduly prominent (*OED* 2).

508. *she what was honour knew* Cp. Heb. 13. 4: 'Marriage is honourable in all, and the bed undefiled'.

509. *obsequious* compliant with the will of a superior (*OED* 1).

511. *blushing like the Morn* Lewis (124) objects to unfallen Eve's 'female bodily shame' and finds it 'most offensive' that her blush should be 'an incentive to male desire'. But not all blushes signify shame. See line 619. M.'s syntax even leaves open 'some tender possibility . . . that Adam too is blushing' (Christopher Ricks, *Keats and Embarrassment*, 1974, 22).

513. *influence* See *Nativity* 71*n*. Stars will not shed bad influence until after the Fall. See x 661–4.

514. *gratulation* rejoicing and congratulation. Cp. Homer, *Il.* xiv 347–51, where the *earth* puts forth flowers as Zeus and Hera make love.

515. *gales* winds.

　airs breezes and melodies. Cp. iv 264.

518. *amorous bird of night* the nightingale.

519. *ev'ning star* Hesperus (Venus), whose rising was the traditional sign for lighting the *bridal lamp* and bringing the bride to the bridegroom. Cp. xi 588–91, Catullus, *Carmina* lxii and Spenser, *Epithalamion* 286–95.

521. *state* original, flourishing, prosperous condition (*OED* 6a), exalted position (*OED* 16).

526. *vehement* both 'ardent' and 'deprived of the mind' (from Latin *vehe mens*).

530. *Transported* enraptured, but 'transport' could also mean 'banish' (*OED* 2c), so Adam speaks with dramatic irony.

531. *Commotion* mental perturbation, excitement (*OED* 5).

535. *proof* impervious.
    sustain withstand (*OED* 8a).

536. *subducting* subtracting.

539. *exact* finished, refined, perfect (*OED* 1).

547. *absolute* complete, perfect (*OED* 4), independent (*OED* 7).

553. *Looses* becomes unstable (*OED* 5), as in: 'the hole frame of the joyntes of his body dissolved and losed' (1526). Many editors modernize to 'loses', but Adam's point is that he goes to pieces even when he wins an argument with Eve.

556. *Occasionally* incidentally (*OED* 2b), on the occasion of Adam's request. Eve was made for Adam, but not as an afterthought.
    consúmmate make perfect (*OED* 3).

562. *diffident* mistrustful (*OED* 1).

563–4. *she . . . her* Wisdom.

565–6. *things / Less excellent* Eve is less excellent than Adam (570–75), but her *outside* (568) is also less excellent than her own inner wisdom (578).

569–70. *thy love / Not thy subjection* i.e. 'love her, don't subject yourself to her'. See x 153 and note.

572. **self-esteem OED*'s earliest instance is from 1657, but M. coined the term in *An Apology for Smectymnuus* (1642), where he boasts of his 'honest haughtinesse, and self-esteem either of what I was, or what I might be' (*YP* 1. 890).

574. *head* Cp. I Cor. 11. 3: 'the head of the woman is the man'.

576. **adorn* adorned (sole adjectival instance in *OED*).

577. *awful* awe-inspiring.

578. *who sees . . . wise* See x 925–7 and xi 163 for instances of Eve's wisdom. Cp. also Ariosto's view that a woman's intuition is a special gift from Heaven (*Orl. Fur.* xxvii 1).

583. *divulged* *imparted generally (*OED* 3, sole instance), with overtones of 'reveal a secret' (love-making as a 'mystery'). See below, 599*n*.

590. *heart enlarges* including 'makes wise'. See i 444*n*.

591. *scale* ladder (the neo-Platonic ladder of love).

598. *genial* nuptial, generative. Cp. iv 712.

599. *mysterious* St Paul describes marriage as 'a great mystery' (Eph. 5. 32), patterned after Christ's union with his Church. Cp. iv 743.

601. *decencies* *decent or becoming acts (*OED* 4).

607. *subject not* do not make me subject to her.

608. *foiled* overcome.

609–10. *from . . . representing* variously represented to me by the senses.

611. *Approve . . . approve* Cp. Ovid's Medea committing herself to evil: 'I see the better, I approve it too: / The worse I follow' (*Met.* vii 20–21, trans. Sandys).

617. *virtual* in essence or effect, though not actually (*OED* 4a).

   immediate involving actual contact (*OED* 2a). Virtual love-making would be limited to *looks*; immediate love-making would include *touch*.

619. *proper* distinctive, morally commendable, comely. M. approved of both sexes blushing in the context of love. See above, 511*n*. Critics have disapproved of Raphael's blush, and Waldock (108) mocks it; but Raphael's blush is 'a delightful touch' (Flannagan), and a natural response to Adam's embarrassing question.

624. *In eminence* eminently, surpassingly.

626. *Easier . . . embrace* Devils had been thought to mate with women (see v 446–50*n*), but amorous encounters between angels were rare in angelology. Editors compare Henry More, *The Immortality of the Soul* (1659), where angels are 'mutual Spectators of the perfect pulchritude of one anothers persons' (III ix 4), but this is at best *virtual* rather than *immediate* love-making. West (172) finds no 'hint' of 'amorous . . . penetration' in More.

628. *restrained conveyance* restricted mode of expression. Raphael might be thinking of monogamy as well as physical *bars* of *joint* or *limb*. Cp. Mark 12. 25: 'the angels which are in heaven' 'neither marry, nor are given in marriage'. Cp. M.'s covert allusion to polygamy at iv 762.

631. *green cape* Cape Verde.

   verdant isles the Cape Verde Islands, off West Africa.

632. *Hesperian* in the west (*OED* 1), suggesting also the Hesperian Isles, with which the Cape Verde Islands were sometimes identified.

634–5. *love . . . command* Cp. I John 5. 3: 'this is the love of God, that we keep his commandments'.

637. *admit* permit (*OED* 2a).

639. *persevering* continuing in a state of grace (*OED* 1e).

641. *arbitrament* free choice (*OED* 1).

642. *require* call upon, look for (*OED* 9).

649. *condescension* See above, 9*n*.

BOOK IX

1–47. The induction to book ix refers to the Muse in the third person (21), but never invokes her. Contrast the invocations at i 1–49 and vii 1–50, and cp. iii 1–55, where M. invokes Light but not the Muse (see iii 19*n*).

1. *No more of talk* both 'no more talk about conversation' and 'no more conversation'.

2. *familiar* both 'on a family footing' (*OED* 2) and 'familiar (guardian) angel' (*OED* 2d).

5. *Venial* permissible, blameless (*OED* 3). Orgel and Goldberg object that *unblamed* 'would make no sense' if Adam were blameless. They conclude that Adam 'is at fault', though 'not seriously', for his 'inquisitiveness about astronomy'. But *unblamed* is a Latin use of the past participle and means 'unblameable'. Cp. iii 4, iv 493, 987 and *A Masque* 793. M. also plays on Latin *venialis*, 'gracious'.

6. *breach* breaking of a command (*OED* 3) and break-up of friendly relations (*OED* 5b).

9. *distance* including 'aloofness'.

   distaste aversion and disrelish.

13 (and 28). *argument* subject-matter (*OED* 6).

14–15. *wrath . . . Achilles* Homer's subject in the *Iliad* (i 1). See *Il.* xxii 136f. for Achilles' pursuit of Hector.

16–17. *rage / Of Turnus* Turnus, King of the Rutuli, was a suitor of *Lavinia*, daughter of King Latinus. He made war on the Trojans when Latinus gave Lavinia to Aeneas (Virgil, *Aen.* vii).

17. **disespoused OED*'s sole instance.

18. *Neptune's ire* Odysseus (*the Greek*) incurred Poseidon's anger when he blinded Poseidon's son, Polyphemus (Homer, *Od.* ix 526–35).

   or Juno's Juno hated Aeneas because his mother Venus (*Cytherea*) had defeated her in the beauty contest judged by Paris (see v 381–2n).

19. *Perplexed* *tormented (*OED* 1b).

20. *answerable* fitting, corresponding.

22. *nightly visitation* See vii 29n.

   *unimplored.

26. *long choosing, and beginning late* See headnote to *PL* (p. 711).

29. *dissect* both 'cut to pieces' and 'anatomize'. Classical and Italian epics give precise details in describing wounds.

33. *races and games* See ii 528–55n.

34–7. Turning from the classical epic, M. now rejects medieval romances and Renaissance romance epics.

34. *tilting furniture* accoutrements for jousting.

   *emblazoned OED's earliest participial instance.

35. *Impreses* heraldic devices (often with a motto).

   quaint cunningly designed (*OED* 3), haughty (*OED* 9).

   caparisons ornamental coverings (or armour) for horses.

36. *Bases* cloth coverings for horses (*OED* sb³ 1).

   tinsel trappings Spenser equips the horses of Duessa (*FQ* I ii 13) and Florimell (*FQ* III i 15) with 'tinsell trappings'.

37. *marshalled feast a feast with the guests placed at table according to rank (*OED* 'marshal' 2). *OED*'s earliest participial instance.

38. sewers attendants at a feast who supervised the seating of the guests. *seneschals* stewards.

39. artifice *mechanic art, artificer's work (*OED* 1b).

43. raise both 'evoke' and 'raise to a new level'.

44. That name of epic.

    age too late In his poem *Naturam non pati senium* M. had argued against the theory that the world is decaying, but in *RCG* he fears that something 'advers in our climat, or the fate of the age' might inhibit the epic poet (*YP* 1. 814).

44-5. cold / Climate Aristotle had said that cold climates dull intelligence (*Politics* VII vii 1) and the idea troubles M. in *Mansus* 24-9, *RCG* and *Of Education* (*YP* 1. 814, 2. 383).

45. years M. was fifty-eight in 1667.

    damp stupefy, benumb (*OED* 2) and dampen (*cold Climate*).

    intended both 'purposed' and 'outstretched' (*wing*).

46. Depressed lowered (*wing*) and dejected (spirits).

49. Hesperus Venus, the evening star.

54. improved augmented, made worse (*OED* 4).

56. maugre despite.

63. seven continued nights Satan experiences a week of darkness by flying in the earth's shadow, thus eluding the eye of Uriel in *the sun* (60). But M. nods when he places Satan in darkness *From pole to pole*. Earth's poles were in perpetual daylight before the Fall (x 680-87). Fowler sees a 'deliberate prolepsis' as Satan describes 'a fallen world', but even in the fallen world darkness extends only to one pole at a time.

65. car of Night the earth's shadow (conceived as the chariot of Nox, goddess of night).

66. colure one of two great circles intersecting at right angles at the poles and dividing the equinoctial circle into four equal segments.

67. coast averse side turned away. The sentries are stationed in the east of Paradise (iv 542); Satan enters from the north (iv 223).

77. Pontus the Black Sea.

78. Maeotis the Sea of Azov. The *river Ob* flows from Siberia into the Arctic Ocean.

80. Orontes a river in Syria.

    ocean barred God sets 'bars and doors' for the sea at Job 38. 10.

81. Darien Panama.

87. irresolute undecided.

89. Fit vessel Cp. Rom. 9. 22: 'What if God, willing to shew his wrath, and to make his power known, endured with much longsuffering the vessels of wrath fitted to destruction'. See also Acts 9. 15, and II Tim. 2. 21.

89. *imp* child of the Devil (*OED* 4a), evil spirit (*OED* 4b).

90. *suggestions* temptations.

95. *Doubt* suspicion.

104–5. *officious . . . for thee alone* Contrast Raphael's words at viii 98–9: 'Yet not to earth are those bright luminaries / Officious, but to thee earth's habitant'.

107–8. *God . . . extends to all* Fowler compares the Renaissance commonplace that 'God is an infinite sphere, whose centre is everywhere, whose circumference nowhere'. Cp. vii 170.

110. *Not . . . appears* Contrast iii 606–12 where the sun's 'elixir pure' arises from its own 'rivers', 'fields and regions'. See also iii 565–71, viii 148–58.

112. *gradual* gradated, in steps.

113. *growth, sense, reason* the vegetable, animal, and rational souls (see v 484–5).

118. *Rocks, dens, and caves* Satan's celebration of the earth's beauty carries a melancholy echo from Hell: 'Rocks, caves, lakes, fens, bogs, dens, and shades of death' (ii 621).

120–1. *siege / Of contraries* Satan is besieged by *Pleasures* which throw his *Torment* into acute contrast. Thus M. inverts the allegorical siege, in which it was 'Satan, with pleasure as his ally, who beleaguered the human soul' (Fowler). One such allegorical siege is found in Spenser, *FQ* II xi 6, where Maleger besieges the castle of Alma with various pleasures, deploying them 'Where each might . . . his contrary object most deface' (*FQ* II xi 6).

123. *Bane* poison, destruction, woe.

144. *to repair his numbers* God does create us to 'repair' a 'detriment' (vii 152–3), but Satan does not constrain our *numbers*. See iii 289 and vii 150–56n.

145. *virtue* power.

148–9. *into our room . . . earth* So Tasso's Satan despises 'Vile man, begot of clay, and born of dust' who will possess Heaven 'in our place' (*Gerus. Lib.* iv 10), trans. Fairfax (1600).

150. *original* origin.

151. *spoils* Satan means 'spoils of war', but Fowler notes a secondary meaning whereby he 'unwittingly prophesies' the Incarnation. Exalted human nature was 'often referred to as "spoil" '. The context evokes a third meaning: 'skin of a snake' (*OED* 6). Man's 'spoil' is exalted, Satan's debased.

156. *flaming ministers* Cp. Ps. 104. 4 ('his . . . ministers a flaming fire') and Heb. 1. 14 ('Are they not all ministering spirits?').

164. *Gods* Most modernizing editors read 'gods' (angels), but Satan is more likely referring to the Father and the Son, for it is they who *sit the highest*. Cp. Lucifer's words at Isa. 14. 13–14: 'I will sit also upon the mount of the congregation . . . I will be like the most High'.

constrained compressed, forced, imprisoned (*OED* 7, 1, 8).

166. *incarnate* the Satanic counterpart to the Messiah's Incarnation.

170. *obnoxious* exposed, liable to punishment (*OED* 1a, 2). Satan is also 'injurious' (*OED* 5) to the serpent, whom he makes noxious or *nocent* (186).

172–4. *recoils . . . well aimed . . . fall short* Cp. the 'devilish engine' that 'recoils' on Satan at iv 17.

173. *reck* care.

174. *higher I fall short* 'I fall short when I aim higher'.

176. *despite* both (God's) 'spite' (*OED* 4) and (Satan's) 'contempt' (*OED* 1).

180. *black mist low creeping* Cp. Lucretius's description of a spreading plague (*De Rerum Nat.* vi 1120–21): *aer inimicus serpere coepit, / ut nebula ac nubes paulatim repit* ('the baleful air begins to creep, and glides like mist or cloud'). The connection with Satan is fortified by *inimicus* and *serpere*. Cp. x 695, where postlapsarian exhalations are 'pestilent'.

183. *labyrinth* home of the monstrous Minotaur.

186. *Nor*] Ed II; *Not* Ed I.

nocent both 'harmful' and 'guilty' (*OED* 1, 2), the opposite of 'innocent'.

188. *brutal* animal.

191. *close* concealed, confined, stifled.

197. *grateful* pleasing, and full of gratitude.

198–9. *choir . . . wanting voice* the musical silence of Paradise. Cp. iv 600–604.

200. *airs* breezes and melodies.

204. *Eve . . . began* Eve has never before spoken *first*. Her plain *Adam* (205) is also unprecedented.

205. *still* continually.

209. *Luxurious* luxuriant (*OED* 4), but the pejorative sense (cp. i 498, 722, xi 711, 784) adds an ominous overtone taken up by *wanton* (211).

213. *hear*] Ed I; *bear* Ed II.

216–17. *direct . . . where to climb* i.e. around the masculine elm. In her new spirit of independence, Eve speaks dismissively about an emblem of wifely dependence. Contrast v 215–16 where she and Adam 'led the vine / To wed her elm'.

218. *spring* grove of young trees.

219. *redress* set upright (*OED* 1a).

227. *Sole . . . sole* Unrivalled . . . only. The same pun as at iv 411, but here the context also suggests 'unaccompanied by another' (*OED* 2a), so *associate sole* is an oxymoron.

229. *motioned* proposed.

249. *solitude . . . society* See viii 427–8*n*.

265. *Or* whether.

270. *virgin majesty* 'Virginity' in Puritan usage included chaste marriage (see *A Masque* 787n).

272. *composure* *calmness, collectedness. The extant sense (*OED* 11). Earlier senses included 'temperament' (*OED* 6c) and 'posture, pose' (*OED* 7).

275–6. *by thee informed . . . overheard* Eve had been 'attentive' to all of Raphael's story about Satan (vii 51), so it is odd that she should now speak as if she had heard only his *parting* words – especially since Raphael did not mention Satan at viii 630–43. Raphael's final warning (*overheard* by Eve?) was about Adam's passion for Eve. Gagen argues that M. is inconsistent about how much Eve heard (*MQ* 20, March 1986, 17–22). See also vi 909n.

292. *entire* unblemished, blameless (*OED* 8).

293. *diffident* mistrustful.

296. *asperses* bespatters, vilifies.

310. *Accéss* increase.

318. *domestic* concerned for his family.

320. *Less* too little.

322–41. *If this . . . exposed* Cp. M.'s *Areopagitica*: 'I cannot praise a fugitive and cloister'd vertue, unexercis'd & unbreath'd, that never sallies out and sees her adversary' (*YP* 2. 515). Eve anticipates *Areopagitica*, but M. had never intended his argument to apply to the unfallen state, but to the 'state of man' as it 'now is' (*YP* 2. 514).

325. *like* equal (to each other and to Satan's attack).

326. *still* always.

328. *affronts* both 'insults' and 'confronts face to face' (*OED* 7). *Front* (330) means 'face'.

329. *integrity* sinlessness (*OED* 3). Eve herself is breaking integrity in the sense 'undivided state' (*OED* 1).

334. *event* outcome.

335. *what is . . . virtue* Cp. *Areopagitica*: 'what were vertue but a name?' (*YP* 2. 527).

341. *no Eden* including 'no pleasure'. See iv 27n.

343. *O woman* Adam gently reminds Eve of his authority: 'she shall be called Woman, because she was taken out of Man' (Gen. 2. 23, cp. viii 496–7).

353. *still erect* always alert (*OED* 'erect' 3), and suggesting man's 'Godlike erect' posture, sign of *reason* (vii 508).

358. *mind . . . mind* remind . . . pay heed to. Perhaps also *take care of (*OED* 11a, cited from 1694).

359. *subsist* stand firm (*OED* 7).

361. *specious* deceptively attractive (*OED* 2). There may be a pun on 'species' (which is etymologically related).

suborned procured in an underhand manner (*OED* 3).

367. *approve* prove.

371. *securer* more careless, overconfident.

386. *light* light-footed, with overtones of 'fickle, ready of belief' (*OED* 16), 'wanton' (*OED* 14b) and 'frivolous' (*OED* 14a), as in 'A sober grave matron . . . will never be light' (1631).

387. *Oread or Dryad* mountain- or wood-nymph. Oreads were mortal and Dryads 'perished with the trees over which they presided' (Fowler).

    Delia Diana (who was born on Delos).

388. *Betook her to the groves* a prolepsis, since 'groves' in the O.T. are associated with idolatry. See i 403n and cp. *PR* ii 289.

388–9. *Delia's self / In gait surpassed* Porter (111) sees a 'strong allusion' to the ill-fated Dido, whom Virgil likens to Diana leading her Oreads out to the hunt (*Aen.* i 500–501): 'she carries her quiver on her shoulder and, stepping along, surpasses those goddesses' (*gradiensque deas supereminet*). See also below, 783n, 1000–1001n.

392. *Guiltless* *having no experience of (*OED* 3). Adam discovers fire only after the Fall (x 1070–80), and it is associated with guilt in the Prometheus story (iv 715–19).

393. *Pales* goddess of flocks and pastures.

    Pomona goddess of fruit-trees. The wood-god *Vertumnus* wooed her, changing his shape in order to seduce her. Ovid makes her a nymph and says that she surrendered with 'answering passion' (*Met.* xiv 623–771).

394. *Likeliest*] Ed II; *Likest* Ed I. *Likeliest* is preferable because 'likely' includes 'seemly, becoming, appropriate' (*OED* 6) as well as 'resembling' (*OED* 1). *Likeliest* might also imply that Eve 'is likely to get in trouble' (Adams 84). Cp. 'where likeliest he might find' (ix 414).

395. *prime* prime of youth, springtime, and first age of the world (*OED* 6b). Autumn and winter were unknown until *Ceres* lost *Proserpina*. See iv 269–72n.

404–5. *O much . . . return* Direct address of a character is a Homeric formula. Cp. *Il.* xvi 787: 'there, Patroklos, the end of your life was shown forth'. Martin Mueller, *CLS* 6 (1969), 292–316 (302), argues that M. has modelled Adam and Eve's parting on that of Achilles and Patroclus. Patroclus entreated 'his own death' when he asked to enter the battle wearing Achilles' armour. Achilles prayed in vain for Patroclus's safe return (Homer, *Il.* xvi 47, 246–52).

405. *event perverse* unexpected outcome (Latin *perversus*, 'turned the wrong way'). Cp. *SA* 737: 'perverse event'.

413. *Mere* entirely and only.

425. *fragrance The older form was 'fragrancy'.

431. *mindless* heedless.

432. *Herself . . . flow'r* echoing iv 270 ('Herself a fairer flow'r'). For Eve as Proserpine, see iv 269–72n and below, 838–42n, and cp. ix 395.

436. *voluble* gliding, undulating (*OED* 3), with proleptic overtones of 'glib, fluent' (*OED* 5a).

437. *arborets* shrubs, small trees.

438. *hand* handiwork.

440. *Adonis* a hunter loved by Venus. After he was killed by a boar, Jupiter (or Proserpine) *revived* him at Venus's request and he spent half the year with Venus and half with Proserpine. Since ancient times, small plots of fast-fading flowers had been called 'gardens of Adonis'. Spenser's Garden of Adonis is a paradise of perpetual spring, but even it is subject to mortality (*FQ* III vi 39–42).

441. *Laertes' son* Odysseus, who visits the miraculous gardens of Alcinous in Homer, *Od.* vii 112–35.

442. *mystic* allegorical (*OED* 1), perhaps also 'mythical'.

  sapient king Solomon.

443. *Egyptian spouse* Solomon married Pharaoh's daughter (I Kings 3. 1). See Song of Sol. 6. 2 for his garden.

446. *annoy* *make noisome (not in *OED*, but 'annoy' and 'noisome' are etymologically related).

450. *tedded spread out to dry (as hay).

  kine cows.

453. *for* because of.

456. *plat* plot of ground.

459–66. *Her graceful . . . revenge* Cp. the effect of the Lady's chastity and beauty on Comus (*A Masque* 244–65).

461. *rapine* like 'rapture' and 'rape', from Latin *rapere*, 'to seize'. The would-be ravisher (393–411) is ravished.

463. *abstracted* drawn off, removed from (*OED* 1).

465. *Stupidly* *in consequence of stupefaction (*OED* 1b), but the modern sense existed (cp. xii 116) and M. might play on it to suggest that Satan is incapable of any positive good. When 'the Arch-Enemy' is *of enmity disarmed* he loses the only identity he has.

471. *recollects* remembers and summons by effort.

472. *gratulating* greeting (*OED* 1), with *thoughts* as object.

474. *transported* both 'entranced' and 'conveyed' (*hither brought us*). Cp. iii 81: 'what rage / Transports our Adversary'.

480. *Occasion* opportunity.

481. *opportune* conveniently exposed to attack (*OED* 4).

484. *haughty* of exalted courage (*OED* 4).

485. *mould* bodily form (*OED* sb³ 10b) and earth regarded as the material of the human body (*OED* sb¹ 4).

486. *informidable Cp. the neologism 'undesirable' (ix 824), which also occurs in a litotes.

488. *to* in comparison with.

490. *terror be in love* Cp. Song of Sol. 6. 4: 'Thou art beautiful, O my love . . . Terrible as an army with banners'. Cp. also *PR* ii 160.

496. *indented* zigzagged.

500. *carbuncle* any red stone, esp. 'a mythical gem said to emit a light in the dark' (*OED*).

501. *erect* upright and alert (*OED* 3). Some biblical exegetes argued that the serpent went upright until God cursed it; others argued that it 'assumed an upright posture only while being used as an instrument by Satan' (Fowler). *As since* (497) favours the former view, but Satan's erectness still implies a novel self-awareness and phallic potency.

502. *spires* coils of a serpent (*OED* 1a).

503. *redundant* *in swelling waves (*OED* 3a) and *copious, plentiful (*OED* 2, citing *SA* 568 as earliest instance).

506. *Cadmus* the legendary founder of Thebes. He was changed into a serpent when he went to *Illyria* in his old age. His wife Harmonia (*Hermione*) became a serpent when she caressed his metamorphosed body (Ovid, *Met.* iv 563f.).

506–7. *god . . . Epidaurus* Aesculapius, god of healing, had a temple in Epidaurus from which he travelled in serpent form to end a plague in Rome (Ovid, *Met.* xv 622–744). Like Satan, he was erect (674), crested (669), and glided fold above fold (721).

508. *Ammonian Jove* Plutarch relates that Philip II of Macedon found his wife *Olympias* in bed with a serpent. The Delphic oracle identifed the serpent as Zeus-Ammon (*Alexander* 2). The historical Olympias did keep pet snakes in her bed – a hazard 'calculated to put even the toughest bridegroom off his stroke' (Peter Green, *Alexander of Macedon, 356–323 BC: a Historical Biography*, 1991, 30).

508–10. *Capitoline . . . Rome* Livy and others relate that Jupiter Capitolinus took serpent form to father Scipio Africanus, who defeated Hannibal.

510–14. Paul J. Klemp (*MQ* 11, 1977, 91–2) sees a deliberate acrostic S-A-T-A-N working in the same *sidelong* manner as the hidden tempter. Satan's name does not appear elsewhere in the temptation. Cp. the possible acrostic M-A-R-S in Virgil, *Aen.* vii 601–4.

510. *tract* course.

513–15. *a ship . . . sail* Cp. the earlier nautical similes with Satan as tenor (ii 636–42, 1043–4, iv 159–65).

517. *wanton* sportive (*OED* 3c), with proleptic overtones of the fallen sense. See Ricks, *Milton's Grand Style*, 112.

522. *Circean . . . disguised* The witch Circe changed men into animals, who fawned on Odysseus's crew like dogs on their master (Homer, *Od.* x 212–19).

525. *enamelled* variegated in colour.

530. *Organic* serving as an organ or instrument (*OED* 1).

impúlse Both 'impelling' (of *air*) and 'suggestion from an evil spirit' (*OED* 3a).

532. *Wonder not* Satan's entreaty not to marvel 'is calculated to produce precisely the opposite effect' (Steadman 108).

536. *I thus single* Satan's apology for coming alone prepares for his dismissal of Adam: *one man . . . what is one?* (545-6).

549. *glozed* fawned, talked smoothly and speciously (*OED* v¹ 3).

proem prefatory part of a speech.

553-4. *What . . . expressed?* M.'s Eve is shrewder than her biblical counterpart, who shows no surprise at hearing a serpent speak. Some exegetes blamed Eve for her lack of surprise. Fish (254) blames M.'s Eve for being surprised. M. recognizes that Eve's surprise is only natural, and ethically neutral.

558. *demur* hesitate about.

563. *speakable* *able to speak (*OED* 2).

576. *A goodly tree* Satan does not at first name the tree and so allows Eve to hope that it might not be the forbidden one.

579. *savoury* See v 84*n*.

580. *Grateful* pleasing.

581. *fennel . . . teats* Fennel and milk sucked from animals' teats were popularly supposed to be the favourite food of serpents.

582. *ewe* Le Comte (80) hears a pun on 'you'. Incubi (see *PR* ii 152*n*) were thought to suck animals' *teats* and women's breasts. See Harry Blamires, *Milton's Creation: a Guide through 'Paradise Lost'* (1971) 225.

586. *defer* delay.

584-99. *To satisfy . . . Strange alteration* Satan's most cunning lie (and M.'s most significant addition to Genesis) is to have the serpent claim that it can speak because it ate the fruit. There were rabbinic versions in which the serpent ate the fruit in front of Eve to reassure her that it was safe to do so, but the serpent in these versions did not claim to have acquired knowledge by eating. Evans (276-7) cites Joseph Beaumont's *Psyche* (1648) as the sole precedent.

585. *apples* Satan alone speaks of 'apples' in *PL*. The good characters always refer to 'fruit', which includes 'consequences'.

601. *Wanted* were lacking.

605. *middle* the air between.

612. *universal dame* mistress of the universe.

613. *spirited* including *possessed by an evil spirit (*OED* 4).

616. *virtue* efficacy.

proved tested.

623. *their provision* what is provided for them.

624. *her bearth* what she bears. The spelling (*Ed I*, *Ed II*) was unusual even in M.'s time.

625. *adder* any serpent (*OED* 1). Satan was often called 'the adder' in medieval times.

629. *blowing* blooming.

632. *made*] *Ed II*; make *Ed I*.

634–42. *wand'ring fire . . . lost* Cp. *A Masque* 205–9, 433, and the earlier bog similes in *PL* (ii 592–4, 939–40).

635. *Compact . . . vapour* composed of oily gas. Milton gives a scientific explanation for the *ignis fatuus*, or will-o'-the-wisp, before turning to the supernatural.

637. *agitation* friction (of gases) and (evil Spirit's) scheming (*OED* 6), as in 'crafty and subtill agitations' (1606).

640. *amazed* including 'led through a maze'. Cp. Shakespeare, *A Midsummer Night's Dream* II i 39: 'Mislead night-wanderers, laughing at their harm'.

642. *swallowed up and lost* echoing Belial: 'swallowed up and lost / In the wide womb of uncreated Night' (ii 149–50).

643. *fraud* *state of being defrauded (*OED* 5) – a passive usage unique to M., from Latin *fraus*. Cp. vii 143, *PR* i 372.

644–5. *tree / Of prohibition* both 'prohibited tree' and 'tree of *all* prohibition' (Ricks, *Milton's Grand Style*, 76).

645. *root* the same silent pun as at ii 383.

648. *Fruitless . . . excess* See Ricks, *Milton's Grand Style*, 73 on the 'jaunty levity' of Eve's pun on *Fruitless*. M.'s voice behind Eve puns on *excess* as 'violation of law', 'intemperance in eating' and 'unrestrained grief' (*OED* 4a, 5b, 2). Cp. xi 111: 'Bewailing their excess'.

653. *daughter of his voice* a Hebraism, *Bath Kol*, 'daughter of a voice'. Hunter (23) cites sources showing that *Bath Kol* (or *filia vocis*) was an inferior form of revelation, lacking real authority. Thus Eve understates the command, which had come from God's own voice and resounded dreadfully in Adam's (but not Eve's) ear (viii 335).

654. *Law to ourselves* Cp. St Paul on the virtuous Gentiles who 'are a law unto themselves' (Rom. 2. 14).

668. *Fluctuates* moves like a wave (*OED* 1).

act including Latin *actio*, an orator's exterior bearing.

669. *Raised* both in posture and rhetoric.

673. *in himself collected* both mentally and physically (the serpent's coils). *part* both 'dramatic role' and 'part of the body'

674. *Motion* gesture, mime, with overtones of 'puppet show' (*OED* 13a). *audience* attention.

675. *in heighth* the high, impassioned style usually reserved for the climax of an oration.

677. *to heighth* *upgrown* both 'standing upright' and 'elevated in rhetorical style'.

680. *science* knowledge.

683–7. *highest agents . . . the Threat'ner* The serpent begins to avoid naming 'God'.

687. *To* both 'in addition to' and 'eventuating in'.

692. *incense* excite, kindle (*OED* v² 2).

694. *virtue* courage (*OED* 7), which Satan identifies with moral virtue.

695. *denounced* threatened.

whatever thing death be Satan had learned about death at ii 781–816. He now feigns innocence. Cp. Adam's 'whate'er death is' (iv 425), but even Adam knew death to be 'Some dreadful thing'.

698–9. *if what is evil / Be real* Many theologians had argued that evil is a privation of good, and so has no real existence. Satan perverts this doctrine into the easy inference that evil is nothing to worry about. He also hints that if evil is real, it must have been created by a malevolent God.

701. *Not just, not God* Satan's final naming of 'God' argues him out of existence. Henceforward he will speak of 'gods' (708–25).

713–14. *putting off . . . gods* Satan perverts a biblical metaphor. See e.g. Col. 3. 9–10: 'ye have put off the old man with his deeds; And have put on the new man'.

717. *participating* partaking of.

722. *they all* i.e. they produce all.

729–30. *can envy dwell / In Heav'nly breasts* echoing Virgil on Juno's anger: *tantaene animis caelestibus irae?* (*Aen.* i 11). Raphael had echoed the same line when describing the devils' desperate resistance in battle (vi 788).

732. *humane* both 'human' and 'benevolent' (the spellings were not yet distinguished). The oxymoron 'human goddess' looks back to 'human gods' (712).

739. *noon* Eve had promised Adam that she would 'be returned by noon' (401).

741. *savoury* See v 84n.

742. *Inclinable* disposed (modifying *desire*) and bending down (modifying *fruit*). Fowler rules out the latter sense, but cp. iv 332 and viii 308. Cp. also Spenser, *FQ* II xii 54 and Marvell, 'The Garden' (printed 1681) 33–40.

754. *infers* implies.

the good Eve omits 'evil', yet evil is what the tree will bring. See below, 1072n.

755. *communicated* See v 72n.

want lack.

758. *In plain* in plain words.

761. *after-bands* subsequent bonds.

770. *envies* begrudges.

771. *author* authority, informant (*OED* 4).

unsuspect above suspicion.

776. *cure of all* Eve means 'remedy', but M. puns on Latin *cura*, 'grief'. Cp. 'all our woe' (i 3, ix 645).

781. *ate*] eat *Ed I*, *Ed II* (past tense, pronounced 'et').

783. *signs of woe* Porter (112) sees an allusion to Virgil, *Aen.* iv 165–70, where earth gave a sign (*signum*) of woe at the moment of Dido's 'fall': 'Primal Earth and nuptial Juno gave the sign; lightning flashed and Heaven was witness to the marriage, and nymphs howled on the mountain-top. That was the first day of death, the first cause of woe.'

792. *knew not eating death* The syntax includes: 'she did not experience death while she ate', 'she did not know that she was eating death', 'she did not acquire knowledge while she ate death', and 'she did not know death, which devours' (Latin *mors edax*).

793. *boon* jolly, jovial.

795. *virtuous, precious* most powerful, most precious (Greek and Latin idiom: the positive for the superlative).

797. *sapience* both 'knowledge' and 'tasting' (Latin *sapere*). Cp. Adam's pun at ix 1018.

infamed slandered.

800. *each morning . . . due praise* Eve now offers the tree the kind of morning hymn she had once offered God (v 153–208).

804. *gods* Editors infer that Eve means 'God' and that she has picked up the plural from Satan (712, 716). But Eve's gods might be 'angels' (cp. v 70), whom she distinguishes from unspecified *others* (the Father and Son).

810–11. *secret . . . secret* uncommunicative (*OED* 2a) . . . hidden. Rather than face the disappointing fact that wisdom is still uncommunicative, Eve takes comfort in the thought that her own doings might be hidden from God. Cp. Ps. 10. 11: 'He [the wicked man] hath said in his heart, God hath forgotten: / He hideth his face; he will never see it'.

815. *safe* both 'not endangered' and 'not at present dangerous'.

820. *odds* equalizing allowance (*OED* 4c), advantage (*OED* 4b).

821. *copartner* both 'sharer' and 'equal' (*OED* 3), as in 'Without a Co-Partner, or any Parallel' (1660).

wants is lacking.

824. **undesirable* See above, 486n.

827. *I shall be no more* A new concept for Eve, who had had no notion of death as annihilation at iv 425 or ix 695. The fruit has brought her some kind of knowledge.

832. *all deaths* Eve is being hyperbolical, but her plural has ominous resonances. The 'second death' was a theological term for damnation.

M. in *CD* i 11–13 distinguishes four deaths: guiltiness, spiritual death, extinction of body and soul, and final damnation. Cp. x 770–844.

835. *low reverence* deep bow.

837. *sciential* granting knowledge.

sap including a pun on Latin *sapere*, 'to know'. See above, 797*n*.

838–42. *Adam . . . harvest queen* Cp. Claudian's Proserpina in Enna: 'she made a flower crown and put it on her brow, / but she did not see this grim prophecy of marriage' (*De Rapt. Pros.* ii 142–3). Cp. also the *garland* worn by Pandora when she comes to Epimetheus full of 'Lies and persuasive words and cunning ways' (Hesiod, *WD* 79). Bush compares Andromache embroidering flowers for Hector, unaware that he is dead (Homer, *Il.* xxii 437f.). See below, 892–3*n*.

845. *divine of* divining (with proleptic overtones of 'divinity', cp. ix 1010). *Misgave him* with proleptic overtones of 'bestow amiss' (*OED* 3). Cp. 'She gave him' (ix 996).

846. *falt'ring measure* Adam's heartbeat; also the 'measured motion' of 'unsteady Nature' (*Arcades* 70–74), which has just been thrown out of rhythm (782–4). *Ed I* and *Ed II* punningly spell 'fault'ring'.

852. *ambrosial* *fragrant (*OED* 1c), and recalling 'nectar, drink of gods' (line 838).

854. *apology* justification (not regret).

855. *bland* mildly coaxing (*OED* 1), flattering (Latin *blandus*).

864–5. *nor to evil unknown / Op'ning the way* i.e. 'this tree does not open the way to evil, which remains unknown', but Eve's syntax admits the opposite meaning: 'this tree is known to evil, to which it opens the way'.

868. *Or . . . or* either . . . or.

876. *erst* formerly.

887. *distemper* disordered state arising from disturbance of bodily humours, intoxication (*OED* 4, 4d).

890. *Astonied* stunned, paralysed (with a pun on 'as stone').

blank discomfited, deprived of speech, resourceless (*OED* 5) and pale (*OED* 1).

892–3. *From his slack hand . . . dropped* Cp. Homer, *Il.* xxii 448, where Andromache hears the sound of mourning and realizes that Hector is dead: 'her limbs spun, and the shuttle dropped from her hand to the ground'. Cp. also Statius, *Thebaid* vii 148–50, where Bacchus, fearing the destruction of Thebes, drops his thyrsus, and unspoiled grapes fall from his garlanded head.

893. *faded roses* 'The first instance of decay in Paradise' (Fowler), but cp. the 'show'red roses' at iv 773.

901. *deflow'red* Cp. Eve as 'unsupported flow'r' (ix 432). Her temptation has also been presented as a sexual seduction (ix 386–96).

devote   doomed (*OED* 'devoted' 3). Porter (111) compares Dido, *pesti devota futurae*, 'doomed to impending ruin' (Virgil, *Aen.* i 712).

905. *unknown* modifies *fraud*, not *Enemy*. Adam knows that Satan beguiled Eve, but he doesn't yet know how he did it. Cp. ix 1172, where Adam clearly knows who 'the lurking enemy' was. Adam has always referred to Satan as 'the Enemy'.

906–7. *with thee . . . to die* Waldock (52) and Empson (189) applaud Adam's decision as springing from 'protectiveness' and 'true love', but Adam chooses to die *with* Eve, for his own sake. He does not die for her. Cp. Eve's selfless offer at x 930–36.

919. *what seemed remédiless* Lewis (123) takes *seemed* to imply that Adam might have found a remedy, and Burden (168) infers that 'the remedy is divorce'. Other critics suggest that Adam, like the Son, might have risked himself to save Eve. See Fish (261–72), Danielson² (121–4), and Leonard (213–32).

922. *hath*] *Ed II*; hast *Ed I*. *Hast* goes better with line 921, but Adam might shift to a more general thought so as not to confront Eve's particular case.

923–5. *to eye . . . touch* Gen. 3. 3 and *PL* vii 46 confirm the *ban* on *touch*, but Adam's claim that it was perilous even to look at the fruit is nowhere supported.

924. *sacred* *set apart, exclusively appropriated (*OED* 2b), with overtones of 'consecrated', 'entitled to veneration' (*OED* 3b). Adam is making an idol of the fruit.

928. *fact* both 'crime' (*OED* 1c) and 'a thing done' (*OED* 1a).

946–50. *loath . . . next* Cp. the Son's plea at iii 156–64.

947. *Adversary* Satan. Adam still refers to him as *the Foe* (951), but now fails to pursue his earlier insight that serpent and 'enemy' are one and the same (see above, 905*n*).

953. *Certain* resolved.

954. *death is to me as life* Cp. Satan's 'Evil be thou my good' (iv 110), but Adam (who did not understand death at iv 425) might not see the paradox. He intends a witty play on *life* as the meaning of Eve's name: 'if death consort with you, then death is to me like Eve'. By *Consort* Adam means 'associate', but the sense 'have sexual commerce with' (*OED* 2) is grimly appropriate to the lustful Death of book ii.

959. *to lose thee were to lose myself* The *Ed I* and *Ed II* spelling 'loose' could indicate 'lose' or 'loose'. *Bond* (956) invites a pun, but the implications are ambiguous. 'Loose' could mean 'set free' (*OED* 1b), 'redeem' (*OED* 10), or 'dissolve, do away with' (*OED* 7a).

961. *O . . . love* Cp. iii 410 ('O unexampled love').

973. *good . . . good* Eve still omits 'evil' from the name 'Tree of Knowledge of good and evil'. Cp. lines 754–9, 864–5.

980. *oblige* make liable to a penalty.

fact crime, deed.

984. *event* outcome.

994-5. *recompense . . . recompense* compensation for a loss . . . retribution for an offence (*OED* 2, 5). Cp. Adam's bitter cry at 1163: 'Is this the love, is this the recompense?'

994. *compliance* unworthy submission (*OED* 6b).

998. *not deceived* Cp. I Tim. 2. 14: 'Adam was not deceived'.

1000-1001. *Earth . . . second groan* Cp. earth's groan at the 'fall' of Dido and Aeneas (Virgil, *Aen.* iv 165-70). See above, 783*n*. Cp. also the mournful groan (*gemitus lacrimabilis*) that comes from beneath the tree plucked by Aeneas at *Aen.* iii 39.

1003-4. *sin / Original* the theological doctrine that all of Adam's descendants 'committed sin in Adam' (*CD* i 12, *YP* 6. 395, trans. Carey). Cp. x 729f.

1016. *dalliance* amorous toying (*OED* 2). Contrast the innocent 'youthful dalliance' of iv 338.

1018. *sapience* wisdom and taste. See above, 797*n*.

1019. *each meaning savour* tastiness (*OED* 1b) and understanding (*OED* 5). Cp. v 84.

we] Ed I; *me* Ed II.

1021. *purveyed* provided food.

1026. *forbidden ten* proleptic of the Ten Commandments.

1027. *play* have sex (*OED* 10c).

1028. *meet* appropriate, with a pun on 'meat' ('human body regarded as an instrument of sexual pleasure', *OED* 3e, cited from 1595). Contrast Eve as a 'help meet' (Gen. 2. 21) and unfallen Adam's judging 'of fit and meet' (viii 448).

1029-32. *For never . . . now* echoing Zeus's amorous invitation to Hera (Homer, *Il.* xiv 314-16) and Paris's to Helen (*Il.* iii 442): 'Never before as now has passion enmeshed my senses'. Zeus and Hera make love on a bed of flowers (including *hyacinth*, *Il.* xiv 346-51), and Zeus falls asleep when *wearied*.

1030-31. *adorned / With all perfections* Flannagan hears a pun on 'Pandora', 'all gifts'. Cp. iv 714-15.

1034. *toy* light caress (*OED* 1).

1037. *a shady bank* Before the Fall Adam and Eve had made love in their bower at night-time (see iv 741). Now they do it anywhere, at any time.

1042-4. *their fill . . . solace* Cp. Prov. 7. 18, where a woman 'with the attire of an harlot' accosts a youth: 'Come, let us take our fill of love until the morning: let us solace ourselves with loves'. Contrast the 'solace' of marriage before the Fall (iv 486, viii 419, ix 844).

1043. *seal* a legal metaphor enlivened by a bawdy pun. Cp. Donne, 'Elegy

19': 'To enter in these bonds, is to be free; / Then where my hand is set, my seal shall be' (32–3).

1047. *bland* *pleasing to the senses (*OED* 2). Contrast the 'temperate vapours bland' that before the Fall bred 'airy light', not *grosser*, sleep (v 5).

1050. *unkindly* unnatural.

conscious guilty (*OED* 4b).

1058. *he* i.e. Shame (who is personified, see line 1097).

1059. *Danite* Samson was of the tribe of Dan (Judges 13. 2). See *SA* 216n on Dalila (Delilah) as a Philistine.

1062. *they* M. likens both Adam and Eve to Samson. Eve is not Adam's Dalila.

1067. *Eve . . . evil* Adam's pun is *constrained* (1066), 'forced as opposed to natural' (*OED* 2). 'Eve' means 'life', and Adam will reaffirm this meaning at xi 159–61.

1068. *of whomsoever taught* Having suppressed his recognition of Satan (see above, 905n), Adam is now genuinely ignorant. But recognition is still within his grasp. See ix 1172–3.

1072. *good lost, and evil got* M. follows most commentators in deriving the tree's name from the event. Cp. iv 222, 774–5, xi 84–9 and *CD* i 10: 'since it was tasted, not only do we know evil, but also we do not even know good except through evil' (trans. Carey, *YP* 6. 352–3).

1078. *evil store* evil in abundance.

1079. *the first* the evil that caused the *shame*.

1083. *this earthly* earthly nature. Cp. viii 453.

1087. *umbrage* shadow, foliage, protective screen (*OED* 1, 2c, 5) and false show (*OED* 6), as in 'Truth will appear from under all the false glosses and umbrages that men may draw over it' (1693). Notice *Hide me.*

1091. *plight* including 'offence, sin' (*OED* sb^1 2) and 'pleat', 'attire' (*OED* sb^2 1, 8). The pun may be borrowed from Spenser (see below, 1116n).

1092–3. Following *Ed I*. *Ed II* wrongly transposes *for* and *from*.

1094. *obnoxious* exposed (*OED* 1a), with possible overtones of the modern sense, which *OED* cites from 1675.

1101. *fig-tree* the banyan (*ficus religiosa*). In fact it has small leaves, but M. has taken his details from contemporary encyclopedists. The *loopholes* (1110) and the Amazon simile (1111) are found in Gerard's *Herbal* (1597) 1330.

1103. *Malabar* south-west coast of India.

Deccan southern India.

1106. *mother tree* Cp. the feminization of the Tree of Knowledge (ix 581–2, 680).

1111. *Amazonian targe* an Amazon's shield.

1115. *naked glory* Cp. Marlowe, *Hero and Leander* (1598), i 12–13: 'Venus in her naked glory strove / To please the careless and disdainful eyes / Of proud Adonis'.

1116. *Columbus . . . girt* Cp. Spenser's simile likening Fancy to a sunburned Indian clad in 'painted plumes' and 'proudest plight' (*FQ* III xii 8). American Indians were sometimes seen as untainted by the Fall, but M. associates them with ruined innocence. See Evans³ 94f.

1117. *cincture* belt.

1121. *sat them down to weep* Cp. Ps. 137. 1: 'By the rivers of Babylon, there we sat down, yea, we wept, when we remembered Zion'.

1131. *distempered* See above, 887n.

1132. *estranged* changed from his normal self (*OED* 4) and alienated (from Eve).

1140. *approve* test.

1141. *owe* both 'own' and 'owe'.

1144. *What words . . . thy lips* echoing Homer (*Il.* xiv 83). Eve is referring specifically to Adam's word *wand'ring* (1136) which has now assumed its fallen meaning. See ii 148n and Fish (140).

   severe another tainted word. It had meant 'austerely simple' (iv 283–4, 845, v 807), but Eve now means 'harsh'. Adam laments the new meaning in line 1169.

1155. *the head* I Cor 11. 3 (cit. above, viii 574n).

1164. *expressed* modifies both (Eve's) *love* (1163) and *mine for thee*. Eve's love was 'declared'; Adam's was 'manifested in actions' (*OED* 'express' 7).

1175. *confidence* overboldness (*OED* 4a).

   secure overconfident.

1183–4. *women . . . her* The grammatical inconsistency is 'in keeping with Adam's agitation' (Bush).

1188. *fruitless* Cp. Eve's pun in line 648.

1189. *no end* inverting 'No more' (ix 1).

BOOK X

3. *perverted* including 'turned from a true to a false religious belief' (*OED* 3b).

10. *Complete* fully equipped (*OED* 5), as in 'complete steel'. Notice *armed* and cp. *A Masque* 420.

12. *still* always.

16. *manifold in sin* sinful in many ways.

19. *by this* by this time.

28–30. *they . . . vigilance* 'Accountable for their actions, they (the *guards*) hasted to the supreme throne to make plain their utmost vigilance with a righteous plea.'

31. *approved* confirmed (*OED* 2). Cp. Argument, 'approve their vigilance, and are approved'.

40. *speed* be successful.

45. *moment* slightest weight sufficient to tip a *scale*.

48. *rests* remains.

49. *denounced* formally proclaimed.

49–52. *that day . . . immediate stroke* God had told Adam that he would die 'in the day' he ate (Gen. 2. 17). See viii 331*n*.

53. *Forbearance no acquittance* 'abstinence from enforcing a debt is not release from the debt' (proverbial expression, *OED* 'forbearance' 3).

54. *Justice . . . scorned* 'My justice must not be scorned as my generosity has been'.

56–7. *to thee . . . All judgement* John 5. 22.

58. *might*] *Ed II*; *may Ed I*.

70–71. *in me . . . well pleased* Matt. 3. 17.

77. *derived* diverted (*OED* 2) and passed on by descent (*OED* 4).

78. *illústrate* set in the best light.

79. *Them* justice and mercy.

80. *Attendance none shall need* no retinue will be necessary.
    train attendants.

82. *the third* Satan.

83. *Convict* proved guilty (*OED* a 2).
    rebel to all law M. had called Charles I a 'rebell to Law' (*YP* 3. 230).

84. *Conviction* both 'proof of guilt' and *'condition of being convinced of sin' (*OED* 8). *OED* cites the latter sense only from 1675, but it was well established in the verb. See John 8. 9 and *PR* iv 308.

86. *collateral* side by side.

87. **ministrant* Cp. Heb. 1. 14: 'Are they not all ministering spirits?'

89. *coast* region of the earth (*OED* 6).

90–91. *the speed . . . winged* The Son's descent is timeless. Raphael had taken most of the morning to travel from Heaven to earth (viii 110–15).

92. *cadence* sinking, with a musical pun taken up by *airs* (Ricks). Cp. iv 264–6.

106. *obvious* coming in the way (*OED* 3), thus 'coming out to meet'. Cp. viii 504.

107–8. *what change . . . what chance* Cp. ii. 222–3 ('what chance, what change / Worth waiting').

112. *apparent* manifest.

120. *still* always.

128. *other self* See viii 450*n*.

135. *Devolved* caused to fall upon.

137–43. *This woman . . . did eat* Cp. Gen. 3. 12: 'The woman whom thou gavest to be with me, she gave me of the tree, and I did eat.' Biblical commentators detected a hint of resentment in 'thou gavest'. To this M. adds irony (*so good, / So fit*), tactlessness (*so divine*) and self-exculpation (*I could suspect no ill*). Contrast Eve's humble directness in lines 159–62.

147. *or but equal* or even equal. Cp. viii 568–75.

151. *real* both 'true' and 'royal' (*OED* a¹).

155–6. *part / And person* role and character (theatrical terms).

157. *few* few words.

165. *unable* modifies *serpent*.

167. *end* purpose.

171. *at last* including 'on the last day' (see line 190).

173. *mysterious* mystical (see x 1030–40).

183. *second Eve* a common patristic idea. Cp. v 385–7.

184. *Satan . . . lightning* When the disciples told Jesus how they had subjected devils, he replied: 'I beheld Satan as lightning fall from heaven. Behold, I give unto you power to tread on serpents and scorpions, and over all the power of the enemy' (Luke 10. 18–19).

185. *Prince of the Air* Satan is 'prince of the power of the air' in Eph. 2. 2. Cp. *PR* i 39–47.

186–7. *Spoiled . . . show* Col. 2. 14–15.

188. *Captivity led captive* Ps. 68. 18, Eph. 4. 8.

190. *tread . . . under our feet* Cp. Rom. 16. 20: 'the God of peace shall bruise Satan under your feet shortly'.

195–6. *thy husband's . . . rule* Cp. Gen. 3. 16: 'thy desire shall be to thy husband, and he shall rule over thee'. Adam has always ruled over Eve in *PL*. See iv 441–8, viii 561–75, x 145–56, etc. M. in *CD* i 10 argues that Adam's authority became 'still greater after the Fall' (trans. Carey, *YP* 6. 355).

210. *denounced* announced as a calamitous event about to take place (*OED* 1b).

214. *the form of servant* Phil. 2. 7.

215. *he washed his servants' feet* John 13. 5.

217. *or . . . Or* either . . . or. If the beasts were *slain*, the Son is 'the immediate cause' of 'the first instance of actual death' (Fowler).

222. *robe of righteousness* Cp. Isa. 61. 10: 'he hath covered me with the robe of righteousness'. Notice the pun *Opprobrious . . . robe*.

236. *author* father (*OED* 2a) and prompter, instigator (*OED* 1d).

241. *avengers*] *Ed II*; avenger *Ed I*.

   like so well as.

243–4. *Methinks . . . Wings growing* Cp. *PL* ix 1009–10, where the fallen and intoxicated Adam and Eve 'fancy that they feel / Divinity within them breeding wings'. Fowler notes that Sin's wings may grow 'simultaneously' with Adam and Eve's, for M. has just taken us back in time. See line 229.

M. thus presents us with the Fall 'twice in the poem, and this second time it is horrific' (Rushdy 130).

246. *sympathy* affinity drawing two things together.

connatural force innate force linking us.

249. *conveyance* communication.

253–323. Prodigies of building or engineering are traditional in epic. In *PL* we have seen Pandaemonium and the Creation. Examples in earlier epics include the wall around the Greek ships (Homer, *Il.* vii 433f.), Carthage (Virgil, *Aen.* i 423f.), Caesar's causeway over the port of Brindisi (Lucan, *Pharsalia* ii 660–79), and Goffredo's siege engines (Tasso, *Gerus. Lib.* xviii).

254. *impervious* through which there is no way (*OED* 1).

257. *main* ocean (of Chaos).

260. *intercourse* passing back and forth.

261. *transmigration* permanent emigration (to earth), but suggesting also 'passage from this life, by death' (*OED* 3). Sin and Death's bridge opens our way to Hell as readily as it opens Hell's way to us.

264. *meagre* emaciated (*OED* 1).

272. *snuffed* *detected by inhaling an odour (*OED* v² 4). *OED*'s earliest instance (from Dryden, 1697) is an obvious imitation of Milton.

274–8. *ravenous fowl . . . bloody fight* Cp. Satan as vulture at iii 431–9. Cp. also Lucan's description of vultures following the Roman armies to Pharsalia (*Pharsalia* vii 831–7).

275. *Against* in anticipation of.

277. *designed* set apart, destined.

279. *feature* form, shape (*OED* 1c).

281. *Sagacious* acute in sense of smell (*OED* 1), with a play on 'wise'. Cp. Adam and Eve's puns on 'savour' and 'sapience' (ix 797, 1018–10).

284. *diverse* in different directions.

285. *Hovering upon the waters* Sin and Death travesty the dove-like Spirit of God at Creation. See i 21–2, vii 235–40.

288. *shoaling* crowding together (*OED* v³ 2).

290. *Cronian Sea* the Arctic Ocean (solid with ice).

291. *th' imagined way* the north-east passage to Cathay. Hudson had tried to find it in 1608, but his way was blocked by ice.

292. *Petsora* Pechora, a river in Siberia.

293. *Cathayan* Milton distinguished Cathay (North China) from China proper. See xi 386–8.

294. *petrific* that turns things to stone.

cold and dry See ii 898n for the four contraries: Hot, Cold, Moist, and Dry. Death employs the qualities productive of melancholy and associated with decay. Fowler contrasts the Son's use of Hot and Moist in Creation (vii 236–9).

296. *Delos floating once* Pregnant by Jupiter (and persecuted by Juno) Latona could find no place in which to give birth to Apollo and Diana until Neptune *fixed* the floating island of *Delos* with his *trident* (Callimachus, *Hymns*, iv, Hyginus, *Fables*, cxl). Cp. v 262-6.

297. *Gorgonian rigor* The Gorgon Medusa turned anything she looked at into stone. See ii 611.

298. *asphaltic slime* bitumen, pitch. Cp. i 729 and xii 40-44.

300. *mole* massive pier or bridge.

302. *wall* the hard outer shell of the universe (see ii 1023-33).

305. *inoffensive* free from obstacles (Latin *inoffensus*), with a play on *fenceless* (303).

307-11. *Xerxes . . . waves* In 480 BC King Xerxes of Persia built a bridge of ships over the Hellespont so that his army could invade Greece. He ordered the sea to be whipped when it destroyed this bridge. As his army passed over a second bridge, Xerxes wept at the thought that all his soldiers would be dead within a hundred years (Herodotus vii 46). Cp. i 620n. Quint (7) traces M.'s simile to Lucan, who compares Caesar's causeway over the port of Brindisi to Xerxes' bridging of 'Europe and Asia' (*Pharsalia* ii 672-7). Quint also notes a pun on *Hellespont* as 'Hell's pont'.

308. *Susa* the biblical Shushan, winter palace of the Persian kings – *Memnonian* because the mythical Prince Memnon lived there, and its acropolis was called the Memnonium (Strabo XV iii 2). On Memnon see *Il Penseroso* 18n.

313. *Pontifical* *bridge-building (*OED* 6), with a pun on 'papal' (*OED* 2) or 'episcopal' (*OED* 1). The Pope's title *Pontifex* was taken to mean that he was a bridge-builder between this world and the next. See below, 348n.

314. *vexed* turbulent.

321. *confines* boundaries.

322. *the left* the 'sinister' evil side. Cp. ii 755, x 886 and Matt. 25. 33.

323. *three several ways* the stair linking the universe to Heaven, the bridge joining the universe to Hell, and the passage through the universe down to the earth (iii 526-39).

327. *Satan . . . bright* Cp. II Cor. 11. 14: 'Satan himself is transformed into an angel of light'.

328. *Betwixt the Centaur and the Scorpion* If *the Centaur* is Sagittarius, Satan is steering his way through Anguis, the Serpent constellation. If *the Centaur* is Centaurus, Satan is steering through Lupus, the Wolf. M. likens Satan to a wolf at iv 181-3.

332. *unminded* unnoticed.

334. *sequel* consequence.

335. *unweeting* unaware.

337. *covertures* garments (see ix 1110-15), concealments (*OED* 7), justifications (*OED* 8; see x 115-17).

342–5. *list'ning . . . future time* refers to Adam's recollection of the curse on Satan (x 1030). Thus x 720–1104 precedes x 345–609 in chronological time. See further below, 716*n*.

344. *understood* (he) understood.

347. *foot* the end of the slope of the bridge (*OED* 18b).

348. **pontifice* bridge (*OED* sb², sole instance), coined from Latin *pons* on the model of 'edifice' – but 'pontifice' (*OED* sb¹) already existed as a variant of 'Pontifex' meaning 'Bishop' or 'Pope'. In this sense, Satan himself is the *wondrous pontifice*.

359. *Still* always.

364. *consequence* relationship of cause to effect.

366. **unvoyageable*.

370. *fortify* grow strong (*OED* I 6) and erect fortifications (the bridge).

371. *portentous* marvellous (*OED* 2) and ominous (*OED* 1).

372. *virtue* manliness, courage, valour (*OED* 7), the only virtue Satan's followers recognize.

374. *odds* advantage, profit.

375. *foil* defeat (*OED* sb²). A 'foil' in wrestling was 'a throw not resulting in a flat fall' (*OED* sb² 1), so Sin punningly hints that Satan's 'foil' was not a 'Fall'. 'Foil' could also mean 'tread under foot' (*OED* v¹ 1) and so anticipate Satan's ultimate fate (cp. x 175–81).

378. *doom* Judgement.

381. *quadrature* Cp. Rev. 21. 16, where the New Jerusalem is 'foursquare'. The sphere was thought to be more perfect than the cube, so Sin's antithesis between God's square and Satan's *orbicular* realm implies a 'subtle sneer' (Fowler). Heaven was 'undetermined square or round' at ii 1048.

382. *try* find by experience to be (*OED* 13).

386. *Satan . . . the name* This is the first and only time that Satan speaks his name in *PL*.

387. *Antagonist* 'Satan' means 'enemy', 'adversary' or 'antagonist'. The latter word originally signified a competitor in athletic games (as in *SA* 1628), so Satan might be looking back to Sin's word 'foil' (375) and boasting of his prowess as a wrestler.

390. *Triumphal . . . triumphal* Sin and Death celebrate Satan's triumph by building a triumphal arch. Cp. *PR* iv 37.

397. *these*] Ed *II*; those Ed *I*.

404. *Plenipotent* having full power.

408. *prevail*] Ed *I*; prevails Ed *II*.

409. *No detriment* echoing the formula by which the Roman Senate would give dictatorial power to two Consuls: *ne quid respublica detrimenta capiat* ('that the state suffer no harm').

    go and be strong So Moses tells Joshua to take possession of the Promised

Land: 'Be strong and of a good courage: for thou must go with these people' (Deut. 31. 7).

412. *bane* poison, destruction.

blasted stricken by malignant astral influences (*OED* 1).

413. *planet-strook* stricken by the malign influence of an adverse planet (*OED*); suggesting also a physical collision. Cp. vi 310–15.

real eclipse not just an obscuration by an intervening body, but a diminution of light at its source.

415. *causey* causeway, arched viaduct (*OED* 2c).

420. *those* Sin and Death.

425. *Lucifer* the morning star. Cp. v 760, vii 131.

allusion metaphor (*OED* 3).

426. *paragoned* compared (*OED* 1).

427. *the grand* 'the grand infernal Peers' (ii 507).

428. *solicitous* anxious (*OED* 1).

431–3. *Tartar . . . Retires* The simile implies Satanic cunning, since Tartars were famous for shooting arrows to the rear while feigning retreat. Cp. Spenser, *FQ* II xi 26, and Phineas Fletcher, *The Purple Island* (1633): 'As when by Russian Volga's frozen banks / The false-back Tartars fear with cunning feign, / And posting fast away in flying ranks, / Oft backward turn, and from their bows down rain / Whole storms of darts; so do they flying fight: / And what by force they lose, they winne by sleight' (xi 48).

432. *Astrakhan* a Tartar khanate on the lower Volga annexed by Ivan the Terrible in 1556. Astrakhan was a mere remnant of the once mighty Golden Horde, so the name implies the devils' decline. But they remain a threat. In 1571 the Tartars 'broke into *Russia*' and 'burnt *Mosco* to the ground' (M.'s *History of Muscovia*, *YP* 8. 515).

433. *Bactrian Sophy* Persian Shah.

433–4. *horns . . . crescent* referring both to the Turkish battle formation and emblem.

435. *realm of Aladule* Armenia (Aladule being the last Persian ruler before the Turkish conquest).

436. *Tauris* Tabriz, in north-west Persia.

Casbeen Kazvin, north of Tcheran.

438. *reduced* led back (*OED* 2), drawn together (*OED* 25), and diminished.

439. *metropolis* including 'parent state of a colony' (*OED* 3). Satan will soon provide *foreign worlds* to colonize (441).

441–55. *he . . . returned* Satan's *invisible* entry, his remaining *unseen*, and his *sudden* blazing *as from a cloud* are taken from Tasso, *Gerus. Lib.* x 32–50, where the Sultan Solimano enters a Saracen council of war concealed in a cloud, and 'Unseen, at will did all the prease behold' (x 35). When morale is at its lowest, Solimano tears the cloud 'like a veil' and 'amid the press he shined' (x 49). M.'s *whom they wished beheld* (454) directly echoes

Fairfax's translation of Solimano's first words on becoming visible: 'Of whom you speake behold the Soldan here' (x 50). Cp. also Homer, *Od.* vii 37–145 and Virgil, *Aen.* i 411–14, 579–94.

444. **Plutonian* infernal, from Pluto, god of the underworld.

445. *state* canopy.

451. *permissive* permitted (by God).

453. *Stygian* Styx, the river of hate in Hades. Cp. ii 506, 577.

457. *Divan* Turkish Council of State. Satan was a 'Sultan' at i 348 and he has just appeared in the manner of Tasso's Sultan Solimano.

458. **Congratulant* saluting (*OED* 'congratulate' 5).

458–9. *with hand / Silence* Cp. Lucan's hero-villain Caesar commanding his legions' attention before leading them into revolt: *dextraque silentia iussit,* 'with his right hand commanded silence' (*Pharsalia,* i 298).

460–62. *Thrones . . . of right* Satan's distinction between *right* and *possession* accords with seventeenth-century notions of ruling *de jure* (by law) or *de facto* (by possession). Thus Charles II claimed to rule *de jure* throughout the Interregnum, but did not rule *de facto* until 1660. See v 773*n* for Satan's fallacy in arguing from angelic titles.

471. *unreal* formless (Chaos has matter but not form).

475. *uncouth* strange and desolate (*OED* 2b, 5).

477. **unoriginal* having no origin, uncreated (*OED* 1, sole instance in this sense).

477–8. *Chaos . . . opposed* Critics object that Chaos and Night did not oppose Satan, and 'Chaos even helped him' (Fowler). But Chaos the place was a formidable obstacle (ii 910–50).

480. *Protesting* both 'appealing to' (*OED* 6) and 'protesting against'. Satan equivocates as to whether *Fate* was for him or against him.

481–2. *fame . . . foretold* See i 651–6, ii 345–76.

487. *an apple* Satan alone speaks of 'apples' in *PL.* Cp. ix 585. The poem's good characters speak of 'fruit', which relates actions to consequences. Cp. i 1, iii 67, etc.

496–7. *that . . . enmity* This is the nearest Satan ever comes to naming himself to the other devils. The Hebrew word translated as 'enmity' at Gen. 3. 15 is not etymologically related to 'Satan', but see x 1030–34 and note.

503. *bliss* Satan's last word in the poem is answered with a rhyming *hiss* (508, 518).

511–14. *His visage . . . prone* Cp. the serpent metamorphoses in Ovid, *Met.* iv 572–603 (alluded to at ix 506) and Dante, *Inf.* xxiv and xxv.

513. *supplanted* tripped up (*OED* 1) and made to fall from power (*OED* 2). Adam and Eve were often said to have been 'supplanted' by Satan. See Ricks, *Milton's Grand Style,* 64 and cp. *PR* iv 607*n*.

515. *Reluctant* struggling, writhing.

517. *doom* judgement (the curse of x 175–81).

521. *riot* rebellion.

523. *complicated* *composite (*OED* 4), tangled (*OED* 2).

524. *amphisbaena* Greek 'going both ways': a mythical snake with a head at either end of its body (Lucan, *Pharsalia* ix 719).

525. *Cerastes* a snake with four horns. The *hydrus* and *ellops* are mythical water snakes.

526. *dipsas* a mythical snake whose bite caused raging thirst. Lucan describes how one of Cato's soldiers, bitten while crossing the Libyan desert, searched for water deep in the sand, drank sea-water ('but there was not enough'), and finally opened his veins so as to drink blood (*Pharsalia* ix 737–60). Cp. the devils' *scalding thirst* (556).

526–7. *soil . . . Gorgon* When Perseus flew over Libya, drops of blood falling from Medusa's severed head became snakes. Lucan and Ovid cite the story to explain why snakes are so abundant in Libya (*Pharsalia* ix 620–732, *Met.* iv 617–20).

528. *Ophiusa* Greek 'full of snakes'. The name was anciently given to several islands.

529. *dragon* Cp. Rev. 12. 9. In Joost van den Vondel's *Lucifer* (1654), Lucifer becomes a dragon at the moment of his expulsion from Heaven (Kirkconnell 414). Cp. also Phineas Fletcher, *The Purple Island* (1633) vii 10–11.

529–31. *the sun . . . Python* The monstrous serpent *Python*, slain by Apollo, was born of the *slime* deposited by Deucalion's flood (Ovid, *Met.* i 438–40). The *Pythian vale* is Delphi.

535. *in station* at their posts.

 in just array on parade.

536. *Sublime* *exalted in feeling, elated (*OED* 3b).

540. *sympathy* both 'compassion' and 'corresponding condition'.

546. *exploding *OED*'s earliest participial instance. The sense includes 'hoot (an actor) off the stage', 'reject with scorn', 'expose the hollowness of' and 'drive out air' (*OED* 1, 2, 3, 4).

550. *penance* punishment (*OED* 5).

 fair fruit] *Ed I*; fruit *Ed II*.

560. *Megaera* one of three snaky-haired Furies, goddesses and avengers of crime. Cp. ii 596.

562. *bituminous lake* the Dead Sea, identified as the site of *Sodom* on the authority of II Esdras 5. 7. Josephus claimed that fruit growing near the Dead Sea contained Sodom's ashes and would dissolve into ashes when plucked (*De Bellis* IV viii 4). M. alludes to this story in *Eikonoklastes*, where he compares King Charles's rhetoric to 'the Apples of *Asphaltis*' that look appealing to the eye, 'but touch them, and they turne into Cinders' (*YP* 3.

552). Cp. Deut. 32. 32: 'their vine is of the vine of Sodom . . . Their wine is the poison of dragons, / And the cruel venom of asps'.

565. *gust* relish.

568. *drugged* *nauseated (*OED* 2b).

572. *triúmphed* triumphed over.

once both 'as soon as' (man fell) and 'a single time' (in contrast to the devils' *oft*-repeated error).

575. *some say* No source has been found for M.'s story of an annual metamorphosis.

579. *purchase* both 'plunder' (*OED* 8) and 'annual return or rent from land' (*OED* 10), 'alluding to the *annual* punishment of the devils' (Fowler). See lines 575–6.

581. *Ophion with Eurynome* the first king and queen of Olympus, overthrown by *Saturn* and *Ops* (Cronus and Rhea), who were ousted in their turn by *Jove* (Apollonius Rhodius, *Argonautica* i 503–9). *Ophion* means 'serpent' and *Eurynome* means 'wide-ruling' (though *wide-Encroaching* suggests 'wide of the law'). Claudian describes Ophion as a serpent and includes him among the Giants who fought against Jove (*De Rapt. Pros.* iii 332–56). The association with Satan was traditional.

584. *Dictaean* Zeus was raised in Crete, either on Mount Dicte or in the Dictaean cave in Mount Ida (see i 515).

587. *actual* 'Actual sin' is a theological term for sin that is freely chosen (as opposed to 'original sin', which is inherited).

in body physically present (Sin's body) and habitually rooted (in all other bodies).

590. *pale horse* Cp. Rev. 6. 8: 'behold a pale horse: and his name that sat on him was Death, and Hell followed with him'.

593. *travail* labour and travel.

595. *Unnamed* Sin had named Death at ii 787, but the name has hitherto been an empty sound in Paradise. See iv 427*n*.

599. *ravin* prey.

601. *unhidebound OED's sole instance. A 'hidebound' animal is one that is so emaciated as to have the 'skin clinging closely to the back and ribs' (*OED* 1). Death is so ravenous that he can never fill his skin.

611. *unimmortal The neologism implies that mortality is not a natural state but a privation.

616–17. *dogs . . . havoc* Cp. Shakespeare, *Julius Caesar* III i 273: 'Cry "Havoc" and let slip the dogs of war'. 'Havoc' was the signal permitting a victorious army to pillage.

624. *conniving* shutting one's eyes to a thing that one dislikes but cannot help (*OED* 'connive' 1).

627. *quitted all* handed everything over (*OED* 'quit' 5b). Cp. iii 307, where

God praises the Son for having 'quitted (i.e. "renounced", "redeemed", "remitted") all'.

630. *draff* dregs.

633. *at one sling* Cp. I Sam. 25. 29: 'The souls of thine enemies, them shall he sling out, as out of the middle of a sling'.

638. *heav'n and earth renewed* II Pet. 3. 7–13.

640. *precedes* both 'takes precedence' and 'goes before'.

642. *hallelujah, as the sound of seas* Rev. 19. 6.

644. *Righteous are thy decrees* Rev. 16. 7.

645. *extenuate* disparage, diminish in honour (*OED* 5).

651. *sorted* suited.

656. *blank* white, pale (*OED* 1).

658. *aspécts* astrological positions (*OED* 4).

sextile, square, trine, and *opposite* are positions of 60, 90, 120, and 180 degrees respectively.

661. *synod* astrological conjunction.

fixed fixed stars.

664. *tempestuous* productive of storms. Cp. i 305–6.

668–78. *Some say . . . seasons* M. imagines that the earth's equator had coincided with the ecliptic, producing the prelapsarian 'eternal spring'. He gives both a heliocentric and a geocentric explanation to account for the loss of this pristine state. Copernican astronomers assume that the earth's axis is now tilted (668–71); Ptolemaic astronomers assume that the plane of the sun's orbit is tilted (671–8). M. typically declines to choose between the two systems.

671. *centric globe* the earth (pivoted on its centre).

672. *equinoctial road* the earth's equator.

673. *Like distant breadth* a like declination (23.5°).

673–7. *Taurus . . . Capricorn* The sun had been in Aries. Now it travels through the zodiac. In spring and summer, it passes through *Taurus* (which includes the Pleiades or *sev'n / Atlantic Sisters*), Gemini (*the Spartan Twins*), and Cancer (*the Tropic Crab*), where it reaches the summer solstice. In late summer and autumn, it moves through *Leo*, Virgo (*the Virgin*), Libra (*the Scales*), eventually reaching the winter solstice in *Capricorn*.

675. *amain* at full speed.

679. *vernant* flourishing in spring.

682. **unbenighted* not overtaken by the darkness of night.

686. *Estoliland* northern Labrador.

687. *Magellan* the straits at the tip of South America.

688. **Thyestean banquet* Thyestes seduced the wife of his brother Atreus. In revenge, Atreus killed one of Thyestes' sons and served him to Thyestes as food. The sun turned from the banquet in horror (Seneca, *Thyestes* 776–8).

693. *sideral blast* malign stellar influence.

694. *exhalation* vapour productive of meteors (see i 710–12).

695. *pestilent* See ix 180n for the tradition that mists carried the plague.

696. *Norumbega* northern New England and maritime Canada.

  Samoed north-eastern Siberia.

697. *brazen dungeon* the cave in which Aeolus imprisoned the winds (Virgil, *Aen.* i 50–59).

698. *flaw* sudden squall.

699–700. *Boreas, Caecias, Argestes,* and *Thrascias* are winds from the N, NW and NE; opposing them are *Notus* (S) and *Afer* (SW), while blowing across (*thwart*) them are *Eurus* (ESE), *Zephyr* (W), *Sirocco* (SE) and *Libecchio* (SW).

703. *Serraliona* Sierra Leone (on the west coast of Africa).

704. *levant . . . ponent* east and west (lit. 'rising' and 'setting'). In the Mediterranean, a 'levant' (or 'levanter') was a strong easterly wind from the Levant.

707–8. *Discord . . . Daughter of Sin* The classical Discordia (Eris) was Death's sister. She was depicted with serpents wreathed about her head.

716. *Already in part* Adam has not yet witnessed the *miseries* of lines 650–715. He first sees animals pursue each other at xi 185–90. Sin and Death have not yet entered our universe, and Satan has not yet left it. Satan is still in Paradise, eavesdropping, at the end of book x. See above, 342–5n.

718. *troubled sea* Cp. Isa. 57. 20: 'The wicked are like the troubled sea, when it cannot rest, whose waters cast up mire and dirt'. Cp. i 304–6, iv 19.

729. *propagated* handed down from one generation to another (*OED* 1d), extended (*OED* 4), increased and multiplied (*OED* 2).

738. *own* own curses.

  bide upon stick to (*OED* 2b).

739. *redound* flow back (*OED* 4) and cast opprobrium (*OED* 8b).

740. *light* both 'alight' and 'not heavy'. *Light / heavy* is a paradox. According to Aristotelian science (still current in M.'s day), heavy objects lost their heaviness, and their tendency to move, once they reached their *natural centre*, the centre of the earth. The curses of Adam's descendants should therefore become light once they reach Adam. Instead, Adam will continue to feel them as *heavy*.

743. *Did I request . . . from my clay* Cp. Isa. 45. 9: 'Woe unto him that striveth with his Maker! Let the potsherd strive with the potsherds of the earth. Shall the clay say unto him that fashioneth it, What makest thou?'

748. *equal* equitable, just.

758. *Thou* Adam himself. In lines 743–55 *thou* referred to God.

760–64. *what if . . . proud excuse* Cp. Isa. 45. 10: 'Woe unto him that saith unto his father, What begettest thou?'

764. *election* choice.

778. *mother's lap* Cp. Spenser, *FQ* V vii 9: 'mother Earths deare lap'. Adam's desire is more poignant for the fact that earth is his only mother.

782–814. *Yet . . . perpetuity* Adam considers three possibilities: (1) the soul will survive the body (782–89), (2) body and soul will both die (789–808), (3) body and soul will survive in *endless misery* (808–16). Editors often confuse (2) with M.'s 'mortalist heresy', which held that body and soul died together, and were resurrected together on the last day (*CD* i 13). Adam intuits the first part of this doctrine, but fails to imagine resurrection or damnation. Even when he speaks of *endless misery* (810), it is misery in Paradise that daunts him. Adam has forgotten (or blocks out) Raphael's warning about 'eternal misery' in Hell (vi 904).

783. *all I* all of me.

795. *be it* even if it is.

804–8. *that . . . sphere* Adam employs a scholastic argument, which held that the action of any agent is limited by the recipient's powers to be acted upon. So while God's *anger* might be *infinite*, man (as a *finite* creature) cannot suffer infinitely.

814. *revolution* recurrence.

815–16. *Death and I / Am* Adam's ungrammatical *Am* reflects his realization that he and death are *incorporate*, 'united in one body' (*OED* 1).

827. *they then*] *Ed II*; they *Ed I*.

831. *conviction* both 'proof of guilt' and *"the condition of being convinced of sin' (*OED* 8). See above, 84*n*.

832. *me, me only* Adam echoes the Son's offer to die for man: 'Behold me then, me for him' (iii 236). See also x 936.

834. *So might the wrath* 'would that the wrath were so confined'.

836. *world* universe.

842–4. *abyss . . . plunged* Cp. Satan's descent into the 'lower deep' of an internal Hell (iv 75–9).

847. *black air* Cp. Satan as a pestilent 'black mist' (ix 180).

853. *denounced* proclaimed as a threat or warning.

860–62. *O woods . . . other song* Adam recalls the morning hymn of v 153–208 (see esp. 203–4).

867. *thou serpent* Clement of Alexandria and Eusebius had claimed that 'Eve' aspirated means 'serpent'. See D. C. Allen, *MLN* 74, 1959, 681–3. Elsewhere in *PL* M. follows a rival tradition which took 'Eve' to mean 'life'. See iv 474–5*n*, v 385–7*n*, xi 159–61*n*. Adam now invents a bad pun and a misogynistic tradition. Cp. ix 1067, where Adam puns on 'Eve' and 'evil'. See further, Leonard 229–30.

869. *wants* is missing.

872. *pretended* held in front as a cover (*OED* 1), with overtones of 'feigned'.

878–9. *him . . . overreach* overconfidently thinking that you could outwit him.

884–5. *rib / Crookèd by nature* a commonplace of misogynistic diatribes. Cp. Joseph Swetnam, *The Araignment of Lewd, idle . . . women* (1615): 'a ribbe is a crooked thing . . . and women are crooked by nature' (1).

886. *siníster* left side (with evil overtones). Cp. Sin's birth from 'the left side' of Satan's head (ii 755).

887. *supernumerary* Calvin and other commentators believed that Adam had been created with an extra rib for the purpose of forming Eve.

888–95. *O why . . . Mankind* echoing the misogyny of Euripides' Hippolytus (*Hippolytus* 616–19) and Ariosto's Rodomonte (*Orl. Fur.* xxvii 120).

890. *Spirits masculine* M. in his own voice has told us that Spirits assume 'either sex . . . or both' (i 424).

891. *defect / Of nature* Aristotle had called the female a defective male.

898. *strait* close, intimate, hard-pressing, tightly-drawn (used of bonds and embraces, *OED* 2). The *Ed I* and *Ed II* spelling 'straight' plays on 'honest, free from crookedness' (*OED* 6a) to contrast honest men with *Crooked* women (885).

conjunction union, including 'marriage', 'sexual union' (*OED* 2a, 2b).

910–13. *tears . . . plaint* Cp. Mary Magdalene washing Jesus's feet with her hair and tears (Luke 7. 38). Cp. v 130–31.

917. *deceived* perhaps including a pun on 'dis-Eved'. Cp. i 35, ix 904, and *PR* i 52 ('Eve / Lost Paradise deceived'). Adam has just wrenched 'Eve' from 'life' to 'serpent' (x 867).

917–18. Eve acts like a *suppliant* in Greek epic or tragedy, clasping Adam's *knees* in a plea for protection.

926. *doom* the judgement at x 175–81. It is fitting that Eve bring this up, since the *enmity* was to be 'between the *woman* and the serpent' (Fowler). Eve does not yet recognize her *foe*, but her words open the way for Adam's recognition in line 1034.

931. *God . . . and thee* Cp. iv 299: 'He for God only, she for God in him'.

936. *Me me only* Eve's cry combines Adam's guilt ('On me, me only', x 832) with the Son's love ('Behold me then, me for him', iii 236). Cp. Abigail's plea for her husband: 'Upon me, my lord, upon me let this iniquity be' (I Sam. 25. 24). Cp. also the plea of Nisus for Euryalus (Virgil, *Aen.* ix 427).

965. *derived* passed on by descent.

969. *event* outcome.

976. *extremes* extremities, hardships.

978. *As in our evils* considering our afflictions.

979. *descent* descendants.

perplex torment.

987. *prevent* forestall, cut off in advance.

989–90. *Childless . . . two* So the first five editions. Most subsequent editions move *So Death* back to the previous line. Fowler argues that the metrical irregularity may 'be intended to mime first the deficiency of childlessness (line 989 defective), then the glut denied to Death (line 990 hypermetrical)'.

990. *deceived* cheated out of.

991. *forced* including 'fattened, crammed with food' (*OED* v³ 2).

993. *Conversing* cohabiting, with overtones of 'have sexual intercourse' (*OED* 2b) even though this is what Eve proposes to abstain from.

996. *the present object* Eve herself.

1000. *make short* lose no time.

1009. *dyed*] 'di'd' *Ed I, Ed II*, with an obvious pun.

1027. *cóntumácy* wilful disobedience, contempt of a court of law.

1028. *make death in us live* M.'s voice behind Adam is referring to eternal damnation, *mors aeterna*. Cp. 'living death' (788).

1030–34. *calling . . . Satan* Recovering his insight of ix 904–6 and ix 1172–3, Adam at last names Eve's tempter. He owes his recognition partly to Eve, who at x 925–7 reminded him of their 'one enmity / Against a foe by doom express assigned us, / That cruel serpent'. Adam now matches *Foe* with *Satan* and with the curse of enmity on the serpent. Justin Martyr and Irenaeus had interpreted *Satan* as *Sata-nas*, 'apostate serpent'. See Leonard (231) and L. W. Barnard, *Justin Martyr: his Life and Thought* (1967), 108.

1045. *Reluctance* resistance, struggling against (*OED* 1).

1051–2. *Pains . . . joy* Adam unwittingly prophesies the Second Coming. Cp. Christ's metaphor at John 16. 20–21: 'ye shall be sorrowful, but your sorrow shall be turned into joy. A woman when she is in travail hath sorrow, because her hour is come: but as soon as she is delivered of the child, she remembereth no more the anguish, for joy that a man is born into the world'.

1053. *Fruit of thy womb* another unwitting allusion to the Son. Cp. Luke 1. 42.

1058. **unbesought*.

1061. *to pity incline* Cp. iii 402, 405.

1066. *shattering* scattering, causing to fall.

1068. *shroud* shelter.

   cherish keep warm (*OED* 6).

1069. *this diurnal star* the sun. The thought that our sun is a star now implies man's insignificance. Cp. 'other suns' (viii 148), where the emphasis is on God's glory.

1071. *sere* dry.

   foment heat, with a play on Latin *fomes*, 'kindling wood'.

1073. *attrite* ground down by friction.

1075. *Tine* ignite.

thwart slanting.

1078. *supply* serve as a substitute for.

1081–2. *of grace / Beseeching him* both 'asking him for grace' and 'beseeching him, having been given the grace to do so'.

1086–1104. *to the place . . . meek* The repetition of 1086–92 in 1098–1104 is a Homeric formula (cp. *Il.* ix 122–57, 264–99), but M. does not repeat 1093–6 and so refrains from presuming that God will *relent and turn from his displeasure.* Adam and Eve have yet to be expelled from Paradise.

1103. *Frequenting* filling.

BOOK XI

1. *stood* Adam and Eve were 'prostrate' at x 1099, but now their *port* is not of *mean suitors* (9). They had stood to pray at iv 720.

2. *mercy-seat* the golden covering of the ark of the Covenant (Exod. 25. 17–22) – a type of divine intercession.

3. *Prevenient grace* grace that is antecedent to human will (theological term).

4. *stony . . . flesh* Cp. Ezek. 11. 19: 'I will take the stony heart out of their flesh, and will give them a heart of flesh'.

6. *Unutterable . . . prayer* Cp. Rom. 8. 26: 'we know not what we should pray for as we ought: but the Spirit itself maketh intercession for us with groanings which cannot be uttered'.

8–9. *port . . . important* Both words are from Latin *portare*, 'to carry'.

12. *Deucalion* the Greek Noah. He and his wife *Pyrrha* survived a universal flood by building an ark. They then prayed to *Themis*, goddess of justice, who told them to restore mankind by throwing stones behind them. The stones became men and women. Notice *stony* and *made new flesh* (4).

15. *envious* malicious, spiteful (*OED* 2).

17. **Dimensionless* without physical extension (*OED* 1a).

18. *incense* Rev. 8. 3.

28. *manuring* cultivating (*OED* 2).

33–4. *advocate / And propitiation* Cp. I John 2. 1: 'We have an advocate with the Father, Jesus Christ the righteous: And he is the propitiation for our sins'.

35. *ingraft* Rom. 11. 16–24. Cp. iii 293*n.*

44. *Made . . . one* Cp. John 17. 22–3: 'that they may be one, even as we are one: I in them, and thou in me'.

52. *purge him off* Cp. ii 141, where Belial predicts that Heaven would 'purge off the baser fire' of Hell (ii 141).

53. *distemper* imbalance of the four humours (*OED* 3) resulting in death and decay.

55. *dissolution* death, with overtones of 'dissolute living'.

59. *fondly* foolishly.

65. *renovation* renewal of the body at the resurrection (*OED* 1b).

67. *synod* assembly.

70. *peccant* sinning.

74. *trumpet . . . Oreb* A trumpet sounded on Mount Horeb when God delivered the Ten Commandments (Exod. 19. 19).

76. *general doom* the Last Judgement. See Matt. 24. 31, I Thess. 4. 16 and I Cor. 15. 52: 'the trumpet shall sound, and the dead shall be raised incorruptible'.

78. **amarantine* See iii 352n.

86. *defended* forbidden (*OED* 3).

91. *motions* stirrings of the soul (*OED* 9b). Cp. *PR* i 290, *SA* 1382.

93. *Self-left* if left to itself.

93–8. *Lest . . . taken* Cp. Gen. 3. 22–3: 'And now, lest he put forth his hand, and take also of the tree of life, and eat, and live for ever: therefore the Lord God sent him forth from the garden of Eden, to till the ground from whence he was taken'. M.'s addition *dream at least to live* implies that Adam could not have cheated God.

102. *Or . . . or* either . . . or.

in behalf of man Empson[2] (165) cites the phrase as evidence of Satan's altruism, but it might mean 'with regard to man' (*OED* 'behalf' 1d) or 'in man's name' (*OED* 2a) rather than 'for man's benefit' (*OED* 2b).

102–3. *invade / Vacant possession* encroach on untenanted property.

105. *remorse* pity, compassion (*OED* 3a).

106. *denounce* announce.

108. *faint* lose heart.

111. *excess* violation of law (*OED* 4), intemperance in eating (*OED* 5b).

126. **Archangelic*.

128–30. *four faces . . . eyes more numerous* Ezek. 1. 18.

129. *double Janus* Janus, the Roman god of gateways, had two faces. Janus Quadrifrons had four faces corresponding to the four seasons and four quarters of the earth.

131. *Argus* a hundred-eyed giant. Juno set him to watch Io, whom Jove had disguised as a heifer. Mercury (*Hermes*) killed him after charming him to sleep with his *pipe* and sleep-inducing wand (*opiate rod*). See Ovid, *Met.* i 568–779.

135. *Leucothea* Roman goddess of the dawn. See *A Masque* 875n.

144. *prevalent* potent, influential.

157–8. *Assures . . . past* echoing the last words of Agag, King of the Amalekites, spoken just before Samuel cut him to pieces: 'surely the bitterness of death is past' (I Sam. 15. 32). Like Agag, Adam has 'spoken too soon' (Fowler), but his hope that Eve's *seed* will bring eternal life is not groundless.

158. *hail to thee* anticipating 'the holy salutation used / Long after to blest Mary, second Eve' (v 386–7).

159–61. *Eve . . . all things live* Cp. Gen. 3. 20: 'And Adam called his wife's name Eve; because she was the mother of all living'. 'Eve' (Hebrew *Chava*) is cognate with *chai*, 'life'. The biblical Eve is not so named until after the Fall. Before then she was 'the woman'. M.'s Adam had named Eve at iv 481. He now affirms that the name was *rightly* given. See iv 474–5n, v 385–7n.

185. *bird of Jove, stooped* the eagle, having swooped.

   tow'r lofty flight.

187. *beast . . . woods* lion.

188. *brace* pair.

196. *too secure* overconfident.

205. *orient* both 'bright' and 'eastern'. The latter sense is paradoxical, for Michael's squadron appears *in yon western cloud*. Cp. Raphael appearing as 'another morn' in the east of Paradise (v 310), and Satan's army arising as a 'fiery region' on Heaven's northern horizon (vi 79–82).

208. *by this* by this time.

209. *lighted* both 'alighted' and 'shone' (*OED* v² 1).

210. *made halt* came to a halt (military term).

214. *Mahanaim* Hebrew 'armies', 'camps' (hence *pavilioned*). Jacob gave the name to the place where he saw an army of angels (Gen. 32. 1–2).

216–20. *flaming . . . unproclaimed* The *Syrian king* besieged the city of *Dothan* in an attempt to capture Elisha (*One man*). When Elisha's servant expressed fear at the Syrian 'horses and chariots', Elisha prayed to God, asking him to open the servant's eyes 'that he may see. And the Lord opened the eyes of the young man; and he saw: and, behold, the mountain was full of horses and chariots of fire' (II Kings 6. 17).

221. *stand* station (military term).

   powers army.

227. *determine* make an end.

237. *thou retire* Contrast v 383 where Eve 'Stood to entertain her guest from Heaven'; but even before the Fall Eve 'sat retired' while Adam and Raphael conversed (viii 41).

240. *Clad to meet man* Raphael had been covered by his wings, but had not worn clothes (v 277–85).

   lucid bright.

242. *Meliboean* The Thessalian town of Meliboea was famous in antiquity for its purple dye.

243. *Sarra* Tyre, also famous for its dye (*grain*).

244. *Iris . . . woof* Cp. the Attendant Spirit's 'sky–robes, spun out of Iris' woof' (*A Masque* 83).

247. *zodiac* belt of constellations.

249. *state* stateliness of bearing.

254. *Defeated of* cheated of (*OED* 7).

  his seizure what he had seized.

256–7. *one . . . cover* Cp. I Peter 4. 8: 'for charity shall cover the multitude of sins'.

264. *gripe* spasm or pang of grief (*OED* sb¹ 2a).

267. *Discovered* revealed.

  retire withdrawal.

270. *native soil* Unlike Adam, Eve was created in Paradise.

272. *respite* delay, extension (*OED* 1).

277. *gave ye names* Eve's naming of the flowers, like Adam's naming of the animals, implies special knowledge (see viii 352–3n). M. here departs from traditional interpretations of Gen. 2. 19, where Adam alone gives names.

283. *to* compared with.

293. *by this* by this time.

  damp stupefied condition (*OED* 4).

298. *Prince among princes* Cp. Dan. 10. 13: 'Michael, one of the chief princes'.

309. *can* both 'knows' (*OED* 1) and 'can perform'.

316. *from . . . hid* Cp. Cain's response to his curse: 'from thy face shall I be hid; and I shall be a fugitive and a vagabond in the earth' (Gen. 4. 14).

323. *grateful* both 'pleasing' and 'expressing gratitude'. Patriarchs built altars where God had spoken to them. See e.g. Gen. 12. 7.

331. *promised race* the human race, whose 'promised Seed' will bruise Satan's head (xi 155, xii 623).

336. *Not this rock only* Cp. Jesus's warning to the woman of Samaria not to localize worship 'in this mountain' (John 4. 21).

338. *Fomented* nurtured, cherished.

  virtual potent.

357. *To show . . . future days* Prophetic visions are frequent in epic. See e.g. Virgil, *Aen.* vi 754–854 (Aeneas's vision of Rome), Ariosto, *Orl. Fur.* xiii 53–74 (Bradamante's vision of the House of Este), and Spenser, *FQ* III iii 29–49 (Britomart's vision of Britain). An angelic subordinate of Michael relates future events to Daniel in Dan. 10–12.

367. *drenched* overwhelmed (*OED* 6). A 'drench' was a soporific potion. Cp. ii 73.

373. **chast'ning OED*'s earliest participial sense.

374. *obvious* exposed, vulnerable (*OED* 2).

377. *visions . . . hill* Cp. Ezek. 40. 2: 'In the visions of God brought he me into the land of Israel, and set me upon a very high mountain'.

379. *ken* view.

380. *the amplest*] *Ed II*; amplest *Ed I*.

381–4. *that hill . . . glory* When Satan tempted Christ he took 'him up into an exceeding high mountain' (Matt. 4. 8). See also Luke 4. 5 and *PR* iii 251ff.

388. *Cambalu* capital of Cathay (north China). M. imagines China and Cathay to be distinct, but the *Cathayan khan* Kubilai had ruled all China from Cambalu (Beijing).

389. *Temir* Timur (Tamburlaine), a descendant of Genghis Khan. His capital *Samarkand* was near the *Oxus* river in modern Uzbekistan.

390. *Paquin* Peking (Beijing).

Sinaean Chinese.

391. *Agra and Lahore* Mogul capitals in northern India and the Punjab (Pakistan).

Great Mogul the Mogul emperor.

392. *golden Chersonese* a vaguely defined area east of India, fabled for its wealth. See *PR* iv 74 and note.

393. *Ecbatan* Ecbatana, capital of Media and a summer residence of the Persian kings. Isfahan (*Hispahan*) replaced Kazvin as the Persian capital in the sixteenth century (hence *since*).

395. *Bizance* Byzantium (Constantinople, Istanbul), capital of the Ottoman Empire after falling to the Turks in 1453.

396. *Turkéstan-born* The Ottoman Turks traced their tribal origins to Turkestan, in central Asia between Mongolia and the Caspian.

397. *Negus* title of the Abyssinian emperors.

398. *Ercoco* Arkiko, a Red Sea port in modern Ethiopia.

399. *Mombaza* Mombasa, in Kenya.

Quiloa Kilwa, in Tanzania.

Melind Malindi, in Kenya. All Muslim colonies on the east African coast.

400. *Sofala* a port in Mozambique, sometimes identified with the biblical *Ophir*, the source of Solomon's gold.

402. *Niger* a river in west Africa.

Atlas the Atlas Mountains in Morocco.

403. *Almansor* Various Muslim rulers were called 'Al-Mansur' ('the victorious'). Here it may be a title (cp. *Khan, Ksar, Great Mogul, Negus*) or a name (cp. *Motezume, Atabalipa*). M. may be thinking of Abu'Amir al Ma-Ma'afiri, Caliph of Cordova (r. 976–1002), known to European writers as 'Almanzor', or Abu Yusuf Ya'qub al-Mansur (r. 1184–99). Both ruled north Africa and much of Spain.

Fez in Morocco.

Sus Tunis.

404. *Tremisen* Tlemcen, part of Algeria.

406. *in spirit* because of the earth's curvature.

407. *Motezume* Montezuma II, the last Aztec ruler. His capital Tenochtitlán (*Mexico*) fell to Cortez in 1520.

409. *Atabalipa* Atahuallpa, the last Inca ruler, murdered in 1533 by Pizarro, who sacked his capital Cuzco (in Peru).

410. *Geryon's sons* the Spanish. Geryon was a mythical three-headed monster (killed by Hercules) who inhabited an island off the Spanish coast. Spenser made him an allegory of the 'huge powre and great oppression' of Spain (*FQ* V x 9).

411. *El Dorado* a mythical city in the New World. Ralegh, who tried to find it in 1595, wrote in *The Discoverie of Guiana*: 'I have beene assured by such of the Spanyardes as have seen *Manoa* the emperiall Citie of *Guiana*, which the *Spanyardes* call *el Dorado*, that for the greatness, for the riches, and for the excellent seat, it farre exceedeth any of the world' (10).

412. *the film removed* So Athena removes the mist from Diomedes' eyes (Homer, *Il.* v 127), Venus clears the eyes of Aeneas (Virgil, *Aen.* ii 604), and Michael clears those of Goffredo (Tasso, *Gerus. Lib.* xviii 92f.).

414. *euphrasy and rue* herbs thought to sharpen the eyesight. Fowler notes that Greek *euphrasia* means 'cheerfulness' and *rue* means 'sorrow', so the two names pun on the 'joy' and 'pious sorrow' (xi 361-2) of Adam's visions.

416. *Well of Life* Cp. Ps. 36. 9: 'With thee is the fountain of life: in thy light shall we see light'.

426. *excepted* forbidden.

427. *that sin*] Ed I; that *Ed II. Sinned thy sin* is biblical idiom (Exod. 32. 30, John 5. 16).

429-60. See Gen. 4 for the story of Cain and Abel. Adam never hears these names in book xi, where all his visions are of unnamed persons. Michael speaks names only after recounting the Confusion of tongues (see xii 140*n*).

430. *tilth* cultivated land.

432. *landmark* boundary marker.

436. **Unculled* picked at random (unlike Abel's 'choicest' offering, 438).

441. *fire from heav'n* Acceptable sacrifices were often consumed by 'fire from heaven' (Lev. 9. 24, I Kings 18. 38, etc.). God 'had respect unto Abel and his offering' (Gen. 4. 4).

442. *nimble glance* quick flash.

grateful pleasing.

443. *sincere* including 'unmixed, uncontaminated' (*OED* 2).

455. *Out of thy loins* As progenitor of all mankind, Adam need not realize that Cain and Abel will be his own sons.

457. *fact* evil deed, crime.

469. *his grim cave* Cp. the 'deep cave' leading to Virgil's underworld (*Aen.* vi 237). Within the cave dwell Grief, Cares, Diseases, Age, Death and other horrors (*Aen.* vi 273f.).

dismal including 'malign, fatal' (*OED* 2).

476. *inabstinence *OED* cites 'abstinence' from 1382.

477–90. Adam's vision of future diseases has no one biblical source.

479. *lazar-house* a hospital for those suffering leprosy or other infectious diseases, named for Lazarus (Luke 16. 20).

485–7. *Demoniac . . . pestilence* Added in *Ed II*. It is odd that *Ed I* should make no mention of *wide-wasting pestilence*. The Great Plague had just killed 60,000 Londoners.

486. *moon-struck madness* lunacy.

487. *Marasmus* wasting away of the body.

496. *not of woman born* Cp. Shakespeare, *Macbeth* IV i 80, V viii 13.

497. *best of man* manliness, courage. Cp. Shakespeare, *Macbeth* V viii 18. When Macduff tells Macbeth that he was not born of woman, Macbeth replies that the news has 'cowed my better part of man'.

502. *Better . . . unborn* a commonplace in classical literature. See e.g., Sophocles, *Oedipus at Colonus* 1224–6, Theognis 425, and Seneca, *Ad Marciam: De Consolatione* xxii 3.

512–14. *Retaining . . . Maker's image* Cp. *CD* i 12: 'it cannot be denied that some traces of the divine image still remain in us' (trans. Carey, *YP* 6. 396).

516. *vilified* lessened in worth, made morally vile (*OED* 1, 1b).

519. *Inductive mainly to* strongly inducing (a repetition of).

528. *passages* deaths (*OED* 2b).

531. *Not too much* This maxim (*rule*) was carved in Apollo's temple at Delphi alongside the inscription 'Know thyself' (Plato, *Protagoras* 343B).

535–7. *ripe . . . mature* The comparison of peaceful death to the dropping of *ripe fruit* goes back to Cicero, *De Senectute* (19). Cyriack Skinner (who is now known to have written the anonymous *Life*) reports that M. died 'with so little pain or Emotion, that the time of his expiring was not perceiv'd by those in the room' (Darbishire 33).

Harshly plucked recalls Eve's Fall: 'she plucked, she ate' (ix 781f.).

536. *mother's lap* Cp. x 778.

544. *damp* depression of spirits (*OED* 5), noxious vapour (*OED* 1).

551–2. So *Ed II*. *Ed I* has only the one line: 'Of rend'ring up. Michael to him replied'.

551. *attend* wait for.

553. *Nor love thy life, nor hate* a classical commonplace. Cp. Martial: 'neither dread thy last day, nor hope for it' (*Epigrams* X xlvii 13).

556–97. Adam's third vision is based on Gen. 4. 19–22 and Gen. 6. 2–4.

557–8. *tents . . . cattle* An indication (to us, not Adam) that these are Cain's descendants: 'such as dwell in tents, and . . . such as have cattle' (Gen. 4. 20). Adam learns the truth at xi 607–10.

560. *who* Jubal, Cain's descendant and 'the father of all such as handle the harp and organ' (Gen. 4. 21).

561. *volant* moving rapidly.

562. *Instinct* *impelled (*OED* 2).

proportions musical rhythms or harmonies (*OED* 10).

563. *fugue* From Latin *fuga*, 'flight'. Notice *Fled*. 'Jubal's race is the fugitive race of Cain' (Fowler). See Gen. 4. 12: 'a fugitive . . . shalt thou be'.

564. *one* Tubal-Cain, Jubal's brother and 'an instructor of every artificer in brass and iron' (Gen. 4. 22).

566. *casual* accidental (*OED* 1).

573. *Fusile* formed by melting or casting.

574. *a different sort* the descendants of Seth. They dwell on the *hither side* because Cain had migrated to 'the east of Eden' (Gen. 4. 16).

578–9. *works / Not hid* Josephus (*Antiquities* I ii 3) credits Seth's descendants with discovering astronomy. M. implicitly contrasts this lawful science with Tubal-Cain's metallurgy – a delving after 'treasures better hid' (i 688). At viii 166 even astronomy is full of 'matters hid'.

584. *amorous ditties* ominously recalling the 'amorous ditties' of i 449.

588. *ev'ning star* Venus, planet of love (cp. viii 519).

591. *Hymen* god of marriage. Cp. *L'Allegro* 125–9.

593. *interview* including 'glance' (*OED* 3b), 'mutual view of each other' (*OED* 2).

event outcome.

595. *symphonies* harmonies.

attached laid hold of (*OED* 3).

607–8. *tents / Of wickedness* Cp. Ps. 84. 10: 'I had rather be a doorkeeper in the house of my God, than to dwell in the tents of wickedness'. Jabal was the father of 'such as dwell in tents' (Gen. 4. 20). Cp. also v 890.

618. *completed* *accomplished, fully equipped (*OED* 3).

619. *appetence* appetite, desire.

620. *troll* not 'wag' (as most editors) but *'move (the tongue) volubly' (*OED* 4b). The gesture implies *lustful appetance*.

622. *sons of God* Cp. Gen. 6. 2: 'the sons of God saw the daughters of men that they were fair; and they took them wives of all which they chose'. M. here follows a patristic tradition identifying the sons of God with Seth's descendants. Elsewhere he adopts a rival tradition that saw the sons of God as fallen angels. See v 446–50 and *PR* ii 178–81 and notes.

624. *trains* wiles, snares (*OED* sb² 1, 2). Cp. *SA* 533.

625. *swim in joy* The expression was idiomatic (cp. 'swim in mirth' ix 1009). Michael's pun (not understood by Adam) resembles Satan's puns on artillery (vi 338–67) which the good angels had at first not understood.

632–3. *man's woe . . . woman* Like his earlier puns on 'Eve' (ix 1067, x 867), Adam's pun on 'woman' is based on a false etymology and is motivated by self-exculpation. It was also a cliché.

638–73. Adam's fourth vision is an elaboration of Gen. 6. 4. The details imitate scenes on the shields of Achilles (Homer, *Il.* xviii 478–540) and Aeneas (Virgil, *Aen.* viii 626–728). Homer begins with a wedding-feast but soon proceeds to an assembly, siege, cattle-raid and pitched battle.

641. *Concourse* hostile encounter (*OED* 1b).

642. *Giants* A hint to the reader (but not to Adam) that Adam is witnessing the consequences of the marriages of lines 585–97. Cp. Gen. 6. 4: 'There were giants in the earth in those days; and also after that, when the sons of God came in unto the daughters of men, and they bare children to them, the same became mighty men which were of old, men of renown'.

emprise martial prowess.

643. *Part . . . steed* Cp. the chivalric devils in Hell: 'Part curb their fiery steeds' (ii 531).

644. *ranged* drawn up in ranks.

651. *makes*] *Ed II*; tacks *Ed I*. The earlier reading may be an error or an aphetic of 'attacks'.

654. **ensanguined* blood-stained (*OED* 1).

656. *scale* scaling-ladder.

665. *one* Enoch, identified more clearly in lines 700 and 707.

669. *Exploded* mocked, drove away (*OED* 1).

670. *a cloud . . . snatched him* Gen. 5. 24 states that God 'took' Enoch, but never mentions a cloud. M. may have indirect access to the pseudepigraphical I Enoch where Enoch says 'clouds invited me' (14. 8).

678. *Ten thousandfold* One of Enoch's prophecies was that 'the Lord cometh with ten thousands of his saints, to execute judgment upon all' (Jude 14).

689–90. *might . . . virtue* 'Virtue' could mean 'physical strength', 'manliness' (*OED* 6, 7), and Latin *virtus* (from *vir*, 'man') meant 'valour'. Contrast 'true virtue' (790).

698. *renown on earth* The biblical giants were 'men of renown' (see above, 642*n*).

700. *seventh from thee* Jude 14 calls Enoch 'the seventh from Adam'. See also Gen. 5. 1–22.

706. *balmy* including alchemical 'balm' – a mythical substance thought to preserve life.

wingèd steeds Cp. the 'horses of fire' that translated Elijah (II Kings 2. 11). Ariosto places Enoch and Elijah together in the earthly Paradise where they dwell 'far beyond our pestilential air' (*Orl. Fur.* xxxiv 59). The *climes of bliss* are presumably Heaven, but at iii 461 M. had conjectured that 'Translated saints' might dwell on the moon.

707. *walk with God* Cp. Gen. 5. 24: 'Enoch walked with God: and he was not; for God took him'.

712–53. Adam's vision of the Flood is based on Gen. 6. 9 – 9. 17. Cp. also Jesus's account at Luke 17. 26–7: 'They did eat, they drank, they married wives, they were given in marriage, until the day that Noe entered into the ark, and the flood came'. The details of lines 738–53 follow Ovid's account of Deucalion's flood (*Met.* i 262–347).

715. *luxury* including 'lust'.

riot debauchery, wanton revel. Cp. i 498–500.

717. *passing fair* both 'pre-eminent beauty' and 'women passing by'.

719. *reverend sire* Noah (like the other biblical characters Adam sees in book xi, he is never named).

724–5. *to souls / In prison* So Christ 'preached unto the spirits in prison' (I Pet. 3. 19). Peter goes on to liken Christ to Noah (3. 20–21).

734. *and insect* M. places insects in the ark in accordance with Gen. 6. 20 ('every creeping thing'). Some commentators thought that insects grew from putrefaction and so need not have been saved by Noah.

740. *supply* assistance (*OED* 1).

741. *exhalation dusk* dark mist.

742. *amain* with main force.

749–50. *sea . . . without shore* Cp. Ovid, *Met.* i 292: 'For, all was Sea, nor had the Sea a shore' (trans. Sandys, 1632).

750–52. *palaces . . . stabled* Cp. Ovid, *Met.* i 299–300: 'Where Mountaine-loving Goats did lately graze, / The Sea-calfe now his ugly body layes' (trans. Sandys).

753. *bottom* boat.

754. *How didst thou grieve then, Adam* The direct address of a character is a Homeric formula. See ix 404–11 and note.

756–7. *flood, / Of tears* The conceit is common in Donne. See 'A Valediction of Weeping' and 'Holy Sonnet 5'.

765–6. *each . . . bear* Cp. Matt. 6. 34: 'Sufficient unto the day is the evil thereof'.

777. *Man is not whom* 'There is no one left'.

797–806. *The conquered . . . depraved* M. is probably alluding to the backsliding Englishmen who had betrayed the English Commonwealth in 1660. Cp. *SA* 268–77.

797. *enslaved *OED*'s earliest participial sense. The verb 'enslave' first appeared in English at the time of the Civil War (*OED*'s earliest instance is from 1643).

815. *denouncing* proclaiming.

821. *devote* doomed.

824. *cataracts* following the Junius-Tremellius version of Gen. 7. 11. Where

A.V. speaks of 'windows of heaven', Junius-Tremellius has *cataractae*, 'flood-gates'. Cp. ii 176.

831. *hornèd flood* Greek and Roman river-gods were depicted as bull-like because of their strength (Homer, *Il.* xxi 237, Virgil, *Georg.* 373, *Aen.* viii 77).

833. *the great river* Cp. Gen. 15. 18: 'the great river, the river Euphrates'. *gulf* the Persian Gulf.

834. *salt* barren (biblical diction). The description and location of dislodged Paradise suit the island of Hormuz, which M. had associated with Satan at ii 2. Paradise is obliterated by the Flood in Sylvester, *DWW* (1592–1608), *Eden* 185–92.

835. *orcs* sea-monsters. Cp. Satan as Leviathan (i 200–202).
sea-mews' clang harsh cries of gulls.

840. *hull* float adrift.

842. *north wind* Gen. 8. 1, Ovid, *Met.* i 328.

843. *Wrinkled . . . decayed* The sea's *face* is wrinkled as with age until it mirrors the sun's *clear* (unwrinkled) face. Fowler hears a pun on *glass* (844) as 'mirror' and 'drinking vessel'. Notice *thirst* and cp. the sun's supping with the ocean at v 426.

847. *tripping* running.

851. *some high mountain* 'the mountains of Ararat' (Gen. 8. 4). See above, 429–60*n* for M.'s avoidance of names in book xi.

854. **retreating OED*'s earliest participial instance.

864. *Grateful* expressing gratitude and pleasing.

866. *three listed colours* the primary colours (red, yellow, blue) arranged in bands.

867. *cov'nant* The rainbow signifies God's covenant with mankind never again to flood the earth (Gen. 9. 8–17).

870. *who*] *Ed II*; *that Ed I*.

880. *Distended* 'spread out' and so 'not contracted in anger' (God's *brow*).

881. *verge* limiting or bounding belt (*OED* 16).

886–7. *repenting . . . Grieved* Cp. Gen. 6. 6: 'And it repented the Lord that he had made man on the earth, and it grieved him at his heart'.

888–9. *violence . . . Corrupting* Cp. Gen. 6. 11: 'The earth also was corrupt before God, and the earth was filled with violence'.

899. *Seed time and harvest* Cp. Gen. 8. 22: 'neither will I again smite any more every thing living, as I have done. While the earth remaineth, seedtime and harvest'.

900. *till fire purge all things new* II Pet. 3. 6–7.

BOOK XII

1–5. *As . . . resumes* These lines were added in 1674 when book x of *Ed I* became books xi and xii of *Ed II*.

1. *baits* of travellers: stops at an inn (*OED* 7).

7. *second stock* Noah, but glancing too at Christ, in whom believers were 'ingrafted'. See iii 293*n*.

24. *one* Nimrod (identified obliquely in lines 30 and 36).

30–32. *Hunting . . . tyrannous* Cp. Gen. 10. 8–10: 'Nimrod . . . began to be a mighty one in the earth. He was a mighty hunter before the Lord. . . . And the beginning of his kingdom was Babel'. Nimrod was the archetypal tyrant. M. in *Eikonoklastes* (1649) calls him 'the first King' (*YP* 3. 598) and John Vicars in *God in the Mount* (1646) praises Cromwell for resisting 'the mighty Nimrods and hunting Furies of our time' (273). Even Salmasius admitted that kingship began with Nimrod, who won his power by 'arms' (see *YP* 4. 1027).

34. *Before the Lord* M. offers two possible interpretations of the phrase (Gen. 10. 9). Either Nimrod openly defied God (*in despite of Heav'n*) or he claimed divine right (*second sov'reignty*), like the Stuart kings.

36. *rebellion . . . name* An ancient (but false) etymology derived 'Nimrod' from Hebrew *marad*, 'to rebel'. M. often employs the paradox that kings are rebels. Cp. 'rebel king' (i 484) and 'rebel Thrones' (vi 199). In *TKM* M. calls Charles I a 'rebell to Law' (*YP* 3. 230).

38–62. See Gen. 11. 1–9 on the Tower of Babel. Genesis does not say that Nimrod built the tower, though it associates him with Babel (10. 10). Josephus first made Nimrod responsible for the Confusion (*Antiquities* I iv 2).

41. **gurge* whirlpool (coined from Latin *gurges*).

42. *mouth of Hell* Cp. Sylvester, *DWW* (1592–1608), *Babilon* (1598): 'there, for their firme foundations / They digg to hell' (154–5).

43. *cast* determine (*OED* 44), scheme (*OED* 43), and throw (anything fluid) into a particular shape (*OED* 49).

45. *get themselves a name* Cp. Gen. 11. 4: 'And they said, Go to, let us build us a city and a tower, whose top may reach unto heaven; and let us make us a name, lest we be scattered abroad upon the face of the whole earth'. *Name* means 'reputation' but also suggests the proper names 'Nimrod' and 'Babel', to which Michael alludes in lines 36 and 62. Cp. the devils who 'got them new names' (i 365).

52. *in derision* Cp. Ps. 2. 4: 'the Lord shall have them in derision'.

53. *various* *'calculated to cause difference' (*OED* 5b).

55. *jangling noise* Cp. Sylvester, *DWW* (1592–1608), *Babilon* (1598): 'Through all the worke . . . A jangling noyse' (190–91).

56–60. *gabble . . . hubbub*   The nonsense words suggest 'Babel', but M. avoids the obvious pun 'babble'. 'Hubbub' was a Gaelic interjection of contempt (*OED*), so the builders (like the metamorphosed devils) cast scorn 'on themselves from their own mouths' (x 546).

62. *Confusion named*   Cp. Gen. 11. 9: 'Therefore is the name of it called Babel; because the Lord did there confound the language of all the earth'. *Babel* (Babylon) means 'gate of the gods' but was punningly related to Hebrew *balal*, 'confound'. See Josephus, *Antiquities* (I iv 3) and A.V. marginal gloss.

81. *affecting* aspiring.

82–101. *yet know . . . inward lost*   Michael roots political in psychological *servitude*. The whole passage implicitly blames the English people for capitulating to monarchy in 1660. Cp. *SA* 268–71.

84. *right reason* conscience, planted by God in all men.

85. *dividual* separate, distinct.

101. *irreverent son*   Ham, who looked on the nakedness of his drunken father, Noah. Noah then cursed Ham's son Canaan and all his descendants: 'Cursed be Canaan; a servant of servants shall he be unto his brethren' (Gen. 9. 25).

104. *vicious* depraved.

race descendants (*OED* 1), tribe (*OED* 2b). *OED* records 'one of the great divisions of mankind' only from 1774, so M. is probably thinking of the Canaanites rather than black Africans (who were also classed among Ham's descendants). But Noah's curse was used to justify black slavery and M. is untroubled by the persecution of '*Slaves* and *Negro's*' in *Of Reformation* (*YP* 1. 617).

111. *peculiar* specially chosen. Cp. Deut. 14. 2: 'the Lord hath chosen thee to be a peculiar people unto himself'.

113. *one faithful man*   Abraham. Lines 113–63 are based on Gen. 11. 27–25. 10.

115. *Bred up in idol-worship*   Abraham's father Terah 'served other gods' (Josh. 24. 2).

117. *the patriarch*   Noah, who lived for 350 years after the Flood (Gen. 9. 28).

119. *their own work in wood and stone*   Cp. Jeremiah's scorn for those who say 'to a stock, Thou art my father; and to a stone, Thou hast brought me forth' (Jer. 2. 27). M. now gives no hint that pagan gods were devils (cp. i 365–75).

125–6. *seed . . . blest*   Cp. Gen. 12. 3: 'in thee shall all families of the earth be blest'. At line 148 Michael connects God's promise with the Messiah.

127. *Not knowing . . . believes*   Cp. Heb. 11. 8: 'By faith Abraham . . . went out, not knowing whither he went'.

130. *Ur* a city on the west bank of the Euphrates.

131. *Haran* a city east of the Euphrates, north-west of Ur.

132. *servitude* slaves and servants.

139-45. *From . . . eastward* The Promised Land is bounded to the north by *Hamath*, a city on the Orontes (Num. 34. 8, Josh. 13. 5), to the south by the *desert* of Zin (Num. 34. 3), to the west by the Mediterranean (Num. 34. 6), and to the east by the *Jordan* (Num. 34. 12) or *Mount Hermon* (Josh. 13. 5).

140. *names . . . yet unnamed* Cp. Virgil, *Aen.* vi 776: 'Names to be heard for places nameless now'.

144. *Mount Carmel* on the Mediterranean, near modern Haifa.

double-founted M. follows an incorrect tradition that the Jordan springs from two streams, named 'Jor' and 'Dan'.

146. *Senir* a peak of Mount Hermon, depicted on seventeenth-century maps as a *ridge*.

152. *faithful Abraham* italicized in *Ed I*, perhaps (as Flannagan notes) to emphasize a phrase instituted by God at Gal. 3. 9. God renames Abram at Gen. 17. 5: 'Neither shall thy name any more be called Abram, but thy name shall be Abraham; for a father of many nations have I made thee'. Cp. Gen. 12. 2: 'I will bless thee, and make thy name great'. 'Abraham' is the first personal name Michael has revealed.

153. *son* Isaac.

grandchild Jacob.

160. *younger son* Joseph (see Gen. 45-6).

161-96. As at i 306-7, M. identifies the Pharaoh of Exod. 1 (who enslaved the Israelites) with the Pharaoh of Exod. 14 (who pursued them).

165. *Suspected to* mistrusted by (*OED* 1b).

sequent successive (to Joseph's Pharaoh) and pursuing (Moses). Latin *sequor* could mean 'pursue'.

166. *overgrowth* too rapid growth.

inmate foreign (*OED* 1b).

168. *kills their infant males* Exod. 1. 16-22.

173. *denies* refuses.

179. *murrain* cattle plague.

180. *Botches* boils, tumours.

blains pustules.

188. *Palpable darkness* See ii 406n.

190. *ten wounds* the ten plagues (Exod. 7-12).

191. *The*] *Ed II*; *This Ed I*.

river-dragon Pharaoh is called 'the great dragon that lieth in the midst of his rivers' at Ezek. 29. 3. Cp. Satan as dragon (x 529) and Leviathan (i 201).

197. *two crystal walls* Cp. Exod. 14. 22: 'the waters were a wall unto them on their right hand, and on their left'. Cp. also vii 293 ('crystal wall') and

M.'s version of Ps. 136 (line 49): 'walls of glass'. Sylvester in *DWW* (1592–1608), *The Lawe* (1606) describes the Red Sea dividing into 'walls of cristall' (690).

199. **rescued* *OED*'s earliest participial instance.

200. *saint* holy person (Moses).

202–3. *Before . . . fire* Exod. 13. 21–4. M.'s view that God was *present in his angel*, not in his own person, is based on Exod. 33. 2–4. See further *CD* i 5 (*YP* 6. 254).

205–13. *king pursues . . . waves return* Exod. 14. 23–31. Cp. i 306–11.

207. *defends* repels, prevents (*OED* 1, 2).

210. *craze* shatter (*OED* 1).

214. *war* *soldiers in fighting array (*OED* 6b).

216. *not the readiest way* M.'s explanation for the Israelites' detour through the desert (lasting thirty-eight years) is from Exod. 13. 17–18.

217. *alarmed* called to arms.

225. *great senate* the Seventy Elders (Exod. 24. 1–9, Num. 11. 16–30). M. in *REW* exalts 'the supreme councel of seaventie call'd the *Sanhedrim*' as a model republican government (*YP* 7. 436).

227–30. *God . . . laws* Exod. 19. 16–20.

232. *types* any person, event or object in the O.T. prefiguring a Christian counterpart. Cp. Heb. 8 and see below, 238–44*n*.

236–8. *they beseech . . . terror cease* Cp. Exod. 20. 19: 'Speak thou with us and we will hear: but let not God speak with us, lest we die'.

238. *what they besought*] Ed II; them their desire, *Ed I*.

238–44. Moses is a type or *figure* of Christ in his office as *mediator*. See Deut. 18. 15–19, Acts 3. 22 and cp. *CD* i 15: 'the office of mediator is also ascribed to Moses, as a type of Christ' (trans. Carey, *YP* 6. 431).

247. *tabernacle* See Exod. 25–6 and Heb. 9.

255. *as in a zodiac* Josephus says the candlestick had *seven lamps* in imitation of the seven planets (*Antiquities* III vi 7).

256–8. *over the tent . . . journey* Exod. 40. 34–8.

263–7. *the sun . . . overcome* When Joshua defeated the Amorites he said: 'Sun, stand thou still upon Gibeon; and thou, Moon, in the valley of Ajalon. And the sun stood still, and the moon stayed, until the people had avenged themselves upon their enemies' (Josh. 10. 12–13). *Gibeon* and *Aialon* were a few miles north of Jerusalem.

264. *adjourn* The context (*a day*) invites a play on French *jour*.

267. *the third* Jacob, named *Israel* ('he wrestles with God') at Gen. 32. 28.

274. *eyes true op'ning* Contrast the false eye-openings of ix 708, 875, 985, 1071, x 1053, xi 412. *True* is an adverb (*OED* C).

277. *His day* Adam means 'Abraham's day', but M.'s voice behind him alludes to John 8. 56: 'Your father Abraham rejoiced to see my day'. When asked if he had seen Abraham, Jesus replied: 'Before Abraham was, I am'

(8. 58). Adam will learn the meaning of Abraham's *seed* (273) at xii 446–50.

287. *evince* make evident (*OED* 5). 'Overcome' (*OED* 1) is a momentary possibility, but it cannot survive line 290 (*law* can reveal sin, but not *remove* it). Cp. Rom. 3. 20: 'by the deeds of the law there shall no flesh be justified in his sight: for by the law is the knowledge of sin'.

288. *natural pravity* Original Sin (theological term).

291-2. *shadowy . . . goats* Cp. Heb. 10. 4: 'it is not possible that the blood of bulls and of goats should take away sins'. Blood sacrifices under the law were 'a shadow of good things to come' (Heb. 10. 1).

293. *blood more precious* I Pet. 1. 18.

294. *Just for unjust* I Pet. 3. 18.

295. *imputed* attributed vicariously (*OED* 2, theological term).

297-8. *law . . . Cannot appease* Cp. Gal. 2. 16: 'A man is not justified by the works of the law, but by the faith of Jesus Christ'.

301. *resign* make over, yield up (*OED* 2).

307-10. *not Moses . . . Joshua* Deut. 34, Josh. 1. Cp. *CD* i 26: 'The imperfection of the law was made apparent in the person of Moses himself. For Moses, who was a 'type' of the law, could not lead the children of Israel into the land of Canaan, that is, into eternal rest. But an entrance was granted to them under Joshua, that is, Jesus' (trans. Carey, *YP* 6. 519).

310. *Joshua . . . Jesus* 'Jesus' is the Greek equivalent of 'Joshua' ('saviour'). Thus the O.T. Joshua was a type of Christ. See above, *232n* on typology.

316. *but* except.

319. *he saves them penitent* ambiguous, since *penitent* could mean 'relenting' (*OED* 2) and so modify *he* as well as *them*. *OED* cites the Douay Bible (1609): 'Thou art our Lord, most highe, benigne, long-suffering, and very merciful, and penitent upon the wickednes of men'.

322-4. *promise . . . endure* See II Sam. 7. 16 for Nathan's promise to David: 'thy throne shall be established for ever'.

325-7. *royal stock . . . son* Messianic prophecies about David's line are frequent in the O.T. (e.g. Isa. 11. 10, Ps. 89. 36) and are applied to Jesus in the N.T. (e.g. Luke 1. 32).

329-30. *of kings / The last* M. in *TKM* (1649) argues that Christ's kingship made other kings redundant (*YP* 3. 256).

332. *next son* Solomon. See I Kings 5–8, II Chron. 2–4 on the Temple. The ark is *clouded* because God spoke from amidst clouds (Exod. 24. 16) and a cloud of glory filled the Temple when the ark was placed there (I Kings 8. 10).

338. *Heaped . . . sum* 'Added to the sum total of the people's sins'.

339-45. *expose . . . seventy years* See II Kings 25, II Chron. 36 and Jer. 39 on the Babylonian Captivity and the destruction of the Temple (sixth century BC). Jeremiah prophesied seventy years of captivity (Jer. 25. 12).

348–50. *Returned . . . re-edify* The Persian kings Cyrus, Darius and Artaxerxes permitted the Jews to return and rebuild the Temple (Ezra, Neh. 1–6).

349. *disposed* put into a favourable mood (*OED* 6).

353–7. *priests . . . sceptre* The apocryphal II Macc. 4–6 tells how *strife* between the priests enabled the Seleucid King Antiochus IV to sack Jerusalem and pollute the Temple, which he dedicated to Zeus (169 BC). *They* (356) are the priestly dynasty of the Maccabees (Hasmoneans), one of whom, Aristobulus I, proclaimed himself king in 104 BC, becoming the first king since the Babylonian Captivity.

357. *sons* descendants.

358. *stranger* Antipater the Idumean. The Romans made him governor of Jerusalem in 61 BC and procurator of Judaea in 47 BC. He was Herod the Great's father.

364. *solemn* holy (*OED* 1), awe-inspiring (*OED* 7).

367. **squadroned OED's* earliest participial instance.

370–71. *bound . . . Heav'ns* Cp. Ps. 2. 8 (which was referred to Christ): 'I shall give thee . . . the uttermost parts of the earth'. Christ's *reign* on *earth* will last throughout the Millennium – the 1,000 years following his Second Coming (Rev. 20). See *CD* i 33 (*YP* 6. 623–4). Cp. also Virgil's prophecy that Augustus will bound his 'empire with Ocean, his glory with the stars' (*Aen.* i 287).

373. *Surcharged* overwhelmed (*OED* 4b) and weighed down with moisture (*OED* 3c). Cp. *SA* 728.

379. *virgin mother, hail* Luke 1. 28. Cp. v 385–7, xi 158.

383. *capital* on the head (*OED* 1), fatal (*OED* 2d).

393. *recure* heal a wound (*OED* 2).

394. *destroying . . . works* Cp. I John 3. 8: 'For this purpose the Son of God was manifested, that he might destroy the works of the devil'.

396. *want* lack.

401. *apaid* satisfied.

402. *exact* rigorous, strict (*OED* 4, 5) and perfect (*OED* 1).

403–4. *love . . . law* Cp. Rom. 13. 10: 'Love is the fulfilling of the law'.

406. *cursèd death* Cp. Gal. 3. 13 (citing Deut. 21. 23): 'Christ hath redeemed us from the curse of the law, being made a curse for us: for it is written, Cursed is every one that hangeth on a tree'.

409. *Imputed* attributed vicariously (*OED* 2, theological term).

410. *though legal works* 'though their works accorded with the (Mosaic) law'. M. shared the general Protestant belief in Justification by Faith. See *CD* i 22.

415–16. *to the cross he nails . . . sins* Col. 2. 14.

419. *satisfaction* payment of penalty (theological term).

422. *stars of morn* literal stars and angels. Cp. Job 38. 7: 'the morning stars sang together'. Christ was also called 'morning star' (Rev. 22. 16), though Michael here presents the resurrected Son as a rising sun (*dawning light*).

432. *in . . . stings* Cp. I Cor. 15. 55: 'O death, where is thy sting?' Flannagan notes that Sin's sting returns to its source in Satan's *head*. Cp. ii 752–8.

433. *temporal* temporary (*OED* 1). M. believed that body and soul died and were resurrected together.

442. *profluent* flowing. M. believed that baptism should be performed in running water (*CD* i 28, *YP* 6. 544).

450. *So . . . blest* Michael now reveals the meaning of God's promise to Abraham that all nations will be blessed in his seed (xii 277, Gen. 12. 3). The *seed* is Christ. Cp. Gal. 3. 8: 'the scripture, foreseeing that God would justify the heathen through faith, preached before the gospel unto Abraham, saying, In thee shall all nations be blessed'.

454. *prince of air* Satan is 'prince of the power of the air' at Eph. 2. 2 and is led captive 'up on high' at Eph. 4. 8. He is led *in chains* at Rev. 20. 1.

460. *quick* living. The N.T. often speaks of judging 'the quick and dead' (e.g. Acts 10. 42, II Tim. 4. 1).

467. *period* consummation, end (*OED* 5).

469–78. *O goodness . . . abound* Much debated. Many hear Adam as articulating the paradox of the 'Fortunate Fall', but Adam says only that God's bringing good out of evil is *more wonderful* than his bringing light out of darkness. He does not say that man will be more happy for sinning. Contrast Fletcher, *CV* (1610) iv 12: 'Such joy we gained by our parentalls, / That good, or bad, whither I cannot wiss, / To call it a mishap, or happy miss / That fell from Eden, and to heav'n did rise'. M. never implies that the Fall is a precondition for man's ascent to Heaven. Adam and Eve could have reached Heaven without sinning (see v 496–503, vii 155–61) and the Son could have become incarnate without man's Fall (see v 839*n* and Danielson 215–27).

469. *immense* unmeasured, infinite (*OED* 1).

478. *wrath . . . abound* Cp. Rom. 5. 20: 'Where sin abounded, grace did much more abound'.

486. *Comforter* the Holy Spirit (John 15. 26).

488–9. *law . . . love* Rom. 3. 27, Gal. 5. 6.

491–2. *spiritual armour . . . fiery darts* Cp. Eph. 6. 11–17: 'Put on the whole armour of God . . . taking the shield of faith, wherewith ye shall be able to quench all the fiery darts of the wicked'.

493. *What . . . afraid* Cp. Ps. 56. 11: 'In God have I put my trust: I will not be afraid / What man can do unto me'.

501. *To speak all tongues* Cp. Mark 16. 17 ('they shall speak with new tongues') and the fulfilment of this promise in Acts 2. 4–7.

505. *race well run* A Pauline metaphor (I Cor. 9. 24, II Tim. 4. 1, etc.)

used by M. in *Areopagitica*: 'the race, where that immortall garland is to be run for' (*YP* 2. 515).

508. *grievous wolves* Cp. Acts 20. 29: 'For I know this, that after my departing shall grievous wolves enter in among you, not sparing the flock'. Cp. iv 183–7, *Lycidas* 113–31, and M.'s sonnet *To the Lord General Cromwell* 14.

511. *lucre* Cp. I Pet. 5. 2: 'Feed the flock of God . . . not for filthy lucre, but of a ready mind'. M. was opposed to a stipendiary clergy.

511–14. *the truth . . . understood* a typical Protestant assertion of the Christian's right to interpret scripture guided solely by the inner light.

515. *names* titles of rank or dignity (*OED* 2b).

520. *pretence* assertion of a right or title (*OED* 1), with overtones of the modern sense.

523. *enrolled* written (in the Bible).

525. *force the Spirit* M. in *CD* i 30 denounces the forcing of conscience as 'a yoke not only upon man but upon the Holy Spirit itself' (trans. Carey, *YP* 6. 590).

526. *His consort Liberty* II Cor. 3. 17.

527. *living temples* Cp. I Cor. 3. 16: 'Know ye not that ye are the temple of God?'

529–30. *Who . . . Infallible* M. attacks papal claims to 'infallibilitie over both the conscience and the scripture' in *A Treatise of Civil Power* (*YP* 7. 248). The doctrine of papal infallibility was not instituted until 1870.

532–3. *worship . . . truth* John 4. 23.

534. *Will*] *Ed I*; Well *Ed II*.

536. *works of faith* See *CD* i 22 for M.'s view that faith is a work and 'not merely infused' (trans. Carey, *YP* 6. 489). Cp. also 'faith not void of works' (xii 427).

539. *groaning* Cp. Rom. 8. 22: 'For we know that the whole creation groaneth and travaileth in pain together until now'.

540. *respiration* respite, breathing space (*OED* 3).

546. *dissolve* not 'annihilate' (as Fowler) but 'destroy the binding power of' (*OED* 11). Annihilation would be a mercy to the devils (ii 155–9), whom God had said that he would punish 'without end' (v 615). M. in *CD* i 33 confirms that Hell is a place of 'endless punishment' and rejects the view that Hell might be destroyed in the final conflagration: 'If this were to happen it would be very nice for the damned, no doubt!' (trans. Carey, *YP* 6. 630). Michael had earlier said that the Son would destroy Satan by destroying his works. See xii 394–5.

547. **perverted* turned from the right way. *OED*'s earliest participial instance.

548–9. *conflagrant . . . earth* See II Pet. 3. 6–13 on the destruction by fire. See Rev. 21. 1 on the *New heavens, new earth*.

551. *fruits* playing on Latin *fruitio*, meaning *joy* or *bliss*.

555. *Till time stand fixed* At Rev. 10. 5-6 an angel swears 'that there should be time no longer'. Cp. *On Time* 1.

559. *this vessel* the entire human nature (mind and body).

565. *Merciful . . . works* Cp. Ps. 145. 9: 'his tender mercies are over all his works'.

566. *overcoming evil* Cp. Rom. 12. 21: 'overcome evil with good'.

567-8. *weak . . . strong* Cp. I Cor. 1. 27: 'God hath chosen the weak things of the world to confound the things which are mighty'. See also vi 137-9*n*.

576-7. *all the stars . . . by name* Cp. Ps. 147. 4: 'He telleth the number of the stars; he calleth them all by their names'.

581-4. *only add . . . charity* II Pet. 1. 5-7.

587. *paradise within* Cp. Satan's 'Hell within' (iv 20).

588-9. *top / Of speculation* both 'hill of extensive view' and 'summit of theological speculation'.

592. *motion* military deployment (*OED* 5).

593. *remove* signal for departure (*OED* 5b).

602. *many days* Adam lived to be 930 (Gen. 5. 5).

608. *found her waked* The Argument to book xii says that Adam 'wakens Eve'.

611. *God is also in sleep* Cp. Num. 12. 6: 'If there be a prophet among you, I the Lord will make myself known unto him in a vision, and will speak unto him in a dream'.

615-18. *with thee . . . all places thou* Cp. Ruth 1. 16: 'And Ruth said, Intreat me not to leave thee, or to return from following after thee: for whither thou goest, I will go; and where thou lodgest, I will lodge: thy people will be my people, and thy God my God'. See also Eve's love poem at iv 641-56.

629. *metéorous raised on high (*OED*). A 'meteor' was any atmospheric phenomenon (*OED* 1) and 'meteoric' meant 'pertaining to the region of mid-air' (*OED* 1a). Richardson contrasts the good angels' lofty, luminous *mist* with Satan as a 'black mist low creeping' (ix 180).

630. *marish* marsh.

631. *the labourer's heel* Adam is now a labourer, and his *heel* is vulnerable to the serpent (Flannagan).

635. *adust* scorched. Patristic tradition interpreted the 'flaming sword' of Gen. 3. 24 as the heat of the uninhabitable torrid zone (hence *Libyan*).

637-8. *In either hand . . . ling'ring parents* Michael's conduct of Adam and Eve recalls the angels' conduct of Lot's family from Sodom: 'And while he lingered, the men laid hold upon his hand, and upon the hand of his wife, and upon the hand of his two daughters; the Lord being merciful unto him: and they brought him forth, and set him without the city' (Gen. 19. 16).

640. *subjected* lying below.

643. *brand* sword (*OED* 8b) or lightning (*OED* 3d). Cp. Gen. 3. 24: 'a flaming sword which turned every way'.

644. *dreadful faces thronged* Martindale (134) compares 'the supreme moment of terror' in Virgil's *Aeneid*, when Venus clears Aeneas's sight and he sees the gods' 'dreadful forms' (*dirae facies*) menacing Troy (ii 622).

648. *hand in hand* See iv 321*n*.

648–9. *wand'ring . . . way* Cp. Ps. 107. 4: 'They wandered in the wilderness in a solitary way; they found no city to dwell in.' But the psalm continues: 'Then they cried unto the Lord . . . and he delivered them out of their distresses. / And he led them forth by the right way' (6–7).

PARADISE REGAINED

Date: 1667–70. *PR* was printed in 1671 in a volume that included *SA*. The precise date of composition is not known, but Edward Phillips records that it 'was begun and finisht and Printed after the other [*PL*] was publisht, and that in a wonderful short space considering the sublimeness of it' (Darbishire 75). Thomas Ellwood, who was M.'s pupil in the early 1660s, claims to have played some part in the engendering of *PR*. M. lent Ellwood the completed manuscript of *PL*, which Ellwood read and returned, commenting: 'Thou hast said much here of *Paradise lost*; but what hast thou to say of *Paradise found*?' M. did not reply, 'but sate some time in a Muse'. Some time later he presented Ellwood with the completed *PR*, saying: 'This is owing to you; for you put it into my head by the question you put to me at Chalfont; which before I had not thought of' (*History of the Life of Thomas Ellwood*, 1714, 233–4).

The plot of *PR* is based upon the Gospels account of Christ's temptation in the wilderness. M. follows Luke 4. 1–13 in the order of temptations, but he follows Matt. 4. 1–11 in placing the temptations after Christ's forty-day fast. In Luke Christ is tempted for forty days. Biblical commentators had long discussed the question of what Satan was trying to accomplish by tempting Christ. One view was that he was trying to discover Christ's identity, and that the temptations were designed to make Christ acknowledge his divinity. Critics disagree about the motives of M.'s Satan and Jesus (who is never called 'Christ' in the poem). Pope argued that Jesus knows his own identity, and deliberately withholds evidence of it from Satan. Allen argued that Satan merely pretends not to know who Jesus is. Lewalski believes that both Jesus and Satan are ignorant of Jesus's true identity until the very end of the poem, when Jesus discovers and reveals his divinity with the words 'Tempt not the Lord thy God' (meaning 'do not tempt me'), and Satan, understanding him, falls in despair. Ashraf H. A. Rushdy, in 'Standing Alone on the Pinnacle: Milton in 1752', *MS* (1990), 193–218, has recently argued that the action of *PR* 'does not constitute an identity test'. Most critics agree that the Satan of *PR* is less impressive than his namesake in *PL*. Ricks describes him as 'shabby and transparent'. Shabby he may be, but the diversity of interpretations as to his motives suggests that he is anything but transparent.

THE FIRST BOOK

1. *I who erewhile* Cp. Virgil, *Aen.* 1a–1d: 'I am he who once piped my song on a slender reed, then, leaving the woods, compelled the neighbouring fields to serve the greedy farmer . . . but now I sing of Mars' bristling'. This opening (rejected by Virgil or his executors) appeared in most Renaissance editions, and biblical epics imitated it (Lewalski 116–17). Cp. also Spenser, proem to *FQ*. Virgil and Spenser look back from mature epic to pastoral or georgic; M. looks back to his earlier epic as if it were apprentice work for 'the true epic subject' (Lewalski 6).

2–4. *one man's . . . obedience* Cp. Rom. 5. 19: 'For as by one man's disobedience many were made sinners, so by the obedience of one shall many be made righteous'.

5. *foiled* including 'trodden underfoot' (*OED* v[1] 1). Cp. God's curse on the serpent (Gen. 3. 15, *PL* x 175–81, 1030–36).

7. *Eden . . . waste wilderness* Cp. Isa. 51.3: 'the Lord shall comfort Zion: he will comfort all her waste places; and he will make her wilderness like Eden'.

8. *Spirit who led'st* Cp. Matt. 4. 1 ('Then was Jesus led up of the spirit into the wilderness') and Luke 4. 1. M. in *CD* i 6 argues that 'spirit' can mean the inner light or 'the actual person of the Holy Spirit' (trans. Carey, *YP* 6. 285).

   eremite *desert-dweller (*OED* 1b) – the Greek meaning.

9. *field* battlefield (though the agricultural sense plays against *desert*).

14. *full-summed* in full plumage (a term from falconry).

16. *unrecorded* Many critics have objected that Christ's temptation is recorded (albeit summarily) in the Gospels. M. might be using 'record' in the sense 'render in song' (*OED* 2b). *OED*'s instances all describe birdsong, but cp. *SA* 983–4. The metaphor of birdsong would in any case be appropriate after *wing full-summed* (14).

18–32. *Now . . . beloved Son* See Matt. 3, Mark 1. 2–11, Luke 3. 1–22, John 1. 6–34.

18. *great proclaimer* John the Baptist.

23. *son of Joseph deemed* Cp. Luke 3. 23: 'being (as was supposed) the son of Joseph'.

24. *as then* as yet.

  obscure Cp. John 1. 26: 'there standeth one among you, whom ye know not'.

26. *divinely warned* Cp. John 1. 33: 'And I knew him not; but he that sent me to baptize with water, the same said unto me, Upon whom thou shalt see the Spirit descending, and remaining on him, the same is he which baptizeth with the Holy Ghost'.

30–32. *Heaven . . . beloved Son* Cp. Matt. 3. 16–17: 'and, lo, the heavens were opened unto him, and he saw the Spirit of God descending like a dove, and lighting upon him: And lo a voice from heaven, saying, This is my beloved Son, in whom I am well pleased'. Cp. Mark 1. 10–11, Luke 3. 21–2, John 1. 32–4.

33. *Adversary* Satan, whose name literally means 'enemy' (cp. *PL* i 82), 'antagonist' (cp. *PL* x 386), or 'adversary' (cp. *PL* ii 629). 'Adversary' has legal overtones suggesting that Satan is to bring an adversary suit.

  still continually.

33–4. *roving . . . the world* Cp. Job 1. 7: 'And the Lord said unto Satan, Whence comest thou? Then Satan answered the Lord and said, From going to and fro in the earth, and from walking up and down in it'; also I Pet. 5. 8: 'your adversary the devil, as a roaring lion, walketh about, seeking whom he may devour'.

37. *attest* testimony, attestation.

39. *his place . . . mid air* Satan's place had been Hell (*PL* vii 135, etc.). Now it is the cold middle air, extending to the mountain-tops (*PL* i 516n). Satan was 'prince of the power of the air' (Eph. 2. 2). Cp. *PL* iv 940, x 189.

40. *peers* nobles.

41. *involved* enfolded (modifying *clouds*) and underhand, crooked (modifying *peers*).

42. *A gloomy cónsistory* Cp. Virgil, *Aen.* iii 679: *concilium horrendum*. The Virgilian analogue bodes ill for the devils, for Aeneas is describing the thwarted Cyclopes who gather on the shore and 'stand impotent with glaring eyes' as the Trojans sail away. *Cónsistory* means 'council', but has satirical overtones of 'ecclesiastical senate of Pope and Cardinals' (*OED* 6) and 'ecclesiastical court' of a Bishop (*OED* 7) or Presbyters (*OED* 9). Cp. the puns on 'conclave', 'synod', 'pontifical' (*PL* i 795, ii 391, x 313).

44. *Powers* rulers (*OED* 6a), pagan deities (*OED* 7), angelic Powers.

48. *as* as reckoned by.

49. *universe* the earth as abode of mankind (*OED* 3a). Satan rules *earth and air* (63), but not the stellar heavens.

possessed inhabited. English law distinguished possession from ownership.

50. *In manner* in some degree (*OED* 'manner' sb¹ 10).

51. *facile* easily led (*OED* 5).

51–2. *Eve . . . deceived* including 'dis-Eved' ('deprived of immortality'). Cp. *PL* i 35–6. Eve's name means 'life' and M. relates it to immortality at *PL* xi 161–71.

53. *attending* awaiting (qualifies *me*).

fatal wound the 'bruise' foretold at Gen. 3. 15 (cp. *PL* x 175–92).

56. *longest time to him is short* Cp. Ps. 90. 4: 'a thousand years in thy sight are but as yesterday'.

57. *the circling hours* Cp. 'the circling Hours' (*PL* vi 3). M. again alludes to the Horae, but Satan's dread is greater for his having waited hour by hour. Cp. Virgil's Venus waiting through the circling years, *volventibus annis* (*Aen.* i 234).

58. *compassed* completed a circuit (*OED* 5), attained (*OED* 11).

59. *bide* endure (*OED* 9) and await (*OED* 6).

60. *At least if so we can* 'If, that is, we are able to endure (and so survive) the stroke'.

62. *infringed* broken, shattered, invalidated (*OED* 1).

64–5. *ill news . . . woman born* Jesus's birth is not news to Satan. He knew of it 'with the first' and has kept watch ever since (iv 504–12). It is unclear whether the other devils knew of it. If they didn't, Satan has kept them in the dark for thirty years.

73. *Pretends* claims (with overtones of the modern sense).

74. *Purified . . . pure* I John 3. 3.

80. *on him rising* as he arose.

83. *dove* Cp. Matt. 3. 16: 'he saw the Spirit of God descending like a dove'. M. in *CD* i 6 identifies this Spirit with 'the actual person of the Holy Spirit' (trans. Carey, *YP* 6. 285). Cp. *PR* i 31.

87. *He who* As in *PL*, Satan avoids naming 'God'. See *PL* i 93n.

obtains holds, possesses (*OED* 6).

89. *first-begot* Messiah as Satan knew him in Heaven. See *PL* v 603 and note.

91. *Who this is we must learn* Pope (36) and Lewalski (159) take Satan at his word, and assume that he genuinely sets out to discover Jesus's identity. Allen (111) believes that Satan merely feigns ignorance. Woodhouse (171–3) argues that Satan knows 'in his heart' that Jesus is the *first-begot*, but clings to his 'assiduously fostered doubt' with 'diminishing conviction and mounting despair'. In *PL*, after his fall from Heaven, Satan had never named the Son or acknowledged his existence (see *PL* iv 36–7n). He would not mention him now unless he suspected the truth. See below, 356n.

93. *glimpses* momentary flashes, traces (*OED* 1, 2).

94–5. *utmost edge / Of hazard* Cp. Shakespeare, *All's Well that Ends Well* III iii 6: 'th' extreme edge of hazard'; also *PL* i 276–7.

96. *sudden* impromptu, extempore (*OED* 7).

97. *well-couched* well-hidden (*OED* 13), well-expressed (*OED* 15).

100. *sole undertook* See *PL* ii 430–66.

103. *calmer voyage* Satan had travelled through Chaos to reach Adam and Eve; now he descends from 'mid air'.

105. *success* result (*OED* 1). Satan will meet with 'bad success' (iv 1).

107. *amazement* overwhelming fear, alarm (*OED* 3).

112. *main* momentous (*OED* 5a).

113. *dictator* the Roman term for a chief magistrate invested with absolute but temporary power in times of crisis.

117. *gods* M. identifies fallen angels with heathen gods. See *PL* i 373*n*.

119. *coast* district (*OED* 6).

120. *easy steps* Cp. Satan's 'uneasy steps' in Hell (*PL* i 295).

girded . . . wiles Cp. Isa. 11. 5: 'righteousness shall be the girdle of his loins'.

122. *This man of men* combining awe (cp. 'King of kings') and contempt (cp. 'this man of clay' *PL* ix 176).

124. *subvert* corrupt, pervert (*OED* 5).

128. *frequence* assembly.

129. *Gabriel* the angel of the Annunciation. See lines 134–40 and Luke 1. 26–38.

130. *proof* act of testing (*OED* 4a).

143. *assay* either 'practise by way of trial' (*OED* 8) or 'try the mettle of', 'accost with arguments', 'tempt' (*OED* 14, 15, 13). The former reading credits Satan, the latter the Son, with *utmost subtlety*.

146. *apostasy* the apostate angels.

147. *overweening* presumption.

Job M. in *RCG* calls the book of Job a 'brief epic', and many critics have seen Job as a model for *PR*. Lewalski (112) traces the comparison between Jesus and Job to Gregory's *Moralia in Job*. Cp. i 369, 425, iii 64–7, 95.

149. *invent* plan, plot (*OED* 2a).

152–3. *at length . . . to Hell* Satan falls to Hell at iv 576, but God may be referring to the Last Judgement.

155. *fallacy* deception, trickery, a lie (*OED* 1).

156. *exercise* tax the powers of, subject to ascetic discipline (*OED* 4a, 3a). M. in *CD* i 8 states that a 'good temptation' can 'exercise' (*exercendam*) the faith or patience of the righteous (*YP* 6. 338). Cp. also *Areopagitica* (1644): 'I cannot praise a fugitive and cloistered virtue, unexercised and unbreathed' (*YP* 2. 515).

157–8. *rudiments . . . warfare* Cp. Virgil, *Aen.* xi 156–7; but Lewalski (117) finds a closer analogue in Jacobus Strasburgus's *Oratorio Prima* (1565) – a 'brief epic' which depicts the tempted Christ as a young warrior learning the *rudimentum* of his warfare with Satan. Cp. ii 245.

161. *His weakness . . . strength* Cp. I Cor. 1. 27: 'God hath chosen the weak things of the world to confound the things which are mighty'.

165. *virtue* from Latin *vir*, 'man' (*perfect man*).

169. *Admiring* regarding with loving wonder (*OED* 1).

171. *the hand* instrumental music.

172. *argument* subject-matter, theme (*OED* 6).

176. *The Father knows the Son* Cp. John 10. 15: 'As the Father knoweth me, even so know I the Father'.

   secure free from anxiety (*OED* 1).

180. *frustrate* frustrated.

182. *vigils* nocturnal prayers (*OED* 2d).

184. *Bethabara* the place of the baptism (John 1. 28).

188. *Publish* make publicly known, disseminate a creed (*OED* 1).

190–91. *converse / With* keep company with (*OED* 2).

193. *bordering desert* See below, 354*n.*

196–7. *thoughts . . . swarm* Cp. Samson's 'deadly swarm' of 'thoughts' (*SA* 19).

200. *sorting* corresponding (*OED* 1).

201. *When I was yet a child* See Luke 2 for Christ's childhood. Jesus's lines recall some autobiographical statements in M.'s prose. See esp. *YP* 4. 612.

203. *Serious* earnestly bent, keen (*OED* 1b).

204–5. *myself . . . truth* Cp. John 18. 37: 'To this end was I born . . . that I should bear witness unto the truth'.

207–8. *Law . . . delight* Cp. Ps. 1. 2 (M.'s translation): 'Jehovah's Law is ever his delight'.

209–14. *ere . . . all* Luke 2. 46–50. M. adds the detail that the twelve-year-old Jesus entered the Temple to teach the doctors. Cp. iv 215–20.

214. *admired* marvelled at.

215–19. *victorious . . . pow'r* The Gospels give no hint that Jesus had ever wished to oppose violence with violence.

223. *persuasion . . . fear* Cp. *RCG* (*YP* 1. 746): 'Persuasion certainly is a more winning, and more manlike way to keepe men in obedience then feare'. Cp. also Plato, *Laws* iv 718.

226. *subdue* destroy *1671*, corr. to *subdue* in the *Errata*. Cp. Luke 9. 56: 'the Son of man is not come to destroy men's lives'.

233. *express* manifest, reveal.

234. *For know* The Gospels give no hint that Mary informed Jesus of his divine nature, or that Jesus needed to be told.

238. *messenger* Gabriel, who appeared to Mary (Luke 1. 26–33) and Joseph (Matt. 1. 20–23). 'Angel' means 'messenger'.

253. *-grav'n* indelibly fixed (*OED* 'grave' v 6b).

255. *Just Simeon* Simeon was 'just and devout' and 'it was revealed unto him by the Holy Ghost, that he should not see death, before he had seen the Lord's Christ'. Simeon recognized the infant Jesus as Messiah (Luke 2. 25–35). See ii 87–91*n*.

prophetic Anna The 'prophetess' Anna saw Jesus in the same 'instant' as Simeon and acknowledged him as the Redeemer (Luke 2. 36–8).

258. This is the last line of Mary's speech.

259. *revolved* studied, read (*OED* 5).

262–3. *of whom they spake / I am* Cp. the divine 'I AM' at Exod. 3. 14, John 8. 58, and *PL* viii 316; also Mark 14. 61–2, where the high priest asks: 'Art thou the Christ, the Son of the Blessed? And Jesus said, I am'.

264. *assay* affliction (*OED* 2).

even to the death Cp. Matt. 26. 38 (Christ's words in Gethsemane): 'My soul is exceeding sorrowful, even unto death'. Isa. 53. 3. 12 prophesies the Messiah's death.

271. *Not knew by sight* Cp. John 1. 33: 'I knew him not'. M. follows Matt. 3. 13–17 in having John recognize the Messiah before the Spirit descends. At John 1. 29–34 the Spirit's descent causes the recognition.

274. *from above* The Bible never hints that Jesus had looked upon John as his superior. When John declared his unworthiness to baptize Jesus, Jesus said 'Suffer it to be so now' (Matt. 3. 15).

279. *hardly won* persuaded with difficulty.

281. *eternal doors* Cp. Ps. 24. 7: 'everlasting doors'.

283. *sum* ultimate end, highest point (*OED* sb¹ 13a).

286–7. *the time / Now full* Cp. Gal. 4. 4: 'When the fulness of the time was come, God sent forth his Son'.

290. *motion* working of God in the soul (*OED* 9b). Cp. Samson's 'rousing motions' (*SA* 1382).

292. *I . . . not know* M. in *CD* i 5 cites Mark 13. 32 as proof that the Son is not omniscient.

294. *Morning Star* Cp. Rev. 22. 16: 'I am the . . . bright and morning star'. The star is in its *rise* because Jesus's ministry is about to begin. The morning-and-evening star symbolized Christ's death and Resurrection.

296. *dusk with horrid shades* gloomy with bristling trees.

302. *solitude . . . society* Cp. *PL* viii 427–8, ix 249 and notes.

303. *forty days* M. follows Matt. 4. 2 in placing the temptation at the end of the forty days. Mark 1. 13 and Luke 4. 2 say that the temptation itself lasted forty days.

309. *hungered then at last* At ii 244 M. says that Jesus first felt hunger during the banquet temptation. Lewalski (202) therefore infers that *then* means 'later', and that Jesus is not hungry now, during the stones-into-bread temptation. See below, 355*n*.

310-13. *wild beasts . . . aloof* Cp. Mark 1. 13: 'he was . . . with the wild beasts'. The beasts grow *mild* in accordance with Ezek. 34. 25: 'evil beasts . . . shall dwell safely in the wilderness'. But the *serpent, lion* and *tiger* do not regain the innocence prophesied at Isa. 11. 6-9 and 65. 25 (cp. *PL* iv 243-4). Contrast Fletcher, *CV* (1610) ii 3-5, where the lion licks Jesus's feet and sports with the lamb.

312. *noxious worm* harmful snake.

314. *an aged man* Renaissance writers and artists often assumed that Satan had appeared in disguise (Pope 43). Spenser's Archimago (*FQ* I i 29-30) and Fletcher's Satan (*CV* ii 15-18) appear as old hermits, but M.'s Satan seems a simple poor old man, with no pretensions to asceticism. As such, he can feign concern for Jesus's welfare 'with an energy that would be highly unbecoming in a pious recluse' (Pope 47). See also ii 299*n*, iv 449*n*.

315. *in quest of some stray ewe* Lewalski (118) sees a reference to Satan as 'a false shepherd' looking for lost souls.

316. *withered sticks* Cp. John 15. 6: 'If a man abide not in me he is cast forth as a branch, and is withered; and men gather them, and cast them into the fire'.

324-5. *dropped . . . carcass* Cp. Num. 14. 29: 'Your carcases shall fall in this wilderness'.

pined wasted.

326. *admire* marvel.

327. *For that* because.

328. *baptizing *OED*'s earliest participial instance.

333-4. *aught . . . What* anything that.

334. *fame* rumour.

337. *swain* rustic.

339. *stubs* stumps of trees, shrubs or plants.

342-50. *But if . . . God* Matt. 4. 3-4 and Luke 4. 3-4.

347. *Is it not written* Deut. 8. 3.

352. *Moses . . . forty days* Exod. 24. 18.

353. *forty days Elijah without food* 1 Kings 19. 8.

354. *the same I now* At i 193 M. had placed Jesus in the Desert of Quarentana between Jerusalem and Jericho. Now he follows a rival tradition which identified Jesus's wilderness with that in which the Jews wandered for forty years and Moses and Elijah fasted for forty days. The former desert suits geography; the latter, typology. See Pope 16, 110-12.

355. *suggest* prompt to evil (*OED* 2a).

distrust The Church Fathers saw the stones-into-bread temptation as an invitation to gluttony. Protestants saw it as an attempt to arouse distrust of God. Cp. Fletcher, *CV* ii 20, where the marginal note states that Satan tempts Jesus 'to despaire of Gods providence, and provide for himselfe'. See Pope (57).

356. *Knowing who I am, as I know who thou art*   Allen (110–12) and Woodhouse (171–2) cite the line as proof that Satan (despite his professed doubts) knows who the Son is. MacCallum (248) (following Carey) thinks that Satan might know Jesus to be 'Son of God' without knowing what the title means. But *as* implies that Satan and the Son know each other in the same way. Cp. Fletcher, *CV* ii 30: 'Well knewe our Saviour this the Serpent was, / And the old Serpent knewe our Saviour well'.

357. *now undisguised*   Satan retains his 'grey dissimulation' (i 498), though Jesus has seen through it.

358. *that Spirit unfortunate*   Satan avoids speaking his name, for he does not want Jesus to think of him as an enemy (see above, 33n, below, 387n). Satan never speaks his name in *PR* and is 'abashed' when Jesus confronts him with it (iv 194).

363. **unconniving*   unwinking (*OED*'s sole instance, from Latin *inconivus*). Satan implies that God has either connived at Satan's misdoings or at least 'shut [His] eyes from neglect' (*OED* 'connive' 4). At *PL* x 624 God denies that he would connive with Satan.

368. *I . . . sons of God*   Cp. Job 1. 6: 'The sons of God came to present themselves before the Lord, and Satan came also among them'. Satan's allusion insinuates his own claim to be a 'son of God'. Cp. iv 517–20.

369. *Uzzéan Job*   Cp. Job 1. 1: 'There was a man in the land of Uz whose name was Job'. See iii 94n.

370. *prove*   put to the test.

illústrate   set in a good light, render illustrious (*OED* 3, 4). Satan's real motive had been to make Job curse God (Job 1. 11, 2. 5).

372–6. *Ahab . . . destruction*   See I Kings 22. 19–35. God sent 'a lying spirit' to King Ahab of Israel and so lured him to defeat and death. A.V.'s marginal note to II Chron. 18. 20 (a cross-reference to Job 1. 6) implicitly identifies the 'lying spirit' with Satan.

372. *fraud*   the state of being defrauded (a passive usage unique to M.). Cp. *PL* vii 143, ix 643.

373. *they demurring*   while they hesitated.

375. *glibbed*   rendered fluent and slippery (*OED* 'glib' v¹ 2, 1).

383–4. *What can be then less in me*   Satan's surface meaning is: 'How can I feel anything less than a desire to see thee?' but his 'opposite and truer meaning' is that he desires 'nothing . . . less than thus to confront and listen to Christ' (Lewalski 351).

385. *attent*   attentive.

387. *Men . . . foe*   Satan again distances himself from his name and identity. See above, 358n, and cp. ii 330, iv 525–7.

393. *disposer*   distributor (*OED* 3) and ruler (*OED* 2). Notice the slipperiness of Satan's *If not*. Satan declines to say whether he distributes anything to his human partners, who may be no more than subjects.

397. *Envy* malice, enmity (*OED* 1).

400. *proof* experience (*OED* 5).

401. *fellowship . . . smart* The thought (and its opposite) was a classical and Renaissance commonplace. See e.g. Seneca, *De Consolatione ad Polybium* xii 2, Shakespeare, *The Rape of Lucrece* 790, Sir Thomas Browne, *Christian Morals* I xviii.

402. *peculiar* own.

407. *composed of lies* Cp. John 8. 44: 'the devil . . . is a liar, and the father of it'.

413. *the prime* the most exalted, highest ranking (angels).

414. *emptied* Jesus means 'devoid of true worth', but M.'s voice behind him might allude to the Greek version of Phil. 2. 7, where it is Christ who 'emptied himself' at the Incarnation. Cp. *On the Circumcision* 20.

418. *representing* displaying to (your) eye (*OED* 4a) and presenting again (*OED* 're-present').

420. *never more in Hell than when in Heaven* Cp. *PL* iv 18–23, ix 119–23, 467–8.

421. *serviceable* both 'useful' and 'willing to be of service' (*OED* 1a), as in Shakespeare, *King Lear* IV iv 257: 'A serviceable villain'.

423. *pleasure to do ill* Cp. *PL* i 159–60.

427. *other service* Satan's deception of Ahab (see above, 372–6n).

428. *four hundred mouths* Ahab's prophets numbered 'about four hundred men' (I Kings 22. 6).

430. *pretend'st* lay claim (with overtones of the modern sense).

430–35. *oracles . . . deluding* The most famous pagan oracles were those of Apollo at Delphi, Zeus at Dodona, and Zeus-Ammon at Siwa. Patristic writers saw them as the work of demons and condemned them for their ambiguity (see *Nativity* 173n). A notable victim was King Croesus of Lydia, who consulted Delphi before invading Persia. He was told: 'if you cross the Halys you will destroy a great realm'. He crossed the Halys and lost his own realm.

433. *vent* utter.

436. *seldom understood* a grudging admission that not all oracles led to disaster. When Xerxes invaded Greece, the Delphic oracle told the Athenians to trust in their 'wooden walls'. Themistocles understood that the walls were ships.

442–3. *justly . . . delusions* Cp. II Thess. 2. 11: 'And for this cause God shall send them strong delusion, that they should believe a lie'. The previous verses speak of 'the working of Satan with all power and signs and lying wonders, and with all deceivableness' (II Thess. 2. 9).

446. *then* i.e. when God declares his Providence. Jesus is drawing a distinction between Satan's false oracles and God's true ones. The distinction is also made by Aquinas, who cites the Sibyl's prophecy of Christ as an instance of a good oracle. See *Summa* II ii 172 (6).

447. *president* presiding. M. in *CD* i 9 thinks it 'probable' that 'angels are put in charge of nations, kingdoms and particular districts' (trans. Carey, *YP* 6. 246).

452. *parasite* including the Greek sense: 'one admitted to the feast after a sacrifice' (*OED* 1b). Notice *temples* (449) and *sacrifice* (457) and cp. the dictionary definition given by M.'s nephew, Edward Phillips: '*Parasite* (among the Ancients) was the Priest's Guest, whom he invited to eat part of the Sacrifice'.

454. *retrenched* cut short, repressed (*OED* v¹ 1).

456. *oracles are ceased* Cp. *Nativity* 173 and Mic. 5. 12. The cessation of the oracles was usually dated to the Nativity (see *Nativity* 173n), or (less often) the Crucifixion. See C. A. Patrides, 'The Cessation of the Oracles: the History of a Legend' (*MLR* 60, 1965, 500–507).

458. *Delphos* Delphi, site of Apollo's oracle.

460. *Oracle* divine teacher (*OED* 3c). The etymology (Latin *orare*, 'to speak') points to Jesus's identity as 'the Word'.

462. *Spirit of Truth* John 16. 13.

466. *disdain* vexation (*OED* 2), loathing (*OED* 3).

474. *Say and unsay* Cp. *PL* iv 947–9: 'To say and straight unsay . . . Argues no leader, but a liar'.

476. *submiss* submissive, lit. 'placed beneath'. Notice *placed above* (475).

477. *quit* both 'free, clear' (*OED* a 1) and 'requited for an injury' (*OED* v 11a).

480. *tuneable* melodious, sweet-sounding.

sylvan woodland.

482–3. *Most men . . . her lore* Cp. Rom. 7. 19: 'For the good that I would I do not: but the evil which I would not, that I do'; also Medea's words in Ovid, *Met.* vii 20–21: 'I see the better, I approve it too: / The worse I follow'. Cp. *PL* viii 611.

485. *I despair to attain* Satan does not say what he despairs to attain. He despairs of salvation, but he also wants to 'detect [Jesus] in an offence' (*OED* 'attain' 3), and so 'attaint' him in the senses: 'accuse of crime', 'infect with corruption', 'condemn to death' (*OED* 10, 7, 6).

487. *atheous* impious (*OED* 1). Cp. *PL* i 495 ('the priest / Turns atheist').

488. *To tread his sacred courts* Cp. Isa. 1. 12: 'who hath required this at your hand, to tread my courts? Bring no more vain oblations'.

491. *Balaam* Balak, King of Moab, ordered Balaam to curse the Israelites, but Balaam blessed them at God's command (Num. 22–4).

reprobate morally corrupt (*OED* 2). M. calls Balaam a 'Reprobate hireling Priest' in *Of Reformation* (*YP* 1. 589).

494. *scope* aim, purpose.

498. *grey dissimulation* Cp. Ford, *The Broken Heart* (1633) IV ii 101: 'Lay by thy whining grey dissimulation'.

499. *Into thin air diffused* Satan vanishes like gods and ghosts in pagan epics (cp. Homer, *Od.* iv 838–9, Virgil, *Aen.* iv 278) or the spirits in Shakespeare's *The Tempest* that melt 'into air, into thin air' (IV i 150).

500. *sullen* gloomy.

  double-shade Cp. *A Masque* 335.

500–502. *Night . . . roam* Cp. Ps. 104. 20: 'Thou makest darkness, and it is night: wherein all the beasts of the forest do creep forth'; also Shakespeare, *Macbeth* III ii 50–53.

THE SECOND BOOK

1–7. In Matthew, Mark, and Luke, Jesus meets his disciples only after Satan has tempted him. M. finds evidence for an earlier meeting in John 1. 35–42, where two disciples, including Andrew, follow Jesus on the day after his baptism.

3–4. *expressly . . . declared* The voice from Heaven called Jesus *Son of God*, not *Messiah*. But Andrew *expressly* called Jesus 'the Messias' at John 1. 41, and John the Baptist implicitly acknowledged him as such at John 1. 27 and 29.

6. *lodged* Cp. John 1. 39: 'They came and saw where he dwelt, and abode with him that day'.

15. *Moses . . . missing long* Exod. 32. 1.

16. *the great Thisbite* Elijah, called 'the Tishbite' at I Kings 17. 1. See II Kings 2. 2 for his ascent to Heaven in a chariot of fire (*fiery wheels*), and cp. *PL* iii 522.

17. *once again to come* Cp. Mal. 4. 5: 'Behold, I will send you Elijah the prophet before the coming of the great and dreadful day of the Lord'.

18. *those young prophets* After Elijah's translation, 'the sons of the prophets' sent fifty men in search of him, 'but found him not' (II Kings 2. 15–17).

20. *Bethabara* the place of Jesus's baptism (John 1. 28).

20–21. *Jericho / The city of palms* Deut. 34. 3.

21. *Aenon . . . Salem old* Cp. John 3. 23: 'And John was also baptizing in Aenon near to Salim'. Patristic tradition identified Salim with the Salem of Gen. 14. 18 (hence *old*).

22. *Machaerus* a fortress to the east of the Dead Sea, the traditional site of John the Baptist's execution.

23. *lake Genezaret* the Sea of Galilee (Luke 5. 1).

24. *Perea* the land east of the Jordan.

27. *Plain fishermen . . . them call* Cp. Spenser, *Shep. Cal.* Januarye 1: 'A shepeheards boye (no better doe him call)', and Phineas Fletcher, *Piscatory Eclogues* (1633) iii 1: 'A fisher-lad (no higher dares he look)'.

34. *full of grace and truth* John 1. 14.

36. *The kingdom . . . restored* In Acts 1. 6 the disciples ask the risen Christ: 'Lord, wilt thou at this time restore again the kingdom to Israel?'

38. *perplexity* distress (*OED* 1b).

40. *rapt* carried off.

44. *the kings of the earth* Cp. Ps. 2. 2: 'The kings of the earth set themselves . . . against the Lord, and against his anointed'.

50. *his Anointed* the Messiah (which means 'the anointed one').

51. *Prophet* John the Baptist.

pointed at John 1. 29–37.

54. *he will not fail* Cp. Joshua 1. 5: 'I will not fail thee'.

67. *salute* Gabriel's salutation (Luke 1. 28).

76. *murd'rous king* Herod. See Matt. 2. 16.

87–91. *old Simeon . . . A sword* Cp. Luke 2. 34–5: 'And Simeon blessed them, and said unto Mary his mother, Behold, this child is set for the fall and rising again of many in Israel; and for a sign which shall be spoken against; (yea, a sword shall pierce through thy own soul also)'. Cp. i 255–6.

92. *My exaltation* Miriam (the Hebrew form of 'Mary') was thought to mean 'exaltation'.

94. *argue* find fault with (*OED* 2).

96–9. *when twelve . . . Father's business* See Luke 2. 49 and i 209–15.

99. *mused* wondered and pondered.

101. *obscures* leaves unexplained.

103–4. *My heart . . . sayings* Cp. Luke 2. 19: 'Mary kept all these things, and pondered them in her heart', and Luke 2. 51: 'his mother kept all these sayings in her heart'.

107. *salutation* Gabriel's greeting (Luke 1. 28).

115. *preface* earlier statement (Latin *praefatio*), i.e. Satan's promise to return (i 483–5).

116. *vacant* at leisure (*OED* 4b).

117. *middle . . . air* See i 39*n* for Satan's association with the cold middle air.

118. *Potentates* leaders, or a synecdoche for all angelic orders.

120. *Solicitous* anxious (*OED* 1).

blank nonplussed (*OED* 5).

122. *Demonian Spirits elemental daemons (see *Il Penseroso* 93*n*), with overtones of 'evil spirits'. Augustine had identified Platonic and Hermetic daemons with wicked demons (*City of God* viii 14–24, ix *passim*).

126–7. *an enemy / Is risen* Cp. the 'enmity' that God placed between Eve's seed and the serpent (Gen. 3. 15, *PL* x 180).

127. *invade* attack, assault (*OED* 5).

130. *frequence* assembly (*OED* 1).

131. *tasted* put to the proof (*OED* 2), had experience of (*OED* 3).

141-2. *Eve . . . Deceive* See i 51-2*n* and cp. iv 6-7.

147. *the old Serpent* Cp. Rev. 12. 9: 'that old serpent, called the Devil, and Satan'.

150. *Belial* See *PL* i 490-505, ii 108-18 and notes.

151. *Asmodai* Hebrew 'the destroyer'. Asmodai (or 'Asmodeus') was associated with lust because he slaughtered Sarah's seven husbands on their wedding nights (Tobit 3. 8). Cp. *PL* iv 167-71, v 221-3.

152. *incubus* a demon that had sexual intercourse with women while they slept. (A succubus took female form to have intercourse with sleeping men.) Augustine (*City of God* xv 23) acknowledged the existence of incubi, and belief in them was still strong in M.'s time. See e.g. King James's *Demonologie* (1597) iii 3.

159. *virgin majesty* Cp. *PL* ix 270: 'the virgin majesty of Eve'.

160. *terrible to approach* Cp. *PL* ix 489-91: 'though terror be in love / And beauty, not approached by stronger hate'. Cp. also Song of Sol. 6. 4.

162. *amorous nets* Cp. *Elegia I* 60, *PL* x 897, xi 586-7 ('in the amorous net / Fast caught') and *SA* 409, 532.

163. *object* The word need not imply contempt. Cp. *PL* x 996 where Eve describes herself as 'the present object'. Carey hears overtones of the older sense: 'Something "thrown" or put in the way so as to interrupt or obstruct the course of a person' (*OED* 2).

164. *Severest* most self-disciplined.

temper temperament.

165. *Enerve* enervate, weaken.

166. *Draw out* allure (men) and prolong (the temptation). *Nets* (162) implies the drawing of a fishing net (*OED* 'draw' 51) and *magnetic* implies drawing 'by physical force, as a magnet' (*OED* 'draw' 25).

168. *magnetic* magnet (*OED* B 1).

170-71. *Solomon . . . wives* Solomon's wives led him into idolatry in his old age (I Kings 11. 1-12). Cp. Phineas Fletcher's Jesuit council in which a devil names Solomon as a victim of sexual temptation (*The Apollyonists* iv 23). See also *PL* i 399-405, 443-6, ix 442-3.

173. *Belial* The name means 'worthlessness', and Satan's immediate use of it is crushing. The devils had never addressed each other by name in *PL*. See *PL* i 361-5*n*.

177. *toys* contemptible trifles (*OED* 8).

178-81. *Before the Flood . . . a race* Cp. Gen. 6. 2-4: 'the sons of God saw the daughters of men that they were fair; and they took them wives of all which they chose . . . There were giants in the earth in those days; and also after that, when the sons of God came in unto the daughters of men, and they bare children to them, the same became mighty men which were of old, men of renown.' Here (and in *PL* v 446–50) M. follows a patristic tradition identifying the *sons of God* as fallen angels. In *PL* xi 573–87 he follows a rival tradition identifying them as Seth's descendants. R. H. West, in *MLN* 65 (1950) 187–91, explains away the inconsistency, and most subsequent editors have followed him, but now see Edward E. Ericson, *MQ* 25 (1991) 79–89.

183. *courts and regal chambers* Cp. Belial's association with 'courts and palaces' in *PL* i 497. The court of Charles II was notorious for debauchery.

186. *Callisto* a nymph of Diana. Jupiter raped her after disguising himself as Diana (Ovid, *Met.* ii 409–40).

Clymene mother of Phaethon by Apollo (*Met.* i 765–75).

187. *Daphne* a virgin nymph, changed into a laurel when Apollo pursued her (Ovid, *Met.* i 452–567).

Semele mother of Bacchus by Jupiter (*Met.* i 253–315).

Antiopa mother of Amphion and Zethus by Jupiter (*Met.* vi 110–11).

188. *Amymone* a sea-nymph ravished by Neptune, after he had saved her from a satyr (Ovid, *Amores* I x 5).

Syrinx an Arcadian nymph, changed into reeds when Pan pursued her (Ovid, *Met.* i 698–706).

189. *Too long* too many to mention.

scapes breaches of chastity (*OED* 2).

191. *Faun . . . Sylvan* Faunus . . . Sylvanus: Roman wood-gods identified with *Pan*.

haunts habits (*OED* 1).

196. *Pelléan conqueror* Alexander the Great, born at Pella in Macedonia. He captured Darius's wife and daughters after the battle of Issus, but treated them honourably, since he considered 'the mastery of himself a more kingly thing than the conquest of his enemies' (Plutarch, *Alexander* 21). Satan praises Alexander's restraint with women, but ignores his homosexuality. Satan will include both women and youths in the banquet temptation (ii 351–61).

198. *slightly* indifferently (*OED* 2b).

199. *he surnamed of Africa* Scipio Africanus. After conquering New Carthage in 210 BC, Scipio (who was twenty-four) was presented with a beautiful captive. He restored her to her Celtiberian fiancé (Livy xxvi 50).

205–6. *wiser far / Than Solomon* Cp. Matt. 12. 42: 'Behold, a greater than Solomon is here'.

211. *fond* foolish.

214. *zone of Venus* the girdle of Aphrodite, worn by Hera when she seduced Zeus (Homer, *Il.* xiv 214–351).

216. *brow* including 'brow of a hill'.

218. *despised* including 'looked down on' (from *Virtue's hill*).

219. *deject* cast down from high estate (*OED* 3).

222. *admire* marvel.

222–3. *plumes . . . toy* Cp. Ovid's peacock (*Ars Amatoria* i 627): 'the bird of Juno displays its feathers if you praise them; but if you look at them in silence, it hides its treasures'. M.'s language might also suggest phallic detumescence.

235. *grant* consent (*OED* 1a).

237. *Spirits likest to himself* Cp. the 'unclean spirit' of Matt. 12. 45: 'Then goeth he, and taketh with himself seven other spirits more wicked than himself'; also Luke 11. 26.

239–40. *active scene . . . part* The theatrical terms imply that Satan's temptations will be presented as if in a play or court masque. See below, 402–3*n*.

242. *shade to shade* either 'shelter to shelter' or 'one night to the next'.

244. *Now hung'ring first* See i 309*n*.

255. *so* provided that.

258. *fed . . . thoughts* Cp. *PL* iii 37: 'Then feed on thoughts'.

259. *hung'ring . . . Father's will* Cp. John 4. 34: 'My meat is to do the will of him that sent me'.

264–83. *dreamed . . . but a dream* Lucretius observes that thirsty men often dream of drinking whole rivers (*De Rerum Nat.* iv 1024–5). Jesus shows restraint even in sleep, eating only such food as Daniel's *pulse* (278). The dream might be caused by *appetite* alone (264), but Satan's prompt reference to Elijah and Daniel (312, 329) suggests that he is at least partly responsible. Cp. Eve's demonic dream (*PL* v 30–93), which also ends with the words *but a dream*.

266. *Him thought* it seemed to him.

266–9. *brook of Cherith . . . brought* Cp. I Kings 17. 5–6: 'For he [Elijah] went and dwelt by the brook Cherith, that is before Jordan. And the ravens brought him bread and flesh in the morning, and bread and flesh in the evening; and he drank of the brook'.

270–76. *He saw . . . forty days* Cp. I Kings 19. 4–8. Fleeing from Jezebel, Elijah slept in the wilderness, where he was twice fed by an angel before fasting for forty days.

278. *Daniel at his pulse* Cp. Dan. 1. 8–21. Daniel rejected Nebuchadnezzar's rich fare for a diet of pulse (beans, lentils, etc.).

286. *ken* scan, descry.

288. *cottage, herd or sheep-cote* Jesus is looking for food. His subsequent rejection will be of Satan as giver (321–2).

289. *bottom* valley.

pleasant grove Jesus as yet sees only a place of natural beauty, but *grove* has ominous overtones from O.T. usage, where 'groves' are places of idolatry. See *PL* i 403*n*, ix 388*n*. Giles Fletcher's Satan tempts Christ in a garden (*CV* ii 39–52).

290. **chant* song. *OED*'s earliest instance of the noun.

292. *noon* the hour of Eve's fall (*PL* ix 739) and Samson's death (*SA* 1612). Cp. Ps. 91. 6: 'the destruction that wasteth at noonday'.

293. *brown* dusky, dark.

294. *a woody scene* Cp. *PL* iv 140–41: 'A sylvan scene . . . a woody theatre'.

295. *Nature's . . . Art* Cp. Art's imitation of Nature in Spenser's Bower of Bliss (*FQ* II xii 58–9).

296. *superstitious* including 'idolatrously devoted' (*OED* 2b).

299. *Not rustic as before* Satan's fine clothes are appropriate to the banquet as his earlier garb was appropriate to a desert-dweller. It is unclear whether Satan appears as the same *man* on both days. See iv 449*n*.

302. *officious* eager to please (*OED* 1), with overtones of the pejorative sense.

308. *fugitive bondwoman* Hagar, mother of Ishmael by Abraham. Sarah and Abraham drove Hagar and Ishmael into the desert after Ishmael mocked the birth of Isaac. Ishmael would have died had not an angel shown Hagar a well (Gen. 21. 9–20). Satan calls Ishmael by the name of his eldest son *Nebaioth* (Gen. 25. 13), perhaps because Ishmael (like Jesus) was named by God (Gen. 16. 11, Matt. 1. 21).

312. *manna* Exod. 16. 35.

Prophet Elijah. See above, 270–76*n*.

313. *Thebèz* a city named at Judges 9. 50. M. is unusual in associating 'Elijah the Tishbite' (I Kings 17. 1) with it rather than with Thisbe, in Gilead.

318. *need . . . none* Jesus had earlier acknowledged his need, but added that God could support it (ii 250–51).

321–2. *as I like / The giver* Cp. *A Masque* 702–3.

324. *right to all created things* Cp. Heb. 1. 2: 'His Son, whom he hath appointed heir of all things'.

328. *Meats . . . unclean* foods prohibited by the Mosaic dietary law (Lev. 11. 2–31, Deut. 14. 3–20). Satan's assurance is false, for shellfish (345) were 'an abomination' (Lev. 11. 9–12). M. Fixler, in *MLN* 70 (1955), 573–7, thinks that so palpable a lie cannot be intended to deceive Jesus. Satan's hope is rather to provoke Jesus into subjecting himself to the law he has come to supersede.

328–9. *offered first / To idols* Cp. I Cor. 10. 20–21: 'The things which the Gentiles sacrifice, they sacrifice to devils, and not to God: and I would not that ye should have fellowship with devils. Ye cannot drink the cup of the Lord, and the cup of devils: ye cannot be partakers of the Lord's table, and the table of devils'.

329. *Daniel* See above, 278*n*.

330. *Nor . . . an enemy* given the lie by Satan's name and the word 'Fiend' (323) which also means 'enemy'. See i 358*n*.

331. *scruple* doubt the goodness of (*OED* 2).

337–67. The banquet scene has no biblical precedent. Cp. Fletcher, *CV* ii 40–60, where Christ is tempted in a garden full of flowing wine and naked ladies. Cp. also the banquets with which Cleopatra beguiles Caesar (Lucan, *Pharsalia* x 107–68) and Armida tries to ensnare the Christian knights (Tasso, *Gerus. Lib.* x 64).

340. *A table richly spread* Lewalski (203) compares the Israelites' presumptuous demand: 'Can the Lord furnish a table in the wilderness?' (Ps. 78. 19). Cp. also I Cor. 10. 21 (cit. above, 328–9*n*).

343. *In pastry built* Renaissance and medieval banquets served large, elaborate pastries.

344. *Grisamber* ambergris, a sweet-smelling substance found floating in tropical seas. Notoriously expensive, it was used as a perfume and in cooking, and was a favourite food of Charles II (Macaulay, *History of England*, 1849, i 442). It is now known to be (and even in M.'s time was suspected of being) sperm whale dung. See *A Masque* 863*n*.

345. *freshet* small stream.

346. *exquisitest* including the original sense 'diligently sought out, far-fetched' (*OED* 1, Latin *exquaerere*).

347. *Pontus* the Black Sea, famous for fine fish (Juvenal iv 41–4).
   Lucrine bay a lagoon near Naples, prized for oysters (Juvenal iv 141).
   Afric coast the Nile, famous for fish (Juvenal x 155–6).

348. *cates* dainties, delicacies.

349. *crude* uncooked (*OED* 2) and sour to the taste (*OED* 4).
   diverted pleasurably excited (*OED* 4) and turned away from the straight (*OED* 6).

350. *sideboard* *drawing-room furniture for holding wine (*OED* 1b).

352. *hue* shape, appearance, aspect (*OED* 1a).

353. *Ganymede* a handsome Trojan boy abducted by Jove to be his cupbearer. His name was a byword for homosexual love. Giles Fletcher includes 'a lewd throng / Of wanton boyes' in his version of Christ's pinnacle temptation (*CV* ii 31).
   Hylas a beautiful youth loved by Hercules. M. names him alongside Ganymede in *Elegia VII* (21–4).

355. *Naiades* nymphs of springs, rivers, and lakes.

356. *Amalthea's horn* the cornucopia ('horn of plenty') with which the nymph Amalthea fed the infant Jupiter (Ovid, *Fasti* v 115–28).

357. *Hesperides* the Garden of the Hesperides, often associated with female beauty. See *A Masque* 393*n*.

360. *Logres* a kingdom in Arthurian Britain (east of the Severn and south of the Humber).

Lyonesse the legendary birthplace of Arthur and Tristram. Camden in *Britannia* (1600) describes it as a now-submerged land, west of Cornwall (150).

361. *Lancelot* Arthur's chief knight. Four *fairy damsels* (including Morgan Le Fay) found him sleeping under the apple tree and tried to seduce him (Malory, *Morte d'Arthur* vi, 3). I owe the source to Matthew Woodcock.

Pelleas another of Arthur's knights. He loved Etarre, who treated him with scorn (Malory iv 22).

Pellenore King of the Isles. Lewalski (225) suggests that M. is referring to Pellenore's son Percival. While seeking the Grail, Percival fasted for three days in a wilderness. A devil disguised as a woman offered him a banquet and sex. Percival ate the food and went to bed with the woman, but her pavilion vanished in smoke when he made the sign of the cross (Malory xiv 9–10).

363. *charming* both 'delightful' and 'exercising magic charms'.

364. *gale* gentle breeze. Cp. *PL* iv 156, viii 515.

Arabian odours Felix Arabia (Yemen) was famous for perfumes and aromatic spices. Cp. *PL* iv 162–3.

365. *Flora* Roman goddess of flowers and springtime.

368. *What doubts* Why fears.

369. *not fruits forbidden* In fact the banquet does contain forbidden food (see above, 328*n*). Christ's temptation had long been seen as counterbalancing Adam and Eve's. See Pope (51–69), Lewalski (225–6).

370. *Defends* forbids (*OED* 3).

375–6. *pay / Thee homage* Satan does not include himself among those who would pay homage. Were Jesus to accept Satan's banquet, he would be implicitly acknowledging Satan's right to give it (380–91). Satan will later ask Jesus to pay him homage in return for his gifts (iv 163–9).

382. *likes* pleases.

384. *Command a table in this wilderness* Cp. Ps. 78. 19: 'They said, Can God furnish a table in the wilderness?' The psalmist is referring to Num. 11. 4–5, where the Israelites yearn for the good food they had left in Egypt.

386. *my cup* Cp. Matt. 26. 39: 'O my Father, if it be possible, let this cup pass from me'; also Matt. 20. 22. Cp. the dramatic irony in 'wreath of thorns' (ii 459).

387. *diligence* persistent endeavour to please (*OED* 1b).

391. *gifts no gifts* M. in *An Apology for Smectymnuus* speaks of 'enemies . . . whose guifts are no guifts, but the instruments of our bane' (*YP* 1. 939). Cp. Sophocles, *Ajax* 665.

397. *apparent* manifest.

401. *far-fet* far-fetched.

402–3. *vanished . . . Harpies' wings* Cp. the stage direction to Shakespeare's *The Tempest* III iii 53: 'enter Ariel like a harpy; claps his wings upon the table; and with a quaint device, the banquet vanishes'. Harpies were monstrous bird-women who snatched food from hungry mortals and defiled their tables (Virgil, *Aen.* iii 225-8).

404. *impórtune* irksomely persistent.

414. *A carpenter thy father known* Cp. i 23 and Matt. 13. 55: 'Is not this the carpenter's son?'

416. *hunger-bit* Cp. Job 18. 12: 'His strength shall be hunger-bitten, / And destruction shall be ready at his side'.

422. *Money brings . . . realms* Cp. Mammon's praise of money in *FQ* II vii 11: 'Sheilds, steeds, and armes, and all things for thee meet / It can purvay in twinckling of an eye; / And crownes and kingdomes to thee multiply'.

423. *Antipater* procurator of Judaea. He and his son *Herod* ('the Great') rose to power by promising money to Julius Caesar and Mark Antony (Josephus, *Antiquities* xiv 1).

429. *Riches are mine* Satan's claim is given the lie by Hag. 2. 8: 'The silver is mine, and the gold is mine, saith the Lord of hosts'.

430. *amain* exceedingly.

439. *Gideon* born to a poor family (Judges 6. 15), he was chosen by God to rout the Midianites with 300 men.

Jephtha a harlot's son, and driven from his father's house, he rose to deliver Israel from the Ammonites (Judges 11).

shepherd lad David, whom God chose 'from the sheepfolds' (Ps. 78. 70-72).

441. *So many ages* David's heirs reigned in Judah for over three hundred years, until the time of Nebuchadnezzar.

441-2. *regain . . . without end* Cp. Luke 1. 32-3: 'The Lord God shall give him the throne of his father David: And he shall reign over the house of Jacob for ever; and of his kingdom there shall be no end'. See also Isa. 9. 6-7, 16. 5, Ezek. 34. 23-4, Amos 9. 11.

446. *Quintius* Lucius Quinctius Cincinnatus, a semi-legendary Roman hero who was called from the plough to be dictator in 458 BC, when the Aequi had blockaded the consul Minucius. He routed the Aequi, resigned his dictatorship after two weeks, and returned to his farm, refusing his share of the booty.

Fabricius Gaius Fabricius Luscinus, a Roman hero in the war with Pyrrhus. Although poor, he rejected Pyrrhus's bribes.

Curius Manius Curius Dentatus, hero of wars against the Sabines, the Samnites, and Pyrrhus. When the Samnites tried to bribe him, he replied that he would rather rule those who possessed gold than possess it himself. He gave all his booty to the Roman Republic and retired to his simple farm.

Regulus Marcus Atilius Regulus was captured by the Carthaginians in the First Punic War. He was sent to Rome with terms of peace, after promising to return to Carthage. Regulus went to Rome, persuaded the

Senate to reject the terms, then returned to Carthage where he was tortured to death.

453. *toil* both 'labour' and 'snare' (*OED* 2).

455. *abate* blunt (*OED* v¹ 8).

458. *yet not for that* yet not because.

459–62. *Golden . . . burden* Cp. *2 Henry IV* III i: 'Uneasy lies the head that wears a crown'; also *Henry V* IV i 235ff.

459. *wreath of thorns* Jesus will one day wear a literal crown of thorns (Matt. 27. 29, Mark 15. 17, John 19. 1–5).

466. *reigns within himself* Cp. Prov. 16. 32: 'he that ruleth his spirit [is better] than he that taketh a city'. Cp. *PL* vi 181, xii 82–96, *PR* iii 71–87.

474. *saving* that delivers from sin (*OED* 4).

480. *sincere* genuine (*OED* 2).

481–3. *to give . . . assume* Cp. Seneca, *Thyestes* 529: 'To have a kingdom is chance; to give one, virtue'.

482–3. *to lay down / Far more magnanimous* Editors have thought that M. is referring to the abdications of Diocletian or Charles V. But Jesus would not praise kings who merely sought release from a burden (see lines 458–65). He is more likely thinking of Gideon (named in line 439) who refused the kingship of Israel (Judges 8. 23). He might also be alluding to Cromwell, who had refused the title of king in December 1653. Cp. *Defensio Secunda* (*YP* 4. 672): 'The name of king you spurned . . . May you then, O Cromwell, increase in your magnanimity' (*magnitudine . . . animi*). Marvell likens Cromwell to Gideon in *The First Anniversary of the Government under O.C.* (1655) 249–64.

THE THIRD BOOK

3. *convinced* overcome in argument (*OED* 2), with overtones of 'suffer a moral conviction of sinfulness' (*OED* 3d).

14. *Urim and Thummim* gems in Aaron's breastplate (Exod. 28. 30, cp. *PL* iii 597). Their purpose is unknown. I Sam. 28. 6 and Num. 27. 21 imply an *oraculous* function. Jesus had said 'oracles are ceased' (i 456–60).

16. *sought to* called upon for.

18. *conduct* military leadership.

19. *sustain* withstand (*OED* 8a).
  subsist stand firm (*OED* 7).

22. *Affecting* seeking to obtain (*OED* 'affect' 1).

23. *savage* uncultivated, wild.

27. *erected* high-souled (*OED* 2). Cp. Mammon as 'the least erected Spirit' (*PL* i 679).

31. *Thy years are ripe* Jesus 'was about thirty' at the time of his baptism (Luke 3. 23).

31-3. *son . . . held* Alexander the Great (356–323 BC) invaded Asia when he was twenty-two, and ruled the Persian empire (founded by *Cyrus*) before he was twenty-six.

34. *young Scipio* Publius Cornelius Scipio Africanus (236–183 BC) ousted the Carthaginians from Spain while still in his twenties. He defeated Hannibal at Zama in 202 BC. M. in *PL* ix 510 calls him 'the heighth of Rome'

35-6. *young Pompey* Gnaeus Pompeius Magnus (106–48 BC) was forty when he defeated the *Pontic king* Mithridates, and forty-five when he celebrated his triumph. Satan therefore exaggerates his youth. But Pompey had been granted two earlier triumphs: in 81 BC (when he was twenty-five), and in 71 BC.

39-41. *Great Julius . . . wept* Plutarch tells how Caesar, aged thirty, wept when he read of Alexander's exploits. Asked the reason, he replied that Alexander, at his age, was king of many peoples, whereas he had yet to achieve a brilliant success (*Caesar* xi 3).

45. *affect* seek to obtain (*OED* 1).

47. *blaze* glory (*OED* sb¹ 5b), with overtones of 'proclaim as with a trumpet' (*OED* v² 2). Cp. the 'sudden blaze' of *Lycidas* 74 (which is also distinguished from 'fame in Heaven'). Cp. also Gal. 5. 26: 'Let us not be desirous of vain glory, provoking one another, envying one another'.

51. *well weighed* if they were judged properly.

56. *to be dispraised . . . praise* Cp. Jonson, *Cynthia's Revels* III iii 15–16: 'of such / To be disprais'd is the most perfect praise' – itself an echo of Seneca, *De remediis fortuitorum* vii 1: *Malis displicere laudari est.*

59. *raised* lauded – a rare sense (*OED* 'raise' 14b) coined by M. in *Arcades* 8.

62. *divulges* proclaims publicly (*OED* 1b). Cp. *Lycidas* 78–84.

67. *Hast . . . Job?* Cp. Job 1. 8: 'Hast thou considered my servant Job, that there is none like him in the earth, a perfect and an upright man, one that feareth God, and escheweth evil?' See also i 369–70.

74. *worthies* heroes of antiquity (*OED* 1b). Satan has mentioned some of the traditional 'nine worthies', consisting of three pagans (Hector, Alexander, Julius Caesar), three Jews (Joshua, David, Judas Maccabeus) and three Christians (Arthur, Charlemagne, Godfrey of Bouillon).

81. *titled gods* Alexander was acclaimed as a god in his lifetime; Julius Caesar was placed among the gods by law after his death. Roman emperors were worshipped as gods.

82. *benefactors* translating the Greek title *Euergetes*, adopted by Hellenistic kings. Cp. Luke 22. 25: 'The kings of the Gentiles . . . are called benefactors'. M. mocks the title in *Defensio* (*YP* 4. 378).

deliverers translating the Greek title *Soter*, adopted by hellenistic kings. It implied divinity and in N.T. usage is used of Christ as Saviour.

84. *son of Jove* Alexander and Scipio both claimed this lineage. See *PL* ix 508*n*, 508–10*n*.

Mars Romulus was called the son of Mars.

86–7. *brutish vices . . . shameful death* Alexander was an alcoholic and died shortly after a drinking-party. Julius Caesar was assassinated.

91–2. *wisdom . . . temperance* II Pet. 1. 6.

94. *a land and times obscure* Job's homeland of Uz was of uncertain location. Job himself was thought to have lived before Moses (Lewalski 11–12).

96–8. *Socrates . . . unjust* Socrates was condemned for corrupting the youth of Athens and for introducing new gods. His accusers asked for the death penalty, but made it easy for him to escape. He chose to die rather than break the city's laws (Plato, *Crito*). Justin Martyr saw Socrates' death as foreshadowing Christ's (*First Apology* v). See Lewalski (240).

101. *African* Scipio Africanus.

106–7. *I seek not mine, but his / Who sent me* Cp. John 5. 30: 'I seek not mine own will, but the will of the Father which hath sent me'; also John 9. 50: 'I seek not mine own glory'.

111. *for his glory all things made* Cp. Rev. 4. 11: 'Thou art worthy, O Lord, to receive glory and honour and power; for thou hast created all things, and for thy pleasure they are and were created'.

118. *Promiscuous* without discrimination.

119. *barbarous* non-hellenic.

120. *foes pronounced* Satan still draws back from admitting that he is the foe, even though that is what his name means. Cp. i 387.

122. *his word* Jesus seems unaware that he himself is the Word (John 1. 1).

127. *benediction* *expression of thanks (*OED* 1d).

138. *recreant* apostate.

140. *sacrilegious* M. in *CD* ii 4 defines 'sacrilege' as 'the appropriation of things . . . dedicated to God' (trans. Carey, *YP* 6. 682).

146. *had not to answer* had nothing to answer.

154. *By mother's side thy father* Matt. 1. 1–16 and Luke 3. 23–38 trace Jesus's descent from David through Joseph, but patristic tradition took Luke 1. 27 to mean that both Joseph and Mary were 'of the house of David'. Jewish law did not recognize descent through the mother, so Satan's exclusion of Joseph is insulting. Some theologians had argued that Jesus was Joseph's heir by adoption. See also iv 500–501*n*.

158–60. *Roman . . . sway* Pompey took Jerusalem in 68 BC, and Mark Antony stormed it in 37 BC. Judaea was added to the Roman province of Syria in AD 6. Pontius Pilate was procurator from AD 25–36. Josephus testifies to his tyrannical acts (*Antiquities* xviii 3). Cp. Luke 13. 1.

160–61. *violated / The Temple* Pompey entered the Holy of Holies in 63 BC and Crassus stole gold from the Holy of Holies. Pilate broke the Jewish *Law* by bringing images of Roman emperors into Jerusalem (*Antiquities* xiv 4–7, xviii 3).

163. *Antiochus* Antiochus IV Epiphanes, Seleucid Emperor of Syria. After capturing Jerusalem (169 BC), he attempted to abolish the Jewish religion and hellenize the Jews. He forced them to build shrines for idols and sacrifice swine at the altar (I Macc. 1. 20–63).

165. *Maccabeus* Judas Maccabeus, leader of a Jewish revolt against Antiochus (I Macc. 2–9). His family were originally priests in *Modin* (I Macc. 2. 1), but later assumed royal power as the Hasmonean dynasty. See *PL* xii 354–8.

166. *Retired into the desert* Judas waged guerilla warfare in and from the desert (I Macc. 2. 29–31, 5. 24–8).

171. *kingdom* the rank of a king (*OED* 1).

173. *Occasion's forelock* a proverbial phrase for an opportunity that must be seized. Occasion (opportunity) was depicted as a woman, bald save for one lock of hair hanging over her forehead, which must be seized from the front. Cp. Spenser, *FQ* II iv 4–12 and Shakespeare, *Othello* III i 50.

174. *occasion* both 'opportunity' (*OED* 1) and 'adequate reason' (*OED* 2a).

175. *Zeal of thy father's house* When Jesus expelled the money-changers from the Temple, his disciples 'remembered that it was written, The zeal of thine house hath eaten me up' (John 2. 17; cp. Ps. 69. 9).

178. *Prophets . . . endless reign* See ii 441–2n.

183. *time . . . for all things* Cp. Eccles. 3. 1: 'To every thing there is a season, and a time to every purpose under the heaven'.

187. *all times and seasons* Cp. Acts 1. 7: 'they asked of him, saying, Lord, wilt thou at this time restore again the kingdom to Israel? And he said unto them, It is not for you to know the times of the seasons, which the Father hath put in his own power'. Cp. also John 2. 4: 'mine hour is not yet come'.

188–91. *What if . . . violence* O.T. prophets (e.g. Isa. 53. 6) had foretold Jesus's death. Cp. i 263–7.

194–5. *who best / Can suffer, best can do* echoing the words spoken by Mutius Scaevola as he thrust his hand into a flaming brazier (see *PL* ii 199n). Cp. also Matt. 20. 26–7: 'whosoever will be chief among you, let him be your servant'.

201. *my rising is thy fall* Simeon had prophesied that Jesus 'is set for the fall and rising again of many in Israel' (Luke 2. 34). MacKellar, *Var.* 4 (1975) 157, sees an image of 'the rising and setting of opposite stars' that continues the figure of Christ as morning star 'then in his rise' (i 294). See Rev. 22. 16 and Isa. 14. 12 for Christ and Satan as morning stars.

206. *no hope . . . no fear* Cp. Satan's words on Mount Niphates in *PL* iv

108: 'So farewell hope, and with hope farewell fear'. Satan is about to carry Jesus to Niphates.

211. *final good* Philosophers and theologians applied the term *summum bonum* ('highest good') to many goals, including riches, bodily delights, virtue, and contemplation. Christians saw man's *summum bonum* as the loving vision of God's perfection.

213. *whatever* both 'whatever the crime was' and 'no matter what punishment may follow'.

215–21. *though . . . cool* See *PL* iv 79*n* for the question of whether Satan might have repented. Critics disagree as to whether Satan's present swerving to repentance is sincere.

218. *aggravate* both 'make worse' and 'bring as a charge or "gravamen" against' (*OED* 3).

219. *stand between . . . ire* Cp. *Fair Infant* 69: 'To stand 'twixt us and our deservèd smart'.

221–2. *shelter . . . summer's cloud* Cp. Isa. 25. 4–5: 'For thou hast been . . . a refuge from the storm, a shadow from the heat . . . even the heat with the shadow of a cloud'.

234. *once a year* Cp. Luke 2. 41: 'Now his parents went to Jerusalem every year at the feast of the passover'.

242. *he who . . . found a kingdom* Saul, first king of Israel, anointed by Samuel while looking for his father's asses (I Sam. 9. 3–10.).

243. **unadvent'rous* *OED* cites 'adventurous' from 1350.

245. *rudiments* initial stages. See i 157–8 and note.

247. *inform* train in some particular course of action (*OED* 4b).

249. *mysteries* skills (*OED* sb^2 2c), secrets of state (*OED* sb^1 5c).

252. *a mountain high* Cp. the 'high mountain' in Matt. 4. 8 and Luke 4. 5. M. probably identifies this mountain with Mount Niphates, which was sometimes thought to be the source of both the Tigris and the Euphrates (see 255–6). Satan had alighted on Niphates in *PL* iii 742, and had there pledged himself to evil (*PL* iv 32–113).

255. *two rivers* Euphrates and Tigris. The former is *winding*, the latter *straight*. They meet and flow into the Persian Gulf.

257. *champaign* flat, open country (Mesopotamia).

259. *glebe* cultivated land.

264. **fountainless* unwatered.

270. *ancient bounds* Satan points out the boundaries of the Assyrian empire at the zenith of its power (722–636 BC).

271. *Araxes* now Aras, a river flowing through Armenia to the Caspian Sea.

274. *drouth* desert (*OED* 3).

275. *Nineveh* capital of Assyria, on the banks of the Tigris.

276. *Several days' journey* Cp. Jonah 3. 3: 'Nineveh was an exceeding great city of three days' journey'.

Ninus the eponymous founder of Nineveh, and mythical king of Assyria.

277. *that first golden monarchy* perhaps alluding to the golden head of the image in Nebuchadnezzar's dream of four empires (Dan. 2. 31-45). Daniel had interpreted the head as a symbol of Nebuchadnezzar and Babylon (2. Dan. 38).

278. *Salmanassar* Shalmaneser, King of Assyria from 727 to 722 BC, carried the ten northern tribes of Israel into captivity in 726 BC (II Kings 17. 6). Cp. iii 374-80, 414-40.

280. *Babylon* on the Euphrates. It was uninhabited in Jesus's time. The supposed founders were Belus and Semiramis, Ninus's father and wife. Thus Babylon is *As ancient* as Nineveh.

wonder of all tongues a pun. Babylon did contain wonders (the temple of Bel, the hanging gardens), but M. in *PL* xii 342-3 had identified it with Babel.

281. *him* Nebuchadnezzar, King of Babylon (which he *rebuilt*) from 604 to 561 BC. He *twice* captured Jerusalem (in 597 and 587 BC) and led the Jews into their Babylonish captivity (II Kings 24. 10-17, II Kings 25. 1-22, Dan. 1. 1-2, Jer. 39. 1-9).

284. *Cyrus* founder of the Persian empire. He conquered Babylon in 538 BC and freed the Jews (Dan. 5, Ezra 1. 1-8).

Persepolis summer capital of the Persian kings. Alexander had burned it in 331 BC.

285. *Bactra* capital of the Persian province of Bactria (now Balkh, in Afghanistan).

286. *Ecbatana* ancient capital of the Medes, and a summer residence of the Persian kings. Herodotus i 98 and Judith 1. 2-4 testify to its *structure vast*. Cp. *PL* xi 393.

287. *Hecatompylos* Greek 'hundred gates', the Parthian capital.

288. *Susa* the winter residence of the Persian kings. Cp. *PL* x 308.

Choaspes a river of Susiana.

289. *The drink of none but kings* Herodotus i 188 says that the Persian king would carry water from the Choaspes with him when he went on campaign, and would drink no other water. Athenaeus says that only the king and his son could drink of the Choaspes (*Deipnosophists* xii 515).

290. *Emathian* Macedonian (the Seleucid successors of Alexander).

291. *great Seleucia* a city on the Tigris, built by Alexander's general Seleucus Nicator (*c*. 358-281 BC). Cp. *PL* iv 212.

Nisibis a Macedonian city in north-western Mesopotamia (now Nusaaybin, on the border of Turkey and Syria).

292. *Artaxata* the ancient capital of Armenia.

Teredon a city near the confluence of the Tigris and the Euphrates.

Ctesiphon the winter capital of the Parthian kings, on the Tigris, near Seleucia.

294–7. *the Parthian . . . won* Parthia was originally a province of the Persian and Seleucid empires, but *Arsaces* threw off the Seleucid yoke in 247 BC. The Parthian Arsacid dynasty fought many wars against Rome, and halted Roman expansion to the east. Parthia was eventually supplanted by the Sassanid Persians (*c.* AD 226). The Parthian king in Jesus's time, Artabanus III, was hostile to Rome.

297. *Antioch* the Seleucid capital, on the Orontes in Syria.

298–336. *just in time . . . war* Satan is describing a typical engagement between Parthians and Scythians, rather than a specific historical campaign.

301. *Scythian* The Scythians were barbarian tribes who lived in what is now Russia and Siberia.

302. *Sogdiana* the most north-eastern province of Alexander's empire (modern Turkestan and Bokhara). It was not a Parthian province in Jesus's time.

303–36. *see . . . war* Editors cite Ammianus Marcellinus (xxv 11–19) as M.'s prime source, but Ammianus is describing Sassanid Persians, not Parthians. Most of M.'s details are found in Plutarch, *Crassus* 24, but the *steel bows* (305) are his own invention. Parthians used the Asian composite bow of sinew and horn.

306. *in flight, or in pursuit* Parthian mounted archers were renowned for their ability to shoot to the rear while feigning flight (the 'Parthian shot'). See lines 322–5.

309. *rhombs* lozenge-shaped formations.

wedges half-rhombs.

311. **outpoured.*

316. *Arachosia* the easternmost Parthian province, west of the Indus river. *Candaor* a province and city in what is now Afghanistan.

317. *Margiana* a region east of the Caspian.

Hyrcanian Hyrcania was a province south-east of the Caspian.

318. *dark Iberian dales* Iberia (modern Georgia) was heavily wooded.

319. *Atropatia* the northern portion of Media.

320. *Adiabéne* one of the plains around Nineveh.

321. *Susiana* the southernmost Parthian province, on the Persian Gulf. *Balsara's hav'n* the confluence of the Euphrates and Tigris (the Chatt-el-Arab). *Balsara* (Basra) was not founded until AD 636.

326. *The field . . . brown* Plutarch describes the Parthians at Carrhae 'blazing in helmets and breastplates' (*Crassus* 24). *Brown* means 'burnished, glistening' (*OED* 4).

327. *clouds of foot* translating Homer, *Il.* iv 274 and Virgil, *Aen.* vii 793. *horn* wing of an army (*OED* 19).

328. *Cuirassiers* heavy armoured cavalry.

329. *endorsed* *carrying on their backs (*OED* 3a).

330. *pioneers* military engineers.

334. *bridges . . . yoke* perhaps alluding to Xerxes' bridge of ships over the Hellespont, which Aeschylus (*Persians* 71-2) and M. (*PL* x 307) had called a 'yoke'.

338-43. *Agrican . . . Charlemagne* See Boiardo's romantic epic *Orlando Innamorato* I x-xiv. The Tartar King *Agrican* brought an army of 2,200,000 men to besiege *Albracca*, the fortress of *Gallaphrone*, King of Cathay. Agrican loved Gallaphrone's daughter *Angelica*. Many paladins of *Charlemagne*, including Orlando, were drawn into the conflict.

342. *prowest* most valiant.

343. *paynim* pagan: a favourite word of Spenser's.

344. *chivalry* army, host (*OED* 2).

347-9. *I seek not . . . thy safety* 'It is not my aim to stir up your valour without taking every precaution for your safety'; but the double negative (*not . . . On no slight grounds*) admits a Satanic ambiguity as to how much protection Satan is offering. At best, Satan offers only slight protection, and he might offer none at all. Cp. Jesus's condemnation of Satan's dark ambiguities in i 434-5.

347-8. *engage / Thy virtue* exhort thy manliness (*OED* 'engage' 8a, 'virtue' 7), but 'engage' could also mean 'ensnare' (*OED* 11), and Satan does mean to ensnare Jesus's moral virtue.

358. *opposite* hostile (*OED* 4a).

359. *Samaritan or Jew* Samaritans and Jews had been enemies since the Jews had returned from captivity in Babylon (Ezra 4). Satan's implication that Jesus might reconcile them is calculated to appeal to the Jesus who will tell the parable of the good Samaritan (Luke 10. 25-37) and preach to Samaritans (John 4. 5-42).

365-7. *invasion . . . bound* The Parthians invaded Judaea in about 40 BC and carried off the Judaean King Hyrcanus II, who was an ally of Rome. But Satan errs in saying that Hyrcanus's nephew Antigonus was led captive. Antigonus allied himself to the Parthians, who made him king. He reigned for three years before Herod and Mark Antony defeated and crucified him (Josephus, *Antiquities* xiv 13-16). Satan might be rewriting history so as to exaggerate Parthian power, or M. might simply be in error.

365. *annoy* injure, harm.

368. *Maugre* in spite of.

373-80. *David's . . . deliver* David ruled all twelve tribes of Israel, but the kingdom was divided after Solomon's death (933 BC). The two southern tribes remained loyal to Solomon's son Rehoboam and formed the kingdom of Judah. The ten northern tribes followed Jeroboam and formed the kingdom of Israel (I Kings 12. 12-20, *PL* i 484). Shalmaneser of Assyria led the ten tribes into captivity (see above, 278*n*), from which they never returned (hence *lost*, 377).

376. *Habor* a tributary of the Euphrates near which the King of Assyria placed the ten lost tribes (II Kings 17. 6).

377. *Ten . . . Joseph* The ten tribes are all descended from Jacob, and two of them (Ephraim and Manasseh) are also descended from Jacob's son Joseph.

384. *From Egypt to Euphrates* Cp. God's covenant with Abraham: 'Unto thy seed have I given this land, from the river of Egypt unto the great river, the river Euphrates' (Gen. 15. 18). Cp. also I Kings 4. 21.

387. *fleshly arm* Cp. II Chron. 32. 8 (on the King of Assyria): 'With him is an arm of flesh; but with us is the Lord our God to help us, and to fight our battles'; also Jer. 17. 5: 'Cursed is the man that trusteth in man, and maketh flesh his arm'. Cp. also Spenser, *FQ* III iv 27: 'So feeble is the powre of fleshly arme'.

391. *policy* political cunning.

393. *Plausible* winning public approval (*OED* 2a).

395. **unpredict* Sole instance in *OED*.

396–7. *My time . . . yet come* Cp. John 7. 6: 'My time is not yet come'.

401. *Luggage* baggage of an army (*OED* 1) and encumbrance (*OED* 2a), as in 'Those uncountable multitudes . . . are . . . rather a luggage than an aid' (1614).

410. *numb'ring Israel* Cp. I Chron. 21. 1–15: 'Satan stood up against Israel, and provoked David to number Israel . . . And God was displeased with this thing; therefore he smote Israel'. The ensuing plague killed 'seventy thousand men'.

414–15. *captive tribes . . . captivity* The ten tribes in Assyria were led captive as a punishment for idolatry (II Kings 17. 7–18).

416–17. *calves . . . Egypt* Jeroboam instituted the worship of calves in Israel. See I Kings 12. 28–9 and *PL* i 482–6.

417. *Baal . . . Ashtaroth* See *PL* i 422*n*, *Nativity* 200*n*.

425. *circumcision vain* Cp. Rom. 2. 25: 'if thou be a breaker of the law, thy circumcision is made uncircumcision'.

428. *patrimony* heritage (*OED* 1c), i.e. the idolatrous religions of the corrupt kings of Israel.

436. *Assyrian flood* the Euphrates. Jesus is recalling Isaiah's prophecy of the delivery of the ten lost tribes: 'the Lord shall . . . shake his hand over the river, and shall smite it in the seven streams, and make men go over dryshod. And there shall be an highway for the remnant of his people, which shall be left, from Assyria; like as it was to Israel in the day that he came up out of the land of Egypt' (Isa. 11. 15–16). Cp. also Rev. 16. 12 and II Esdras 13. 40–46.

438. See Exod. 14. 21–2 for the cleaving of the *Red Sea*, and Josh. 3. 14–17 for the cleaving of *Jordan*.

THE FOURTH BOOK

1. *Perplexed* sorely distressed.
   success outcome.
5. *sleeked* rendered smooth with flattering speech (*OED* 3b).
6–7. *Eve . . . deceived* See i 51–2n and cp. ii 141–2.
7. *This* Jesus.
   who Satan (referring back to *his*). Cp. the ambiguous syntax at iv 581f.
15–17. *flies . . . humming sound* Spenser (*FQ* II ix 51) compares 'idle thoughts' to buzzing flies, Homer (*Il.* ii 469–71, xvi 641–3) likens warriors to flies swarming over milk pails, and Ariosto (*Orl. Fur.* xiv 109) likens Moors attacking Christians to flies attacking ripe grapes. M.'s *wine-press* is also proleptic of Christ as vine (John 15. 1).
16. *must* new wine.
18–20. *surging waves . . . bubbles end* The simile of rock and waves is common in epic. Cp. Homer, *Il.* xv 618–22, Virgil, *Aen.* vii 586–90, Tasso, *Gerus. Lib.* ix 31. Vida (*Christiad* iv 634–6) and Giles Fletcher (*CV* iii 23) apply it to Christ resisting Satan's temptations. Cp. also Matt. 7. 24–5 (the house built upon a rock).
23. *desperate* despairing.
27. *Another plain* Latium (Lazio).
29. *ridge of hills* the Apennines.
31. *Septentrion blasts* north winds (named from the seven stars of the Great Bear).
32. *a river* the Tiber.
36. *Porches* porticos.
37. *trophies* spoils of war.
   arcs arches.
40. *parallax* an apparent change in the position of an object.
41. *multiplied* magnified optically.
42. *telescope* Cp. Fletcher, *CV* (1610) ii 58–60, where Pangloretta tempts Christ by showing him 'all the world' in a 'hollowe globe of glasse', and Christ shatters the 'optique glasses'. 'Optic glass' was a term for 'telescope' (cp. *PL* i 288).
   curious unduly inquisitive.
47. *the Capitol* the smallest of Rome's seven hills, on which stood the temple of Jove, Juno, and Minerva.
49. *Tarpeian rock* the steep cliffs of the Capitoline hill.
50. *Mount Palatine* another of the seven hills.
51. *imperial palace* the Domus Tiberiana, on the west corner of the Palatine. M. had seen the ruins of Domitian's palace on the hill's centre.

54. Roman palaces may have had *terraces*, but the *turrets* and *spires* owe more to English architecture.

57. *microscope* See above, 42*n*.

59. *hand* handiwork.

63. *Praetors* Roman magistrates acting as provincial governors in the year following their term of office at Rome. There were about sixteen praetors in Tiberius's time.

    proconsuls governors of senatorial provinces.

65. *Lictors* attendants on a magistrate. They walked before him carrying *rods* (*fasces*) as a symbol of his power.

66. *legion* the largest unit in the Roman army, with a nominal strength of 6,000 infantry.

    cohort a tenth part of a legion.

    wings cavalry formations flanking the infantry. A *turm* was a tenth part of a wing, about thirty in number.

68. *Appian road* the Via Appia, Rome's principal road to south Italy, running from Rome to Brundisium.

69. *Aemilian* the Via Aemilia, leading north from Rome.

70. *Syene* modern Aswan in Egypt, the southernmost limit of the Roman Empire.

    where the shadow both way falls i.e. at the equator, where shadows fall to the south in summer and to the north in winter.

71. *Meroë* the capital of Ethiopia, on a peninsula in the Nile, bounded by the Nile, the Atbara, and the Blue Nile.

72. *realm of Bocchus* ancient Mauretania (modern Morocco and coastal Algeria). Bocchus (Jugurtha's father-in-law) was King of Mauretania at the time of the Jugurthine War (111–106 BC).

    Blackmoor sea the Mediterranean off Morocco, by the Barbary coast.

74. *golden Chersoness* a region east of India, sometimes identified with the Malay peninsula. The usual spelling is 'Chersonese' (cp. *PL* xi 392); M. may be avoiding a rhyme with *these*.

75. *Tapróbanè* an island in the far east (Pliny, *Natural History* VI xxiv 81–91), in M.'s time identified with Ceylon or Sumatra.

77. *Gallia* Gaul.

    Gades Cadiz.

    British west Armorica (Brittany). Britain itself was not yet conquered.

78. *Scythians* See iii 301*n*.

    Sarmatians a barbarian tribe related to the Scythians. Inhabiting what is now Poland, they were never subject to Rome.

79. *Danubius* the Danube, the north-eastern border of the Roman Empire in Jesus's time.

    Tauric pool Sea of Azov.

90. *This emperor* Tiberius (42 BC–AD 37) reigned from AD 14. He had *no* *son* because his sons were dead by AD 23. In AD 26 he retired from active government and took up residence on the isle of Capri (*Capreae*). Suetonius, *De Vita Caesarum* iii 43–5, and Tacitus, *Annales* vi 1, describe his *horrid lusts* there.

95. *wicked favourite* Sejanus. He was executed in AD 31 after Tiberius denounced him to the Senate.

103–4. *to me the power / Is given* Cp. Luke 4. 6: 'And the devil said unto him, All this power will I give thee, and the glory of them: for that is delivered unto me; and to whomsoever I will I give it'.

115. *citron tables* Citrus wood was famed for its hardness and the beauty of its grain.

Atlantic stone marble from the Atlas Mountains.

117. *Setia, Cales, and Falerne* famous wine-growing districts south of Rome.

118. *Chios and Crete* Aegean islands famous for wine.

119. *Crystal and myrrhine cups* Pliny xxxiii 2, and Juvenal vi 155–6, mention cups of crystal and myrrhine as luxuries prized by the Romans. Myrrhine was probably Chinese porcelain imported from Parthia.

130. *Conscience* Tacitus, *Annales* vi 6, testifies that Tiberius was tortured by guilt.

132. *That people victor once* the Romans, who had been free and victorious under the Republic, but were now vassals of the emperors.

133. *Deservedly made vassal* M. believed that external enslavement was the inevitable punishment of those who became slaves to their own passions. Cp. *PL* xii 82–104.

136. *Peeling* plundering, pillaging.

138. *insulting* exulting proudly or contemptuously.

139. *sports* gladiatorial combats.

142. *scene* theatrical performance (*OED* 3a). Plato, the Christian Fathers, and the Puritans thought that the theatre was morally corrupting. M. defends tragedy in his preamble to *SA*, so Jesus is probably not condemning all drama. M. might be alluding to the Restoration theatre.

147. *like a tree* Jesus sees himself as the fulfilment of Nebuchadnezzar's dream of a tree that 'reached unto heaven, and the sight thereof to the end of all the earth' (Dan. 4. 10–12). Daniel had interpreted the tree as a sign of Nebuchadnezzar, but Christian exegesis made it a symbol of Christ's Church (Lewalski 277–8). Cp. the parable of the mustard seed (Matt. 13. 21–2).

149. *as a stone* Jesus refers to Nebuchadnezzar's dream of a stone that smashed an idol and then became a mountain (Dan. 2. 31–5). Daniel saw the stone as a sign of God's kingdom that would break all other kingdoms and 'stand for ever' (Dan. 2. 44). Christian exegesis interpreted the stone as Christ or his kingdom (Lewalski 279).

151. *kingdom . . . no end* Luke 1. 33.

152–3. *Means there shall be* Jesus never does tell Satan what the *means* to his kingdom will be. Rushdy (237) thinks that he is referring to 'the "paradise within"', but Jesus has just referred to his kingship over *all the earth* (148). One means to this, as yet unsuspected by Satan, is the Crucifixion (see *PL* iii 333–42, xii 386–465). Satan will soon read Jesus's death in the stars (iv 382–93), but he nowhere imagines that this will be the means whereby Jesus will fulfil his kingship.

157. *nice* fastidious, difficult to please.

158. *still* always.

164. *giv'n to me* Allan H. Gilbert, in *JEGP* 15 (1916) 606, points out that Satan does not include Athens among the gifts under his personal control. See also Pope (67).

166–7. *if . . . lord* Cp Matt. 4. 9: 'All these things will I give thee, if thou wilt fall down and worship me'.

175–7. *It is written . . . serve* Cp. Luke 4. 8: 'Get thee behind me, Satan: for it is written, Thou shalt worship the Lord thy God, and him only shalt thou serve'. Jesus is referring to the first of the Ten Commandments (Exod. 20. 3, Deut. 6. 13). Cp. Matt. 4. 10.

184. *donation* bestowal of property (*OED* 1).

185. *King of kings* The title could be used either of God (I Tim. 6. 15) or Christ (Rev. 17. 14, 19. 16). Jesus here uses it of the Father, but he also makes his own implicit claim in calling Satan's kingdoms *my own* (191).

193. *Get thee behind me* Luke 4. 8 (cit. above, 175–7n).

194. *That Evil One, Satan* Jesus had recognized Satan at i 356, but this is the first and only time that he addresses him by name. The name declares the enmity that Satan has so far denied or tried to conceal (see i 387, ii 330). Satan will not admit to being Jesus's enemy until iv 525–7.

197. *Sons of God both angels are and men* Angels (including Satan) are called *sons of God* at Job 1. 6 and 2. 1. John 1. 12 and Rom. 8. 14 state that *men* may become sons of God. Cp. also Ps. 82. 6: 'I have said, Ye are gods; and all of you are children of the most High'. Many critics take Satan at his word when he professes not to know how Jesus bears the title. See i 91, iv 517 and notes.

199. *proposed* presented to view (*OED* 1), handed to someone for him to take (*OED* 3a).

201. *Tetrarchs* subordinate rulers, rulers of a fourth part (*OED* 2a). The Roman province of Judaea was divided into four tetrarchies (Luke 3. 1). Satan applies the term to demonic rulers of the four elements (201) and rulers of all human nations from the *quartered winds* (202).

203. *God of this world* Satan's title in II Cor. 4. 4.

215. *that early action* See i 209–14n.

217. *wast*] was *1671*. The emendation has been widely adopted since the eighteenth century.

218. **disputant* engaged in controversy (*OED*'s earliest adjectival instance).

219. *fitting Moses' chair* regarding the law. Cp. Matt. 23. 2: 'The scribes and the Pharisees sit in Moses' seat'. Moses 'sat to judge the people' in Exod. 18. 13-16.

225. *couched* comprised, included (*OED* v¹ 14).

226. *Pentateuch* the first five books of the O.T.

228. *To admiration* in an excellent manner (*OED* 2b).

231. *Without their learning* Satan assumes that a man brought up as a carpenter must be ignorant of Greek philosophy, but Jesus soon shows himself to be conversant with it (iv 286-321). Thus Satan's offer is not so much 'rejected' as it is shown to be redundant.

234. *idolisms* *fallacies (*OED* 3) or idolatries. Sylvester had coined the word in *DWW* (1592-1608), *The Decay* (1608), where it means 'idolatries' (491, 507). Satan might be punning.

   paradoxes used by the Stoics to teach moral philosophy.

235. *evinced* confuted (*OED* 2b).

236. *specular* *affording an extensive view (*OED* 7). Cp. 'top / Of speculation' (*PL* xii 588-9).

239. *pure the air* Plato and Cicero attributed the Athenians' intelligence to the clear air of their city (*Timaeus* 24C, *De Fato* iv 7). Cp. *PL* ix 44-5 and note.

240. *the eye* the seat of intelligence or light (*OED* 3e). Athens and Sparta were anciently described as the 'eyes' of Greece (see e.g. Aristotle, *Rhetoric* III x 7).

242. *recess* place of retirement.

244. *Academe* an olive grove and gymnasium west of Athens, near the hill of Colonus. Plato established his school there.

245. *Attic bird* the nightingale. Colonus was the home of many nightingales (Sophocles, *Oedipus at Colonus* 671).

247. *Hymettus* a range of hills to the south-east of Athens, famous for honey.

249. *Ilissus* a small river flowing from Hymettus through the Attic plain to the sea. Plato's *Phaedrus* is set there.

251. *who* Aristotle, Alexander's tutor.

253. *Lyceum* a grove and gymnasium where Aristotle taught. M. errs in placing it *within the walls*; it lay to the east of Athens, near the Ilissus. *painted Stoa* the northern colonnade of the Athenian market-place, decorated with frescoes. Zeno taught there, and his followers were known as 'Stoics'.

255. *numbers* groups of notes (*OED* 18).

257. *Aeolian charms* songs in the Aeolic dialect (e.g. the lyric poems of Sappho and Alcaeus).

Dorian lyric odes Pindar, Alcman and Stesichorus wrote odes in the Doric dialect.

258. *his who gave them breath* Homer, anciently seen as the origin of all poetry.

259. *Melesigenes* a name sometimes applied to Homer in allusion to his alleged birthplace near the banks of the river Meles in Ionia.

thence from his blindness. According to an ancient etymology, 'Homer' was the Cumaean word for 'blind'.

260. *challenged* laid claim to (*OED* 5). Apollo claims authorship of Homer's poems in an epigram in *The Greek Anthology* ix 455.

262. *chorus or iambic* The chorus in Greek tragedy is written in various metres; the dialogue is usually in iambic trimeter. See M.'s preface to *SA*.

264. *sententious precepts* aphoristic maxims. M. in *Defensio* (1651) cites maxims from Aeschylus, Sophocles, Euripides and Seneca. He concludes that poets place their own opinions in the mouths only of their great characters. Other characters (such as the royalist chorus in Aeschylus's *Suppliants*) do not speak for their authors (*YP* 4. 446).

266. *passions* including 'sufferings' (*OED* 3).

268. *resistless* irresistible.

269. *Wielded* ruled.

democraty democracy.

270. *Shook the Arsenal* caused the dockyards to reverberate. Athenian orators addressed large crowds in the Piraeus, and their oratory could stir men into making noisy preparations for a naval expedition. Aristophanes imagines just such an event in *Acharnians* 550f., where he says that 'all the arsenal had rung with noise'. In 415 BC, Alcibiades' eloquence was decisive in launching the Sicilian expedition (Thucydides vi 15–19).

fulmined thundered. Aristophanes says that Pericles thundered and lightened over Greece (*Acharnians* 530). Cicero describes Demosthenes as *fulmina* (*Ad Atticum* xv 1a).

271. *Artaxerxes* name of several Persian kings hostile to Athens.

273. *low-roofed* Socrates lived in a modest home. See Xenophon, *Oeconomicus* II iii, and Aristophanes, *Clouds* 92.

275–6. *oracle . . . men* When Chaerephon asked the Delphic oracle if any man was wiser than Socrates, the oracle replied that none was (Plato, *Apology* 21).

278. *Academics old and new* Ancient writers divided the Academy's history into three phases: old, under Plato (d. 347 BC); middle, under Arcesilas (d. 242 BC); and new, under Carneades (d. 128 BC).

279. *Peripatetics* Aristotle's school derived its name from a covered walk (*peripatos*) in the Lyceum, or from Aristotle's habit of walking about (*peripatein*) while lecturing.

279-80. *sect / Epicurean*   The teaching of Epicurus (341-271 BC derived from Aristippus, a pupil of Socrates. See 299*n*, below.

Stoic severe   See *A Masque* 707*n*.

281. *revolve*   turn over in your mind.

289. *fountain of light*   a traditional image for God the Father. See *PL* iii 7-8*n*.

293. *the first*   Socrates.

294. *To know . . . nothing knew*   Socrates was puzzled when he learned that the Delphic oracle had pronounced him the wisest of men (see above, 275-6*n*). After searching Athens for a man wiser than himself, he concluded that he was the wisest – but only because he knew that he knew nothing (Plato, *Apology* 21-3).

295. *The next*   Plato. The contempt for his *fabling* is itself Platonic. Plato banished the poets from his ideal city because they were fablers (*Republic* x 595-607), yet he is one himself. M. in *Idea* 38 calls him *fabulator maximus*, 'the greatest storyteller'.

smooth conceits   specious, fanciful notions.

296. *third sort*   the Sceptics, founded by Pyrrhon of Elis (*c*. 365-*c*. 270 BC). They held that knowledge was unattainable, either by reason or the senses, and that the opposite to any statement is no less true than the statement itself.

297. *Others*   the Peripatetics. Aristotle had argued that both virtue and external goods were necessary for happiness (*Nicomachean Ethics* i 11).

299. *he*   Epicurus. He taught that pleasure was the chief good – but by 'pleasure' he meant the pleasure of a virtuous mind, not *corporal pleasure*. Jesus is repeating slanders levelled at the Epicureans by the Stoics.

300-307. *The Stoic . . . boast*   The Stoics (founded by Zeno of Citium, *c*. 333 262 BC) believed in the absolute freedom of the individual will. The wise man's aim was to accept whatever happened and live in harmony with divine reason. M. sees Stoicism as flawed because it ignores Original Sin. Cp. his contempt in *CD* ii 10 for the Stoics' 'hypocritical patience' (trans. Carey, *YP* 6. 740).

303. *shames not to prefer*   'is unashamed to prefer himself to God'.

305-6. *life . . . he leaves*   Stoics permitted suicide in some circumstances. Nero forced Seneca to commit suicide.

308. *conviction*   including 'consciousness of sin' (*OED* 8).

316-17. *usual names . . . Fate*   M. in *CD* i 2 explains that 'fate or *fatum* is only what is *fatum*, spoken, by some almighty power' (trans. Carey, *YP* 6. 131). Cp. *PL* vii 173.

321. *empty cloud*   alluding to Ixion, who embraced a cloud instead of Juno. Cp. M.'s veiled allusions to the same myth in *The Passion* 56 and *PL* iv 499-500.

321-2. *many books . . . wearisome*   Cp. Eccles. 12. 12: 'of making many books there is no end; and much study is a weariness of the flesh'. In *Areopagitica* M. adds: 'but neither he, nor any other inspired author, tells us that . . . reading is unlawful' (*YP* 2. 514). Some pagan philosophers agreed with Jesus. Cp. Marcus Aurelius, *Meditations* ii 3: 'cast away the thirst after books'.

328. *Crude* lacking power to digest (*OED* 3b).

329. *worth a sponge* both *'worth very little' (*OED* 'sponge' 1b) and 'fit to be expunged' (*OED* 4a).

334. *story* the historical books of the O.T.

335. *artful terms* either 'artistic expressions' or 'technical terms' (such as appear in the headings of certain psalms).

336–7. *Our . . . victors' ear* Cp. Ps. 137. 1–3: 'By the rivers of Babylon, there we sat down, yea, we wept, when we remembered Zion . . . For there they that carried us away captive required of us a song . . . saying, Sing us one of the songs of Zion.'

338. *Greece from us these arts derived* It was a patristic and Renaissance commonplace that the Jews invented the arts and passed them on to the Egyptians and Greeks.

341. *personating* both 'representing in writing' (*OED* 5) and 'imitating the example of' (*OED* 4).

343. *swelling* bombastic, turgid (*OED* 8).

343–4. *thick-laid . . . harlot's cheek* Cp. Shakespeare, *Hamlet* III i 51: 'The harlot's cheek, beautied with plast'ring art'.

344. *varnish* cosmetics, outward show.

346–7. *unworthy to compare / With Sion's songs* M. in *RCG* (1642) affirms that biblical poets are superior to all others 'in the very critical art of composition' (*YP* 1. 816). Sidney also believed that biblical poets were superior to the Greeks. See *A Defence of Poesie*, in *Works*, ed. Feuillerat (1923) iii 9.

347. *tastes* *faculty of perceiving what is excellent in art or literature (*OED* 8a).

351. *Unless* refers back to 'unworthy' (346).

352. *light of Nature* reason, God's image in man.

354. *statists* statesmen.

366. *all his darts were spent* Cp. Eph. 6. 16: 'the shield of faith, wherewith ye shall be able to quench all the fiery darts of the wicked'.

377. *Nicely* fastidiously.

380. *fulness of time* Cp. Gal. 4. 4: 'when the fulness of time was come, God sent forth his Son'.

382. *contrary* on the contrary.

382–93. *read . . . rubric set* Satan casts Jesus's horoscope. Astrology was controversial in seventeenth-century England. Cp. Jer. 10. 2: 'Learn not the way of the heathen, and be not dismayed at the signs of heaven'. M.

cites this verse in *CD* ii 5, but he also points to the Magi and their star as evidence that 'there is some astrology which is neither useless nor unlawful' (trans. Carey, *YP* 6. 696).

384. *Voluminous* forming a large book.

characters stars regarded as individual letters in the book, with a pun on 'astrological symbol of a planet' (*OED* 5). Cp. Marlowe, *Faustus* II i 168: 'a book where I might see all characters and planets of the heavens'.

385. *conjunction* the apparent proximity of two stars or planets.

spell comprehend by study (*OED* 2a), with a pun on 'spell out letter by letter'.

387. *Attends* are in store for (*OED* 14). The matching of plural subject with singular verb was not unusual in seventeenth-century English.

injuries including 'insults' (*OED* 2).

391–2. *eternal . . . Without beginning* Satan sarcastically plays on the notion that eternity has neither beginning nor end.

393. *rubric* a chapter-title printed in red letters (*OED* 2a), continuing the book metaphor (384–5).

399. *unsubstantial* Darkness and night are merely the absence of light. Cp. *PL* ii 439: 'unessential Night'.

400. *mere* including the modern sense and 'absolute, entire' (*OED* 4). Darkness is no less total for being privative.

402. *jaunt* fatiguing or troublesome journey (*OED* 1).

407. *at his head* See *PL* viii 292n.

409. *either tropic* the northern and southern skies (Cancer and Capricorn). The *ends of heav'n* are the east and west.

410–19. *thunder . . . sheer* As 'prince of the power of the air' (Eph. 2. 2), Satan can raise storms (Burton, *Anatomy of Melancholy* I ii I 2). Cp. the storms raised by malevolent deities to harass particular mortals in Homer, *Od.* v 291–6, Virgil, *Aen.* i 82–123, and Tasso, *Gerus. Lib.* vii 115–17.

411. *abortive* The clouds are imagined to be wombs that miscarry the elements of fire and water. Cp. the 'abortive gulf' of Chaos (*PL* ii 441), which also brings contraries together and so fails to deliver the four elements.

412–13. *water with fire . . . reconciled* Cp. Aeschylus, *Agamemnon* 650–52: 'fire and sea, once bitterest enemies, swore alliance and conspired to ruin the Greek fleet'.

413. *ruin* both 'destruction' and 'falling'.

414. *caves* Aeolus kept the winds imprisoned in a vast cavern. See Virgil, *Aen.* i 52–4, Lucan, *Pharsalia* v 608–10.

415. *hinges* cardinal points (Latin *cardo*, 'hinge').

419. *shrouded* sheltered. Lewalski (312) sees a premonition of Jesus's death and burial.

420. *only* solitary (*OED* 1).

423. *some howled, some yelled, some shrieked* Cp. Tasso, *Gerus. Lib.* xvi 67:

'Some spirits howld, some barkt, some hist, some cride' (trans. Fairfax).

424. *fiery darts* See above, 366n.

426–7. *morning . . . amice grey* Cp. 'the grey-hooded Ev'n, / Like a sad votarist in palmer's weed' (*A Masque* 188–9). An *amice* was an ecclesiastical hood lined with grey fur.

428. *radiant finger* Cp. Homer's 'rosy-fingered dawn'.

437. *Cleared up* sang out clearly.

438. *gratulate* greet (*OED* 1) and show thanks for (*OED* 4).

446. *despite* hatred, spite.

449. *in wonted shape* either 'in his accustomed disguise (as an old man)' or 'in his own shape (as the Devil)'. The former reading would mean that Satan has retained the same human disguise (but not the same clothes) throughout his temptations. See ii 299n. Pope (46–50) finds precedents for both readings.

452. *rack* gale, storm (*OED* sb¹ 2), *crash as of something breaking (*OED* sb⁵ 1b).

453. *earth and sky would mingle* Cp. Virgil, *Aen.* i 133–4: *caelum terramque . . . miscere.*

454. *flaws* squalls.

455. *pillared* Cp. Job 26. 11: 'the pillars of heaven tremble'.

457. *main* the universe (macrocosm) as opposed to the microcosm of *man's less universe* (459).

458. *sneeze* Renaissance medicine adopted Aristotle's belief that sneezing purged the brain and so was therapeutic.

467. *Did I not tell thee* See iv 375ff.

470. *push* exertion of influence to promote a person's advancement, critical juncture (*OED* sb¹ 1c, 6).

481. *ominous* attended by evil omens.

496. *storm'st* both 'rage' and 'raise a storm'.

500–501. *Son . . . doubt* Satan mockingly implies that the titles *Son of David* and *Son of God* are incompatible. Behind the sneer lies an old debate as to whether Jesus was descended from David through Joseph alone, or both Joseph and Mary (see iii 154n). Satan might even imply that Jesus is Joseph's biological son. As such, he would be David's heir, but not the *virgin-born* Messiah prophesied at Isa. 7. 14.

503–4. *thy birth . . . with the first I knew* Satan has given some indication that he is familiar with Jesus's early life (see ii 413–15, iv 215–21), but this is his first open admission that he has been watching him since birth.

518. *The Son of God I also am* Cp. Job 1. 6: 'Now there was a day when the sons of God came to present themselves before the Lord, and Satan came also among them'.

520. *All men are Sons of God* Cp. Ps. 82. 6–7: 'all of you are children of the most High'.

524. *collect* infer.

525. *fatal* both 'deadly' and 'decreed by fate'.

529. *parle* parley.

composition truce, terms of surrender (*OED* 23). Satan is evasive as to who would surrender.

534. *adamant* a mythical substance of impenetrable hardness.

centre fixed point at the centre of rotation.

542. *hippogriff* a fabulous creature (half horse, half griffin) on which Ariosto's heroes fly around the world and ascend to the moon (*Orl. Fur.* ii 37–55, iv 4, x 66–7, xxii 26–8, xxxiv 48–51, 68–81).

sublime raised aloft (*OED* 1).

546. *Temple* the Temple built by Herod the Great (on the site of Solomon's Temple). Cp. the description in Josephus, *De Bellis* V v 6.

547. *pile* lofty building.

549. *highest pinnacle* Satan sets Christ on a 'pinnacle of the temple' at Matt. 4. 5 and Luke 4. 9. The nature of this 'pinnacle' was much debated. In M.'s time it was variously identified as a projecting cornice, a parapet, a flat roof and a sharp spire (Pope 84–5). M.'s pinnacle is presumably one of the *golden spires*. Critical opinion is divided as to whether Jesus stands by human effort alone or by a miracle. See below, 584*n*.

554. *progeny* lineage, parentage (*OED* 5).

555. *Cast thyself down* Cp. Matt 4. 6 and Luke 4. 10: 'If thou be the Son of God, cast thyself down'. Biblical commentators assumed that Christ had a choice and that Satan was tempting him to presumption. But Pope (92–5) and Lewalski (315–16) argue that M.'s Satan does not intend Jesus to choose. Rather, 'he expected him to fall, and by falling to settle the problem of his identity. If he were the Son of God, the angels would save him; if he were not, he would die' (Pope 94–5). Other critics see Satan as tempting Jesus. See esp. Ashraf H. A. Rushdy, 'Standing Alone on the Pinnacle: Milton in 1752', *MS* (1990) 193–218.

556. *it is written* See Ps. 91. 11–12: 'For he shall give his angels charge over thee, to keep thee in all thy ways. / They shall bear thee up in their hands, lest thou dash thy foot against a stone.' Both in *PR* and in the Gospels (Matt. 4. 6, Luke 4. 10) Satan omits the words 'in all thy ways'. Biblical exegetes saw the omission as a twisting of Psalm 91, where God's protection is conditional (Pope 82). Psalm 91 continues: 'the dragon shalt thou trample under feet'. Cp. God's curse on the serpent (i 53–65).

560–61. *Also . . . thy God* Cp. Luke 4. 12 and Matt. 4. 7: 'It is written again, Thou shalt not tempt the Lord thy God'. Jesus is citing Deut. 6. 16: 'Ye shall not tempt the Lord your God, as ye tempted him in Massah'. At Massah the Jews had 'tempted' (i.e. made trial of) God by demanding a miracle (Exod. 17. 1–7). Jesus therefore hints that he will not give Satan the miracle he is asking for. Many critics hear an additional (or alternative) meaning: 'Do not tempt *me*, your God'. There was some precedent for reading the Gospels in this way (Pope 103), but several critics reject that meaning here since it 'would give Satan the answer that he seeks' (MacCallum 260). This objection fails to recognize that ambiguities are not clear answers (see i 434–41). M. in his divorce pamphlets had argued that Christ speaks ambiguously to those who would tempt him (see *YP* 2. 329, 2. 642–3).

561–2. *stood . . . fell* Both words have moral overtones. Cp. *PL* iii 102: 'Freely they stood who stood, and fell who fell'. Satan does not fall in the Gospels. Cp. Giles Fletcher, *CV* ii 38, where Presumption 'tombled headlong'.

563. *Antaeus* a Libyan giant, son of Neptune and Earth. Wrestling with Hercules, he drew strength from contact with his mother Earth, and so arose stronger from each fall. Seeing this, Hercules throttled him in the air (Lucan, *Pharsalia* iv 593–660). Jesus vanquishes the 'prince of the power of the air' in his own element (see i 39*n*).

563–4. *to compare . . . greatest* Virgil had compared 'great things with small' (*Ecl.* i 24) and 'small things with great' (*Georg.* iv 176), and M. echoes Virgil in *PL* ii 921, vi 310, and x 306. He now overgoes Virgil with a superlative.

565. *Jove's Alcides* Hercules, Jove's son by Alcmene. Alcmene's husband Amphitryon was the son of Alcaeus (hence *Alcides*). As Jove's son, Hercules was not Alcaeus's grandson, but M. gives him the patronymic perhaps to imply that Jesus is David's legal heir even though he is not Joseph's son. See iii 154*n*, iv 500–1*n*. Hercules was a 'type' of Christ (see *Nativity* 227–8*n*).

568. *expired* both 'breathed his last' (referring to Antaeus) and 'became void through lapse of time' (referring to Satan's power). Cp. iv 174–5 ('I endure the time, till which expired / Thou hast permission on me') and iv 394–5 ('he knew his power / Not yet expired').

569. *foil* including 'a throw not resulting in a flat fall' (*OED* 1, wrestling term).

572. *Theban monster* the Sphinx. She leapt to her death from the Theban acropolis (*Ismenian steep*) after Oedipus answered her riddle: 'What creature walks on four legs in the morning, on two at noon, and on three at evening?' Oedipus answered: 'Man'. Stanley Fish, *MS* 17 (1983) 182, notes that this is also the answer to Satan's question about Jesus (iv 538–40), who resists temptation as a man. Cp. i 150–67.

578. *triumphals* *tokens of triumph (*OED* 2, sole instance).

581. *globe* compact body of persons (*OED* 8). Giles Fletcher coined this sense (from Latin *globus*) to describe Christ's ascension amidst 'A globe of winged Angels' (*CV* iv 13). Both poets may also suggest a spherical formation of flying angels. Cp. *Nativity* 110 and *PL* ii 512.

582-3. *angels . . . received him soft* Cp. Fletcher, *CV* ii 38: 'But him the Angels on their feathers caught, / And to an ayrie mountaine nimbly bore'. M.'s *him* at first seems to be Satan, the last figure named, but turns out to be Jesus. Carey calls this 'a splendid dismissal of Satan, now fallen, from the poem. He ceases to count even as a grammatical referent'.

583. *vans* *wings (*OED* sb¹ 3), a sense coined by M. in *PL* ii 927.

584. *uneasy station* Carey in his note to iv 560-61 takes these words to mean that Jesus stood by human skill, not a miracle. MacCallum (258) replies: 'it is the station which is . . . "uneasy", not the stander'. MacCallum assumes that *station* means 'a place to stand' (*OED* 7a), but it might mean 'manner of standing' (*OED* 1), as in 'Nature . . . allowes us two feet for the firmer station' (1650).

587-8. *set before him . . . food* Cp. Matt. 4. 11: 'angels came and ministered unto him'. Fletcher describes the angels as presenting Christ with a banquet (*CV* ii 61).

589. *Ambrosial* M.'s Jesus eats ambrosia only at the end of his temptation. Cp. Fletcher's Christ, who throughout his fast 'upon ambrosia daily fed' (*CV* ii 29).

Tree of Life Cp. Rev. 22. 14: 'Blessed are they that do his commandments, that they may have right to the tree of life'. Jesus's eating from the Tree of Life signifies his regaining of the Paradise that Adam lost by eating from the Tree of Knowledge.

590. *Fount of Life* Rev. 21. 6.

596. *True image of the Father* Heb. 1. 2-3.

597. *bosom of bliss* John 1. 18, *PL* iii 169, 239, 279, x 225.

597-8. *light of light / Conceiving* receiving light from the source of all light (the Father). Cp. *PL* iii 1-12.

599. *tabernacle* the human body regarded as the abode of the soul (*OED* 3c). The metaphor is common in the Bible (Cp. II Pet. 1. 14, II Cor. 5. 1), but the Son's *fleshly tabernacle* specifically recalls the Tabernacle as God's dwelling-place (Exod. 35-40).

601. *habit* outward form (*OED* 1e), with overtones of 'deportment, posture' (*OED* 4) suggesting that the Son has retained divine dignity even when balancing on the tower (notice *place* and *motion*).

605. *debel* put down in fight (*OED*), a rare word coined in the sixteenth century from Latin *debellare*.

607. *Supplanted* dispossessed by treachery (*OED* 3), caused to fall from a position of power (*OED* 2), as in 'He set upon our fyrst parentes in paradyse and by pride supplanted them' (1522). The etymology (Latin *sub*, 'under', and *planta*, 'sole of the foot') anticipates the treading underfoot that Satan had dreaded at i 53-63 and which the angels prophesy explicitly in lines 620-21. *OED*'s earliest participial instance (but see *PL* x 513).

611. *his snares are broke* Cp. Ps. 124. 7: 'The snare is broken, and we are escaped'.

612. *be failed* be absent (i.e. 'has disappeared').

613. *A fairer Paradise* Cp. *PL* xii 587: 'A Paradise within thee, happier far'.

619. *autumnal star* a comet or meteor. Such bodies were thought to be generated in the atmosphere, so the simile is apt to Satan's expulsion from *the clouds*. Cp. *PL* ii 708–11.

620. *lightning . . . from heav'n* Cp. Christ's words at Luke 10. 18: 'I beheld Satan as lightning fall from heaven'.

620–21. *trod down / Under his feet* Cp. Rom. 16. 20 ('the God of peace shall bruise Satan under your feet shortly'), Mal. 4. 3 ('ye shall tread down the wicked . . . under the soles of your feet') and Luke 10. 19 ('I give unto you power to tread on serpents and scorpions, and over all the power of the enemy'). All of these texts recall God's curse on the serpent at Gen. 3. 15. Cp. *PL* x 190.

622. *thy last and deadliest wound* After his final defeat, Satan will be cast into 'the lake of fire' where he will be 'tormented day and night for ever and ever' (Rev. 20. 10).

624. *Abaddon* Hell, place of destruction. This is the O.T. meaning of the Hebrew word, which A.V. usually renders as 'destruction' (Job 26. 6, Prov. 15. 11, 27. 20) and which M. renders as 'perdition' in his translation of Ps. 88. 11. At Rev. 9. 11 Abaddon is the angel of the bottomless pit.

628. *holds* places of refuge, strongholds (*OED* sb¹ 9, 10). Babylon is 'the hold of every foul spirit' at Rev. 18. 2.

possession both military (of *holds*) and demonic.

630–32. *herd of swine . . . before their time* In Matt. 8. 28–34 Jesus meets two people possessed of devils, and the devils cry out: 'art thou come hither to torment us before the time?' The devils then ask permission to enter a herd of swine, Jesus consents, and the swine plunge into the sea and are drowned. Cp. Mark 5. 1–13, Luke 8. 26–33.

636. *meek* Cp. Matt. 11. 29: 'I am meek and lowly in heart'.

SAMSON AGONISTES

SA appeared in 1671, in the same volume as *PR*. The date of composition is not known. The traditional dating is 1666–70, but W. R. Parker has argued for the late 1640s or early 1650s. He has convinced several editors. Edward Phillips informs us that *PR* was written between 1667 and 1670, but of *SA* he says only that the date of composition 'cannot certainly be concluded' (Darbishire 75). It is possible that different parts were written at different times. Some lines were almost certainly written after 1660, for they have a strong topical relevance. See esp. 678–704 and note. In the title, *agonistes* is a Greek word meaning 'contestant in the games' or 'champion'. Here it refers to Samson's display of strength in Dagon's temple, and so (in the manner of such Greek titles as *Prometheus Bound* or *Oedipus at Colonus*) indicates which episode in the hero's life the drama will present. Edward Phillips compiled a dictionary, in which he defines 'agonize' as 'play the champion'. M.'s chorus call Samson God's 'champion' (705, 1152, 1751). *Agon* is also a term from Greek tragedy, where it denotes a set-piece (usually a distinct scene) in which two hostile characters confront each other with opposing speeches of about equal length. See Michael Lloyd, *The Agon in Euripides* (1992). Samson's confrontations with Dalila and Harapha are agones in this sense. In Christian usage, the word implied a spiritual struggle. Jesus's 'agony' at Luke 22. 44 is called an *agonia* in the Greek. The name 'Samson' was thought to mean 'there the second time'. Phillips so derives it in his dictionary. This (false) etymology may have suggested M.'s idea of a second encounter with Dalila (not found in Judges).

Preface: OF THAT SORT OF DRAMATIC POEM . . .
3. *Aristotle* See *Poetics* vi on tragic catharsis.
8–10. *so in physic . . . humours* The analogy between tragic catharsis and homoeopathic medicine ('like cures like') is not Aristotelian, but is found in such Renaissance critics as Minturno, Guarini, and Heinsius. Minturno and Guarini are less hospitable than M. to *pity and fear*, which they maintain is driven out, not reduced *to just measure*. Heinsius is closer to M. but he limits the catharsis to pity and fear, not *other such like passions*.
14. *a verse of Euripides* 'Evil communications corrupt good manners' (I Cor. 15. 33), quoted by St Paul from a Euripidean fragment that had become proverbial.
15. *Paraeus* David Paraeus (1548–1622), a German Calvinist. M. refers to chapter 8 of his *In Divinam Apocalypsin* (1618), which had been translated by Elias Arnold as *On the Divine Apocalypse* (1644).
20. *Dionysius* Dionysius I of Syracuse (*c.* 430–367 BC, Tyrant from 405). He was a patron of the arts, and bought the writing tablets of Aeschylus. His own poems were often ridiculed, but his tragedy *The Ransoming of Hector* won first prize at the Athenian Lenaea in the year of his death.
21. *Augustus Caesar* Suetonius reports that Augustus destroyed his unfinished tragedy *Ajax* (*Caesars* ii 85).
23. *Seneca* Lucius Annaeus Seneca (4 BC–AD 65). Seneca the Stoic philosopher was the same person as Seneca the tragedian, but this was not yet known in M.'s time, hence M.'s caution in identifying them.

25. *Gregory Nazianzen* Bishop of Constantinople (329–389). He was long thought to have written *Christus Patiens* (*Christ Suffering*), but his authorship is now doubted.

30. *interludes* comic stage-plays.

32. *sadness* seriousness (*OED* 2).

   trivial commonplace (*OED* 5).

35. *prologue* a prefatory address (the modern sense), not to be confused with Aristotle's sense (part of a tragedy preceding the chorus's entrance).

37. *Martial . . . epistle* Martial prefaces five of his twelve books of *Epigrams* with prose epistles. The epistle to *Epig.* ii notes that tragedies and comedies may need epistles since 'they cannot speak for themselves'.

45. **monostrophic* repeating one strophic (stanzaic) arrangement.

   apolelymenon Greek 'freed' (from the obligation to repeat stanzaic patterns).

46. *strophe* (lit. 'turning') the stanza sung by the Greek chorus as it danced from right to left across the orchestra. The *antistrophe* ('counter-turning') was a metrically identical stanza sung by the chorus as it moved back again. The chorus then stood still to sing the *epode* in a different metre, to a different tune. M. is correct in thinking that these metrical divisions were *framed only for the music*.

50. **alloeostropha* Greek 'of irregular strophes'.

54. *the fifth act* Greek tragedies did not strictly adhere to a five-act structure, but they are generally divided by choruses into four or five episodes. *SA* can be so divided into five acts: Act I (lines 1–325), Act II (lines 326–709), Act III (lines 710–1060), Act IV (lines 1061–1296), Act V (lines 1297–end).
   produced prolonged, extended in time (*OED* 2c).

   style and uniformity diction and consistency of characterization (see Aristotle, *Poetics* xxii and xv).

55. *explicit* *simple (*OED* 1). Aristotle (*Poetics* vi) classes plots as either simple or complex (*intricate*). His preference was for complex plots in which an action brings about the opposite of what was intended. *SA* fits this description.

56. *economy* *arrangement of a poem (*OED* 7), the 'putting together of the incidents' (Aristotle, *Poetics* vi).

57. *decorum* literary propriety (*OED* 1), as in *Of Education* (1644): 'what the laws are of a true *Epic* poem, what of a *Dramatic*, what of a *Lyric*, what decorum is, which is the grand master peece to observe' (*YP* 2. 405).

61. *circumscription of time* Aristotle's 'unity of time', whereby tragedy 'tries' to confine itself to one day. Renaissance neo-classical critics hardened Aristotle's 'unity of time' into a *rule*, even though several Greek tragedies do not accord with it.

Argument

2. *workhouse* where vagrants and the unemployed poor were forced to work in return for food and shelter (*OED* 1).

6. *equals* people of about the same age (*OED* B 1c).

20. *second time* The Public Officer gives Samson two opportunities (1310, 1390) to obey him. There may be a pun on 'Samson' (thought to mean 'there the second time').

25. *catastrophe* the change (Greek 'overturning') that produces the conclusion of a drama: the dénouement.

26. *by accident* as a secondary effect (as in Latin *per accidens*). M. might be justifying Samson's suicide (which had been an obstacle to his sainthood). See below, 503-15n, 1584n, 1664-5n and Krouse (49).

1-2. *A little . . . on* Cp. the blind Oedipus led by Antigone in Sophocles, *Oedipus at Colonus* 1-13, and the blind Tiresias led by his daughter in Euripides, *Phoenician Women* 834-5.

5. *servile* befitting a slave.

6. *else enjoined me* otherwise imposed on me.

9. *draught* inhaled air.

11. *day-spring* daybreak.

13. *Dagon their sea-idol* the chief Philistine god, a 'sea-monster, upward man / And downward fish' (*PL* i 462-3).

15. *superstition* idolatrous religion (*OED* 2).

16. *popular* made by the populace.

19-20. *thoughts . . . hornets* Cp. *PR* i 196-7. Spenser likens 'thoughts' to 'flyes' (*FQ* II ix 51).

22. *what once I was, and what am now* Cp. Satan's 'bitter memory / Of what he was, what is' (*PL* iv 24-5).

23-4. *foretold / Twice* Judges 13. 3-5 and 13. 10-23.

27. *charioting* Cp. Judges 13. 20: 'the angel . . . ascended in the flame of the altar'. Josephus, *Antiquities* v 8, says that the angel ascended 'by means of the smoke, as by a vehicle'.

31. *separate to God* Cp. Judges 13. 7: 'the child shall be a Nazarite to God'. 'Nazarite' derives from Hebrew *nazar*, 'to separate oneself'. Cp. Num. 6. 2-5: 'When either man or woman shall separate themselves to vow a vow of a Nazarite, to separate themselves unto the Lord: he shall separate himself from wine and strong drink . . . All the days of the vow of his separation there shall no razor come upon his head'.

34. *gaze* spectacle, gazing stock.

35. *task* compulsion (*OED* 4c).

38-9. *Promise . . . deliver* See Judges 13. 5. Samson misrepresents the prophecy. The angel did not say that Samson would deliver Israel; he said that Samson would 'begin to deliver Israel'.

41. *Gaza* one of the chief Philistine cities (called Azza in 147).

45. *but through* were it not for.

53–6. *what is strength . . . subtleties* Cp. Sophocles, *Ajax* 1250–54. Horace, *Odes* III iv 65, Ovid, *Met.* xiii 365.

55. *secure* overconfident (*OED* 1).

57. *subserve* *serve as a subordinate (*OED* 3a).

61. *dispensation* divine providence (*OED* 5).

63. *Suffices* it suffices for me to know.
 bane ruin.

67. *complain* including 'lament'.

70. *prime work* first creation.
 extinct extinguished.

70–71. *Light . . . delight* punningly suggesting that *objects of delight* give pleasure because they reflect *light*.

72. *Annulled* reduced to nothingness. Cp. 'unessential Night' (*PL* ii 438–40). M. did not believe in creation *ex nihilo*.

77. *still* always.

82. *all* any whatever (*OED* 4).

87. *silent* of the moon: not shining (*OED* 5a, first recorded 1646). *Luna silens* was a Latin phrase for a dark moon (cp. Virgil, *Aen.* ii 255). The metaphor is pathetically appropriate to Samson, who can hear, but not see.

89. *vacant* at leisure (*OED* 4). The ancients supposed that the moon rested in a *cave* during the *interlunar* period between old and new moons. *Vacant* also implies empty space.

93. *She all in every part* The idea that the soul was diffused throughout the body was a patristic and neo-Platonic commonplace. M. accepts the doctrine in *CD* i 7 (*YP* 6. 321).

95. *obvious* exposed, liable (*OED* 2).
 quenched deprived of sight (a sense coined by M. in *PL* iii 25).

103. *exempt* both 'not liable to' and 'taken away from' (*OED* 1a), as in: 'exempt from Mortal Earth' (1697).

106. *obnoxious* liable, exposed to (*OED* 1a).

115. *This, this is he* Cp. *Arcades* 5 and 17: 'This this is she'.

118. *at random* without care (*OED* 3).
 diffused *extended, spread out (*OED* v 3).

119. *languished* drooping.

122. *In slavish habit* dressed like a slave.
 weeds clothes.

123. *O'erworn* shabby, threadbare.

124. *Can this be he* Cp. *PL* i 84: 'If thou beest he'.

128. *tore the lion* Judges 14. 6.

129. *embattled* drawn up in battle array.

131. *forgery* the craft of forging metal (with a hint that forged weapons merely counterfeit Samson's authentic strength).

132. *cuirass* breastplate.

133. **Chalybean* The Chalybes were a Black Sea tribe famous for their forging of iron.

134. **Adamantean proof* proof armour (*OED* 10c) as strong as (or capable of resisting) adamant – a mythical substance of impenetrable hardness.

136. **insupportably* irresistibly.

137. *tools* weapons, swords (*OED* 1b).

138. *Spurned* trampled (*OED* 5).

Ascalonite Ascalon was one of five Philistine cities.

139. **ramp* act of ramping (*OED* sb³). Lions were said to 'ramp' when they stood on their hind legs and raised their forepaws in the air (a threatening posture).

142. *trivial* both 'paltry' and 'found at a place where three roads meet' (*OED* 3, from Latin *trivium*). In Judges 15. 15–16 Samson finds the *jaw of a dead ass* and kills a thousand Philistines with it.

144. *foreskins* uncircumcised Philistines. Israelites collected their enemies' foreskins as military trophies (Flannagan).

145. *Ramath-lechi* The marginal note to A.V. Judges 15. 17 takes the name to mean the 'lifting up' or 'casting away of the jawbone'.

147. *Azza* Gaza. See Judges 16. 3 for Samson's lifting of the gates.

148. *Hebron, seat of giants* Hebron had been settled by 'the sons of Anak, which come of the giants' (Num. 13. 33).

149. *No journey of a sabbath day* Jewish law restricted travel on the sabbath to about three-quarters of a mile (Jerusalem Targum on Exod. 16. 29). Samson carried the massive gates from Gaza to Hebron – about forty miles.

150. *whom . . . heaven* the Titan Atlas, who bore heaven on his shoulders.

156–8. *thy soul . . . Imprisoned* Pythagorean and Platonic philosophy held that the soul was imprisoned in the body. Such dualistic complaints are *without cause* because M.'s materialist God did not create the body as a prison. But Samson is *imprisoned now indeed* in his blind body.

161. *incorporate* unite with so as to form one body (*OED* 5). Cp. *PL* x 816, where Adam becomes 'incorporate' with Death.

163. *Puts forth no visual beam* It was thought that eyes saw by emitting a beam. Cp. Uriel's 'visual ray' (*PL* iii 620).

165. *Since man on earth unparalleled* 'unparalleled since man was on earth'.

170. *high estate* Aristotle thought that the tragic hero should come from an illustrious family (*Poetics* xiii).

172. *sphere of fortune* Fortune's wheel (here imagined to be a globe).

181. *Eshtaol and Zora* Samson was born at Zora (Judges 13. 2), and he was first moved by the Spirit 'in the camp of Dan between Zorah and Eshtaol' (Judges 13. 25). He was buried between the two towns (Judges 16. 31).

184. *swage* assuage.

185. *tumours* the 'swellings' of passion (*OED* 4a). See below, 605*n*, for the proverbial healing power of *words* in tragedy.

186. *balm* aromatic ointment used for healing wounds (*OED* 5).

190. *superscription* inscription on a coin.

190–91. *of the most / I would be understood* i.e. 'what I say is true of most people'.

197. *heave the head* Cp. the fallen Satan at *PL* i 210–11: 'nor ever thence / Had ris'n or heaved his head'.

203. *proverbed* Cp. Ps. 69. 11: 'I became a proverb to them', and Job 30. 9: 'And now am I their song, yea, I am their byword' (Vulgate and Junius-Tremellius have *proverbium*).

209. *transverse* off course (continuing the nautical metaphor).

210. *Tax* blame.

   disposal divine management of events.

212. *pretend they ne'er so wise* 'however wise they claim to be'.

216. *wed Philistian women* Samson's first wife, the woman of Timna, was a Philistine (Judges 14. 1). The Bible does not say that Delilah was a Philistine, or that she was married to Samson. M.'s interpretation had strong patristic support, but there was a rival exegetical tradition which saw Delilah as Samson's concubine. Cajetan had even argued that she was an Israelite. See Krouse (76).

219. *Timna* the biblical Timnath (Judges 14. 1), a Philistine city.

222. *motioned* proposed, recommended as a marriage partner (*OED* 1, 1c). Samson also plays on 'motion' as 'a working of God in the soul' (*OED* 9b). Cp. his 'rousing motions' (1382). The biblical Samson does not claim to have been prompted to the marriage by a divine motion. He says: 'Get her for me; for she pleaseth me well'. But the next verse adds: 'his father and his mother knew not that it was of the Lord, that he sought an occasion against the Philistines' (Judges 14. 3–4). *1671* prints 'mentioned', but the *Errata* correct to 'motioned'.

223. *intimate* *proceeding from one's inmost self (*OED* 2).

   impúlse strong suggestion supposed to come from a good or evil spirit (*OED* 3a), as in 'An immediate Revelation or Divine Impulse' (1674).

227. *She proving false* The woman of Timna betrayed Samson by telling her countrymen the answer to his riddle (Judges 14. 16–18). Samson then left her, and she was given to his 'companion, whom he had used as his friend' (Judges 14. 20). The Philistines later burned the woman and her father.

   to wife See above, 216*n*.

228. *fond* foolish.

229. *in the vale of Sorec, Dálila* Cp. Judges 16. 4: 'He loved a woman in the valley of Sorek, whose name was Delilah'.

230. *specious* deceptively attractive.

accomplished both 'full of accomplishments' and 'fully informed' (*OED* 3), as in 'she, who was perfectly accomplished in all his qualities, advised him to lye with her' (1603).

231. *I thought it lawful from my former act* Notice that Samson does not say that he received a divine 'motion' to marry Dalila; he thought his first marriage had given him a permanent dispensation to marry Philistines. Dalila's betrayal of Samson is therefore no indication that Samson's divine motions are spurious. See below, 422*n* and 1382*n*.

235. *peal* appeal (*OED* 1) and discharge of guns in a salute (*OED* 5). Guns 'were not weapons of attack when pealing' (Carey), so Samson's surrender of his *fort* is all the more shameful.

237. *provoke* challenge, summon to fight (*OED* 3).

242. *Israel's governors* The biblical Samson himself 'judged Israel twenty years' (Judges 15. 20, 16. 32). M. may be glancing at the English Parliamentary leaders who failed to prevent the Restoration in 1660. Cp. *REW* (*YP* 7. 458): 'But let our governors beware in time'.

247. *ambition* canvassing, solicitation of honours (*OED* 5).

253. *rock of Etham* After the Philistines had burned his first wife (see above, 227*n*), Samson 'smote them hip and thigh with a great slaughter: and he went and dwelt in the top of the rock Etam' (Judges 15. 8).

254. *forecasting* planning.

256−64. These events are related in Judges 15. 9−15.

258. *on some conditions* Samson surrendered to the men of Judah on the condition that they would not attack him themselves (Judges 15. 12).

261−2. *cords . . . flame* Cp. Judges 15. 14: 'the cords that were upon his arms became as flax that was burnt with fire, and his bands loosed from off his hands'. Samson then killed a thousand men with the ass's jawbone (see above, 142*n*).

266. *by this* by now (*OED* 'by' 21b).

Gath one of five Philistine cities, here used as a synecdoche for Philistia.

268−76. *But . . . deeds* M.'s general statement about *nations grown corrupt* carries implications for the England that had recalled Charles II. Cp. M.'s contempt in *REW* for those who would turn back to servitude out of a false belief 'that they then livd in more plenty and prosperity' (*YP* 7. 462). The antithesis between *bondage with ease* and *strenuous liberty* echoes Sallust, *Speech of the Consul Lepidus* 26: *potiorque visa est periculosa libertas quieto servitio* ('I looked upon freedom united with danger as preferable to peace with slavery'). Cp. *PL* ii 255−7.

275. *frequent* common, usual.

280. *Gideon* See Judges 8. 5−9. The ungrateful Israelites of *Succoth* and *Penuel* refused to give bread to Gideon's 300 soldiers when he was pursuing Zebah and Zalmunna, the *vanquished kings* of Midian.

282. *ingrateful Ephraim* See Judges 11. 12−33, 12. 1−6. The Ephraimite

Jews refused to help Jephtha fight the Ammonites. After Jephtha had defeated the Ammonites in argument and battle, the Ephraimites threatened to burn him in his house. Jephtha's Gileadites then fought the Ephraimites and slaughtered the survivors as they tried to cross the Jordan. The Ephraimites revealed themselves by their inability to pronounce the word *shibboleth*. St Paul names Gideon and Jephtha alongside Samson as examples of exemplary faith (Heb. 11. 32).

291. *mine* my fellow Hebrews.

293. *Just are the ways of God* Cp. Rev. 15. 3: 'just and true are thy ways'.

294. *justifiable to men* Cp. *PL* i 26.

295. *think* believe in the existence of (*OED* 13).

296. *obscure* intellectually dark (*OED* 1c) and frequenting the darkness to elude sight (*OED* 2). Cp. Eccles. 2. 14: 'the fool walketh in darkness'. Atheists had to *walk obscure* when atheism was punishable by law.

298. *heart of the fool* Cp. Ps. 14. 1: 'The fool hath said in his heart, There is no God'.

299. *doctor* teacher, learned divine.

305. *ravel* inquire (*OED* v¹ 4) and become entangled (*OED* v¹ 1). There is also an implied metaphor of a maze. A clue was said to 'ravel' as it came off the reel (*OED* v¹ 3). Notice *wand'ring* and *involved* and cp. 'in wand'ring mazes lost' (*PL* ii 561).

resolved freed from doubt (*OED* 3a).

306. *self-satisfying.

312. *obstriction legal obligation (prohibiting marriages with Gentiles). Carey notes: 'seemingly no O.T. prohibition bans marriage with Philistines', but Deut. 7. 4 implies that any marriage between Jew and Gentile will lead to idol worship, and Deut. 7. 6 states that God has chosen the Jews as 'a special people unto himself'. See also below, 319*n*.

313. *legal debt* duty to the (Mosaic) law.

319. *strictest purity* The chorus is referring to the impurity of mixed marriages. The Nazarite *vow* did not require celibacy (Num. 6. 1–21). Carey claims that 'marriage with Gentiles was not impurity until after the reformation of Ezra', but Ezra advocated a return to the Mosaic law. See Ezra 9–10, esp. 9. 14, where Ezra refers to Deut. 7. 3–5. M. cites these verses (and Neh. 13. 30) in *DDD* (*YP* 2. 262).

320. *fallacious* deceitful.

bride Samson's first wife, the woman of Timna.

321. *Unclean* as a Gentile.

325. *Unchaste was subsequent* Samson's first wife became *unchaste* when she was 'given to his companion' (Judges 14. 20).

327. *careful* anxious, troubled.

333. *uncouth* unfamiliar (*OED* 2).

334. *gloried *OED*'s sole instance of the past participle.

335. *informed* guided (*OED* 4d) – a sense coined by M. in *A Masque* 180.

338. *signal* conspicuous.

dejected abased, humbled (*OED* 2).

339. *erst* formerly.

340. *miserable change* Cp. Shakespeare, *Antony and Cleopatra* IV xv 51: 'The miserable change now at my end / Lament nor sorrow at'.

345. *Duelled their armies* engaged entire armies in single combat as if they were equal antagonists.

357. *pomp* the splendour of the angel who ascended 'in the flame of the altar' after announcing Samson's birth (Judges 13. 20).

360. *graces* favours, including 'individual excellencies, divinely given' (*OED* 11e).

scorpion's tail Cp. Luke 11. 12: 'if [a son] shall ask [of his father] an egg, will he offer him a scorpion?'

363. *sacred* including 'set apart' (as a 'Nazarite', see above, 31*n*).

373. *Appoint* both 'blame' (*OED* 18) and 'prescribe' (*OED* 8).

377. *profaned* including 'disclosed, revealed' (Latin *profano*).

380. *Canaanite* 'no true Israelite' (*OED* 1). The Philistines had immigrated into Canaan from Caphtor (Amos 9. 7).

384. *secret* the answer to Samson's riddle, which his first wife betrayed to her countrymen. See 227 and Judges 14.

388. *prime* both 'beginning' and 'most desirable part'.

389. *vitiated* corrupted – with overtones of 'deflower or violate a woman' (*OED* 3). Samson's *rivals* seduced Dalila with the mere *scent* of money, which sufficed to make her conceive treason as her illegitimate (*spurious*) first-born child.

390. *Though offered only* Cp. Judges 16. 5: 'And we will give thee every one of us eleven hundred pieces of silver'.

394. *capital* chief, fatal, and pertaining to the head (*OED* 6d, 4, 1). Cp. 'capital bruise' (*PL* xii 383).

395. *summed* concentrated. The context also implies the image of a stag, whose head was 'summed' when full of antlers (*OED* 1). Contrast Samson as a shorn 'wether' (538).

396. *Thrice I deluded her* Judges 16. 6–15.

400. *undissembled* *not disguised or concealed (*OED* 2). Dalila did not hide her *contempt* for Samson even when she dissembled her love for him.

403. **blandished* invested with flattery (sole instance in *OED*).

405. *over-watched* wearied with too much watching (*OED*).

408. *grain* the smallest unit of weight (*OED* 8).

422. *Divine impulsion* the 'intimate impulse' of line 223. Manoa speaks as if Samson had claimed divine impulsion for both marriages. But Samson claims an 'intimate impulse' for his first marriage only. See above, 231*n*. At stake is the authenticity of the 'rousing motions' that bring about the catastrophe (1382). Manoa implies that Samson is an unreliable interpreter of divine motions. Samson never doubts their authenticity.

423–5. *occasion . . . occasion* excuse, pretext (*OED* 2b) . . . opportunity (to attack).

infest attack (*OED* 1a).

424. *state* *have an opinion upon (*OED* 2b, sole instance). Manoa is doing his best not to say 'I told you so'.

426. *triumph* *subject of triumph (*OED* 2b, sole instance).

433. *rigid score* unchanging debt.

434. *popular* public.

439. *Them out of thine* the Philistines out of Samson's *hands*.

slew'st them many a slain 'slew many of them, to their cost'. The *them* imitates the Latin dative of disadvantage.

442. *Disglorified* deprived of glory.

453. *idolists* idolators.

scandal including 'discredit to religion occasioned by the conduct of a religious person' (*OED* 1a).

454. *diffidence* distrust (*OED* 1).

455. *propense* inclined, willing, ready.

456. *fall off* revolt, withdraw from allegiance (*OED* 92e). Cp. *PL* i 42–3: 'to fall off / From their Creator'.

463. *enter lists with* enter a place enclosed for tilting, hence: challenge to fight.

464–5. *preferring / Before* both 'liking (his own deity) better than God's' and 'laying (his deity) before God formally for consideration, approval, or sanction' (*OED* 'prefer' 5).

466. *connive* remain inactive (*OED* 5). *OED* cites only this and *PL* x 624 as instances of this sense. Latin *conniveo* means 'close the eyes'.

468. *stoop* 'bow' to superior power (*OED* 2). Samson's words are indeed a *prophecy* (473), for Dagon's idol will soon fall flat on its face. See 471*n*, below.

469. *discomfit* defeat.

471. *blank* disconcert, 'shut up' (*OED* 2). *Blank his worshippers* recalls *PL* i 461, where Dagon 'fell flat, and shamed his worshippers', who had placed the ark of the Covenant in his temple. See I Sam. 5. 4.

475. *vindicate* assert or make good by means of action (*OED* 4) and *claim as properly belonging to himself (*OED* 5).

483. *ransom* There is no precedent either in the Bible or the Samson tradition for Manoa's attempted ransoming of Samson.

by this by now. Cp. 266.

493. *fact* evil deed, crime (*OED* 1c).

496. *front* forehead.

500–501. *Gentiles . . . confined* Tantalus was condemned to eternal punishment in Hades because he had revealed the gods' secrets (Euripides, *Orestes* 10).

503-15. *But . . . offended* Cp. Adam's argument against suicide in *PL* x 1013-28; also *CD* ii 8, where M. argues that suicides are guilty of 'a perverse hatred' of self (trans. Carey, *YP* 6. 719). There was much debate as to whether the biblical Samson was guilty of suicide. See below, 1664-5*n*.

509. *quit thee all his debt* remit all your debt to him.

513. *self-rigorous* both 'strict in judging oneself' and 'being oneself a strict judge' (when the truly penitent sinner would submit the judgement to God).

514. *argues over-just* proves one to be excessively just.

515. *self-offence* injury against oneself (*OED* 1). Manoa implies that Samson is more concerned with the injury (*OED* 'offence' 4a) he has brought upon himself than with his sin (*OED* 'offence' 7a) against God.

516. *what . . . knows* 'whatever means are offered, which (who knows?) . . .'

518. *his sacred house* the Tabernacle – a curtained tent which held the ark of the Covenant and served as the portable sanctuary of the Israelites until Solomon built the Temple.

526. *instinct* impulse (*OED* 1), as in 'he began to have many instincts and strong motions from God' (1633). Cp. Samson's 'intimate impulse' (223) and 'rousing motions' (1382).

528. *sons of Anak* giants. See above, 148*n*.

blazed celebrated.

530. *admired* wondered at.

531. *affront* attack, assault (*OED* 3).

533. *fallacious* deceitful.

venereal trains sexual snares.

535. *pledge* sign of (God's) favour (*OED* 3), i.e. Samson's hair, which he had pledged never to cut (Judges 13. 5).

537. *concubine* Some biblical commentators saw Delilah as a concubine, but M. follows a tradition that saw her as Samson's wife (see above, 216*n*). Samson is reluctant to acknowledge the marriage (cp. 725, 929), but does acknowledge it at 227, 755, 885, etc.

shore me The biblical Delilah called for a man to shave off Samson's locks (Judges 16. 19); M.'s Dalila shaved them herself.

538. *wether* castrated ram.

541. *wine* As a Nazarite Samson was required to 'separate himself from wine and strong drink' (Num. 6. 3; cp. Judges 13. 4).

543. *dancing ruby* red wine.

545. *cheers the heart of gods and men* Cp. Judges 9. 13: 'wine, which cheereth God and man'.

547-8. *fountain . . . eastern ray* Ancient belief held that the most wholesome

water was that which rose from a spring in the face of the rising sun. Cp.
Ezek. 47. 8 and Tasso, *Il Mondo Creato* iii 133–40.

549. *fiery rod* sunbeam. Cp. Euripides, *Suppliants* 650: 'fiery shaft'.

550. *milky juice* fresh water. Cp. *PL* v 306: 'milky stream'. Cp. also Song
of Sol. 5. 12: 'rivers of water, washed with milk'.

557. *liquid* clear, transparent, bright (*OED* 2).

558. *complete* fully armed.

560. *What boots it* of what use is it.

562. *Effeminately* *through degrading passion for a woman (*OED* 2, sole
instance).

567. *gaze* that which is gazed at.

568. *redundant* *plentiful, exuberant (*OED* 2) and superfluous.

569. *Robustious* strong or healthy-looking.

571. *craze* render decrepit (*OED* 5).

574. *draff* pig-swill.

  servile food food fit for slaves.

578. *annoy* molest, injure.

580. *unemployed* *idle (a sense coined by M. in *PL* iv 617).

581–98. *But God . . . rest* Cp. Apollonius Rhodius, *Argonautica* ii 438–48.
When Jason expresses the hope that a god might restore Phineus's sight,
Phineus replies that there is no remedy for his eyes, and that death is his
only hope.

581. *fountain* See Judges 15. 18–19. In A.V. the water comes from the
jawbone. But the Hebrew is ambiguous, and M. follows a rival tradition,
in which the water comes from the *dry ground* named 'Lehi' after the
jawbone.

589. *frustrate* ineffectual, useless (*OED* 2).

591. *treat with* have to do with.

593. *double darkness* of blindness and death.

594. *genial* pertaining to 'genius' or natural disposition (*OED* 6). *Genial
spirits* here means vital energy, will to live.

599. *suggestions* including 'promptings to evil' (*OED* 1a).

600. *humours black* black bile (an imaginary fluid associated with melancholy
in the old physiology).

601. *fancy* imagination.

603. *prosecute* persevere in.

605. *healing words* The healing power of words is proverbial in Greek
tragedy. Cp. Aeschylus, *Prometheus Bound* 379, Euripides, *Hippolytus* 478.
Cp. also the chorus's promise to cure Samson with words (183–6). Adam
speaks 'healing words' in *PL* ix 290.

609. *reins* kidneys.

612. *accidents* medical symptoms (*OED* 3).

615. *answerable* corresponding.

622. *mortification* gangrene, necrosis (*OED* 2).

624. *apprehensive* pertaining to mental impressions.

625. *Exasperate* increase the fierceness of a disease (*OED* 2) and provoke to anger (*OED* 4).

exulcerate cause ulcers.

628. *alp* any high, snow-capped mountain. Cp. *PL* ii 620.

637. *Abstemious* abstaining from wine.

amain vigorously.

639. *nerve* strength (*OED* 3a).

643. *appointment* direction.

645. *repeated* made repeatedly.

651. *balm* aromatic ointment used for soothing pain (*OED* 5) and aromatic preparation for embalming the dead (*OED* 2).

657. *Consolatories* consoling treatises.

659. *Lenient of* soothing to.

661–2. *tune . . . complaint* Cp. Ecclesiasticus 22. 6: 'A tale out of season is as music in mourning'.

662. *mood* both 'state of mind' and 'mode of music'.

667. *what is man* Cp. Job 7. 17: 'What is man, that thou shouldest magnify him?' and Ps. 8. 4: 'What is man, that thou art mindful of him?'

668. *various* *acting in different ways (*OED* 6b, sole instance).

669. *contrarious* self-contradictory (*OED* 2). Cp. M.'s only other instance, in *DDD*: 'the righteous and all wise judgements and statutes of God; which are not variable and contrarious' (*YP* 2. 321).

670. *Temper'st* regulate, control (*OED* 7).

671. *evenly* *without fluctuations (*OED* 4a).

678–704. *But . . . end* Most of the details in these lines could apply to biblical heroes, but the specific mention of *unjust tribunals* and *change of times* (695) strongly suggests that M. is alluding to the treatment of Commonwealth leaders after the Restoration. Charles II's tribunals punished both the living and the dead. The *carcasses* (693) of Cromwell, Bradshaw and Ireton were exhumed and decapitated, and the heads were placed on poles at Westminster Hall, where they remained for several years. (Cromwell's skull was buried only in 1960.) The Parliamentary generals Lambert and Martin were imprisoned (*captived*), while Sir Henry Vane was hanged, drawn and quartered (a fate that M. narrowly escaped). The *ingrateful multitude* applauded these acts.

678. *elected* chosen by God to be the recipient of a temporal or spiritual blessing (*OED* 4).

682. *dignified* raised to positions of dignity.

687. *remit* consign again to a previous condition (*OED* 11b).

700. *crude* premature (*OED* 4).

701–2. *Though . . . days* 'Even though they have not themselves been immoderate (*disordinate*), they suffer, without cause, the same punishment as those who have led dissolute lives'. M. himself suffered from blindness and gout, despite having refrained from intemperance.

702. *in fine* in conclusion.

706. *minister* servant, agent.

709. *peaceful end* tranquil death.

711–18. *female . . . Sails filled* Tudor and Stuart writers often compared women to ships. Hughes cites Lady Pecunia in Jonson's *The Staple of News* (Act II), who appears 'like a galley, Gilt in the prow'. There is much nautical imagery in *SA*. Cp. 198–200, 710–24, 960–64, 1044–5, 1061–3, 1070, 1647–51.

714–15. *ship / Of Tarsus* 'Ships of Tarshish' is a common O.T. phrase connoting worldly vanity. Cp. Isa. 23. 1: 'Howl, ye ships of Tarshish', and Ps. 48. 7: 'Thou breakest the ships of Tarshish'. Tarshish is usually identified with Tartessus in Spain rather than Tarsus in Cicilia.

715–16. *isles / Of Javan* Aegean isles. On Javan, see *PL* i 508*n*.

716. *Gadier* the Phoenician city of Gadera (now Cadiz, in Spain).

717. *bravery* finery.

tackle trim rigging in good order. 'Tackle' was also a slang term for 'mistress' (*OED* 7), and 'trim' could mean 'finely arrayed, "got up"' (*OED* 2).

719. *hold them play* keep them moving.

720. *amber* ambergris, an aromatic substance found in the sea and used as a perfume. See *A Masque* 863*n*.

729. *addressed* made ready.

731. *makes address* makes ready.

734. *merited* deserved an evil estimation (*OED* 2).

736. *fact* evil deed (*OED* 1c).

737. *perverse event* unexpected outcome.

738. *penance* penitence.

748. *hyena* A note to Ecclesiasticus 8.18 in the Geneva Bible (1560) explains that the hyena 'counterfaiteth the voyce of men, and so entiseth them out of their houses and devoureth them'. Cp. Jonson, *Volpone* IV vi 2–3: 'Now thine eyes / Vie tears with the hyena'.

752. *move* urge, request (*OED* 12a).

754. *try* make trial of (his *virtue*) and afflict (his *patience*).

763. *bosom snake* combining the proverb 'to cherish a viper in one's bosom' with the idiom 'bosom friend'.

769. *aggravations* extrinsic circumstances which increase the guilt of a crime (*OED* 7b). In Latin *aggravare* means 'make heavier' (notice *weighed*, *surcharged*, *counterpoised*).

775. *importune* irksome through persistency of request.

779. *naught* both 'nothing' and 'wickedness' (*OED* 2), as in 'From doing nothing proceed to doing naught' (1656).

785. *parle* parley.

795. *her at Timna* Samson left his first wife after she revealed the answer to his riddle. See above, 227n.

800-802. *I was assured ... safe custody* Dalila might not be lying. In the LXX version of Judges 16. 5 the Philistine lords tell Dalila that they plan to 'humiliate' Samson. In the Vulgate the Greek word for 'humiliate' becomes *affligare*. In A.V. the Philistines say 'Entice him ... that we may bind him to afflict him', but the marginal note gives 'humble' as an alternative to 'afflict'.

803. *That made for me* 'that counted with me' (*OED* 'make' 25) or 'that worked to my advantage' (*OED* 78).

809. *Whole* both 'unshared' and 'unwounded'.

812. *fond* foolishly tender, doting (*OED* 5a).

826. *which* i.e. *pardon* (825).

840. *Knowing* knowing myself to be.

841-2. *to cover shame ... uncover'st more* Cp. *PL* ix 1057-61, where Adam and Eve are 'naked left / To guilty Shame: he covered, but his robe / Uncovered more. So rose the Danite strong / Herculean Samson from the harlot-lap / Of Philistéan Dálila'.

857. *priest* There is no priest in the biblical account.

859. *meritorious* entitling to divine reward (*OED* 1, theological term). There may be a pun on Latin *meritorius*, 'earning money (by prostitution)'.

865. *grounded* firmly established.

866. *rife* frequently heard.

868. *Private respects* personal considerations.

878-9. *loved ... Too well* Cp. Shakespeare, *Othello* V ii 345: 'loved not wisely, but too well'.

881. *could deny thee nothing* Cp. Shakespeare, *Othello* III iii 83: 'I will deny thee nothing'.

885-6. *thou wast to leave / Parents* Cp. Gen. 2. 24: 'Therefore shall a man leave his father and his mother'. M.'s own first wife had returned to her parents shortly after marrying M.

890. *law of nature, law of nations* echoing the title of John Selden's *De Jure Naturali et Gentium* (1640), which M. cites in *DDD* as *Of the Law of Nature and of Nations* (*YP* 2. 350).

891. *crew* gang, mob (*OED* 4). M. often employs this pejorative sense. Cp. *PL* vi 49, 370 ('Godless crew', 'Atheist crew').

894. *our country* Israel, as opposed to *thy country* (884, 889, 891). Cp. 238, 518, 851.

897. *acquit themselves* perform their offices, avenge themselves, prove themselves to be (*OED* 'acquit' 2, 6, 13b). Samson withholds the expected complement 'gods', since that is what Philistine gods *cannot be*.

prosecute persecute (*OED* 9).

901. *varnished colours* specious pretences.

906. *worried* *pestered with reiterated demands (*OED* v 6a).

peals noisy appeals.

910. *Afford me place to* give me a chance to.

913. *sensibly* acutely, intensely (*OED* 2a).

916. *other senses* Dalila hints at the pleasures of sex. See below, 951*n*.

want lack.

926. *grateful* pleasing.

932. *trains* snares and the bait leading to them (*OED* sb² 2, 3).

933. *dearly* at great cost and from the heart.

gins snares.

toils hunting nets. Cp. Orestes' description of the robe in which Clytemnestra caught Agamemnon: 'what shall I call it . . . ? Trap for an animal or . . . net . . . May no such wife as she was come to live with me' (Aeschylus, *Libation Bearers* 998–1005).

934. *enchanted cup* alluding to Circe and the whore of Babylon. See *A Masque* 51*n*.

charms songs, spells.

936. *adder's wisdom* deafness. Cp. Ps. 58. 4–5: 'the deaf adder that stoppeth the ear; / Which will not hearken to the voice of charmers'.

944. *insult* exult proudly or contemptuously (*OED* 1).

948. *gloss upon* make unfavourable comments upon (*OED* 1b).

censuring, frown or smile 'finding fault with me, both when you frown and when you smile'.

950. *To* compared to.

951. *Let me . . . touch* Greek tragedy places great significance on touch. See e.g. Sophocles, *Oedipus the King* 1467, *Oedipus at Colonus* 1112, 1130–35, *Philoctetes* 810–20. Samson's spurning of Dalila recalls Philoctetes' rejection of Neoptolemus (*Philoctetes* 761–2), but Dalila's offered touch has sexual overtones.

953. *tear thee joint by joint* Cp. Samson's tearing of the lion (128); also Euripides, *Hecuba* 1125, where Polymestor, blinded by Hecuba, threatens to 'claw her to pieces with these bare hands'. See further Lieb² 252–3.

958. *Cherish* cheer, gladden (*OED* 4).

967. *evil omen* Dalila means Samson's sarcastic prediction about her future fame (956–7).

969. *concernments* affairs.

971–4. *Fame . . . flight* the goddess Fama (Rumour) was often depicted as flying or blowing a trumpet, but Dalila makes *Fame* a god, not a goddess.

The black and white wings are also M.'s invention, though Silius Italicus depicts *Infamia* as flying with black wings (*Punica* xv 6–9).

971. *double-mouthed* with two mouths and mouthing duplicities.

975. *circumcised* Israelites.

976. *Dan* a city in the territory of the Danites, Samson's tribe.

979. *traduced* passed on to posterity (*OED* 2) and maligned.

981. *Ecron . . . Gath* Philistine cities.

983. *solemn* including 'grand, sumptuous' (*OED* 4a).

984. *recorded* sung about (*OED* 2b) and recorded in history.

987. *odours* incense. Cp. Jer. 34. 5: 'So shall they burn odours for thee'.

988–90. *Mount Ephraim . . . nailed* See Judges 4. 21. Defeated by the Israelites, the Canaanite general *Sisera* sought refuge in the tent of *Jael*, wife of the Kenite Heber. Jael told Sisera 'fear not', then killed him by driving a nail through his head while he slept. The prophetess Deborah, who lived in *Mount Ephraim*, sang Jael's praises (hence *renowned*). See Judges 5. 24–7.

995–6. *At this . . . my own* Cp. Teucer's words in Sophocles' *Ajax* 1038–9: 'But if anyone should find my thought at fault, / Let him keep his opinion, and I mine'.

1000. *aggravate* make more grievous (*OED* 6).

1012. *inherit* hold, possess.

1015. *refer* consider.

1016. *thy riddle* the riddle that Samson set his Philistine guests when he married the woman of Timna: 'Out of the eater came forth meat, and out of the strong came forth sweetness' (Judges 14. 14). The 'eater' was a lion, and 'sweetness' honey in the lion's carcass. After *seven* days, the Philistines learned the answer from Samson's wife, whom they had threatened with death (Judges 14. 15–18).

1020. *paranymph* 'best man' (*OED* 1). After Samson left his wife, she 'was given to his companion, whom he had used as his friend' (Judges 14. 20). Junius-Tremellius has *pronubus* for 'friend'.

1022. *both* both wives.

disallied dissolved, cancelled.

1025. *Is it for that* Is it because.

1030. *affect* prefer (*OED* 2).

1035–7. *under virgin veil . . . a thorn* Cp. *DDD*: 'who knows not that the bashfull mutenes of a virgin may oft-times hide all the unlivelines & naturall sloth which is really unfit for conversation' (*YP* 2. 249).

1037. *joined* married.

1037–8. *a thorn / Intestine* Cp. Num. 33. 55: 'if ye will not drive out the inhabitants of the land from before you . . . those which ye let remain of them shall be . . . thorns in your sides'. Cp. also II Cor. 12. 7: 'a thorn in the flesh'. *Intestine* includes 'domestic' (*OED* 1a).

1038. *within defensive arms* 'having penetrated his defences' and 'within his embrace'.

1039. *cleaving* both 'clinging to' and 'splitting apart'. Cp. *Areopagitica* (1644): 'good and evill as two twins cleaving together' (*YP* 2. 514). Cp. also *Tetrachordon* on Gen. 2. 24: '*Cleav to a Wife*, but let her bee a wife . . . not an adversary, not a desertrice; can any law or command be so unreasonable as to make men cleav to calamity?' (*YP* 2. 605).

1044–5. *What pilot . . . helm* Cp. Samson as shipwrecked pilot (197–200).

1046. *Favoured of Heav'n who finds* 'That man is favoured by Heaven who finds'. See Proverbs 31. 10–28 on the virtues of a good wife.

1055. *in due awe* primarily 'her awe of him', but perhaps also 'his awe of her'. Cp. *PL* viii 558: 'an awe / About her', and viii 577: 'So awful, that with honour thou may'st love / Thy mate'.

1059. *swayed* ruled, governed.

1060. *female usurpation* Cp. I Tim. 2. 12: 'I suffer not a woman to . . . usurp authority over the man'. M. cites this verse approvingly in *DDD* (*YP* 2. 324).

1062. *contracted* incurred.

1064. *riddling days* See above, 1016*n*.

1068. *Hárapha* No such character appears in Judges, but in the A.V. of II Sam. 21. 16, David fights 'the sons of the giant'. Some commentators took 'the giant' (Hebrew *ha rapha*) to be a name. See also 1249*n* below.

1069. *pile* *lofty mass (*OED* 4b, earliest figurative instance).

1073. *His habit carries peace* 'he is dressed as if for peace'.

1075. *fraught* cargo of a ship (*OED* 2), continuing the nautical imagery. Harapha is also 'big with menace' (*OED* ppl. a 3b). Cp. Satan 'fraught with mischievous revenge' (*PL* ii 1054).

1076. *condole thy chance* lament your misfortune.

1080. *Og . . . Anak . . . Emims* biblical giants (see Deut. 2. 10–11, 3. 11; Num. 13. 33 and 21. 33–35).

1081. *Kiriathaim* home of the Emims (Gen. 14. 5).

1081–2. *thou know'st . . . art known* Cp. Satan's 'Not to know me argues yourselves unknown' (*PL* iv 830).

1087. *camp* field of battle (Latin *campus*).
  listed *provided with lists, for tilting (*OED* a² 2).

1088. *noise* report, rumour (*OED* 2a).

1091. *taste* explore by touch, put to the proof (*OED* 1, 2).

1092. *single* pick out (*OED* 4), 'challenge to single combat'.

1093. *Gyves* shackles, fetters.

1099. *Palestine . . . Philistine* The two words are etymologically related.

1105. *in thy hand* within easy reach.

1109. *Afford* allow.
  assassinated wounded by treachery (*OED*).

1113. *Close-banded* both 'secretly banded together' and 'fighting in close-ranks'.

1115. *circumvent* take prisoner (*OED* 1) and outwit.

1116. *shifts* evasions, excuses.

1120. *brigandine* chain-mail or plates sewn on canvas or leather.
     habergeon sleeveless coat of mail.

1121. *Vant-brace* armour for the forearm.

1121-2. *spear / A weaver's beam* Goliath's spear was 'like a weaver's beam' (I Sam. 17. 7, I Chron. 20. 5) – the heavy roller used to keep threads taut in a loom.

1122. *seven-times-folded shield* Cp. the shield of Ajax, made of seven layers of bull's hide (Homer, *Il.* vii 200), and the sevenfold shield of Turnus (Virgil, *Aen.* xii 925).

1123. *staff* David 'took his staff in his hand' when he faced Goliath, who said: 'Am I a dog, that thou comest to me with staves?' (I Sam. 17. 40, 43). Hill (437) notes that the staff 'was the traditional weapon of the English lower classes'.

1138. *chafed* angered.
     ruffled angry and stiffened (quills).

1139. *I know no spells* echoing the judicial oath taken by medieval knights before engaging in trial by combat: 'I do swear that I have not upon me, nor upon any of the arms I shall use, words, charms, or enchantments, to which I trust for help to conquer my enemy, but that I do only trust in God, in my right, and in the strength of my body and arms' (Todd).

1144. *pledge* Cp. the apple as a 'pledge' of Adam and Eve's obedience (*PL* viii 325).

1147. *spread before him* explain to him.

1153. *seconded* both 'assisted' and 'supported as by a "second" in a duel'. Cp. *PL* iv 929.

1157-8. *cut off / Quite* Cp. *PL* iii 46-50: 'from the cheerful ways of men / Cut off . . . quite shut out'.

1164. *boist'rous* coarse-growing, rank (*OED* 6).

1169. *thine* thy people.

1186-8. *murder . . . robes* Samson had wagered 'thirty change of garments' that the Philistines could not answer his riddle (see above, 1016*n*). When his wife betrayed his secret (see above, 227*n*), he paid his wager in this way: 'And the Spirit of the Lord came upon him, and he went down to Ashkelon, and slew thirty men of them, and took their spoil, and gave change of garments unto them which expounded the riddle' (Judges 14. 19).

1192-3. *Among . . . no foe* In fact Samson married the woman of Timna precisely because he sought an 'occasion' against the Philistines. See 222-5, 423 and Judges 14. 4.

1195. *politician* craftily plotting.

1197. *await* wait upon (*OED* 5) and watch stealthily with hostile purpose (*OED* 1).

thirty spies Cp. Judges 14. 11: 'And it came to pass, when they saw him, that they brought thirty companions to be with him'. The Bible does not call these men *spies*, but Josephus says they were sent 'in pretence to be his companions, but in reality to be a guard upon him' (*Antiquities* V viii 6).

1198. *threat'ning cruel death* The Philistines threatened to burn Samson's wife (Judges 14. 15).

1201–3. *When . . . hostility* 'When I saw that the Philistines were all set on enmity, I treated them as enemies, wherever I came upon them'.

1204. *underminers* insidious assailants.

1206–7. *force . . . conquered can* Cp. *Brief Notes Upon a Late Sermon* (1660): 'if [kings rule] by conquest, that conquest we have now conquerd' (*YP* 7. 483).

1208. *But I a private person* 'But you call me a private person'. Samson is not conceding the point. See line 1211.

1210. *Single* perhaps including 'free from duplicity' (*OED* 14a). Contrast the tricks of the 'politician lords' (1195).

1211. *private* person not holding any public office (*OED* B 1a).

1218. *my known offence* 'my offence of making [God's secret] known'. Some editors conjecture that M. dictated 'mine own offence'.

1220. *shifts* evasions.

appellant one who challenges another to single combat to prove upon his body the felony of which he 'appealed' him (*OED* B 1b).

1221. *attempts* warlike enterprises (*OED* 3a).

1222. *defies thee thrice to single fight* In judicial combats it was customary to repeat a challenge three times. Samson has openly challenged Harapha in lines 1151 and 1175.

1223. *enforce* effort, exertion.

1224. *enrolled* named on a list, as a criminal or slave. Only nobles or soldiers could participate in judicial combat.

1228. *descant* comment at length.

1231. *Baäl-zebub* the name under which Baal was worshipped in the Philistine city of Ekron (II Kings 1. 2). He appears as Beëlzebub in *PL*. *unused* unaccustomed.

1234. *van* vanguard (i.e. 'start fighting').

1237. *baffled* publicly disgraced (*OED* I 1). When a knight was 'baffled', he (or his image) was hung by the heels and he could never again fight in duels. See *The Gentleman's Calling* (1660): 'he that has once been baffled, is ever after an incompetent Challenger' (v 71).

1238. *bulk without spirit vast* both 'vast bulk without courage' and 'bulk without an aspiring spirit' (*OED* 'vast' 3), as in 'the Prince of Orange and Count Egmont . . . were of vaster spirits than the rest' (1650).

1242. *Astaroth* See *PL* i 422n.

1243. *braveries* boasts (*OED* 1).

1244. **giantship* a mocking echo of 'his worship', a title of honour used of persons of note.

crestfall'n punning on 'crest' as the plume on a knight's helmet (*OED* 2).

1245. *unconscionable* excessive (*OED* 2b).

1246. *sultry* *hot with anger (*OED* 2b).

chafe rage.

1249. *Goliah* Goliath of Gath. He and his brothers are 'sons of the giant' (Hebrew *ha rapha*) in II Sam. 21. 19 and I Chron. 20. 5. See above, 1068n. M. may have identified him with the Goliath slain by David (I Sam. 17).

1263. *rid* set free (*OED* 2a) and kill (*OED* 6c).

1273. *boist'rous* violent.

1277. *ammunition* military supplies (of any kind).

1278. *feats . . . defeats* both words derive from Latin *facere*, and 'defeat' could mean 'undo' (*OED* 1).

1283. *expedition* prompt execution of justice (*OED* 1).

1286. *distracted* crazed, mad, insane (*OED* 5).

1287. *patience* including 'suffering', as in 'patience and heroic martyrdom' (*PL* ix 32).

1288. *saints* holy persons (the Protestant sense).

1294. *sight bereaved* loss of sight.

1298. *Labouring* imposing labour upon (*OED* 9a).

1300. *behind* still to come (*OED* 4).

1303. *quaint* skilfully made (*OED* 4). The Public Officer is carrying a wand of office like a Greek herald.

1304. *amain* at full speed.

1305. *habit* clothing.

1307. *voluble* fluent.

1309. *remark* mark out, distinguish (*OED* 1).

1312. *triumph* procession honouring a victory.

1317. *heartened* strengthened with food (*OED* 3).

1320. *Our Law forbids* The second commandment forbids idol-worship (Exod. 20. 4–5). Cp. Exod. 23. 24: 'Thou shalt not bow down to their gods, nor serve them, nor do after their works: but thou shalt utterly overthrow them, and quite break down their images'.

1324. *gymnic* gymnastic.

1325. *antics* clowns.

mummers . . . mimics mimes.

1328. *activity* gymnastics, athletics (*OED* 3).

1333. *Regard thyself* look out for your own interests.

1342. *Joined* enjoined, imposed.

1344. *Brooks* endures.

1346. *stoutness* rebelliousness (*OED* 4), courage (*OED* 2).

1358. *prostituting* including 'expose to shameful view' (*OED* 3c).

1362. *profane* from Latin *profanus*, 'outside the temple'. Samson's acts would be all the more 'profane' for taking place inside Dagon's temple.

1369. *sentence holds* maxim holds true.

1375. *his jealousy* Cp. Exod. 20. 5: 'I the Lord thy God am a jealous God'.

1377. *dispense with* grant (a person) special exemption or release from a law (*OED* 9).

1380. *come off* escape (a sense coined by M. in *A Masque* 647).

1382. *rousing* *awakening (*OED* 3).

motions workings of God in the soul (*OED* 9b). Some critics doubt whether Samson's motions really do come from God, and 'motions' could be inner promptings of any kind (*OED* 9a). Cp. Shakespeare, *Othello* I iii 330: 'we have reason to cool our raging motions'. M. was nevertheless drawn to the positive sense. Cp. *A Treatise of Civil Power*: 'the inward perswasive motions of his spirit' (*YP* 7. 261). See above, 222n and 422n.

1387–9. *If . . . last* Cp. Sophocles, *The Women of Trachis* 1169–72, where Heracles realizes that the oracle which foretold 'release from all toil' actually foretold his death. Samson imagines that this day will be either *remarkable* or his *last*. He does not yet know it will be both.

1390. *In time thou hast resolved* Greek tragic protagonists rarely change their minds 'in time'. Creon in Sophocles' *Antigone* repents too late to save Antigone, Haemon and Eurydice. Cp. also Shakespeare, *King Lear* V iii 248: 'Nay, send in time'.

1396. *engines* means, contrivances (*OED* 3) and physical engines of war or torture (*OED* 5).

1397. *hamper* bind, fetter, entangle.

1400. *pernicious* fatal.

1402. *Because* so that.

1410. *resolution* decision (*OED* 11). The Officer is praising Samson's *compliance*, not his earlier stubborn resolution.

1419. *well-feasted sole instance in *OED*.

1420. *if aught* if in any way.

1422. *insolent* including 'immoderate, going beyond the bounds of propriety' (*OED* 3).

1431–3. *angel . . . flames* See above, 23–4n, 27n.

1435. *Spirit . . . rushed on thee* Cp. Judges 13. 25: 'the Spirit of the Lord began to move him at times in the camp of Dan'. Cp. also Judges 14. 6: 'the Spirit of the Lord came mightily upon him'.

1450. *I had no will* I had no desire to go there.

1453. *give ye part* let you share.

1454. *good success* happy outcome. Manoa's *hope* for Samson typifies the

'false dawn' which often precedes the catastrophe in Greek tragedy. See
e.g. Hecuba's hope for Astyanax in Euripides' *The Trojan Women* 700f.

1457. *attempted* sought to influence by entreaty (*OED* 7).

1459. *prone* either 'grovelling' (*OED* 4), suggesting that Manoa has 'pros-
trated himself' (Carey), or 'bending forward' (*OED* 1).

1461–71. *Some . . . proposed* These lines might allude to the various
attitudes the Royalists held towards Commonwealth figures such as M.

1467. *civil* humane, gentle (*OED* 11).

1470. *The . . . remit* 'It would be magnanimous to give up the rest of their
revenge'.

1471. *convenient* of befitting size (*OED* 3b).

1478. *numbered down* paid out (*OED* 3b).

1479. *richest* The Book of Judges never says that Manoa was rich.

1484. *wanting* lacking.

1503. *to* in addition to.

1507. *next* next of kin (as Danites).

1512. *inhabitation* population (*OED* 3), perhaps imitating a Greek phrase
meaning 'the inhabited earth, the world'.

1515. *ruin* the act of giving way and falling down, on the part of a building
(*OED* 1a).

1519. *dismal* fatal, calamitous (*OED* 2, 3), from Latin *dies mali*, 'evil days'.

1520–22. *Best . . . mouth* imitating the catastrophe in a Greek tragedy.
When a cry is heard off-stage, the chorus will move about distractedly,
wondering what to do. See e.g. Aeschylus, *Agamemnon* 1346–71, Euripides,
Hippolytus 782–5, *Medea* 1275–6, *The Bacchae* 576–603.

1529. *dole* the dealing of blows, death (*OED* sb¹ 5b) – with puns on 'sorrow'
(*OED* sb² 1) and 'that which is charitably dealt out' (*OED* sb¹ 5a). Cp. *PL*
iv 893–4.

1534. *doubt* hesitate, scruple (*OED* 3).

1535. *would fain subscribe* would willingly agree.

1536. *stay* pause, delay.

   notice news.

1538. *rides post* travels quickly (as on post horses).

   baits delays (at an inn, to feed the horses).

1539. *to our wish* just as we would wish.

1541–51. An excited messenger brings dreadful news in many Greek
tragedies. The Argument says that the Hebrew messenger speaks 'confus-
edly at first'.

1543. *erst* just now (*OED* 5b).

1552. *accident* as yet unexplained occurrence (*OED* 1).

   here heard *1671*, corrected to 'here' in *Errata*.

1556. *distract* confused in mind, shocked.

1557. *the sum* the gist.

1567. *irruption* bursting in.

1570. *in brief, Samson is dead* Cp. Sophocles, *Electra* 673: 'in short, Orestes is dead'.

1574. *windy* vain, worthless (*OED* 5).

1574–5. *conceived . . . delivery* imagined . . . release (with puns on conception and birth). Notice *Abortive, first-born*.

1576–7. *first-born . . . frost* Cp. Shakespeare, *Love's Labour's Lost* I i 100–101: 'An envious-sneaping frost, / That bites the first-born infants of the spring'.

1584. **self-violence* a euphemism for self-murder (*OED*). Cp. 'self-preservation', 'self-rigorous', 'self-displeased' and 'self-offence' in Manoa's earlier argument against suicide (503–15). On Samson's suicide, see below, 1664–5*n*.

1596. *Occasions* business (*OED* 6a).

1599. *dispatched* accomplished, got done.

1603. *minded* intended (*OED* 6a).

1605. *theatre* implying tiers of seats. The Hebrew, LXX, Vulgate, and A.V. of Judges 16. 27 call the building a house.

1608. *sort* high rank (*OED* sb² 2b).

   in order by rank.

1609. *The other side was open* Judges mentions no open space, but instead says that 3,000 men and women 'were upon the roof' (16. 27). M. places the common people in an open area so as to spare them. See below, 1659*n*.

1610. *banks* benches (*OED* sb² 1).

   scaffolds stands for spectators (*OED* 5).

1616. *livery* uniform of a retainer.

1617. *timbrels* tambourines.

1619. *cataphracts* *soldiers in full armour (*OED* 2), heavy cavalry (Latin *cataphracti*).

   spears spearmen.

1621. *Rifted* split.

1626. *still* on each occasion.

1627. *stupendious* stupendous.

1628. *antagonist* challenger to the 'agonist' (contender in the games).

1630. *his guide* a 'lad' in Judges 16. 26.

1637. *as one who prayed* Cp. Judges 16. 28–30: 'And Samson called unto the Lord, and said, O Lord God, remember me, I pray thee, and strengthen me, I pray thee, only this once, O God, that I may be at once avenged of the Philistines for my two eyes . . . Let me die with the Philistines'.

1643. *my own accord* Wittreich (143) takes this to mean that Samson's final act is self-motivated, not prompted by God. But the antithesis is between Samson's *own* deeds and the Philistines' *commands* (1640), not between

Samson's will and God's. The biblical Samson also employs 'all his might' (Judges 16. 30).

1645. *strike all who behold* Critics hostile to Samson compare the devils' puns on artillery in *PL* vi 557–627. But M. had his own taste for cruel or gloating puns. Cp. 'swim' in *PL* xi 625–6 and 'neck' in M.'s sonnet *To the Lord General Cromwell* (5).

1647. *winds . . . pent* Subterranean winds were thought to cause earthquakes. See *PL* i 231*n*.

1659. *The vulgar only 'scaped* only the common people escaped. The Bible says that 3,000 common people were standing on the roof which fell 'upon the lords, and upon all the people' (Judges 16. 30). M. has redesigned the temple in order to save the common people. See above, 1609*n*.

1664. *self-killed* Theologians had defended Samson's suicide by arguing that God prompted him to it. See e.g. Augustine, *City of God* I xxi, xxvi. See further Krouse (37, 49).

1665. *Not willingly* not eagerly. 'Willingly' had 'several shades of meaning, from "with acquiesence" to "wishfully, eagerly"' (*OED* 2). Samson acquiesces in God's will, but he is not eager to die.

tangled in the fold suggesting a serpent's coils (*OED* 'fold' sb³ 1e).

1667. *in number more* Cp. Judges 16. 30: 'the dead which he slew at his death were more than they which he slew in his life'.

1669. *sublime* exalted in feeling, elated (*OED* 3b), a sense coined by M. in *PL* x 536, *OED*'s sole other instance.

1671. *fat* Mosaic law forbade the eating of fat (Lev. 3. 17).

regorged *gorged to repletion. Not in *OED*, but the Latin prefix *re* could be an intensive.

1674. *Silo* Shiloh, site of the ark of the Covenant at this time.

1682. *fond* foolish.

1685. *Insensate . . . reprobate* 'left without reason, or left to a depraved reason'. Cp. Rom. 1. 28: 'God gave them over to a reprobate mind'.

1690. *virtue* strength, courage.

1692. *dragon* not the flying, fire-breathing kind, but a large snake (*OED* 1), such as might enter a barnyard by stealth to prey upon domestic *fowl*. Samson entered the temple like a cunning snake, but he struck the Philistines like an *eagle*.

1693. *perchèd* *furnished with perches (*OED* 2a).

1695. *villatic belonging to a farm (Latin *villaticus*).

1696. *cloudless thunder* unexpected thunder from a clear sky.

1699. *self-begotten bird* the phoenix, a mythical bird that was consumed by fire every 500 years, then rose from its own ashes. See *PL* v 272*n*.

1700. *embossed* imbosked, hidden in a wood (*OED* 1b).

1702. *holocaust* something consumed by fire (*OED* 2c).

1703. *teemed* born.

1707. *secular* living for an age or ages (*OED* 6).

1709. *hath quit himself* both 'has borne himself' (*OED* 3a) and 'has left his life'.

1713. *sons of Caphtor* the Philistines, who had immigrated from Caphtor (Jer. 47. 4, Amos 9. 7), thought to be Crete.

1715. *hath* he hath.

　let but them if only they would.

1727. *lavers* large wash-basins used in Jewish ritual (*OED* 1b).

1728. *what speed* as much speed as possible.

1729. *plight* condition.

1730–33. *Will . . . house* Cp. Judges 16. 31: 'Then his brethren and all the house of his father came down, and took him, and brought him up, and buried him between Zorah and Eshtaol in the burying-place of Manoah his father'.

1735. *laurel . . . palm* Both plants symbolized victory, and laurel was also an emblem of distinction in poetry.

1736. *enrolled* recorded with honour (*OED* 6).

1737. *legend* inscription, perhaps suggesting the story of a saint's life (*OED* 1).

1745–58. 'The last choral speech is a Petrarchan sonnet rhyming ABAB, CDCD, EFEFEF' (Flannagan).

1745–8. *All is best . . . close* Cp. the closing choruses in Euripides' *Alcestis*, *Medea*, *The Bacchae*, *Andromache*, and *Helen*, all of which insist that the gods' will is inscrutable.

1746. *dispose* ordering of things (*OED* 2).

1749. *hide his face* Cp. Ps. 30. 7: 'Thou didst hide thy face, and I was troubled' (also 27. 9, 104. 29).

1751. *in place* at hand (*OED* 19b).

1755. *acquist* acquisition.

THE LATIN AND GREEK POEMS

1645 was divided into two sections with separate title-pages. The poems in the first section were in English (or Italian); those in the second section were in Latin (or Greek). The second section was further subdivided into a book of elegies (*Elegiarum Liber*), and a miscellany (*Silvarum Liber*). Two Latin poems were added in 1673, and the Greek poem *In Effigiei eius Sculptorem* (which had appeared on the frontispiece of *1645*) was placed after the other two Greek poems in the main body of the text.

ELEGIARUM LIBER [A BOOK OF ELEGIES]

These poems are called 'elegies' because they are written in the elegiac metre (see *Elegia I* 92*n*, *Elegia VI* 8*n*). The term 'elegy' does not imply that the poems are poems of mourning (even though two of them are).

Elegia Prima. Ad Carolum Diodatum [Elegy I, To Charles Diodati]

Date: spring 1626. Charles Diodati, the son of Italian Protestants living in London, had been M.'s closest friend at St Paul's School. Their friendship continued into early manhood, and M. mourned Diodati's premature death in *Epitaphium Damonis* (1639). Diodati went up to Oxford in 1623; M. was admitted to Christ's College, Cambridge, two years later on 12 February 1625. Near the end of his first year, in the Lent term of 1626, M. was apparently rusticated (suspended) after a misunderstanding with his tutor, William Chappell. M. wrote this poem during his temporary exile.

4. *Vergivium . . . salum* [*Vergivian Sea*] the Irish Sea.
14. *Phoebicolis* [*votaries of Phoebus*] poets.
15. *duri . . . magistri* [*stern tutor*] William Chappell. Aubrey reports M.'s brother Christopher as saying that M. received 'some unkindness' from Chappell. Aubrey adds that 'he whipped him' (Darbishire 10). M. was assigned a new tutor, Nathaniel Tovey, on his return to Cambridge.
21. *vates* [*poet*] Ovid. He was banished to Tomis on the Black Sea by Augustus in 8 AD, partly due to his notorious *Ars Amatoria*, and partly due to a mysterious scandal involving Augustus's family. He died in exile ten years later.
23. *Ionio . . . Homero* [*Ionian Homer*] Homer wrote in the Ionic dialect, and was often supposed to be a native of Ionia.
24. *Maro* Virgil.
27. *theatri* Although M. speaks as a spectator, the details of lines 29–46 recall Greek and Roman, rather than English, drama.
37. *furiosa Tragoedia sceptrum* [*raging Tragedy . . . sceptre*] Cp. *Il Penseroso* 97–100 and Ovid's description of 'raging Tragedy' (*violentia Tragoedia*) wielding her sceptre (*Amores* III i 11–13).
45. *Pelopeia domus* [*house of Pelops*] Pelops's descendants Atreus, Thyestes, Agamemnon, Orestes, Electra and Iphigeneia appear in many ancient tragedies. Cp. *Il Penseroso* 99–100.
    Ili [*Ilus*] the mythical founder of Troy (Ilium).
46. *aula Creontis* [*Creon's palace*] the royal house of Thebes. The incestuous forebears are Jocasta (Creon's sister) and her son Oedipus.

57. *bis vivi Pelopis* [*twice-living Pelops*] The gods restored Pelops to life after his father Tantalus had served him to them in a stew. They gave Pelops a shoulder of ivory to replace the one Demeter had eaten (Ovid, *Met.* vi 403–11). Marlowe compares beautiful white skin to Pelops's shoulder in *Hero and Leander* (1598) i 64–5.

62. *floris* [*flower*] the anemone, which sprang from Adonis's blood (Ovid, *Met.* x 735–9). The hyacinth (61) was also once a beautiful youth. See *Fair Infant* 23–7 and *Lycidas* 105–7.

63. *Heroides* alluding to Ovid's poem of that name.

65. *Achaemeniae* Persian (from Achaemenes, the legendary founder of the Persian royal house).

turrita fronte [*turreted foreheads*] the goddess Cybele wore a towered crown (see *Arcades* 21–2n). Women in the seventeenth century also wore a high head-dress called a 'tower' (*OED* 6b).

66. *Susa* the winter capital of the Persian kings.

Ninon Nineveh, the Syrian capital. Strictly speaking, Susa (not Nineveh) was associated with Memnon. See *PL* x 308n.

67. *Danaae* [*Danaan*] a Homeric term for 'Greek'.

69. *Tarpeia Musa* [*Tarpeian Muse*] Ovid. He lived near the Tarpeian rock (*Tristia* I iii 29–30) and recommended Pompey's colonnade and the theatre as places to meet women (*Ars Amatoria* i 67, iii 387).

70. *Ausoniis* [*Ausonian*] Italian.

73. *Dardaniis* [*Dardanian*] Trojan. Britain was supposedly colonized by Trojan exiles. See *Q Nov* 2n.

78. *Endymioneae . . . deae* [*Endymion's goddess*] Selene, goddess of the moon.

83–4. *Cnidon . . . Cypron* Cnidos (on the coast of Asia Minor) and Cyprus were sacred to Venus, who was born from sea-foam at the Cypriot city of Paphos. The Simois flows from Mount Ida, where the Trojan Paris awarded Venus the prize for beauty in preference to Juno and Minerva.

85. *pueri . . . caeci* [*blind boy*] Cupid.

88. *Molyos* [*Moly*] the herb that saved Odysseus from being turned into a beast by Circe (Homer, *Od.* x 305). It was a traditional symbol of temperance. See *A Masque* 636n.

92. *alternos . . . modos* [*alternate measures*] the alternate pentameters and hexameters of the elegiac couplet.

Elegia Secunda. In Obitum Praeconis Academici Cantabrigiensis
[Elegy II. On the death of the Cambridge University Beadle]

Date: autumn 1626. The caption *Anno aetatis* 17 means 'at the age of seventeen' (not 'in his seventeenth year'). Richard Ridding, Beadle of Cambridge University, died on or shortly after 19 September 1626. M.

turned eighteen on 9 December 1626. M.'s method of dating was not unusual in the seventeenth century. See Parker (785) and cp. the dating of *Elegia III* and *In Obitum Praesulis Eliensis*.

1. *baculo* the Beadle's mace, carried in academic processions.
2. *Palladium . . . gregem* [*flock of Pallas*] members of the university, seen as devotees of Athena, goddess of wisdom.
6. Jove assumed the shape of a swan when he raped Leda. The swan's whiteness was proverbial. Cp. Spenser, *Prothalamion* (1596) 42-3.
7. *Haemonio . . . succo* [*Haemonian drugs*] Medea used drugs from Thessaly (Haemonia) to rejuvenate Jason's father Aeson (Ovid, *Met.* vii 251-93). Cp. the herb 'haemony' in *A Masque* 638.
10. *Coronides* Aesculapius, god of medicine (the son of Apollo and Coronis). He restored Hippolytus to life at Diana's request (Ovid, *Fasti* vi 743-56).
12. *Phoebo . . . tuo* [*your Phoebus*] the Vice-Chancellor.
13. *Cyllenius* Mercury (born on Mount Cyllene in Arcadia). See Homer, *Il.* xxiv 336-467 for his message to Priam.
15. *Eurybates* one of two heralds sent by Agamemnon (*Atrides*) to seize Achilles' captive, Briseis. M.'s reference is inaccurate. Far from delivering Atrides' stern command, the heralds were too terrified to speak (Homer, *Il.* i 318-44).
17. *Magna . . . regina* [*Great queen*] Mors, goddess of death. Avernus (a lake near Naples) was a fabled entrance to Hades. Poets used the name for Hades itself.

Elegia Tertia. In Obitum Praesulis Wintoniensis [Elegy III. On the death of the Bishop of Winchester]

Date: late 1626. The caption *Anno aetatis* 17 means 'at the age of seventeen' (see previous headnote). Lancelot Andrewes, Bishop of Winchester, died on 25 September 1626. He was a staunch defender of the Anglican Church and one of the translators of the King James Bible. M. was later highly critical of him. In *The Reason of Church Government* (1641) he refutes Andrewes' arguments defending episcopacy (*YP* 1. 768-74).

4. *Libitina* Italian goddess of corpses. Her temple at Rome contained registers of the dead. At least 35,000 Londoners (one sixth of the population) died in the plague of 1625.
9. *ducis, fratrisque* The leader and his brother are usually identified as Duke Christian of Brunswick (d. June 1626) and his 'brother in arms' Count Ernst von Mansfeld, who was killed while fighting for the Protestant cause in the Thirty Years War (29 November 1626). Douglas Bush proposes

King James I (d. March 1625) and his royal 'brother' Maurice, Prince of Orange (d. April 1625) as a more likely pair (*Var.* 1. 66–8).

12. *Belgia* Protestant leaders who died in the Low Countries included the Earls of Southampton (1624) and Oxford (1625), as well as Duke Christian and Prince Maurice. Breda fell to the Spaniards in May 1625.

16. *Tartareo . . . Iovi* [*Tartarean Jove*] Pluto, ruler of the underworld. See *A Masque* 20n.

20. *Cypridu* [*Cypris*] Venus (named Cypris because she rose from the sea near Cyprus).

26. *Proteos* Proteus was herdsman of Neptune's seals (see *Ep. Dam.* 99n).

32. *Roscidus* the evening star.

33. *Tartessiaco . . . aequore* [*Tartessian sea*] the Atlantic Ocean. Tartessus was an ancient city in Spain.

41. *Thaumantia proles* [*daughter of Thaumas*] Iris, goddess of the rainbow.

44. *Chloris* the Roman goddess of flowers. Her name was changed to 'Flora' after she was wooed by Zephyrus, god of the west wind (Ovid, *Fasti* v 195–378). See *PL* v 341n and ix 441n on the miraculous gardens of Alcinous.

46. *Tago* [*Tagus*] a river in Spain and Portugal, famous for its golden sand.

47. *Favoni* [*Favonius*] Zephyrus, the west wind.

50. Lucifer ('light-bearer') is here the sun, whose palace was east of India (Ovid, *Met.* i 778–9).

54. Cp. the shining face of Moses (Exod. 34. 29–35).

64. Cp. Rev. 14. 13: 'they may rest from their labours'.

67. *Cephaleia pellice* [*Cephalus's paramour*] Aurora, goddess of the dawn. See *Il Penseroso* 124n.

68. *Talia . . . mihi* [*May such dreams often befall me*] M. daringly paraphrases Ovid, *Amores* I v 26 (also a last line). Ovid wishes that he may have many more sultry siestas like the one he has just spent in bed with Corinna.

Elegia Quarta. Ad Thomam Iunium, Preaeceptorem Suum [Elegy IV. To Thomas Young, his tutor]

Date: March–April 1627? If the caption *Anno aetatis* 18 accords with M.'s usual method of dating, the poem should have been written 'at the age of eighteen' (i.e. between 9 December 1626 and 8 December 1627). Lines 33–8 date the poem to March or April.

Thomas Young (*c.* 1587–1655) was a Scottish schoolmaster and clergyman who acted as M.'s boyhood tutor from 1618 to 1620. He moved to Hamburg in 1620, where he was chaplain to the community of English merchants. In 1628 he returned permanently to England where he was presented to a Church living in Stowmarket, Suffolk. He became a prominent Presbyterian opponent of episcopacy, and was the 'ty' of Smectymnuus, the group of Puritan divines whom M. supported in his prose pamphlets of 1641-2. M.'s relations with him cooled thereafter. Young disapproved of M.'s views on divorce; M. disapproved of Young's views on Church government (Young was nominated to the Westminster Assembly in 1643).

1. M.'s instructions to his letter imitate Ovid, *Tristia* III vii 1-2.

7. *Dorida* [*Doris*] wife of Nereus and mother of the fifty sea-nymphs, the Nereids.

10. *Colchis* [*the Colchian*] Medea, who fled from Jason in a chariot drawn by dragons after she had killed their children.

11. *Triptolemus* the hero chosen by Demeter to give agriculture to the world. Ovid tells how he arrived in Scythia in a chariot drawn by dragons (*Met.* v 642-61).

15. *Hama* a mythical Saxon hero slain by Starcaterus, a Danish giant.

19. *pars altera* [*other half*] See Plato, *Symposium* 189d-193e for the conceit that close friends are two halves of one soul. Cp. also Horace, *Odes* I iii 8 and *PL* iv 488.

23. *doctissime Graium* [*wisest of the Greeks*] Socrates. Cliniades is Alcibiades, son of Clinias. He claims descent from Telamon, Ajax's father, in Plato, *Alcibiades* 121a.

25. *Stagirites* [*the Stagirite*] Aristotle (who was born at Stagira). Alexander the Great was his pupil.

26. *Chaonis* [*woman of Chaonia*] Alexander's mother Olympias came from Chaonia in Epirus. Plutarch (*Alexander* 2-3) says that Zeus-Ammon fathered Alexander on her in the form of a snake. Cp. *PL* ix 508.

28. *Myrmidonum Regi* [*king of the Myrmidons*] Achilles. His two tutors were Phoenix, son of Amyntor, and the centaur Chiron, son of the nymph Philyra.

30. *bifidi ... iugi* [*twin-peaked mountain*] Parnassus, sacred to Apollo and the Muses, in Aonia (Boeotia). The Castalian spring, also sacred to the Muses, was at its foot. Pieria, near Mount Olympus, was the Muses' birthplace.

31. *Clio* one of the Muses, in Roman times the Muse of history.

33. *Aethon* one of the horses of the sun (Ovid, *Met.* ii 153). Chloris (35) was the Greek name for Flora, whose festival at Rome began on 28 April. The sun has entered Aries three times since M. last saw Young, but Chloris has brought spring only twice. Hence the poem was written between 21 March (when the sun enters Aries) and 28 April.

36. *Auster* the south wind.

39. *Eurus* the east wind.

51. *praelia* [*battles*] of the Thirty Years War.

56. *lento ... viro* [*tardy husband*] Odysseus.

74. *Saxonicos ... duces* [*Saxon leaders*] the sons of Duke John of Saxe-

Weimar. They had served with Mansfeld against the Imperial forces, and would soon join Gustavus Adolphus.

75. *Enyo* goddess of war, Homer's 'sacker of cities' (*Il.* v 333).

78. *Odrysios* [*Odrysian*] Thracian. Thrace was the traditional home of Ares or Mars, the god of war (Homer, *Od.* viii 361).

80. *diva* [*goddess*] Eirene, goddess of peace.

81–2. *virgo . . . iusta* [*virgin of Justice*] Astraea, goddess of justice, the last of the gods to flee the earth. See *Nativity* 142n.

97. *vates . . . Thesbitidis* [*Tishbite prophet*] Elijah, who fled from Ahab and Jezebel (I Kings 19. 1–18).

102. *Paulus . . . Cilix* St Paul, from Tarsus in Cicilia, was scourged in Philippi in Macedonia (Acts 16. 22–40).

104. See Matt. 8. 28–34.

114. In II Kings 19. 35–6 God destroys Sennacherib's Assyrian army before the walls of Jerusalem.

122. In II Kings 7. 6–7 God terrifies Ben-hadad's Syrian army by causing them to hear 'the noise of a great host'.

Elegia Quinta. In adventum veris [*Elegy V. On the coming of spring*]

Date: spring 1629. The caption *Anno aetatis 20* presumably means 'at the age of twenty' (see headnote to *Elegia II*).

9. *Castalis . . . cacumen* [*Castalian . . . mountain*] See *Elegy IV* 30n.

10. *Pirenen* [*Pirene*] a fountain in Corinth, sacred to the Muses.

13. *Delius* [*the Delian*] Apollo (born on the island of Delos).

Peneide lauro [*Daphne's laurel*] Daphne, daughter of the river-god Peneus, was changed into a laurel by her father so that she might escape Apollo. Apollo thereafter wore laurel leaves in his hair (Ovid, *Met.* i 452–567).

25. *Philomela* the nightingale.

30. *perennis*] *1673*; *quotannis 1645*. M. changed the word after Salmasius (*Responsio* (1660) 5), pointed out the false quantity in *1645*.

31. *Aethiopas* The sun flees the Ethiopians in spring because it then rises north of the equator (called 'the Ethiop line' in *PL* iv 282).

Tithoniaque arva [*Tithonus's fields*] the east (Tithonus being husband of Aurora, goddess of the dawn).

35. *Lycaonius* [*Lycaonian*] northern. Lycaon, King of Arcadia, was father of Callisto, who became the constellation known as Ursa Major (the Great Bear) or the Wain (*plaustrum*).

40. *Giganteum* The Giants attacked the gods during the Iron Age, when Justice had fled the earth. See Ovid, *Met.* i 151f.

46. *Cynthia* the moon-goddess Diana, Apollo's sister.

50. *effoeto ... toro* [*bed of impotence*] Tithonus, Aurora's husband, was made impotent by old age. Aurora had granted him immortality, but he forgot to ask for eternal youth.

51. *Aeolides* Cephalus. Aurora loved him when she saw him spreading nets on Mount Hymettus (Ovid, *Met.* vii 700–713).

60. *Paphiis* [*Paphian*] Paphos, in Cyprus, was sacred to Venus.

62. *Idaeam ... Opim* [*Idaean Ops*] Cybele, a Phrygian fertility-goddess (worshipped in Rome as Ops) was associated with Mount Ida, near Troy. She wore a turreted crown.

66. *diva Sicana* [*Sicanian goddess*] Proserpine, whom Pluto abducted in Sicily (Sicania). Pluto is 'the Taenarian god' because Taenarus, in Laconia, was a fabled entrance to Hades.

83. *Tethy* [*Tethys*] wife of Oceanus and mother of the rivers.

Tartesside lympha [*Tartessian flood*] the Atlantic Ocean. See *Elegia III* 33*n*.

91. *Semeleia fata* [*Semele's fate*] Semele was destroyed by fire when Jupiter complied with her request that he make love to her in his full glory. See Ovid, *Met.* iii 252–315.

92. *Phaetonteo ... equo* [*Phaethon's chariot*] Phaethon, son of Apollo (or Helios), almost destroyed the earth when he tried to drive the chariot of the sun. Jupiter saved the earth by killing Phaethon with a thunderbolt. See Ovid, *Met.* ii 1–400.

101–2. *Dianam ... Vesta* Diana and Vesta were virgin goddesses. Vesta's priestesses were the vestal virgins.

104. Venus was born of sea-foam.

106. Hymen was god of marriage. The cry *io Hymen Hymenaee* is the refrain in an epithalamium by Catullus (lxi).

112. *Cytherea* a common name for Venus, who landed on the island of Cythera after being born from sea-foam.

114. *Phyllis* a stock pastoral name for a shepherdess. Cp. *L'Allegro* 86.

116. Dolphins were thought to be fond of music and known to be friendly to men. Cp. Pliny IX viii 24–8 and Ovid, *Fasti* ii 83ff., and see *Lycidas* 164*n*.

122. Silvanus, the Roman god of uncultivated land, wore cypress leaves in memory of the boy Cyparissus, whom he had loved, and who died of grief after Silvanus killed his pet deer.

125. *Maenalius Pan* [*Maenalian Pan*] Maenalus was an Arcadian mountain, sacred to Pan.

126. *Cybele* the great mother, identified with Rhea and Ops. See above, 62*n*. *Ceres* was her daughter.

127. *Faunus* a Roman wood-god. See *PL* iv 707–8*n*. An Oread is a mountain-nymph.

131–40. Contrast the banishing of the pagan gods in *Nativity* 173ff.

Elegia Sexta. Ad Carolum Diodatum, ruri commorantem [Elegy VI. To Charles Diodati, staying in the country]

Date: from M.'s prose heading, and from the reference to the composition of *Nativity* (79–90), it is clear that this elegy was written a few days after Christmas, 1629.

8. *claudos . . . pedes* [*limping feet*] the alternating hexameters and pentameters of elegy. The joke about limping is borrowed from Ovid, *Tristia* III i 11–12.

18. The Nine are the Muses. Bacchus is called *Thyoneus* because his mother Semele was called Thyone. *Euoe* was the cry of Bacchic revellers.

20. See *Elegy I* 21*n* for Ovid's banishment to the Black Sea. The Coralli were a local Germanic tribe. In *Ex Ponto* IV viii 80–83 Ovid complains that the Coralli have no wine, and in *Ex Ponto* IV ii 15–22 he admits that his poems have suffered.

21. *Lyaeum* Bacchus was known as Lyaeus, 'the releaser'.

22. *Teia Musa* [*Teian poet*] Anacreon, a Greek lyric poet, born *c.* 570 BC in Teos on the coast of Asia Minor.

23. *Teumesius Euan* Boeotian Bacchus.

27. *lyricen Romanus* [*Roman lyrist*] Horace. Glycera and blonde Chloe both appear in his *Odes* (e.g. I xix and xxiii).

31. *Massica* Mount Massicus in Campania was famous for its wine.

37. *Thressa . . . barbitos* [*Thracian lyre*] Orpheus was a Thracian.

43. *ebur . . . plectrum* [*ivory key*] of the harpsichord or virginal, although the plectrum used to strike a lyre might also be meant.

48. *Thalia* the Muse of comedy and (according to Ovid, *Odes* IV vi 25) lyric poetry.

51. *Erato* the Muse of lyric, especially erotic, poetry.

58. *cane* [*dog*] Cerberus, the watchdog of Hades.

59. *Samii . . . magistri* [*the Samian master*] Pythagoras, the ascetic philosopher born at Samos *c.* 580 BC.

68. *Tiresian* [*Tiresias*] the Theban prophet. He had been (at different times) a man and a woman, and Juno blinded him when he revealed that sex was more pleasurable for women than for men. Jove compensated him with prophetic powers.

Linon Linus, a mythical bard of Thebes (Ogygia), and Orpheus' teacher.

69. *Calchanta* [*Calchas*] the Greek prophet in the Trojan War. M. follows medieval tradition in making him a Trojan who defected to the Greeks.

70. Orpheus tamed wild beasts after he had failed to rescue Eurydice from Hades. Virgil, *Georg.* iv 516, and Ovid, *Met.* x 79–82, say that he then shunned all women. (Ovid adds that he consoled himself with 'tender boys'.)

71. Boccaccio had depicted Homer as living an ascetic life (*De Genealogiis Deorum* XIV xix). Contrast Horace's view that Homer must have loved wine (*Epistulae* I xix 1–6).

72. The island of *Dulichium* was part of Odysseus's realm.

73. *Perseiae Phoebados* [*daughter of Phoebus and Perseis*] Circe, who turned Odysseus's men into swine (Homer, *Od.* x 274–574).

76. Homer describes the Sirens' song in *Od.* xii 184–92 and Odysseus' descent to Hades in *Od.* xi.

89. *Te quoque* [*For you too*] My translation assumes that M. is still referring to *Nativity* in lines 89–90 and that *quoque* means that that poem is a gift for Diodati as well as for Christ. Carey thinks that *quoque* refers to some other poems that M. has written, and that these are the Italian sonnets composed in Diodati's (not M.'s) ancestral language (*patriis cicutis*).

Elegia Septima [Elegy VII]

Date: summer 1628? The caption *Anno aetatis undevigesimo* is puzzling. M.'s usual method of dating would suggest that the phrase means 'at the age of nineteen' (see headnote to *Elegia II*). The caption is unique, however, in using the ordinal. M. normally employs arabic numerals. M. might therefore mean that the poem was composed in his nineteenth year (9 December 1626 – 8 December 1627). If (as seems likely) he is describing a real incident, the poem was written after May Day (14), perhaps in the summer when attractive young women were accustomed to walk in the fields in and around London (51). If *Elegia VII* was written in either 1627 or 1628 it must antedate *Elegia VI*. Parker (754) tries to save the *1645* chronology by arguing that *undevigesimo* is a misreading of M.'s manuscript *uno & vigesimo*, 'twenty-one'.

1. *Amathusia* Venus, after her shrine at Amathus in Cyprus.

2. *Paphio* [*Paphian*] Venus had a temple at Paphos, in Cyprus.

11. *Cyprius* [*Cyprian lad*] Cupid, whose mother Venus was called 'Cypris' from her association with Cyprus. Classical authors do not apply the epithet to Cupid.

21. *iuvenis Sigeius* [*Sigeian youth*] Ganymede, the Trojan boy abducted by Jove to be his cupbearer. Sigeum was near Troy.

24. *Hylas* a beautiful youth loved by Hercules. Sent by the Argonauts to fetch water from a pool, he was dragged to the bottom by amorous nymphs (Theocritus xiii).

31. Having killed the monstrous Python with his arrows, Apollo taunted

Cupid for presuming to use the bow. Cupid then turned his bow on Apollo, causing him to love Daphne (Ovid, *Met.* i 452–567).

36. *Parthus eques* [*Parthian horseman*] Parthian mounted archers were famous for their ability to shoot to the rear while feigning retreat. Cp. *PR* iii 322–5.

37. *Cydonius* [*Cydonian*] Cretan. Cretans were famous archers.

38. Cephalus, while hunting, mistook his wife Procris for a beast rustling in the bushes, and unwittingly killed her with his javelin. See Ovid, *Met.* vii 835–62.

39. *Orion* a giant hunter who pursued the Pleiades, daughters of Atlas. He and they were turned into constellations.

40. *Herculeaeque manus* [*the hands of Hercules*] Hercules had many sexual adventures, and his strong hands were subjected to love when Queen Omphale dressed him in women's clothes and made him spin for her.

comes [*companion*] Hercules had many companions. Cupid probably means Jason or Theseus.

46. *anguis* [*serpent*] Aesculapius, god of healing, took the form of a snake when he came to Rome to end a plague. See Ovid, *Met.* xv 626–744 and cp. *PL* ix 506–7.

47. Cupid used gold-tipped arrows to excite love, lead-tipped ones to excite hate. See Ovid, *Met.* i 468–71.

64. *regina deum* [*queen of the gods*] Juno. M. is referring to the judgement of Paris.

81. *proles Iunonia* [*Juno's son*] Vulcan (Hephaestus, Mulciber) was thrown from heaven by Jove and fell for a whole day before landing in Lemnos (Homer, *Il.* i 590–94). Cp. *PL* i 739–47.

84. *Amphiaraus* an Argive seer and one of the seven against Thebes. In the midst of battle, the earth opened to swallow him and his chariot. Statius, *Thebaid* vii 820–22, describes his last longing look at the vanishing sky.

'Haec ego mente . . .' [Epilogue to the Elegies]

Appended to *Elegia VII* in *1645* and *1673*, these verses act as an epilogue to the whole series. They were clearly written after the other elegies (see line 1) but before M.'s marriage in 1642 (see lines 7–10).

5. *Academia* [*Academy*] Platonic philosophy. See *PR* iv 244–6.

10. Diomedes wounded Aphrodite (Venus) when she went to the aid of her son, Aeneas. See Homer, *Il.* v 334–51.

In Proditionem Bombardicam [On the Gunpowder Plot]

Date: unknown. M.'s four epigrams on the Gunpowder Plot, and his epigram on the inventor of gunpowder, may have been written at various times or at the same time. The second epigram on the Gunpowder Plot alludes to King James's death and so must have been written after it (see 6n).

7. *ille* Elijah, who was swept up to Heaven while still alive. See II Kings 2. 7. The *Parcae* are the Fates.

In eandem [On the same]

2. *Belua* [*Beast*] Protestants often identified the seven-headed Beast of Rev. 13. 1 with the Roman Church.
6. James I died on 27 March 1625.
7. Cp. the Paradise of Fools in *PL* iii 473–94.

In eandem [On the same]

1. James had ridiculed the idea of Purgatory in the preface to the second edition of his *Apology for the Oath of Allegiance* (1609).
3. *Latiale* Roman (from Latium, home of the Latins). The triple-crowned monster is the Pope.
4. *cornua dena* The Beast of Rev. 13. 1 has ten horns.

In eandem [On the same]

1. James had been baptized a Roman Catholic but raised as a Protestant. In the eyes of Rome he was therefore excommunicate.
2. *Taenarioque sinu* [*Taenarian abyss*] See *Elegia V* 66n.

In Inventorem Bombardae [On the Inventor of Gunpowder]

Parker (732) thinks that M.'s praise for the inventor of gunpowder 'may be intended literally instead of ironically', but the fact that M. published this epigram alongside the Fifth of November verses strongly suggests that

his praise is ironic. Gunpowder was traditionally seen as a devilish invention.
See *PL* vi 484*n*.

1. *Iapetionidem* [*son of Iapetus*] Prometheus, who stole fire from heaven.
Cp. the devils' scorn for God's thunder in *PL* vi 632, after Satan has
invented gunpowder.

Ad Leonoram Romae canentem [To Leonora singing at Rome]

Leonora Baroni was a famous Neapolitan singer. M. heard her sing on one
of his two visits to Rome: either October–November 1638 or January–
February 1639.

5. *mens tertia* [*third mind*] perhaps the third person of the Trinity, the Holy
Ghost (I John 5. 7). Carey thinks that M. is referring to the neo-Platonic
World-Soul.

· Ad eandem [To the same]

See headnote to previous poem.

1. *Torquatum* Torquato Tasso (1544–95) suffered from insanity which
caused him to be confined (1579–86). He was said to have loved Leonora
d'Este, the sister of his patron, the Duke of Ferrara, and this alleged love
was fancifully supposed to be the cause of his illness.
5. *Pieria* the birthplace of the Muses, in Macedonia.
6. Leonora's mother was a musician.
7. *Dircaeo* Theban.
    Pentheo Pentheus, King of Thebes, opposed the Dionysian rites.
Dionysus then deprived him of his sanity and caused him to be torn to
pieces by the Bacchantes.

Ad eandem [To the same]

2. *Parthenopes* one of the Sirens, drowned near Naples. See *A Masque*
879*n*. The river-god Achelous was the Sirens' father.
4. *Chalcidico* [*Chalcidian*] Neapolitan. See *Ep. Dam.* 182*n*.
6. *Pausilipi* Mount Posillipo, near Naples, was pierced by a tunnel through
which passed much noisy traffic. The hoarse roar (*rauci murmura*) might
be caused by this traffic or by the waves crashing at the foot of the mountain.

SILVARUM LIBER [A BOOK OF
MISCELLANEOUS POEMS]

Latin *silvae* was used, by Statius for example, as a title for collections of occasional poems. Jonson had used the English equivalent as the title of his *The Forest* (1616).

In Obitum Procancellarii Medici [On the death of the
Vice-Chancellor, a Physician]

Date: autumn 1626. Dr John Gostlin, Master of Caius College, Professor of Medicine, and Vice-Chancellor of Cambridge University, died on 21 October 1626, when M. was seventeen. The heading *Anno aetatis* 16 is therefore an error.

2. *Parcae* [*goddess of destiny*] Atropos, the Fate who cut the thread of life.
3. *pendulum telluris orbem* [*pendulous globe of the earth*] Cp. *PL* iv 1000: 'The pendulous round earth'.
4. *Iapeti* Iapetus was the father of Prometheus, the creator of man.
5. *Taenaro* Taenarus, in Laconia, was fabled to be an entrance to Hades.
12. Hercules died after putting on the robe of Nessus, which had been poisoned by the Hydra's blood. See *PL* ii 542-6n.
14. Disguised as Hector's brother Deiphobus, Pallas Athene caused Hector's death by shaming him into fighting Achilles (Homer, *Il*. xxii 226-404). When Achilles failed to hit Hector with his first cast, Athene invisibly retrieved his spear, and so ensured his victory (*Il*. xxii 276-7).
16. Zeus wept tears of blood when his son Sarpedon was killed by the Locrian Patroclus, who was wearing Achilles' armour (Homer, *Il*. xvi 419-507).
18. *Telegoni parens* [*Telegonus's mother*] Circe. She had Telegonus by Odysseus. Hecate was goddess of witchcraft.
20. *Aegiali soror* [*Aegialeus's sister*] Medea. She murdered her brother and scattered his dismembered body on the sea to delay her father's pursuit of the Argonauts.
24. Machaon, son of Aesculapius, was a surgeon in the Greek army at Troy. Quintus Smyrnaeus reports his death at the hands of another Greek, Eurypylus (*Posthomerica* vi 390-429).
25. *Philyreie* [*son of Philyra*] Chiron the centaur, son of Cronos and the nymph Philyra. He was skilled in medicine, and tutored Aesculapius, but was unable to heal himself when one of Hercules' arrows scratched him.
28. *puer* Aesculapius, whom his father Apollo cut from the womb of his

mother Coronis. His medical skill was so great that he revived even the dead, so Jupiter killed him with a thunderbolt.

31. *Cirrha* a very ancient town near Delphi, sacred to Apollo.

33. *Palladio gregi* [*Pallas's flock*] the students and Fellows of Cambridge University. Pallas Athene was goddess of wisdom.

35. *Charontis* Charon ferried the dead over the river Styx.

37. *Persephone* queen of hell. In line 46 M. calls her by her Latin name *Proserpina*.

45. *Aeaci* Aeacus. After his death he became, with Minos and Rhadamanthys, a judge of the dead in Hades.

46. *Aetnaea* Sicilian (from Mount Etna). Proserpine had been abducted by Pluto from the Sicilian meadow of Enna. Cp. *PL* iv 268f.

In Quintum Novembris [On the Fifth of November]

The heading *Anno aetatis* 17 almost certainly means 'at seventeen years of age' (see headnote to *Elegia II*). M.'s miniature epic may have been written for Cambridge festivities celebrating Guy Fawkes Day (5 November) in 1626. The Gunpowder Plot (to assassinate King James in Parliament) had been exposed on 5 November 1605. Many critics have detected in M.'s poem the influence of Phineas Fletcher's *Locustae* (1627), which M. might have seen in manuscript. M.'s early English poems contain many probable echoes of poems by Fletcher that M. could have seen only in manuscript. See *Nativity* 239n.

2. *Teucrigenas populos* [*Troy-descended people*] The Britons were thought to be descendants of Trojan exiles led by Brutus, Aeneas's grandson. The myth is found in Nennius's eighth-century *Historia Brittonum* as well as in Geoffrey of Monmouth's *Historia Regum Britanniae*.

7. *ignifluo . . . Acheronte* [*Acheron's fiery waves*] Phlegethon, not Acheron, was the infernal river of fire. Acheron was the river of sorrow. But 'Acheron' could also denote Hell in general, so the fiery waves might be the 'lake of fire' of Rev. 19. 20 and 20. 14. The tyrant is Satan.

10. *vernas* [*slaves by birth*] implying Calvinist predestination. M. was not yet an Arminian in 1626.

12. *medio . . . aere* [*middle air*] Satan's abode as 'prince of the power of the air' (Eph. 2. 2). Cp. *PR* i 39, ii 117.

23. *Summanus* an obscure god of midnight storms. He was identified with Pluto as prince of the dead (*summus manium*), and Jove's thunderbolts were said to be in his power at night. See Ovid, *Fasti* vi 731.

27. *Neptunia proles* [*Neptune's son*] Albion, the legendary king of Britain, who gave the island his own name. He was killed fighting Hercules in Gaul.

28. *Amphitryoniaden* [*Amphitryon's son*] Hercules, son of Jove and Alcmene, wife of Amphitryon. Classical poets often call Hercules 'Amphitryoniades'.

37. See *PL* i 198–9n on the monster Typhoeus, his war against the gods, and imprisonment under Etna.

52. *Thetidi* Thetis, the sea-nymph, here stands for the sea, which Tiber flows into.

53. *Quirini* Romulus was called Quirinus after his deification.

55. *Tricoronifer* the Pope, with his triple crown.

56. *Panificosque deos* [*gods made of bread*] the Eucharist, which Roman Catholics see as the body of Christ.

60. *Cimmeriis* Cimmeria was a land of perpetual darkness visited by Odysseus (Homer, *Od.* xi 13–22).

62. St Peter's feast is on 28 June.

64. *Bromius* 'the noisy one', a surname of Bacchus.

65. *Echionio Aracyntho* the Boeotian mountain Aracynthus. Echion was a Theban hero who sprang from the dragons' teeth sown by Cadmus.

66. *Asopus* a Boeotian river.

67. *Cithaeron* a mountain near Thebes, sacred to Dionysus, whose orgies take place there in Euripides' *The Bacchae*.

69. *Erebus* the husband and brother of Night.

71–3. The Greek names of Night's horses are M.'s invention. Typhon means 'blind', Melanchaetes means 'long, black hair', Siope means 'silence', and Phrix means 'shuddering'.

74. *regum domitor* [*tamer of kings*] the Pope.

79–85. Satan appears disguised as a Franciscan friar.

88. *Silvestri . . . genti* [*forest folk*] birds.

92. *Dormis . . .* [*Are you sleeping . . .*] echoing many previous epics, where heroes or villains are roused from peaceful sleep by a voice which lures them into performing rash deeds. Cp. Homer, *Il.* ii 23, Virgil, *Aen.* iv 560, vii 421, Tasso, *Gerus. Lib.* x 8, and M.'s *PL* v 38 and 673.

95. *Hyperboreo* Diodorus Siculus II xlvii 1 locates the blessed island of the Hyperboreans in the northern sea, beyond the land of the Celts.

101. *Apostolicae . . . clavis* [*Apostolic key*] the keys of Heaven given to Peter by Christ (Matt. 16. 19).

102. *Hesperiae . . . classem* [*Hesperian fleet*] the Spanish Armada, defeated in 1588.

105. *Thermodoontea . . . puella* [*Amazonian virgin*] Elizabeth I had persecuted Catholics in England. The Amazons lived near the river Thermodon, in Pontus.

108. *Tyrrhenum . . . Pontum* [*Tyrrhenian Sea*] the Mediterranean west of Italy.

109. *Aventino . . . colle* The Aventine is the southernmost of Rome's seven hills.

117. *Patricios* [*patricians*] members of the Commons.

procerum de stirpe creatos [*the men of high descent*] the Lords.

118. *patres* bishops, as members of the House of Lords.

127. *Saecula . . . Mariana* [*the Marian age*] Mary Tudor had burned many Protestant martyrs during her reign (1553–8). In ancient Latin usage *Mariana* referred to the brutal age of Marius and Sulla. M.'s friend Alexander Gill had used the pun in his anti-Catholic poem *In ruinam Camerae Papisticae* (1625).

132. *Lethen* [*Lethe*] the river of oblivion in Hades.

133. *Tithonia* [*wife of Tithonus*] Aurora, goddess of dawn.

135. *nigri . . . nati* [*black son*] Memnon, an Ethiopian hero slain by Achilles at Troy. Aurora's tears are the dew.

137. *ianitor* the Pope, as keeper of Heaven's keys.

139–54. Cp. the personified inhabitants of hell's vestibule in Virgil, *Aen.* vi 273–81 and Spenser, *FQ* II vii 21–5.

143. *praeruptaque*] *1673*; semifractaque *1645*. M. changed the word after Salmasius (*Responsio* (1660) 5) pointed out the false quantity in *1645*.

150. *Exululat*] *1673*; Exululant *1645*.

conscia Latin *conscius* could imply guilty knowledge, as could English 'conscious' (*OED* 4b). Cp. 'conscious Night' in *PL* vi 521.

156. *Babylonius* English Protestants identified Rome with the Babylon of Rev. 14. 8 and 17. 5.

168. *ridet* Cp. God's laughing at his enemies in Ps. 2. 4 and in *PL* ii 731 and v 736–7.

170–93. M.'s description of the tower of *Fama* (Rumour) draws upon Ovid, *Met.* xii 39–63, Virgil, *Aen.* iv 173–88, and Chaucer, *The House of Fame* iii.

171. *Mareotidas* Lake Mareotis, near Alexandria. M. might be referring by synecdoche to Africa in general, which forms a third continent alongside Asia (170) and Europe (171). D. T. Starnes, in *N&Q* 196 (1951) 515–18, plausibly argues that *Mareotidas* is a misprint for *Maeotidas* (lake Maeotis, the Sea of Azov), the traditional centre of the world (see e.g. Lucan, *Pharsalia* iii 271–8).

172. *Titanidos* [*daughter of the Titaness*] Virgil's Fama was the daughter of Terra (Earth), and the younger sister of the Giants (*Aen.* iv 178–80).

174. Athos, Pelion and Ossa are Greek mountains. The Giants piled Pelion on Ossa when they attacked the gods. See Homer, *Od.* xi 313–16 and Ovid, *Met.* i 151–5.

178–9. Homer uses the simile of flies buzzing around milk-pails to describe the mustering Greeks (*Il.* ii 469–73) and the Greeks and Trojans fighting over Sarpedon's corpse (*Il.* xvi 641–3). Cp. also *PR* iv 15–17.

181. *ultrix matris* [*her mother's avenger*] Terra gave birth to Rumour to avenge the defeat of the Giants, her sons (Virgil, *Aen.* iv 178–80).

185. *Aristoride* [*Arestor's son*] Argus, the hundred-eyed herdsman whom Juno set to guard Io, daughter of Inachus. Jove had changed Io into a heifer in a vain attempt to hide their love. Ancient tradition identified Io (who was restored to human form in Egypt) with the Egyptian goddess Isis.

194–8. The Gunpowder Plot was thwarted because one of the plotters warned Lord Monteagle not to attend the opening of Parliament.

207. *Temesaeo* Temesa, in southern Italy, was famous for its copper mines.

In Obitum Praesulis Eliensis [*On the death of the Bishop of Ely*]

Date: October 1626. Dr Nicholas Felton (1556 – 5 October 1626) followed Lancelot Andrewes as Bishop of Ely (1619–26) and died ten days after Andrewes. He and Andrewes were friends, and both were translators of the A.V.

1–6. M. is referring to *Elegia III*, his tribute to Andrewes.

10. Neptune was the father of Albion, founder of Britain.

11. *ferreis sororibus* [*cruel sisters*] the Parcae (Fates).

14. *Anguillae* [*Eel*] Ely means 'eel-isle'.

17. *deam* [*goddess*] Libitina (Roman goddess of funerals), or Mors (Death), or Proserpina.

18. *Ibida* Ovid's *Ibis* (*The Crane*) is an invective against an enemy.

20. *Graiusque vates* [*Greek poet*] Archilochus of Paros, a Greek poet of around the mid-seventh century BC. Ancient tradition says that he loved Neobule, daughter of Lycambes. When Lycambes forbade the marriage, Archilochus wrote such biting satires that father and daughter hanged themselves.

27–8. *vitream / Bilemque* [*gleaming bile*] Greek medical theory held that black bile, the source of melancholy, would gleam in mad persons.

32. Hesiod calls Death daughter of Night (*Theog.* 758–9).

39. *Horae* [*the Hours*] goddesses of the seasons. They were the daughters of Zeus and Themis, goddess of justice.

49. *Vates* [*prophet*] Elijah. See II Kings 2. 11 for his ascent to Heaven in a chariot of fire.

56. *deam* [*goddess*] Luna, goddess of the moon. She is *triformis* because she was called Luna in heaven, Diana on earth, and Hecate or Proserpina in hell. Hecate is associated with a dragon-drawn chariot in Ovid, *Met.* vii 218–19. Cp. *Il Penseroso* 59 and *A Masque* 131.

Naturam non pati senium *[That Nature does not suffer from old age]*

Date: unknown. These verses are usually taken to be an academic exercise from M.'s Cambridge days. M. wrote a letter to Alexander Gill, dated 2 July 1628, in which he mentions a poem that he had recently written for a Fellow of the College to use in a Commencement disputation. Many editors think that this poem was *Naturam non pati senium*, and that the date of composition was therefore June 1628. But M. in his letter describes the poem as *leviculas . . . nugas* ('trivial nonsense'). The phrase may simply be false modesty, but Carey plausibly conjectures that M. in his letter is referring to the lighthearted *De Idea Platonica*. *Naturam non pati senium* has a serious subject, which might have been inspired by George Hakewill's *Apology of the Power and Providence of God* (1627). Hakewill's *Apology* was a rebuttal of the theory – recently expressed by Godfrey Goodman in *The Fall of Man* (1616) – that Nature is in a process of continual decay. Goodman did not invent the idea. It was familiar to Spenser (see proem to book V of *FQ*) and to Donne (see his *Anniversaries*). M. himself was later to describe the postlapsarian world as groaning under its own weight (*PL* xii 539). In the present poem, however, he expresses optimism about the unchanging goodness of Nature.

3. *Oedipodioniam . . . noctem* *[Oedipean night]* self-inflicted blindness. See Sophocles, *Oedipus the King* 1298f.

9. *mater* Ge, Mother Earth, the common ancestor of gods and men. *Omniparens* was one of her titles.

14–15. Cronos, son of Uranus and Ge (Heaven and Earth), devoured his children at birth. Cronos was sometimes identified with Chronos (Time), which devours its own offspring. M. imagines a decay so universal that Time runs backwards to devour its own father, Heaven.

19. *sono . . . tremendo* *[tremendous crash]* Cp. II Pet. 3. 10: 'The heavens shall pass away with a great noise'.

22. *Gorgone* Pallas Athene wore the head of the Gorgon Medusa on her shield. Whoever saw it uncovered was turned to stone.

23. *proles Iunonia* *[Juno's son]* Vulcan. See *Elegia VII* 81*n*.

25. *tui . . . nati* *[your son]* Phaethon. See *Elegia V* 92*n*.

27. *Nereus* the Old Man of the Sea, father of the Nereids.

29. *Haemi* *[Haemus]* a high mountain range in Thrace. Ovid says that it was burned by Phaethon's chariot (*Met.* ii 219).

31–2. The Ceraunian mountains are in Epirus. M. might have confused these with the Thessalian mountains Pelion and Ossa, (see note to line 174, '*In Quintum Novembris*'). See Ovid, *Met.* i 151–5.

33–4. *Pater omnipotens . . . Consuluit rerum summae* *[the omnipotent Father has consulted on the sum of things*] echoing Ovid, *Met.* ii 300, where Earth begs Jove (*Pater omnnipotens*) to place the public interest first (*rerum consule summae*) and kill Phaethon so as to save the world from conflagration. Cp. *PL* vi 673.

37. *rota prima* [*prime wheel*] the *primum mobile* or 'first moved' in the Ptolemaic system: the outermost sphere of the universe which makes a complete revolution in twenty-four hours, imparting movement to all the lower spheres.

41–4. A supposed shift in the sun's orbit was often cited as evidence that Nature suffered from decay. Thus Spenser claims that the sun had 'declyned . . . Nigh thirtie minutes' to the south in the 1,400 years since Ptolemy's day (*FQ* V proem 7).

45–8. The planet Venus is both Lucifer, the morning star, and Hesperus, the evening star.

49. *Delia* Diana, goddess of the moon.

cornu both the moon's 'horns' and the bow held by Diana, goddess of the hunt (50).

53. *Corus* the north-west wind.

55. *Aquilo* the north-east wind.

56. *Pelori* Pelorus (Cape Faro), near Mount Etna in Sicily. Neptune (the king of the sea) batters the region as god of earthquakes. Cp. *PL* i 230–37.

58. *tubicen* [*trumpeter*] Triton, Neptune's herald.

59. *Aegaeona* a hundred-armed Giant, called Briareos by gods, Aegaeon by men (Homer, *Il.* i 403–4). Ovid depicts Aegaeon as clasping huge whales in his arms (*Met.* ii 9–10). M. likens Satan to Briareos and a whale in *PL* i 199–201.

61. *Narcissus* the beautiful youth transformed into a flower (Ovid, *Met.* iii 402–510).

63. Apollo's beloved boy is Hyacinthus, whom Apollo transformed into a flower after he had accidentally killed him with a discus (Ovid, *Met.* x 162–216). Cypris is Venus. Her beloved boy is Adonis. She transformed him into an anemone after he was killed by a boar (*Met.* x 728–39).

67–9. The final conflagration is prophesied at II Pet. 3. 10.

De Idea Platonica quemadmodum Aristoteles intellexit [On the Platonic form as Aristotle understood it]

Date: June 1628? See previous headnote. The poem is light in manner, but it has a serious subject: Aristotle's critique (in *Metaphysics* I ix, VII viii) of Plato's doctrine of the ideal Forms. M. poses as a literal-minded Aristotelian, asking where the ideal Form of man is to be found. M.'s irony is aimed at Aristotle, not Plato.

1. *deae* [*goddesses*] either the Muses, to whom Numa dedicated a grove (Livy I xxi 3), or Diana and her nymphs, who attend at births. Virgil calls Diana 'guardian of the groves' (*Aen.* ix 405).

2. *noveni . . . numinis* [*ninefold deity*] the Muses.

3. *Memoria* [*Memory*] Mnemosyne, mother of the Muses.

4–6. Cp. the cave of Time (an old man who keeps Jove's records) in Claudian, *De Consulatu Stilichonis* ii 424–8 and Boccaccio, *De Genealogiis Deorum* I ii.

12. Pallas Athene sprang fully armed from the head of Jove.

20. The Pythagorean doctrine of reincarnation is found in Plato, *Phaedo* 70–72 and *Republic* x 617–18. Virgil's Aeneas sees crowds of souls waiting to drink from Lethe, river of forgetfulness, before being reborn (*Aen.* vi 710–15).

24. *Atlante* Atlas carried the heavens on his shoulders.

26. *Dircaeus augur* [*Dircean seer*] Tiresias, the blind Theban prophet. See *Elegia VI* 68n.

27. *Pleiones nepos* [*Pleione's grandson*] Mercury. His mother was Maia, daughter of Atlas and Pleione.

29. *sacerdos . . . Assyrius* [*Assyrian priest*] perhaps one of the sages who informed Herodotus (I i) about the Assyrian king Ninus; but Carey plausibly suggests that M. is referring to the Assyrian priest Hierombalus – the ancient oral source of a lost history of Phoenicia, fragments of which survive in Eusebius, *Praeparationis Evangelicae* I ix and are quoted by John Selden in *De Dis Syris* (1617) 111.

30. *Nini* [*Ninus*] founder of the Assyrian monarchy.

31. *Priscumque Belon* [*primeval Belus*] See George Sandys, *Relation of a Journey* (1615) 207: 'Belus Priscus, reputed a God and honoured with Temples, called *Bel* by the Assyrians, and *Baal* by the Hebrewes'. See also *PL* i 720n.

   Osiridem [*Osiris*] an Egyptian god. See *Nativity* 216–20n.

33. *Ter magnus Hermes* [*thrice-great Hermes*] See *Il Penseroso* 88n.

34. *Isidis cultoribus* [*worshippers of Isis*] Egyptians.

35. *Academi decus* [*glory of the Academy*] Plato, who excluded poets from his ideal state on the grounds that fables are mere imitations (*Republic* x 595–607).

Ad Patrem [*To his Father*]

Date: much disputed. Suggested dates range from 1631 to 1645. The poem clearly arose from some kind of conflict between M. and his father about M.'s failure to choose a career. As Bush points out, the problem of a profession 'would have come up between father and son before the son left

Cambridge, certainly by his last year, 1631–32'. Bush feels that the present tenses in 71–6 tell for an early date, and concludes that the *secessibus* (seclusion) of 74 refers to Cambridge (which would date the poem before 1632). Others feel that the seclusion is that of Hammersmith or Horton (1632–8). *Ad Patrem* has been well described as M.'s 'Apology for Poetry'.

1. *Pierios . . . fontes* [*Pierian fountains*] Pieria, in Macedonia, was the birthplace of the Muses.

3. *gemino . . . vertice* [*twin peaks*] of Mount Parnassus, which was sacred to the Muses. See *Elegia IV* 30n.

14. *Clio* one of the Muses, in Roman times the Muse of history.

20. *Prometheae . . . flammae* Prometheus stole fire from heaven and brought it to man. The fire was sometimes allegorized as philosophic wisdom. See e.g. Natale Conti, *Mythologiae* (1567) IV vi.

25. *Phoebades* priestesses of Apollo, especially the Pythia at Delphi.

Sibyllae prophetesses inspired by Apollo. The most famous was the Cumaean Sibyl, who guided Aeneas through Hades (Virgil, *Aen.* vi). Virgil describes her as pale and shaking while she prophesies to Aeneas (*Aen.* vi 46–51).

32–3. Cp. St John's vision of the four and twenty elders wearing 'crowns of gold' (Rev. 4. 4), and playing harps (Rev. 5. 8). Cp. also Rev. 14. 1–5, where the 144,000 male virgins who 'were not defiled with women' sing a 'new song' accompanied by harps. Many critics have thought that the young M. made a pledge of sacrificial celibacy, but here he includes his father among those who will wear a crown and play a harp. In *An Apology for Smectymnuus* (1642) he remarks that the 144,000 virgins of Rev. 14 include married men, 'For mariage must not be call'd a defilement' (*YP* 1. 893). See *Ep. Dam.* 214n and *A Masque* 787n.

35. *Spiritus* identified by John Carey as M.'s own spirit, which has been released from his body to sing amid the stars. Carey traces the theory of this release to Macrobius's commentary on Cicero's *Somnium Scipionis*. See *RES* n.s. 15 (1964) 180–84. M. N. K. Mander (*MQ* 23, December 1989, 158–65) agrees that Macrobius is the source, but argues that *Spiritus* is 'unspecific' so as to include 'Milton, his father, and any bard reading the poem' (162).

37. *inenarrabile carmen* [*inexpressible song*] Cp. *Lycidas* 176.

38. *Serpens* the constellation.

48. *Reptantesque deos* [*crawling gods*] The bard is presumably singing of the gods' infancy.

glandes [*acorns*] Ovid says that men who lived during the Golden Age fed on acorns fallen from the tree of Jove (*Met.* i 106).

49. The Golden Age ended when Jupiter, armed with thunderbolts,

dethroned Saturn. Virgil describes the Cyclopes forging thunderbolts in a cave under Etna (*Georg.* iv 170–75).

52–5. Orpheus entrances oak-trees with his song in Virgil (*Georg.* iv 510) and moves the ghosts to tears in Ovid (*Met.* x 41).

60. *Arionii* Arion saved himself from drowning when he charmed a dolphin with his lyre (Herodotus i 23–4). M.'s father was a talented musician.

64. Phoebus Apollo was god both of poetry and music.

75. *Aoniae ... ripae* [*Aonian stream*] The fountains of Aganippe and Hippocrene, on Mount Helicon in Aonia (Boeotia), were thought to inspire those who drank from them. The Muses were called Aonides.

94. *Austriaci gazas* the wealth of the Holy Roman Empire.

Peruanaque regna Spain conquered the fabulously wealthy Inca empire of Peru in the 1530s.

98. *nato* [*son*] Phaethon. See *Elegia V* 92n.

99. Hyperion was father of Helios, the sun. M. here follows Homer (*Il.* viii 480, *Od.* i 24) in calling Helios 'Hyperion'.

102. *hederas ... laurosque* [*ivy and laurel*] See *Lycidas* 1–2n.

111–14. Cicero argues that the way to pay a moral debt is to acknowledge it (*Pro Plancio* xxviii 68). Cp. *PL* iv 50–57.

118. *Orco* [*Orcus*] Hades, the underworld.

Psalm CXIV

This is almost certainly the poem referred to in M.'s letter to Alexander Gill, dated 4 December 1634. M. tells Gill that he has recently translated one of the psalms into Greek heroic verse and is enclosing it with the letter (*YP* 1. 321). M. also apologizes for any errors that Gill might find, and points out that this is the first poem he has written in Greek since leaving school.

Philosophus ad Regem [A Philosopher to a King]

Date: unknown. This epigram may be a grammar-school exercise. If not written at St Paul's, it was probably written after 1634, for M. in a letter dated 4 December 1634 says that *Psalm CXIV* was the first thing he had written in Greek since leaving school (see previous headnote). Parker (144) dates the poem in 1634 and conjectures (without evidence) that M. might be referring to Gill's clash with Star Chamber and his pardon by King Charles (30 November 1630). M.'s epigram would be oddly belated if it were making a topical reference four years after the event.

4. Μαψιδίως ... οδυρῃ,] *1673*; Μὰψ ἄυτως δ' ἀρ' ἔπειτα χρόνῳ μάλα πολλὸν ὀδύρῃ 1645. The earlier version means: 'and in time then you lament grievously, all in vain'.

Ad Salsillum poetam Romanum aegrotantem. Scazontes [To Salzilli, the Roman poet, when he was ill. Scazons]

Date: late 1638 or early 1639. M. met Giovanni Salzilli in Rome, either during his first visit (October–November 1638) or his second (January–February 1639). The earlier date is more likely, for *Ad Salsillum* precedes *Mansus* in *1645*, and M. implies that he has only recently arrived in Italy (10). Salzilli wrote an extravagant Latin quatrain in which he praised M. above Homer, Virgil, and Tasso. M.'s poem is a reply to this quatrain (which was printed in *1645* alongside other commendatory verses by M.'s Italian friends). Nothing is known about Salzilli's illness. Salzilli had contributed poems to a volume called *Poesie de'Signori Accademici Fantastici* (Rome 1637).
Title. Scazontes. a modification of iambic trimeter in which a spondee or trochee takes the place of the final iamb.

1. *claudum [lame]* punning on the literal sense of 'scazon', which is Greek for 'limping'.
2. *Vulcanioque ... incessu* Vulcan was lame after his fall from heaven. See *Elegia VII* 81*n*.
4. *Deiope* Juno promised Deiopea, the loveliest of her nymphs, to Aeolus as a reward for harassing Aeneas's fleet (Virgil, *Aen.* i 65–75).
22. *Lesbium ... melos [poetry of Lesbos]* Alcaeus and Sappho were natives of Lesbos. Salzilli had evidently adapted their Greek lyric tradition to Latin or Italian.
23. *Salus [Health]* a Roman goddess.
   Hebe goddess of youth.
25. *Paean* Apollo's title as god of healing. Salzilli is his priest (*sacerdos*) because Apollo was also god of poetry. The Python was a monstrous serpent slain by Apollo.
27. *Fauni* Faunus, a Roman god of woods and pastures, identified with Pan.
28. *Evandri sedes [Evander's home]* Evander was an Arcadian Greek who founded the city of Pallanteum on the site where Rome would later stand. He welcomed Aeneas and aided him in his war against the Latins (Virgil, *Aen.* viii 51–584).
34. *Numa* Numa Pompilius, the second of Rome's legendary kings. He

would frequent the groves where he met the goddess Egeria, who taught him divine wisdom (Plutarch, *Numa* 4).

38–9. The left bank of the Tiber was prone to floods. Horace tells how such a flood overwhelmed the *monumenta regis* (*Odes* I ii 15). Ovid means the Regia, the official headquarters of the Pontifex Maximus. M. may have confused this with the Mausoleum of Augustus.

41. *Portumni* Portumnus was god of harbours. He is 'curving' because the shore curves, or perhaps because Ovid describes the sea as *curvus* (*Met.* xi 505).

Mansus [Manso]

Date: December 1638 – January 1639. M. sent Manso the poem before leaving Naples (see M.'s headnote). Giovanni Battista Manso (*c.* 1560–1645) was a generous patron of the arts, and a friend of the poets Torquato Tasso and Giambattista Marino. He also wrote his own volume of poems (1635), some philosophical dialogues (1608, 1618), and a *Life of Tasso* (1619). He addressed a Latin couplet to M., which was printed as one of the commendatory verses in *1645*. M. recalled their acquaintance in *Defensio Secunda* (1654), where he relates that Manso received him with great warmth, conducted him over Naples, and visited him more than once at his lodgings. When M. left the city, Manso apologized for not showing him more attention, and said that he would have been a better host had M. been more guarded about his religious beliefs.

M.'s headnote. Tasso's *Gerusalemme Conquistata* (1593) was a revised version of his *Gerusalemme Liberata* (1580–81).

1. *quoque* [*too*] Manso had received many other poetic tributes before M.'s.

2. *Pierides* the Muses, named from their birthplace, Pieria in Macedonia.

4. *Galli* Cornelius Gallus (d. 26 BC), a poet and friend of Virgil, who commemorates him in *Ecl.* vi and x.

Mecaenatis Maecenas (d. 8 BC), the famous literary patron and friend of Virgil, Horace, Propertius and others.

6. See *Lycidas* 1–2n on ivy and laurel as emblems of poetry. Cp. also *Ad Patrem* 102, with which this line is almost identical.

9. *Marinum* the poet Giambattista Marino (1569–1625).

11. Marino's poem *L'Adone* (1623) is a version of the story of Venus and Adonis.

Assyrios Venus and Adonis were identified with the Semitic Astarte and Babylonian Thammuz. Cp. *A Masque* 1002 and *PL* i 446–57.

16. *aere* [*bronze*] Marino's monument in Naples.

18. *Orco* [*Orcus*] the underworld.

21. Manso wrote a *Life of Tasso* (1619). His life of Marino (known only from M.'s lines) has not survived.

22. *illius* Herodotus, who was born at Halicarnassus, not far from the mountainous promontory of Mycale in Ionia.

23. Herodotus is not now credited with the *Life of Homer*. M. calls Homer 'Aeolian' because northern Asia Minor was settled by Aeolian Greeks.

24. *Clius* [*Clio*] one of the nine Muses.

26. *Hyperboreo* See *Q Nov* 95n.

30. *Cygnos* [*swans*] English poets. Jonson calls Shakespeare 'Sweet swan of Avon' in his famous tribute in the First Folio.

34. *Tityrus* Chaucer. The name, from Virgil's *Eclogues*, had been given Chaucer by Spenser (*Shep. Cal.* February 92, June 81, December 4). Chaucer visited Italy in 1372 and 1378.

37. *Booten* [*Boötes*] a northern constellation, the Wagoner (or Bear-Ward), driver of the Wain (or Great Bear).

38–48. Callimachus tells how the three Hyperborean maidens, Loxo, Upis and Hecaerge, brought gifts of corn to Apollo at Delos (*Hymn* iv 283–99). Cp. also Herodotus, iv 33–5.

43. See *Lycidas* 53n on the connection between Druids and Bards.

46. *Corineida* [*daughter of Corineus*] Corineus accompanied the Trojan Brutus to Britain, where he governed Cornwall. See Geoffrey of Monmouth, *Historia Regum Britanniae* I xii. M. invents his parentage of Loxo.

55. *Cynthius* Apollo (from Mount Cynthius, on Delos, his birthplace).

57. *Pheretiadai* [*Pheretiades*] Admetus, son of Pheres and King of Pherae. When Zeus killed Apollo's son Aesculapius, Apollo killed the Cyclopes who had forged Zeus's thunderbolt. Zeus then punished Apollo by making him serve for a year as herdsman to Admetus.

58. *Alciden* [*Alcides*] Hercules. While staying as a guest in Admetus's house, he rescued Admetus's wife Alcestis, who had died in Admetus's place. See *Sonnet XIX* 2n. Ancient sources (including Euripides, *Alcestis*) place this event after Apollo's servitude. M.'s lines imply an earlier visit by Hercules.

60. *Chironis* Chiron the centaur, tutor of many Greek heroes. M. may have invented the story of Apollo's visits to his cave.

66. *Trachinia rupes* [*Trachinian cliff*] Mount Oeta in Thessaly.

69. Cp. Euripides, *Alcestis* 570f., where Apollo, tending Admetus's flocks, charms wild lynxes with his lyre.

72. *Atlantisque nepos* [*grandson of Atlas*] Mercury, god of eloquence. His mother Maia was Atlas's daughter.

75. Medea restored Jason's father Aeson to youth.

76. *frontis honores* [*honours of your brow*] Mansus's hair. Mansus was bald by 1638, but he wore a wig, and M. may have been deceived by it.

81. *etiam sub terris bella moventem* [*waging war even under the earth*] Carey suggests that M. may have been influenced by the Welsh *Spoils of Annwfn*

(*Book of Taliesin* xxx), in which Arthur and his men try to carry off the magic cauldron of the Otherworld. But descents to the underworld are so common in epic that M. would almost certainly have included one whether or not he was influenced by Welsh sources.

84. *phalanges* [*shield-wall*] The Saxon *scildweall*, like the Greek phalanx, was a body of infantry fighting with interlocked shields. Geoffrey of Monmouth (*Historia Regum Britannniae* IX i–vi) describes Arthur's victories over the invading Anglo-Saxons.

92. *Paphia myrti* [*Paphian myrtle*] Myrtle was sacred to Venus, who had a famous temple at Paphos, in Cyprus.

Parnasside lauri [*Parnassian laurel*] Mount Parnassus was sacred to Apollo, one of whose attributes was the laurel.

Epitaphium Damonis [Damon's Elegy]

Date: autumn 1639. Charles Diodati, M.'s closest friend, died in London in August 1638 while M. was in Italy. M. returned to England in the summer of 1639 and wrote this poem shortly thereafter (13–17), probably in the autumn (58–61). It was privately printed in 1640 or later, and was reprinted with no verbal variants in *1645*. Like *Lycidas*, it is a pastoral elegy, and follows many of the same conventions. There is no procession of mourners (see 69–90n), but there is a refrain (see 18n).

1. *Himerides* [*Nymphs of Himera*] pastoral Muses. The Himera is a river in Sicily, home of the Greek pastoral poets Theocritus, Bion and Moschus. *Daphnin* [*Daphnis*] a young shepherd mourned in Theocritus i, the earliest pastoral elegy.

Hylan [*Hylas*] a youth drowned by amorous nymphs (Theocritus xiii). 2. *Bionis* Bion, author of the *Lament for Adonis*, is himself mourned in the *Lament for Bion* (Moschus iii), the first pastoral elegy on the death of a fellow poet.

4. *Thyrsis* M. gives himself the name of the shepherd who mourns for Daphnis in Theocritus i. The name is common in pastoral. See *L'Allegro* 83n.

7. *Damona* Damon is a common pastoral name (see Virgil, *Ecl.* iii and viii). M. might also be thinking of the famous Sicilian friends Damon and Pythias.

9. *bis* [*twice*] John Shawcross, *MLN* 71 (1956) 322–4, points out that M. is referring to Italian crops, which are harvested twice a year (in March and August). Diodati died in August 1638, so two Italian harvests would have passed by April 1639, when M. was in Florence (the Tuscan city of line 13).

18. *Ite domum . . .* [*Go home . . .*] Refrains are common in pastoral elegy. Cp. Theocritus i, Bion, *Lament for Adonis* and Moschus, *Lament for Bion.* M.'s refrain echoes Virgil, *Ecl.* vii 44 and the last line of Virgil, *Ecl.* x (neither of which is a refrain).

23. *ille* [*he*] Mercury, guide of the dead. He used his wand (*virga*) to summon some ghosts from Orcus and send others to Tartarus (Virgil, *Aen.* iv 242-3).

27. Ancient superstition held that a man would be struck dumb if a wolf saw him before he saw it (Virgil, *Ecl.* ix 53-4).

31. *post Daphnin* [*next after Daphnis*] M. is ranking himself, as poet, below Theocritus.

32. *Pales* Roman goddess of shepherds. See *PL* ix 393. See *Ad Salsillum* 27 on *Faunus*.

34. Pallas Athene was goddess of wisdom. Diodati had studied at Oxford and Geneva.

56. *Cecropiosque sales* [*Attic wit*] Cecrops was the first king of Athens. Attic wit was famous.

65. *Innuba . . . uva* [*unwedded grapes*] Vines were said to be 'wedded' to the trees that propped them. See *PL* v 215-19*n*.

66. *myrteta* [*myrtle groves*] sacred to Venus, goddess of love.

69-90. A procession of mourners is conventional in pastoral elegy. Cp. *Lycidas* 88-112. M. replaces this convention with a procession of friends who try to comfort Thyrsis. Cp. the would-be comforters of Gallus in Virgil, *Ecl.* x 19-30.

69. *Tityrus* a stock pastoral name, found in Theocritus iii and vii, and Virgil, *Ecl.* i and viii.

Alphesiboeus Damon's rival in a singing contest in Virgil, *Ecl.* viii.

70. *Aegon* The name is found in Theocritus iv and Virgil *Ecl.* iii.

Amyntas the (male) beloved of Menalcas in Virgil, *Ecl.* iii. Cp. also Theocritus vii, Virgil, *Ecl.* ii, v and x.

75. *Mopsus* a shepherd in Virgil, *Ecl.* v and viii. A Mopso who understands the language of birds is mentioned in Tasso, *Aminta* I ii 459.

79. The planet Saturn was thought to cause melancholy.

88-90. The classical names might here refer to real acquaintances of M. and Diodati. Except for Aegle (who is a lovely nymph in Virgil, *Ecl.* vi 21) none of the names occurs in the pastoral poetry of Theocritus or Virgil.

90. *Idumanii . . . fluenti* [*Idumanian river*] the Blackwater, in Essex.

99. *Proteus* a sea-god, the herdsman of Neptune's seals. He knew all things and could change his shape at will so as not to answer questions. These 'protean' changes made his name a byword for inconstant or fickle love.

101. *Passer* [*sparrow*] notorious for lechery.

117. *Tityrus* not Chaucer (as in *Mansus* 34), but Virgil's Tityrus, who went to Rome in the days of its splendour (*Ecl.* i). Virgil's Tityrus might be

Virgil himself, who went to Rome and appealed successfully to Octavian against the confiscation of his farm.

129. *Arni* [*Arno*] the river of Florence.

132. Singing matches are a pastoral convention. Lycidas and Menalcas compete (not against each other) in Theocritus vii and viii. M. is here referring to real poetical contests in the Florentine academies, where everyone was expected to 'give some proof of his wit and reading' (*YP* 1. 809).

134. *munera* [*gifts*] M. received books and verse encomia from his Italian hosts.

137. *Datis, et Francinus* Carlo Dati (1619–76) was only nineteen when M. met him in Italy. He addressed a panegyric to M. which preceded M.'s Latin poems in *1645*. One of M.'s letters to him and two of his to M. survive (*YP* 2. 762–75). Antonio Francini wrote a long Latin ode to M. which also appeared among the commendatory verses in *1645*.

138. *Lydorum sanguinis* [*of Lydian blood*] Herodotus (i 94) relates that Tuscany was settled by Lydian colonists from Asia Minor.

149. The Colne is a river near Horton, where M. had lived before departing for Italy. Horton was in the territory of the ancient British chieftain Cassivelaunus, who had resisted Julius Caesar's second invasion of Britain in 54 BC.

150–52. Diodati had studied medicine at Oxford.

155–60. M. is referring to his planned epic on a British subject. He outlines his plans in lines 162–70. Cp. *Mansus* 81–4. His pastoral pipe has proved inadequate for the high style of epic.

160. *vos cedite silvae* [*Give place, woodlands*] echoing Gallus's farewell to pastoral poetry in Virgil, *Ecl.* x 63: *concedite silvae*.

162. *Rutupina . . . aequora* [*Rutupian Sea*] the English Channel. The Trojan ships are those of Brutus. See *A Masque* 828*n*.

163. Pandrasus was a king in Greece. He gave his daughter Inogen (or Ignoge) in marriage to Brutus after Brutus had defeated him. See M.'s *History of Britain* (*YP* 5. 11–13) and Geoffrey of Monmouth, I ix–xi.

164. *Brennumque . . . Belinum* Brennus and Belinus were legendary kings of Britain who conquered Rome. In his *History of Britain* M. follows Holinshed in conjecturing that Brennus might be the historical Brennus, a Gallic chieftain who took Rome in 390 BC (*YP* 5. 30). Arviragus was King Cymbeline's son. He married Claudius's daughter, but then rebelled against Rome (Geoffrey of Monmouth, *Historia Regum Britanniae* IV xii–xvi, Spenser, *FQ* II x 52). M. in his *History of Britain* rejects this legend and names Caractacus as Cymbeline's son (*YP* 5. 64–7).

165. M. in his *History of Britain* relates a tradition that Armorica (Brittany) was first colonized by Constantine's British veterans. When the Saxons invaded Britain, the Armoricans welcomed British refugees.

166–8. Uther Pendragon, aided by Merlin's magic, assumed the appearance of Gorlois, Duke of Cornwall, and so was admitted to the bed of Gorlois's wife Igraine, on whom he begot Arthur (Geoffrey of Monmouth, *Historia Regum Britanniae* VIII xix, Malory, *Morte d'Arthur* I ii).

175. *Usa* the Ouse, first in a list of English rivers. Cp. *FQ* IV xi.

Alauni [*Alne*] Camden, in *Britannia*, mentions a river Alne in Northumberland and another in Hampshire.

180. The laurel bark is used as a writing surface. Cp. Virgil, *Ecl.* v 13-14.

181. *Mansus* See headnote to *Mansus*. Manso's gift of two cups might represent books or poems (as the baskets of line 135 represented literary tributes). Pindar (*Olympian Ode* vii), refers to a poem as a cup. Whether books or cups, Manso's gifts speak of resurrection. The cups in Theocritus i 29-56 and Virgil, *Ecl.* iii 36-48 depict earthly delights only.

182. *Chalcidicae* [*Chalcidian*] Neapolitan. Naples had been settled by Greek colonists from Chalcis in Euboea.

187. *Phoenix* a symbol of resurrection, since it rose from its own ashes. See *PL* v 272n.

191. *Amor* [*Cupid*] not the irresponsible boy-god of *Elegia VII* but the 'Celestial Cupid' of *A Masque* 1004. Cp. Plato's distinction between the common and the heavenly Aphrodite (*Symposium* 180-82).

208. *quicunque vocaris* [*by whatever name you are called*] Cp. the cautious addressing of divine beings in *PL* iii 7 and vii 1-2. Pagan gods were often invoked 'by whatever name you wish to be called'.

210. *divino nomine* [*divine name*] Diodati means 'God-given'. The righteous will be given a 'new name' in Heaven (Rev. 3. 12), so Diodati's retention of his own name (210-11) might imply that he was always heavenly, even when on earth.

213. *quod nulla tori libata voluptas* [*because you never tasted the pleasure of the bed*] Almost all editors translate *torus* as 'marriage bed' or 'marriage'. There is classical precedent for such a usage, but *torus* usually meant 'bed' and could refer to any bed of pleasure, licit or illicit. Thus while M. applauds Diodati's abstention from unchastity, he need not view marriage as unchaste. See next note.

214. *virginei . . . honores* [*virginal honours*] At Rev. 14. 1-4 St John sees 144,000 male virgins singing 'a new song' before the Lamb. They can sing the song because they 'were not defiled with women; for they are virgins'. M. implies that the unmarried Diodati will join this choir, but he need not be degrading marriage. In *An Apology for Smectymnuus* (1642) M. assumes that St John's virgins include married men, 'For mariage must not be call'd a defilement' (*YP* 1. 893). Puritans called marriage 'pure virginitie'. See *A Masque* 787n and *Ad Patrem* 32-3n, and cp. the married Eve's 'virgin majesty' (*PL* ix 270).

216. *palmae* Cp. Rev. 7. 9: 'a great multitude, which no man could number

. . . stood before the throne, and before the Lamb, clothed with white robes, and palms in their hands'.

217. *hymenaeos* [*marriage-rite*] alluding to the marriage supper of the Lamb (Rev. 19. 5–7). Numerous Miltonists (confusing Rev. 14 and 19) have claimed that only virgins take part in the Lamb's nuptials. But the Lamb's marriage is celebrated by 'all' God's servants, 'both small and great' (Rev. 19. 5). Cp. *Lycidas* 176–8, where 'all the saints' sing the 'nuptial song'.

219. *thyrso* [*thyrsus*] the vine- and ivy-wreathed wand of Bacchic revellers.

GREEK AND LATIN POEMS ADDED IN 1673

Apologus de Rustico et Hero [A fable of a Peasant and his Landlord]

Date: 1624? Although printed only in *1673*, this poem was probably a grammar-school exercise. The story is from Aesop's Fables, but its poetic model is a version of the fable by Mantuan, *Opera* (Paris 1513) 194ᵛ. The poem was placed last of the Latin elegies in *1673*.

In Effigiei eius Sculptorem [On the Engraver of his Portrait]

Date: 1645. The poem appeared engraved beneath M.'s portrait on the *1645* frontispiece, and was printed between *Philosophus ad Regem* and *Ad Salsillum* in *1673*. The engraver of M.'s portrait was William Marshall. M., who was proud of his handsome appearance, had cause to dislike Marshall's unflattering picture, and he took his revenge in this poem. The Greekless Marshall, suspecting no malice, engraved the words that condemned his own skill. Thomas O. Mabbott (*Explicator* 8, 1950, item 58) detects an intentional ambiguity in M.'s last phrase, which means that the rotten picture has been engraved either *by* or *of* a rotten artist. Thus M. implies that Marshall's engraving is a self-portrait.

Ad Ioannem Rousium Oxoniensis Academiae Bibliothecarium [To John Rous, Librarian of Oxford University]

Date: 23 January 1647 (M.'s date of 1646 is Old Style). M. had sent a copy of *1645* to Rous, together with copies of the eleven prose pamphlets he had so far published. The volume of poems was lost or stolen in transit, so M. sent a replacement with this Pindaric ode. The manuscript of the poem is still in the Bodleian, placed between the English and Latin poems in a copy of *1645* that might be the replacement copy referred to in the poem. The poem was placed last in *1673*.

1. *Gemelle . . . liber* [*Twin-born book*] The English and Latin poems in *1645* formed a 'twin' volume with separate title-pages and pagination.

10. *Daunio* [*Daunian*] Italian. M. might be referring to his Italian poems, which were written in England (see *Canzone*).

18. *Thamesis* a name sometimes given to the upper reaches of the river Thames above the point where it is joined by the river Thame. Oxford lies at the confluence of the Thames and the Cherwell.

21. *Aonidum* The Muses were called 'Aonides' from their home on Mount Helicon in Aonia.

thyasusque [*Bacchic dance*] the Bacchic throngs are here Oxford scholars (Bacchus being a god of learning).

25-36. Cp. Ovid's appeal to an unnamed god or hero who might atone for Rome's past misdoings and help her to recover from civil war (*Odes* I ii 25 52).

29. *civium tumultus* M. was writing in the fourth year of the Civil War, which had broken out in 1642. Oxford was the King's headquarters.

33-6. The filthy birds are the Harpies, whom Zeus sent to defile the food of the blind prophet Phineus. Phineus was delivered by the Argonauts (not Apollo), but Apollo suits M.'s purposes as god of poetry. The winged horse Pegasus was a symbol for poetry. See *PL* vii 4*n*.

45. *Lethen* [*Lethe*] the river of oblivion in Hades.

56. *Ion* the guardian of Apollo's shrine and treasury at Delphi. He was the son of Apollo and Creusa (daughter of Erectheus, King of Athens). See Euripides, *Ion* 54-8.

60. *Actaea* [*Actaean*] Athenian (*Acte* being an early name for Attica).

65-6. *Delo* Delos, in the Cyclades, was Apollo's birthplace. Parnassus was sacred to Apollo and the Muses.

77. *Hermes* god of learning and guide of the dead.

endnote. The Phaleucian line consisted of a spondee, a dactyl and three spondees.

LATER POEMS FROM THE PROSE WORKS

Epigram from Pro Populo Anglicano Defensio

Date: 1650. M.'s pamphlet was published in 1651 but entered in the Stationers' Register in December 1650. It was a reply to Claudius Salmasius (Claude de Saumaise, 1588-1653), who had attacked the English regicides in his *Defensio Regia Pro Caroli I* (1649). Salmasius in his tract had laboured the English term 'hundred' (a subdivision of a county). M. in his reply mocks Salmasius and adds this poem, which makes punning reference to the hundred gold Jacobuses Salmasius was allegedly paid by the exiled Charles II. M.'s poem imitates the Roman satirist Persius (*Prologus* 8–14). M. indicates his borrowings by italicizing those words that he has taken directly from the original.

3. *Iacobei* [*Jacobuses*] 'Jacobus' was the unofficial name of a gold coin issued in 1603. It was worth one pound at the time of issue.
6. *primatum Papae* [*supremacy of the Pope*] Salmasius, a Protestant, had challenged papal supremacy in *De Primatu Papae* (1645).

Epigram from Defensio Secunda

Date: 1653. Salmasius died in 1653; M.'s *Defensio Secunda* was published in 1654. M. in his pamphlet (*YP* 4. 581) says that he wrote these verses when he still expected that Salmasius would reply to his *Pro Populo Anglicano Defensio*. The poem turns on an ancient joke that worthless books are good only to wrap fish. See e.g. Martial, *Epigrams* III ii 1–5.

3. *Salmasius* Bush notes a pun on Latin *salmo*, 'salmon'.
eques [*knight*] Louis XIII had made Salmasius a knight of the Order of St Michael – an order held in low esteem in France.
6. *cucullos* both 'cowls' and 'conical wrappers for merchandise'. Martial makes the same pun in *Epigrams* III ii 5.
10. It was an ancient Roman jibe that fishmongers wiped their noses on their sleeves.

UNPUBLISHED LATIN POEMS

Carmina Elegiaca [Elegiac Verses]

An autograph copy of these verses was discovered in 1874, along with M.'s Commonplace Book, a short Latin essay on early rising, and the Asclepiad verses on the same theme (see next poem). The two poems are probably grammar-school exercises written when M. attended St Paul's.

5. *Titan* the sun.
7. *Daulias* [*Daulian bird*] the swallow, called *Daulias ales* by Ovid (*Her.* xv 154). Procne was turned into a swallow at Daulis, in central Greece.

11. *Zephyritis* [*Zephyr's consort*] Flora, goddess of spring. She covers the ground with pasture in Ovid, *Fasti* v 208.

[*Asclepiads*]

See headnote to previous poem. This poem (written in the lesser Asclepiad metre) is untitled in M.'s autograph copy.

3. *Dauni . . . filius* [*Daunus's son*] Turnus, King of the Rutuli and leader of the Latins against Aeneas. The Trojans Nisus and Euryalus attack his camp in Virgil, *Aen.* ix 176–449.

4. *toro* a conjectural restoration. The MS is damaged.

INDEX OF TITLES

INDEX OF FIRST LINES

READ MORE IN PENGUIN

In every corner of the world, on every subject under the sun, Penguin represents quality and variety – the very best in publishing today.

For complete information about books available from Penguin – including Puffins, Penguin Classics and Arkana – and how to order them, write to us at the appropriate address below. Please note that for copyright reasons the selection of books varies from country to country.

In the United Kingdom: Please write to *Dept. EP, Penguin Books Ltd, Bath Road, Harmondsworth, West Drayton, Middlesex UB7 ODA*

In the United States: Please write to *Consumer Sales, Penguin Putnam Inc., P.O. Box 999, Dept. 17109, Bergenfield, New Jersey 07621-0120.* VISA and MasterCard holders call 1-800-253-6476 to order Penguin titles

In Canada: Please write to *Penguin Books Canada Ltd, 10 Alcorn Avenue, Suite 300, Toronto, Ontario M4V 3B2*

In Australia: Please write to *Penguin Books Australia Ltd, P.O. Box 257, Ringwood, Victoria 3134*

In New Zealand: Please write to *Penguin Books (NZ) Ltd, Private Bag 102902, North Shore Mail Centre, Auckland 10*

In India: Please write to *Penguin Books India Pvt Ltd, 210 Chiranjiv Tower, 43 Nehru Place, New Delhi 110 019*

In the Netherlands: Please write to *Penguin Books Netherlands bv, Postbus 3507, NL-1001 AH Amsterdam*

In Germany: Please write to *Penguin Books Deutschland GmbH, Metzlerstrasse 26, 60594 Frankfurt am Main*

In Spain: Please write to *Penguin Books S. A., Bravo Murillo 19, 1° B, 28015 Madrid*

In Italy: Please write to *Penguin Italia s.r.l., Via Benedetto Croce 2, 20094 Corsico, Milano*

In France: Please write to *Penguin France, Le Carré Wilson, 62 rue Benjamin Baillaud, 31500 Toulouse*

In Japan: Please write to *Penguin Books Japan Ltd, Kaneko Building, 2-3-25 Koraku, Bunkyo-Ku, Tokyo 112*

In South Africa: Please write to *Penguin Books South Africa (Pty) Ltd, Private Bag X14, Parkview, 2122 Johannesburg*

A CHOICE OF CLASSICS

Armadale Wilkie Collins

Victorian critics were horrified by Lydia Gwilt, the bigamist, husband-poisoner and laudanum addict whose intrigues spur the plot of this most sensational of melodramas.

Aurora Leigh and Other Poems Elizabeth Barrett Browning

Aurora Leigh (1856), Elizabeth Barrett Browning's epic novel in blank verse, tells the story of the making of a woman poet, exploring 'the woman question', art and its relation to politics and social oppression.

Personal Narrative of a Journey to the Equinoctial Regions of the New Continent Alexander von Humboldt

Alexander von Humboldt became a wholly new kind of nineteenth-century hero – the scientist–explorer – and in *Personal Narrative* he invented a new literary genre: the travelogue.

The Pancatantra Visnu Sarma

The Pancatantra is one of the earliest books of fables and its influence can be seen in the *Arabian Nights*, the *Decameron*, the *Canterbury Tales* and most notably in the *Fables* of La Fontaine.

A Laodicean Thomas Hardy

The Laodicean of Hardy's title is Paula Power, a thoroughly modern young woman who, despite her wealth and independence, cannot make up her mind.

Brand Henrik Ibsen

The unsparing vision of a priest driven by faith to risk and witness the deaths of his wife and child gives *Brand* its icy ferocity. It was Ibsen's first masterpiece, a poetic drama composed in 1865 and published to tremendous critical and popular acclaim.

READ MORE IN PENGUIN

A CHOICE OF CLASSICS

Sylvia's Lovers Elizabeth Gaskell

In an atmosphere of unease the rivalries of two men, the sober tradesman Philip Hepburn, who has been devoted to his cousin Sylvia since her childhood, and the gallant, charming whaleship harpooner Charley Kinraid, are played out.

The Republic Plato

The best-known of Plato's dialogues, *The Republic* is also one of the supreme masterpieces of Western philosophy, whose influence cannot be overestimated.

Ethics Benedict de Spinoza

'Spinoza (1632–77),' wrote Bertrand Russell, 'is the noblest and most lovable of the great philosophers. Intellectually, some others have surpassed him, but ethically he is supreme.'

Virgil in English

From Chaucer to Auden, Virgil is a defining presence in English poetry. Penguin Classics' new series, Poets in Translation, offers the best translations in English, through the centuries, of the major Classical and European poets.

What is Art? Leo Tolstoy

Tolstoy wrote prolifically in a series of essays and polemics on issues of morality, social justice and religion. These culminated in *What is Art?*, published in 1898, in which he rejects the idea that art reveals and reinvents through beauty.

An Autobiography Anthony Trollope

A fascinating insight into a writer's life, in which Trollope also recorded his unhappy youth and his progress to prosperity and social recognition.

A CHOICE OF CLASSICS

Matthew Arnold	**Selected Prose**
Jane Austen	**Emma**
	Lady Susan/The Watsons/Sanditon
	Mansfield Park
	Northanger Abbey
	Persuasion
	Pride and Prejudice
	Sense and Sensibility
William Barnes	**Selected Poems**
Anne Brontë	**Agnes Grey**
	The Tenant of Wildfell Hall
Charlotte Brontë	**Jane Eyre**
	Shirley
	Villette
Emily Brontë	**Wuthering Heights**
Samuel Butler	**Erewhon**
	The Way of All Flesh
Lord Byron	**Selected Poems**
Thomas Carlyle	**Selected Writings**
Arthur Hugh Clough	**Selected Poems**
Wilkie Collins	**Armadale**
	The Moonstone
	No Name
	The Woman in White
Charles Darwin	**The Origin of Species**
	Voyage of the *Beagle*
Benjamin Disraeli	**Sybil**
George Eliot	**Adam Bede**
	Daniel Deronda
	Felix Holt
	Middlemarch
	The Mill on the Floss
	Romola
	Scenes of Clerical Life
	Silas Marner

READ MORE IN PENGUIN

A CHOICE OF CLASSICS

Charles Dickens	**American Notes for General Circulation**
	Barnaby Rudge
	Bleak House
	The Christmas Books (in two volumes)
	David Copperfield
	Dombey and Son
	Great Expectations
	Hard Times
	Little Dorrit
	Martin Chuzzlewit
	The Mystery of Edwin Drood
	Nicholas Nickleby
	The Old Curiosity Shop
	Oliver Twist
	Our Mutual Friend
	The Pickwick Papers
	Selected Short Fiction
	A Tale of Two Cities
Elizabeth Gaskell	**Cranford/Cousin Phillis**
	The Life of Charlotte Brontë
	Mary Barton
	North and South
	Ruth
	Sylvia's Lovers
	Wives and Daughters
Edward Gibbon	**The Decline and Fall of the Roman Empire** (in three volumes)
George Gissing	**New Grub Street**
	The Odd Women
William Godwin	**Caleb Williams**

READ MORE IN PENGUIN

A CHOICE OF CLASSICS

Thomas Hardy	**Desperate Remedies**
	The Distracted Preacher and Other Tales
	Far from the Madding Crowd
	Jude the Obscure
	The Hand of Ethelberta
	A Laodicean
	The Mayor of Casterbridge
	A Pair of Blue Eyes
	The Return of the Native
	Selected Poems
	Tess of the d'Urbervilles
	The Trumpet-Major
	Two on a Tower
	Under the Greenwood Tree
	The Well-Beloved
	The Woodlanders
Lord Macaulay	**The History of England**
Henry Mayhew	**London Labour and the London Poor**
John Stuart Mill	**The Autobiography**
	On Liberty
William Morris	**News from Nowhere** and **Other Writings**
John Henry Newman	**Apologia Pro Vita Sua**
Robert Owen	**A New View of Society and Other Writings**
Walter Pater	**Marius the Epicurean**
John Ruskin	**Unto This Last and Other Writings**
Walter Scott	**Ivanhoe**
	Heart of Mid-Lothian
	Old Mortality
	Rob Roy
	Waverley

READ MORE IN PENGUIN

A CHOICE OF CLASSICS

Robert Louis Stevenson

Kidnapped
Dr Jekyll and Mr Hyde and Other Stories
The Master of Ballantrae
Weir of Hermiston

William Makepeace
  Thackeray

The History of Henry Esmond
The History of Pendennis
The Newcomes
Vanity Fair

Anthony Trollope

An Autobiography
Barchester Towers
Can You Forgive Her?
The Duke's Children
The Eustace Diamonds
Framley Parsonage
He Knew He Was Right
The Last Chronicle of Barset
Phineas Finn
The Prime Minister
Rachel Ray
The Small House at Allington
The Warden
The Way We Live Now

Oscar Wilde

Complete Short Fiction
De Profundis and Other Writings
The Picture of Dorian Gray

Mary Wollstonecraft

A Vindication of the Rights of Woman
Mary and **Maria** (includes Mary Shelley's
Matilda)

Dorothy and William
  Wordsworth

Home at Grasmere

READ MORE IN PENGUIN

A CHOICE OF CLASSICS

Adomnan of Iona	**Life of St Columba**
St Anselm	**The Prayers and Meditations**
St Augustine	**Confessions**
	The City of God
Bede	**Ecclesiastical History of the English People**
Geoffrey Chaucer	**The Canterbury Tales**
	Love Visions
	Troilus and Criseyde
Marie de France	**The Lais of Marie de France**
Jean Froissart	**The Chronicles**
Geoffrey of Monmouth	**The History of the Kings of Britain**
Gerald of Wales	**History and Topography of Ireland**
	The Journey through Wales and **The Description of Wales**
Gregory of Tours	**The History of the Franks**
Robert Henryson	**The Testament of Cresseid and Other Poems**
Walter Hilton	**The Ladder of Perfection**
St Ignatius	**Personal Writings**
Julian of Norwich	**Revelations of Divine Love**
Thomas à Kempis	**The Imitation of Christ**
William Langland	**Piers the Ploughman**
Sir John Mandeville	**The Travels of Sir John Mandeville**
Marguerite de Navarre	**The Heptameron**
Christine de Pisan	**The Treasure of the City of Ladies**
Chrétien de Troyes	**Arthurian Romances**
Marco Polo	**The Travels**
Richard Rolle	**The Fire of Love**
François Villon	**Selected Poems**

READ MORE IN PENGUIN

A CHOICE OF CLASSICS

Francis Bacon	**The Essays**
Aphra Behn	**Love-Letters between a Nobleman and His Sister**
	Oroonoko, The Rover and Other Works
George Berkeley	**Principles of Human Knowledge/Three Dialogues between Hylas and Philonous**
James Boswell	**The Life of Samuel Johnson**
Sir Thomas Browne	**The Major Works**
John Bunyan	**The Pilgrim's Progress**
Edmund Burke	**Reflections on the Revolution in France**
Frances Burney	**Evelina**
Margaret Cavendish	**The Blazing World and Other Writings**
William Cobbett	**Rural Rides**
William Congreve	**Comedies**
Thomas de Quincey	**Confessions of an English Opium Eater**
	Recollections of the Lakes and the Lake Poets
Daniel Defoe	**A Journal of the Plague Year**
	Moll Flanders
	Robinson Crusoe
	Roxana
	A Tour Through the Whole Island of Great Britain
Henry Fielding	**Amelia**
	Jonathan Wild
	Joseph Andrews
	The Journal of a Voyage to Lisbon
	Tom Jones
John Gay	**The Beggar's Opera**
Oliver Goldsmith	**The Vicar of Wakefield**
Lady Gregory	**Selected Writings**

READ MORE IN PENGUIN

A CHOICE OF CLASSICS

William Hazlitt	**Selected Writings**
George Herbert	**The Complete English Poems**
Thomas Hobbes	**Leviathan**
Samuel Johnson/	
James Boswell	**A Journey to the Western Islands of Scotland** and **The Journal of a Tour of the Hebrides**
Charles Lamb	**Selected Prose**
George Meredith	**The Egoist**
Thomas Middleton	**Five Plays**
John Milton	**Paradise Lost**
Samuel Richardson	**Clarissa**
	Pamela
Earl of Rochester	**Complete Works**
Richard Brinsley	
Sheridan	**The School for Scandal and Other Plays**
Sir Philip Sidney	**Selected Poems**
Christopher Smart	**Selected Poems**
Adam Smith	**The Wealth of Nations** (Books I–III)
Tobias Smollett	**The Adventures of Ferdinand Count Fathom**
	Humphrey Clinker
	Roderick Random
Laurence Sterne	**The Life and Opinions of Tristram Shandy**
	A Sentimental Journey Through France and Italy
Jonathan Swift	**Gulliver's Travels**
	Selected Poems
Thomas Traherne	**Selected Poems and Prose**
Henry Vaughan	**Complete Poems**